D0203160

IMPORTANT

HERE IS YOUR REGISTRATION CODE TO ACCESS MCGRAW-HILL PREMIUM CONTENT AND MCGRAW-HILL ONLINE RESOURCES

For key premium online resources you need THIS CODE to gain access. Once the code is entered, you will be able to use the web resources for the length of your course.

Access is provided only if you have purchased a new book.

If the registration code is missing from this book, the registration screen on our website, and within your WebCT or Blackboard course will tell you how to obtain your new code. Your registration code can be used only once to establish access. It is not transferable.

To gain access to these online resources

1. **USE** your web browser to go to: **www.mhhe.com/nolen4**

2. **CLICK** on "First Time User"

3. **ENTER** the Registration Code printed on the tear-off bookmark on the right

4. After you have entered your registration code, click on "Register"

5. **FOLLOW** the instructions to setup your personal UserID and Password

6. **WRITE** your UserID and Password down for future reference. Keep it in a safe place.

If your course is using WebCT or Blackboard, you'll be able to use this code to access the McGraw-Hill content within your instructor's online course.

To gain access to the McGraw-Hill content in your instructor's WebCT or Blackboard course simply log into the course with the user ID and Password provided by your instructor. Enter the registration code exactly as it appears to the right when prompted by the system. You will only need to use this code the first time you click on McGraw-Hill content.

These instructions are specifically for student access. Instructors are not required to register via the above instructions.

Higher Education

Thank you, and welcome to your McGraw-Hill Online Resources.

ISBN 13: 978-0-07-322477-0
ISBN 10: 0-07-322477-4 T/A NOLEN-HOEKSEMA: ABNORMAL PSYCHOLOGY, 4/E

Abnormal Psychology

Abnormal Psychology

4th Edition

Susan Nolen-Hoeksema
Yale University

Boston   Burr Ridge, IL   Dubuque, IA   Madison, WI   New York   San Francisco   St. Louis
Bangkok   Bogotá   Caracas   Kuala Lumpur   Lisbon   London   Madrid   Mexico City
Milan   Montreal   New Delhi   Santiago   Seoul   Singapore   Sydney   Taipei   Toronto

Higher Education

ABNORMAL PSYCHOLOGY

Published by McGraw-Hill, a business unit of The McGraw-Hill Companies, Inc., 1221 Avenue of the Americas, New York, NY 10020. Copyright © 2007, 2004, 2001, 1998 by The McGraw-Hill Companies, Inc. All rights reserved. No part of this publication may be reproduced or distributed in any form or by any means, or stored in a database or retrieval system, without the prior written consent of The McGraw-Hill Companies, Inc., including, but not limited to, in any network or other electronic storage or transmission, or broadcast for distance learning.
Some ancillaries, including electronic and print components, may not be available to customers outside the United States.

This book is printed on acid-free paper.

1 2 3 4 5 6 7 8 9 0 DOW/DOW 0 9 8 7 6 5

ISBN-13: 978-0-07-313369-0
ISBN-10: 0-07-313369-8

Editor in Chief: *Emily Barrosse*
Publisher: *Beth Mejia*
Senior Developmental Editor: *Judith Kromm*
Permissions Editor: *Marty Granahan*
Marketing Manager: *Melissa Caughlin*
Managing Editor: *Jean Dal Porto*
Project Manager: *Emily Hatteberg*
Art Director: *Jeanne Schreiber*
Design Manager: *Laurie J. Entringer*
Art Editor: *Emma C. Ghiselli*
Cover and Interior Designer: *Amanda Kavanagh*
Photo Research Coordinator: *Nora Agbayani*
Photo Researcher: *Toni Michaels/PhotoFind, L.L.C.*
Cover Credit: © *David Muir/Masterfile*
Illustrators: *Joanne Brummett, Kathryn Rathke*
Senior Media Producer: *Stephanie George*
Media Project Manager: *Kathleen Boylan*
Senior Supplement Producer: *Louis Swaim*
Senior Production Supervisor: *Carol A. Bielski*
Composition: *10/12 Minion, by Cenveo*
Printing: *45 # Pub Matte Plus, R. R. Donnelley/Willard, OH*

Credits: The credits section for this book begins on page C-1 and is considered an extension of the copyright page.

Library of Congress Cataloging-in-Publication Data
Nolen-Hoeksema, Susan, 1959-
      Abnormal psychology / Susan Nolen-Hoeksema. — 4th ed.
         p. cm.
      Includes bibliographical references and indexes.
      ISBN-13: 978007313690 (alk. paper)
      ISBN-10: 0-07-313369-8 (alk. paper)
      1. Psychology, Pathological. 2. Mental illness. I. Title.
RC454.N64 2007
616.89—dc22
                                                          2005053359

The Internet addresses listed in the text were accurate at the time of publication. The inclusion of a Web site does not indicate an endorsement by the authors or McGraw-Hill, and McGraw-Hill does not guarantee the accuracy of the information presented at these sites.

www.mhhe.com

To Michael and Richard

CONTENTS IN BRIEF

Preface   xix
About the Author   xxix

1. **Looking at Abnormality**   3
2. **Contemporary Theories of Abnormality**   33
3. **The Research Endeavor**   71
4. **Assessing and Diagnosing Abnormality**   99
5. **Treatments for Abnormality**   133
6. **Stress Disorders and Health Psychology**   171
7. **Anxiety Disorders**   217
8. **Somatoform and Dissociative Disorders**   267
9. **Mood Disorders**   301
10. **Suicide**   351
11. **Schizophrenia**   375
12. **Personality Disorders**   421
13. **Childhood Disorders**   459
14. **Cognitive Disorders and Life-Span Issues**   509
15. **Eating Disorders**   539
16. **Sexual Disorders**   573
17. **Substance-Related Disorders**   619
18. **Mental Health and the Law**   675

Glossary   G-1
References   R-1
Credits   C-1
Name Index   NI-1
Subject Index   SI-1

CONTENTS

Preface   xix
About the Author   xxix

1   Looking at Abnormality   3

Extraordinary People—Clifford Beers:
A Mind That Found Itself   4

Defining Abnormality   5

Cultural Relativism   6
Unusualness   8
Discomfort   9
Mental Illness   9
Maladaptiveness   9
■ *Taking Psychology Personally: When You
   Wonder If You Are Abnormal*   11

Historical Perspectives on Abnormality   11

Ancient Theories   11
Medieval Views   14
The Spread of Asylums During the
Renaissance   17
Moral Treatment in the Eighteenth
Century   19

The Emergence of Modern Perspectives   21

The Beginnings of Modern Biological
Perspectives   21
The Psychoanalytic Perspective   22
The Roots of Behaviorism   23
The Cognitive Revolution   23

Modern Mental-Health Care   24

Deinstitutionalization   24
Managed Care   25

Professions Within Abnormal Psychology   26

Chapter Integration   26

Extraordinary People: Follow-Up   27

Chapter Summary   28
Key Terms   29

2   Contemporary Theories of Abnormality   33

Extraordinary People—Albert Ellis:
The Phobic Psychologist   34

Biological Approaches   36

Structural Brain Abnormalities   37
Biochemical Causes of Abnormality   39
Genetic Factors in Abnormality   42
■ *Taking Psychology Personally: Do "Bad
   Genes" Doom You to a Disorder?*   43
Assessing the Biological Theories   45

Psychological Approaches   46

Psychodynamic Theories of Abnormality   46
Behavioral Theories of Abnormality   53
Cognitive Theories of Abnormality   55
Humanistic and Existential Theories of
Abnormality   58

Social and Interpersonal Approaches   60

Interpersonal Theories of Abnormality   60
Family Systems Theories of Abnormality   62
Social Structural Theories of Abnormality   63

Chapter Integration   65

Extraordinary People: Follow-Up   66

Chapter Summary   66
Key Terms   67

3   The Research Endeavor   71

Extraordinary People—The Old Order Amish of
Pennsylvania   72

The Scientific Method   73

Defining the Problem and Stating a Hypothesis   73
Choosing and Implementing a Research Method   73

Case Studies   74

Evaluating Case Studies   76

Correlational Studies   76

Measuring the Relationship Between Variables   77
Selecting a Sample   79
Evaluating Correlational Studies   80

Epidemiological Studies   81

Evaluating Epidemiological Research   82

Experimental Studies   82

Human Laboratory Studies   82
■ *Taking Psychology Personally: Your Rights as a Research Participant   85*

Therapy Outcome Studies   85
Single-Case Experimental Designs   87
Animal Studies   88

Cross-Cultural Research   90

Meta-Analysis   91

Evaluating Meta-Analysis   92

Chapter Integration   92

Extraordinary People: Follow-Up   93

Chapter Summary   94

Key Terms   96

4   Assessing and Diagnosing Abnormality   99

Extraordinary People—Michael J. Fox: *Lucky Man*   100

Gathering Information   101

Symptoms and History   101
Physiological and Neurophysiological Factors   102
Sociocultural Factors   102

Assessment Tools   104

Clinical Interviews   104
Cognitive, Symptom, and Personality Tests   104
■ *Taking Psychology Personally: Is Self-Assessment a Good Idea?   111*

Behavioral Observation and Self-Monitoring   114

Problems in Assessment   115

Evaluating Children   115
Evaluating Clients from Other Cultures   117

Diagnosis   118

Diagnostic and Statistical Manual of Mental Disorders (DSM)   119
The Dangers of Diagnosis   125

Chapter Integration   127

Extraordinary People: Follow-Up   128

Chapter Summary   129

Key Terms   130

5   Treatments for Abnormality   133

Extraordinary People—The Inside Story on Coping with Schizophrenia   134

Biological Treatments   136

Drug Therapies   136
Herbal Medicines   140
Electroconvulsive Therapy   142
Psychosurgery   142
Repetitive Transcranial Magnetic Stimulation   143
The Social Impact of the Biological Approach to Treatment   143

Psychological Therapies   144

Psychodynamic Therapies   145
■ *Taking Psychology Personally: How to Look for a Therapist   146*
Humanistic Therapy   148
Behavior Therapies   149
Cognitive Therapies   151

Interpersonal and Social Approaches   154

Interpersonal Therapy   154
Family Systems Therapy   155
Group Therapy   157
Community Treatment   158
Cross-Cultural and Gender Issues in Treatment   159

Evaluating Treatments   163

Special Issues in Treating Children   164

Psychotherapies Matched to Children's Developmental Levels   165
The Effects of Drugs on Children and Adolescents   165
The Need to Treat the Child's Family   165
Children's Unwillingness to Seek Therapy   166

Chapter Integration   167

Extraordinary People: Follow-Up   167

Chapter Summary   168

Key Terms   169

6   Stress Disorders and Health Psychology   171

Extraordinary People—Norman Cousins: *Healing with Laughter*   172

Physiological Responses to Stress   174

Health Psychology   176
Stress, Coronary Heart Disease, and Hypertension   177
Stress and the Immune System   178

Sleep and Health   180

Sleep Deprivation   181
Sleep Disorders   181

Personality and Health   184

Pessimism   184
The Type A Behavior Pattern   185
Social Support   188

Interventions to Improve Health   188

Guided Mastery Techniques   189
Biofeedback   190
Sociocultural Interventions   190

Posttraumatic Stress Disorder, Acute Stress Disorder, and Adjustment Disorder   191

The Role of Trauma in PTSD   194
■ *Taking Psychology Personally: What to Do If You've Been Sexually Assaulted   197*

Explanations of PTSD Vulnerability   199
Treatments for PTSD   204

Chapter Integration   211

Extraordinary People: Follow-Up   212

Chapter Summary   212

Key Terms   214

7   Anxiety Disorders   217

Extraordinary People—Marc Summers:
Everything in Its Place   218

Panic Disorder   221

Theories of Panic Disorder   223
Treatments for Panic Disorder   227
■ *Taking Psychology Personally:
Relaxation Exercises*   230

Phobias   232

Agoraphobia   232
Specific Phobias   233
Social Phobia   235
Theories of Phobias   236
Treatments for Phobias   241

Generalized Anxiety Disorder   245

Theories of Generalized Anxiety
Disorder   246
Treatments for Generalized Anxiety
Disorder   249

Obsessive-Compulsive Disorder   251

OCD Symptoms   252
Theories of OCD   254
Treatments for OCD   257

**Social Approaches to the Anxiety
Disorders   259**

Gender Differences   259
Cross-Cultural Differences   260

Chapter Integration   261

Extraordinary People: Follow-Up   261

Chapter Summary   262

Key Terms   264

8   Somatoform and
Dissociative Disorders   267

Extraordinary People—Anna O.   268

Somatoform Disorders   269

Distinction Between Somatoform and
Related Disorders   269
Conversion Disorder   271
Somatization Disorders and Pain
Disorders   274
Hypochondriasis   278
Body Dysmorphic Disorder   279

Dissociative Disorders   281

■ *Taking Psychology Personally:
Dissociation in Everyday Life*   281

Dissociative Identity Disorder   283
Dissociative Fugue   290
Dissociative Amnesia   291
Depersonalization Disorder   293
Controversies Around the Dissociative
Disorders   293

Chapter Integration 296

Extraordinary People: Follow-Up 296

Chapter Summary 297

Key Terms 298

9 Mood Disorders 301

Extraordinary People—Kay Redfield Jamison: *An Unquiet Mind* 302

Unipolar Depression 303

Symptoms of Depression 303
The Diagnosis of Unipolar Depressive Disorders 304
Prevalence and Course of Depression 306
Depression in Childhood and Adolescence 307

Bipolar Mood Disorders 309

Symptoms of Mania 309
The Diagnosis of Mania 310
Prevalence and Course of Bipolar Disorder 311
Creativity and Bipolar Disorder 311

Biological Theories of Mood Disorders 313

The Role of Genetics 313
Neurotransmitter Dysregulation 315
Brain Abnormalities 315
Neuroendocrine Factors 317

Psychological Theories of Mood Disorders 319

Behavioral Theories 319
Cognitive Theories 321

Psychodynamic Theories 324
Interpersonal Theories 325

Social Perspectives on Mood Disorders 327

The Cohort Effect in Depression 327
Social Status 328
Cross-Cultural Differences 328

Mood Disorders Treatments 330

Biological Treatments for Mood Disorders 330
■ *Taking Psychology Personally: Primary Care Physicians Treating Depression 333*

Psychological Treatments for Depression 336
Comparisons of Cognitive-Behavioral, Interpersonal, and Drug Therapies 342
Depression Prevention 343

Chapter Integration 345

Extraordinary People: Follow-Up 346

Chapter Summary 346

Key Terms 348

10 Suicide 351

Extraordinary People—William Styron: *Darkness Visible* 352

Defining and Measuring Suicide 353

Types of Suicide 353
Suicide Rates 354

Understanding Suicide 359

Suicide Notes 359

Social Perspectives on Suicide   361
Psychological Theories of Suicide   363
Biological Theories of Suicide   366

Treating and Preventing Suicidal Tendencies   367

■ *Taking Psychology Personally: What to Do If a Friend Is Suicidal   368*

Drug Treatments   368
Psychological Treatments   369
Social Approaches and Prevention   369

Chapter Integration   371

Extraordinary People: Follow-Up   372

Chapter Summary   372
Key Terms   373

11 Schizophrenia   375

Extraordinary People—John Nash: *A Beautiful Mind*   376

■ *Taking Psychology Personally: Helping Families Cope with Schizophrenia   380*

Symptoms, Diagnosis, and Prognosis of Schizophrenia   380

Symptoms   380
Diagnosis   389
Prognosis   392

Biological Theories of Schizophrenia   394

Genetic Contributors to Schizophrenia   394
Structural Brain Abnormalities   397
Birth Complications   399
Prenatal Viral Exposure   399
Neurotransmitters   399
An Integrative Model   401

Psychosocial Perspectives on Schizophrenia   402

Social Drift and Urban Birth   402
Stress and Relapse   403
Psychodynamic Theories   403
Communication Patterns   404
Expressed Emotion   404
Cognitive and Behavioral Perspectives   405
Cross-Cultural Perspectives   406

Treatments for Schizophrenia   407

Biological Treatments: Drug Therapy   407
Psychological and Social Treatments   409

Chapter Integration   414

Extraordinary People: Follow-Up   415

Chapter Summary   416
Key Terms   417

12 Personality Disorders   421

Extraordinary People—Susanna Kaysen: *Girl, Interrupted*   422

Defining and Diagnosing Personality Disorders   423

Problems with the DSM Categories   424
■ *Taking Psychology Personally: Seeing Yourself in the Personality Disorders   425*

Gender and Ethnic Biases in Construction and Application   426

Odd-Eccentric Personality Disorders   428

Paranoid Personality Disorder   428
Schizoid Personality Disorder   431
Schizotypal Personality Disorder   432

Dramatic-Emotional Personality Disorders   435

Antisocial Personality Disorder   435
Borderline Personality Disorder   440
Histrionic Personality Disorder   444
Narcissistic Personality Disorder   445

Anxious-Fearful Personality Disorders   447

Avoidant Personality Disorder   447
Dependent Personality Disorder   449
Obsessive-Compulsive Personality Disorder   451

Alternative Conceptualizations of Personality Disorders   452

Five-Factor Model   453
Evaluations of Dimensional Models   454

Chapter Integration   454

Extraordinary People: Follow-Up   455

Chapter Summary   456

Key Terms   457

13 Childhood Disorders   459

Extraordinary People—Temple Grandin: *Thinking in Pictures*   460

Behavior Disorders   464

Attention-Deficit/Hyperactivity Disorder   464
Conduct Disorder and Oppositional Defiant Disorder   470

Separation Anxiety Disorder   478

Biological Contributors to Separation Anxiety Disorder   479

Psychological and Sociocultural Contributors to Separation Anxiety Disorder   480
Treatments for Separation Anxiety Disorder   481

Elimination Disorders   483

Enuresis   483
Encopresis   484

Disorders of Cognitive, Motor, and Communication Skills   485

Learning Disorders   485
Motor Skills Disorder   486
Communication Disorders   487
Causes and Treatment of Disorders of Cognitive, Motor, and Communication Skills   487

■ *Taking Psychology Personally: College Students with Mental Disorders*   488

Mental Retardation   488

Biological Causes of Mental Retardation   490
Social Contributors to Mental Retardation   493
Treatments for Mental Retardation   493

Pervasive Developmental Disorders   496

The Diagnosis of Autism   498
Pervasive Developmental Disorders Other Than Autism   499
Contributors to Autism   500
Treatments for Autism   502

Chapter Integration   503

Extraordinary People: Follow-Up   504

Chapter Summary   504

Key Terms   506

14 Cognitive Disorders and Life-Span Issues 509

Extraordinary People—Iris Murdoch: *Elegy for Iris* 510

Dementia 512

Symptoms of Dementia 513
Types of Dementia 515
Treatments for Dementia 522
The Impact of Gender and Culture on Dementia 522
■ *Taking Psychology Personally: How Does Dementia Affect Caregivers?* 524

Delirium 525

Causes of Delirium 526
Treatments for Delirium 527

Amnesia 527

Mental Disorders in Later Life 529

Anxiety Disorders 529
Depression 530
Substance Use Disorders 532

Chapter Integration 534

Extraordinary People: Follow-Up 535

Chapter Summary 536
Key Terms 537

15 Eating Disorders 539

Extraordinary People—Diana, Princess of Wales 540

Anorexia Nervosa 544

Diagnosis, Prevalence, and Prognosis of Anorexia Nervosa 544
Types of Anorexia Nervosa 545

Bulimia Nervosa 547

Cultural and Historical Trends 550

Binge-Eating Disorder 552

Understanding Eating Disorders 553

Biological Theories 553
Sociocultural and Psychological Factors 554

Treatments for Eating Disorders 562

Psychotherapy for Anorexia Nervosa 562
■ *Taking Psychology Personally: Is There Such a Thing as a Healthy Diet?* 564
Psychotherapy for Bulimia Nervosa 564
Biological Therapies 567

Chapter Integration 567

Extraordinary People: Follow-Up 569

Chapter Summary 569
Key Terms 570

16 Sexual Disorders 573

Extraordinary People—David Reimer: *The Boy Who Was Raised as a Girl* 574

Sexual Dysfunctions 575

The Sexual Response Cycle 576
Sexual Desire Disorders 578
Sexual Arousal Disorders 581
Orgasmic Disorders 582
Sexual Pain Disorders 583
Causes of Sexual Dysfunctions 583
Treatments for Sexual Dysfunctions 590

■ *Taking Psychology Personally: Practicing Safe Sex* 593

Paraphilias 598

Fetishism 600
Sexual Sadism and Sexual Masochism 602
Voyeurism, Exhibitionism, and Frotteurism 602
Pedophilia 603
Causes of Paraphilias 604
Treatments for Paraphilias 605

Gender Identity Disorder 607

Contributors to Gender Identity Disorder 610
Treatments for Gender Identity Disorder 611

Chapter Integration 612

Extraordinary People: Follow-Up 613

Chapter Summary 613

Key Terms 615

17 Substance-Related Disorders 619

Extraordinary People—Celebrity Drug Users 620

Society and Substance Use 621

Definitions of Substance-Related Disorders 623

Intoxication 625
Withdrawal 626
Abuse 626
Dependence 626

Depressants 628

Alcohol 628
Benzodiazepines, Barbiturates, and Inhalants 636

Stimulants 638

Cocaine 640
Amphetamines 641
Nicotine 643
Caffeine 645

Opioids 646

Hallucinogens and PCP 648

Cannabis 650

Club Drugs 651

Theories of Substance Use, Abuse, and Dependence 653

Biological Theories 654
Psychological Theories 656
Sociocultural Approaches 657

Treatments for Substance-Related Disorders 659

Biological Treatments 659
Behavioral and Cognitive Treatments 661
Alcoholics Anonymous 664
Prevention Programs for College Students 666
Gender-Sensitive Treatment Programs 667

Chapter Integration 668

■ *Taking Psychology Personally: Tips for Responsible Drinking* 669

Extraordinary People: Follow-Up 669

Chapter Summary   670

Key Terms   672

18 Mental Health and the Law   675

Extraordinary People—One Family's Struggle with Schizophrenia and the "System"   676

Judgments About People Accused of Crimes   678

Competence to Stand Trial   679
Insanity Defense   679

Involuntary Commitment and Civil Rights   685

Civil Commitment   685
Civil Rights   690

Clinicians' Duties to Clients and Society   691

Chapter Integration   692

■ *Taking Psychology Personally: Guidelines for Ethical Service to Culturally Diverse Populations   693*

Extraordinary People: Follow-Up   694

Chapter Summary   695

Key Terms   696

Glossary   G-1

References   R-1

Credits   C-1

Name Index   NI-1

Subject Index   SI-1

Abnormal Psychology, fourth edition, is about people— people who suffer and struggle and sometimes triumph over their mental-health problems. Beginning with the first edition of this book, my goal has been to bring readers face to face with people diagnosed with mental disorders, to increase their understanding and compassion. The voices of these people are heard loudly and clearly throughout this book, giving us glimpses of the personal experience of mental disorders. I have also dealt directly with the fact that many readers of this book will have experienced mental disorders in themselves or close family members or friends. These concerns with the personal experience of mental disorders continue in the fourth edition.

As our understanding and treatment of many types of abnormality progress, we are beginning to understand how biological and psychosocial factors interact to create psychological disorders. These interactions are a major focus of *Abnormal Psychology*. In this edition, I have highlighted theoretical models and new research that integrate biological and psychosocial approaches to mental disorders. I have also incorporated research on how biological treatments affect psychosocial functioning and how psychosocial treatments change biological processes. As a result, *Abnormal Psychology*, fourth edition, provides readers with the most advanced integrative perspectives in the field.

EMPHASIS ON EMPIRICAL RESEARCH

Empirical research is the gold standard for evaluating theories and treatments of mental disorders. In *Abnormal Psychology*, fourth edition, I have updated the reviews of research on theories and treatments for each disorder. Moreover, I have stated clearly when particular theories or treatments have not been supported empirically or have not been tested adequately. These reviews of recent research have benefited greatly from the many pre-prints and in-press manuscripts sent to me by some of the most respected researchers in the field. As a result, I have been able to provide readers with a sense of what the best and brightest researchers believe is the most important new work and where the field is going.

EMPHASIS ON INTEGRATION

Students often come to a course in abnormal psychology asking whether mental disorders are the result of biological factors *or* psychosocial factors. It is increasingly clear that this is the wrong question and that both biological and psychosocial factors are involved in most disorders. I highlighted integrative models of biological and psychosocial factors in previous editions of this book, but, in the fourth edition, these integrative models are central. In every chapter, a new section called *Chapter Integration* describes an integrative approach to the disorders discussed in that chapter and illustrates this approach with a new figure. In addition, specific disorders are often discussed in terms of integrative bio-psycho-social models. Thus, the fourth edition features an enhanced emphasis on how biology, psychology, and social contexts come together to create vulnerability to disorders.

EMPHASIS ON CLARITY

I have always attempted to write clearly, so that readers can comprehend the vast array of theories, research, and treatments available for various disorders. This emphasis on clarity continues in the fourth edition. Because students sometimes find biological theories and research especially difficult to understand, in this edition I have made a major effort to make this material clear and comprehensible. Toward this end, throughout the book I have added small diagrams of the brain, highlighting structures in which abnormalities have been associated with a particular disorder. These standardized illustrations will help students learn the parts of the brain and identify areas relevant to particular disorders.

EMPHASIS ON CULTURE AND GENDER

Beginning with the first edition of *Abnormal Psychology*, I have tried to help readers understand how culture and gender play a role in mental disorders, influencing people's vulnerability to a disorder, expression of a disorder, or response to treatment. I have relied as much as possible on empirical research in describing how culture and gender impact a disorder. In the fourth edition, I have updated the discussions of the research on culture and gender and have highlighted new debates, such as the debate on how culture influences the diagnosis of personality disorders. As always, my coverage of gender and cultural issues is not marginalized into "boxes" but is integrated as critical material readers should know about the disorders being discussed.

EMPHASIS ON UNDERSTANDING PERSONAL EXPERIENCE

Whenever I teach abnormal psychology, students approach me to talk about their own experience with mental disorders in their family, friends, or themselves. Often, these students begin by saying, "I've never told anyone else at school this, but . . ." They have many questions and concerns about these experiences—what can be done to help them, what it means for their future, how they can be supportive of family members or friends who suffer from a mental disorder.

I want students to come away from this book with the power of knowledge. I want them to be empowered not to suffer in silence, feeling victimized and helpless, but to understand better the sources of their distress and to make good choices that help them overcome this suffering. This knowledge comes, in part, from learning about research on explanations and treatments for disorders.

In addition, the feature titled *Taking Psychology Personally* directly addresses the personal questions and concerns students bring to a course on abnormal psychology, such as questions on how to find a therapist and how to support a loved one. In consultation with the major organizations that serve mental-health consumers (such as the American Psychological Association), I present ideas for how students can think about the meaning of the research they are reading for their own lives and how they can find appropriate help for their concerns.

EMPHASIS ON THE VOICES OF PEOPLE WITH DISORDERS

How can students understand what it is like to suffer from a mental disorder? They can read the crite-ria for diagnosing the disorder. But these criteria are often no more than lists of symptoms that are foreign and incomprehensible to students. In each chapter of this book, I let people who have experienced these symptoms describe them in their own words. Every chapter of the fourth edition begins with the feature *Extraordinary People*, which highlights the experiences of people who suffer from mental disorders and gives us a window into the hearts and minds of these people. Some of these extraordinary people, including Nobelist John Nash and psychology researcher and professor Kay Redfield Jamison, have achieved tremendous success despite their mental disorders. Others have led more ordinary lives, which in itself is a great accomplishment for people with serious mental disorders. These stories take students far beyond lists of diagnostic criteria and into the subjective experience of a disorder.

Also, within the text of each chapter are features called *Voices*, first-person accounts from people with mental disorders. These quotes give students a subjective sense of the symptoms of each disorder, allowing people who suffer these symptoms to describe their experiences. The quotes also illustrate key points about a disorder, such as how it affects the functioning of the individual or his or her family members or friends. This feature helps students get inside the experiences of people with mental disorders to gain a deeper understanding of the symptoms and the impact of the symptoms on people's lives.

MAJOR CHANGES ACROSS ALL CHAPTERS IN THE FOURTH EDITION

The fourth edition of *Abnormal Psychology* includes a number of major changes that were implemented in all chapters. These changes, some of which I have already mentioned, reflect a greater emphasis on integrated approaches to abnormal psychology and a concerted effort to make biological information clear to students.

1. *Integrative bio-psycho-social models* of mental disorders are featured in each chapter of the fourth edition. Where appropriate, these models are discussed and illustrated with regard to individual disorders. Then, at the end of each chapter, a new section called *Chapter Integration* describes an integrative approach to the group of disorders discussed in that chapter and illustrates this approach with a new figure. Color-coding helps students distinguish among the biological, psychological, and social factors in these figures and others.
2. *Extraordinary People,* a feature that usually highlights an individual diagnosed with a mental disorder, now opens and closes each chapter. The individual's own words and experiences introduce the characteristics of a mental disorder discussed in the chapter. Where appropriate, I refer to that individual in the chapter to illustrate important points about the disorder, its causes and treatments. At the end of the chapter, the *Extraordinary People* follow-up gives the reader a sense of how the individual is living with the mental disorder and its consequences. In some cases, the individual highlighted in *Extraordinary People* is a celebrity; in others, he or she is generally unknown but provides a compelling account of living with a mental disorder.
3. New *standardized brain diagrams* in most chapters help students understand which parts of the brain are implicated in a disorder. These small diagrams of the brain highlight areas where abnormalities have been associated with a particular disorder. These standardized illustrations will help students learn the parts of the brain and identify areas relevant to particular disorders.
4. The *biological theories* of mental disorders and evidence for these theories have been thoroughly updated. I have also rewritten much of the material on biological approaches to make it more accessible.
5. *Concept Overviews* in each chapter highlight, summarize, and illustrate the main "take-home" messages about theories of and treatments for disorders. Some of these *Concept Overviews* are tables; others are figures.
6. The *Chapter Summary* now includes references to relevant *Concept Overviews,* tables, and figures. These references point students to the summary material that will be most helpful in reviewing the material.

PROVEN FEATURES RETAINED IN THE FOURTH EDITION

Instructors and students liked a number of features in the third edition of *Abnormal Psychology.* I have kept—and strengthened—these popular features in the fourth edition:

1. *Taking Psychology Personally* addresses in each chapter the personal issues and questions students often bring to a course on abnormal psychology. Some examples include how to look for a therapist, how to cope with a family member who has a mental disorder, and what to do if a friend is suicidal.
2. *Voices* excerpts bring alive the characteristics of mental disorders in the words of people who live with them.
3. *Case Studies* illustrate the disorders, possible contributors to the disorders, and treatments for the disorders.
4. Several *learning tools* help students identify the most important information, organize it, understand it, and remember it:
    - **a.** A *Chapter Overview* at the beginning of each chapter previews and frames the main sections of the chapter, including the *Chapter Integration* section.
    - **b.** *Summing Up* provides a bulleted summary of key points at the end of each major section.

c. *DSM-IV-TR tables* list the symptoms and criteria for diagnosis of each major disorder.

d. *Concept Overviews* summarize key material in table form or as figures, which provide a more visual summary.

e. *Key Terms* are listed at the end of each chapter, with page references, for easy review.

CHAPTER-BY-CHAPTER CHANGES IN THE FOURTH EDITION

In addition to the major changes across all the chapters, I have made the following key changes in individual chapters:

Chapter 1: Looking at Abnormality

■ Added a discussion of how various criteria for abnormality can be summarized and remembered as the 3Ds: distress, dysfunction, and deviance

■ Expanded and updated the discussion of managed care

Chapter 2: Contemporary Theories of Abnormality

■ Revised the sections on biological theories for greater clarity and added new figures on the brain and other biological systems

■ Added more information on the empirical support for various theories

Chapter 3: The Research Endeavor

■ Clarified the meanings and roles of theory and hypothesis in the scientific method

■ Added a section on epidemiological research

■ Added discussions of prevalence and incidence

■ Added a section on single-case experimental designs

■ Added discussions of efficacy and effectiveness in therapy outcome research

■ Added a section on meta-analysis

Chapter 4: Assessing and Diagnosing Abnormality

■ Revised the *Extraordinary People* feature to focus on Michael J. Fox's autobiography and used examples from this autobiography throughout the chapter to illustrate how clinicians would assess his symptoms

■ Expanded and updated sections on neuroimaging technologies in assessment

■ Expanded and updated section on concerns about the DSM-IV-TR

■ Added a section in differential diagnosis

Chapter 5: Treatments for Abnormality

■ Added a section on the multiple caregivers often involved in the treatment of an individual diagnosed with a mental disorder

■ Updated the section on herbal medicines to reflect recent evidence questioning their safety and efficacy

■ Added a section on repetitive transcranial magnetic stimulation

■ Revised the section on evaluating therapies for greater clarity and to reflect recent critiques of the lack of data on the efficacy of therapies across ethnic groups

■ Added a discussion of recent concerns about the safety of antidepressant drugs for children and adolescents

Chapter 6: Stress Disorders and Health Psychology

■ Integrated material on the effects of stress on physical health (formerly in Chapter 18) with material on posttraumatic stress disorder (formerly in Chapter 7) to create one chapter on stress-related disorders

■ Expanded the discussion of acute stress disorder

■ Added a discussion of adjustment disorder

■ Added information on PTSD in the survivors of recent disasters and wars

- Updated the section on the biological factors in PTSD to reflect substantial new research in this field, including on the role of early childhood trauma on the development of the physiological stress response

Chapter 7: Anxiety Disorders

- Gathered material on all anxiety disorders except PTSD into this chapter
- Clarified the distinctions between adaptive fear and maladaptive anxiety
- Added a discussion of the role of interoceptive awareness in panic disorder
- Added a discussion of the role of negative reinforcement in phobias
- Reduced the number of *Voices* segments in the section on obsessive-compulsive disorder to improve the flow of that section

Chapter 8: Somatoform and Dissociative Disorders

- Reversed the order of discussion of somatoform and dissociative disorders, so that the more typical disorders are discussed first
- Clarified the distinctions among malingering, factitious disorders, and psychosomatic disorders
- Updated the section on the repressed or false memory debate

Chapter 9: Mood Disorders

- Updated epidemiology based on new data from the National Comorbidity Survey
- Added a section on the neurobiological changes accompanying early abuse that could contribute to risk for mood disorders
- Added a discussion of the role of excessive reassurance seeking in depression
- Added discussions of repetitive transcranial magnetic stimulation in the treatment of depression

- Added a section on vagus nerve stimulation in the treatment of depression

Chapter 10: Suicide

- Updated epidemiology of suicide with new data from the Centers for Disease Control and Prevention and the World Health Organization

Chapter 11: Schizophrenia

- Added a discussion of research on smooth pursuit eye movement in schizophrenia
- Added a discussion of deficits in working memory in schizophrenia
- Added a discussion of the integrative model of Barch on how neuropsychological deficits may contribute to schizophrenia
- Condensed the discussion on older and unsupported theories of schizophrenia

Chapter 12: Personality Disorders

- Emphasized empirically supported theories and treatments for personality disorders and deemphasized unsupported theories and treatments
- Clarified the distinction between antisocial personality disorder and psychopathy
- Expanded the discussions of problems with the DSM-IV-TR conceptualization of personality disorders, including possible gender and cultural bias
- Emphasized the trend toward dimensional models of personality disorders

Chapter 13: Childhood Disorders

- Added a section on college students coping with mental disorders
- Expanded the discussion of the subtypes of attention-deficit/hyperactivity disorder,

including information on the role of sluggish cognitive tempo

- Expanded the discussion of the distinctions between conduct disorder and oppositional defiant disorder
- Added a section on Asperger's disorder

Chapter 14: Cognitive Disorders and Life-Span Issues

- Added information on the causes of and treatments for Alzheimer's disorder

Chapter 15: Eating Disorders

- Expanded the section on binge-eating disorder
- Updated the research on social pressures toward eating disorders, including new experimental work
- Added a discussion of dieting subtype versus depressive subtype binge eating
- Reorganized and updated the section on the psychosocial factors in eating disorders

Chapter 16: Sexual Disorders

- Extensively revised the entire chapter to reflect new research and treatments
- Expanded the discussion of the role of Viagra and similar drugs in the treatment of sexual dysfunctions
- Clarified the role of sex therapy in the psychotherapy of sexual dysfunction
- Added a discussion of the history of thought on homosexuality
- Clarified the characteristics of the paraphilias
- Substantially updated the section on gender identity disorder

Chapter 17: Substance-Related Disorders

- Updated epidemiology and historical trends of drug use
- Added a section on club drugs

- Expanded the discussion of the role of GABA in drug effects
- Expanded and updated the section on the explanations for gender differences in alcohol use

Chapter 18: Mental Health and the Law

- Added a discussion of the "Zoloft defense" as a type of insanity defense
- Added new data on violence among people with mental illness

SUPPLEMENTS

The text has an outstanding ancillary package to support student learning and classroom teaching.

For the Student

Student Study Guide (prepared by Jennifer Boothby, Indiana State University)   This study tool provides students with a comprehensive review of the material in the textbook. Each chapter of the study guide includes learning objectives, a list of essential ideas from each chapter, a guided review through all of the major sections, a 20-item practice multiple-choice exam with answers, and a practice essay exam with answers.

MindMap Student CD-ROM   A rich resource for students, this CD-ROM includes short video excerpts from McGraw-Hill's *Faces of Abnormal Psychology* series and other sources with wrap-around pedagogy, interactive exercises, chapter quizzes, and other valuable tools to help students master the concepts of abnormal psychology.

Online Learning Center for Students (updated by Gail Edmunds)   The official Web site for the text contains PowerWeb articles, *New York Times* news feeds, chapter outlines, practice quizzes that can be e-mailed to the professor, key term flashcards, interactive exercises, Internet activities, Web links to relevant abnormal psychology sites, an Internet primer, a career appendix, and a statistics primer. www.mhhe.com/nolen4

PowerWeb   This unique online tool provides students with current articles, curriculum-based materials, weekly updates with assessment, informative and timely world news, refereed Web links, research tools, study tools, and interactive exercises. A PowerWeb access password is bound into the front of each new copy of the text.

For the Instructor

Instructor's Manual (revised by Linda Raasch, Normandale Community College, and NiCole Buchanan, Michigan State University)   This comprehensive guide includes an overview of each chapter, learning objectives, suggestions and resources for lecture topics, classroom activities, projects, suggestions for video and multimedia lecture enhancements, and a media integration guide to help link the electronic resources to the syllabus. For this edition, NiCole Buchanan has provided ideas for addressing in the classroom differences in gender and culture that affect the way individuals experience psychological disorders in a diverse society. The *Instructor's Manual* is available on the password-protected Instructor's Center of the text Web site and on the *Instructor's Resource CD-ROM.*

Test Item File (revised by Brenda Flippen, Durham Technical Community College)   Available on the *Instructor's Resource CD-ROM,* the *Test Item File* provides a wide variety of book-specific test questions. Available as Word files, the questions in the *Test Item File* are also provided in EZ Test. McGraw-Hill's EZ Test is a flexible and easy-to-use electronic testing program that allows instructors to create tests from book-specific items. It accommodates a wide range of question types and allows instructors to add their own questions. Multiple versions of a test can be created and any test can be exported for use with course management systems such as WebCT, BlackBoard, or PageOut. EZ Test Online is a new service that gives instructors a place to easily administer EZ Test–created exams and quizzes online. The program is available for Windows and Macintosh environments.

PowerPoint Lectures (revised by Crystal Park, University of Connecticut, Storrs)   Available on the text Web site as well as on the *Instructor's Resource CD-ROM,* these presentations cover the key points of the chapter and include graphics. Helpful lecture guidelines are provided in the "notes" section for each slide. They can be used as-is or modified to meet the instructor's needs.

Classroom Performance System (CPS)   The Classroom Performance System (CPS) from **eInstruction** allows instructors to gauge immediately what students are learning during lectures. With CPS, instructors can ask questions, take polls, or host classroom demonstrations and get instant feedback. In addition, CPS makes it easy to take attendance, give and grade pop quizzes, or give formal, paper-based class tests with multiple versions of the test using CPS for immediate grading.

For instructors who want to use CPS in their classroom, McGraw-Hill is pleased to offer text-specific multiple-choice questions and polling questions created by Elisabeth Sherwin (University of Arkansas, Little Rock) for in-class use. The questions are available on the *Instructor's Resource CD-ROM* and can be downloaded from the Web site for *Abnormal Psychology,* fourth edition.

Instructor's Resource CD-ROM   This comprehensive CD-ROM includes the *Instructor's Manual, Test Item Files,* PowerPoint slides, CPS questions, and an image gallery. An easy-to-use interface is provided for the design and delivery of multimedia classroom presentations.

Faces of Abnormal Psychology, **Volumes I and II**   This series of 20 8- to 10-minute video short clips suitable for classroom viewing is available on DVD and VHS for instructors who adopt this text. Each video features an interview with an individual who has experienced a mental disorder. Schizophrenia, posttraumatic stress disorder, bulimia nervosa, obsessive-compulsive disorder, and Asperger's disorder are some of the conditions covered.

Taking Sides: Clashing Views on Controversial Issues in Abnormal Psychology   This debate-style reader introduces students to controversial viewpoints on important issues in the field. Each topic is carefully framed for students, and the pro and con essays represent the arguments of leading scholars and commentators in their fields. An instructor's guide containing testing materials is also available.

Online Learning Center for Instructors The password-protected instructor side of the text Web site contains the *Instructor's Manual,* a sample chapter from the text, PowerPoint presentations, Web links, *New York Times News* feeds, and other teaching resources. www.mhhe.com/nolen4

PageOut™ With this tool from McGraw-Hill, instructors can build their own course Web sites in less than an hour. PageOut™ requires no prior knowledge of HTML, no long hours of coding, and no design skills. With PageOut™, even the most inexperienced computer user can quickly and easily create a professional-looking course Web site. Instructors simply fill in templates with their information and with content provided by McGraw-Hill, then choose a design, to create a Web site specifically designed for their course. Instructors can visit www.pageout.net to find out more about this free course management system.

Populated **WebCT and Blackboard** course cartridges are also available for use with this text. Instructors should contact their McGraw-Hill sales representative for details.

ACKNOWLEDGMENTS

I greatly appreciate the hard work and creativity of the McGraw-Hill staff who have contributed to this fourth edition. I especially wish to thank Anne Reid for her careful and patient editing of the manuscript, as well as for her creativity in helping me develop new features for this edition. I also wish to thank Judith Kromm, John Wannemacher, Melissa Caughlin, Laura Kuhn, Emily Hatteberg, Laurie Entringer, Emma Ghiselli, Nora Agbayani, Alex Rohrs, Stephanie George, Louis Swaim, and Carol Bielski at McGraw-Hill. Laura Lawrie coordinated the development of the supplements. I also thank Richard Liu and Thomas Flanagan for being diligent research assistants during this revision.

Many colleagues reviewed sections of the book and provided invaluable feedback for the fourth edition. My heartfelt thanks go to

Carol Shaw Austad
Central Connecticut State University

Jason Bowman
University of Florida, Gainesville

Seth Brown
University of Northern Iowa

Michael Connor
California State University, Long Beach

Miriam Ehrenberg
John Jay College, CUNY

Timothy R. Elliott
University of Alabama, Birmingham

Tom Ersfeld
Central Lakes College

Marc Feldman
University of Alabama, Birmingham (retired)

Karen Freiberg
University of Maryland, Baltimore County

Debra Hollister
Valencia Community College

Gloria Lawrence
Wayne State College

Dianne Leader
Georgia Institute of Technology

Karsten Look
Columbus State University

Terri Messman-Moore
Miami University of Ohio

Kurt Michael
Appalachian State University

Crystal Park
University of Connecticut, Storrs

Karen Pfost
Illinois State University

Brady Phelps
South Dakota State University

Mirjam Quinn
Purdue University

Linda Raasch
Normandale Community College

Kim Renk
University of Central Florida

Carolyn Roecker Phelps
University of Dayton

Esther Rothblum
University of Vermont

David Sbarra
University of Arizona

Glenn Shean
College of William
and Mary

Elisabeth Sherwin
University of Arkansas,
Little Rock

**Persephanie
Silverthorn**
University of New
Orleans

Ari Solmon
Williams College

Marian Underwood
University of Texas
at Dallas

As always, my family provided tremendous support as I worked on this edition, particularly given that we moved halfway across the country just before work on the revision began. I thank Richard Nolen-Hoeksema and Michael Hoeksema, John Nolen, and Renze and Marjorie Hoeksema.

Susan Nolen-Hoeksema
New Haven, Connecticut

Susan Nolen-Hoeksema, Ph.D., is professor of psychology at Yale University. She has also been a professor at Stanford University and the University of Michigan. She received her B.A. from Yale University and her Ph.D. from the University of Pennsylvania. Her research focuses on mood regulation and on gender differences in psychopathology. The recipient of two major teaching awards, Professor Nolen-Hoeksema has received research funding from the National Institutes of Health, the National Science Foundation, and the William T. Grant Foundation. She was awarded the Leadership Award from the Committee on Women, as well as the Early Career Award from the American Psychological Association. She lives near New Haven, Connecticut, with her husband, Richard, and her son, Michael.

Abnormal Psychology: The Intersection of Science and Humanity

Challenging Material with Pedagogy that Motivates Learning

Sometimes students find it difficult to appreciate the scientific side of abnormal psychology as well as the human side. Susan Nolen-Hoeksema took special care to make the content as clear and precise as possible and to provide engaging pedagogy that promotes understanding of abnormal psychology as a science.

TABLE 12.3 Concept Overview

Dramatic-Emotional Personality Disorders

People with dramatic-emotional personality disorders tend to have unstable emotions and to engage in dramatic and impulsive behavior.

Label	Key Features	Similar Disorders on Axis I
Antisocial personality disorder	Pervasive pattern of criminal, impulsive, callous, or ruthless behavior; disregard for the rights of others; no respect for social norms	Conduct disorder (diagnosed in children)
Borderline personality disorder	Rapidly shifting and unstable mood, self-concept, and interpersonal relationships; impulsive behavior; transient dissociative states; self-effacement	Mood disorders
Histrionic personality disorder	Rapidly shifting moods, unstable relationships, and intense need for attention and approval; dramatic, seductive behavior	Somatoform disorders, mood disorders
Narcissistic personality disorder	Grandiose thoughts and feelings of one's own worth; obliviousness to others' needs; exploitative, arrogant demeanor	Manic symptoms

Source: Reprinted with permission from the *Diagnostic and Statistical Manual of Mental Disorders*, Fourth Edition, Text Revision. Copyright © 2000 American Psychiatric Association.

CONCEPT REVIEW TABLES AND FIGURES

summarize the major conceptual points, such as the leading theories of what causes a disorder and the principal treatment options. These visual displays organize the material in ways that make it easier to retain.

TABLE 12.1 DSM-IV-TR

Personality Disorders

The DSM-IV-TR groups personality disorders into three clusters.

Cluster A: Odd-Eccentric Personality Disorders

People with these disorders have symptoms similar to those of people with schizophrenia, including inappropriate or flat affect, odd thought and speech patterns, and paranoia. People with these disorders maintain their grasp on reality, however.

Cluster B: Dramatic-Emotional Personality Disorders

People with these disorders tend to be manipulative, volatile, and uncaring in social relationships. They are prone to impulsive, sometimes violent behaviors that show little regard for their own safety or the safety or needs of others.

Cluster C: Anxious-Fearful Personality Disorders

People with these disorders are extremely concerned about being criticized or abandoned by others and, thus, have dysfunctional relationships with others.

Source: Reprinted with permission from the *Diagnostic and Statistical Manual of Mental Disorders*, Fourth Edition, Text Revision. Copyright © 2000 American Psychiatric Association.

DSM-IV-TR TABLES list the symptoms and diagnostic criteria of each major disorder.

CASE STUDIES illustrate the disorders, possible contributing factors to the disorders, and treatments for the disorders.

CASE STUDY

Debbie was a 26-year-old woman who worked as a salesclerk in a trendy clothing store and who sought therapy for panic disorder with agoraphobia. She dressed flamboyantly, with an elaborate and dramatic hairdo. Her appearance was especially striking, since she was quite short (under 5 feet tall) and at least 75 pounds overweight. She wore sunglasses indoors throughout the evaluation and constantly fiddled with them, taking them on and off nervously and waving them to emphasize a point. She cried loudly and dramatically at various points in the interview, going through large numbers of tissue. She continually asked for reassurance. ("Will I be OK?" "Can I get over this?") She talked nonstop throughout the evaluation. When gently interrupted by the evaluator, she was very apologetic, laughing and saying, "I know I talk too much"; yet she continued to do so throughout the session.

SUMMING UP

- People diagnosed with the odd-eccentric personality disorders—paranoid, schizoid, and schizotypal personality disorders—have odd thought processes, emotional reactions, and behaviors similar to those of people with schizophrenia, but they retain their grasp on reality.
- People diagnosed with paranoid personality disorder are chronically suspicious of others but maintain their grasp on reality.
- People diagnosed with schizoid personality disorder are emotionally cold and distant from others and have great trouble forming interpersonal relationships.
- People diagnosed with schizotypal personality disorder have a variety of odd beliefs and perceptual experiences but maintain their grasp on reality.
- These personality disorders, especially schizotypal personality disorder, have been linked to familial histories of schizophrenia and some of the biological abnormalities of schizophrenia.

SUMMING UP SECTIONS provide a bulleted review of key points at the end of each major section in a chapter.

CHAPTER INTEGRATIONS at the end of each chapter emphasize how biology, psychology, and social context come together to create vulnerability to disorders and illustrate this approach with a figure.

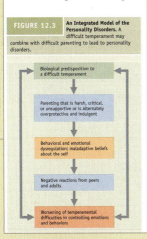

CHAPTER INTEGRATION

Although the empirical research on the personality disorders is too lacking to allow a clear integration

> **FIGURE 12.3**　**An Integrated Model of the Personality Disorders.** A difficult temperament may combine with difficult parenting to lead to personality disorders.
>
> Biological predisposition to a difficult temperament
> ↓
> Parenting that is harsh, critical, or unsupportive or is alternately overprotective and indulgent
> ↓
> Behavioral and emotional dysregulation; maladaptive beliefs about the self
> ↓
> Negative reactions from peers and adults
> ↓
> Worsening of temperamental difficulties in controlling emotions and behaviors

of the biological, psychological, and social factors impinging on these disorders, some theoretical models have attempted this integration. They serve as the basis for current research (Millon et al., 2000; Siever & Davis, 1991; Trull & Durrett, 2005). According to these models, at the root of many of the personality disorders may be a biological predisposition to a certain kind of difficult temperament (see Figure 12.3).

For example, in the case of avoidant, dependent, and obsessive-compulsive personality disorders, an anxious and fearful temperament may be involved. In narcissistic and antisocial personality disorders, an impulsive and aggressive temperament may contribute. In borderline and histrionic personality disorders, a unstable, overly emotional temperament may be involved.

Children born with any of these temperaments are difficult to parent effectively. If parents can be supportive of these children yet set appropriate limits on their behavior, the children may never develop severe enough behavior or emotional problems to be diagnosed with a personality disorder. If parents are unable to counteract children's temperamental vulnerabilities or if they exacerbate these vulnerabilities with harsh, critical, unsupportive parenting or overprotective, indulgent parenting, then the children's temperamental vulnerabilities may grow into severe behavior and emotional problems, as well as maladaptive beliefs about the self. These problems will influence how others—teachers, peers, and eventually employers and mates—interact with the individuals, perhaps in ways that further exacerbate their temperamental vulnerabilities.

In this way, a lifelong pattern of dysfunction, called a personality disorder, may emerge out of the interaction between a child's biologically based temperament and others' reactions to that temperament.

Extraordinary People

Susanna Kaysen: *Girl, Interrupted*

Susanna Kaysen was 18 and depressed, drifting through life and endlessly oppositional toward her parents and teachers. She tried to commit suicide. She began having strange perceptions:

> I was having a problem with patterns. Oriental rugs, tile floors, printed curtains, things like that. Supermarkets were especially bad, because of the long, hypnotic checkerboard aisles. When I looked at these things, I saw other things within them. That sounds as though I was hallucinating, and I wasn't. I knew I was looking at a floor or a curtain. But all patterns seemed to contain potential representations, which in a dizzying array would flicker briefly to life. That could be . . . a forest, a flock of birds, my second grade class picture. Well, it wasn't—it was a rug, or whatever it was, but my glimpses of the other things it might be were exhausting. Reality was getting too dense. (Kaysen, 1993, pp. 40–41)

Kaysen went to see a psychiatrist for a routine evaluation. At the end of one session, he put her in a taxi and sent her to McLean Hospital outside Boston. When she signed herself in, she was told that her stay would be about two weeks. Instead, Kaysen was not released for nearly two years.

Years after she was released from the hospital, Kaysen discovered that her diagnosis had been borderline personality disorder. In her autobiography, *Girl, Interrupted,* she raises many questions about this disorder:

> . . . I had to locate a copy of the *Diagnostic and Statistical Manual of Mental Disorders* and look up Borderline Personality to see what they really thought about me.
>
> It's a fairly accurate picture of me at eighteen, minus a few quirks like reckless driving and eating binges. . . . I'm tempted to try refuting it, but then I would be open to the further charges of "defensiveness" and "resistance."
>
> All I can do is give the particulars: an annotated diagnosis.
>
> . . . "Instability of self-image, interpersonal relationships, and mood . . . uncer-

tainty about . . . long-term goals or career choice. . . ." Isn't this a good description of adolescence? Moody, fickle, faddish, insecure: in short, impossible.

> "Self-mutilating behavior (e.g., wrist-scratching). . . ." I've skipped forward a bit. This is the one that caught me by surprise as I sat on the floor of the bookstore reading my diagnosis. Wrist-scratching! I thought I'd invented it. Wrist-banging, to be precise. . . .
>
> I had a butterfly chair. In the sixties, everyone in Cambridge had a butterfly chair. The metal edge of its upturned seat was perfectly placed for wrist-banging. I had tried breaking ashtrays and walking on the shards, but I didn't have the nerve to tread firmly. Wrist-banging—slow, steady, mindless—was a better solution. It was cumulative injury, so each bang was tolerable. . . .
>
> I spent hours in my butterfly chair banging my wrist. I did it in the evenings, like homework. I'd do some homework, then I'd spend half an hour wrist-banging, then finish my homework, then back in the chair for some more banging before brushing my teeth and going to bed.
>
> I was trying to explain my situation to myself. My situation was that I was in pain and nobody knew it; even I had trouble knowing it. So I told myself, over and over, You are in pain. It was the only way I could get through to myself ("counteract feelings of 'numbness'"). I was demonstrating, externally and irrefutably, an inward condition. . . .

Understanding Brings Compassion and Choices

EXTRAORDINARY PEOPLE VIGNETTES at the beginning of each chapter highlight the experiences of people who suffer from one of the disorders discussed in the chapter. Within the chapter, these vignettes are used to illustrate key points about the disorder. At the end of the chapter, a follow-up section places the chapter content in the personal context of these Extraordinary People.

VOICES quotations throughout each chapter allow individuals to speak from their own experience about their disorder and put a human face on the clinical aspects of abnormal psychology.

compulsions may often seem purposeful, they are not functional. In some cases, the family members of people with OCD become accomplices in the disorder, as did the husband of writer Emily Colas, who has written about her OCD (Colas, 1998, pp. 70–72).

VOICES

> My husband and I generally kept a pile of about twenty garbage bags in one corner of our apartment. Which may seem out of character, for me to let them stay, but it was our trash and I knew nothing bad was in there. It was the communal trash that made me shake. So when it was time to take the bags out to the dumpster, my husband had to follow the whole hygienic procedure. To keep the neighbors' germs out of our place. First the water had to be turned on and left that way because if he touched the garbage and then the spigot, the spigot would get contaminated. Next he'd take one bag in his right hand and open the door with his left. Then he'd shut the door behind him and lock it so that no one could get into the house. I guess I could have monitored, but he wanted me upstairs so I couldn't critique him. He'd take the bag down, stand a few feet from the dumpster to be sure not to touch it, and throw the bag in. Then he'd unlock the door, open it, slip his shoes off, come inside, and wash his hands. He used a pump soap so

that he could use his clean wrist to pump some in the palm of his hand and not contaminate the dispenser. The water would stay on, and he'd move to the next bag. He went through this procedure twenty times, once for each bag, until they were gone.

Theories of OCD

The biological theories of OCD have dominated research in recent years, and they have provided some intriguing hypotheses about its sources. Psychodynamic and cognitive-behavioral theories of OCD have also been proposed. These theories are summarized in the Concept Overview in Table 7.10.

Biological Theories

Biological theories of obsessive-compulsive disorder view it as a neurobiological disorder. Much of this research has focused on a circuit in the brain that is involved in the execution of primitive patterns of behavior, such as aggression, sexuality, and bodily excretion (Baxter et al., 2001; Rapoport, 1990; Saxena & Rauch, 2000). This circuit begins in the orbital region of the frontal cortex (see Figure 7.11). These impulses are then carried to a part of the basal ganglia called the **caudate nucleus,** which allows only the strongest of these impulses to carry through to the thalamus. If these impulses reach the thalamus, the person is motivated to think further about and possibly act on these impulses. The action might involve a set of stereotyped behaviors appropriate to the impulse. Once these behaviors are executed, the impulse diminishes.

Taking Psychology Personally

Seeing Yourself in the Personality Disorders

In Chapter 1, we discussed the tendency for students reading an abnormal psychology textbook to see signs of many mental disorders in themselves or in the people in their lives. Students may be especially prone to see personality disorders in themselves or in others. Indeed, people are considerably more likely to diagnose themselves on self-report questionnaires as having a personality disorder than are clinicians to diagnose them in the context of psychiatric interviews (Weissman, 1993).

Why might this be so? It may occur because people tend to attribute behaviors to personality traits and to ignore the influence of situations on those behaviors (see Ross & Nisbett, 1991). This tendency is often referred to as *fundamental attribution error.*

A classic study demonstrating how strongly people discount situational influences over personality influences was conducted by Jones and Harris (1967). They asked participants to read essays presumably written by other participants. The participants were told that the persons writing the essays had been assigned to present a particular viewpoint on the topic of the essay. For example, they were told that a political science student had been assigned to write an essay defending communism in Cuba or that a debate student had been assigned to attack the proposition that marijuana should be legalized. Despite the fact that the participants were told that the essay writers had been assigned to take a particular viewpoint (and had not chosen that viewpoint), they tended to believe that the essay writers actually held the viewpoint they presented in their essays.

If you think you see signs of one or more personality disorders in yourself or someone close to you, stop and ask yourself the following questions:

■ *What are the situational influences that might be driving my behavior or my friend's or relative's behavior?* For example, let's say that you are concerned that your brother has developed an obsessive-compulsive personality disorder (see pp. 451–452) since he has taken on two jobs to try to help your family with finances. He is preoccupied with schedules and always has lists of things to do; he has become a workaholic; he has become a perfectionist to the point of not being able to get things done; and he has become even more moralistic than he was in high school.
It is true that certain situations can exaggerate the already dysfunctional behaviors of people with obsessive-

compulsive personality disorder. However, consider the possibility that your brother's behaviors, particularly the ones that he has developed since taking these two jobs, are largely driven by the demands of his life rather than by enduring personality traits. Your brother's preoccupation with lists and schedules and his working 20 hours a day are probably behaviors that he believes are necessary, given the demands of the situation. This kind of pressure can cause many people to try to be perfectionists but to become so anxious about the possibility of failing that they cannot do their work. When you find yourself wondering if you or someone you care about has developed a personality disorder, stop to consider the aspects of the situation that might really be responsible for the behaviors you observe.

■ *Am I selectively remembering behaviors that are signs of a personality disorder and selectively forgetting behaviors that contradict the diagnosis of a personality disorder?* One of the strongest reasons people overestimate the influence of personality traits on behaviors is that they selectively pay attention to and remember behaviors that are consistent with personality traits and ignore or forget behaviors that are inconsistent with the traits. For example, if you fear that you are an overly dependent person, you will probably find it quite easy to remember times in the past when you have had trouble making decisions without much advice from others, have felt uncomfortable and helpless when alone, or have been passive in voicing your opinions or needs to others. You will probably forget the many more times when you made decisions with no help from others, actually enjoyed being alone, or spoke up to express your opinions or needs.

It can be helpful to write down all the times in the recent or distant past when you behaved in ways that contradicted the troubling personality trait you think you have. Or you might want to ask a trusted friend to help you sort out whether your behaviors are always consistent with a negative personality trait.

■ *Are the behaviors I am observing part of a longtime pattern of behavior, or do they occur only occasionally?* Most of us occasionally act in dysfunctional or plainly stupid ways. Sometimes, these actions are driven by the situations in which we find ourselves, but sometimes we act in stupid ways even when there is no apparent situational excuse for doing so. A personality disorder is a pattern of behavior that has existed most of a person's life and that the person demonstrates across a range of situations.

(continued)

TAKING PSYCHOLOGY PERSONALLY boxes address personal questions and concerns that sometimes come up in the abnormal psychology course, such as concern about one's own mental health and questions about how to get help for oneself or others.

Electronic Resources to Enhance Teaching and Learning

ONLINE LEARNING CENTER www.mhhe.com/nolen4

STUDENT RESOURCES include chapter outlines and practice quizzes keyed to learning goals, flashcards, interactive review exercises, Abnormal Psychology Box Office guide to related movies, and access, via **PowerWeb**, to current news about psychology, research tools, and other valuable study tools.

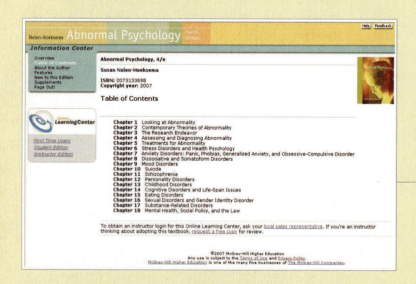

The **MINDMAP CD-ROM** for students comes with new copies of the text. This CD-ROM contains numerous video exercises featuring short excerpts from McGraw-Hill's *Faces of Abnormal Psychology* series and other sources, interactive exercises, chapter quizzes, and other valuable study tools.

> Chapter 1

People Flying
by Peter Sickles

*Who, except the gods, can live time through forever
without any pain.*

—Aeschylus

Looking at Abnormality <

Extraordinary People

- **Clifford Beers:** *A Mind That Found Itself*

Defining Abnormality

The context for a behavior often determines whether it is considered abnormal. Criteria that have been used to determine the abnormality of behaviors are cultural norms for behaviors, how unusual the behaviors are, whether the behaviors cause the person discomfort, the presence of an identifiable illness, and whether the behaviors interfere with the person's functioning. Today, mental-health professionals tend to view behaviors as maladaptive or abnormal if they cause distress or dysfunction or if they are deviant.

Taking Psychology Personally

- **When You Wonder If You Are Abnormal**

Historical Perspectives on Abnormality

Theories of abnormality across the ages have included biological theories, supernatural theories, and psychological theories. In prehistoric times, supernatural theories of abnormality may have dominated, and a primitive form of brain surgery designed to release demons may have been performed. Some of the most ancient writings about abnormality are in Chinese texts from around 2674 B.C. Other prominent writings include the papyri of Egypt and Mesopotamia, the Old Testament, and the works of Greek and Roman philosophers and physicians. In the Middle Ages, many people with mental disorders may have been accused of being witches and killed out of fear. Throughout history, people who acted abnormally have been imprisoned, tortured, or cast out. In the eighteenth and nineteenth centuries, however, several advocates of more gentle treatment of people with mental disorders helped establish facilities where they could be treated with kindness.

The Emergence of Modern Perspectives

Biological and psychosocial theories of abnormality dominate in mainstream science and practice in abnormal psychology. Some people still take their own lay and supernatural theories of abnormality into their interactions with therapists, however.

Modern Mental-Health Care

Major breakthroughs in drug therapies for serious mental disorders in the mid-twentieth century made it possible to move many people out of institutional care and into community-based care. Deinstitutionalization never lived up to its lofty goals, however, because the resources to support people in the community were never adequate. The late twentieth century saw the rise of managed care systems, some of which severely limit access to mental-health care.

Professions Within Abnormal Psychology

Mental-health professionals treat people with psychological problems and do research on these problems. Several professions are available in the field.

Chapter Integration

Modern approaches to abnormality emphasize the integration and interaction of biological, psychological, and social factors.

Extraordinary People

Clifford Beers: *A Mind That Found Itself*

Clifford Beers was always an energetic child, moody with little self-control. Still, he was intelligent and ambitious enough to do well in school and eventually to graduate from a university. Beers' moodiness increased with time, however, particularly after his brother Sam began to have severe convulsive seizures. These seizures were diagnosed as epilepsy (but were probably due to a massive brain tumor discovered after the brother's death). Clifford Beers developed a morbid fear that he would be overcome with epilepsy.

In March 1890, as his brother lay dying in the family home, Beers' moodiness grew to despair, accompanied by deep paranoia. By June, Beers' despair had become so great that he was unable to speak. He began contemplating suicide and eventually jumped out a fourth-floor window. He escaped with only broken bones. Beers' obsession with becoming epileptic passed with this incident but was replaced with other paranoid and grandiose beliefs. Beers was hospitalized, first in a private mental hospital and later in public mental hospitals when his family ran out of money. His mood alternated between depression and manic excitement.

In the early 1900s, there were no drugs that significantly affected symptoms such as those suffered by Clifford Beers. He endured some of the drugs of the day—strychnine and arsenic tonics. He also was beaten; choked; locked away for long periods in dark, cold cells with no clothes; and put in a straitjacket for up to 21 days. Beers wrote volumes about the hospital conditions, describing the need for better care for the "insane." Over those three years of hospitalization, Beers' mood swings became less severe, and in 1903 he was declared recovered enough to be released.

Clifford Beers survived the harsh treatment he received in early twentieth-century mental hospitals and recovered from his symptoms of fear, depression, and paranoia, perhaps despite these treatments. Later in this chapter, we will pick up the story of Clifford Beers and will see how he transformed his terrible experience into a social movement to improve the treatment of people with mental-health problems. The study of abnormal psychology is the study of people, like Clifford Beers, who suffer mental, emotional, and often physical pain as a result of some form of psychological or mental disorder, often referred to as **psychopathology**. Sometimes the experiences of people with psychopathology are as unusual as the experiences of a young woman named Julia, whose voice we listen to in the following.

VOICES

My illness began slowly, gradually, when I was between the ages of 15 and 17. During that time reality became distant and I began to wander around in a sort of haze, foreshadowing the delusional world that was to come later. I also began to have visual hallucinations in which people changed into different characters, the change indicating to me their moral value. For example, the mother of a good friend always changed into a witch, and I believed this to be indicative of her evil nature. Another type of visual hallucination I had at this time is exemplified by an occurrence during a family trip through Utah: The cliffs along

(continued)

the side of the road took on a human appearance, and I perceived them as women, bedraggled and weeping. At the time I didn't know what to make of these changes in my perceptions. On the one hand, I thought they came as a gift from God, but on the other hand, I feared that something was dreadfully wrong. However, I didn't tell anyone what was happening; I was afraid of being called insane. I also feared, perhaps incredibly, that someone would take it lightly and tell me nothing was wrong, that I was just having a rough adolescence, which was what I was telling myself. (Anonymous, 1992, pp. 333–334)

Sometimes, however, people with psychopathology have experiences that are familiar to many of us but more extreme, as Jamison (1995, p. 110) describes:

VOICES

From the time I woke up in the morning until the time I went to bed at night, I was unbearably miserable and seemingly incapable of any kind of joy or enthusiasm. Everything—every thought, word, movement—was an effort. Everything that once was sparkling now was flat. I seemed to myself to be dull, boring, inadequate, thick brained, unlit, unresponsive, chill skinned, bloodless, and sparrow drab. I doubted, completely, my ability to do anything well. It seemed as though my mind had slowed down and burned out to the point of being virtually useless. The wretched, convoluted, and pathetically confused mass of gray worked only well enough to torment me with a dreary litany of my inadequacies and shortcomings in character and to taunt me with the total, the desperate hopelessness of it all.

In this book, we explore the lives of people with troubling psychological symptoms to understand how they think, what they feel, and how they behave. We investigate what is known about the causes of and treatments for various types of symptoms. The purpose of this book is not only to provide you with information, facts and figures, theories, and research. It is also to take you into the lives of people with psychological symptoms and to

help you understand their experience. You may recognize yourself in some of these people, and you may attain the knowledge you need to seek effective treatment. The good news is that, thanks to an explosion of research in the last few decades, there *are* effective biological and psychological treatments for many of the mental-health problems we discuss in this book.

DEFINING ABNORMALITY

Let us start by defining what is meant by *psychopathology*, or, more generally, by *abnormality*. This key step is often more difficult than it might seem at first glance. Consider the following behaviors:

1. A man kissing another man
2. A woman slapping a child
3. A man driving a nail through his hand
4. A woman refusing to eat for several days
5. A man barking like a dog and crawling on the floor on his hands and knees
6. A woman building a shrine to her dead husband in a corner of her living room and leaving food and gifts for him at the altar

Do you think these behaviors are abnormal? You may reply, "It depends." In some circumstances, several of these behaviors may seem perfectly normal. In many European cultures, for example, men commonly greet other men with a kiss. In many religious traditions, refusing to eat for a period, or fasting, is a common ritual of cleansing and penitence. You might expect that some of the other listed behaviors, such as driving a nail through one's hand or barking like a dog, are abnormal in all circumstances, yet even these behaviors are accepted by some people and indeed are prescribed for specific situations. In Mexico, some Christians have themselves nailed to crosses at Easter to commemorate the crucifixion of Jesus. Among the Yoruba of Africa, traditional healers act as dogs, barking and crawling on the floor, during healing rituals (Murphy, 1976). In Shinto and Buddhist religions, it is customary to build altars to dead loved ones, to offer them food and gifts, and to speak with them as if they were in the room (Stroebe et al., 1992). Thus, the **context,** or circumstances surrounding a behavior, influences whether a behavior is viewed as abnormal.

Some theorists have gone so far as to argue that deviation from cultural or societal norms is the only criterion for labeling a behavior as abnormal (see Mezzich et al., 1999). A parallel perspective argues that behaviors become defined as abnormal if they

In Mexico, some Christians have themselves nailed to a cross to commemorate the crucifixion of Jesus.

violate a culture's **gender roles,** which are expectations for the behavior of an individual based on his or her gender. For example, a woman crying in public is not viewed as terribly abnormal in our culture, but a man crying in public is seen as abnormal, because this violates gender roles for men's display of emotions.

Other theorists have argued for what might appear, on the surface, to be more objective criteria, or standards, for defining abnormality. Such standards do not rely on cultural traditions or gender roles. Instead, they focus on the *unusualness* of the behavior, the *discomfort* of the person exhibiting the behavior, the presence of *mental illness,* and the *maladaptiveness* of the behavior. Each of these standards has its advantages and disadvantages, as we will see in the following sections.

Cultural Relativism

The **cultural relativism** perspective holds that there are no universal standards or rules for labeling a behavior as abnormal. Instead, behaviors can only be abnormal relative to cultural norms (Snowden & Yamada, 2005). Cultural relativists believe that there are different definitions of abnormality across different cultures.

Bereavement practices provide a good example of cultural relativism. In Western countries, bereaved people are expected to mourn their dead loved ones for a period of time, perhaps a few weeks or months, then to "let go" of the loved ones and move on in their lives (Stroebe et al., 1992). People who continue to think and talk about their dead loved ones a great deal after the specified period of mourning are thought to have "compli-

cated bereavement" and may be encouraged to seek counseling. More often, their family members and friends simply tell them to "get over it." The norm in these cultures is to break emotional bonds with dead loved ones, and people who seem not to have adequately broken those bonds may be labeled as abnormal.

In contrast, people in other cultures believe that we cannot and should not break psychological ties with dead loved ones. For example, in Japan, maintaining emotional bonds with deceased loved ones is not only normal but also prescribed for bereaved people (Yamamoto, 1970). In Egypt, the bereaved are encouraged to dwell profusely on their grief, and other people support them by recounting their own losses and openly expressing their sorrow in emotional outpourings (Wikan, 1991).

Even in Western countries, during the romantic age of the nineteenth century, expectations of the bereaved were radically different from current expectations (Rosenblatt, 2001; Stroebe et al., 1992). People's close relationships were at the center of their self-definitions, and the loss of a loved one was a critical defining moment in the survivor's life. "To grieve was to signal the significance of the relationship, and the depth of one's own spirit. Dissolving bonds with the deceased would not only define the relationship as superficial, but would deny as well one's own sense of profundity and self-worth" (Stroebe et al., 1992, p. 1208). People clung to the lost loved one and wrote about their grief in poetry, diaries, and fiction.

Opponents of cultural relativism argue that dangers arise when societal norms are allowed to dictate what is normal and abnormal. In particular, psychiatrist Thomas Szasz noted that, throughout history, societies have labeled individuals and groups abnormal in order to justify controlling or silencing them. Hitler branded Jews abnormal and used this as one justification for the Holocaust. The former Soviet Union branded political dissidents mentally ill and jailed them in mental hospitals.

When the slave trade was active in the United States, slaves who tried to escape their masters could be diagnosed as having *drapetomania,* a sickness that caused them to desire freedom. This provided a justification for capturing them and returning them to their masters (Szasz, 1971). In 1851, Dr. Samuel Cartwright, a prominent physician, published an essay in the prestigious *New Orleans Medical and Surgical Journal* titled "Report on the Diseases and Physical Peculiarities of the Negro Race," in which he argued that

the cause, in most cases, that induces the Negro to run away from service, is as

When the slave trade was active, slaves who tried to escape were sometimes labeled as having a mental illness and beaten to "cure" them.

much a disease of the mind as any other species of mental alienation, and much more curable, as a general rule. With the advantages of proper medical advice, strictly followed, this troublesome practice that many Negroes have of running away, can be almost entirely prevented.

Cartwright also described a disease called *dysaesthesia Aethiopis*, the refusal to work for one's master. To cure this "disease," Cartwright prescribed the following:

The liver, skin and kidneys should be stimulated to activity, and be made to assist in decarbonising the blood. The best means to stimulate the skin is, first, to have the patient well washed with warm water and soap; then to anoint it all over with oil, and to slap the oil with a broad leather strap; then to put the patient to some hard kind of work in the open air and sunshine, that will compel him to expand his lungs, as chopping wood, splitting rails, or sawing with the cross-cut or whip saw.

According to Cartwright, whipping slaves who refused to work and then forcing them to do hard labor would "revitalize" their lungs and bring them back to their senses. We might like to believe that Cartwright's essay represented the extreme views of just one person, but he was writing on behalf of a prestigious medical association.

As noted earlier, in our modern society, gender-role expectations heavily influence the labeling of behaviors as normal or abnormal (Hartung & Widiger, 1998). Men who display sadness or anxiety, who choose to stay home to raise their children while their wives work, or who otherwise violate the male gender role are at risk for being labeled as abnormal. Women who are too aggressive, who don't want to have children, or who otherwise violate the female gender role are at risk for being labeled as abnormal. On the other hand, aggression in men and chronic anxiety or sadness in women are often dismissed as normal, because they do not violate gender roles—we expect these behaviors, so we label them as normal.

The cultural relativist perspective creates many difficulties in defining abnormality. Most psychologists these days do not take an extreme relativist view on abnormality, recognizing the dangers of completely accepting society's definitions of what is normal and abnormal. There is increasing sensitivity, however, to the reality that cultural norms and gender roles strongly influence people's feelings and actions.

Unusualness

A second standard that has been used for designating behaviors as abnormal is **unusualness.** Behaviors that are unusual, or rare, are considered abnormal, whereas behaviors that are typical, or usual, are considered normal. This criterion has some ties to the relativist criterion, because the unusualness of any behavior depends in part on a culture's norms for that behavior. For example, how unusual it is for a bereaved person to be wailing in public? The answer depends on whether that person is in Minneapolis or Cairo.

The unusualness criterion for abnormality has two other problems. First, although the criterion may seem objective, someone still has to decide how rare a behavior must be in order to call it abnormal. Are behaviors that only 10 percent of the population exhibits abnormal? Or do we want to set a more strict cutoff and say that only behaviors that 1 percent or less of the population exhibits are abnormal? Choosing a cutoff is as subjective as relying on personal opinions as to what is abnormal and normal.

The second problem with the unusualness criterion is that many rare behaviors are positive for the individual and for society, and most people would object to labeling such behaviors as abnormal. For example, we don't label the playing of a piano virtuoso abnormal; we label it gifted. Other people have hobbies or activities that are rare but are a source of great joy for them and do no harm to others. These people are often referred to as *eccentrics.* For example, consider Gary Holloway, an environmental planner who works for the city of San Francisco and who is described in the following case study.

"Do people hate us because we dress this way or do we dress this way because people hate us?" © *Sidney Harris, courtesy ScienceCartoonsPlus.com*

He is fascinated by Martin Van Buren, the eighth president of the United States. Eighteen years ago, he discovered that Van Buren was the only president not to have a society dedicated to his memory, so he promptly founded the Martin Van Buren Fan Club. "This man did absolutely nothing to further the course of our national destiny," Holloway told us proudly, "yet hundreds of people now follow me in commemorating him." Holloway has served as the club's president for eighteen consecutive terms, and he has also been the winner for eighteen consecutive years of the Marty, its award for excellence in Van Burenism. Holloway is also a lifelong devotee of St. Francis of Assisi, and frequently dresses in the habit of a Franciscan monk. "It's comfortable, fun to wear, and I like the response I get when I wear it," he explained. "People always offer me a seat on the bus." Holloway has an obsession with the British Commonwealth and has an encyclopedic knowledge of places such as Tristan da Cunha and Fiji. During the Falklands war he passionately espoused the cause of the islanders, to the point of flying the Falklands flag on the flagpole on his front lawn. After the war he celebrated Britain's victory by renaming his home Falklands House, where he continues to fly its flag. His bedroom at Falklands House still has everything in it that it had when he was a boy. He calls it the Peanuts Room because of his huge collection of stuffed Snoopies and other memorabilia pertaining to the comic strip *Peanuts*. He has slept on the same twin bed there for forty years. He has dozens of toy airplanes, relics of his boyhood, and the walls are covered with pennants. "As a monk," he explained, "I'm always doing pennants"—thereby demonstrating the sly sense of humor that many eccentrics possess. (Weeks & James, 1995, pp. 36–37)

Gary Holloway's activities certainly are eccentric, but would we call them abnormal?

One of the few studies of eccentrics estimates that only about 1 in 10,000 people is a true eccentric. This study found that eccentrics certainly have unusual tastes but are generally very happy and function well in society (Weeks & James, 1995). Indeed, the rate of serious dysfunction among the eccentrics in this study was lower than the rate among noneccentrics.

Discomfort

Proponents of a **discomfort** criterion for abnormality suggest that behaviors should be considered abnormal only if the individual suffers discomfort and wishes to be rid of the behaviors. This criterion avoids, to some extent, the problems of using societal norms as the criterion for abnormality. If a person's behaviors violate societal norms but do not cause him or her any discomfort, then the behaviors should not be considered abnormal.

This viewpoint has contributed to a change in how psychologists and psychiatrists viewed one behavior pattern—homosexuality. Gay men and lesbians have argued that their sexual orientation is a natural part of themselves and a characteristic that causes them no discomfort and that they don't wish to alter or eliminate. Partly because of these arguments, in 1973 the American Psychiatric Association removed homosexuality from its list of recognized psychological disorders (Spitzer, 1981).

Some therapists object to the subjective discomfort criterion, however, because people are not always aware of problems their behaviors create for themselves or for others. For example, some

people who have lost touch with reality wander the streets aimlessly, not eating or taking care of themselves, in danger of starvation or exposure to the elements. These people may not be fully aware that they have severe problems and do not seek help. If we require that people acknowledge and seek help for their behaviors before we call those behaviors abnormal, some people who could benefit greatly from help might never get it.

In addition, the behaviors of some people cause great discomfort in others, if not in themselves. An example is people who engage in highly antisocial behavior, lying, cheating, and even being violent toward others. They may suffer no discomfort, and even may experience pleasure, at causing others great pain. Thus, we may want to call their behaviors abnormal.

Mental Illness

A fourth way of defining abnormality is as behaviors that result from mental disease or illness. This **mental illness** criterion implies that there is a clear, identifiable physical process that differs from "health" and that leads to specific behaviors or symptoms. For example, when many people say that an individual "has schizophrenia," they imply that he or she has a disease that should show up on some sort of biological test, just as hypertension shows up when a person's blood pressure is taken.

To date, however, there is no biological test available to diagnose any of the types of abnormality we will discuss in this book. This may be simply because we do not yet have the right biological tests. But many theorists believe that most mental-health problems are due to a number of complex biological and psychosocial factors, rather than to single abnormal genes or disease processes.

When we give a person's psychological symptoms a diagnosis, it is simply a label for that set of symptoms. For example, when we say someone "has" obsessive-compulsive disorder, we can mean only that he or she is exhibiting a set of symptoms, including obsessive thoughts and compulsive behaviors. The term *obsessive-compulsive disorder* does not refer to an identifiable physical process that is found in all people who exhibit these symptoms.

Maladaptiveness

How do the majority of researchers and clinicians in the mental-health field decide whether a set of behaviors is abnormal? The consensus is that behaviors and feelings that are **maladaptive**—that cause people to *suffer distress* and that *prevent them from functioning in daily life*—are abnormal and should be the focus of research and intervention (Spitzer, 1981). In addition, mental-health professionals tend

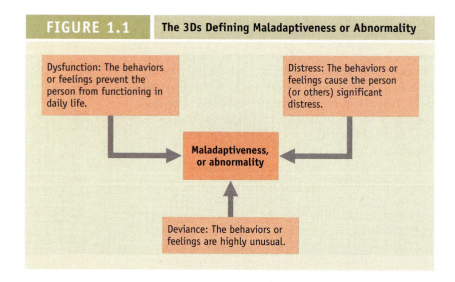

FIGURE 1.1   **The 3Ds Defining Maladaptiveness or Abnormality**

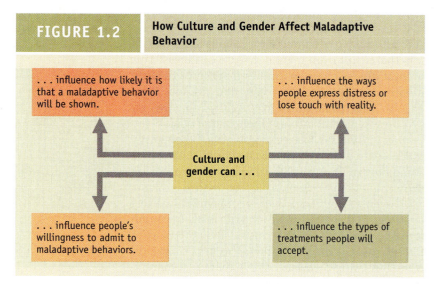

FIGURE 1.2   **How Culture and Gender Affect Maladaptive Behavior**

to reserve the label *maladaptive* for behaviors and feelings that are highly unusual or deviant.

Thus, the three components of maladaptiveness can be remembered with the heuristic of the *3Ds: dysfunction, distress,* and *deviance* (see Figure 1.1). Julia's experiences and the feelings described by Jamison, presented at the beginning of this chapter, would be labeled as abnormal by these criteria because they caused them suffering, they interfere with their ability to function in daily life, and they are highly unusual.

The maladaptiveness criteria have attracted widespread support among mental-health professionals, because they seem to capture what most of us mean when we call something abnormal, while avoiding some of the problems of using only the cultural relativism, unusualness, discomfort, and illness criteria. Still, the maladaptiveness criteria call for subjective judgments—how much emotional pain or harm must a person be suffering?

How much should the behaviors be interfering with daily functioning? Who determines what is adequate functioning? And the criteria still depend on societal norms. Many behaviors are physically damaging but are accepted by society, such as smoking cigarettes. There are also many beliefs that some people think are "crazy," such as the belief in an afterlife, but that are accepted by society. Throughout this book, as we apply the maladaptiveness criteria to specific types of behavior, we will keep in mind the subjectivity of these criteria and the fuzziness of definitions of abnormality.

Even when the maladaptiveness criteria can be used confidently to identify a certain group of behaviors as abnormal, culture and gender can still influence the expression of those behaviors and the way those behaviors are treated (see Figure 1.2). First, culture and gender influence how likely it is that a given maladaptive behavior will be shown. For example, men are twice as likely as women to suffer problems related to alcohol use. This fact suggests that something about being male—male biology, male personality, or the social pressures put on men—contributes to the development of alcoholism.

Second, culture and gender can influence the ways people express distress or lose touch with reality. People who lose touch with reality often believe that they have divine powers, but whether an individual believes he or she is Jesus Christ or Buddha depends on his or her religious background.

Third, culture and gender can influence people's willingness to admit to certain types of maladaptive behaviors (Snowden & Yamada, 2005). People in Eskimo and Tahitian cultures may be reluctant to admit to angry feelings because of strong cultural norms against the expression of anger. However, the Kaluli of New Guinea and the Yanamamo of Brazil value the expression of anger and have elaborate and complex rituals for expressing anger (Jenkins, Kleinman, & Good, 1991).

Fourth, culture and gender can influence the types of treatments that are deemed acceptable or helpful for maladaptive behaviors (Snowden & Yamada, 2005). For example, women may be more willing than men to accept psychological treatments for problems. Throughout this book, we will explore these influences of culture and gender on maladaptive behaviors.

Many students take a course on abnormal psychology, wondering if they are abnormal, because they feel unusual, are uncomfortable with themselves, or fear they have inherited a mental illness. *Taking Psychology Personally: When You Wonder If You Are Abnormal* addresses this concern and what to do about it.

Taking Psychology Personally

When You Wonder If You Are Abnormal

As you read in this book about behaviors labeled as abnormal, you may find yourself thinking, "That's me!" or "That's someone I know!" You should be aware that many of the behaviors discussed in this book occur occasionally, in mild form, in many people. For example, many people between the ages of 18 and 25, even when not under the influence of a drug, have brief "out-of-body" experiences, in which they feel their "soul" or "self" is floating out of their body. It is even more common for people of all ages to have periods of sad or anxious moods or times when they feel that life is "out of control." For most people, these periods are relatively brief, and these behaviors or feelings do not severely interfere with their

ability to function in life. If, however, you have been behaving in ways that interfere with daily functioning or that cause you or others much suffering, it is a good idea to talk with a professional about these experiences. Your instructor may be willing to speak with you or to provide you with referrals to professionals with whom you may speak. Many colleges offer confidential counseling for students at no cost or minimal cost. Some counties have mental-health associations that provide information on professionals or groups that serve people with specific types of problems. The phone number for your local mental-health association may be in the *Yellow Pages* or available through an operator.

SUMMING UP

- Cultural relativism is a perspective on abnormality that argues that the norms of a society must be used to determine the normality or abnormality of a behavior.

- The unusualness criterion for abnormality suggests that unusual, or rare, behaviors should be labeled abnormal.

- The discomfort criterion suggests that only behaviors or emotions that an individual finds distressing should be labeled abnormal.

- The mental illness criterion for abnormality suggests that only behaviors resulting from mental illness are abnormal.

- The consensus among professionals in the mental-health field is that behaviors that cause people to suffer distress, that prevent them from functioning in daily life, and that are unusual are abnormal. Often these behaviors are referred to as *maladaptive* and can be remembered as the 3Ds: distress, dysfunction, and deviance.

HISTORICAL PERSPECTIVES ON ABNORMALITY

References to madness, insanity, or other forms of abnormal behavior can be found throughout human history. Three types of theories of the causes of abnormal behaviors have competed for dominance across time. The **biological theories** saw abnormal behavior as similar to physical diseases, caused by

the breakdown of systems in the body. The appropriate cure for mental disorders, according to the biological theories, was the restoration of the body to good health. The **supernatural theories** saw abnormal behavior as a result of divine intervention, curses, demonic possession, and personal sin. To rid the person of the disorder, religious rituals, exorcisms, confessions, and atonement were prescribed. The **psychological theories** saw abnormal behavior as a result of traumas, such as bereavement, or chronic stress. According to these theories, rest, relaxation, a change of environment, and certain herbal medicines were sometimes helpful to the afflicted person. These three types of theories influenced how people afflicted with disorders were regarded in the society. A person thought to be insane because he or she was a sinner would be regarded differently than would a person thought to be insane because of a medical disorder.

Ancient Theories

Our understanding of prehistoric people's conceptions of abnormality is based on inferences from archeological artifacts—fragments of bones, tools, artwork, and so on. Ever since humans developed written language, they have been writing about abnormal behavior. It seems that humans have always viewed abnormality as something needing special explanation.

Evil Spirits of the Stone Age

Historians speculate that even prehistoric people had a concept of insanity, probably one rooted in supernatural beliefs (Selling, 1940). Demons and ghosts were the cause of abnormal behavior. When a person acted oddly, he or she was suspected of being possessed by evil spirits.

The typical treatment for abnormality, according to supernatural beliefs, was exorcism—driving the evil spirits from the body of the suffering person. Shamans, or healers, would say prayers or incantations, try to talk the spirits out of the body, or make the body an uncomfortable place for the spirits to reside, often through extreme measures, such as starving or beating the person. At other times, the person thought to be possessed by evil spirits would simply be killed.

One treatment for abnormality in the Stone Age may have been to drill holes in the skulls of people displaying abnormal behavior to allow the spirits to depart. Archeologists have found skulls dating back to the Stone Age a half-million years ago, in which circular sections of the skull had been drilled away (Maher & Maher, 1985). The tool used for this drilling is called a trephine and the operation is called **trephination.** Some historians believe that people who were seeing or hearing things that were not real and people who were chronically sad were subjected to this prehistoric form of brain surgery (Selling, 1940). Presumably, if the person survived this surgery, the evil spirits would have been released and his or her abnormal behavior would have declined. However, we cannot know with certainty that trephination was used to drive away evil spirits. Some historians suggest that trephination was used primarily to remove blood clots caused by stone weapons during warfare and for other medical purposes (Maher & Maher, 1985). It is clear, however, that supernatural theories of abnormality have been around for a very long time.

Ancient China: Balancing Yin and Yang

Some of the earliest written sources on abnormality are ancient Chinese texts on medicine (Tseng, 1973). *Nei Ching* (*Classic of Internal Medicine*) was probably written around 2674 B.C. by Huang Ti, the third legendary emperor of China.

Ancient Chinese medicine was based on the concept of yin and yang. The human body was said to contain a positive force (yang) and a negative force (yin), which confronted and complemented each other. If the two forces were in balance, the individual was healthy. If not, illness, including insanity, could result. For example, *excited insanity* was considered the result of an excessive positive force:

The person suffering from excited insanity initially feels sad, eating and sleeping

Some scholars believe that holes found in ancient skulls are from trephination, a crude form of brain surgery performed on people acting abnormally.

less; he then becomes grandiose, feeling that he is very smart and noble, talking and scolding day and night, singing, behaving strangely, seeing strange things, hearing strange voices, believing that he can see the devil or gods, etc. As treatment for such an excited condition withholding food was suggested, since food was considered to be the source of positive force and the patient was thought to be in need of a decrease in such force. (Tseng, 1973, p. 570)

Another theory in ancient Chinese medical philosophy was that human emotions were controlled by internal organs. When the "vital air" was flowing on one of these organs, an individual experienced a particular emotion. For example, when air flowed on the heart, a person felt joy; when on the lungs, sorrow; when on the liver, anger; when on the spleen, worry; and when on the kidney, fear. This theory encouraged people to live in an orderly and harmonious way, so as to maintain the proper movement of vital air.

Although the ancient Chinese perspective on psychological symptoms was largely a biological theory in ancient times, the rise of Taoism and Buddhism during the Chin and T'ang dynasties (A.D. 420 to 618) led to some religious interpretations of abnormal behavior. Evil winds and ghosts were blamed for bewitching people, and for people's erratic emotional displays and uncontrolled behavior. Religious theories of abnormality declined in China after this period.

Some of the earliest medical writings on mental disorders came from ancient Chinese texts. The illustration shows a healer at work.

Ancient Egypt, Greece, and Rome: Biological Theories Dominate

Other ancient writings on abnormal behavior are found in the papyri of Egypt and Mesopotamia (Veith, 1965). The oldest of these is a document known as the Kahun Papyrus, after the ancient Egyptian city in which it was found, and it dates from about 1900 B.C. This document lists a number of disorders, each followed by a physician's judgment of the cause of the disorder and the appropriate treatment.

Several of the disorders apparently left people with unexplainable aches and pains, sadness or distress, and apathy about life. Some examples are "a woman who loves bed; she does not rise and she does not shake it"; "a woman who is pained in her teeth and jaws; she knows not how to open her mouth"; and "a woman aching in all her limbs with pain in the sockets of her eyes" (Veith, 1965, p. 3). These disorders were said to occur only in women and were attributed to a "wandering uterus." Apparently, the Egyptians believed that the uterus could become dislodged and wander throughout a woman's body, interfering with her other organs and causing these symptoms. Later the Greeks, holding to the same theory of the anatomy of women, named this disorder hysteria (from the Greek word hysteria, which means "uterus"). These days, the term hysteria is used to refer to physiological symptoms that are probably the result of psychological processes. In the Egyptian papyri, the prescribed treatment for this disorder involved the use of strong-smelling substances to drive the uterus back to its proper place.

Another, more complete papyrus, the Papyrus Ebers, recommends a combination of physiological interventions and incantations to the gods to assist in the healing process (Veith, 1965). One astounding feature of the Papyrus Ebers is that it provides a detailed description of the brain and clearly ascribes mental functioning to the brain. The ancient Egyptians' perspective on abnormal behavior was clearly driven by biological theories of these disorders, but they also believed that supernatural powers could intervene in the cure (and perhaps cause) of disorders.

The Old Testament makes several references to madness. In Deuteronomy, which dates from the seventh century B.C., Moses warns his people that if they "will not obey the voice of the Lord your God or be careful to do all his commandments and his statutes . . . the Lord will smite you with madness and blindness and confusion of the mind . . ." (Deuteronomy 28:15, 28). Thus, the Hebrews saw madness as a punishment from God. People stricken with madness were to confess their sins and repent in order to achieve relief. There are several passages in the Old Testament in which people thought to be mad were also attended by physicians, however (e.g., Job 13:4), so the Hebrews believed that physicians could at least comfort people, if not cure them of madness.

Beginning with Homer, the Greeks wrote frequently of people thought to be mad (Veith, 1965). Flute music played an important role in religious rituals, and there are accounts of people hearing and seeing phantom flute players by day and night. Physician Hippocrates (460–377 B.C.) described a case of a common phobia. A man could not walk alongside a cliff, pass over a bridge, or jump over even a shallow ditch without feeling unable to control his limbs and having his vision impaired. Another physician, Aretaeus (A.D. 50–130), described an artisan who appears to have had symptoms of what we now call agoraphobia (people with this disorder become housebound because they experience episodes of panic when away from their safe abodes): "If at any time he went away to the market, the bath, or on any other engagement, having laid down his tools, he would first groan, then shrug his shoulders as he went out. But when he had got out of sight of the domestics, or of the work and the place where it was performed, he became completely mad; yet if he returned speedily he recovered his reason again" (cited in Veith, 1965, p. 96).

The traditional interpretation of madness throughout much of Greek and Roman history was

Hippocrates argued that mental disorders are caused by imbalances in the body's essential humors, or elements.

that it was an affliction from the gods. The afflicted retreated to temples honoring the god Aesculapius, where priests held healing ceremonies. Plato (429–347 B.C.) and Socrates (384–322 B.C.) argued that some forms of madness were divine and could be the source of great literary and prophetic gifts.

For the most part, however, Greek physicians rejected supernatural explanations of abnormal behavior. Hippocrates, often regarded as the father of medicine, argued that abnormal behavior was like other diseases of the body. According to Hippocrates, the body was composed of four basic humors: blood, phlegm, yellow bile, and black bile. All diseases, including abnormal behavior, were caused by imbalances in the body's essential humors, typically an excess of one of the humors. Based on careful observation of his many patients, including listening to their dreams, Hippocrates classified abnormal behavior into epilepsy, mania, melancholia, and brain fever. He also recognized hysteria, although he did not view it as a mental disease. Like others, he thought that this was a disorder confined to women and caused by a wandering uterus.

The treatments prescribed by the Greek physicians were intended to restore the balance of the humors. Sometimes these treatments were physiological and intrusive; for example, bleeding a patient was a common practice for disorders thought to result from an excess of blood. Other treatments were rest, relaxation, a change of climate or scenery, a change of diet, and a temperate life. Some of the nonmedical treatments prescribed by these physicians sound remarkably like prescriptions made by

modern psychotherapists. Hippocrates, for example, believed that removing a patient from a difficult family could help restore mental health. Plato took a decidedly psychological view of abnormal behavior. He argued that madness arose when the rational mind was overcome by impulse, passion, or appetite. Sanity could be restored by a restoration of the rational process through a discussion with the individual designed to induce emotional control (Maher & Maher, 1985).

Throughout ancient times, the relatives of people considered mad were encouraged to confine the afflicted people to the home. The state claimed no responsibility for insane people; there were no asylums or institutions, other than the religious temples, to house and care for them. The state could, however, take rights away from people declared mad. Relatives could bring suit against those they considered mad, and the state could award the property of insane people to their relatives. People declared mad could not marry or acquire or dispose of their own property. Poor people who were considered mad were simply left to roam the streets if they were not violent. If they were violent, they were locked away in stocks and chains. The general public greatly feared madness of any form, and people thought to be mad, even if divinely mad, were often shunned or even stoned.

Medieval Views

The Middle Ages (around A.D. 400–1400) are often described as a time of backward thinking, dominated by an obsession with witchcraft and supernatural forces, yet even within Europe supernatural theories of abnormal behavior did not dominate until late in the Middle Ages, between the eleventh and fifteenth centuries. Prior to the eleventh century, witches and witchcraft were accepted as real but considered merely nuisances that were overrated by superstitious people. Severe emotional shock and physical illness and injury were most often seen as the causes of bizarre behaviors. For example, English court records on persons thought to be mentally ill attributed their illnesses to factors such as a "blow received on the head," explained that symptoms were "induced by fear of his father," or noted that "he has lost his reason owing to a long and incurable infirmity" (Neugebauer, 1979, p. 481). Laypeople probably did believe in demons and curses as causes of abnormal behavior, but there is strong evidence that physicians and government officials attributed abnormal behavior to physical causes or traumas.

Witchcraft

Beginning in the eleventh century, the power of the Church was threatened by the breakdown of feudalism and rebellions caused by the economic and political inequalities of the times. The Church chose to interpret these threats in terms of heresy and satanism. The Inquisition was established originally to rid the earth of religious heretics, but eventually those practicing witchcraft or satanism were also the focus of hunts. The witch hunts continued long after the Reformation and were perhaps at their height during the fifteenth to seventeenth centuries, the period known as the Renaissance (Kroll, 1973).

Some psychiatric historians have argued that persons accused of witchcraft must have been mentally ill (Veith, 1965; Zilboorg & Henry, 1941). Accused witches sometimes confessed to speaking with the devil, flying on the backs of animals, and engaging in other unusual behaviors. Such people may have been experiencing delusions (false beliefs) or hallucinations (unreal perceptual experiences), which are signs of some psychological disorders.

Accused witches were also said to have a devil's mark on their bodies, which was often invisible but was insensitive to even the most severe pain. Professional "witch prickers" poked accused witches all over their bodies to find the devil's mark, and areas of insensitivity were found in some of the accused. Psychiatric historians have interpreted this insensitivity as a sign of hysteria or self-hypnosis.

The accused witches' supposed insensitivity to pain indeed could have been real but may have been due to poor nutrition and ill health, common in medieval times, as opposed to any influence of the devil. Professional witch prickers were also known to use techniques to make it falsely appear that a person was insensitive to pain. For example, some witch prickers used collapsible needles attached to hollow shafts, making it appear that the needle pierced deeply into the accused's flesh without inducing pain. However, many of the confessions of accused witches may have been extracted through brutal torture or under the promise of a stay of execution in exchange for a confession (Spanos, 1978).

Accusations of witchcraft were also used as a means of social punishment or control. For example, in 1581, Johann Klenke was accused of witchcraft by the mayor of his town. This accusation came after Klenke had lent the mayor money and then insisted on having it paid back (Rosen, 1968). In England, during the sixteenth and seventeenth centuries, persons accused of being witches were

Some people burned at the stake as witches may have been suffering from mental disorders that caused them to act abnormally.

typically older women, unmarried and poor, who often begged for food and money and were considered by their neighbors to be foul-mouthed and disgusting. These women sometimes cultivated the myth that they were witches to frighten their neighbors into giving them money. This ploy could backfire, however, if their neighbors attributed some misfortune to a spell cast by the self-acclaimed witch. The woman would be arrested and the neighbor could be rid of her.

Some people truly believed themselves to be witches. These people may have been suffering from abnormal behavior. Indeed, even during the witch hunts, some physicians risked condemnation by the Church and even death by arguing that accused witches were suffering from mental illnesses.

In 1563, Johann Weyer published *The Deception of Dreams*, in which he argued that the people accused of being witches were suffering from melancholy (depression) and senility. The Church banned Weyer's writings, however, and he was scorned by many of his peers. Twenty years later, Reginald Scot, in his *Discovery of Witchcraft* (1584), supported Weyer's beliefs: "These women are but diseased wretches suffering from melancholy, and their words, actions, reasoning, and gestures show that sickness has affected their brains and impaired their powers of judgment" (Castiglioni, 1946, p. 253). Again, the Church, and this time the state, refuted the arguments and banned Scot's writings.

As is often the case, change came from within. In the sixteenth century, Teresa of Avila, a Spanish nun who was later canonized, explained that the mass hysteria that had broken out among a group of nuns was not the work of the devil but the effect of infirmities or sickness. She argued that these nuns were *comas enfermas*, or "as if sick." She sought out natural causes for the nuns' strange behaviors and concluded that they were due to melancholy, a weak imagination, or drowsiness and sleepiness (Sarbin & Juhasz, 1967).

It is also possible that some people who truly believed they were witches were not suffering from abnormal behavior. The culture in which they lived so completely accepted the existence of witches and witchcraft that these people may simply have used these cultural beliefs to explain their own feelings and behaviors, even when these feelings and behaviors were not components of a mental disorder. In addition, most writings of medieval and Renaissance times, as well as writings from the witch hunt period in Salem, Massachusetts, clearly distinguish between people who were mad and people who were witches. This distinction between madness and witchcraft continues to this day in cultures that believe in witchcraft.

Psychic Epidemics

Psychic epidemics are defined today as a phenomenon in which large numbers of people begin to engage in unusual behaviors that appear to have a psychological origin. During the Middle Ages, reports of dance frenzies or manias were frequent. A monk, Peter of Herental, described a rash of dance frenzies that broke out over a four-month period in 1374 in Germany:

> Both men and women were abused by the devil to such a degree that they danced in their homes, in the churches and in the streets, holding each other's hands and leaping in the air. While they danced they called out the names of demons, such as Friskes and others, but they were unaware of this nor did they pay attention to modesty even though people watched them. At the end of the dance, they felt such pains in the chest, that if their friends did not tie linen clothes tightly around their waists, they cried out like madmen that they were dying. (cited in Rosen, 1968, pp. 196–197)

Other instances of dance frenzy were reported in 1428 during the feast of Saint Vitus, at Schaffhausen, at which a monk danced himself to death. Again, in 1518, a large epidemic of uncontrolled dance frenzy occurred at the chapel of Saint Vitus at Hohlenstein, near Zabern. According to one account, more than 400 people danced during the four-week period the frenzy lasted. Some writers of the time began to call the frenzied dancing *Saint Vitus' dance*.

A similar phenomenon was *tarantism*, which was seen in Italy as early as the fourteenth century but became prominent in the seventeenth century. People suddenly developed an acute pain, which they attributed to the bite of a tarantula. They jumped around and danced wildly in the streets, tearing at their clothes and beating each other with whips. Some people dug holes in the earth and rolled on the ground; others howled and made obscene gestures. At the time, many people interpreted dance frenzies and tarantism as the results of possession by the devil. The behaviors may have been the remnants of ancient rituals performed by people worshipping the Greek god Dionysus.

Although dance frenzies and similar psychic epidemics were observed frequently in the Middle Ages, this phenomenon is not confined to that period in history. Dance frenzies and similar behavior patterns were observed later, in the eighteenth century, in some religious sects. These sects included the Shakers; the mystical Russian sects, such as the Chlysti; certain Jewish sects; congregations of the early Methodist movement; and the Quakers. During religious services, members of these sects might become so emotionally charged that they would jerk around violently, running, singing, screaming, and dancing. This type of religious service tended to be more popular among people suffering great economic and social deprivation and alienation. The enthusiastic expression of religious fervor can act as a welcome release from the tensions and stresses of simply trying to survive in a hostile world.

Even today, we see episodes of psychic epidemics. On February 8, 1991, a number of students and teachers in a high school in Rhode Island thought they smelled noxious fumes coming from the ventilation system. The first person to detect these fumes, a 14-year-old girl, fell to the floor, crying and saying that her stomach hurt and her eyes stung. Other students and the teacher in that room then began to experience symptoms. They were moved into the hallway with a great deal of commotion. Soon, students and teachers from adjacent rooms, who could clearly see into the hallway, began to experience symptoms. Eventually, 21 people (17 students and 4 teachers) were admitted to the local hospital emergency room. All were hyperventilating, and most complained of dizziness, headache, and nausea. Although some of them initially showed symptoms of mild carbon monoxide intoxication in blood tests, no evidence of toxic gas in the school could be found. The physicians treating the children and teachers concluded that the outbreak was a case of mass hysteria prompted by the fear of chemical warfare during the Persian Gulf War (Rockney & Lemke, 1992).

Psychic epidemics are no longer viewed as the result of spirit possession or the bite of a tarantula. Rather, psychologists attempt to understand them using research from social psychology about the influence of others on individuals' self-perceptions. The social context can affect even our perceptions of our own bodies, as we will see when we discuss people's differing reactions to psychoactive substances, such as marijuana (see Chapter 17) and people's interpretations of physiological arousal in their bodies (see Chapters 6 and 7).

The Spread of Asylums During the Renaissance

As early as the twelfth century, many towns in Europe took some responsibility for housing and caring for people considered mentally ill (Kroll, 1973). Remarkable among these towns was Gheel, in Belgium, where townspeople regularly took into their homes the mentally ill who visited the shrine of Saint Dymphna for cures.

General hospitals began to include special rooms or facilities for people with abnormal behavior in about the eleventh or twelfth century. In 1326, a *Dollhaus* (madhouse) was constructed as part of the Georgehospital at Elbing. In 1375, a *Tollkiste* (mad cell) was mentioned in the municipal records of Hamburg (Kroll, 1973). Unlike the humane treatment people with abnormal behavior received in such places as Gheel, the treatment in these early hospitals was far from humane. The mentally ill were little more than inmates, housed against their will, often in extremely harsh conditions.

One of the most famous of these hospitals was the Hospital of Saint Mary of Bethlehem, in London, which officially became a mental hospital in 1547. This hospital, nicknamed *Bedlam*, was famous for its deplorable conditions, which were highlights in Shakespeare's *King Lear*:

> Bedlam beggers, who, with roaring voices
> . . . sometimes with lunatic bans, sometimes with prayers enforce their charity.
> (*King Lear*, Act II, Scene iii)

Shakespeare is referring to the practice of forcing patients at this hospital to beg in the streets for money. At Bedlam and other mental hospitals established in Europe in the sixteenth, seventeenth, and eighteenth centuries, patients were exhibited to the public for a fee. They lived in filth and confinement, often chained to walls or locked in small boxes. The following description of the treatment of patients in La Bicêtre Hospital, an asylum for male patients in Paris, provides an example of typical care:

> The patients were ordinarily shackled to the walls of their dark, unlighted cells by iron collars which held them flat against the wall and permitted little movement. Ofttimes there were also iron hoops around the waists of the patients and both their hands and feet were chained. Although these chains usually permitted enough movement that the patients could feed themselves out of bowls, they often kept them from being able to lie down at night. Since little was known about dietetics, and the patients were presumed to be animals anyway, little attention was paid to whether they were adequately fed or whether the food was good or bad. The cells were furnished only with straw and were never swept or cleaned; the patient remained in the midst of all the accumulated

Bedlam—the Hospital of St. Mary of Bethlehem—was famous for the chaotic and deplorable conditions in which people with mental disorders were kept.

ordure. No one visited the cells except at feeding time, no provision was made for warmth, and even the most elementary gestures of humanity were lacking. (adapted from Selling, 1940, pp. 54–55)

The laws regarding the confinement of the mentally ill in Europe and the United States were concerned with the protection of the public and the ill person's relatives (Busfield, 1986; Scull, 1993). For example, Dalton's 1618 edition of the *Common Law* states that "it is lawful for the parents, kinsmen or other friends of a man that is mad, or frantic . . . to take him and put him into a house, to bind or chain him, and to beat him with rods, and to do any other forcible act to reclaim him, or to keep him so he shall do no hurt" (Allderidge, 1979).

The first *Act for Regulating Madhouses* in England was not passed until 1774, with the intentions of cleaning up the deplorable conditions in hospitals and madhouses and protecting people from being unjustly jailed for insanity. This act provided for the licensing and inspection of madhouses and required that a physician, a surgeon, or an apothecary sign a certificate before a patient could be admitted. These provisions applied only to paying patients in private madhouses, however, and not to the poor people confined to workhouses for lunatics.

The conditions of asylums in America were not much better. In 1756, Benjamin Franklin helped establish the Pennsylvania Hospital in Philadelphia, which included some cells or wards for mental patients. In 1773, the Public Hospital in Williamsburg, Virginia, became the first hospital exclusively for the mentally ill. The treatment of patients, although designed to restore health and balance to the mind, included powerful electrical shocks, plunging of the person into ice water or hot water, starvation, and the heavy use of restraints (Bennett, 1947).

It is worth noting that these asylums typically were established and run by people who thought that abnormal behaviors were medical illnesses. For example, Benjamin Rush (1745–1813), one of the founders of American psychiatry, believed that abnormal behavior was caused by excessive blood in the brain and prescribed bleeding the patient—drawing huge amounts of blood from the body. Thus, although the demonology and witchcraft theories of the Middle Ages have often been decried as leading to brutal treatment of people with mental illnesses, the medical theories of those times and of the next couple of centuries did not always lead to much more gentle treatment. These treatments were based on beliefs and understandings about anatomy and physiology that we now know to be incorrect.

Moral Treatment in the Eighteenth Century

Fortunately, the eighteenth and nineteenth centuries saw the growth of a movement toward a more humane treatment of the mentally ill. This new form of treatment was based on the psychological view that people became mad because they were separated from nature and succumbed to the stresses imposed by the rapid social changes of the period (Rosen, 1968). This was a heavily psychological theory of abnormal behavior, which suggested that the appropriate treatment for madness was rest and relaxation in a serene and physically appealing place.

In 1796, Quaker William Tuke (1732–1819) opened an asylum in England called The Retreat, in direct response to the brutal treatment he saw being delivered to people with abnormal behavior at other facilities. Tuke's intent was to provide a "mild system of treatment," which he referred to as **moral treatment** (Busfield, 1986). This treatment was designed to restore patients' self-restraint by treating them with respect and dignity and encouraging them to exercise self-control.

One of the most militant crusaders for moral treatment of the insane was Dorothea Dix (1802–1877). A retired schoolteacher living in Boston in 1841, Dix visited a jail on a cold Sunday morning to teach a Sunday School class to women inmates. There she discovered the negligence and brutality that characterized the treatment of poor people with abnormal behavior, many of whom were simply warehoused in jails:

> Following the lesson, Miss Dix focused her attention on conditions in the jail. Prostitutes, drunks, criminals, retarded individuals, and the mentally ill were housed together in unheated, unfurnished, and foul-smelling quarters. Inmates without adequate clothing were huddled and shivering in the chill March New England climate. The conditions offended all the senses. When Dorothea Dix asked why heat was not provided, she was informed that the insane do not feel heat and cold. (Viney & Zorich, 1982, p. 212)

That encounter began Dix's tireless quest to improve the treatment of people with abnormal behavior. Dix was armed with dogged determinism and considerable political savvy, and she went from state to state, speaking to legislators and laypeople about the conditions in mental hospitals. Dix's lobbying efforts led to the passage of laws and appropriations to fund the clean-up of mental hospitals and the training of mental-health professionals dedicated to the moral treatment of patients. Be-

Dorothea Dix crusaded for the moral treatment of mental patients in the United States.

tween 1841 and 1881, Dix personally helped establish more than 30 mental institutions in the United States, Canada, Newfoundland, and Scotland. Hundreds more public hospitals for the insane were established during this period by others and were run according to humanitarian perspectives.

Another leader of the moral treatment of people with abnormality was Philippe Pinel (1745–1826), a French physician, who was put in charge of La Bicêtre in Paris in 1793. Pinel argued, "To detain maniacs in constant seclusion and to load them with chains; to leave them defenceless, to the brutality of underlings . . . in a word, to rule them with a rod of iron . . . is a system of superintendence, more distinguished for its convenience than for its humanity or success" (Grob, 1994, p. 27). Pinel rejected supernatural theories of abnormality and believed that many forms of abnormality could be cured by restoring the dignity and tranquility of patients.

Pinel ordered that patients be released from their chains and allowed to walk freely around the asylum. They were provided with clean and sunny rooms, comfortable sleeping quarters, and good food. Nurses and professional therapists were trained to work with the patients, to help them restore their sense of tranquility, and to help them engage in planned social activities. Although many other physicians thought Pinel himself was mad for releasing the patients, his approach was remarkably successful. Many people who had been locked away in darkness for decades became able to control their behavior and reengage in life. Some improved so much that they could be released. Pinel later reformed a mental hospital in Paris for female patients, La Salpetrière, and had remarkable success there as well.

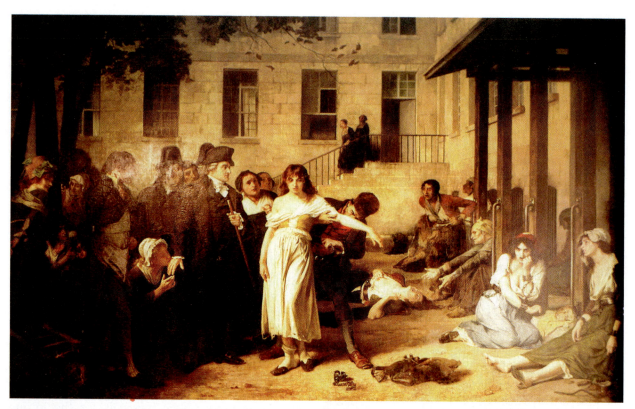

Philippe Pinel, a leader in the moral movement in France, helped free mental patients from the horrible conditions of the hospitals.

Unfortunately, the moral treatment movement grew too fast. As more asylums were built, and more people went into these asylums, the capacity of the asylums to recruit mental-health professionals and to maintain a humane, individual approach to each patient declined (Grob, 1994; Scull, 1993). The physicians, nurses, and other caretakers simply did not have enough time to give each patient the calm and dedicated attention he or she needed. The fantastic successes of the early moral treatment movement gave way to more modest successes, and many outright failures, as patients remained impaired or even got worse. Even some patients who received the best of moral treatment could not benefit from it, because their problems were not due to a loss of dignity or tranquility. Because so many patients were being given the moral treatment, the number of patients who failed to benefit from it increased, and questions about the effectiveness of moral treatment grew louder.

At the same time, the rapid pace of immigration into the United States in the late nineteenth century meant that an increasing percentage of its asylum patients were from different cultures and often were of lower socioeconomic classes. Prejudice against these "foreigners," combined with increasing attention to the failures of moral treatment

to cure many patients, led to declines in public support for funding these institutions. This reduced funding led to even greater declines in the quality of care given to patients. At the turn of the twentieth century, many public hospitals were no better than warehouses, where patients were kept in restraints for long periods of time simply to control their behavior (Grob, 1994; McGovern, 1985; Scull, 1993).

Effective biological treatments were not developed for most major psychological disorders until well into the twentieth century. Until these treatments were developed, mental patients who could not afford private care were basically warehoused in large state institutions and not given the psychological and social rehabilitation prescribed by the moral management theories. Many of these institutions were overcrowded and isolated far from cities or towns. The physical isolation of the mental hospitals contributed to the slow progress in the application of medical advances to the treatment of abnormal behavior (Deutsch, 1937). Clifford Beers, highlighted at the beginning and ending of this chapter, was one extraordinary man who suffered the conditions of mental hospitals at the turn of the twentieth century, survived them, and worked to change them.

SUMMING UP

- Three types of theories have influenced the definition and treatment of abnormality over the ages: the biological theories, the supernatural theories, and the psychological theories.

- Stone Age people probably viewed abnormal behavior as a result of supernatural forces. They may have drilled holes in the skulls of sufferers—a procedure known as trephination—to release the evil forces causing the abnormal behavior.

- Some of the earliest written references to abnormal behavior can be found in Chinese medical texts around 2674 B.C. and then in the papyri of Egypt and Mesopotamia, in the Old Testament, and in the writings of ancient Greek and Roman philosophers and physicians. Abnormal behaviors were often described as medical disorders in these ancient writings, although there is also evidence that they were viewed as due to supernatural forces.

- The witch hunts began in the late Middle Ages. Some accused witches may have suffered from abnormal behavior.

- Psychic epidemics have occurred throughout history. They were formerly explained as due to spirit possession but are now seen as a result of the effects of social conditions on people's self-perceptions.

- In the eighteenth and nineteenth centuries, advocates of more gentle treatment of people with abnormal behavior began to establish asylums for these people.

THE EMERGENCE OF MODERN PERSPECTIVES

Although the quality of the treatment of people with abnormal behavior had declined somewhat at the turn of the twentieth century, tremendous advances in the scientific study of disorders took place in the early twentieth century. These advances laid the groundwork for the biological, psychological, and social theories of abnormality that now dominate psychology and psychiatry.

The Beginnings of Modern Biological Perspectives

Basic knowledge of the anatomy, physiology, neurology, and chemistry of the body increased rapidly in the late nineteenth century. With the advancement of this basic knowledge came increasing focus on biological causes of abnormality. In 1845, Ger-

Emil Kraepelin (1856–1926) developed a classification system for mental disorders that remains very influential today.

man psychiatrist Wilhelm Griesinger (1817–1868) published *The Pathology and Therapy of Psychic Disorders*, the first systematic argument that all psychological disorders can be explained in terms of brain pathology. In 1883, one of Griesinger's followers, Emil Kraepelin (1856–1926), also published a textbook emphasizing the importance of brain pathology in psychological disorders. More important, Kraepelin developed a scheme of classifying symptoms into discrete disorders that has stood the test of time and is the basis for our modern classification systems, as we will discuss in Chapter 4. Having a good classification system gives investigators a common set of labels for disorders, as well as a set of criteria for distinguishing between disorders. This contributes immensely to the advancement of the scientific study of the disorders.

One of the most important discoveries underpinning modern biological theories of abnormality was the discovery of the cause of general paresis, a disease that leads to paralysis, insanity, and eventually death. In the mid-1800s, reports that patients with paresis also had a history of syphilis led to the suspicion that syphilis might be a cause of paresis. In 1897, Viennese psychiatrist Richard Krafft-Ebing conducted a daring experiment that would not pass scientific ethics boards today. He injected paretic patients with matter from syphilis sores. None of the patients developed syphilis, and Krafft-Ebing concluded that they must already have been infected with syphilis. The discovery that syphilis is the cause of one form of insanity lent great weight to the idea that biological factors can cause abnormal behaviors.

As we will discuss in more detail in Chapter 2, modern biological theories of the psychological disorders have focused on the role of genetics, structural abnormalities in the brain, and biochemical imbalances. The advances in our understanding of the biological aspects of psychological disorders have contributed to the development of a large number of medications that are useful in the treatment of these disorders, as we will discuss in Chapter 5.

The Psychoanalytic Perspective

The development of psychoanalytic theory begins with the odd story of Franz Anton Mesmer (1734–1815), an Austrian physician who believed that people had a magnetic fluid in the body that must be distributed in a particular pattern in order to maintain health. The distribution of magnetic fluid in one person could be influenced by the magnetic forces of other people, as well as by the alignments of the planets. In 1778, Mesmer opened a clinic in Paris to treat all sorts of diseases by "animal magnetism."

The psychological disorders that were the focus of much of Mesmer's treatment were the hysterical disorders, in which people lose functioning or feeling in some part of the body for no apparent physiological reason. The patients sat in darkness around a tub containing various chemicals, the affected areas of their bodies prodded by iron rods emerging from the tub. With music playing, Mesmer emerged in an elaborate robe, touching each patient as he passed by, supposedly realigning people's magnetic fluids through his own powerful magnetic force. This process, Mesmer said, cured illness, including psychological disorders.

Mesmer was eventually labeled a charlatan by a scientific review committee, which included Benjamin Franklin, yet his methods, known as **mesmerism,** continued to fuel debate long after he had faded into obscurity. The "cures" Mesmer caused in his psychiatric patients were attributed to the trancelike state that Mesmer seemed to induce in his patients. Later, this state was relabeled *hypnosis.* Under hypnosis, Mesmer's patients appeared very suggestible, and the suggestion that their ailments would disappear seemed enough to make them actually disappear.

The connection between hypnosis and hysteria fascinated several leading scientists of the time, although not all scientists accepted this connection. In particular, Jean Charcot (1825–1893), head of La Salpetrière Hospital in Paris and the leading neurologist of his time, argued that hysteria was caused by degeneration in the brain and had nothing to do with hypnosis. The work of two physicians practicing in the French town of Nancy, Hippolyte-Marie Bernheim (1840–1919) and Ambroise-Auguste Liebault (1823–1904), eventually won Charcot over, however. Bernheim and Liebault argued that hysteria was caused by self-hypnosis. They showed that they could induce the symptoms of hysteria, such as paralysis in an arm or the loss of feeling in a leg, by suggesting these symptoms to patients who were hypnotized. Fortunately, they could also remove these symptoms under hypnosis. Charcot was so impressed by the evidence that hysteria has psychological roots that he became a leading researcher of the psychological causes of abnormal behavior. The experiments of Bernheim and Liebault, and the leadership of Charcot, did a great deal to advance psychological perspectives on abnormality.

One of Charcot's students was Sigmund Freud (1856–1939), a Viennese neurologist. He went to study with Charcot in 1885 and, in this work, became convinced that much of the mental life of an individual remains hidden from consciousness. This view was further supported by Freud's interactions with Pierre Janet (1858–1947) in Paris, who was investigating multiple personality disorder, in which people appear to have multiple, distinct personalities, each of which operates independently of the others, often not knowing the others exist (Matarazzo, 1985).

When he returned to Vienna, Freud worked with another physician who was interested in

Anton Mesmer's (1734–1815) work on animal magnetism set the stage for the study of hypnosis.

hypnosis and the unconscious processes behind psychological problems, Josef Breuer (1842–1925). Breuer had discovered that encouraging patients to talk about their problems while under hypnosis led to a great upswelling and release of emotion, which was eventually called catharsis. The patient's discussion of his or her problems under hypnosis was less censored than conscious discussion, allowing the therapist to elicit important psychological material more easily.

Breuer and Freud collaborated on a paper published in 1893 as *On the Psychical Mechanisms of Hysterical Phemonena*, which laid out their discoveries about hypnosis, the unconscious, and the therapeutic value of catharsis. This paper proved to be a foundation stone in the development of **psychoanalysis,** the study of the unconscious. Freud introduced his ideas to America in a series of lectures in 1909 at Clark University in Worcester, Massachusetts, at the invitation of G. Stanley Hall, one of the founders of American psychology.

Freud went on to write dozens of papers and books describing his theory of psychoanalysis, and he became the best-known figure in psychiatry and psychology. The impact of Freud's theories on the development of psychology over the next century cannot be overestimated. Freudian ideas not only influenced the professional literature on psychopathology but also are used heavily in literary theory, anthropology, and other humanities. They pervade popular notions of psychological processes to this day.

The Roots of Behaviorism

In what seems now like a parallel universe, while psychoanalytic theory was being born, the roots of behaviorism were being planted in Europe and then the United States. Wilhelm Wundt (1832–1920) established the first experimental psychology laboratory in 1879 in Leipzig, Germany. His work focused on memory and sensation, but he and others developed many of the basic experimental techniques that are the mainstay of behavioral experimentation. In 1896, one of Wundt's students, Lightner Witmer (1867–1956), established the first psychological clinic at the University of Pennsylvania to study the causes and treatment of mental deficiency in children. Witmer thus brought the experimental techniques of the new behaviorism to bear on an important clinical issue—the functioning of children.

Ivan Pavlov (1849–1936), a Russian physiologist, was also developing methods and theories to understand behavior in terms of stimuli and responses, rather than in terms of the internal workings of the unconscious mind. He discovered that dogs could be conditioned to salivate to stimuli other than food if the food was paired with these other stimuli—a process later called *classical conditioning*. Pavlov's discoveries inspired American John Watson (1878–1958) to study important human behaviors, such as phobias, in terms of classical conditioning (see Chapter 7). Watson rejected psychoanalytic and biological theories of abnormal behaviors, such as phobias, and explained them entirely on the basis of the individual's history of conditioning. Watson went so far as to boast that he could train any healthy child to become any kind of adult one wished:

> Give me a dozen healthy infants, well-formed, and my own specified world to bring them up in, and I'll guarantee to take any one at random and train him to be any type of specialist I might select—doctor, lawyer, artist, merchant-chief, and yes, even beggar-man and thief, regardless of his talents, penchants, tendencies, abilities, vocations, and the race of his ancestors. (Watson, 1930, p. 104)

In the meantime, two other psychologists, E. L. Thorndike (1874–1949) and B. F. Skinner (1904–1990), were studying how the consequences of behaviors shape their likelihood of recurrence. They argued that behaviors that are followed by positive consequences are more likely to be repeated than behaviors followed by negative consequences. This process came to be known as *operant*, or *instrumental, conditioning*. This idea may seem simple to us now (which is one sign of how much it has influenced thinking over the past century), but at the time it was radical to argue that even complex behaviors, such as violence against others, can be explained by the reinforcement or punishment these behaviors have had in the past.

Behaviorism—the study of the impact of reinforcements and punishments on behavior—has had as profound an impact on psychology and on our common knowledge of psychology as has psychoanalytic theory. Behavioral theories have led to many of the effective psychological treatments for disorders that we will discuss in this book.

The Cognitive Revolution

In the 1950s, some experimental psychologists began to argue that behaviorism is limited in its explanatory power by its refusal to look at some of the internal thought processes that mediate the relationship between stimulus and response. It wasn't until the 1970s that psychology shifted its focus substantially to the study of **cognitions**—thought processes that influence behavior and emotion. An important player in this cognitive revolution was Albert Bandura, a clinical psychologist trained in behaviorism who had contributed a great deal to the application of behaviorism to psychopathology (see Chapters 2 and 7). Bandura argued that people's beliefs about their ability to execute the behaviors necessary to control important events—which he called **self-efficacy beliefs**—are crucial in determining their well-being. Again, this idea seems obvious to us now, but that is only because it took hold of both professional psychology and lay notions of psychology.

Another key figure in cognitive perspectives was Albert Ellis, who argued that people prone to psychological disorders are plagued by irrational negative assumptions about themselves and the world. Ellis developed a therapy for emotional problems based on his theory, called rational-emotive therapy. This therapy was controversial, because it required therapists to challenge, sometimes quite harshly, their patients' irrational belief systems. It became very popular, however, and moved psychology into the study of the thought processes behind serious emotional problems. Another therapy focused on the irrational thoughts of people with psychological problems was developed by Aaron Beck. Beck's cognitive therapy has become one of the widest used therapies for many disorders (see Chapters 2 and 5). Since the 1970s, theorists have continued to emphasize cognitive factors in psychopathology, although behavioral theories have remained strong, and interpersonal theories, which we will examine in the next chapter, have become more prominent.

SUMMING UP

- Modern biological theories and therapies began with the development of Kraepelin's classification scheme for psychological disorders and the discovery that syphilis causes general paresis, a disease with symptoms including loss of touch with reality.

- The roots of psychoanalytic theory can be found in the work of Mesmer and the suggestion that psychological symptoms can be relieved through hypnosis. Jean Charcot, Sigmund Freud, and Josef Breuer are among the founders of modern psychoanalytic theory, which focuses on the role of the unconscious in psychological symptoms.

- Behavioral approaches to psychopathology began with the development of basic experimental techniques to study the effects of reinforcement and punishment in producing normal, and abnormal, behavior.

- Cognitive approaches to abnormality emerged in the mid-twentieth century, when theorists began arguing that the way people think about events in their environment determines their emotional and behavioral responses to those events.

MODERN MENTAL-HEALTH CARE

Halfway through the twentieth century, major breakthroughs were made in drug treatments for some of the major forms of abnormality. In particular, the discovery of a class of drugs that can reduce the symptoms of schizophrenia, known as the phenothiazines (see Chapter 5), made it possible for many people who had been institutionalized for years to be released from asylums and hospitals. Since then, there has been an explosion of new drug therapies for psychopathology. In addition, as we will discuss in Chapter 5, several types of psychotherapy have been developed, and continue to be developed, that have proven effective in treating a wide range of psychological problems. Still, there are significant problems in the delivery of mental-health care, some of which began with the deinstitutionalization movement of the mid-twentieth century.

Deinstitutionalization

By 1960, a large and vocal movement, known as the **patients' rights movement,** had emerged. Patients' rights advocates argued that mental patients can recover more fully or live more satisfying lives if they are integrated into the community, with the support of community-based treatment facilities—a process known as **deinstitutionalization.** Many of these patients would continue to need around-the-clock care, but it could be given in treatment centers based in neighborhoods, rather than in large, impersonal institutions. The **community mental-health movement** was officially launched in 1963 by President John Kennedy as a "bold new approach" to mental-health care. This movement attempted to provide coordinated mental-health services to people in community-based centers.

The deinstitutionalization movement had massive effects on the lives of people with serious psychological problems. Between 1955 and 1998, the number of patients in state psychiatric hospitals went from a high of 559,000 to about 57,000—almost a 90 percent reduction (Lamb & Weinberger, 2001). Many former mental patients who had lived for years in cold, sterile facilities, receiving little useful care, experienced dramatic increases in the quality of life on their release. Moreover, they suddenly had the freedom to live where they wanted to, as they saw fit.

Unfortunately, the resources to care for all the mental patients released from institutions were never adequate. There were not enough halfway houses built or community mental-health centers funded to serve the thousands of men and women who were formerly institutionalized or who would have been if the movement had not happened. In the meantime, the state psychiatric hospitals to which they would have retreated were closed down by the hundreds. These men and women began living in nursing homes and other types of group homes, where they received little mental-health treatment, or with their families, many of whom were ill-equipped to handle serious mental illness (Lamb, 2001). Some of these people began living on the streets. Certainly not all homeless people are mentally ill, but some researchers estimate that one-third to one-half of all long-term homeless adults in the United States have a major mental disorder, and up to four-fifths have a mental disorder, a severe substance use disorder (such as alcoholism), or both (Baum & Burnes, 1993). In emergencies, these people end up in general or private hospitals that are not equipped to treat them appropriately (Kiesler & Sibulkin, 1983). Many end up in jail (Torrey, 1997). It is estimated that 10 to 15 percent of the prison population has a serious mental disorder (Lamb & Weinberger, 2001).

Thus, deinstitutionalization began with laudatory goals, but many of these goals were never fully reached, leaving many people who formerly would have been institutionalized in mental hospitals no better off. In recent years, the financial strains on local, state, and federal governments have led to the closing of many more community mental-health centers.

Managed Care

The entire system of private insurance for health care underwent a revolution in the second half of the twentieth century. Managed care emerged as the dominant means for organizing health care. The exact nature of managed care systems varies greatly from one company to another, but **managed care** is generally a loose collection of methods for organizing health care that ranges from simple monitoring all the way to total control over what care can be provided and paid for. The goals are to coordinate services for an existing medical problem and to prevent future medical problems before they arise. Often, health care providers are given a set amount of money per member (patient) per month and then must determine how best to serve their patients with that money.

Under managed care, some of the problems created by deinstitutionalization can be solved. For example, instead of leaving it up to people with a serious psychological problem, or their families, to find appropriate care, the primary provider might find this care and ensure that patients have access to it. Say an individual patient reported to his physician that he was hearing voices when there was no one around. The physician might refer the patient to a psychiatrist for an evaluation, to determine if the patient might be suffering from schizophrenia. In some cases, the primary care physician might coordinate care offered by other providers, such as drug treatments, psychotherapy, and rehabilitation services. And the primary provider might ensure continuity of care, so that patients did not "fall through the cracks." Thus, theoretically, managed care could have tremendous benefits for people with long-term, serious mental-health problems. For people with less severe psychological problems, the availability of mental-health care through managed care systems and other private insurance systems has led to a tremendous increase in the number of people seeking psychotherapy and other types of mental-health care.

Unfortunately, however, mental-health care is often not covered, or covered fully, by health insurance. For people who need hospitalization, insurance often pays for a very limited stay. For those who need outpatient care, insurance may pay for only a few sessions of psychotherapy and often pays only for drugs, not psychotherapy. Then, of course, many people do not have any kind of health insurance, because they are not employed or their employer does not offer it.

The Medicaid Program, which covers one-fifth of all mental-health care spending in the United States, has been a target for reductions in recent years. Many states have reduced or restricted eligibility and benefits for mental-health care, have increased copayments, have controlled drug costs, and have reduced or frozen payments to providers (Mechanic & Bilder, 2004). In the meantime, the number of people seeking mental-health care has risen. For example, the Veterans Administration provides health care for poor and disabled veterans, and the number of people seeking mental-health care has increased by 4 percent per year since 1990 (Rosenheck, 1999). At the same time, reductions in state and city welfare programs and other community services to the poor have made daily life more difficult for poor people in general, and in particular for people with serious mental disorders, who often have exhausted their financial resources. At the turn of the millennium, it was estimated that about 50 percent of the people in the United States with serious psychological problems were not receiving stable mental-health treatment (Kessler et al., 2001). This situation is particularly distressing, given that effective biological and psychosocial treatments now exist for the majority of mental-health problems, as we will discuss throughout this book.

PROFESSIONS WITHIN ABNORMAL PSYCHOLOGY

In our times, a number of professions are concerned with abnormal or maladaptive behavior. Psychiatry is a branch of medicine that focuses on psychological disorders. *Psychiatrists* have an M.D. degree and have specialized training in the treatment of psychological problems. Psychiatrists can prescribe medications for the treatment of these problems, and some also have been trained to conduct psychotherapies that involve talking with people about their problems.

Clinical psychologists typically have a Ph.D. in psychology, with a specialization in psychological problems. Clinical psychologists can conduct psychotherapy, but in most states they do not currently prescribe medications (although they do have limited prescription privileges in some programs and many psychologists are lobbying for prescription privileges in many states).

Marriage and family therapists specialize in helping families, couples, and children overcome problems that are interfering with their well-being. *Clinical social workers* have a master's degree in social work and often focus on helping people with psychological problems overcome the social conditions contributing to their problems, such as joblessness or homelessness. *Psychiatric nurses* have a degree in nursing, with a specialization in the treatment of people with severe psychological problems. They often work on inpatient psychiatric wards in hospitals, delivering medical care and certain forms of psychotherapy, such as group therapy to increase patients' contacts with one another. They have privileges to write prescriptions for psychotherapeutic drugs in some states.

Dramatic changes are currently taking place in the field of mental health, due to changes in the funding of mental-health care. There have been some increases in insurance funding for psychiatric medications, but many people in the United States either have no insurance to cover mental-health care or have only limited coverage. The practice of psychiatry has declined in status somewhat over the past two decades, and fewer and fewer students with new M.D.s are pursuing psychiatry

(Appelbaum, 2003). In contrast, there has been a substantial increase in the number of clinical psychologists, clinical social workers, and marriage and family therapists (Mechanic & Bilder, 2004). The increased competition for the mental-health dollar has led to political disagreements between the types of mental-health professionals over who has the right to treat which kinds of disorders.

Each of these professions has its rewards and its limitations. Students who are interested in one or more of these professions often find it helpful to volunteer to be a research assistant in studies of psychological problems or to volunteer to work in a psychiatric clinic or hospital, to learn more about these professions. This type of volunteering can help students determine what type of work within abnormal psychology is most comfortable for them. Some students find tremendous gratification working with people with psychological problems, whereas others find it more gratifying to conduct research that might answer important questions about psychological problems. Many mental-health professionals of all types combine clinical practice and research in their careers.

SUMMING UP

- The goal of the deinstitutionalization movement was to move mental patients from custodial mental-health facilities, where they were isolated and received little treatment, to community-based mental-health centers. Thousands of patients were released from mental institutions. Unfortunately, community-based mental-health centers have never been fully funded or supported, leaving many former mental patients with few resources in the community.

- Managed care systems are meant to provide coordinated, comprehensive medical care to patients. This can be a great asset to people with long-term, serious disorders. Coverage for mental-health problems tends to be limited, however, and many people have no insurance at all.

- A number of professions provide care to people with mental-health problems, including psychiatrists, psychologists, marriage and family therapists, clinical social workers, and psychiatric nurses.

CHAPTER INTEGRATION

Although the biological, psychological, and social theories of abnormality have traditionally been viewed as competing with each other to explain psychological disorders, many clinicians and researchers now believe that theories that integrate biological, psychological, and social perspectives on abnormality will prove most useful (see Figure 1.3). For example, in Chapter 7, we will discuss theories of anxiety disorders that take into account individuals' genetic and biochemical vulnerabilities, the impact of stressful events, and the role of cognitions in explaining why some people suffer debilitating anxiety. Throughout this book, we will first examine the biological, psychological, and social theories of a given disorder, but we will focus on how these factors interact and influence each other to produce and maintain mental-health problems. In other words, we will take an **integrationist approach** to psychological problems. Note that the color-coding scheme in Figue 1.3 reinforces this approach and will be used in other figures throughout the book, with green for biological factors, blue for social factors, and orange for psychological factors.

What about supernatural theories? Most cultures still have *spiritual healers*. Throughout this book, we will consider cross-cultural perspectives on psychological disorders, and we will note the supernatural theories some cultures hold about abnormality and the healing rituals that emerge from these theories. Even in cultures in which most healers do not subscribe to supernatural theories of abnormality, however, laypeople often still believe in the power of supernatural forces to cause or cure their psychological problems. These beliefs influence the type of healer a person with a psychological problem might seek out and how he or she might present the psychological problem to a potential therapist. Thus, supernatural theories arise in the practice of treating people with psychological problems, because these clients take them into discussions with their therapists. In turn, therapists must work within a client's framework to help the client understand his or her mental-health problems.

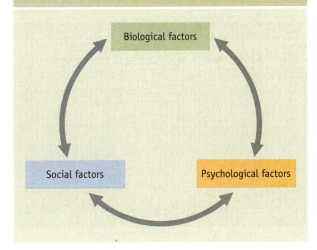

FIGURE 1.3 **The Integrationist Approach to Understanding Mental Health.** Many mental health theories today strive to integrate biological, psychological, and social factors in understanding mental-health issues, and this integrationist approach will be emphasized in this book.

Extraordinary People: Follow-Up

At the beginning of this chapter, we met Clifford Beers, a young man whose paranoia of becoming epileptic evolved into a three-year nightmare of depression, a break from reality, and horrific treatments in mental hospitals in the early 1900s. One of the extraordinary things about Beers is that this experience did not break him—instead, it inspired him to start a movement for the reform of mental-health treatment, which he called the **mental hygiene movement.** After his release from the mental hospital, Beers wrote a personal account of his time there, which was published in 1908 as *A Mind That Found Itself.* This book changed how physicians and the lay public viewed mental patients and hospitals. He argued that all psychological disorders are medical diseases and should be treated biologically. Beers outlined a plan for reforms in the treatment of the mentally ill and for the prevention of mental illness. He advocated public education about mental illness and early treatment for those who were afflicted. One of Beers' supporters was Dr. Adolph Meyer, who was himself revolutionizing the treatment of mental patients by advocating the treatment of the "whole individual," including assisting former mental patients in their reintegration into society. Beers eventually founded the National and International Committees on Mental Hygiene and became a fund-raiser and lobbyist for the rights of mental patients.

In *A Mind That Found Itself*, Beers explained his motivations and drive to use his experiences to change the lives of others who suffered from psychological disorders:

> When I set out upon a career of reform, I was impelled to do so by motives in part like those which seem to have possessed Don Quixote when he set forth, as Cervantes says, with the intention "of righting every kind of wrong, and exposing himself to peril and danger, from which in the issue he would obtain eternal renown and fame." In likening myself to Cervantes' mad hero my purpose is quite other than to push myself within the charmed circle of the chivalrous. What I wish to do is to make plain that a man abnormally elated may be swayed irresistibly by his best instincts, and that while under the spell of an exaltation, idealistic in degree, he may not only be willing, but eager to assume risks and endure hardships which under normal conditions he would assume reluctantly, if at all. In justice to myself, however, I may remark that my plans for reform have never assumed quixotic, and therefore impracticable, proportions. At no time have I gone a-tilting at windmills. A pen rather than a lance has been my weapon of offense and defense; for with its point I have felt sure that I should one day prick the civic conscience into a compassionate activity, and thus bring into a neglected field earnest men and women who should act as champions for those afflicted thousands least able to fight for themselves.

Beers' biographer, Norman Dain, writes:

> [Beers] significantly contributed toward making public discussion of psychological disorders legitimate, informed, and matter-of-fact. The movement helped to introduce mental health considerations into many aspects of American life, such as the schools and the courts, not for sensational exploitation but to develop systematic means of dealing with children's emotional problems. On a personal plane, Clifford Beers was a living refutation of the view that mental disorder forever incapacitated a person for useful public activity. His life experience educated people to the complexities and surprising possibilities that lie within so many men and women whom society tends to discard. (Dain, 1980, p. 331)

Chapter Summary

- Cultural relativists argue that the norms of a society must be used to determine the normality of a behavior. Others have suggested that unusual behaviors, or behaviors that cause subjective discomfort in a person, should be labeled abnormal. Still others have suggested that only behaviors resulting from mental illness or disease are abnormal. All these criteria have serious limitations, however.

- Currently, the consensus among professionals is that behaviors that cause people to suffer distress, that prevent them from functioning in daily life, and that are unusual are abnormal. These behaviors are often referred to as maladaptive and can be remembered with the heuristic of the 3Ds: distress, dysfunction, and deviance (review Figure 1.1).

- Historically, theories of abnormality have fallen into one of three categories. Biological theories saw psychological disorders as similar to physical diseases, caused by the breakdown of a system of the body. Supernatural theories saw abnormal behavior as a result of divine intervention, curses, demonic possession, and personal sin. Psychological theories saw abnormal behavior as a result of stress. These three types of theories led to very different types of treatment of people who acted abnormally.

- In prehistoric times, people probably had largely supernatural theories of abnormal behavior, attributing it to demons or ghosts. A treatment for abnormality in the Stone Age may have been to drill holes in the skull to allow demons to depart, a procedure known as trephination.

- Ancient Chinese, Egyptian, and Greek texts suggest that these cultures took a natural, or biological, view of abnormal behavior, although references to supernatural and psychological theories also can be found.

- During the Middle Ages, abnormal behavior may have been interpreted as due to witchcraft.

- History provides many examples of psychic epidemics and mass hysterias. Groups of people have shown similar psychological and behavioral symptoms, which usually have been attributed to common stresses or beliefs.

- Even well into the nineteenth and twentieth centuries, many people who acted abnormally were shut away in prisonlike conditions, tortured, starved, and ignored.

- As part of the mental hygiene movement, the moral management of mental hospitals became more widespread. Patients in these hospitals were treated with kindness and the best biological treatments available. Effective biological treatments for most psychological problems were not available until the mid-twentieth century, however.

- Modern biological perspectives on psychological disorders were advanced by Kraepelin's development of a classification system and the discovery that the syndrome known as general paresis is caused by a syphilis infection.

- The psychoanalytic perspective began with the odd work of Anton Mesmer, but then it grew as Jean Charcot, and eventually Sigmund Freud, became interested in the role of the unconscious in producing abnormality.

- Behaviorist views on abnormal behavior began with the basic research of John Watson and B. F.

Skinner, who used principles of classical and operant conditioning to explain both normal and abnormal behavior.

- The cognitive revolution was spurred by theorists such as Albert Ellis, Albert Bandura, and Aaron Beck and focused on the role of thinking processes in abnormality.

- The deinstitutionalization movement attempted to move mental patients from mental-health facilities, where they were isolated and received little treatment, to community-based mental-health centers. Unfortunately, community-based mental-health centers have never been fully funded or supported, leaving many former mental patients with few resources in the community.

- Managed care systems are meant to provide coordinated, comprehensive medical care to patients. This can be a great asset to people with long-term, serious psychological disorders. Insurance coverage for mental-health problems tends to be limited, however, and many people have no insurance at all.

- The professions within abnormal psychology include psychiatrists, psychologists, marriage and family therapists, clinical social workers, and psychiatric nurses.

MindMap CD-ROM

The following resources on the MindMap CD-ROM that came with this text will help you to master the content of this chapter and prepare for tests:

- Video: History of Mental Illness
- Chapter Timeline
- Chapter Quiz

Key Terms

psychopathology 4

context 5

gender roles 6

cultural relativism 6

unusualness 8

discomfort 9

mental illness 9

maladaptive 9

biological theories 11

supernatural theories 11

psychological theories 11

trephination 12

psychic epidemics 16

moral treatment 19

general paresis 21

mesmerism 22

psychoanalysis 23

behaviorism 23

cognitions 23

self-efficacy beliefs 24

patients' rights movement 24

deinstitutionalization 24

community mental-health movement 24

managed care 25

integrationist approach 27

mental hygiene movement 27

Chapter 2

Heart of the Hunter
by Michelle Puleo

It can be no dishonor to learn from others when they speak good sense.

—Sophocles, *Antigone*
(442–441 B.C.; translated by Elizabeth Wyckoff)

Contemporary Theories of Abnormality <

Extraordinary People

■ **Albert Ellis:** *The Phobic Psychologist*

Biological Approaches

Biological theories suggest that psychological symptoms are due to structural abnormalities in the brain, poor functioning of brain neurotransmitter systems, or faulty genes. These three types of biological abnormalities may work independently to create psychological symptoms, or genetic abnormalities are often the cause of other abnormalities.

Taking Psychology Personally

■ **Do "Bad Genes" Doom You to a Disorder?**

Psychological Approaches

Psychodynamic theories of abnormality suggest that psychological symptoms are due to unconscious conflicts. Newer psychodynamic theories focus on concepts of the self that develop from early experiences. Behavioral theories say symptoms result from the reinforcements and punishments people have received for their behaviors. Cognitive theories say that people's ways of interpreting situations determine their emotional and behavioral symptoms. Humanist and existential theories suggest that symptoms arise when people are not allowed to pursue their potential and, instead, try to conform to others' wishes.

Social and Interpersonal Approaches

Interpersonal theorists focus on the role of interpersonal relationships in shaping normal and abnormal behavior. Family systems theories suggest that psychopathology within individual family members is the result of dysfunctional patterns of interaction within families that encourage and maintain the psychopathology within the individual members. Social structural theorists focus on the influence of the environment and culture on individuals' behavior.

Chapter Integration

Many scientists believe that only models that *integrate* biological, psychological, and social factors can provide comprehensive explanations of psychological disorders. Integrated models are often called vulnerability-stress models.

Extraordinary People

Albert Ellis: *The Phobic Psychologist*

Albert Ellis is best known as the psychologist who developed a cognitive theory of emotional problems called rational-emotive theory, as well as a form of therapy based on this theory. According to Ellis' theory, which we will discuss in more detail in this chapter, emotional problems are the result of irrational beliefs. In rational-emotive therapy, therapists confront clients with their irrational beliefs in an attempt to change those beliefs (see Chapter 5).

What most people don't know about Albert Ellis is that he suffered from a fear of public speaking that was so severe that it could have prevented his career. Fortunately, Ellis was a born psychologist. He devised methods for treating himself that hadn't been discovered by psychologists at the time but now are part of many therapists' tool kit:

> At 19, Ellis became active in a political group but was hampered by his terror of public speaking. Confronting his worst demons in the first of many "shame-attacking" exercises he would devise, Ellis repeatedly forced himself to speak up in any political context that would permit it. "Without calling it that, I was doing early desensitization on myself," he says. "Instead of just getting good at this, I found I was very good at it. And now you can't keep me away from a public platform." After mastering his fear of public speaking, Ellis decided to work on the terrors of more private communication. "I was always . . . interested in women," he says. "I would see them and flirt and exchange glances, but I always made excuses not to talk to them and was terrified of being rejected. Since I lived near The New York Botanical Garden in the Bronx, I decided to attack my fear and shame with an exercise in the park. I vowed that whenever I saw a reasonably attractive woman up to the age of 35, rather than sitting a bench away as I normally would, I would sit next to her with the specific goal of opening a conversation within one minute. I sat next to 130 consecutive women who fit my criteria. Thirty of the women got up and walked away, but about 100 spoke to me—about their knitting, the birds, a book, whatever. I made only one date out of all these contacts—and she stood me up. According to learning theory and strict behavior therapy, my lack of rewards should have extinguished my efforts to meet women. But I realized that throughout this exercise no one vomited, no one called a cop, and I didn't die. The process of trying new behaviors and understanding what happened in the real world instead of in my imagination led me to overcome my fear of speaking to women." (Warga, 1988, p. 56)

Thus, rational-emotive therapy was born.

Albert Ellis was able to integrate his personal perspective with contemporary theory and research on anxiety to develop a new theory of his own. A **theory** is a set of ideas that provides a framework for asking questions about a phenomenon, as well as gathering and interpreting information about that phenomenon.

Ellis believed that his fears were due to irrational beliefs, but other theories suggest alternative causes of his fears. If you took a **biological approach** to abnormality, you would suspect that Ellis' symptoms were caused by a biological factor, such as a genetic vulnerability to anxiety, inherited from his parents. Ellis' own rational-emotive theory is a **psychological approach** to abnormality, which suggests that symptoms are rooted in psychological factors, such as belief systems or early childhood experiences. If you took a **social approach** to understanding Ellis' symptoms, you would look to his interpersonal relationships and the social environment in which he lived.

Traditionally, biological, psychological, and social approaches have been seen as incompatible with one another. People frequently ask, "Is the cause of this disorder biological *or* psychological *or* social?" This question is often called the *nature-nurture question*—is the cause of the disorder something in the *nature*, or biology, of the person or in the person's *nurturing*, or history of events to which the person was exposed? This question implies that there has to be one cause of a disorder, rather than multiple causes. Indeed, most theories of psychological disorders over history have searched for the one factor—the one gene, the one traumatic experience, the one personality trait—that causes people to develop that disorder.

Many contemporary theorists recognize that there are often many pathways that all lead to the same end—namely, the development of a specific disorder. In some cases, it takes only one of these factors to cause a disorder. In most cases, however, it takes an accumulation of several factors before an individual develops the disorder. Just one or two of the factors working together may not be enough to create the disorder, but, when multiple factors are present in the life of an individual, a threshold is reached and the disorder develops.

Biological, psychological, and social approaches are being integrated to develop comprehensive models of the many factors that lead some people to develop a given mental disorder (e.g., Caspi, 1993; Cicchetti & Rogosch, 1996). These integrated models are sometimes referred to as **vulnerability-stress models** (see Figure 2.1). According to these models, a person must carry a vulnerability to the disorder in order to develop it. This vulnerability can be a biological one, such as a genetic predisposition to the disorder. It can also be a psychological one, such as a personality trait that increases the person's risk of developing the disorder or a history of poor interpersonal relationships.

In order for the person to develop the disorder, however, he or she has to experience some type of stress, or trigger. Again, this trigger can be a biological one, such as illness that changes the person's balance of certain hormones. Or the trigger can be a psychological or social one, such as a traumatic event. Only when the vulnerability and the stress come together in the same individual does the full-blown disorder emerge. Although Ellis may indeed have had a genetic vulnerability to anxiety, he may have experienced stressers that triggered this vulnerability.

How do vulnerability and stress interact to cause a disorder? Another feature of contemporary theories of abnormality is that they recognize the *feedback effects* that biological and psychosocial factors have on each other. Feedback effects develop, so that changes in one factor result in changes in a second factor, but then those changes in the second factor feed back to change the first factor again (see Figure 2.2 on page 36). For example, a change in a person's biology, such as an increase in the levels of certain brain chemicals, might make the person angry and irritable. The person acts angrily and irritably around her friends, and in turn her friends react angrily toward her and begin to avoid her. The rejection of her friends only makes her more angry and irritable, which then causes even greater changes in her brain chemistry.

In this chapter, we examine the major biological, psychological, and social theories of

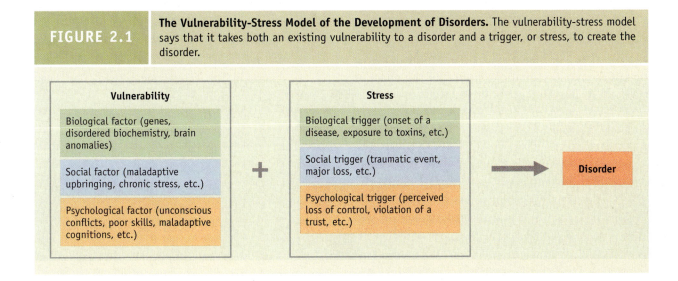

FIGURE 2.1   **The Vulnerability-Stress Model of the Development of Disorders.** The vulnerability-stress model says that it takes both an existing vulnerability to a disorder and a trigger, or stress, to create the disorder.

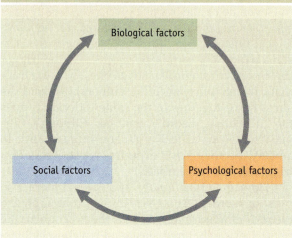

FIGURE 2.2   **Feedback Effects Among Biological, Social, and Psychological Factors.** Some integrative models of psychopathology suggest that biological, social, and psychological factors all affect each other in feedback loops that maintain and enhance psychopathological processes.

abnormality that have dominated the field in its modern history. They provide a background for understanding specific disorders and their treatments. Then in Chapter 5 we explore the treatments and therapies deriving from these theories. We look at the theories and treatments one at a time, so that they are easier to understand. Keep in mind, however, that most mental-health professionals now take an integrated approach to understanding mental disorders, viewing them as the result of a combination of biological, psychological, social vulnerabilities, and stresses that come together and feed off one another. We will return to this integrationist theme at the end of this chapter.

BIOLOGICAL APPROACHES

Let's start by considering the story of Phineas Gage, one of the most dramatic examples of the effect of biological factors on psychological functioning.

On 13 September 1848, Phineas P. Gage, a 25-year old construction foreman for the Rutland and Burlington Railroad in New England, became the victim of a bizarre accident. In order to lay new rail tracks across Vermont, it was necessary to level the uneven terrain by controlled blasting. Among other tasks, Gage was

in charge of the detonations, which involved drilling holes in the stone, partially filling the holes with explosive powder, covering the powder with sand, and using a fuse and a tamping iron to trigger an explosion into the rock. On the fateful day, a momentary distraction let Gage begin tamping directly over the powder before his assistant had had a chance to cover it with sand. The result was a powerful explosion away from the rock and toward Gage. The fine-pointed, 3-cm-thick, 109-cm-long tamping iron was hurled, rocket-like, through his face, skull, and brain, and then into the sky. Gage was momentarily stunned but regained full consciousness immediately thereafter. He was able to talk and even walk with the help of his men. The iron landed many yards away.

   Phineas Gage not only survived the momentous injury, in itself enough to earn him a place in the annals of medicine, but he survived as a different man, and therein lies the greater significance of this case. Gage had been a responsible, intelligent, and socially well-adapted individual, a favorite with peers and elders. He had made progress and showed promise. The signs of a profound change in personality were already evident during the convalescence under the care of his physician, John Harlow. But as the months passed, it became apparent that the transformation was not only radical but difficult to comprehend. In some respects, Gage was fully recovered. He remained as able-bodied and appeared to be as intelligent as before the accident; he had no impairment of movement or speech; new learning was intact, and neither memory nor intelligence in the conventional sense had been affected. On the other hand, he had become irreverent and capricious. His respect for the social conventions by which he once abided had vanished. His abundant profanity offended those around him. Perhaps most troubling, he had taken leave of his sense of responsibility. He could not be trusted to honor his commitments. His employers had deemed him "the

(continued)

most efficient and capable" man in their "employ" but now they had to dismiss him. In the words of his physician, "the equilibrium or balance, so to speak, between his intellectual faculty and animal propensities" had been destroyed. In the words of his friends and acquaintances, "Gage was no longer Gage." (Damasio et al., 1994, p. 1102)

As a result of damage to his brain from the accident, Gage's basic personality seemed to change. He was transformed from a responsible, socially appropriate man to an impulsive, emotional, and socially inappropriate man. Almost 150 years later, researchers using modern neuroimaging techniques on Gage's preserved skull and a computer simulation of the tamping-iron accident determined the precise location of the damage to Gage's brain (see Figure 2.3). (We will discuss neuroimaging techniques, such as MRI, CT, and PET scanning, in Chapter 4.)

Studies of people today who suffer damage to the same area of the brain as Gage's injury reveal that they have trouble making rational decisions in personal and social matters and have trouble processing information about emotions. They do not have trouble, however, with the logic of an abstract problem, with arithmetic calculations, or with memory. Like Gage, their basic intellectual functioning remains intact, but their emotional control and judgment in personal and social matters are impaired (Damasio et al., 1994).

Gage's psychological changes were the result of damage to his brain. *Structural damage to the brain* is one of three causes of abnormality on

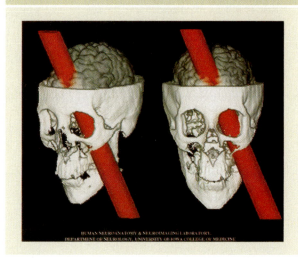

FIGURE 2.3   **Phineas Gage's Brain Injury.** Modern neuroimaging techniques have helped identify the precise location of damage to Phineas Gage's brain.

HUMAN NEUROANATOMY & NEUROIMAGING LABORATORY,
DEPARTMENT OF NEUROLOGY, UNIVERSITY OF IOWA COLLEGE OF MEDICINE

which biological approaches to abnormality often focus (see Figure 2.4). The other two are *biochemical imbalances* and *genetic abnormalities.* Structural abnormalities, biochemical imbalances, and genetic abnormalities can all influence each other. For example, structural abnormalities may be the result of genetic factors and may cause biochemical imbalances. We explore these three biological causes of abnormality in this section.

Structural Brain Abnormalities

It may seem obvious to us today that damage to the areas of the brain responsible for personality

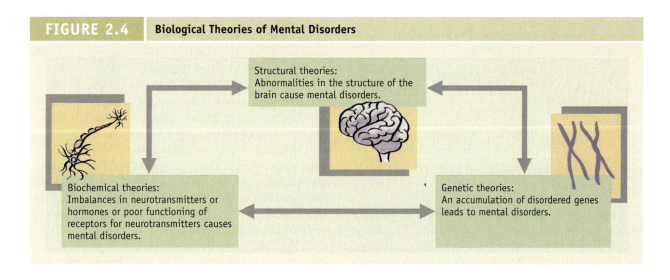

FIGURE 2.4   **Biological Theories of Mental Disorders**

Structural theories:
Abnormalities in the structure of the brain cause mental disorders.

Biochemical theories:
Imbalances in neurotransmitters or hormones or poor functioning of receptors for neurotransmitters causes mental disorders.

Genetic theories:
An accumulation of disordered genes leads to mental disorders.

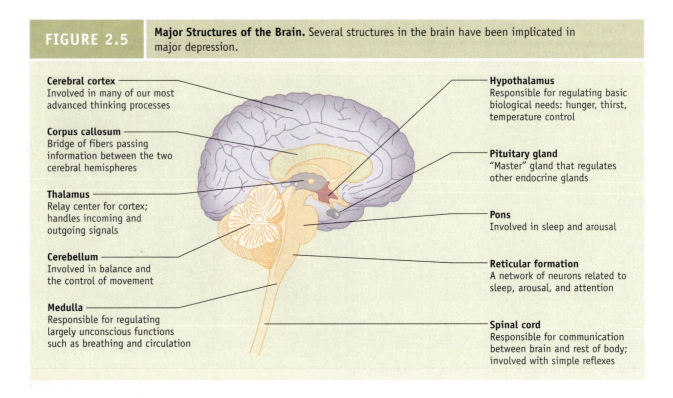

FIGURE 2.5   **Major Structures of the Brain.** Several structures in the brain have been implicated in major depression.

Cerebral cortex
Involved in many of our most advanced thinking processes

Corpus callosum
Bridge of fibers passing information between the two cerebral hemispheres

Thalamus
Relay center for cortex; handles incoming and outgoing signals

Cerebellum
Involved in balance and the control of movement

Medulla
Responsible for regulating largely unconscious functions such as breathing and circulation

Hypothalamus
Responsible for regulating basic biological needs: hunger, thirst, temperature control

Pituitary gland
"Master" gland that regulates other endocrine glands

Pons
Involved in sleep and arousal

Reticular formation
A network of neurons related to sleep, arousal, and attention

Spinal cord
Responsible for communication between brain and rest of body; involved with simple reflexes

FIGURE 2.6   **Structures of the Limbic System.** The limbic system is a collection of structures that are closely interconnected with the hypothalamus. They appear to exert additional control over some of the instinctive behaviors regulated by the hypothalamus, such as eating, sexual behavior, and reactions to stressful situations.

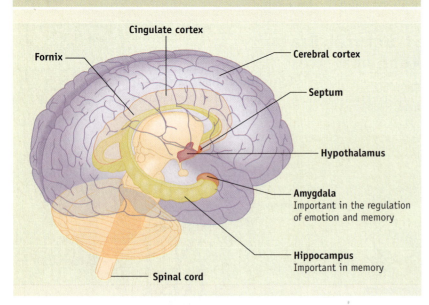

Cingulate cortex

Fornix

Cerebral cortex

Septum

Hypothalamus

Amygdala
Important in the regulation of emotion and memory

Hippocampus
Important in memory

Spinal cord

and emotional functioning will result in psychological changes. In the days of Phineas Gage and for many years thereafter, however, this was not a popular perspective. More precisely, it was unpopular to believe that a person's character and control over his or her behavior rest, at least in part, in biology and are not completely the result of will and upbringing.

We now know that people who suffer damage to the brain (often referred to as *lesions*) or who have major abnormalities in the structure of the brain often show problems in psychological functioning. The location of the structural damage influences the specific psychological problems they have. Figure 2.5 shows some of the major structures in the brain. The damage that Phineas Gage suffered was primarily to the **cerebral cortex,** an area of the brain involved in many of our most advanced thinking processes. Some of the brain structures shown in Figure 2.5 are clearly separated. Others gradually merge into each other, leading to debates about their exact boundaries and the functions they control.

Another key structure shown in Figure 2.5 is the **hypothalamus,** which regulates eating, drinking, and sexual behavior. Abnormal behaviors that involve any of these activities may be the result of dysfunction in the hypothalamus. The hypothalamus also influences basic emotions. For example, the stimulation of certain areas of the hypothalamus produces sensations of pleasure, whereas the stimulation of other areas produces sensations of pain or unpleasantness.

The **limbic system,** shown in Figure 2.6, is a collection of structures that are closely interconnected with the hypothalamus and appear to exert additional control over some of the instinctive behaviors regulated by the hypothalamus, such as eating, sexual behavior, and reactions to stressful situations. Monkeys with damage to the limbic system sometimes become chronically aggressive, reacting with rage to the slightest provocation. At other times, they become excessively passive and do not react even to direct threats.

Structural damage to the brain can result from injury, such as from an automobile accident, and from diseases that cause deterioration. In schizophrenia, a severe disorder in which people lose touch with reality, the cerebral cortex does not function effectively or normally. In this book, we will encounter other examples of psychological disorders that appear to be associated with structural abnormalities in the brain.

Often, even modern neuroimaging techniques detect no structural abnormalities in the brains of people with psychological disorders, including some severe disorders. Instead, these disorders may be tied to biochemical processes in the brain.

Biochemical Causes of Abnormality

The brain requires a number of chemicals to work efficiently and effectively. Chief among these are **neurotransmitters,** biochemicals that act as messengers, carrying impulses from one *neuron*, or nerve cell, to another in the brain and in other parts of the nervous system (see Figure 2.7). Each neuron has a *cell body* and a number of short branches, called *dendrites*. The dendrites and cell body receive impulses from adjacent neurons. The impulse then travels down the length of a slender, tubelike extension, called an *axon*, to small swellings at the end of the axon, called *synaptic terminals*. Here the impulse stimulates the release of neurotransmitters.

The synaptic terminals do not actually touch the adjacent neurons. There is a slight gap between the synaptic terminals and the adjacent neurons. This gap is called the *synaptic gap*, or **synapse.** The neurotransmitter is released into the synapse. It then binds to **receptors,** which are molecules on the membranes of adjacent neurons. This binding works somewhat as a key fits into a lock. The binding stimulates the adjacent neurons to initiate the impulse, which then runs through the neuron's dendrites and cell body and down the axon to cause the release of more neurotransmitter between that neuron and other neurons.

Neurotransmitter Theories

Many of the biochemical theories of psychopathology suggest that too much or too little of certain neurotransmitters in the synapses causes specific types of psychopathology. The amount of a neurotransmitter available in the synapse can be affected by two processes. The process of **reuptake** occurs when the initial neuron releasing the neurotransmitter into the synapse reabsorbs the neurotransmitter, decreasing the amount left in the synapse. Another process, called **degradation,** occurs when the receiving neuron releases an enzyme into the synapse that breaks down the neurotransmitter into other biochemicals. The reuptake and degradation of neurotransmitters happens naturally. When one or both of these processes malfunction, abnormally high or low levels of neurotransmitter in the synapse result.

Psychological symptoms may also be linked to the number and functioning of the receptors for neurotransmitters on the dendrites. If there are too few receptors or the receptors are not sensitive

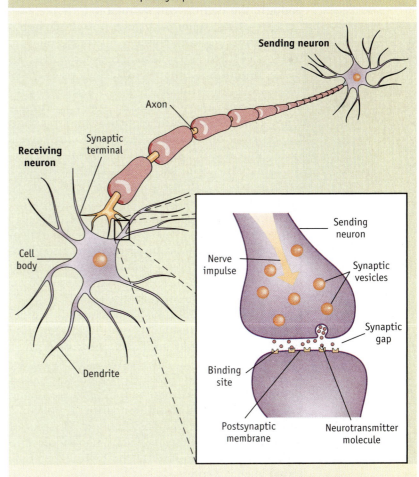

FIGURE 2.7   **Neurotransmitters and the Synapse.** The neurotransmitter is released into the synapic gap. There it may bind with receptors on the postsynaptic membrane.

Sending neuron

Axon

Synaptic terminal

Receiving neuron

Cell body

Dendrite

Sending neuron

Nerve impulse

Synaptic vesicles

Synaptic gap

Binding site

Postsynaptic membrane

Neurotransmitter molecule

FIGURE 2.8   **Some Major Neurotransmitter Systems.** Serotonin and dopamine are two neurotransmitters important in many mental disorders.

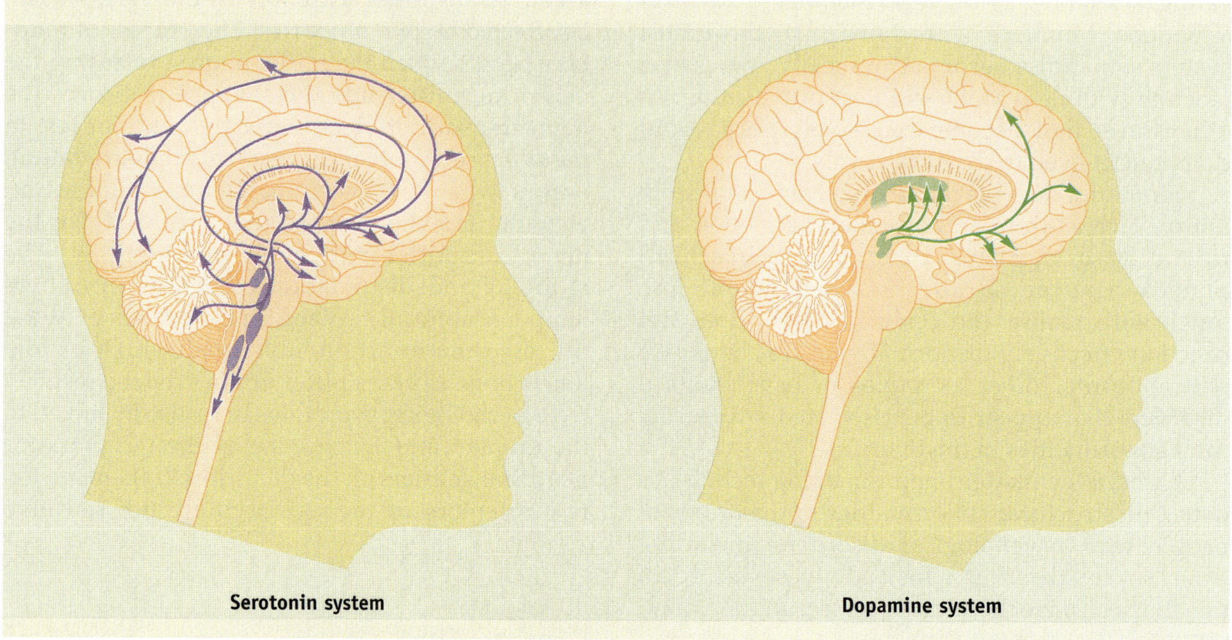

Serotonin system

Dopamine system

enough, the neuron will be unable to make adequate use of the neurotransmitter available in the synapse. If there are too many receptors or they are too sensitive, the neuron may be overexposed to the neurotransmitter that is in the synapse.

Scientists have identified more than 100 neurotransmitters. *Serotonin* plays a particularly important role in mental health, regulating emotions and impulses, such as aggression. Serotonin travels through many key areas of the brain, affecting the function of those areas (see Figure 2.8).

Dopamine is a neurotransmitter that is prominent in the areas of the brain that regulate our experience of reinforcements or rewards (see Figure 2.8), and it is affected by substances, such as alcohol, that we find rewarding. Dopamine also is important to the functioning of muscle systems, and it plays a role in disorders involving control over muscles, such as Parkinson's disease.

Norephinephrine (also known as noradrenaline) is a neurotransmitter that is produced mainly by neurons in the brain stem. Two well-known drugs, cocaine and amphetamines, prolong the action of norepinephrine by slowing its reuptake process. Because of the delay in the reuptake, the receiving neurons are activated for a longer period of time, causing the stimulating psychological effects of these drugs. On the other hand, when there is too little norepinephrine in the brain, the person's mood level is depressed.

Another prominent neurotransmitter is *gamma-aminobutyric acid*, or *GABA*, which inhibits the action of other neurotransmitters. Certain drugs have a tranquilizing effect because they increase the inhibitory activity of GABA. GABA is thought to play an important role in anxiety symptoms, so one contributor to Albert Ellis' anxiety could have been a dysfunction in his GABA system.

These are but a few of the neurotransmitters we discuss in this book. You will find that some neurotransmitters are implicated in a number of disorders. This is probably because each neurotransmitter plays crucial roles in the functioning of several basic systems in the brain. Several functions in the brain can go awry when the level of a particular neurotransmitter is too high or low, when receptors for that neurotransmitter are not working properly, or when there are too few receptors or too many.

The Endocrine System

Other biochemical theories of psychopathology focus on the body's **endocrine system** (see Figure 2.9). This system of glands produces many different chemicals called *hormones,* which are released directly into the blood. A **hormone** carries messages throughout the body, potentially affecting a person's moods, levels of energy, and reactions to stress.

FIGURE 2.9   **The Endocrine System.** The hypothalamus regulates the endocrine system, which produces most of the major hormones of the body.

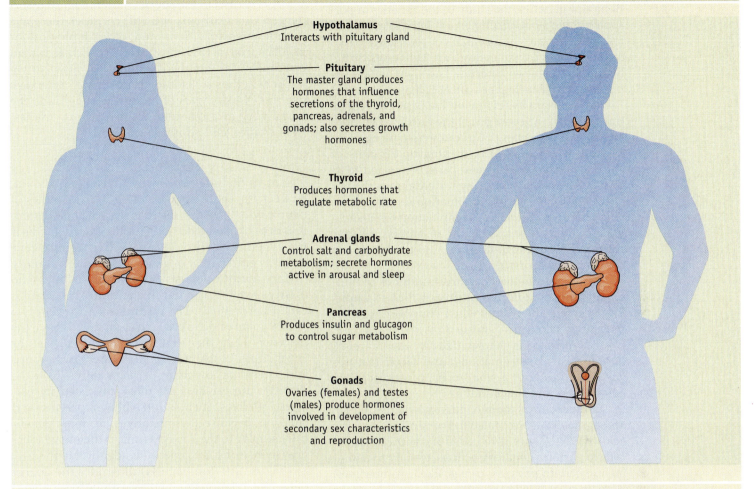

Hypothalamus
Interacts with pituitary gland

Pituitary
The master gland produces hormones that influence secretions of the thyroid, pancreas, adrenals, and gonads; also secretes growth hormones

Thyroid
Produces hormones that regulate metabolic rate

Adrenal glands
Control salt and carbohydrate metabolism; secrete hormones active in arousal and sleep

Pancreas
Produces insulin and glucagon to control sugar metabolism

Gonads
Ovaries (females) and testes (males) produce hormones involved in development of secondary sex characteristics and reproduction

Source: From Goldstein and Noble, *Psychology,* 1st edition. Copyright © 1994. Reprinted with permission of Wadsworth, a division of Thomson Learning: www.thomsonrights.com. Fax 800-730-2215.

One of the major endocrine glands, the **pituitary,** has been called the "master gland" because it produces the largest number of different hormones and controls the secretion of other endocrine glands. It is partly an outgrowth of the brain and lies just below the hypothalamus (review Figure 2.5).

The relationship between the pituitary gland and the hypothalamus illustrates the complex interactions that take place between the endocrine system and the nervous system. For example, in response to stress (fear, anxiety, pain, and so forth), certain neurons on the hypothalamus secrete a substance called corticotropin-release factor (CRF). CRF is carried from the hypothalamus to the pituitary through a channel-like structure. The CRF stimulates the pituitary to release the body's major stress hormone, adrenocorticotrophic hormone (ACTH). In turn, ACTH is carried by the bloodstream to the adrenal glands and to various other organs of the body, causing the release of about 30 hormones, each of which plays a role in the body's adjustment to emergency situations.

As we discuss in Chapters 7, 8, and 9, some theories of anxiety and depression suggest that these disorders result from dysregulation of this relationship, called the *hypothalamic-pituitary-adrenal axis* (or *HPA axis*). People who have a dysregulated HPA axis may have abnormal physiological reactions to stress, which make it more difficult for them to cope psychologically with the stress resulting in symptoms of anxiety and depression.

The proper working of neurotransmitter and endocrine systems requires a delicate balance, and many forces can upset this balance. One of these is a genetic abnormality, which can affect biochemical systems as well as brain development. The end result can be a psychological disturbance.

Genetic Factors in Abnormality

Behavior genetics, the study of the genetics of personality and abnormality, is a relatively new and fast-growing area of research concerned with two questions: (1) To what extent are behaviors or behavioral tendencies inherited and (2) what are the processes by which genes affect behavior?

Let us begin by reviewing the basics of genetic transmission. At conception, the fertilized embryo has 46 chromosomes, 23 from the female egg and 23 from the male sperm, making up 23 pairs of chromosomes. One of these pairs is referred to as the *sex chromosomes* because it determines the sex of the embryo: The XX combination results in a female embryo, and the XY combination results in a male embryo. The mother of an embryo always contributes an X chromosome, and the father can contribute an X or a Y.

Alterations in the structure or number of chromosomes can cause major defects. For example, Down syndrome results when chromosome 21 is present in triplicate instead of as the usual pair. Down syndrome is characterized by mental retardation, heart malformations, and facial features such as a flat face, a small nose, protruding lips and tongue, and slanted eyes.

Chromosomes contain individual genes, which are segments of long molecules of deoxyribonucleic acid (DNA). Genes give coded instructions to the cells to perform certain functions, usually to manufacture certain proteins. Genes, like chromosomes, come in pairs. One half of the pair comes from the mother, the other from the father. Abnormalities in genes that make up chromosomes are much more common than are major abnormalities in the structure or number of chromosomes.

Although you may often hear of scientists having discovered "the gene" for a major disorder, most disorders are not the result of single faulty genes but of combinations of altered genes. Each of these altered genes makes only a small contribution to a vulnerability for the disorder. However, when a critical number of these altered genes come together, the individual may develop the disorder. This is known as a multigene, or **polygenic** process—it takes multiple genetic abnormalities coming together in one individual to create a disorder. Most of the genetic models of the major types of mental disorders are also polygenic. A number of physiological disorders, such as diabetes, coronary heart disease, epilepsy, and cleft lip and palate, result from such polygenic processes. As we discuss in *Taking Psychology Personally: Do "Bad Genes" Doom You to a Disorder?*, genetic fac-

tors increase vulnerablility to a disorder rather than determining whether it occurs.

As we discuss the specific psychological disorders in this textbook, we will consider the ways genetic predispositions and other biological or psychosocial factors may interact to increase an individual's risk for the disorder. But how do we know whether a disorder is heritable? Scientists use three basic types of studies to determine the heritability of a disorder: family history studies, twin studies, and adoption studies.

Family History Studies

Disorders that are genetically transmitted should, on average, show up more often in the families of people who have the disorder than they do in families of people who do not have the disorder. This is true whether the disorder is caused by a single gene or by a combination of genes. To conduct a **family history study,** scientists first identify people who clearly have the disorder in question. This group is called the *probands*. The researchers also identify a *control group* of people who clearly do not have the disorder. They then trace the *family pedigrees*, or family trees, of the individuals in these two groups and determine how many of their relatives have the disorder. Researchers are most interested in *first-degree* relatives, such as full siblings, parents, and children, because these relatives are most genetically similar to the subjects (unless they have identical twins, who are genetically identical to them).

Figure 2.10 (on page 44) illustrates the degree of genetic relationship between an individual and various categories of relatives. This figure gives you an idea of why the risk of inheriting the genes for a disorder quickly decreases as the relationship between an individual and the relative with the disorder becomes more distant: The percentage of genes the individual and relative with the disorder have in common decreases greatly with distance.

Although family history studies provide very useful information about the possible genetic transmission of a disorder, they have their problems. The most obvious one is that families share not only genes but also environment. Several members of a family might have a disorder because they share the same environmental stresses. Family history studies cannot tease apart genetic and environmental contributions to a disorder. Researchers often turn to twin studies to do that.

Twin Studies

Notice in Figure 2.10 that identical, or **monozygotic (MZ), twins** share 100 percent of their genes. This is

Taking Psychology Personally

Do "Bad Genes" Doom You to a Disorder?

The media are full of stories about scientists discovering the genes that contribute to serious mental disorders. These stories are fascinating, and the advances in our understanding of the genetics of mental disorders over the last decade or two are critical to the development of more effective biological treatments for these disorders.

In the general public, however, there is widespread misunderstanding of the meanings of genetic findings. First, people usually don't understand, and the media don't make clear, that mental disorders, like most physical disorders, are rarely the result of a single "bad gene." Instead, they are usually the result of polygenic processes, in which a number of irregular genes must come together in an individual to produce a disorder.

People who have disorders caused by polygenic processes often wonder why they have no family history of the disorder. It may be because none of their relatives accumulated all the different genes necessary for the disorder to develop fully. It just happened that, when the people with disorders were conceived, all the genes necessary for the disorders were present in the chromosomes contributed by their mothers and fathers. When their brothers or sisters were conceived, however, different sets of chromosomes were contributed by their mothers and fathers, and these may not have contained all the necessary genes for the disorders, so their siblings did not develop the disorders.

Conversely, many people who have relatives with disorders that are heritable worry that they will inevitably develop the disorders. In most cases, however, the odds of an individual's inheriting all the genes necessary for a disorder are fairly low, even if a relative who has the disorder is a parent or sibling. For example, the sibling of a person with schizophrenia, which is probably the psychological disorder in which genes play the strongest role, has only about a 9 percent chance of developing schizophrenia at some point in his or her life (see Chapter 11).

Another widely misunderstood characteristic of polygenic disorders involves what is inherited. A person inherits the **predisposition** to the disorder—a tendency to develop it. The disorder is not inevitable. Often the predisposition must interact with other biological or environmental influences for the individual to fully develop the disorder. A good example from the medical field is coronary heart disease. A person can inherit a predisposition to coronary heart disease by inheriting the genes for hypertension, diabetes, or hyperlipidemia (too much fat in the blood). Whether he or she actually develops coronary heart disease depends, however, on a number of environmental and behavioral factors, such as obesity, smoking, exercise, alcohol abuse, a hard-driving personality, and life in an industrialized society.

The same characteristic may be true of many psychological disorders. What is inherited is a predisposition to the disorder. Whether an individual ever fully develops the disorder may depend on exposure to other biological risks (such as malnutrition or negative intrauterine experiences) and other psychosocial risks (such as growing up in a dysfunctional family).

If you have a family history of a particular psychological disorder, or worry that you may carry the genes for a disorder, you are not "doomed" to develop the disorder. You may have an increased risk for the disorder, but there may also be steps you can take to reduce that risk. You can learn about these steps by talking with a mental-health professional.

because they come from a single fertilized egg, which splits into two identical parts. In contrast, nonidentical, or **dizygotic (DZ), twins** share, on average, 50 percent of their genes, because they come from two separate eggs fertilized by separate sperm, just as regular siblings do.

Researchers have capitalized on this difference between MZ and DZ twins to investigate through **twin studies** the contribution of genetics to many disorders. If a disorder is determined *entirely* by ge-netics, when one member of a monozygotic (MZ) twin pair has a disorder, the other member of the pair should always have the disorder. This probability that both twins have the disorder if one twin has the disorder is called the **concordance rate** for the disorder. Thus, if a disorder is entirely determined by genes, the concordance rate among MZ twins should be 100 percent. The concordance rate for the disorder among dizygotic (DZ) twins should be much lower than 100 percent. Even when a disorder

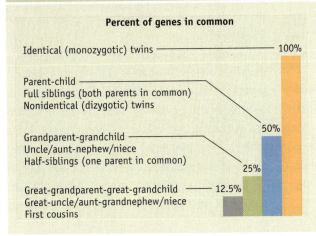

FIGURE 2.10   **Degrees of Genetic Relationship.** People with whom you share 50 percent of your genes are your first-degree relatives. People with whom you share 25 percent of your genes are your second-degree relatives. People with whom you share 12.5 percent of your genes are your third-degree relatives.

is transmitted only partially by genetics, the concordance rate for MZ twins should be considerably higher than the concordance rate for DZ twins, because MZ twins are genetically identical, but DZ twins share only about half the same genes.

For example, let us say that the concordance rate for Disorder X for MZ twins is 48 percent, whereas the concordance rate for DZ twins is 17 percent. These concordance rates tell us two things. First, because the concordance rate for MZ twins is considerably higher than the concordance rate for DZ twins, we have evidence that Disorder X is genetically transmitted. Second, because the concordance rate for MZ twins is well under 100 percent, we have evidence that it takes a combination of a genetic predisposition and other factors (biological or environmental) for an individual to develop Disorder X.

By now, you may be objecting that twin studies do not fully tease apart genetic factors from environmental factors, because MZ twins may have much more similar environments and experiences than do DZ twins. For example, MZ twins typically look alike, whereas DZ twins often do not look alike, and physical appearance can strongly affect other people's reactions to an individual. MZ twins may also be more likely than DZ twins to share talents that influence the opportunities they are given in life. For instance, MZ twins may both be athletic or very talented academically or musically, which then affects their treatment by others and their opportunities in life. In contrast, DZ twins much less often share the same talents and thus are less likely to be treated similarly by others. Finally, parents may simply treat MZ twins more similarly than they do DZ twins, for a variety of reasons. To address these problems, researchers have turned to a third method for studying heritability, adoption studies.

Adoption Studies

An **adoption study** can be carried out in a number of ways. Most commonly, researchers first identify people who have the disorder of interest who were adopted shortly after birth. Then they determine the rates of the disorder in the biological relatives of these adoptees and the adoptive relatives of the adoptees. If a disorder is strongly influenced by genetics, researchers should see higher rates of the disorder among the biological relatives of the adoptee than among the adoptive relatives. If the disorder is strongly influenced by environment, they should see higher rates of the disorder among the adoptive relatives than among the biological relatives.

Some of the most interesting studies of the genetics of personality combine the strategies of adoption studies and the twin studies. Researchers at the University of Minnesota identified several dozen pairs of MZ and DZ twins who had been reared apart and brought them together to assess their personalities. Some of the twins reared apart had never met each other and had not even known that they had a twin. The personalities and behavioral patterns of the MZ twins reared apart were compared with the personalities of the DZ twins reared apart and with MZ and DZ twins reared in the same households.

The results of this study have provided evidence that some aspects of personality and everyday behavior are substantially affected by genetics. Some of the characteristics affected by genetics will not surprise you, nor have they surprised many other scientists. For example, it appears that traits such as shyness and the tendency to become easily upset are heavily influenced by genetics (Bouchard & Loehlin, 2001; Johnson et al., 2004).

What stunned the world of behavior genetics, however, was evidence that even the most mundane behaviors, which were thought to be shaped by circumstance and rearing, are heavily influenced by genetics, such as the amount of television we watch and what we snack on while we're watching TV (Bouchard, 1994; Hur, Bouchard, & Eckert, 1998). There are startling examples of iden-

Studies of identical twins reared apart have revealed amazing similarities. Jim Lewis and Jim Springer were reared apart but, when reunited, found that they were identical in more than appearance.

tical twins reared apart who are amazingly similar, even though they have never met. Consider, for example, the "Jim twins" (Holden, 1980). Jim Lewis and Jim Springer were identical twins reunited at the age of 39 after being separated since infancy. Both had married and later divorced women named Linda. Their second wives were both named Betty. Both had sons named James Allan and dogs named Toy. Both chain-smoked Salem cigarettes, worked as sheriffs' deputies, drove Chevrolets, chewed their fingernails, enjoyed stock car racing, had basement workshops, and had built circular white benches around trees in their yards.

Genetic researchers do not argue that there are genes for marrying women named Linda or Betty or genes for having basement workshops. Given similar circumstances, however, people with identical genes may choose the same activities and have the same likes and dislikes.

Not surprisingly, the work on behavior genetics has been controversial. Some scientists believe that behavior geneticists are underestimating the role of the environment as they overestimate the role of genetics. This work clearly has stimulated a lively and interesting discussion, however, about how deeply and broadly genes affect our behavior.

In sum, adoption studies, twin studies, and family history studies all help to determine whether a characteristic or disorder is influenced by genetics and the degree of this influence. Each type of study has its limitations. Family history and twin studies cannot fully tease apart the impacts of genetics and shared environment. Adoption studies suffer from the fact that it is difficult to find large numbers of adoptees with the disorder

of interest, so the sample sizes in these studies tend to be very small.

Assessing the Biological Theories

Modern biological theories have greatly advanced our understanding of the human mind and the biological influences on behavior. Research on these theories seems to be advancing at a rapid pace, with new discoveries about the role of biology in mental disorders in the news every day. These theories have led to new treatments, which have restored the lives of people who suffer with disorders.

The biological theories have their flaws, however. They often seem reductionistic, boiling down the complex human behavior called psychopathology into the firing of neurons and abnormal genes. Some of these theories ignore the influence of social factors and the environment in shaping the behavior of people who may carry a biological risk for psychopathology. More generally, the biological theories often have trouble explaining why not everyone who carries a biological risk for a disorder, such as an unusual level of a hormone or neurotransmitter, eventually develops the disorder.

Although we may think of biological research as "harder science" than the research done to test the psychosocial theories of abnormality, biological research is often at least as messy and nondefinitive as psychosocial research (Valenstein, 1998). Most of the processes thought to cause psychopathology, such as changes in neurotransmitter levels, can be measured only indirectly and quite imprecisely in the brains of live humans. As a result, much of the evidence for the biological theories comes from studies of animals rather than humans. Although animal studies can be informative, it is sometimes difficult to generalize from animals to humans.

Many of the biological theories of psychopathology were based on accidental discoveries that certain drugs change behavior in animals or humans. Reasoning backward from the effects of drugs on behavior to a theory of what causes that behavior is a tricky business, particularly because the drugs that are used to alleviate psychopathology have widespread effects on many areas and systems in the brain (Valenstein, 1998).

The biological theories of abnormality have many proponents, however, and seem to have captured the hearts of the general public. Many people find biological theories of psychopathology appealing, because they seem to take away any stigma or blame on the individual sufferer for having the disorder. Indeed, many organizations for people with psychological disorders explicitly advocate a biological view of these disorders, emphasizing that people with the disorders need to stop blaming themselves, accept the fact that they have a "disease," and obtain the appropriate medical treatment. In addition, many insurance companies will pay only for biological treatments, even though psychological treatments have longer-lasting positive effects for some disorders.

SUMMING UP

- The biological theories of psychopathology hold that psychological symptoms and disorders are caused by structural abnormalities in the brain, disordered biochemistry, or faulty genes.

- Structural abnormalities in the brain can be caused by injury or disease processes. The location of brain damage influences the type of psychological symptoms shown.

- Most biochemical theories focus on neurotransmitters, the biochemicals that facilitate the transmission of impulses in the brain. Some theories say that psychological symptoms are caused by too little or too much of a particular neurotransmitter in the synapses of the brain. Other theories focus on the number of receptors for neurotransmitters.

- Some people may be genetically predisposed to psychological disorders. Most of these disorders are probably linked not to a single faulty gene but to an accumulation of faulty genes.

- Three methods of determining the heritability of a disorder are family history studies, twin studies, and adoption studies.

PSYCHOLOGICAL APPROACHES

Psychological theories of abnormality vary greatly. Some theories focus on unconscious conflicts and anxiety, some focus on the effects of rewards and punishments in the environment, some focus on thought processes, and others focus on the difficulties humans have in striving to realize their full potential in a capricious world (see Figure 2.11). In this book, we will discuss the psychological theories that have had the largest and most enduring impacts on how psychologists view abnormality and on the types of psychological therapies that are currently used to treat people.

Psychodynamic Theories of Abnormality

The **psychodynamic theories** of abnormality suggest that all behavior, thoughts, and emotions, whether normal or abnormal, are influenced to a large extent by unconscious processes (McWilliams & Weinberger, 2003). The psychodynamic theories began with Sigmund Freud in the late nineteenth century and have expanded to include several newer theories. These theories accept many of Freud's basic assumptions about the working of the human mind but emphasize different processes from those that Freud emphasized.

Freud developed **psychoanalysis,** which is (1) a theory of personality and psychopathology, (2) a

FIGURE 2.11   **Psychological Theories of Mental Disorders.** Psychological theories of mental disorders describe a variety of causes of symptoms.

Psychodynamic theories: Unconscious conflicts between primitive desires and constraints on those desires cause symptoms of mental disorders.

Behavioral theories: Symptoms of mental disorders are due to reinforcements and punishments for specific behaviors.

Cognitive theories: People's ways of interpreting situations, their assumptions about the world, and their self-concepts cause negative feelings and behaviors.

Humanistic and existential theories: Mental disorders arise when people do not pursue their own values and potentials and, instead, feel they must conform to the demands of others.

Sigmund Freud believed that normal and abnormal behaviors are driven by needs and drives, most of which are unconscious.

method of investigating the mind, and (3) a form of treatment for psychopathology (McWilliams & Weinberger, 2003). As we noted in Chapter 1, Freud was a Viennese neurologist who became interested in unconscious processes while working with Jean Charcot in Paris in the late nineteenth century. He then returned to Vienna and worked with physician Josef Breuer, most notably on the case of "Anna O."

Anna O. had extensive symptoms of hysteria—physical ailments with no apparent physical cause—including paralysis of the legs and right arm, deafness, and disorganized speech. Breuer attempted to hypnotize Anna O., hoping he could cure her symptoms by suggestion. Anna O. began to talk about painful memories from her past, which were apparently tied to the development of her hysterical symptoms. She expressed a great deal of distress about these memories, but, following the recounting of the memories under hypnosis, many of her symptoms went away. Breuer labeled the release of emotions connected to these memories **catharsis,** and Anna O. labeled the entire process her "talking cure." (Later Anna O., whose real name was Bertha Pappenheim, rejected the psychoanalytic explanation for her symptoms and believed Breuer's treatment had had no positive effects.)

Breuer and Freud published papers on their cases together and suggested that hysteria is the result of traumatic memories that have been repressed from consciousness because they are too painful. **Repression** was defined as the motivated forgetting of a difficult experience, such as being abused as a child, or an unacceptable wish, such as

the desire to hurt someone. Repression does not dissolve the emotion associated with the memory or wish. Instead, this emotion is "dammed-up" and emerges as symptoms.

Freud went on to develop these ideas about dynamic processes within the unconscious into an elaborate and comprehensive theory of human thought and behavior. Freud was a passionate reader of history, archeology, philosophy, and many other fields, and he developed theories reaching far beyond psychology and psychiatry. In this book, we will review the central assumptions of Freudian theory that are most pertinent to abnormal behavior. Some of these ideas are summarized in the Concept Overview in Table 2.1 (on page 48).

The Id, Ego, and Superego
Freud believed that the two basic drives that motivate human behavior are the sexual drive, which he referred to as **libido,** and the aggressive drive. The energy from these drives continually seeks to be released but can be channeled or harnessed by various psychological systems. Most of Freud's writings focused primarily on libido (or libidinal drive), so our discussion will do so as well.

According to Freud, the three systems of the human psyche that help regulate the libido are the id, the ego, and the superego. The **id** is the system from which the libido emerges, and its drives and impulses seek immediate release. The id operates by the **pleasure principle**—the drive to maximize pleasure and to minimize pain, as quickly as possible. A number of reflex actions, such as an infant's turning to the mother's breast for milk, are direct expressions of the pleasure principle. When direct action cannot be taken, humans may use fantasies or memories to conjure up the desired object or

© Sidney Harris, courtesy ScienceCartoonsPlus.com

TABLE 2.1   Concept Overview

Key Concepts in Freudian Theory

Freudian theory includes a number of complex concepts.

Name	Description
Repression	The motivated forgetting of memories or desires that cause anxiety
Catharsis	The release of energy bound up in painful emotions
Libido	Psychical energy emerging from sexual drive
Id	The most primitive part of the unconscious, which consists of drives and impulses seeking immediate gratification
Ego	The part of the psyche that channels libido into activities that balance the demands of society and the superego
Superego	The part of the unconscious that consists of absolute moral standards internalized from one's parents and culture
Pleasure principle	The principle that desires and wishes should be immediately gratified, without concern for the constraints of society
Primary process thinking	Thinking oriented toward satisfying primitive urges, perhaps through fantasy
Reality principle	The realization that primitive urges cannot always be immediately gratified because of the constraints of society
Secondary process thinking	Rational deliberation about how to satisfy primitive urges within the constraints of society
Introjection	Incorporating or internalizing the standards or view of others into one's own ways of thinking
Unconscious	The vast area of the psyche holding desires, memories, and emotions of which we are not aware
Preconscious	The "way station" between the unconscious and conscious, holding material that is somewhat accessible to consciousness
Conscious	The aspect of the psyche holding material of which we are aware
Defense mechanisms	Strategies for transforming unacceptable desires, thoughts, and feelings into a more acceptable form
Neurotic paradox	When an individual's defense mechanisms become maladaptive and distressing
Oedipus complex	The stage of development in which a boy desires his mother and hates his father
Castration anxiety	Anxiety a little boy feels when he fears his father will castrate him in retaliation for his desire for his mother
Electra complex	The stage of development in which a girl becomes attached to her father in hopes he will provide her with a replacement for the penis she lacks
Penis envy	A female's desire to have a penis

action. This is known as **primary process thinking,** or *wish fulfillment*. A hungry infant, for example, may imagine the mother's breast when she is not readily available.

As children grow older, they become aware that they cannot always quickly satisfy their impulses without paying a price. They cannot immediately satisfy sexual urges and cannot carry out

aggressive impulses without being punished by society. A part of the id splits off and becomes the **ego,** the force that seeks to gratify wishes and needs in ways that remain within the rules of society for their appropriate expression. The ego follows the **reality principle**—the drive to satisfy our needs within the realities of society's rules—rather than the pleasure principle. **Secondary process**

thinking, or *rational deliberation*, is the ego's primary mode of operation, rather than primary process thinking. A preschooler, who may wish to suckle at the mother's breast but is aware that this is no longer allowed, may satisfy himself with cuddling in his mother's lap.

The **superego** develops from the ego a little later in childhood. It is the storehouse of rules and regulations for the conduct of behavior that are learned from one's parents and from society. These rules and regulations are in the form of absolute moral standards. We **introject,** or *internalize*, these moral standards, because following them makes us feel good and reduces anxiety. The superego is made up of two components, the conscience and the ego ideal. The *conscience* constantly evaluates whether we are conforming our behavior to our internalized moral standards. The *ego ideal* is an image of the person we wish to become, formed from images of those people with whom we identified in our early years, usually our parents.

Most of the interactions among the id, ego, and superego occur in the **unconscious**—completely out of our awareness. The **preconscious** is a way station, or buffer, between the unconscious and the **conscious.** Wishes, needs, and memories from the unconscious can make their way into the preconscious, but they rarely reach the conscious level. The ego deflects this material back into the unconscious or changes the material in such a way as to protect the conscious from being fully aware of the unconscious material. This pushing material back into the unconscious is repression.

Why must the conscious be protected from unconscious material? In their raw form, unconscious wishes, needs, and memories represent our basic instincts and drives, seeking to be satisfied in the quickest and fullest way possible. Because these unconscious desires are often unacceptable to the individual or society, they cause anxiety if they seep into the conscious, prompting the ego to push the material back into the unconscious.

The psychoanalytic explanation for depression illustrates how repression can lead to symptoms. Freud argued that at the root of depression is a deep rage against important people in your life, such as your caregivers. Expressing, or even consciously acknowledging, this rage causes anxiety, however, so the rage is repressed and made unconscious. The ego turns this rage on itself, leading to the self-criticism and even suicidal behaviors of depression.

Freud—and later his daughter, Anna Freud described certain strategies, or **defense mechanisms,** that the ego uses to disguise or transform unconscious wishes. The particular defense mechanisms that a person regularly uses shape his or her behav-

Anna Freud, daughter of Sigmund Freud, was a major contributor to psychodynamic theory and described the basic defense mechanisms people use to control anxiety.

ior and personality. Table 2.2 (on page 50) provides a list and examples of the basic defense mechanisms. Everyone uses defense mechanisms to a degree, because everyone must protect against an awareness of unacceptable wishes and conform his or her behavior to societal norms.

When a person's behavior becomes ruled by defense mechanisms or when the mechanisms themselves are maladaptive, the defense mechanisms can result in abnormal, pathological behavior. Freud called this situation the **neurotic paradox.** For example, a man whose father physically abused him as a child may develop the tendency to displace his rage—to transfer his feelings to another target—because it is too dangerous to express his anger directly against his father. This displacement may take the form of beating his wife or getting into frequent fist fights with other men. The displacement behavior is maladaptive in itself, and the man is stuck in the neurotic paradox.

Psychosexual Stages

Psychoanalytic theory argues that the nurturance a child receives from his or her early caregivers strongly influences personality development. Freud proposed that, as children develop, they pass through a series of universal **psychosexual stages.** In each stage, sexual drives are focused on the stimulation of certain body areas, and particular psychological issues can arouse anxiety. The id, ego, and superego must negotiate and develop successfully through these stages for the child to become a psychologically healthy adult.

The responses of caregivers, usually parents, to the child's attempts to satisfy basic needs and wishes can greatly influence whether a given stage is negotiated successfully. If the parents are not

TABLE 2.2   Defense Mechanisms

These defense mechanisms were described by Sigmund and Anna Freud.

Defense Mechanism	Definition	Example
Regression	Retreating to a behavior of an earlier developmental period to prevent anxiety and satisfy current needs	A woman abandoned by her lover curls up in a chair, rocking and sucking her fingers.
Denial	Refusing to perceive or accept reality	A husband whose wife recently died denies she is gone and actively searches for her.
Displacement	Discharging unacceptable feelings against someone or something other than the true target of these feelings	A woman who is angry at her children kicks a dog.
Rationalization	Inventing an acceptable motive to explain unacceptably motivated behavior	A soldier who killed innocent civilians rationalizes that he was only following orders.
Intellectualization	Adopting a cold, distanced perspective on a matter that actually creates strong, unpleasant feelings	An emergency room physician who is troubled by seeing young people with severe gunshot wounds every night has discussions with colleagues that focus only on the technical aspects of treatment.
Projection	Attributing one's own unacceptable motives or desires to someone else	A husband who is sexually attracted to a colleague accuses his wife of cheating on him.
Reaction formation	Adopting a set of attitudes and behaviors that are the opposite of one's true dispositions	A man who cannot accept his own homosexuality becomes extremely homophobic.
Identification	Adopting the ideas, values, and tendencies of someone in a superior position in order to elevate self-worth	Prisoners adopt the attitudes of their captors toward other prisoners.
Sublimation	Translating wishes and needs into socially acceptable behavior	An adolescent with strong aggressive impulses trains to be a boxer.

appropriately responsive, helping the child learn acceptable ways of satisfying and controlling drives and impulses, the child can become *fixated* at a stage, trapped in the concerns and issues of that stage, never successfully moving beyond that stage and through the subsequent stages.

According to Freud, the earliest stage of life, the **oral stage,** lasts for the first 18 months following birth. In the oral stage, libidinal impulses are best satisfied through stimulation of the mouth area, usually through feeding or sucking. At this stage, the child is entirely dependent on caregivers for gratification, and the central issues of this stage are issues of one's dependence and the reliability of others. If the child's caregiver, typically the mother,

is not adequately available to the child, he or she can develop deep mistrust and fear of abandonment. Children fixated at the oral stage develop an "oral character"—a personality characterized by excessive dependence on others but mistrust of their love. A number of habits focused on the mouth area—for example, smoking or excessive drinking and eating—are said to reflect an oral character.

The **anal stage** lasts from about 18 months to 3 years of age. During this phase, the focus of gratification is the anus. The child becomes very interested in toilet activities, particularly the passing and retaining of feces. Parents can cause a child to become fixated at this stage by being too harsh or critical during toilet training. People with an "anal personality" are said to be stubborn, overcontrolling, stingy, and too focused on orderliness and tidiness.

During the **phallic stage,** lasting from about ages 3 to 6, the focus of pleasure is the genitals. During this stage, one of the most important conflicts of sexual development occurs, and it occurs differently for boys and girls. Freud believed that boys become sexually attracted to their mothers and hate their fathers as rivals. Freud labeled this the **Oedipus complex,** after the character in Greek mythology who unknowingly kills his father and marries his mother. Boys fear that their fathers will retaliate against them by castrating them, however. This fear arouses **castration anxiety,** which is then the motivation for putting aside their desire for their mothers and aspiring to become like their fathers. The successful resolution of the Oedipal complex helps instill a strong superego in boys, because it results in boys' identifying with their fathers and their fathers' value systems.

Freud believed that, during the phallic stage, girls recognize that they do not have a penis and are horrified at this discovery. They also recognize that their mothers do not have a penis and disdain their mothers and all other females for this deficit. Girls develop an attraction for their fathers, in hopes that their fathers will provide the penis they lack. He labeled this the **Electra complex,** after the character in Greek mythology who conspires to murder her mother to avenge her father's death. Girls cannot have castration anxiety, because, according to Freud, they feel they have already been castrated. As a result, girls do not have as strong a motivation as boys to develop a superego. Freud argued that females never do develop superegos as strong as males' and this leads to a greater reliance on emotion than on reason in the lives of women. Freud also thought that much of women's behavior is driven by **penis envy**—the wish to have the male sex organ.

The unsuccessful resolution of the phallic stage can lead to a number of psychological problems in children. If children do not fully identify with their same-sex parents, they may not develop "appropriate" gender roles or a heterosexual orientation. They also may not develop a healthy superego and may become either too self-aggrandizing or too self-deprecating. If children's sexual attraction to their parents is not met with gentle but firm discouragement, they may become overly seductive or sexualized and have a number of problems in romantic relationships.

After the turmoil of the phallic stage, children enter the **latency stage,** during which libidinal drives are quelled somewhat. Their attention turns

to developing skills and interests and becoming fully socialized into the world in which they live. They play with friends of the same sex and avoid children of the opposite sex. This is the time when girls hate boys and boys hate girls.

At about the age of 12, children's sexual desires emerge again as they enter puberty, and they enter the **genital stage.** If they have successfully resolved the phallic stage, their sexual interests turn to heterosexual relationships. They begin to pursue romantic alliances and learn to negotiate the world of dating and early sexual encounters with members of the opposite sex.

Later Psychodynamic Theories

Freud's theories are some of the most intriguing and enduring in psychology, but they have had critics, even among Freud's followers. Freud viewed behavior and thought as the products of energies that were either contained or released. Where, many people asked, was the person, the self, in Freud's human being?

Several of Freud's followers developed new theories, which emphasized the role of the ego as an independent force striving for mastery and competence (e.g., Jacobson, 1964; Mahler, 1968). Others talked explicitly about the concept of a self and argued that the development of a positive sense of the self is an individual's primary aim (e.g., Kohut, 1984). Freud downplayed the roles of the environment and interpersonal relationships in the development of personality, and several of his contemporaries believed this was a mistake. In the section "Interpersonal Theories of Abnormality," we will review the interpersonal theories, which view social relationships as the driving force of psychological development within individuals. These interpersonal theories grew out of splits between Freud and his followers.

One new school of thought within psychodynamic theory retained significant aspects of Freud's drive theory but integrated them with the role of early relationships in the development of self-concept and personality. This theory is known as object relations theory. According to proponents of this school, such as Melanie Klein, Margaret Mahler, Otto Kernberg, and Heinz Kohut, our early relationships create images, or representations, of ourselves and others. We carry these images throughout adulthood and they affect all our subsequent relationships.

According to this theory, there are four fundamental stages in the development of the self-concept. In the first stage, known as the *undifferentiated stage,* the newborn has only an image of the self and no sense that other people and

Melanie Klein questioned some of the principles of Freudian psychoanalytic theory and helped develop object relations theory.

Otto Kernberg is one of the leaders of the object relations school.

objects are separate from the self. The infant believes that the caregiver and itself are one and that everything the infant feels or wants the caregiver feels or wants.

In the second stage, known as *symbiosis*, the infant still does not distinguish between self and other but does distinguish between good and bad aspects of the self-plus-other image. That is, the child has an image of the good self-plus-other and an image of the bad self-plus-other. These images are either all good or all bad.

In the third stage, the *separation-individuation stage,* the child begins to differentiate between the self and the other. The child's images of the good self and the bad self are not integrated, however. The child focuses on either the good self or the bad self exclusively. Similarly, the child's images of the good other and the bad other are not integrated, and the child focuses on only the good other or the bad other. A child who is frustrated with a parent may say, "I hate you!" and mean it with all her heart, because she is focusing only on the bad image of the parent at the time.

In the fourth stage, the *integration stage,* the child is able to distinguish clearly between the self and the other and to integrate the good and bad images of the self and the other into complex representations. This new ability allows a frustrated child to say to a parent, "I am really mad at you, but I still love you."

According to the object relations theorists, many people with psychopathology never fully resolve Stage 2 or 3 and are prone to seeing the self and others as all good or all bad. This tendency is known as **splitting,** because the image of the self

and other is split into the good image and the bad image, with no appreciation for the mixed qualities of good and bad that are true of all people. Also, a person stuck in Stage 2 or 3 never fully differentiates between the self and other and expects others to know what he or she feels and wants.

As we will see, the notion of splitting provides an intriguing explanation for the syndrome known as *borderline personality disorder.* People with this disorder tend to view themselves and other people as either all good or all bad and vacillate between these two images. They either idealize themselves and others or hate themselves and others to the point of wanting to hurt themselves or others. People with borderline personality disorder also tend to have trouble accepting the boundaries between themselves and others. When even slightly rejected by another, they feel completely abandoned and empty.

Assessing Psychodynamic Theories

Freud and the psychodynamic theorists who came after him were the first to establish a systematic explanation of abnormal behavior in terms of psychological principles rather than purely biological or supernatural principles. They were truly the founders of a psychological approach to the study of psychopathology. Moreover, psychodynamic theories are probably the most comprehensive theories of human behavior established to date. For some people, they are also the most satisfying theories. They explain both normal and abnormal behavior with similar processes. And they have an "aha!" quality about them that leads us to believe they hold important insights.

Karen Horney was an early critic of Freud's assertions that personality is fixed in childhood and that women suffer from penis envy.

Psychodynamic theories also have many limitations and weaknesses. One of the earliest critics of Freud's conceptualization of female development was Karen Horney, who was trained in Berlin by Freud's colleagues, Abraham and Sachs, in the early 1900s. Using research from anthropology, sociology, and her own therapy practice, Horney (1934/1967) challenged several assumptions and methods in classical psychoanalysis. These included (1) the emphasis on sexual drives and anatomy in personality and the exclusion of environmental and cultural influences on personality development, (2) the view that the male is the prototypical human being, and (3) the claim that one can describe a universally applicable psychology based on a small sample.

Another major problem with most psychodynamic theories is that it is difficult or impossible to scientifically test their fundamental assumptions (Erdelyi, 1992; although see Westen, 1998). The processes described by these theories are abstract and difficult to measure. The theories themselves often provide ways of explaining away the results of studies that seem to dispute their fundamental assumptions. Perhaps as a result, there is little controlled research testing traditional psychodynamic theories or the newer theories.

Finally, Freud believed that personality is essentially fixed in childhood, with little opportunity for significant change later on, even with therapy. Many of his early critics believed that human personality continues to grow and change in response to changes in the environment and in personal relationships. They believed that therapy does

offer significant hope for people who want to change fundamental aspects of their personalities.

In spite of their weaknesses, psychodynamic theories have played a major role in shaping psychology and psychiatry in the past century. The fundamental assumption of traditional psychodynamic theory that unconscious processes drive our behaviors has become a fundamental assumption of laypeople's views of human behaviors. When we find ourselves questioning the "real" motives behind our own or others' behaviors, when we "realize" we are attracted to a certain person because we know our mother would disapprove, or when we recall a traumatic event from the past that we believe we have been repressing, we are applying psychodynamic theories.

Behavioral Theories of Abnormality

Behavioral theories reject claims that unconscious conflicts drive human behavior. Instead, behaviorists focus on the influences of reinforcements and punishments in producing behavior. Like the psychodynamic theorists, behavioral theorists seek to explain both normal and abnormal behavior through the same principles. The principles of behaviorism, however, focus on how behaviors are learned through experiences in the environment. The two core principles or processes of learning according to behaviorism are *classical conditioning* and *operant conditioning*. In later developments of the theory behaviorists acknowledged that learning can occur through *modeling* and *observational learning*.

Classical Conditioning

Ivan Pavlov, a Russian physiologist, was conducting experiments on the salivary glands of dogs when he made discoveries that would revolutionize psychological theory. Not surprisingly, his dogs salivated when Pavlov or an assistant put food in their mouths. Pavlov noticed that, after a while, the dogs began to salivate when he or his assistant simply walked into the room. This process gained the name **classical conditioning.**

Pavlov had paired a previously neutral stimulus (himself) with a stimulus that naturally leads to a certain response (the dish of food, which leads to salivating), and eventually the neutral stimulus (Pavlov) was able to elicit that response (salivation). He named the stimulus that naturally produced the desired response the **unconditioned stimulus (US),** and he named the response created by the unconditioned stimulus the **unconditioned response (UR).** Thus, in Pavlov's experiments, the dish of food was the US and salivation in response

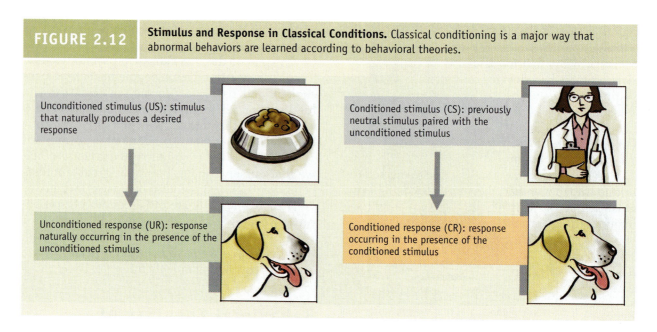

FIGURE 2.12   **Stimulus and Response in Classical Conditions.** Classical conditioning is a major way that abnormal behaviors are learned according to behavioral theories.

to this food was the UR. He named the previously neutral stimulus the **conditioned stimulus (CS)** and the response that it elicited the **conditioned response (CR).** Thus, Pavlov was the CS, and, when the dogs salivated in response to seeing him, this salivation became the CR (see Figure 2.12).

Classical conditioning has been used to explain people's seemingly irrational responses to a host of neutral stimuli. For example, a college student who failed a test in a particular classroom may break out in a cold sweat when she enters that room again—this response is the result of classical conditioning. The room has become a conditioned stimulus, eliciting a response of anxiety, because it was paired with an unconditioned stimulus (failing an exam) that elicited anxiety.

Classical conditioning can also explain why heroin addicts, if they simply see a syringe, sometimes have physiological responses similar to those they have had when they have injected heroin in the past. They have developed a conditioned physiological response to syringes (which have become a conditioned stimulus), because of the frequent pairing of the syringes with the physiological action of the drugs.

Operant Conditioning

E. L. Thorndike observed that behaviors that are followed by a reward are strengthened, whereas behaviors that are followed by a punishment are weakened. This simple but important observation, which Thorndike labeled the *law of effect,* led to the development of the principles of **operant conditioning**—the shaping of behaviors by providing rewards for desired behaviors and punishments for undesired behaviors.

B. F. Skinner is the psychologist most strongly associated with operant conditioning. In the 1930s, he showed that a pigeon will learn to press on a bar if pressing it is associated with the delivery of food, and it will learn to avoid pressing another bar if pressing it is associated with an electric shock. Similarly, a child will learn to make his bed if he receives a hug and kiss from his mother each time he makes the bed, and he will learn to stop hitting his brother if, every time he hits his brother, he is not allowed to watch his favorite television show that week.

In operant conditioning, behaviors will be learned most quickly if they are paired with the reward or punishment every time the behavior is emitted. This consistent response is called a **continuous reinforcement schedule.** Behaviors can be learned and maintained, however, on a **partial reinforcement schedule,** in which the reward or punishment occurs only sometimes in response to the behavior. **Extinction**—the elimination of a learned behavior—is more difficult when the behavior has been learned through a partial reinforcement schedule than it is when the behavior has been learned through a continuous reinforcement schedule. This is because the behavior has been learned under conditions of occasional reward, so a constant reward is not needed to maintain the behavior. A good example is gambling behavior. People who frequently gamble are seldom rewarded, but they continue to gamble in anticipation of that occasional, unpredictable win.

Combinations of classical and operant conditioning can help explain responses people develop to avoid situations that arouse fear in them. For example, consider a woman who developed a fear of bridges through classical conditioning: She fell off a bridge into icy waters as a child, and now anytime she nears a bridge, she feels very anxious. This woman has developed elaborate means of getting around her hometown without having to cross any bridges. Avoiding the bridges reduces her anxiety, and thus her avoidant behavior is reinforced. This woman has developed a *conditioned avoidance response* through operant conditioning. As a result, however, she never exposes herself to a bridge and never has the opportunity to extinguish her initial fear of bridges. As we will see, many of the therapeutic techniques developed by behavioral theorists are designed to extinguish conditioned avoidance responses, which can interfere greatly with a person's ability to function in everyday life.

Modeling and Observational Learning

Skinner and other "pure" behaviorists have argued that humans and animals learn behaviors only by directly experiencing the rewards or punishments for these behaviors. In the 1950s, however, psychologist Albert Bandura argued that people can also learn behaviors by watching other people, a view that came to be known as **social learning theory.** First, in **modeling,** people learn new behaviors from imitating the behaviors modeled by important people in their lives, such as their parents. Learning through modeling is more likely to occur when the person modeling the behavior is seen as an authority figure or is perceived to be like oneself. For example, Bandura (1969) argued that children are most likely to imitate the behaviors modeled by their same-sex parent, because this parent is an authority figure and because the same-sex parent seems more similar to them than does the opposite-sex parent.

Second, **observational learning** takes place when a person observes the rewards and punishments that another person receives for his or her behavior and then behaves in accord with those rewards and punishments. For example, a child who views her sibling being punished for dropping food on the floor will learn, through observation, the consequences of dropping food on the floor and will be less likely to engage in this behavior herself. Some theorists argue that even extremely negative behaviors, such as teenagers going on a shooting rampage, are also due to observational learning. Teenagers see heroes in the media being rewarded for violent behavior and thus learn that behavior. They also are directly rewarded for violent behavior in certain video games.

The behavioral theory of anxiety would suggest that Albert Ellis' symptoms were the result of experiences of being punished in some way for his public speaking—for example, being ridiculed by an audience member. He learned, through operant conditioning, that he could reduce his anxiety by avoiding speaking engagements.

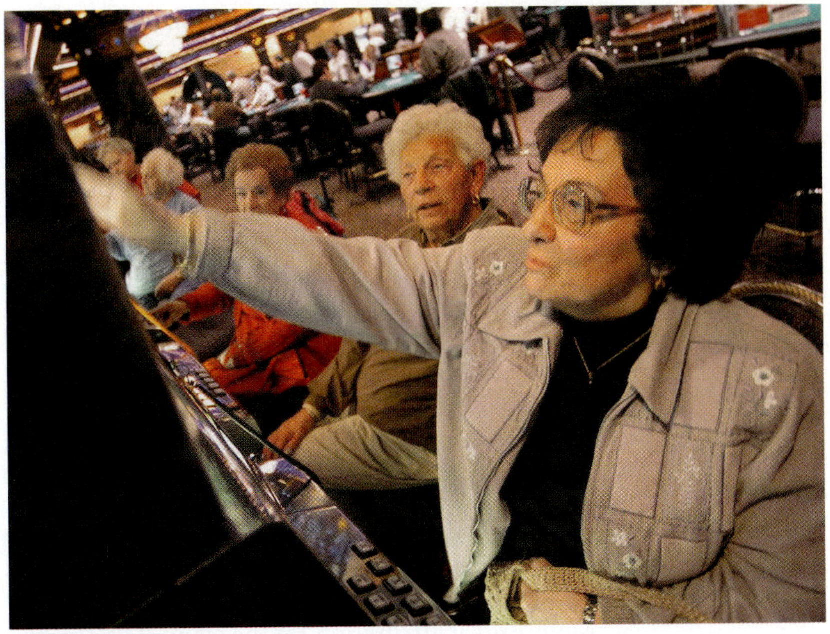

Gambling is reinforced only occasionally by wins, but this makes it more difficult to extinguish the behavior.

Assessing Behavioral Theories

The behavioral theorists set the standard for scientifically testing hypotheses about how normal and abnormal behaviors develop. The hypotheses developed from these theories are precise, and the studies that have been done to test these hypotheses are rigorously controlled and exact. These studies have provided strong support for behavioral explanations of many types of abnormal behavior.

The behavioral theories have limitations, however. Certain types of abnormal behaviors can be created in the laboratory, but is this how they develop in the real world? Laboratory studies are artificial and cannot capture the complexity of environmental experiences that shape people's behavior. Like the psychodynamic theories, the behavioral theories have been criticized for not recognizing free will in people's behaviors—the active choices they make to defy the external forces upon them.

Cognitive Theories of Abnormality

The movement that followed the development of the behavioral theories is now known as the cognitive revolution in psychology. Cognitive psychologists made great strides in understanding the processes of memory, attention, and information processing and, by the late 1960s and early 1970s, much of the theorizing about the causes of abnormal behavior had focused on the role of cognitions. The cognitive theorists argued that it is not just rewards, punishments, or even drives that motivate human behavior. Instead, humans actively construct meaning out of their experiences and act in accord with their interpretations of the world.

Cognitive theories of abnormality argue that **cognitions**—thoughts and beliefs—shape our behaviors and the emotions we experience. Several theories of abnormal behavior have focused on three types of cognitions: causal attributions, control beliefs, and dysfunctional assumptions.

When something happens to us, we ask ourselves why that event happened (Abramson, Metalsky, & Alloy, 1989; Abramson, Seligman, & Teasdale, 1978). The answer to this "why" question is our **causal attribution** for the event. The attributions we make for events can influence our behavior, because they influence the meaning we give to events and our expectations for similar events in the future.

For example, if we attribute a friend's rude behavior to temporary or situational factors (he is under a lot of pressure), we do not evaluate that friend too harshly, and we do not expect the friend to act rudely again in the future. However, if we attribute the friend's behavior to personality factors (he is a mean guy), our evaluations of the friend will be more harsh, and we will expect the friend to act rudely again. A personality attribution for the friend's behavior might lead us to avoid the friend or even break up the relationship, whereas a situational attribution would not.

The attributions we make for our own behavior can have a strong effect on our emotions and self-concept. For example, if we act meanly toward another person and attribute this behavior to situational factors (the other person acted meanly first), we may feel slightly guilty but we may also feel justified. However, if we attribute this behavior to personality factors (we are mean), we may feel quite guilty and lose self-esteem. Our attributions for our performance in achievement settings can also affect our self-esteem, our emotions, and our willingness to continue striving. Attributing failure on an exam to situational factors (the exam was too hard) will result in less negative emotion than attributing failure on an exam to personality factors (a lack of intelligence).

A **control theory** focuses on people's expectations regarding their abilities to control important events (Bandura, 1977; Rotter, 1954; Seligman, 1975). When people believe they can control an important event, they behave in ways to control that event. When they believe they are unable to control an event, they do not attempt to control it or easily give up when they have difficulty controlling it. Martin Seligman (1975) argued that repeated experiences with uncontrollable events lead a person to develop *learned helplessness*, the general expectation that future events will be uncontrollable. He described a set of learned helplessness deficits that result from this expectation, including lowered self-esteem, lowered persistence and motivation, and the inability to see opportunities for control when they do arise.

In an update of his social learning theory, Albert Bandura (1977) argued that a major contributor to people's sense of well-being, motivation, and persistence is their sense of *self-efficacy*. Self-efficacy is a person's belief that he or she can successfully execute the behaviors necessary to control desired outcomes. A good example of high self-efficacy is "the little engine that could," which kept saying, "I think I can! I think I can! I think I can!" People with high self-efficacy in a given situation exert more control over that situation, try harder, are more per-

Garfield © *Paws, Inc. Reprinted with permission of Universal Press Syndicate. All Rights Reserved.*

sistent, and are more successful in that situation than are people with low self-efficacy (Bandura, 1986). High self-efficacy also protects a person against negative emotional reactions to a situation. For example, consider a person whose home has been ruined in a flood. If she has high self-efficacy, she will maintain her motivation to rebuild her home, will make better decisions about how to rebuild, and will be less likely to become depressed over the loss of her home than if she has a low sense of self-efficacy.

A different set of cognitive theories of psychopathology suggests that we have broad beliefs about how things work, which can be either positive and helpful to us or negative and destructive. These broad beliefs are called **global assumptions.** Two of the prominent proponents of this view are Albert Ellis, whom we met in the Extraordinary People opening segment, and Aaron Beck. They argued that most negative emotions and maladaptive behaviors are the result of one or more of the dysfunctional global assumptions that guide a person's life. Some of the most common dysfunctional assumptions are:

1. I should be loved by everyone for everything I do.
2. Things should turn out the way I want them to turn out.
3. I should be terribly upset by dangerous situations.
4. It is better to avoid problems than to face them.
5. I need someone stronger and more powerful than me to rely on.
6. I should be completely competent, intelligent, and achieving in all I do.
7. Once something affects my life, it will affect it forever.
8. I must have perfect self-control.
9. I have no control over my emotions and cannot help feeling certain feelings.

People who hold such beliefs will often react to situations with irrational thoughts and behaviors and negative emotions. For example, someone who believes that she must be completely competent, intelligent, and achieving in all areas in her life will be extremely upset by even minor failures or bad events, such as tearing her blouse or forgetting to return a phone call. If she were to score poorly on an exam, she could have thoughts such as "I am a total failure. I will never amount to anything. I should have gotten a perfect score on that exam." Similarly, someone who believes that things should

always turn out the way he wants them to may be unable to respond flexibly to the obstacles and setbacks that inevitably stand in the way of achieving goals in daily life. Rather than finding a way around these obstacles, he may focus on the obstacles, distressed that things are not going his way.

In the 1960s and 1970s, effective therapies were developed for the mood and anxiety disorders, based on Beck's and Ellis' theories, and we will discuss these therapies in Chapter 5. These cognitive therapies help clients identify and challenge these negative thoughts and dysfunctional belief systems.

Assessing the Cognitive Theories

The cognitive theories may seem the most comfortable or familiar to you of all the theories we have discussed thus far. If so, that is probably because they are a product of our times and dominate much of current clinical, personality, and social psychology. The cognitive theories are also attractive because they focus on that distinctly human process of abstract thinking. Cognitive theorists have worked hard to provide scientific evidence for their explanations of specific disorders and have been successful in many domains. Particularly in studies of mood disorders and anxiety disorders, and increasingly in studies of sexual disorders and substance use disorders, the cognitive theories have helped explain how unwanted emotions, thoughts, and behaviors develop and are maintained.

The greatest limitation of the cognitive theories has been the difficulty of proving that maladaptive cognitions precede and cause disorders, rather than being the symptoms or consequences

Aaron Beck is one of the founders of cognitive theories of psychopathology.

of the disorders. For example, it is clear that depressed people think depressing thoughts. But is this a cause of their depression or a symptom of it? It turns out to be harder than you might think to answer this question definitively (Coyne & Gotlib, 1983). Even if cognitions can cause changes in mood and behavior, it is clear that changes in mood and behavior can also cause cognitions (Bower, 1981). In other words, there are reciprocal effects, or feedback loops, among cognitions, behaviors, and moods, making it difficult to distinguish cause from effect.

The cognitive theories have also been criticized for assuming that negative beliefs are always irrational and for ignoring the negative lives that some people truly lead. People who believe they have little control over their environments, that they are not good at most things, or that no one loves them may be correct in their beliefs and not distorting reality. Many cognitive theorists would argue, however, that reality is always in the eye of the beholder to some extent and that there are more and less adaptive ways of viewing even the most difficult circumstances.

Humanistic and Existential Theories of Abnormality

More than any of the other theories of abnormality, **humanistic theories** and **existential theories** focus on what we might call "the person" behind the cognitions, the behaviors, and the unconscious conflicts. These theories are based on the assumption that humans have an innate capacity for goodness and for living a full life. Pressure from society to conform to certain norms, rather than to seek one's most developed self, interferes with the fulfillment of this capacity.

The humanistic theories emerged in the 1950s and 1960s, partly in reaction to the pessimistic and deterministic view of human behavior provided by traditional psychodynamic theory and to the claims of traditional behavioral theory that humans are only products of their environment. The humanistic theorists recognized that we are often not aware of the forces shaping our behavior and that the environment can play a strong role in our happiness or unhappiness. But they were optimistic that, once people were made aware of these forces and freed to make choices about the direction of their lives, they would naturally make good choices and be happier.

Carl Rogers (1951) developed the most widely known version of humanistic theory. Rogers believed that, without undue pressure from others, individuals naturally move toward personal growth, self-acceptance, and **self-actualization,** which is the

Carl Rogers (1902–1987) was one of the founders of humanistic theory.

fulfillment of one's potential for love, creativity, and meaning. We can develop a set of values that is all our own, as well as an identity that is free from the expectations of others. Under the stress of pressure from society and family, however, people can develop rigid and distorted perspectives of the self and can lose touch with their own values and needs. This can lead to emotional distress, unhealthy behaviors, and even loss of touch with reality. Rogers developed a form of therapy, called **client-centered therapy,** that is designed to help people realize their genuine selves, accept themselves entirely, and begin growing toward self-actualization (see Chapter 5).

Abraham Maslow, another key figure in the development of the humanistic perspective, argued that humans have a hierarchy of needs, and self-actualization can occur only after lower-order needs are satisfied (see Figure 2.13). The most basic needs are physiological needs, such as hunger. At the highest level of the hierarchy is the need to fulfill one's own personal values and to reach self-actualization. Maslow said that people who are at this highest level of the hierarchy "no longer strive in the ordinary sense, but rather develop. They attempt to grow to perfection and to develop more and more fully in their own style" (Maslow, 1954, p. 211). Maladaptive behavior and general distress can result from a person's inability to fulfill lower-order needs and reach a point of growth instead of striving.

The existential theories of Fritz Perls, Martin Heidegger, and Soren Kierkegaard were based on many of the same beliefs as the humanistic theories. Humans are in control—they have the capacity and the responsibility to direct their lives in meaningful and constructive ways. They also believed that the

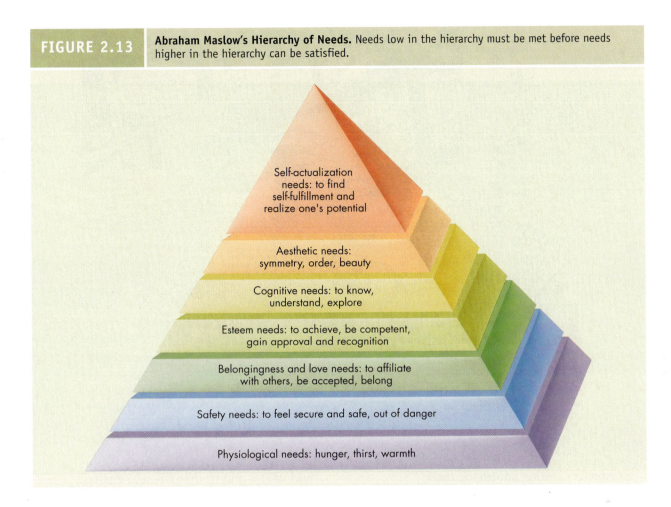

ultimate goals in human growth are the discovery of one's own values and meaning and the living of one's life by these values.

The existentialists, however, put more emphasis on the difficulties inherent in self-actualization, recognizing that society puts many obstacles in the way of living according to one's own values. *Existential anxiety*, created by the realization of our ultimate death, leads many people to abandon their personal growth and search for meaning. We must overcome this anxiety by choosing to live full and meaningful lives, or our lives will be wasted and corrupted and likely will be filled with misery and maladaptive behaviors.

Assessing Humanistic and Existential Theories

The humanistic theories struck a positive chord in the 1960s and still have many proponents, especially among self-help groups and peer counseling programs. The optimism and attribution of free will of these theories is a refreshing change from the emphasis on pathology and external forces in other theories. These theories change the focus from what is wrong with people to questions about how people can be helped to achieve their greatest potential.

The humanistic and existential theories have been criticized, however, for being vague and impossible to test scientifically. And, as we discuss in Chapter 5, the humanistic therapies may be helpful and interesting to people who are generally healthy and functioning in society, but it is not clear they can help people with serious psychopathology.

SUMMING UP

- Psychodynamic theories of psychopathology focus on unconscious conflicts that cause anxiety and result in maladaptive behavior.

- The ways people handle their conflicts are defined by the types of defense mechanisms they use. Children can become fixated on certain needs or concerns if their transitions through psychosexual stages are not managed well.

- More recent psychodynamic theories focus less on the role of unconscious impulses and more on the development of the individual's self-concept in the context of interpersonal relationships. They describe a greater role for the environment in the shaping of personality

Calvin and Hobbes © *Watterson. Dist. By Universal Press Syndicate. Reprinted with permission. All Rights Reserved.*

and provide more hope for change in personality during adulthood than Freud did.

- The behavioral theories of abnormality focus only on the rewards and punishments in the environment that shape and maintain behavior. Classical conditioning takes place when a previously neutral stimulus is paired with a stimulus that naturally creates a certain response. Eventually the neutral stimulus will also elicit the response.

- Operant conditioning involves rewarding desired behaviors and punishing undesired behaviors.

- People also learn by imitating the behaviors modeled by others and by observing the rewards and punishments others receive for their behaviors.

- Cognitive theories suggest that people's attributions for events, their perceptions of control and self-efficacy, and their global assumptions about themselves and the world influence their behaviors and emotions in reaction to situations.

- Humanistic and existential theories suggest that all humans strive to fulfill their potential for good and to self-actualize. The inability to fulfill one's potential arises from the pressures

of society to conform to others' expectations and values and from existential anxiety.

SOCIAL AND INTERPERSONAL APPROACHES

The psychological theories we have discussed so far focus primarily on the individual. They attribute problematic psychological symptoms to unconscious conflicts, negative cognitions, existential anxiety, and other factors within the individual. Although these theories may suggest that the environment plays a role in creating these problems, they still consider the individual to be the primary focus of analysis. The social approaches to abnormality focus more on the larger social structures within which an individual lives (see Figure 2.14). These structures can include the individual's marriage or family and his or her neighborhood, social class, or culture.

Interpersonal Theories of Abnormality

Humans are social beings. The **interpersonal theories** put this fact at the center of their explanations of the development of normal and abnormal behavior more than any of the theories we have discussed so far. Contemporary interpersonal theories grew out of a split between Freud and one of his students,

FIGURE 2.14   **Social Approaches to Mental Disorders.** Social approaches to mental disorders look to an individual's relationships to others and place in society for the source of mental disorders.

Interpersonal theories: Mental disorders are the result of long-standing patterns of negative relationships, which have their roots in early experiences with caregivers.

Social structural theories: Societies create mental disorders in individuals by putting them under unbearable stress and by sanctioning abnormal behavior.

Family systems theories: Families create and maintain mental disorders in individual family members to maintain the status quo.

Alfred Adler. Adler disagreed with Freud's singular focus on unconscious processes within the individual as the force behind human behavior, as well as on Freud's concern with instinctual drives. Adler argued that the primary motivation of humans is to belong to and participate in social groups. Later, other psychodynamic theorists also split with Freud and emphasized social motives and social forces more than sexual drives in shaping humans' behaviors. These theorists included Erich Fromm, Karen Horney, and Erik Erikson.

Erik Erikson proposed a series of stages of psychosocial development that are not concerned with gratifying sexual needs, as in Freud's stages, but with resolving crises in our understanding of the world, ourselves, and our relationships (see Figure 2.15 on page 62). We never fully resolve all of these issues, but some people make better resolutions than others, and these people tend to be happier and better adjusted.

Harry Stack Sullivan (1953) developed ideas similar to those of the object relations school about the roles of important others in the development of self-concept, but he used very different language. He noted that children constantly receive feedback from others for their behaviors—criticism for some behaviors and praise for others. The behaviors and aspects of self that are continually criticized become part of the child's self-concept as the *bad-me*, and the aspects of self that are praised become part of the self-concept as the *good-me*. The bad-me arouses anxiety, so the child develops ways of averting attention from those aspects of the self. If enough anxiety is aroused by those aspects of the self, the child may develop it as the *not-me*, blocking it from consciousness.

All of us have aspects of ourselves we wish to deny—perhaps our anger, our sexual urges, or our competitiveness. Even when these not-me aspects are repressed, they still exert influence on our behavior. We may deny we are angry, but everyone else knows we are angry, for instance. People with severe psychopathology have images of the self and others that are so painful that they engage in self-destructive behavior to avoid these images. For example, a woman whose father secretly abused her as a child may be completely unable to confront these truths about herself and her father and may drink heavily to numb her feelings.

The child's self-concept is part of a broader system of **prototypes**—images of the self and others in relation to the self—that are formed from experiences with family members during childhood. Throughout life, our reactions to others reflect these prototypes. The influence of these prototypes can lead to irrational and exaggerated reactions. For example, an innocent remark by our boss can lead to extreme anxiety or anger because it activates our prototype of our father, who was constantly critical.

More recently, interpersonal theorists have focused on the "scripts" people develop for their relationships—the sets of expectations for how each person in a relationship should behave toward the other. Wives and husbands each have implicit scripts for how the other should behave in the marriage, parents and children have implicit scripts for each other's behaviors, and so on. When these expectations are violated, people can become confused, angry, and frightened, and relationships can dissolve. Other relationships are filled with conflict because patterns of communication break down and the methods partners use to negotiate common goals do not work (Leary, 1957; Wiggins, 1982).

Finally, several theorists have formulated theories of normal and abnormal behavior based on the

FIGURE 2.15	**Erikson's Stages of Psychosocial Development.** Erickson proposed eight stages of psychosocial crises, which can lead to positive or negative development across the life span.

Stage of life	Psychosocial crisis	Favorable outcome
I. Infancy	Trust vs. mistrust	Trust and hope
II. Early childhood	Autonomy vs. shame, doubt	Self-control, sense of adequacy
III. Years 3 to 5	Initiative vs. guilt	Purpose and direction, initiative
IV. Years 6 to puberty	Industry vs. inferiority	Competence
V. Adolescence	Identity vs. confusion	Integrated view of self as unique
VI. Early adulthood	Intimacy vs. isolation	Ability to form close relationships
VII. Middle adulthood	Generativity vs. stagnation	Concern for family, society
VIII. Old age	Integrity vs. despair	Fulfillment and satisfaction, willingness to face death

work of John Bowlby (1969), whose ideas were influenced by psychodynamic thought but also by *ethology*—the study of animal behavior. Bowlby argued that early in life we form strong attachments to our caregivers, and the quality of these attachments then determines our expectations for ourselves and our relationships. On one hand, children who form *secure attachments* are confident that their caregivers will be there when they need them. This confidence gives them the courage to explore their environment, returning to their caregivers for comfort and assistance when necessary. As they mature, children expect other relationships to be secure and seek out and form positive, strong relationships with others.

On the other hand, children who have *insecure attachments* do not have confidence in their caregivers, because their caregivers have not been consistently trustworthy. They may be anxious and clinging to their caregivers, refusing to leave their side. Or they may be hostile and avoidant of caregivers. In either case, these children then have negative expectations for future relationships, which essentially become self-fulfilling prophecies. Children with anxious, insecure attachments become adults who are prone to anxiety, depression, and excessive dependence on others. Children with avoidant, insecure attachments may become adults who are hostile, isolated, and even violent. When we discuss childhood disorders in Chapter 13, we will see that the field of developmental psychopathology, which focuses on how normal development goes awry to produce psychopathology in children, has incorporated attachment theory into several of its theories of the development of specific disorders.

A number of empirical studies have tested the interpersonal theories in recent years. Some of the hypotheses about the importance of prototypes, or "mental models," of early relationships in shaping adult relationships have been supported (Banse, 2004; Fraley & Bonanno, 2004; Roisman, Tsai, & Chiang, 2004). In addition, new therapies based on the interpersonal theories are proving helpful in several disorders, as we discuss in Chapter 5.

Family Systems Theories of Abnormality

Most of the theories we have discussed thus far have implicated the family in the development of both normal and abnormal behavior. The **family systems theories** and therapies focus on the family in quite a different manner from the other theories, however (Minuchin, 1981; Mirsalimi et al., 2003; Satir, 1967). These theories see the family as a complex system, which works to maintain the status quo or *homeostasis*. Each family has its own hierarchy and set of rules, which govern the behavior of the members and help maintain homeostasis. The family system can function well and be healthy for its individual members, supporting their growth and accepting their change. Or the family system can be dysfunctional, in essence requiring psychopathology in one or more members in order to maintain the status quo.

When a member of the family has a psychological disorder, family systems theorists see it not as a problem within the individual but as an indication of a dysfunctional family system. Psychopathology in an individual reflects pathology or dysfunction in the family, according to family systems theory. The particular form that any individual's psychopathology takes depends on the complex interactions among the family's cohesiveness, adaptability to change, and communication style.

For example, an *inflexible family* is resistant to and isolated from all forces outside the family and does not adapt well to changes within the family, such as a child moving into adolescence. In an *enmeshed family*, each member is too greatly involved in the lives of the other members, to the point that individuals do not have personal autonomy and can feel controlled. In contrast, a *disengaged family* is one in which the members pay no attention to each other and operate as independent units isolated from other family members. And in *pathological triangular relationships*, parents avoid dealing with conflicts with each other by always keeping their children involved in their conversations and activities (Mirsalimi et al., 2003). Thus, a family theorist trying to understand Albert Ellis' anxiety would examine how his family functioned as he grew up and how that continued to influence him an adult.

Some of the research on family systems theories of psychopathology has focused on disorders in the children in the family, particularly eating disorders (e.g., Minuchin, Rosman, & Baker, 1978). This research suggests that many young girls who develop eating disorders are members of enmeshed families. The parents of these girls are overcontrolling and overinvested in their children's success, and in turn the children feel smothered and dependent on their parents. Anorexia nervosa, a disorder in which an individual refuses to eat and becomes emaciated, may be a girl's way of claiming some control over her life. The family system of these girls maintains and supports the anorexia, rather than working to help her overcome her anorexia. The anorexia becomes a focal point and excuse for the family's enmeshment.

As we discuss in Chapter 5, the family systems theories have led to therapeutic approaches that have proven useful for some types of disorders. Family systems therapies may be particularly appropriate in the treatment of children, because children are so much more entwined in their families than adults. Although the details of many family systems theories have not been thoroughly tested in research, it is clear that families can contribute to or help diminish psychological symptoms in their members (e.g., Mirsalimi et al., 2003).

Social Structural Theories of Abnormality

Social structural theories suggest that we need to look beyond the family to the larger society to find

Family therapists believe that individuals' problems are rooted in patterns of interaction among family members.

the causes of psychopathology in individuals. First, society can create stresses on individuals that increase their risk for psychopathology. These stresses may come in the form of a massive reorganization of the society, such as the industrialization of America in the early twentieth century or the great increases in the presence of people of Hispanic origins in the American West in the past decade. Such societal reorganization changes people's roles and relationships to the society—from factory worker to unemployed person or from member of the majority culture to member of a multicultural society. Societies undergoing significant social change often experience increases in the rates of mental disorders. This is especially true if the change is generally seen as a negative one, as during an economic depression.

Second, some people live in more chronically stressful circumstances than others, and these people appear to be at greater risk for psychopathology. For example, people living in poverty-stricken urban neighborhoods experience more problems, especially substance abuse, juvenile delinquency, depression, and anxiety (Belle & Doucet, 2003). Just what makes some neighborhoods toxic is a matter of debate among researchers.

One model for the effects of neighborhoods on mental health is given in Figure 2.16 (on page 64). Certain characteristics of neighborhoods seem important, such as high rates of poverty, the frequent experience of prejudice and discrimination due to ethnic minority status, families moving in and out of neighborhoods frequently, a lack of cultural or

FIGURE 2.16	**A Social Structural Model of Mental Health.** Social structural theories focus on the effects of the larger society on individuals' mental health.

Neighborhood characteristics
Widespread poverty
Prejudice and discrimination
Lack of cultural or ethnic ties
High residential turnover
High child-to-adult ratio

\+

Social organization
Lack of common values
Lack of social control
Open conflict

Psychological stress
Insufficient resources
Chronic agitation and fear

Subcultural influences
Development of gangs
and drug use

Mental-health outcomes
Child maltreatment
Juvenile delinquency
Behavioral disorders
Depression
Anxiety
Schizophrenia
Substance abuse

Source: Based on Wandersman & Nation, 1998.

ethnic ties among neighbors, and high numbers of children relative to the numbers of adults (Earls, 2001; Leventhal & Brooks-Gunn, 2003). These characteristics contribute to a scarcity of financial resources for individual families, a lack of cohesion and common values in the neighborhood, an unwillingness of neighbors to monitor and constrain the behavior of each other's children, and often open conflict between neighbors. In such neighborhoods, subcultures often emerge that offer members a means of coping with the stresses they face, but in maladaptive ways, such as through drugs and crime. Other people are chronically agitated and afraid, seeing no way out. All these forces then result in high rates of a number of mental-health problems, from behavioral disorders to depression (Wandersman & Nation, 1998).

Finally, societies may influence the types of psychopathology their members show by having implicit or explicit rules about what types of abnormal behavior are acceptable and in what circumstances. Throughout this book, we will see that the rates of disorders vary from one culture or ethnic group to another and between males and females. For example, people from "traditional" cultures, such as the Old Order Amish in the United States, appear to have less depression than people in modern cultures (Egeland & Hostetter, 1983). In addition, the particular manifestations of disorders seem to vary from one culture to another. For example, the symptoms of anorexia nervosa, the disorder in which people refuse to eat, appear to be different in Asian cultures than in American culture. Finally, there may be many disorders that are specific to certain cultures.

Assessing Social Approaches

The social approaches to abnormality argue that we should analyze the larger social and cultural forces that may be influencing people's behavior. It is not enough to look only at what is going on within individuals or their immediate surroundings. Social approaches are often credited for not "blaming the victim," as other theories seem to do, by placing responsibility for psychopathology within the individual. The social approaches also raise our consciousness about our responsibility within families and as a society to change the social conditions that put some individual members at risk for psychopathology.

The social structural theories can be criticized, however, for being somewhat vague about the exact ways in which social and cultural forces lead to psychological disturbance in individuals. Just how is it that social change or stress leads to depression, schizophrenia, and so on? Why does it lead to depression in some people but to drug abuse in others? Why do most people exposed to social stress and change develop no psychological disturbance at all? These theories and the studies testing them are becoming more complex as they attempt to answer such questions.

SUMMING UP

- The interpersonal theories assert that our self-concepts and expectations of others are based on our early attachments and relationships to caregivers.

- Family systems theories suggest that families form cohesive systems, which regulate the behavior of each member in the system. Sometimes these systems support and enhance the well-being of their members but sometimes they do not.

- Social structural theories suggest that society contributes to psychopathology in some people by creating severe stresses for them, then allowing or encouraging them to cope with these stresses with psychological symptoms. People living in chronically stressful environments have higher rates of psychopathology.

CHAPTER INTEGRATION

Surely, you might be saying to yourself, after decades of research and with the modern scientific techniques available, we must know which of the many theories covered in this chapter is right or correct. Or at least we should know which of these theories best explains specific disorders. As we go through each disorder, we will discuss which theories have been supported best by modern scientific methods.

As we noted at the beginning of this chapter, however, many scientists believe that only models that *integrate* biological, psychological, and social factors can provide comprehensive explanations of psychological disorders. Only integrated models can explain why many people with disordered genes or deficiencies in neurotransmitters do *not* develop painful emotional symptoms or bizarre thoughts. Similarly, only integrated models can suggest how traumatic experiences and toxic interpersonal relationships can cause changes in the basic biochemistry of the brain, which then cause changes in a person's emotions, thoughts, and behaviors.

Figure 2.17 illustrates how some of the biological, psychological, and social factors discussed in this chapter might come together to contribute, for example, to symptoms of depression. First, some people are born with certain genetic characteristics that lead to poor functioning of the hypothalamic-pituitary-adrenal axis. Chronic arousal of this axis may lead individuals to be overly responsive to stress. If they tend to interpret their reactions to stress in terms of "I can't cope!" this can lead them

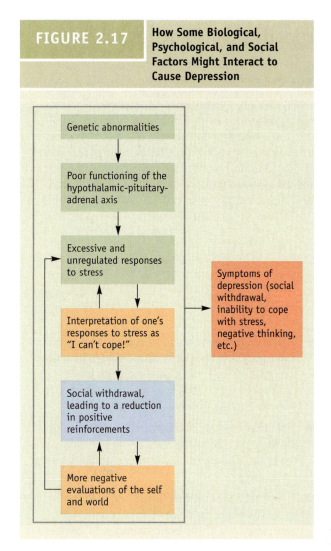

FIGURE 2.17 How Some Biological, Psychological, and Social Factors Might Interact to Cause Depression

to develop a negative thinking style. This negative thinking style then can cause them to withdraw socially, leading to a reduction in positive reinforcements. This could feed negative evaluations of themselves and the world, further contributing to depression. Then, when they are confronted with new stressors, they might not have good strategies for coping with them and might overreact psychologically as well as physiologically. All these processes come together to produce the key symptoms of depression—social withdrawal, an inability to cope with stress, negative thinking, and so on.

Extraordinary People: Follow-Up

After Ellis had his personal insights into the sources of his own anxiety symptoms, he received his doctorate in psychology from Columbia Teacher's College and took training to become a psychoanalyst. He soon rejected psychoanalytic thinking and, by the late 1950s, had established the Institute for Rational-Emotive Therapy. Over the subsequent 50 years, he has written many books on this type of therapy, as well as on sexuality, has treated thousands of clients, and has given thousands of public lectures. He says, "I love my work . . . I like helping people." (Warga, 1988, p. 58)

Chapter Summary

■ Vulnerability-stress models suggest that people must carry a vulnerability to a disorder (usually biological or psychological) and must be confronted with social stresses for a disorder to develop (review Figure 2.1).

■ Biological theories of psychopathology typically attribute symptoms to structural abnormalities in the brain, disordered biochemistry, or faulty genes (review Figure 2.4).

■ Structural abnormalities in the brain can be caused by faulty genes, by disease, or by injury. The particular area of the brain damaged influences the symptoms individuals show.

■ Many biological theories attribute psychopathology to imbalances in neurotransmitters or to the functioning of receptors for neurotransmitters.

■ Genetic theories of abnormality usually suggest that it takes an accumulation of faulty genes to cause a psychopathology. Genetic theories are tested with family history studies, twin studies, and adoption studies.

■ Psychodynamic theories of psychopathology focus on unconscious conflicts that cause anxiety in the individual and result in maladaptive behavior (review Concept Overview in Table 2.1). Freud argued that these conflicts arise when the libidinal impulses of the id clash with the constraints on behavior imposed by the ego and superego.

■ Psychodynamic theories say that the ways people handle their conflicts are defined by the types of defense mechanisms they use (review Table 2.2). How caregivers handle children's transitions through the psychosexual stages determines the concerns or issues the children may become fixated upon.

■ More recent psychodynamic theorists focus less on the role of unconscious impulses and more on the development of the individual's self-concept in the context of interpersonal relationships. They see a greater role for the environment in shaping personality and have more hope for change during adulthood than Freud did.

■ The behaviorist theories of abnormality reject notions of unconscious conflicts and focus only on the rewards and punishments in the environment that shape and maintain behavior.

■ Classical conditioning takes place when a previously neutral stimulus is paired with a stimulus that naturally creates a certain response; eventually, the neutral stimulus will also elicit the response (review Figure 2.12).

■ Operant conditioning involves rewarding desired behaviors and punishing undesired behaviors.

■ People also learn by imitating the behaviors modeled by others and by observing the rewards and punishments others receive for their behaviors.

■ Cognitive theories suggest that people's attributions for events, their perceptions of control and self-efficacy, and their global beliefs and assumptions influence the behaviors and emotions they have in reaction to situations.

■ Humanist and existential theories suggest that all humans strive to fulfill their potential for good and to self-actualize. The inability to fulfill one's potential arises from the pressures of society to conform to others' expectations and values and from existential anxiety.

- Interpersonal theories suggest that children develop internal models of the self and others through their attachments and relationships with early caregivers. These models then affect their behaviors and later relationships, sometimes in unhealthy ways.

- Family systems theories suggest that psychopathology in individual family members is due to dysfunctional patterns of interaction within families, which create and maintain the abnormal behaviors.

- Social structural theories suggest that societies create severe stresses for some people, and then subcultures can sanction maladaptive ways of coping with these stresses. Cultures also have implicit and explicit rules for the types of abnormal behavior that are permissible in the society.

MindMap CD-ROM

The following resources on the MindMap CD-ROM that came with this text will help you to master the content of this chapter and prepare for tests:

- Interactive segment: Parts of the Brain
- Video: Functions of Neurotransmitters
- Interactive segment: Identifying Psychological Perspectives
- Chapter Timeline
- Chapter Quiz

Key Terms

theory 34
biological approach 34
psychological approach 34
social approach 34
vulnerability-stress models 35
cerebral cortex 38
hypothalamus 38
limbic system 38
neurotransmitters 39
synapse 39
receptors 39
reuptake 39
degradation 39
endocrine system 40
hormone 40
pituitary 41
behavior genetics 42
polygenic 42
family history study 42
monozygotic (MZ) twins 42
predisposition 43
dizygotic (DZ) twins 43
twin studies 43
concordance rate 43

adoption study 44
psychodynamic theories 46
psychoanalysis 46
catharsis 47
repression 47
libido 47
id 47
pleasure principle 47
primary process thinking 48
ego 48
reality principle 48
secondary process thinking 48
superego 49
introject 49
unconscious 49
preconscious 49
conscious 49
defense mechanisms 49
neurotic paradox 49
psychosexual stages 49
oral stage 50
anal stage 50
phallic stage 51
Oedipus complex 51

castration anxiety 51

Electra complex 51

penis envy 51

latency stage 51

genital stage 51

object relations 51

splitting 52

behavioral theories 53

classical conditioning 53

unconditioned stimulus (US) 53

unconditioned response (UR) 53

conditioned stimulus (CS) 54

conditioned response (CR) 54

operant conditioning 54

continuous reinforcement schedule 54

partial reinforcement schedule 54

extinction 54

social learning theory 55

modeling 55

observational learning 55

cognitive theories 56

cognitions 56

causal attribution 56

control theory 56

global assumptions 57

humanistic theories 58

existential theories 58

self-actualization 58

client-centered therapy 58

interpersonal theories 60

prototypes 61

family systems theories 62

social structural theories 63

> Chapter 3

The Global Seat
by Christian Pierre

There's no limit to how complicated things can get, on account of one thing always leading to another.

—E. B. White

The Research Endeavor <

Extraordinary People

■ **The Old Order Amish of Pennsylvania**

The Scientific Method

Conducting scientific research involves defining a problem; specifying a hypothesis, or a statement about what you believe will happen in a study; and defining the variables.

Case Studies

Case studies are detailed histories of individuals. They are rich in detail and honor the uniqueness of individuals. They help in generating new ideas and in illuminating rare problems. It is difficult to generalize from the experiences of one person, however, and case studies are open to bias.

Correlational Studies

Correlational studies examine the relationship between two variables without manipulating them. Correlational studies can show that two variables are related but cannot show that one causes the other. A correlation coefficient is a statistic used to describe the relationship between variables.

Epidemiological Studies

Epidemiological studies attempt to determine the rates of certain types of psychopathology in a population.

Experimental Studies

Experimental studies attempt to create conditions to test hypotheses in which variables are controlled or manipulated. Experimental studies may involve humans or ani-mals. A special type of experimental study is the therapy outcome study, in which people with psychopathology are given therapy meant to reduce their symptoms, and their outcomes are compared with those of people who receive no therapy or an alternative therapy. In a single-case experimental design, an individual participant or small group of participants is evaluated intensively before and after receiving an intervention or a treatment. Experimental studies may not generalize to the real world and can raise ethical issues.

Taking Psychology Personally

■ **Your Rights as a Research Participant**

Cross-Cultural Research

Cross-cultural research examines the similarities and differences in abnormality across cultures. Some special challenges of cross-cultural research include applying theories across cultures and translating concepts across cultures.

Meta-Analysis

Meta-analysis is a statistical procedure for combining the results of several studies to determine the overall trends across studies.

Chapter Integration

Modern thinking about psychopathology increasingly integrates biological, psychological, and social concepts using a vulnerability-stress perspective. Researchers taking an integrationist approach must gather information about people's biological, psychological, and social vulnerabilities and strengths. To carry out this work, more and more researchers are working in teams and seeking specialized training.

Extraordinary People

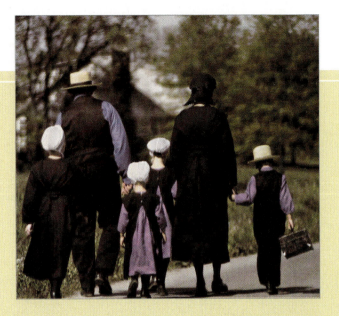

The Old Order Amish of Pennsylvania

Imagine that you live in a quiet, close-knit rural community, surrounded by family and friends. You purposely live a simple life and shun notoriety and attention.

Then imagine having a team of investigators come into your community, asking detailed questions about the most distressing, embarrassing, and intimate experiences of your life and the lives of your family members and closest friends. The team also asks community leaders to report on unusual behaviors by members of the community.

Most of us would not agree to such an experience. We value our privacy and don't want anyone making public the problems that we or our loved ones have faced, yet one extraordinary community agreed to open itself to researchers, and from that research has come some of the most interesting and important work on the mood disorders—depression and mania (see Chapter 9)—that has been published in the scientific literature. That community is the Old Order Amish of southeastern Pennsylvania.

The Amish are a religious sect who avoid contact with the "modern" world and live a simple, agrarian life, much as people lived in the eighteenth century. The Amish use horse and buggy as transportation, most of their homes do not have electricity or telephones, and there is little movement of people into or out of this culture. It is a theocratic society, with the community divided according to church districts and led by church elders. The Amish are pacifists, and they avoid involvement with local and national politics and practices. The rules of social behavior among the Amish are very strict, and roles within the community are clearly set. Members who do not comply with community norms are isolated or shunned.

Despite their self-enforced isolation from mainstream American society, the Amish of southeastern Pennsylvania welcomed researcher Janice Egeland and several of her colleagues to conduct some of the most intensive studies of depression and mania ever done (Egeland, 1986, 1994; Egeland & Hostetter, 1983; Pauls, Morton, & Egeland, 1992). These researchers first attempted to ascertain how common depression and mania were among the Amish. They searched the records of local hospitals for Amish people who had been hospitalized for psychological problems. They also interviewed thousands of members of this community (which, in total, numbered about 12,000) to discover people with mood disorders who had not yet been hospitalized.

Thanks to this closed community, which opened itself to research on psychological disorders, and to the tireless work by researcher Janice Egeland and colleagues, researchers have come a long way in understanding the major mood disorders.

Research in abnormal psychology is similar in many ways to research in many other fields. There are some special challenges in studying psychopathology, however. One of the greatest is that the populations of interest—such as the Old Order Amish in the *Extraordinary People* feature, or people who are paranoid and hearing voices—can be difficult to convince to participate in research.

Another challenge is that abnormal behaviors and feelings are extremely difficult to measure accurately. We cannot see, hear, or feel other people's emotions and thoughts. Researchers must often rely on people's own accounts, or *self-reports*, of their internal states and experiences. Self-reports can be distorted in a number of ways, intentionally or unintentionally. Similarly, relying on an observer's assessments of a person also has pitfalls. The observer's assessments can be biased by stereotypes involving gender and culture, idiosyncratic biases, and lack of information.

A third challenge is that most forms of abnormality probably have multiple causes. Unless a single study can capture the biological, psychological, and social causes of the abnormality of interest, it cannot fully explain the causes of that abnormality. Rarely can a single study accomplish so much. Instead, we are usually left with partial answers to the question of what causes a certain abnormality, and we must piece together the partial answers from several studies to get a full picture of that abnormality.

Despite these challenges, tremendous strides have been made in our understanding of many forms of abnormality in the past 50 years or so, thanks to the cleverness and persistence of researchers. Researchers overcome many of the challenges of researching abnormality by using a *multimethod approach*, which means they use a variety of methodologies. Each method may have some limitations, but taken together, the various methods can provide convincing evidence concerning an abnormality.

In this chapter, we discuss the most common methods of doing research on abnormality. We consider one very common psychological problem, depression, and talk about how to test a simple idea about this problem—the idea that stress is a cause of depression—using various research methods. Of course, the research methods we discuss can be used to test many different ideas, but, by applying all the methods to one idea, we can see how many tools researchers have at their disposal to test a given idea.

THE SCIENTIFIC METHOD

Any research project involves a basic series of steps. These steps are designed to obtain and evaluate information relevant to a problem in a systematic way—a process often called the **scientific method.**

The first step is to select and define a problem. In our case, the problem is to determine the relationship between stress and depression. Then, a testable statement of what is predicted to happen in the study must be formulated. Next, the method for testing the prediction must be chosen and implemented. Once the data have been collected and analyzed, the researcher draws the appropriate conclusions. Finally, the results are written in a research report.

Defining the Problem and Stating a Hypothesis

Throughout this chapter, we examine the idea that stress causes depression. Even this simple idea is too broad and abstract to test directly. Thus, we must state a hypothesis based on this idea. A **hypothesis** is a testable statement of what we predict will happen in the study.

To generate a hypothesis, we might ask, "What kind of evidence would support the idea that stress causes depression?" If we find that people who had recently experienced stress are more likely to be depressed than people who had not recently experienced stress, this evidence would support our idea. One hypothesis, then, is that people who have recently experienced stress are more likely to be depressed than people who have not. This hypothesis can be tested by a number of research methods.

If we find support for this hypothesis, we will have support for our idea. Our idea will not be proven correct, however. No one study can do that. However, a series of studies supporting our idea will bolster our confidence in the idea, particularly if these studies have different methodologies.

The alternative version of our hypothesis is that people who experience stress are *not* more likely to develop depression than are people who do not experience stress. This expectation, that there is *no relationship* between the phenomena being studied—in this case, stress and depression, is called the **null hypothesis.** Results often support the null hypothesis instead of the researcher's primary hypothesis.

Does support for the null hypothesis mean that the underlying idea has been disproved? No. The null hypothesis can be supported for many reasons. Most important, the study may not be designed well enough to provide support for the primary hypothesis. Researchers will often continue to test their primary hypothesis, using a variety of methodologies. If the null hypothesis continues to get much more support than the primary hypothesis, they eventually either modify or drop the primary hypothesis.

Choosing and Implementing a Research Method

Once we have stated a hypothesis, the next step in testing our idea that stress leads to depression is to choose how we are going to define the phenomena we are studying.

A **variable** is a factor or characteristic that can vary within an individual or between individuals. Weight, mood, neurotransmitter levels, and attitudes toward one's mother are all factors that can vary over time, so they are considered variables. Similarly, height, sex, and ethnicity are factors that do not vary for an individual over time, but they can vary from one individual to another, so they, too, can be considered variables.

A **dependent variable** is the factor being predicted in a study. In our studies of stress and depression, we will be trying to predict depressive symptoms, so depression is our dependent variable.

An **independent variable** is the factor that is believed to affect the dependent variable. In our studies, stress is our independent variable.

In order to research depression and stress, we must define what we mean by these terms. As we will discuss in Chapter 9, *depression* is a syndrome or collection of the following symptoms: sadness, loss of interest in one's usual activities, weight loss or gain, changes in sleep, agitation or slowing down, fatigue and loss of energy, feelings of worthlessness or excessive guilt, problems in concentration or indecisiveness, and suicidal thoughts (American Psychiatric Association, 2000). Some researchers define depressed people as those who can be diagnosed with a depressive disorder. Anyone who had some of these symptoms of depression but has not been diagnosed with a depressive disorder would be considered not depressed. Other researchers focus on the full range of depressive symptoms, from no symptoms to moderate symptoms to the most severe symptoms. They divide people into those who show depressive symptoms, those who show moderately severe depressive symptoms, and those who show severe depressive symptoms.

Stress is more difficult to define, because the term has been used in so many ways in research and the popular press. *Stressor* refers to an *event* that is uncontrollable, is unpredictable, and challenges the limits of people's abilities to cope. *Stress* has been used to refer to people's *emotions and behaviors* in response to such stressful events.

Operationalization is the way a researcher measures or manipulates the variables in a study. Our definitions of depression and stress will influence how we operationalize these variables. For example, if we define depression as symptoms meeting criteria for a depressive disorder, then we will operationalize depression as diagnoses. If we define depression as symptoms along the entire range of severity, then we might operationalize depression as scores on a depression questionnaire.

In operationalizing stress, we must first decide whether to focus on stressful events or on people's stress reactions to these events. Then we must devise a measure of what we define as stress or a way of manipulating or creating stress, so that we can then examine people's reactions to this stress. As

we discuss different research methods in this chapter, we examine several operationalizations of stress. In the remaining sections of the book, we discuss various methods of testing hypotheses, as well as the conclusions one can and cannot draw from these methods.

SUMMING UP

- The scientific method is a set of steps designed to obtain and evaluate information relevant to a problem in a systematic way.

- A hypothesis is a testable statement of what a researcher expects to happen in a study.

- A null hypothesis is the statement that the outcome of the study will contradict the primary hypothesis of the study. Usually, the null hypothesis says that the variables (such as stress and depression) are unrelated to one another.

- A variable is a factor that can vary within an individual or between individuals.

- A dependent variable is the factor that is being predicted in a study.

- An independent variable is the factor being used to predict the dependent variable.

- Operationalization is the way the variables of interest are measured or manipulated.

CASE STUDIES

Throughout this book, you will see **case studies**—detailed histories of individuals who have suffered a form of psychological disorder. Case studies have been used for centuries as a way of trying to understand the experiences of individuals and to make more general inferences about the sources of psychopathology.

If we wanted to use a case study to test our idea that stress causes depression, we would focus on an individual, interviewing him or her at length to discover the links between periods of depression and stressful events in his or her life. We might also interview close friends and family to obtain additional information. Based on the information we gathered, we would create a detailed description of the causes of his or her depressive episodes, with an emphasis on the role of stressful events in these episodes. For example, the following brief case study describes singer Kurt Cobain of the hit 1990s rock band Nirvana. It was written by a reporter a week after Cobain committed suicide.

Cobain always had a fragile constitution (he was subject to bronchitis, as well as the recurrent stomach pains he claimed drove him to a heroin addiction). The image one gets is that of a frail kid batted between warring parents. "[The divorce] just destroyed his life," Wendy O'Connor tells Michael Averred in the Nirvana biography *Come As You Are*. "He changed completely. I think he was ashamed. And he became very inward—he just held everything [in]. . . . I think he's *still* suffering." As a teen, Cobain dabbled in drugs and punk rock and dropped out of school. His father persuaded him to pawn his guitar and take an entrance exam for the navy. But Cobain soon returned for the guitar. "To them, I was wasting my life," he told the *Los Angeles Times*. "To me, I was fighting for it." Cobain didn't speak to his father for 8 years. When Nirvana went to the top of the charts, Don Cobain began keeping a scrapbook. "Everything I know about Kurt," he told Azerrad, "I've read in newspapers and magazines."

The more famous Nirvana became, the more Cobain wanted none of it. . . . Nirvana—with their stringy hair, plaid work shirts, and torn jeans—appealed to a mass of young fans who were tired of false idols like Madonna and Michael Jackson and who'd never had a dangerous rock-and-roll hero to call their own. Unfortunately, the band also appealed to the sort of people Cobain had always hated: poseurs and band wagoneers, not to mention record company execs and fashion designers who fell over themselves cashing in on the new sights and sounds. Cobain, who'd grown up as an angry outsider, tried to shake his celebrity. . . .

By 1992, it became clear that Cobain's personal life was as tangled and troubling as his music. The singer married [Courtney] Love in Waikiki—the bride wore a moth-eaten dress once owned by actress Frances Farmer—and the couple embarked on a self destructive pas de deux widely referred to as a 90s version of *Sid and Nancy*. As Cobain put it, "I was going off with Courtney and we were scoring drugs and we were f—king up against a wall and stuff . . . and causing scenes just to do it. It was fun to be with someone who would stand up all of a sudden and smash a glass on the table." In September 1992, *VanityFair* reported that Love had used heroin while she was pregnant with [their daughter] Frances Bean. She and Cobain denied the story (the baby is healthy). But authorities were reportedly concerned enough to force them to surrender custody of Frances to Love's sister, Jamie, for a month, during which time the couple was, in Cobain's words, "totally suicidal.". . .

[T]hose who knew the singer say there was a real fragility buried beneath the noise of his music and his life. . . . If only someone had heard the alarms ringing at that rambling, gray-shingled home near the lake. Long before there was a void in our hearts, there was a void in Kurt Cobain's. (Giles, 1994, pp. 46–47)

In-depth histories of troubled people, such as, Kurt Cobain, may be rich in detail but not generalizable.

Case studies are a time-honored method of research for several reasons. No other method captures the uniqueness of the individual as much as a case study. The nuances of an individual's life and experiences can be detailed, and the individual's own words can be used to describe his or her experiences. Exploring the unique experiences of individuals and honoring their own perspectives on these experiences are important goals for many researchers, and in-depth case studies of individual lives have become more popular in recent years.

Case studies are sometimes the only way to study rare problems, because there simply are not enough people with that problem to study through any other method. For example, much of the research on people with multiple personalities has come from case studies, because this form of psychopathology has historically been quite rare.

Case studies can be invaluable in helping generate new ideas and provide tentative support for those ideas. Most of Freud's theories came from his case studies of people he treated. Freud would listen for hours to his patients' descriptions of their lives, their dreams, and their memories and would notice themes in these reports, which he speculated were related to the psychological symptoms they were suffering. Freud was often quite hesitant in stating his ideas in his reports of his work, encouraging further research to test his ideas.

Today one of the most common uses of case studies is in drug treatment research to report unusual reactions patients have had to certain drugs. These reports can alert other clinicians to watch for similar reactions in their patients. If enough case reports of these unusual reactions emerge in the literature, larger-scale research to study the sources of these reactions may be warranted.

Evaluating Case Studies

Case studies have their drawbacks, however. The first involves **generalizability**—the ability to apply what has been learned to other individuals or groups. The conclusions drawn from the study of an individual may not apply to many other individuals. This limitation is especially true when case studies focus on people whose experiences have been dramatic but unusual. For example, the circumstances leading to Kurt Cobain's death may be very interesting, but they may not tell us anything about why other people commit suicide. As we noted in Chapter 2, even some of Freud's contemporaries criticized him for attempting to generate universal theories of human psychological functioning based on the experiences of his patients who were suffering from psychopathology.

Case studies also suffer from a lack of *objectivity* on the part of both the people telling their stories and the therapists or researchers listening to the stories. The people telling their stories might have biased recollections of their pasts and may selectively report events that happen to them in the present. The therapists or researchers listening to the stories filter them through their own beliefs and assumptions about the causes of human behavior and might selectively remember the parts of the stories that support their beliefs and assumptions and selectively forget the parts that do not. Thus, two case studies of the same person, if conducted by two researchers, may come to very different conclusions about the motivations and key events in that person's life.

Researchers bring their own perspectives to a case study; as a result, one case study may not *replicate*—repeat the conclusions of—another. **Replication** is a key feature of the scientific method. Difficulties in replication are one of the major drawbacks of case studies.

SUMMING UP

- Case studies are in-depth histories of the experiences of individuals.
- The advantages of case studies are their richness in detail, their attention to the unique experiences of individuals, their ability to focus on rare problems, and their ability to generate new ideas.
- The disadvantages of case studies are their lack of generalizability, their lack of objectivity, and difficulties in replication.

CORRELATIONAL STUDIES

Correlational studies examine the relationship between an independent variable and a dependent variable without manipulating either variable. Correlational studies are the most common type of study in psychology and medicine. For example, you will often read about studies of the relationship between television watching and violence, smoking and heart disease, or Internet use and depression, in which researchers have not manipulated any variables but have examined the naturally occurring relationships between the variables.

There are many kinds of correlational studies. The most common type in abnormal psychology is a study of two or more continuous variables. A **continuous variable** is measured along a continuum. For example, on a scale measuring the severity of depression, scores might fall along a continuum from 0 (no depression) to 100 (extreme

Calvin and Hobbes   by Bill Watterson

depression). On a scale measuring the number of recent stressors, scores might fall along a continuum from 0 (no stressors) to 20 (20 or more recent stressors). If we measured severity of depression and number of recent stressors in the same group of people and then looked at the relationship between these two continuous variables, we would be doing a continuous variable correlational study.

Another type of correlational study is a **group comparison study.** In this type of study, researchers are interested in the relationship between people's membership in a particular group and their scores on some other variable. For example, we might be interested in the relationship between depression and whether or not people have experienced a specific type of stress, such as the loss of a loved one. In this case, the groups of interest are bereaved and nonbereaved people. We would find people who represented these two groups, then measure depression in both groups. This is still a correlational study because we are only observing the relationship between two variables—bereavement and depression—not manipulating any variable. In this type of study, however, at least one of the variables—group membership—is not a continuous variable.

Both continuous variable studies and group comparison studies can be either **cross-sectional**—they observe people at only one point in time—or **longitudinal**—they observe people on two more occasions over time. Longitudinal studies have a major advantage over cross-sectional studies, because they can show that the independent variable precedes and predicts changes in the dependent variable over time. For example, a longitudinal study of stress and depression can show that people who are not depressed at the beginning of the study are much more likely to be depressed later in the study if they have experienced a stressful event in the interim than if they have not.

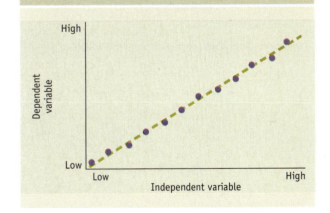

FIGURE 3.1   **A Positive Correlation.** A positive correlation indicates that, as values of the independent variable increase, values of the dependent variable increase. This graph illustrates a correlation of +1.00.

Measuring the Relationship Between Variables

In most correlational studies, the relationship between the variables is indicated by a correlation coefficient. Let us review what this statistic is and how to interpret it.

Correlation Coefficient

A **correlation coefficient** is a statistic used to represent the relationship between variables, and it is usually denoted with the symbol r. A correlation coefficient can fall between -1.00 and $+1.00$. A positively valued correlation coefficient indicates that, as values of the independent variable increase, values of the dependent variable increase (see Figure 3.1). For example, a *positive correlation* between stress and depression would mean that people who reported more stressors had higher levels of depression.

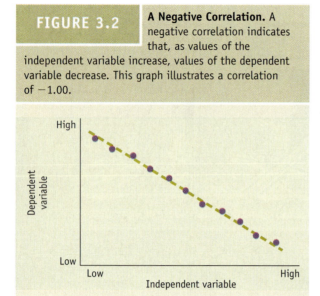

FIGURE 3.2 **A Negative Correlation.** A negative correlation indicates that, as values of the independent variable increase, values of the dependent variable decrease. This graph illustrates a correlation of −1.00.

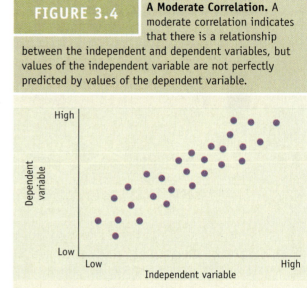

FIGURE 3.4 **A Moderate Correlation.** A moderate correlation indicates that there is a relationship between the independent and dependent variables, but values of the independent variable are not perfectly predicted by values of the dependent variable.

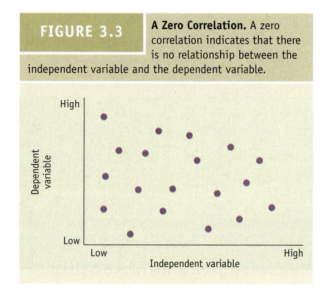

FIGURE 3.3 **A Zero Correlation.** A zero correlation indicates that there is no relationship between the independent variable and the dependent variable.

A negatively valued correlation coefficient indicates that, as values of the independent variable increase, values of the dependent variable decrease (see Figure 3.2). If we were still measuring stressors and depression, a *negative correlation* would mean that people who reported more stressors actually had lower levels of depression. This is an unlikely scenario, but there are many instances of negative correlations between variables. For example, people who have more positive social support from others typically have lower levels of depression.

The magnitude (size) of a correlation is the degree to which the variables move in tandem with each other. It is indicated by how close the correla-

tion coefficient is to either −1.00 or +1.00. A correlation (r) of 0, a zero correlation, indicates no relationship between the variables (see Figure 3.3). An r of −1.00 or +1.00 indicates a perfect relationship between the two variables (as illustrated in Figures 3.1 and 3.2). The value of one variable is perfectly predictable by the value of the other variable—for example, every time people experience stress, they become depressed.

Seldom do we see perfect correlations in psychological research. Instead, correlations are often in the low to moderate range, indicating some relationship between the two variables, but far from a perfect relationship (see Figure 3.4). Many relationships between variables happen by chance and are not meaningful. Scientists evaluate the importance of correlation coefficient by examining its statistical significance.

Statistical Significance

The **statistical significance** of a result such as a correlation coefficient is an index of how likely that result occurred simply by chance. You will often see statements in research studies such as "The result was statistically significant at $p < .05$." This means that the probability (p) is less than 5 in 100 that the result occurred only by chance. Researchers typically accept results at this level of significance as support of their hypotheses, although the choice of an acceptable significance level is somewhat arbitrary.

Whether a correlation coefficient will be statistically significant at the $p < .05$ level is determined by its magnitude and the size of the sample on which it is based. Both larger correlations and larger sample sizes increase the likelihood of achieving statistical significance. A correlation of .30 will be significant if it is based on a large sample, say 200 or more, but will not be significant if it is based on a small sample, such as 10 or fewer participants. On the other hand, a correlation of .90 will be statistically significant even if the sample is as small as 30 people.

Correlation versus Causation

One of the most important things to understand about correlations is that they do not tell us anything about causation. That is, even though we may find that an independent and a dependent variable are highly correlated, this correlation does not tell us that the independent variable caused the dependent variable. In other words, even if we found a strong positive correlation between stress and depression, we could not conclude that stress causes depression.

All that a positive correlation could tell us is that there is a relationship between stress and depression. It could be that depression causes stress. Or some other variable might cause both stress and depression. This latter situation is called the **third variable problem**—the possibility that variables not measured in a study are the real cause of the relationship between the variables measured in the study. For example, perhaps some people with difficult temperaments both generate stressful experiences in their lives by being difficult to live with and are prone to depression. If we measure only stress and depression, we might observe a relationship between them because they co-occur within the same individuals. But this relationship is actually due to their common relationship to temperament.

Selecting a Sample

One of the critical choices in a correlational study is the choice of the sample. A **sample** is a group of people taken from the population that we want to study.

Representativeness

A *representative sample* is a sample that is highly similar to the population of interest in terms of sex, ethnicity, age, and other important variables. If a sample is not representative—for example, if there are more women or people of color in the sample than in the general population of interest—then the sample is said to have *bias*. The representativeness of a sample is important to the generalization we want to make from the study. If the sample represents only a small or an unusual group of people, then we cannot generalize the results of the study to the larger population. For example, if all of the people in our study are white, middle-class females, we cannot know whether our results generalize to males, people of color, or people in other socioeconomic classes.

Some methods of recruiting participants into a study create more representative samples than do others. For example, in our study of stress and depression, we could put an advertisement in the local newspaper, asking people who had recently experienced stressful experiences to volunteer for our study. This would bias our sample in favor of people who have experienced stress, however, and leave out people who have not. Perhaps many people who have not experienced stress are depressed. This is important information we need in order to evaluate our hypothesis that stress causes depression.

An effective way of obtaining a representative sample of a population is to generate a random sample of that population. For example, some studies have obtained random samples of the entire U.S. population by randomly dialing phone numbers throughout the country and then recruiting the people who answered the phone into the study. Often, researchers can settle for random samples of smaller populations, such as random samples of particular cities. When a sample is truly random, the chances are high that it will be similar to the population of interest in ethnicity, sex, age, and all the other important variables in the study.

Selection of a Comparison Group

In a group comparison study, we are interested in comparing the experiences of one group with those of another. For example, we may be interested in the depression levels of bereaved and nonbereaved people. We might begin by recruiting our sample of bereaved people, attempting to make this sample as representative as possible of bereaved people in our community.

In selecting the comparison group of nonbereaved people, it is a good idea to match our bereaved group with this comparison group on any variable (other than stress) we think might influence levels of depression, so that the two groups are alike on these variables. If we did not do this matching process, any differences we found between the two groups on levels of depression could be attributable to variables for which we did not match—the third variable problem again.

For example, women are generally more likely to be depressed than men. If we happen to have more women in our bereaved group than in our comparison group, higher levels of depression in the bereaved group might be attributable to a third

Some studies of depression have focused on people who have experienced the stressor of bereavement.

variable—the fact that there are more women in that group—not to the fact that the group has recently been bereaved. For this reason, we need to match our bereaved and comparison groups on all third variables that might influence our dependent variable of depression.

If we decide to match our two groups on sex, age, ethnicity, and socioeconomic status, we can then generate the comparison group by consulting the local census records. For every person in our bereaved group, we can recruit a person of the same sex, age, ethnicity, and socioeconomic status from the local area into our comparison group. Although not a simple task, this is good way to generate a matched comparison group.

Evaluating Correlational Studies

Correlational studies have provided much important information for abnormal psychology. One of the major advantages of correlational studies is that they focus on situations occurring in the real world, rather than those manipulated in a laboratory. This gives them relatively good **external validity,** the extent to which a study's results can be generalized to the phenomena in real life. In other words, the results of these studies are generalizable to wider populations and to people's actual experiences in life.

Longitudinal correlational studies have several advantages over cross-sectional correlational studies. In longitudinal correlational studies, researchers can determine whether there are differences between the groups before the crucial event occurs. If there are no differences before the event but significant differences after the event, researchers can have more confidence that it was the event that actually led to the differences between the groups. Longitu-

dinal designs also allow researchers to follow groups long enough to assess both short-term and long-term reactions to the event.

The most significant disadvantage of all correlational studies is that they cannot tease apart what is a cause and what is a consequence. For example, many stressful events that depressed people report may be the consequences of their depression, rather than the causes. In addition, the symptoms of depression can cause stress by impairing interpersonal skills, interfering with concentration on the job, and causing insomnia. The same problem exists for many types of psychopathology. The symptoms of schizophrenia can disrupt social relationships, alcoholism can lead to unemployment, and so on. Some psychological symptoms may even cause physiological changes in people. For example, people who have recently experienced psychological trauma often develop medical diseases, because the traumas reduce the effectiveness of their immune systems, which help fight disease (Schneiderman, Ironson, & Siegel, 2005).

Another disadvantage of correlational studies is their potential for bad timing. Stress may indeed cause depression, but if we do not assess these two variables at the right point in time, we may not observe this relationship. For example, in our study of bereavement, we could miss many of the depressed people in our bereaved group if we measured depression either before they developed it or after they had recovered from it.

Longitudinal studies can be time-consuming and expensive to run. Chapter 11 reports studies in which children at high risk for schizophrenia were studied from their preschool years to their early adult years to determine what characteristics could predict who would develop schizophrenia and who would not (Erlenmeyer-Kimling et al., 1991). Some longitudinal studies have been going on for more than 25 years and have cost millions of dollars. They are producing extremely valuable data but at a high cost in researchers' time and research dollars.

Finally, all correlational studies suffer from the third variable problem. Researchers seldom can measure all the possible influences on their participants' levels of depression or other psychopathologies.

SUMMING UP

- A correlational study examines the relationship between two variables without manipulating either variable.

- A correlation coefficient is an index of the relationship between two variables. It ranges from −1.00 to +1.00. The magnitude of the correlation indicates how strong the relationship between the variables is.

■ A positive correlation indicates that, as values of one variable increase, values of the other variable increase. A negative correlation indicates that, as values of one variable increase, values of the other variable decrease.

■ A result is said to be statistically significant if it is unlikely to have happened by chance. The convention in psychological research is to accept results that have a probability of less than 5 in 100 of happening by chance.

■ A correlational study can show that two variables are related, but it cannot show that one variable caused the other.

■ All correlational studies suffer from the third variable problem—the possibility that variables not measured in the study actually account for the relationship between the variables measured in the study.

■ Continuous variable studies evaluate the relationship between two variables that vary along a continuum.

■ A sample is a subset of a population of interest. A representative sample is similar to the population on all important variables. One way to generate a representative sample is to obtain a random sample.

■ Cross-sectional studies assess a sample at one point in time, and longitudinal studies assess a sample at multiple points in time.

■ Group comparison studies evaluate differences between key groups, such as a group that has experienced a specific type of stressor and a comparison group that has not experienced the stressor but is matched on all important variables.

■ Potential problems in correlational studies include the potential for bad timing and the expense of longitudinal studies.

EPIDEMIOLOGICAL STUDIES

Epidemiology is the study of the frequency and distribution of a disorder, or a group of disorders, in a population. An epidemiological study asks how many people in a population have the disorder and how this number varies across important groups within the population, such as men and women or people with high and low incomes.

Epidemiological research focuses on three types of data: the prevalence of a disorder, the incidence of a disorder, and the risk factors for a disorder. The

TABLE 3.1 Lifetime and 12-Month Prevalence of Major Depressive Disorder		
	Lifetime Prevalence (%)	12-Month Prevalence (%)
Males	12.7	7.7
Females	21.3	12.9
Total	17.1	10.3

Source: Kessler et al., 1994.

prevalence of a disorder is the proportion of the population that has the disorder at a given point or period in time. For example, a study might report the *lifetime prevalence* of a disorder, or the number of people who will have the disorder at sometime in their lives. The *12-month prevalence* of a disorder is the proportion of the population who will be diagnosed with the disorder in any 12-month period.

Table 3.1 shows the lifetime prevalence and 12-month prevalence of one of the more severe forms of depression, major depressive disorder, from a nationwide epidemiological study conducted in the United States (Kessler et al., 1994). Not surprisingly, the proportion of the population who will be diagnosed with major depressive disorder at sometime in their lives is larger than the proportion who will be diagnosed with the disorder in any 12-month period. Another interesting thing seen in Table 3.1 is that the prevalence of major depression is greater for women than for men. As we will discuss in Chapter 9, this fact, revealed by many epidemiological studies, has been an important focus of research in depression.

Epidemiological research also seeks to determine the **incidence** of a disorder, the number of new cases of the disorder that develop during a specific period of time. The one-year incidence of a disorder is the number of people who develop the disorder during a one-year period.

Finally, epidemiological research is concerned with the **risk factors** for a disorder—conditions or variables that are associated with a higher risk of having the disorder. Thus, if women are more likely than men to have a disorder, being a woman is a risk factor for the disorder. In terms of our interest in the relationship between stress and depression, an epidemiological study might show that people who live in high-stress areas of a city are more likely to have depression than are people who live in low-stress areas of a city.

How do researchers determine the prevalence of, incidence of, and risk factors for a disorder? Epidemiological researchers first identify the population of interest, then identify a random sample of that population—for example, by randomly phoning residential telephone numbers. They then use *structured clinical interviews,* in which interviewers use a specific set of questions with every participant to assess whether he or she has the symptoms that make up the disorders and risk factors, such as gender or socioeconomic status, being studied. We will discuss structured clinical interviews more in Chapter 4. From these data, epidemiologists are able to estimate how many people in different categories of risk factors have the disorder.

Evaluating Epidemiological Research

Epidemiological studies have provided valuable information on the prevalence of, incidence of, and risk factors for disorders, and we will discuss evidence from some of the major nationwide studies throughout this book. This research can give us important clues as to who is at highest risk for a disorder, and this information can then be used to test hypotheses about why those people are at higher risk.

Epidemiological studies suffer many of the same limitations as correlational studies. First and foremost, they cannot establish that any risk factor causes a disorder. That is, even though a study may show that people living in higher-stress neighborhoods are more likely to have a disorder, this finding does not mean that the high stress of the neighborhoods caused the disorder. Similarly, as in correlational studies, third variables may explain the relationship between any risk factor and the rates of a disorder.

SUMMING UP

- Epidemiology is the study of the frequency and distribution of a disorder in a population.
- The prevalence of a disorder is the proportion of the population that has the disorder at a give point or period in time.
- The incidence of a disorder is the number of new cases of the disorder that develop during a specific period of time.
- Risk factors for a disorder are conditions or variables that are associated with a higher risk of having the disorder.

EXPERIMENTAL STUDIES

The hallmark of **experimental studies** is control. Researchers attempt to control the independent variable and any potentially problematic third variables, rather than simply observing them as they naturally occur.

We turn now to the various types of experimental studies we could do to test our idea that stress leads to depression. We will examine three types in particular. The first, the *human laboratory study,* has the goal of inducing the conditions that we predict will lead to our outcome of interest (e.g., increasing stress to cause depression) in people. The second, the *therapy outcome study,* also is conducted with humans but has the opposite focus of the first type of study. In a therapy outcome study, the researcher wants to reduce the conditions leading to the outcome of interest so as to reduce that outcome (e.g., decreasing stress to decrease depression). The third, the *animal study,* attempts to model what happens in humans by manipulating animals in a laboratory.

Human Laboratory Studies

One experimental method for testing our hypothesis that people exposed to stress will become depressed, whereas those not exposed will not become depressed, is to expose participants to a stressor in a laboratory and then determine whether it causes an increase in depressed mood—a method known as a **human laboratory study.**

Several experimental studies on stress and depression have been done (see Peterson & Seligman, 1984). The stressor that is often used in these studies is an unsolvable task or puzzle, such as an unsolvable anagram. If we chose this as the type of stress we would induce, our operationalization would be participants' exposure to unsolvable anagrams. We would be manipulating stress, not just measuring it. This would give us the advantage of knowing precisely what type of stress participants were exposed to and when.

A human laboratory study is also called an **analogue study,** because researchers are attempting to create conditions in the laboratory that resemble certain conditions in the real world but that are not exactly like those real conditions. We cannot create in the laboratory many of the types of stress that may cause depression in the real world, such as the destruction of a person's home in a hurricane or continual assaults. Instead, we can create analogues—situations that capture some of the key characteristics of these real-world events, such as their uncontrollability and unpredictability.

Internal Validity

Researchers want to ensure that the experiment has **internal validity,** meaning that changes in the dependent variable can be confidently attributed to the manipulation of the independent variable, not

Researchers cannot reproduce some kinds of stress, such as losing a home in a hurricane, in the laboratory, so they must settle for creating analogues of these stressors.

to other factors. For example, people who participate in our experiment using anagrams might become more depressed over the course of the experiment simply because participating in an experiment is a negative experience, not because of the unsolvable anagrams. This threat to internal validity is basically the same type of third variable problem we encountered in correlational studies.

To control third variables, researchers create a **control group,** or a *control condition*, in which participants have all the same experiences as the group of main interest in the study, except that they do not receive the key manipulation—in our case, the experience of the unsolvable puzzles. The control group for our study could be made to do puzzles very similar to the unsolvable anagrams the other group works on, but the control group's anagrams could be solvable. Thus, the control group's experience would be identical to that of the other group—the **experimental group,** or *experimental condition*—except that the control group would not receive the stressor of unsolvable anagrams.

Another threat to internal validity can arise if the participants for our experimental group (the one that does the unsolvable anagrams) and for our control group (the one that does the solvable anagrams) differ in important ways before they begin the experiment. Because of such differences, we could not be sure that our manipulation was

the cause of any changes in our dependent variable. To safeguard internal validity, random assignment to the experimental and control groups is a critical step. **Random assignment** occurs when each participant has an equal chance of being assigned to the experimental or the control group. Often, a researcher will use a table of random numbers to assign participants to groups.

Yet another threat to internal validity is the presence of **demand characteristics**—situations that cause participants to guess the hypothesis of the study and change their behavior as a result. For example, if our measure of depression were too obvious, participants could guess what hypothesis we were testing. To avoid demand characteristics, we could use more subtle measures of depression, such as those illustrated in Figure 3.5 on page 84, embedded in other measures, so as to obscure the real purpose of our study. These other measures are often called *filler measures*. Researchers also often use *cover stories:* Participants are told false stories to prevent them from guessing the true purpose of the experiment and changing their behavior accordingly.

In order to reduce demand characteristics further, the experimenters who actually interact with the participants should be *unaware* of which condition the participants are in, the experimental condition or control condition, so that the experimenters do not give off subtle cues as to what they expect

FIGURE 3.5 **Scales to Measure Depression, Embedded in Other Scales.** The researcher may be interested only in participants' answers on the scales measuring happiness and depression but may embed these scales in other scales to obscure the purpose of the study.

Instructions: On each scale, mark off how you feel right now.

Happy		--	--	--	--	--	--	--		Unhappy
Curious		--	--	--	--	--	--	--		Not curious
Thoughtful		--	--	--	--	--	--	--		Not thoughtful
Depressed		--	--	--	--	--	--	--		Not depressed
Smart		--	--	--	--	--	--	--		Not smart

the participants to do in the experiment. For example, if experimenters know that a participant is in the experimental condition, they might suggest to the participant in subtle ways that the anagrams are unsolvable. This creates demands for the participant to behave in ways he or she otherwise might not.

Assume that we have instituted a number of safeguards for internal validity on our study: The participants have been randomly selected and assigned, and the experimenters they interact with are unaware of the hypothesis of our study and of the condition that participants are in. Now the study can be conducted. When our data have been collected and analyzed, we find that, as we predicted, the participants given the unsolvable anagrams showed greater increases in depressed mood than did participants given the solvable anagrams.

What can we conclude about our idea of depression, based on this study? Our experimental controls have helped us rule out third variable explanations, so we can be relatively confident that it was the experience of the uncontrollable stressor that led to the increases in depression in the experimental group. Thus, we can say that we have supported our hypothesis that people exposed to uncontrollable stress will show more depressed mood than will people not exposed to uncontrollable stress.

Evaluating Human Laboratory Studies

The primary advantage of human laboratory studies is control. Researchers have more control over

third variables, the independent variable, and the dependent variable in these studies than they do in any other type of study they can do with humans. However, human laboratory studies have their own limitations.

Generalizability The primary limitation of human laboratory studies is that we cannot know if our results generalize to what happens outside the laboratory. For this reason, their external validity can be low. Is being exposed to unsolvable anagrams anything like being exposed to major, real-world, uncontrollable stressors, such as the death of a loved one? Clearly, there is a difference in the severity of the two types of experiences, but is this the only important difference? Similarly, do the increases in depressed mood in the participants in our study, which were probably small increases, tell us anything about why some people develop extremely severe, debilitating episodes of depression? Experimental analogue studies such as ours have been criticized for the lack of generalizability of their results to the major psychopathology that occurs in everyday life.

Ethical Issues Apart from posing the problems of generalizability, human laboratory studies sometimes pose serious ethical issues. Is it ethical to induce distress, even mild distress, in people? Participants in an experiment can be warned of possible discomfort or distress and told that they can end their participation at any time. Even so, participants rarely stop experiments, even if they are uncomfortable, because of the subtle pressures of the social situation. (See *Taking Psychology Personally: Your Rights as a Research Participant* for further discussion.)

What if participants, even after being told that the stressful experience they had (e.g., being given an unsolvable anagram) was completely out of their control, believe that they should have been able to control the situation or solve the tasks? It turns out that many participants, especially college students, continue to believe that they should have been able to solve unsolvable tasks or that negative feedback they received in an experiment was a true indication of their abilities, even after being told that they were deceived by the experimenter. The researchers who discovered this phenomenon recommended conducting a *process debriefing* with participants following any potentially upsetting experiments (Ross, Lepper, & Hubbard, 1975). In such debriefings, experimenters slowly draw out the participants' assumptions about the experiments

Taking Psychology Personally

Your Rights as a Research Participant

You may participate in a research study at sometime. You have certain basic rights, which you should expect to be honored, regardless of the type of research being conducted:

- *Understanding of the study*. You have the right to understand the nature of the research you are participating in, particularly any factors that might influence your willingness to participate. For example, if you are likely to experience discomfort (psychological or physical) as a result of participating in the study or if there are any risks to your well-being as a result of participation, the researcher should spell these out in plain language to you.

- *Confidentiality*. You should expect your identity and any information gathered from you in the study to be held in strict confidence. This usually means that the researcher will report data from the study aggregated across participants, rather than reporting data from individual participants. If the researcher intends to report data from individual participants, he or she should explain this to you and obtain your explicit permission.

- *Right to refuse participation*. You should be allowed to refuse to participate in the study, or to withdraw from participation once the study has begun, without suffering adverse consequences. If you are participating as a course requirement or as an opportunity for extra credit for a class, you should be given the choice of equitable alternative activities if you choose not to participate in the study. If you are offered payment or other inducements for participating in the study, they should not be so great that you basically cannot afford to refuse to participate.

- *Informed consent*. Usually, your consent to participate in the study should be documented in writing. In some cases, a written informed consent document is not used, as when you are filling out an anonymous survey (in this case, your willingness to complete the survey is taken as your consent to participate).

- *Deception*. Researchers should use deception in studies only when such techniques are absolutely essential and justified by the study's potential contributions. Participants should not be deceived about the aspects of the research that might affect their willingness to participate, such as physical risks, discomfort, or unpleasant emotional experiences. Researchers should explain the deception to the participants once the research is complete.

- *Debriefing*. At the end of the study, researchers should explain the purpose of the research and answer any questions you have about the research.

Colleges and universities have institutional review boards (IRBs), which review proposed research studies to ensure that they honor the rights of participants; IRBs also handle complaints from participants about research. If you have any concerns about a study you have participated in, you can contact the IRB at your school to discuss these concerns. Some IRBs also have student members who assist in reviewing proposed research studies. This is a good way of learning about the variety of research going on at your college or university.

and their performances. They conduct extended conversations with the participants about the purposes and procedures of the experiments, explaining how their behavior was beyond their control and certainly not a reflection of their abilities.

Experimenters must always be aware of the ethical concerns raised by experiments of this sort and take all possible means to limit dangers to participants. All colleges and universities have a human participants committee, which reviews the procedures of studies done with humans to ensure that the benefits of the study substantially outweigh any risks to the participants and that the risks to the participants have been minimized.

Therapy Outcome Studies

The ethical concerns surrounding human laboratory studies have led some researchers to advocate studies that attempt to *reduce* psychopathology by reducing the factors believed to cause it. Applying this type of study to our idea would mean intervening with depressed participants to reduce stress, which should, in turn, decrease depression, according to our idea. This type of study is called a **therapy outcome study.**

Therapy outcome studies are appealing because they involve helping people while obtaining information. The goal of therapy outcome studies is to determine the effectiveness of an experimental therapy over no therapy or as compared with other, often established therapies. We discuss many therapy outcome studies in this book, including some that have compared psychological therapies with drug therapies in the treatment of specific disorders.

Control Groups

Sometimes, people get better simply because of the passage of time. Thus, researchers need to compare the experiences of people who receive an experimental therapy with those of a control group of people who do not receive the therapy to see if the experimental group's improvement has anything to do with the therapy. Sometimes, researchers use a *simple control group* consisting of participants who do not receive the experimental therapy but are tracked for the same period of time as the participants who do receive the therapy.

A variation on this simple control group is the **wait list control group.** The participants in this type of group do not receive the therapy when the experimental group does, but they go onto a wait list to receive the intervention at a later date when the study is complete. Both groups of participants are assessed at the beginning and end of the study, but only the experimental group receives the therapy as part of the study.

Another type of control group is the **placebo control group.** This type of group is used most often in studies of the effectiveness of drugs. The participants in this group have the same interactions with experimenters as do the participants in the experimental group, but they take pills that are *placebos* (inactive substances) rather than the real drug. Usually, to prevent demand effects, both the participants and the experimenters in these studies are unaware of what condition the participants are in. In this case, the experiment is known as a **double-blind experiment.**

A placebo control group can also be used to control for the possibility that the simple interaction with the therapist affected the outcome of the participants. This placebo group interacts with a therapist for the same amount of time but receives no therapy. However, some theorists have objected to the idea that interacting with a warm and caring therapist without experiencing any other experimental conditions is a placebo. They suggest that the active ingredient in therapy is receiving unconditional support and encouragement from a warm and caring therapist, not the actual program of therapy (Rogers, 1951). Indeed, psychological placebo interventions have been found to be quite effective with some types of problems (Elkin et al., 1989). It seems that a little bit of human caring goes a long way in helping people overcome their distress. It also seems nearly impossible to construct a true psychological placebo.

Evaluating Therapy Outcome Studies

Although therapy outcome studies might seem the most ethical way of conducting research on people in distress, they carry their own methodological challenges and ethical issues. Most psychological therapies involve a package of techniques for responding to people's problems. For example, depressed people in an experimental therapy group might be taught assertiveness skills, social problem-solving skills, and skills in changing self-defeating thinking. Which of these skills was most responsible for alleviating their depression? Even when a therapy works, researchers often cannot know exactly what it is about the therapy that works.

This uncertainty has practical implications, because we need to know what the effective elements of a therapy are in order to bolster those elements and to reduce other elements that may be useless or even harmful. The uncertainty also has important theoretical and scientific implications. If we conduct a therapy outcome study to test a particular idea about the cause of a psychopathology, we need to know whether the therapy works for the reasons we have theorized. For example, if we are testing our idea that stress causes depression, we need to know that our intervention reduced depression because it reduced stress, not because it provided the participants with an opportunity to ventilate their feelings, because it provided social support in the form of a therapist, or because of some other factor unrelated to our idea.

Ethical Issues Ethical problems arise in using simple control groups, wait list control groups, and placebo control groups in therapy outcome research. Some researchers believe it is unethical to withhold treatment or to provide a treatment they believe is ineffective for people in distress. For example, many depressed participants assigned to a control group may be in severe distress or in danger of harming themselves or someone else and, therefore, require immediate treatment.

In response to this concern, many therapy outcome studies now compare the effectiveness of two or more therapies that are expected to have positive effects. These studies basically are a competition between rival therapies and the theories behind these therapies. There is reason to believe that all the participants in such a study will benefit from participation in the study but that the study

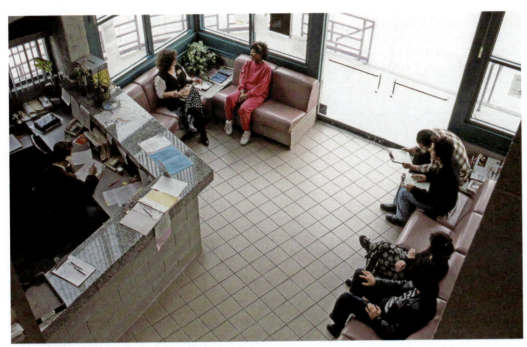

Real-world settings where therapy is delivered, such as busy mental-health clinics, may differ substantially from the controlled conditions of a therapy outcome study.

will yield useful information about the most effective type of therapy for the participants.

Another ethical issue concerns the therapist's obligation to respond to the patients' needs. How much can a therapy be modified to respond to a specific participant's needs without compromising the scientific element of the study? Therapists may feel the need to vary the dosage of a drug or to deviate from a study's procedure for psychological intervention. If they depart too far from the standard therapy, however, there will be great variation in the therapy that participants in the intervention group receive, which could compromise the results of the study.

Generalizability A related methodological issue has to do with generalizing results from therapy outcome studies to the real world. In these studies, the therapeutic intervention is usually delivered to patients in a controlled, high-quality atmosphere by the most competent therapists. The patients are usually screened, so that they fit a narrow set of criteria for inclusion in the study, and often only the patients who stick with the therapy to its end are included in the final analyses.

In the real world, mental-health services are not always delivered in controlled, high-quality atmospheres by the most competent therapists. Patients are who they are, with their complicated symptom pictures and lives that may not fit neatly

into the criteria for an "optimal patient." Patients often leave and return to therapy and may not receive "full trials" of the therapy before they drop out for financial or personal reasons.

Therapy outcome research that tests how well a therapy works in highly controlled settings with a narrowly defined group of people is said to test the **efficacy** of a therapy. In contrast, therapy outcome research that tests how well a therapy works in real-world settings with all the complications we've just discussed is said to test the **effectiveness** of a therapy.

Single-Case Experimental Designs

Another type of experimental study is the **single-case experimental design,** in which one individual or a small group of people is studied intensively. This design may sound like the case studies we discussed earlier. The major difference is that, in a single-case experimental design, the individual is put through a manipulation or an intervention, and his or her behavior is examined before and after this to determine the effects. (In a case study, usually no manipulation or intervention is attempted.) In addition, in a single-case experimental design, the participants' behaviors are measured through a standard method, repeatedly over time, whereas a case study is often based on the researcher's

FIGURE 3.6

Effects over Time of Drug Treatment for Depression in an Individual. This graph shows an individual's level of depression during a 4-week baseline assessment (A), during 4 weeks of drug treatment (B), when the drug treatment is withdrawn for 4 weeks (A), and when the drug treatment is reinstated for 4 weeks (B).

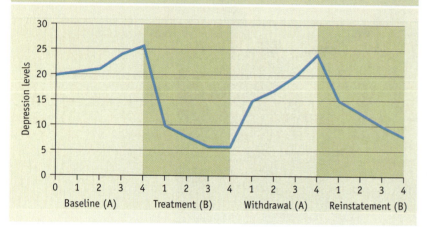

The major disadvantage of single-case experimental designs is that their results may not generalize to the wider population. One individual's experience on or off a treatment may not be the same as others experiences. In addition, not all hypotheses can be tested with single-case experimental designs. Some treatments have lingering effects after they end. For example, if a person is taught new skills at coping with stress during the treatment, these skills might continue to be present after the treatment has been withdrawn.

Animal Studies

Researchers sometimes try to avoid the ethical issues involved in experimental studies with humans by conducting such studies with animals. Animal research has its own set of ethical issues, but many researchers feel it is acceptable to subject animals to situations in the laboratory that would not be ethical to impose on humans. **Animal studies** thus provide researchers with even more control over laboratory conditions and third variables than is possible in human laboratory studies.

In a well-known series of animal studies designed to investigate depression (discussed in Chapter 9), Martin Seligman, Bruce Overmier, Steven Maier, and their colleagues subjected dogs to an uncontrollable stressor in the laboratory (Overmier & Seligman, 1967; Seligman & Maier, 1967). They did not ask the dogs to do unsolvable anagrams. Instead, they used a stressor over which the researchers could have complete control: a painful electric shock. The experimental group of dogs received a series of uncontrollable shocks. Let us call this *Group E* for *experimental*.

In addition, there were two control groups. One control group of dogs received shocks of the same magnitude as the dogs in the experimental group, but they could control the shocks by jumping over a short barrier in their cage (see Figure 3.7). Let us call this *Group J* for *jump*. The dogs in this control group and the dogs in Group E received exactly the same number and duration of shocks. The only difference between the groups was that the dogs in Group E could not control their shocks, whereas the dogs in control Group J could. The second control group of dogs received no shock. Let us call this *Group N* for *none*.

The dogs in Group E initially responded to the shocks by jumping around their cages and protesting loudly. Soon, however, the majority became passive and simply hovered in one part of their cages, whimpering. Later, when the researchers provided the dogs with the opportunity to escape the shock by jumping over a barrier, these dogs did not learn to do this. It seemed that they had an ex-

impressions of the participant and the factors that are affecting him or her.

A specific type of single-case experimental design is the **ABAB,** or **reversal design,** in which an intervention is introduced, withdrawn, and then reinstated, and the behavior of the participant is examined on and off the treatment. For example, in a study on the effect of a drug for depression, a depressed person might be assessed for her level of depression each day for 4 weeks. This is the baseline assessment (A) (see Figure 3.6). Then the participant is given the drug for 4 weeks (B), and her level of depression assessed each day during that period. Then the drug is withdrawn for 4 weeks (A), and her level of depression assessed each day during that time. Finally, the drug is reinstated for 4 weeks (B), and her level of depression reassessed each day during that period. If the participant's levels of depression follows the pattern seen in Figure 3.6, this result suggests that her depression level was much lower during the periods when she was taking the drug (B) than when she was not taking the drug (A).

Evaluating Single-Case Experimental Designs

A major advantage of single-case experimental designs is that they allow for much more intensive assessment of participants than might be possible if there were many more participants. For example, an individual child could be observed for hours each day as he was put on, then taken off, a treatment. This intensity of assessment can allow researchers to pinpoint the types of behaviors that are and are not affected by their interventions.

pectation that they could not control the shock, so they were unable to recognize the opportunities for control that arose. They seemed to have given up. The researchers labeled this set of behaviors *learned helplessness deficits* and argued that the dogs had learned they were helpless to control their situation.

The dogs in controllable shock Group J, however, quickly learned how to control the shock and did not develop the learned helplessness deficits shown by the dogs in the uncontrollable shock group. The fact that the two groups of dogs experienced the same amount of shock suggests that lack of control, not the shock alone, led to the learned helplessness deficits in the experimental group. The dogs in control Group N, which received no shock, also did not develop learned helplessness deficits.

Seligman and his colleagues likened the learned helplessness deficits shown by the dogs to the symptoms of depression in humans: apathy, low initiation of behavior, and the inability to see opportunities to improve one's environment (see Seligman, 1975). They argued that many human depressions result from people learning they have no control over important outcomes in their lives. This learned helplessness theory of depression seems useful in explaining the depression and passivity seen in chronically oppressed groups, such as battered spouses and some people who grow up in poverty.

A second type of animal study is similar to therapy outcome studies. In studies of the effectiveness of drugs, animals are often given the drugs to determine the effects of the drugs on different bodily systems and behaviors. Sometimes, the animals are sacrificed after receiving the drugs, so that detailed physiological analyses of the effects of the drugs can be determined. Obviously, such studies could not be done with humans. Animal studies of drugs are particularly useful in the early stages of research, when the possible side effects of the drugs are unknown.

Evaluating Animal Studies

There clearly are problems with animal studies. First, some people believe it is no more ethical to conduct painful, dangerous, or fatal experiments with animals than it is to do so with humans. Second, from a scientific vantage point, we must ask whether we can generalize the results of experiments with animals to humans. Are learned helplessness deficits in dogs really analogous to human depression? The debate over the ethical and scientific issues of animal research continues, sometimes leading to violent clashes between proponents and opponents of animal research. Particularly in the case of research on drug effectiveness, however,

FIGURE 3.7 **Shuttle Box for Learned Helplessness Experiments.** Researchers used an apparatus like this to deliver controllable or uncontrollable shocks to dogs in order to investigate the phenomenon of learned helplessness.

animal research is crucial to the advancement of our knowledge of how to help people overcome psychopathology.

SUMMING UP

- Experimental studies attempt to control all the variables affecting the dependent variable.
- In human laboratory studies, the independent variable is manipulated and the effects on people participating in the study are examined. To control for the effects of being in the experimental situation and the passage of time, researchers use control groups, in which participants have all the same experiences as the group of main interest in the study, except that they do not receive the key manipulation.
- Demand characteristics are aspects of the experimental situation that cause participants to guess the purpose of the study and change their behavior as a result.
- The disadvantages of human laboratory studies are their lack of generalizability and the ethical issues involved in manipulating people.
- Therapy outcome studies assess the impact of an intervention designed to relieve symptoms.

Simple control groups, wait list control groups, and placebo control groups are used to compare the effects of the intervention with other alternatives.

■ It can be difficult to determine what aspects of a therapy resulted in changes in participants. Therapy outcome studies also can suffer from lack of generalizability, and assigning people who need treatment to control groups holds ethical implications.

■ Single-case experimental designs involve the intensive investigation of single individuals or small groups of individuals, before and after a manipulation or intervention.

■ In an ABAB, or reversal, design, an intervention is introduced, withdrawn, and then reinstated, and the behavior of the participant is examined on and off the treatment.

■ Animal studies involve exposing animals to conditions thought to represent the causes of a psychopathology and then measuring changes in the animals' behavior or physiology. The ethics of exposing animals to conditions that we would not expose humans to can be questioned, as can the generalizability of animal studies.

CROSS-CULTURAL RESEARCH

Not long ago, most psychological research was conducted with college students, many of whom were White and middleclass, and researchers believed that any results they obtained from these samples could be generalized to any other relevant sample. Only anthropologists and a handful of psychologists and psychiatrists argued that what is true of one ethnic group, culture, or gender is not necessarily true of others.

In the past two decades, however, there has been an explosion of cross-cultural research in abnormal psychology. Researchers are investigating the similarities and differences across culture in the nature, causes, and treatment of psychopathology. Cross-cultural researchers face their own special challenges in addition to the ones common to all research.

First, gaining access to the people one wants to study can be difficult. People who have never participated in research may be wary of cooperating with researchers. In addition, some cultures explicitly shun contact with outsiders. An example was described in *Extraordinary People: The Old Order Amish of Pennsylvania* at the beginning of this chapter. Researcher Janice Egeland spent 20 years gaining the trust of the Amish, and eventually they

allowed her to bring in a research team to study major psychopathology in the culture (Egeland & Hostetter, 1983). The result was some of the most exciting research ever published on cross-cultural similarities and differences in bipolar disorder.

Most of us do not have 20 years to gain the trust of the people we want to study and thus will not choose to study populations that are that difficult to access. Nevertheless, most groups of people need some time to warm up to research. Researchers can usually do some things to facilitate this warming up. For example, they can enlist the support of important leaders in the group, provide things that the group needs or wants in exchange for its participation, and learn the group's customs and adhere to these customs in all interactions with the group.

The second challenge is that researchers must be careful in applying theories or concepts developed in one culture to another culture (Rogler, 1999). Because the manifestations of disorders can differ across cultures, researchers who insist on narrow definitions of disorders may fail to identify many people suffering from disorders in culturally defined ways. Similarly, theoretical variables can have different meanings or manifestations across cultures.

A good example is the variable known as *expressed emotion*. Families high in expressed emotion are highly critical and hostile toward other family members and emotionally overinvolved with each other. Several studies of the majority cultures in America and Europe have shown that people with schizophrenia whose families are high in expressed emotion have higher rates of relapse than do those whose families are low in expressed emotion (Brown, Birley, & Wing, 1972; Vaughn & Leff, 1976). The meaning and manifestation of expressed emotion can differ greatly across cultures, however:

> Criticism within Anglo-American family settings, for example, may focus on allegations of faulty personality traits (e.g., laziness) or psychotic symptom behaviors (e.g., strange ideas). However, in other societies, such as those of Latin America, the same behaviors may not be met with criticism. Among Mexican-descent families, for example, criticism tends to focus on disrespectful or disruptive behaviors that affect the family but not on psychotic symptom behavior and individual personality characteristics. Thus, culture plays a role in creating the content or targets of criticism. Perhaps most importantly, culture is influential in determining *whether* criticism is a

prominent part of the familial emotional atmosphere. (Jenkins & Karno, 1992, p. 10)

For this reason, today's researchers are more careful to search for culturally specific manifestations of the characteristics of interest in their studies and for the possibility that the characteristics or variables that predict psychopathology in one culture are irrelevant in other cultures.

Third, even if researchers believe they can apply their theories across cultures, they may have difficulty translating their questionnaires or other assessment tools into different languages (Rogler, 1999). A key concept in English may not be precisely translated into another language. Subtle problems can arise because many languages contain variations on pronouns and verbs whose usage is determined by the social relationship between the speaker and the person being addressed. For example, in Spanish, the second-person pronoun *usted* (you) connotes respect, establishes an appropriate distance in a social relationship, and is the correct way for a young interviewer to address an older respondent (Rogler, 1989). By contrast, when a young interviewer addresses a young respondent, the relationship is more informal, and the appropriate form of address is *tú* (also *you*). If an interviewer violates the social norms implicit in a language, he or she can alienate a respondent and impair the quality of the research.

Fourth, there may be cultural or gender differences in people's responses to the social demands of interacting with researchers. For example, people of Mexican origin, older people, and people of lower socioeconomic class are more likely to answer yes to researchers' questions, regardless of the content, and to attempt to answer questions in socially desirable ways than are Anglo Americans, younger people, and people of higher socioeconomic class. These differences appear to result from differences among groups in deference to authority figures and concern over presenting a proper appearance (Ross & Mirowsky, 1984). Similarly, it is often said that men are less likely than women to admit to "weaknesses," such as symptoms of distress or problems in coping. If researchers do not take biases into account when designing assessment tools and analyzing data, erroneous conclusions can result.

Fifth, researchers may face pressure to designate one culture as the healthy, or normative, one and another culture as the unhealthy, or aberrant, one. Researchers must constantly guard against such assumptions and must be willing to interpret differences simply as differences, acknowledging that each culture and gender has its healthy and unhealthy characteristics. Despite the difficulties

in conducting cross-cultural research, the need for such research is clear as our understanding of the diversity of human experience of psychopathology becomes greater.

SUMMING UP

- Cross-cultural research has expanded greatly in recent decades.
- Some special challenges of cross-cultural research include difficulty in accessing populations, in applying theories appropriate in one culture to other cultures, in translating concepts and measures across cultures, in predicting the responses of people in different cultures to being studied, and avoiding defining "healthy" and "unhealthy" cultures.

META-ANALYSIS

Often there are a large number of studies in the research literature that have investigated a particular idea (for example, that stress leads to depression) by testing various hypotheses that are based on it. Some of these studies have supported their hypothesis; some have not. An investigator may want to find out the overall trend of the results across all the studies, as well as what factors might account for some studies' supporting their hypothesis and others' failing to do so. One way to determine the overall trend is simply to read all the studies and draw conclusions about whether most of them support or do not support their hypothesis. These conclusions can be biased, however, in the reader's assumptions about the hypotheses and impressions of the studies.

A more objective way to draw conclusions about a body of research is to conduct a **meta-analysis,** a statistical technique for summarizing the results across several studies. The first step in a meta-analysis is to do a thorough literature search, usually with the help of computer search engines that identify all studies with certain key words. Studies often use different methods and measures for testing a hypothesis, so the second step of a meta-analysis is to transform the results of each study into a statistic that is common across all the studies. This statistic is called the *effect size*, and it gives an indication of how big the differences are between two groups (such as a group that received a specific form of therapy and one that did not), or how large the relationship between two continuous variables is (such as the correlation between levels of stress and levels of depression). Researchers can then examine the average effect size across studies and relate the effect size to characteristics of the study, such as the year it was published, the type of measures used, or the age or gender of the participants.

Evaluating Meta-Analysis

As we noted, a major advantage of meta-analysis is that it removes much of the bias that can be introduced when individual investigators read various studies and try to draw conclusions. It also allows researchers to examine the characteristics of studies that can account for differences in effect sizes. For example, in a meta-analysis of studies of children's depression levels, Twenge and Nolen-Hoeksema (2002) found that studies done in more recent years tend to find lower depression scores than studies done several years ago. This finding suggests that levels of depression may be going down in more recent groups of children.

In addition, meta-analysis can overcome some of the problems of small numbers of participants in an individual study by pooling the data from thousands of participants, providing more power to find significant effects. The studies examined by Twenge and Nolen-Hoeksema (2002) generally have small numbers of ethnic minority children, making it difficult to compare their depression scores with those of other children. By pooling studies, however, the overall sample size of Hispanic and African American children was large enough to do comparisons by race/ethnicity. The meta-analysis found that the Hispanic children generally had higher depression scores than the African American or White children.

Meta-analyses have their problems, however. First, some studies have methodological flaws but still are published. These flawed studies may be included in a meta-analysis, along with methodologically stronger studies, influencing the overall results.

Second, is the *file drawer effect*—studies that do not support the hypothesis they are designed to test are less likely to get published than studies that do. For example, a study that finds that a psychotherapy is not any more effective than a wait list control is less likely to get published than a study that finds that the same psychotherapy is more effective than the wait list control. Note that some studies do not support the investigator's hypothesis because they are methodologically flawed, so you wouldn't want them to be published. But the bias toward publishing studies with positive results means that many perfectly good studies that fail to find the expected effects do not get published and therefore do not end up in meta-analyses. This file drawer effect biases the results of meta-analyses toward finding an overall posi-

tive effect of a treatment, or another type of difference between groups.

SUMMING UP

- Meta-analysis is a statistical technique for summarizing results across several studies.
- In a meta-analysis, the results of individual studies are standardized into a statistic called the effect size. Then the magnitude of the effect size and its relationship to characteristics of the study are examined.
- Meta-analyses reduce the bias that can occur when investigators draw conclusions across studies in a more subjective manner; however, they can include studies that have poor methods and can exclude good studies that were not published because they did not find significant effects.

CHAPTER INTEGRATION

We noted in Chapter 2 that theories and models of psychopathology are increasingly based on the integration of concepts from biological, psychological, and social approaches. These concepts are often viewed from a vulnerability-stress perspective. The characteristics that make a person more vulnerable to abnormality might include biological characteristics, such as genetic predisposition, or psychological characteristics, such as maladaptive styles of thinking about the world. These personal characteristics must interact with characteristics of the situation or environment to create the abnormality. For example, a woman with a genetic predisposition to depression may never develop the disorder in its full form if she has a supportive family and never faces major stressors.

Conducting research that reflects this integrationist perspective on abnormality is not easy. Researchers must gather information about people's biological, psychological, and social vulnerabilities and strengths. This work may require specialized equipment or expertise. It may also require following participants longitudinally to observe what happens when people with vulnerabilities face stressors that may trigger episodes of their disorders.

Increasingly, researchers are working together in teams to share their expertise in specialized research methods and to share resources that make multidisciplinary longitudinal research possible (see Figure 3.8). Researchers are also receiving training in disciplines and methods that are not their primary disciplines. For example, psychologists are learning to use magnetic resonance imaging (MRI), positron-emission tomography (PET)

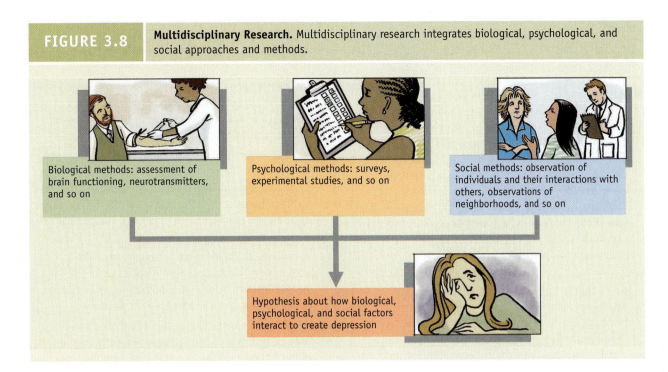

FIGURE 3.8   **Multidisciplinary Research.** Multidisciplinary research integrates biological, psychological, and social approaches and methods.

Biological methods: assessment of brain functioning, neurotransmitters, and so on

Psychological methods: surveys, experimental studies, and so on

Social methods: observation of individuals and their interactions with others, observations of neighborhoods, and so on

Hypothesis about how biological, psychological, and social factors interact to create depression

scans, and other advanced biological methods to investigate abnormality.

If you pursue a career researching abnormality, you may find yourself integrating methods from psychology (which have been the focus of this chapter), sociology, and biology to create the most comprehensive picture of the disorder you are investigating. This task may seem daunting right now, but the interactionist approach holds the possibility of producing breakthroughs that greatly improve the lives of people vulnerable to psychopathology.

Extraordinary People: Follow-Up

The researchers who studied the Old Order Amish quickly realized that they would have to adjust their definitions of depression and mania to take into account the cultural context of the Amish. As we discuss in more depth in Chapter 9, the manifestations of mood problems, particularly mania, among the Amish were quite different from the manifestations in mainstream culture, due to the strong social norms for behavior among the Amish. This realization alone brought the study of cross-cultural differences in psychiatric disorders into the mainstream psychiatric literature and gave cross-cultural research a legitimacy in that literature it had not had before (Egeland, Hostetter, & Eshleman, 1983).

Egeland and colleagues did not simply describe and count cases of mood disorders among the Amish, however. They took advantage of the fact that the Amish are a closed society, with little movement of individuals in or out, and that the Amish keep extensive genealogical records on their members. In addition, the Amish have essentially only one social class—everyone has the same level of education and similar occupational pursuits, and there is little variation in income. This setting was perfect for genetic studies of mood disorders. Egeland and colleagues conducted groundbreaking work that shaped how researchers think about the role of heritability in depression and mania (e.g., Ginns et al., 1996, 1998).

This study of the Old Order Amish set important precedents for how cross-cultural work is done in psychology and psychiatry. The researchers entered this study with respect and understanding for this culture's norms for behavior and relationships to the outside world, and they worked within these expectations as much as possible. As a result, they accomplished extraordinary research that has had important effects on the field of mood disorders and on cross-cultural research in general.

Chapter Summary

- Researchers of abnormal behavior face certain special challenges. First is the challenge of convincing the population of interest to participate in research. Second, abnormal behaviors and feelings are difficult to measure objectively and must rely to a large extent on people's self-reports. Third, most forms of abnormality probably have multiple causes, and no one study can investigate all possible causes simultaneously. These challenges require a multimethod approach.

- A hypothesis is a testable statement of what is predicted to happen in a study. The primary hypothesis is the one believed to be true based on the idea. The null hypothesis is the alternative to the primary hypothesis, stating there is no relationship between the independent variable and the dependent variable.

- The dependent variable is the factor being predicted in a study. The independent variable is the factor being used to predict the dependent variable.

- In any study, the variables of interest must be operationalized: The researcher must decide how to measure or manipulate the variables.

- A sample is a group of people taken from the population of interest to participate in the study. The samples for the study must be representative of the population of interest, and the research must be generalizable to the population of interest.

- A control group consists of people who are similar in most ways to the primary group of interest but who do not experience the variable the theory says causes changes in the dependent variable. Matching the control group to the group of primary interest can help control third variables, which are variables unrelated to the theory that may still have some effect on the dependent variable.

- Case studies of individuals provide rich and detailed information about their subjects. They are helpful in the generation of new ideas and the study of rare problems. Case studies suffer from problems in generalizability and in the subjectivity of both the person being studied and the person conducting the study.

- Correlational studies examine the relationship between two variables without manipulating the variables. A correlation coefficient is an index of the relationship between two variables. It ranges from -1.00 to $+1.00$. The magnitude of the correlation indicates how strong the relationship between the variables is.

- A positive correlation indicates that, as values of one variable increase, values of the other variable increase. A negative correlation indicates that, as values of one variable increase, values of the other variable decrease (review Figures 3.1 and 3.2).

- A result is said to be statistically significant if it is unlikely to have happened by chance. The convention in psychological research is to accept results for which there is a probability of less than 5 in 100 that they happened by chance.

- A correlational study can show that two variables are related, but it cannot show that one variable caused the other. All correlational studies suffer from the third variable problem—the possibility that variables not measured in the study actually account for the relationship between the variables measured in the study.

- Continuous variable studies evaluate the relationship between two variables that vary along a continuum.

- A representative sample is similar to the population of interest on all important variables. One way to generate a representative sample is to obtain a random sample.

- Whereas cross-sectional studies assess a sample at one point in time, longitudinal studies assess a sample at multiple points in time. Group comparison studies evaluate differences between key groups, such as a group that has experienced a certain stressor and a matched comparison group that has not.

- Epidemiology is the study of the frequency and distribution of a disorder in a population. The prevalence of a disorder is the proportion of the population that has the disorder at a give point or period in time. The incidence of a disorder is the number of new cases of the disorder that develop during a specific period of time. Risk factors for a disorder are conditions or variables that are associated with a higher risk of having the disorder.

- Experimental studies can provide evidence that a given variable causes psychopathology. The goal of a human laboratory study is to induce the conditions that are hypothesized to lead to the outcome of interest (for example, increasing stress to cause depression) in people in a controlled setting. Participants are randomly assigned to either the experimental group, which receives a manipulation, or a control group, which does not.

- Generalizing experimental studies to real-world phenomena is sometimes not possible. In addition, manipulating people who are in distress in an experimental study can create ethical problems.

- A special type of experimental study is the therapy outcome study. It allows researchers to test a hypothesis about the causes of a psychopathology while providing a service to participants.

- Difficult issues associated with therapy outcome studies include problems in knowing what elements of therapy were effective, questions about the appropriate control groups to use, questions about whether to allow modifications of the therapy to fit individual participants' needs, and the lack of generalizability of the results of these studies to the real world.

- In therapy outcome studies, researchers sometimes use wait list control groups, in which control participants wait to receive the interventions after the studies are complete. Alternatively, researchers may try to construct psychological placebo control groups, in which participants receive the general support of therapists but none of the elements of the therapy thought to be active. Both of these types of control groups have practical and ethical limitations.

- Single-case experimental designs involve the intensive investigation of single individuals or small groups of individuals, before and after a manipulation or an intervention. In an ABAB, or reversal, design, an intervention is introduced, withdrawn, and then reinstated, and the behavior of a participant is examined on and off the treatment (review Figure 3.6).

- Animal studies allow researchers to manipulate their subjects in ways that are not ethically permissible with human participants, although many people feel that such animal studies are equally unethical. Animal studies suffer from problems in generalizability to humans.

- In doing cross-cultural research, researchers face special challenges. Access to the populations of interest can be difficult. Theories and concepts that make sense in one culture may not be applicable to other cultures. Questionnaires and other assessment tools must be translated accurately. Culture can affect how people respond to the social demands of research. Finally, researchers must be careful not to build into their research assumptions that one culture is healthy and another culture is deviant.

- Meta-analysis is a statistical technique for summarizing the results across several studies. In a meta-analysis, the results of individual studies are standardized into a statistic called the effect size. Then the magnitude of the effect size and its relationship to characteristics of the study are examined.

- Meta-analyses reduce bias that can occur when investigators draw conclusions across studies in a more subjective manner but can include studies that have poor methods and exclude good studies that were not published because they did not find significant effects.

MindMap CD-ROM

The following resources on the MindMap CD-ROM that came with this text will help you to master the content of this chapter and prepare for tests:

- Interactive Segments: Self-Report Bias in Surveys; Correlational Research; Samples and Populations; Independent and Dependent Variables; Reliability, Validity, and Variability
- Chapter Timeline
- Chapter Quiz

scientific method 73

hypothesis 73

null hypothesis 73

variable 73

dependent variable 74

independent variable 74

operationalization 74

case studies 74

generalizability 76

replication 76

correlational studies 76

continuous variable 76

group comparison study 77

cross-sectional 77

longitudinal 77

correlation coefficient 77

statistical significance 78

third variable problem 79

sample 79

external validity 80

epidemiology 81

prevalence 81

incidence 81

risk factors 81

experimental studies 82

human laboratory study 82

analogue study 82

internal validity 82

control group 83

experimental group 83

random assignment 83

demand characteristics 83

therapy outcome study 85

wait list control group 86

placebo control group 86

double-blind experiment 86

efficacy 87

effectiveness 87

single-case experimental design 87

ABAB (reversal) design 88

animal studies 88

meta-analysis 91

> Chapter 4

Essor
by André Rouillard

Beauty cannot disguise nor music melt
A pain undiagnosable but felt.

—Anne Morrow Lindbergh, *The Unicorn and Other*
Poems, 1935–1955 (1956)

Assessing and Diagnosing Abnormality <

Extraordinary People

■ **Michael J. Fox:** *Lucky Man*

Gathering Information

Assessment is the process of gathering information about the symptoms people are suffering and the possible causes of these symptoms. Many types of information are gathered during an assessment, including information about current symptoms and ways of coping with stress, recent events and physical condition, drug and alcohol use, personal and family history of psychological disorders, cognitive functioning, and sociocultural background. This information helps in planning treatment.

Assessment Tools

Clinicians use many types of assessment tools. An assessment tool should provide valid and reliable information. Neuropsychological tests can help detect neurological problems that may be causing symptoms. Intellectual tests indicate cognitive functioning. Structured clinical interviews and symptom questionnaires provide direct information about symptoms. Personality inventories, behavioral observations, self-monitoring, and projective tests can indicate personality styles and behavioral deficits. At some point in the future, brain-imaging techniques may prove useful in assessing psychopathology, but the technology does not allow this today.

Taking Psychology Personally

■ **Is Self-Assessment a Good Idea?**

Problems in Assessment

Clients may be resistant to providing information. Some clients may be unable to provide information because of cognitive impairment or youth. Children's manifestation of distress can change significantly with age. Cultural biases can impair the accuracy of clinicians' assessments of clients from other cultures.

Diagnosis

The *Diagnostic and Statistical Manual of Mental Disorders* (DSM) provides the primary set of rules used for diagnosing psychological disorders in the United States. The first two editions of the DSM had diagnostic criteria that were vague and based on theory. In the third edition of the DSM in 1980, the diagnostic criteria were revised to be as observable and atheoretical as possible. The current edition, DSM-IV-TR, specifies five axes to be used in making diagnoses. Critics of the DSM have charged that it reflects Western, masculine ideals for a "healthy" person and thus pathologizes the normal behaviors of women and people from other cultures. In addition, the subjectivity inherent in psychiatric diagnoses and the stigma attached to these diagnoses raise concerns about the application of these diagnoses, yet having clear criteria for diagnosis is necessary for the progress of research on psychological disorders and for communication among clinicians.

Chapter Integration

Understanding the context and possible sources of a person's psychological symptoms requires a comprehensive, integrated assessment of biological, psychological, and social factors.

Extraordinary People

Michael J. Fox: *Lucky Man*

Michael J. Fox was one of the most successful movie and television actors of the late twentieth century. He starred in the long-running sitcom *Family Ties* and in the blockbuster movies *Back to the Future*, *The Secret of My Success*, and *Doc Hollywood*. When he was just 30 years old and at the height of his career, however, Fox began to have strange symptoms, which he could not control. It started with a twitching in his pinkie finger. Over the next few months, the twitching progressed to his ring and middle fingers, and he began to have weakness in his left hand, stiffness in his shoulder, and aches in the muscles on one side of his chest.

Fox attributed these symptoms to having accidentally been hanged for a few moments in a botched scene in *Back to the Future* and tried his best to ignore them. Over the next few years, Fox's symptoms progressed, so that at their worst he was experiencing rigidity, shuffling, a lack of balance, difficulty in expressing his feelings and ideas, and a weakening of his voice. He felt terrific frustration over his difficulties of expression, finding that he could form his thoughts and ideas into words and sentences but had trouble getting them out of his mouth. He spoke in a halting monotone and his face became expressionless.

Fox attempted to drown his symptoms, and his fear of them, in alcohol. He describes one of the binges he and his film crew went on after finishing the taping of his movie *For Love or Money*. They had already consumed three pitchers of Margaritas on the set, but the party continued at a local restaurant and bar as the group switched from tequila to beer and finally to vodka. After each shot, they threw their glasses into the fireplace. Well after closing time and yet more beer, Fox was driven home, where he grabbed another beer from the refrigerator and passed out on the couch.

Fox eventually went to see a neurologist for an evaluation of his tremors and difficulties in moving and speaking. At first, the neurologist dismissed the symptoms as insignificant, but, the more testing he did, the more grave his expression became. At the end of the appointment, he dropped a bombshell—Fox had a rare, early-onset form of Parkinson's disease, a progressive, degenerative, and incurable neurological disease. He probably had 10 years left of being able to function normally.

Suppose that Michael J. Fox showed up at your clinic, asking you to determine what was wrong with him before he had the diagnosis of Parkinson's disease. How would you do this? The assessment and diagnosis of symptoms is the focus of this chapter.

Assessment is the process of gathering information about people's symptoms and the possible causes of those symptoms. The information gathered in an assessment is used to determine the appropriate diagnosis for a person's problems. A **diagnosis** is a label attached to a set of symptoms that tend to occur with one another. Michael J. Fox

was diagnosed with Parkinson's disease. If his alcohol use had come under the scrutiny of a clinician, he might also have been diagnosed with alcohol abuse or dependence (which is discussed in Chapter 17).

In this chapter, we discuss the modern tools of assessment and how they are used to determine the proper diagnosis of psychological symptoms and to understand the nature and causes of psychological problems. Some of these tools are very new, but others have been around for many years. These tools provide information on personality characteristics, cognitive deficits (such as learning disabilities or problems in maintaining attention), emotional well-being, and biological functioning. Increasingly, comprehensive assessments that take into account a person's biological, psychological, and social functioning are being done so that the contribution of each of these factors to symptoms can be understood.

We also consider modern systems of diagnosing psychological problems. There are a number of dangers and problems in applying a psychiatric diagnosis to a person, such as the stigmatizing effects of having a psychiatric diagnosis. We will discuss these dangers. Still, having a standardized system of diagnosis is crucial to communication among mental-health professionals and to good research on psychological problems. Clinicians must agree on what diagnostic labels mean, and a standardized diagnostic system provides agreed-upon definitions of disorders.

First, however, we explore the types of information to be gathered during an assessment. Then we review several methods that can be used to gather this information. Throughout the process of gathering information, the clinician must watch for many pitfalls in the assessment process, and we examine several of these in the following sections.

GATHERING INFORMATION

Let's look at three types of information—symptoms and history, physiological and neurophysiological factors, and sociocultural factors—that guide the formation of a diagnosis and treatment plan.

Symptoms and History

If you were Michael J. Fox's clinician, you would want to ask about his *current symptoms*, including their severity and chronicity. You would try to ascertain how much the symptoms are interfering with Fox's *ability to function* in the various domains of his life (e.g., in his work, his relationships with others, and his role as a parent). Is Fox experiencing the symptoms across a wide variety of situations or only in specific types of situations? The criteria for diagnosing most of the major psychological disorders require that the symptoms be severe and pervasive enough that they are interfering with the person's ability to function in daily life. If the symptoms are not that severe and are specific to one situation, then a diagnosis may not be warranted. Information about the pervasiveness and duration of Fox's symptoms will also help you formulate a plan for treatment that addresses all the areas in which he is having problems.

"I was beginning to think of myself as a visionary. Turned out they were hallucinations." © *Sidney Harris, courtesy ScienceCartoonsPlus.com*

In Fox's case, it would also be very helpful to know how he is *coping* with the stress of his life and his symptoms. Rather than seeking out people with whom he trusted to talk about his stresses, Fox initially turned to alcohol to drown his awareness of them. As is frequently the case, his way of coping with his symptoms and stressors created significant problems over and above his initial symptoms. Indeed, it turned out that his symptoms were the result of a neurological disorder, but he developed psychological symptoms of alcohol abuse in response to his neurological symptoms.

You would want to know about any *recent events* in Fox's life and whether the onset of the symptoms is tied to these life events. Fox thought his symptoms were due to his accidental hanging on a movie set. Symptoms that arise in response to a specific event are often given a different diagnosis (or, in some cases, no diagnosis) from the same symptoms when they arise with no apparent trigger.

For example, a child who becomes depressed after his or her parents separate might be given a diagnosis of adjustment disorder with depressed mood, whereas a child who gradually becomes more and more depressed for no apparent reason might be given a diagnosis of major depressive disorder. This distinction is made because symptoms that are triggered by a specific event often have a different prognosis and require different treatment than do symptoms that arise "out of the blue." A child whose symptoms of depression are triggered by a specific event is more likely to recover from these symptoms after a few talks with a supportive counselor than is a child who gradually becomes more and more depressed for no apparent reason.

An individual's *history of psychological problems* is also important in the assessment. For example, if Fox had a history of heavy drinking, his bout of

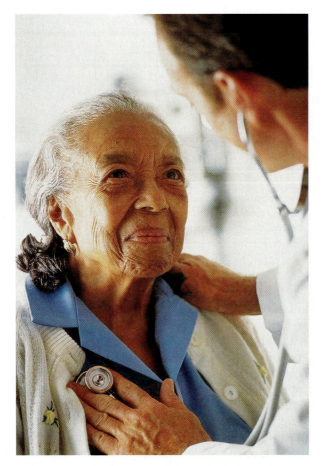

It is important for clients to receive a physical examination to determine whether medical problems are affecting their mental health.

drinking in response to his neurological symptoms might not just be a reaction to a stressor but rather, a longer-standing problem with alcohol abuse. It is also helpful to know an individual's *family history of disorders*. As we will discuss repeatedly in this book, many disorders appear to have genetic roots, so knowing that an individual has a family history of a particular disorder can assist in diagnosing that disorder.

Physiological and Neurophysiological Factors

Michael J. Fox's story is an interesting one from the perspective of assessment, because he was experiencing both severe neurological symptoms (tremors and weakness) and significant psychological symptoms (heavy drinking). It would be easy for a clinician to focus on one set of symptoms and to ignore the other.

When clients seek an assessment of what appear to be primarily psychological symptoms, it is still a good idea for the clinician to have them obtain a complete *physical examination* to determine if they are suffering from any medical conditions that can create psychological symptoms. For example, some brain tumors can create disorientation and agitation that are similar to symptoms of the psychological disorder schizophrenia.

Unfortunately, there are no definitive biological tests for any of the psychological disorders. What biological tests can sometimes tell, however, is whether there is a medical disease that is causing psychological symptoms as side effects. For example, thyroid disorders can cause people to experience the classic symptoms of depression, but most people who get depressed do not have a thyroid disorder. However, if an individual's depression is caused by a thyroid disorder, clinicians can often simply treat the thyroid disorder and the symptoms of depression will also disappear without any additional antidepressant treatment. For this reason, it is important to determine whether a medical disease, such as a thyroid disorder, might be causing a person's psychological symptoms.

Clinicians also need to know about any *drugs*—legal or illegal—their clients are taking. Many drugs can induce distressing psychological symptoms as side effects during drug use or withdrawal from the drug. In such cases, a different diagnosis is given from that given when the symptoms are not the consequence of a drug. Clinicians also need to know about any drugs a client is taking to protect against interactions between those drugs and medications the clinician might prescribe.

Clinicians often assess their clients' *cognitive functioning* and *intellectual abilities*. This information can be relevant to making a **differential diagnosis**—a determination of which of several possible disorders an individual may be suffering. For example, symptoms of paranoia can be the result of several psychological disorders, such as paranoid personality disorder or schizophrenia. They can also be the result of difficulties in short-term memory. People who cannot remember conversations they have had or where they have left items sometimes begin to believe that other people are doing things behind their backs. Determining whether or not symptoms of paranoia are due to cognitive deficits, such as memory loss, can have a major impact on the diagnosis and type of treatment the person receives.

Sociocultural Factors

Clients' social environment and cultural background can influence their symptoms and thus need to be assessed. Clinicians often ask about the *social resources* their clients have available—the number of friends and family members they have contact with and the quality of their relationships with these people. Michael J. Fox was fortunate to have tremendous support from his wife, Tracy. Social isolation can make it much more difficult for people to overcome psychological problems. On the other hand, friends and family members can also be burdens when these relationships are marked by conflict or create unreasonable demands.

An important step for clinicians working with a culturally diverse clientele is to obtain information on clients' *sociocultural background.* For immigrant clients, this background includes the specific culture in which they were raised, the number of years they have been in this country, the circumstances that brought them to this country (e.g., to escape war or oppression or to seek work), their continuing connections to their homeland, and whether they are currently living with people from their homeland (Dana, 2001; Westermeyer, 1993). As we will see, immigrants who left their homeland under difficult circumstances and who do not have a strong support system of people from their culture in their new homes are at especially high risk for disorders such as posttraumatic stress disorder (see Chapter 7). It is also useful to know as much as possible about the clients' socioeconomic status and occupation in their homeland—perhaps they were physicians in their homeland but now are street cleaners—because the contrast between their lives in the homeland and their current lives can be a source of difficulty.

Immigrants and other members of ethnic minority groups differ in their levels of acculturation. **Acculturation** is the extent to which a person identifies with his or her group of origin and its culture or with the dominant, mainstream culture (Dana, 2000). Some members of ethnic minority groups retain as much of their culture of origin as possible and reject the dominant, mainstream culture. They may continue to speak their language of origin and refuse to learn the dominant language. Other members fully identify with the dominant culture and reject their culture of origin. Still others are bicultural—they continue to identify with their culture of origin and celebrate it but also assimilate as necessary into the dominant culture.

Clinicians need to understand their clients' level of acculturation, because it can affect how clients talk about and present their problems, the kinds of stresses clients will be exposed to, and clients' responses to interventions (Lopez & Guarnaccia, 2000). We discuss these issues in more depth in Chapter 5, but let's briefly examine three examples. First, members of some cultures experience psychological distress in somatic symptoms, such as headaches and stomachaches (Kirmayer, 2001).

Parents and children can have different levels of acculturation, leading to conflicts.

Knowing that a client remains fully identified with a culture that tends to present psychological symptoms in somatic terms can help a clinician interpret a client's complaints. Second, when members of a family differ in their levels of acculturation, this difference can cause significant stress for family members. For example, an adolescent who is fully acculturated to the dominant culture may have many conflicts with a parent who remains identified with his or her culture of origin and does not want the adolescent to adopt the mainstream culture. Third, a client who is acculturated to the mainstream American culture will respond differently to certain suggestions a clinician makes, such as to confront an abusive boss, than will a client who remains identified with a culture in which authority figures are never questioned.

SUMMING UP

- Information concerning clients' symptoms and history is obtained in an assessment. This information includes the details of their current symptoms, their ability to function, their coping strategies, recent events, their history of psychological problems, and their family history of psychological problems.

- Clients' physiological and neurophysiological functioning is assessed as well. Clients may be asked to undergo a physical examination to detect medical conditions, questioned about their drug use, and tested for their cognitive functioning and intellectual abilities.

- Clients' sociocultural background—including their social resources and cultural heritage—is important to ascertain in an assessment.

ASSESSMENT TOOLS

A number of assessment tools have been developed to ensure that clinicians gather all the information needed for an accurate assessment.

Clinical Interviews

Much of the information for an assessment is gathered in an initial interview, often called an *intake interview,* or a *mental status exam,* when the clinician first meets the client. The interview may be an **unstructured interview,** with only a few questions that are open-ended, such as "Tell me about yourself." The clinician will listen to the client's answers to the questions and observe how the client answers—whether the client hesitates when talking about her marriage, whether she avoids questions about her drinking habits, whether she looks sad when talking about her career—to obtain nonverbal indicators of what is bothering her.

The clinician may also interview the client's family members for information about the family's history of psychological problems, the client's history, and the client's current symptoms. Information from family members is especially important if the client is a child, because children cannot always state what they are feeling or thinking. In addition, some adults are so impaired that they cannot provide adequate information to the assessor. They may be so depressed, anxious, or confused that they cannot properly answer questions. In such cases, an assessor often must rely entirely on family members and friends for information about a client's functioning.

Unstructured interviews have an important place in an assessment. The specific questions asked in an unstructured interview may vary from one assessor to the next, however, making comparisons of the information gathered by different assessors difficult. Increasingly, clinicians and researchers are using what is known as a **structured interview** to gather information about clients. In a structured interview, the clinician asks the respondent a series of questions about symptoms he or she is experiencing or has experienced in the past. The format of the questions and the entire interview is highly structured and standardized, and the clinician uses concrete criteria to score the person's answers to each question (see Table 4.1). At the end of the interview, the clinician should have enough information from the respondent to determine whether he or she has symptoms that qualify for a diagnosis of any of the major types of psychological problems.

Several such structured interviews have been developed in recent decades, including the Diag-

nostic Interview Schedule, or DIS (Robins et al., 1981), and the Structured Clinical Interview for the DSM (First et al., 1997). Structured interviews have also been adapted for diagnosing children's problems. Much of the information about a child's symptoms must often come from parents and other sources.

Structured and unstructured interviews can be valuable tools in assessment, but they have limitations. One of the greatest can be **resistance** on the part of the client who is being interviewed. Sometimes, the individual being assessed does not want to be assessed or treated. For example, the parents of a teenager may have forced him to see a psychologist because they are worried about recent changes in his behavior. This teenager may be resistant to providing any information to the assessor. Because much of the information a clinician needs must come directly from the person being assessed, resistance can be a formidable problem.

Even when the client is not completely resistant to being assessed, he or she may have a strong interest in the outcome of that assessment and thus may be highly selective in the information provided, may bias his or her presentation of the information, or may even lie to the assessor. Such problems often arise when assessments are being done as part of a legal case, such as when parents are fighting for custody of their children in divorce. Each parent will want to present him- or herself in the best light but may negatively bias his or her reports on the other parent when speaking to psychologists who have been appointed to assess each parent's fitness for custody of the children.

Cognitive, Symptom, and Personality Tests

Clinicians have a number of tests they use to aid in gathering information from clients. Before we discuss several of these tests, let's define two criteria that are used to evaluate the quality of any test: validity and reliability.

Validity

If you administer a test to determine what is wrong with a client, you want to be sure that the test is an accurate measure. The *accuracy* of a test in assessing what it is supposed to measure is called its **validity.** The best way to determine the validity of a test is to see if the results of the test yield the same information as an objective and accurate indicator of what the test is supposed to measure. For example, if there was a blood test that definitively proved

TABLE 4.1	Sample Structured Interview

Anxiety Disorders

Panic Disorder Questions	Panic Disorder Criteria
Have you ever had a panic attack, when you *suddenly* felt frightened, anxious, or extremely uncomfortable? If Yes: Tell me about it. When does that happen? (Have you ever had one that just seemed to come out of the blue?) IF PANIC ATTACKS IN EXPECTED SITUATIONS: Did you ever have one of these attacks when you weren't in (EXPECTED SITUATION)? Have you ever had four attacks like that in a four-week period? If No: Did you worry a lot about having another one? (How long did you worry?) When was the last bad one (EXPECTED OR UNEXPECTED)? Now I am going to ask you about that attack. What was the first thing you noticed? Then what? During the attack . . . . . . were you short of breath? (have trouble catching your breath?) . . . did you feel dizzy, unsteady, or as if you might faint? . . . did your heart race, pound, or skip? . . . did you tremble or shake? . . . did you sweat? . . . did you feel as if you were choking? . . . did you have nausea, upset stomach, or the feeling that you were going to have diarrhea? . . . did things around you seem unreal or did you feel detached from things around you or detached from part of your body?	A. At some time during the disturbance, one or more panic attacks (discrete periods of intense fear or discomfort) have occurred that were (1) unexpected, i.e., did not occur immediately before or on exposure to a situation that almost always causes anxiety, and (2) not triggered by situations in which the person was the focus of others' attention. B. Either four attacks, as defined in criterion A, have occurred within a four-week period, or one or more attacks have been followed by a period of at least a month of persistent fear of having another attack. C. At least four of the following symptoms developed during at least one of the attacks: 1. Shortness of breath (dyspnea) or smothering sensations 2. Dizziness, unsteady feelings, or faintness 3. Palpitations or accelerated heart rate (tachycardia) 4. Trembling or shaking 5. Sweating 6. Choking 7. Nausea or abdominal distress 8. Depersonalization or derealization

Source: Data from First et al., 1997.

whether a person had a particular psychological disorder, you would want any other test for that disorder (such as a questionnaire) to yield the same results when administered to the person. (You may remember that we talked about internal and external validity in Chapter 3 in reference to experimental studies. The types of validity we discuss here refer specifically to the validity of questionnaires or tests.)

So far, there are no definitive blood tests, brain scans, or other objective tests for any of the psychological disorders we discuss in this book. Fortunately, the validity of a test can be estimated in a number of other ways (see Figure 4.1 on page 106). A test is said to have **face validity** when, on face value, the items seem to be measuring what the test is intended to measure. For example, a questionnaire for anxiety that includes questions such

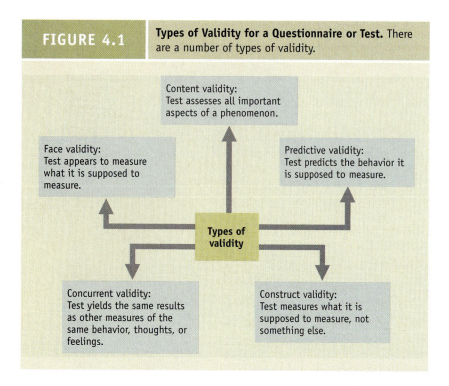

FIGURE 4.1 | **Types of Validity for a Questionnaire or Test.** There are a number of types of validity.

Content validity:
Test assesses all important aspects of a phenomenon.

Face validity:
Test appears to measure what it is supposed to measure.

Predictive validity:
Test predicts the behavior it is supposed to measure.

Types of validity

Concurrent validity:
Test yields the same results as other measures of the same behavior, thoughts, or feelings.

Construct validity:
Test measures what it is supposed to measure, not something else.

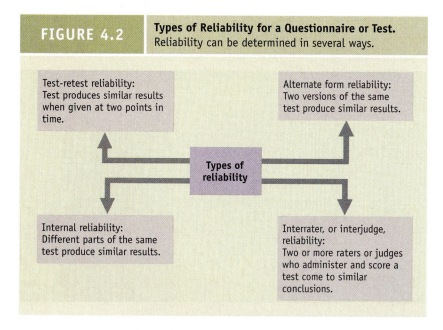

FIGURE 4.2 | **Types of Reliability for a Questionnaire or Test.** Reliability can be determined in several ways.

Test-retest reliability:
Test produces similar results when given at two points in time.

Alternate form reliability:
Two versions of the same test produce similar results.

Types of reliability

Internal reliability:
Different parts of the same test produce similar results.

Interrater, or interjudge, reliability:
Two or more raters or judges who administer and score a test come to similar conclusions.

hensions about the future, anticipation of negative events), then we might question whether it is a good measure of anxiety.

Concurrent validity is the extent to which a test yields the same results as other measures of the same behavior, thoughts, or feelings. A person's scores on our anxiety questionnaire should bear some relation to information gathered from the client's family members and friends about his or her typical level of anxiety. Information from family members and friends may not be completely accurate or valid, so it is not a definitive standard against which to judge our anxiety questionnaire. However, the notion behind concurrent validity is that any new measure of a variable should yield results similar to established measures of that variable.

A test that has **predictive validity** is good at predicting how a person will think, act, or feel in the future. Our anxiety measure has good predictive validity if it correctly predicts which people will behave in anxious ways when confronted with stressors in the future and which people will not be anxious.

Construct validity is the extent to which the test measures what it is supposed to measure, not something else altogether (Cronbach & Meehl, 1955). Consider the construct validity of multiple-choice exams given in courses. These exams are supposed to measure a student's knowledge and understanding of what has been taught in a course. What they may often measure, however, is the student's ability to take multiple-choice examinations—to determine what the instructor is trying to get at with the questions and to recognize any tricks or distractors in the questions.

Reliability

It is important that a test provide consistent information about a client. The **reliability** of a test is an indicator of the *consistency* of a test in measuring what it is supposed to measure. As with validity, there are several types of reliability (see Figure 4.2). **Test-retest reliability** is an index of how consistent the results of a test are over time. If a test supposedly measures an enduring characteristic of a person, then the person's scores on that test should be similar when he or she takes the test at two different points in time. For example, if our anxiety questionnaire is supposed to measure people's general tendencies to be anxious, then their scores on this questionnaire should be similar if they complete the questionnaire once this week and then again next week. On the other hand, if our anxiety questionnaire is a measure of people's current symptoms of anxiety (with questions such as "Do you

as "Do you feel jittery much of the time?" "Do you feel as if you can't sit still?" and "Do you worry about many things?" has face validity, because it seems to assess the symptoms of anxiety.

Content validity is the extent to which a test assesses all the important aspects of a phenomenon that it purports to measure. For example, if our measure of anxiety included only questions about the physical symptoms of anxiety (nervousness, restlessness, stomach distress, rapid heartbeat) and none of the cognitive symptoms of anxiety (appre-

feel jittery right now?"), then we might expect low test-retest reliability on this measure. Typically, measures of general and enduring characteristics should have higher test-retest reliability than measures of momentary, or transient, characteristics.

When people take the same test a second time, they may remember their answers from the first time and try to repeat these answers to seem consistent. For this reason, researchers often develop two or more forms of a test. When people's answers to these different forms of a test are similar, the tests are said to have **alternate form reliability.** Similarly, a researcher may simply split a test into two or more parts to determine if people's answers to one part of a test are similar to their answers to another part of the test. When there is similarity in people's answers among different parts of the same test, the test is said to have high **internal reliability.**

Finally, many of the tests we examine in this chapter are not self-report questionnaires but interviews or observational measures that require a clinician or researcher to make judgments about the people being assessed. These tests should have high **interrater,** or *interjudge,* **reliability.** That is, different raters or judges who administer and score the interview or test should come to similar conclusions when they are evaluating the same people.

Neuropsychological Tests

If the clinician suspects neurological impairment in a client, paper-and-pencil **neuropsychological tests** may be useful in detecting specific cognitive and fine-motor deficits, such as an attentional problem or a tendency to ignore items in one part of the visual field (Golden & Freshwater, 2001). One frequently used neuropsychological test is the Bender-Gestalt Test (Bender, 1938). This test assesses clients' sensorimotor skills by having them reproduce a set of nine drawings (see Figure 4.3). Clients with brain damage may rotate or change parts of the drawings or be unable to reproduce the drawings. When asked to remember the drawings after a delay, they may show significant memory deficits. The Bender-Gestalt Test appears to be good at differentiating people with brain damage from those without brain damage, but it does not reliably identify the specific type of brain damage a person has (Goldstein & Hersen, 1990).

More extensive batteries of tests have been developed to pinpoint types of brain damage. Two of the most popular batteries are the Halstead-Reitan Test (Reitan & Davidson, 1974) and the Luria-Nebraska Test (Luria, 1973). These batteries contain several tests that provide specific information about an individual's functioning in several skill

| FIGURE 4.3 | **The Bender-Gestalt Test.** On the left are the figures presented to clients. On the right are the figures as copied by a child with a brain tumor that is creating perceptual-motor difficulties. |

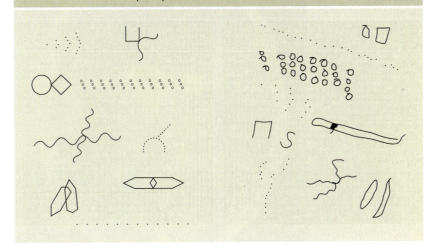

areas, such as concentration, dexterity, and speed of comprehension.

Brain-Imaging Techniques

Increasingly, neuropsychological tests are being used in conjunction with brain-imaging techniques to identify specific deficits and possible brain abnormalities. Clinicians use brain scans to determine if a patient has a brain injury or tumor. Blood tests can detect medical problems (such as low blood sugar) that might be contributing to certain psychological symptoms. Researchers use brain scans and blood tests to search for differences in biochemicals or in brain activity or structure between people with a psychological disorder and people with no disorder. Ideally, this research will reveal enough about the biology of psychological disorders that researchers can develop valid and reliable biological tests for these disorders in the future.

Indeed, both technology and clinicians' understanding of the biology of disorders are advancing so rapidly that there will probably be major breakthroughs in biological techniques for assessing and diagnosing psychological disorders in the near future. Let's review existing brain-imaging technologies and what they can tell us now. This technology is providing some of the most exciting new findings in the search for biological underpinnings of psychological disorders. Michael J. Fox underwent several of these procedures when his physicians were trying to determine the sources of his symptoms.

Computerized tomography (CT) is an enhancement of X-ray procedures. In CT, narrow

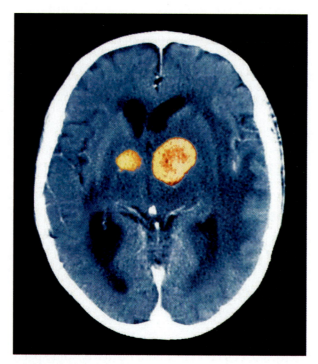

CT scan of a patient with a tumor in the tissues near the basal ganglia (tumor appears orange).

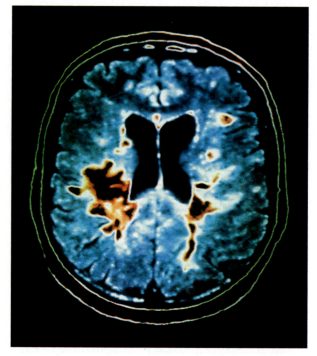

Magnetic resonance imaging (MRI) scan of a patient with multiple sclerosis. The orange/black areas are lesions of the myelin sheaths around axon nerve fibers.

X-ray beams are passed through the person's head in a single plane from a variety of angles. The amount of radiation absorbed by each beam is measured, and from these measurements a computer program constructs an image that looks like a slice of the brain. By taking many slices of the brain, the computer can reconstruct a three-dimensional image, showing the major structures of the brain. A CT scan can reveal brain injury, tumors, and structural abnormalities. The two major limitations of CT technology are that it exposes patients to X rays, which can be harmful, and it provides only an image of the *structure* of the brain, rather than an image of the *activity* in the brain.

Positron-emission tomography (PET) can provide a picture of activity in the brain. PET requires injecting the patient with a harmless radioactive isotope, such as fluorodeoxyglucose (FDG). This substance travels through the blood to the brain. The parts of the brain that are active need the glucose in FDG for nutrition, so FDG accumulates in the active parts of the brain. Subatomic particles in FDG, called *positrons*, are emitted as the isotope decays. These positrons collide with electrons, and both are annihilated and converted to two photons, traveling away from each other in opposite directions. The PET scanner detects these photons and the point at which they are annihilated and constructs an image of the brain, showing the areas that are most active.

PET scans can be used to show differences in the activity level of specific areas of the brain between people with a psychological disorder and people without a disorder.

Magnetic resonance imaging (MRI) holds several advantages over both CT and PET technology. It does not require exposing the patient to any form of radiation or injection of radioisotopes. It is safe to use repeatedly in the same patient. It provides much more finely detailed pictures of the anatomy of the brain than do other technologies, and it can image the brain at any angle. It can also provide pictures of the activity and functioning in the brain.

MRI involves creating a magnetic field around the brain that is so powerful that it causes a realignment of hydrogen atoms in the brain. When the magnetic field is turned off and on, the hydrogen atoms change position, causing them to emit magnetic signals. These signals are read by a computer, which reconstructs a three-dimensional image of the brain. Researchers are using MRI to study functional and structural brain abnormalities in almost every psychological disorder.

Intelligence Tests

In clinical practice, **intelligence tests** are used to get a sense of a client's intellectual strengths and weaknesses, particularly when mental retardation or brain damage is suspected (Ryan & Lopez, 2001).

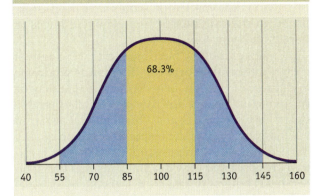

IQ Distribution. If the entire population took an IQ test, the scores would fall into a bell-shaped curve around the most frequent score of 100. More than two-thirds of all people score between 85 and 115 on IQ tests.

Intelligence tests are also used in schools to identify children with intellectual difficulties and to place children in "gifted" classrooms. They are used in occupational settings and the military to evaluate adults' capabilities for certain jobs or types of service. Some examples of these tests are the *Wechsler Adult Intelligence Scale*, the *Stanford-Binet Intelligence Test*, and the *Wechsler Intelligence Scale for Children*.

These tests were designed to measure basic intellectual abilities, such as the ability for abstract reasoning, verbal fluency, and spatial memory. The term *IQ* is used to describe a method of comparing an individual's score on an intelligence test with the performance of individuals of the same age group. An IQ score of 100 means that the person performed similarly to the average performance of other people his or her age (see Figure 4.4).

Intelligence tests are controversial in part because there is little consensus as to what is meant by intelligence (Sternberg, 2004). The most widely used *intelligence* tests assess verbal and analytical abilities but do not assess other talents or skills, such as artistic and musical ability. Some psychologists argue that success in life is as strongly influenced by social skills and other talents not measured by intelligence tests as by verbal and analytical skills (Gardner, 2003; Sternberg, 2004).

Another important criticism of intelligence tests is that they are biased in favor of middle- and upper-class, educated European Americans because these people have more familiarity with the kinds of reasoning that are assessed on the intelligence tests (Sternberg, 2004). In addition, educated European Americans may be more comfortable in taking intelligence tests, because testers are often also European Americans, and the testing situation resembles testing situations in their educational experience. In contrast, different cultures within the United States and in other countries may emphasize other forms of reasoning over those assessed on intelligence tests and may not be comfortable with the testing situations of intelligence tests.

A "culture-fair" test would have to include items that are equally applicable to all groups or items that are different for each culture but are psychologically equivalent for the groups being tested. Attempts have been made to develop culture-fair tests, but the results have been disappointing. Even if a universal test were created, it would be difficult to make statements about intelligence in different cultures, because different nations and cultures vary in the emphasis they place on "intellectual achievement."

So far, we have focused on tests to assess brain abnormalities and cognitive and intellectual functioning. Much of the information that must be gathered in an assessment, however, has to do with the client's emotional, social, and behavioral

Garfield ® by Jim Davis

TABLE 4.2 Sample Items from the Beck Depression Inventory®—Second Edition (BDI®—II)

Unhappiness

0   I do not feel unhappy.

1   I feel unhappy.

2   I am unhappy.

3   I am so unhappy that I can't stand it.

Changes in Activity Level

0   I have not experienced any change in activity level.

1a I am somewhat more active than usual.

1b I am somewhat less active than usual.

2a I am a lot more active than usual.

2b I am a lot less active than usual.

3a I am not active most of the day.

3b I am active all of the day.

Source: Beck Depression Inventory®—Second Edition. Copyright © 1996 by Aaron T. Beck. Reproduced with permission of Publisher, Harcourt Assessment, Inc. All rights reserved. Beck Depression Inventory and BDI are trademarks of Harcourt Assessment, Inc. registered in the United States and/or other jurisdictions.

Information concerning the BDI®—II is available from:
Harcourt Assessment, Inc.
Attn: Customer Service
19500 Bulverde Road
San Antonio, TX 78259
Phone: (800) 211-8378
Fax: (800) 232-1223
Web site: www.harcourtassessment.com
Email: Customer_Service@harcourt.com

functioning. Now let's turn to tools that help the clinician assess these characteristics.

Symptom Questionnaires

Often, when a clinician or researcher wants a quick way to assess what symptoms a person is experiencing, he or she will ask the person to complete a **symptom questionnaire.** Some questionnaires cover a wide variety of symptoms, representing several different disorders. Others focus on the symptoms of specific disorders.

One of the most common questionnaires used to assess the symptoms of depression is the *Beck Depression Inventory*, or *BDI* (Beck & Beck, 1972).

The most recent form of the BDI has 21 items, each of which describes four levels of a given symptom of depression (see Table 4.2). The respondent is asked to indicate which of the descriptions best fits how he or she has been feeling in the past week. The items are scored to indicate the level of the depressive symptoms. Cutoff scores have been established to indicate moderate and severe levels of depressive symptoms.

Critics of the BDI have argued that it does not clearly differentiate between the clinical syndrome of depression and the general distress that may be related to an anxiety disorder or several other disorders (see Kendall et al., 1987). The BDI also cannot indicate whether the respondent would qualify for a diagnosis of depression. But the BDI is extremely quick and easy to administer and has good test-retest reliability. Hence, it is widely used, especially in research on depression.

Clinicians treating depressed people also use the BDI to keep track of their clients' symptom levels from week to week. They use it as a monitoring tool rather than as a diagnostic tool. A client may be asked to complete the BDI at the beginning of each therapy session, and both the client and the clinician then have a concrete indicator of the progress of the client's symptoms.

Personality Inventories

Personality inventories are usually questionnaires that are meant to assess people's typical ways of thinking, feeling, and behaving. These inventories are used as part of an assessment procedure to obtain information on people's well-being, self-concept, attitudes and beliefs, ways of coping, perceptions of their environment and social resources, and vulnerabilities. You have probably seen versions of personality inventories in popular magazines, although often these versions have not undergone much scientific scrutiny, as we discuss in *Taking Psychology Personally: Is Self-Assessment a Good Idea?*

The most widely used personality inventory in professional clinical assessments is the *Minnesota Multiphasic Personality Inventory (MMPI)*, which has been translated into more than 150 languages and used in more than 50 countries (Dana, 1998). The original MMPI was first published in 1945 and contained 550 items. In 1990, an updated version, published under the name MMPI-2, contained 567 items (Butcher, 1990). Both versions of the MMPI present respondents with sentences describing moral and social attitudes, behaviors, psychological states, and physical conditions and ask them to respond "true," "false," or "can't say" to each sentence.

Taking Psychology Personally

Is Self-Assessment a Good Idea?

Self-help books and magazine articles often feature questionnaires that allow readers to assess their own personal characteristics or weaknesses or the characteristics of their relationships with others. These self-assessment tools typically involve a set of questions that help readers "diagnose" problems and some guidelines on how to interpret the scores on the questionnaires. Are these self-assessment tools a good idea?

In this chapter, we have discussed the problems with the reliability and validity of many assessment tools. The tools described in this chapter are the "best of the bunch"—those most widely used and accepted by professional psychologists and psychiatrists—yet even these tools have many critics. The self-assessment questionnaires in books and magazines are often not as well tested or well conceived as those we discuss in this chapter. In addition, the writers of these questionnaires often make claims about the diagnoses they produce that are overly conclusive and extreme, such as "If you scored between 10 and 20 on the Relationship Diagnostic Inventory, then your relationship is definitely going to fail. You might as well dump him and find someone else now!"

This does not mean that all self-assessment tools are a bad idea. People often want to deny their problems or are not aware that their symptoms are part of syndromes that can be treated successfully, and self-assessment tools can help people recognize their troubles and seek help. For example, questionnaires that lead people to recognize that they consume much more alcohol than the average person and that withdrawal from the effects of alcohol often interferes with their daily functioning can help these people moderate their alcohol consumption or seek treatment for alcohol addiction if necessary. Similarly, questionnaires or guidelines that make people aware that the symptoms they have been experiencing add up to the syndrome of an anxiety disorder can lead these people into therapy.

One of the most important points to remember about any self-assessment tool is that the information it provides is only suggestive, not conclusive. If you are concerned about the outcome of any self-assessment tool—your score on a questionnaire or how you have answered individual questions—it is a good idea to consult with a professional counselor about your concerns. Doing so would enable you to obtain a more thorough and expert assessment of how you are doing.

The MMPI was developed *empirically*, meaning that a large group of possible items were given to psychologically "healthy" people and to people suffering from various psychological problems. Then the items that reliably differentiated among the groups of people were included in the inventory.

The items on the original MMPI cluster into 10 scales, which measure different types of psychological characteristics or problems, such as paranoia, anxiety, and social introversion. An additional 4 scales were added to the MMPI-2 to assess vulnerability to eating disorders, substance abuse, and poor functioning at work. A respondent's scores on each of the scales are compared with scores from the normal population, and a profile of the respondent's personality and psychological problems is derived. There are also 4 validity scales that determine whether the person tends to respond to the items on the scale in an honest and straightforward manner or tends to distort his or her answers in a way that might invalidate the test (see Table 4.3 on page 112). For example, the Lie scale measures the respondent's tendency to respond to items in a socially desirable way that makes him or her look unusually positive or good.

Because the items on the MMPI were chosen for their ability to differentiate people with specific types of psychological problems from people without psychological problems, the concurrent validity of the MMPI scales was built in during their development. The MMPI may be especially useful as a general screening device for detecting people who are functioning very poorly psychologically. The test-retest reliability of the MMPI has also proven to be quite high (Dorfman & Leonard, 2001).

Many criticisms have been raised about the use of the MMPI in culturally diverse samples (Dana, 1998; Tsai et al., 2001). The norms for the original MMPI—the scores considered "healthy" scores—were based on samples of people in the United States that were not representative of people from a wide range of ethnic backgrounds, age groups, and social classes. In response to this problem, the publishers of the MMPI established new norms based

TABLE 4.3   Clinical and Validity Scales of the Original MMPI

The MMPI is one of the most widely used questionnaires to assess people's symptoms and personalities. It also includes scales to assess whether respondents are lying or trying to obfuscate their answers.

CLINICAL SCALES

SCALE NUMBER	SCALE NAME	WHAT IT MEASURES
Scale 1	Hypochondriasis	Excessive somatic concern and physical complaints
Scale 2	Depression	Symptomatic depression
Scale 3	Hysteria	Hysterical personality features and tendency to develop physical symptoms under stress
Scale 4	Psychopathic deviate	Antisocial tendencies
Scale 5	Masculinity-femininity	Sex role conflict
Scale 6	Paranoia	Suspicious, paranoid thinking
Scale 7	Psychasthenia	Anxiety and obsessive behavior
Scale 8	Schizophrenia	Bizarre thoughts and disordered affect
Scale 9	Hypomania	Behavior found in mania
Scale 0	Social introversion	Social anxiety, withdrawal, overcontrol

VALIDITY SCALES

SCALE NAME	WHAT IT MEASURES
Cannot say scale	Total number of unanswered items
Lie scale	Tendency to present favorable image
Infrequency scale	Tendency to falsely claim psychological problems
Defensiveness scale	Tendency to see oneself in unrealistically positive manner

Source: Clinical and Validity Scales of the Original MMPI Minnesota Multiphasic Personality Inventory (MMPI). Copyright © 1942, 1943, 1951, 1967 (renewed 1970), 1983. Reprinted by permission of the University of Minnesota. "MMPI" and "Minnesota Multiphasic Personality Inventory" are trademarks owned by the University of Minnesota.

on more representative samples of eight communities across the United States. Still, there are concerns that the MMPI norms do not reflect variations across cultures in what is considered normal or abnormal. In addition, the linguistic accuracy of the translated versions of the MMPI and the comparability of these versions to the English version have been questioned (Dana, 1998).

Projective Tests

A **projective test** is based on the assumption that, when people are presented with an ambiguous stimulus, such as an oddly shaped inkblot or a captionless picture, they will interpret the stimulus in line with their current concerns and feelings, their relationships with others, and their conflicts or desires. The people are said to project these issues as they describe the content of the stimulus, hence the name *projective tests*. Proponents of these tests argue that they are useful in uncovering the unconscious issues or motives of a person or in assessing a person who is resistant or heavily biasing the information he or she presents to the assessor. Four of the most frequently used projective tests are the Rorschach Inkblot Test, the Thematic Apperception Test (TAT), the Sentence Completion Test, and the Draw-a-Person Test.

The *Rorschach Inkblot Test*, commonly referred to simply as the *Rorschach*, was developed in 1921 by Swiss psychiatrist Hermann Rorschach. The test consists of 10 cards, each containing a symmetrical inkblot in black, gray, and white or in color (see Figure 4.5). The examiner tells the respondent something like "People may see many different things in these inkblot pictures; now tell me what you see, what it makes you think of, what it means

"Rorschach! What's to become of you?" © *Sidney Harris, courtesy ScienceCartoonsPlus.com*

the inkblot as a whole or the clients' hesitations in responding to certain inkblots (Exner, 1993).

The *Thematic Apperception Test (TAT)* consists of a series of pictures. The client is asked to make up a story about what is happening in the pictures (Murray, 1943). Proponents of the TAT argue that clients' stories reflect their concerns and wishes and their personality traits and motives. As with the Rorschach, clinicians are interested in both the content and the style of clients' responses to the TAT cards. Some cards may stimulate more emotional responses than others or no responses at all. These cards are considered to tap the clients' most important issues. The following is a story that a person made up about a picture of a man and young woman (Allison, Blatt, & Zimet, 1968).

to you" (Exner, 1993). Clinicians are interested in both the content of the clients' responses to the inkblots and the style of their responses. In the content of responses, they look for particular themes or concerns, such as the frequent mention of aggression or fear of abandonment. Important stylistic features may include the clients' tendency to focus on small details of the inkblot rather than

This looks like a nice man and—a sweet girl— They look like this is a happy moment—Looks like he's telling her that he loves her—or something that's tender and sweet. She looks very confident and happy! It looks nice; I like it. Hm! Wait now! Maybe—well—that's right—he looks kind of older—but she looks efficient—

(continued)

FIGURE 4.5   **Projective Tests.** Clinicians analyze people's answers to projective tests for particular themes or concerns.

and sweet. [Efficient?] Yes [laughs]. Doesn't look particularly efficient at the moment, but I imagine—[puts card away]. [What led up to this?] Well—I think maybe he taught school nearby, and she was a girl in the village—It strikes me as a sort of sweet, old fashioned romance. Maybe she's seen him a long time, and now it has just come to the state where he tells her that he loves her. [What will the outcome be?] I think they will get married, get some children and be happy—not that they will live happily ever after, not like a fairy tale. They look like ordinary people.

In interpreting the client's story, the clinician might note that it exhibits a romanticized, naive, and childlike quality. The client presents a very conventional scenario but with moral themes and much emotional expression. The clinician might interpret these tendencies as part of the client's basic personality style (Allison et al., 1968).

A third test that is based on the idea that people project their concerns and wishes onto ambiguous stimuli is the *Sentence Completion Test*. Sentence Completion Tests have been designed for children, adolescents, and adults. The tests provide a "stem," which is the beginning of a sentence, such as "My mother is . . ." or "I wish. . . ." The individual is asked to complete the sentence. Although more structured than the Rorschach and TAT, Sentence Completion Tests are also interpreted subjectively by the examiner. Clinicians might look for indications of the person's concerns in both what he or she says in response to the sentence stem and what he or she avoids saying in response to the stem. For example, a clinician might find it interesting that the person seems unable to come up with any response to the stem "Sex is. . . ."

A fourth test is the *Draw-a-Person Test* (Machover, 1949). The client is asked to draw a picture of him- or herself and then to draw a picture of another person of the opposite sex. The clinician examines how the client depicts him- or herself: Does he draw himself as a small figure, huddled in the corner of the page, or as a large figure, filling the page? The drawings of self are thought to reflect the client's self-concept as a strong person or weak person, a smart person or unintelligent person, and so on. The drawing of the other person is thought to reflect the client's attitudes toward the opposite sex and his or her relationships with important members of the opposite sex.

Clinicians from psychodynamic perspectives see projective tests as valuable tools for assessing the underlying conflicts and concerns that clients cannot or will not report directly. Clinicians from other perspectives question the usefulness of these tests. The validity and reliability of all of the projective tests have not proven strong in research (Garb, Florio, & Grove, 1998; Kline, 1993). In addition, because these tests rely so greatly on subjective interpretations by clinicians, they are open to a number of biases. Finally, criteria for interpreting the tests do not take into account the cultural context from which an individual comes (Dana, 2001).

Behavioral Observation and Self-Monitoring

Clinicians often use **behavioral observation** of clients to assess deficits in their skills or ways of handling situations. For example, a clinician might watch a child interact with other children to determine what situations seem to provoke the child to act aggressively. The clinician can then use information from behavioral observation to help the client learn new skills, stop negative habits, and understand and change the way he or she reacts to certain situations. A couple seeking marital therapy might be asked to discuss with each other a topic on which they disagree. The clinician observes this interaction, noting the specific ways that the couple handles conflict. For example, one member of the couple may lapse into statements that blame the other for problems in their marriage, escalating conflict to a boiling point.

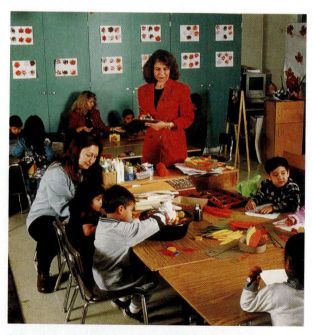

Behavioral observation is a good way to gather data, but these observations should be reliable.

The advantages of direct behavioral observation are that it does not rely on the clients' reporting and interpretation of their behaviors. Instead, the clinician sees just how skilled a client is or is not in handling important situations. One disadvantage is that different observers may draw different conclusions about an individual's skills. That is, direct behavioral observations may have low interrater reliability, especially when no standard means of making the observations are established. In addition, any individual rater may have difficulty catching everything that is happening in a situation, particularly when he or she is observing two or more people interacting.

It can be time-consuming and sometimes impossible for a clinician to observe a client's behaviors in key situations. If direct observation is not possible, the clinician may require client **self-monitoring**—that is, may ask the client to keep track of the number of times per day he or she engages in a specific behavior (e.g., smoking a cigarette) and the conditions under which this behavior happens. The following is an example (adapted from Thorpe & Olson, 1997, p. 149):

> Steve, a binge drinker, was asked to self-monitor his drinking behavior for two weeks, noting the situational context of urges to drink and his associated thoughts and feelings. These data revealed that Steve's drinking was completely confined to bar situations, where he drank in the company of friends. Gaining relief from stress was a recurring theme.

Self-monitoring is open to biases in what the client notices about his or her behavior and is willing to report. However, the client can gain valuable insight into the triggers of unwanted behaviors through self-monitoring, which can lead to changing these behaviors.

SUMMING UP

- Paper-and-pencil neuropsychological tests can help identify specific cognitive deficits that may be tied to brain damage.
- CT, PET, and MRI technologies are used to investigate the structural and functional differences between the brains of people with psychological disorders and those of people without disorders. We cannot yet use these technologies to diagnose specific psychological disorders in individual patients.
- Intelligence tests can indicate a client's general level of intellectual functioning in verbal and analytic tasks.

- Structured interviews provide a standardized way to assess, in an interview format, people's symptoms.
- Symptom questionnaires allow for the mass screening of large numbers of people to determine self-reported symptoms.
- Personality inventories assess stable personality characteristics.
- Projective tests are used to uncover unconscious conflicts and concerns but are open to interpretive biases.
- Behavioral observation and self-monitoring can help detect behavioral deficits and the environmental triggers for symptoms.

PROBLEMS IN ASSESSMENT

Some of the problems that arise in assessing clients' problems include the client's inability to provide information or resistance to providing information and the weaknesses of the tests used to gain information. In this section, we examine the challenges that arise in assessing certain groups of clients—children and people from cultures different from the assessor's culture.

Evaluating Children

Consider the following conversation between a mother and her 5-year-old son, Jonathon, who has been sent home from preschool for fighting with another child.

Mom: Jonathon, why did you hit that boy?
Jonathon: I dunno. I just did.
Mom: But I want to understand what happened. Did he do something that made you mad?
Jonathon: Yeah, I guess.
Mom: What did he do? Did he hit you?
Jonathon: Yeah.
Mom: Why did he hit you?
Jonathon: I dunno. He just did. Can I go now?
Mom: I need to know more about what happened.
Jonathon: [Silence]
Mom: Can you tell me more about what happened?
Jonathon: No. He just hit me and I just hit him. Can I go now?

Anyone who has tried to have a conversation with a distressed child about why he or she misbehaved has a sense of how difficult it can be to engage a child in a discussion about emotions or behaviors. Even when a child talks readily, his or

It can be difficult to talk with a distressed child or teenager who doesn't want to talk about his or her feelings.

her understanding of the causes of his or her behaviors or emotions may not be very well developed. Children, particularly preschool-age children, cannot describe their feelings, or the events associated with these feelings, as easily as adults can. Young children do not differentiate among different types of emotions, often just saying that they feel "bad," for example (Harter, 1983). When distressed, children may talk about physical aches and pains rather than the emotional pain they are feeling. Or a child might not verbalize that he or she is distressed and show this distress only in nonverbal behavior, such as making a sad face, withdrawing, or behaving aggressively. Children who have behavior problems, such as excessive distractibility or lack of control over their anger, may not believe that they have problems and thus may deny that anything is wrong (Kazdin, 1991).

These problems with children's self-reporting of emotional and behavior problems have led clinicians and researchers to rely on other people, usually adults in children's lives, to provide information about children's functioning. Parents are often the first source of information about a child's functioning. A clinician may interview a child's parents when the child is taken for treatment, asking the parents about changes in the child's behavior and corresponding events in the child's life. A researcher studying children's functioning may ask parents to complete questionnaires assessing the children's behavior in a variety of settings.

Because parents typically spend more time with their child than any other person does, they potentially have the most complete information about the child's functioning and a sense of how the child's behavior has or has not changed over time. Unfortunately, however, parents are not always accurate in their assessments of their children's functioning. One study found that the parents and children disagreed as to what prob-

lems had brought the child to a psychiatric clinic in 63 percent of the cases (Yeh & Weisz, 2001). Parents' perceptions of their children's well-being can be influenced by their own symptoms of psychopathology and their expectations for their children's behavior (Nock & Kazdin, 2001). Indeed, sometimes parents take children for assessment and treatment of psychological problems as a way of seeking treatment for themselves.

Parents may also be the source of a child's psychological problems and, as a result, unwilling to acknowledge or seek help for the child's problems. The most extreme example is parents who are physically or sexually abusing a child. These parents are unlikely to acknowledge the psychological or physical harm they are causing the child or to seek treatment for that harm. A less extreme example is parents who do not want to believe that an action they have taken, such as filing for a divorce or moving the family across the country, is the cause of the child's emotional or behavior problems. Again, such parents may be slow in taking a child who is distressed to a mental-health professional or in admitting to the child's problems when asked by a researcher.

Cultural norms for children's behaviors differ, and parents' expectations for their children and their tolerance of "deviant" behavior in children are affected by these norms. For example, Jamaican parents appear more tolerant than American parents of unusual behaviors in children, including both aggressive behavior and behavior indicating that a child is shy and inhibited. In turn, Jamaican parents have a higher threshold than American parents in terms of the appropriate time to take a child to a clinician (Lambert et al., 1992).

Teachers are another source of information about children's functioning. Teachers and other school personnel (such as guidance counselors and coaches) are often the first to recognize that a child has a problem and to initiate an intervention for the problem. Teachers' assessments of children, however, are often different from the assessments by other adults, including parents and trained clinicians (Weisz et al., 1995). Such discrepancies may arise because these other adults are providing invalid assessments of the children, whereas the teachers are providing valid assessments. The discrepancies may also arise because children function at different levels in different settings. At home a child may be well behaved, quiet, and withdrawn, but at school the same child may be impulsive, easily angered, and distractible. These differences in a child's behavior in different settings might make it seem that either a parent's report of the child's behavior or the teacher's report is invalid, when the truth is that the child simply acts differently, depending on the situation.

Evaluating Clients from Other Cultures

A number of challenges to assessment arise when there are significant cultural differences between the assessor and the person being assessed (Dana, 2000; Tsai et al., 2001; Tseng, 2001). Imagine having to obtain all the information needed to assess what is wrong with someone from a culture very different from your own. The first problem you may run into is that the client does not speak the same language you do or speaks your language only partially (and you do not speak his or hers at all). There is evidence that symptoms can go both underdiagnosed and overdiagnosed when the client and assessor do not speak the same language (Okazaki & Sue, 2003). Overdiagnosis often occurs because a client tries to describe his or her symptoms in the assessor's language, but the assessor interprets a client's slow and somewhat confused description of symptoms as indicating more pathology than is really present. Underdiagnosis can occur when the client cannot articulate complex emotions or strange perceptual experiences in the assessor's language and thus does not even try.

One solution is to find an interpreter to translate between the clinician and the client. Interpreters can be invaluable to good communication. However, interpreters who are not trained assessors themselves can misunderstand and mistranslate a clinician's questions and the client's answers, as in the following example (Marcos, 1979, p. 173):

Clinician to Spanish-speaking patient: "Do you feel sad or blue, do you feel that life is not worthwhile sometimes?"

Interpreter to patient: "The doctor wants to know if you feel sad and if you like your life."

Patient's response: "No, yes, I know that my children need me, I cannot give up, I prefer not to think about it."

Interpreter to clinician: "She says that no, she says that she loves her children and that her children need her."

In this case, the interpreter did not accurately reflect the client's answer to the clinician's question, giving the clinician a sense that the client was doing much better than the client reported she was. In addition, different people from the same country can speak different dialects of a language or can have different means of expressing feelings and attitudes. Mistranslation can occur when the interpreter does not speak the client's dialect or comes from a different subculture than the client.

Cultural differences between clients and clinicians can lead to misinterpretations of clients' problems.

Even when mistranslation is not a problem, some of the questions that the assessor asks or that appear on a test or questionnaire may be so culture-bound that they do not make sense to the client, or they can be interpreted by the client in ways the assessor did not anticipate. This can happen on even the most objective of tests. For example, several assessment tests ask whether a client ever believes that forces or powers other than herself control her behavior or if she ever hears voices talking in her head. According to Western conceptualizations, these are signs of psychosis, yet many cultures, such as the Xhosa of South Africa, believe that ancestors live in the same psychic world as living relatives and that ancestors speak to the living and advise them on their behavior (Gillis et al., 1982). Thus, members of this culture might answer yes to questions intended to assess psychotic thinking, when they are really reporting on the beliefs of their culture.

Cultural biases can arise when everyone is supposedly speaking the same language but each person comes from a unique cultural background. There is evidence that African Americans in the United States are overdiagnosed as suffering from schizophrenia (Neighbors et al., 2003). For example, African Americans are more likely than European Americans to be misdiagnosed as schizophrenic when their symptoms actually fit the diagnosis of bipolar disorder (Mukherjee et al., 1983). Some investigators believe that cultural differences in the presentation of symptoms play a role (Neighbors, 1984). African Americans may present more intense symptoms than European Americans, and these symptoms are then misunderstood by European American assessors as representing more severe psychopathology. Another possibility is that some European American assessors are too quick to diagnose severe psychopathology in African Americans because of negative stereotypes of them.

Finally, even when clinicians avoid all these biases, they are still left with the fact that people from other cultures often think about and talk about their psychological symptoms quite differently than do members of their own culture. We discuss several examples of cultural differences in the presentation of symptoms throughout this book. One of the most pervasive differences is in whether cultures experience and report psychological distress in emotional symptoms or in somatic (physical) symptoms. European Americans tend to view the body and mind separately, whereas many other cultures do not make sharp distinctions between the experiences of the body and the experiences of the mind (Okazaki & Sue, 2003). Following a psychologically distressing event, European Americans tend to report that they feel anxious or sad, but members of many other cultures report having physical aches and maladies. To conduct an accurate assessment, clinicians must know about cultural differences in the manifestation of disorders and in the presentation of symptoms, and they must use this information correctly in interpreting the symptoms that their clients report. Cultural differences are further complicated by the fact that not every member of a culture conforms to what is known about that culture. That is, within every culture, people differ in their acceptance of cultural norms for behavior.

SUMMING UP

- It is often difficult to obtain accurate information on children's problems because children are unable to report their thoughts and feelings. Parents and teachers may provide information about children, but they can be biased in their own assessments of children's symptoms and needs.

- When the clinician and client are from different cultures, language difficulties and cultural expectations can make assessment difficult. Interpreters can help in the assessment process but must be well trained in psychological assessment.

DIAGNOSIS

Recall that a *diagnosis* is a label attached to a set of symptoms that tend to occur together. This set of symptoms is referred to as a **syndrome.** In medical models of psychological disorders, a syndrome is thought to be the observable manifestation of an underlying biological disorder. Thus, if you have the symptoms that make up the syndrome *schizophrenia*, you are thought also to have a biological disorder called *schizophrenia*. As we have noted, however, there are no definitive biological tests for psychological disorders. For this reason, it is impossible to verify whether a given person *has* schizophrenia by giving him or her a biological test for schizophrenia.

We are left to observe humans and identify what symptoms typically occur together in them, and then we call those co-occurring symptoms a *syndrome*. Identifying naturally occurring syndromes is no easy task. Typically, several symptoms make up a syndrome, but people differ in which of these symptoms they experience most strongly. Think about the last time you were in a sad or depressed mood. Did you also feel tired and have trouble sleeping? Do you always feel tired and have trouble sleeping every time you are in a sad or depressed mood or just sometimes? Does everyone you know also experience fatigue and sleeplessness when in a sad mood? Or do some of them simply lose their appetite and their ability to concentrate?

Thus, syndromes are not lists of symptoms that all people have all of the time, if they have any of the symptoms at all. Rather, they are lists of symptoms that tend to co-occur within individuals. There may be overlap between the symptoms of one syndrome and the symptoms of another. Figure 4.6 shows the overlap in the symptoms that make up two common psychological disorders, major depressive disorder (see Chapter 9) and generalized anxiety disorder (see Chapter 7). Both disorders include the symptoms fatigue, sleep disturbances, and concentration problems. Each disorder has symptoms that are more specific to it, however.

For centuries, people have tried to organize the confusing array of psychological symptoms into a limited set of syndromes. This set of syndromes and the rules for determining whether an individual's symptoms are part of one of these syndromes constitute a **classification system.**

One of the first classification systems for psychological symptoms was proposed by Hippocrates in the fourth century B.C. Hippocrates divided all mental disorders into mania (states of abnormal excitement), melancholia (states of abnormal depression), paranoia, and epilepsy. Modern classification systems divide the world of psychological symptoms into a many more syndromes than did Hippocrates. Let's focus on the classification system most widely used in the United States. Then we will examine the dangers of *diagnosis*.

Diagnostic and Statistical Manual of Mental Disorders (DSM)

For more than 50 years, the official manual for diagnosing psychological disorders in the United States has been the ***Diagnostic and Statistical Manual of Mental Disorders* (DSM)** of the American Psychiatric Association. The first edition of the DSM was published in 1952. It outlined the diagnostic criteria for all the mental disorders recognized by the psychiatric community at the time. These criteria were somewhat vague descriptions heavily influenced by psychoanalytic theory. For example, the diagnosis of *anxiety neurosis* could have been manifested in a great variety of specific behavioral and emotional symptoms. The key to the diagnosis was whether the clinician inferred that unconscious conflicts were causing the client to experience anxiety. The second edition of the DSM (DSM-II), published in 1968, included some new disorders that had been recognized since the publication of the first edition but was not much different.

Because the descriptions of disorders were so abstract and theory based in the first and second editions of the DSM, the reliability of the diagnoses was low. For example, one study found that 4 experienced clinicians using the first edition of the DSM to diagnose 153 patients agreed on their diagnoses only 54 percent of the time (Beck et al., 1962). This low reliability eventually led psychiatrists and psychologists to call for a radically new system of diagnosing mental disorders.

DSM-III, DSM-IIIR, DSM-IV, and DSM-IV-TR

In response to the reliability problems of the first and second editions of the DSM, in 1980 the American Psychiatric Association published the third edition of the DSM, known as DSM-III. The third edition was followed by a revised third edition, known as DSM-IIIR, published in 1987, and a fourth edition, known as DSM-IV, originally published in 1994 and revised as DSM-IV-TR in 2000.

In the newer editions of the DSM, the developers replaced the vague descriptions of disorders with specific and concrete criteria for each disorder. These criteria are in the form of behaviors people must show and experiences or feelings they must report in order to be given a diagnosis. The developers tried to be as atheoretical and descriptive as possible in listing the criteria for each disorder. Good examples are the diagnostic criteria for panic disorder in the DSM-IV-TR, which are given

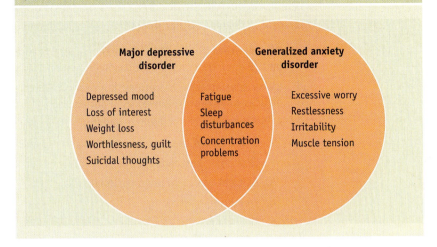

FIGURE 4.6 **Syndromes as Clusters of Symptoms.** Syndromes are clusters of symptoms that frequently co-occur. The symptoms of one syndrome, such as major depressive disorder, can overlap with the symptoms of another syndrome, such as generalized anxiety disorder.

in Table 4.4. As you can see, a person must have 4 of 13 possible symptoms in order to be given the diagnosis of panic disorder. These criteria reflect the fact that not all the symptoms of panic disorder will be present in every assessed individual.

Two other elements distinguish the DSM-III, DSM-IIIR, DSM-IV, and DSM-IV-TR from their predecessors. First, the later editions specify how long a person must show symptoms of the disorder to be given the diagnosis (see Table 4.4 on page 120, item B). Second, the criteria for most disorders require that the symptoms interfere with occupational or social functioning for the person to be diagnosed. This emphasis on symptoms that are long-lasting and severe reflects the consensus among psychiatrists and psychologists that abnormality should be defined in terms of the impact of behaviors on the individual's ability to function and on his or her sense of well-being (see Chapter 1).

Reliability of the DSM

Despite the use of explicit criteria for disorders, the reliability of many of the diagnoses listed in the DSM-III and DSM-IIIR was disappointing. On average, experienced clinicians agreed on their diagnoses using these manuals only about 70 percent of the time (Kirk & Kutchins, 1992). The reliability of some of the diagnoses, particularly the personality disorder diagnoses, was much lower.

Low reliability of diagnoses can be caused by many factors. Although the developers of the DSM-III and DSM-IIIR attempted to make the criteria for each disorder explicit, many of the criteria were still vague and required the clinician to make

TABLE 4.4	DSM-IV-TR

Diagnostic Criteria for Panic Disorder

These are the DSM-IV-TR criteria for a diagnosis of panic disorder. They specify core symptoms that must be present and several other symptoms, a certain number of which must be present, for the diagnosis.

A. At some time during the disturbance, one or more panic attacks have occurred that were (1) unexpected, and (2) not triggered by situations in which the person was the focus of another's attention.

B. Either four attacks, as defined in criterion A, have occurred within a four-week period, or one or more attacks have been followed by a period of at least a month of persistent fear of having another attack.

C. At least four of the following symptoms developed during at least one of the attacks:

   1. Shortness of breath or smothering sensations

   2. Dizziness, unsteady feelings, or faintness

   3. Palpitations or accelerated heart rate

   4. Trembling or shaking

   5. Sweating

   6. Choking

   7. Nausea or abdominal distress

   8. Depersonalization or derealization

   9. Numbness or tingling sensations

   0. Flushes or chills

  11. Chest pain or discomfort

  12. Fear of dying

  13. Fear of going crazy or doing something uncontrolled

D. During at least some of the attacks, at least four of the C symptoms developed suddenly and increased in intensity within 10 minutes of the beginning of the first C symptom.

E. It cannot be established that an organic factor initiated the disturbance, such as caffeine intoxication.

Source: Reprinted with permission from the *Diagnostic and Statistical Manual of Mental Disorders,* Fourth Edition, Text Revision. Copyright © 2000 American Psychiatric Association.

inferences about the client's symptoms or to rely on the client's willingness to report symptoms. For example, most of the symptoms of the mood disorders and anxiety disorders (e.g., sadness, apprehensiveness, hopelessness) are subjective experiences, and only clients can report whether they have these symptoms and how severe they are. To diagnose any of the personality disorders, the clinician must establish that the client has a lifelong history of specific dysfunctional behaviors or ways of relating to the world. Unless the clinician has known the client all his or her life, the clinician must rely on the client and the client's family to provide information about the client's history, and different sources of information can provide very different pictures of the client's functioning.

In an effort to increase the reliability of diagnoses in the DSM-IV, the task force that developed the DSM-IV conducted numerous field trials, in which the criteria for most of the diagnoses to be included in the DSM-IV were tested in clinical and research settings. In a field trial, testing determines if diagnostic criteria can be applied reliably and if they fit clients' experiences. As a result, the reliability of the DSM-IV diagnoses are higher than the reliability of the predecessors, although clearly they are not perfectly reliable (Widiger, 2002).

Multiaxial System

In a system introduced in the third edition of the DSM, the manual specifies five *axes,* or dimensions, along which a clinician evaluates a client's behavior (see Table 4.5). Only the first two axes list actual disorders and the criteria required for their diagnoses. The other three axes are meant to provide information on physical conditions that might

TABLE 4.5	DSM-IV-TR

The DSM-IV-TR has five axes, along which each client should be evaluated.

Axis I	Clinical disorders
Axis II	Personality disorders
	Mental retardation
Axis III	General medical conditions
Axis IV	Psychosocial and environmental problems
Axis V	Global assessment of functioning

Source: Reprinted with permission from the *Diagnostic and Statistical Manual of Mental Disorders,* Fourth Edition, Text Revision. Copyright © 2000 American Psychiatric Association.

TABLE 4.6	Disorders Listed on Axis I

These disorders, most of which we discuss in this book, represent conditions that typically cause people significant distress or impairment.

Disorders usually first diagnosed in infancy, childhood, or adolescence

- Attention-deficit disorder
- Hyperactivity
- Conduct and oppositional disorder
- Separation anxiety disorder
- Pervasive developmental disorder
- Learning disorders
- Feeding, tic, and elimination disorders

Delirium, dementia, and amnesic or other cognitive disorders

Substance-related disorders

Schizophrenia and other psychotic disorders

Mood disorders

Anxiety disorders

Somatoform disorders

Factitious disorders

Dissociative disorders

Sexual and gender identity disorders

Eating disorders

Sleep disorders

Adjustment disorders

Other conditions that may be a focus of clinical attention

Source: Reprinted with permission from the *Diagnostic and Statistical Manual of Mental Disorders,* Fourth Edition, Text Revision. Copyright © 2000 American Psychiatric Association.

be affecting the person's mental health (Axis III), psychosocial and environmental stressors in the person's life (Axis IV), and the degree of impairment in the person's mental health and functioning (Axis V). Let's take a look at these five axes, one by one, and then apply them to a case study.

On Axis I, a clinician lists any major disorders for which the person qualifies, with the exclusion of mental retardation and personality disorders (see Table 4.6). The clinician also notes whether these disorders are chronic or acute. *Chronic* disorders last for long periods of time. *Acute* disorders have a more recent and abrupt onset of severe symptoms.

On Axis II, the clinician lists mental retardation or any personality disorders for which the person qualifies (see Table 4.7 on page 122). Mental retardation is listed on Axis II instead of Axis I because it is a lifelong condition, whereas most of the disorders on Axis I tend to wax and wane across the life span. Similarly, a personality disorder is characterized by a chronic and pervasive pattern of dysfunctional behavior that the person has shown since at least adolescence. For example, a person with an antisocial personality disorder has a lifelong pattern of being abusive toward others and violating basic norms of social relationships.

On Axis III, the clinician notes any medical or physical diseases from which the person is suffering. These diseases may or may not be directly related to the psychological disorders from which the person is also suffering. For example, a person may have lung cancer, which has nothing to do with the fact that he or she also has schizophrenia. However, it is important for the clinician to know about any physical diseases for two reasons. First, these diseases could be related to the person's mental health.

For example, Michael J. Fox was abusing alcohol in part because he was distressed over his neurological symptoms. Also, a clinician must guard against any interactions between the drugs the patient is taking for the physical disease and the drugs the clinician will prescribe for the mental disorder.

On Axis IV, the clinician rates the severity of the psychosocial stressors the client is facing, such as those listed in Table 4.8 on page 122. Again, these psychosocial stressors may be related to the client's mental disorder, as causes or consequences. Or they may merely be coincidental with the disorder. However, it is important for the clinician to know what

TABLE 4.7   Disorders Listed on Axis II

These disorders typically represent lifelong disorders that pervade every area of the person's life.

Mental retardation
Personality disorders
- Paranoid personality disorder
- Schizoid personality disorder
- Schizotypal personality disorder
- Antisocial personality disorder
- Borderline personality disorder
- Histrionic personality disorder
- Narcissistic personalty disorder
- Avoidant personality disorder
- Dependent personality disorder
- Obsessive-compulsive personality disorder

Source: Reprinted with permission from the *Diagnostic and Statistical Manual of Mental Disorders,* Fourth Edition, Text Revision. Copyright © 2000 American Psychiatric Association.

TABLE 4.8   Axis IV Psychosocial and Environmental Problems to Note

These are some of the important problems people might face that should be noted on Axis IV.

Problems with primary support group
Problems related to the social environment
Education problems
Occupational problems
Housing problems
Economic problems
Problems with access to health care services
Problems related to interaction with the legal system and to crime

Source: Reprinted with permission from the *Diagnostic and Statistical Manual of Mental Disorders,* Fourth Edition, Text Revision. Copyright © 2000 American Psychiatric Association.

types of stressors the client is facing in order to provide a successful treatment plan.

On Axis V, the clinician rates the level at which the client is able to function in daily life on the scale given in Table 4.9. This helps the clinician quantify and communicate the degree to which the disorder is impairing the client's functioning.

Consider the following case study of a woman who is seeking help for some distressing symptoms. Think about how the clinician would incorporate all five of the DSM-IV-TR axes in making a diagnosis.

CASE STUDY

Jonelle is a 35-year-old African American woman who works as a manager of a large bank. She reports at least a dozen incidents from the past six weeks in which she suddenly felt her heart pounding, her pulse racing, and her breathing become rapid and shallow; she felt faint and dizzy; and she was sure that she was about to die. These attacks lasted for several minutes. Jonelle consulted with her physician, who conducted a complete physical checkup and concluded that there was no evidence of cardiac problems or other physical problems that could be causing her symptoms. Jonelle is becoming so afraid of having one of these attacks that it is interfering with her ability to do her job. She is constantly vigilant for signs of an impending attack, and this vigilance is interfering with her concentration and her ability to converse with customers and employees. When she feels an attack may be coming on, she rushes to the rest room or out to her car and remains there, often for over an hour, until she is convinced she will not have an attack. Jonelle reports that the attacks began shortly after her mother died of a heart attack. She and her mother were extremely close, and Jonelle still feels devastated by her loss.

In consulting the five axes, Jonelle's clinician would likely come up with the following list:

Axis I: Panic disorder

Axis II: None

Axis III: None

Axis IV: Psychosocial and environmental stressors: recent bereavement

Axis V: Global functioning: 60 (moderate difficulty)

TABLE 4.9   Axis V Global Assessment of Functioning Scale

This is the scale for indicating how well the person is functioning across the domains of his or her life.

Code

100	Superior functioning in a wide range of areas
90	Absent or minimal symptoms; good functioning in all areas
80	If symptoms present, they are transient and expectable reactions to psychosocial stressors; only slight impairment in functioning
70	Some mild symptoms or difficulty in functioning
60	Moderate symptoms and difficulty in functioning
50	Serious symptoms and difficulty in functioning
40	Some impairment in reality testing or communication or major impairment in several domains
30	Considerable delusions and hallucinations or serious impairment in communication and judgment
20	Some danger of hurting self or others or gross impairment in communication
10	Persistent danger of severely hurting self or others

Source: Reprinted with permission from the *Diagnostic and Statistical Manual of Mental Disorders*, Fourth Edition, Text Revision. Copyright © 2000 American Psychiatric Association.

What is particularly interesting is that this case study provides a good example of the importance of Axes III (physical conditions) and IV (psychosocial and environmental stressors). The clinician would certainly want to know if Jonelle had a physical condition that was creating her panic attacks before diagnosing them as a psychological disorder. Similarly, knowing that the panic attacks began to occur shortly after the death of Jonelle's mother from a heart attack gives the clinician a good clue about their possible psychological origins. It is fairly common for people suffering from panic attacks to have lost a close relative or friend to a heart attack or stroke and then to experience symptoms mimicking a heart attack or stroke.

Continuing Concerns About the DSM-IV-TR

Although the past two decades have seen substantial improvement in the scheme for diagnosing mental disorders now represented by the DSM-IV-TR, many researchers believe there is much more room for improvement (Widiger, 2002).

Where to Draw the Line   One of the greatest controversies concerns the assumption in the DSM-IV-TR that it is possible to define where normality ends and psychopathology begins. This is an old controversy, which we highlighted at the beginning of Chapter 1. It has gained momentum, however, based on recent research supporting the claim that

there is no clear demarcation between "normal" responses and "pathological" responses in many domains.

For example, the predictors of mild depression are highly similar to the predictors of severe depression (e.g., Judd et al., 1996; Klein, Lewinsohn, & Seeley, 1996). Another example, which we discuss in Chapter 12, concerns the personality disorders. According to the DSM-IV-TR, these disorders represent pathologies that are qualitatively different from normal human personality. Several researchers have argued, however, that it is more useful and valid to conceptualize personality disorders as extreme variants of normal personality traits (Widiger & Coker, 2003).

In sum, many believe that it would be better to have a diagnostic system that recognizes many disorders as the extremes of continuums, rather than implying that they are categories of thought, behavior, and mood that are qualitatively different from normal functioning.

Differentiating Mental Disorders from Each Other   Another ongoing problem with the DSM-IV-TR is the difficulty in differentiating the mental disorders from each other (Widiger & Clark, 2000). Most people who are diagnosed with one DSM-IV-TR disorder also meet the criteria for a diagnosis of at least one other disorder (Kessler et al., 1994). This overlap occurs, in part, because certain symptoms show up in the criteria for several disorders. For

TABLE 4.10 Culture-Bound Syndromes

Certain syndromes appear to occur only in some cultures.

Syndrome	Cultures Where Found	Symptoms
Amok	Malaysia, Laos, Philippines, Polynesia, Papua New Guinea, Puerto Rico	Brooding followed by an outburst of violent, aggressive, or homicidal behavior
Ataque de nervios	Latin American and Latin Mediterranean cultures	Uncontrollable shouting, attacks of crying, trembling, heat in the chest rising into the head, verbal or physical aggression, a sense of being out of control
Dhat	India, Sri Lanka, China	Severe anxiety about the discharge of semen, whitish discoloration of the urine, feelings of weakness and exhaustion
Ghost sickness	Native American cultures	Preoccupation with death and the deceased; manifested in dreams and in severe anxiety
Koro	Malaysia, China, Thailand	Episode of sudden and intense anxiety that the penis (or, in women, the vulva and nipples) will recede into the body and possibly cause death
Mal de ojo	Mediterranean cultures	Fitful sleep, crying without apparent cause, diarrhea, vomiting, fever
Shinjing shuairuo	China	Physical and mental fatigue, dizziness, headaches, other pains, concentration difficulties, sleep disturbance, memory loss
Susto	U.S. Latinos, Mexico, Central America, South America	Appetite disturbances, sleep problems, sadness, lack of motivation, low self-worth, aches and pains; follows a frightening experience
Taijin kyofusho	Japan	Intense fear that one's body displeases, embarrasses, or is offensive to other people

example, irritability or agitation can be part of depression, mania, anxiety, and schizophrenia; some of the personality disorders; and some of the childhood disorders.

We might want to "clean up" the diagnostic criteria for disorders to make them more distinct from each other, but recent research suggests that much of the overlap (or *comorbidity,*) among disorders represents how problems in mood, behavior, and thought co-occur in nature (Krueger, 2002). This finding suggests that there are some fundamental dimensions of functioning and that people vary in where they fall along these dimensions, with the extremes being "maladaptive" or "dysfunctional." Diagnostic systems of the future might specify how these dimensions come together to create different types of psychopathology, as well as how and why these psychopathologies are related to each other. This dimensional approach to diagnosis is very different from the DSM-IV-TR, which designates discrete categories of disorders, which supposedly represent distinct types of pathology.

Cultural Issues A third concern many researchers and clinicians have with the DSM-IV-TR is with its treatment of culture. We noted in Chapter 1 that different cultures have different ways of conceptualizing mental disorders. There are some disorders defined in one culture that do not seem to occur in other cultures. The developers of the DSM-IV-TR included an appendix that lists many of these culture-specific disorders and brief guidelines for gathering information during the assessment process regarding a client's culture. Table 4.10 describes some of these culture-bound syndromes.

The DSM-IV-TR also includes short descriptions of cultural variation in the presentation of the each of the major mental disorders recognized in the manual. For example, it notes differences among cultures in the content of delusions (beliefs out of touch with reality) in schizophrenia. Some critics do not believe it goes nearly far enough in recognizing cultural variation in what is healthy or unhealthy (see Kirmayer, 2001; Tsai, et al., 2001). Throughout the remainder of this book, we comment on cultural variations in the experience and prevalence of each of the disorders recognized by the DSM.

How the DSM Was Developed A final issue has to do with the process by which recent editions of the DSM were developed. The diagnostic criteria for the DSM-III, DSM-IIIR, DSM-IV, and DSM-IV-TR were derived by committees of experts on each of the disorders. These committees conducted reviews of the published literature to determine the evidence for and against the existence of the syndromes being considered for inclusion in the DSM. The developers of the DSM-IV and DSM-IV-TR also conducted field trials to determine the reliability and usefulness of criteria sets in clinical and research settings. Despite the efforts of the developers of the DSM to be objective and accurate in their definitions of disorders, these definitions represent a process of consensus building and compromise among experts with different opinions. The opportunity for political, cultural, and ideological influences on the establishment of the diagnostic criteria for disorders in such a process is considerable (Widiger, 2005).

One good example of the politicization of the DSM process was the debate over the addition of two personality disorders in an earlier version of the DSM, the DSM-IIIR. Some members of the committee revising the DSM-IIIR argued for the inclusion of a disorder that they felt was very common and was distinct from all the disorders that were already recognized in the DSM-IIIR. People with this proposed disorder had a lifelong practice of getting themselves into and remaining in situations in which other people used and abused them. The proponents of this disorder suggested that it be labeled *masochistic personality disorder.*

When news of this proposed disorder became public, some psychologists and psychiatrists strongly objected to it (Caplan & Gans, 1991). They argued that it would be used to pathologize women who, because of their lack of power and their social upbringing, found themselves trapped in abusive relationships, such as wife-battering relationships. They demanded a hearing before the committee to discuss the scientific merits of the masochistic personality disorder diagnosis and the social implications of including it as a disorder in the DSM. To address the concerns of the opponents of the masochistic personality disorder diagnosis, some of the committee members suggested adding yet another disorder, called sadistic personality disorder, which then would pathologize the behavior of the abusers in wife-battering relationships. Soon, however, several people pointed out that one of the political implications of this

"solution" was that some wife batterers could plead "not guilty" by reason of a mental disorder when charged with beating their wives.

In the end, the committee could not reach consensus and simply voted on what to do. The masochistic personality disorder was relabeled *self-defeating personality disorder,* and both it and sadistic personality disorder were included in an appendix of the DSM-IIIR as "Proposed Diagnostic Categories Needing Further Study." The further study of these diagnoses after the publication of the DSM-IIIR did not strongly support the reliability or validity of the diagnoses. For this reason, they were dropped altogether from the DSM-IV.

The Dangers of Diagnosis

One influential critic of psychiatry, Thomas Szasz, has argued that there are so many biases inherent in who is labeled as having a mental disorder that the entire system of diagnosis is corrupt and should be abandoned. Szasz (1961) believes that people in power use psychiatric diagnoses to label and dispose of people who do not "fit in." He suggests that mental disorders do not really exist and that people who seem to be suffering from mental disorders are suffering only from the oppression of a society that does not accept their alternative ways of behaving and looking at the world.

Even psychiatrists and psychologists who do not fully agree with Szasz's perspective on labeling recognize the great dangers of labeling behaviors or people as abnormal. A person labeled abnormal is treated differently by society, and this treatment can continue long after the person stops exhibiting behaviors labeled abnormal. This point was made in a classic study of the effects of labeling by psychologist David Rosenhan (1973). He and a group of seven colleagues had themselves admitted to 12 different mental hospitals by reporting to hospital staff that they had been hearing voices saying the words *empty, hollow,* and *thud.* When they were questioned by hospital personnel, they told the truth about every other aspect of their lives, including the fact that they had never experienced mental-health problems before. All eight were admitted to the hospital, all but one with a diagnosis of schizophrenia (see Chapter 11).

Once they were admitted to the hospital, the pseudopatients stopped reporting they were hearing voices and behaved as "normally" as they usually did. When asked how they were doing by hospital staff, the pseudopatients said they felt fine and they no longer heard voices. They cooperated in activities. The only thing they did differently than other patients was to write down their observations on notepads occasionally during the day.

Not one of the pseudopatients was ever detected as normal by the hospital staff, although they remained in the hospital for an average of 19 days each. Several of the other patients in the mental hospital detected the pseudopatients' normality, however, making comments such as "You're not crazy, you're a journalist, or a professor [referring to the continual note taking]. You're checking up on the hospital" (Rosenhan, 1973). When the pseudopatients were discharged, they were given the diagnosis of schizophrenia in remission, meaning that the physicians still believed they had schizophrenia but the symptoms had subsided for the time being.

Rosenhan concluded, "It is clear that we cannot distinguish the sane from the insane in psychiatric hospitals. The hospital itself imposes a special environment in which the meanings of behavior can be easily misunderstood" (Rosenhan, 1973, p. 257). He also noted that, if mental-health professionals cannot distinguish sanity from insanity, the dangers of diagnostic labels are even greater in the hands of nonprofessionals: "Such labels, conferred by mental health professionals, are as influential on the patient as they are on his relatives and friends, and it should not surprise anyone that the diagnosis acts on all of them as a self-fulfilling prophecy. Eventually, the patient himself accepts the diagnosis, with all of its surplus meanings and expectations, and behaves accordingly" (Rosenhan, 1973, pp. 253–254).

Not surprisingly, Rosenhan's study created a furor in the mental-health community. How could seasoned professionals have made such mistakes—admitting mentally healthy people to a psychiatric hospital on the basis of one symptom (hearing voices), not recognizing the pseudopatients' behavior as normal, and allowing them to be discharged carrying a diagnosis that suggests they still had schizophrenia? Even today, Rosenhan's study is held up as an example of the abuses of power—the power to label people as sane or insane, normal or abnormal, good or bad.

The label *abnormal* may be even more dangerous when it is applied to children, as is illustrated by one study of boys in grades 3 through 6 (Harris et al., 1992). Researchers paired boys who were the same age but who were previously unacquainted. In half of the pairs, one of the boys was told that his partner had a behavior problem that made him disruptive. In reality, only some of the boys labeled as having a behavior problem actually had a behavior problem. In the other half of the pairs, the boys were not told anything about each other, although some of the boys actually did have behavior problems. All the pairs worked together on a task while researchers videotaped their interaction. After the interaction, the boys were asked several questions about each other and about their enjoyment of the interaction.

The boys who had been told that their partners had a behavior problem were less friendly toward their partners during the task, talked with them less often, and were less involved in the interaction than were the boys who had been told nothing about their partners. In turn, the boys who had been labeled as having a behavior problem enjoyed the interaction less, took less credit for their performance on the task, and said their partners were less friendly toward them than did the boys who had not been labeled as having a behavior

Children who are labeled as "different" can be ostracized by other children.

problem. Most important, labeling a boy as having a behavior problem influenced his partner's behaviors toward him and his enjoyment of the task, regardless of whether he actually had a behavior problem. These results show that labeling a child as abnormal strongly affects other children's behaviors toward him or her, even when there is no reason for the child to be labeled as abnormal.

Should we avoid psychiatric diagnoses altogether? Probably not—despite the potential dangers of diagnostic systems, they serve vital functions. The primary role of diagnostic systems is to organize the confusing array of psychological systems in an agreed-upon manner. This facilitates communication from one clinician to another and across time.

For example, if Dr. Jones reads in a patient's history that he was diagnosed with schizophrenia according to the DSM-IV-TR, she knows what criteria were used to make that diagnosis and can compare the patient's diagnosis then with his symptoms now. Such information can assist Dr. Jones in making an accurate assessment of the patient's current symptoms and in determining the proper treatment for his symptoms. For example, if the patient's current symptoms also suggest schizophrenia and the patient responded to Drug X when he had schizophrenia a few years ago, this suggests that the patient might respond well to Drug X now.

Having a standard diagnostic system also greatly facilitates research on psychological disorders. For example, if a researcher at State University is using the DSM-IV-TR criteria to identify people with obsessive-compulsive disorder, and a researcher at Private University is using the same criteria for the same purpose, the two researchers will be better able to compare the results of their research than if they were using different criteria to diagnose obsessive-compulsive disorder. This can lead to faster advances in our understanding of the causes of and effective treatment for disorders.

SUMMING UP

- The *Diagnostic and Statistical Manual of Mental Disorders* (DSM) provides criteria for diagnosing all psychological disorders currently recognized in the United States.

- The first two editions of the DSM provided vague descriptions of disorders based on psychoanalytic theory; thus, the reliability of the diagnoses made according to these manuals was low. More recent editions of the DSM contain more specific, observable criteria that are not as strongly based on theory for the diagnosis of disorders.

- Five axes, or dimensions, of information are specified in determining a DSM diagnosis:

  - On Axis I, clinicians list all significant clinical syndromes.
  - On Axis II, clinicians indicate if the client is suffering from a personality disorder or mental retardation.
  - On Axis III, clinicians list the client's general medical condition.
  - On Axis IV, clinicians list the psychosocial and environmental problems the client is facing.
  - On Axis V, clinicians indicate the client's global level of functioning.

- Many critics of the DSM argue that it reflects Western, male perspectives on abnormality and pathologizes the behavior of women and other cultures. The DSM-IV-TR includes descriptions of culture-bound syndromes— groups of symptoms that seem to occur only in specific cultures.

- Diagnoses can be misapplied for political or social reasons. The negative social implications of having a psychiatric diagnosis can be great, but having a standard diagnostic system helps in treatment and research.

CHAPTER INTEGRATION

Assessment is inherently a process of biopsychosocial integration of pieces of information about an individual. After clinicians administer a battery of assessment tests to a client, they must then integrate the information from these tests to form a coherent picture of the client's strengths and weaknesses. This picture weaves together information on the client's biological functioning (major illnesses, possible genetic vulnerability to psychopathology), psychological functioning (personality, coping skills, intellectual strengths), and social functioning (support networks, work relationships, social skills), as depicted in Figure 4.7 on page 128. The clinician comments on ways in which strengths or deficits in one area are influencing functioning in another area.

For example, Michael J. Fox had increasing difficulties performing his job as his neurological symptoms got worse; as a result, he became anxious and depressed. To cope with that anxiety and depression, he began drinking heavily. This drinking caused conflict in his marriage, which then made him even more anxious and depressed.

The latest editions of the DSM were revised to reflect a more integrated and dynamic view of how biology, psychology, and social factors influence each other. The manual now includes information on cultural differences and similarities for each disorder and biological symptoms associated with

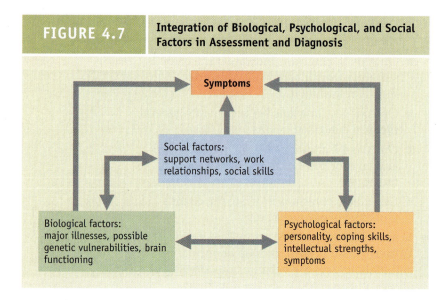

FIGURE 4.7   **Integration of Biological, Psychological, and Social Factors in Assessment and Diagnosis**

each disorder. In addition, the DSM-IV changed the label for an entire set of disorders to enhance an integrated biopsychosocial view of disorders. The editions prior to the DSM-IV included a category called *organic disorders*, which included delirium, dementia, and amnesia. These disorders were included in the DSM-IV, but not under the label *organic disorders*. The DSM-IV developers dropped the label *organic disorders* because labeling one category of disorders as organic implied that these disorders were caused by biological factors but that other disorders listed under other labels were not. This philosophy continued in the DSM-IV-TR.

Thus, both the assessment process and the DSM-IV-TR itself reflect a biopsychosocial approach to psychopathology. As we will see as we discuss each of the major disorders recognized by the DSM-IV-TR, this type of approach appears warranted.

Extraordinary People: Follow-Up

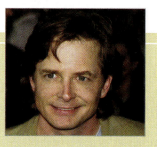

What happened to Michael J. Fox after receiving his diagnosis of early-onset Parkinson's disease? Over the 10 years following his diagnosis, Fox attempted to hide his Parkinson's symptoms from all but his family and closest friends and to drown out his own consciousness of it in alcohol abuse. His autobiography, *Lucky Man*, takes us through that decade as he hit bottom with alcohol, recovered with a great deal of help from his wife and a psychotherapist, and finally was forced to admit his Parkinson's publicly.

He fought against the Parkinson's even while sitting with his therapist. During their sessions, he sometimes punched his own tremoring left arm until he raised bruises on it. But they worked on his denial and, with time, Fox gained the courage to acknowledge his Parkinson's, at least to his wife, Tracy, and his young son, Sam. His family's loving acceptance of his disorder gave him the courage to accept it himself.

Fox's left-side tremors eventually became so severe that his arm flapped uncontrollably, shaking his entire body. It couldn't be controlled by drugs any longer, so in 1998 he underwent brain surgery to lesion a small part of his thalamus, which was responsible for the tremor. This was at the end of the second season of his hit sitcom, *Spin City*. The surgery was successful in eliminating the tremor in his left side, but that only made the emerging tremor in his right side more evident.

Fox revealed his Parkinson's disease publicly in November 1998 and was overwhelmed by the outpouring of support he received from the public. He continued on *Spin City* until May 2000, when he retired from acting to take care of himself and to advocate for Parkinson's patients and research. Fox's book, *Lucky Man*, is a story of personal triumph, not so much over the disease he has but over his former approach to life. He writes that, if he could trade the years since his diagnosis for "more years as the person [he] was before," he would not do so.

Chapter Summary

- Assessment is the process of gathering information about people's symptoms and the causes of the symptoms. A diagnosis is a label attached to symptoms that tend to co-occur with one another.

- During an assessment, a clinician gathers information about an individual's symptoms and history. This includes information about the nature, duration, and severity of the symptoms, as well as the person's ability to function, coping strategies, recent life events, history of psychological problems, and family history of psychological problems.

- An assessment also obtains information about physiological and neurophysiological functioning. This includes any medical conditions from which the client is suffering, any drugs the client is taking, and the client's cognitive and intellectual abilities.

- An assessment should also examine the client's social resources and cultural background.

- The validity and reliability of assessment tools are indices of their quality. Validity is the accuracy of a test in assessing what it is supposed to assess. Five types of validity are face validity, content validity, concurrent validity, predictive validity, and construct validity (review Figure 4.1). Reliability is the consistency of a test. The types of reliability are test-retest reliability, alternate form reliability, internal reliability, and interrater reliability (review Figure 4.2).

- Paper-and-pencil neuropsychological tests can assess specific cognitive deficits that may be related to brain damage in patients. Intelligence tests provide a more general measure of verbal and analytical skills.

- Brain-imaging techniques, such as CT, MRI, and PET scans, are being used primarily for research purposes but in the future may contribute to the assessment of psychological disorders.

- To assess emotional and behavioral functioning, clinicians use structured clinical interviews, symptom questionnaires, personality inventories, behavioral observation and self-monitoring, and projective tests. Each test has its advantages and disadvantages.

- During the assessment procedure, many problems and biases can be introduced. Clients may be resistant to being assessed and thus distort the information they provide. Clients may be too impaired by cognitive deficits, distress, or a lack of development of verbal skills to provide information.

Finally, many biases can arise when the clinician and client are from different cultures.

- A classification system is a set of definitions for syndromes and rules for determining when a person's symptoms are part of each syndrome. The predominant classification system for psychological problems in the United States is the *Diagnostic and Statistical Manual of Mental Disorders* (DSM) of the American Psychiatric Association. Its most recent editions provide specific criteria for diagnosing each of the recognized psychological disorders, as well as information on the course and prevalence of disorders.

- The explicit criteria in the DSM have increased the reliability of diagnoses, but there is still room for improvement.

- The DSM provides five axes, along which clinicians should assess client (review Table 4.5). On Axis I, major clinical syndromes are noted. Axis II contains diagnoses of mental retardation and personality disorders. On Axis III, the clinician notes any medical conditions that clients have. On Axis IV, psychosocial and environmental stressors are noted. On Axis V, clients' general levels of functioning are assessed.

- Critics have charged that the DSM reflects cultural and gender biases in its views of what is psychologically healthy and unhealthy. They also point to many dangers in labeling people with psychiatric disorders, including the danger of stigmatization. Diagnosis is important, however, to communication between clinicians and researchers. Only when a system of definitions of disorders is agreed upon can communication about disorders be improved.

MindMap CD-ROM

The following resources on your MindMap CD-ROM that came with this text will help you to master the content of this chapter and prepare for tests:

- Interactive Segment: DSM-IV-TR
- Chaper Timeline
- Chapter Quiz

Key Terms

assessment 100

diagnosis 100

differential diagnosis 102

acculturation 103

unstructured interview 104

structured interview 104

resistance 104

validity 104

face validity 105

content validity 106

concurrent validity 106

predictive validity 106

construct validity 106

reliability 106

test-retest reliability 106

alternate form reliability 107

internal reliability 107

interrater reliability 107

neuropsychological tests 107

computerized tomography (CT) 107

positron-emission tomography (PET) 108

magnetic resonance imaging (MRI) 108

intelligence tests 108

symptom questionnaire 110

personality inventories 110

projective test 112

behavioral observation 114

self-monitoring 115

syndrome 118

classification system 118

Diagnostic and Statistical Manual of Mental Disorders (DSM) 119

Chapter 5

Window of Opportunity
by Christian Pierre

The wish for healing has ever been the half of health.

—Seneca

Treatments for Abnormality <

Extraordinary People

- **The Inside Story on Coping with Schizophrenia**

Taking Psychology Personally

- **How to Look for a Therapist**

Biological Treatments

Biological therapies most often involve the prescription of drugs. Antipsychotic medications help reduce unreal perceptual experiences, unreal beliefs, and other symptoms of psychosis. Antidepressant drugs help reduce symptoms of depression. Lithium, anticonvulsants, and calcium channel blockers help reduce mania. Barbiturates and benzodiazepines help reduce anxiety. Herbal medicines have been popular for psychological symptoms, but their effectiveness has not been proven in many cases and they can be dangerous. Electroconvulsive therapy is used to treat severe depression. Psychosurgery is used in rare circumstances. A new therapy is repetitive transcranial magnetic stimulation (rTMS), in which magnets are used to stimulate specific areas of the brain.

Psychological Therapies

Psychodynamic therapies focus on uncovering and resolving unconscious conflicts. Humanistic therapy seeks to help people discover their greatest potentials and self-heal. Behavior therapies try to reshape people's maladaptive behaviors. Cognitive therapies attempt to change people's maladaptive ways of thinking.

Interpersonal and Social Approaches

Interpersonal therapy is a short-term version of psychodynamic therapies focused more on current relationships. Family systems therapists attempt to change maladaptive systems of behavior within families. Prevention programs attempt to stop or retard the development of disorders or to help people reduce the impact of disorders on their daily lives. Culturally specific therapies use the beliefs and rituals of a culture in treating clients of that culture.

Evaluating Treatments

It is very difficult to conduct good, ethical research on the effectiveness of treatments. Many studies have compared the various treatments for mental disorders. Some have found that they are equally effective; others have found that certain therapies are more effective than others for specific disorders. All successful psychotherapies share certain components, although their specific techniques may differ greatly. These common components include the development of a positive relationship with a therapist and the client's belief that the therapy will help.

Special Issues in Treating Children

A number of special issues arise in the treatment of children with psychological problems. First, therapies must be adapted so that they are appropriate to children's developmental levels. Second, there are concerns about the long-term effects of drug therapies on children's physical development. Third, it is often necessary to treat a child's family as well as the child. Fourth, children typically do not seek treatment for themselves but are taken to treatment by others.

Chapter Integration

A comprehensive, integrated approach to treatment for people with psychological problems involves teams of mental-health professionals with different specializations, including psychologists, psychiatrists, and social workers. In addition, some theorists are arguing for the integration of the elements of various therapies.

Extraordinary People

The Inside Story on Coping with Schizophrenia

"In lectures on antipsychotic drugs I want to tell the faculty and fellow students what it feels like to take these medicines and have to depend on them to function 'outside' and what it is like to be titrated as an individual to the proper medication and dosage and the problems involved. . . .

"During my first semester of pharmacy school I was on 2 mg of Haldol (haloperidol) and 2 mg of Cogentin (benztropine, an anticholinergic drug used to reduce such side effects of antipsychotic drugs, such as speech slurring, rigid neck muscles, and fixed gaze) h.s. (at bedtime) as prescribed for me after hospitalization the summer before entry to school. My condition improved psychologically and I seemed to be in remission until I entered school. I found I could neither read the board nor my notes; everything was blurred no matter where I sat. I called the psychiatrist who had prescribed the drugs and remembered his suggesting that I should take 2 more mg of Cogentin. . . . I complied and the next few days I not only had blurry vision, but I could not even see the lines on my notebook paper nor my writing—it was all one blur. In fact, the paper looked colorless. After 2 to 3 days of this, I called the physician back and told him I just could not take this medicine anymore, because I could not read or see with it. I could not even tell if I was taking notes on the lines. This side effect, he said, was as he expected; his recommendation now was to drop down to only 2 mg of Cogentin and switch from Haldol to Stelazine (trifluoperazine) 6 mg every day h.s. This was a compromise solution because, although I could now read and write, my schizophrenia was not so well-controlled. I wanted to drop out of school 3 weeks into the semester; I was afraid to go outside and felt as though I did not belong in pharmacy school or would not be able to overcome the stresses to be faced there. Fellow students were remarking to me that I seemed to be more impatient, hyperactive, and depressed. I also had problems with what a friend of mine called the 'Stelazine stroll'—akathesia (restlessness). I continued to go out of the city once a week to see my psychologist, who helped me with aspects of the pressures I could not face alone or with only the drugs. . . .

"In my first semester of my second year . . . I had just restarted Stelazine (after going off it by myself) at 8 mg h.s., an increased dose, and began having what I thought were seizures. In my classes I experienced an aura and then a wave hit me. I felt overstimulated and could hear a lecture but not process the information and take notes. My hand tremor was so bad during these episodes that I could not write. My psychologist suggested a consultation with the psychiatrist who had supervised my previous hospitalizations and prescribed the medications.

"Although the psychiatrist was hesitant to give me the label for what was happening, I insisted, and he said it was 'transient psychotic episodes.' The problem with this development was that it began after I had already been taking an increased amount of the medication. Where could we go from here? The psychiatrist recommended titration, increasing the dose of Stelazine. However, it didn't work. He then suggested taking Stelazine along with another antipsychotic drug with more milligram potency (Navane [thiothixene] 5 mg h.s.), but I was still having acute psychotic episodes in my classes. I had taken to sitting in the back of the classroom, although I could not see the board, because I needed to be able to leave the room when this occurred. When I got up in the morning, I could predict that the episodes would occur and where—I had a prodrome (a premonitory symptom). There were many frantic long distance calls to my psychologist after these episodes. I had to tell someone who could help me with what was happening to me. I, at this point, felt scared enough that never again would I have a compliance problem. I didn't want to lose all I had worked for in pharmacy school. I noticed the episodes were worse when emotionally volatile material was discussed in classes, such as antipsychotic agents, characteristics of schizophrenia, depression—all problems I had to cope with daily and that remained unresolved for me. . . .

"As a consequence of the psychotic episodes and occasionally having to leave the classroom, I missed a lot of notes in my classes. All this work had to be made up. This increased the pressure I was under, which in turn worsened the schizophrenic symptoms and almost forced me into hospitalization. I did not
(continued)

want to drop out of school or receive too many incomplete grades, which would have been the result of 4 to 8 weeks of hospitalization to get properly titrated on the medication and to decrease disease symptoms. However, most of my instructors had rigid rules about missing exams and taking makeup exams. To reduce the pressure, I told the professor with whom I was doing independent study that for medical reasons I would not be able to finish the paper due in that course. I decided to tell him why and he allowed me the Incomplete grade without requiring a medical letter on file, saving me the possible consequences of having this information on written record. And, most importantly, he did not treat me differently as a result of knowing. This reduced my stress and gave me time to make up work and take my final examinations. It also allowed me to work on my independent study paper during vacation and to do a good job on it while I was finally beginning to get a positive response to the medication.

"When classes started, I still felt overstimulated and again had prodromes of psychotic episodes. I could not process information when people were talking; everything just seemed like noise. I was now on 5 mg of Navane b.i.d. (twice daily) and 2 mg

of Cogentin h.s. I got enough courage to sit in front of the class again, but I was very fearful. My psychologist explained that I had begun to associate that classroom with these episodes and that extreme anxiety was causing dissociation reactions in me: I felt I was outside my body; I was watching everything. I wanted an antianxiety agent to get rid of these feelings and that constant impending feeling that a psychotic episode would begin. The psychiatrist prescribed 5 mg of Valium (diazepam) in the morning and at bedtime when necessary. I took it only in the morning when I could not restructure my environment and situation to reduce the anxiety. For the first several weeks I was falling asleep in my first class and had double vision because I could not keep my eyes open. Finally, I became tolerant to the sedative effect. So this is the answer right now for me: a neuroleptic, an antianxiety agent, an anti-Parkinsonian agent, and intense long-term psychotherapy with my psychologist. And I still look around at my fellow students and say to myself, 'They do it without medicine, or doctors, or going to a psychiatric ward,' but I needed all these things to cope with the pressure and stress of pharmacy school and life." (Anonymous, 1983, pp. 152–155)

When we read about the treatments for mental disorders, particularly the biological treatments, they can seem very straightforward. You determine what is wrong with a person, prescribe a medication and/or a psychotherapy, administer it competently, and the person gets better. As this young pharmacy student's story illustrates, however, it often isn't that straightforward.

As was the case with this pharmacy student, multiple caregivers are often involved in the treatment of any one individual. The system of mental-health services has four major sectors. The *specialty mental-health* sector includes psychiatrists, psychologists, psychiatric nurses, and psychiatric social workers who are trained specifically to treat people with mental disorders. The *general medical* or *primary care* sector includes health care professionals, such as internists, pediatricians, and nurse practitioners, who may not be specifically trained in mental-health treatment, but are often the initial point of contact, or the only source of mental-health

services, for people with mental-health problems. The *human services* sector includes social services, school-based counseling services, residential rehabilitation services, criminal justice services, and religious professional counselors. Finally, the *voluntary support network* sector, which consists of self-help groups such as Alcoholics Anonymous, is a growing component of the mental-health treatment system. In all, about 15 percent of adults in the United States use one or more of these services in any given year (U.S. Department of Health and Human Services, 1999).

Unfortunately, however, most people who might benefit from treatment are getting no treatment at all (see Figure 5.1 on page 136). About 28 percent of the U.S. population has a diagnosable mental-health problem, but only 8 percent of the population receives professional treatment in a given year (U.S. Department of Health and Human Services, 1999). Although they may eventually seek out treatment, they typically delay telling a health

FIGURE 5.1

Mental-Health Care. The majority of people with diagnosable mental disorders do not seek treatment in a given year, whereas about half of people who do seek treatment do not have a diagnosis of a mental disorder.

28%
Percent of population with mental/addictive disorders (in one year)

15%
Percent of population receiving mental-health services (in one year)

20%
Diagnosis and no treatment

8%
Diagnosis and treatment

7%
Treatment and no diagnosis

care professional about their psychological symptoms for several years after these symptoms first appear (Kessler, Olfson, & Berglund, 1998). Almost half of the people who receive treatment in any given year don't have symptoms that would qualify for a diagnosis.

What does mental-health treatment consist of? That depends greatly on the theoretical approach of the person providing the treatment. Proponents of biological theories of mental disorders most often prescribe *medication,* although several other types of biological treatments are discussed in this chapter and throughout this book. Proponents of psychological and some social approaches to abnormality most often prescribe **psychotherapy.** There are many forms of psychotherapy, but most involve a therapist (psychiatrist, psychologist, clinical social worker, or marriage or family counselor) talking with the person suffering from the disorder (typically called a patient or client) about his or her symptoms and what is contributing to these symptoms. The specific topic of these conversations depends on the therapist's theoretical approach. Many of the psychotherapies have been adapted for work with couples or families, or with groups of people who have something in common, usually the experience of specific symptoms or disorders.

Both drug therapies and psychotherapy have proven effective in the treatment of many disorders. Drugs and psychotherapy may work on different aspects of a disorder, and they are increasingly being used together in an integrated approach to disorders, as we discuss in the Chapter Integration at the end of this chapter.

BIOLOGICAL TREATMENTS

Most of the biological treatments for abnormality are drug therapies (see Table 5.1). These drugs are thought to relieve psychological symptoms by correcting imbalances of neurotransmitters in the brain. They may also compensate for structural deficits in the brain or the effects of genetic abnormalities. Other biologically based therapies include electroconvulsive therapy, psychosurgery, and transcranial magnetic stimulation. Some people turn to herbal remedies for psychological problems, and we will discuss these here.

Drug Therapies

You might imagine that most drugs used to treat psychopathology were discovered through a perfectly rational and systematic application of basic science. A clever scientist did the basic research to discover which systems of the body and brain are responsible for a particular form of psychopathology and then, using his or her understanding of basic biology, developed a drug that would reverse the bodily processes known to cause the disorder. In truth, most of the drugs now used to treat mental disorders were discovered in roundabout ways, typically by accident.

Antipsychotic Drugs

The beginning of modern drug treatment is generally thought to have occurred with the discovery of **chlorpromazine,** a drug now used to treat the symptoms of psychosis (Valenstein, 1998). *Psychosis involves the loss of touch with reality, hallucinations (unreal perceptual experiences), and delusions (fantastic, unrealistic beliefs).* The pharmacy student at the beginning of this chapter was suffering from psychotic symptoms.

Chlorpromazine belongs to a group of chemical compounds called **phenothiazines.** While working to produce synthetic dyes in 1883, August Bernthsen, a research chemist in Heidelberg, synthesized a phenothiazine, which has a chemical structure very similar to that of synthetic violet and blue dye products. Later, it was discovered that phenothiazine compounds have a number of biological effects on humans. They can act as antihistamines and thus were initially thought useful in the treatment of allergies.

In the 1940s, researchers in a pharmaceutical company in Paris learned that phenothiazines also result in a decrease in muscle tone, the reduction of nausea, and in some cases either sedation or euphoria. At first, these effects were considered unwanted side effects. Some physicians began to use phenoth-

TABLE 5.1 Drug Therapies for Mental Disorders

These are the major types of drugs used to treat several kinds of mental disorders.

Type of Drug	Purpose	Examples
Antipsychotic drugs	Reduce symptoms of psychosis (loss of reality testing, hallucinations, delusions)	Thorazine (a phenothiazine) Haldol (a butyrophenone) Clozaril (an atypical antipsychotic)
Antidepressant drugs	Reduce symptoms of depression (sadness, loss of appetite, sleep disturbances)	Parnate (an MAO inhibitor) Elavil (a tricyclic) Prozac (a selective serotonin reuptake inhibitor)
Lithium	Reduce symptoms of mania (agitation, excitement, grandiosity)	Lithobid Cibalith-S
Antianxiety drugs	Reduce symptoms of anxiety (fearfulness, worry, tension)	Nembutal (a barbiturate) Valium (a benzodiazepine)

iazines to calm agitated patients, however, and to reduce tremors in patients with Parkinson's disease.

Shortly after World War II, French surgeon Henri Laborit became interested in using phenothiazines as a presurgery drug to reduce postsurgical shock, a neuroendocrine response to stress that can be fatal. Laborit found that the administration of a phenothiazine called promethazine creates a "euphoric quietude. . . . Patients are calm and somnolent, with a relaxed and detached expression" (Swazey, 1974, p. 79). Pain was reduced so greatly in some patients that they did not require morphine. Laborit went back to the pharmaceutical company that had produced promethazine to ask for a phenothiazine with even greater central nervous system effects. The company suggested he try a compound it had recently synthesized, which was eventually called chlorpromazine.

In the early 1950s, Laborit and a number of other researchers were investigating the effects of chlorpromazine on psychological symptoms. Reports were published that chlorpromazine reduces the hallucinations and delusions of some psychiatric patients. Particularly influential were reports in 1952 by French psychiatrists Jean Delay and Pierre Deniker that chlorpromazine reduces agitation, excitation, confusion, and paranoia in psychotic patients (Delay, Deniker, & Harl, 1952; Valenstein, 1998). Delay labeled chlorpromazine a **neuroleptic,** implying that this drug depresses the activity of the nervous system. In 1953, Delay and Deniker in France, and other physicians in Switzerland and Great Britain, were reporting that chlorpromazine was having such remarkable effects on

psychotic patients that it was transforming psychiatric hospitals.

Soon, chlorpromazine was introduced to North American psychiatrists. American drug company Smith Kline & French began marketing the drug for use in psychiatry in 1954 under the name Thorazine. At that time, there was little regulation of the prescription drug market, compared with today's standards, so Thorazine was introduced before much research had been done on its effectiveness or side effects.

Word spread quickly about the remarkable effects of Thorazine on patients with psychotic disorders, however. Within a year of the introduction of Thorazine on the market, more than 2 million prescriptions for the drug were written in the United States. By 1965, chlorpromazine had been the subject of about 10,000 publications worldwide (Valenstein, 1998). By 1970, Smith Kline & French's Thorazine sales had totaled over $116 million.

The success of chlorpromazine led other drug companies to develop and patent similar drugs. Some of the more successful phenothiazines that were developed were thioridazine (Mellaril) and trifluoperazine (Stelazine). During the 1950s, researcher Paul Janssen discovered another class of drugs that can reduce psychotic symptoms, **butyrophenone.** The first drug in this class to be marketed was haloperidol (Haldol), in 1957, and it proved at least as effective as chlorpromazine.

Unfortunately, both the phenothiazines and butyrophenone also produce a number of dangerous side effects. These side effects are detailed in Chapter 11 and include severe sedation, visual disturbances, and tardive dyskinesia, a neurological disorder characterized by involuntary movements of the tongue, face, mouth, or jaw. The pharmacy student we met at the beginning of this chapter was suffering several of these side effects. Fortunately, new drugs, such as clozapine and risperidone, which are part of a class referred to as the *atypical antipsychotics*, seem to be effective in treating psychosis without inducing some of the serious side effects of the phenothiazines and butyrophenone (see Chapter 11).

How do these drugs work to reduce psychotic symptoms? The answer to this question is less clear than you might think. Indeed, their use became widespread before researchers had any evidence of how they work (Valenstein, 1998). The leading theories today, however, suggest that these drugs reduce levels of the neurotransmitter dopamine or influence receptors for dopamine in the brain.

Antipsychotic drugs—drugs that relieve the symptoms of psychosis—led to a revolution in the treatment and lives of people with psychosis, who had been locked away in mental hospitals and state institutions, perhaps for life, often completely out of touch. These are the major types of drugs used to treat several kinds of mental disorders.

Antidepressant Drugs

The discovery of drugs to treat the symptoms of depression—sadness, low motivation, and sleep and appetite disturbances—was just as fortuitous as the discovery of the antipsychotic drugs (Valenstein, 1998). One of the fuels used by the Germans for the V-2 rocket during World War II was hydrazine. When the war ended, drug companies acquired much of the leftover hydrazine, believing that modifications of the chemical could make it useful for medical purposes. In 1951, researchers in the Hoffman-LaRoche pharmaceutical company in New Jersey found that two hydrazine compounds, isoniazid and iproniazid, were effective in treating tuberculosis. One of the side effects of these drugs, however, seemed to be euphoria—the tuberculosis patients were dancing with joy in the hospital corridors after treatment with these drugs.

French psychiatrist Jean Delay, who also played a role in the discovery of chlorpromazine for psychiatric uses, suspected that isoniazid and iproniazid could be useful as **antidepressants**—drugs to treat the symptoms of depression. The initial tests done by him and other physicians, however, proved unsuccessful, probably because they did not allow enough time for the drugs to have any effect. Several years passed before enough research was done to establish that isoniazid and iproniazid truly do have antidepressant effects. These drugs are part of

a class of drugs now called the **monoamine oxidase inhibitors,** or **MAOIs.**

Some trade names of the MAOIs are Nardil and Parnate. These drugs inhibit the enzyme monoamine oxidase in the brain, which results in higher levels of a number of neurotransmitters, such as norepinephrine. Unfortunately, the MAOIs have potentially dangerous side effects, including throbbing headaches, jaundice, and a precipitous rise in blood pressure, especially when mixed with certain foods (see Chapter 9). Because of these side effects, other drugs are used more often.

Until the 1980s, the antidepressants most often used were **tricyclic antidepressants.** In the 1950s, Swiss psychiatrist Roland Kuhn was trying different drugs in an attempt to improve sleep in mental patients. One drug he tried was imipramine, which has a chemical structure similar to that of a phenothiazine. Imipramine did not induce sleep but, rather, energized patients and elevated their moods. Kuhn treated more than 500 psychiatric patients with imipramine over the next three years and reported that imipramine is not simply a stimulant but a true antidepressant:

> The patients get up in the morning of their own accord, they speak louder and more rapidly, their facial expression becomes more vivacious. They commence some activity on their own, again seeking contact with other people, they begin to entertain themselves, take part in games, become more cheerful and are once again able to laugh. . . . The patients express themselves as feeling much better, fatigue disappears, the feeling of heaviness in the limbs vanishes, and the sense of oppression in the chest gives way to a feeling of relief. The general inhibition, which led to retardation, subsides. They declare that they are now able to follow other persons' train of thought, and that once more new thoughts occur to them, whereas previously they were continually tortured by the same fixed idea. . . . Instead of being concerned about imagined or real guilt in their past, they become occupied with plans concerning their own future. Actual delusions of guilt, or loss, or hypochondriacal delusions become less evident. The patients declare "I don't think of it anymore" or "the thought doesn't enter my head now." Suicidal tendencies also diminish, become more controllable or disappear altogether. . . . Not infrequently the cure is complete, sufferers and their relatives confirming the fact that

they had not been so well for a long time. (Kuhn, 1958, pp. 459–460)

The Geigy pharmaceutical company started marketing imipramine (Tofranil) in 1958. Other tricyclic antidepressants, such as Elavil and Anafranil, were soon introduced by other pharmaceutical companies. By 1980, approximately 10 million prescriptions for antidepressant drugs were being written annually in the United States, and most of these were for tricyclic antidepressants (Valenstein, 1998). Tricyclic antidepressants quickly became favored over MAOIs because they seemed more effective and had fewer dangerous side effects. Tricyclics do have their side effects, however, including sedation, dry mouth, and blurred vision.

The tricyclic antidepressants were thought to work by inhibiting the reuptake of the neurotransmitters norepinephrine, serotonin, and perhaps dopamine in the brain. Because they have effects on so many neurotransmitter systems, the tricyclic antidepressants are sometimes referred to as "dirty drugs." Researchers thought that, if they could synthesize drugs that had more specific effects on individual neurotransmitter systems, these drugs could be more effective in treating depression. By the 1980s, the technology for synthesizing drugs that bind to specific neurotransmitter subtypes had advanced enough to make it possible to test many new drugs.

In 1986, pharmaceutical company Eli Lilly introduced the drug fluoxetine, under the trade name Prozac, as an antidepressant. Prozac is one of the **selective serotonin reuptake inhibitors (SSRIs),** which means that it is thought to act more selectively on serotonin receptors than do the tricyclic antidepressants. Some psychiatrists have touted Prozac as the "SCUD missile of psychopharmacology," able to zero in on its target with amazing precision (Slater, 1998, p. 10). Other SSRIs, including Zoloft and Paxil, were soon introduced by other drug companies. In the 12 months between August 1996 and August 1997, more than 3.5 million prescriptions were written for SSRIs. Lilly's sales of Prozac alone were over $1.8 billion, and Pfizer's sales of Zoloft were almost $1.2 billion. Today, more than 40 million people worldwide have taken Prozac, and many more millions have taken one of the other SSRIs.

Why did the SSRIs become so popular so fast? It is not because they are more effective than the tricyclic antidepressants. Most studies comparing the two classes of drugs find they are equally effective in treating depression (Thase, Jindal, & Howland, 2002). One reason the SSRIs became so popular is that many people can tolerate the side effects of the

Media stories about so-called "wonder drugs," including Prozac, touted their ability to alleviate a wide range of problems beyond the treatment of serious psychological disorders.

SSRIs better than the side effects of the tricyclics. Some of the common side effects of the SSRIs are nausea, diarrhea, headache, tremor, daytime sedation, failure to achieve orgasm, nervousness, and insomnia. Another reason for the rapid proliferation of the SSRIs is that they seem useful in the treatment of a number of other psychological problems in addition to depression, including anxiety, poor impulse control, and eating disorders.

Finally, the impact of stories in the media on the SSRIs cannot be underestimated. These drugs enjoyed unprecedented coverage as "wonder drugs" in their early days, and several popular books have promoted these drugs as the cures not only for depression but also for lack of self-confidence, shyness, impulsiveness, and a host of other problems.

Some of the newest antidepressant drugs are designed to target both serotonin and norepinephrine; they include venlafaxine (Effexor) and mirtazapine (Remeron). In addition, people with depression are often given combinations of antidepressant drugs and lithium or an antianxiety drug.

Lithium and Other Mood Stabilizers

Lithium is a metallic element that is present in the sea, in natural springs, and in animal and plant tissue. It has been used to treat a number of medical disorders, with weak results. In the middle of the nineteenth century, it was widely used to treat rheumatism and gout, and several physicians thought there was a relationship between these disorders and mania—a condition in which people experience agitated, excited, and grandiose ideas. Indeed, mania was often referred to as "brain gout." In 1871, William Hammand, a neurologist at Bellevue Hospital in New York and a former surgeon general of the United States, recommended lithium as a treatment for mania. His recommendation got little attention, however.

The introduction of lithium as a treatment followed a rather unusual path. During World War II, Australian physician John Cade was captured by the Japanese and spent three and a half years in a military prison. He observed the onset of mania in some of his fellow prisoners and wondered if it was caused by an excessive accumulation of a metabolite that had a toxic effect on the brain (Valenstein, 1998). Cade did not know what the metabolite was, but he pursued this idea vigorously when he was released after the war. His research subjects were guinea pigs. A series of unusual experiments led Cade to discover, quite accidentally, that lithium had a powerful calming effect on the guinea pigs: The animals remained fully awake, but after about two hours they became so calm that they lost their "startle-reaction" and frantic righting-reflex when placed on their backs. It was this observation that prompted the trial of lithium salts in that overexcitable state of mania (Cade, 1949, pp. 70–71).

Cade proceeded to experiment on himself to determine the safety of lithium. After being convinced of its safety, he tried a lithium regimen on 19 patients, 10 of whom had frequent bouts of mania. He published his report of the successful treatment of these patients with lithium in 1949. Unfortunately, however, this was published in an Australian medical journal not widely read outside of Australia, and Cade was an unknown psychiatrist with no research training working in a small hospital. Thus, Cade's work went unnoticed for the most part.

It wasn't until a Danish psychiatrist, Mogens Schou, published a series of studies on the effectiveness of lithium in 1970 that lithium was legitimized as a treatment for mania. Schou had come across Cade's report in the early 1950s and had begun experimenting with lithium in a more carefully controlled research procedure. His initial findings had shown lithium to be effective in treating mania. But lithium is a dangerous substance and can have many severe side effects, even death. American and European psychiatrists had been reluctant to accept lithium because of its toxicity. Schou's 1970 paper had such convincing evidence of the effectiveness of lithium, however, that psychiatrists were forced to consider using it, especially because there were no effective alternatives in the treatment of mania.

Lithium continues to be widely used in the treatment of mania today. Other drugs, known as the **anticonvulsants,** and **calcium channel blockers** are also being used in the treatment of mania (see Chapter 9). Fortunately, these newer drugs appear to have fewer side effects than lithium.

Antianxiety Drugs

Anxiety and insomnia are the symptoms for which drugs are most often prescribed. The first group of **antianxiety drugs** were the **barbiturates,** introduced at the beginning of the twentieth century. Barbiturates suppress the central nervous system, decreasing the activity of a variety of types of neurons. Although these drugs are effective for inducing relaxation and sleep, they are quite addictive, and withdrawal from them can cause life-threatening symptoms, such as increased heart rate, delirium, and convulsions.

The other major class of anxiety-reducing drugs, the **benzodiazepines,** was discovered in the 1940s, but these drugs were not widely available until the 1960s, when drug companies began selling them under names such as Librium, Valium, and Serax. These drugs appear to reduce the symptoms of anxiety without interfering substantially with an individual's ability to function in daily life. The most frequent use of benzodiazepines, accurately referred to as minor tranquilizers, is as sleeping pills. As many as 70 million prescriptions are written each year in the United States for benzodiazepines. The pharmacy student featured in *Extraordinary People* was using benzodiazepines to quell her symptoms of anxiety.

Unfortunately, benzodiazepines are also highly addictive, and up to 80 percent of the people who take them for six weeks or more show withdrawal symptoms, including heart rate acceleration, irritability, and profuse sweating. The active metabolites of benzodiazepines remain in the body for days and can create toxic interaction effects with alcohol and other drugs.

Herbal Medicines

You have probably heard of St. John's wort (technically known as *Hypericum perforatum*). This little roadside weed became big news in the mid-1990s, when the media became aware of studies in Europe suggesting that St. John's wort is an effective treatment for depression. Psychiatrist Harold Bloomfield published the book *Hypericum & Depression,* which reviewed the European studies and concluded that St. John's wort is a reasonable alternative to medications in the treatment of mild or moderate depression. Since then, sales of St. John's wort, which can be bought without prescription in

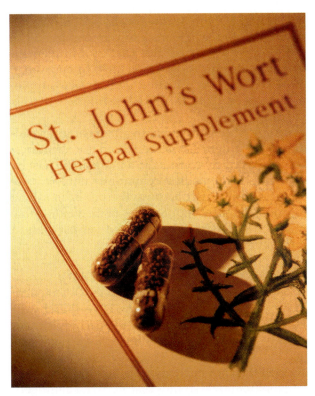

St. John's Wort became a popular treatment for depression in the 1990s, but studies have raised questions about its safety and efficacy.

most pharmacies, have soared, hitting $48 million in the United States in 1997.

American researchers jumped to action to test whether St. John's wort is effective for depression on this side of the ocean. They actually had serious questions about how depression was defined in many of the European studies and differences between the people studied in Europe and those who might seek out St. John's wort in the United States. The National Institutes of Health initiated a large study in America comparing St. John's wort with a placebo in treating serious depression (Hypericum Depression Trial Study Group, 2002). St. John's wort did not fare well in this study—it proved no more effective than placebo on several measures of depression (but, then, neither did the selective serotonin reuptake inhibitor it was compared with).

One reason people had hoped that St. John's wort would prove helpful for depression is that its side effects tend to be less severe than the side effects of antidepressant drugs. One study found that less than 3 percent of the people taking St. John's wort experienced any side effects (Woelk, Burkard, & Grunwald, 1994). The most common side effects are gastrointestinal irritation, allergic reactions, dry mouth, sedation, headache, and increased sensitivity to light.

In the past few years, however, the safety of St. John's wort has been seriously questioned by evidence that it can interact with a number of medications people take for medical ailments (Zhou et al., 2004). For example, there are several reports that St. John's wort interferes with the efficacy of drugs used to treat patients who have recently received organ transplants, resulting in the rejection of the new organs. It may also interfere with drugs used to treat heart disease, seizures, and certain cancers. Thus, there are increasing concerns about the widespread use of St. John's wort, because people may be exposing themselves to potential drug-drug interactions with little reason for hope that they will gain relief from depressive symptoms.

What about other "natural" remedies for psychological problems? These have been referred to as phytomedicines, and their use dates back to the beginning of civilization. For example, *Rauwolfia serpentina* was used at least 3,000 years ago by Hindu Ayurvedic healers as a treatment for insanity. In the twentieth century, it was "rediscovered," and chemical analysis of the root extracts of *R. serpentina* led to the discovery of dopamine and its role in Parkinson's disease and schizophrenia.

Phytomedicines are a regular part of modern mainstream medicine in Asia and parts of Western Europe, particularly Germany (Beaubrun & Gray, 2000). Herbal products account for over $4 billion in sales in the United States annually, with as many as 40 percent of Americans reporting they use herbal products at least occasionally (Astin, 1998; Brevoort, 1998). These products are typically sold as foods. They can range from simple and mild products, such as chamomile and peppermint, to products with potent pharmacological activity, such as foxglove, from which digitalis is derived. Two of the most common ailments for which people take herbal products are anxiety and depression (Astin, 1998). People also use herbals to treat chronic pain, chronic fatigue syndrome, addictions, and memory problems.

What is the effectiveness of these products? Only a few of them have been tested in rigorous research. We have already discussed the research on St. John's wort for depression. Two products used to treat anxiety, valerian and kava, have also undergone close scientific scrutiny. Valerian is made from the root of *Valeriana officinalis,* a common herb native to both Europe and Asia (Cott, 1995). Valerian appears to be a safe, mild sedative that produces no morning hangover (Fugh-Berman & Cott, 1999). Kava is the psychoactive member of the pepper family, widely used in Polynesia, Micronesia, and Melanesia as a ceremonial, tranquilizing beverage, as well as in Europe and the United

States for anxiety and insomnia. Several placebo-controlled studies have shown that kava is a safe herb for short-term relief from stress and anxiety (Fugh-Berman & Cott, 1999; Volz & Kieser, 1997). Although most people who take kava report no side effects, some report mild gastrointestinal complaints or allergic skin reactions. Kava may also interact with benzodiazepines.

Ginkgo biloba is the most widely prescribed phytomedicine in Germany. It is an antioxidant, and some reports suggest it enhances cognitive functioning in people with Alzheimer's disease and other memory impairments (Le Bars et al., 1997). One review of studies of the cognitive effects of ginkgo biloba concluded that it enhances cognitive functions, but weakly and inconsistently across studies (Gold, Cahill, & Wenk, 2002). Although it is rare for humans to experience significant side effects from gingko, it does have anticoagulant effects and in rare cases has been associated with serious bleeding problems, usually in people who are already taking anticoagulant drugs.

Concerns have been raised that many people are using the more potent substances without any supervision from a physician, putting themselves at risk for side effects or interactions with drugs or other substances, when sufficient research on their efficacy and safety has not been done. In addition, even for the products that do seem to be effective, little is known about how they work. Unfortunately, it is unlikely that herbal products will ever be researched to the degree that drugs produced by pharmaceutical companies are researched.

Doing sufficient research to have herbal products approved as drugs is extremely expensive in the United States. Meanwhile, botanicals are not patentable and are chemically very complex. The U.S. Congress passed the Dietary Supplement Health and Education Act in 1994 to encourage more research on nutrition and dietary supplements, as well as increased regulation of this industry.

Thus, although herbal treatments for psychological disorders have been used for centuries, they were largely considered a thing of the past by the mainstream medical community until very recently. Now, in part because the public is asking for more "natural" approaches in medicine, these products are becoming one of the newest tools in the treatment of mental disorders.

Electroconvulsive Therapy

An alternative to drug therapies in the treatment of some disorders is **electroconvulsive therapy,** or **ECT.** ECT was introduced in the early twentieth century, originally as a treatment for schizophrenia. Italian physicians Ugo Cerletti and Lucio Bini decided to experiment with the use of ECT to treat schizophrenia, reasoning that ECT can calm people with schizophrenia, much as experiencing an epileptic seizure can calm and sedate people with epilepsy. Eventually, clinicians found that ECT is not effective for schizophrenia, but it is effective for depression.

ECT consists of a series of treatments in which a brain seizure is induced by passing electrical current through the patient's brain. Patients are first anesthetized and given muscle relaxants, so that they are not conscious when they have the seizure and so that their muscles do not jerk violently during the seizure. Metal electrodes are taped to the head and a current of 70 to 150 volts is passed through one side of the brain for about one-half of a second. Patients typically have a convulsion, which lasts about one minute. The full series of treatments consists of 6 to 12 sessions.

In Chapter 9, we discuss the use of ECT in the treatment of depression. Although many mental-health professionals believe that ECT can be useful, it remains a controversial treatment. The idea of passing electrical current through the brain of a person to relieve psychiatric symptoms seems somewhat bizarre. And some critics argue that ECT results in significant and permanent cognitive damage, even when done according to modern guidelines (Breggin, 1997). For some seriously depressed people who do not respond to medications, however, ECT may be the only effective alternative.

Psychosurgery

In Chapter 1, we examined theories that prehistoric people performed crude brain surgery, called

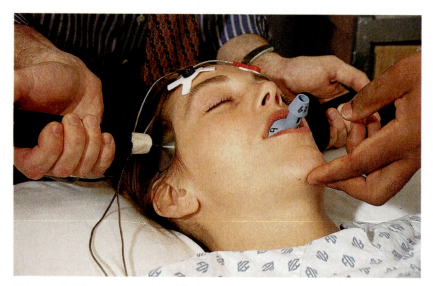

Electroconvulsive therapy has been controversial for much of its history but can be effective for certain disorders in its present form.

trephining, on people with mental disorders in order to release evil spirits thought to be causing the mental disorders. In modern times, brain surgery did not become a mode of treatment for mental disorders until the early twentieth century. A Portuguese neurologist named Antonio de Egas Moniz introduced a procedure in 1935 in which the frontal lobes of the brain were severed from the lower centers of the brain in people suffering from psychosis. This procedure eventually developed into the procedure known as **prefrontal lobotomy.** Although Moniz won the Nobel Prize for his work, prefrontal lobotomies were eventually criticized as a cruel and ineffective means of treating psychosis (Valenstein, 1986). Many patients suffered severe and permanent side effects, including either an inability to control impulses or a loss of the ability to initiate activity, extreme listlessness and loss of emotions, seizures, and sometimes even death.

By the 1950s, the use of **psychosurgery** had declined dramatically, especially in countries outside the United States. These days, psychosurgery is used rarely, and only with people who have severe disorders that do not respond to other forms of treatment. Modern neurological assessment and surgical techniques make psychosurgery more precise and safer than it was, although it remains highly controversial, even among professionals. Neurosurgeons attempt to lesion, or destroy, minute areas of the brain thought to be involved in a patient's symptoms. One of the greatest remaining problems in psychosurgery, however, is that it is not yet known what areas of the brain are involved in the production of most psychiatric symptoms, and it is likely that many areas of the brain are involved in any given disorder (Valenstein, 1986).

Repetitive Transcranial Magnetic Stimulation

One of the newest biologically based therapies uses powerful magnets, such as those used in magnetic resonance imaging (see Chapter 4), to stimulate targeted areas of the brain. The procedure, known as **repetitive transcranial magnetic stimulation (rTMS),** exposes patients to repeated, high-intensity magnetic pulses, which are focused on particular brain structures. When treating depressed people, researchers have targeted the left prefrontal cortex, which tends to show abnormally low metabolic activity in some depressed people.

Several studies have suggested that depressed patients given rTMS daily for at least a week tend to experience relief from their symptoms (Chae et al., 2001; George et al., 2003; Jorge et al., 2004; Martin et al., 2003). In addition, rTMS relieved auditory hallucinations (hearing voices that aren't there) in patients in some studies (Hoffman et al., 2000, 2003).

How does rTMS work? Electrical stimulation of neurons can result in long-term changes in neurotransmission across synapses (George et al., 2003). Neurotransmission can be enhanced or blunted, depending on the frequency of the stimulation. Patients who receive rTMS report few side effects, usually only minor headaches treatable by aspirin. Patients can remain awake, rather than having to be anesthetized, as in electroconvulsive therapy (ECT), thereby avoiding possible complications of anesthesia. Thus, there is a great deal of hope that rTMS will be an effective and safe alternative therapy, particularly for people who do not respond to drug therapies and cannot tolerate ECT.

The Social Impact of the Biological Approach to Treatment

The biological therapies have revolutionized the treatment of people with psychological disorders. At the beginning of the twentieth century clinicians were able only to warehouse and comfort people with severe psychological disturbances. We entered the twenty-first century able to treat many of these people so successfully that they can lead

Peanuts: © United Features Syndicate.

normal lives, thanks to many of the biological therapies that have been developed in recent decades.

Many people find the biological theories appealing, because they seem to erase any blame or responsibility that might be put on the sufferer of a disorder. Indeed, many organizations that advocate for people with mental disorders argue vehemently that mental disorders should be seen as medical diseases, just like diabetes or high blood pressure. They argue that people who suffer these disorders simply must accept they have a disease and obtain the appropriate medical treatment.

Despite their current popularity, the biological therapies are not a panacea. They do not work for everyone. Indeed, significant percentages of people with psychological disorders do not respond to any of the drugs or other biological treatments currently available. With time, new and more effective treatments may be developed that help these people, too.

Most of the biological therapies have significant side effects. Often, these side effects are tolerable, and people endure them because they are getting relief from their psychological disorder. For some people, however, the side effects are worse than the disorder itself. For others, the side effects can be dangerous and even deadly.

Some critics of biological theories and drug therapies worry that people will turn to the drugs rather than dealing with the difficult issues in their lives that are causing their psychological problems. If people can rid themselves of troubling symptoms by popping a pill, they may never make changes in their lives that could have permanent positive effects on their own psychological health and their relationships with others. As we will discuss later, there are several highly effective psychological therapies, and the combination of drug treatment and psychotherapy can be especially effective for some disorders.

Finally, the widespread use of some drugs, such as the SSRIs and the benzodiazepines, by people who are not suffering from severe depression or anxiety, but who just want a little help getting through the day, has raised many questions about the appropriateness of "changing your personality with a pill." We are grappling with the ethical and philosophical issues raised by the availability of drugs that offer us the opportunity to be smarter, more confident, less shy, and more energetic. Is this how we want these drugs to be used? Writer Lauren Slater, whose own symptoms of obsessions and compulsions (see Chapter 7) were relieved by Prozac, writes the following.

VOICES Much has been said about the meanings we make of illness, but what about the meanings we make out of cure? Cure is complex, disorienting, a revisioning of the self, either subtle or stark. Cure is the new, strange planet, pressing in. (Slater, 1998, p. 9)

No doubt these issues will continue to be debated for many years to come. Biological science is advancing at a rapid pace, presenting us with more alternatives in the treatment of mental disorders and more questions about how we view the relationship between the body and the mind.

SUMMING UP

- Antipsychotic drugs, such as phenothiazines and butyrophenone, help reduce the symptoms of psychosis.
- Antidepressant drugs, including the monoamine oxidase inhibitors, the tricyclic antidepressants, and the selective serotonin reuptake inhibitors, help reduce the symptoms of depression.
- Lithium is used to treat the symptoms of mania.
- Anticonvulsant drugs and calcium channel blockers also help treat mania.
- Antianxiety drugs include the barbiturates and the benzodiazepines.
- Herbal medicines are popular, but the efficacy and safety of some of these drugs has not been definitively shown.
- Electroconvulsive therapy (ECT) is useful in treating severe depression.
- Psychosurgery is used on rare occasions to help people with severe psychopathology that is not affected by drugs or other treatments.
- Repetitive transcranial magnetic stimulation (rTMS) is a new technique that involves exposing the brain to magnets. It may be helpful in the treatment of depression.

PSYCHOLOGICAL THERAPIES

Drug treatments can go a long way toward helping people with psychological problems. For many disorders, however, psychotherapy is an effective alternative to drugs; in addition, psychotherapy and drug therapy in combination can be particularly helpful for some disorders. There are many types of psychotherapy, which we dis-

TABLE 5.2 Psychological Therapies for Mental Disorders

These are some of the most commonly used psychologically based therapies used to treat mental disorders.

Type of Therapy	Description
Psychodynamic therapies	Help clients gain insight into unconscious motives and conflicts, through analysis of free associations, resistances, dreams, and transferences
Humanistic therapy	Helps clients explore their own values and potentials and fulfill their potential more fully by providing a warm and supportive relationship
Behavior therapies	Help clients extinguish unwanted behaviors or teach clients new, desired behaviors, with techniques such as systematic desensitization and response shaping
Cognitive therapies	Help clients change maladaptive thought patterns by challenging irrational thoughts and learning new skills

cuss in this section (see Table 5.2). In the remaining chapters of this book, you will see how these therapies are applied to treat specific disorders. In *Taking Psychology Personally: How to Look for a Therapist*, we discuss how people go about finding a clinician who will provide them with the kind of treatment they believe they need.

Psychodynamic Therapies

Psychodynamic therapies focus on uncovering and resolving unconscious conflicts that are thought to drive psychological symptoms. The goal is to help clients recognize the maladaptive ways in which they have been trying to cope and the sources of their unconscious conflicts. These insights are thought to free clients from the grip of the past and give them a sense of agency in making changes in the present (Vakoch & Strupp, 2000). Another goal is to help clients integrate aspects of their personality that have been split off or denied into a unified sense of self. As Freud stated in 1923,

> It may be laid down that the aim of the treatment is to remove the patient's resistances and to pass his repressions in review and thus to bring about the most far-reaching unification and strengthening of his ego, to enable him to save the mental energy which he is expending on internal conflicts, to make the best of him that his inherited capacities will allow and so to make him as efficient and as capable of enjoyment as possible. The removal of the symptoms of the illness is not specifically aimed at, but is achieved, as it were, as a by-product if the analysis is properly carried through. (Freud, 1923, p. 251)

It is not easy to uncover unconscious conflicts. Freud and others developed the method of **free association,** in which a client is taught to talk about whatever comes to mind, trying not to censor any thoughts. By "turning off" the censor, a client might find herself talking about subjects or memories that she did not even realize were on her mind. The therapist notices what themes seem to recur in a client's free associations, just how one thought seems to lead to another thought, and the specific memories that a client recalls.

The material that the client is reluctant to talk about during psychotherapy—that is, the client's **resistance** to certain material—is an especially important clue to the client's most central unconscious conflicts, because the most threatening conflicts are the ones the ego tries hardest to repress. The therapist eventually puts together these pieces of the puzzle into a suggestion or an interpretation of a conflict the client might be facing and voices this interpretation to the client. Sometimes, the client accepts this interpretation as a revelation. Other times, the client is resistant to this interpretation. The therapist might interpret this resistance as a good indication that the interpretation has identified an important issue in the client's unconscious.

The client's **transference** to the therapist is also a clue to unconscious conflicts and needs. A transference occurs when the client reacts to the therapist as if the therapist were an important person in the client's early development, such as his father or mother. For example, a client may find himself reacting with rage or extreme fear when a therapist is just a few minutes late for an appointment, and this might stem from his feelings of having been emotionally abandoned by a parent during childhood. The therapist might point out the ways the client

Taking Psychology Personally

How to Look for a Therapist

How do you know when you or someone you care about needs a therapist? How do you find a therapist once you decide to seek one? The American Psychological Association has published the following guidelines for evaluating whether you should seek a therapist and for finding a therapist (from *Choosing a Therapist Who Is Right for You,* distributed by the Practice Directorate of the American Psychological Association).

Consider Therapy If . . .

- You feel helpless and problems do not seem to get better despite your efforts.
- You feel sad or blue, nervous, or tense for a prolonged period of time.
- You or others notice changes in your mood or behavior or a decrease in your ability to carry out everyday activities.
- You are concerned about the emotional health of a family member or partner.
- You want to look at life and make decisions in a different way.
- You want to find ways of changing your life to feel more satisfied.

How Do You Find a Therapist?

- Talk to friends and family.
- Call your local or state psychological association.
- Contact your community mental-health center.
- Inquire at your church, synagogue, or mosque.
- Ask your physician or other health professional.
- Consult counseling centers at local colleges and universities.
- Consult your local *Yellow Pages.*

What Should You Consider When Making a Choice?

A therapist and client work together. The right match is important. Also, as you will see in later chapters of this book,

some therapies have been shown to be more effective than others in treating certain disorders. The following are sample interview questions that may be useful when considering a particular psychologist:

- Are you a licensed psychologist?
- How many years have you been practicing psychology?
- I've been feeling (anxious, tense, depressed, etc.). I'm having problems (with my job, my marriage, eating, sleeping, etc.). What kind of experience do you have in helping people with these types of problems?
- What are your specialty areas (children, marriage, etc.)?
- What might I expect during our sessions?
- What are your fees? (Fees are usually based on a 45-minute to 50-minute session.)
- Do you use a sliding-fee scale? Please explain how this works.
- What types of insurance do you accept?
- Do you accept Medicare/Medicaid patients?
- How do you bill for services? Will you bill my insurance company directly, or do I bill for reimbursement?

Interview several therapists—by telephone or in person—before making a choice. Following the initial contact, you may want to meet two or three times before you decide to work together. These sessions, called *consultation sessions,* will help you determine if the therapist is right for you. It may also be recommended that you work with therapists with different specializations to create a comprehensive treatment plan.

For further information on choosing a therapist, you can contact the American Psychological Association, Practice Directorate, 1200 17th Street NW, Washington, DC 20036, or visit www.apa.org.

behaves that represent a transference and might help the client explore the roots of his behavior in his relationships with significant others.

Following is a simulation of how a psychodynamic therapist might use transference to help the

pharmacy student at the beginning of this chapter understand the sources of her ambivalence about her studies.

Therapist: Each time I notice that you are doing well in school, you get tearful and cry.

Pharmacy student [crying]: I worry that your praise is not sincere. Father said I would never amount to anything because of my illness.

Therapist: I see, so you feel you have some well-established old reasons for feeling that way with me.

Some psychodynamic therapists also have their clients recount their dreams, and they use this material in the analysis of their conflicts. Freud believed that, during sleep, the ego loosens its control over the unconscious, and some unconscious material slips out in the form of dreams. These dreams are seldom direct representations of unconscious material, however, because this would be too threatening. Instead, dreams symbolize unconscious material in fascinating and creative ways.

By **working through,** or going over and over, painful memories and difficult issues, clients are able to understanding them and weave them into their self-definition in ways that are acceptable. This allows them to move forward in their lives. Many therapists believe that **catharsis,** or the expression of emotions connected to memories and conflicts, is also central to the healing processes in psychodynamic therapies. Catharsis unleashes the energy bound in unconscious memories and conflicts, allowing this material to be incorporated into more adaptive self-views.

An important issue in psychodynamic therapies is the **therapeutic alliance.** By being empathic and supportive, and by listening nonjudgmentally, the therapist creates a relationship of trust with the client, which gives the client the freedom and

"Have a couple of dreams, and call me in the morning."
© Sidney Harris, courtesy ScienceCartoonsPlus.com

courage to explore difficult issues. This does not mean that the therapist never confronts the client about issues he or she may be avoiding. But the therapist carefully times confrontations and interpretations, so that the client can receive and respond to these without undue anxiety. Several studies have shown that the strength of the therapeutic alliance between a therapist and a client, even in the early sessions of therapy, is a strong predictor of whether or not the client will benefit from therapy (Luborsky & Crits-Christoph, 1990). Indeed, clients who do not experience their therapists as supportive are prone to quit therapy altogether.

What is the difference between **psychoanalysis** and psychodynamic therapies? Psychoanalysis typically involves three or four sessions per week over a period of many years. The focus of psychoanalysis is primarily on the interpretation of transferences and resistances, as well as on experiences in the client's past (Wolitzky, 1995). Psychodynamic therapies may also go on for years, but they can be as short-term as 12 weeks (Crits-Christoph & Barber, 2000). Transferences, resistances, and the client's relationship with early caregivers are also the focus of psychodynamic therapies, but the psychodynamic therapist, compared with the psychoanalyst, may focus more on current situations in the client's life.

Many people report that the self-exploration of psychodynamic therapies has been valuable to them. The long-term, intensive nature of psychodynamic therapies makes them unaffordable for many people, however. In addition, people suffering from acute problems, such as severe depression or anxiety, often cannot tolerate the lack of structure in traditional psychodynamic therapies and need more immediate relief from their symptoms (Bachrach et al., 1991). Finally, it is unclear whether traditional psychodynamic therapies are effective in the treatment of many mental disorders, largely because the therapies last so long that studies have not been conducted to test their effectiveness empirically (Wolitzky, 1995).

For these reasons, modern psychodynamic therapists have developed some shorter-term, more structured versions of psychodynamic therapies (Luborsky, 1984). In these short-term therapies, the therapist and patient contract with each other for a limited number of sessions, usually fewer than 30, and focus on a limited set of problems the client identifies as causing him or her the most trouble. The few studies conducted on the effectiveness of these short-term therapies suggest they can result in significant improvement in symptoms for many clients (Crits-Christoph, 1992).

Some of these new therapies have incorporated the revisions in psychodynamic thought offered by object relations theorists and other theorists who argued that interpersonal relationships throughout the life span can shape people's behaviors and self-concepts (Anderson & Lambert, 1995). Interpersonal therapies explicitly focus on people's roles and relationships within their network of relationships with friends, family, and the larger community.

Humanistic Therapy

The stated goal of **humanistic therapy,** often referred to as **person-centered therapy,** is to help clients discover their greatest potential through self-exploration. Person-centered therapy is unique in the extent to which it emphasizes the self-healing capacities of the person (Bohart, 1995). The job of the therapist in person-centered therapy is not to act as an authority or expert who provides healing to the client. Rather, the therapist's job is to provide the optimal conditions for the client to heal him- or herself.

This therapy rests on the assumption that the natural tendency for humans is toward growth. When obstacles toward growth are removed, then the client will let go of symptoms and move forward in his or her life. Person-centered therapists do not push clients to uncover repressed painful memories or unconscious conflicts. Instead, they believe that, when clients are supported and empowered to grow, they will eventually face their past when it is necessary for their further development (Bohart, 1995).

The best known of this type of therapy is Carl Rogers' **client-centered therapy (CCT).** Rogers (1951) said there are three essential ingredients of CCT. First, the therapist communicates a genuineness in his or her role as helper to the client, acting as an authentic, real, living, behaving person rather than as an authority figure. Second, the therapist shows **unconditional positive regard** for the client. Third, the therapist communicates an empathic understanding of the client by making it clear that he or she understands and accepts the client's underlying feelings and search for self.

Through these conditions, the therapist helps the client know that he or she understands what the client is experiencing and feeling and what the client is trying to bring forth and understand. Rogers believed that this experience of being understood helps clients bring forth their own self-healing powers and have the courage to recognize and pursue their potential.

The main strategy for accomplishing these goals is the use of reflection. **Reflection** is a method of responding in which the therapist expresses an attempt to understand what the client is experiencing and trying to communicate (Bohart, 1995). The therapist does not attempt to interpret the unconscious aspects of the client's experience. Rather, the therapist tries to communicate an understanding of the client and explicitly asks for feedback from the client about this understanding.

Following is an example of the difference between how a humanistic therapist would use reflection and how a psychodynamic therapist would use interpretation to respond to the pharmacy student's feelings about her schoolwork and career (adapted from Bohart, 1995, p. 101).

VOICES

Pharmacy student: I'm feeling so lost in my career. Every time I seem to be getting close to doing something really good, like acing a class, I somehow manage to screw it up. I never feel like I am really using my potential. There is a block there.

Reflection: It's really frustrating to screw up and kill your chances; and it feels like it's something in you that's making that happen again and again.

A psychodynamic interpretation: It sounds like every time you get close to success you unconsciously sabotage yourself. Perhaps success means something to you that is troubling or uncomfortable, and you are not aware of what that is.

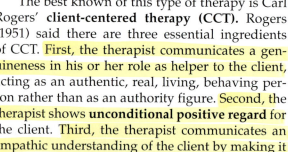

GARFIELD © *Paws, Inc. Reprinted with permission of Universal Press Syndicate. All Rights Reserved.*

The psychodynamic interpretation may be true, but the client-centered therapist would view it as inappropriate, because it brings to the client's attention something that is not currently in the client's awareness.

Client-centered therapy has been used to treat people with a wide range of problems, including depression, alcoholism, schizophrenia, anxiety disorders, and personality disorders (Bohart, 1990). An analysis of more than 20 studies comparing client-centered and other humanistic therapies with more structured therapies found that the humanistic therapies were generally as effective as the more structured therapies for a variety of disorders (Greenberg, Elliot, & Lietaer, 1994). For example, Borkovec and Mathews (1988) found client-centered therapy to be as effective as behavior and cognitive therapies in the treatment of anxiety disorders.

Not all studies find client-centered therapy to be an effective treatment, however (Bohart, 1990). Some therapists believe that CCT may be appropriate and sufficient for people who are moderately distressed, but not sufficient for people who are seriously distressed.

Behavior Therapies

Just as behavior *theories* of psychopathology are radically different from psychodynamic and humanistic *theories,* **behavior therapies** seem to be the polar opposite of these other therapies. Whereas psychodynamic therapies focus on uncovering unconscious conflicts and relational issues that develop during childhood and humanistic therapy focuses on helping the client discover the inner self, behavior therapies focus on identifying the reinforcements and punishments contributing to a person's maladaptive behaviors and on changing specific behaviors.

The foundation for behavior therapy is the **behavioral assessment** of the client's problem. The therapist works with the client to identify the specific circumstances that seem to elicit the client's unwanted behavior or emotional responses: What situations seem to trigger anxiety symptoms? When is the client most likely to begin heavy drinking? What types of interactions with other people make the client feel most distressed? The therapist may ask the client to use some of the techniques of self-monitoring described in Chapter 4 to identify triggers for symptoms. For example, the pharmacy student in *Extraordinary People* may be asked to keep a journal in which she notes each time she feels anxious and specifically what is happening in those situations.

The therapist may also **role-play** situations with the client, with the therapist taking the role of a person to whom the client feels she reacts badly. The therapist would observe the client's behavior in the role-play to assess what aspects of that behavior need to change for the client to be effective in interpersonal interactions.

Although there are many specific techniques for behavior change (see Table 5.3 on page 150), they can be grouped into two main categories: techniques that extinguish unwanted behaviors and techniques for teaching a person new, desired behaviors. We discuss some examples of each category in this chapter. The application of the other techniques, listed in Table 5.3, to specific disorders is discussed in the later chapters on those disorders.

Techniques for Extinguishing Unwanted Behaviors

Systematic desensitization therapy is based on Mowrer's (1939) two-factor model, which suggests that people develop fear and anxiety responses to previously neutral stimuli through classical conditioning. Then, through operant conditioning, they develop behaviors designed to avoid triggers for that anxiety. It is a gradual method for extinguishing anxiety responses to stimuli and the maladaptive behavior that often accompanies this anxiety.

In systematic desensitization, the client first creates a hierarchy of feared stimuli, ranging from stimuli that would cause him or her only mild anxiety to stimuli that would cause severe anxiety or panic. A person with a snake phobia might generate the hierarchy in Table 5.4 on page 150. Then the therapist would help the person proceed through this hierarchy, starting with the least feared stimulus. The person would be instructed to vividly imagine the feared stimulus or would even be exposed to the feared stimulus for a short period, while implementing relaxation exercises to control the anxiety. When the person gets to the point where he or she can imagine or experience the first and least feared stimulus without feeling anxious, the person moves on to the next most feared stimulus, imagining or experiencing it while implementing relaxation exercises. This proceeds until he or she reaches the most feared stimulus on the list and is able to experience this stimulus without feeling extremely anxious. Thus, by the end of systematic desensitization therapy, a person with a snake phobia should be able to pick up and handle a large snake without becoming very anxious.

Often, systematic desensitization therapy is combined with **modeling**—the client might watch a therapist pick up a snake, pet it, and play with it, observing that the therapist is not afraid, is not bitten or choked, and seems to enjoy playing with the snake. Eventually, the client is encouraged to imitate the therapist's behaviors with and reactions to

TABLE 5.3   Behavior Change Techniques

These are some of the methods used in behavior therapy.

Label	Description
Removal of reinforcements	Removes the individual from the reinforcing situation or environment
Aversion therapy	Makes the situation or stimulus that was once reinforcing no longer reinforcing
Relaxation exercises	Helps the individual voluntarily control physiological manifestations of anxiety
Distraction techniques	Helps the individual temporarily distract from anxiety-producing situations; diverts attention from physiological manifestations of anxiety
Flooding, or implosive, therapy	Exposes the individual to the dreaded or feared stimulus while preventing avoidant behavior
Systematic desensitization	Pairs the implementation of relaxation techniques with hierarchical exposure to the aversive stimulus
Response shaping through operant conditioning	Pairs rewards with desired behaviors
Behavioral contracting	Provides rewards for reaching proximal goals
Modeling and observational learning	Models desired behaviors, so that the client can learn through observation

TABLE 5.4   Hierarchy of Fears for Snake Phobia

This is a hierarchy of feared stimuli for a person with a snake phobia, ranging from the least feared stimulus to the most feared stimulus.

1. Hearing the word *snake*
2. Imagining a snake in a closed container at a distance
3. Imagining a snake uncontained at a distance
4. Imagining a snake nearby in a closed container
5. Looking at a picture of a snake
6. Viewing a movie or video of a snake
7. Seeing a snake in a container in the same room
8. Seeing a snake uncontained in the same room
9. Watching someone handle a snake
10. Touching a snake
11. Handling a snake
12. Playing with a snake

the snake. In some cases, people undergoing systematic desensitization are asked only to imagine experiencing the feared stimuli. In other cases, they are asked to experience these stimuli directly, actually touching and holding the snake, for example. The latter method is known as **in vivo expo-**sure, and it generally has stronger results than exposure only in the client's imagination (Follette & Hayes, 2000).

Another technique for extinguishing unwanted behaviors is **flooding,** or **implosive therapy,** which involves exposing clients to feared stimuli or situations to an excessive degree while preventing them from avoiding that situation. One example is having a person with a deep fear of germs soil her hands with dirt and then not wash her hands for several hours. This may sound relatively benign to you, but, for person with a germ obsession, that would arouse a great deal of anxiety. Over time, however, the anxiety tends to extinguish.

Techniques for Learning Desirable Behaviors

The techniques we have just discussed are designed to extinguish maladaptive responses or behaviors. Often, however, a person wishes to learn a new set of behaviors. A student of B. F. Skinner's, named Ogden Lindsley, first conceived of using the methods of operant conditioning to create new, positive behaviors in people with serious mental disorders. He began working with severely impaired mental patients in the Metropolitan State Hospital just outside Boston, setting up a system whereby they were given rewards for positive, nonpsychotic behavior, whereas rewards were withheld when they exhibited psychotic behavior. This method of shaping the responses of severely impaired people proved extremely successful.

Soon, during the 1950s and 1960s, whole wards of state hospitals were being turned over to behavior therapists. In these wards, a **token economy** was often set up, in which a patient would receive a small chip or token each time he or she exhibited a desired behavior (e.g., spoke to another person, made his or her bed). These tokens could be exchanged for privileges, such as a walk on the hospital grounds, or desired objects, such as special food. This technique is credited, along with the introduction of antipsychotic drugs, with helping cut the population of inpatient mental hospitals by 67 percent between 1955 and 1980 (Bellack, Morrison, & Mueser, 1992). This type of operant conditioning is frequently used to treat children with severe disorders, such as autism.

Response shaping through operant conditioning is also an effective tool in working with children who have behavior problems in the normal range for children. For example, suppose that a child tends to have tantrums in his school class. A behavior therapist might observe that the child initiates these tantrums when it appears he wants, but is not receiving, the teacher's attention. The therapist might prescribe that the teacher put the child in a small, empty room for three or four minutes each time he begins to tantrum—in other words, to give the child a time-out. At the same time, the therapist might train the child to ask the teacher in an appropriate manner to come and look at his drawing or another accomplishment, rather than to tantrum. At first, the child may use these new communication skills poorly, but even a minor attempt at using them instead of tantruming would be rewarded by the teacher's attention. Over time, only completely appropriate communications with the teacher would be rewarded. This is a form of **social skills training,** which has been adapted to help people with a variety of problems in interacting and communicating with others.

Behavior therapies have proven effective for a wide range of psychological problems, including several of the anxiety disorders, and behavior problems, particularly in children (Thorpe & Olson, 1997). Many therapists combine behavioral strategies with cognitive strategies.

Cognitive Therapies

Cognitive therapies focus on challenging people's maladaptive interpretations of events or ways of thinking and replacing them with more adaptive ways of thinking. Cognitive therapists also help clients learn more effective problem-solving techniques to deal with the concrete problems in their lives.

One of the most widely used cognitive therapies was developed by Aaron Beck (1976). There are many specific techniques in cognitive therapies (see Table 5.5 on page 152). They reflect three main goals.

The first goal is to assist clients in identifying their irrational and maladaptive thoughts. People often do not recognize the negative thoughts that are swirling in their minds and affecting their emotions and behaviors. Cognitive therapists encourage clients to pay attention to the thoughts that are associated with their moods or with unwanted behaviors, to write down these thoughts, and to bring the thoughts into the therapy session. If the pharmacy student we have been discussing did this, she would discover that every time she begins to feel somewhat anxious in class, thoughts such as "I'll never succeed! I can't do this! My illness is too debilitating!" rush through her mind.

The second goal is to teach clients to challenge their irrational or maladaptive thoughts and to consider alternative ways of thinking. Many of the specific techniques listed in Table 5.5 are designed to challenge clients' irrational thoughts.

These techniques tend to be implemented through a Socratic method of asking questions that help clients come to insights about their thoughts on their own. For example, a therapist might ask the pharmacy student, "What's the evidence for your belief that you'll never finish pharmacy school?" Sometimes, a client will have no evidence for his or her belief about a situation. For example, the pharmacy student may be pulling straight *A*s and have little evidence that she is about to flunk out of school. Other times, a client will have identified pieces of evidence for his or her perspective.

The therapist might ask a second question: "Are there other ways of looking at this evidence or this situation?" The therapist is encouraging the client to think of alternative perspectives to his or her own. The pharmacy student might answer, "Well, I have been bouncing back each time I have a setback, I guess, so it's not a sure thing that I will flunk out of school."

The third goal of the cognitive therapist is to get the client to face his or her worst fears about a situation and recognize ways the client could cope with them. The therapist might ask the pharmacy student, "What's the worst that could happen?" and "What could you do if the worst did happen?" The point of these questions is to get clients to generate ways they can cope with their worst fears, diminishing the fears and developing a set of coping strategies they can use if these fears come to pass. The pharmacy student may say that her worst fear is that she will have a psychotic episode in class, which everyone will see, and she will be forced to

TABLE 5.5 Techniques in Cognitive Therapies

Cognitive therapists use many different techniques to challenge clients' thinking.

Label	Description	Example
Challenge idiosyncratic meanings	Explore personal meaning attached to the client's words and ask the client to consider alternatives	When a client says he will be "devastated" by his spouse leaving, ask just how he would be devastated and ways he could avoid being devastated.
Question the evidence	Systematically examine the evidence for the client's beliefs or assertions	When a client says she can't live without her spouse, explore how she lived without the spouse before she was married.
Reattribution	Help the client distribute responsibility for events appropriately	When a client says that her son's failure in school must be her fault, explore other possibilities, such as the quality of the school.
Examine options and alternatives	Help the client generate alternative actions to maladaptive ones	If a client considers leaving school, explore whether tutoring or going part-time to school are good alternatives.
Decatastrophize	Help the client evaluate whether he or she is overestimating the nature of a situation	If a client states that failure in a course means he must give up the dream of medical school, question whether this is a necessary conclusion.
Fantasize consequences	Explore fantasies of a feared situation; if unrealistic, the client may recognize this; if realistic, work on effective coping strategies	Help a client who fantasizes "falling apart" when asking the boss for a raise to role-play the situation and develop effective skills for making the request.
Examine advantages and disadvantages	Examine advantages and disadvantages of an issue, to instill a broader perspective	If a client says she "was just born depressed and will always be that way," explore the advantages and disadvantages of holding that perspective versus other perspectives.
Turn adversity to advantage	Explore ways that difficult situations can be transformed into opportunities	If a client has just been laid off, explore whether this is an opportunity for him to return to school.
Guided association	Help the client see connections between different thoughts or ideas	Draw the connections between a client's anger at his wife for going on a business trip and his fear of being alone.
Scaling	Ask the client to rate his or her emotions or thoughts on scales to help gain perspective	If a client says she was overwhelmed by an emotion, ask her to rate it on a scale from 0 (not at all present) to 100 (fell down in a faint).
Thought stopping	Provide the client with ways of stopping a cascade of negative thoughts	Teach an anxious client to picture a stop sign or hear a bell when anxious thoughts begin to snowball.
Distraction	Help the client find benign or positive distractions to take attention away temporarily from negative thoughts or emotions	Have a client count to 200 by 13s when he feels himself becoming anxious.
Labeling of distortions	Provide labels for specific types of distorted thinking to help the client gain more distance and perspective	Have a client keep a record of the number of times per day she engages in all-or-nothing thinking—seeing things as all bad or all good.

Source: Freeman & Reinecke, 1995.

drop out of pharmacy school. The therapist would then help her explore ways of coping with this if it were true. For example, the therapist might work with the pharmacy student to identify the early signs of her anxiety attacks and psychotic symptoms and to develop a specific plan for leaving class and contacting the therapist at this time.

Behavioral Assignments

An important component of cognitive therapies is the use of **behavioral assignments** to help the client gather evidence concerning his or her beliefs, to test alternative viewpoints about a situation, and to try new methods of coping with different situations. These assignments are presented to the client as ways of testing hypotheses and gathering information that will be useful in therapy, regardless of the outcome. The assignments can also involve trying out new skills, such as skills at communicating more effectively, between therapy sessions.

The following simulation illustrates how a therapist might use behavioral assignments to provide the *Extraordinary People* pharmacy student with opportunities to practice new skills and to gather information about thoughts that contribute to negative emotions:

A socially anxious client may be given the behavioral assignment to talk to a clerk in a checkout line.

> **CASE STUDY**
>
> The pharmacy student was unable to complete her degree because she feared meeting with a professor to discuss an incomplete grade she had received in a course. She was quite convinced that the professor would "scream at her" and had been unable to complete a homework assignment to call the professor's secretary to arrange a meeting. An in vivo task was agreed on, in which she called the professor from her therapist's office. Her thoughts and feelings before, during, and after the call were carefully examined. As might be expected, the professor was quite glad to hear from his former student and was pleased to accept her final paper. The origins of her beliefs about how others feel toward her were then reviewed and she was able to see that these beliefs were both maladaptive and erroneous. (Adapted from Freeman & Reinecke, 1995, pp. 203–204)

Therapists also often use role-plays during therapy sessions to elicit the client's reactions to feared situations and to help the client rehearse positive responses to such situations. For example, a therapist might engage the pharmacy student in a role-play in which the therapist plays the part of the student's professor and the client rehearses how she might talk with him about her concerns about her homework assignment.

Taking Control

Cognitive therapists attempt to teach clients skills, so that clients can become their own therapists (Beck et al., 1979). Therapists try to get clients to take responsibility for and control over their own thoughts and actions, rather than looking to the therapist to tell them what to do, or only reacting to external forces. By learning these strategies and gaining a sense of control over their thinking and emotions, clients not only can overcome current problems but also can handle new problems that arise more effectively.

Do cognitive therapists ever get around to exploring the "deeper" meanings of clients' emotions and irrational thoughts? Most cognitive therapists are not against exploring the origins of clients' negative ways of thinking in their earlier experiences in life. Most believe, however, that clients must first learn how to manage and control these thoughts and emotions. Once clients have become effective at challenging their irrational thoughts and coping with negative emotions and difficult situations, cognitive therapists may then help them investigate the roots of these patterns.

Cognitive therapies are designed to be short-term, 12 to 20 weeks in duration, with one or two sessions per week (Beck et al., 1979). They have been compared with drug therapies and interpersonal therapy in the treatment of depression, anxiety, substance use problems, and eating disorders and have been shown to be highly effective (Hollon, Haman, & Brown, 2002).

SUMMING UP

- Psychodynamic therapies focus on uncovering the unconscious motives and concerns behind psychopathology through free association and the analysis of transferences and dreams.

- Humanistic, or client-centered, therapy attempts to help clients find their own answers to problems by supporting them and reflecting back these concerns, so they can self-reflect and self-actualize.

- Behavior therapies focus on altering the reinforcements and punishments people receive for maladaptive behavior. Behavior therapists also help clients learn new behavioral skills.

- Cognitive therapies focus on changing the maladaptive cognitions behind distressing feelings and behaviors.

INTERPERSONAL AND SOCIAL APPROACHES

The psychological therapies focus primarily on changing the ways people think and behave. The interpersonal and social approaches to treatment view the individual as part of a larger system of relationships, influenced by social forces and culture, and hold that this larger system must be addressed in therapy.

The treatments discussed in this section vary greatly in how broadly they reach beyond the individual into the social system in attempting to alleviate the individual's symptoms. *Interpersonal therapists* work primarily with individuals to help them understand their place in their social system and change their behaviors and roles in that social system. *Family systems therapists* insist that the whole family needs to be part of therapy, because the dynamics that cause and maintain psychopathology rise from the family unit, not from the individual. *Group therapies* capitalize on the presence of other group members to help individuals learn to cope with their problems more effectively. The *community mental-health movement* was designed to be a wholistic approach to the treatment of mental disorders that involves the entire community in an individual's treatment. *Cultural perspectives* on treatment acknowledge the impact of cultural values and norms on people's experiences of mental disorders.

Interpersonal Therapy

As we noted in Chapter 2, **interpersonal therapy,** or **IPT,** emerged out of modern psychodynamic theories of psychopathology, which shifted their focus from the unconscious conflicts of the individual to the client's pattern of relationships with important people in his or her life (Klerman et al., 1984; Weissman & Markowitz, 2002). IPT differs from psychodynamic therapies in that the therapist is much more structuring and directive in the therapy, offering interpretations much earlier and focusing on how to change current relationships. In addition, IPT is designed to be a short-term therapy, often lasting only about 12 weeks. An example of the application of IPT and some of the differences between an IPT approach and a traditional psychodynamic approach comes in the following case study (adapted from Klerman et al., 1984, pp. 155–182).

CASE STUDY

Mrs. C. was an older woman whose husband died a year earlier after a long and painful illness. Mrs. C. had been extremely dependent on her husband prior to his illness, relying on him to lead their social life and manage all their finances. Over the course of his illness, Mrs. C. became resentful both that her husband was "abandoning her" by becoming incapacitated by his illness at a time they were supposed to be enjoying their retirement and that he was becoming a severe burden on her. Following his death, she still felt a great deal of anger toward him, but also a great deal of guilt for her anger. She came into therapy suffering from unshakable sadness, preoccupation with memories of her husband's death and her guilty feelings, problems in sleeping, and complete social withdrawal. The IPT therapist began by reassuring Mrs. C. that her feelings were not unusual and telling her that the goal of therapy would be to help her confront all that she has lost and learn to manage her new life better. Much of the therapy then focused on eliciting Mrs. C.'s feelings about her husband and her loss, helping her clarify the reasons for these feelings and accept these feelings. At the end of the first session, the therapist said:

One of the reasons why people sometimes have difficulty starting up again after losing a loved one is be-

(continued)

cause it's been hard to really look the loss straight in the face, and to really think about what it means, and allow yourself to feel the painful feelings. I think one of the things we can do in therapy is to try to look at what's happened with you and your husband, to look at what he meant to you. . . . The other side of trying to look at what's happened with the loss of your husband is for us to look into the ways you can start enjoying life again. And it seems that in fact you've made a start as far as that kind of thing is concerned. However, it also seems that you have a number of long-term attitudes that to some extent you realize aren't realistic, such as the difference between the way things turn out and the way you anticipate them. Also, you have a lot of fears, that somehow people won't like you, that they're avoiding you or perhaps going to exploit you. We will spend some time trying to look at just what makes these things seem so powerful and likely to happen. Also we'll look at ways you can overcome these hesitations.

Like a psychodynamic therapist, the IPT therapist believed that Mrs. C.'s inability to accept the anger she felt against her husband caused her depression. The therapy focused on helping Mrs. C. express her guilt and anger. Unlike a psychodynamic therapist, who would have focused on the roots of Mrs. C.'s relationship with her husband and feelings about that relationship in her early childhood, the IPT therapist was concerned primarily with Mrs. C.'s recent and current relationships. In addition, the IPT therapist was directive in gently but consistently urging Mrs. C. to increase her social contacts and her activities. The following interchange between the therapist and Mrs. C. illustrates how the therapist focused on helping Mrs. C. express and clarify her feelings but stayed in the present:

> **Mrs. C.:** I like Christmas. I like decorating the house. So . . . I-I just, when my husband isn't there, I still will . . . decorate.
>
> **Therapist:** It's still hard to think about doing things for yourself.
>
> **Mrs. C.:** Well, I think that's where the guilt comes in, that he isn't here, you know. I get

CASE STUDY

this pang of guilt, thinking, well, gee, you shouldn't be, you shouldn't be so happy about things.

Therapist: Because if you're enjoying things, that means you can't be thinking about him?

Mrs. C.: I think about him less and less, but I don't . . . suddenly, all of a sudden, when I'm doing something that I'm enjoying, the thought intrudes that, you know, you shouldn't be so happy [chuckles]. I'm sure he wouldn't want me to be—sad. . . .

Therapist: But in a way, hanging on to those sad thoughts . . . is a little like hanging on to him?

Mrs. C.: Probably.

Because IPT is short-term, it has been relatively easy for its proponents to test its effectiveness and to compare its effectiveness with that of a number of other treatments. IPT has been shown effective in the treatment of depression, anxiety, drug addiction, and eating disorders (Weissman & Markowitz, 2002). In addition, it appears as effective as drug treatments for most of these disorders.

Family Systems Therapy

Family systems therapy is based on the belief that an individual's problems are always rooted in interpersonal systems, particularly in the systems called *families*. According to this viewpoint, a therapist cannot help an individual without treating the entire family system that created and is maintaining the individual's problems. In fact, family systems theorists argue that the individual may not actually have a problem but has become the "identified patient" in the family, carrying the responsibility or blame for the dysfunction of the family system.

Two of the most frequently used types of family systems therapy are Virginia Satir's Conjoint Family Therapy (Satir, 1967) and Salvador Minuchin's Structural Family Therapy (Minuchin, 1981). Satir's therapy focuses on the patterns and processes of communication among family members. The therapist identifies and points out dysfunctional communication patterns and teaches family members to communicate better by modeling for them effective communication and by teaching members to be clear and to refrain from inferring meaning.

Minuchin's Structural Family Therapy focuses more on the role each member of the family has

Family therapists work with the entire family rather than only the "identified patient."

come to play in the family system and on changing the structure and dynamics of the relationships among family members. The therapist attempts to "join" with the family, becoming a part of the family so as to exert influence over the processes by which family members interact. By questioning family members about their feelings about one another's behaviors and commenting on the behaviors and feelings of the members, the therapist attempts to bring the family dynamics into the open. What follows is an example of an interchange between Minuchin and a husband and wife with whom he was working (1981, adapted from pp. 35–36).

VOICES

Husband: I think when something irritates me, it builds up and I hold it in until some little thing will trigger it, and then I'll be very, very critical and get angry. Then I'll tell her that I just don't understand why it has to be this way. But then I try to be very careful not to be unreasonable or too harsh because, when I'm harsh, I feel guilty about it.

Minuchin: So, sometimes the family feels like a trap.

Husband: It's not the family so much; it's just—[indicates wife].

Minuchin [completing husband's gesture]: Your wife?

Husband [looking at wife]: No, not her either. It's just the things she doesn't do versus the things she does in terms of how she

spends her time. Sometimes I think her priorities should be changed.

Minuchin: I think you are soft-pedaling.

Wife: About being trapped?

Minuchin: Yes, about being trapped. I think people sometimes get depressed when they are, like your husband, unable to be direct. He's not a straight talker. There's a tremendous amount of indirection in your family, because you are essentially very good people who are very concerned not to hurt one another. And you need to tell white lies a lot. . . .

Wife [to husband]: Am I indirect?

Husband: I don't really know. Sometimes you seem very direct, but I find myself wondering if you are telling me everything about what's bothering you. You know, if you seem upset, I'm not always sure that I know what's bugging you.

Wife: That I can be upset for something like that because it wouldn't upset you?

Husband: Maybe that's part of it.

Wife [smiling, but at the same time her eyes are watering]: Because you always seem to know better than I do what is really upsetting me, what my problem is at the moment.

Minuchin [to husband]: You see what's happening now? She's talking straight, but she's afraid that, if she talks straight, you will be hurt, so she begins to cry and she begins to smile, so she's saying, "Don't take my straight talk seriously, because it is just the product of a person who is under stress." And that is the kind of thing you do to each other, so you cannot change too much. Because you don't tell each other in what direction to change.

The goal of the family systems therapist is to challenge and disrupt the current dysfunctional dynamics of the family, so that the family is forced to change these dynamics, ideally toward more adaptive dynamics. The following are the three primary strategies of family systems therapy:

1. To challenge the family's assumption that "the problem" lies in one member of the family, rather than in the family dynamics

2. To challenge dysfunctional family structures, such as those in which the family members are overinvolved with each other and do not allow each other sufficient autonomy

3. To challenge the family's defensive conception of reality, such as in challenging the parents' belief that there is nothing wrong with their daughter, when she is suffering from a serious eating disorder

If the pharmacy student we have been discussing had family systems therapy to deal with her anxiety symptoms, the therapist might explore how these symptoms are part of a larger system of the family's seeing her as weak and damaged, possibly communicating their low expectations to her. The therapist might work with her and her family, so that the family provides her with the support she needs without undermining her attempts at autonomy.

Group Therapy

Most of the psychotherapies we have discussed in this chapter have been applied in **group therapy** as well as in one-on-one interactions between a therapist and a client. Often, the members of the group share an experience, such as a history of sexual abuse, severe problems in social interactions, or the diagnosis of a life-threatening disease. The pharmacy student we have been discussing might join a group of people with serious mental-health problems who are attempting to finish their education, to obtain support and understanding from people having some of the same life experiences she is.

Group therapy offers many potential benefits over individual therapy. Groups provide individuals with unique opportunities to view their problems from a broader perspective than their own, as well as to practice new attitudes and skills in a safe environment. Group therapy also is an efficient, cost-effective way for therapists to provide their services to larger numbers of clients. Many studies of group therapies for specific disorders have found them to be effective (Forsyth & Corazzini, 2000), as we will discuss in their application to the specific disorders.

Many group therapy sessions are not led by professional therapists, however. Many **self-help groups**—people who come together to deal with a common experience or need—organize themselves without the help of mental-health professionals. Many of these groups subscribe to the perspective of Rogers' client-centered therapy that it does not necessarily require a professional to help people in self-exploration—what it really takes is a listening, caring person. In colleges, client-centered approaches are taught in many courses on *peer coun-*

Group therapies bring together people experiencing a common problem to learn from and support each other.

seling, in which students learn to counsel other college students. Client-centered therapy is considered appropriate for such situations, because it does not require years of training for the counselor and is based on the premise that the counselor and client are equals.

Self-help groups are extremely popular, with as many as 15 million people in the United States alone attending these groups. One popular type of self-help group is the *bereavement support group* for people who have recently experienced a loss. The loss of a loved one can be an overwhelming experience, and grief can involve frightening symptoms, such as severe problems in concentration or the sense that the deceased loved one is present. Bereavement support groups provide a safe place for the expression of grief, education on grief, and validation of members' experiences of grief. Support groups can also help decrease the isolation that many bereaved people feel. Group members may learn new coping strategies as they hear about how others have approached the tasks of mourning. Many people find bereavement support groups helpful, as the following 65-year-old man who lost his wife describes (Nolen-Hoeksema & Larson, 1999, p. 171).

VOICES

I've been going to the support group they have once a week, for all the people who lost their loved ones—over a year now. With some other people, we sit around, you know, and everybody tells their problems. You feel then you're not the only one, that some other people are hurting, too.

Evaluating the effectiveness of bereavement groups and other self-help groups has not been easy. These groups tend to be fluid, with members coming and going, getting different "dosages" of the group. The effectiveness of one of the most widespread and popular self-help groups, Alcoholics Anonymous, has been evaluated, and it appears that this form of self-help group therapy can be quite effective in the treatment of alcoholism (see Chapter 17).

Community Treatment

As we noted in Chapter 1, *the community mental-health movement* was officially launched in 1963 by President John Kennedy to provide coordinated mental-health services to people in community-based centers. Let's take a look at some of these community treatment centers.

Community Treatment Centers

Community mental-health centers are intended to provide mental-health care based in the community, often from teams of social workers, therapists, and physicians who coordinate care. **Halfway houses** offer people with long-term mental-health problems the opportunity to live in a structured, supportive environment while they are trying to reestablish a job and ties to family and friends. **Day treatment centers** allow people to obtain treatment all day, as well as occupational and rehabilitative therapies, but to live at home at night.

People who have acute problems that require hospitalization may go to inpatient wards of general hospitals or specialized psychiatric hospitals. Sometimes, their first contact with a mental-health professional is in the emergency room of a hospital. Once their acute problems have subsided, however, they often are released back to their community treatment center, rather than remaining for the long term in a psychiatric hospital.

Deinstitutionalization was successful in getting patients out of psychiatric hospitals. The number of patients in large state psychiatric hospitals decreased by 75 percent in the 1960s and 1970s after the movement was launched (Lamb & Weinberger, 2001). Unfortunately, the resources to care for all the mental patients released from institutions were never adequate. Not enough halfway houses were built or community mental-health centers funded to serve the thousands of men and women who had been institutionalized or who would have been if the movement had not happened.

The mental-health care system in the United States has hit another turning point in the early twenty-first century (Torrey, 1997). Mental-health services are expensive, because mental-health prob-

lems are sometimes chronic and mental-health treatment can take a long time. Many people are not insured, and those who have insurance often find that their mental-health coverage is limited (Rosenheck, 1999). People with long-term, severe mental disorders, such as schizophrenia, often exhaust all sources of funding for their mental-health care, and many end up homeless or incarcerated for crimes they commit while not being treated.

Although 50 to 60 percent of people with a severe mental illness receive some sort of care, that leaves about half who receive none (Kessler et al., 2001; Narrow et al., 1993; Torrey, 1997). Sometimes, people refuse care that might help them; other times, they fall through holes in the medical safety net because of bureaucratic rules designed to shift the burden of the cost of mental-health care from one agency to another, as in the case of Rebecca J. (Torrey, 1997, pp. 105–106):

CASE STUDY

Because of severe schizoaffective disorder, Rebecca J., age 56, had spent 25 years in a New York State psychiatric hospital. She lived in a group home in the community but required rehospitalization for several weeks approximately once a year when she relapsed despite taking medications. As a result of the reduction in state hospital beds (for people with mental disorders) and attempts by the state to shift readmissions for fiscal reasons, these rehospitalizations increasingly took place on the psychiatric wards of general hospitals that varied widely in quality. In 1994, she was admitted to a new hospital because the general hospital where she usually went was full. The new hospital was inadequately staffed to provide care for patients as sick as Rebecca J. In addition, the psychiatrist was poorly trained and had access to only a small fraction of Rebecca J.'s complex and voluminous past history. During her 6-week hospitalization, Rebecca J. lost 10 pounds because the nursing staff did not help her eat, had virtually all her clothing and personal effects lost or stolen, became toxic from her lithium medication, which was not noticed until she was semicomatose, and was prematurely discharged while she was still so psychotic that she had to be rehospitalized in another hospital less than 24

(continued)

hours later. Meanwhile, less than a mile away in the state psychiatric hospital where she had spent many years, a bed sat empty on a ward with nursing staff and a psychiatrist who knew her case well and with her case records readily available in a file cabinet.

As we discuss the research showing the effectiveness of various treatments for specific disorders throughout the remainder of the book, it is important to keep in mind that those treatments can work only if people have access to them. A critical question for society is whether we will ensure that the people who can benefit from the treatments researches have worked so hard to develop will get access to them.

Community Prevention Programs

It would be better to prevent people from developing psychopathology in the first place than to treat it once it had developed. This approach is known as **primary prevention**—stopping the development of disorders before they start. Some primary prevention strategies for reducing drug abuse and delinquency might include changing some of the neighborhood characteristics that seem to contribute to delinquency and drug use. Education is a big part of primary prevention. For example, researchers in the Stanford Heart Disease Program educated townspeople through the local media about how they could reduce their risk for cardiovascular disease (for example, by stopping smoking and reducing fat in their diets). This effort led to measurable decreases in blood pressure and cholesterol in the townspeople (Maccoby & Altman, 1988).

Secondary prevention is focused on catching disorders in their earliest stages and providing treatment designed to reduce their development. Secondary prevention usually focuses on people at high risk for the disorder. For example, one highly successful study targeted people in low-income minority groups who were suffering from physical ailments (Munoz, 1997; Munoz, Mrazek, & Haggerty, 1996). The people in these groups also were at high risk for serious depression. This program provided cognitive-behavioral therapy to the people in these groups, teaching them strategies for overcoming or preventing the symptoms of depression. It also helped them learn skills for coping more effectively with their physical illnesses and for dealing with medical professionals. The people who went through this program were less likely to develop serious de-

pression over the year they were followed than was a control group of people who did not go through the program. The program participants were also physically healthier at the end of their follow-up year.

Cross-Cultural and Gender Issues in Treatment

A number of assumptions or values are inherent in the psychological therapies we have discussed. They can clash with the values and norms of cultures different from the Western cultures that created those psychotherapies (Sue & Lam, 2002, Snowden & Yamada, 2005). First, most psychotherapies are focused on the individual—the individual's unconscious conflicts, dysfunctional ways of thinking, maladaptive behavior patterns, and so on. In contrast, many cultures focus on the group, or collective, rather than the individual (Sue & Sue, 2003). The identity of the individual is not seen apart from the groups to which that individual belongs—his or her family, community, ethnic group, and religion. If therapists fail to recognize this when working with clients from collectivist cultures, they may make recommendations that are useless or perhaps even harmful, leading to conflicts between clients and important groups in the clients' lives that clients cannot handle.

Second, most psychotherapies value the expression of emotions and the disclosure of personal concerns, whereas the restraint of emotions and personal concerns is valued in many cultures, such as Japanese culture (Sue & Sue, 2003). Some counselors may see this restraint as a problem and try to encourage clients to become more expressive. Again, this effort can clash badly with the self-concepts of clients and with the norms of their culture.

Third, in many psychotherapies, clients are expected to take the initiative in communicating their concerns and desires to the therapist and in generating ideas about what is causing their symptoms and what changes they might want to make. These expectations can clash with cultural norms that require deference to people in authority (Sue & Sue, 2003). A client from a culture in which one speaks only when spoken to and never challenges an elder or authority figure may be extremely uncomfortable with a therapist who does not tell the client what is wrong and how to fix it in a very direct manner.

In addition, many clients who are in ethnic minority groups may also be in lower socioeconomic groups, whereas their therapists are likely to be in middle- or upper-class socioeconomic groups. This can create tensions due to class differences as well as cultural differences.

Some studies suggest that people from Latino, Asian, and Native American cultures are more comfortable with structured and action-oriented therapies, such as behavior and cognitive-behavioral therapies, than with the less structured therapies (see Miranda et al., 2005). The specific form of therapy may not matter as much as the cultural sensitivity the therapist shows the client. Sue and Zane (1987, pp. 42–43) give the following example of the importance of cultural sensitivity in the interaction between a client and a therapist. First, they describe the problems the client faced; second, they describe how the therapist (one of the authors of the study) responded to these problems.

CASE STUDY

At the advice of a close friend, Mae C. decided to seek services at a mental health center. She was extremely distraught and tearful as she related her dilemma. An immigrant from Hong Kong several years ago, Mae met and married her husband (also a recent immigrant from Hong Kong). Their marriage was apparently going fairly well until six months ago when her husband succeeded in bringing over his parents from Hong Kong. While not enthusiastic about having her parents-in-law live with her, Mae realized that her husband wanted them and that both she and her husband were obligated to help their parents (her own parents were still in Hong Kong).

After the parents arrived, Mae found that she was expected to serve them. For example, the mother-in-law would expect Mae to cook and serve dinner, to wash all the clothes, and to do other chores. At the same time, she would constantly complain that Mae did not cook the dinner right, that the house was always messy, and that Mae should wash certain clothes separately. The parents-in-law also displaced Mae and her husband from the master bedroom. The guest room was located in the basement, and the parents refused to sleep in the basement because it reminded them of a tomb.

Mae would occasionally complain to her husband about his parents. The husband would excuse his parents' demands by indicating "They are my parents and they're getting old." In general, he avoided any potential conflict; if he took sides, he supported his parents. Although Mae realized that she had an obligation to his parents, the situation was becoming intolerable to her.

I (the therapist) indicated (to Mae) that conflicts with in-laws were very common, especially for Chinese, who are obligated to take care of their parents. I attempted to normalize the problems because she was suffering from a great deal of guilt over her perceived failure to be the perfect daughter-in-law. I also conveyed my belief that in therapy we could try to generate new ideas to resolve the problem—ideas that did not simply involve extreme courses of action such as divorce or total submission to the in-laws (which she believed were the only options).

I discussed Mae during a case conference with other mental health personnel. It is interesting that many suggestions were generated: Teach Mae how to confront her parents-in-law; have her invite the husband for marital counseling so that husband and wife could form a team in negotiation with his parents; conduct extended family therapy so that Mae, her husband, and her in-laws could agree on contractual give-and-take relationships. The staff agreed that working solely with Mae would not change the situation. . . . Confronting her in-laws was discrepant with her role of daughter-in-law, and she felt very uncomfortable in asserting herself in the situation. Trying to involve her husband or in-laws in treatment was ill advised. Her husband did not want to confront his parents. More important, Mae was extremely fearful that her family might find out that she had sought psychotherapy. Her husband as well as her in-laws would be appalled at her disclosure of family problems to a therapist who was an outsider. . . . How could Mae's case be handled? During the case conference, we discussed the ways that Chinese handle interpersonal family conflicts which are not unusual to see. Chinese often use third-party intermediaries to resolve conflicts. The intermediaries obviously have to be credible and influential with the conflicting parties. At the next ses-

(continued)

sion with Mae, I asked her to list the persons who might act as intermediaries, so that we could discuss the suitability of having someone else intervene. Almost immediately, Mae mentioned her uncle (the older brother of the mother-in-law) whom she described as being quite understanding and sensitive. We discussed what she should say to the uncle. After calling her uncle, who lived about 50 miles from Mae, she reported that he wanted to visit them. The uncle apparently realized the gravity of the situation and offered to help. He came for dinner, and Mae told me that she overheard a discussion between the uncle and Mae's mother-in-law. Essentially, he told her that Mae looked unhappy, that possibly she was working too hard, and that she needed a little more praise for the work that she was doing in taking care of everyone. The mother-in-law expressed surprise over Mae's unhappiness and agreed that Mae was doing a fine job. Without directly confronting each other, the uncle and his younger sister understood the subtle messages each conveyed. Older brother was saying that something was wrong and younger sister acknowledged it. After this interaction, Mae reported that her mother-in-law's criticisms did noticeably diminish and that she had even begun to help Mae with the chores.

If Mae's therapist had not been sensitive to Mae's cultural beliefs about her role as a daughter-in-law and had suggested some of the solutions put forward by his colleagues in the case conference, Mae might have dropped out of therapy. People from ethnic minority groups in the United States are much more likely than European Americans to drop out of psychosocial therapy (Snowden & Yamada, 2005). Ethnic minority clients often find therapists' suggestions strange, unhelpful, and even insulting. Because Mae's therapist was willing to work within the constraints of her cultural beliefs, he and Mae found a solution to her problem that was acceptable to her.

In treating children, cultural norms about child-rearing practices and the proper role of doctors can make it difficult to include the family in a child's treatment. For example, in a study of behavior therapy for children, Hong Kong Chinese parents were very reluctant to be trained to engage

Therapists working with children must be sensitive to parents' expectations concerning the role of the therapist.

in behavioral techniques, such as responding with praise or ignoring certain behaviors. Such techniques violated the parents' views of appropriate child-rearing practices and their expectations that the therapist should be the person "curing" the child. However, several clinicians argue that family-based therapies are more appropriate than individual therapy in cultures that are highly family-oriented, including Native American, Hispanic, African American, and Asian American cultures (Hall, 2001; Tharp, 1991).

Rosselló and Bernal (2004) adapted both cognitive-behavioral therapy and interpersonal therapy to be more culturally sensitive in the treatment of depressed Puerto Rican adolescents. The Puerto Rican value of *familism*, a strong attachment to family, was incorporated into the therapy. Issues of the balance between dependence and independence were explicitly discussed in family groups. The adapted therapies proved effective in treating the adolescents' depression.

Matching Therapist and Client

Must a therapist come from the same culture as the client to understand the client fully? A review of several studies suggests that ethnic matching is not an important predictor of how long clients remain in therapy or of the outcomes of therapy (Maramba & Nagayama Hall, 2002).

Cultural sensitivity can probably be acquired through training and experience to a large degree (D'Andrea & Daniels, 1995; Sue et al., 1998). In fact, just because a therapist is from the same ethnic group as the client does not mean that the therapist and client share a value system (Teyber & McClure, 2000). For example, a fourth-generation Japanese American who has fully adopted American competitive and individualistic values may clash with a recent immigrant from Japan who subscribes to the self-sacrificing, community-oriented values of

Japanese culture. These value differences among people of the same ethnic group may explain why studies show that matching the ethnicity or gender of the therapist and client does not necessarily lead to a better outcome for the client (Maramba & Nagayama Hall, 2002). On the other hand, the relationship between a client and a therapist and a client's beliefs about the likely effectiveness of a therapy contribute strongly to a client's full engagement in the therapy and the effectiveness of the therapy.

As for gender, there is little evidence that women or men do better in therapy with a therapist of the same gender (Garfield, 1994; Huppert et al., 2001; Teyber & McClure, 2000). In the largest study of the treatment of depression, for example, clients who were matched with a therapist of their gender did not recover more quickly or more fully than clients who were matched with a therapist of the other gender (Zlotnick, Elkin, & Shea, 1998). This was true whether the client received cognitive-behavioral therapy, interpersonal therapy, or drug therapy.

Women and men do tend to report that they prefer a therapist of the same gender, however (Garfield, 1994; Simons & Helms, 1976). Again, because the client's comfort with a therapist is an important contributor to a client's seeking therapy and remaining in therapy for an entire course, gender matching may still be important in therapy.

Culturally Specific Therapies

Our review of the relationships among culture and therapy has focused on the forms of therapy most often practiced in modern, industrialized cultures, such as psychodynamic, behavior, and cognitive therapies. Cultural groups, even within modern, industrialized countries, often have their own forms of therapy for distressed people, however (Hall, 2001). Let's examine two of these.

Native American healing processes simultaneously focus on the physiology, psychology, and religious practices of the individual (LaFromboise, Trimble, & Mohatt, 1998). "Clients" are encouraged to transcend the self and experience the self as embedded in the community and as an expression of the community. Family and friends are brought together with the individual in traditional ceremonies involving prayers, songs, and dances that emphasize the Native American cultural heritage and the reintegration of the individual into the cultural network. These ceremonies may be supplemented by a variety of herbal medicines, used for hundreds of years to treat people with physical and psychological symptoms.

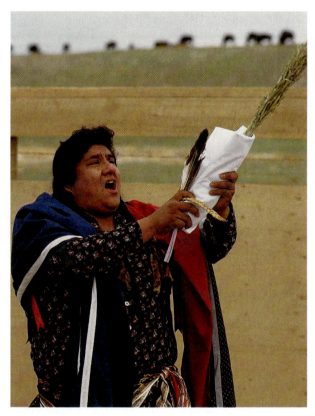

Several cultures have healing rituals that have been part of their cultural traditions for generations.

Hispanics in the southwestern United States and in Mexico suffering from psychological problems may consult folk healers, known as *curanderos* or *curanderas* (Koss-Chioino, 1995; Rivera, 1988). One survey of urban Hispanic American women in Colorado found that 20 percent had consulted a curandero for treatment (Rivera, 1988). Curanderos use religion-based rituals to overcome the folk illnesses believed to cause psychological and physical problems. These illnesses may be the result of hexes placed on the individual, soul loss, or magical fright. The healing rituals include prayers, the use of holy palm, and incantations. Curanderos may also apply healing ointments or oils and prescribe herbal medicines.

Native Americans and Hispanics often seek both folk healers and psychiatric care from mental-health professionals practicing the therapies described in this chapter. Mental-health professionals need to be aware of the practices and beliefs of folk healing when treating clients from these cultural groups. They need to keep in mind the possibility that clients will combine these forms of therapy, following some of the recommendations of both types of healers.

SUMMING UP

- Interpersonal therapy is a short-term therapy that focuses on clients' current relationships and concerns but explores the roots of their problems in past relationships.

- Family systems therapists focus on changing maladaptive patterns of behavior within family systems to reduce psychopathology in individual members.

- In group therapy, people who share a problem come together to support each other, learn from each other, and practice new skills. Self-help groups are a form of group therapy that does not involve a mental-health professional.

- The community mental-health movement was aimed at deinstitutionalizing people with mental disorders and treating them through community mental-health centers, halfway houses, and day treatment centers. The resources for these community treatment centers have never been adequate, however, and many people do not have access to mental-health care.

- Primary prevention programs aim to stop the development of disorders before they start.

- Secondary prevention programs provide treatment to people in the early stages of their disorders, in the hope of reducing the development of the disorders.

- The values inherent in most psychotherapies that can clash with the values of certain cultures include the focus on the individual, the expression of emotions and disclosure of personal concerns, and the expectation that clients take initiative.

- People from minority groups may be more likely to remain in treatment if matched with a therapist from their own cultural group, but there are large individual differences in these preferences.

- There are a number of culturally specific therapies designed by cultural groups to address psychopathology within the traditions of those cultures.

EVALUATING TREATMENTS

In 1952, well-known British psychologist Hans Eysenck stunned the field when he reviewed studies evaluating the effectiveness of psychotherapy and concluded that psychotherapy does not work. People who had received psychotherapy apparently fared no better than people who were untreated or who were placed on a waiting list.

The number and quality of studies evaluating psychotherapies prior to 1952 were limited. Not surprisingly, Eysenck's review prompted a great deal of new research. Several reviews of this research over the past five decades have concluded that psychotherapy does, indeed, have positive effects and is better than no treatment at all or than various placebos (see Westen, Novotny, & Thompson-Brenner, 2004).

Are some psychotherapies clearly better than others? Some reviews have concluded the answer is no (see Wampold et al., 1997). Rosenweig (1936) called this the *Dodo bird verdict*—"Everybody has won and all must have prizes"—quoting from the Dodo bird in *Alice in Wonderland*. Other reviews suggest that some therapies are better than others, at least for some disorders (Crits-Christoph, 1997; Dobson, 1989; Engels, Garnefski, & Diekstra, 1993; Lambert & Bergen, 1994; Shadish et al., 1993; Smith, Glass, & Miller, 1980).

Some theorists argue that one therapy is unlikely to win over another in therapy outcome studies, because all therapies share certain components that make them successful. This may seem an outrageous idea—on the surface, the different types of therapy described in this chapter may seem radically different. Indeed, proponents of a given approach have often been loud in their opposition to other approaches, decrying these other approaches as useless or even harmful to clients. There is increasing evidence, however, that there are some common components to successful therapies, even when the specific techniques of the therapies differ greatly (see Table 5.6).

The first of these components is a *positive relationship* with the therapist (Norcross, 2002). Clients

TABLE 5.6 Common Components of Successful Therapies

All successful therapies may share certain components that contribute to their success.

Component	Result
Positive relationship with therapist	Affirmation and safety to explore difficult issues or to make difficult changes
Explanation for symptoms	Insight into symptoms and a plan for how to alleviate them
Confrontation of negative emotions	Habituation to emotions and/or catharsis

who trust their therapists and believe that the therapists understand them are more willing to reveal important information, to engage in homework assignments, and to try new skills or coping techniques that the therapists suggest. In addition, simply having a positive relationship with a caring, understanding human being goes a long way toward helping people overcome distress and change behaviors.

Second, all therapies provide clients with an *explanation or interpretation* of why they are suffering (Ingram, Hayes, & Scott, 2000). Simply having a label for painful symptoms and an explanation for those symptoms seems to help many people feel better, much as having a diagnosis for a physical ailment can bring relief. This may suggest that insight provides relief. In addition, however, the explanations that therapies provide for symptoms are usually accompanied by a set of recommendations for how to overcome those symptoms. Following these recommendations may provide the main relief from the symptoms.

In any case, it seems clear that a client has to believe the explanation given to him or her for the symptoms in order for the therapy to help (Frank, 1978). For example, studies of cognitive-behavioral therapy for depression have found that the extent to which clients believe and accept the rationale behind this therapy is a significant predictor of the effectiveness of the therapy (Fennell & Teasdale, 1987). Clients to whom the rationale behind cognitive therapy makes sense engage more actively in therapy and are less depressed after a course of therapy than are those who don't accept the rationale for the therapy from the outset. A major problem in drug therapies is the high dropout rate from these therapies. Often, people drop out either because they do not experience quick enough relief from the drugs and therefore believe the drugs will not work or because they feel they need to talk about problems to overcome them.

A number of other common components across psychotherapies have been suggested (Frank, 1978; Prochaska, 1995; Snyder et al., 2000). For example, most therapies encourage clients to *confront painful emotions* and have techniques for helping them become less sensitive to these emotions. In behavior therapy, systematic desensitization or flooding might be used. In psychodynamic therapies, interpretation of transference and catharsis might be used. Whatever technique is used, the goal is to help the client stop denying, avoiding, or repressing the painful emotions and become able to accept and experience the emotions without being debilitated by them.

Finally, the treatment outcome literature has essentially ignored the question of whether the efficacy of treatments varies by cultural group or ethnicity (Miranda et al., 2005). An analysis conducted for the report of the surgeon general entitled "Mental Health: Culture, Race and Ethnicity" (U.S. Department of Health and Human Services [USDHHS], 2001) found that, of 9,266 participants involved in efficacy studies forming the major treatment guidelines for bipolar disorder, schizophrenia, depression and attention deficit/hyper-activity disorder (ADHD), only 561 African Americans, 99 Latinos, 11 Asian American/Pacific Islanders, and 0 American Indian/Alaskan Natives were included. Few of these studies had the power necessary to examine the impact of care on specific minorities. The need for more studies specifically examining the cultural variation in the efficacy of therapy is obvious.

SUMMING UP

- Some reviews of studies of the effectiveness of psychological treatments find they are all equally effective, but others suggest that certain treatments are more effective than others in treating specific disorders.

- Methodological and ethical problems make doing good research on the effectiveness of therapy difficult.

- Most successful therapies establish a positive relationship between a therapist and client, provide an explanation or interpretation to the client, and encourage the client to confront painful emotions.

SPECIAL ISSUES IN TREATING CHILDREN

Every therapy described in this chapter has probably been used to treat children and adolescents with psychological disorders. Studies of the effectiveness of biological, psychological, and interpersonal, and social therapies generally show that children and adolescents receiving therapy have better outcomes than do those receiving no therapy (Kazdin, 2003a; Kazdin & Weisz, 2003). The effectiveness of any type of therapy may depend largely on the type of disorder the child or adolescent has.

Designing and applying effective therapies for children and adolescents involve problems similar to those that arise in assessing and diagnosing disorders in children and adolescents (refer to Chapter 4). These problems include the need to match the therapy to the child's developmental level; the possibility that a therapy, especially a drug therapy, will have long-term negative effects on the child's development; the fact that children are embedded in families that often need to be treated as well; and the fact that children and adolescents seldom refer themselves for treatment and thus often are not motivated to engage in treatment.

Psychotherapies Matched to Children's Developmental Levels

As we discussed in Chapter 4, children can have difficulty expressing their feelings and concerns in words, particularly when they are very distressed. Therapists use a variety of methods to elicit information from children about their feelings. For example, they may have children draw pictures or engage in play that symbolizes how they are feeling.

Psychodynamically oriented therapists believe that expressing feelings and concerns through play can help the child master these feelings and concerns and overcome negative behaviors. Their therapy with a child may consist primarily of helping the child engage in this indirect expression and exploration of feelings and concerns. Other therapists use play or other projective techniques only as tools to assess a child's feelings and concerns.

Can children participate in talking therapies, such as cognitive-behavioral therapy? It seems that the answer is yes, although the conversations between the therapist and child must be at a level that is appropriate for the child's age (Roberts, Vernberg, & Jackson, 2000). However, many therapists believe that, for children, behavior-oriented therapies are more appropriate than are talking therapies, because behavior therapies are not as dependent on children's verbal abilities. Moreover, children may have trouble changing their behaviors only by changing their thinking—it may take repeated practicing of new behaviors and reinforcement of these behaviors for children to learn them. Comparisons of behavior and nonbehavior therapies for children have suggested that behavior therapies produce a larger and more reliable effect, although nonbehavior therapies do have positive effects on children (Weisz & Hawley, 2002).

The Effects of Drugs on Children and Adolescents

Drug therapies are becoming increasingly popular in treating children and adolescents with psychological problems (Martin, et al., 2002). Drugs were initially used to treat only the most severe disorders in children, such as autism, but they are now being used to treat disorders such as depression and phobias. The use of drugs in children has been extremely controversial, largely because of fears that drugs will have toxic effects both in the short term and in the long term. Finding a safe dosage of drugs for children is initially tricky, because body size, age, and hormones all affect the metabolism of drugs, and there is more variability in the proper dosage of a drug among children than there is among adults.

Most of the drugs used to treat psychological problems in children and adolescents are not approved for use in these populations. Fears of possible negative effects of these drugs were heightened by reports that the serotonin reuptake inhibitors (SSRIs), which are widely prescribed for depression, anxiety, and other conditions in children and adolescents, increase the risk of children committing suicide (see Couzin, 2004; Ramchandani, 2004; Wessely & Kerwin, 2004). Close monitoring is clearly needed when children or adolescents must use psychotherapeutic drugs.

The Need to Treat the Child's Family

Most children live in some sort of family, whether in the traditional two-parent family, with a single parent or perhaps a grandparent, in a foster-care family, or in some other configuration. Many clinicians believe that children's disorders cannot be treated effectively outside the context of the family (Mirsalimi et al., 2003). The family may be the direct cause of a child's disorder, such as when one parent is physically abusive to the child and perhaps to other members of the family. In such cases, treating the child without correcting the cause of

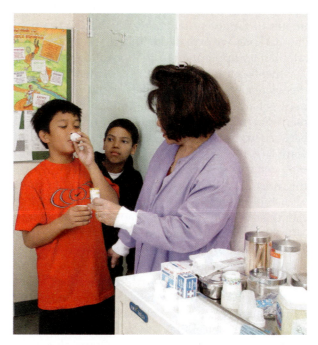

The use of medications to treat children with mental-health problems is controversial.

"Don't you realize, Jason, that when you throw furniture out the window and tie your sister to a tree, you make mommy and daddy very sad?" *© Sidney Harris, courtesy ScienceCartoonsPlus.com*

the child's problem (i.e., the parental abuse) is ineffective. Indeed, sometimes the parent needs therapy even more than the child.

In other cases, the family may not have directly caused the child's problem but may be reinforcing or supporting it in some way. For example, a child may have trouble controlling aggressive behavior, perhaps because of a biological dysfunction, but the family reinforces the child's aggressivity by allowing her to have what she wants when she threatens to lose control. In such cases, teaching family members how to extinguish the child's aggressive behavior can help the child gain control over that behavior, even if the initial cause of the behavior is biological (Estrada & Pinsof, 1995). Children and their families are sometimes treated with the techniques of family systems therapy, but all the psychotherapies we explored in this chapter have been adapted for application to children and families.

Incorporating the family into a child's treatment creates many difficulties, however. A child may not want his or her family involved in treatment. For example, an adolescent who is depressed because his mother is emotionally abusive may not want to confront his mother in therapy and instead may want an exclusive relationship with the caring therapist. The therapist may still choose to meet with the parent, apart from the adolescent, if the therapist believes the parent must be dealt with in order for the adolescent's problems to be overcome. The adolescent must know the therapist is meeting with the parent, however, and must be helped to trust that his relationship with the therapist is not compromised by these meetings with the parent. Family members may not want to join therapy, particularly if they feel they are being blamed for the child's problems. If they do join therapy, they may not cooperate with the therapist in overcoming the child's and family's problems.

Therapists are sometimes faced with extremely difficult decisions about whether to remove children from their families, such as when a therapist believes a family poses a danger to a child. They also must decide when to allow a child to return to a family from which he or she has been removed because of a perceived danger. A therapist's perceptions of the danger a family poses to a child can be influenced by the therapist's biases against the ethnicity or culture of the family or by misunderstandings of the parenting practices of that ethnic or cultural group. For example, Gray and Cosgrove (1985) note that spanking is an accepted form of discipline in some ethnic and socioeconomic groups in the United States but can be taken as evidence of child abuse by social workers and therapists who do not believe spanking is appropriate. Certain cultures may accept some parenting practices that therapists never want to endorse, but therapists must be careful to take into account the cultural context of a parent's behaviors before passing judgment.

Children's Unwillingness to Seek Therapy

Most children and adolescents who enter therapy do not seek it for themselves (Yeh & Weisz, 2001). They may be taken by their parents, who are overwhelmed by their children's behavior or emotional difficulties. Often, troubled children are first identified by school officials, by their pediatricians, by social service agents (e.g., welfare workers), or by the criminal justice system (Snowden & Yamada, 2005). Children who enter psychotherapy through any of these avenues may enter it reluctantly and thus may not participate wholeheartedly in therapy. Little research has been done on the effects of the relationship between a child and a therapist on the outcome of child psychotherapy, but it is likely that a warm, positive relationship with a therapist is as important in therapy with children as it is in therapy with adults. Therapists usually must work against a child's initial reluctance to enter therapy in order to establish a good therapeutic relationship.

Unfortunately, most children who could benefit from therapy do not receive it. Treatment facilities specializing in children's problems are unavailable in many parts of the United States and other industrialized countries and are nonexistent in other parts of the world. The child welfare system sees many troubled children, often the victims of abuse and neglect. Such children are increasingly placed in long-term foster care, rather than given specialized psychological treatment. Many children in the juvenile justice system suffer from psychological disorders, including conduct disorders, depression, and drug addiction, but few receive long-term, intensive treatment (Cauce et al., 2002). There is much room for expanding services to children with psychological problems.

SUMMING UP

- Treatments for children must take into account their cognitive skills and developmental levels and must adapt to their ability to comprehend and participate in therapy.

- There are reasons to be concerned about the possible toxic effects of drugs on children.

- Often, a child's family must be brought into therapy, but the child or the family may object.

- Most children who enter therapy do not seek it out themselves but are taken by others, raising issues about children's willingness to participate in therapy.

CHAPTER INTEGRATION

Many theorists have argued for integration of the different psychotherapies (e.g., Norcross, Beutler, & Caldwell, 2002). Although it may be difficult to integrate the theories behind the therapies because these theories disagree too profoundly on the causes of psychopathology, it may be possible to integrate the techniques of the therapies into a group of strategies used as the therapist sees fit (see Figure 5.2). Indeed, therapists commonly see themselves as eclectics—using the techniques of various therapies depending on the specific issues needing to be addressed. For example, a psychologist might use behavioral techniques for treating phobias but more psychodynamic techniques for treating people who have chronic moderate anxiety.

In addition, team approaches to treatment are becoming increasingly common. A psychologist may provide psychotherapy to clients, with a psychiatrist available to prescribe medications if warranted. A team approach to treatment is especially important for people with chronic mental disorders that can be debilitating, such as schizophrenia. As we discuss in Chapter 11, people with schizophrenia often need drug therapies, psychotherapy that helps them cope with their illnesses, and community-oriented interventions that help them find jobs and housing and reintegrate into society. The pharmacy student in *Extraordinary People* is working with a team such as this. Those people who are able to receive comprehensive care often can live full, productive lives.

FIGURE 5.2	Integrated treatments capitalize on the most effective elements of different therapies.

"I utilize the best from Freud, the best from Jung and the best from my uncle Marty, a very smart fellow." © *Sidney Harris, courtesy ScienceCartoonsPlus.com*

Extraordinary People: Follow-Up

"What I have been trying to express here is the actual reality of what being 'individually titrated to an antipsychotic medicine' and having schizophrenia means to someone personally going through it as opposed to how objectively and easily it is expressed in pharmacy classes. My instructors have stated that 'antipsychotics alleviate symptoms but do not cure psychoses,' but this matter-of-fact statement has very personal meaning for me. It involves internal conflicts and many complicated adjustments—getting to a psychologist outside the city, or if the necessity of hospitalization occurs, getting hospitalized outside the city so fellow students and the pharmacy

school will not have access to that information about me. It means never being able to see well because of the side effects of the medication. It also means enormous medical bills and debts. . . .

"Finally, I heard a teacher in one class talk about long-term chronic illness such as schizophrenia in a way that suggested the teacher knew something about the disease and had looked beyond the myths. Through this class, I began to understand a little better my own noncompliance with the psychotropic drugs; how unacceptable my illness was not only to me, but would have been to others if they had known my diagnosis. I didn't take the medicine at times because I didn't want the disease, its problems, and its stigma. I wanted to be normal. And even now in a professional pharmacy school it would probably shock many people to know a schizophrenic was in their class, would be a pharmacist, and could do a good job. And knowledge of it could cause loss of many friends and acquaintances. So even now I must write this article anonymously. But I want people to know I have schizophrenia, that I need medicine and psychotherapy, and at some times I have required hospitalization. But, I also want them to know that I have been on the dean's list, and have friends, and expect to receive my pharmacy degree from a major university.

"When you think about schizophrenia next time, try to remember me; there are more people like me out there trying to overcome a poorly understood disease and doing the best they can with what medicine and psychotherapy have to offer them. And some of them are making it." (Anonymous, 1983, pp. 152–155).

Chapter Summary

- A wide variety of biological and psychological approaches to the treatment of psychological disorders have been developed in line with different theories of the causes of these disorders. Biological therapies most often involve drugs intended to regulate the functioning of the brain neurotransmitters associated with a psychological disorder or to compensate for structural brain abnormalities or the effects of genetics (review Table 5.1).

- Antipsychotic medications help reduce unreal perceptual experiences, unreal beliefs, and other symptoms of psychosis. Antidepressant drugs help reduce the symptoms of depression. Lithium, anticonvulsants, and calcium channel blockers help reduce mania. Barbiturates and benzodiazepines help reduce anxiety.

- Herbal medicines have been used for centuries to treat psychological symptoms and have increased in popularity in recent years. Most herbal medicines have not been sufficiently tested, however, and some have been shown not to be very effective.

- Electroconvulsive therapy is used to treat severe depression. Psychosurgery is used in rare circumstances.

- Repetitive transcranial magnetic stimulation (rTMS) is a technique in which powerful magnets are used to stimulate the brain. It has proven useful for some psychological disorders.

- Psychological therapies can be delivered to individual clients or used in a group setting. They include

  1. Psychodynamic therapies, which focus on unconscious conflicts and interpersonal conflicts that lead to maladaptive behaviors and emotions

  2. Behavior therapies, which focus on changing specific maladaptive behaviors and emotions by changing the reinforcements for them

  3. Cognitive therapies, which focus on changing the way clients think about important situations

  4. Humanistic therapy, which intends to help clients realize their potential for self-actualization (review Table 5.2)

- Two types of treatment focus on the individual's relationships and roles in social systems. Interpersonal therapies are based on psychodynamic theories but focus more on current relationships and concerns. Family systems therapies attempt to break maladaptive patterns of relating among family members.

- The community mental-health movement intended to coordinate community services for people with mental disorders. Patients were deinstitutionalized and treated in community mental-health centers, day treatment centers, and halfway houses. Because adequate resources were never put into this movement, its goals were never fully realized.

- Prevention programs focus on preventing disorders before they develop, retarding the development of disorders in their early stages, and reducing the impact of disorders on people's functioning.

- Some clients may wish to work with therapists of the same culture or gender, but it is unclear whether matching a therapist and client in terms of culture and gender is necessary for therapy to be effective. It is important for therapists to be sensitive to the influences of culture and gender on a client's attitudes toward therapy and various solutions to problems.

- Some studies comparing different therapies suggest they are equally effective, whereas others suggest that certain therapies are more effective than others in the treatment of specific disorders. Common components of effective therapy seem to be a good therapist-client relationship, an explanation for symptoms, and the confrontation of negative emotions.

- Therapy with children has its own set of challenges. First, a therapy must be matched to a child's developmental level for the child to be able to participate fully. Second, therapists must be concerned about the short-term and long-term effects of drugs on children's development. Third, children's families may need to be brought into therapy. Fourth, children do not tend to seek

therapy for themselves and thus are sometimes reluctant to participate.

MindMap CD-ROM

The following resources on the MindMap CD-ROM that came with this text will help you to master the content of this chapter and prepare for tests:

- Interactive Segment: Systematic Desensitization
- Chapter Timeline
- Chapter Quiz

Key Terms

psychotherapy 136

chlorpromazine 136

phenothiazines 136

neuroleptic 137

butyrophenone 137

antipsychotic drugs 138

antidepressants 138

monoamine oxidase inhibitors (MAOIs) 138

tricyclic antidepressants 138

selective serotonin reuptake inhibitors (SSRIs) 139

lithium 139

anticonvulsants 140

calcium channel blockers 140

antianxiety drugs 140

barbiturates 140

benzodiazepines 140

electroconvulsive therapy (ECT) 142

prefrontal lobotomy 143

psychosurgery 143

repetitive transcranial magnetic stimulation (rTMS) 143

psychodynamic therapies 145

free association 145

resistance 145

transference 145

working through 147

catharsis 147

therapeutic alliance 147

psychoanalysis 147

humanistic therapy (person-centered therapy) 148

client-centered therapy (CCT) 148

unconditional positive regard 148

reflection 148

behavior therapies 149

behavioral assessment 149

role-play 149

systematic desensitization therapy 149

modeling 149

in vivo exposure 150

flooding (implosive therapy) 150

token economy 151

response shaping 151

social skills training 151

cognitive therapies 151

behavioral assignments 153

interpersonal therapy (IPT) 154

family systems therapy 155

group therapy 157

self-help groups 157

community mental-health centers 158

halfway houses 158

day treatment centers 158

primary prevention 159

secondary prevention 159

> Chapter 6

The Dream Tree
by Daniel Nevins

If the mind, which rules the body, ever forgets itself so far as to trample upon its slave, the slave is never generous enough to forgive the injury; but will rise and smite its oppressor.

—Longfellow, *Hyperion* (1839)

Stress Disorders and Health Psychology <

CHAPTER OVERVIEW

Extraordinary People

■ **Norman Cousins:** *Healing with Laughter*

Physiological Responses to Stress

Our bodies have a natural physiological response to stress, known as the fight-or-flight response. In the short term, this physiological response is adaptive, because it helps the body fight or flee from a threat. When this physiological response is prolonged, however, it causes wear and tear on the body, potentially contributing to ulcers, asthma, headaches, coronary heart disease, high blood pressure, and impairment of the immune system. Events that people perceive as stressful are often uncontrollable or unpredictable.

Sleep and Health

Stress can affect health indirectly by leading people to engage in less healthy behaviors, such as not sleeping enough. Some people develop sleep disorders, which the DSM-IV-TR divides into four categories: sleep disorders due to another mental disorder, sleep disorders due to a general medical condition, substance-induced sleep disorders, and primary sleep disorders. The most well-known primary sleep disorder is insomnia.

Personality and Health

Some personality styles that have been linked to poor physical health include dispositional pessimism and the Type A behavior pattern. Each of these may contribute to poor health by causing a chronic hyperarousal of the fight-or-flight response or by causing people to engage in unhealthy behaviors. One coping style associated with better health is seeking positive social support.

Interventions to Improve Health

Health psychologists have designed a variety of cognitive and behavioral interventions to improve people's physical health, including guided mastery techniques that help people learn healthy behaviors and biofeedback. Social interventions for health focus on helping people use or change their social environment to improve their health.

Posttraumatic Stress Disorder, Acute Stress Disorder, and Adjustment Disorder

Posttraumatic stress disorder (PTSD) is a set of symptoms—including hypervigilance, reexperiencing of trauma, and emotional numbing—experienced by trauma survivors. Acute stress disorder has the same symptoms as PTSD but is experienced for a short time after the trauma. Adjustment disorder is diagnosed when people experience depressive or anxiety symptoms or antisocial behavior in the 3 months following a stressor. Some predictors of people's vulnerability to PTSD are the proximity, duration, and severity of the stressor; the availability of social support; pretrauma distress; and coping strategies. Treatment generally involves exposing people to their fears, challenging their cognitions, and helping them manage ongoing problems. Eye movement desensitization and reprocessing therapy is a controversial intervention for PTSD. Drug therapies may be used to quell distress.

Taking Psychology Personally

■ **What to Do If You've Been Sexually Assaulted**

Chapter Integration

Social factors, such as the experience of trauma; psychological factors, such as personality and health-related behaviors; and biological factors, such as the physiological stress response, have reciprocal effects on each other that contribute to an individual's vulnerability to a stress-related disorder.

Extraordinary People

Norman Cousins: *Healing with Laughter*

In 1964, Norman Cousins, a successful writer at the *Saturday Review,* was diagnosed with ankylosing spondylitis, a painful collagen disease. After many medical tests and days in the hospital, doctors gave him a 1 in 500 chance of living.

Cousins refused to believe that he would succumb to the disease and set out to find a course of action that might reverse its progression. His 1979 book *Anatomy of an Illness* describes his use of comedy and movies to raise his levels of positive emotions and thereby affect the functioning of his adrenal and endocrine systems. Cousins eventually recovered from his illness and became known for his view that laughter cured his fatal disease.

Although many scientists criticized Cousins' conclusions about the role of laughter in his recovery, Cousins objected that these criticisms tended to oversimplify his theorizing about the role of positive emotions in recovery and the scientific evidence that positive emotions have healing powers. After returning to his career as a writer for several years, Cousins spent the last 12 years of his life at the UCLA Medical School, working with researchers to find scientific proof for his beliefs. It is clear that Cousins played a pivotal role in the movement toward more holistic approaches to patient care by physicians and hospitals. Following is an excerpt of an essay Cousins wrote, based on his experience:

> A good place to begin, I thought, was with amusing movies. Allen Funt, producer of the spoofing television program "Candid Camera," sent films of some of his "CC" classics, along with a motion-picture projector. The nurse was instructed in its use.
>
> It worked. I made the joyous discovery that ten minutes of genuine belly laughter had an anesthetic effect and would give me at least two hours of pain-free sleep. When the painkilling effect of the laughter wore off, we would switch on the motion-picture projector again, and not infrequently, it would lead to another pain-free sleep interval. Sometimes the nurse read to me out of a trove of humor books.
>
> How scientific was it to believe that laughter—as well as the positive emotions in general—was affecting my body chemistry for the better? If laughter did in fact have a salutary effect on the body's chemistry, it seemed at least theoretically likely that it would enhance the system's ability to fight the inflammation. So we took sedimentation-rate readings just before as well as several hours after the laughter episodes. Each time, there was a drop of at least five points. The drop by itself was not substantial, but it held and was cumulative.
>
> I was greatly elated by the discovery that there is a physiological basis for the ancient theory that laughter is good medicine. . . . (Cousins, 1976, pp. 1458–63)

Many years have passed since Cousins' discovery that laughter was good medicine for him. Since then, there has been considerable new evidence that positive emotions speed physiological and psychological recovery from stress (Fredrickson & Joiner, 2002; Fredrickson et al., 2003). These findings evoke the ancient mind-body question: Does the mind affect the body, or does the body affect the mind?

In this chapter, we will review research on how stress affects us psychologically and physiologically. We will examine the psychological and social factors that make it harder or easier to cope with stress, as well as interventions to help people who have been exposed to considerable stress. Finally, we will consider two diagnosable psychological disorders, acute stress disorder and posttraumatic stress disorder (PTSD), as well as possible treatments.

First, what is stress? In general terms, experiencing **stress** means experiencing events that we perceive as endangering our physical or psychological well-being. These events are usually referred to as *stressors,* and people's reactions to them are labeled *stress responses* (Schneiderman, Ironson, & Siegel, 2005).

What makes some events especially stressful? Uncontrollable negative events, such as the loss of a job, the sudden death of a loved one, or the loss of one's home to a natural disaster, are perceived by most people as stressful. Indeed, any negative event is perceived as more stressful if it is *uncontrollable.* For example, in a classic experimental study, participants were shown vivid photographs of victims of violent deaths. One group of participants, the experimental group, could terminate their viewing by pressing a button. The other group, the control group, could not terminate their viewing by pressing a button. Both groups of participants saw the same photographs for the same duration of time. The level of anxiety in both groups was measured by their *galvanic skin response (GSR),* a drop in the electrical resistance of the skin, which is an index of physiological arousal. The experimental group showed much less anxiety while viewing the photographs than did the control group, even though the only difference between the groups was their control over their viewing (Geer & Maisel, 1972).

Similarly, a person who has a traffic accident because he or she is not wearing glasses while driving may experience the accident as less stressful than if he or she had not perceived a reason for the accident. An accident that happens because a person has forgotten to wear glasses can presumably be prevented from happening again by wearing glasses. An accident that appears to have no explanation cannot be prevented from happening again.

Unpredictability also makes some events especially stressful. Experimental studies have confirmed that unpredictable events are more stressful than predictable events. These studies show that both rats and human participants prefer mild but painful electric shocks or loud bursts of noise that are preceded by a warning tone (and therefore are predictable) to electric shocks or noise that is preceded by no warning tone (Abbott, Schoen, & Badia, 1984; Glass & Singer, 1972; Katz & Wykes, 1985).

Having sufficient warning of upcoming aversive events may allow people to prepare themselves in ways that reduce the impact of those events. Predictable aversive events may also be less stressful because people know they can relax until they get the warning that the events are about to occur. With unpredictable events, people feel they can never relax, because the events may occur at any time, so they remain anxious all the time. This explanation has been called the *safety signal hypothesis* (Seligman & Binik, 1977).

For example, perhaps a woman's boss occasionally flies into a rage, criticizing her in front of others. If these outbursts are completely unpredictable, then the employee is always on guard and may chronically feel stressed. If, however, she knows these outbursts happen only around the end of each fiscal quarter, when her boss is upset because he has to prepare a fiscal account for the firm, then she can relax to some extent during the remainder of the fiscal year.

Finally, any *change* in life that requires numerous readjustments—even a positive change—can be perceived as stressful. A positive change can challenge our self-concept or the limits of our capabilities (Holmes & Rahe, 1967). For example, most people think of marriage as a positive event, but it requires many readjustments in daily life and self-concept as two people go from living as single individuals to living as lifetime partners.

Nevertheless, negative events are more likely than positive events to be perceived as stressful and to have impacts on physical and psychological health (e.g., Sarason, Johnson, & Siegel, 1978). This may be because of the different consequences of positive and negative events. Although some positive events require people to make adjustments and to change their self-concepts, these changes tend to be for the better. The person affected usually gains

Unpredictable and uncontrollable negative events are often perceived as stressful.

something from the events and from the new roles that he or she takes. In contrast, negative events often involve loss and can threaten a person's self-esteem or sense of mastery of the world (Monroe & Hadjiyannakis, 2002).

PHYSIOLOGICAL RESPONSES TO STRESS

How do we respond to stress? When we face any type of stressor—a saber-toothed tiger, a burglar with a weapon, a first bungee jump—the body mobilizes to handle the stressor. The liver releases extra sugar (glucose) to fuel our muscles, and hormones are released to stimulate the conversion of fats and proteins to sugar. The body's metabolism increases in preparation for expending energy on physical action. Heart rate, blood pressure, and breathing rate increase and the muscles tense. At the same time, less essential activities, such as digestion, are curtailed. Saliva and mucus dry up, increasing the size of the air passages to the lungs.

FIGURE 6.1   **The Fight-or-Flight Response.** The body's fight-or-flight response is initiated by the part of the brain known as the hypothalamus. The hypothalamus stimulates the sympathetic division of the autonomic nervous system, which acts on smooth muscles and internal organs to produce the bodily changes shown in the figure. The hypothalamus also releases corticotropin-release factor (CRF), which triggers the pituitary gland to release adrenocorticotropic hormone (ACTH). In turn, ACTH then stimulates the adrenal glands to release about 30 other hormones. These hormones act on organs and muscles to prepare the body to fight or flee.

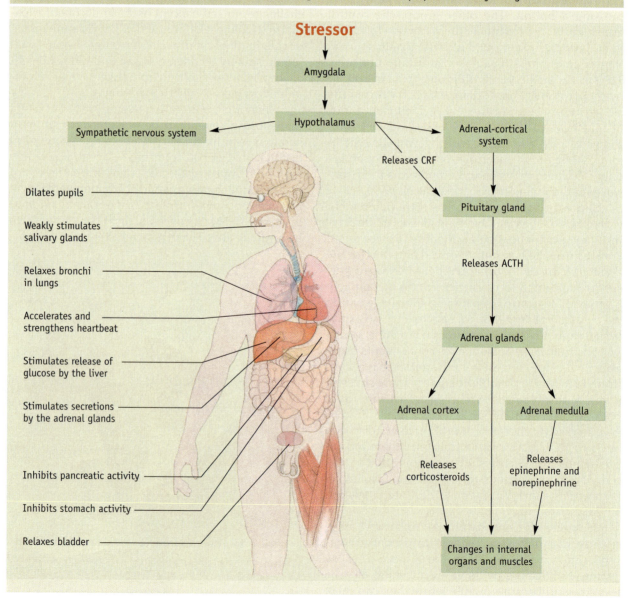

The body's natural painkillers, endorphins, are secreted, and the surface blood vessels constrict to reduce bleeding in case of injury. The spleen releases more red blood cells to help carry oxygen.

Most of these physiological changes result from the activation of two systems controlled by the hypothalamus, as shown in Figure 6.1: the *autonomic nervous system* (in particular, the sympathetic division of this system) and the *adrenal-cortical system* (a hormone-releasing system). These physiological responses have developed through evolution to prepare the body to fight a threat or to flee from it—to attack a saber-toothed tiger or to run away from it—and have been labeled **fight-or-flight response.** The hypothalamus first activates the sympathetic division of the autonomic nervous system. The sympathetic system acts directly on the smooth muscles and internal organs to produce some of the bodily changes—for example, increased heart rate and elevated blood pressure. The sympathetic system also stimulates the release of a number of hormones, including epinephrine (adrenaline) and norepinephrine, which perpetuate a state of physiological arousal.

The hypothalamus activates the adrenal-cortical system by releasing corticotrophin-release factor (CRF), which signals the pituitary gland to secrete adrenocorticotrophic hormone (ACTH), the body's major stress hormone. ACTH stimulates the outer layer of the adrenal glands (the adrenal cortex), resulting in the release of a group of hormones, the major one being **cortisol.** The amount of cortisol in blood or urine samples is often used as a measure of stress. ACTH also signals the adrenal glands to release about 30 other hormones, each of which plays a role in the body's adjustment to emergency situations. Eventually, the hormones signal the hippocampus, a part of the brain that helps regulate emotions, to turn off this physiological cascade when the threatening stimulus has passed. The fight-or-flight system thus has its own feedback loop, which normally regulates the level of physiological arousal experienced in response to a stressor.

This response is very adaptive when the stressor or threat is immediate and fight or flight is possible and useful. However, when a stressor is chronic and a person or an animal cannot fight it or flee from it, the chronic physiological arousal that results can be severely damaging to the body (Schneiderman et al., 2005).

In groundbreaking work that continues to be influential today, researcher Hans Selye (1979) described such physiological changes as part of the **general adaptation syndrome** that all organisms show in response to stress. The general adaptation syndrome consists of three phases (see Figure 6.2).

In the first phase, *alarm,* the body mobilizes to confront a threat by triggering sympathetic nervous system activity. In the second phase, *resistance,* the organism makes efforts to cope with the threat, by fighting it or fleeing from it. The third phase, *exhaustion,* occurs if the organism is unable to fight or flee from the threat and depletes physiological resources while trying to do so.

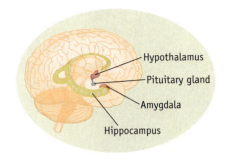

These structures of the brain are involved in activating or turning off the fight-or-flight response.

Selye argued that a wide variety of physical and psychological stressors trigger this response pattern. He also argued that the repeated or prolonged exhaustion of physiological resources, due to exposure to prolonged stressors that one cannot fight or flee from, is responsible for a wide array of physiological diseases. He conducted laboratory studies in which he exposed animals to several types of prolonged stressors—such as extreme cold and fatigue—and found that, regardless of the stress, certain bodily changes inevitably occurred: enlarged adrenal glands, shrunken lymph nodes, and stomach ulcers (Selye, 1979). Although some of Selye's specific hypotheses have not been supported in subsequent work, his general assertion that stress is an important determinant of the degree of physiological damage in several diseases has been supported (Schneiderman et al., 2005).

Taylor, Iacono, and McGue (2000) have suggested that, due to evolutionary pressures, there are gender differences in responses to stressful circumstances. Instead of engaging in fight or flight when faced with a threat, females engage in a

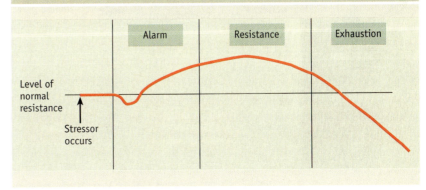

FIGURE 6.2   **The General Adaptation Syndrome.** According to Hans Selye, the body reacts in three phases to a stressor. In the first phase, alarm, the body mobilizes to confront the threat, which temporarily expends resources and lowers resistance. In the resistance phase, the body is actively confronting the threat and resistance is high. If the threat continues, the body moves into exhaustion.

Alarm   Resistance   Exhaustion

Level of normal resistance

Stressor occurs

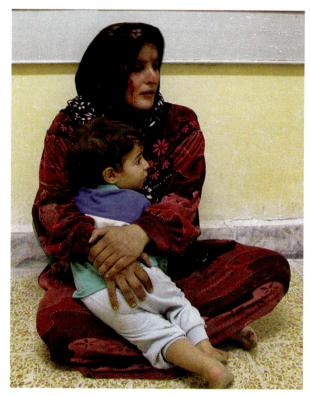

When confronted with an extremely stressful situation, some women focus on caring for others.

| **FIGURE 6.3** | **Three Models for the Effects of Psychological Factors on Disease.** These three models posit quite different pathways by which psychological factors, such as stress or personality style, might affect physical disease. |

a. The direct effects model

| Psychological factors (stress, personality styles) | → | Physiological changes | → | Disease |

b. The interactive model

| Psychological factors |
| **X** | } | → | Physiological changes | → | Disease |
| Vulnerability to disease |

c. The indirect effects model

| Psychological factors | → | Health-related behaviors (smoking, sleep) | → | Disease |

pattern they term "tend and befriend." Females are not as physically capable of fighting off many aggressors as men, and across evolutionary history they have had more responsibility than men for their offspring. As a result, rather than attempting to fight or flee from an aggressor, females join social groups to reduce their vulnerability and to gain resources, and they focus on caring for their offspring. This gender difference does not mean that stress has less impact on the physical health of women; in some cases, it may have more. It does suggest that the ways in which stress affects health in women may be different from those in men.

Health Psychology

Selye's work inspired the development of an entire field of psychology, known as **health psychology,** which investigates the effects of stress and other psychological factors on physical illness. This field has grown considerably over the past 30 years or so. Health psychologists are concerned with the roles of personality factors, coping styles, stressful events, and health-related behaviors, such as maintaining good sleep and diet habits, in the development and progress of physical disease. They also study whether changing a person's psychology—for example, by teaching stress-reduction techniques or inducing positive emotions—can influence the course of a physical disease and whether diseases can be prevented by helping people adopt healthy lifestyles and attitudes about the world.

Three models of the ways in which psychological factors affect physical disease drive most of the work in health psychology. The *direct effects model* suggests that psychological factors, such as stressful experiences or certain personality characteristics, directly cause changes in the physiology of the body, which in turn cause or exacerbate disease (see Figure 6.3a).

The *interactive model* suggests that psychological factors must interact with a preexisting biological vulnerability to a disease in order for an individual to develop the disease. According to this model, prolonged stress contributes to disease only in people who already have a biological vulnerability to the disease or perhaps have already developed mild forms of the disease (see Figure 6.3b).

The *indirect effects model* suggests that psychological factors affect disease largely by influencing whether people engage in health-promoting behaviors (see Figure 6.3c). Our diets, the amount of exercise we get, and whether we smoke can all influence our vulnerability to certain diseases, such as heart disease or lung cancer, and can influence the progression of many diseases once we have developed them. People under stress or with certain personality characteristics may be less prone to engage in healthy behaviors and more prone to engage in unhealthy behaviors. According to this model, psychological factors do not directly affect health but, rather, affect health indirectly by influencing health-related behaviors. Similarly, Norman Cousins' use of laughter to reduce his symptoms is an example of how health-promoting behaviors may help reduce physical disease.

Now let's examine some of the research into stress and disorders that modern health psychology has been particularly concerned with, such as coronary heart disease, hypertension, colds, and cancer.

Stress, Coronary Heart Disease, and Hypertension

CASE STUDY

Orrin was so mad he could scream. He had been told at 3:00 that afternoon to prepare a report on the financial status of his division of the company in time for a meeting of the board of directors the next morning. On the way home from work, someone rear-ended him at a stoplight and caused several hundred dollars in damage to his new car. When he got home from work, there was a message from his wife, saying she had been delayed at work and would not be home in time to cook dinner for the children, so Orrin would have to do it. Then, at dinner, Orrin's 12-year-old son revealed that he had flunked his math exam that afternoon.

After finishing the dishes, Orrin went to his study to work on the report. The kids had the TV on so loud he couldn't concentrate. Orrin yelled to the kids to turn off the TV, but they couldn't hear him. Furious, he stalked into the family room and began yelling at the children about the television and anything else that came to his mind.

Then, suddenly, Orrin began to feel a tremendous pressure on his chest, as if a truck were driving across it. Pain shot through his chest and down his left arm. Orrin felt dizzy and terrified. He collapsed onto the floor. His 7-year-old began screaming. Luckily, his 12-year-old called 911 for an ambulance.

Coronary heart disease occurs when blood vessels supplying the heart are blocked by plaque; complete blockage causes a myocardial infarction—a heart attack.

Orrin was having a *myocardial infarction*—a heart attack. A myocardial infarction is one endpoint of **coronary heart disease,** or **CHD.** CHD occurs when the blood vessels that supply the heart muscles are narrowed or closed by the gradual buildup of a hard, fatty substance called *plaque,* blocking the flow of oxygen and nutrients to the heart. This can lead to pain, called *angina pectoris,* which radiates across the chest and arm. When the oxygen to the heart is completely blocked, it can cause a myocardial infarction.

Coronary heart disease is the leading cause of death and chronic illness in the United States today, accounting for 20 percent of all deaths, most before the age of 65 (American Heart Association, 2002). CHD is also a chronic disease, and more than 12 million Americans live daily with its symptoms. Men are more prone to CHD than are women, but CHD is still the leading cause of death of women. African Americans and Hispanic Americans have higher rates of CHD than European Americans. People with family histories of CHD are more susceptible to CHD. CHD has been linked to high serum cholesterol, diabetes, smoking, and obesity.

People who live in chronically stressful environments over which they have little control appear to be at increased risk for CHD. For example, one study followed about 900 middle-aged men and women for over 10 years, tracking the emergence of coronary heart disease (Karasek, Russell, & Theorell, 1982). These people worked in a variety of jobs, and the researchers categorized these jobs in terms of how demanding they were and how much control they allowed a worker. Over the 10 years of this study, workers in jobs that were highly demanding but low in control had a risk for coronary heart disease that was one and one-half times greater than that of those in other occupations.

Hypertension, or high blood pressure, is a condition in which the supply of blood through the vessels is excessive, putting pressure on the vessel walls. Chronic high blood pressure can cause hardening of the arterial walls and deterioration of the cell tissue, leading eventually to coronary heart disease, kidney failure, and stroke. Approximately 50 million people in the United States have hypertension, and about 16,000 die each year due to hypertensive disease. Genetics appears to play a role in the predisposition to hypertension, but only about 10 percent of all cases of hypertension can be traced to genetics or to specific organic causes, such as kidney dysfunction. The other 90 percent of cases are known as *essential hypertension*, meaning the causes are unknown.

Because part of the body's response to stress—the fight-or-flight response—is to increase blood pressure, it is not surprising that people who live in chronically stressful circumstances are more likely to develop hypertension (Schneiderman et al., 2005). As an example, persons who move from quiet rural settings to crowded, noisy urban settings show increases in rates of hypertension.

One group that lives in chronically stressful settings and has particularly high rates of hypertension is low-income African Americans (American Heart Association, 2002). Many do not have adequate financial resources for daily living, are poorly educated and have trouble finding good employment, live in neighborhoods racked with violence, and are frequently exposed to racism. All these conditions have been linked to higher blood pressure. In addition, African Americans may be genetically prone to a particular pattern of cardiovascular response to stress that contributes to the development of hypertension (Anderson et al., 1989; Light & Sherwood, 1989).

Persons with hypertension and the children of parents with hypertension tend to show a stronger blood pressure response to a wide variety of stressors. In experimental situations, solving arithmetic problems and immersing their hands in ice water, people with no personal or family histories of hypertension showed much less response than those with a history of hypertension (Harrell, 1980). In addition, it takes longer for the blood pressure of persons with hypertension to return to normal following stressors than it does the blood pressure of those without hypertension.

This information suggests that people with hypertension and people with family/genetic histories of hypertension may have a heightened physiological reactivity to stress. If they are exposed to chronic stress, their chronically elevated blood pressure can lead to hardening and narrowing of the arteries, which creates a physiologically based hypertension (Harrell, 1980). Low-income African Americans may have both this physiological predisposition to heightened reactivity to stress *and* chronic exposure to stressful environments, making them doubly vulnerable to hypertension.

Stress and the Immune System

The **immune system** protects the body from disease-causing microorganisms. This system affects our susceptibility to infections, diseases, allergies, cancer, and autoimmune disorders, such as rheumatoid arthritis, in which the immune cells attack normal tissues of the body. Many components of the immune system fight disease. One of the fastest-growing areas of health psychology is *psychoneuroimmunology*, the study of the effects of psychological factors on the functioning of the immune system. Stress can affect the immune system in several ways. In particular, some of the biochemicals released as part of the fight-or-flight response, such as the corticosteroids, may suppress the immune system.

The most controlled research linking stress and immune system functioning has been conducted with animals. They are experimentally exposed to stressors and then the functioning of their immune system is measured directly. Studies have shown that **lymphocytes,** the cells of the immune system that attack viruses, are suppressed in animals that have been exposed to loud noise, electric shock, separation from their mothers as infants, separation from peers, and a variety of other stressors (Segerstrom & Miller, 2004).

Animals are most likely to show impairment of their immune system if exposed to stressors that are uncontrollable. In one experiment, one group of rats was subjected to electric shock that they could turn off by pressing a lever (Laudenslager et al., 1983). Another group received an identical sequence of shocks but could not control the shocks by pressing the lever. A third group received no shock. The investigators examined how well the rats' *T-cells*, lymphocytes that secrete chemicals that kill harmful

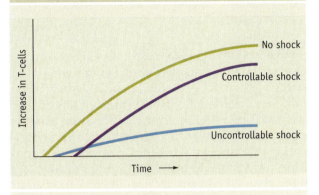

FIGURE 6.4   **The Effects of Controllable and Uncontrollable Shock on Rats' Immune Systems.** In one study, rats given uncontrollable shocks showed less increase in T-cells, which kill harmful cells, than did rats given controllable shocks or no shock.

Source: Laudenslager et al., 1983.

Studies suggest that immune-related diseases, such as colds, are more common among those who are under stress.

cells, multiplied when challenged by invaders. They found that the T-cells in the rats that could control the shock multiplied, as did those in the rats that were not shocked at all (see Figure 6.4). The T-cells in the rats exposed to uncontrollable shock multiplied only weakly, however. In another study following the same experimental design, investigators implanted tumor cells into rats, gave them controllable or uncontrollable shocks, and examined whether the rats' natural defenses rejected the tumors. Only 27 percent of the rats given uncontrollable shock rejected the tumors, whereas 63 percent of the rats given controllable shock rejected the tumors (Visintainer, Volpicelli, & Seligman, 1982).

Uncontrollable stress also is related to impaired immune system functioning in humans (Schneiderman et al., 2005). In one study, investigators exposed about 400 healthy volunteers either to a nasal wash containing one of five cold viruses or to an innocuous salt solution (Cohen, Tyrrell, & Smith, 1991). Each participant was assigned a stress score ranging from 3 (lowest stress) to 12 (highest stress), based on the number of stressful events they had experienced in the past year, the degree to which they felt able to cope with daily demands, and their frequency of negative emotions, such as anger and depression. The participants were examined daily for cold symptoms and for the presence of cold viruses or virus-specific antibodies in their upper respiratory secretions. About 35 percent of the volunteers who reported the highest stress in their lives developed colds, compared with about 18 percent of those with the lowest stress scores.

Most other studies of humans simply have compared the functioning of the immune system in persons undergoing particular stressors with that of persons not undergoing these stressors (see Cohen, 1996). For example, a study of people who survived Hurricane Andrew in 1992 found that those who had experienced more damage to their homes or whose lives had been more threatened by the storm showed poorer immune system functioning than people whose homes and lives had been safer (Ironson et al., 1997). Similarly, following the 1994 Northridge earthquake in the Los Angeles area, people whose lives had been more severely disrupted showed more decline in immune system functioning than those who had not experienced as much stress as a result of the earthquake (Solomon et al., 1997). People who worried more about the impact of the earthquake on their lives were especially likely to show detriments in *natural killer cells*, a type of T-cell that seeks out and destroys cells that have been infected with a virus (Segerstrom et al., 1998).

More common events have also been linked to deficits in immune system functioning. For example, students often complain that they become ill during exam times. Studies have verified the idea that college students and medical students are more prone to infectious illness during exam periods than at other times of the academic year (Glaser et al., 1986).

Negative interpersonal events seem particularly likely to affect immune system functioning. Married couples who have more conflictual interactions with each other show poorer immunological functioning than married couples with fewer conflictual interactions (Kiecolt-Glaser & Newton, 2001). Men and women who have recently been separated or divorced show poorer immune functioning than matched control subjects who are still married (Robles & Kiecolt-Glaser, 2003). However, the partner who has more control over the divorce or separation—that is, the partner who initiated the divorce or separation—shows better immune system functioning and better health than does the partner who has less control over the divorce or separation. This is one example of how perceptions of the controllability of a stressor can influence the impact of that stressor on health.

Several studies have examined whether stress can contribute to the development or progression of cancer in humans (see Segerstrom & Miller, 2004). The results of these studies have been mixed, some showing that people who are more stressed are more vulnerable to developing cancer or have faster progressions of their cancer than people who are less stressed. Again, it may be that people's perceptions or appraisals of stressors, not the presence of the stressors alone, determine the impact of the stressors on immune system functioning. For example, one study of women with breast cancer found that those who felt they had little control over their cancer and over other aspects of their lives were more likely to develop new tumors over a five-year period were women who felt more in control, even though the two groups of women did not differ in the type or initial seriousness of their cancers (Levy & Heiden, 1991; Watson et al., 1999). Similarly, although studies have not shown conclusively that stress contributes to the progression of acquired immune deficiency syndrome (AIDS), perceptions of control may be related to the progression of this disease (Baum & Posluszny, 2001).

SUMMING UP

- The body has a natural response to stress that prepares it for fight or flight. In the short term, this response is highly adaptive but, if it is chronically aroused, it can cause physical damage.
- There is substantial evidence that stress, particularly uncontrollable stress, increases the risks for coronary heart disease and hypertension, probably through chronic hyperarousal of the body's fight-or-flight response.
- There is mounting evidence from animal and human studies that stress impairs the functioning of the immune system, possibly leading to higher rates of infectious diseases.

SLEEP AND HEALTH

One of the first things to go when you are under stress is sleep. In 1993, the National Commission on Sleep Disorders Research estimated that at least one-third of all U.S. adults suffer from chronic sleep disturbances, especially chronic sleep deprivation due to busy schedules. Over the past century, the average night's sleep time has declined by more than 20 percent, as people have tried to fit more and more into the 24-hour day.

The costs to society of sleep disorders and sleepiness include lost lives, lost income, disabilities, accidents, and family dysfunction (Drake, Roehrs, & Roth, 2003; Léger, et al., 2002; McConnell, Bretz, & Dwyer, 2003). For example, each year in the United States, there are 200,000 sleep-related automobile accidents, and 5,000 of these are fatal. Twenty percent of automobile drivers admit to having fallen asleep at the wheel at least once. Some of the most serious disasters in modern history have been caused by mistakes made by sleepy people (Mitler & Miller, 1995). In 1979, the worst nuclear plant accident in the United States resulted from fatigued workers at Three Mile Island failing to respond to a mechanical problem at the plant. In 1986, the world's worst nuclear disaster happened in Chernobyl in the former Soviet Union while a test was being conducted by an exhausted team of engineers.

Young adults will sleep, on average, 9.2 hours per day when they have no environmental influences to interfere with sleep patterns, yet most young adults sleep 7.5 or fewer hours per day (Wolfson & Carskadon, 1998). Similarly, most middle-aged adults seem to need at least 7 or 8 hours of sleep per day but, on average, get less than 7 hours. People who work rotating shifts or in jobs demanding long periods of activity, such as nurses, doctors, firefighters, police, and rescue personnel, are often chronically sleep deprived. Even when they have time to sleep, they have trouble doing so, because their bodies' natural rhythms that promote sleep are disrupted by their irregular schedules. The effects of sleep deprivation are cumulative: A person builds up an increasing sleep debt for every 24-hour period in which he or she does not get adequate sleep.

Sleep Deprivation

Lack of sleep can impair health. In addition to the increased risk for accidents due to sleepiness, lack of sleep also appears to impair the immune system (Cruess et al., 2003). People who sleep fewer than six hours per night have a 70 percent higher mortality rate than do those sleeping at least seven or eight hours per night (Kryger, Roth, & Dement, 1994). This is true for both men and women, for people of many ethnicities, and for people with many different health backgrounds. People who work rotating shifts have higher rates of illness, including cardiovascular and gastrointestinal disease, than do people who do not work such shifts. Traumatic events can also cause loss of sleep, and the sleep deprivation then can affect the immune system. One study of people who survived Hurricane Andrew found that those with the most sleep problems also had the greatest decreases in immune system functioning (Ironson et al., 1997).

Sleep deprivation also has a number of psychological effects. Cognitive impairments caused by sleep deprivation include impairments in memory, learning, logical reasoning, arithmetic skills, complex verbal processing, and decision making. For example, reducing the amount of sleep to five hours per night for just two nights significantly reduces performance on math problems and creative thinking tasks. Thus, staying up to study for exams for just a couple of nights can significantly impair your ability to do as well as possible on those exams. A study of more than 3,000 high school students found that those who were getting Cs, Ds, and Fs in school were getting significantly less sleep than those getting As and Bs (Wolfson, 2002). Sleep deprivation also causes irritability, emotional ups and downs, and perceptual distortions, such as mild hallucinations.

How can people reduce sleepiness and the effects of sleep deprivation? First of all, they can get enough sleep. Although the social lives of college students often begin at 10 P.M. or later, it is important to keep in mind that the sleep lost on the weekend can affect performance and health for the rest of the week. Students who have families and/or jobs are especially prone to skipping sleep in order to get everything done. Good time-management skills can help people find more time in their days to accomplish all their tasks without having to give up much sleep. Avoiding alcohol, nicotine, and caffeine in the evening can also help people fall asleep and sleep well.

In addition to its direct positive effects on health, adequate sleep helps us feel more in control of the stressful events that befall us during the day. When we are alert and rested, challenging events may not seem so overwhelming, because we can marshal our best coping responses. Indeed, when we are rested, we may be better able to prevent stressful events from happening, because we are alert enough to anticipate them and to take action before they occur. Thus, sleep has both direct and indirect effects on our health by enhancing our ability to prevent or cope with stressful events.

Sleep Disorders

Some people experience so much difficulty in sleeping that they may be diagnosed with a sleep disorder. The DSM-IV-TR recognizes four general types of sleep disorders. *Sleep disorders related to another mental disorder* are sleep disturbances that are directly attributable to psychological disorders, such as depression or anxiety. *Sleep disorders due to a general medical condition* are sleep disturbances that result from the physiological effects of a medical condition. Many medical conditions can disturb sleep, including degenerative neurological illnesses (such as Parkinson's disease), cerebrovascular disease (such as vascular lesions to the upper brain stem), endocrine conditions (such as hypo- or hyperthyroidism), viral and bacterial infections (such as viral encephalitis), pulmonary diseases (such as chronic bronchitis), and pain from musculoskeletal diseases (such as rheumatoid arthritis or fibromyalgia). Norman Cousins mentioned that pain kept him awake many nights and that his laughter treatments helped him get a few hours of pain-free sleep.

Substance-induced sleep disorders are sleep disturbances due to the use of substances, including

Busy students are often sleep deprived.

TABLE 6.1   Concept Overview

Dyssomnias

These are the primary sleep disorders known as dyssomnias. Each condition must not be due to a general medical condition or substance use and must cause significant impairment in functioning to be diagnosed.

Type	Definition
Primary insomnia	Difficulty initiating or maintaining sleep, or nonrestorative sleep, for at least a month
Primary hypersomnia	Excessive sleepiness for at least one month, as evidenced by either prolonged sleep episodes or daytime sleep episodes that occur almost daily
Narcolepsy	Irresistible attacks of refreshing sleep that occur daily over at least three months plus either sudden loss of muscle tone or recurrent intrusions of elements of rapid eye movement (REM) sleep
Breathing-related sleep disorder	Sleep disruption leading to excessive sleepiness or insomnia that is due to a sleep-related breathing condition, such as apnea
Circadian rhythm sleep disorder	Sleep disruption leading to excessive sleepiness or insomnia that is due to a mismatch between the sleep-wake schedule required by a person's environment and his or her circadian sleep-wake pattern

Source: Reprinted with permission from the *Diagnostic and Statistical Manual of Mental Disorders,* Fourth Edition, Text Revision. Copyright © 2000. American Psychiatric Association.

prescription medications (such as medications that control hypertension or cardiac arrhythmias) and nonprescription substances (such as alcohol and caffeine).

The fourth category of sleep disorders is *primary sleep disorders*. These are further subdivided into **dyssomnias** (see the Concept Overview in Table 6.1), which involve abnormalities in the amount, quality, or timing of sleep, and **parasomnias** (see the Concept Overview in Table 6.2), which involve abnormal behavioral and physiological events occurring during sleep.

Insomnia

Probably the most familiar dyssomnia is **insomnia,** difficulty in initiating or maintaining sleep or sleep that chronically does not restore energy and alertness. People with insomnia usually report a combination of difficulty falling asleep and intermittent wakefulness during the night. A vicious cycle often develops in people with insomnia. The longer they lie in bed, unable to go to sleep, the more distressed and aroused they become. This arousal makes it even more difficult for them to fall asleep. Their arousal then becomes conditioned to their environment—to their bed and bedroom—so that their arousal levels go up when they try to go to bed the

next night. In addition, they may consciously worry about having trouble falling asleep, which adds more to their arousal level. Many people with insomnia report that they sleep better when they are in unfamiliar settings, such as hotel rooms. In contrast, people without insomnia report they sleep worse in unfamiliar settings (Hauri & Fisher, 1986).

Occasional problems with insomnia are extremely common, with as many as 50 percent of adults reporting they have had insomnia sometime in their lives and one in three adults complaining they have had insomnia in the past year (Nowell et al., 1998). Complaints of insomnia increase with age but decrease with socioeconomic status.

To be diagnosed with primary insomnia, people must have the symptoms of insomnia for at least one month, and the sleep disturbance must cause significant distress or impairment in their functioning. In addition, the insomnia must not be due to another mental disorder, to a medical condition, or to substance use. It is unclear how prevalent diagnosable insomnia is in the general population, but in one long-term study of young adults, 9 percent reported chronic insomnia (Angst et al., 1989).

Various medications are used to treat insomnia, including antidepressants, antihistamines, tryptophan, delta-sleep-inducing peptide (DSIP), mela-

TABLE 6.2   Concept Overview

Parasomnias

These are the primary sleep disorders known as parasomnias. Each condition must not be due to a general medical condition or substance use and must cause significant impairment in functioning to be diagnosed.

Type	Definition
Nightmare disorder	Repeated awakenings with detailed recall of extended and extremely frightening dreams, usually involving threats to survival, security, or self-esteem; on awakening, the person is alert and oriented.
Sleep terror disorder	Repeated, abrupt awakenings beginning with a panicky scream; intense fear and signs of autonomic arousal; relative unresponsiveness to the efforts of others to comfort the person; no detailed dream is recalled and there is amnesia for the episode.
Sleepwalking disorder	Repeated episodes of rising from the bed during sleep and walking about; while sleepwalking, the person has a blank, staring face, is relatively unresponsive to others, and can be awakened only with great difficulty; on awakening, the person has amnesia for the episode; within several minutes after awakening, there is no impairment of mental activity or behavior, although there may initially be a short period of confusion and disorientation.

Source: Reprinted with permission from the *Diagnostic and Statistical Manual of Mental Disorders,* Fourth Edition, Text Revision. Copyright © 2000. American Psychiatric Association.

tonin, and benzodiazepines (Dündar et al., 2004). All of these have proven effective in at least some studies, although the number of studies done on most of these agents is small. The agents that have proven most reliably effective are the benzoidiazepines and zolpidem (trade name Ambien). Those that have the least clear benefit are antihistamines and tryptophan (Lee, 2004; Nowell et al., 1998).

Several studies have shown that cognitive-behavioral interventions for insomnia can be highly effective (e.g., Bastien et al., 2004). These interventions have a number of components. **Stimulus-control therapy** involves a set of instructions designed to curtail behaviors that might interfere with sleep and to regulate sleep-wake schedules (Bootzin & Perlis, 1992):

1. Go to bed only when sleepy.
2. Use the bed and bedroom only for sleep and sex, not for reading, television watching, eating, or working.
3. Get out of bed and go to another room if you are unable to sleep for 15 to 20 minutes, and do not return to bed until you are sleepy.
4. Get out of bed at the same time each morning.
5. Don't nap during the day.

Sleep restriction therapy involves initially restricting the amount of time insomniacs can try to sleep in the night (Smith, 2001). Once their sleep becomes more efficient, the amount of time they are allowed to spend in bed is gradually increased, until they reach the greatest total amount of sleep possible while maintaining efficient sleep. In addition, people are often taught relaxation exercises (see the *Taking Psychology Personally* feature in Chapter 7) and are educated about the effect of diet, exercise, and substance use on sleep. Cognitive-behavioral interventions may be used to help counteract people's maladaptive cognitions about sleep, such as "There's no way I can go to sleep quickly." Although these behavioral and cognitive interventions typically take longer than the drug therapies to begin working with insomniacs, they tend to have more long-lasting effects (Nowell et al., 1998).

Other Sleep Disorders
Primary **hypersomnia** is the opposite of insomnia. People with hypersomnia are chronically sleepy and sleep for long periods at a time. They may sleep 12 hours at a stretch and still wake up sleepy. A nap during the day may last for an hour or more, and people may wake up unrefreshed. If their environment is not stimulating (for example, they are sitting in a boring lecture), they are sure to fall asleep.

They may even fall asleep at the wheel while driving. To qualify for a diagnosis, the hypersomnia must be present for at least a month and must cause significant distress or impairment in functioning. Again, the prevalence of hypersomnia in the general population is not known, but about 5 to 16 percent of people who go to sleep disorders clinics are diagnosed with primary hypersomnia (APA, 2000).

Narcolepsy involves irresistible attacks of sleep. People must experience these attacks for at least three months to be diagnosed. These sleep attacks are most likely to come during low-stimulation, low-activity situations but may also occur while the person is carrying on a conversation or driving a car. Sleep episodes generally last 10 to 20 minutes but can last up to an hour, and people may dream during the episodes. They wake up from these sleep attacks refreshed but then become sleepy again after several hours and may have chronic sleepiness. Narcolepsy most often starts in adolescence and is quite rare, affecting less than .05 percent of the general population.

If untreated, people with narcolepsy typically have two to six episodes of sleep per day. In addition to sleepiness, people diagnosed with narcolepsy must experience (1) cataplexy or (2) recurrent intrusions of elements of rapid eye movement (REM) sleep into the transition between sleep and wakefulness. **Cataplexy** consists of episodes of sudden loss of muscle tone, lasting from a few seconds to minutes. It occurs in about 70 percent of people with narcolepsy. They may suddenly drop objects, buckle at the knees, or even fall to the ground. Cataplexy is usually triggered by a strong emotion, such as anger or surprise. The intrusions of REM sleep often involve the experience of intense, dreamlike imagery just before falling asleep or just after awakening. Sometimes, these hallucinations are accompanied by a sense of paralysis, so people report seeing or hearing unusual things but being unable to move.

The most common *breathing-related sleep disorder* is obstructive **sleep apnea,** which involves repeated episodes of upper-airway obstruction during sleep. People with sleep apnea typically snore loudly, go silent and do not breathe for several seconds at a time, then gasp for air. Apnea occurs in up to 10 percent of the population and can begin anytime throughout the life span. It is most common, however, in overweight, middle-aged men and prepubertal children with enlarged tonsils.

Other primary sleep disorders include circadian rhythm sleep disorder, nightmare disorder, sleep terror disorder, and sleepwalking disorder (review Tables 6.1 and 6.2). Occasional problems with the symptoms of these disorders are very common, but only a small percentage of the population ever develops one of these sleep disorders. For example, most children have occasional nightmares but do not develop a disorder.

SUMMING UP

- The sleep disorders are divided into sleep disorders related to another mental disorder, sleep disorders due to a general medical condition, substance-induced sleep disorders, and primary sleep disorders.

- The primary sleep disorders are further divided into dyssomnias and parasomnias.

- The most common dyssomnia is insomnia. Hypersomnia, narcolepsy, and breathing-related sleep disorders, such as sleep apnea, are also dyssomnias.

- Sleep disorders, particularly insomnia, can be treated with a variety of drugs or through behavioral and cognitive-behavioral therapies that change sleep-related behavior and thinking patterns.

PERSONALITY AND HEALTH

In recent years, psychologists have explored certain personality characteristics and coping strategies that seem to be associated with an increased risk for a variety of diseases. Individuals with these characteristics or strategies appraise a wider range of events as stressful or do not readily engage in behaviors that reduce the stressfulness of events. Thus, these people are more chronically stressed, and their bodies are more chronically in the fight-or-flight response.

Pessimism

Being pessimistic appears to be bad for your health. In one study of 412 patients with human immunodeficiency virus (HIV), those who were pessimistic at a baseline assessment had a greater load of the virus 18 months later than those who were less pessimistic (Milam et al., 2004). Similarly, a study of gay men who were HIV-positive found that those who blamed themselves for negative events and those with more negative expectations showed more decline in immune functioning and greater development of HIV symptoms over time than those who were more optimistic (Reed et al., 1999; Segerstrom et al., 1996).

Pessimists' vulnerability to illness seems to be lifelong. In a long-term study of men in the Harvard classes of 1939 and 1940, those who were pessimistic in college were more likely to develop physical illness over the subsequent 35 years than were the men who were more optimistic (Peterson, Seligman, & Vaillant, 1988; see also Peterson et al., 1998). Other studies have found that pessimists recover more slowly from coronary bypass surgery and have more severe angina than optimists (Fitzgerald et al., 1993; Scheier et al., 1989). Also, pessimistic cancer patients are more likely than optimistic patients to die during the first few years after their diagnosis (Schulz et al., 1996).

How does pessimism affect health? People who are pessimistic tend to feel they have less control over their lives than people who are more optimistic and, therefore, may appraise more events as stressful. Thus, pessimism may contribute to poor health by causing chronic arousal of the body's fight-or-flight response, resulting in physiological damage (see Figure 6.5).

Several studies have found evidence for this explanation. In one, the blood pressure of pessimists and optimists was monitored daily for three days. The pessimists had chronically higher blood pressure levels than the optimists across the three days (Raikkonen et al., 1999). Another study found that older adults who were pessimistic showed poorer immune system functioning on two biological indices than those were optimistic, even after the researchers statistically controlled for differences between the pessimists and optimists on current health, depression, medication, sleep, and alcohol use (Kamen-Siegel et al., 1991).

A pessimistic outlook may also impair health by leading people to engage in unhealthy behaviors. In the previously mentioned work with people who were HIV-positive, researchers found that those who were more pessimistic were less likely to be engaging in healthy behaviors, such as maintaining proper diets, getting enough sleep, and exercising (Milam et al., 2004; Taylor et al., 1992). These behaviors are particularly important for HIV-positive people, because these healthy behaviors can reduce the risk of developing AIDS.

In short, a pessimistic outlook may affect health directly by causing hyperarousal of the body's physiological response to stress or indirectly by reducing positive coping strategies and, more specifically, reducing healthy behaviors. In contrast, an optimistic outlook, such as Norman Cousins attempted to create in himself through laughter, may promote physical health by reducing physiological stress responses and promoting positive coping strategies.

The Type A Behavior Pattern

Like the word *stress*, the term **Type A behavior pattern** is often used loosely to describe friends, colleagues, and family members. Let's try to pin down the definition of this important personality style. The Type A pattern was initially identified by two physicians, Meyer Friedman and Ray Rosenman, who noticed that the chairs in the waiting room of their offices seemed to wear out very quickly (Friedman & Rosenman, 1974). Specifically, the edges of the seats became threadbare, as if their patients were sitting on the edges, anxiously waiting to spring up. These patients were most frequently cardiology patients who had histories of coronary artery disease. Friedman and Rosenman eventually described a personality pattern seen in many of their cardiology patients, which was given the label Type A behavior pattern.

The three components of the Type A pattern, according to these physicians, are a sense of time urgency, easily aroused hostility, and competitive achievement strivings. People who are Type A are always in a hurry, setting unnecessary deadlines for themselves and trying to do multiple things at once. They are competitive, even in situations in

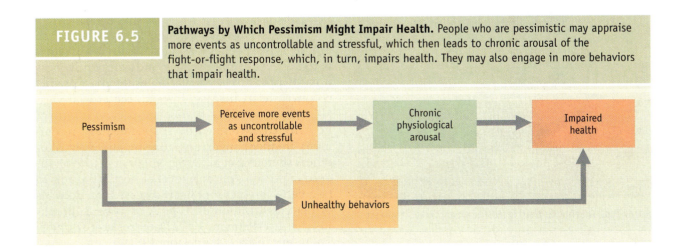

FIGURE 6.5 **Pathways by Which Pessimism Might Impair Health.** People who are pessimistic may appraise more events as uncontrollable and stressful, which then leads to chronic arousal of the fight-or-flight response, which, in turn, impairs health. They may also engage in more behaviors that impair health.

which it is ridiculous to be competitive. For example, they rush to be the first in line at a restaurant or at the movies, even when the wait would be only two or three minutes if they were last in line. They are also chronically hostile and fly into a rage with little provocation. Persons who are not Type A are referred to as *Type B*. They are able to relax without feeling guilty, are able to work without feeling pressured or becoming impatient, and are not easily aroused to hostility.

Although we tend to think of Type A people as angry and aggressive, always fighting to get their way and to accomplish a great deal, there is evidence that they are often anxious and depressed and that these negative emotions may contribute to their risk for disease (Kiecolt-Glaser et al., 2002). Type As may be anxious and depressed because they tend to be dissatisfied with their careers; they tend to spend little time with their families and, thus, jeopardize their home lives; and their social lives in general are not as satisfying as they might be. Regardless of the source of their negative emotions, it appears that these emotions are risk factors for both coronary heart disease and death as the result of a variety of other diseases (Kiecolt-Glaser et al., 2002).

Type A Personality and Coronary Heart Disease

One of the most compelling studies to demonstrate the relationship between Type A behavior and coronary heart disease followed more than

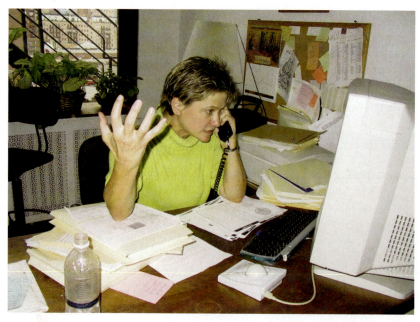

Hostility is the component of Type A behavior that is most strongly linked to heart disease.

3,000 healthy, middle-aged men for 8½ years (Rosenman et al., 1976). At the beginning of the study, the men were evaluated for the Type A pattern by means of an interview that was designed to be irritating. The interviewer kept the participants waiting without explanation and then asked a series of questions about being competitive, hostile, and pressed for time: Do you ever feel rushed or under pressure? Do you eat quickly? Would you describe yourself as ambitious and hard driving or relaxed and easygoing? Do you resent it if someone is late?

The interviewer interrupted participants, asked questions in a challenging manner, and threw in non sequiturs. A participant's level of Type A behavior was determined more on the way he behaved in answering the questions and responding to the interviewer's rudeness than on his answers to the questions themselves. For example, a man was labeled as extremely Type A if he spoke loudly in an explosive manner, talked over the interviewer so as not to be interrupted, appeared tense and tight-lipped, and described hostile incidents with great emotional intensity. The Type B men tended to sit in a relaxed manner, spoke slowly and softly, were easily interrupted, and smiled often.

Over the 8½ years of the study, the Type A men had twice as many heart attacks or other forms of coronary heart disease than did the Type B men. These results held up even after diet, age, smoking, and other variables associated with coronary heart disease were taken into account. Other studies have confirmed this twofold risk and have linked Type A behavior to heart disease in both men and women (Haynes, Feinleib, & Kannel, 1980; Schneiderman et al., 2001). In addition, Type A behavior correlates with severity of coronary artery blockage as determined at autopsy or in X-ray studies (Friedman et al., 1968; Williams et al., 1988). Based on such evidence, in 1981 the American Heart Association classified Type A behavior as a risk factor for coronary heart disease.

More recent research suggests that the definition of Type A behavior, as originally formulated, is too diffuse. Time urgency and competitiveness do not appear to be the variables that best predict coronary heart disease. Instead, the crucial variable may be hostility, particularly a cynical form of hostility characterized by suspiciousness, resentment, frequent anger, antagonism, and distrust of others (Barefoot et al., 1989; Miller et al., 1996). Indeed, a person's chronic level of hostility seems to be a better predictor of heart disease than does his or her classification as Type A or Type B (Booth-Kewley & Friedman, 1987; Dembroski et al., 1985; Thoresen, Telch, & Eagleston, 1981).

For example, a 25-year study of 118 male lawyers found that those who scored high on hostility traits on a personality inventory taken in law school were five times more likely to die before the age of 50 than were classmates who were not hostile (Barefoot et al., 1989). Similarly, in a study of physicians, hostility scores obtained in medical school predicted the incidence of coronary heart disease as well as mortality from all causes (Barefoot, Dahlstrom, & Williams, 1983). In both studies, the relationship between hostility and illness was independent of the effects of smoking, age, and high blood pressure.

How does Type A behavior—or, more specifically, hostility and related negative emotions—lead to coronary heart disease? Again, overarousal of the sympathetic nervous system may play a role (see Figure 6.6). Hostile people show greater physiological arousal in the anticipation of stressors and in the early stages of dealing with stressors (Benotsch, Christensen, & McKelvey, 1997; Lepore, 1995): Their heart rates and blood pressures are higher and they have greater secretion of the stress-related biochemicals known as *catecholamines*. They also return more slowly to baseline levels of sympathetic nervous system activity following stressors than do nonhostile people. This hyperreactivity may cause wear and tear on the coronary arteries, leading to coronary heart disease. Alternately, the excessive secretion of catecholamines in response to stress in hostile people may exert a direct chemical effect on blood vessels. The frequent rise and fall of catecholamine levels may cause frequent changes in blood pressure, which reduce the resilience of the blood vessels. Finally, hostile people may also

engage in behaviors that increase their propensity for heart disease, including smoking, heavy drinking, and high-cholesterol diets (Schneiderman et al., 2001).

Gender Differences

Some research has suggested that men are more likely than women to have the Type A personality pattern and to be chronically hostile (Barefoot et al., 1987; Haynes et al., 1980). Men also are more likely than women to carry three other risk factors for CHD: smoking, hypertension, and elevated cholesterol. In turn, among young and middle-aged people, far more men than women die of cardiovascular disease (Stoney, 2003).

Newer research, however, suggests that women may carry as much anger and hostility as men—they just don't express it as readily (Kring, 2000; Lavoie et al., 2001; Nolen-Hoeksema & Rusting, 2002). In addition, excessive hostility and anger—whether expressed or suppressed—are associated with risk factors for coronary heart disease in both women and men (Matthews et al., 1995). Depression and anxiety are also risk factors for coronary heart disease, and women are more likely than men to suffer these negative emotions (see Chapters 7 and 9).

Coronary heart disease is the number one killer of women, as well as men, and the rates of CHD in women go up dramatically after menopause (Stoney, 2003). Women are less likely than men to recognize the signs of a heart attack, possibly in part because the signs in women are different from those in men. They are also less likely than men to seek help for heart attack symptoms and, even after

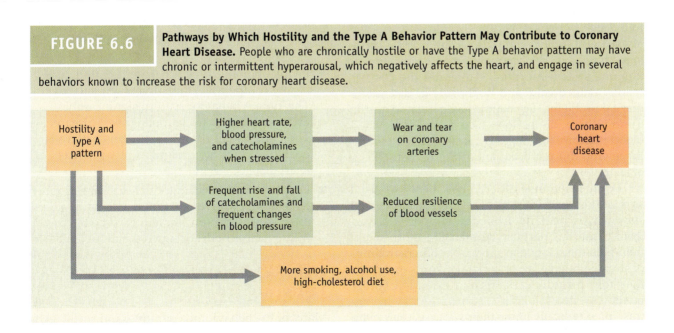

FIGURE 6.6   **Pathways by Which Hostility and the Type A Behavior Pattern May Contribute to Coronary Heart Disease.** People who are chronically hostile or have the Type A behavior pattern may have chronic or intermittent hyperarousal, which negatively affects the heart, and engage in several behaviors known to increase the risk for coronary heart disease.

they seek help, they are less likely to be given aggressive treatment. After a heart attack, women are more likely than men to die, to have chronic impairment, to have a lower quality of life, and to drop out of rehabilitative therapy. The sources of these gender differences are currently unknown, but cardiac disease in women is a fast-growing area of research.

Social Support

So far, we have discussed psychosocial factors that may contribute to poorer health. What about factors that contribute to better health? One such factor that appears to promote adjustment to stressors is social support. A wide variety of studies have found that people who seek and receive positive emotional support from others show more positive health outcomes, both on micro-level measures, such as natural killer cell activity, and on macrolevel outcomes, such as the progression of major diseases (Pennebaker, 1990). For example, studies of women with breast cancer found that those who actively sought social support from others had higher natural killer cell activity (Levy et al., 1990; Turner-Cobb et al., 2000). Similarly, Dixon and colleagues (2001) found that HIV-positive men who experienced declines in social support and increases in loneliness showed biological signs of poorer control over the virus.

One of the main sources of social support is a partner or spouse. Married people have less physical illness and are less likely to die from a variety of conditions, including cancer, heart disease, and surgery, compared with nonmarried people (see Kiecolt-Glaser & Newton, 2001). When a marriage is conflictual, however, it can be a major detriment to health. Experimental studies of married couples found that those who became hostile and negative toward each other while discussing marital problems showed more decrements in four indicators of immune system functioning than did the couples who remained calm and nonhostile in discussing marital problems. The couples who became hostile during these discussions also showed elevated blood pressure for longer periods of time than did those who did not become hostile (Kiecolt-Glaser et al., 1993).

Women and men differ in how they use social support and in the benefits they derive from social support, particularly from the support derived from a marital partner. Women are more likely than men to seek out support from others in times of stress and have larger social networks on whom they rely, including friends and extended family members (Kiecolt-Glaser & Newton, 2001). In contrast, men typically name their wives as their main source of support and the only person in whom

they confide. Marriage is greatly beneficial to men's health—unmarried men have a 250 percent higher mortality rate than married men, compared with a 50 percent difference in mortality rates between unmarried and married women (Ross, Mirowsky, & Goldsteen, 1990).

Why would women not benefit from marriage as much as men do? Women are more physiologically reactive to marital conflict than men (Kiecolt-Glaser & Newton, 2001). This may be because women's self-concepts, as well as their financial well-being, tend to be more closely tied to their marital partner than are men's (Cross & Madson, 1997). Women are more emotionally tuned to their partners and are more conscious of conflict in their relationships than are men. For these reasons, women may be more emotionally, cognitively, and physiologically sensitive to marital conflict, and this sensitivity may counteract any positive health effects they could derive from the support provided to them by their partners (Kiecolt-Glaser & Newton, 2001).

Psychologists can work with people facing stress and illness to help them identify their sources of positive social support and use these resources better. This might involve helping people organize their time, so that they have opportunities for quiet walks or evenings with a friend. Or a psychologist might help an individual whose relationships with important others are conflictual to deal more effectively with those relationships, so that they are a source of strength, rather than a burden.

SUMMING UP

- People who are chronically pessimistic may show poorer physical health because they appraise more events as uncontrollable or because they engage in poorer health-related behaviors.

- People with the Type A behavior pattern are highly competitive, time urgent, and hostile. The Type A behavior pattern significantly increases the risk for coronary heart disease. The most potent component of this pattern is hostility, which alone significantly predicts heart disease.

- People who receive high-quality social support have more positive physical health outcomes in stressful situations than those who have little social support or much social friction.

INTERVENTIONS TO IMPROVE HEALTH

Many of the behavioral, cognitive, and social techniques that are useful in the treatment of psychological disorders (see Chapter 5) can also improve physical health.

Guided Mastery Techniques

When told what they have to do to protect or improve their health, people often feel unable or unwilling to engage in these behaviors. **Guided mastery techniques** provide people with explicit information about how to engage in positive health-related behaviors and with opportunities to engage in these behaviors in increasingly challenging situations (Taylor, 1999). The goals are to increase people's skills at engaging in the behaviors and their beliefs that they can engage in the behaviors.

A guided mastery program for teaching women how to negotiate safe sexual practices in sexual encounters with men could begin with information on condom use. A counselor could then model how a woman can tell a man that she wants him to use a condom when they have sex. The women would watch the counselor and then practice insisting on condom use in role-plays with the counselor or other group participants. In these role-plays, the women would face increasingly difficult challenges to their insistence on condom use, receive feedback on effective means for meeting these challenges, and practice meeting these challenges. The women could also be taught techniques for determining when it is useless to argue with their partners any longer about condom use and skills for withdraw-

ing from sexual encounters in which their partners want to practice unsafe sex.

Guided mastery techniques have been used successfully in AIDS prevention programs with African American female and male adolescents (Jemmott & Jemmott, 1992). In the programs with the young women, researchers gave participants information about the cause, transmission, and prevention of AIDS. The young women then participated in guided mastery exercises to increase their skills and self-confidence for negotiating condom use by their male partners. The young women were also given instruction on how to eroticize condom use—how to incorporate putting on condoms into foreplay and intercourse in ways that increase positive attitudes toward condoms. Compared with young women who received only information, not guided mastery exercises, these young women showed a greater sense of efficacy in negotiating condom use, more positive expectations for sexual enjoyment with condoms, and stronger intentions to use condoms. These effects were found in a similar program with sexually active African American female adolescents drawn from the inner city (Jemmott & Jemmott, 1992).

In a program with African American male adolescents, the young men were first given information about the cause, transmission, and prevention of AIDS. Then they participated in guided mastery exercises that taught them how to negotiate condom use with their partners and to eroticize

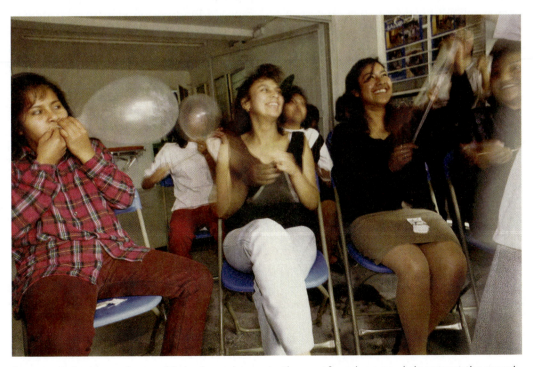

Programs to increase safe sexual behavior and promote the use of condoms may help prevent the spread of sexually transmitted diseases, especially if the programs are culturally sensitive.

condom use. Follow-up assessments showed that, compared with a control group, these adolescents were more knowledgeable about the risks for AIDS, were less accepting of risky practices, and engaged in lower-risk sexual behavior with fewer sexual partners (Jemmott et al., 1992).

Biofeedback

Biofeedback has been used to treat a wide variety of health problems—most frequently, migraine headaches, chronic pain, and hypertension. Biofeedback actually involves several techniques designed to help people change bodily processes by learning to identify signs that the processes are going awry and then learning ways of controlling the processes. For example, a person with hypertension might be hooked up to a machine that converts his heartbeats to tones. He sits quietly, listening to his heart rate and trying various means to change it, such as breathing slowly or concentrating on a pleasant image. The goal in biofeedback is for people to detect early signs of dysfunction in their bodies, such as signs that their blood pressure is rising, and to use the techniques they learned while hooked up to machines to control their bodies even when they are independent of the machines. Several controlled studies have found that biofeedback training can significantly reduce blood pressure among people with hypertension (Glasgow, Engel, & D'Lugoff, 1989; Glasgow, Gaader, & Engel, 1982; Nakao et al., 1997).

Biofeedback also seems to be successful in reducing tension-related headaches (Gannon et al., 1987). Headache sufferers learn to detect when they are tensing the muscles in their heads. They then use techniques for reducing this tension, thus relieving their headaches.

Biofeedback is used for migraine sufferers to increase the blood flow to the body's periphery, thereby decreasing the blood flow to the head and reducing pressure on the arteries. Migraine patients are hooked up to machines that give them temperature readings from their head and fingers. They are taught to relax fully and to notice the effects of relaxation on their temperatures. Then they may be encouraged to increase the temperature of their fingers, using the machine's feedback as an aid. It is not clear just how patients do this—it is a matter of using trial and error to find a way of changing their temperatures. Eventually, patients attempt to use these techniques to control headaches at home. When they feel headaches coming on, they concentrate on warming their fingers to divert blood flow from the arteries in their head to the periphery (see Turk, Meichenbaum, & Berman, 1979).

Although biofeedback can be successful in treating hypertension and pain conditions, such as headaches, it is not clear that it works the way its proponents believe it works. For example, although biofeedback can reduce migraine headaches, the evidence that it does so by temperature control is mixed. In addition, biofeedback appears to be no more successful than simple relaxation techniques in reducing headaches, pain, and hypertension (see Chapter 7 for a description of relaxation techniques). Indeed, biofeedback may work largely because individuals often learn relaxation techniques as a part of biofeedback training. Relaxation techniques have the advantage over biofeedback of being much less expensive and time-consuming to learn.

Sociocultural Interventions

Many people facing stressors, including physical illness, participate in support groups. A provocative study of breast cancer patients found evidence that support groups may not only help women cope emotionally with their cancer but also prolong their lives (Spiegel et al., 1989). Several years ago, researchers began a study in which they randomly assigned women with advanced breast cancer either to a series of weekly support groups or to no support groups. All the women received standard medical care for their cancer. The focus in the groups was on facing death and learning to live one's remaining days to the fullest. The researchers did not expect to alter the course of the cancer; they wanted only to improve the quality of life for the women with advanced cancer. They were quite surprised when, 48 months after the study began, all the women who had not been

Biofeedback helps people learn to detect when bodily processes are going awry and to counteract these processes.

in the support groups were dead from their cancer but a third of the women in the support groups were still alive. From the time the study began, the average survival time for the women in the support groups was about 40 months, compared with about 19 months for the women who were not in the support groups. There were no differences between the groups other than their participation in the weekly support meetings that could explain the differences in the average survival times. It appears that the support groups actually increased the number of months that the women in the support groups lived. Some subsequent studies have found similar results (e.g., Fawzy et al., 1990; Richardson et al., 1990), whereas others have not (e.g., Goodwin et al., 2001).

If support groups can improve the physical health of cancer patients, how might this work? In the Spiegel et al. (1989) study, the women in the support groups had lower levels of emotional distress, and they learned how to control their physical pain better than the women who did not participate in the support groups. This lowering of distress may have improved the functioning of their immune systems. The ways in which the lowering of distress can affect immune functioning are not yet known, but one possibility is that reducing distress reduces levels of stress-related hormones, including the corticosteroids. Excessive levels of corticosteroids promote the growth of some cancers (Spiegel, 2001).

SUMMING UP

- Guided mastery techniques help people learn positive health-related behaviors by teaching them the most effective ways of engaging in these behaviors and by giving them an opportunity to practice the behaviors in increasingly challenging situations.
- Biofeedback is used to help people learn to control their own negative physiological responses.
- Support groups are one source of social support for some people. Some research suggests that they can improve both psychological and physical well-being.

POSTTRAUMATIC STRESS DISORDER, ACUTE STRESS DISORDER, AND ADJUSTMENT DISORDER

We've considered the effects of stressful experiences on physical health, but stress also takes a toll on emotional health. Three psychological disorders, **posttraumatic stress disorder (PTSD)**, **acute stress disorder**, and **adjustment disorder**, are by definition the consequences of more extreme stressors and are the focus of the remainder of this chapter.

Here one survivor of the terrorist attacks on the World Trade Center on September 11, 2001, describes many of the core symptoms of PTSD and acute stress disorder:

VOICES

I just can't let go of it. I was working at my desk on the 10th floor of the World Trade Center when the first plane hit. We heard it but couldn't imagine what it was. Pretty soon someone started yelling, "Get out—it's a bomb!" and we all ran for the stairs.

The dust and smoke were pouring down as we took step by step. It seemed to take an eternity to get down to the ground. When I got outside, I saw people running away but also people just standing, looking up, in pure horror. When I looked up and saw that the top of the tower was on fire, I just froze; I couldn't move. Then the second plane hit. Someone grabbed my arm and we started running. Concrete and glass began to fly everywhere. People were falling down, stumbling. Everyone was covered in dust. When I got far enough away, I just stood and stared as the towers fell. I couldn't believe what I was seeing. Other people were crying and screaming, but I just stared. I couldn't believe it.

Now, I don't sleep very well. I try, but just as I'm falling asleep, the images come flooding into my mind. I see the towers falling. I see people with cuts on their faces. I see the ones who didn't make it out, crushed and dead. I smell the dust and smoke. Sometimes, I cry to the point that my pillow is soaked. Sometimes, I just stare at the ceiling, as I stared at the towers as they fell. During the day, I go to work, but often it's as if my head is in another place. Someone will say something to me, and I won't hear them. I often feel as if I'm floating around, not touching or really seeing anything around me. But if I do hear a siren, which you do a lot in the city, I jump out of my skin.

Traumatic events such as the attacks on the World Trade Center can lead to posttraumatic stress.

Studies done immediately after the World Trade Center attacks found that about 20 percent of the people living very nearby had symptoms meeting the diagnosis of PTSD (Galea et al., 2002). Even people who were not present at the World Trade Center attack were traumatized by it. Nationwide studies showed that, just after September 11, 2001, 44 percent of adults reported symptoms of PTSD (Schuster et al., 2001). Two months later, in November 2001, 21 percent of adults nationwide still reported being "quite a bit" or "extremely" bothered by one of five distress symptoms (Stein et al., 2004). Those with persistent distress reported accomplishing less at work (65 percent); avoiding public gathering places (24 percent); and using alcohol or other drugs to quell worries about terrorism (38 percent).

A wide range of traumas can induce posttraumatic stress disorder or acute stress disorder, ranging from extraordinary events, such as a terrorist attack, to common events, such as a traffic accident. About 20 percent of women and 8 percent of men exposed to trauma will suffer from posttraumatic stress disorder at sometime in their lives (Kessler et al., 1995). The symptoms can be mild to moderate, and some people function adequately with these symptoms without seeking treatment. For other people, however, the symptoms can be immobilizing, causing deterioration in their work, family, and social lives (Putnam, 1996).

The diagnosis of PTSD requires that three types of symptoms be present (see Table 6.3). The first set of PTSD symptoms is repeated *reexperiencing of the traumatic event.* PTSD sufferers may experience intrusive images or thoughts, recurring nightmares, or flashbacks in which they relive the event. They react psychologically and physiologically to stimuli that remind them of the

event. One survivor of war atrocities in Bosnia in the 1990s said films of traumas constantly play in his head, and, although he tries to look away from them, they continue to intrude on his consciousness (Weine et al., 1995). The quoted World Trade Center survivor vividly remembers her traumatic event to the point of reliving it. Memories of the attack intrude into her consciousness against her will, particularly when she encounters something that reminds her of the event. She

TABLE 6.3   DSM-IV-TR
Symptoms of Posttraumatic Stress Disorder
Three categories of symptoms characterize PTSD.
Reexperiencing of the Traumatic Event
Distressing memories of the event
Distressing dreams about the event
Reliving of the event by acting or feeling as if the event were recurring
Intense psychological and physiological distress when exposed to situations reminiscent of the event
Emotional Numbing and Detachment
Avoidance of thoughts, feelings, or conversations about the event
Avoidance of activities, places, or people associated with the event
Trouble recalling important aspects of the event
Loss of interest in activities
Feelings of detachment from others
Inability to have loving feelings toward others and a general restriction of feelings
Sense that the future is bleak
Hypervigilance and Chronic Arousal
Difficulty falling or staying asleep
Irritability or outbursts of anger
Difficulty concentrating
Hypervigilance
Exaggerated startle response

Source: Reprinted with permission from the *Diagnostic and Statistical Manual of Mental Disorders,* Fourth Edition, Text Revision. Copyright © 2000. American Psychiatric Association.

also relives her emotional reaction to the event, and since the event she has chronically experienced negative emotions, which have not diminished with time.

The second set of symptoms in PTSD is *emotional numbing and detachment*. People become withdrawn, reporting that they feel numb and detached from others. Especially just after the trauma, they may also feel detached from themselves and their ongoing experiences, with a general sense of unreality, as does the quoted World Trade Center survivor.

The third set of symptoms involves *hypervigilance* and *chronic arousal*. PTSD sufferers are always on guard for the traumatic event to recur. Sounds or images that remind them of their trauma can instantly create panic and flight. A war veteran, on hearing a car backfire, may jump into a ditch and begin to have flashbacks of the war, reexperiencing the terror he felt on the front lines. PTSD sufferers may report "survivor guilt," painful guilt feelings over the fact that they survived the traumatic event or about things that they had to do to survive. Many Holocaust survivors report guilt for having survived when their families did not or for not having fought more strongly against the Nazis (Krystal, 1968).

Children can experience PTSD in much the same way that adults can, but they may have their own ways of manifesting it (Fremont, 2004; LaGreca et al., 1996; Pfefferbaum et al., 2000; Ruggiero, Morris, & Scotti, 2001). Children's memories and fears of a traumatic event may generalize to fears of a wide range of stimuli (Baker & Shalhoub-Kevorkian, 1999). One 12-year-old girl who had been kidnapped, along with several of her friends, spoke of her feelings several months later (Terr, 1981, p. 18):

VOICES

I don't like to turn off the lights. I'm afraid someone would come in and shoot and rob us. When I wake up I turn on the light. . . . I've been in Bakersfield helping my brother. . . . At night in Bakersfield it feels like someone broke in. Nothing is there. I hear footsteps again. I keep going to check. . . . I check where the sound is coming from. . . . I'm very frightened of the kitchen because no one's there at all. I completely avoid it. At home I kept feeling someone was looking in and watching me. I kept the light on. I was afraid they'd come in and kill us all or take us away again.

Acute stress disorder occurs in response to traumas, as does PTSD, and it has symptoms simi-

lar to those of PTSD (see Table 6.4). The main difference is that acute stress disorder occurs within one month of exposure to the stressor and is short-lived, not lasting more than four weeks. Also, in acute stress disorder, **dissociative symptoms**—symptoms that indicate a detachment from the trauma and from ongoing events—are especially prominent. People may become emotionally unresponsive, finding it impossible to experience pleasure. They may have difficulty concentrating, feel detached from their bodies, experience the world as unreal or dreamlike, and have increasing difficulty recalling the details of the trauma. In addition, as in PTSD, the sufferer of acute stress disorder persistently reexperiences the trauma through flashbacks, nightmares, and intrusive thoughts; avoids reminders of the trauma; and is constantly aroused.

TABLE 6.4   DSM-IV-TR

Symptoms of Acute Stress Disorder

Acute stress disorder has symptoms similar to those of PTSD but occurs within one month of a stressor and is less than four weeks in duration.

A. While experiencing or after experiencing a traumatic event, the individual has three or more of the following dissociative symptoms:

  1. sense of numbing, detachment, or emotional unresponsiveness

  2. reduced awareness of one's surroundings ("being in a daze")

  3. sense that things are not real

  4. sense that one's body and mind are not connected

  5. inability to recall an important aspect of the trauma

B. Reexperiencing the traumatic event through recurrent images, thoughts, dreams, illusions, flashbacks, or sense of reliving the experience; distress when exposed to reminders of the trauma

C. Avoidance of stimuli that arouse recollections of the trauma

D. Symptoms of anxiety or increased arousal (such as difficulty sleeping, irritability, poor concentration, hypervigilance, exaggerated startle response, motor restlessness)

Source: Reprinted with permission from the *Diagnostic and Statistical Manual of Mental Disorders*, Fourth Edition, Text Revision. Copyright © 2000. American Psychiatric Association.

Although acute stress disorder is defined as a short-term response to trauma, it appears that people who experience acute stress disorder are at high risk of continuing to experience posttraumatic stress symptoms for many months following the trauma (Classen et al., 1998).

Another stress-related diagnosis is adjustment disorder, which consists of emotional and behavioral symptoms (depressive symptoms, anxiety symptoms, and/or antisocial behaviors) that arise within three months of the onset of a stressor. Adjustment disorder differs from PTSD and acute stress disorder in that the stressors that lead to adjustment disorder can be of any severity, whereas the stressors that lead to PTSD and acute stress disorder are extreme. In addition, PTSD and acute stress disorder have some specific symptoms that do not occur in adjustment disorder, including re-experiencing of the traumatic event. Adjustment disorder is a residual category in DSM-IV-TR, used for people who are experiencing emotional and behavioral symptoms following a stressor but who do not meet the criteria for a diagnosis of PTSD, acute stress disorder, or another anxiety or mood disorder (which are described in Chapters 7 and 9) that is the result of the stressful experience.

The Role of Trauma in PTSD

A wide variety of traumatic events can induce posttraumatic stress disorder. We will focus on four types of events: natural disasters, abuse, combat- and war-related traumas, and common traumatic events, such as the loss of a loved one in a car accident. These are the traumatic events that have been researched most thoroughly.

Natural Disasters

Natural disasters, such as floods, tsunami, earthquakes, fires, hurricanes, and tornadoes, can trigger a wave of PTSD among the survivors. A study of Florida children who lived through Hurricane Andrew in 1992 found that nearly 20 percent were still suffering from PTSD a year after the disaster (LaGreca et al., 1996). Another study of children in South Carolina who survived Hurricane Hugo in 1993 found that, three years after the hurricane, one-third still experienced a sense of detachment and avoided thoughts or feelings associated with the hurricane, one-quarter were irritable and angry, and one-fifth experienced physiological arousal (Garrison et al., 1995).

Other studies have focused on survivors of major earthquakes. For example, a study of survivors of an earthquake in Turkey found that

Survivors of natural disasters, such as the tsunami in Asia in 2004 or Hurricane Katrina in 2005, often experience posttraumatic stress disorder.

23 percent of those who were at the epicenter had PTSD 14 months later, and 16 percent had PTSD plus depression (Basoglu et al., 2004). Similar rates of PTSD were found in survivors of a large earthquake in Taiwan (Lai et al., 2004).

Rescue workers are at high risk for PTSD and acute stress disorder. Another study of the Taiwan earthquake found that 20 percent of professional rescuers and 32 percent of nonprofessional rescuers had significant symptoms of PTSD one month following the disaster (Guo et al., 2004).

Culture and gender appear to interact in interesting ways to influence vulnerability to PTSD. One study compared random community samples of survivors of Hurricane Andrew, which hit Florida in 1992, with survivors of Hurricane Paulina, which hit Acapulco, Mexico, in 1997 (Norris et al., 2001). These two hurricanes were similar in many ways, rated as Category 4 hurricanes and causing widespread property damage, physical injury, and death. Rates of PTSD symptoms were high in both countries. Women had more symptoms than men in both countries (see Figure 6.7), yet the difference in PTSD symptoms between Mexican women and men was much greater than the difference between American women and men. In addition, within the American sample, the difference in PTSD symptoms between non-Hispanic White women and men was significantly greater than the difference between African American women and men.

The researchers suggest that the relative strength of traditional sex roles across these three cultures (Mexican, non-Hispanic White, and African American) influenced the magnitude of sex differences in PTSD symptoms. There is more social pressure in Mexican culture than in American culture for women to be passive, self-sacrificing, and compliant and for men to be dominant, fearless, and strong (Vazquez-Nuttall, Romero-Garcia, & DeLeon, 1987). This may lead Mexican women to feel more helpless following a trauma and to be less able to get the material support they need, compared with Mexican men. Within American culture, there is some evidence that sex roles are more egalitarian among African Americans than among non-Hispanic Whites (Davenport & Yurich, 1991). Thus, African American women did not suffer much more PTSD than African American men. It is noteworthy that African Americans in the Norris et al. (2001) study generally had higher rates of PTSD than non-Hispanic Whites, perhaps because they had fewer financial and material resources to cope with the disaster. Many of the victims of Hurricane Katrina in 2005 were poor African Americans, and future studies may reveal high rates of PTSD in this group.

Abuse

There are many kinds of abuse—physical abuse (such as in battering relationships), sexual abuse (as in rape and incest), and emotional abuse (as when parents continually ridicule their children). Each of these forms of abuse can contribute to long-term PTSD. Studies of rape survivors have found that about 95 percent experience posttraumatic stress symptoms severe enough to qualify for a diagnosis of the disorder in the first two weeks following the rape (see Figure 6.8 on page 196). About 50 percent still qualify for the diagnosis three months after the rape. As many as 25 percent still suffer from PTSD four to five years after the rape (Faravelli et al., 2004; Foa & Riggs, 1995; Resnick et al., 1993; Rothbaum et al., 1992).

In the United States alone, more than 200,000 cases of verified child sexual abuse and more than 380,000 cases of physical abuse are reported each year. Studies of children who have been sexually and/or physically assaulted show that they remain at increased risk for PTSD, as well as other anxiety disorders, depression, substance abuse, and sexual dysfunction, well into adulthood (Cicchetti & Toth, 2005; Kessler et al., 1997; Saunders et al., 1992). Indeed, over 60 percent of childhood rape survivors develop PTSD at sometime in their lives (Saunders et al., 1992).

The risk of long-term PTSD can be reduced when a child or an adult receives compassionate support from family members and friends and

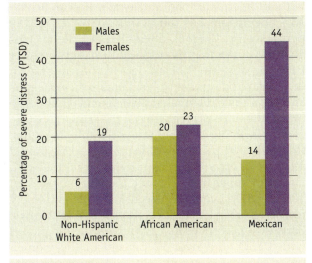

FIGURE 6.7 **Cultural and Sex Differences in PTSD.** Sex differences in rates of PTSD were greatest among Mexicans, followed by non-Hispanic White Americans, then least among African Americans in a study of reactions to a hurricane.

Source: Norris et al., 2001.

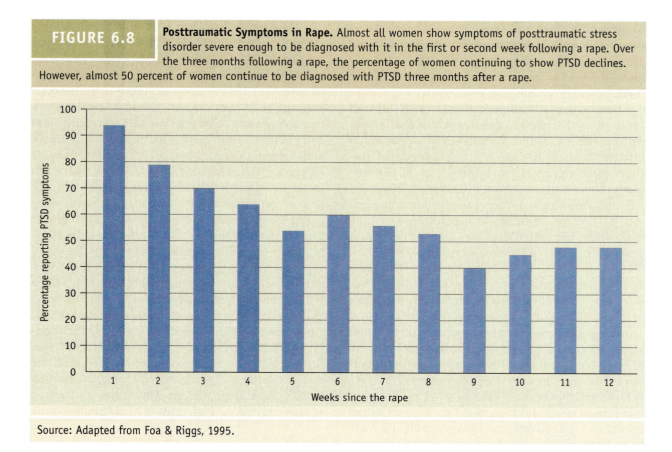

FIGURE 6.8   **Posttraumatic Symptoms in Rape.** Almost all women show symptoms of posttraumatic stress disorder severe enough to be diagnosed with it in the first or second week following a rape. Over the three months following a rape, the percentage of women continuing to show PTSD declines. However, almost 50 percent of women continue to be diagnosed with PTSD three months after a rape.

Source: Adapted from Foa & Riggs, 1995.

professional mental-health care as needed. PTSD and other psychological problems are more likely when abused people try to hide or deny their abuse. *Taking Psychology Personally: What to Do If You Have Been Sexually Assaulted* describes what people who have been sexually abused can do to get the help they need.

Combat- and War-Related Traumas

Much of what is known about PTSD comes from studies of men and women who fought in wars and were taken as prisoners of war. There are well-documented cases of "combat fatigue syndrome," "war zone stress," and "shell shock" among soldiers and former prisoners of the two world wars and the Korean War. Follow-up studies of some of these people show chronic posttraumatic stress symptoms for decades after the war (Elder & Clipp, 1989; Sutker, Allain, & Winstead, 1993; Sutker et al., 1991). PTSD came into the national limelight after the Vietnam War, when it was revealed that large numbers of Vietnam veterans suffered PTSD shortly after the war, and as many as half a million still suffered PTSD 15 years after their service had ended (Schlenger et al., 1992).

Recent and ongoing wars and conflicts have left thousands of sufferers of PTSD in their wake. A study of U.S. army soldiers and Marines deployed to Iraq found that approximately 13 percent could be diagnosed with PTSD (Hoge et al., 2004).

The citizens of countries besieged by war are at even higher risk for PTSD. The Afghan people have endured decades of war and occupation, the repressive regime of the Taliban, and then the bombing of their country by the United States after the attacks on the World Trade Center and the Pentagon. Thousands of Afghanis have been killed, injured, or displaced from their homes. Thousands still live in make-shift tents on a barren landscape without adequate food and water. Research with Afghani citizens has found that approximately 20 percent can be diagnosed with PTSD (Scholte et al., 2004). Women may be especially likely to suffer PTSD because the Taliban deprived them of even the most basic human rights, killed their husbands and other male relatives, and then made it impossible for them to survive without these men. A study of women living in Kabul under the Taliban regime found that 84 percent had lost at least one family member in war, 69 percent reported that they or a family member had been detained and abused by Taliban militia, and 68 percent reported extremely restricted social activities (Rasekh et al., 1998). Forty-two percent of these women were diagnosed with PTSD, and over 90 percent of the women reported some symptoms of PTSD (see also Scholte et al., 2004).

Taking Psychology Personally

What to Do If You've Been Sexually Assaulted

You probably don't want to think about how you would cope with being sexually assaulted. One study estimated that, across the globe, one woman in three has been beaten, coerced into sex, or otherwise abused in her lifetime (Heise, Ellsberg, & Gottemuller, 1999). Large studies in the United States suggest that about 13 to 15 percent of women are the victims of completed rape at sometime in their lives, and over half of these women experience their first sexual assault during childhood and adolescence (Kilpatrick, Edmunds, & Seymour, 1992; Kilpatrick & Saunders, 1996).

Sexual assault can be defined as unwanted sexual contact obtained without consent or obtained through the use of force, threat of force, intimidation, or coercion. It includes unwanted sexual contact that occurs after the administration of intoxicants to lower the victim's resistance. Following are some tips from the Sexual Assault Prevention and Awareness Center of the University of Michigan on what to do if you have been sexually assaulted.

- *Believe in yourself.* Don't blame yourself; take care of yourself.

- *Tell someone you can trust.* Sexual assaults can be terrifying and traumatic. It is an enormous burden to bear alone. Think about whom you might trust to tell—maybe a friend, relative, or faculty member. You may also be able to call a 24-hour sexual assault crisis line in your community—it should be listed in your phone book.

- *Have a medical examination.* Even if you don't think you have been physically hurt, you may want to be checked for internal injuries; sexually transmitted diseases; and, if you are a woman, pregnancy as soon as possible. Also, a medical exam within 72 hours is the best time for collecting physical evidence of the rape. Even if you are not sure about pressing charges, it can be reassuring to have the evidence in case you decide to do so.

- *Report it to the police.* Choosing whether or not to report the assault is your right. Whether to press charges is a decision you do not have to make immediately, but making a criminal report sooner may help if the case is prosecuted. Your local sexual assault counseling center may be able to help you make a third-party report. If you are making an immediate criminal report, do not clean yourself up or touch anything in the area where the assault took place.

- *Seek additional supportive counseling.* Regardless of whether you get a medical exam or report the assault, you may need help to deal with the consequences of the assault. Recovering from a sexual assault may take time and professional counseling.

People from Southeast Asia (Vietnamese, Cambodians, Laotians, and Hmong) have undergone decades of civil war, invasions by other countries, and death at the hands of despots. In the few years that Pol Pot and the Khmer Rouge ruled Cambodia (1975–1979), perhaps one-third of Cambodia's 7 million people died. Many others were tortured, starved, and permanently separated from their families. Hundreds of thousands of Southeast Asians fled to Thailand, Europe, the United States, and Canada. Unfortunately, many of these refugees faced further trauma, being imprisoned in refugee camps for years, often separated from their families (Kinzie, 2001). Studies of refugees who have relocated to the United States suggest that as many as half suffer PTSD, and these symptoms may persist for years if untreated (Kinzie, 2001).

The wars in the former Yugoslavia in the 1990s were marked by "ethnic cleansing"—the torture and slaughter of thousands and displacement of millions of former Yugoslavians. This campaign was one of the most brutal in history, with many atrocities, concentration camps, organized mass rapes, and neighbors murdering neighbors. A survey of a random sample of 1,358 Kosovar Albanians done in 1998–1999 found that one-quarter had experienced the murder of a family member or friend, two-thirds had been in a combat situation during the war, and over 80 percent had been displaced from their homes during the war (Cardozo et al., 2000). Seventeen percent of these people had symptoms that met the criteria for posttraumatic stress disorder in 1999, and a follow-up survey in 2000 found that 25 percent reported PTSD symptoms (Cardozo, et al., 2003).

People who have been forced to flee their country, never to return, may be even more likely to suffer PTSD: A study of Bosnian refugees just after they had resettled in the United States found that 65 percent suffered from posttraumatic stress disorder (Weine et al., 1995). The following woman's story is far too common.

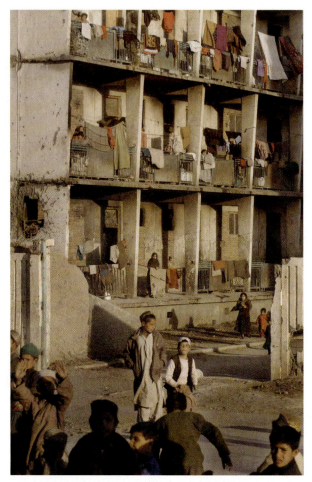

The people of Afghanistan have lived in desperate conditions for many years and many suffer PTSD.

CASE STUDY

A woman in her 40s worked the family farm in a rural village until the day the siege began, when mortar shells turned most of their house to rubble. A few months before, she and her husband had sent their son away to be with relatives in Slovenia. The morning after the shelling, the Chetniks—Serbian nationalist forces—came and ordered everyone to leave their houses at once. Many neighbors and friends were shot dead before the woman's eyes. She and her husband were forced to sign over the title to their house, car, and bank deposits—and watched as the looting began. Looters included neighbors who were their friends. Over the next few days they traveled back from the Muslim ghetto to their land to feed the animals. One day, as she and her husband stood in the garden, the Chetniks cap-

tured them. Her husband was taken away with other men. For the next 6 months she did not know if he was dead or alive. She spent days on transport trains with no food or water, where many suffocated to death beside her. On forced marches she had to step over the dead bodies of friends and relatives. Once her group was forced across a bridge that was lined with Chetnik machine gunners randomly shooting to kill and ordering them to throw all valuables over the edge into nets. She spent weeks in severely deprived conditions in a big tent with many women and children, where constant sobbing could be heard. When she herself could not stop crying she thought that something had broken in her head and that she had gone "crazy." Now she says, "I will never be happy again." When alone, everything comes back to her. But when she is with others or busy doing chores, she can forget. "My soul hurts inside, but I'm able to pull it together." She is able to sleep without nightmares only by using a nightly ritual: "I lie down and go through every step of the house in Bosnia—the stable, everything they took, the rugs, the horses, the doors. I see it all again." (Weine et al., 1995, p. 540)

A follow-up of the Bosnian refugees one year later found that 44 percent still suffered from PTSD, with the older refugees more vulnerable to PTSD than the younger refugees (Weine et al., 1998). Many refugees from Bosnia and other war-torn countries were tortured before they escaped their homeland, and the experience of torture significantly increases the chance that an individual will develop PTSD (Basoglu et al., 1997; Shrestha et al., 1998). Torture survivors who have been political activists appear less prone to develop PTSD than those who have not been political activists (Basoglu et al., 1997). Political activists appear more psychologically prepared for torture than nonactivists, because they expect at sometime to be tortured, often have previous experience with torture, and have a belief system whereby torture is viewed merely as an instrument of repression.

Common Traumatic Events

PTSD can occur following more common events: being in an automobile accident or another serious accident; experiencing the sudden, unexpected death of a loved one; learning that one's child has a life-threatening disease; or observing someone else being severely injured or killed. Studies of people who attended an emergency room shortly after a motor vehicle accident found that half of them reported intrusive reexperiencing of the accident, hyperarousal, or distress (Ehlers, Mayou, & Bryant, 1998; Mayou, Bryant, & Ehlers, 2001). Over 20 percent suffered symptoms severe enough to meet the diagnostic criteria for PTSD 3 months after the accident, and 17 percent were diagnosed with PTSD 1 year after the accident. Another study found that adults who had lost children or spouses in fatal car accidents were still experiencing high levels of anxiety and depression 4 to 7 years after their losses, and those who had lost children were more likely than people in a control group to have divorced (Lehman, Wortman, & Williams, 1987). As these studies illustrate, PTSD symptoms can last a long time after a trauma. About half the people experiencing a trauma appear to recover from PTSD within 3 months of the trauma, but many others continue to experience symptoms for at least 12 months or much longer (APA, 2000).

Explanations of PTSD Vulnerability

The cause of PTSD seems obvious: trauma. It seems perfectly understandable for PTSD to develop in assault or torture victims, people who have lost a loved one in a car accident, people who have lost their homes in a hurricane, and so on. But just what is it about traumatic events that can cause long-term, severe psychological impairment in some people? And why do some people develop PTSD in the wake of a trauma, whereas others do not? Researchers have identified a number of social, psychological, and biological factors that seem to contribute to PTSD (Scheiderman et al., 2005) (see the Concept Overview in Table 6.5).

TABLE 6.5 Concept Overview

Contributors to PTSD

A number of social, psychological, and biological factors may contribute to vulnerability to PTSD.

Contributor	Description	Example
Social factors		
1. Severity, duration, and proximity of trauma	1. More severe and longer traumas, and traumas directly affecting people, are more likely to lead to PTSD.	1. War veterans who were on the front lines for months at a time are more prone to PTSD.
2. Social support	2. Good social support protects against PTSD.	2. Women whose husbands commit suicide are less prone to PTSD if they can discuss it with friends.
Psychological factors		
1. Shattered assumptions	1. People whose basic assumptions are shattered are more prone to PTSD.	1. People who believe that bad things happen to others may be more traumatized when they experience a trauma.
2. Preexisting distress	2. People who are already distressed before a trauma are at greater risk for PTSD.	2. People distressed before a natural disaster are more at risk for PTSD after the disaster.
3. Coping styles	3. Use of avoidance, rumination, or dissociation or inability to make sense of trauma increases risk for PTSD.	3. People who cannot make sense of the loss of a loved one are more prone to PTSD.
Biological factors		
1. Physiological hyperreactivity	1. PTSD sufferers show greater arousal of neurotransmitters, hormones, and brain regions associated with stress response.	1. While imaging combat scenes, combat veterans with PTSD show greater blood flow in areas of the brain involved in emotion and memory.
2. Genetics	2. Vulnerability to PTSD may be influenced by genetic factors.	2. Identical twins show higher concordance for PTSD than fraternal twins.

Environmental and Social Factors

Not surprisingly, the nature of a traumatic event plays an important role in determining people's likelihood of developing PTSD in response to the event. In addition, the response of family members and friends to a trauma survivor is a critical influence on the survivor's vulnerability to PTSD.

Severity, Duration, and Proximity of Trauma The most potent predictors of people's reactions to trauma are the *severity* and *duration* of the trauma and the individual's *proximity* to the trauma (Cardozo et al., 2000; Ehlers, Mayou, et al., 1998; Hoge et al., 2004; Kessler et al., 1995). That is, people who experience more severe and longer-lasting traumas and are directly affected by a traumatic event are more prone to develop PTSD. For example, soldiers are more likely to experience PTSD if they were on the front lines of the war for an extended period of time or if they were taken prisoner of war than if they were not (Hoge et al., 2004; Schlenger et al., 1992; Wolfe et al., 1999). People who were at Ground Zero during the World Trade Center attacks were more likely to develop PTSD than those who were not (Galea et al., 2002). Rape survivors who are violently and repeatedly raped over an extended period are more likely to experience PTSD than are those whose experiences are shorter and less violent (Epstein, Saunders, & Kilpatrick, 1997; Merrill et al., 2001; Resick, 1993). Victims of natural disasters who lose their homes or loved ones or are themselves injured are more likely to experience PTSD than are those whose lives are less affected by the natural disaster (Basoglu et al., 2004; Nolen-Hoeksema & Morrow, 1991; Norris & Uhl, 1993).

Social Support Another predictor of people's vulnerability to PTSD following trauma is the *social support* available to them (Shalev, Tuval-Mashiach, & Hadar, 2004). People who have others who will support them emotionally through recovery from their traumas, allowing them to discuss their feelings and memories of the traumas, recover more quickly than do those who do not (Kendall-Tackett, Williams, & Finkelhor, 1993; King et al., 1999; La-Greca et al., 1996; Sutker et al., 1995). For example, women whose husbands have committed suicide show better physical and emotional health and fewer intrusive thoughts about the suicides if they are able to discuss the suicides with supportive friends than if they had not discussed the suicides with others (Pennebaker & O'Heeron, 1984).

Some events may be more difficult to discuss with others and less likely to engender social support from others because of social stigmas against people who experience such events. Examples are the suicides of family members, sexual assault, and the loss of loved ones to AIDS, particularly if the loved ones were homosexual. Some theorists have argued that veterans of the Vietnam War were more likely than veterans from previous wars to experience PTSD, because they received less social support from friends and family members on returning from combat, due to the social controversy over the war (Figley & Leventman, 1980). Similarly, one reason women are more likely than men to develop PTSD may be because the types of traumas women most frequently suffer (for example, sexual abuse) are stigmatized, whereas men are more likely to suffer traumas that don't carry as much stigma, such as exposure to war (Resick & Calhoun, 2001).

Differences among ethnic or cultural groups in vulnerability to PTSD may also be linked to differences in the social support available to members of these groups before and after traumas. Groups in which individuals have strong social support networks may be less prone to PTSD than those with weaker networks. For example, Southeast Asian refugees who are able to move into existing communities of people from their homeland when emigrating to a new country are less likely to show PTSD than are those who do not have existing communities in their new home (Beiser, 1988).

Psychological Factors

People facing the same circumstances around a trauma vary greatly in their risk for PTSD. At least three psychological factors have been identified to explain differences between people in response to trauma. First, for some people, a trauma shatters certain basic assumptions about life, and the shattering of these assumptions can contribute to long-term psychological distress. Second, some people are already distressed before a trauma occurs and they appear at greater risk for PTSD. Third, certain coping styles seem to increase people's chances of developing PTSD.

Shattered Assumptions We tend to go through life with a number of assumptions about ourselves and how the world works that help us feel good most of the time but can be shattered by a trauma (Janoff-Bulman, 1992). The first is the assumption of *personal invulnerability*. Most people believe that bad things happen to other people and that they are relatively invulnerable to traumas, such as being in a severe car accident, having their homes destroyed in natural disasters, or being kidnapped or raped. When such events do happen, people lose their illusion of invulnerability. Chronically feeling vulnerable, they are hypervigilant for signs of new traumas and may show signs of chronic anxiety (Janoff-Bulman, 1992).

The second basic assumption is that *the world is meaningful and just and that things happen for a good reason* (Lerner, 1980). This assumption can be shattered by events that seem senseless, unjust, or perhaps evil, such as the terrorist bombing of a children's day-care center or teenagers randomly shooting their classmates.

The third assumption is that *people who are good, who "play by the rules," do not experience bad things.* Trauma victims often will say that they have lived a good life, have been good people, and thus can't understand how the trauma happened to them (Janoff-Bulman & Frieze, 1983). A study of refugees from Bhutan, a region near Nepal, who had been forced from their homes and often tortured, found that many saw their misfortune as a result of past deeds, in line with cultural beliefs (Shrestha et al., 1998). A study of rape survivors found that those who engaged in self-blame involving their character—saying there was something bad about themselves that resulted in their being raped—showed greater distress than those who did not engage in such self-blame (Boeschen et al., 2001). Blaming themselves for causing a trauma can shatter people's views of themselves as good people (Janoff-Bulman & Frieze, 1983).

Preexisting Distress Another predictor of people's vulnerability to PTSD is the level of *distress* they were experiencing *before* the trauma hit (Shalev et al., 2004). People who are already experiencing increased symptoms of anxiety or depression are more likely to develop PTSD than are those who were not anxious or depressed (Blanchard et al., 1996; Cardozo et al., 2003; Hoge et al., 2004; Mayou et al., 2001). For example, a study of the victims of Hurricane Andrew found that the children who had already been anxious before the hurricane were more likely to develop posttraumatic stress reactions than were those who had not been anxious prior to the hurricane (LaGreca, Silverman, & Wasserstein, 1998). War veterans who have psychological problems or poor interpersonal relationships before they enter combat are more likely to develop symptoms of PTSD (Chemtob et al., 1990; King et al., 1999; Orsillo et al., 1996). African American, Hispanic American, and Native American combat veterans from the Vietnam and Persian Gulf wars appear to have been more vulnerable to PTSD than White veterans (Manson et al., 1996). This may be because they faced discrimination in the United States both before and after the war, increasing their base levels of distress and making it more likely they would respond to the traumas of combat with PTSD.

Coping Styles People's styles of *coping* with stressful events and with their own symptoms of

distress may also influence their vulnerability to PTSD. Several studies have shown that people who use self-destructive or avoidant coping strategies, such as drinking and self-isolation, are more likely to experience PTSD (Fairbank, Hansen, & Fitterling, 1991; Merrill et al., 2001; Sutker et al., 1995).

A similar form of coping that may increase the likelihood of PTSD is the use of dissociation (Foa & Hearst-Ikeda, 1996; Spiegel, 1991). Dissociation involves a range of psychological processes that indicate a detachment from the trauma and from ongoing events. People who dissociate following a trauma may feel they are in another place or in someone else's body, watching the trauma and its aftermath unfold. Studies have shown that people who dissociate shortly after a trauma are at increased risk to develop PTSD (Ehlers, Mayou et al., 1998; Fauerbach et al., 2000; Koopman, Classen, & Spiegel, 1994; Mayou et al., 2001; Shalev et al., 1996). Some studies suggest that Latinos are more prone to dissociate in response to severe stress, and this may increase their vulnerability to PTSD (Hough et al., 1996; Marshall & Orlando, 2002).

On the other hand, many studies have found that, following a trauma, most people try to *make sense* of the trauma somehow as a way of coping (Lehman et al., 1987; Silver, Boon, & Stones, 1983). They try to find a reason or purpose for the trauma or to understand what the trauma means in their lives. Psychodynamic and existential theorists have argued that searching for meaning in a trauma is a healthy process, which can lead people to gain a sense of mastery over their traumas and to integrate their traumas into their understanding of themselves (Frankl, 1963; Freud, 1920; Horowitz, 1976). They suggest that people who are able to make sense of their traumas are less likely to develop PTSD or other chronic emotional problems and may recover more quickly from their traumas than do people who cannot make sense of their traumas (Bulman & Wortman, 1977; Silver et al., 1983).

How do people make sense of traumas? Some people have religious or philosophical beliefs that assist them. For example, many recently bereaved people who are religious say that God needed their loved ones in heaven or had a special purpose for taking their loved ones, and this view seems to help them understand their losses (McIntosh, Silver, & Wortman, 1993; Nolen-Hoeksema & Larson, 1999). Other people say that the deaths of loved ones made them reevaluate their lives and their relationships with others and make positive changes, and this process helped them deal with the loss. For example, the following are some comments from a person who had lost a close loved one in recent months (Nolen-Hoeksema & Larson, 1999, p. 143).

Thinking back on it, if I had not done this, look at all I would have missed—all this growth, all this understanding. I tend to look at it generally as if all the things that happen in my life are a gift, for whatever reason, or however they happen. It doesn't necessarily have to be only pleasant gifts, but everything that happens . . . there's a meaning. I've had a lot of suffering in my life . . . and through that I've learned a great deal. While I wouldn't want to go back and relive that, I'm grateful for that because it makes me who I am. There's a lot of joys and sorrows, but they all enrich life. I like who I am now because I find at 44 that I really like myself. If I didn't go through a lot of the hardships that I had, I wouldn't be who I am. So in a lot of ways, it's been an OK journey. And if I hadn't had people like that in my life, I wouldn't have a good sense of humor, which is one of the things that helps us get through, right? I feel extremely fortunate lately.

Some people are never able to make sense of their losses or other traumas, and these people are more likely to experience chronic and severe symptoms of PTSD and depression. For example, researchers questioned 77 women who were the survivors of incest an average of 20 years after the incest had ended. They found that 50 percent of the women were still actively searching for meaning in their incest. These women said things such as "I always ask myself why, over and over, but there is no answer" and "There is no sense to be made. This should not have happened to me or any child" (Silver et al., 1983). The more actively a woman was still searching for meaning in her incest, the more likely she was to be experiencing recurrent and intrusive thoughts about the incest experience, the more distress she was experiencing, and the lower her level of social functioning was. Because those who search for meaning are ruminating about the past, perhaps they are also less able to focus coping efforts on the present and the future. In trying to understand, they may, in effect, get stuck in the past. Finding meaning may be particularly difficult in traumas such as sexual assault or genocide, in which the nature of the event violates basic moral codes and destroys people's basic trust in others (Resick, 1993; Silver et al., 1983).

Biological Factors

In recent years, researchers have been searching for biological factors that determine whether an individual will develop PTSD following a trauma. That search has focused on differences between PTSD sufferers and nonsufferers in the functioning of the brain and biochemical systems involved in the stress response. Some research also suggests that genetics play a role in vulnerability to PTSD.

Physiological Hyperreactivity Studies using neuroimaging techniques, such as positron-emission tomography (PET) and functional magnetic resonance imaging (MRI) (see Chapter 3), have found differences between PTSD sufferers and nonsufferers. The differences occur in activity levels in the parts of the brain involved in the regulation of emotion and the fight-or-flight response and in memory, including the amygdala and hippocampus (Ballenger et al., 2004; Nutt & Malizia, 2004). The *amygdala* appears to be hyperreactive to trauma-related stimuli in PTSD sufferers. In one study, combat veterans with PTSD show increased blood flow in the amygdala while imagining combat-related scenes, compared with when they were imagining neutral scenes (Liberzon & Phan, 2003; Shin et al., 1997) (see Figure 6.9). Similar results have been found in studies comparing survivors of childhood sexual assault with and without PTSD (Shin et al., 1999).

FIGURE 6.9 **Amygdala Activity in PTSD.** Combat veterans with PTSD showed increased blood flow in the amygdala when asked to imagine combat scenes in studies using positron-emission tomography.

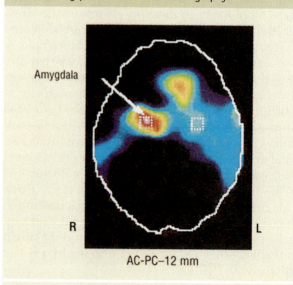

Amygdala

R   L

AC-PC–12 mm

Source: Shin et al., 1997.

FIGURE 6.10   **Hippocampal Deterioration in PTSD.** Studies using magnetic resonance imaging show deterioration in the hippocampus of people with PTSD (right), compared to someone without PTSD (left).

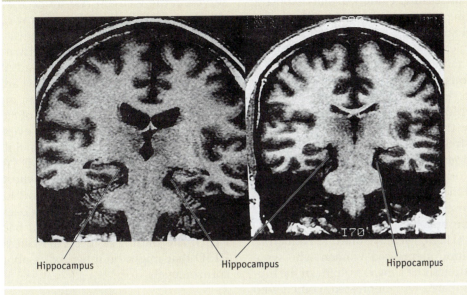

Hippocampus   Hippocampus   Hippocampus

Source: Bremner, 1998.

Some studies also show shrinkage in the *hippocampus* among PTSD patients (Bremner et al., 2000; Villarreal et al., 2002) (see Figure 6.10). The hippocampus is involved in memory. Damage to it may result in some of the memory problems that PTSD sufferers report. In addition, the hippocampus plays a role in the extinction of fear responses, so damage could interfere with an individual's ability to overcome fearful responses to stimuli reminiscent of the trauma.

Recall that one of the major hormones released as part of the fight-or-flight response is *cortisol* and that high levels of cortisol usually indicate an elevated stress response. Interestingly, resting levels of cortisol among PTSD sufferers (when they are not being exposed to reminders of their trauma) tend to be *lower* than among people without PTSD (Ballenger et al., 2004; Yehuda, 2004). Cortisol shuts down sympathetic nervous system activity after stress, so the lower levels of cortisol among PTSD sufferers may result in prolonged activity of the sympathetic nervous system following stress. As a result, they may more easily develop a conditioned fear of stimuli associated with the trauma and subsequently develop PTSD.

One longitudinal study assessed cortisol levels in people who had been injured in a traffic accident one to two hours previously (Yehuda, McFarlane, & Shalev, 1998). Six months later, these people were evaluated for the presence of PTSD. Those who developed the disorder had had signif-

icantly lower cortisol levels immediately after the trauma than had the people who did not develop the disorder. Similar results were found in a study of rape survivors (Resnick et al., 1995). These data suggest that people who develop PTSD have lower baseline levels of cortisol before they experience their trauma and possibly that abnormally low cortisol levels contribute to the development of PTSD.

Although PTSD sufferers have low levels of cortisol, some of their other physiological responses to stress are exaggerated, including elevated heart rate and increased secretion of the neurotransmitters epinephrine and norepinephrine (Ballenger et al., 2004; Yehuda, 2004). One possibility is that people who are vulnerable to the development of PTSD in the wake of trauma show a decoupling, or dissociation, among the various regulators of the tress response, including the hypothalamic-pituitary-adrenal (HPA) axis and the sympathetic nervous system. The HPA axis may be unable to shut down the response of the sympathetic nervous system to a trauma by secreting the necessary levels of cortisol, resulting in the brain's overexposure to epinephrine, norepinephrine, and other neurochemicals. This overexposure then may lead

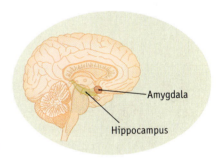

Amygdala

Hippocampus

These structures of the limbic system have been implicated in PTSD.

to memories of the traumatic event being "over-consolidated," or inappropriately remembered (Pitman, 1989).

There is increasing evidence that exposure to trauma during childhood may permanently alter children's biological stress response, making them more vulnerable to PTSD and to other anxiety disorders and depression throughout their lives (Cicchetti & Toth; 2005; Nemeroff, 2004). Studies of children who have been maltreated (severely neglected or physically, emotionally, or sexually abused) show that they have abnormal cortisol responses to stressors (Cicchetti, Toth, & Rogosch, 2001) and a diminished startle response (Klorman et al., 2003). Studies of adults who were abused as children show that they continue to have abnormal cortisol responses to laboratory stressors, even if they do not continue to show symptoms of PTSD or depression (Heim, Meinlschmidt, & Nemeroff, 2003). In addition, depressed women who were abused as children show a lower volume of the hippocampus, compared with depressed women who were not abused as children (Vythilingam et al., 2002). Thus, early childhood trauma may leave permanent physical scars, as well as emotional scars, that predispose individuals to later psychological problems.

Genetics There is some evidence that a vulnerability to PTSD can be inherited (Segman & Shalev, 2003). One study of about 4,000 twins who had served in the Vietnam War found that, if one twin developed PTSD, the other twin was much more likely also to develop PTSD if he was an identical twin than if he was a fraternal twin (True et al., 1993). Fascinating studies of the adult children of Holocaust survivors find that they are three times more likely to develop PTSD than matched comparison groups, and the children of Holocaust survivors who developed PTSD are even more likely to develop the disorder than the children of survivors who did not develop PTSD (Yehuda et al., 1998). In turn, the adult children whose parents developed PTSD have abnormally low levels of cortisol, whether or not they had ever been exposed to traumatic events themselves and had developed PTSD. This finding suggests that one risk factor for PTSD that might be inherited is abnormally low cortisol levels.

Treatments for PTSD

Psychotherapies for PTSD generally have three goals: exposing clients to what they fear in order to extinguish that fear, challenging distorted cognitions that are contributing to symptoms, and

---

TABLE 6.6 Concept Overview

Treatments for PTSD

Treatments for PTSD focus on exposing clients to feared images, challenging distorted cognitions, managing stressful circumstances, and reducing painful anxiety symptoms.

Treatment	Description	Example
Cognitive-behavioral therapy	Systematic desensitization is used to extinguish fear reactions to memories; cognitive techniques are used to challenge irrational thoughts.	Rape survivor works through hierarchy of feared memories of rape using relaxation techniques; therapist helps her confront self-blaming thoughts.
Stress management	Therapist helps the client solve concrete problems to reduce stress; may use thought-stopping strategies to quell intrusive thoughts.	Disaster survivor is helped to find a new home and job.
Biological therapies	Antianxiety and antidepressant drugs are used to quell symptoms.	Person uses Valium (a benzodiazeine) to help induce sleep at night.
Sociocultural approaches	PTSD symptoms are understood and treated within the norms of people's culture.	Culture-specific rituals might be used to help a PTSD sufferer make peace with the trauma and reintegrate into the community.

helping clients manage their ongoing life problems to reduce the stress in their lives. These goals are addressed in cognitive-behavioral therapy for PTSD and in stress-management therapies. Some people with PTSD also benefit from the use of antianxiety and antidepressant medications (see the Concept Overview in Table 6.6). After we discuss psychotherapies and drug therapies for PTSD, we will address social perspectives on PTSD and its treatment.

Cognitive-Behavioral Therapy

Cognitive-behavioral therapy has proven effective in the treatment of PTSD in adults (Davidson, 2004; Resick & Calhoun, 2001; Van Etten & Taylor, 1998) and in children (Cohen et al., 2004). A major element of cognitive-behavioral treatment for PTSD is **systematic desensitization therapy.** The client identifies thoughts and situations that create anxiety, ranking them from most anxiety-provoking to least. The therapist then begins to take the client through this hierarchy, using relaxation techniques to quell anxiety. The focus of anxiety in PTSD is the memory of the traumatic event and stimuli that remind the person of the event. It is impossible to return to the actual event that triggered the PTSD in many cases, so imagining the event vividly must replace actual exposure to the event. A combat veteran being treated for PTSD imagines the bloody battles and scenes of killing and death that haunt him; a rape survivor imagines the minute details of the assault. The therapist also watches for distorted thinking patterns, such as survivor guilt, and helps the client challenge these thoughts, as in the following interchange between a therapist and a woman named Cindy, who developed PTSD after being raped (adapted from Resick & Calhoun, 2001, p. 81).

VOICES

Cindy: Why did this have to happen? Why? Why?

Therapist: Why did the rape have to happen?

Cindy: Yeah. Why did he do that to me? Why should I have to feel this? I'm a product of my environment. I really feel like that.

Therapist: We all are to a certain extent.

Cindy: Yeah. We are.

Therapist: What answer have you given yourself up to this point to that "why" question?

Cindy: Because, just, that's my life, that was my past. That is what happened.

Therapist: But you still keep asking why.

Cindy: I think my "why" question just stems from, you know, you stupid idiot, you don't take that from people. [Long pause] You know, it's not why did he take it from me. One thing I get mad at myself is [crying], why did I let him?

Therapist: You didn't let him.

Cindy: I know.

Therapist: Did you? He just did it.

Cindy: It happened. I was 15. I was so scared.

Therapist: And confused.

Cindy: Yeah, and alone. I think that's why I'm mad. Because I was so alone and I walked away from so many people. It kind of wiped away all the good memories.

Therapist: It's a scary decision for a 15-year-old to try to reach out to people when she's feeling bad about herself. At times a person in that position is going to pull away, because she's so afraid of compounding the trauma by other people rejecting her. It seems almost better to walk away yourself than let other people reject you. So you were rejecting them first.

Repeatedly and vividly imagining and describing the feared events in the safety of the therapist's office, the client has an opportunity to habituate to his or her anxiety and to distinguish the memory from present reality (Foa & Jaycox, 1999; Resick & Calhoun, 2001). Repeatedly imagining and discussing the traumatic events may also allow the client to work through them and integrate them into his or her concepts of the self and the world (Foa & Jaycox, 1999; Horowitz, 1976).

Studies of rape survivors, combat veterans, survivors of road traffic collisions, and refugees have found that this kind of repeated exposure therapy significantly decreases PTSD symptoms and helps prevent relapse (Foa et al., 1991, 1999; Keane et al., 1992; Paunovic & Öst, 2001; Resick & Schnicke, 1992; Tarrier et al., 1999; Taylor et al., 2001). In another type of imagery intervention, rape survivors who had repeated nightmares about their rape experience were taught to use positive imagery to change the content of their nightmares. Even after only a few sessions of imagery training, these women showed decreases in nightmares, improved sleep quality, and decreased PTSD symptoms (Krakow et al., 2000, 2001).

Stress Management

What about those people who are constantly ruminating about their traumas, even years after they are over? Will intensive exposure to thoughts about the traumas help them? Some theorists argue that, for PTSD sufferers who cannot find any meaning in their traumas or cannot "resolve" their traumas and who experience very frequent, intrusive thoughts, it may be more useful to help them find ways of blocking their intrusive thoughts (Ehlers, Clark, et al., 1998; Horowitz, 1976; Silver et al., 1983). **Thought-stopping techniques** include the client's yelling "No!" loudly when realizing he or she is thinking about the trauma, as well as learning to engage in positive activities that distract thoughts away from the trauma (Rachman, 1978). These thought-stopping techniques are often combined with **stress-management interventions** that teach clients skills for overcoming problems in their lives that are increasing their stress and that may be the result of PTSD, such as marital problems or social isolation (Keane et al., 1992; Wolfsdorf & Zlotnick, 2001). The following case study illustrates the use of several stress-management interventions with a combat veteran suffering from PTSD (Keane et al., 1992, p. 91):

CASE STUDY

D. P. was a male Vietnam veteran referred to the PTSD unit of his local DVA [Department of Veterans Affairs] Medical Center. D. P. reported feeling extremely stressed over the past six months because of problems on his job. He complained of sleep disturbance, angry outbursts, intrusive thoughts, nightmares, and avoidance of movies, books, and television shows associated with Vietnam. He also was experiencing marital difficulties, constriction of affect, and numbing of emotions. Since his discharge from the military, D. P. had avoided discussing Vietnam (his friends over the past 20 years were unaware that D. P. had even been in the military), and he stated that he did not want to discuss Vietnam in treatment. Respecting his wishes, treatment began by addressing sleep disturbance and interpersonal difficulties. D. P. learned progressive muscle relaxation and began using the technique to prepare for sleep, to get back to sleep after awakening, and at

times throughout the day when he felt himself becoming stressed. Interpersonal difficulties were then addressed in couples sessions using communication and problem-solving skills. D. P. and his wife had developed a relatively noncommunicative style over a number of years. Mrs. P. complained about a lack of intimacy in their relationship and being overburdened with decisions that were better made by both of them. In therapy, the couple learned to listen to one another and to give constructive positive and negative feedback. As is common among combat veterans with PTSD, D. P. was afraid of his anger, even though he had not been violent in over 17 years. To address this concern, he was taught several strategies for anger control. For example, D. P. was given permission by the therapist to remove himself from a situation or discussion that created stress for him. He was taught to request a time and place to later continue working on that specific problem. This allowed D. P. to work on problem-solving skills while titrating his exposure to aversive, arousing circumstances. Initially, problem solving was conducted only during the session; however, after several weeks, the couple began problem solving at home and reviewed the contracts and solution processes in the following session. As D. P. learned a variety of new skills that enhanced his ability to manage his stress and his interpersonal problems, he became less defensive about Vietnam and began to address those issues more directly in therapy.

Wolfsdorf and Zlotnick (2001) recommend a variation on stress-management therapy for survivors of sexual abuse, which they call *affect-management therapy*. This therapy uses a variety of behavioral and cognitive methods to help clients manage their negative moods better, with the hope that eventually they will be able to confront the overwhelming memories of their abuse. An interchange between a therapist and client who is self-destructive in response to her negative feelings goes like this (adapted from Wolfsdorf & Zlotnick, 2001, pp. 178–179):

V O I C E S

Client: Once I'm upset, that's it. There's nothing I can do. I just sit on the floor and chain smoke.

Therapist: Then what?

Client: I usually end up bingeing. If it's really bad, I burn myself with a cigarette.

Therapist: Does that work for you?

Client: Kind of. I mean, it does usually stop me from doing something more drastic. But I'm getting fat, and I'm sick of all these little scars. I end up feeling worse the next day because I did it again.

Therapist: Yes, that's hard. I think it's important for you to have other options for feeling better when you are in a crisis. Something that could help you feel better in the moment and also longer term. What do you think?

Client: Well, it *sounds* okay.

Therapist: One thing that can be very important at those times is to have a plan of healthy things you could do. If you have a crisis plan, then you don't have to come up with other options when you're upset; it's already done for you. Does that make sense?

Client: Yes.

Therapist: Okay, good. So what kinds of things could you do in a crisis instead of hurting yourself?

Client: I could get away. Take a trip. That would really help. To be able to just get on a plane and go visit a friend.

Therapist: Yes, visiting friends is a great idea. It can really help deal with stress. But I'm concerned that you might not always be able to do that in a crisis. And for a crisis plan to work, we need to focus on things you could do any time. Does that make sense?

Client: I guess.

Therapist: So what could you do that would help you feel better any time you were in crisis? What do you enjoy doing?

Client: I like to go for walks in the park near my house. There are some beautiful trees in that park. And I like to give my dog a bath. He loves the water, so it's fun.

Therapist: Those are great ideas. Do you think that would help if you were in crisis?

Client: Yes. They're both distracting, and they get me out of the house, which is good.

Therapist: Excellent. Now, if you needed to do something else, what else could you do?

Client: I could call a friend and let her know how I'm feeling.

Therapist: Okay, do you have someone specific in mind?

Studies find that these affect- and stress-management interventions are helpful both to combat veterans with PTSD and to persons suffering PTSD after rape (Foa et al., 1999; Kilpatrick, Veronen, & Resick, 1979; Meichenbaum & Jaremko, 1983; Veronen & Kilpatrick, 1983; Wolfsdorf & Zlotnick, 2001). There is still much work to do, however, before it is known just how to treat persons with PTSD.

Eye Movement Desensitization and Reprocessing

Eye movement desensitization and reprocessing, or **EMDR,** is a highly controversial therapy for trauma survivors that evolved from a personal observation. The originator of this therapy, Francine Shapiro (1995), noticed that her troubling thoughts were resolved when her eyes followed the waving of leaves during a walk in the park. She suggested that lateral eye movements facilitate the cognitive processing of trauma and developed EMDR from this hypothesis.

During a session of EMDR, a client attends to the image of the trauma, thoughts about the trauma, and the physical sensations of anxiety aroused by the trauma. At the same time, the therapist quickly moves a finger back and forth in front of the client's eyes to elicit a series of repeated, rapid, jerky, side-to-side eye movements ("saccades"). During the session, the client provides ratings of his or her anxiety level and how strongly he or she believes negative thoughts pertaining to the trauma.

In its early days, EMDR was described as a one-session cure for PTSD and related disorders. More recently, proponents have suggested that it requires multiple sessions. The fantastic claims made by early proponents of EMDR led to a flurry of studies of its effectiveness. A statistical summary, or meta-analysis (review Chapter 3), of 34 studies examining EMDR with a variety of populations and measures concluded that EMDR is significantly more effective at reducing PTSD symptoms than no treatment or nonspecific treatments that do not expose people to their traumatic memories (Davidson & Parker, 2001). EMDR had effects similar to those of behavior therapies focused on exposing people to their traumatic memories and cognitive-behavioral therapies.

Interestingly, this meta-analysis also compared EMDR with a form of the therapy that has all the components of EMDR except the eye movements (i.e., directing clients' attention to images and thoughts of the trauma), and it concluded that the eye movements are unnecessary for reducing PTSD symptoms. This analysis suggests that the active components of EMDR are the exposure and habituation of clients to their traumas and the cognitive restructuring of their thoughts about the traumas—not the eye movements (see also Resick & Calhoun, 2001).

Biological Therapies

Studies have shown the selective serotonin reuptake inhibitors (SSRIs) and, to a lesser extent, the benzodiazepines, to be useful in treating the symptoms of PTSD, particularly the sleep problems, nightmares, and irritability (Ballenger et al., 2004; Brady et al., 2000; Davidson, 2004; Marshall et al., 2001). One study showed that PTSD patients who had had a successful treatment with an SSRI were more likely to be symptom-free for five months, compared with patients who had not received an SSRI (Martenyi et al., 2002). Patients who continue to take an SSRI after their acute symptoms have subsided are even more likely to remain symptom-free (Davidson, Rothmaum, et al., 2001).

Sociocultural Approaches

Treatments for PTSD often must consider the cultural context for this disorder. Some cultural groups have suffered a tremendous number of traumas and, thus, are more likely to have high rates of PTSD. The appropriateness of any given treatment for PTSD, however, may depend on the norms and values of that culture. In addition, when whole communities have been the victims of traumas, treatment must often be at a community level as well as at an individual level.

Cross-Cultural Issues Southeast Asians may be especially vulnerable to PTSD because of the chronic and severe traumas to which many of them have been exposed. When they do seek treatment for psychological distress, Southeast Asians often have bodily symptoms, such as pain, poor sleeping, and stomachaches, rather than the psychological symptoms of posttraumatic stress disorder. They often do not believe that the primary symptoms of PTSD, such as startle reaction, nightmares, reexperiencing of the trauma, and irritability, are worth mentioning to a physician, and they steadfastly avoid thinking about or talking about the traumas they experienced (Kinzie & Leung, 1993). Dissociative experiences, such as transient hallucinations or loss of physical functioning for no medical reason, are also common. What follows is a case history of a Cambodian woman with PTSD (adapted from Kinzie & Leung, 1993, p. 292).

CASE STUDY

When originally seen, S. A. was 38 years old. She was a Cambodian refugee brought because she believed she was possessed by her dead mother. During the original evaluation, the patient was so distressed and agitated that no real history could be obtained. A subsequent evaluation showed that she had recently been angry and depressed much of the time and actually felt that her mother had entered her body. This intrusion caused her to become very irritable and angry, and during these episodes, she would lose control. . . . S. A.'s past history was very disturbing. She was born in a rural area in Cambodia, the third of five children. She worked as a secretary for 1½ years and married at the age of 17. During the Pol Pot regime, she was subjected to 4 years of forced labor. Her father died, and her husband was executed at the time she was in labor with her second child. S. A.'s child died of starvation, and her mother died of disease and starvation. She felt most distressed about the death of her mother, who was the person closest to her and who had helped her with the delivery of her child. In 1979, she left Cambodia and lived in refugee camps for 1½ years before coming to the United States. . . . At her original presentation, S. A. was extremely agitated and appeared to be in a dissociated state. However, in the second interview, after a week of benzodiazepine treatment, she demonstrated a good fund of knowledge and a good memory for past events. She appeared to be numb and saddened about what she had suffered. Her symptoms included frequent nightmares, intrusive

(continued)

thoughts about the past, startle reaction, irritability, and marked attempts to avoid all memories of the past or any events that would remind her of Cambodia. . . .

The treatment of PTSD in Southeast Asian refugees, such as S. A., can be especially delicate. They may never have told anyone about the traumas they experienced in their homeland because of strong cultural taboos against discussing these traumas in their families. Thus, therapists must be highly sensitive and supportive in encouraging the refugee to tell his or her own story (Kinzie, 2001). The therapist must be careful to avoid any suggestion of interrogating the client, as he or she might have been interrogated in the homeland.

These refugees may need to protect themselves against the agony that memories of their severe traumas arouse and focus more on solving current problems. For example, the therapist treating S. A. might want to ensure that she is getting all the financial support and education available to her to stabilize her income and living situation. Although refugees may be having significant problems in their marital and family relationships due to their PTSD symptoms and the amount of stress their families are facing, they may be reluctant to talk to the therapist about these, due to cultural taboos against doing so.

Some cultures have their own treatments for PTSD-like symptoms. For example, some Native American groups have cleansing rituals that absolve combat veterans from their actions during combat and reintegrate veterans into the community and with the values of his or her group. The Navajo have a healing ceremony called the *Enemy Way*, which is explicitly oriented toward returning combat veterans. The ceremony lasts for seven days and seven nights. The veteran, his or her family and community members, and a tribal healer actively participate in ritual song designed to return balance and harmony to the veteran and the entire community (Manson et al., 1996).

Community-Level Interventions Often, whole communities are ravaged by traumas—a tornado might wipe out most businesses in a community or a flood might make most of the homes in a community uninhabitable. Human-made disasters can also ravage whole communities, such as the atrocities committed under "ethnic cleansing" and apartheid. Hundreds of thousands of people in many communities around the world—Afghanistan, Kosovo, Bosnia, Rwanda, South Africa, Eritrea—have been forced from their homes, driven out of their countries, tortured, raped, and killed. Mental-health professionals have been on the front lines of these conflicts, attempting to help survivors cope with the traumas they have suffered.

A community-level intervention helped women refugees in Kwazulu-Natal, South Africa cope with the traumas they suffered.

Following is the story of one of these helpers, a psychologist in South Africa (Burnette, 1997, pp. 10–11).

When the civil strife started two years ago, the men of Bhambayi went off to fight and the women were forced to move from their middle-class homes into rundown shacks on barren land. The war, fought by two factions in conflict over apartheid, drastically altered the lives of the people in Bhambayi, a town in KwaZulu-Natal, South Africa. Hundreds of people were killed and the people's homes were destroyed.

Psychologist Craig Higson-Smith, a 27-year-old South African native, became aware of the region's problems while teaching at the University of Natal and founded the KwaZulu-Natal Program for Survivors of Violence. He first brought a team of South African community researchers to help the beleaguered people there in 1992 and their work continues today.

Before the war, most of the families owned their own homes, benefited from two incomes and had gardens where they grew their own vegetables. So, as one of the first priorities, the staff of the KwaZulu-Natal Program for the Survivors of Violence secured a 3,000-square-foot piece of land from the government. While the women toiled, they discussed how the violence had affected their lives and how it felt to lose their husbands and their children.

The garden fulfilled many needs. The 25 women turned the once-barren soil into a flourishing vegetable patch. The garden also became a therapeutic oasis as the women supported each other, and spoke with program staff about their experiences, and gained self-esteem from being productive.

"What happened was the same interaction that psychologists think of as group therapy," says Higson-Smith. "But it happened in a different context and was facilitated by a process that we wouldn't have necessarily thought of using."

The program is geared primarily toward communities, although staff conduct some work at the individual, small group, and societal levels. With individuals, they conduct traditional psychotherapy to help people cope psychologically in their war-torn environment. At the small group level, they work with families, schools, and churches to restore support systems and foster community empowerment.

And at the societal level, they advocate for government funding for their program, discuss the violence in the region with lawmakers, and advocate for conflict resolution programs in the school curricula.

"The interventions we conduct mean rethinking what we as psychologists understand as our role, particularly in underdeveloped countries," Higson-Smith says. "Our job often includes facilitating, promoting and networking so that the structures [that already exist in the community] can mobilize.

"Even the most fragmented communities contain structures," Higson-Smith said. Church groups, stokvels (savings clubs), social clubs and paramilitary units are examples of such networks. His group works with those structures to link people in the communities.

Higson-Smith's team worked with a paramilitary group whose members had become involved in criminal activities, such as stealing and selling drugs. The researchers facilitated discussion among the group members about their problems and helped them come up with concrete strategies they could use to improve their lives, such as getting job training.

At the same time, Higson-Smith and his group were working with nurses at a local clinic, training them in trauma management. The team connected the two groups and now some of the group members are volunteering at the clinic.

Higson-Smith and his staff also have programs designed specifically for the young people whose lives have been ravaged by the war. They recruit youth who have been involved in the conflict to help them resume normal lives and use group discussions to explore topics such as unemployment and coping with anger and grief. They also focus on other issues young people must face, including peer pres-

(continued)

sure and substance abuse, and explore how those issues relate to the violence they have experienced.

"Political violence is the most salient feature of their lives. Most of the teens there have killed someone, know someone who's been killed or have been forced to leave their homes," Higson-Smith says. "So in the groups we discuss how the violence relates to these other issues they must contend with as adolescents."

The youth groups play games and work on projects aimed at teaching life skills. Last year when the youth group organized a community sports day, they learned to communicate with each other as well as youth from other communities, and take responsibility by seeing the event through to completion.

Higson-Smith and his colleagues also conduct psychodrama, art and music groups that serve as a venue for the youth to express how it felt to live through the conflict. The youth write poems, for example, to express their feelings, some of which were published in a book, *On Common Ground* (KwaZulu-Natal Program for Survivors of Violence, 1996).

Higson-Smith says the team's work is difficult yet rewarding. He also emphasizes that he and his colleagues are not the sole cause of healing in these devastated communities. "Before we came, the people here survived, coped, and found joy in their lives," he said.

Therapists who work with refugees and other groups that have undergone tremendous, chronic stressors emphasize the need for flexibility—adapting therapeutic methods to the cultural norms of the groups—and for respect and recognition of the resilience of these people in the face of overwhelming conditions (Eisenbruch, de Jong, & van de Put, 2004; Lemaire & Despret, 2001).

SUMMING UP

- People with posttraumatic stress disorder repeatedly reexperience the traumatic event, avoid situations that might arouse memories of their trauma, and are hypervigilant and chronically aroused.
- PTSD may be most likely to occur following traumas that shatter people's assumptions that

they are invulnerable, that the world is a just place, and that bad things do not happen to good people.

- People who experience severe and long-lasting traumas, who have lower levels of social support, who experience socially stigmatizing traumas, who were already depressed or anxious before the trauma, or who have maladaptive coping styles may be at increased risk for PTSD.
- People who are unable to make sense of a trauma appear more likely to have chronic PTSD symptoms.
- PTSD sufferers show greater physiological reactivity to stressors, greater activity in the areas of the brain involved in emotion and memory, but lower resting cortisol levels.
- Effective psychotherapy for PTSD involves exposing the person to memories of the trauma and extinguishing his or her anxiety over these memories through systematic desensitization and flooding.
- Some people cannot tolerate such exposure, however, and may do better with supportive therapy focused on solving current interpersonal difficulties and life problems.
- Benzodiazepines and antidepressant drugs can quell some of the symptoms of PTSD.
- Clinicians must be sensitive both to the extraordinary circumstances that may have led to PTSD and to the cultural norms of the person or group being treated.

CHAPTER INTEGRATION

This chapter amply illustrates the reciprocal effects of the body, the mind, and the environment (see Figure 6.11 on page 212). Psychological and social factors can have direct effects on the physiology of the body and indirect effects on health by leading people to engage in behaviors that either promote or impair health. On the other hand, our physical health affects our emotional health and self-concept. People with life-threatening or debilitating physical illnesses are at a much increased risk for depression and other emotional problems. At a more subtle level, physiology may influence many characteristics we think of as personality, such as how quick we are to react with anger when someone confronts us or how adaptable we are to new situations. For these reasons, health psychologists begin with the assumption that biology, psychology, and the social environment have reciprocal influences on each other. Then they attempt to characterize these influences and determine their importance.

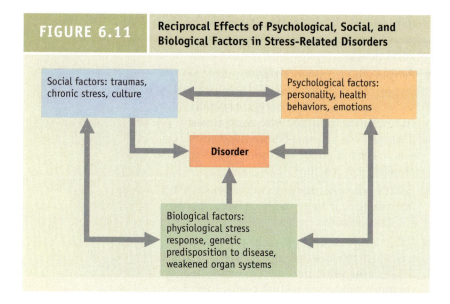

FIGURE 6.11 Reciprocal Effects of Psychological, Social, and Biological Factors in Stress-Related Disorders

Social factors: traumas, chronic stress, culture

Psychological factors: personality, health behaviors, emotions

Disorder

Biological factors: physiological stress response, genetic predisposition to disease, weakened organ systems

By definition, posttraumatic stress disorder is the result of a psychological experience of trauma, yet new research is showing just how much traumatic experiences can permanently change an individual's biology. As we discussed in this chapter, people with PTSD show changes in how their brains function and how they respond to stimuli. Studies of young children who have suffered traumas, such as emotional or sexual abuse, show that their brains develop differently than do the brains of children who have not suffered traumas (Cicchetti & Toth, 2005). In turn, the risk of developing serious PTSD following a trauma may be influenced by genetics or by other types of predisposing vulnerability factors.

Does the mind affect the body, or does the body affect the mind? The work in health psychology and the research on PTSD show that this ancient mind-body question can only be answered with *"Both."*

Extraordinary People: Follow-Up

We end this chapter with powerful encouragement from Norman Cousins for anyone who has faced serious disease or the impact of traumatic events on the mind and body.

What we are talking about essentially, I suppose, is the chemistry of the will to live. If I had to guess, I would say that the principal contribution made by my doctor to the taming, and possibly the conquest, of my illness was that he encouraged me to believe I was a respected partner with him in the total undertaking. He fully engaged my subjective energies. He may not have been able to define or diagnose the process through which self-confidence (wild hunches securely believed) was somehow picked up by the body's immunologic mechanisms and translated into anti-morbid effects. But he was acting, I believe, in the best tradition of medicine in recognizing that he had to reach out in my case beyond the usual verifiable modalities. . . .

Something else I have learned. I have learned never to underestimate the capacity of the human mind and body to regenerate—even when the prospects seem most wretched. The life-force may be the least understood force on earth. William James (1948) said that human beings tend to live too far within self-imposed limits. It is possible that those limits will recede when we respect more fully the natural drive of the human mind and body toward perfectibility and regeneration. Protecting and cherishing that natural drive may well represent the finest exercise of human freedom. (Cousins, 1976, pp. 1458–63)

Chapter Summary

■ Events that are uncontrollable or unpredictable are perceived as more stressful. Stress can have a direct effect on health by causing chronic arousal of the physiological responses that make up the fight-or-flight response. These physiological

responses result from the activation of the sympathetic nervous system and the adrenal-cortical system. Although these physiological changes are useful in helping the body fight or flee from a threat, they can cause damage to the body if they are chronically aroused due to stress. (Review Figures 6.1 and 6.2.)

- Health psychologists are concerned with the roles of personality factors, coping styles, stressful events, and health-related behaviors in the development of physical disease and in the progress of disease. Health psychologists use three models for explaining how psychological factors affect health (review Figure 6.3):

  1. The direct effects model suggests that psychological factors, such as stressful experiences or certain personality characteristics, directly cause changes in the physiology of the body, which, in turn cause or exacerbate disease.
  2. The interactive model suggests that psychological factors must interact with a pre-existing biological vulnerability to disease in order for a disease to develop.
  3. The indirect effects model suggests that psychological factors affect disease largely by influencing whether people engage in health-promoting behaviors.

- Chronic physiological arousal in response to stress can contribute to coronary heart disease, hypertension, and possibly impairment of the immune system.

- Many of us give up sleep when we are under stress. The amount and quality of sleep we get on a daily basis have a significant impact on our physical health and psychological functioning.

- Some people develop sleep disorders. Dyssomnias, such as insomnia, involve abnormalities in the amount, quality, or timing of sleep. Parasomnias involve abnormal behavioral and psychological events during sleep. (Review Tables 6.1 and 6.2.)

- Pessimism is a personality characteristic that has been linked to poor health. (Review Figure 6.5.)

- The Type A behavior pattern is strongly related to a high risk for coronary heart disease and possibly other diseases. People who have the Type A pattern have a sense of time urgency, are easily made hostile, and are competitive in many situations. The component of this pattern that has been most consistently linked to coronary heart disease is a cynical form of hostility. (Review Figure 6.6.)

- People who seek and receive positive social support appear to fare better after stressful experiences.

- Guided mastery techniques have been effective in increasing self-efficacy for engaging in healthy behaviors and skill in conducting healthy behaviors. They include modeling and role-playing to provide people with new skills and opportunities to practice them in increasingly challenging circumstances.

- Biofeedback is sometimes used to help people gain control over the bodily processes that contribute to disease. It is unclear how biofeedback works, but it has been shown to be useful in reducing hypertension and headaches.

- Sociocultural interventions focus on changing and using people's social networks to improve their health. Some research suggests that support groups may improve physical well-being.

- Posttraumatic stress disorder (PTSD) occurs after a person experiences a severe trauma. It involves three types of symptoms: (1) repeatedly reexperiencing of the traumatic event through intrusive images or thoughts, recurring nightmares, flashbacks, and psychological and physiological reactivity to stimuli that remind the person of the event; (2) withdrawal, emotional numbing, and avoidance of anything that might arouse memories of the event; and (3) hypervigilance and chronic arousal. In addition to having these symptoms, PTSD sufferers report survival guilt. (Review Table 6.3.)

- Acute stress disorder has symptoms similar to those of PTSD but occurs within one month of a stressor and lasts less than four weeks. (Review Table 6.4.)

- Adjustment disorder is diagnosed when depressive or anxiety symptoms or antisocial behavior occurs within three months after a stressor.

- Social factors appear involved in the risk for PTSD. The more severe and longer-lasting a trauma and the more involved a person is in the trauma, the more likely he or she is to show PTSD. People who have lower levels of social support and who experience socially stigmatizing traumas are at increased risk for PTSD.

- Psychological factors also play a role in PTSD. People who are already depressed or anxious before a trauma, cope through dissociation, or have difficulty making sense of the trauma may be at increased risk for PTSD.

- The biological factors involved in vulnerability to PTSD may include abnormally low cortisol levels and a genetic risk. In addition, people with PTSD show hyperarousal of the amygdala, atrophy in the hippocampus, and exaggerated heart rate responses to stressors. (Review Table 6.5.)

- An effective treatment for PTSD involves exposing a person to his or her memories of a trauma, through systematic desensitization and flooding, to extinguish his or her anxiety over these memories. Some people cannot tolerate such exposure, however, and may do better with supportive therapy focused on solving current interpersonal difficulties and life problems.

■ Benzodiazepines and antidepressant drugs can quell some of the symptoms of PTSD. (Review Table 6.6.)

■ Alternative approaches to the treatment of PTSD include eye movement desensitization and reprocessing as well as culturally specific practices.

MindMap CD-ROM

The following resources on the MindMap CD-ROM that came with this text will help you to master the content of this chapter and prepare for tests:

■ Interactive Segments: Stress and Life Events; Type A Behavior

■ Video: PTSD

■ Chapter Timeline

■ Chapter Quiz

Key Terms

stress 173

fight-or-flight response 175

cortisol 175

general adaptation syndrome 175

health psychology 176

coronary heart disease (CHD) 177

hypertension 178

immune system 178

lymphocytes 178

dyssomnias 182

parasomnias 182

insomnia 182

stimulus-control therapy 183

sleep restriction therapy 183

hypersomnia 183

narcolepsy 184

cataplexy 184

sleep apnea 184

Type A behavior pattern 185

guided mastery techniques 189

biofeedback 190

posttraumatic stress disorder (PTSD) 191

acute stress disorder 191

adjustment disorder 191

dissociative symptoms 193

systematic desensitization therapy 205

thought-stopping techniques 206

stress-management interventions 206

eye movement desensitization and reprocessing (EMDR) 207

Chapter 7

Birddog
by Diana Ong

*All emotions are pure which gather you and lift you up;
that emotion is impure which seizes only one side of
your being and so distorts you.*

—Rainer Maria Rilke, *Letters to a Young Poet*
(1904, November 4; translated by M. D. Herter)

Anxiety Disorders <

Extraordinary People

■ **Marc Summers:** *Everything in Its Place*

Panic Disorder

People with panic disorder experience sudden bursts of anxiety symptoms, feel out of control, and think they are dying. They may have an overreactive autonomic nervous system, which easily turns on a fight-or-flight response. They also tend to catastrophize their symptoms and have an excessive sensitivity to anxiety. Antidepressant and antianxiety drugs can reduce symptoms of panic, and cognitive-behavioral treatments are effective for panic disorder.

Taking Psychology Personally

■ **Relaxation Exercises**

Phobias

People with agoraphobia fear being in places where they might be trapped or unable to get help in an emergency. The emergency they often fear is having a panic attack. The specific phobias focus on animals, elements of the environment (such as water), certain situations (such as flying), blood, injections, and injuries. Social phobia involves a pervasive fear of scrutiny by others.

Psychodynamic theories attribute phobias to the displacement of unconscious conflicts onto symbolic objects. Behavioral theories argue that phobias develop from classical and operant conditioning. Cognitive theories of social phobia suggest that this disorder develops in people who have excessively high standards for their social performance, assume that others are judging them harshly, and are hypervigilant to signs of rejection from others. Biological theories attribute phobias to genetics. The most effective treatments for phobias are behavioral treatments that expose people to their phobic objects and teach them skills for reducing their anxiety.

Generalized Anxiety Disorder

People with generalized anxiety disorder have chronic and pervasive anxiety about most aspects of their lives. Both consciously and unconsciously, they are hypervigilant for threat. They worry constantly about both important and unimportant things. Cognitive-behavioral therapies have proven effective for generalized anxiety disorder. Antianxiety drugs and antidepressants can also reduce anxiety symptoms.

Obsessive-Compulsive Disorder

Obsessive-compulsive disorder (OCD) is classified as an anxiety disorder but has many distinct characteristics. Obsessions are unwanted, intrusive thoughts that the individual feels are uncontrollable. Compulsions are ritualized behaviors that the individual feels forced to engage in. Biological theories attribute obsessive-compulsive disorder to genetics and to dysfunction in areas of the brain regulating impulses. Psychodynamic theories view obsessions and compulsions as symbols of unconscious conflicts. Cognitive-behavioral theories attribute obsessions to rigid thinking and compulsions to operant conditioning. Treatment for obsessive-compulsive disorder generally involves a combination of drug therapy and cognitive-behavioral therapy.

Social Approaches to the Anxiety Disorders

Sociocultural theorists focus on group differences in anxiety disorders and look to environmental demands and social and cultural norms to explain these differences. Sociocultural perspectives shed some light on the fact that women are more likely than men to have any of the anxiety disorders discussed in this chapter. They also help explain cross-cultural differences in the manifestation of anxiety.

Chapter Integration

Vulnerability-stress models of the anxiety disorders argue that individuals who develop these disorders have underlying biological or psychological vulnerabilities to anxiety, which may be due in part to past experiences with traumas, and these vulnerabilities interact with new stressors to produce anxiety symptoms.

Extraordinary People

Marc Summers: *Everything in Its Place*

Marc Summers has had a successful television career as the host of the game show Double Dare and the Food TV show Unwrapped. He is funny, self-confident, and good on his feet.

Marc Summers is also a man with a significant anxiety disorder called obsessive-compulsive disorder. In his autobiography, *Everything in Its Place* (Summers, 2000), Marc Summers describes how his obsession with orderliness and cleanliness has plagued him all his life. On Sunday afternoons, when the other children in the neighborhood were playing outside together, Marc Summers was in his room, cleaning it from top to bottom (pp. 33–34):

> This was no ordinary cleaning. First I'd strip my bunk bed, and dust the woodwork behind the bed and the bed itself. I'd walk around and around the bed as I made it, back and forth, until the bedding was perfectly smooth and symmetrical. The bedspread couldn't touch the floor. It had to be perfectly even along the bottom. I put the bed back into its indentations in our dark green carpet so I wouldn't make new ones. If by chance, the bed had left any slight indentations in its temporary position, I would get down on my hands and knees and rub them out.
>
> I then turned my attention to our bookshelf. I dusted each book with a rag—the cover, binding, spine, bottom, top, every surface. I dusted and Pledged the shelves, put each book back in its place, taking care that the edges were exactly flush with the lip of the bookshelf. The bookshelf alone could take an hour to clean. . . .
>
> Once a month, I'd binge, moving everything away from the walls and dusting behind the furniture. . . . There was nothing in my room that wasn't Pledged to death,

wiped, Windexed, vacuumed. Nothing. Everything was shiny and perfect. I loved the way a clean room smelled. Cleaning gave me an incredible feeling of satisfaction. It fulfilled a very deep inner need.

So far, you may be saying that Marc Summers was just a quirky little boy who liked a clean room. That's what his parents thought. But he harbored a terrible sense of responsibility for the welfare of his family, which could be allayed only by compulsive rituals (p. 42):

> I thought my parents would die if I didn't do everything in exactly the right way. When I took my glasses off at night I'd have to place them on the dresser at a particular angle. Sometimes I'd turn on the light and get out of bed seven times until I felt comfortable with the angle. If the angle wasn't right, I felt that my parents would die. The feeling ate up my insides.
>
> If I didn't grab the molding on the wall just the right way as I entered or exited my room; if I didn't hang a shirt in the closet perfectly; if I didn't read a paragraph a certain way; if my hands and nails weren't perfectly clean, I thought my incorrect behavior would kill my parents.

Ever since he was a boy, Marc Summers had wanted to be on television, and he credits his perfectionism and drive with helping him become a success in the hypercompetitive world of TV. Ironically, his first big hit, *Double Dare*, was a show in which the goal was to get the guests and the host (Marc Summers) as dirty as possible with the slimiest, most disgusting substances the producers could imagine. On every show, he ended up covered in gooey globs of green slime, swimming in vats of baked beans, or otherwise covered with something revolting. After each show, Marc Summers took multiple showers at the studio and then went home and showered again until he finally felt clean.

His obsessions about others being hurt and his compulsions to try to prevent this harm continued into adulthood. Marc Summers lived in New York for a couple of years when he hosted a talk show called *Biggers and Summers*, and he developed a set of compulsions that involved street signs (pp. 133–134):

> I'd walk up and down Madison when I returned to Manhattan after a day in the Queens studio. I would read the signs in the shop windows over and over again.

If I didn't read the signs correctly, I was convinced that Meredith [his daughter] wouldn't get a part in the school play or Matthew [his son] wouldn't make the sports team. I was afraid that if I didn't read the sign just right, the plane I took every Thursday to California would crash.

I obsessed endlessly about those Thursday flights, following strict rituals to ensure that disaster didn't strike. I was especially drawn to the window of one particular watch store. I vividly remember standing in front of the store's window one blustery fall evening. A sale was on for Breitling watches. There was a sign in the window that explained the watches' special features: dual time zones, perpetual calendar, day-and-date display. I read the sales pitch from top to bottom at least 25 times, a sickening feeling gripping my stomach and chest, utterly convinced that if I didn't read the ad copy perfectly my plane would hurtle downward in a ball of flame somewhere over Missouri.

We all have our fears, but they usually are mild, short-term, or reasonable, given the circumstances. People with anxiety disorders, like Marc Summers, live with fears that are not mild, short-term, or reasonable. The fears of people with anxiety disorders are severe and ultimately lower the quality of their lives. Their fears are chronic and frequent enough to interfere with their functioning. Finally, their fears are out of proportion to the dangers that they truly face. In the following segment, one man named Harry describes his debilitating fears:

VOICES

> My wife keeps telling me to calm down. If only I could. There is something wrong with me, I just know it. I feel tense all the time, even when I try to relax. My heart skips beats, or I think it's going to jump out of my chest. I have a constant stomachache. I need to pee all the time. If only the doctor could find a diagnosis. I have a lot of reasons to be tense. My father had a heart attack last year, and, although his cardiologist says he's doing well, I worry that he will have another one. I go over to Dad's house every day to check on him, and I call him several times a day. He gets annoyed and tells me he's okay, but I have to check to make sure. And then there's my job. Supposedly, the company is in good shape, but I worry constantly about being laid off. If that happened, I don't know what I'd do. My wife probably wouldn't put up with my being unemployed. She'd probably leave me. I worry she'll leave me just because I'm tense. Lately, I just can't stand to go out with her. The noise and bustle of stores and

(continued)

restaurants make me feel worse. Sometimes, I get dizzy and think I'm going to faint right on the street. I feel better when I'm home. But she doesn't want to stay home all the time. I don't know what I'll do if she leaves me.

Harry is experiencing four types of symptoms that make up **anxiety** (see Table 7.1). First, he has *physiological,* or *somatic, symptoms,* including muscle tension, heart palpitations, stomach pain, and the need to urinate. Second, he has *emotional symptoms*—primarily a sense of fearfulness and watchfulness. Third, he has *cognitive symptoms,* including unrealistic worries that something bad is happening (that his father is ill) or is about to happen (that he will lose his job). Finally, he has *behavioral symptoms*—he avoids situations because of his fears.

The physiological and behavioral symptoms listed in Table 7.1 are similar to those those of the *fight-or-flight response,* which we discussed in Chapter 6. In addition, Harry is experiencing the emotion of fear. These physiological, behavioral, and emotional symptoms can occur whether we are facing a poisonous snake or a midterm exam.

We can draw several distinctions between an adaptive response to a threat, which we will refer to as *adaptive fear,* and a *maladaptive anxiety* response, although these distinctions are often not sharp:

- In adaptive fear, people's concerns are realistic, given the circumstances, but, in maladaptive anxiety, their concerns are *unrealistic.* What they are anxious about cannot hurt them or is very unlikely to come about. For example, people having a panic attack may fear they will suddenly keel over and die, although this is highly unlikely.

- In adaptive fear, the amount of fear people experience is in proportion to the reality of the threat, but, in maladaptive anxiety, the amount of fear experienced is *out of proportion* to the harm the threat could cause. For example, a person with a social phobia may become absolutely panicked over the thought that she could say something that would embarrass her if she were called on in class, so she therefore avoids going to class at all.

- In adaptive fear, people's fear response subsides when the threat ends, but, in maladaptive anxiety, people's concern is *persistent* when a threat passes, and they may have a great deal of *anticipatory anxiety* about the future. For example, the man previously quoted continues to worry about his father's health after his heart attack, even though his father now seems healthy.

Anxiety is a prominent feature in many psychological disorders. For example, the majority of people with serious depression also report bouts of anxiety (Kessler et al., 1994; Lewinsohn et al., 1997). People with schizophrenia often feel anxious when

TABLE 7.1   Symptoms of Anxiety

Somatic	Emotional	Cognitive	Behavioral
Goosebumps	Sense of dread	Anticipation of harm	Escape
Tense muscles	Terror	Exaggeration of danger	Avoidance
Increased heart rate	Restlessness	Problems in concentrating	Aggression
Accelerated respiration	Irritability	Hypervigilance	Freezing
Deepened respiration		Worried, ruminative thinking	Decreased appetitive responding
Spleen contraction		Fear of losing control	Increased aversive responding
Dilated peripheral blood vessels		Fear of dying	
Widened bronchioles		Sense of unreality	
Dilated pupils			
Increased perspiration			
Adrenaline secretion			
Inhibited stomach acid			
Decreased salivation			
Bladder relaxation			

they believe they are slipping into a new episode of psychosis. Many people who abuse alcohol and other drugs do so to dampen anxious symptoms. In addition, the anxiety disorders are highly comorbid with each other, meaning that they co-occur (Craske & Waters, 2005), so people who have one of the anxiety disorders appear to be at increased risk for another.

Freud and many other early theorists believed that anxiety was the underlying cause of most forms of psychopathology. He used the term **neurosis** to refer to disorders in which the anxiety aroused by unconscious conflicts could not be quelled or channeled by defense mechanisms. This anxiety could be experienced more or less directly as conscious symptoms of anxiety. It could also take a number of maladaptive forms, such as depression or hypocondriasis (unrealistic worry about one's health).

The DSM no longer uses the term *neurosis*. Instead, it classifies disorders in which the predominant symptoms are anxiety as anxiety disorders. Depression, hypocondriasis, and other disorders are classified separately, and it is no longer assumed that anxiety underlies these disorders.

Research suggests that some people do have a general tendency toward anxiety from a very early age (Biederman et al., 1993). This tendency is sometimes referred to as neuroticism (Eysenck, 1967), negative affectivity (Watson & Clark, 1984), or behavioral inhibition (Gray, 1987). Children and adults who have high levels of neuroticism, negative affectivity, or behavioral inhibition become anxious or depressed easily in response to stressors, and they may chronically carry a low level of anxiety. High levels of these characteristics in childhood have been shown to predict several of the anxiety disorders in adulthood (see Craske & Waters, 2005).

Children who are neurotic or behaviorally inhibited may not develop a full-blown anxiety disorder unless they also experience parenting that exacerbates their anxious tendencies rather than quells them (Craske & Waters, 2005; Neal & Edelmann, 2003). The parents of anxious children tend to be overprotective, controlling, and intrusive (Hudson & Rapee, 2001; Siqueland, Kendall, & Steinberg, 1996). Anxious children perceive their parents as being less accepting of them, compared with nonanxious children (Siqueland et al., 1996). Parents may be overinvolved and controlling with their anxious children in an attempt to prevent the children's distress, but this behavior promotes their children's perceptions that the world is a dangerous place over which they have no control (Craske & Waters, 2005).

In addition, the parents of anxious children tend to be anxious themselves. Anxious mothers

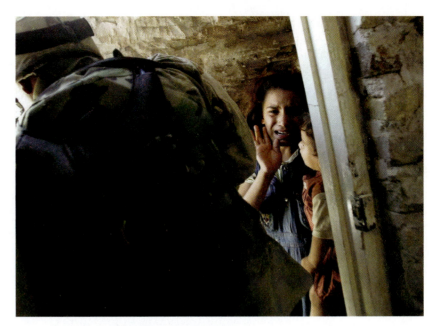

Fear is adaptive in truly dangerous situations.

interacting with their children tend to catastrophize and criticize more, are less likely to grant autonomy, and display less warmth than nonanxious mothers (e.g., Whaley, Pinto, & Sigman, 1999). In turn, these parenting behaviors foster anxiety in their children. Thus, the interactions between anxious parents and anxious children may be reciprocal, feeding the anxiety of both.

In this chapter, we focus on disorders classified in the DSM-IV-TR as anxiety disorders. We begin with a discussion of panic, which can be a part of many of the anxiety disorders or, when frequent, can be a disorder in itself. We then discuss agoraphobia, which usually develops in response to a history of panic attacks, and then simple phobias and social phobias. We discuss generalized anxiety disorder (GAD), which is characterized not by acute panic attacks but by chronic, diffuse anxiety. Finally, we discuss obsessive-compulsive disorder, which is categorized as an anxiety disorder but has some intriguing features that distinguish it from the other anxiety disorders. (Posttraumatic stress disorder, which we discussed in Chapter 6 in the context of responses to stress, is also classified as an anxiety disorder.)

PANIC DISORDER

The first time Celia had a panic attack, she was working at McDonald's. It was two days before her 20th birthday. As she was handing a customer a Big Mac, she had the worst experience

(continued)

CASE STUDY

of her life. The earth seemed to open up beneath her. Her heart began to pound, she felt she was smothering, she broke into a sweat, and she was sure she was going to have a heart attack and die. After about twenty minutes of terror, the panic subsided. Trembling, she got in her car, raced home, and barely left the house for the next three months.

Since that time, Celia has had about three attacks a month. She does not know when they are coming. During an attack she feels dread, searing chest pain, smothering and choking, dizziness, and shakiness. She sometimes thinks this is all not real and she is going crazy. She also thinks she is going to die. (Seligman, 1993, p. 61)

Celia is suffering from **panic attacks,** short but intense periods in which she experiences many symptoms of anxiety: heart palpitations, trembling, a feeling of choking, dizziness, intense dread, and so on (see Table 7.2). Celia's panic attacks appear to come out of the blue, in the absence of any environmental triggers. Simply handing a customer a hamburger should not cause such terror. This is one of the baffling characteristics of some panic attacks.

Some people have panic attacks that are triggered by specific situations or events. For example, people with a social phobia may have panic attacks when forced into a social situation. Most commonly, panic attacks are related to certain situations: The person is more likely to have them in certain situations but does not always have them when in those situations. In all cases, however, a panic attack is a terrifying experience, causing a person intense fear or discomfort, the physiological symptoms of anxiety, and the feeling of losing control, going crazy, or dying.

As many as 40 percent of all young adults have occasional panic attacks, especially during times of intense stress, such as exams week (King, Gullone, & Tonge, 1993). Similarly, many people facing a severely traumatic event will have a panic attack. For most of these people, the panic attacks are annoying but isolated events and do not change how they live their lives. When panic attacks become a common occurrence, when the panic attacks are usually not provoked by any particular situation, and when a person begins to worry about having attacks and changes behaviors as a result of this worry, a diagnosis of **panic**

TABLE 7.2   Symptoms of a Panic Attack

These are the common symptoms of a panic attack. Occasional experiences of these symptoms are common. When four or more symptoms occur frequently and interfere with daily living, the individual may be diagnosed with panic disorder.

Heart palpitations

Pounding heartbeat

Numbness or tingling sensations

Chills or hot flashes

Sweating

Trembling or shaking

Sensations of shortness of breath or smothering

Feeling of choking

Chest pain or discomfort

Nausea and upset stomach

Dizziness, unsteadiness, lightheadedness, or faintness

Feelings of unreality or being detached from oneself

Fear of losing control or going crazy

Fear of dying

disorder may be given (American Psychiatric Association [APA], 2000).

Some people with panic disorder have many attacks in a short period of time, such as every day for a week, and then go for weeks or months without having another attack, followed by another period in which the attacks come often. Other people have attacks less frequently but more regularly, such as once every week for months. Between full-blown panic attacks, they might have more minor bouts of panic.

People who have panic disorder often fear that they have life-threatening illnesses, and they are more likely to have a history of serious chronic illness in themselves or family members (Craske & Waters, 2005). However, even after such illnesses are ruled out, people with panic disorder may continue to believe that they are about to die of a heart attack, a seizure, or another physical crisis. They may seek medical care frequently, going from physician to physician to find out what is wrong with them. Another common but erroneous belief among people with panic disorder is that they are going crazy or losing control. Many people with panic disorder feel ashamed of their disorder and try to hide it from others. If the disorder is left untreated, they may become demoralized and depressed.

Each year, about 7 percent of people experience a panic attack, and 3 to 4 percent of people will develop panic disorder at sometime in their lives (Craske & Waters, 2005; Culpepper, 2004). Most people who develop panic disorder usually do so between late adolescence and their mid-thirties. The disorder tends to be chronic once it begins. One study found that 92 percent of patients with panic disorder continued to experience panic attacks for at least one year, and, among those whose symptoms subsided at sometime during the year, 41 percent relapsed into panic attacks within the year (Ehlers, 1995).

Panic disorder can be debilitating in its own right. Many people with panic disorder also suffer from chronic generalized anxiety, depression, and alcohol abuse (Wilson & Hayward, 2005). People with panic disorder who are also depressed or abuse alcohol may be at increased risk for suicide attempts (Hornig & McNally, 1995; McNally, 1994). And one-third to one-half of people diagnosed with panic disorder develop agoraphobia, as we discuss in the section "Phobias."

Theories of Panic Disorder

The biological and psychological theories of panic disorder have been integrated into a model (see Figure 7.1) to clarify how these factors work together to create the disorder (Bouton, Mineka, & Barlow, 2001; Craske & Waters, 2005; White & Barlow, 2002). We will review each of the components of this model.

The Role of Genetics

Panic disorder appears to run in families (Craske & Waters, 2005). A review of family history studies of panic disorder found that about 10 percent of the first-degree relatives of people with panic disorder also have panic disorder. In comparison, only about 2 percent of the first-degree relatives of people without panic disorder have the disorder (Hettema, Neale, & Kendler, 2001). In particular, the children of parents with panic disorder are at increased risk of developing panic disorder (Biederman et al., 2001). Twin studies of panic disorder report a broad range of concordance rates for monozygotic and dizygotic twins, but generally find that 30 to 40 percent of the variation in rates of panic disorder is due to genetics (e.g., Kendler, Neale, Kessler, & Heath, 1993; Scherrer et al., 2000; also see a review by Hettema et al., 2001). These studies suggest that a bio-

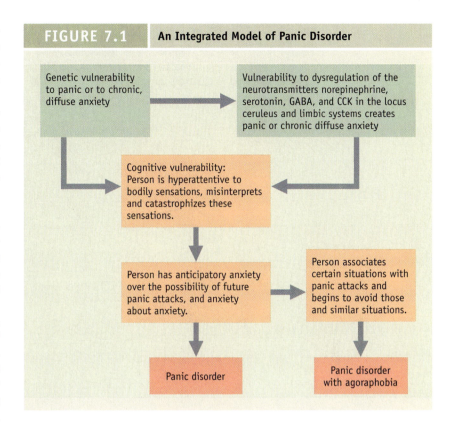

FIGURE 7.1   **An Integrated Model of Panic Disorder**

logical vulnerability to panic disorder, or to a chronic diffuse anxiety that predisposes one to panic disorder, may be transmitted at least in part through genes.

Neurotransmitters and the Brain

Most of the modern neurological theories of panic disorder are the result of the fortuitous discovery by psychiatrist Donald Klein in the 1960s that antidepressant medications reduce panic attacks (Klein, 1964). Because these medications affect the levels of the neurotransmitter **norepinephrine** in the brain, Klein and others reasoned that norepinephrine may be involved in panic disorder. Over the years, evidence has mounted that norepinephrine may be poorly regulated in people with panic disorder, especially in an area of the brain stem called the **locus ceruleus** (see Figure 7.2 on page 224). Electrical stimulation of this brain area in monkeys produces paniclike responses, and the destruction of this area in monkeys renders them unable to experience fear, even in the presence of real threats (Redmond, 1985).

. Other research suggests that, when people are given drugs that alter the activity of norepinephrine, particularly in the locus ceruleus, this alteration can induce panic attacks (Bourin, Baker, & Bradwejn, 1998; Charney et al., 2000). For example, the drug yohimbine alters norepinephrine, but not other neurotransmitters, in the locus ceruleus.

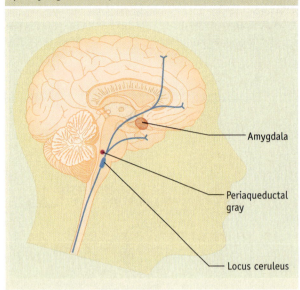

FIGURE 7.2   **Areas of the Brain Involved in Panic.** The locus ceruleus, a part of the brain stem, may be poorly regulated in panic disorder.

Amygdala

Periaqueductal gray

Locus ceruleus

Amygdala

Hypothalamus

Hippocampus

Locus ceruleus

The locus ceruleus and these structures of the limbic system may be involved in panic attacks.

When people with panic disorder take this drug, they typically have a panic attack immediately. On the other hand, other drugs that alter norepinephrine activity have been shown to reduce panic attacks in people who suffer from the disorder (Charney et al., 2000). This, and other evidence, suggests that abnormal activity of norepinephrine, particularly in the locus ceruleus, is involved in human panic attacks.

Other neurotransmitters, particularly serotonin, gamma-aminobutyric acid (GABA), and cholecystokinin (CCK), have been implicated in panic disorders (Bell & Nutt, 1998; Bourin et al., 1998; Charney et al., 2000). Research also has focused on serotonin, following evidence that drugs that alter the functioning of serotonin systems are helpful in reducing panic attacks (Bell & Nutt, 1998). Some theories suggest that panic disorder is due to excessively high levels of serotonin in key areas of the brain, but other theories suggest it is due to deficiencies in serotonin levels (Bell & Nutt, 1998; Bourin et al., 1998). It may be that acute panic attacks have a different association with serotonin than does anticipatory anxiety. Animal studies suggest that increases in serotonin in certain areas of the brain stem (specifically the *periaqueductal gray*) reduce paniclike responses in animals, whereas increases in serotonin in the amygdala increase anxiety, particularly anticipatory anxiety (review Figure 7.2) (Graeff et al., 1996).

Some women with panic disorder report increases in anxiety symptoms during their premenstrual periods and the postpartum period (Brawman-Mintzer & Yonkers, 2001). It may be that the ovarian hormones, particularly progesterone, play a role in vulnerability to panic attacks. Progesterone can affect the activity of both the serotonin and the GABA neurotransmitter systems. Fluctuations in progesterone levels with the menstrual cycle or in the postpartum period thus might lead to imbalances in or dysfunctioning of the serotonin or GABA system, thereby influencing their susceptibility to panic. In addition, increases in progesterone can induce mild, chronic hyperventilation. In women prone to panic attacks, this may be enough to induce full panic attacks.

Gorman and colleagues (Gorman, Papp, & Coplan, 1995) have suggested a "kindling" model of panic disorder, which suggests that the anticipatory anxiety that many people with the disorder have chronically kindles, or sets the stage for, the experience of panic attacks (see Figure 7.3). This link has to do with two parts of the brain, the locus ceruleus and the **limbic system,** which have well-defined pathways between them. Gorman and colleagues argue that, whereas the locus ceruleus is involved in the production of panic attacks, the limbic system is involved in diffuse, anticipatory anxiety. Poor regulation in the locus ceruleus causes panic attacks, which then stimulate and kindle the limbic system, lowering the threshold for the activation of diffuse and chronic anxiety. This anticipatory anxiety, in turn, may increase the likelihood of dysregulation of the locus ceruleus and thereby a new panic attack.

One thing is clear—people with panic disorders can be easily induced into a panic attack through a number of procedures. For example, researchers may have them hyperventilate, inhale a small amount of carbon dioxide, ingest caffeine, breathe into a paper bag, or take infusions of sodium lactate, a substance that resembles the lactate produced by the body during exercise (Craske & Barlow, 2001; McNally, 1999b). In contrast, people without a history of panic attacks may experience some physical discomfort while doing these activities but rarely experience a full panic attack (see Figure 7.4).

What these panic-inducing procedures may have in common is that they initiate the physiological changes of the fight-or-flight response. People who develop panic disorder appear to have a poorly regulated fight-or-flight response, perhaps due to poor regulation of norepinephrine or serotonin in the brain circuits that regulate this response (Gorman et al., 1986; Margraf, 1993). The fight-or-flight response can be initiated without the provocation of a fear stimulus. Once the fight-or-flight response gets going, it operates out of control.

The Cognitive Model

Although many people who develop panic disorder may have a biological vulnerability to this disorder, psychological factors also appear to play a heavy role in determining who will develop the disorder. Cognitive theorists argue that people prone to panic attacks tend to (1) pay very close attention to their bodily sensations, (2) misinterpret bodily sensations in a negative way, and (3) engage in snowballing catastrophic thinking, exaggerating their symptoms and the consequences of the symptoms (Beck & Emery, 1985; Clark, 1988; Craske & Barlow, 2001). For example, when a person prone to panic disorder feels a bit dizzy because she has stood up too quickly, she might think, "I'm really dizzy. I think I'm going to faint. Maybe I'm having a seizure. Oh God, what's happening?" This kind of thinking increases the subjective sense of anxiety and sympathetic nervous system activity. These feelings then are interpreted catastrophically, and the person is on her way into a full panic attack. Between full panic attacks, the person is hypervigilant for any bodily sensations. She worries about her health generally and about having more panic attacks specifically. This constant arousal makes it more likely that she will have more panic attacks.

The belief that bodily symptoms have harmful consequences has been labeled **anxiety sensitivity** (McNally, 1999a). Several studies have shown that

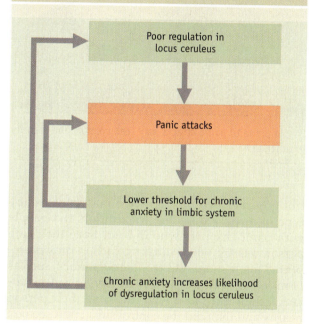

FIGURE 7.3 | **The Kindling Model of Panic Disorder.** This model suggests that poor regulation in the locus ceruleus initiates panic attacks, lowering the threshold for chronic anxiety in the limbic system. This chronic anxiety then increases the likelihood of dysregulation in the locus ceruleus, inducing more frequent panic attacks.

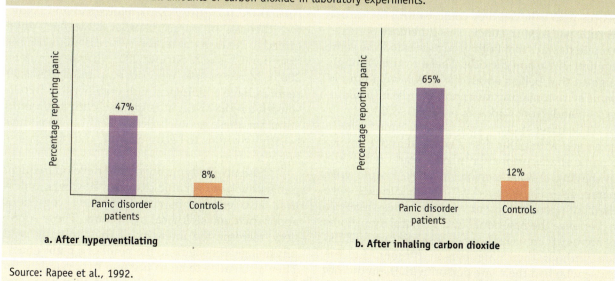

FIGURE 7.4 | **Panic Attacks of Patients and Controls.** People with panic disorder are much more likely than people without panic disorder to have a panic attack when made to hyperventilate or inhale small amounts of carbon dioxide in laboratory experiments.

a. After hyperventilating

b. After inhaling carbon dioxide

Source: Rapee et al., 1992.

people high in anxiety sensitivity are more likely to have panic disorder already, to have more frequent panic attacks, or to develop panic attacks over time, compared with people low in anxiety sensitivity (Hayward et al., 2000; Pauli et al., 1997; Shipherd, Beck, & Ohtake, 2001; Zoellner, Craske, & Rapee, 1996).

People prone to panic attacks also appear to have increased **interoceptive awareness**—a heightened awareness of bodily cues that a panic attack may soon happen. Slight sensations of arousal or anxiety become conditioned stimuli for more severe symptoms of anxiety or panic (Bouton, et al., 2001). Thus, slight changes in relevant bodily functions that are not necessarily consciously recognized may elicit conditional fear due to previous pairings with panic, thereby accounting for the apparent spontaneity of panic attacks (Craske & Waters, 2005).

Evidence for the role of psychological factors in panic disorder comes from several studies (see Craske & Waters, 2005). In one study, researchers examined the influence of beliefs about the controllability of panic symptoms on the actual experience of panic in the laboratory. Two groups of people with panic disorder were asked to wear breathing masks, which delivered air that was slightly enriched with carbon dioxide. They were warned that inhaling carbon dioxide could induce a panic attack. One group was told that they could not control the amount of carbon dioxide that came through their masks. The other group was told they could control the amount of carbon dioxide that came through their masks by turning a knob. Actually, neither group had any control over the amount of carbon dioxide they inhaled. Eighty percent of the people who believed they had no control experienced a panic attack, but only 20 percent of the people who believed they could control the carbon dioxide had a panic attack. This difference occurred despite the fact that both groups inhaled the same amount of carbon dioxide. These results strongly suggest that beliefs about the uncontrollability of panic symptoms play an important role in panic attacks (Sanderson, Rapee, & Barlow, 1989).

In another study, researchers examined whether people with panic disorder could avoid having a panic attack, even after inhaling carbon dioxide, by having a "safe person" nearby. People with panic disorder exposed to carbon dioxide with their safe person present were much less likely to experience the emotional and physical symptoms of anxiety than were those exposed to carbon dioxide without their safe person present. Indeed, those who had their safe person with them did not experience significantly more anxiety than a con-

People prone to panic attacks may seek comfort and security in others.

trol group of people who were not prone to any type of anxiety disorder. In addition, the people with panic disorder who did not have their safe person nearby when inhaling carbon dioxide reported many more catastrophic cognitions, such as "I'm losing control" and "I'm having a heart attack," than did those who did have their person nearby and than did the control subjects. It seemed that having the safe person nearby reduced the tendency to interpret the bodily changes they were experiencing as dangerous (Carter et al., 1995).

The Integrated Model

As shown in Figure 7.5, the biological and cognitive theories of panic disorder have been integrated to create a vulnerability-stress model of this disorder (Craske & Barlow, 2001; Craske & Waters, 2005). Many people who develop panic disorder seem to have a biological vulnerability to a hypersensitive fight-or-flight response. With just a mild stimulus, these people's hearts begin to race, their breathing begins to become rapid, and their palms begin to sweat.

These people typically do not develop frequent panic attacks or a panic disorder, however, unless they also engage in catastrophizing cognitions about their physiological symptoms. These cognitions increase the intensity of their initially mild physiological systems to the point of a panic attack. They also cause them to become hypervigilant for signs of another panic attack, which puts them con-

FIGURE 7.5 — The Vulnerability-Stress Model of Panic Disorder.

The vulnerability-stress model of panic disorder suggests that a biological vulnerability to a hypersensitive fight-or-flight response interacts with the tendency to engage in catastrophizing cognitions to create panic attacks and panic disorder.

Biological vulnerability to hypersensitive fight-or-flight response

X

Tendency to engage in catastrophizing cognitions about physiological symptoms

↓

Panic attacks and hypervigilance for signs of panic

TABLE 7.3 — Concept Overview

Treatments for Panic Disorder

A number of biological treatments and one psychological treatment help people with panic disorder.

Treatment	How It Works
Tricyclic antidepressants	Increase levels of norepinephrine and a number of other neurotransmitters
Selective serotonin reuptake inhibitors	Increase levels of serotonin
Benzodiazepines	Suppress the central nervous system and influence functioning in the GABA, norepinephrine, and serotonin neurotransmitter systems
Cognitive-behavioral therapy	Teaches clients ways to reduce anxiety symptoms, to reinterpret these symptoms in a more positive way; systematic desensitization used to expose clients gradually to feared situations as they use new skills to quell anxiety symptoms

stantly at a mild to moderate level of anxiety. This anxiety level increases the probability that they will become panicked again, and the cycle continues. As we will discuss in more detail later, some people then begin to associate certain places or situations with symptoms of anxiety and panic. If they then avoid those situations, and generalize to a wide range of situations, they may also develop agoraphobia, which we will discuss shortly.

Treatments for Panic Disorder

Both biological and psychological treatments have been developed for panic disorder (see the Concept Overview in Table 7.3). Some of the most effective drugs for the treatment of panic disorder are classified as antidepressant drugs. These include the tricyclic antidepressants and selective serotonin reuptake inhibitors. In addition, the benzodiazepines, which are antianxiety drugs, help some people. Antidepressant drugs and benzodiazepines quell the immediate symptoms of panic disorder, but most people relapse if they discontinue the drugs. Relapse rates can be greatly diminished, however, if cognitive-behavioral therapies are combined with the benzodiazepines or antidepressants (Doyle & Pollack, 2004).

Tricyclic Antidepressants

The **tricyclic antidepressants,** such as imipramine, can reduce panic attacks in the majority of patients (Doyle & Pollack, 2004). Recall that one of the neurotransmitters that may be involved in panic disorder is norepinephrine. The tricyclic antidepressants are thought to improve the functioning of the norepinephrine system, and this may be why they are effective in treating panic. These drugs also may affect the levels of a number of other neurotransmitters, including serotonin, thereby affecting anxiety levels.

The disadvantages of the tricyclic antidepressants are their side effects and the relapse rate once patients discontinue the drugs. Possible side effects include blurred vision, dry mouth, difficulty urinating, constipation, weight gain, and sexual dysfunction.

Selective Serotonin Reuptake Inhibitors

Another type of drug used to treat people with panic disorder is the **selective serotonin reuptake inhibitors (SSRIs).** Some commonly used SSRIs include Paxil, Prozac, Zoloft, and Celexa. These drugs increase the functional levels of the neurotransmitter serotonin in the brain. The possible side effects of these drugs include gastrointestinal upset and irritability, initial feelings of agitation, insomnia, drowsiness, tremor, and sexual dysfunction. Studies suggest that the SSRIs are more effective than placebo and about as effective as the tricyclic antidepressants in reducing acute anxiety symptoms (Culpepper, 2004; Doyle & Pollack, 2004).

Benzodiazepines

The third type of drugs used to treat panic disorder is the **benzodiazepines,** which suppress the central nervous system and influence functioning in the GABA, norepinephrine, and serotonin neurotransmitter systems. The benzodiazepines approved to treat panic are alprazolam and clonazepam. These drugs work quickly to reduce panic attacks and general symptoms of anxiety in most people with panic disorder (Culpepper, 2004).

Unfortunately, the benzodiazepines have three major disadvantages (Chouinard, 2004). First, they are physically and psychologically addictive. People build up a tolerance to these drugs, so that they need increasing dosages of the drug to get a positive effect. In turn, when they stop using the drug, they experience difficult withdrawal symptoms, including irritability, tremors, insomnia, anxiety, tingling sensations, and, more rarely, seizures and paranoia. These withdrawal symptoms can occur even if people are tapered off the drug gradually.

The second major disadvantage of benzodiazepines is that they can interfere with cognitive and motor functioning. People's ability to drive or to avoid accidents is impaired, and their performance on the job, at school, and in the home suffers. These impairments can be especially severe if the benzodiazepines are combined with alcohol.

The third major disadvantage of the benzodiazepines is that about half of the patients begin having panic attacks again shortly after discontinuing treatment with these drugs, and 90 percent of the patients eventually relapse into panic disorder after being taken off these drugs (Fyer et al., 1987; Spiegel, 1998).

Cognitive-Behavioral Therapy

Cognitive-behavioral therapy (CBT) for all the anxiety disorders, including panic disorder, involves getting clients to confront the situations or thoughts that arouse anxiety in them. Confrontation seems to help in two ways: Irrational thoughts about these situations can be challenged and changed, and anxious behaviors can be extinguished.

Cognitive-behavioral therapy appears to be at least as effective in eliminating panic disorder as drug therapies, and it is more effective in preventing relapse following treatment (Barlow et al., 2000; Clark et al., 1999; Kenardy et al., 2003; Telch et al., 1993). There are a number of components to cognitive-behavioral interventions.

First, clients are taught relaxation and breathing exercises, such as those described in *Taking Psychology Personally: Relaxation Exercises.* These exercises are useful in therapy for anxiety disorders because they give clients some control over their symptoms, which then permits them to engage in the other components of the therapy.

Second, the clinician guides clients in identifying the catastrophizing cognitions they have about changes in bodily sensations. Clients may do this by keeping diaries of the thoughts they have about their bodies on days between therapy sessions, particularly when they begin to feel they are going to panic. Figure 7.6 shows the entries in one man's panic thoughts diary. He noted that he had had mild symptoms of panic while in his office at work but more severe symptoms while riding the subway home. In both situations, he had had thoughts about feeling trapped and suffocating and had thought he was going to faint.

Many clients need to experience panic symptoms in the presence of their therapist before they can begin to identify their catastrophizing cognitions. They are too overwhelmed by their symptoms when they are having them outside the therapy office to pay attention to their thoughts. For this reason, the therapist may try to induce panic symptoms in clients during therapy sessions by having them exercise to elevate their heart rates, spin to get dizzy, or put their heads between their knees and then stand up quickly to get lightheaded (due to sudden changes in blood pressure). None of these activities is dangerous, but all are likely to produce the kinds of symptoms that clients catastrophize. As clients are experiencing these symptoms and their catastrophizing cognitions, the therapist helps them collect these thoughts.

Third, clients practice using their relaxation and breathing exercises while experiencing panic symptoms in the therapy session. If the panic attacks occur during sessions, the therapist talks clients through them, coaching them in the use of relaxation and breathing skills, suggesting ways of improving their skills, and noting successes clients have in using these skills to stop the attacks.

Fourth, the therapist challenges clients' catastrophizing thoughts about their bodily sensations and teaches them to challenge their thoughts for themselves, using the cognitive techniques described in Chapter 5. The therapist might help clients reinterpret bodily sensations accurately. For example, the client whose thoughts are illustrated in Figure 7.6 frequently felt he was choking. His therapist could explore whether his choking sensation might be due to the stuffiness of a small office or a subway on a warm summer day. If he interprets the increase in his heart rate as a heart attack, the therapist might have him collect evidence from his physician that he is in perfect cardiac health.

FIGURE 7.6   **A Panic Thoughts Diary.** This man recorded the thoughts he had had during panic attacks and then worked on these thoughts in cognitive therapy.

SITUATION	SYMPTOMS AND SEVERITY	THOUGHTS
Office at work	Choking (mild)	Oh, I can't have an attack
	Dizziness (mild)	here. People will see me
	Heart racing (mild)	and I might get fired. I'm
		suffocating! I'm going to
		faint.
Riding subway home	Sweating (severe)	I can't stand this! I've got to
	Choking (severe)	get out of here. I'm going to
	Shaking (severe)	choke to death. I'm trapped.
	Heart racing (severe)	I'm going to faint!
	Dizziness (severe)	
At home	Sweating (mild)	I can't believe I made it
	Heart still racing (moderate)	home.
	A little faintness	

The therapist and client might also explore the client's expectations that he is sure to die of a heart attack because a relative of his did. If the therapist induces panic symptoms in the client during a therapy session, and the client is able to reduce these symptoms with relaxation or breathing skills, the therapist will use this success to challenge the client's belief that there is nothing that can be done to control the panic symptoms once they begin.

Fifth, the therapist uses **systematic desensitization therapy** to expose the client gradually to the situations they most fear while helping them maintain control over their panic symptoms. The client and therapist compose a list of panic-inducing situations, from most threatening to least threatening. Then, after learning relaxation and breathing skills and perhaps gaining some control over panic symptoms induced during therapy sessions, the client begins to expose him- or herself to the panic-inducing situations, beginning with the least threatening. The therapist may accompany the client on trips to the panic-inducing situations, coaching the client in the use of relaxation and breathing skills and skills in challenging catastrophic cognitions that arise in these situations. The following is an example of an interchange between a therapist and a client as they ride together in the client's car.

VOICES

Client: I really don't think we should be doing this. I might have a panic attack while I'm driving. I wouldn't want to be responsible for an accident while you're in the car.

Therapist: Do you think I would have gotten in the car if I thought that it was likely you would have a panic attack and wreck the car?

Client: No, probably not, but I'm really scared.

Therapist: Yes, I understand. Have you ever had a car wreck?

Client: No, I just always worry about one.

Therapist: Remember, our worries are not reality. Tell me what else is going through your mind.

Client: I feel like my chest is about to cave in. I'm having trouble breathing. Oh no, here I go.

Therapist: Okay, let's begin using some of your exercises. Try counting backward from one hundred by sevens. Breathe in deeply the

(continued)

Taking Psychology Personally

Relaxation Exercises

Therapists often teach clients with anxiety disorders to use relaxation exercises to quell their anxiety. These exercises can also be used to combat the everyday anxiety and tension associated with anger. Following are a few exercises that you can use when you feel tense or anxious (Rimm & Masters, 1979; Schafer, 1992).

Six-Second Quieting Response

This is a simple breathing technique that you can use very quickly (it takes only six seconds) and in almost any situation to relax when you feel anxious or angry. (1) Draw a long, deep breath. (2) Hold it for two or three seconds. (3) Exhale slowly and completely. (4) As you exhale, let your jaw and shoulders drop. Feel relaxation flow into your arms and hands.

Quick Head, Neck, and Shoulder Relaxers

The remainder of the exercises described involve tensing or stretching certain muscles. (If you have had a significant injury, such as whiplash or an injured back, you should not try these exercises without first consulting your physician or physical therapist.)

Some of the muscles that most commonly tense up when we are anxious or angry are the neck and shoulder muscles. A quick way to release some of this tension is first to tighten the neck and shoulder muscles as much as possible and then hold this tension for 5 to 10 seconds. Then completely release the muscles. Repeat this exercise a number of times, focusing on the contrast between the tension and the relaxation.

You can also release some neck and shoulder tension by gently rotating your shoulders, first forward and then backward. You can also gently rotate your head from side to side and from front to back in a circular motion. Then repeat the movements in the opposite direction. Continue this exercise a number of times until you feel more relaxed. Perform this exercise very slowly and gently to avoid straining your neck muscles.

The muscles on the forehead are also tensed when you are anxious or angry, and your teeth may be clenched. To relax your forehead, lift your eyebrows gently and release lines of tension or fatigue. Then relax your forehead as you use the six-second quieting response.

Check to see if your teeth are clenched and, if so, relax your jaw while breathing deeply and slowly.

Progressive Muscle Relaxation

Progressive muscle relaxation is a set of techniques for successively tensing and then relaxing voluntary muscles in an orderly sequence until all the muscles are relaxed. Before beginning this exercise, you should get as comfortable as possible, sitting down, with any tight clothing loosened. You might also want to begin by using the six-second quieting response to start you down the path to relaxation.

Go through each of the following steps in the order given. Spend 10 seconds tensing each muscle group, then at least 10 to 15 seconds relaxing. Repeat the 10 seconds of tensing that muscle group, followed by another 10 to 15 seconds of relaxation. During the relaxation period, focus on the positive sensations of relaxation and try not to worry about anything else. If you feel that muscle group has relaxed sufficiently, move on to the next one. As you progress through the muscle groups, concentrate hard on tensing only the muscle group you are working on in that step. Try not to let any of the other muscle groups, particularly the ones you have already tensed and relaxed, become tense again (Rimm & Masters, 1979):

- *Hands.* Tense your fists and then relax them. Extend your fingers as far as possible and then relax them.
- *Biceps and triceps.* Tense your biceps and then relax. Tense your triceps and then relax.
- *Shoulders.* Pull your shoulders back and then relax. Push your shoulders forward and then relax.
- *Neck.* Slowly roll your head on your neck's axis three or four times in one direction, then in the opposite direction.
- *Mouth.* Open your mouth as widely as possible and then relax. Purse your lips in an exaggerated pout and then relax.
- *Tongue.* With your mouth open, extend your tongue as far as possible and then relax. Next bring your tongue back into your throat as far as possible and then relax. Next dig your tongue into the roof of your mouth as hard as possible and then relax. Finally, dig your tongue into the floor of your mouth as hard as possible and then relax.
- *Eyes and forehead.* Close your eyes and imagine you are looking at something pleasant far away. Focus your eyes so that you can see and enjoy the distant object. Continue this for about one minute.
- *Breathing.* Take as deep a breath as possible and then relax.
- *Back.* With your shoulders resting against a chair, push the trunk of your body forward so as to arch your entire back

Taking Psychology Personally (*continued*)

and then relax. Do this very slowly; if you experience any pain, relax immediately and do not repeat this exercise.

- *Midsection*. Raise your midsection slightly by tensing your buttocks and then relax. Lower your midsection slightly by digging your buttocks into the seat of your chair and then relax.
- *Thighs*. Extend and raise your legs about 6 inches off the floor, trying not to tense your stomach muscles, and then relax. Dig your heels or the backs of your feet into the floor and then relax.
- *Stomach*. Pull your stomach in as hard as possible and then relax. Extend your stomach out as much as possible and then relax.

- *Calves and feet*. Support your legs, bend your feet so that your toes are pointed toward your head, and then relax. Next bend your feet in the opposite direction and then relax. If your muscles cramp during this exercise, relax them and shake them loose.
- *Toes*. With your legs supported and your feet relaxed, dig your toes into the bottoms of your shoes and then relax. Then bend your toes in the opposite direction until they dig into the tops of your shoes and then relax.
- *Breathing*. Breathe slowly and deeply for two to three minutes. Each time you exhale, say the word *calm* to yourself.

first count, then out with the second count, and so on.

Client: Okay, I'll try. [Breathes in] One hundred. [Breathes out] Ninety-three. [Breathes in] Eighty-six. [Breathes out]

Therapist: How are you feeling now?

Client: Better. I'm not as panicked. Oh, my gosh, here comes a bridge. I hate bridges.

Therapist: What do you hate about bridges?

Client: If I ever had an accident on a bridge, I'd be more likely to die.

Therapist: What do you think is the likelihood that you are going to have an accident on a bridge?

Client: Well, sometimes it feels like it's 100 percent!

Therapist: But what do you think it really is?

Client: Probably very low. Hey, we're already over that bridge!

Therapist: Okay, there's another bridge coming up in a couple of miles. I want you to decide what strategies you're going to use to help yourself feel less panicked as we approach the bridge.

A large-scale, multisite study compared cognitive-behavioral therapy (CBT) with tricyclic antidepressants in the treatment of 312 people with panic disorder and found the two treatments to be equally effective in eliminating panic symptoms (Barlow et al., 2000). Several other studies have found that 85 to 90 percent of panic disorder patients treated with CBT experience complete relief from their panic attacks within 12 weeks (Addis et al., 2004; Barlow et al., 1989; Clark et al., 1994; Klosko et al., 1990; Westen & Morrison, 2001). Follow-up studies of patients receiving CBT found that nearly 90 percent were classified as panic-free two years after the treatment (Craske, Brown, & Barlow, 1991; Fava et al., 2001; Margraf et al., 1993; Westen & Morrison, 2001). Cognitive-behavioral therapy appears to be considerably better than antidepressants at preventing relapse after treatment ends (Barlow et al., 2000), probably because this therapy teaches people strategies to prevent the recurrence of panic symptoms.

SUMMING UP

- Panic disorder is characterized by sudden bursts of anxiety symptoms, a sense of loss of control or unreality, and the sense that one is dying.
- Several neurotransmitters, including norepinephrine, serotonin, GABA, and CCK, have been implicated in panic disorder.
- Panic disorder runs in families, and twin studies suggest that genetics plays a role.
- The cognitive model suggests that people with panic disorder are hypersensitive to

bodily symptoms and tend to catastrophize these symptoms.

- The vulnerability-stress model suggests that people who develop panic disorder are born with a biological predisposition to an overactive fight-or-flight response, but they don't develop the disorder unless they also tend to catastrophize their bodily symptoms.

- Tricyclic antidepressants, selective serotonin reuptake inhibitors, and benzodiazepines can be helpful in reducing symptoms, but these symptoms tend to recur once the drugs are discontinued.

- Cognitive-behavioral therapy has proven as useful as antidepressants in reducing panic symptoms and more useful in preventing relapse in panic disorder.

PHOBIAS

People can develop phobias of many things. In this section, we consider three groups of phobias: agoraphobia, specific phobias about objects or situations, and social phobia about social situations in particular (see Figure 7.7).

Agoraphobia

The term *agoraphobia* comes from the Greek for "fear of the marketplace." People with **agoraphobia** fear crowded, bustling places, such as the marketplace or, in our times, the shopping mall. They also fear enclosed spaces, such as buses, subways, and elevators. Also, they fear wide open spaces, such as open fields, particularly if they are alone. In general, people with agoraphobia fear any places where they might have trouble escaping or getting help in an emergency. The emergency that they often fear is a panic attack. Thus, the person with agoraphobia thinks, "If I have a panic attack while I'm in this mall [or on this airplane, or in this movie theater, or on this deserted beach], it will be hard for me to get away quickly or to find help." People with agoraphobia also often fear that they will embarrass themselves if others see their symptoms of panic or their frantic efforts to escape during a panic attack. Actually, other people can rarely tell when a person is having a panic attack.

Agoraphobia can occur in people who do not have panic attacks, but most people who seek treatment for agoraphobia do experience full-blown panic attacks, more moderate panic attacks, or severe social phobia, in which they experience panic-

FIGURE 7.7	Phobic Disorders. These are the phobic disorders recognized in the DSM-IV-TR.

Phobic Disorder	Description	Example
Agoraphobia	Fear of places where help might not be available in case of emergency	Person becomes housebound because anyplace other than the person's home arouses extreme anxiety symptoms.
Specific phobias	Fear of specific objects, places, or situations	
Animal type	Specific animals or insects	Person has extreme fear of dogs, cats, or spiders.
Natural environment type	Events or situations in the natural environment	Person has extreme fear of storms, heights, or water.
Situational type	Public transportation, tunnels, bridges, elevators, flying, driving	Person becomes extremely claustrophobic in elevators.
Blood-injection-injury type	Blood, injury, injections	Person panics when viewing a child's scraped knee.
Social phobia	Fear of being judged or embarrassed by others	Person avoids all social situations and becomes a recluse for fear of encountering others' judgment.

like symptoms in social situations (Craske & Barlow, 2001). In most cases, agoraphobia begins within one year after a person begins experiencing frequent anxiety symptoms.

The lives of people with agoraphobia can be terribly disrupted, even brought to a complete halt. Think how difficult it would be to carry on daily life if you could not ride in a car, a bus, a train, or an airplane; if you could not go into a store; or if you could not stand being in any kind of crowd. Lia's case illustrates how debilitating agoraphobia can be:

People with agoraphobia may become housebound.

CASE STUDY

Lia was a graduate student who was conducting research on children's styles of learning in the classroom. For her research, Lia needed to travel to local elementary schools and observe children in classrooms for a couple of hours each day. Lia had spent months developing good relationships with the schools, teachers, and children who were participating in her research. Everyone was excited about the potential for Lia's research to improve classroom teaching. It seemed that Lia was on her way toward a promising career as an educational researcher.

The problem was that Lia could not leave her apartment. Over the past year, she had become terrified at the idea of driving her car, convinced that she would have a fatal car accident. She had tried to ride the public bus instead, but, when she got onto the bus, she felt as if she was choking, and she was so dizzy she almost missed her stop, so she began walking everywhere she went. The elementary schools participating in her research were too far away for her to walk to them, however. Moreover, Lia was becoming afraid even when she stepped out of her apartment. When she walked onto her street, it seemed to open into a big chasm. The thought of being confined in a small elementary school classroom for two hours was just intolerable.

Lia was beginning to believe that she was going to have to abandon her research and her degree. She could not see any way to finish her work. Even if she did get her degree, how could she possibly hold a job if she could not even leave her apartment?

Like Lia, people with agoraphobia often get to the point at which they will not leave their own homes. Sometimes, they can venture out with a close family member who makes them feel safe. However, family members and friends often have trouble understanding their anxiety and may not be willing to chaperone them everywhere they go. People with agoraphobia may force themselves to enter situations that frighten them, as Lia had been forcing herself to travel for her research. The persistent and intense anxiety they experience in these situations can be miserable, however, and, like Lia, many people give up and remain confined to their homes. Some people with this disorder turn to alcohol and other substances to dampen these anxiety symptoms.

Agoraphobia strikes people in their youth. In one large study, more than 70 percent of the people who developed agoraphobia did so before the age of 25, and 50 percent developed the disorder before the age of 15 (Bourden et al., 1988).

Specific Phobias

Agoraphobia is different from many people's conception of a phobia, because people with agoraphobia fear such a wide variety of situations. In contrast, the **specific phobias** conform more to popular conceptions of phobia. Most specific phobias fall into one of four categories (APA, 2000): animal type, natural environment type, situational type, and blood-injection-injury type. When people with these phobias encounter their feared objects or situations, their anxiety is immediate and intense, and they may even have full panic attacks. They also become anxious if they believe there is any chance they will encounter their feared objects or situations, and they will go to great lengths to avoid the objects or situations.

Most phobias develop during childhood. Adults with phobias recognize that their anxieties are illogical and unreasonable. Children, however, may not have this insight and just have the anxiety. As many as 1 in 10 people will have a specific phobia at sometime, making it one of the most common disorders (Kessler et al., 1994). Almost 90 percent of people with a specific phobia never seek treatment (Regier et al., 1993).

Animal type phobias are focused on specific animals or insects, such as dogs, cats, snakes, or spiders. A snake phobia appears to be the most common type of animal phobia in the United States (Agras, Sylvester, & Oliveau, 1969). Other animals or insects, such as scorpions, may be more commonly feared in other countries. Many people who come across a feared animal or insect may startle and move away quickly. Most of these people would not be diagnosed with a phobia, however, because they can get through daily life without worrying constantly about encountering a feared animal or insect. People with phobias go to great lengths to avoid the objects of their fears. For example, one woman with a severe spider phobia sprayed powerful insecticide around the perimeter of her apartment (which was in a new, pristine apartment building) once a week to prevent spiders from coming in. The fumes from this insecticide made her physically ill, and her neighbors complained of the smell. However, this woman was so fearful of encountering a spider that she withstood the fumes and her neighbors' complaints, remaining vigilant for any signs of a spider web in her apartment. She refused to go into older buildings, because she believed they were more likely to hold spiders. Since she lived in a city with many old buildings, this meant that she could not enter the homes of many of her friends or establishments where she might want to do business.

Natural environment type phobias are focused on events or situations in the natural environment, such as storms, heights, or water. As with fears of animals or insects, mild to moderate fears of these natural events or situations are ex-

tremely common and, of course, adaptive in that they prevent people from getting into dangerous situations. Again, however, these fears do not usually cause people much inconvenience or concern in their daily lives and thus are not considered phobias. It is only when people begin reorganizing their lives to avoid their feared situations or having severe anxiety attacks when confronted with the situations that a diagnosis of phobia is warranted.

Situational type phobias usually involve a fear of public transportation, tunnels, bridges, elevators, flying, and driving. *Claustrophobia*, the fear of enclosed spaces, is a common situational type phobia. People with situational type phobias believe they might have panic attacks in their phobic situations. Indeed, they often have had panic attacks when forced into those situations. Unlike people with agoraphobia, people with situational type phobias tend to have panic attacks only in the specific situations they fear. Situational type phobias often arise in people between 2 and 7 years of age, but another common period of onset is the mid-twenties.

The final type, **blood-injection-injury type phobias,** was first recognized in the DSM-IV-TR. People with this type of phobia fear seeing blood or an injury:

CASE STUDY

When her son José was born, Irene decided to quit her job and become a full-time mother. She enjoyed José's infancy tremendously. He was a happy baby and had hardly been ill for the first two years of his life. Now that he was a toddler, however, José was beginning to get the usual skinned knees and bumps and bruises that small children do. Irene had always been squeamish about blood, but she thought she could overcome this when it came to caring for her son. The first time José scraped his knee seriously enough for it to bleed, however, Irene became dizzy on seeing it and fainted. José screamed and cried in terror at seeing his mother faint. Fortunately, a neighbor saw what happened and quickly went over to comfort José and to see that Irene was okay. Since then, Irene has fainted three more times on seeing José injured. She has begun to think that she will not be able to care for José by herself any longer.

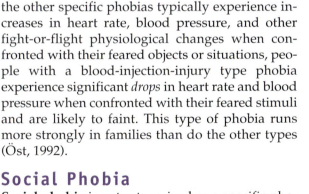

Fear of heights is a common specific phobia.

Irene's reaction to seeing José's scraped knee illustrates the unusual physiological reaction of people with blood-injection-injury type phobias to their feared objects. Whereas people with one of the other specific phobias typically experience increases in heart rate, blood pressure, and other fight-or-flight physiological changes when confronted with their feared objects or situations, people with a blood-injection-injury type phobia experience significant *drops* in heart rate and blood pressure when confronted with their feared stimuli and are likely to faint. This type of phobia runs more strongly in families than do the other types (Öst, 1992).

Social Phobia

Social phobia is not categorized as a specific phobia because, rather than fearing a specific (often inanimate) object or situation, people with social phobia fear being judged or embarrassing themselves in front of other people. Social phobia also differs from the specific phobias in that it is more likely to severely disrupt a person's daily life (Kessler, 2003). It is easier in most cultures to avoid snakes or spiders than it is to avoid social situations in which one might embarrass oneself. Con-

sider the inner pain that this man with social phobia suffered and the way that he has organized his life to avoid social situations:

CASE STUDY

Malcolm was a computer expert who worked for a large software firm. One of the things he hated to do most was ride the elevator at the building where he worked when other people were on it. He felt that everyone was watching him, commenting silently on his ruffled clothes and noticing every time he moved his body. He held his breath for almost the entire elevator ride, afraid that he might say something or make a sound that would embarrass him. Often, he walked up the eight flights of stairs to his office, rather than take the risk that someone would get on the elevator with him.

Malcolm rarely went anywhere except to work and home. He hated even to go to the grocery store for fear he would run his cart into someone else or say something stupid to

(continued)

a grocery clerk. He found a grocery store and several restaurants that allowed customers to send orders for food over the computer to be delivered to their homes. He liked this service, because he could use it to avoid even talking to someone over the phone to place the order.

In the past, Malcolm's job had allowed him to remain quietly in his office all day, without interacting with other people. Recently, however, his company was reorganized, and it took on a number of new projects. Malcolm's supervisor said that everyone in Malcolm's group needed to begin to work together more closely to develop these new products. Malcolm was supposed to make a presentation to his group on some software he was developing, but he called in sick the day of the presentation, because he could not face it. Malcolm was thinking that he had to change jobs and that perhaps he would go into private consulting, so that he could work from his home, rather than having to work with anyone else.

Many people get a little nervous when speaking in front of a group of people or when they must join a group of people already engaged in conversation (see Table 7.4). In one study of college students, 48 percent could be classified as "shy" (Heiser, Turner, & Beidel, 2003). Only 18 percent of these shy students, however, had symptoms qualifying for a diagnosis of social phobia.

People with social phobia, like Malcolm, get more than a little nervous in social situations. They may begin trembling and perspiring, feel confused and dizzy, have heart palpitations, and eventually have a full panic attack. They are sure that others see their nervousness and judge them as inarticulate, weak, stupid, or "crazy." Malcolm avoided speaking in public and having conversations with others for fear of being judged. People with a social phobia may avoid eating or drinking in public, for fear they will make noises when they eat, drop food, or otherwise embarrass themselves. They may avoid writing in public, including signing their names, for fear that others will see their hands tremble. Many with social phobia avoid urinating in public bathrooms for fear of embarrassing themselves.

People with social phobia tend to fall into three groups (Eng et al., 2000). Some people with social phobia fear only public speaking. Others have moderate anxiety about a variety of social situations. Finally, people who have severe fear of many social situations, from speaking in public to having a conversation with another person, are said to have a generalized type of social phobia.

Social phobia is relatively common, with lifetime prevalence rates of about 7 percent across countries (Neal & Edelmann, 2003; Wittchen & Fehm, 2003). Women are somewhat more likely than men to develop this disorder (Lang & Stein, 2001). In addition, one study found that women with social phobia have more severe social fears than men, particularly with regard to performance situations, such as giving a presentation (Turk, Heimberg, & Hope, 2001).

There are two periods in life when social phobia tends to develop—in the early preschool years and in the adolescent years, when many people become excessively self-conscious and concerned about others' opinions of them (Lang & Stein, 2001; Turk et al., 2001). Some people report having had humiliating experiences that triggered their social phobia, but others report having felt extremely uncomfortable in social situations all their lives. Social phobia often co-occurs with mood disorders, other anxiety disorders, and antisocial personality disorder (Neal & Edelmann, 2003; Wittchen & Fehm, 2003). Once it develops, social phobia tends to be a chronic problem if untreated. Most people with a social phobia do not seek treatment for their symptoms (Kessler, 2003).

Theories of Phobias

The phobias have been the battleground for various psychological approaches to abnormality, as

TABLE 7.4 Lifetime Prevalence of Social Fears in a National Survey	
Social Fear	Percentage of People Saying They Experienced the Fear in Their Lifetimes
Public speaking	30.2%
Talking in front of a small group	15.2
Talking with others	13.7
Using a toilet away from home	6.6
Writing while someone watches	6.4
Eating or drinking in public	2.7
Any social fear	38.6

Source: Kessler, Stein, & Berglund, 1998, p. 614.

well as the focus of some of the most revolutionary psychological theories developed in the past century. Biological theories have also been proposed. The Concept Overview in Table 7.5 summarizes the theories reviewed in this section.

Psychodynamic Theories

Freud's theory of the development of phobias is one of his most well known. He argued that phobias result when unconscious anxiety is displaced onto a neutral or symbolic object (Freud, 1909). That is, people become phobic of objects not because they have any real fear of the objects but because they have displaced their anxiety over other issues onto the object.

This theory is detailed in a 150-page case history of a little boy named Hans, who had a phobia of horses after seeing a horse fall on the ground and writhe around violently. How did Hans' phobia develop? According to Freud, young boys have a sexual desire for their mothers and jealously hate their fathers, but they fear that their fathers will castrate them in retaliation for this desire. As we

discussed in Chapter 2, this phenomenon is known as the Oedipus complex. In Freud's interpretation, Hans found the anxiety created by this conflict so unbearable that he unconsciously displaced this anxiety onto horses, which somehow symbolized his father for him. Freud's evidence for this formulation came from Hans' answers to a series of leading questions asked by Freud and by Hans' father. After long conversations about horses and what Hans was "really" afraid of, Hans reportedly became less fearful of horses, because, according to Freud, he had gained insight into the true source of his anxiety.

There is little reason to accept Freud's theory of phobias, either in the case of Hans or in general. Hans never provided any spontaneous or direct evidence that his real concerns were Oedipal concerns instead of a fear of horses. In addition, Hans' phobia of horses decreased slowly over time, rather than suddenly in response to an insight. Many children have specific fears that simply fade with time with no intervention. In general, psychodynamic therapies for phobias are not highly effective, suggesting

---

TABLE 7.5 Concept Overview

Theories of Phobias

The psychodynamic, behavioral, biological, and cognitive theories of phobias take very different approaches to explaining these disorders.

Theory	Description	Example
Psychodynamic theories	Phobias result when unconscious anxiety is displaced onto a neutral object.	Little Hans developed a horse phobia, which represented his Oedipal fears of his father.
Behavioral theories	1. Classical conditioning leads to fear of the object when it is paired with a naturally frightening event.	1. A child who falls into a river and cannot swim develops a fear of water.
	2. Avoidance of the object reduces anxiety; thus, it is reinforced through operant conditioning.	2. A person with agoraphobia learns that, by staying in her apartment, panic attacks are less likely, and thus staying in her apartment is reinforced.
	3. Humans are prepared through evolutionary history to develop phobias to objects or situations that were dangerous to our ancient ancestors.	3. Humans develop phobias to spiders and heights more easily than to guns or powerlines.
Cognitive theories (of social phobia)	Social phobia develops in people with excessively high standards for their social performance, who assume others judge them harshly, and who are attentive to signs of social rejection.	A man who believes that he always stammers in conversations and that others think he is stupid as a result might develop a social phobia.
Biological theories	Genetics contribute to risk for phobias, either directly or by creating certain temperaments that are more prone to phobias.	Children with phobias often have relatives with the same phobia, or the children tend to be excessively timid or shy.

that insight into unconscious anxieties is not what is needed in treating phobias.

Behavioral Theories

In contrast to the psychodynamic theories, the behavioral theories have been very successful in explaining phobias. According to these theories, classical conditioning leads to the fear of the phobic object, and operant conditioning helps maintain that fear (Mowrer, 1939). Recall that, in classical conditioning, a previously neutral object (the conditioned stimulus) is paired with an object that naturally elicits a reaction (an unconditioned stimulus that elicits an unconditioned response) until the previously neutral object elicits the same reaction (which is now called the conditioned response). For example, when a tone is paired with an electric shock, the conditioned stimulus is the tone, the electric shock is the unconditioned stimulus, the unconditioned response is anxiety in response to the shock, and the conditioned response is anxiety in response to the tone.

The first application of these theories to phobias came in a series of studies done 80 years ago by a philosopher turned behaviorist, John Watson, and a graduate student named Rosalie Raynor (1920). Their subject in these studies was an 11-month-old boy named Little Albert. One day, Watson and Raynor placed a white rat in front of Little Albert. As Little Albert playfully reached for the white rat, they banged a metal bar loudly just above his head. Naturally, Little Albert was completely startled,

nearly jumped out of his diapers, quickly pulled his hand away from the rat, and then broke down, whimpering. This only encouraged Watson and Raynor to continue their study, however. After several more pairings of the white rat with the loud noise from the metal bar, Little Albert would have nothing to do with the creature—in effect, developing a fear of the white rat. When presented with it, he retreated and showed distress. Little Albert's fear also generalized to other white, furry animals—he would not approach white rabbits, either.

Although by today's standards this experiment with Little Albert would raise serious ethical questions, it laid the groundwork for the behavioral theories of phobias by showing powerfully that a phobia can easily be created through classical conditioning. In the case of Little Albert, the unconditioned stimulus (US) was the loud noise from the banged bar, and the unconditioned response (UR) was his startle response to the loud noise. The conditioned stimulus (CS) was the white rat, and the conditioned response (CR) was the startle and fear response to the white rat (see Figure 7.8). If Little Albert had been subsequently presented with the white rat several times without the bar being banged behind his head, his fear of white rats should have been extinguished, according to what we know about classical conditioning.

Most people who develop a phobia, however, try to avoid being exposed to their feared object. Thus, they avoid the exposure that could extinguish their phobia. In addition, if they are suddenly confronted with their feared object, they experience extreme anxiety and run away as quickly as possible. The running away, or avoidance, is reinforced by the subsequent reduction of their anxiety—a process known as **negative reinforcement**. In this way, behaviors that help maintain the phobia are negatively reinforced through operant conditioning.

For example, Malcolm, the person with social phobia described in the section "Social Phobia," had developed a wide array of avoidant behaviors to prevent him from exposing himself to what he feared most: the possibility of scrutiny by others. He walked up several flights of stairs rather than be trapped in an elevator for a few minutes with another person who might notice something odd about Malcolm's clothes or mannerisms. He paid a great deal of money to have his groceries delivered, rather than risk going to a crowded grocery store, where he might embarrass himself in front of other people. He was even prepared to quit his job to avoid having to make presentations or work closely with others on projects. These avoidant behaviors created much hardship for Malcolm, but

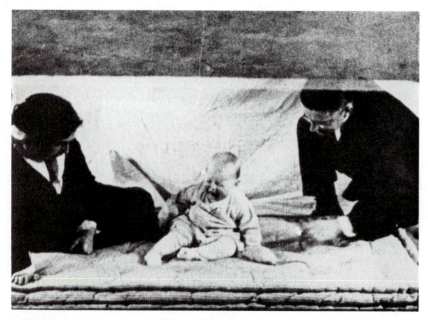

Little Albert, shown in this photo, developed a fear of white rats through classical conditioning.

they reduced his anxiety and therefore were greatly reinforced. Also, as a result of this avoidance, Malcolm never had the opportunity to extinguish his anxiety about social situations.

Behavioral theory also does a good job of explaining why agoraphobia so often develops in people with panic disorder (see Figure 7.9). The fear of panic attacks leads the individual to search for safe people and places that are associated with a low risk for panic attacks. These safe people and places have been referred to as *safety signals*, which we discussed briefly in Chapter 6. According to the *safety signal hypothesis* (Seligman & Binik, 1977), people remember vividly the places in which they have had panic attacks, even if the panic attacks have come on by surprise, with no obvious environmental triggers. They associate these places with their symptoms of panic and may begin to feel these symptoms again if they return to these places. By avoiding these places, they reduce their

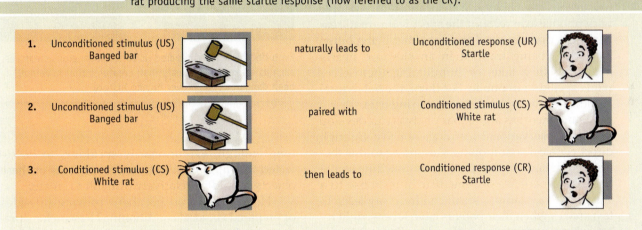

FIGURE 7.8   **The Behavioral Account of Little Albert's Phobia.** The pairing of the banged bar (the US), which naturally leads to a startle response (the UR), and the white rat (the CS) leads eventually to the white rat producing the same startle response (now referred to as the CR).

1. Unconditioned stimulus (US)
   Banged bar   naturally leads to   Unconditioned response (UR)
   Startle

2. Unconditioned stimulus (US)
   Banged bar   paired with   Conditioned stimulus (CS)
   White rat

3. Conditioned stimulus (CS)
   White rat   then leads to   Conditioned response (CR)
   Startle

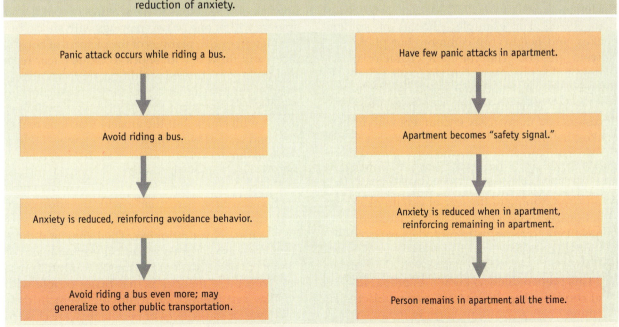

FIGURE 7.9   **How Agoraphobic Behaviors Develop in Panic Disorder.** Behavioral theories argue that agoraphobic behaviors develop when avoiding situations in which panic has often occurred and remaining in situations where panic has occurred less often are reinforced by the reduction of anxiety.

Panic attack occurs while riding a bus.
↓
Avoid riding a bus.
↓
Anxiety is reduced, reinforcing avoidance behavior.
↓
Avoid riding a bus even more; may generalize to other public transportation.

Have few panic attacks in apartment.
↓
Apartment becomes "safety signal."
↓
Anxiety is reduced when in apartment, reinforcing remaining in apartment.
↓
Person remains in apartment all the time.

symptoms; thus, their avoidance behavior is highly reinforced. If a man has a panic attack while sitting in a theater, he may later associate a theater with his panic symptoms and begin to feel anxious whenever he is near the theater. He can reduce his anxiety by avoiding the theater. In addition, other places, such as his own home or a specific room in his home, may become associated with lowered anxiety levels, and being in these places is thus reinforcing. Through classical and operant conditioning, the person's behavior becomes shaped in ways that lead to the development of agoraphobia.

The behavioral theories of phobias are one of the most elegant examples of the application of basic learning principles to the understanding of a mysterious psychological disorder. Many people with phobias can recount the specific traumatic experiences that triggered their phobias: being bitten by a dog, being trapped in an elevator, nearly drowning in a lake, or humiliating themselves while speaking in public. For them, the behavioral accounts of their phobias seem to ring true.

Some theorists argue that phobias can develop through observational learning, not just through direct classical conditioning. According to this theory, people can develop phobias by watching someone else experience extreme fear in response to a situation. For example, small children may learn to fear snakes when their parents have severe fright reactions on seeing snakes (Bandura, 1969; Mineka et al., 1984).

An extension of the behavioral theories of phobias seems to answer an interesting question about phobias: Why do humans develop phobias to some objects or situations but not to others (deSilva, Rachman, & Seligman, 1977; Mineka, 1985; Seligman, 1970)? For example, phobias of spiders, snakes, and heights are common, but phobias of flowers are not. The common characteristic of many phobic objects appears to be that these are things whose avoidance, over evolutionary history, has been advantageous for humans. Our distant ancestors had many nasty encounters with insects, snakes, heights, loud noises, and strangers. Those who learned quickly to fear and avoid these objects or events were more likely to survive and bear offspring. Thus, evolution may have selected for the rapid conditioning of the fear of certain objects or situations. Although these objects or situations are not as likely to cause us harm today, we carry the vestiges of our evolutionary history and are biologically prepared to learn certain associations quickly.

This preparedness is known as **prepared classical conditioning.** In contrast, many objects that are more likely to cause us harm in today's world (such as guns and knives) have not been around

Evolution may have prepared us to fear dangerous creatures, such as snakes, more easily than creatures that have not been dangerous to us over human history.

long enough, evolutionarily speaking, to be selected for rapid conditioning, so phobias of these objects should be relatively difficult to create.

How would you go about proving this idea of prepared classical conditioning? Researchers presented subjects with pictures of objects that theoretically should be evolutionarily selected for conditioning (snakes or spiders) and objects that should not be selected (houses, faces, and flowers) and paired the presentation of these pictures with short but painful electric shocks. The subjects developed anxiety reactions to the pictures of snakes and spiders within one or two pairings with shock, but it took four or five pairings of the pictures of houses, faces, and flowers with shock to create a fear reaction to these pictures. In addition, it was relatively easy to extinguish the subjects' anxiety reactions to houses and faces once the pictures were no longer paired with shock, but the anxiety reactions to spiders and snakes were difficult to extinguish (Hugdahl & Ohman, 1977; Ohman et al., 1976).

As we have seen, the behavioral theories of phobias seem to provide a compelling explanation for this disorder, particularly with the addition of the principles of observational learning and prepared classical conditioning. The behavioral theories have also led to very effective therapies for phobias, as we will see. The most significant problem with these theories is that many people with phobias can identify no traumatic event in their own lives or in the lives of people they are close to that triggered their phobias. Without conditioned stimuli, it is hard to argue that they developed their phobias through classical conditioning or observational learning. Craske and Waters (2005) argue that many individuals who develop phobias have a chronic low-level anxiety or reactivity, which makes them more susceptible to the development of phobias, given even mild aversive experiences.

Cognitive Theories

The cognitive theories of phobias have primarily focused on the development of social phobia (Clark & Wells, 1995; Rapee & Heimberg, 1997; Turk et al., 2001). According to these theories, people with social phobia have excessively high standards for their social performance—for example, believing that they should be liked by everyone they meet and never do anything embarrassing in front of others. Unfortunately, they also tend to focus on what is going wrong in social interactions instead of what is going right, and they evaluate their own behavior extremely harshly. They enter social situations assuming that others will find them boring, peculiar, or unattractive. People with social phobia also show biases in attention, picking up on socially threatening cues (such as a grimace on the face of the person they are speaking to) and then interpreting them in self-defeating ways (Heinrichs & Hofman, 2001). They are exquisitely attuned to their own self-presentation and their internal feelings, and they tend to assume that, if they feel anxious, it is because the social interaction is not going well (Clark & Wells, 1995).

Several studies have supported the claims of the cognitive theories that people with social phobia have biases in attention and in evaluating social situations (see Heinrichs & Hofman, 2001; McNally, 1996; Turk et al., 2001). Where do these biases come from? Adults with social phobia often describe their parents as having been overprotective and controlling but also critical and negative (see Craske & Waters, 2005; Neal & Edelmann, 2003). These are retrospective accounts, however, and could be incorrect. To date, there are no prospective studies of the family environments of people who develop social phobia. In addition, studies have not yet established whether the beliefs and cognitive biases described by the cognitive theories are the causes of social phobia or only the symptoms. Cognitive-behavioral therapies based on these theories, however, can help people with social phobia overcome their avoidant and anxious symptoms.

Biological Theories

The first-degree relatives of people with phobias are three to four times as likely to have a phobia as the first-degree relatives of people without pho-

bias, and twin studies suggest that this is due, at least in part, to genetics (Hettema et al., 2001; Merikangas et al., 2003). For example, family history studies of agoraphobia find that 10 to 11 percent of the first-degree relatives of people with this disorder also have the disorder, compared with 3 to 4 percent of the relatives of people without the disorder (Fyer et al., 1995; Noyes et al., 1986).

There is an interesting gender difference in the heritability of agoraphobia. The female relatives of people with this disorder are even more likely than the male relatives to have the disorder (Crowe, 1990). In addition, twin studies of females find evidence for a genetic contribution to agoraphobia (Kendler, Myers, Prescott, & Neale, 2001), whereas twin studies of males do not (Kendler et al., 2001). This evidence suggests that the genetic vulnerability to agoraphobia is sex-linked.

Several researchers suggest that a particular phobia in itself is not strongly heritable but that the general tendency toward anxiety is heritable, leading to a temperament that makes it easier for phobias to be conditioned (Eysenck, 1967; Gray, 1987; Pavlov, 1927). Children who, as toddlers, are behaviorally inhibited—that is, excessively timid and shy—are at higher risk to develop specific phobias and social phobia than are those who are not inhibited (Biederman et al., 2001; Craske & Waters, 2005; Turner, Beidel, & Wolff, 1996). For example, one study found that children who were socially inhibited were four times more likely to develop social phobia in high school than those who were not socially inhibited (Hayward et al., 1998). Again, however, children with a genetic predisposition toward anxiety or who are behaviorally inhibited may not develop social phobia, or a specific phobia, unless the parenting they receive exacerbates their anxiety (Craske & Waters, 2005; Neal & Edelmann, 2003).

Treatments for Phobias

A number of behavioral techniques are used to treat phobias. In addition, some therapists add cognitive techniques and certain drug therapies to their treatment regime for people with phobias (see the Concept Overview in Table 7.6 on page 242).

Behavioral Treatments

The goal of behavior therapies for phobias is to extinguish the fear of the object or situation by exposing the person to the object or situation. The majority of phobias can be cured with these therapies (Christopherson & Mortweet, 2001; Emmelkamp, 1994; Wolpe, 1997). Some studies suggest that just one session of behavior therapy leads to major reductions in phobic behaviors and anxiety (Öst et al., 2001). There are three basic components of behavior

TABLE 7.6 Concept Overview

Treatments for Phobias

A number of treatments have proven useful for phobias.

Treatment	Description	Example
Behavioral treatments	Focus on extinguishing fear by exposing the person to the feared object or situation.	
1. Systematic desensitization therapy	1. It gradually exposes the person to a hierarchy of fears while the person practices techniques to reduce the fear response.	A person with agoraphobia ventures out to the least feared situation (such as the local grocery) first, practicing relaxation, and then gradually ventures to more and more fearful situations.
2. Modeling	2. Therapist models behaviors most feared by the client before asking the client to engage in behaviors.	Therapist handles a snake before asking the person with a snake phobia to do so.
3. Flooding	3. It intensively exposes the client to the feared object until anxiety extinguishes.	Person with a fear of heights may look out the window of the 100th floor of a building until her anxiety passes.
Cognitive-behavioral therapy	It helps clients identify and challenge negative, catastrophizing thoughts about feared situations.	Therapist accompanies a person with agoraphobia to the local grocery, helping him challenge thoughts that he is about to have a panic attack.
Biological treatments	They reduce symptoms of anxiety generally, so that they do not arise in the feared situation.	Benzodiazepines, monoamine oxidase inhibitors, and selective serotonin reuptake inhibitors are used.

therapy for phobias: *systematic desensitization therapy, modeling,* and *flooding.*

Systematic Desensitization In systematic desensitization therapy, clients formulate lists of situations or objects they fear, ranked from most feared to least feared. They learn relaxation techniques, which will reduce the symptoms of anxiety they will experience when they are exposed to their feared objects. They then begin to expose themselves to the items on their hierarchy of fears, beginning with the least feared item. For example, a person with a severe dog phobia might have as the first item on his list "seeing a picture of a dog in a magazine." This client might then first visualize a picture of a dog. As the client begins to feel anxious, the therapist coaches him to use his relaxation techniques to quell his anxious feelings. The point is to help the client replace his anxious reaction with the calm that comes with the relaxation techniques. When the client can visualize a picture of a dog without experiencing anxiety, he might move on to looking at a picture of a dog in a magazine, again using relaxation techniques to lower his anxiety reaction and replace it with a calm reac-

tion. Gradually, the client and therapist move through the entire list, until the client is able to pet a big dog without feeling overwhelming anxiety.

One of the specific phobias, blood-injection-injury type phobia, requires a different approach than the other phobias (Öst & Sterner, 1987). Recall that, unlike people with other specific phobias, whose blood pressure and heart rate increase when they confront their phobic objects, people with a blood-injection-injury type phobia experience severe decreases in heart rate and blood pressure when confronted with their phobic objects. Sometimes, because less blood is circulating to their head, they faint. Relaxation techniques would only worsen these people's natural response to their phobic object, because such techniques also decrease blood pressure and heart rate. Thus, therapists must take the opposite approach, teaching them to tense the muscles in their arms, legs, and chest until they feel the warmth of their blood rising in their face. This **applied tension technique** increases blood pressure and heart rate. When a person with a blood-injection-injury type phobia learns this technique, she can use it when confronted with her phobic object to counteract her typical biological

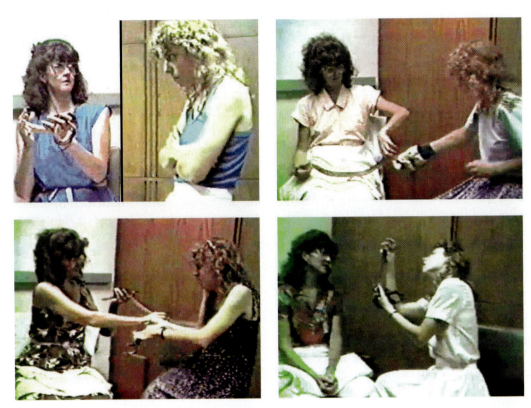

The therapist first models handling a snake for this woman with a snake phobia, then gradually she is able to handle it herself.

response and prevent fainting. Then systematic desensitization therapy can be implemented to extinguish her fear of blood, injury, or injections.

Modeling Techniques of **modeling** are often used in conjunction with systematic desensitization therapy in the treatment of phobias. The therapist models the behaviors most feared by clients before they attempt behaviors themselves. For example, if a therapist is treating a person with a snake phobia, the therapist may perform each of the behaviors on the client's hierarchy of fears before asking the client to perform them. The therapist stands in the room with the snake before asking the client to do so, touches the snake before asking the client to do so, and holds the snake before the client does. Eventually, the therapist allows the snake to crawl around on her before asking the client to attempt this. Through observational learning, the client begins to associate these behaviors with a calm, nonanxious response in the therapist, which reduces the client's own anxiety about engaging in the behaviors. Modeling is as effective as systematic desensitization therapy in reducing phobias (Bandura, 1969; Thorpe & Olson, 1997).

Flooding The idea behind **flooding** (also called implosive therapy) is to intensively expose a client to his or her feared object until anxiety extinguishes. In a flooding treatment, a person with claustrophobia might lock himself in a closet for several hours, a person with a dog phobia might spend the night in a dog kennel, and a person with social phobia might volunteer to teach a class that meets every day for a semester. The therapist typically prepares clients with relaxation techniques they can use to reduce their fear during the flooding procedure. Flooding is as effective as systematic desensitization therapy or modeling and often works more quickly. It is more difficult to get clients to agree to this type of therapy, though, because it is frightening to contemplate (Thorpe & Olson, 1997).

Cognitive-Behavioral Therapy

Many therapists combine behavioral techniques with cognitive techniques that help clients identify and challenge the negative, catastrophizing thoughts they are having when they are anxious (Beck & Emery, 1985; Turk et al., 2001). For example, when a person with a snake phobia is saying, "I just can't do this. I can't stand this anxiety. I'll never get over this," the therapist might point out the progress the client has already made on his hierarchy of fears and the client's previous statements that the relaxation techniques have been a great help to him. Creating the expectations in clients that they can master their problems, known as *self-efficacy expectations,* is a potent factor in curing phobias (Bandura, 1986).

In the treatment of social phobia, cognitive-behavioral therapy (CBT) is more effective than the SSRIs both in the short term and in 6-month and 1-year follow-ups (Clark et al., 2003; Hofmann, 2004). CBT can be implemented in a group setting, where all the members, except the therapist, suffer from a social phobia (Coles, Hart, & Heimberg, 2005; Heimberg, 2001; Turk et al., 2001). The group members are an audience for one another, providing exposure to the very situation each member fears. An individual group member can practice her feared behaviors in front of the other members while the therapist coaches her in the use of relaxation techniques to calm her anxiety. The group can also help the individual challenge her negative, catastrophizing thoughts about her behavior, as in the following excerpt from a group cognitive therapy session with Gina, a woman with social phobia (adapted from Turk et al., 2001, pp. 124–125):

VOICES

Therapist: So your automatic thought is "I don't know how to have a conversation," is that right?

Gina: Yeah, I always screw it up.

Therapist: All right, let's ask the rest of the group what they think about that. Who has had a conversation with Gina or noticed her talking with someone else?

Ed: We walked out to our cars together last week and talked in the parking lot for a while. [Several other group members list similar conversations.]

Therapist: So it sounds like you have had a number of conversations with the rest of the group.

Gina: I guess so.

Therapist: Group, how did she do? How did the conversations go?

Sally: It was fine. She was asking me about my car, because she has been looking for a new one, so we talked mostly about that.

[Other group members provide similar answers.]

Therapist: Well, Gina, the rest of the group doesn't seem to agree that you don't know how to have conversations.

Gina: I guess I have always been so nervous that I never stopped to think that sometimes the conversations go OK.

Through observational learning, the group members' cognitions about incompetence and embarrassment are challenged as they challenge one another. Group-administered cognitive-behavioral therapy has proven effective even for people with generalized social phobia (Heimberg, 2001; Turk et al., 2001). For example, in one study, 133 people with social phobia were randomly assigned to receive group cognitive-behavioral therapy (CBT), to take an antidepressant, to receive a pill placebo, or simply to meet in a group to receive support and education about social phobia (Heimberg et al., 1998). After 12 weeks of treatment, 75 percent of the group cognitive-behavioral therapy -patients were significantly improved in their symptoms, compared with 77 percent of the people who had received the antidepressant. These response rates were similar, but both the CBT group and the antidepressant group had significantly better recovery than the pill placebo group or the education/support group. A follow-up showed that cognitive-behavioral therapy was much better at preventing relapse into social phobia than the antidepressant treatment: Only 17 percent of the CBT group had relapsed one year later, compared with 50 percent of the antidepressant treatment group (Heimberg, 2001).

Biological Treatments

Some people use the benzodiazepines to reduce their anxiety when forced to confront their phobic objects. For example, when people with a phobia of flying are forced to take a flight, they might take a high dose of the benzodiazepine Valium or drink alcohol to relieve their anxiety. Many people who become very nervous in public presentations take a benzodiazepine to reduce their anxiety before giving a speech or a performance. These drugs produce temporary relief (Jefferson, 2001), but the phobia remains.

Antidepressants, particularly the monoamine oxidase inhibitors and the selective serotonin reuptake inhibitors, are more effective than placebos in the treatment of social phobia (Davidson, 2003; Schneier, 2001; Van Ameringen et al., 2001). However, follow-up studies suggest that people soon relapse into social phobia after discontinuing their use of the drug (Davidson, 2003). Of course, these drugs also have potential significant side effects, and the benzodiazepines are addictive.

In contrast, the vast majority of people can be cured of phobias with behavioral techniques after only a few hours of treatment (Öst et al., 2001), and cognitive-behavioral therapy is effective in the treatment of social phobia (Zaider & Heimberg, 2003). For now, it appears that the old advice to "confront your fears" through behavior therapy is the best advice for people with phobias.

SUMMING UP

- People with agoraphobia fear a wide variety of situations in which they might have an emergency but not be able to escape or get help. Many people with agoraphobia also suffer from panic disorder.

- The specific phobias include animal type phobias, natural environment type phobias, situational type phobias, and blood-injection-injury type phobias.

- People with social phobia fear social situations in which they might be embarrassed or judged by others.

- Psychodynamic theories of phobias suggest that they represent unconscious anxiety that has been displaced. These theories have not been supported, however.

- Behavioral theories of phobias suggest that they develop through classical conditioning and are maintained by operant conditioning. Humans may be evolutionarily prepared to develop some types of phobias more easily than others.

- Cognitive theories have focused on social phobia and suggest that this disorder develops in people who have excessively high standards for their social performance, assume that others are judging them harshly, and are hypervigilant to signs of rejection from others.

- Biological theories of phobias attribute their development to heredity.

- Behavioral treatments for phobias include systematic desensitization therapy, modeling, and flooding.

- Cognitive techniques are used to help clients identify and challenge the negative, catastrophizing thoughts they have when anxious. Group cognitive therapy has proven highly effective in the treatment of social phobia and in preventing relapse.

- The benzodiazepines and antidepressant drugs can help quell anxiety symptoms, but people soon relapse into phobias after the drugs are discontinued.

GENERALIZED ANXIETY DISORDER

The phobias, panic, and agoraphobia involve periods of anxiety that are acute, usually short-lived, and more or less specific to certain situations. Some people are anxious all the time, however, in almost all situations. These people may be diagnosed with a **generalized anxiety disorder (GAD)** (see Table 7.7 on page 246). People with GAD worry about many things in their lives, as Claire describes in the following excerpt (adapted from Brown, O'Leary, & Barlow, 2001, p. 187):

VOICES

I just feel anxious and tense all the time. It all started in high school. I was a straight-A student, and I worried constantly about my grades, whether the other kids and the teachers liked me, being prompt for classes—things like that. . . . My husband thinks I'm neurotic. For example, I vacuum four times a week and clean the bathrooms every day. There have even been times when I've backed out of going out to dinner with my husband because the house needed to be cleaned. Generally, my husband is supportive, but it has caused a strain on our marriage.

I get so upset and irritated over minor things, and it'll blow up into an argument. . . . I still worry about being on time to church and to appointments. Now I find I worry a lot about my husband. He's been doing a tremendous amount of traveling for his job, some of it by car, but most of it by plane. Because he works on the northeastern seaboard, and because he frequently has to travel in the winter, I worry that he'll be stuck in bad weather and get into an accident or, God forbid, a plane crash. It's just so scary.

Oh, and I worry about my son. He just started playing on the varsity football team, so he's bound to get an injury sometime. It's

(continued)

so nerve-wracking to watch him play that I've stopped going to his games with my husband. I'm sure my son must be disappointed that I'm not watching him play, but it's simply too much for me to take.

People with GAD may worry about their performance on the job, about how their relationships are going, and about their own health. Like Claire, they also may worry about minor issues, such as whether they will be late for an appointment, whether the hair stylist will cut their hair the right way, or whether they will have time to mop the kitchen floor before dinner guests arrive. The focus of their worries may shift frequently, and they tend to worry about many different things, instead of just focusing on one issue of concern.

Their worry is accompanied by many of the physiological symptoms of anxiety, including muscle tension, sleep disturbances, and a chronic sense of restlessness. Claire's worries give her a chronically upset stomach and sense of nausea. People with GAD report feeling tired much of the time, probably due to their chronic muscle tension and sleep loss.

GAD is a relatively common type of anxiety disorder, with cross-national studies showing lifetime prevalences of about 5 percent of women and 3 percent of men (Kessler et al., 2002). Many people with this disorder report they have been anxious all their lives, and the disorder most commonly first appears in childhood or adolescence. Over half of people with GAD also develop another anxiety disorder, such as phobias or panic disorder. Over 70 percent experience a mood disorder, and a third have a substance use disorder as well (Craske & Waters, 2005; Kessler et al., 2002). Many recent psychological theories, and the biological theories, have come to view generalized anxiety disorder as a distinct disorder that has many differences even from other anxiety disorders (see the Concept Overview in Table 7.8).

Theories of Generalized Anxiety Disorder

Many of the earliest psychological theories saw chronic, generalized anxiety not only as a problem in itself but also as the core issue behind many other disorders.

Psychodynamic Theories

Freud (1917) developed the first psychodynamic theory of generalized anxiety. He distinguished among three kinds of anxiety: realistic, neurotic,

and moral. **Realistic anxiety** occurs when we face a real danger or threat, such as an oncoming tornado. **Neurotic anxiety** occurs when we are repeatedly prevented from expressing our id impulses. The energy of those impulses is not allowed release, and it causes anxiety. For example, a person who feels she can never act on her sexual urges may experience neurotic anxiety. **Moral anxiety** occurs when we have been punished for expressing our id impulses, and we come to associate those impulses with punishment, causing anxiety. For example, a child who is harshly punished for fondling his genitals may, as an adult, have moral anxiety over any sexual impulses.

Generalized anxiety occurs when our defense mechanisms can no longer contain either the id impulses or the neurotic or moral anxiety that arises from these impulses. We are anxious all the time because we cannot find healthy ways to express our id impulses and greatly fear the expression of those impulses.

Because more recent psychodynamic theories focus more on the development of self-concept through early close relationships, it is not surprising that these theories have attributed generalized anxiety to poor upbringing, which results in fragile and conflicted images of the self and others (Zerbe, 1990). Children whose parents are not sufficiently

TABLE 7.7 DSM-IV-TR

Symptoms of Generalized Anxiety Disorder

People diagnosed with GAD must show excessive anxiety and worry, difficulty in controlling the worry, and at least three of the other symptoms on this list chronically for at least six months.

Excessive anxiety and worry
Difficulty in controlling the worry
Restlessness or feeling keyed-up or on edge
Easily fatigued
Difficulty concentrating, mind goes blank
Irritability
Muscle tension
Sleep disturbance

Source: Reprinted with permission from the *Diagnostic and Statistical Manual of Mental Disorders*, Fourth Edition, Text Revision. Copyright © 2000. American Psychiatric Association.

TABLE 7.8	Concept Overview

Theories of Generalized Anxiety Disorder

These are the major theories of generalized anxiety disorder.

Theory	Description
Psychodynamic theories	
Freud's theory	GAD results when impulses are feared and cannot be expressed.
Newer psychodynamic theories	Children whose parents are not warm and nurturing develop images of the self as vulnerable and images of others as hostile, which results in chronic anxiety.
Humanistic theory	GAD occurs in children who develop a harsh set of self-standards they feel they must achieve in order to be acceptable.
Existential theory	GAD is due to existential anxiety, a universal fear of the limits and responsibilities of one's existence.
Cognitive theories	Both the conscious and unconscious thoughts of people with GAD are focused on threat, leading to chronic anxiety.
Biological theories	
GABA theory	People with GAD have a deficiency in GABA receptors, resulting in excessive firing in the limbic system.
Genetic theory	A biological vulnerability to GAD is inherited.

warm and nurturing, and may have been overly strict or critical, may develop images of the self as vulnerable and images of others as hostile. As adults, their lives are filled with frantic attempts to overcome or hide their vulnerability, but stressors often overwhelm their coping capacities, causing frequent bouts of anxiety.

These psychodynamic formulations have been studied in some empirical research (Eisenberg, 1958; Jenkins, 1968; Luborsky, 1973). Most of these studies are open to multiple interpretations and do not really get at the heart of the causal factors implicated in psychodynamic theories of generalized anxiety disorder.

Humanistic and Existential Theories

Carl Rogers' humanistic explanation of generalized anxiety suggests that children who do not receive unconditional positive regard from significant others become overly critical of themselves and develop **conditions of worth,** harsh self-standards they feel they must meet in order to be acceptable. Throughout their lives, these people then strive to meet these conditions of worth by denying their true selves and remaining constantly vigilant for the approval of others. They typically fail to meet their self-standards, causing them to feel chronically anxious or depressed.

Existential theorists attribute generalized anxiety disorder to **existential anxiety,** a universal hu-

man fear of the limits and responsibilities of one's existence (Bugental, 1997; May & Yalom, 1995; Tillich, 1952). Existential anxiety arises when we face the finality of death, the fact that we may unintentionally hurt someone, or the prospect that our lives have no meaning. We can avoid existential anxiety by accepting our limits and striving to make our lives meaningful, or we can try to silence that anxiety by avoiding responsibility or by conforming to others' rules. Failing to confront life's existential issues only leaves the anxiety in place, however, and leads us to "inauthentic lives."

Neither the humanistic nor the existential theory of generalized anxiety disorder has been extensively researched. Instead, most research attention these days is focused on the cognitive theories of GAD.

Cognitive Theories

The cognitive theories of GAD suggest that the cognitions of people with GAD are focused on threat, at both the conscious and nonconscious levels (Beck, 1997; Beck & Emery, 1985; Borkovec, 1994; Ellis, 1997; Mathews & MacLeod, 2005). At the conscious level, people with GAD have a number of maladaptive assumptions that set them up for anxiety, such as "I must be loved or approved of by everyone," "It's always best to expect the worst," and "I must anticipate and prepare myself at all times for any possible danger" (Beck & Emery, 1985; Ellis, 1997).

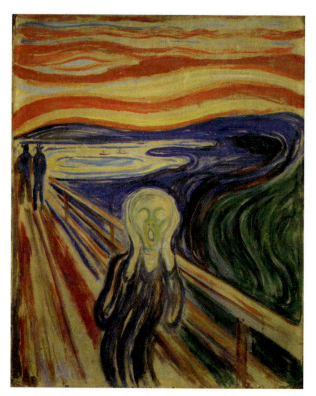

Munch's painting *The Scream* seems to capture the experiences of generalized anxiety.

Many of these assumptions reflect issues of being in control and losing control.

People with GAD believe that worrying can prevent bad events from happening. Many of these beliefs are superstitious, but people with GAD also believe that worrying motivates them and facilitates their problem solving, yet people with GAD seldom get around to problem solving. Although they are always anticipating a negative event, they do not tend to think through this anticipated event and vividly imagine it happening to them (Borkovec, 2002). Indeed, they actively avoid visual images of what they worry about, perhaps as a way of avoiding the negative emotion associated with those images. By avoiding fully processing those images, while anticipating that something bad is going to happen, people with GAD do not allow themselves to consider the ways they might cope with an event if it were to happen. Neither do they allow themselves to habituate to the negative emotions associated with the image of an event.

Their maladaptive assumptions lead people with GAD to respond to situations with **automatic thoughts,** which directly stir up anxiety, cause them to be hypervigilant, and lead them to overreact to situations. For example, when facing an exam, a person with GAD might reactively think, "I don't think I can do this," "I'll fall apart if I fail

this test," and "My parents will be furious if I don't get good grades."

The unconscious cognitions of people with GAD also appear to be focused on detecting possible threats in the environment (Mathews & MacLeod, 2005). One paradigm in which this has been shown is the Stroop color naming task. In this task, a participant is presented with words printed in color on a computer screen (see Figure 7.10). The participant's task is to say what color the word is printed in. Some of the words have special significance for a person with chronic anxiety, such as *disease* or *failure,* whereas other words have no special significance. In general, participants are slower in naming the color of words that have special significance to them than in naming nonsignificant words. The reason is that they are paying more attention to the content of the significant words than to the colors in which the words are printed.

One study presented threatening and nonthreatening words to GAD patients and nonpatient controls on the computer screen for only 20 milliseconds, too short a period for the subjects to consciously process the content of the word. The GAD patients were slower in naming the colors of the threatening words than were the nonpatients, but the two groups of subjects did not differ in the time it took them to name the colors of the nonthreatening words. This suggests that people suffering from GAD are always vigilant for signs of impending threat, even at an unconscious level (Mathews & MacLeod, 2005).

Why do some people become vigilant to signs of threat? One theory is that they have had experiences in which they have been confronted with stressors or traumas that were uncontrollable and came on without warning (Mineka & Kelly, 1989; Mineka & Zinbarg, 1998). Animal studies show that animals given unpredictable and uncontrollable shock often show symptoms of chronic fear or anxiety (Mineka, 1985). People who have had unpredictable and uncontrollable life experiences—such as an unpredictably abusive parent—may also develop chronic anxiety. Although these ideas are difficult to test in humans, studies of monkeys have shown that the level of control and predictability in an infant monkey's life is related to the monkey's symptoms of anxiety as an adolescent or adult (Mineka, Gunnar, & Champoux, 1986).

Biological Theories

Recall that the discovery that antidepressant medications reduce panic attacks led to the hypothesis that norepinephrine is involved in panic disorder. Similarly, the discovery in the 1950s that the benzodiazepines provide relief from generalized anxiety has led to theories about the neurotransmitters involved in generalized anxiety. The benzodiazepines increase the activity of **gamma-aminobutyric acid (GABA),** a neurotransmitter that carries inhibitory messages from one neuron to another. When GABA binds to a neuronal receptor, the neuron is inhibited from firing. One theory is that people with generalized anxiety disorder may have a deficiency of GABA or GABA receptors, which results in the excessive firing of neurons through many areas of the brain, but particularly in the limbic system, which is involved in emotional, physiological, and behavioral responses to threat (Charney, 2004; LeDoux, 1995). As a result of excessive and chronic neuronal activity, the person experiences chronic, diffuse symptoms of anxiety.

Genetic studies suggest that GAD, as a specific disorder, has a modest heritability (Kendler et al., 1992; Rapee & Barlow, 1993). The more general trait of anxiety is much more clearly heritable, and it puts individuals at risk for the diagnosis of GAD (Craske & Waters, 2005).

Treatments for Generalized Anxiety Disorder

The effective treatments for GAD are cognitive-behavioral or biological.

Cognitive-Behavioral Treatments

Cognitive-behavioral treatments focus on helping people with GAD confront the issues they worry most about; challenge their negative, catastrophizing thoughts; and develop coping strategies. We see in the following excerpt how a cognitive-behavioral therapist helps Claire challenge her tendency to overestimate the probability that her son will have an injury playing football (Brown, O'Leary, & Barlow, 2001, pp. 193–194):

VOICES

Therapist: Claire, you wrote that you were afraid about your son playing in his football game. What specifically were you worried about?

Claire: That he'd get seriously hurt. His team was playing last year's state champions, so you know that those boys are big and strong. My son is good, but he hasn't been playing for years and years.

Therapist: How specifically do you imagine your son getting hurt?

FIGURE 7.10 **The Stroop Color Naming Task.** In this task, words are flashed on a computer screen for a brief period of time, and the person is asked to name the color the word is printed in. People with generalized anxiety disorder are slower to name the color of words with threatening content than of neutral words, presumably because they are attending to the content of the threatening words.

DISEASE   CHAIR

Claire: Getting a broken back or neck. Something that will result in paralysis or death. It happened to two NFL players this past year, remember?

Therapist: What happened to your son when he played in the game?

Claire: Nothing, really. He came home that afternoon with a sore thumb, but that went away after a while. He said he scored a touchdown and had an interception. I guess he played really well.

Therapist: So what you're saying is that you had predicted that he would be injured during the game, but that didn't happen. When we're anxious, we tend to commit a common cognitive error, called "probability overestimation." In other words, we overestimate the likelihood of an unlikely event. While you were feeling anxious and worried, what was the probability in your mind that your son would be hurt, from 0 to 100%?

Claire: About 75%.

Therapist: And now what would you rate the probability of your son getting hurt in a future game?

Claire: Well, if you put it that way, I suppose around a 50% chance of him getting injured.

Therapist: So that means for every two times that your son plays football, he gets hurt once. Is that correct?

(continued)

Claire: Umm, no. I don't think it's that high. Maybe about 30%.

Therapist: That would be one out of every three times that your son gets hurt. To counter the tendency to overestimate the probability of negative future events, it's helpful to ask yourself what evidence from the past supports your anxious belief. What evidence can you provide from your son's playing history to account for your belief that he'll get hurt one out of every three games?

Claire: Well, none. He had a sprained ankle during summer training, but that's it.

Therapist: So what you're saying is that you don't have very much evidence at all to prove that your son has a 30% chance of getting hurt in a game.

Claire: Gee, I never thought of it that way.

Therapist: What are some alternatives to your son getting seriously hurt in a football game? . . .

Claire: He could get a minor injury, like a sprained ankle or something of that nature.

Therapist: Right. And what would be the probability of your son getting a minor versus a major injury?

Claire: Probably higher, like 60% or 70%.

Therapist: To go back to your original worry, what would you rate the probability of your son getting seriously injured during a football game?

Claire: Low, about 10%.

Therapist: So 1 out of every 10 times your son will get seriously hurt playing football. How many times has your son played football?

Claire: He just started varsity this year and he's a junior. But he's been playing since he got to high school, about 3 years. All in all, about 25 games.

Therapist: And how many times in those 3 years has he been seriously injured?

Claire: Not once. I see what you're doing.

Cognitive-behavioral therapy has been shown to be more effective than benzodiazepine therapy, placebos, or humanistic therapy in the treatment of GAD (Borkovec, Newman, & Castonguay, 2003;

Borkovec & Ruscio, 2001; Borkovec & Whisman, 1996; Butler et al., 1991; Harvey & Rapee, 1995). In one study, the positive effects of cognitive-behavioral therapy remained in a two-year follow-up of GAD clients (Borkovec et al., 2002).

Biological Treatments

The benzodiazepine drugs (such as Xanax, Librium, Valium, and Serax) provide short-term relief from the symptoms of anxiety (Gorman, 2003). The side effects and addictiveness of the benzodiazepines preclude their long-term use. Once people discontinue using these drugs, their anxiety symptoms return (Davidson, 2001).

A drug named **buspirone** (trade name BuSpar) appears to alleviate the symptoms of generalized anxiety for some people; it has few side effects and is unlikely to lead to physical dependence (Gorman, 2003). Buspirone is not a benzodiazepine but one of a class of drugs called azaspirones. It appears to reduce anxiety by blocking serotonin receptors.

Both the tricyclic antidepressant imipramine (trade name Tofranil) and the selective serotonin reuptake inhibitor paroxetine (trade name Paxil) have been shown to be better than placebo in reducing anxiety symptoms in GAD, and paroxetine improves anxiety more than a benzodiazepine does (Rocca et al., 1997). Venlafaxine (trade name Effexor), which is a serotonin-norepinephrine reuptake inhibitor, has also been shown to reduce the symptoms of anxiety in GAD better than placebo and in some studies better than busiprone (Davidson et al., 1999; Gelenberg et al., 2000; Rickels et al., 2000; Stocchi et al., 2001).

SUMMING UP

- Generalized anxiety disorder is characterized by chronic symptoms of anxiety across most situations.

- Freud suggested that GAD develops when people cannot find ways to express their impulses and fear the expression of these impulses. Newer psychodynamic theories suggest that children whose parents are not sufficiently warm and nurturing develop images of the self as vulnerable and images of others as hostile, which results in chronic anxiety. Neither of these theories has been supported empirically.

- Humanistic theory suggests that generalized anxiety results in children who develop a harsh set of self-standards they feel they must achieve in order to be acceptable.

- Existential theory attributes generalized anxiety to existential anxiety, a universal fear of the limits and responsibilities of one's existence.

- Cognitive theories suggest that both the conscious and unconscious thoughts of people with GAD are focused on threat.

- Biological theories suggest that people with GAD have a deficiency in GABA or GABA receptors. They may also have a genetic predisposition to generalized anxiety.

- Cognitive-behavioral treatments for people with GAD focus on helping them confront their negative thinking.

- Drug therapies have included the use of benzodiazepines and a newer drug called buspirone, as well as the tricyclic antidepressants and the selective serotonin reuptake inhibitors.

OBSESSIVE-COMPULSIVE DISORDER

Recall the obsessions and compulsions of Marc Summers, whom we met at the beginning of the chapter. **Obsessions** are thoughts, images, ideas, or impulses that are persistent, that the individual feels intrude upon his or her consciousness without control, and that cause significant anxiety or distress. **Compulsions** are repetitive behaviors or mental acts that an individual feels he or she must perform.

Obsessive-compulsive disorder (OCD) is classified as an anxiety disorder because people with OCD experience anxiety as a result of their obsessional thoughts and when they cannot carry out their compulsive behaviors (see Table 7.9 on page 252). This disorder has quite a different character than the other anxiety disorders we have discussed and may eventually be declassified as an anxiety disorder. Children can suffer OCD, just as adults can, and the little boy's personal account of OCD in the following excerpt illustrates how overwhelming this disorder can be (Rapoport, 1990, pp. 43–44). His name is Zach.

VOICES

When I was 6 I started doing all these strange things when I swallowed saliva. When I swallowed saliva I had to crouch down and touch the ground. I didn't want to lose any saliva—for a bit I had to sweep the ground with my hand—and later I had to blink my eyes if I swallowed. I was frustrated because I couldn't stop the compulsions. Each time I swallowed I had to do something. For a while I had to touch my shoulders to my chin. I don't know why. I had no reason. I was afraid. It was just so unpleasant if I didn't. If I tried not to do these things, all I got was failure. I had to do it, and no matter how hard I tried, I just *still* had to.

I tried to tell my ma. I told her I had to do it. She ways, "You're doing some strange things, why do you do it?" I said, "Cause I don't want to lose any saliva," and she says, "Maybe you'll want to talk about it later." I don't want to lose any saliva and there's no good reason. I just don't want to. I was afraid to tell anybody. People would think I was crazy or something. I don't want to tell Dr. Kaufman. I was nervous when I first came to him and then I just didn't want to talk about it. It just bothered me to talk about it. I felt ashamed. I didn't want anyone to know. I wanted it to be just for me to know, no one else.

It wrecked my life. It took away all the time. I couldn't do anything. If you put it all together I did it maybe an hour and a half or sometimes three hours a day.

I had bathroom problems too. I had to take some toilet paper and rip them up a lot of times into teeny pieces that had to be just the right size—only about a millimeter. They had to be torn perfect and then I'd flush them away.

I had to do all kinds of things with my fingers and my mouth. I had to touch all my fingers to my lips a few times if I swallowed saliva. Swallowing was one of the first things.

You may be thinking that the thoughts and behaviors that Zach describes, as well as those of Marc Summers, are "crazy"—that they are out of touch with reality. The thoughts and behaviors of people with OCD are not considered psychotic, however, because these people are very aware of how irrational their thoughts and behaviors are, yet they cannot seem to control them.

OCD often begins at a young age, as it did for Marc Summers. The peak age of onset for males is between 6 and 15 years, and for females it is between 20 and 29 years (Angst et al., 2004; Foa & Franklin, 2001). Children often hide their symptoms, even from their parents; as a result, their symptoms can go undetected for years (Rapoport

---

TABLE 7.9 DSM-IV-TR

Symptoms of Obsessive-Compulsive Disorder

Obsessive-compulsive disorder is classified as an anxiety disorder but differs from other anxiety disorders in many ways.

The person must show either obsessions or compulsions, which he or she recognizes are excessive or unreasonable.

Obsessions are defined as

1. recurrent and persistent thoughts, impulses, or images that are experienced as intrusive and inappropriate and that cause anxiety or distress

2. thoughts, impulses, or images that are not simply excessive worries about real-life problems

3. thoughts, impulses, or images that the person attempts to ignore or suppress or to neutralize with some other thought or action

4. obsessional thoughts, impulses, or images that the person recognizes are a product of his or her own mind

Compulsions are defined as

1. repetitive behaviors (such as handwashing, ordering, checking) or mental acts (such as praying, counting, repeating words silently) that the person feels driven to perform in response to an obsession or according to rules that must be applied rigidly

2. behaviors or mental acts that are aimed at preventing or reducing distress or preventing some dreaded event or situation; however, these behaviors or mental acts either are not connected in a realistic way with what they are designed to neutralize or prevent or are clearly excessive

Source: Reprinted with permission from the *Diagnostic and Statistical Manual of Mental Disorders,* Fourth Edition, Text Revision. Copyright © 2000. American Psychiatric Association.

---

et al., 2000). Marc Summers' parents thought he just liked a clean room.

OCD tends to be a chronic disorder if left untreated. Obsessional thoughts are very distressing to people with OCD, and engaging in compulsive behaviors can take a great deal of time and can even be dangerous (e.g., washing your hands so often that they bleed). As many as 66 percent of people with OCD are also significantly depressed (Foa & Franklin, 2001). Panic attacks, phobias, and substance abuse are also common in OCD.

Between 1 and 3 percent of people will develop OCD at sometime in their lives (Angst et al., 2004; Hewlett, 2000; Robins et al., 1984). In the United States, European Americans show a higher prevalence of OCD than do African Americans or Hispanic Americans (Hewlett, 2000). The prevalence of OCD does not seem to differ greatly across countries that have been studied, including the United

States, Canada, Mexico, England, Norway, Hong Kong, India, Egypt, Japan, and Korea (Escobar, 1993; Insel, 1984; Kim, 1993). Although some studies have found slightly higher rates of OCD in women than in men (Angst et al., 2004), other studies have not (Edelmann, 1992; Karno & Golding, 1991).

OCD Symptoms

Zach's and Marc Summers' obsessions involve dirt. The focus of obsessive thoughts seems to be similar across cultures, with the most common type of obsession focusing on dirt and contamination (Akhtar et al., 1975; Hewlett, 2000; Rachman & Hodgson, 1980). Other common obsessions include aggressive impulses (such as to hurt one's child), sexual thoughts (such as recurrent pornographic images), impulses to do something against one's moral code (such as to shout obscenities in church), and repeated doubts (such as worrying that one has not turned off the stove). Although thoughts of this kind occur to most people occasionally, most of us can turn them off by dismissing or ignoring them. People with OCD cannot turn off these thoughts.

People with OCD do not carry out the impulses they have (e.g., hurting a baby or shouting obscenities in church), but they are so bothered by the fact that they even have these thoughts that they feel extremely guilty and anxious. Most people who have severe and persistent obsessions engage in compulsions to try to erase their thoughts and the anxiety they create. Sometimes, an individual's compulsion is tied to his or her specific obsession by obvious logic. The compulsive behavior becomes so extreme and repetitive, however, that it is irrational. For example, Zach washes his hands 35 times a day, until they crack and bleed, to rid himself of contamination obsessions. "Checking" compulsions, which are extremely common, are tied to obsessional doubts, as is illustrated in the following story (Rapoport, 1990, pp. 21–22).

VOICES

I'm driving down the highway doing 55 MPH. I'm on my way to take a final exam. My seat belt is buckled and I'm vigilantly following all the rules of the road. No one is on the highway—not a living soul.

Out of nowhere an obsessive-compulsive disorder (OCD) attack strikes. It's almost magical the way it distorts my perception of reality. While in reality no one is on the road, I'm intruded with the heinous thought that I *might* have hit someone . . . a human being! God knows where such a fantasy comes from.

(continued)

I think about this for a second and then say to myself, "That's ridiculous. I didn't hit anybody." Nonetheless, a gnawing anxiety is born. An anxiety I will ultimately not be able to put away until an enormous emotional price has been paid.

I try to make reality chase away this fantasy. I reason, "Well, if I hit someone while driving, I would have *felt* it." This brief trip into reality helps the pain dissipate . . . but only for a second. Why? Because the gnawing anxiety that I really did commit the illusionary accident is growing larger—so is the pain.

The pain is a terrible guilt that I have committed an unthinkable, negligent act. At one level, I know this is ridiculous, but there's a terrible pain in my stomach telling me something quite different.

Again, I try putting to rest this insane thought and that ugly feeling of guilt. "Come on," I think to myself, "this is *really* insane!"

But the awful feeling persists. The anxious pain says to me, "You Really Did Hit Someone." The attack is now in full control. Reality no longer has meaning. My sensory system is distorted. I have to get rid of the pain. Checking out this fantasy is the only way I know how.

I start ruminating, "Maybe I did hit someone and didn't realize it. . . . Oh, my God! I might have killed somebody! I have to go back and check." Checking is the only way to calm the anxiety. It brings me closer to truth somehow. I can't live with the thought that I actually may have killed someone—I have to check it out.

Now I'm sweating . . . literally. I pray this outrageous act of negligence never happened. My fantasies run wild. I desperately hope the jury will be merciful. I'm particularly concerned about whether my parents will be understanding. After all, I'm now a criminal. I must control the anxiety by checking it out. Did it really happen? There's always an infinitesimally small kernel of truth (or potential truth) in all my OC fantasies.

I think to myself, "Rush to check it out. Get rid of the hurt by checking it out."

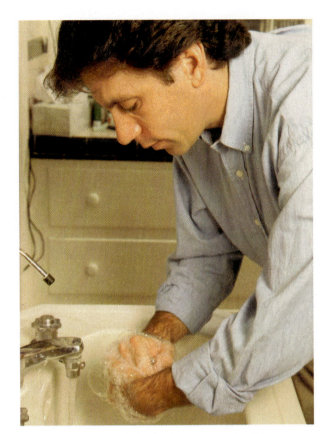

Handwashing is one of the most common compulsions in OCD.

This man's compulsive checking makes some sense, given what he is thinking. However, what he is thinking—that he hit someone on the road without knowing it—is highly improbable. The compulsive checking quells obsessional thoughts briefly, but the obsessional thoughts come back with even more force.

Often, the link between the obsession and the compulsion is the result of "magical thinking." For example, many people with OCD believe that repeating a ritual a certain number of times will ward off danger to themselves or others. Their rituals often become stereotyped and rigid, and they develop obsessions and compulsions about not performing the rituals correctly. For example, Marc Summers felt compelled to read the advertisement for a watch 25 times perfectly, and he feared something would happen to his family if he didn't.

At times, there is no discernible link between the specific obsession a person has and the specific compulsion that helps dispel the obsession. Recall that Zach engages in several behaviors, such as touching the floor and touching his shoulders to his chin, when he has an obsession about losing his saliva. He cannot even say how these behaviors are related to his obsession; he just knows he has to engage in them. Thus, although compulsions may often seem purposeful, they are not functional. In some cases, the family members of people with OCD become accomplices in the disorder, as did the husband of writer Emily Colas, who has written about her OCD (Colas, 1998, pp. 70–72).

VOICES

My husband and I generally kept a pile of about twenty garbage bags in one corner of our apartment. Which may seem out of character, for me to let them stay, but it was our trash and I knew nothing bad was in there. It was the communal trash that made me shake. So when it was time to take the bags out to the dumpster, my husband had to follow the whole hygienic procedure. To keep the neighbors' germs out of our place. First the water had to be turned on and left that way because if he touched the garbage and then the spigot, the spigot would get contaminated. Next he'd take one bag in his right hand and open the door with his left. Then he'd shut the door behind him and lock it so that no one could get into the house. I guess I could have monitored, but he wanted me upstairs so I couldn't critique him. He'd take the bag down, stand a few feet from the dumpster to be sure not to touch it, and throw the bag in. Then he'd unlock the door, open it, slip his shoes off, come inside, and wash his hands. He used a pump soap so

that he could use his clean wrist to pump some in the palm of his hand and not contaminate the dispenser. The water would stay on, and he'd move to the next bag. He went through this procedure twenty times, once for each bag, until they were gone.

Theories of OCD

The biological theories of OCD have dominated research in recent years, and they have provided some intriguing hypotheses about its sources. Psychodynamic and cognitive-behavioral theories of OCD have also been proposed. These theories are summarized in the Concept Overview in Table 7.10.

Biological Theories

Biological theories of obsessive-compulsive disorder view it as a neurobiological disorder. Much of this research has focused on a circuit in the brain that is involved in the execution of primitive patterns of behavior, such as aggression, sexuality, and bodily excretion (Baxter et al., 2001; Rapoport, 1990; Saxena & Rauch, 2000). This circuit begins in the orbital region of the frontal cortex (see Figure 7.11). These impulses are then carried to a part of the basal ganglia called the **caudate nucleus,** which allows only the strongest of these impulses to carry through to the thalamus. If these impulses reach the thalamus, the person is motivated to think further about and possibly act on these impulses. The action might involve a set of stereotyped behaviors appropriate to the impulse. Once these behaviors are executed, the impulse diminishes.

TABLE 7.10	Concept Overview

Theories of OCD

The biological theories of OCD have been dominant in recent years, but psychodynamic and cognitive-behavioral theories have also been proposed.

Theory	Description
Biological theories	People with OCD suffer from a dysfunction in the circuits in the brain regulating primitive impulses, possibly due to deficiencies in serotonin, which cause OCD.
Psychodynamic theories	The obsessions and compulsions of people with OCD represent unconscious wishes or conflicts.
Cognitive-behavioral theories	People with OCD have difficulty turning off intrusive thoughts because of chronic distress, a tendency toward rigid thinking, and the belief they should be able to control their thoughts.

FIGURE 7.11 **OCD in the Brain.** A three-dimensional view of the human brain (with parts shown as they would look if the overlying cerebral cortex were transparent) clarifies the locations of the orbital frontal cortex and the basal ganglia—areas implicated in obsessive-compulsive disorder. Among the basal ganglia's structures are the caudate nucleus, which filters powerful impulses that arise in the orbital frontal cortex, so that only the most powerful ones reach the thalamus. Perhaps the orbital frontal cortex, the caudate nucleus, or both are so active in people with obsessive-compulsive disorder that numerous impulses reach the thalamus, generating obsessive thoughts or compulsive actions.

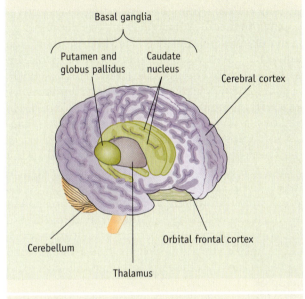

Source: Adapted from Rapoport, 1989, p. 85.

FIGURE 7.12 **PET Scans of OCD.** PET scans of people with OCD show more activity in the frontal cortex, basal ganglia, and thalamus than do PET scans of people without OCD.

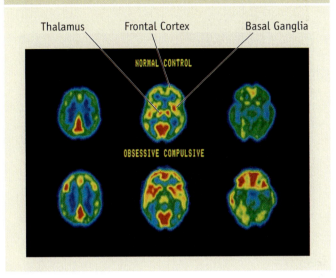

For people with OCD, dysfunction in this circuit may result in the system's inability to turn off these primitive impulses or to turn off the execution of the stereotyped behaviors once they are engaged. For example, when most of us have the thought that we are dirty, we engage in a fairly stereotyped form of cleansing: We wash our hands. People with OCD, however, continue to have the impulse to wash their hands, because their brains do not shut off their thoughts about dirt or their behavior when the behavior is no longer necessary. Proponents of this theory have pointed out that many of the obsessions and compulsions of people with OCD have to do with contamination, sex, aggression, and the repetition of behavior patterns—all issues with which this primitive brain circuit deals.

PET scans of people with OCD show more activity in the areas of the brain involved in this primitive circuit than do PET scans of people without

OCD (Micallef & Blin, 2001; Saxena et al., 1998) (see Figure 7.12). In addition, people with OCD often get some relief from their symptoms when they take drugs that better regulate the neurotransmitter serotonin, which plays an important role in the proper functioning of this primitive circuit in the brain (Micallef & Blin, 2001; Saxena et al., 1998). OCD patients who do respond to serotonin-enhancing drugs tend to show more reductions in the rate of activity in these brain areas than do OCD patients who do not respond well to these drugs (Baxter et al., 1992; Saxena et al., 1999, 2003). Interestingly, OCD patients who respond to behavior therapy also tend to show decreases in rate of activity in the caudate nucleus and thalamus (Schwartz et al., 1996) (see Figure 7.13 on page 256).

Piecing together these studies, researchers have argued that people with OCD have a fundamental dysfunction in the areas of the brain regulating primitive impulses, perhaps due to a depletion of serotonin in these systems. As a result, primitive impulses about sex, aggression, and cleanliness break through to their consciousness and motivate the execution of stereotyped behaviors much more often than in people without OCD (Baxter et al., 2001; Rapoport, 1989, 1991). Whether these differences in brain functioning are a cause or a consequence of OCD is not clear.

Finally, there is evidence that genes may play a role determining who is vulnerable to OCD (Hettema et al., 2001; Jonnal, Gardner, & Prescott, 2000; Nestadt et al., 2000). Family history studies clearly show that OCD runs in families, and twin studies

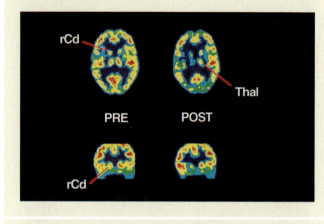

FIGURE 7.13 **The Effects of Behavior Therapy.** PET scans show decreases in metabolic activity in the caudate nucleus (rCd) and thalamus (Thal) in OCD patients after they have received behavior therapy.

Source: Schwartz et al., 1996.

provide evidence for a substantial genetic effect on obsessive and compulsive behaviors (Eley et al., 2003; Hudziak et al., 2004).

Psychodynamic Theories

Psychodynamic theorists suggest that the particular obsessions and compulsions of people with OCD are symbolic of unconscious conflicts that they are guarding against (Freud, 1909). These conflicts create such anxiety for people that they can confront them only indirectly, by displacing the anxiety created by the conflict onto a more acceptable thought or behavior.

According to these theories, the reason that so many obsessions and compulsions involve contamination, sex, and aggression is that unconscious conflicts have to do with sexual and aggressive impulses. Psychodynamic theories suggest that the way to cure people of their OCD is to help them gain insight into the conflicts their obsessions and compulsions symbolize and to help them better resolve these conflicts. Psychodynamic therapy generally is not considered effective for the most OCD patients, however (Salzman, 1980).

Cognitive-Behavioral Theories

Most people, including people who do *not* have OCD, occasionally have negative, intrusive thoughts (Angst et al., 2004; Rachman & deSilva, 1978). People are more prone to have negative, intrusive thoughts and to engage in rigid, ritualistic behaviors when they are distressed (Clark & Purdon, 1993; Rachman, 1997). For example, many new mothers, exhausted from sleep deprivation

and the stresses of caring for a newborn, have thoughts about harming their newborn, even though they are horrified by such thoughts and would never carry them out.

According to the cognitive-behavioral theories of OCD, what differentiates people with OCD from people without the disorder is the ability to turn off these negative, intrusive thoughts (Clark, 1988; Rachman & Hodgson, 1980; Salkovskis, 1998). People who do not develop OCD are able to turn them off by ignoring or dismissing them, attributing them to their distress, and simply letting them subside with the passage of time.

Why do people who develop OCD have trouble turning off their thoughts, according to cognitive-behavioral theories? First, they may be depressed or generally anxious much of the time, so that even minor negative events are more likely to invoke intrusive, negative thoughts (Clark & Purdon, 1993). Second, people with OCD may have a tendency toward rigid, moralistic thinking (Rachman, 1993; Salkovskis, 1998). They judge their negative, intrusive thoughts as more unacceptable than most people would and become more anxious and guilty over having them. This anxiety then makes it even harder for them to dismiss the thoughts (Salkovskis, 1998). In addition, people who feel more responsible for events that happen in their lives and in the lives of others than other people do have more trouble dismissing thoughts such as "Did I hit someone on the road?" and thus might be more likely to develop OCD.

Third, people with OCD appear to believe that they *should* be able to control all thoughts, and they have trouble accepting that everyone has horrific thoughts from time to time (Clark & Purdon, 1993; Freeston et al., 1992). They tend to believe that having these thoughts means they are going crazy, or they equate having the thoughts with actually engaging in the behaviors (e.g., "If I'm thinking about hurting my child, I'm as guilty as if I actually did hurt my child"). Of course, this just makes them that much more anxious when they have the thoughts, which makes it harder for them to dismiss the thoughts.

How do compulsions develop, according to these theories? They develop largely through operant conditioning. People with anxiety-provoking obsessions discover that, if they engage in certain behaviors, their anxiety is reduced. The reduction in anxiety negatively reinforces the behaviors. Each time the obsessions return and they use the behaviors to reduce the obsessions, the behaviors are reinforced. Compulsions are born.

As with the biological theories of OCD, research has supported pieces of the cognitive-

TABLE 7.11	Concept Overview	

Treatments for OCD

Often, drug therapies and cognitive-behavioral therapies are combined in the treatment of OCD.

Treatment	Description	Example
Biological treatments	Use serotonin-enhancing drugs.	Paxil, Prozac
Cognitive-behavioral treatments	Expose the client to obsessions until anxiety about obsessions decreases; prevent compulsive behaviors and help the client manage anxiety that is aroused.	Systematic desensitization therapy to help a person with a germ obsession gradually tolerate exposure to "dirty" materials

behavioral view of OCD, but much more research needs to be done. In particular, it is not clear whether the dysfunctions that the biological and cognitive-behavioral theories point to are the causes or the consequences of OCD. The reason is that almost all studies investigating these theories have compared people who already have OCD with those who do not.

Treatments for OCD

Just as biological theories dominate research on OCD, biological therapies have come to dominate the treatment of OCD. Cognitive-behavioral therapies also appear very helpful in treating OCD (see the Concept Overview in Table 7.11).

Biological Treatments

Until the 1980s, there were few effective biological treatments for OCD. The antianxiety drugs, the benzodiazepines, were not useful in most cases of OCD. This is one clue that OCD is not like the other anxiety disorders.

Then, it was discovered that antidepressant drugs that affect levels of the neurotransmitter serotonin helped relieve symptoms of OCD in many patients (Abramowitz, 1997; Rapoport, 1989, 1991). These drugs include clomipramine (trade name Anafranil), fluoxetine (trade name Prozac), paroxetine (trade name Paxil), sertraline (trade name Zoloft), and fluvoxamine (trade name Luvox). Controlled studies suggest that 50 to 80 percent of OCD patients experience decreases in their obsessions and compulsions when on these drugs, compared with only 5 percent of patients on placebos (March et al., 1998; Riddle et al., 2001).

These drugs may work by inhibiting the reuptake of the neurotransmitter serotonin, increasing the functional levels of serotonin in the brain. Recall that the latest biological theories of OCD sug-

gest that this disorder involves dysfunctioning of the areas of the brain rich in serotonin.

These drugs are not the complete answer for people with OCD, however. A substantial number of patients do not respond to SSRIs, and, even among people who respond to the drug, obsessions and compulsions are reduced by only 40 or 50 percent, and people tend to relapse if the drugs are discontinued (Hewlett, 2000). Also, the drugs have significant side effects, including drowsiness, constipation, and loss of sexual interest, which prevent many people from taking them. Recent studies suggest that adding an atypical antipsychotic (a new form of antipsychotic drug described in Chapter 11) to an SSRI can further help people who do not respond fully to the SSRI (Bystritsky et al., 2004).

As writer Emily Colas observes, after living a lifetime with OCD, she needed to learn how to live a normal life once the drugs removed her symptoms (Colas, 1998, p. 138):

VOICES

You can try really hard not to get better. Use all your strength and will. But when you're on the pill, you get better and there's not a whole lot you can do about it. It takes a little while to kick in, so there are about four or five weeks when you're basically taking medication for the sheer benefit of the side effects. Tired, spacey, constipated. But then it happens. Not dramatically. It comes on slowly, but you can tell. The thoughts and worries become less gripping. I guess I figured that once that began to happen I'd instantly become happy. But the startling realization I made as I was coming to my senses was that life's kind of a

(continued)

drag. There didn't seem to be much to it. And my rituals had been a nice diversion. Without them, I wasn't quite sure what to do with myself. This thought made my head ache. I got anxious, nervous, wondering if I was destined to live this dull and uninteresting life. But because of those damn pills, I wasn't even able to obsess about *that*.

Cognitive-Behavioral Treatments

Many clinicians believe that drugs must be combined with cognitive-behavioral therapies in order to help people recover completely from OCD. The cognitive-behavioral therapies for OCD focus on repeatedly exposing the client to the focus of the obsession and preventing compulsive responses to the anxiety aroused by the obsession (Foa & Franklin, 2001; Marks & Swinson, 1992; Rachman & Hodgson, 1980). The repeated exposure to the content of the obsession is thought to habituate the client to obsession, so that it does not arouse as much anxiety as it formerly did. Preventing the person from engaging in compulsive behavior allows this habituation to take place. In addition, the person comes to learn that not engaging in the compulsive behavior does not lead to a terrible result. To implement this repeated exposure and response prevention, the therapist might first model the behavior he or she wants the client to practice.

For example, if the client has an obsession about contamination and a washing compulsion, the therapist might model rubbing dirt on his hands and then not wash his hands during the therapy session. At the next session, the therapist might again rub dirt on his hands but this time encourage the client to get her hands dirty as well. As the client's compulsion to wash her hands grows, the therapist encourages her not to do so but sits with her and uses relaxation techniques to control her anxiety. After several such sessions, the client may be able to sit with dirty hands without feeling anxious and to control her washing compulsion herself.

The client may also be given homework assignments that help her confront her obsession. For example, early in therapy, she might be assigned simply to refrain from cleaning the house every day of the week, as she normally does, and clean it only every three days. Later in therapy, she might be assigned to drop a cookie on a dirty kitchen floor and then pick it up and eat it or drop the kitchen knives on the floor and then use them to prepare food.

These behavior therapies have been shown to lead to significant improvement in obsessions and compulsive behavior in 60 to 90 percent of OCD clients (Abramowitz, 1997; Fals-Stewart, Marks, & Schafer, 1993; Foa & Franklin, 2001; Marks & Swinson, 1992; McLean et al., 2001; Steketee & Frost, 2003). Moreover, these improvements are maintained in most clients over periods of up to six years (Foa & Franklin, 2001; Foa & Kozak, 1993). Unfortunately, however, this therapy does not eliminate all obsessions and compulsions in OCD patients, and a substantial minority are not helped at all. Much work remains to be done to find a universally and completely effective therapy for OCD. The treatments available now, however, are great improvements over what was available only a few years ago.

SUMMING UP

- Obsessions are thoughts, images, ideas, or impulses that are persistent, are intrusive, and cause distress, and they commonly focus on contamination, sex, violence, and repeated doubts.

- Compulsions are repetitive behaviors or mental acts that the individual feels he or she must perform to erase his or her obsessions.

- Biological theories of OCD speculate that the areas of the brain involved in the execution of primitive patterns of behavior, such as washing rituals, may be impaired in people with OCD. These areas of the brain are rich in the neurotransmitter serotonin, and drugs that regulate serotonin have proven helpful in the treatment of OCD.

- Psychodynamic theories of OCD suggest that the obsessions and compulsions symbolize unconscious conflict or impulses and that the proper therapy for OCD involves uncovering these unconscious thoughts. These theories have not been supported.

- Cognitive-behavioral theories suggest that people with OCD are chronically distressed, think in rigid and moralistic ways, judge negative thoughts as more acceptable than other people do, and feel more responsible for their thoughts and behaviors. This makes them unable to turn off the negative, intrusive thoughts that most people have occasionally.

- Compulsive behaviors develop through operant conditioning. People are reinforced for compulsive behaviors by the fact that they reduce anxiety.

- Effective therapies for OCD involve a combination of selective serotonin reuptake inhibitors and cognitive-behavioral therapy.

SOCIAL APPROACHES TO THE ANXIETY DISORDERS

Social theorists have drawn attention to the fact that some groups and cultures are more prone than others to panic disorders, phobias, and generalized anxiety disorder (although there are not large cultural differences in OCD). They have tried to understand these differences in light of the environmental demands faced by these groups and their cultural norms for behavior.

Studies across the world show that people living in countries undergoing rapid societal change, political oppression, and war are much more likely to show anxiety symptoms than are those in more stable countries (Compton et al., 1991). In the United States, anxiety disorders are more common among people in disadvantaged minority groups and those in lower educational and socioeconomic groups than among Whites and people in higher educational and socioeconomic groups (Manson et al., 1996; Schlenger et al., 1992; Sheikh, 1992).

The stressful environment in which disadvantaged people live may create a chronic and pervasive anxiousness, which increases their risk for the development of anxiety disorders (Barlow, 1988; Manson et al., 1996). For example, consider a woman living in poverty who is anxious about the unsafe neighborhood in which she lives. Her chronic apprehensiveness could make it easier for even minor events, such as being trapped briefly in the elevator of her apartment building, to create paniclike symptoms. She would then be likely to associate her panic symptoms with elevators or, perhaps more generally, with enclosed spaces. Claustrophobia might develop.

Gender Differences

Women are more prone than men to develop most of the anxiety disorders we have discussed in this chapter. Compared with men, women have two or three times the rate of panic with agoraphobia, three or four times more specific phobias, one and one-half times more social phobias, and two times more generalized anxiety disorder (Kessler et al., 1995; Yonkers & Gurguis, 1995). Why would women be more likely than men to develop these disorders?

Some social theories suggest that women have a greater risk for anxiety disorders because of their place in society and the nature of their relationships with others (Chodorow, 1978; Horney, 1934/1967; Miller, 1976). Women generally have less power in society than do men, and their status is typically tied to the men they are related to. This causes women to cling to others, to play passive and subservient roles in relationships, to have a sense of be-

ing vulnerable and defenseless, and to be hypervigilant to any signs of problems in their relationships. This suppression of their own desires and fearfulness of loss, however, leave women chronically anxious, as in generalized anxiety disorder. Panic attacks and phobias are simply extreme expressions of these women's ongoing anxiety. Agoraphobia may be another way to express vulnerability and to conform to the passive role. This intriguing and popular theory has not been extensively studied in empirical research.

A different but related perspective is that sex-role socialization and pressures influence how men and women cope with symptoms of distress and thus whether they develop anxiety disorders. First, men may feel it is socially unacceptable to express anxiety and thus may be more prone to confront their feared situations and thereby extinguish their anxiety (Bruch & Cheek, 1995). Second, men appear more likely than women to seek medical help for anxiety symptoms, especially panic attacks (Yonkers & Gurguis, 1995). Men may view these symptoms as annoying medical problems, rather than as signs that there is something wrong in their lives or in their personalities. As a result, men may be more likely than women to receive effective treatment in the early stages of possible anxiety disorders.

Not all men who have anxiety symptoms seek appropriate help for them, however. Many men who have panic attacks appear to self-medicate by consuming large amounts of alcohol to decrease their panic symptoms, a coping behavior that is more acceptable for men than for women (Chambless et al., 1987; Johannessen et al., 1989). In contrast, because it is more acceptable for women to remain home and to avoid the kinds of situations that people with agoraphobia avoid, women may be more likely than men to develop agoraphobia as a way of coping with their panic attacks.

Women in many cultures face threats in daily life that quite reasonably would lead them to be chronically anxious and more prone to all of the anxiety disorders. In particular, women are more likely than men to be the targets of physical and sexual abuse. Girls and women who have been physically or sexually abused are at increased risk for most anxiety disorders (Burnam et al., 1988).

Victimization has a tragic, cyclical nature. Women are more at risk for abuse when they have very low incomes and are newly divorced. In turn, women who have been abused are more likely to become unemployed, to have reduced income, and to become divorced. Thus, these women suffer a host of circumstances that are difficult to control, may be unpredictable, and may contribute to anxiety. Even women who have not yet been victimized may be chronically anxious due to the pervasive threat of violence.

Cross-Cultural Differences

Culture appears to strongly influence the manifestation of anxiety. People in Latino cultures report a syndrome known as *ataque de nervios* (attack of the nerves). A typical *ataque de nervios* might include trembling, heart palpitations, a sense of heat in the chest rising into the head, difficulty moving limbs, loss of consciousness or mind going blank, memory loss, a sensation of needles in parts of the body (paresthesia), chest tightness, difficulty breathing (dyspnea), dizziness, and faintness. Behaviorally, the person begins to shout, swear, and strike out at others. The person then falls to the ground and either experiences convulsive body movements or lies "as if dead" (Guarnaccia et al., 1996).

When *ataque de nervios* comes out of the blue, it is often attributed to the stresses of daily living or to spiritual causes. Like panic attacks, *ataque de nervios* is more common among recent trauma victims. A study of Puerto Ricans after the 1985 floods and mudslides in Puerto Rico found that 16 percent of the victims reported experiencing *ataque de nervios* (Guarnaccia et al., 1993).

More chronic anxiety-like symptoms, known as *nervios,* are quite common in Latino communities, particularly among the poor and uneducated. The term *nervios* encompasses a broad array of symptoms, including physical ailments (e.g., headaches, stomach problems, dizziness) and emotional symptoms (sadness, irritability, anger, absent-mindedness), as well as the presence of intrusive worries or negative thoughts. One study of 942 adults in rural Mexico found that 21 percent of the women and 10 percent of the men had chronic *nervios* (de Snyder, Diaz-Perez, & Ojeda, 2000). The authors suggest that, among the underprivileged, particularly women, *nervios* is a way of expressing the anger and frustration of "being at the bottom" and provides temporary release from grinding, everyday burdens of life (see also Lopez & Guarnaccia, 2000).

In Japan, the term *taijin kyofu-sho* has been used to describe an intense fear of interpersonal relations. *Taijin kyofu-sho* is characterized by shame about and persistent fears of causing others offense, embarrassment, or even harm through one's own inadequacies. It is most frequently encountered, at least in treatment settings, among young males. People with this disorder may fear blushing, emitting body odor, displaying unsightly body parts, speaking one's thoughts aloud, or irritating others (Chapman, Manuzza, & Fyer, 1995). Although *taijin kyofu-sho* may share some features with social phobia, it

In Latino cultures, *ataque de nervios* is a common anxiety syndrome.

reflects concerns about offending others, rather than embarrassing oneself. This is in line with the emphasis in Japan on deference to others (Kirmayer, 2001).

Are these just different manifestations of disorders that we call panic attacks or social phobias? Or are they truly culture-bound disorders that don't exactly match any disorders in the DSM? The study of people with *ataque de nervios* following the Puerto Rican mudslides found that most of these people could also be diagnosed with anxiety or depressive disorders, according to DSM criteria (Guarnaccia et al., 1993). The authors of this study noted, however, that these people conceptualized their symptoms as *ataque de nervios,* and accepting their conceptualization may be more useful and respectful than imposing a DSM diagnosis on them.

Clinicians are only beginning to understand such differences in the anxiety disorders. The sociocultural perspective draws attention to these differences, as well as differences between other groups, and suggests that we look to factors within the environment, and within interpersonal relationships and culture, for their causes.

SUMMING UP

- Social perspectives on anxiety disorders suggest that group differences are tied to environmental pressures and to social and cultural norms.

- Women are more prone than men to panic disorder, phobias, and generalized anxiety disorder. This tendency may be tied to women's roles in society and to gender roles.

- The manifestation of anxiety may differ across cultures. As examples, Latino cultures have *ataque de nervios* and more chronic *nervios,* and the Japanese culture has *taijin kyofu-sho.* These difficulties may represent culturally acceptable forms of panic attacks, generalized anxiety disorder, and social phobia, respectively, or they may be true culture-bound syndromes.

CHAPTER INTEGRATION

Biology is clearly involved in the experience of anxiety. Evolution has prepared our bodies to respond to threatening situations with physiological changes that make it easier for us to flee from or fight an attacker. For some people, this natural physiological response may be impaired, leading to chronic arousal, to overreactivity, or to poorly regulated arousal. These people may be more prone to severe anxiety reactions to threatening stimuli and to the anxiety disorders.

Psychological and social factors also clearly play a role in anxiety and the anxiety disorders. People differ in what they perceive as threatening, and these differences in perception lead to differences in the level of anxiety people fear when faced with potentially threatening situations. These differences in perception may be due to upbringing. For example, a child may develop a phobia of dogs because her mother modeled a fearful response to dogs. Another child may be chronically anxious and may believe he must be perfect because his parents punish him severely if he makes any type of mistake. Differences in perceptions of what is threaten-

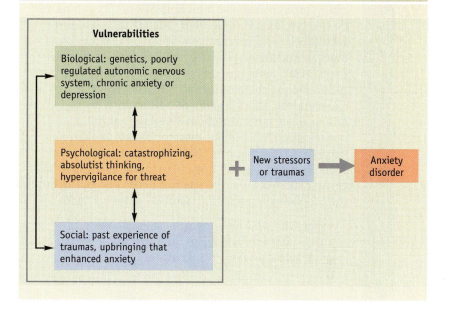

FIGURE 7.14 **Vulnerability-Stress Models.** Vulnerability-stress models of anxiety disorders describe how biological, psychological, and social factors work together to create these disorders.

ing may also be due to specific traumatic experiences that some people have suffered.

Some of the most successful models of the anxiety disorders are vulnerability-stress models (see Figure 7.14). These models stipulate that a person who develops an anxiety disorder has preexisting biological or psychological vulnerabilities, which are due in part to a history of trauma or severe stress. These vulnerabilities interact with new stressors to create the symptoms of anxiety disorders. These models go far in explaining why some people, but not others, experience anxiety that is so severe and chronic that it develops into a disorder.

Extraordinary People: Follow-Up

Marc Summers never knew he had OCD, had never heard of the disorder, until a psychiatrist went on his talk show one day to discuss the disorder, along with Mariette Hartley, an actress who was a spokesperson for the Obsessive Compulsive Foundation. As Marc Summers was reading about the disorder in preparation for interviewing the psychiatrist, he suddenly realized that he had it. He was both extremely relieved to find that what he had experienced all his life was a treatable disorder and extremely distressed at the thought of going on national television to discuss the disorder he now realized he had. He did go on the air with the psychiatrist, and in the middle of the program he admitted that he thought he had OCD. The psychiatrist and everyone else in the studio were supportive of him and congratulated him on his courage.

It was six more months before Marc Summers sought any help. He felt that just having a label for his troubles somehow made them manageable. When his talk show was abruptly canceled, however,

Marc Summers went into a tailspin of OCD symptoms and developed a serious episode of depression. His symptoms caused a great deal of agitation and distress in his family as well: His teenage daughter would be in her room with a friend, and Marc Summers would come in and insist on cleaning around them. After several overwhelming weeks, he finally called the psychiatrist he had interviewed on his TV show to talk about treatment. Eventually, he began taking a selective serotonin reuptake inhibitor and participating in behavior therapy. This treatment has helped him gain substantial control over his symptoms, but vestiges still linger. He thinks of OCD as a chronic disorder that he has not overcome but is in the process of overcoming (Summers, 2000 p. 209):

> My wife and kids have seen the change in me—that I'm better. But there are still things I'm working on. I want people to walk into our house and feel comfortable, but I'm still uptight, and it gnaws at me. I still get antsy when there are little children in the house; I think they're going to put their hands on the walls, or toddle around with a mouth full of cookies, dribbling crumbs on the floor. And I'm still waiting for the day when I'll be able to say to [my daughter] Meredith, "Why don't you invite fifty of your friends over for a party?" That's my goal: to feel comfortable with fifty teenagers partying hard late into the night in our house, leaning against the walls, dancing on the carpets, their jackets tossed hither and yon, bowls of chips knocked over on the living room floor, glasses spilled, glasses broken, chaos and mayhem, everything out of place.

Chapter Summary

- Anxiety has physiological and somatic, emotional, cognitive, and behavioral symptoms. (Review Table 7.1.)

- A panic attack is a short, intense experience of several of the physiological symptoms of anxiety, plus cognitions that one is going crazy, losing control, or dying. (Review Table 7.2.) The diagnosis of panic disorder is given when a person has spontaneous panic attacks frequently, begins to worry about having attacks, and changes his or her ways of living as a result of this worry. About one-third to one-half of people diagnosed with panic disorder also develop agoraphobia.

- One biological theory of panic disorder is that these people have overreactive autonomic nervous systems, which put them into a full fight-or-flight response with little provocation. This may be the result of imbalances in norepinephrine or serotonin or in hypersensitivity to feelings of suffocation. There also is some evidence that panic disorder may be transmitted genetically.

- Psychological theories of panic suggest that people who suffer from panic disorder pay very close attention to their bodily sensations, misinterpret bodily sensations in a negative way, and engage in snowballing, catastrophic thinking. This thinking then increases physiological activation, and a full panic attack ensues.

- Antidepressants and benzodiazepines are effective in reducing panic attacks and agoraphobic behavior, but people tend to relapse into these disorders when they discontinue these drugs. (Review Table 7.3.)

- An effective cognitive-behavioral therapy has been developed for panic and agoraphobia. (Review Table 7.3.) Clients are taught relaxation exercises and then learn to identify and challenge their catastrophic styles of thinking, often while having panic attacks induced in the therapy sessions. Systematic desensitization techniques are used to reduce agoraphobic behavior.

- People with agoraphobia fear places from which they might have trouble escaping or where they might have trouble getting help if they should have a panic attack.

- The specific phobias involve fears of specific objects or situations. Most fall into one of four categories: animal type, natural environment type, situational type, and blood-injection-injury type.

Social phobia involves fears of being judged or embarrassed. (Review Figure 7.8.)

■ There is little support for Freud's theory that phobias symbolize unconscious conflicts and fears that have been displaced onto neutral objects or for psychoanalytic treatment of phobias.

■ Behavioral theories suggest that phobias develop through classical and operant conditioning. (Review Table 7.5.) This fear is maintained because, through operant conditioning, the person has learned that avoiding the phobic object reduces the fear, so the avoidance is negatively reinforced. Phobias can also develop through observational learning. Finally, it appears that, through classical conditioning, humans develop phobias more readily to objects that our distant ancestors had reason to fear, such as snakes and spiders.

■ Cognitive theories have focused on social phobia and suggest that this disorder develops in people who have excessively high standards for their performance in social situations, assume that others will judge them harshly, and have biased attention to signs of social rejection. (Review Table 7.5.)

■ Behavioral treatments focus on extinguishing fear responses to phobic objects and have proven quite effective. (Review Table 7.6.) People with blood-injection-injury type phobias must also learn to tense up when they confront their phobic objects to prevent the decreases in blood pressure and heart rate they experience. Drug therapies have not proven useful for phobias.

■ Group cognitive-behavioral therapy has proven highly effective in the treatment of social phobia.

■ Benzodiazepines and antidepressant drugs can reduce acute symptoms of anxiety in people with phobias, but these symptoms return when the drugs are discontinued. (Review Table 7.6.)

■ People with generalized anxiety disorder (GAD) are chronically anxious and worried in most situations. (Review Table 7.7.) Psychodynamic theories attribute GAD to the inability to quell neurotic and moral anxiety. Humanistic theory attributes GAD to being compelled to meet conditions of worth in order to feel good about oneself. Existential theory attributes GAD to existential or death anxiety. Cognitive theories argue that people with GAD appear more vigilant for threatening information, even on an unconscious level. (Review Table 7.8.)

■ Benzodiazepines can produce short-term relief for some people with GAD but are not suitable in the long-term treatment of GAD. A new drug called buspirone and the antidepressants appear helpful in treating GAD.

■ Cognitive-behavioral therapies focus on changing the catastrophic thinking styles of people with GAD and have been shown to reduce acute symptoms and to prevent relapse in the majority of people.

■ Obsessions are thoughts, images, ideas, or impulses that are persistent, are intrusive, and cause distress, and they commonly focus on contamination, sex, violence, and repeated doubts. (Review Table 7.9.) Compulsions are repetitive behaviors or mental acts that the individual feels he or she must perform to erase his or her obsessions.

■ One biological theory of obessive-compulsive disorder (OCD) speculates that the areas of the brain involved in the execution of primitive patterns of behavior, such as washing rituals, may be impaired in people with OCD. These areas of the brain are rich in the neurotransmitter serotonin, and drugs that regulate serotonin have proven helpful in the treatment of OCD. (Review Table 7.10 and Figure 7.12.)

■ Psychodynamic theories of OCD suggest that obsessions and compulsions symbolize unconscious conflicts or impulses. Psychodynamic therapies, which focus on helping clients gain insight into these unconscious conflicts or impulses, are not effective with OCD, however.

■ Cognitive-behavioral theories suggest that people with OCD think in ways that make them unable to turn off the negative, intrusive thoughts that most people have occasionally. Compulsive behaviors develop through operant conditioning when people are reinforced for behaviors that reduce anxiety. (Review Table 7.10.)

■ The most effective drug therapies for OCD are the antidepressants known as selective serotonin reuptake inhibitors.

■ Cognitive-behavioral therapies have also proven helpful for OCD. These therapies expose OCD clients to the content of their obsessions while preventing compulsive behavior, so that the anxiety over the obsessions and the compulsions to do the behaviors are extinguished.

■ Social perspectives on the anxiety disorders focus on differences between groups in the rates and expression of anxiety disorders. Women have higher rates of almost all the anxiety disorders than do men.

- Social theorists suggest that women are chronically anxious because they fear separation from others or because they truly are in greater danger of sexual or physical abuse than are men. Another theory is that men are punished for exhibiting signs of anxiety, whereas women are not, so men cope with their anxiety through adaptive or maladaptive activities, whereas women go on to develop anxiety disorders.

- Cultures may differ in their expression of anxiety disorders, or they may have distinct types of anxiety disorders not found in other cultures.

MindMap CD-ROM

The following resources on the MindMap CD-ROM that came with this text will help you to master the content of this chapter and prepare for tests:

- Interactive Segment: Measuring Anxiety
- Videos: Agoraphobia; OCD
- Chapter Timeline
- Chapter Quiz

Key Terms

anxiety 220

neurosis 221

panic attacks 222

panic disorder 222

norepinephrine 223

locus ceruleus 223

limbic system 224

anxiety sensitivity 225

interoceptive awareness 226

tricyclic antidepressants 227

selective serotonin reuptake inhibitors (SSRIs) 227

benzodiazepines 228

systematic desensitization therapy 229

agoraphobia 232

specific phobias 234

animal type phobias 234

natural environment type phobias 234

situational type phobias 234

blood-injection-injury type phobias 234

social phobia 235

negative reinforcement 238

prepared classical conditioning 240

applied tension technique 242

modeling 243

flooding 243

generalized anxiety disorder (GAD) 245

realistic anxiety 246

neurotic anxiety 246

moral anxiety 246

conditions of worth 247

existential anxiety 247

automatic thoughts 248

gamma-aminobutyric acid (GABA) 249

buspirone 250

obsessions 251

compulsions 251

obsessive-compulsive disorder (OCD) 251

caudate nucleus 254

Chapter 8

Day Dream
by Daniel Nevis

*The image of myself which I try to create in my own
mind in order that I may love myself is very different
from the image which I try to create in the minds of
others in order that they may love me.*

—W. H. Auden, "Hic et Ille," *The Dyer's Hand* (1963)

Somatoform and Dissociative Disorders <

Extraordinary People

■ Anna O.

Somatoform Disorders

People with conversion disorder completely lose functioning in a part of their bodies, apparently for psychological reasons. These disorders arise most commonly in response to extreme stress. Psychodynamic treatments involve helping people make the links between their symptoms and traumatic memories. Behavioral treatments focus on relieving people's anxiety about the initiating traumas through desensitization and exposure treatments.

People with somatization disorder have histories of multiple physical complaints for which there are no organic causes but for which they have sought a great deal of medical help. People with pain disorder focus their complaints on pain symptoms. These disorders may represent acceptable ways of expressing distress, especially for people in certain cultures. Cognitive theories of these disorders suggest that they are due to the catastrophization of physical symptoms. Treatment for these disorders involves helping people cope more adaptively with the stresses they face.

People with hypochondriasis worry chronically that they may be ill, even when they have no physical symptoms and have been thoroughly checked by medical professionals. The causes and treatments for hypochondriasis are similar to those for somatization disorder.

People with body dysmorphic disorder are excessively preoccupied with a part of their bodies and go to elaborate means to change that part of their bodies. This disorder may be a form of obsessive-compulsive disorder.

Dissociative Disorders

People with dissociative identity disorder (DID) develop multiple separate personalities. Dissociative identity disorder may develop in people who experience severe traumas, especially during childhood, and who use self-hypnosis to create "alters" to help them cope with these traumas. Treatment for dissociative identity disorder involves discovering the functions of all the personalities and helping the individual integrate these personalities and find more adaptive ways of coping with stress.

People with dissociative fugue move away from home and assume a new identity, with complete amnesia for their previous lives. Fugue states may arise following major traumas.

People with dissociative amnesia lose their memory for important facts about their lives and personal identities, apparently for psychological reasons. Psychologically based amnesias most frequently occur following traumatic events, such as sexual assaults. Depersonalization experiences involve a sense that one is detached from one's own mental processes or body.

Taking Psychology Personally

■ Dissociation in Everyday Life

Chapter Integration

The somatoform and dissociative disorders provide several examples of how psychological factors can influence apparent physical functioning.

Extraordinary People

Anna O.

One of the most famous single cases in the annals of psychology and psychiatry was that of Anna O., a young Viennese woman whose real name was Bertha Pappenheim. She was born in Vienna on February 27, 1859, in a wealthy Orthodox Jewish family. Pappenheim became ill in 1880 at the age of 21, around the time of her father's serious illness and eventual death. Josef Breuer, a colleague of Freud's who had treated Pappenheim, wrote about her:

> Up to the onset of the disease, the patient showed no sign of nervousness, not even during pubescence. She had a keen, intuitive intellect, and a craving for psychic fodder, which she did not, however, receive after she left school. She was endowed with a sensitiveness for poetry and fantasy, which was, however, controlled by a very strong and critical mind. . . . Her will was energetic, impenetrable, and persevering, sometimes mounting to selfishness; it relinquished its aim only out of kindness and for the sake of others. . . . Her moods always showed a slight tendency to an excess of merriment or sadness, which made her more or less temperamental. . . . With her puritanically-minded family, this girl of overflowing mental vitality led a most monotonous existence. . . .
>
> Upon her father's illness, in rapid succession there seemingly developed a series of new and severe disturbances.
>
> Left-sided occipital pain; convergent strabismus (diplopia), which was markedly aggravated through excitement. She complained that the wall was falling over (obliquus affection). Profound analyzable visual disturbances, paresis of the anterior muscles of the throat, to the extent that the head could finally be moved only if the patient pressed it backward between her raised shoulders and then moved her whole back. Contractures and anesthesia of the right upper extremity, and somewhat later of the right lower extremity. . . . (Quoted in Edinger, 1963)

Bertha Pappenheim, a patient of Breuer's and Freud's, had several conversion symptoms. Breuer treated Pappenheim by asking her to talk about her symptoms under hypnosis, and after 18 months she seemed to be losing her symptoms. Pappenheim dubbed this the "talking cure." After Breuer told Pappenheim he thought she was well and he would not be seeing her again, later that evening he was called back to her house, where he found Pappenheim thrashing around in her bed, going through imaginary childbirth. Pappenheim claimed that the baby was Breuer's. He calmed her down by hypnotizing her but soon fled the house and never saw her again. Pappenheim remained ill intermittently for six years but, by age 30, had recovered. Breuer collaborated with Sigmund Freud in writing about Anna O., and their descriptions of the talking cure launched psychoanalysis as a form of psychotherapy.

Bertha Pappenheim, or Anna O., appeared to suffer from what is now called a *somatoform disorder*— she experienced physiological symptoms that Breuer argued were the result of painful memories or emotions she was not able to confront. In this chapter, we discuss the somatoform disorders, as well as the *dissociative disorders*, in which people develop multiple separate personalities or completely lose their memory for significant portions of their lives.

Some theorists consider both of these sets of disorders to be the result of an extreme form of escape used by some people facing traumatic experiences or intolerable distress. This form of escape is known as dissociation, a process in which different parts of an individual's identity, memories, or consciousness become split off from one another.

The somatoform and dissociative disorders have a long history in psychology. As the story of Bertha Pappenheim illustrates, these phenomena were the material for much of the early theorizing by Breuer, Freud, and other psychoanalysts. In recent years, these disorders, and the idea that people can completely lose conscious access to painful memories and emotions through dissociation, have become very controversial, and we will discuss that controversy at the end of this chapter. First, however, let's explore the nature of somatoform disorders.

SOMATOFORM DISORDERS

The **somatoform disorders** are a group of disorders in which people experience significant physical symptoms for which there is no apparent organic cause. Often, these symptoms are inconsistent with possible physiological processes, and there is strong reason to believe that psychological factors are involved. People with somatoform disorders usually do not consciously produce or control the symptoms. Instead, they truly experience the symptoms, and the symptoms pass only when the psychological factors that led to the symptoms are resolved.

One of the great difficulties in diagnosing somatoform disorders is the possibility that an individual has a real physical disorder that is simply difficult to detect or diagnose. Many of us have friends or relatives who complained to their physicians for years about specific physical symptoms, which the physicians attributed to "nervousness" or "attention seeking" but which later were determined to be early symptoms of serious disease. The diagnosis of somatoform disorder is easier when the psychological factors leading to the development of the symptoms can clearly be identi-

fied or when physical examination can prove that the symptoms cannot be physiologically possible. For example, when a child is perfectly healthy on weekends but has terrible stomachaches in the morning on school days, the stomachaches may be due to distress over going to school. A more extreme example of a somatoform disorder is *pseudocyesis*, or false pregnancy, in which a woman believes she is pregnant but physical examination and laboratory tests confirm that she is not.

Distinction Between Somatoform and Related Disorders

The somatoform disorders are not the same as the **psychosomatic disorders**, which are medical disorders in which people have an actual physical illness or defect, such as high blood pressure, that can be documented with medical tests and that is being worsened by psychological factors. Instead, a person with a somatoform disorder does not have any illness or defect that can be documented with tests (see the Concept Overview in Table 8.1).

Somatoform disorders are also different from **malingering,** in which people fake a symptom or disorder in order to avoid an unwanted situation, such as military service, or in order to gain something, such as insurance payments. Again, an individual with a somatoform disorder subjectively experiences the symptoms, but there is no organic basis for the symptoms.

Finally, somatoform disorders are different from **factitious disorders,** in which a person deliberately fakes an illness to gain medical attention. Factitious disorders are also referred to as *Munchhausen's syndrome*. Note that the major difference between malingering and factitious disorders is the motivation for faking symptoms—in malingering the symptoms help an individual avoid an unwanted situation, whereas in factitious disorders

TABLE 8.1 Concept Overview

Distinctions Between Somatoform and Related Syndromes

Somatoform Disorders	Psychosomatic Disorders	Malingering	Factitious Disorders
Subjective experience of many physical symptoms, with no organic cause	Actual physical illness present and psychological factors seem to be contributing to the illness	Deliberate faking of physical symptoms to avoid an unpleasant situation, such as military duty	Deliberate faking of physical illness to gain medical attention

the symptoms are intentionally created to gain medical attention.

In recent years, several cases of **factitious disorder by proxy** have come to light. In these tragic cases, parents have faked or even created illnesses in their children in order to gain attention for themselves. They act as devoted and long-suffering protectors of their children, drawing praise for their dedicated nursing. Their children are subjected to unnecessary and often dangerous medical procedures and may actually die from their parents' attempts to make them ill. Seven-year-old Jennifer Bush appeared to be one victim of factitious disorder by proxy:

Sitting beside Hillary Clinton at a meeting on Capitol Hill, Jennifer Bush cut a heart-breaking figure. The 7-year-old Coral Springs, Florida, girl with big eyes and a perky red bow atop her little Dutch-boy coif seemed the perfect poster child for the Administration's health-care reform plan. Chronically ill almost from birth, Jennifer had already endured nearly 200 hospitalizations and 40 operations, and her $2 million–plus medical bill had exhausted the family's health-insurance benefits. Not surprisingly, Jennifer became a media darling, appearing on the *Today* show and on the front page of many newspapers.

Now it appears that Jennifer's suffering may have been much worse than was ever reported. Florida officials arrested Jennifer's seemingly devoted mother Kathleen Bush and charged her with aggravated child abuse and fraud. According to authorities, Bush, 38, deliberately caused her daughter's ailments by dosing her with unprescribed drugs, tampering with her medications, and even contaminating her feeding tube with fecal bacteria. As a result, say officials, Jennifer was subjected to dozens of needless operations and invasive procedures. Bush has denied all charges.

Almost as shocking as the charges against Jennifer's mother, however, is the fact that it took more than 4 years of warnings before state authorities placed the child under protective custody. Nurses at Coral Springs Medical Center began noticing as early as 1991—when Jennifer was just 4—that her condition seemed to worsen whenever her mother visited. . . .

State officials reopened the investigation last April, after receiving an anonymous complaint. According to the arrest affidavit, once her mother was informed of the inquiry, Jennifer's condition improved dramatically. In the preceding 9 months she had been hospitalized seven times for a total of 83 days. In the 9 months afterward she was admitted just once for 4 days. (Toufexis, 1996, p. 70)

Why would it take so long for authorities to intervene in a case such as this? Parents with factitious disorder by proxy may be very adept at hiding what they are doing to their children, especially if they have a medical background. Also, authorities must be extremely cautious about accusing a parent of causing harm to his or her children because of the great repercussions of falsely accusing parents, including the destruction of reputations, careers, and family relationships.

There are five types of somatoform disorders: conversion disorder, somatization disorder, pain disorder, hypochondriasis, and body dysmorphic disorder (see the Concept Overview in Table 8.2). Except for body dysmorphic disorder, each of these is characterized by the experience of one or

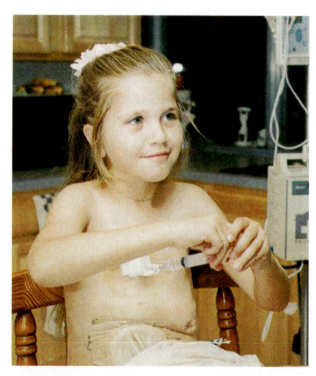

Jennifer Bush has endured hundreds of medical treatments and surgeries in her young life. Her mother was accused of causing Jennifer's illness to gain attention of physicians and the media.

TABLE 8.2 Concept Overview

Somatoform Disorders

The somatoform disorders are characterized by physical symptoms or complaints that appear to have psychological causes.

Disorders	Key Features
Conversion disorder	Loss of functioning in a part of the body for psychological rather than the physical reasons
Somatization disorder	History of complaints about physical symptoms, affecting many different areas of the body, for which medical attention has been sought but that appear to have no physical cause
Pain disorder	History of complaints about pain for which medical attention has been sought but that appears to have no physical cause
Hypochondriasis	Chronic worry that one has a physical disease in the absence of evidence that one does; frequent seeking of medical attention
Body dysmorphic disorder	Excessive preoccupation with a part of the body the person believes is defective

more physical symptoms. Body dysmorphic disorder involves a preoccupation with an imagined defect in one's appearance that is so severe that it interferes with one's functioning in life.

One study of 294 patients admitted to a hospital for medical symptoms examined the prevalence of somatoform disorders (excluding body dysmorphic disorder) and found them quite common. About 20 percent of patients were diagnosed with one or more somatoform disorders (Fink, Hansen, & Oxhøj, 2004). About one-third of these patients also had another psychiatric diagnosis, most often depression or anxiety. These patients were four times more likely than patients without somatoform disorders to have frequently been admitted to the hospital in the past and six times more likely to be heavy users of outpatient primary care facilities.

Conversion Disorder

The most dramatic type of somatoform disorder is **conversion disorder.** People with this disorder lose functioning in a part of their bodies, apparently due to neurological or other medical causes. Some of the most common conversion symptoms are paralysis, blindness, mutism, seizures, hearing loss, severe loss of coordination, and anesthesia in a limb. Conversion disorder typically involves one specific symptom, such as blindness or paralysis, but a person can have repeated episodes of conversion involving different parts of the body. Usually, the symptom develops suddenly following an extreme psychological stressor. A fascinating but

TABLE 8.3 DSM-IV-TR

Diagnostic Criteria for Conversion Disorder

Conversion disorder is diagnosed when individuals lose functioning in a part of their bodies apparently due to neurological or other medical conditions.

A. One or more symptoms or deficits affecting voluntary motor or sensory function that appear due to a neurological or medical condition.

B. Pyschological factors appear to be associated with the onset worsening of the symptoms or deficit.

C. The symptom or deficit is not intentionally produced or faked.

D. The symptom of deficit cannot be fully explained by a condition, the effects of drugs.

Source: Reprinted with permission from the *Diagnostic and Statistical Manual of Mental Disorders,* Fourth Edition, Text Revision. Copyright © 2000 American Psychiatric Association.

controversial feature of conversion disorders is *la belle indifference*, "the beautiful indifference"— people appear completely unconcerned about the loss of functioning they are experiencing (see the DSM-IV-TR criteria in Table 8.3).

Conversion disorder is relatively rare. One study of nearly 300 hospital patients estimated that 2.7 percent of the men and none of the women were suffering from a conversion disorder (Fink et al., 2004).

Theories of Conversion Disorder

Conversion disorder was formerly referred to as *conversion hysteria,* after the Greek word *hystera,* for "womb." Centuries ago, physicians believed that only women develop conversion symptoms and that these symptoms arose when a woman's desires for sexual gratification and children were not fulfilled, causing her womb to dislodge and wander (Veith, 1965). The theory was that the womb wandered into various parts of the body, such as the throat or the leg, causing related symptoms, such as a sensation of choking or paralysis. It is known now that conversion symptoms have nothing to do with wandering wombs and that, although they are more common in women than in men, men as well as women can develop these symptoms (Phillips, 2001).

Sigmund Freud became fascinated with conversion symptoms early in his career. One particularly dramatic conversion symptom is **glove anesthesia,** in which people lose all feeling in one hand, as if they were wearing a glove that wiped out physical sensation. This pattern of feeling loss cannot be caused physiologically, however, because the nerves in the hand do not provide feeling in a glovelike pattern. Freud found that these people tended to regain feeling in their hands when, usually under hypnosis, they recalled painful memories or emotions that had been blocked from consciousness.

The study of patients with severe dissociative experiences contributed much to Freud's theory of the structure of the mind and the role of repression in serious psychopathology. Freud and his contemporaries viewed conversion symptoms as results of the transfer of the psychic energy attached to repressed emotions or memories into physical symptoms. The symptoms often symbolized the specific concerns or memories that were being repressed.

It is difficult to prove the psychoanalytic theory, but some studies have provided evidence that could be interpreted as supporting it. Conversion symptoms were apparently quite common during the two world wars, when soldiers inexplicably became paralyzed or blind and therefore were unable to return to the front (Ironside & Batchelor, 1945). Many of the soldiers seemed unconcerned about their paralysis or blindness, showing *la belle indifference.* Sometimes, the physical symptoms represented traumas the soldiers had witnessed. For example, a soldier who has stabbed a civilian in the throat might lose the ability to talk.

Children can have conversion symptoms as well. Most often, their symptoms mimic those of someone they are close to who has a real illness

(Grattan-Smith, Fairly, & Procopis, 1988; Spierings et al., 1990). For example, a child whose cherished grandfather has had a stroke and has lost functioning on his right side may become unable to use his right arm.

Conversion symptoms may be more common among sexual abuse survivors (Anderson, Yasenik, & Ross, 1993). Consider the following case of a woman who was raped and later developed both posttraumatic stress disorder (see Chapter 6) and conversion mutism.

CASE STUDY

At the time she sought treatment, Jane was a 32-year-old woman living with her 15-year-old son and employed as a lower-level executive. When she was 24, two men entered her home after midnight, held a knife to her throat, and threatened to kill her if she made a sound or struggled. They raped her orally and vaginally in front of her son, who was 7 at the time, and then locked them in the basement before leaving. Several weeks after the rape, Jane's mother, to whom she was very close, died of cancer. Jane felt she had to be "the strong one" in the family and prided herself because she "never broke down."

At the age of 31, during an abusive relationship with a live-in boyfriend, Jane developed conversion mutism. In the midst of attempting to ask her boyfriend to leave her house, she was unable to produce any sound. After several months of treatment with a speech therapist, Jane became able to whisper quietly but did not regain her normal speech. The speech therapist referred Jane to a clinic for the treatment of rape-related PTSD.

The pretreatment interview confirmed that Jane suffered from chronic PTSD as a result of the rape. She presented with fears, panicky reactions, nightmares, flashbacks, and intrusive thoughts about the assault. She reported attempts to avoid thinking about the assault and situations that reminded her of it and feelings of detachment from others. She also complained of sleep problems, exaggerated startle, and hyperalertness. Jane was moderately depressed and quite anxious. During the intake interview, Jane indicated that

(continued)

she had never verbally expressed her feelings about the assault and believed that this constriction underlied her inability to speak. (Rothbaum & Foa, 1991, pp. 453–454)

Recent research suggests that people with conversion symptoms are highly hypnotizable (Roelofs et al., 2002). This supports the idea that conversion symptoms result from spontaneous self-hypnosis, in which sensory or motor functions are dissociated, or split off, from consciousness in reaction to extreme stress.

A behavioral theory of conversion disorder was proposed by Ullman and Krasner (1975), who argued that people with this disorder attempt to behave in accord with their conception of how a person with a neurological disease would act in order to secure some end. Thus, this theory views conversion disorder as being created by an individual to gain attention or support, or to avoid an aversive situation, such as being returned to combat duty.

Distinguishing Conversion Disorder from Physical Disorders

For a conversion disorder to be diagnosed, it must be shown that there is no physiological cause for the individual's symptoms. Sometimes, a physiological cause of symptoms can be definitively ruled out, as in false pregnancy. Often, however, physiological tests cannot give definitive proof that a person's symptoms do not have physical causes.

Over the years, a number of studies have suggested that many people diagnosed with conversion disorder were actually suffering from a physical disorder that the diagnostic tests of the times could not identify. For example, one study found that 62.5 percent of people diagnosed with conversion symptoms later were found to have a medical disease, compared with only 5.3 percent of people not diagnosed with conversion symptoms (Watson & Buranen, 1979). The most common medical problem found in the conversion group was head injury, which usually occurred about six months before the conversion symptoms began. Other common problems were stroke, encephalitis, and brain tumors (see also Fishbain & Goldberg, 1991; Watson & Buranen, 1979).

If diagnostic tests cannot establish a physical cause for puzzling symptoms, then clinicians will try to determine whether the conversion symptoms are consistent with the way the body works. For example, recall that glove anesthesia violates what is known about the innervation of the hand, because the anesthesia usually begins abruptly at the wrist and extends throughout the hand. As Figure 8.1 shows, however, the nerves in the hand are distributed in a way that makes this pattern of anesthesia highly unlikely. Similarly, a person with a conversion paralysis from the waist down may not show the deterioration of the muscles in the legs that a person with a physical paralysis typically shows over time. Still, distinguishing conversion disorder from a physical disorder that is simply difficult to diagnose can be tricky.

With increases in the sophistication of tests to diagnose physical disorders, such as the use of neuroimaging techniques to identify pathologies that are not detectable by other methods, physicians have become better able to differentiate physical disorders from conversion symptoms. Interestingly, a few investigators are using neuroimaging techniques to try to understand how conversion symptoms occur (Ron, 2001).

For example, Vuilleumier and colleagues (2001) used single photon emission computerized tomography (SPECT) to examine seven patients for whom no organic cause could be found for their loss of functioning. They applied a vibration to both hands, a stimulus that typically causes widespread activity in the sensory and motor areas of the brain. The SPECT recorded activity in sensory and motor areas on both sides of the brain but recorded reduced activity in the thalamus and basal ganglia on the sides of the brain opposite the side of the body in which the patient had loss of

FIGURE 8.1   **Glove Anesthesia.** In the conversion symptom called glove anesthesia, the entire hand from finger tips to wrist become numb. Actual physical damage to the ulnar nerve, in contrast, causes anesthesia in the ring finger and little finger and beyond the wrist partway up the arm; damage to the radial nerve causes insensitivity only in parts of the ring, middle, and index fingers and the thumb and partway up the arm.

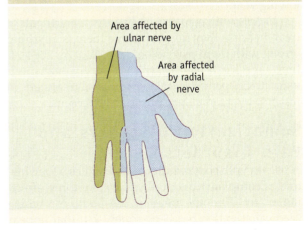

Area affected by ulnar nerve

Area affected by radial nerve

functioning. The authors suggested that emotional stressors can inhibit the circuits between sensorimotor areas of the brain and areas more involved in emotions (such as the thalamus and basal ganglia), resulting in loss of sensation or motor control.

Treating Conversion Disorder

Psychoanalytic treatment for conversion disorder focuses on the expression of painful emotions and memories and insight into the relationship between these and the conversion symptoms (Temple, 2001). Chronic conversion disorder is more difficult to treat. When symptoms are present for more than a month, the person's history often resembles somatization disorder (discussed in the section "Somatization Disorders and Pain Disorders") and is treated as such.

Behavioral treatments focus on relieving the person's anxiety around the initial trauma that caused the conversion symptoms and on reducing any benefits the person is receiving from the conversion symptoms. For example, the treatment of Jane, the woman in the case study, involved both systematic desensitization therapy and exposure therapy (refer to Chapter 6). A hierarchy of situations that Jane avoided, mostly situations that reminded her of her rape, was constructed. For the exposure, Jane was aided in approaching the situations that made her feel anxious and in progressing up her hierarchy to increasingly more feared situations, while practicing relaxation techniques. During the imagery sessions, Jane recounted the details of the assault first in general terms and later in great detail, including the details of the situation and the details of her physiological and cognitive reactions to the assault. At first, Jane was able to describe the assault in only a whisper, but she cried in full volume. After crying, Jane's speech became increasingly louder, with occasional words uttered in full volume. Eventually, she regained a full-volume voice. Following treatment, Jane's PTSD symptoms also decreased and diminished further over the following year.

People with conversion disorder are difficult to treat, because they do not believe there is anything wrong with them psychologically (Brown, 2004). If they have *la belle indifference,* they are not even motivated to cooperate with psychological treatment in order to overcome their physical symptoms.

Somatization Disorders and Pain Disorders

A person with **somatization disorder** has a long history of complaints about physical symptoms, affecting many different areas of the body, for which medical attention has been sought but that appear to have no physical cause (see the DSM-IV-TR crite-

TABLE 8.4   DSM-IV-TR

Diagnostic Criteria for Somatization Disorder

Somatization is diagnosed when individuals have a history of numerous physical complains for which no medical causes can be found.

A. A history of many physical complaints over a period of several years, for which the person seeks treatment

B. Symptoms in each of the following areas must occur at some time during the course of the disorder:
   a. Pain symptoms in at least four areas of the body (e.g., head, back, rectum, legs)
   b. At least two gastrointestinal symptoms other that pain (e.g., nausea, diarrhea)
   c. At least one sexual symptom
   d. At least one apparently neurological symptom (e.g., paralysis, double vision, deafness)

C. The symptom or deficit cannot be fully explained by a medical condition, the effects of drugs.

Source: Reprinted with permission from the *Diagnostic and Statistical Manual of Mental Disorders,* Fourth Edition, Text Revision. Copyright © 2000 American Psychiatric Association.

ria in Table 8.4). To receive a diagnosis of somatization disorder, a person has to complain of pain symptoms in at least four areas of the body, including two gastrointestinal symptoms (such as nausea and diarrhea), a sexual symptom (such as menstrual difficulties or painful intercourse), and an apparent neurological symptom (such as double vision or paralysis) (APA, 2000). A person with somatization disorder often goes from physician to physician, looking for attention and sympathy and for that one test that will prove that he or she really is sick.

People with somatization disorder may also report loss of functioning in a part of the body, as do people with conversion disorder. In somatization disorder, this loss of functioning is just one of a multitude of physical complaints, but, in conversion disorder, the loss of functioning may be the person's only complaint.

People who complain only of chronic pain may be given the diagnosis of **pain disorder.** In contrast, people with somatization disorder must report symptoms in each of four areas in order to be diagnosed with this disorder. Because most of what is known about pain disorder is encompassed in what is known about somatization disorder, we will discuss these two disorders together in this section.

It is extremely important for physicians not to assume that an individual has a psychological problem just because he or she cannot identify the cause of the physical complaints. Somatization disorder should be diagnosed only when the person has a clear history of multiple physical complaints for which no organic causes can be found. These complaints are usually presented in vague, dramatic, or exaggerated ways, and the individual may have insisted on medical procedures, even surgeries, that clearly were not necessary. One study of 191 persons in a general medicine outpatient clinic found that about 40 percent who had physical symptoms for which no organic causes could be found met the diagnostic criteria for a somatization disorder, meaning they had long histories of vague and multiple physical complaints with no apparent organic causes (Van Hemert et al., 1993).

As with conversion disorder, people with somatization or pain disorder may be prone to periods of anxiety and depression that they cannot express or cope with adaptively. They either somatize their distress or mask the distress in alcohol abuse or antisocial behavior. One large study of people with somatization disorder found that 76 percent had lifetime histories of episodes of major depression (Rief, Hiller, & Margraf, 1998; see also Feder et al., 2001; Katon, Sullivan, & Walker, 2001). In addition, people with the disorder frequently have histories of anxiety disorders, drug abuse, and personality disorders (Noyes et al., 2001).

Moderate degrees of somatization are apparently quite common. Very few people tend to meet the diagnostic criteria for somatization disorder (Katon et al., 2001). For example, one study found that 4.40 percent of a randomly selected sample of adults had a history of significant somatization, but only 0.03 percent met the criteria for somatization disorder (Escobar et al., 1987). A more recent study of hospital patients found that 3.3 percent of the women but none of the men qualified for a diagnosis of somatization disorder (Fink et al., 2004). Somatization tends to be more common in women than in men (Feder et al., 2001). Women have more periods of depression and anxiety than do men but are not always comfortable in expressing their distress directly, instead experiencing it in physical symptoms.

There also appear to be cultural variations in the prevalence of somatization disorder. Studies in China, Latin America, and Rwanda and studies of Asian and Hispanic/Latino groups in the United States have found that persons from these cultures are more likely to have somatization disorder than are European Americans (Canino, Rubio-Stipec, & Bravo, 1988; Escobar et al., 1987; Hagengimana et al., 2003; Jun-mian, 1987; Shrout et al., 1992; Westermeyer et al., 1989). People from these cultures may have higher rates of somatization disorder because of norms of expressing distress in physical complaints rather than admitting to negative emotions. Traumatic events contributing to somatization and pain disorders may also be more common in people from these ethnic groups.

In the United States, somatization disorder also appears more common in older adults than in middle-aged adults (Feder et al., 2001). The cultural norms with which older adults were raised often prohibited admitting to depression or anxiety. For this reason, older adults who are depressed or anxious may be more likely to express their negative emotions in somatic complaints, which are acceptable and expected in old age. Young children also often express their distress in somatic complaints (Garber, Walker, & Zeman, 1991). They may not have the language to express difficult emotions but can say that they feel "bad" or that they have stomachaches or headaches. Ten to 30 percent of children and adolescents report having headaches or abdominal pain on a weekly basis (Fritz, Fritsch, & Hagino, 1997).

Somatization disorder tends to be a long-term problem. In a two-year study of people with somatization disorder and people with similar physical complaints for which an organic cause could be found, Craig and colleagues (1993) found that the symptoms of the people with somatization disorder lasted longer than the symptoms of those with medical illnesses. Moreover, changes in the symptoms of

Children sometimes express distress through somatic symptoms.

the people with somatization disorder mirrored their emotional well-being: When they were anxious or depressed, they reported more physical complaints than when they were not anxious or depressed.

It can be extremely difficult to differentiate between somatization disorder and organic disorders for which there are no definitive tests. For example, one disorder that is often confused with, or overlaps with, somatization disorder is chronic fatigue syndrome. Chronic fatigue syndrome involves a persistent, debilitating fatigue accompanied by symptoms resembling those of common viral infections (Manu, Lane, & Matthews, 1992). Chronic fatigue syndrome is a real medical syndrome, probably caused by infections and a poorly

functioning immune system. It is difficult to diagnose, and it involves many of the symptoms identified by people diagnosed with somatization disorder. In one study of 100 adults complaining of chronic fatigue syndrome, 15 met the diagnostic criteria of somatization disorder, meaning they had long histories of vague physical complaints involving many parts of their bodies (Manu, Lane, & Matthews, 1989). However, 85 percent had no history of somatic complaints.

Theories of Somatization Disorders and Pain Disorders

Family history studies of somatization and pain disorders find that the disorders run in families, primarily among female relatives (Phillips, 2001). Anxiety and depression are also common in the female relatives of people with somatization disorder (Garber et al., 1991). The male relatives of persons with somatization disorder also have higher than usual rates of alcoholism and personality disorder. Similarly, patients with pain disorder tend to have family histories of psychological problems, most often pain disorder in the female relatives and alcoholism in the male relatives (Phillips, 2001).

It is not clear that the transmission of somatization or pain disorder in families has to do with genetics. A large study of over 3,400 twins could not determine whether genetics or shared environments were responsible for the aggregation within families of somatization (Gillespie et al., 2000). The children of parents with somatization or pain disorder may model their parents' tendencies to somatize distress (Craig et al., 1993). Parents who are somatizers also are more likely to neglect their children, and the children may learn that the only way to receive care and attention is to be ill. This finding is in accord with a behavioral account of somatization and pain disorders, which views them as the result of reinforcements for "sickness behavior" that the individual has received over much of his or her lifetime (Ullman & Krasner, 1975).

A cognitive theory of somatization and pain disorders suggests that persons with these disorders tend to experience bodily sensations more intensely than other people, to pay more attention than others to physical symptoms, and to catastrophize these symptoms (Kirmayer & Taillefer, 1997) (see Figure 8.2). For example, such a person might have a slight case of indigestion but experience it as severe chest pain and interpret the pain as a sure sign of a heart attack. The person's interpretation of his experience may have a direct influence on his physiological processes, by increasing his heart rate or blood pressure, thereby maintaining and exacerbating his pain. Further, his cognitions will influence the way he presents symptoms to

FIGURE 8.2   **A Model of Somatization Disorder.** Biological and psychosocial factors may combine to lead to somatization disorder.

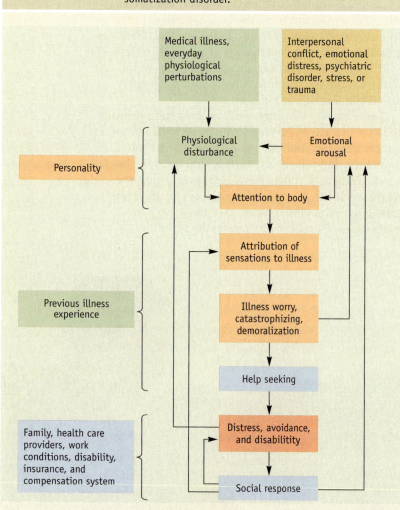

Source: Reprinted from p. 353 of "Somatoform Disorders,"by L. J. Kirmayer and S. Taillefer. In S. M. Turner and M. Hersen (Eds.), *Adult Psychopatholgy and Diagnosis*, 3rd ed., 1997, pp. 333–383. Copyright © 1997 John Wiley & Sons, Inc. Reprinted with permission of John Wiley & Sons, Inc.

his physician and family. As a result, physicians may prescribe more potent medication or order more diagnostic tests, and family members may express more sympathy, excuse the person from responsibilities, and otherwise encourage passive behavior (Turk & Ruby, 1992). In this way, the person's misinterpreting and catastrophizing of his symptoms are reinforced by his physician and family, increasing the likelihood that he will interpret future symptoms in similar ways.

As with conversion disorder, somatization disorder may be part of posttraumatic stress disorder experienced by a person who has experienced a severe stressor. Many people with somatization disorder have histories of physical or sexual abuse or other severe childhood adversity (Katon et al., 2001; Pribor et al., 1993).

Refugees and recent immigrants also have an increased risk for somatization disorder. For example, a study of Bhutanese refugees found that over half of those who had been tortured, and over one-fourth of those who had not been tortured, had a persistent pain disorder (van Ommeren et al., 2001). Another study found that immigrants to the United States from Central America and Mexico had higher rates of posttraumatic stress disorder and somatization disorder than either U.S.–born Mexican Americans or European Americans. Fifty-two percent of the Central Americans who had fled to the United States to escape war or political unrest had posttraumatic stress disorder and somatization disorder (Cervantes, Salgado de Snyder, & Padilla, 1989). Similarly, a study of Hmong immigrants to the United States, who had fled Cambodia during the Khmer Rouge regime, found 17 percent to have posttraumatic stress disorder characterized by moderate to severe somatizing symptoms (Westermeyer et al., 1989).

Treatments for Somatization and Pain Disorders

Convincing people with somatization or pain disorder that they need psychological treatment is not easy. These people have held tightly to the belief that they are physically ill despite dozens of physicians' telling them they are not and hundreds of medical tests' failing to establish a physical illness. If they do agree to psychological treatment, people with these disorders appear to respond well to intervention that teaches them to express negative feelings or memories and to understand the relationship between their emotions and their physical symptoms (Beutler et al., 1988).

Psychodynamic therapies focus on providing this insight into the connections between emotions and physical symptoms by helping people recall events and memories that may have triggered the symptoms. Behavior therapies attempt to determine the reinforcements the individual receives for his or her symptoms and to eliminate these reinforcements while increasing positive rewards for healthy behavior. Cognitive therapies for these disorders help people learn to interpret their physical symptoms appropriately and to avoid catastrophizing physical symptoms, much as in the cognitive treatment of panic symptoms (see Chapter 6 and Campo & Fritz, 2001). One study found that antidepressant medications (selective serotonin reuptake inhibitors) led to significant improvement in somatization symptoms in a sample of 15 people with somatization disorder (Menza et al., 2001).

Some clinicians use the belief systems and cultural traditions of the clients they are treating to motivate the clients to engage in therapy and to help them overcome their physical complaints. Following is an example of the use of cultural beliefs to treat a Hispanic woman with somatization disorder.

CASE STUDY Ellen was a 45-year-old woman who consulted many doctors for "high fever, vomiting, diarrhea, inability to eat, and rapid weight loss." After numerous negative lab tests, her doctor told her, "I can't go on with you; go to one of the *espiritistas* or a *curandera* (traditional healers)." A cousin then took her to a Spiritist center "for medicine." She was given herbal remedies: some baths and a tea of *molinillo* to take in the morning before eating. But the treatment focused mainly on the appearance of the spirit of a close friend who had died a month earlier from cancer. The spirit was looking for help from Ellen who had not gone to help during her friend's illness because of her own family problems. The main thrust of the healers' treatment plan was to help Ellen understand how she had to deal with the feelings of distress related to the stress of a paralyzed husband and caring for two small daughters alone. The spirit's influence on Ellen's body was an object lesson that was aimed at increasing her awareness of how her lifestyle was causing her to neglect the care of her own body and feelings much as she had neglected her dying friend. (Adapted from Koss, 1990, p. 82)

The spiritual healer in this case recognized the cause of Ellen's somatic complaints as stress, anger, and guilt; helped her link her physical symptoms with these emotions; and helped her find ways to cope more adaptively with the emotions. The context for this intervention was not cognitive therapy or another type of psychotherapy used by the dominant, non-Hispanic culture. Instead, the context was the cultural belief system concerning the role of spirits in producing physical symptoms.

Hypochondriasis

Somatization disorder and **hypochondriasis** are quite similar and may be variations of the same disorder. The primary distinction in the DSM-IV-TR between the two disorders is that people with somatization disorder actually experience physical symptoms and seek help for them, whereas people with hypochondriasis worry that they have a serious disease but do not always experience severe physical symptoms. However, when they do have any physical complaints, people with hypochondriasis are more likely to believe they should seek out medical attention immediately, whereas people with somatization disorder are more likely to wait and see how the bodily sensations develop (Rief et al., 1998). People with hypochondriasis may go through many medical procedures and float from physician to physician, sure that they have a dreaded disease. Often, their fears focus on a particular organ system. For example, a woman may be totally convinced that she has heart disease, even though the most sophisticated medical diagnostic tests have shown no evidence of heart disease. Carlos, in the following case study, was convinced something was wrong with his bowels.

CASE STUDY

Carlos, a married man of 39, came to the clinic, complaining, "I have trouble in my bowels and then it gets me in my head. My bowels just spasm on me, I get constipated." The patient's complaints dated back 12 years to an attack of "acute indigestion," in which he seemed to bloat up and pains developed in his abdomen and spread in several directions. He traced some of these pathways with his finger as he spoke. Carlos spent a month in bed at this time and then, based on an interpretation of something the doctor said, rested for another 2 months before working again. Words of reassurance from his doctor failed to take effect. He felt "sick, worried, and scared," feeling that he really would never get well again.

Carlos became very dependent upon the woman he married when he was 22 years old. He left most of the decisions to her and

showed little interest in sexual relations. His wife was several years older than he and did not seem to mind his totally passive approach to life. His attack of "acute indigestion" followed her death, 5 years after marriage, by 3 months during which he felt lost and hopeless. In time, he moved to a rural area and remarried. His second wife proved less willing to assume major responsibilities for him than the first, and she made sexual demands upon him that he felt unable to meet. He became more and more preoccupied with his gastrointestinal welfare. In the complete absence of community facilities for psychological assistance where he lived, prognosis for recovery from chronic partially disabling hypochondria was deemed poor. (Adapted from Cameron & Rychlak, 1985)

Diagnosable hypochondriasis is not very common. A study of 1,456 patients in a general medical practice found that only 3 percent met the diagnostic criteria for hypochondriasis (Escobar et al., 1998). Another study of hospital patients found that 2.1 percent of the men and 7.8 percent of the women were diagnosed with hypochondriasis (Fink et al., 2004).

Most studies of hypochondriasis have grouped people who have this disorder with people who have somatization disorder, in part because many people qualify for the diagnosis of both disorders. Thus, most of what is known about the causes of somatization disorder also applies to the causes of hypochondriasis. In particular, people with hypochondriasis appear very prone to chronic depression and anxiety and have family histories of these disorders (Barsky, Wyshak, & Klerman, 1992; Escobar et al., 1998). Their fears about their health often stem from general distress and an inability to cope with that distress in adaptive ways. People with hypochondriasis also tend to have dysfunctional beliefs about illness, assuming that serious illnesses are common, and they tend to misinterpret any physical change in themselves as a sign for concern (Marcus & Church, 2003).

As is the case with people who have somatization disorder, people who have hypochondriasis do not appreciate suggestions that their problems are caused by psychological factors and thus tend not to seek psychological treatment. When they do receive psychological treatment, it focuses on helping them understand the association between their symptoms and emotional distress and on helping

Dial 123-SICK and reach out to your fellow hypochondriacs.
© *The New Yorker Collection 1989 J.B. Handelsman from cartoon-bank.com. All rights reserved.*

them find more adaptive ways of coping with their distress.

Body Dysmorphic Disorder

People with **body dysmorphic disorder** are excessively preoccupied with a part of their bodies that they believe is defective. Although it is not clear whether there are gender differences in the prevalence of this disorder, men and women with body dysmorphic disorder tend to obsess about different parts of their bodies (Perugi et al., 1997; Phillips & Diaz, 1997). Women seem to be more concerned with their breasts, legs, hips, and weight, whereas men tend to be preoccupied with a small body build, their genitals, excessive body hair, and hair thinning. People with this disorder spend hours looking at their "deformed" body parts, perhaps in a mirror, and perform elaborate rituals to try to improve the parts or hide them. For example, they may spend hours styling their hair to hide the defects in their ears or wear heavy makeup to hide their defects. Many people with this disorder also seek out plastic surgery to change the offensive body parts (Phillips, 2001).

Case studies of some people with this disorder indicate that their perceptions of deformation can be so severe and bizarre as to be considered out of touch with reality (Phillips, 1991). Even if they do not lose touch with reality, some people with body

dysmorphic disorder have severe impairment in their functioning due to the disorder. For example, a study of 188 people with this disorder found that 98 percent avoided social activities because of their "deformity," 30 percent had become housebound, and about 20 percent had attempted suicide (Phillips & Diaz, 1997). Approximately 25 percent attempt suicide (Phillips, Kim, & Hudson, 1995).

Body dysmorphic disorder tends to begin in the teenage years and to become chronic if untreated. The average age of onset of this disorder is 16 years; on average, these people have four or more bodily preoccupations. Those who seek treatment wait an average of 6 years from the onset of their concerns before seeking treatment (Cororve & Gleaves, 2001).

CASE STUDY

Sydney was a popular 17-year-old who attended a suburban high school near Washington, DC. During the spring of her senior year, Sydney became preoccupied with her appearance and began to look constantly for her own image in windows and mirrors. In particular, Sydney began to notice that her nose was abnormally shaped. Her friends all told her that she was crazy when she expressed her concern, so she stopped talking about it to them. She began to apply makeup in an attempt to offset what she believed to be the contemptible contour of her nose. She started wearing her hair loosely, holding her head down much of the time, so that her face was partially obscured, and brushing her hair excessively to encourage it to fall forward around her face. Her distress grew, and she repeatedly begged her parents to let her have surgery to correct the shape of her nose, which she regarded as hideous. Her pleas turned to volatile arguments when her parents told her that her nose was fine and that they would not agree to surgery. Sydney started finding excuses not to go out with her friends and refused to date, because she could not stand the thought of anyone looking at her up close. She stayed home in her room, staring for hours in the mirror. She refused to attend her senior prom or graduation ceremony.

After high school, Sydney got a job as a night security guard, so that she could isolate herself as much as possible and not be seen by others. During the next seven years, she had

(continued)

five surgeries to change the shape of her nose. Each time, she became even more dissatisfied and obsessed with her appearance. Although everyone who knew Sydney thought she looked fine, she remained obsessed and tormented by her "defect," which dominated her life.

Although clinicians in Europe have frequently written about body dysmorphic disorder, it has been relatively ignored in the United States (Corove & Gleaves, 2001). The diagnosis was introduced in the DSM in the 1987 edition. Body dysmorphic disorder is highly comorbid with several disorders, including anxiety and depressive disorders, personality disorders, and substance use disorders (Corove & Gleaves, 2001).

One anxiety disorder that is relatively common among people with body dysmorphic disorder is obsessive-compulsive disorder (Phillips & Diaz, 1997). Some theorists believe that body dysmorphic disorder may be a form of obsessive-compulsive disorder, in which the person obsesses about a part of the body and engages in compulsive behaviors to change that part (see Corove & Gleaves, 2001; Phillips, 2001). An MRI study of the brains of eight women with body dysmorphic disorder found that they showed some of the same abnormalities in the caudate nucleus as are seen in obsessive-compulsive disorder (Rauch et al., 2003).

Other theorists point out the commonalities between body dysmorphic disorder and eating disorders, particularly the extreme overvaluing of

People with body dysmorphic disorder spend a great deal of time examining the parts of their body they feel are defective.

appearance, and suggest they are both variants of a body image disorder (Rosen & Ramirez, 1998). For now, body dysmorphic disorder remains classified as a somatoform disorder because it involves a preoccupation with bodily complaints.

Psychoanalytically oriented therapy for body dysmorphic disorder focuses on helping clients gain insight into the real concerns behind their obsession with a body part. Cognitive-behavioral therapies focus on challenging clients' maladaptive cognitions about the body, exposing them to feared situations concerning their bodies, extinguishing anxiety about their body parts, and preventing compulsive responses to those body parts (Corove & Gleaves, 2001). For example, a client may identify her ears as her deformed body part. The client could develop her hierarchy of things she would fear doing related to her ears, ranging from looking at herself in the mirror with her hair fully covering her ears to going out in public with her hair pulled back and her ears fully exposed. After the client has learned relaxation techniques, she would begin to work through the hierarchy, engaging in the feared behaviors, beginning with the least feared and using the relaxation techniques to quell anxiety. Eventually, the client would work up to the greatly feared situation of exposing her ears in public. At first, the therapist might contract with the client that she cannot engage in behaviors intended to hide the body part (such as putting her hair over her ears) for at least five minutes after going out in public. The eventual goal in therapy would be for the client's concerns about the body part to diminish totally and not affect her behavior or functioning. Empirical studies have supported the efficacy of cognitive-behavioral therapies in treating body dysmorphic disorder (Corove & Gleaves, 2001).

Finally, studies suggest that selective serotonin reuptake inhibitors (SSRIs) can be effective in some cases in reducing obsessional thought and compulsive behavior in persons with this disorder (Phillips & Najjar, 2003; Saxena, Winegrad, Duncan et al., 2001). This finding fuels theories that body dysmorphic disorder is a form of obsessive-compulsive disorder, because SSRIs are effective in treating obsessive-compulsive disorder as well (see Chapter 7).

SUMMING UP

- Somatoform disorders are a group of disorders in which people experience significant physical symptoms for which there is no apparent organic cause.

- Conversion disorder involves loss of functioning in a body part for no organic reason. Conversion symptoms often occur after trauma or stress, perhaps because the person cannot face memories or emotions associated with the trauma. Treatment for conversion disorder focuses on the expression of emotions or memories associated with the symptoms.

- Somatization disorder involves a long history of multiple physical complaints for which people have sought treatment but for which there is no apparent organic cause. Pain disorder involves only the experience of chronic, unexplainable pain. These disorders appear to be common, particularly among women, young children, the elderly, and people of Asian or Hispanic heritage.

- Hypochondriasis is a condition in which people worry chronically about having a dreaded disease, despite evidence that they do not. This disorder appears to be rare.

- In somatization disorder, pain disorder, and hypochondriasis, individuals often have a history of anxiety and depression. These disorders may represent acceptable ways of expressing emotional pain.

- Cognitive theories of the disorders say that they are due to excessive focus on physical symptoms and the tendency to catastrophize symptoms. Treatment for these disorders involves helping people identify the feelings and thoughts behind the symptoms and find more adaptive ways of coping.

- People with body dysmorphic disorder have an obsessional preoccupation with some parts of their bodies and make elaborate attempts to change these body parts. Treatments for body dysmorphic disorder include psychodynamic therapies to reveal underlying concerns, systematic desensitization therapy to reduce obsessions and compulsions about the body, and the use of selective serotonin reuptake inhibitors.

DISSOCIATIVE DISORDERS

Most of us occasionally have mild dissociative experiences (Aderibigbe, Bloch, & Walker, 2001; Seedat, Stein, & Forde, 2003). Daydreaming is a dissociative experience. When we daydream, we can lose consciousness of where we are and of what is going on around us. Becoming absorbed in a movie is also a dissociative experience.

Dissociative experiences are especially common when we are sleep-deprived and under stress. For example, a study of mentally healthy soldiers undergoing survival training in the U.S. Army found that over 90 percent reported dissociative symptoms, such as feeling as if they were separated from what was happening, as if they were watching themselves in a movie, in response to the stress of the training (Morgan et al., 2001). We discuss common dissociative symptoms in *Taking Psychology Personally: Dissociation in Everyday Life.*

Scientific interest in dissociative experiences has waxed and waned for more than a century (Kihlstrom, 2005). There was a great deal of interest in dissociation in nineteenth-century France and in the United States among neurologists and psychologists. French neurologist Pierre Janet viewed dissociation as a process in which systems of ideas are

Taking Psychology Personally

Dissociation in Everyday Life

You are driving down a familiar road, thinking about a recent conversation with a friend. Suddenly, you realize that you've driven several miles and don't remember traveling that section of the road. How did you get where you currently are? Obviously, you must have driven there, but you have no memory of passing the usual landmarks.

This kind of dissociative experience is quite common (Aderibigbe et al., 2001; Seedat et al., 2003). Researcher Colin Ross (1997) asked more than 1,000 adults, randomly selected from the community of Winnipeg in Canada, about a number of different dissociative experiences. The accompanying table on page 282 presents some of Ross' findings. Miss-

ing part of a conversation appears to be the most common dissociative experience, followed by being unsure whether you have actually carried through with something (such as brushing your teeth) or have only thought about it. These experiences seem quite benign. Farther down the list are somewhat more bizarre experiences, such as hearing voices in your head, feeling as though your body is not your own, and not recognizing objects or other people as real. As the table shows, even these rather bizarre experiences are reported as happening at least occasionally by a substantial percentage of "normal" people.

(continued)

Taking Psychology Personally (*continued*)

Dissociative Experiences in the General Population

These are the percentages of people in a random sample of 1,055 adults in Winnipeg, Canada who acknowledged ever having experienced each item and who fell into the pathological range for frequency of experiences of the item.

Experience	Percentage Acknowledging	Percentage in Pathological Range
Missing part of a conversation	83	29
Not sure whether one has done something or only thought about it	73	25
Remembering the past so vividly one seems to be reliving it	60	19
Talking out loud to oneself when alone	56	18
Not sure if remembered event happened or was a dream	55	13
Feeling as though one were two different people	47	12
So involved in fantasy that it seems real	45	11
Driving a car and realizing that one doesn't remember part of the trip	48	8
Finding notes or drawings that one must have done but doesn't remember doing	34	6
Seeing oneself as if looking at another person	29	4
Hearing voices inside one's head	26	7
Other people and objects do not seem real	26	4
Finding unfamiliar things among one's belongings	22	4
Feeling as though one's body is not one's own	23	4
Finding oneself in a place but unaware of how one got there	19	2
Finding oneself dressed in clothes one doesn't remember putting on	15	1
Not recognizing one's reflection in a mirror	14	1

Source: From C. A. Ross, *Dissociative Identity Disorder.* Copyright © 1997 John Wiley & Sons, Inc. Reprinted with permission of John Wiley & Sons, Inc.

How can we explain everyday dissociative experiences? They can be caused by many factors. Fatigue and stress are probably the most common causes. Binge drinking alcohol or taking other psychoactive drugs can cause many of the memory lapses shown in the table. Older adults whose short-term memories are fading often forget having done things, and, as we discuss in Chapter 14, several cognitive disorders can lead to memory lapses, even the inability to recognize faces. Most of the time, however, dissociative experiences are transient and do not signal any long-term problems.

Some people have dissociative experiences frequently enough that they interfere with their functioning. Ross (1997) categorized these people as in the "pathological range" of dissociative experiences. The percentage of people in his sample falling in this range for each of the experiences he studied is given in the righthand column of the table. You can see that occasional dissociative experiences are extremely common, but most of the more bizarre dissociative experiences occur infrequently enough that only a small percentage of people are categorized in the pathological range.

The next time you find yourself wondering how you got to where you are standing, or not remembering dressing in the clothes you are wearing, don't panic. Chances are that it is one of those everyday dissociative experiences we all have.

split off from consciousness but accessible through dreams and hypnosis. One case he investigated was that of a woman named Irene, who had no memory of the fact that her mother had died. However, during her sleep, Irene physically dramatized the events surrounding her mother's death.

After about 1910, interest in dissociative phenomena waned, partly because of the rise of behaviorism and biological approaches within psychology, which rejected the concept of repression and the use of techniques such as hypnosis in therapy. Ernest Hilgard (1977/1986) revitalized interest in dissociation in his experiments on the "hidden observer" phenomenon. He argued that there is an *active mode* to consciousness, which includes our conscious plans and desires and voluntary actions. In its passive *receptive mode*, the conscious registers and stores information in memory without being aware that the information has been processed, as if hidden observers were watching and recording events in people's lives without their awareness.

Hilgard and his associates (Hilgard, 1977/1986) conducted experimental studies in which participants were hypnotized and given a suggestion that they would feel no pain during a painful procedure but that they would remember the pain when the hypnotist gave them a specific cue. These participants, indeed, showed no awareness of pain during the procedure. When cued, they reported memories of the pain in a matter-of-fact fashion, as if a lucid, rational observer of the event had registered the event for the participant.

Other research has shown that some anesthetized surgical patients can later recall, under hypnosis, specific pieces of music played during the surgery. Again, it is as if a "hidden observer" is registering the events of the operations even while the patients are completely unconscious under anesthesia (see Kihlstrom, 2001; Kihlstrom & Couture, 1992; Kirsch & Lynn, 1998).

For most of us, the active and receptive modes of consciousness weave our experiences together so seamlessly that we do not notice any division between them. People who develop dissociative disorders may have chronic problems integrating their active and their receptive consciousness (Hilgard, 1992; Kihlstrom, 2001). That is, different aspects of consciousness in these people do not communicate with each other in normal ways but, rather, remain split and operate independently of each other.

We begin our discussion of specific dissociative disorders with dissociative identity disorder (DID), formerly known as *multiple personality disorder*. We then move to dissociative fugue, dissociative amnesia, and depersonalization disorder (see

the Concept Overview in Table 8.5). All these disorders involve frequent experiences in which various aspects of a person's "self" are split off from each other and felt as separate.

TABLE 8.5   Concept Overview

Key Features of the Dissociative Disorders in DSM-IV-TR

The dissociative disorders represent extreme experiences in which aspects of people identities split apart.

Disorder	Key Features
Dissociative identity disorder	There are separate, multiple personalities in the same individual. The personalitites may be aware of each other or may have amnesia for each other.
Dissociative fugue	The person moves away and assumes a new identity, with amnesia for the previous identity. There is no switching among personalities, as there is in dissociative identity disorder.
Dissociative amnesia	The person loses memory for important personal facts, including personal identity, with no apparent organic cause.
Depersonalization disorder	There are frequent episodes in which the individual feels detached from his or her mental state of body. The person does not develop new identities or have amnesia for these episodes.

Dissociative Identity Disorder

CASE STUDY

Eve White was a quiet, proper, unassuming woman, a full-time homemaker and devoted mother of a young daughter. She sought help from a psychiatrist for painful headaches that were occurring with increasing frequency. The psychiatrist decided that her headaches were related to arguments she was having with her husband over whether to raise their young daughter in the husband's church (Catholic) or in her church (Baptist). After undergoing some marital therapy, Mrs. White's marriage improved and her headaches subsided for a year or so.

Then, her husband recontacted her therapist, alarmed over changes in his wife's behavior. She had gone to visit a favorite cousin in a town 50 miles away and during the visit

(continued)

had behaved in a much more carefree and reckless manner than she usually did. Mrs. White told her husband over the phone that she was not going to return home, and the two had a terrible fight, which ended in an agreement to divorce. When Mrs. White did return home a few days later, however, she said she had no memory of the fight with her husband or, for that matter, of the visit with her cousin.

Shortly thereafter, Mrs. White apparently went shopping and bought hundreds of dollars worth of elaborate clothing, which the couple could not afford. When confronted by her husband about her expenditures, Mrs. White claimed to have no memory of buying the clothing.

At the urging of her husband, Mrs. White made an appointment with the therapist whom she had originally consulted about her headaches. In the session, she admitted that her headaches had returned and were much more severe now than before. Eventually, she also tearfully admitted that she had begun to hear a voice other than her own speaking inside her head and that she feared she was going insane. The therapist asked her more questions about the clothes-buying spree, and Mrs. White became more tense and had difficulty getting words out to discuss the incident. Then, as her therapist reported,

> The brooding look in her eyes became almost a stare. Eve seemed momentarily dazed. Suddenly her posture began to change. Her body slowly stiffened until she sat rigidly erect. An alien, inexplicable expression then came over her face. This was suddenly erased into utter blankness. The lines of her countenance seemed to shift in a barely visible, slow, rippling transformation. For a moment there was the impression of something arcane. Closing her eyes, she winced as she put her hands to her temples, pressed hard, and twisted them as if to combat sudden pain. A slight shudder passed over her entire body.
>
> Then the hands lightly dropped. She relaxed easily into an attitude of

comfort the physician had never before seen in this patient. A pair of blue eyes popped open. There was a quick reckless smile. In a bright, unfamiliar voice that sparked, the woman said, "Hi, there, Doc!"

Still busy with his own unassimilated surprise, the doctor heard himself say, "How do you feel now?"

"Why just fine—never better! How you doing yourself, Doc?"

Eve looked for a moment straight into his eyes. Her expression was that of one who is just barely able to restrain laughter. Her eyes rolled up and to one side for an instant, then the lids flicked softly before opening wide again. She tossed her head lightly with a little gesture that threw the fine dark hair forward onto her shoulder. A five-year-old might have so reacted to some sudden, unforeseen amusement. In the patient's gesture there was something of pert sauciness, something in which the artless play of a child and a scarcely conscious flirtatiousness mingled. . . .

"She's been having a real rough time. There's no doubt about that," the girl said carelessly. "I feel right sorry for her sometimes. She's such a damn dope though. . . . What she puts up with from that sorry Ralph White— and all her mooning over that little brat . . . ! To hell with it, I say!"

The doctor asked, "Who is 'she'?"

"Why, Eve White, of course. Your longsuffering, saintly, little patient."

"But aren't you Eve White?" he asked.

"That's for laughs," she exclaimed, a ripple of mirth in her tone. . . . "Why, I'm Eve Black," she said. . . . "I'm me and she's herself," the girl added. "I like to live and she don't. . . . Those dresses—well, I can tell you about them. I got out the other day, and I needed some dresses. I like good clothes. So I just went into town and bought what I wanted. I charged 'em to her husband, too!" She began to laugh softly. "You ought've seen the look on her silly face when he showed her what was in the cupboard!"

In later sessions, Eve Black told the psychiatrist of escapades in which she had stayed out all night, drinking, and then had gone "back in" in the morning to let Eve White deal with the hangover. At the beginning of therapy, Eve White had no consciousness of Eve Black or of more than 20 personalities eventually identified during therapy.

This story of *The Three Faces of Eve* is one of the most detailed and gripping accounts of someone diagnosed with dissociative identity disorder. Eve White eventually recovered from her disorder, integrating the aspects of her personality represented by Eve Black and her other personalities into one entity and living a healthy, normal life.

Dissociative identity disorder (DID) is one of the most controversial and fascinating disorders recognized in clinical psychology and psychiatry. People with this disorder have more than one distinct identity or personality, and many people have more than a dozen personalities. Each personality appears to have different ways of perceiving and relating to the world. Some theorists claim the alternate personalities, or *alters,* can have distinct facial expressions, speech characteristics, physiological responses, gestures, interpersonal styles, and attitudes (Miller, 1989; Putnam, 1991). They often are different ages and different genders and perform specific functions.

The movie *The Three Faces of Eve* depicted the story of a woman with dissociative identity disorder, who discovered extravagant articles of clothing in her closet that she didn't remember buying.

Reliable estimates of the prevalence of dissociative identity disorder are hard to come by. One study of psychiatric inpatients found that 1 percent could be diagnosed with DID (Rifkin et al., 1998). The vast majority of persons diagnosed with this disorder are adult women. It may be that the conditions leading to dissociative identity disorder are more commonly experienced by women than by men (Peterson, 1991). Among children diagnosed with dissociative identity disorder, however, the numbers of females and males appear to be more equal (Dell & Eisenhower, 1990). It may be that boys with dissociative identity disorder are more likely to be taken for treatment than are girls, so, as adults, males are less likely to continue to have the disorder than are females (Dell & Eisenhower, 1990). Or girls may be more likely than boys to experience traumas in adolescence that lead to dissociative identity disorder, which continues into adulthood.

There are some differences between the characteristics of the personalities of males and females with dissociative identity disorder. Males with dissociative identity disorder appear to be more aggressive than females with the disorder. In one study, 29 percent of male dissociative identity disorder patients had been convicted of crimes, compared with 10 percent of female dissociative identity disorder patients (Ross & Norton, 1989). Case reports suggest that females with dissociative identity disorder tend to have more somatic complaints than do males and may engage in more suicidal behavior (Kluft, 1985).

Symptoms of Dissociative Identity Disorder

The cardinal symptom in dissociative identity disorder is the presence of multiple alters with distinct qualities. These alters can take many forms and perform many functions. *Child alters*—alters who are young children, who do not age as the individual ages—appear to be the most common type (Ross, Norton, & Wozney, 1989). Childhood trauma is often associated with the development of dissociative identity disorder. A child alter may be created during a traumatic experience to become the victim of the trauma, while the "host" personality escapes into the protection of psychological oblivion. Alternately, an alter may be created as a type of big brother or sister to protect the host personality from traumas. When a child alter is "out," or in control of the individual's behavior, the adult may speak and act in a childlike way.

A second type of alter is the *persecutor personality.* These alters inflict pain or punishment on the

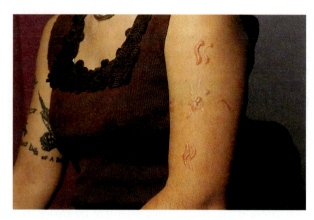

People with dissociative identity disorder may engage in self-mutilative behavior

other personalities by engaging in self-mutilative behaviors, such as self-cutting or -burning and suicide attempts (Coons & Milstein, 1990; Ross, Norton & Wozney, 1989). A persecutor personality may engage in a dangerous behavior, such as taking an overdose of pills or jumping in front of a truck, and then "go back inside," leaving the host personality to experience the pain. Persecutors may have the belief that they can harm other personalities without harming themselves.

A third type of alter is the protector, or *helper, personality*. The function of this personality is to offer advice to other personalities or to perform functions the host personality is unable to perform, such as engaging in sexual relations or hiding from abusive parents. Helpers sometimes control the switching from one personality to another or act as passive observers who can report on the thoughts and intentions of all the other personalities (Ross, 1989).

People with dissociative identity disorder typically claim to have significant periods of amnesia, or blank spells. They describe being completely amnesic for the periods when other personalities are in control or having one-way amnesia between certain personalities. In these instances, one personality is aware of what the other is doing, but the second personality is completely amnesic for periods when the first personality is in control. As with Eve White, people with dissociative identity disorder may suddenly discover unknown objects in their homes, or they may lose objects. People they do not recognize might approach them on the street, claiming to know them. They may consistently receive phone calls or mail addressed to someone with a different first or last name. Verifying claims of amnesia is difficult, but some studies by cognitive psy-

chologists suggest that information and memories tend to transfer between identities, even in individuals who believe certain personalities experience amnesia (Allen & Iacono, 2001). Other studies support claims of amnesic barriers between personalities (Dorahy, 2001).

Self-destructive behavior is very common among people with dissociative identity disorder and is often the reason they seek or are taken for treatment (Ross, 1999). This behavior includes self-inflicted burns or other injuries, wrist slashing, and overdoses. About three-quarters of patients with dissociative identity disorder have a history of suicide attempts, and over 90 percent report recurrent suicidal thoughts (Ross, 1997).

Like adults, children with dissociative identity disorder exhibit a host of behavior and emotional problems (Putnam, 1991). Their performance in school may be erratic, sometimes very good and sometimes very poor. They are prone to antisocial behavior, such as stealing, fire-setting, and aggression. They may engage in sexual relations and abuse alcohol or illicit drugs at an early age. They tend to show many symptoms of posttraumatic stress disorder (see Chapter 6), including hypervigilance, flashbacks to traumas they have endured, traumatic nightmares, and an exaggerated startle response. Their emotions are unstable, alternating among explosive outbursts of anger, deep depression, and severe anxiety.

Most children and many adults with dissociative identity disorder report hearing voices inside their heads. Some report being aware that their actions or words are being controlled by other personalities. For example, Joe, an 8-year-old boy with dissociative identity disorder, described how "a guy inside of me," called B. J. (for Bad Joey), would make him do "bad things" (Hornstein & Putnam, 1992, p. 1081):

VOICES

Well, say B. J. hears someone call me names, then he would strike me to do something, like I'd be running at the other kid, but it wouldn't be my legs, I'd be saying to my legs, "no . . . , stop . . . ," but they'd keep going on their own because that's B. J. doing that. Then my arm would be going at the other kid, hitting him, and I could see my arm doing that, but I couldn't stop it, and it wouldn't hurt when my hand hit him, not until later when B. J. goes back in and then my arm is my own arm. Then it starts hurting.

Issues in Diagnosis

Dissociative identity disorder was rarely diagnosed before about 1980, but there was a great increase in the number of reported cases after 1980 (APA, 2000; Braun, 1986; Coons, 1986). This is due in part to the fact that dissociative identity disorder was first included as a diagnostic category in the DSM in its third edition, published in 1980. The availability of specific diagnostic criteria for this disorder made it more likely that it would be used as a diagnosis. At the same time, the diagnostic criteria for schizophrenia were made more specific in the 1980 version of the DSM, possibly leading to some cases that would have been diagnosed as schizophrenia being diagnosed as dissociative identity disorder. One final, and important, influence on trends in diagnosis was the publication of a series of influential papers by psychiatrists describing persons with dissociative identity disorder whom they had treated (Bliss, 1980; Coons, 1980; Greaves, 1980; Rosenbaum, 1980). These cases aroused interest in the disorder in the psychiatric community.

Still, most mental-health professionals are reluctant to give this diagnosis. Most people diagnosed with dissociative identity disorder have already been diagnosed with at least three other disorders (Kluft, 1987). Some of the other disorders diagnosed may be secondary to or the result of the dissociative identity disorder. For example, one study of 135 patients with dissociative identity disorder found that 97 percent could also be diagnosed with major depression; 90 percent had an anxiety disorder, most often posttraumatic stress disorder; 65 percent were abusing substances; and 38 percent had an eating disorder (Ellason, Ross, & Fuchs, 1996). In addition, most people with dissociative identity disorder also are diagnosed with a personality disorder (Dell, 1998).

Many of the earler diagnoses may be misdiagnoses of the dissociative symptoms, however. For example, when people with dissociative identity disorder report hearing voices talking inside their heads, they are often misdiagnosed as having schizophrenia (Kluft, 1987). The voices that people with schizophrenia hear, however, often are experienced as coming from outside their heads. Conversely, people with dissociative identity disorder do not show schizophrenic symptoms, such as flat or inappropriate affect or loose or illogical associations (Ellason et al., 1996).

There are substantial cross-national differences in rates of diagnosed dissociative identity disorder. This disorder is diagnosed much more frequently in the United States than in Great Britain, Europe, India, or Japan (Ross, 1989; Saxena & Prasad, 1989;

Takahashi, 1990). Some studies suggest that Latinos, both within and outside the United States, may be more likely than other ethnic groups to experience dissociative symptoms in response to traumas. For example, a study of Vietnam veterans found that Latino veterans were more likely than non-Latino veterans to have dissociative symptoms (Koopman et al., 2001). Another study, conducted with Latino survivors of community violence in the United States, found that those who were less acculturated to mainstream U.S. culture were more likely to have dissociative symptoms than those who were more acculturated (Marshall & Orlando, 2002). This finding suggests that something about the Latino culture may increase vulnerability to dissociation. Dissociative symptoms may be part of the syndrome of *ataque de nervios*, a culturally accepted reaction to stress among Latinos that involves transient periods of loss of consciousness, convulsive movements of a psychological origin, hyperactivity, assaultive behaviors, and impulsive suicidal or homicidal acts (see the discussion of *ataque de nervios* in Chapter 7). The following case study describes a Hispanic woman believed to experience *ataque de nervios* but later diagnosed with dissociative identity disorder by a non-Hispanic psychiatrist (adapted from Steinberg, 1990, pp. 31–32).

CASE STUDY

Mrs. C., a 40-year-old divorced Hispanic woman, contacted a Hispanic clinic in Connecticut on the suggestion of her previous psychiatrist in Puerto Rico. Over an 18-year period Mrs. C. had made numerous emergency room and follow-up visits to a Puerto Rican psychiatric hospital. Her previous diagnoses included psychotic depression, schizophrenia, posttraumatic stress disorder, schizoaffective disorder, and hysterical personality. A variety of neuroleptics and antidepressants in therapeutic dosages had been prescribed but had provided no relief.

Mrs. C. was the youngest of three daughters born to indigent parents in Puerto Rico and was raised among numerous relatives in an overcrowded setting. Mrs. C. suffered extreme physical and emotional abuse from her mother, including administration of enemas and emetics every other day as punishment "if she was bad." Mrs. C. also recalled being sexually abused by her father and suffered recurrent dreams of this abuse.

(continued)

Married at age 17, she had three children by her first husband, who was physically abusive. After 4 years, Mrs. C. left him and shortly thereafter married another man, whom she described as physically and emotionally abusive. They separated 4 months later. Recently, she moved to Connecticut to be near her grown daughter.

Mrs. C.'s first presentation in Connecticut was with a classic episode of *ataque*. She described an acute onset of distressing auditory and visual hallucinations, stating that the voices were commanding her to harm herself. The initial diagnostic impression at the clinic was of a psychotic depression and she was given a prescription for an antipsychotic drug. Four days later, in a follow-up visit, she had not used the medication, denied having had auditory or visual hallucinations, and was free of any psychotic symptoms. She described rapid mood swings, "out of body experiences," and amnesic episodes, which she had experienced since childhood.

At this time, Mrs. C. was scheduled for biweekly supportive therapy with a mental-health worker. She attended sessions irregularly. Her demeanor, level of functioning, and symptoms fluctuated radically. Several times she spontaneously began acting as though she were a child. Frequently she came to therapy referring to herself by another name and did not remember previous sessions.

During this period, Mrs. C. was brought to the Hispanic clinic by her boyfriend for an emergency consultation due to the acute onset of bizarre behavior. She was childlike and disoriented, suffered auditory and visual hallucinations of a suicidal and homicidal nature, and rapidly became restless and agitated. She stated her name was *Rosa*. At that time the emergency room psychiatrist noted the similarity of her symptoms to the *ataque* and described her behavior: "When she came into the screening area, she took one of the balloons and began to play with it and asked me if I had a doll for her; she also said she was hungry and wanted some cookies and milk."

His diagnostic impression was "atypical psychosis." Re-evaluation several hours later revealed a "dramatic change in state." She said she was not Rosa, was not 6 years old, had no interest in playing with a doll, and she did not feel like someone was following her or was telling her to hurt herself.

At this time Mrs. C. began a new course of weekly psychotherapy sessions, which she attended fairly regularly. Mrs. C.'s sense of identity, her demeanor, and the content of each session varied significantly. During this treatment, five distinct personalities emerged with different names, ages, memories, and characteristic behaviors. Frequently she would state that she was "unable to remember" what she had discussed in a previous session. Recurrent themes included identity confusion and severe abuse by both parents. Throughout this year she remained off medication.

Some researchers have argued that psychiatrists in the United States are too quick to diagnose dissociative identity disorder, and others have argued that psychiatrists in other countries misdiagnose it as another disorder (Coons et al., 1990; Fahy, 1988).

Explanations of Dissociative Identity Disorder

Many theorists who study dissociative identity disorder view it as the result of coping strategies used by persons faced with intolerable trauma, most often childhood sexual and/or physical abuse, which they are powerless to escape (Bliss, 1986; Kluft, 1987). As Ross (1997, p. 64) describes,

> The little girl being sexually abused by her father at night imagines that the abuse is happening to someone else, as a way to distance herself from the overwhelming emotions she is experiencing. She may float up to the ceiling and watch the abuse in a detached fashion. Now not only is the abuse not happening to her, but she blocks it out of her mind—that other little girl remembers it, not the original self. In this model, DID is an internal divide-and-conquer strategy in which intolerable knowledge and feeling is split up into manageable compartments. These compartments are personified and take on a life of their own.

In most studies, the majority of people diagnosed with dissociative identity disorder self-report having been the victims of sexual or physical abuse

Children who are abused may dissociate and even develop alter personalities as a way of dealing with their abuse.

---

during childhood (Coons, 1994; Dell & Eisenhower, 1990; Hornstein & Putnam, 1992), and dissociative experiences are commonly reported by survivors of child sexual abuse (Butzel et al., 2000; Kisiel & Lyons, 2001). For example, in a study of 135 persons with dissociative identity disorder, 92 percent reported having been sexually abused and 90 percent reported having been repeatedly physically abused (Ellason et al., 1996; see also Putnam et al., 1986). Similar results have been found in studies in which patients' reports of abuse were corroborated by at least one family member or by emergency room reports (Coons, 1994; Coons & Milstein, 1986). This abuse was most often carried out by parents or other family members and was chronic over an extended period of childhood. Other types of trauma that have been associated with the development of dissociative identity disorder include kidnapping, natural disasters, war, famine, and religious persecution (Ross, 1999).

People who develop dissociative identity disorder tend to be highly suggestible and hypnotizable and may use self-hypnosis to dissociate and escape their traumas (Kihlstrom, Glisky, & Angiulo, 1994). They may create the alter personalities to help then cope with their traumas, much as a child might create imaginary playmates to ease pangs of loneliness. These alter personalities can provide the safety, security, and nurturing that they are not receiving from their real caregivers. People with dissociative identity disorder may become trapped in their own defense mechanisms. Retreating into their alter personalities or using these personalities

to perform frightening functions may become a chronic way of coping with life.

There is evidence from a few family history studies that dissociative identity disorder runs in some families (Coons, 1984; Dell & Eisenhower, 1990). In addition, studies of twins and of adopted children have found evidence that the tendency to dissociate is substantially affected by genetics (Becker-Blease et al., 2004). Perhaps the ability and tendency to dissociate as a defense mechanism is, to some extent, biologically determined.

Treatment of Dissociative Identity Disorder

Treating dissociative identity disorder can be extremely challenging (Ross & Ellason, 1999). The goal of treatment is the integration of all the alter personalities into one, coherent personality. This integration is done by identifying the functions or roles of each personality, helping each personality confront and work through the traumas that led to the disorder and the concerns each one has or represents, and negotiating with the personalities for fusion into one personality who has learned adaptive styles of coping with stress. Hypnosis is used heavily in the treatment of dissociative identity disorder to contact alters (Putnam & Lowenstein, 1993).

Patients who have been treated successfully report a sense of unity in their personality, no longer report hearing voices, and are consistent in their expression of one personality. In treating children with dissociative identity disorder, it is often necessary to work with their parents to improve the children's family life, and it is sometimes necessary to remove the children from abusive homes (Dell & Eisenhower, 1990). Antidepressants and antianxiety drugs are sometimes used as adjuncts to supportive psychotherapy.

Experts in the treatment of dissociative identity disorder argue that treatment is successful in most cases (Coons & Bowman, 2001; Kluft, 1987; Ross, 1999), particularly if the treatment is begun in childhood shortly after a child first develops alter personalities (Peterson, 1991). One of the few studies that has empirically evaluated the treatment of DID found that patients who were able to integrate their personalities through treatment remained relatively free of symptoms over the subsequent two years (Ellason & Ross, 1997). These patients also reported few symptoms of substance abuse and depression, and they were able to reduce their use of antidepressant and antipsychotic medications. In contrast, patients who had not achieved integration during treatment continued to show DID symptoms and a number of other disorders. This study did not compare the outcome of the patients who received therapy with that of those who did not, and it did not compare different types of therapy.

Dissociative Fugue

A person in the midst of a **dissociative fugue** will suddenly pick up and move to a new place, assume a new identity, and have no memory for his previous identity. He will behave quite normally in his new environment, and it will not seem odd to him that he cannot remember anything from his past. Just as suddenly, he may return to his previous identity and home, resuming his life as if nothing had happened, with no memory for what he did during the fugue. A fugue may last for days or years, and a person may experience repeated fugue states or a single episode. An extreme and classic case of fugue was that of Reverend Ansel Bourne, reported by American philosopher and psychologist William James (1890, pp. 391–393).

CASE STUDY

The Rev. Ansel Bourne, of Greene, R.I., was brought up to the trade of a carpenter; but, in consequence of a sudden temporary loss of sight and hearing under very peculiar circumstances, he became converted from Atheism to Christianity just before his thirtieth year, and has since that time for the most part lived the life of an itinerant preacher. He has been subject to headaches and temporary fits of depression of spirits during most of his life, and has had a few fits of unconsciousness lasting an hour or less. He also has a region of somewhat diminished cutaneous sensibility on the left thigh. Otherwise his health is good, and his muscular strength and endurance excellent. He is of a firm and self-reliant disposition, a man whose yea is yea and his nay, nay; and his character for uprightness is such in the community that no person who knows him will for a moment admit the possibility of his case not being perfectly genuine.

On January 17, 1887, he drew 551 dollars from a bank in Providence with which to pay for a certain lot of land in Greene, paid certain bills, and got into a Pawtucket horse-car. This is the last incident which he remembers. He did not return home that day, and nothing was heard of him for two months. He was published in the papers as missing, and foul play being suspected, the police sought in vain his whereabouts. On the morning of March 14th, however, at Norristown, Pennsylvania, a man calling himself A. J. Brown, who had rented a

small shop six weeks previously, stocked it with stationery, confectionery, fruit, and small articles, and carried on his quiet trade without seeming to anyone unnatural or eccentric, woke up in a fright and called the people of the house to tell him where he was. He said that his name was Ansel Bourne, that he was entirely ignorant of Norristown, and that he knew nothing of shop-keeping, and that the last thing he remembered—it seemed only yesterday—was drawing the money from the bank, etc. in Providence. He would not believe that two months had elapsed. The people of the house thought him insane; and so, at first, did Dr. Louis H. Read, whom they called in to see him. But on telegraphing to Providence, confirmatory messages came, and presently his nephew, Mr. Andrew Harris, arrived upon the scene, made everything straight, and took him home. He was very weak, having lost apparently over twenty pounds of flesh during his escapade, and had such a horror of the idea of the candy-store that he refused to set foot in it again.

The first two weeks of the period remained unaccounted for, as he had no memory, after he had once resumed his normal personality, of any part of the time, and no one who knew him seems to have seen him after he left home. The remarkable part of the change is, of course, the peculiar occupation which the so-called Brown indulged in. Mr. Bourne has never in his life had the slightest contact with trade. "Brown" was described by the neighbors as taciturn, orderly in his habits, and in no way queer. He went to Philadelphia several times, replenished his stock; cooked for himself in the back shop, where he also slept; went regularly to church; and once at prayer-meeting made what was considered by the hearers as a good address, in the course of which he related an incident which he had witnessed in his natural state of Bourne.

This was all that was known of the case up to June 1890, when I induced Mr. Bourne to submit to hypnotism, so as to see whether, in the hypnotic trance, his "Brown" memory would not come back. It did so with surprising

(continued)

readiness; so much so indeed that it proved quite impossible to make him whilst in the hypnosis remember any of the facts of his normal life. He had heard of Ansel Bourne, but "didn't know as he had ever met the man." When confronted with Mrs. Bourne he said that he had "never seen the woman before," etc. On the other hand, he told of his peregrinations during the lost fortnight, and gave all sorts of details about the Norristown episode. The whole thing was prosaic enough; and the Brown-personality seems to be nothing but a rather shrunken, dejected, and amnesic extract of Mr. Bourne himself. He gives no motive for the wandering except that there was "trouble back there" and "he wanted rest." During the trance he looks old, the corners of his mouth are drawn down, his voice is slow and weak, and he sits screening his eyes and trying vainly to remember what lay before and after the two months of the Brown experience. "I'm all hedged in," he says: "I can't get out at the other end. I don't know what set me down in the Pawtucket horse-car, and I don't know how I ever left that store, or what became of it." His eyes are practically normal, and all his sensibilities (save for tardier response) about the same in hypnosis as in waking. I had hoped by suggestion, etc., to run the two personalities into one, and make the memories continuous, but no artifice would avail to accomplish this, and Mr. Bourne's skill to-day still covers two distinct personal selves.

Some, but not all, persons who experience fugue episodes do so after traumatic events. Many others, such as the Reverend Bourne, seem to escape into a fugue state in response to chronic stress in their lives that is within the realm of most people's experience. People are typically depressed before the onset of fugues (Kopelman, 1987). As in dissociative identity disorder, fugue states may be more common in people who are highly hypnotizable. Unlike a person with dissociative identity disorder, however, a person in a fugue state actually leaves the scene of the trauma or stress and leaves his or her former identity behind.

Fugue states appear to be more common among people who have histories of amnesia, including amnesias due to head injuries (Kopelman, 1987). There is no accurate estimate of the preva-

lence of fugue states, although they appear to be quite rare, and not much is known about the causes of fugue states, in part because of their rarity. Clinicians who treat people with this disorder tend to use many of the same techniques used to treat dissociative identity disorder, but, again, because the disorder is rare, little is known about the outcomes of treatment.

Dissociative Amnesia

In both dissociative identity disorder and dissociative fugue states, individuals may have amnesia for the periods of time when their alter personalities are in control or when they have been in fugue states, yet some people have significant periods of amnesia but do not assume new personalities or identities. They cannot remember important facts about their lives and their personal identities and are typically aware that there are large gaps in their memory or knowledge of themselves. These people are said to have **dissociative amnesia.**

Amnesia is considered either organic or psychogenic (see the Concept Overview in Table 8.6 on page 292). **Organic amnesia** is caused by a brain injury resulting from disease, drugs, accidents (such as blows to the head), or surgery. Organic amnesia often involves the inability to remember new information, known as **anterograde amnesia.**

Psychogenic amnesia arises in the absence of any brain injury or disease and is thought to have psychological causes. Psychogenic amnesia rarely involves anterograde amnesia. The inability to remember information from the past, known as **retrograde amnesia,** can have both organic and psychogenic causes. For example, people who have been in serious car accidents can have retrograde amnesia for the few minutes just before the accident. This retrograde amnesia can be due to a brain injury resulting from blows to the head during accidents, or it can be a motivated forgetting of the events leading up to traumatic accidents. Retrograde amnesia can also occur for longer periods of time than just a few minutes.

When such amnesias are due to organic causes, people usually forget everything about the past, including both personal information, such as where they lived and who they knew, and general information, such as who was president and major historical events of the period. They typically retain memory of their personal identities, however. They may not remember their children, but they know their own names. When long-term retrograde amnesias are due to psychological causes, people typically lose their identities and forget personal information but retain memories for general information.

TABLE 8.6   Concept Overview

Differences Between Psychogenic and Organic Amnesia

There are several important differences between psychogenic amnesia and organic amnesia.

Psychogenic Amnesia	Organic Amnesia
Caused by psychological factors	Caused by biological factors (such as disease, drugs, and blows to the head)
Seldom involves anterograde amnesia (inability to learn new information acquired since onset of amnesia)	Often involves anterograde amnesia
Can involve retrograde amnesia (inability to remember events from the past)	Can involve retrograde amnesia
Retrograde amnesia often only for personal information, not for general information	Retrograde amnesia usually for both personal and general information

The following is a case study of a man with a psychogenic retrograde amnesia (Hilgard, 1977/1986, p. 68).

CASE STUDY

Some years ago a man was found wandering the streets of Eugene, Oregon, not knowing his name or where he had come from. The police, who were baffled by his inability to identify himself, called in Lester Beck . . . , a psychologist they knew to be familiar with hypnosis, to see if he could be of assistance. He found the man eager to cooperate and by means of hypnosis and other methods was able to reconstruct the man's history. . . .

Following domestic difficulties, the man had gone on a drunken spree completely out of keeping with his earlier social behavior, and he had subsequently suffered deep remorse. His amnesia was motivated in the first place by the desire to exclude from memory the mortifying experiences that had gone on during the guilt-producing episode. He succeeded in forgetting all the events before and after this behavior that reminded him of it. Hence the amnesia spread from the critical incident to events before and after it, and he completely lost his sense of personal identity.

Loss of memory due to alcohol intoxication is common, but usually the person forgets only the events occurring during the period of intoxication.

Severe alcoholics can develop a more global retrograde amnesia, known as *Korsakoff's syndrome* (see Chapter 17), in which they cannot remember much personal or general information for a period of several years or decades. However, the type of retrograde amnesia in the previous case study, which apparently involved only one episode of heavy drinking and the loss of only personal information, typically has psychological causes.

Some theorists argue that psychogenic amnesias may be the result of using dissociation as a defense against intolerable memories or stressors (Freyd, 1996; Gleaves et al., 2004). Psychogenic amnesias most frequently occur following traumatic events, such as wars or sexual assaults. Alternately, amnesia for specific events may occur because individuals were in such a high state of arousal during the events that they did not encode and store information during the period of the event and thus were unable to retrieve the information later.

A third explanation for amnesia for specific events is that information about events is stored at the time of the events but is associated with a high state of arousal of painful emotions. Later on, people avoid these emotions and therefore do not gain access to the information associated with them (Bower, 1981).

Amnesias for specific periods of time around traumas appear to be fairly common, but generalized retrograde amnesias for people's entire pasts and identities appear to be very rare. Studies of people in countries that have been the site of attempted genocides, "ethnic cleansings," and wars have suggested that the rate of dissociative amnesias in these country may be elevated. For example, a study of 810 Bhutanese refugees in Nepal found that almost 20 percent of those who had been tortured during

Lorena Bobbit cut off her husband's penis, after years of experiencing his abuse. She claimed to have amnesia for the act of cutting it off.

conflicts in their country could be diagnosed with a dissociative disorder (van Ommeren et al., 2001).

One complication that arises in diagnosing amnesias is the possibility that amnesias are being faked by people trying to escape punishment for crimes committed during the periods for which they claim to be amnesic. True amnesias can occur in conjunction with the commission of crimes. Many crimes are committed by persons under the influence of alcohol or other drugs, and the drugs can cause blackouts for the periods of intoxication (Kopelman, 1987). Similarly, people who incur head injuries during the commission of crimes—for example, by falling while trying to escape the scene of a crime—can have amnesia for the commission of the crimes. Psychogenic amnesias can also occur for the commission of crimes, particularly if the criminals feel extremely guilty about the crimes. For example, a man who beat his wife may feel so guilty for doing so that he develops amnesia for the beating.

Amnesia is most often seen in homicide cases, with between 25 and 45 percent of persons arrested for homicide claiming to have amnesia for the killings (Kopelman, 1987). In most of these cases, the victims are closely related to the killers (as lovers, spouses, close friends, or family members), the offenses appear to be unpremeditated, and the killers are in states of extreme emotional arousal at the time of the killings. More rarely, the killers appear to have been in psychotic states at the time of the killings.

There is no clear-cut way to differentiate true amnesias from feigned ones. Head injuries leading to amnesia may be detectable through neuroimag-

ing of the brain. Some clinicians advocate the use of hypnosis to assist people in remembering events around crimes, if it is suspected that the amnesia is due to psychological causes. However, the possibility that hypnosis will "create" memories through the power of suggestion leads many courts to deny the use of hypnosis in such cases (Kopelman, 1987). In most cases, it is impossible to determine whether the amnesia is true.

Depersonalization Disorder

People with **depersonalization disorder** have frequent episodes in which they feel detached from their own mental processes or bodies, as if they are outside observers of themselves. Occasional experiences of depersonalization are common, particularly when people are sleep-deprived or under the influence of drugs (Baker et al., 2003). Approximately half of all adults report having at least one brief episode of depersonalization, usually following a severe stressor (APA, 2000).

Depersonalization disorder is diagnosed when episodes of depersonalization are so frequent and distressing that they interfere with individuals' ability to function. One study of people diagnosed with depersonalization disorder found that the average age of onset was about 23 years, and two-thirds reported they had chronic experiences of depersonalization since the onset (Baker et al., 2003). Seventy-nine percent reported impaired social or work functioning, and the majority also had another psychiatric diagnosis, most often depression. People diagnosed with depersonalization disorder often report a history of childhood emotional, physical, or sexual abuse (Simeon et al., 2001).

Controversies Around the Dissociative Disorders

Surveys of psychiatrists in the United States and Canada find that fewer than one-quarter of them believe that there is strong empirical evidence that the dissociative disorders represent valid diagnoses (Lalonde et al., 2001; Pope et al., 1999a). Skeptics argue that the disorders are artificially created in suggestible clients by clinicians who reinforce clients for "admitting" to symptoms of dissociative identity disorder and who induce the symptoms of the disorder through hypnotic suggestion (see Kihlstrom, 2005; Lilienfeld et al., 1999; Weekes, Spanos, & Bertrand, 1985). Even clinicians who believe dissociative identity disorder exists and is more common than was originally believed acknowledge that some clinicians are too quick to diagnose DID and can badger clients into believing that they have it (Ross, 1997).

Controversy over the diagnosis of dissociative amnesia has become particularly heated in recent years because of increased attention to claims that some survivors of childhood sexual abuse repressed their memories of the abuse for years and then eventually recalled these memories, often in the context of psychotherapy. These *repressed memories* represent a form of dissociative amnesia. Believers in repressed memories argue that the clinical evidence for dissociative or psychogenic amnesia is ample and the empirical evidence is increasing (Brown, Scheflin, & Whitfield, 1999). Nonbelievers argue that the empirical evidence against the validity of dissociative amnesia is ample and the clinical evidence is biased (Kihlstrom, 2005).

Most of the evidence for repressed memories comes from studies of people who are known to have been abused or who self-report abuse. Researchers then typically look for evidence that these people have forgotten or repressed their abuse. For example, Williams (1995) surveyed 129 women who had documented histories of having been sexually abused sometime between 1973 and 1975. These women, who were between 10 months and 12 years old at the time of their abuse, were interviewed about 17 years after their abuse. Williams found that 49 of these 129 women had no memory of the abuse events that were documented.

Briere and Conte (1993) located 450 therapy patients who identified themselves as abuse victims. They asked the patients if there had ever been a time before their eighteenth birthdays when they "could not remember" their abuse. Fifty-nine percent answered yes. As a final example, Herman and Harvey (1997) examined interviews of 77 women who had reported memories of childhood trauma and found that 17 percent had spontaneously reported they had had some delayed recall of the trauma, and 16 percent had said there had been a period of complete amnesia following the trauma.

Critics of repressed memories have raised questions about the methods and conclusions of these studies (Kihlstrom, 2005; Loftus, 2003; McNally, 2003). For example, regarding the Williams (1995) study, it turns out that 33 of the 49 women who said they could not remember the specific abuse incidents they were asked about could remember other abuse incidents during their childhoods. Thus, they had not completely forgotten or repressed all memories of abuse. Instead, they simply could not remember the specific incident about which they were being asked. Williams did not give any additional information about the 16 women who could remember no incidents of molestation in their childhoods. They may have been too young to remember these incidents, because memory for anything that happens before the age of about 3 tends to be very bad.

Critics of repressed memories also cite numerous studies from the literature on eyewitness identification and testimony indicating that people can be made to believe that events occurred, when, in fact, they never did (Ceci & Bruck, 1995; Loftus, 1993; Read & Lindsay, 1997). For example, Elizabeth Loftus and her colleagues developed a method for instilling a specific childhood memory of being lost on a specific occasion at the age of 5 (Loftus, 1993, 2003). This method involved a trusted family member engaging the subject in a conversation about the time he or she was lost (Loftus, 1993, p. 532):

> Chris (14 years old) was convinced by his older brother Jim that he had been lost in a shopping mall when he was 5 years old. Jim told Chris this story as if it were the truth: "It was 1981 or 1982. I remember that Chris was 5. We had gone shopping in the University City shopping mall in Spokane. After some panic, we found Chris being led down the mall by a tall, oldish man (I think he was wearing a flannel shirt). Chris was crying and holding the man's hand. The man explained that he had found Chris walking around crying his eyes out just a few moments before and was trying to help him find his parents." Just two days later, Chris recalled his feelings about being lost: "That day I was so scared that I would never see my family again. I knew that I was in trouble." On the third day, he recalled a conversation with his mother: "I remember Mom telling me never to do that again." On the fourth day: "I also remember that old man's flannel shirt." On the fifth day, he started remembering the mall itself: "I sort of remember the stores." In his last recollection, he could even remember a conversation with the man who found him: "I remember the man asking me if I was lost." . . . A couple of weeks later, Chris described his false memory and he greatly expanded on it. "I was with you guys for a second and I think I went over to look at the toy store, the Kay-bee Toy and uh, we got lost and I was looking around and I thought, 'Uh-oh, I'm in trouble now.' You know. And then I . . . I thought I was never going to see my family again. I was really scared you know. And then this old man, I think he was wearing a blue flannel, came up to me. . . . He was kind of old. He was kind

of bald on top. . . . He had like a ring of gray hair . . . and he had glasses."

Other studies have found that repeatedly asking adults about childhood events that never actually happened leads some (perhaps 20 to 40 percent) eventually to "remember" these events and even explain them in detail (Hyman & Billings, 1998; Schacter, 1999). In addition, Mazzoni and Loftus (1998) found that, if a psychologist suggests that an individual's dreams reflect repressed memories of childhood events, a majority of subjects subsequently report that the events depicted in their dreams actually happened.

Believers in repressed memories question the application of these studies to claims of repressed memories of sexual abuse (Gleaves & Freyd, 1997; Gleaves, Hernandez, & Warner, 2003). They argue that people might be willing to go along with experimenters or therapists who try to convince them that they were lost in a shopping mall as a child, but it is unlikely that people would be willing to go along with therapists or experimenters trying to convince them they were sexually abused if this abuse did not happen.

Freyd (1996) further argues that childhood abuse and incest are exactly the kinds of events that might be blocked, repressed, or forgotten for a period of time, because they so greatly violate a child's expectations that caregiving adults can be trusted. To survive, the child may dissociate from the ongoing experience of abuse and thus form no explicit memory of the abuse, although an implicit memory lies blocked from consciousness.

Recently, researchers have been using paradigms from cognitive psychology to test hypotheses about the reality of repressed memories. In a series of studies, Richard McNally and colleagues (McNally, 2003; McNally, Clancy, & Schacter, 2001; McNally et al., 2000a, 2000b) have found that individuals reporting recovered memories of either childhood sexual abuse or abduction by space aliens are characterized by a heightened proneness to form false memories in certain laboratory tasks. For example, one task required participants to say whether they recognized words that are similar to words they previously learned but are not exactly the same. Women with recovered memories of abuse, and people who had recovered memories of alien abductions, were more prone than control groups to falsely recognize words that had not appeared on the first list (Clancy et al., 2000, 2002). The researchers argue that these people are characterized by an information-processing style that may render them prone to believing they experienced specific events (such as childhood abuse)

when, in fact, they experienced other, broadly similar events (such as physical abuse or emotional neglect).

Freyd and colleagues have argued that the kinds of cognitive tasks McNally and colleagues have used in their studies do not tap the specific cognitive phenomena that are associated with repressed memories. Specifically, they suggest that women who dissociate from, and forget, their abusive experiences are most likely to perform differently than other women on cognitive tasks that require divided attention—attending to more than one thing at a time—because dividing one's attention is critical to dissociation (DePrince & Freyd, 1999, 2001; Freyd et al., 1998). One divided attention task requires participants to press a key on a keyboard in response to a secondary task while attending to words on a computer screen and committing them to memory. Researchers have shown that, under these divided attention conditions, women who score high on measures of dissociation recall fewer trauma-related words but more neutral words that they had previously been instructed to remember, compared with low-dissociation participants, who show the opposite pattern (DePrince & Freyd, 1999, 2001; Freyd et al., 1998). They suggest that women high in dissociation are better able to keep threatening information from explicit awareness, particularly if they can turn that attention to other things they are doing or that are going on in their environment at the time.

The repressed memory debate will not go away or be resolved soon. Not only are basic researchers in the middle of this debate but psychotherapists are often called upon to testify in court cases involving claims of recovered memories of abuse. People trying to understand their distressing symptoms are at the center of this scientific maelstrom.

SUMMING UP

- The dissociative disorders include dissociative identity disorder (DID), dissociative fugue, dissociative amnesia, and depersonalization disorder.

- In all the dissociative disorders, people's conscious experiences of themselves become fragmented, they may lack awareness of core aspects of themselves, and they may experience amnesia for important events.

- The distinctive feature of dissociative identity disorder is the development of multiple separate personalities within the same person. The personalities take turns being in control.

- People with dissociative fugue move away from home and assume entirely new identities, with complete amnesia for their previous identities. They do not switch back and forth between personalities.

- People with dissociative amnesia lose important memories due to psychological causes.

- People with depersonalization disorder have frequent experiences of feeling detached from their mental processes or their bodies.

- These disorders are often, although not always, associated with traumatic experiences.

- Therapists often treat these disorders by helping people explore past experiences and feelings that they have blocked from consciousness and by supporting them as they develop more integrated experiences of self and more adaptive ways of coping with stress.

- Significant controversy exists over the validity of the diagnoses of dissociative disorders and the notion of repressed memories.

| FIGURE 8.3 | Mind and Body in the Somatoform Dissociative Disorders |

Social factors: trauma, role models who express distress through physical symptoms, reinforcement for physical symptoms ⟷ Psychological factors: inability to cope with, or express distress, exaggerated physical symptoms

→ Physical symptoms ←

CHAPTER INTEGRATION

As we noted in Chapter 6, philosophers and scientists have long debated the *mind-body problem*—does the mind influence bodily processes? Do changes in the body affect a person's sense of "self"? Exactly how do the body and the mind influence each other?

The somatoform and dissociative disorders are excellent evidence that the mind and body are complexly interwoven (see Figure 8.3). In a person with dissociative identity disorder, different personalities may actually have different physiological characteristics, such as different heart rates or blood pressure, even though they reside in the same body. In conversion disorder, psychological stress causes the person to lose eyesight, hearing, or functioning in another important physiological system. In somatization and pain disorders, a person under psychological stress experiences physiological symptoms, such as severe headaches. An underlying theme of these disorders is that it is easier or more acceptable for some people to experience psychological distress through changes in their bodies than to express it more directly as sadness, fear, or anger, perhaps because of cultural or social norms.

We all somatize our distress to some degree—we feel more aches and pains when we are upset about something than when we are happy. People who develop somatoform and perhaps dissociative disorders may somatize their distress to an extreme degree. Their tendency to differentiate between what is going on in their minds and what is going on in their bodies may be low, and they may favor an extreme bodily expression of what is going on in their minds.

Extraordinary People: Follow-Up

Although Bertha Pappenheim eventually lost her painful and mysterious physical symptoms, she did not credit psychoanalysis with her cure. She stated, "Psychoanalysis in the hands of the physician is what confession is in the hands of the Catholic priest. It depends on its user and its use, whether it becomes a beneficial tool or a two-edged sword" (Edinger, 1963, p. 12). Apparently, Pappenheim did not think much of Breuer's use of psychoanalysis in her case.

The remainder of Pappenheim's life after psychoanalysis, however, was not spent bashing Breuer or Freud but serving the poor and afflicted of Vienna.

Pappenheim became a social worker and a tireless advocate for the poor and for the Jewish minority in Europe. She was director of the Jewish Orphanage for Girls and founded other welfare organizations to help the poor, homeless, and outcast and to lift prostitutes out of their hopeless lives. Pappenheim was a strong proponent of emancipation and education for women. She wrote plays on women's rights and translated Mary Wollstonecraft's book *A Vindication of the Rights of Women* (1792).

Many theorists—psychoanalytic ones and feminist ones—have reinterpreted Breuer's and Freud's case history of Anna O., and many have analyzed Pappenheim's life after psychoanalysis. Was her fight for women's rights a fight against Breuer and Freud? Was her advocacy of the poor and outcasts—which was seen as unusual and inexplicable behavior for a wealthy Viennese socialite—a repudiation of her parents, who were strict and deprived her of opportunities to exercise her own capabilities as a youngster?

Bertha Pappenheim described her own motivations in a prayer she wrote, which was published after her death (Pappenheim, 1936):

I am grateful that I can dam up
As in a cool mill-pond
Whatever power grows in my mind
Unintentionally and unforced,
Solely for my own pleasure.
I thank also for the hour
In which I found the words
For what moves me, so that I could
Move others by them.
To feel strength is to live—to live is to wish
  to serve. Allow me to . . .

Chapter Summary

- The somatoform disorders are a group of disorders in which the individual experiences or fears physical symptoms for which no organic cause can be found. (Review Table 8.2.) These disorders may result from the dissociation of painful emotions or memories and the reemergence of these emotions or memories as cries for help or for the secondary gain people receive for these symptoms.

- One of the most dramatic somatoform disorders is conversion disorder, in which the individual loses all functioning in a part of the body, such as the eyes or legs. (Review Table 8.3.) Conversion symptoms often occur after trauma or stress. People with conversion disorder tend to have high rates of depression, anxiety, alcohol abuse, and personality disorder. Treatment for the disorder focuses on the expression of emotions or memories associated with the symptoms.

- Somatization disorder involves a long history of multiple physical complaints for which people have sought treatment but for which there is no apparent organic cause. (Review Table 8.4.) Pain disorder involves only the experience of chronic, unexplainable pain. People with these disorders show high rates of anxiety and depression. The disorders are apparently common and are more common in women, in Asians and Hispanics, and among the elderly and children.

- Somatization and pain disorders run in families. The cognitive theory of these disorders is that affected people focus excessively on physical symptoms and catastrophize these symptoms. People with these disorders often have experienced recent traumas. Treatment involves understanding the traumas and helping the person find adaptive ways of coping with distress.

- Hypochondriasis is a disorder in which the individual fears he or she has a disease, despite medical proof to the contrary. Hypochondriasis shares many of the features and causes of somatization disorder and is typically comorbid with somatization disorder.

- In body dysmorphic disorder individuals have an obsessional preoccupation with parts of their bodies and engage in elaborate behaviors to mask or get rid of these body parts. They are frequently depressed, anxious, and suicidal. This disorder may be a feature of an underlying depression or anxiety disorder or may be a form of obsessive-compulsive disorder. Treatment includes psychodynamic therapies to uncover the emotions driving the obsession about the body, systematic desensitization therapy to decrease obsessions and compulsive behaviors focused on the body part, and the use of selective serotonin reuptake inhibitors to reduce obsessional thought.

■ In the dissociative disorders, the individual's identity, memories, and consciousness become separated, or dissociated, from one another. (Review Table 8.5.) In dissociative identity disorder (DID), the individual develops two or more distinct personalities, which alternate in their control over the individual's behavior. Persons with dissociative identity disorder often engage in self-destructive and mutilative behaviors.

■ The vast majority of diagnosed cases of dissociative identity disorder are women, and recent cases tend to have histories of childhood sexual and/or physical abuse. The alter personalities may have been formed during the traumatic experiences as a way of defending against these experiences, particularly among people who are highly hypnotizable. The treatment of dissociative identity disorder has typically involved helping the various personalities integrate into one functional personality.

■ Fugue is a disorder in which the person suddenly moves away from home and assumes an entirely new identity, with complete amnesia for the previous identity. Fugue states usually occur in response to a stressor and can disappear suddenly, with the person returning to his or her previous identity. Little is known about the prevalence or causes of fugue states.

■ Dissociative, or psychogenic, amnesia involves the loss of memory due to psychological causes. It is different from organic amnesia, which is caused by brain injury and in which a person may have difficulty remembering new information (anterograde amnesia), which is rare in psychogenic amnesia. (Review Table 8.6.) In addition, with organic amnesia, loss of memory for the past (retrograde amnesia) is usually complete, whereas, with psychogenic amnesia, it is limited to personal information.

■ Psychogenic amnesia typically occurs following traumatic events. It may be due to motivated forgetting of events, to poor storage of information during events due to hyperarousal, or to avoidance of the emotions experienced during events and of the associated memories of events.

■ Depersonalization disorder involves frequent episodes in which the individual feels detached from his or her mental processes or body. Transient depersonalization experiences are common, especially under the influence of drugs or sleep deprivation. The causes of depersonalization disorder are unknown.

MindMap CD-ROM

The following resources on the MindMap CD-ROM that came with this text will help you to master the content of this chapter and prepare for tests:

■ Video: Dissociative Features
■ Chapter Timeline
■ Chapter Quiz

Key Terms

somatoform disorders 269

psychosomatic disorders 269

malingering 269

factitious disorders 269

factitious disorder by proxy 270

conversion disorder 271

la belle indifference 271

glove anesthesia 272

somatization disorder 274

pain disorder 274

hypochondriasis 278

body dysmorphic disorder 279

dissociative identity disorder (DID) 285

dissociative fugue 290

dissociative amnesia 291

organic amnesia 291

anterograde amnesia 291

psychogenic amnesia 291

retrograde amnesia 291

depersonalization disorder 293

> Chapter 9

Watching from the Steps
by Hyacinth Manning-Carner

*How much pain have cost us the evils which have
never happened.*

—Thomas Jefferson, letter to Thomas Jefferson Smith
(February 21, 1825)

Mood Disorders <

CHAPTER OVERVIEW

Extraordinary People

■ **Kay Redfield Jamison:** *An Unquiet Mind*

Unipolar Depression

People with unipolar depression experience sadness, loss of interest in their usual activities, changes in sleep and activity levels, and thoughts of worthlessness, hopelessness, and suicide.

Bipolar Mood Disorders

People with bipolar disorder experience both periods of depression and periods of mania, during which their mood is elevated or irritable, and they have great energy and self-esteem. Bipolar disorder is much less common than is unipolar depression.

Biological Theories of Mood Disorders

There clearly is a heritable component to bipolar disorder and for some forms of unipolar depression. Biochemical theories suggest that imbalances in certain neurotransmitters or the malfunctioning of receptors for these neurotransmitters contributes to mood disorders. People with depression show disturbances on neuroimaging scans. They also show chronic hyperactivity of the bodily system that regulates stress responses.

Psychological Theories of Mood Disorders

Behavioral theories suggest that a lack of positive reinforcements and the presence of many aversive circumstances lead to depression. Cognitive theories suggest that people with depression interpret stressful experiences in negative and distorted ways, contributing to their depression. Psychodynamic theories describe depression as anger turned inward on the self. Interpersonal theories of depression attribute it to maladaptive social roles and patterns of relationships.

Social Perspectives on Mood Disorders

Sociologists have examined the large age, gender, and cross-cultural differences in depression for clues to its origins.

Mood Disorders Treatments

Several drugs are effective in the treatment of depression. Electroconvulsive therapy is also used to treat serious depression. The newest treatments include repetitive transcranial magnetic stimulation (rTMS) and vagus nerve stimulation. Lithium, anticonvulsants, antipsychotics, and calcium channel blockers are used to treat mania. The psychological therapies aim to reverse the processes that specific theories say lead to depression. Prevention programs intervene with high-risk groups to prevent first onsets of depression.

Taking Psychology Personally

■ **Primary Care Physicians Treating Depression**

Chapter Integration

New models of mood disorders describe how genetics may affect both the individual's biological sensitivity to stress and personality characteristics that heighten reactivity to stress, contributing to depression.

Extraordinary People

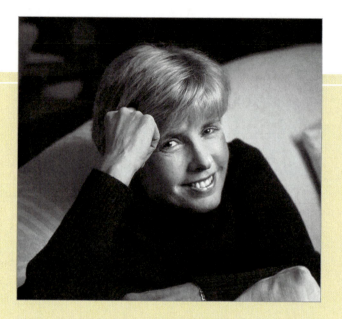

Kay Redfield Jamison: *An Unquiet Mind*

I was a senior in high school when I had my first attack. At first, everything seemed so easy. I raced about like a crazed weasel, bubbling with plans and enthusiasms, immersed in sports, and staying up all night, night after night, out with friends, reading everything that wasn't nailed down, filling manuscript books with poems and fragments of plays, and making expansive, completely unrealistic plans for my future. The world was filled with pleasure and promise; I felt great. Not just great, I felt *really* great. I felt I could do anything, that no task was too difficult. My mind seemed clear, fabulously focused, and able to make intuitive mathematical leaps that had up to that point entirely eluded me. Indeed, they elude me still. At the time, however, not only did everything make perfect sense, but it all began to fit into a marvelous kind of cosmic relatedness. My sense of enchantment with the laws of the natural world caused me to fizz over, and I found myself buttonholing my friends to tell them how beautiful it all was. They were less than transfixed by my insights into the webbings and beauties of the universe although considerably impressed at how exhausting it was to be around my enthusiastic ramblings: You're talking too fast, Kay. Slow down, Kay. You're wearing me out, Kay. Slow down, Kay. And those times when they didn't actually come out and say it, I still could see it in their eyes: For God's sake, Kay, slow down.

I did, finally, slow down. In fact, I came to a grinding halt. The bottom began to fall out of my life and my mind. My thinking, far from being clearer than a crystal, was tortuous. I would read the same passage over and over again only to realize that I had no memory at all for what I had just read. My mind had turned on me: It mocked me for my vapid enthusiasms; it laughed at all my foolish plans; it no longer found anything interesting or enjoyable or worthwhile. It was incapable of concentrated thought and turned time and again to the subject of death: I was going to die, what difference did anything make? Life's run was only a short and meaningless one; why live? I was totally exhausted and could scarcely pull myself out of bed in the mornings. It took me twice as long to walk anywhere as it ordinarily did, and I wore the same clothes over and over again, as it was otherwise too much of an effort to make a decision about what to put on. I dreaded having to talk with people, avoided my friends whenever possible, and sat in the school library in the early mornings and late afternoons, virtually inert, with a dead heart and a brain as cold as clay. (Jamison, 1995, pp. 35–38)

So writes author Kay Redfield Jamison in her autobiography, *An Unquiet Mind: A Memoir of Moods and Madness.* In *An Unquiet Mind*, Jamison describes her moods, her psychotic episodes, her suicide attempts, some outrageous things she did while manic, and her resistance to taking medication. It is an intimate look inside the life of a person with severe bipolar disorder, in all its mystery and tragedy.

When Jamison published this book in 1995, it garnered a great deal of attention in both the professional psychology and psychiatry literatures as well as in the general public media. This was because it was one of the most eloquent accounts of the experience of bipolar disorder published in years. It was also because Dr. Jamison is one of the most prolific and respected researchers of mood disorders in the field. Seldom does a person in Jamison's position—a

(continued)

professor of psychiatry at Johns Hopkins Medical School, a leading researcher and author in the field of mood disorders, an active clinician who specializes in treating people with mood disorders, and a winner of a MacArthur Foundation "genius" award— reveal that she suffers from the very disorder she researches and treats. Throughout this chapter, we will hear more of Jamison's powerful descriptions of what it is like to have a serious mood disorder.

The emotional roller-coaster ride Kay Jamison describes is known as **bipolar disorder,** or *manic-depression*. First, Jamison had **mania,** with great energy and enthusiasm for everything, fizzing over with ideas, talking and thinking so fast that her friends could not keep up with her. Eventually, though, she crashed into a **depression.** Her energy and enthusiasm were gone, and she was slow to think, to talk, and to move. The joy was drained from her life. Bipolar disorder is one of the two major types of mood disorders. The other type is **unipolar depression.** People with unipolar depression experience only depression, no mania.

The symptoms of unipolar depression and bipolar disorder may, at first glance, seem very familiar. We often talk of feeling depressed when something bad happens. And some people get a "fizzing over" feeling of exuberance and invincibility when things are going really well in their world. People who develop mood disorders, however, experience highs and lows that most of us can only imagine.

UNIPOLAR DEPRESSION

VOICES From the time I woke up in the morning until the time I went to bed at night, I was unbearably miserable and seemingly incapable of any kind of joy or enthusiasm. Everything—every thought, word, movement—was an effort. Everything that once was sparkling now was flat. I seemed to myself to be dull, boring, inadequate, thick brained, unlit, unresponsive, chill skinned, bloodless, and sparrow drab. I doubted, completely, my ability to do anything well. It seemed as though my mind had slowed down and burned out to the point of being virtually useless. The wretched, convoluted, and pathetically confused mass of gray worked only well enough to torment me with a dreary litany of my inadequacies and shortcomings in character and to taunt me with the total, the desperate hopelessness of it all. (Jamison, 1995, p. 110)

Symptoms of Depression

Depression takes over the whole person—emotions, bodily functions, behaviors, and thoughts (see DSM-IV-TR criteria in Table 9.1 on page 304).

Emotional Symptoms

The most common emotion in depression is *sadness*. This sadness is not the garden variety type, which we all feel sometimes, but is a deep, unrelenting pain. As Kay Jamison wrote, she was "unbearably miserable and seemingly incapable of any kind of joy or enthusiasm." In addition, many people diagnosed with depression report that they have lost interest in everything in life—a symptom referred to as *anhedonia*. Even when they try to do something enjoyable, they may feel no emotional reaction.

Physiological and Behavioral Symptoms

In depression, many bodily functions are disrupted. These *changes in appetite, sleep, and activity levels* can take many forms. Some people with depression lose their appetite, but others find themselves eating more, perhaps even binge eating. Some people with depression want to sleep all day. Others find it difficult to sleep and may experience a form of insomnia known as *early morning wakening*, in which they awaken at 3 or 4 A.M. every day and cannot go back to sleep.

Behaviorally, many people with depression are slowed down, a condition known as *psychomotor retardation*. They walk more slowly, gesture more slowly, and talk more slowly and quietly. They

TABLE 9.1	DSM-IV-TR

Symptoms of Depression

Depression includes a variety of emotional, physiological, behavioral, and cognitive symptoms.

Emotional Symptoms

Sadness

Depressed mood

Anhedonia (loss of interest or pleasure in usual activities)

Irritability (particularly in children and adolescents)

Physiological and Behavioral Symptoms

Sleep disturbances (hypersomnia or insomnia)

Appetite disturbances

Pyschomotor retardation or agitation

Catatonia (unusual behaviors ranging from complete lack of movement to excited agitation)

Fatigue and loss of energy

Cognitive Symptoms

Poor concentration and attention

Indecisiveness

Sense of worthlessness or guilt

Poor self-esteem

Hopelessness

Suicidal thoughts

Delusions and hallucinations with depressing themes

Source: Reprinted with permission from the *Diagnostic and Statistical Manual of Mental Disorders,* Fourth Edition, Text Revision. Copyright © 2000 American Psychiatric Association.

have more accidents, because they cannot react to crises as quickly as necessary to avoid them. Many people with depression *lack energy* and report feeling chronically *fatigued.* A subset of people with depression have *psychomotor agitation* instead of retardation. They feel physically agitated, cannot sit still, and may move around or fidget aimlessly.

Cognitive Symptoms

The thoughts of people with depression may be filled with themes of *worthlessness, guilt, hopelessness,* and even *suicide.* They often have trouble concentrating and making decisions. Again, as Kay

Jamison described, "It seemed as though my mind had slowed down and burned out to the point of being virtually useless."

In some severe cases, the cognitions of people with depression lose complete touch with reality, and they experience delusions and hallucinations. **Delusions** are beliefs with no basis in reality, and **hallucinations** involve seeing, hearing, or feeling things that are not real. The delusions and hallucinations that people with depression experience usually are depressing and negative in content. For example, people have delusions that they have committed a terrible sin, that they are being punished, or that they have killed or hurt someone. They may have auditory hallucinations in which voices accuse them of having committed an atrocity or instruct them to kill themselves.

The Diagnosis of Unipolar Depressive Disorders

Depression takes several forms. The DSM-IV-TR recognizes two categories of unipolar depression: **major depression** and **dysthymic disorder.** The diagnosis of major depression requires that a person experience either depressed mood or loss of interest in usual activities, plus at least four other symptoms of depression chronically for at least two weeks. In addition, these symptoms have to be severe enough to interfere with the person's ability to function in everyday life.

Dysthymic disorder is a less severe form of depressive disorder than is major depression, but it is more chronic. To be diagnosed with dysthymic disorder, a person must be experiencing depressed mood plus two other symptoms of depression for at least *two years.* During these two years, the person must never have been without the symptoms of depression for more than a two-month period. Said one woman with dysthymic disorder, "It just goes on and on. I never feel really good; I always feel kind of bad, and it seems it's never going to end."

Some unfortunate people experience both major depression and dysthymic disorder. This has been referred to as **double depression.** People with double depression are chronically dysthymic, then occasionally sink into episodes of major depression. As the major depression passes, however, they return to dysthymia rather than recover to a normal mood. As one might imagine, people with double depression are even more debilitated than are people with major depression or dysthymia. One study that followed people with double depression over about nine years found that they remained free of the symptoms of minor or severe depression only about one-third of that time (Judd

TABLE 9.2   DSM-IV-TR

Subtypes of Major Depression (and the Depressive Phase of Bipolar Disorder)

The DSM-IV-TR specifies a number of subtypes of major depression and the depressive phase of bipolar disorder.

Subtype	Characteristic Symptoms
With melancholic features	Inability to experience pleasure, distinct depressed mood, depression regularly worse in morning, early morning awakening, marked psychomotor retardation or agitation, significant anorexia or weight loss, excessive guilt
With psychotic features	Presence of depressing delusions or hallucinations
With catatonic features	Catatonic behaviors: catalepsy, excessive motor activity, severe disturbances in speech
With atypical features	Positive mood reactions to some events, significant weight gain or increase in appetite, hypersomnia, heavy or laden feelings in arms or legs, long-standing pattern of sensitivity to interpersonal rejection
With postpartum onset	Onset of major depressive episode within four weeks of delivery of child
With seasonal pattern	History of at least two years in which major depressive episodes occur during one season of the year (usually the winter) and remit when the season is over

Source: Reprinted with permission from the *Diagnostic and Statistical Manual of Mental Disorders*, Fourth Edition, Text Revision. Copyright © 2000 American Psychiatric Association.

et al., 1998). People with double depression also are less likely to respond to treatments.

Over half of the people diagnosed with major depression or dysthymia also have another psychological disorder. The most common disorders to co-occur with depression are substance abuse, such as alcohol abuse; anxiety disorders, such as panic disorder; and eating disorders (Blazer et al., 1994). Sometimes, the depression precedes and perhaps causes the other disorder. In other cases, depression follows and may be the consequence of the other disorder.

The DSM-IV-TR also recognizes several subtypes of depression—different forms the disorder can take (see DSM-IV-TR criteria in Table 9.2). These subtypes apply both to major depression and to the depressive phase of a bipolar disorder.

The first subtype of depression is *depression with melancholic features*, in which the physiological symptoms of depression are particularly prominent. Second is *depression with psychotic features*, in which people experience delusions and hallucinations during a major depressive episode. Third, people with *depression with catatonic features* show the strange behaviors collectively known as *catatonia*, which can range from a complete lack of movement to excited agitation. Fourth, there is *depression with atypical features*. The criteria for this subtype are an odd assortment of symptoms (review Table 9.2).

The fifth subtype is *depression with postpartum onset*. This diagnosis is given to women when the onset of a major depressive episode occurs within four weeks of the delivery of a child. More rarely, women develop mania postpartum and are given the diagnosis of *bipolar disorder with postpartum onset*. As many as 30 percent of women experience the *postpartum blues*—emotional lability (unstable and quickly shifting moods), frequent crying, irritability, and fatigue—in the first few weeks after giving birth. For most women, these symptoms are only annoying and pass completely within two weeks of the birth. Only about 1 in 10 women experience postpartum depressions serious enough to warrant a diagnosis of a depressive disorder (Steiner, Dunn & Born, 2003).

The final subtype of major depressive disorder is *depression with seasonal pattern*, sometimes referred to as **seasonal affective disorder,** or **SAD.** People with SAD have a history of at least two years of experiencing major depressive episodes and fully recovering from them. The symptoms seem to be tied to the number of daylight hours in a day. People become depressed when the daylight hours are short and recover when the daylight hours are long. In the northern hemisphere, this means people are depressed November through February and not depressed the remainder of the year. Some people with this disorder actually develop mild forms of mania or have full manic episodes during the summer months and are diagnosed with *bipolar disorder with seasonal pattern*. In order to be diagnosed with seasonal affective disorder, a person's mood

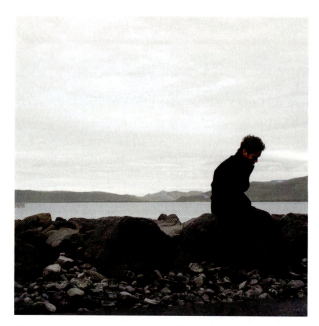

People in northern latitudes have higher rates of seasonal affective disorder.

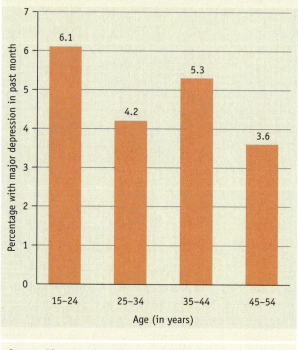

FIGURE 9.1 **Age Differences in Depression.** Shown are the percentages, in one study, of people in each age group who were diagnosed with major depression in a one-month period. Those 15 to 24 years old have the highest rates of depression, and those 45 to 54 years old have the lowest rates.

Source: Blazer et al., 1994.

changes cannot be the result of psychosocial events, such as regularly being unemployed during the winter. Rather, the mood changes must seem to come on without reason or cause.

Although many of us may feel our mood changes with the seasons, only about 1 percent of the U.S. population experiences a diagnosable seasonal affective disorder (Blazer, Kessler, & Swartz, 1998). This disorder is more common in latitudes where there are fewer hours of daylight in the winter months (Rosen et al., 1990). For example, people in Norway and Sweden are more prone to SAD than are people in Mexico and southern Italy.

Prevalence and Course of Depression

Depression is one of the most common psychological problems. At sometime in their lives, 16 percent of Americans experience an episode of major depression (Kessler et al., 2003). Among adults, 15- to 24-year-olds are most likely to have had a major depressive episode in the past month (Blazer et al., 1994; Kessler et al., 2003) (see Figure 9.1). There are lower rates among 45- to 54-year-olds, and other studies have found even lower rates in people 55 to 70 years of age, with only about 2 percent diagnosable with a major depression (Kessler et al., 2003; Newmann, 1989; Zisook & Downs, 1998). The rates of depression go up, however, among the "old-old," those over 85 years of age. When they do occur, depressions in older people tend to be quite severe, chronic, and debilitating (Lyness, 2004).

Perhaps it is surprising that the rate of depression is so low among older adults. The diagnosis of depression in older adults is complicated (Lyness, 2004). First, older adults may be less willing than younger adults to report the symptoms of depression, because they grew up in a society less accepting of the disorder.

Second, depressive symptoms in the elderly often occur in the context of a serious medical illness, which can interfere with making an appropriate diagnosis. Third, older people are more likely than younger people to have mild to severe cognitive impairment, and it is often difficult to distinguish between a depressive disorder and the early stages of a cognitive disorder.

Although these factors are important, some researchers suggest that the low rate is valid and have offered explanations. The first is quite grim: Depression appears to interfere with physical health; as a result, people with a history of depression may be more likely to die before they reach old age (Lyness, 2004). The second explanation is more hopeful: As people age, they may develop more adaptive coping skills and a psychologically healthier outlook on life, and this may lead them to experience fewer episodes of depression (Elder, Liker, & Jaworski, 1984).

Most studies show that women are about twice as likely as men to experience both mild depressive symptoms and severe depressive disorders (Nolen-Hoeksema, 2002). This gender difference in depression has been found in many countries, in most ethnic groups, and in all adult age groups. Could it be that females are more willing to admit to depression than males? The gender difference in depression is found even in studies that use relatively objective measures of depression that do not rely much on self-reports, such as clinicians' ratings of depression, or the reports of family members or friends. As we discuss the various theories of depression in this chapter, we will explore how these theories explain this gender difference in depression.

Depression appears to be a long-lasting, recurrent problem for some people (Boland & Keller, 2002). One nationwide study found that people with major depression spent an average of 16 weeks during the previous year with significant symptoms of depression (Kessler et al., 2003). The picture one gets is of a depressed person spending much of his or her time at least moderately depressed (Judd & Akiskal, 2000). Then, even after the depressed person recovers from one episode of depression, he or she remains at high risk for relapses into new episodes. People with a history of multiple episodes of depression are even more likely to remain depressed for long periods of time.

Depression is a costly disorder to the individual and to society. A study of over 1,100 employed people found that those who had significant symptoms of depression lost an average of 5.6 hours per week in productive work time, compared with 1.5 hours per week in those not depressed. The authors suggest that depression in workers costs employers an estimated $44 billion per year in lost productivity alone (not including the costs of treatment) (Stewart et al., 2003).

The good news is that, once people undergo treatment for their depression, they tend to recover much more quickly and their risk for relapse is reduced. The bad news is that many people with depression never seek care, or they wait years after their symptoms have begun to seek care (Kessler et al., 2003). Why don't people suffering the terrible symptoms of depression seek treatment? It may be because they do not have the money or insurance to pay for care. But often it is because they feel they should be able to get over their symptoms on their own. They believe that the symptoms are

just a phase they are going through, that they will pass with time and won't affect their lives in the long term.

Depression does sometimes pass without treatment, and without long-term consequences. Some people seem to be left with scars from their bouts of depression, however. Their ways of thinking, their views of themselves, their social relationships, and their academic and work histories may be changed for the worse by the depression and may remain impaired long after the symptoms of depression have passed. Even if they do not relapse into additional major depressive episodes, people with previous episodes of major depression tend to have enduring problems in many areas of their lives (Boland & Keller, 2002). Their functioning on the job tends to remain impaired even after their depression has subsided. They report that they are not interested in sex or do not enjoy sex as much as they used to, and there is chronic conflict and dissatisfaction in their intimate relationships (Joiner, 2002).

Depression in Childhood and Adolescence

Depression is less common among children than among adults. At any point in time, as many as 2.5 percent of children and 8.3 percent of adolescents can be diagnosed with major depression, and as many as 1.7 percent of children and 8.0 percent of adolescents can be diagnosed with dysthymic disorder (for reviews, see Garber & Horowitz, 2002; Lewinsohn & Essau, 2002). Between 15 and 20 percent of youth will experience an episode of major depression before the age of 20 (Lewinsohn & Essau, 2002).

Depressive symptoms that don't quite meet the diagnostic criteria for major depression are even more common in adolescents. A study of 9,863 students in grades 6, 8, and 10 in the United States found that 25 percent of the girls versus 10 percent of the boys reported elevated depressive symptoms. The highest rates were among American Indians (29 percent), followed by 22 percent of Hispanics, 18 percent of Whites, 17 percent of Asian Americans, and 15 percent of African Americans. Youth who were using substances were more likely to be depressed (Saluja et al., 2004).

The Scars of Childhood Depression

Depression may be most likely to leave psychological and social scars if it occurs initially during childhood, rather than during adulthood (Cole et al., 1998). Self-concept is still being developed in childhood and adolescence, much more so than in adulthood. A period of significant depressive symptoms while one's self-concept is undergoing substantial change can have long-lasting effects on the content or structure of one's self-concept. Similarly, the development of skills and abilities in school is cumulative during childhood and adolescence. For this reason, a bout of depression that interferes with learning can have long-term effects on children's achievement. Finally, children and adolescents are dependent on and connected with other people to a greater extent than are adults, so a bout of depression that impairs social skills can have long-term effects on social relationships.

Depression may also increase negative thinking, because it brings with it a host of new negative events. Stress-generation models suggest that the symptoms of depression—such as low motivation, fatigue, problems in concentration, low self-esteem, and decreases in social interactions and skills—can interfere with youngsters' functioning in all domains of their lives (Hammen, 1991, 1992). Because depression affects so many domains of functioning in a youngster's life, it may lead to increases in many kinds of stressors. For example, having a depressed child in the family can cause strains on parents, which may affect their relationships, perhaps putting a fragile marriage or partnership over the edge and contributing to separation. Or the cost of treatment for a depressed child may cause significant financial strain in a family.

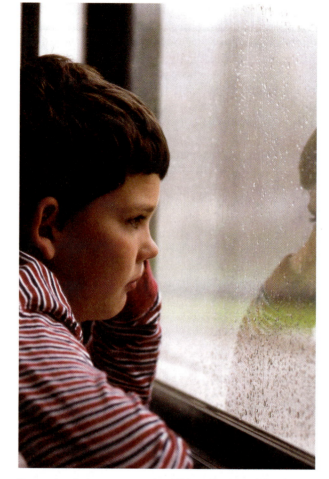

Depression in less common in children than in adults, but can be debilitating and have long-term consequences.

FIGURE 9.2

Emergence of a Gender Difference in Depression. In childhood, boys and girls have relatively equal levels of depression, but, beginning around age 13, girls' levels of depression rise, whereas boys' levels do not.

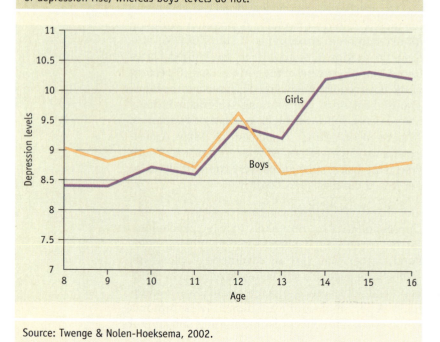

Source: Twenge & Nolen-Hoeksema, 2002.

The Effects of Puberty

Girls' rates of depression escalate dramatically over the course of puberty, but boys' rates do not (Twenge & Nolen-Hoeksema, 2002) (see Figure 9.2). Although there is some evidence that girls' increase in depressive symptoms is correlated with the hormonal changes of puberty (Angold, Costello, & Worthman, 1998), the observable physical changes of adolescence may have more to do with the emotional development of girls and boys than with hormonal development, because these characteristics affect boys' and girls' self-esteem differently. Girls appear to value the physical changes that accompany puberty much less than do boys. In particular, girls dislike the weight they gain in fat and their loss of the long, lithe look that is idealized in modern fashions. In contrast, boys like the increase in muscle mass and other pubertal changes their bodies undergo (Dornbusch et al., 1984). Body dissatisfaction appears to be more closely related to low self-esteem and depression in girls than in boys (Allgood-Merten, Lewinsohn, & Hops, 1990).

The pubertal increase in depression for girls may occur only among European American girls, however, not among African American and Latino girls (Hayward et al., 1999). It may be that African American and Latino girls do not accept the pressures to be thin as much as European American girls do, and this protects them against declines in their self-image and well-being with the onset of puberty. The social environment of African American and Latino girls may also protect them against depression in other ways, although currently there is too little research to determine what factors are important.

SUMMING UP

- Depression includes disturbances in emotion (sadness, loss of interest), bodily function (loss of sleep, appetite, and sexual drive), behavior (retardation or agitation), and thought (worthlessness, guilt, suicidality).

- The two primary categories of unipolar depression are major depression and dysthymic disorder. There are several subtypes of major depression.

- Young adults have the highest rates of depression.

- Many people who become depressed remain so for several months or more and have multiple relapses over their lifetimes.

BIPOLAR MOOD DISORDERS

VOICES

There is a particular kind of pain, elation, loneliness, and terror involved in this kind of madness. When you're high it's tremendous. The ideas and feelings are fast and frequent like shooting stars and you follow them until you find better and brighter ones. Shyness goes, the right words and gestures are suddenly there, the power to seduce and captivate others a felt certainty. There are interests found in uninteresting people. Sensuality is pervasive and the desire to seduce and be seduced irresistible. Feelings of ease, intensity, power, well-being, financial omnipotence, and euphoria now pervade one's marrow.

But, somewhere, this changes. The fast ideas are far too fast and there are far too many; overwhelming confusion replaces clarity. Memory goes. Humor and absorption on friends' faces are replaced by fear and concern. Everything previously moving with the grain is now against—you are irritable, angry, frightened,

TABLE 9.3   DSM-IV-TR

Symptoms of Mania

A diagnosis of mania requires that a person show an elevated, expansive, or irritable mood for at least one week, plus at least three of the other symptoms listed here.

Elevated, expansive, or irritable mood
Inflated self-esteem or grandiosity
Decreased need for sleep
More talkative than usual, a pressure to keep talking
Flight of ideas or sense that your thoughts are racing
Distractibility
Increase in activity directed at achieving goals
Excessive involvement in potentially dangerous activities

Source: Reprinted with permission from the *Diagnostic and Statistical Manual of Mental Disorders,* Fourth Edition, Text Revision. Copyright © 2000 American Psychiatric Association.

uncontrollable, and enmeshed totally in the blackest caves of the mind. You never knew those caves were there. It will never end. (Goodwin & Jamison, 1990, pp. 17–18)

This person is describing an episode of bipolar disorder. When she is manic, she has tremendous energy and vibrancy, her self-esteem is soaring, and she is filled with ideas and confidence. Then, when she becomes depressed, she is despairing and fearful, she doubts herself and everyone around her, and she wishes to die. This alternation between periods of mania and periods of depression is the classic manifestation of bipolar disorder.

Symptoms of Mania

We have already discussed the symptoms of depression in detail, so let's focus on the symptoms of mania (see the DSM-IV-TR criteria in Table 9.3). The moods of people who are manic can be *elated,* but that elation is often mixed with *irritation* and *agitation.*

First and foremost comes a general sense of intense well-being. I know of course that this sense is illusory and transient—

(*continued*)

Although, however, the restrictions of confinement are apt at times to produce extreme irritation and even paroxysms of anger, the general sense of wellbeing, the pleasurable and sometimes ecstatic feeling-tone, remains as a sort of permanent background of all experience during a manic period. (Goodwin & Jamison, 1990, pp. 25–26)

The manic person is filled with a *grandiose self-esteem,* meaning that his view of himself is unrealistically positive and inflated. *Thoughts* and *impulses* race through his mind. At times, these grandiose thoughts are delusional and may be accompanied by grandiose hallucinations. A manic person may *speak rapidly* and *forcefully,* trying to convey the rapid stream of fantastic thoughts he is having. He may become agitated and irritable, particularly with people he perceives as "getting in his way." He may engage in a variety of *impulsive behaviors,* such as ill-advised sexual liaisons or spending sprees. He may have *grand plans* and *goals,* which he pursues frenetically.

The Diagnosis of Mania

In order to be diagnosed with mania, an individual must show an elevated, expansive, or irritable mood for at least one week, plus at least three of the other symptoms listed in Table 9.3. These symptoms must impair the individual's ability to function in order to qualify for the diagnosis.

People who experience manic episodes meeting these criteria are said to have **bipolar I disorder.** Most of these people eventually fall into a depressive episode. For some people with bipolar I disorder, the depressions are as severe as major depressive episodes, whereas others have episodes of depression that are relatively mild and infrequent. People with **bipolar II disorder** experience severe episodes of depression that meet the criteria for major depression, but their episodes of mania are milder and are known as **hypomania** (see the DSM-IV-TR criteria in Table 9.4). Hypomania has the same symptoms as mania. The major difference is that, in hypomania, these symptoms are not severe enough to interfere with daily functioning and do not involve hallucinations or delusions.

Just as dysthymic disorder is the less severe but more chronic form of unipolar depression, there is a less severe but more chronic form of bipolar disorder, known as **cyclothymic disorder.** A person with cyclothymic disorder alternates between episodes of hypomania and moderate depression chronically over at least a two-year period. During the periods of hypomania, the person may be able to function reasonably well in daily life. Often, however, the periods of depression significantly interfere with daily functioning, although these periods are not as severe as those qualifying as major depressive episodes.

About 90 percent of people with bipolar disorder have multiple episodes or cycles during their lifetime (APA, 2000). The length of an individual episode of bipolar disorder varies greatly from one person to the next. Some people are in a manic state for several weeks or months before moving into a depressed state. More rarely, people switch from mania to depression and back within a matter of days. The number of lifetime episodes also varies tremendously from one person to the next,

---

TABLE 9.4 DSM-IV-TR

Criteria for Bipolar I and Bipolar II Disorders

Bipolar I and II disorders differ in the presence of major depressive episodes, episodes meeting the full criteria for mania, and hypomanic episodes.

Criteria	Bipolar I	Bipolar II
Major depressive episodes	Can occur but are not necessary for diagnosis	Are necessary for diagnosis
Episodes meeting full criteria for mania	Are necessary for diagnosis	Cannot be present for diagnosis
Hypomanic episodes	Can occur between episodes of severe mania or major depression but are not necessary for diagnosis	Are necessary for diagnosis

Source: Reprinted with permission from the *Diagnostic and Statistical Manual of Mental Disorders,* Fourth Edition, Text Revision. Copyright © 2000 American Psychiatric Association.

but a relatively common pattern is for episodes to become more frequent and closer together over time. If a person has four or more cycles of mania and depression within a year, this is known as **rapid cycling bipolar disorder.**

Prevalence and Course of Bipolar Disorder

Bipolar disorder is less common than unipolar depression. About 1 or 2 in 100 people experience at least one episode of bipolar disorder at sometime in their lives (Judd & Akiskal, 2003; Kessler et al., 1994; Lewinsohn, Klein, & Seeley, 2000). Men and women seem equally likely to develop the disorder, and there are no consistent differences among ethnic groups in the prevalence of the disorder (Weissman et al., 1996). Most people who develop bipolar disorder do so in late adolescence or early adulthood (Lewinsohn, Seeley, Klein, 2003). About half of the people who eventually develop a bipolar disorder have experienced their first episode by early adulthood (Judd & Akiskal, 2003).

Like people with unipolar depression, people with bipolar disorder often face chronic problems on the job and in their relationships between their episodes (Keck et al., 1998). One study, which followed people who had been hospitalized for an episode of bipolar disorder, found that, over the year following their hospitalization, only about one in four recovered fully from their symptoms and were able to lead a relatively normal life (Keck et al., 1998). The best predictors of recovery were full compliance with medication taking and higher social class, which may have afforded people better health care and social support. Judd and colleagues (2002) followed 146 patients with bipolar I disorder for almost 13 years and found that they experienced significant symptoms during 47 percent of the weeks. Depressive symptoms were more common, occurring 32 percent of the weeks, than manic symptoms, which occurred about 9 percent of the weeks, or cycling/mixed symptoms of depression and mania, which occurred 6 percent of the weeks. The presence of symptoms, even if they do not meet the criteria for an episode of mania or depression, is associated with deficits in both social and occupational functioning, and the symptoms appear to increase the risk for relapse (Marangell, 2004). In addition, people with bipolar disorder often abuse substances (such as alcohol and hard drugs), which also impairs their control over their disorder, their willingness to take medications, and their functioning in life (Goodwin & Ghaemi, 1998; Keck et al., 1998; van Gorp et al., 1998).

A controversial issue in research on bipolar disorder is the extent to which it exists and can be diagnosed reliably in children and young adolescents. One longitudinal study followed 86 prepubertal children who had been diagnosed with bipolar disorder using strict criteria (Geller et al., 2004). They found that, over a two-year period, these children continued to show the symptoms of mania or hypomania for an average of 57 weeks and the symptoms of depression for an average of 47 weeks. These data supported the initial diagnosis of bipolar disorder and suggest that pediatric bipolar disorder tends to be chronic.

Creativity and Bipolar Disorder

Could there possibly be anything good about suffering from a bipolar disorder? Some theorists have argued that the symptoms of mania—increased self-esteem, a rush of ideas, the courage to pursue these ideas, high energy, little need for sleep, hypervigilance, and decisiveness—can actually benefit certain people, especially highly intelligent or talented people. In turn, the melancholy of depression is often seen as inspirational for artists. Indeed, some of the most influential people in history have suffered, and perhaps to some extent benefited, from a mood disorder.

Some political leaders, including Abraham Lincoln, Alexander Hamilton, Winston Churchill, Napoleon Bonaparte, and Benito Mussolini, and some religious leaders, including Martin Luther and George Fox (founder of the Society of Friends, or Quakers), have been posthumously diagnosed by psychiatric biographers as having periods of mania, hypomania, or depression (Jamison, 1993). Although during periods of depression these leaders were often incapacitated, during periods of mania and hypomania they accomplished extraordinary feats. While manic, they devised brilliant and daring strategies for winning wars and solving domestic problems and had the energy, self-esteem, and persistence to carry out these strategies. The Duke of Marlborough, a great English military commander, was able to put his chronic hypomania to great use:

> No one can read the whole mass of the letters which Marlborough either wrote, dictated, or signed personally without being astounded at the mental and physical energy which it attests. . . . After 12 or 14 hours in the saddle on the long reconnaissances often under cannon-fire; after endless inspections of troops in camp and garrison; after ceaseless calculations about food and supplies, and all the anxieties of direct command in war, Marlborough

would reach his tent and conduct the foreign policy of England, decided the main issues of its Cabinet, and of party politics at home. (Rowse, 1969, pp. 249–250)

Marlborough was an ancestor of Winston Churchill, who was also able to put his cyclothymic temperament to use in his career. However, Churchill's biographer also documented how the grandiosity, scheming, and impulsiveness that are part of mania can be a liability in a leader:

All those who worked with Churchill paid tribute to the enormous fertility of his new ideas, the inexhaustible stream of invention which poured from him, both when he was Home Secretary, and later when he was Prime Minister and director of the war effort. All who worked with him also agreed that he needed the most severe restraint put upon him, and that many of his ideas, if they had been put into practice, would have been utterly disastrous. (Storr, 1988, pp. 14–15)

Writers, artists, and composers of music have a higher than normal prevalence of mania and depression. For example, a study of 1,005 famous twentieth-century artists, writers, and other professionals found that the artists and writers experienced two to three times the rate of mood disorders, psychosis, and suicide attempts than did comparably successful people in business, science, and public life. The poets in this group were most likely to have been manic (Ludwig, 1992).

Does mania simply enhance (and depression inhibit) productivity in naturally creative people? Or is there a deeper link between creativity and bipolar disorder? This is a difficult question to answer by simply examining how many creative people are also manic. However, one group of researchers found an ingenious way to address this question (Richards et al., 1988). They hypothesized that the genetic abnormalities that cause bipolar disorder are in close proximity to the genetic abnormalities that cause great creativity. According to this hypothesis, the close relatives of patients with bipolar disorder should be more creative, even if they do not have bipolar disorder, than the close relatives of people without bipolar disorder. The participants in this study were patients with bipolar disorder or cyclothymia, their first-degree relatives (siblings, parents, and children), a control group of people with no psychiatric disorders, and their first-degree relatives. The relatives in both

Winston Churchill had periods of manic symptoms that may have been both an asset and a liability.

Abraham Lincoln suffered periods of severe depression.

these groups had no history themselves of mood disorders, so any creativity they showed was in the absence of mania or depression.

To measure creativity, the researchers examined the lives of these participants for evidence that they had used their special talents in original, and creative ways. For example, one participant who was rated as extremely creative was an entrepreneur who had advanced from a chemist's apprentice to an independent researcher of new products. He then had started a major paint manufacturing company, and, during the Danish Resistance of World War II, he had surreptitiously manufactured and smuggled explosives for the Resistance. A participant who was rated as low in creativity had been a bricklayer for 20 years and then inherited a large trust fund and retired to a passive life on a country estate. An advantage of this measure of creativity is that it did not require that a person receive social recognition to be considered creative.

The results of this study suggested that the relatives of the people with bipolar disorder or cyclothymia were more creative than the participants with no history of bipolar disorder or cyclothymia or their relatives. The people with cyclothymia and the healthy relatives of those with bipolar disorder had somewhat higher creativity scores than did the patients who had bipolar disorder. This suggests that creativity that is associated with a predisposition toward bipolar disorder is more easily expressed in people who do not suffer from full episodes of mania and depression but may suffer from milder mood swings (Richards et al., 1988).

We should not overemphasize the benefits of bipolar disorder. Although many creative people with bipolar disorder may have been able to learn from their periods of depression and to exploit their periods of mania, many also have found the highs and lows of the disorder unbearable and have attempted or completed suicide. As Wurtzel (1995, p. 295) notes,

While it may be true that a great deal of art finds its inspirational wellspring in sorrow, let's not kid ourselves in how much time each of those people wasted and lost by being mired in misery. So many productive hours slipped by as paralyzing despair took over. This is not to say that we should deny sadness its rightful place among the muses of poetry and of all art forms, but let's stop calling it madness, let's stop pretending that the feeling itself is interesting. Let's call it depression and admit that it is very bleak.

SUMMING UP

- The symptoms of mania include elation, irritation and agitation, grandiosity, impulsivity, and racing thoughts and speech. People with bipolar disorder experience periods of both mania and depression.
- The two major diagnostic categories of bipolar mood disorders are bipolar disorder and cyclothymic disorder.
- Bipolar mood disorders are less common than unipolar depression, but they are equally common in men and women.
- The onset of bipolar disorder is most often in late adolescence or early adulthood. Most people with bipolar disorder have multiple episodes.
- There is some evidence that people with bipolar disorder are more creative.

BIOLOGICAL THEORIES OF MOOD DISORDERS

Most of the modern biological theories of the causes of mood disorders focus on genetic abnormalities or dysfunctions in certain neurobiological systems. These two types of theories complement each other: Genetic abnormalities may cause mood disorders by altering a person's neurobiology. In this section, we first review the evidence for a genetic contribution to depression and mania. Second, we review the evidence that neurotransmitters play a role in depression and mania. Third, we examine a variety of abnormalities that have been found in the brains of people with mood disorders. Fourth, we explore hypotheses that the neuroendocrine system, which regulates hormones throughout the body, becomes dysregulated in the mood disorders (see the Concept Overview in Table 9.5 on page 314).

The Role of Genetics

Family history and twin studies suggest that the mood disorders can be transmitted genetically (Southwick, Vythilingam, & Charney, 2005; Wallace, Schneider, & McGuffin, 2002).

Family History Studies

Family history studies of people with bipolar disorder find that their first-degree relatives (i.e., parents, children, and siblings) have rates of both bipolar disorder and unipolar depression at least two to three times higher than the rates of relatives of people without bipolar disorder (MacKinnon, Jamison, & DePaulo, 1997; Wallace et al., 2002) (Figure 9.3 on page 314).

TABLE 9.5 Concept Overview

Biological Theories of Mood Disorders

A number of biological factors have been implicated in the mood disorders.

Theory	Description
Genetic theory	Disordered genes predispose people to depression or bipolar disorder.
Neurotransmitter theories	Dysregulation of neurotransmitters and their receptors causes depression and mania. The monoamine neurotransmitters—norepinephrine, serotonin, and dopamine—have been most researched.
Neurophysiological abnormalities	Abnormalities in the structure and functioning of the prefrontal cortex, hippocampus, anterior cingulate cortex, and amygdala.
Neuroendocrine abnormalities	Depressed people show chronic hyperactivity in the hypothalamic-pituitary-adrenal axis and slow return to baseline after a stressor, which affects the functioning of neurotransmitters.

FIGURE 9.3 **Risk for Bipolar Disorder in Relatives of People with Bipolar Disorder and in the General Population.** The risk of developing bipolar disorder decreases as the genetic similarity between an individual and a relative with bipolar disorder decreases.

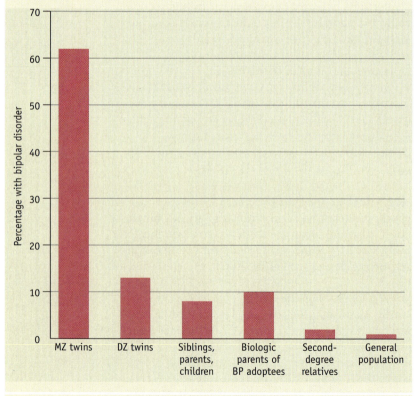

Source: With permission, from *Annual Review of Neuroscience*, Volume 20, copyright © 1997, by Annual Reviews, www.AnnualReviews.org

Does this mean that, if you have a close relative with bipolar disorder, you are destined to develop the disorder? No—most studies find that fewer than 10 percent (and often less than 5 percent) of the first-degree relatives of people with bipolar disorder develop the disorder themselves (MacKinnon et al., 1997) (review Figure 9.3). In other words, the risk is higher for people with a bipolar relative, but only a minority of them develop the disorder.

Unipolar depression also clearly runs in families. Family history studies find that the first-degree relatives of people with unipolar depression are two to three times more likely also to have depression, compared with the first-degree relatives of people without the disorder (Klein et al., 2001). Interestingly, the relatives of people with depression do *not* tend to have any greater risk for bipolar disorder than do the relatives of people with no mood disorder. This suggests that bipolar disorder has a genetic basis different from that of unipolar depression.

Twin Studies

Twin studies of bipolar disorder have shown that the probability that both twins will develop the disorder, or its *concordance rate,* is about 60 percent among monozygotic (identical) twins, compared with about 13 percent among dizygotic (nonidentical) twins (MacKinnon et al., 1997; McGuffin & Katz, 1989; Wallace et al., 2002). This finding suggests that genetics plays a substantial role in vulnerability to bipolar disorder.

Twin studies of major depression also find higher concordance rates for monozygotic twins than for dizygotic twins (e.g., Kendler et al., 2001). Some twin studies of major depression suggest that genetics plays a heavier role in this disorder for women than for men (Kendler et al., 2001). Other twin studies, however, have found no gender difference in the heritability of depression (Eaves et al., 1997; Kendler & Prescott, 1999; Rutter et al., 1999). Still other studies suggest that the types of genes responsible for depression may differ between women and men (Zubenko et al., 2002).

Specific Genetic Abnormalities

What kinds of genetic abnormalities might play a role in these disorders? One specific genetic abnormality that some studies suggest may be involved in the vulnerability to depression is on the serotonin transporter gene (Southwick et al., 2005). As we will discuss shortly, serotonin is one of the neurotransmitters implicated in depression. Abnormalities on the serotonin transporter gene could lead to dysfunction in the regulation of serotonin, which in turn could affect the stability of individuals' moods. In a longitudinal study, Caspi and colleagues (2003) found that people with abnormalities on the serotonin transporter gene were at increased risk for depression when they faced negative life events.

It is likely that there is no single location on a gene that leads to mood disorders. Many researchers believe that the genetic predisposition to mood disorders is *multifactorial*—it involves many factors. That is, a particular configuration of several disordered genes may be necessary to create a mood disorder.

Neurotransmitter Dysregulation

Most of the biochemical theories of mood disorders have focused on neurotransmitters, the biochemicals that facilitate the transmission of impulses across the synapses between neurons. Many different neurotransmitters may play a role in the mood disorders, but the neurotransmitters that have been implicated most often in the mood disorders are the **monoamines.**

The specific monoamines that have been implicated are **norepinephrine, serotonin,** and, to a lesser extent, **dopamine.** These neurotransmitters are found in large concentrations in the *limbic system,* a part of the brain associated with the regulation of sleep, appetite, and emotional processes. These neurotransmitters are thought to cause both depression and mania—imbalances in one direction may cause depression and imbalances in the other direction may cause mania.

The early theory of the roles of these neurotransmitters in mood disorders was that depression was caused by a reduction in the amount of norepinephrine or serotonin in the synapses between neurons (Glassman, 1969; Schildkraut, 1965). This depletion could occur for numerous reasons: decreased synthesis of the neurotransmitter from its precursors, increased degradation of the neurotransmitter by enzymes, or impaired release or reuptake of the neurotransmitter (see Chapter 2 to review these processes). Mania was thought to be caused by an excess of the monoamines or perhaps dysregulation of the levels of these amines, especially dopamine. Taken together, these theories are known as the **monoamine theories** of mood disorders (Bunney & Davis, 1965; Schildkraut, 1965).

More recent studies of the monoamine theories have focused on the number and functioning of receptors for the monoamines on neurons in people suffering from mood disorders (Southwick et al., 2005). Recall from Chapter 2 that neurotransmitters and their receptors interact, somewhat as locks and keys do. Each neurotransmitter fits a particular type of receptor on the nerve cell membrane. If there is the wrong number of receptors for a given type of neurotransmitter or if the receptors for that neurotransmitter are too sensitive or not sensitive enough, then the neurons do not efficiently use the neurotransmitter that is available in the synapse.

Several studies suggest that people with major depression or bipolar disorder may have abnormalities in the number and sensitivity of receptors for the monoamine neurotransmitters (Hasler et al., 2004; Southwick et al., 2005). In major depression, receptors for serotonin and norepinephrine appear to be too few or insensitive. In bipolar disorder, the picture is less clear, but it is likely that receptors for the monoamines undergo poorly timed changes in sensitivity, which are correlated with mood changes (Kujawa & Nemeroff, 2000).

Most of the neurotransmitter abnormalities found in people with mood disorders are state-dependent. That is, these differences are present when the mood disorder is present but tend to disappear when the mood disorder subsides. Certain neurotransmitter abnormalities may be correlated with, but may not necessarily cause, the mood disorders. As the technology for determining the functioning of neurotransmitter systems develops, our understanding of the relationship between neurotransmitters and mood disorders will no doubt increase.

Brain Abnormalities

Neuroimaging studies using computerized tomography (CT) scans, positron-emission tomography

Brain Areas That May Be Involved in Mood Disorders. *(a)* Orbital prefrontal cortex *(green)* and ventromedial prefrontal cortex *(red)*. *(b)* Dorsolateral prefrontal cortex *(purple)*. *(c)* Hippocampus *(pink)* and amygdala *(orange)*. *(d)* Anterior cingulated cortex *(yellow)*.

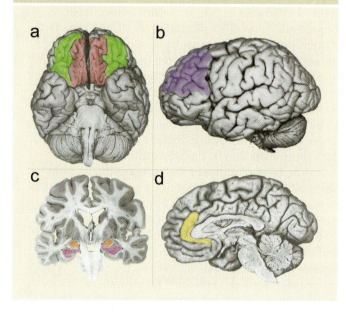

(PET), and magnetic resonance imaging (MRI) have found consistent abnormalities in at least four areas of the brain in people with mood disorders. These areas are the prefrontal cortex, the hippocampus, the anterior cingulate cortex, and the amygdala (Davidson et al., 2002; Southwick et al., 2005) (see Figure 9.4).

Both reductions in metabolic activity and a reduction in the volume of gray matter in the *prefrontal cortex*, particularly on the left side, have been found in people with serious depression or bipolar disorder (review Figure 9.4a, green and red areas, and b, purple areas) (Buchsbaum et al., 1997; Drevets, 2001; Drevets et al., 1997). Davidson, Pizzagalli, Nitschke, and Putnam (2002) have suggested that the left prefrontal cortex is more involved in approach-related goals and that inactivity in this region is associated with the lack of motivation and goal orientation in depression. The successful treatment of depression with antidepressant medications is associated with increases in metabolic activity in the left prefrontal cortex (Kennedy et al., 2001).

The *anterior cingulate* plays an important role in the body's response to stress, in emotional expression, and in social behavior, as well as in the processing of difficult information (Davidson et al., 2002) (review Figure 9.4d, yellow area). Peo-ple with depression show decreased activity in the anterior cingulate relative to controls (Buchsbaum et al., 1997; Drevets et al., 1997). This lack of activity may be associated with problems in attention, in the planning of appropriate responses, and in coping, as well as with anhedonia found in depression. Again, activity increases in this region of the brain when people are successfully treated for their depression (Mayberg et al., 1997; Pizzagalli et al., 2001).

The *hippocampus* is critical in memory and in fear-related learning (review Figure 9.4c, purple area). MRI studies show a smaller volume in the hippocampus of people with major depression or bipolar disorder (Bremner et al., 2000; Noga, Vladar, & Torrey, 2001). Similarly, PET studies show lower metabolic activity in the hippocampus in people with major depression (Saxena, Brody, et al., 2001). Damage to the hippocampus could be the result of chronic arousal of the body's stress response. People with depression show chronically high levels of the hormone cortisol, particularly in response to stress, indicating that their bodies overreact to stress and do not return to normal levels of cortisol as quickly as the bodies of healthy people do. The hippocampus contains many receptors for cortisol, and chronically elevated levels of cortisol may inhibit the development of new neurons in the hippocampus (see Pariante & Miller, 2001; Sapolsky, Krey, & McEwen, 1986).

Abnormalities in the structure and functioning of the amygdala are found in several disorders involving mood (Davidson et al., 2002) (review Figure 9.4c, orange area). The amygdala helps direct attention to stimuli that are emotionally salient and have major significance for the individual. Studies of people with mood disorders show an enlargement of the amygdala (Altshuler et al., 1998; Mervaala et al., 2000) and increased activity in this part of the brain (Drevets, 2001). Activity in the amygdala has been observed to decrease to normal values in people successfully treated for depression (Drevets, 2001). The effects of overactivity in the amygdala are not yet entirely clear, but Drevets (2001) and Davidson and colleagues (2002) suggest that it may bias people toward aversive or emotionally arousing information and lead to rumination over negative memories and negative aspects of the environment.

It is not known whether any of these abnormalities in the structure or functioning of the brain are causes of the mood disorders or the consequences of these disorders (Davidson, Pizzagalli, & Nitschke, 2002; Thase et al., 2002). Animal studies suggest that many of these brain abnormalities can be caused by conditions in the environment, including chronic stress and chronic lack of control (Leverenz et al., 1999). Thus, for some people with mood disorders, the initial cause of their disorder may have been environmental, but the disorder may cause changes in the brain that increase their vulnerability to future episodes. For other people with mood disorders, brain dysfunction may be caused by abnormal genes.

Neuroendocrine Factors

Hormones have long been thought to play a role in mood disorders, especially depression. The *neuroendocrine system* regulates a number of important hormones, which in turn affect basic functions, such as sleep, appetite, sexual drive, and the ability to experience pleasure (to review the neuroendocrine system, see Chapter 2). These hormones also help the body respond to environmental stressors.

Three key components of the neuroendocrine system—the hypothalamus, pituitary, and adrenal cortex—work together in a biological feedback system that is richly interconnected with the limbic system and the cerebral cortex. This system is often referred to as the **hypothalamic-pituitary-adrenal axis,** or **HPA axis**, and is involved in the fight-or-flight response, as discussed in Chapter 6.

Normally, when we are confronted with a stressor, the HPA axis becomes more active (see Figure 9.5). It increases the body's levels of major stress hormones, such as **cortisol**, which help the body respond to the stressor by making it possible to fight the stressor or flee from it. Once the stressor is gone, the HPA axis activity returns to its baseline levels. Thus, this biological feedback loop both helps activate the HPA system during stress and calms the system when the stress is over.

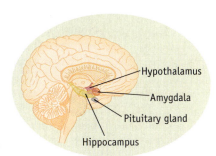

The hypothalamic-pituitary-adrenal (HPA) axis and structures of the limbic system may be involved in the development of depression.

People with depression tend to show chronic hyperactivity in the HPA axis and an inability for the HPA axis to return to normal functioning following a stressor (Southwick et al., 2005; Young & Korzun, 1998). In turn, the excess hormones produced by heightened HPA activity seem to have an inhibiting effect on receptors for the monoamines. One model for the development of depression is that people exposed to chronic stress may develop poorly regulated neuroendocrine systems. Then, when they are exposed even to minor stressors later in life, the HPA axis overreacts and does not easily return to baseline. This overreaction creates change in the functioning of the monoamine neurotransmitters in the brain, and an episode of depression is likely to ensue (Southwick et al., 2005).

Women's Hormonal Cycles as a Factor

Many people have argued over the years that women's greater vulnerability to depression is tied to hormones—specifically, the so-called ovarian hormones, estrogen and progesterone. The main fuel for this idea comes from evidence that women are more prone to depression during the premenstrual period of the menstrual cycle, the postpartum period, and menopause. These are times when estrogen and progesterone levels change dramatically.

Research over the past several decades has shown that most women do not experience significant changes in their moods during times of hormonal change (Nolen-Hoeksema, 2002; Young &

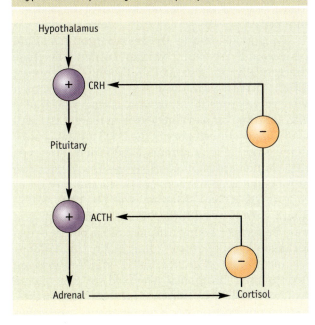

FIGURE 9.5	**The Hypothalamic-Pituitary-Adrenal Axis.** The

hypothalamus synthesizes corticotropin-releasing hormone (CRH). CRH is transported to the pituitary gland, where it stimulates the synthesis and release of adrenocorticotropic hormone (ACTH), which then circulates to the adrenal glands, producing cortisol. Cortisol then inhibits the production of further ACTH and CRH. Normally, this process prevents too much or too prolonged physiological arousal following a stressor. In major depression, however, people often show abnormal cortisol functioning, suggesting that there is dysregulation in the hypothalamic-pituitary-adrenal (HPA) axis.

Korszun, 1998). However, there is a small group of women, about 3 percent of the population, who frequently experience increases in depressive symptoms during the premenstrual phase. Many of these women also have a history of frequent major depressive episodes or anxiety disorders with no connection to the menstrual cycle or of other psychiatric disorders (Steiner et al., 2003). This history suggests that these women have a general vulnerability to depression or anxiety, rather than a specific vulnerability to premenstrual depression.

This information has led many researchers to argue that depressions during the premenstrual period should not be given a separate diagnosis, such as **premenstrual dysphoric disorder,** but, rather, should be considered only exacerbations of major depression or dysthymia. Others argue that premenstrual depression should be recognized separately, with its own diagnosis, because it is different from depression that has no link with the menstrual cycle and therefore should be studied separately. The authors of the DSM-IV-TR dealt with this controversy by putting diagnostic criteria for premenstrual dysphoric disorder in an appendix, rather than in the main body of its text with other officially recognized diagnoses.

Even among women who clearly do have premenstrual symptoms (PMS), there is little evidence that their symptoms are due to changes in estrogen or progesterone levels across the menstrual cycle (Steiner et al., 2003; Young & Korzun, 1998). Many studies have found no differences in estrogen or progesterone levels between women with PMS and those without PMS. There clearly is something about the menstrual cycle that is worsening mood in women with PMS, but it appears that estrogen or progesterone does not have consistent direct effects on mood.

About 1 in 10 women experience a severe postpartum depression in the first few months after giving birth. This might seem like strong evidence that hormonal changes play a role in women's depressions, because this is a period of great hormonal change in women's bodies. However, studies comparing rates of depression in women who are and are not postpartum have tended not to find differences in rates of depression (O'Hara & Swain, 1996). Even among women who do become seriously depressed during the postpartum period, depressions do not seem to be linked to any specific imbalances in hormones (Hendrick, Altshuler, & Suri, 1998).

Postpartum depressions are often linked to severe stress in women's lives, such as financial strain, marital difficulties, lack of social support, and fussy babies (Brugha et al., 1998; Hendrick et al., 1998; O'Hara & Swain, 1996). In addition, women who

About 1 in 10 women suffer postpartum depression.

have a history of depression clearly are at increased risk for postpartum depression (Steiner et al., 2003). These women may carry a general vulnerability to depression, which is triggered by either the physiological or the environmental changes of the postpartum period.

Menopause marks the cessation of menstrual periods, and circulating ovarian hormones decrease dramatically at menopause (Young & Korzun, 1998). Twenty years ago, the belief that women were more prone to depression during menopause was so strong among clinicians that there was a separate diagnostic category in the DSM for this type of depression. Several studies have found, however, that women are no more likely to show depression around the time of menopause than at any other time in their lives (Matthews et al., 1990; Nicol-Smith, 1996). In addition, there are no consistent mood effects of taking estrogen replacement drugs for menopausal women (Young & Korzun, 1998).

In sum, the evidence that women's moods are tied to their hormones is mixed, at best. Some women clearly do experience more depression during the postpartum period, menopause, and other times when their hormone levels change rapidly.

The extent to which these experiences of depression account for the generally higher rates of depression among women compared with men is less clear.

Early Stress as a Cause of Neurobiological Vulnerability to Depression

There is increasing evidence that early traumatic stress, such as being the victim of incest, severe neglect, or other serious, chronic stress, can lead to some of the neurobiological abnormalities that may predispose people to depression (Southwick et al., 2005). Studies of children who have been abused or neglected show that their biological responses to stress, particularly the response of their HPA axis, often are either exaggerated or blunted (Cicchetti & Toth, 2005). Heim and colleagues (Heim & Nemeroff, 2002; Heim, Plotsky, & Nemeroff, 2004) have found that women who were sexually abused as children show altered HPA responses to stress as adults, even when they are not depressed. Similarly, animal studies show that early stress (such as separation from their mothers) promotes exaggerated neurobiological stress reactivity and vulnerability to depression-like responses to future stressors (see Southwick et al., 2005). These neurobiological vulnerabilities can be reduced in animals by providing them with subsequent supportive maternal care and/or pharmacological interventions.

SUMMING UP

- Genetic factors clearly play a role in bipolar disorder, although it is somewhat less clear what role genetics plays in many forms of unipolar depression.

- The neurotransmitter theories suggest that imbalances in levels of norepinephrine or serotonin or the dysregulation of receptors for these neurotransmitters contribute to depression, and dysregulation of norepinephrine, serotonin, or dopamine is involved in bipolar disorder.

- Neuroimaging studies have shown abnormalities in the structure and functioning of the prefrontal cortex, hippocampus, anterior cingulate cortex, and amygdala in people with mood disorders.

- People with depression have chronic hyperactivity of the hypothalamic-pituitary-adrenal (HPA) axis, which helps regulate the body's response to stress.

- Abnormalities in the biological stress response may result from early stressors in some people and contribute to depression.

PSYCHOLOGICAL THEORIES OF MOOD DISORDERS

Psychological theories have focused almost exclusively on depression, because the evidence that bipolar disorder is caused by biological factors is strong. However, new episodes of bipolar disorder may be triggered by experiencing stressful events or living in an unsupportive family (Frank, Schwartz, & Kupfer, 2000; Hlastsala et al., 2000). This pattern suggests a diathesis-stress model of bipolar disorder, in which the *diathesis*, or vulnerability, is a biological one, such as a genetic predisposition to the disorder, and stressors, such as the loss of a job, can trigger new episodes. In this section, however, we focus on depression and the psychological theories that have tried to explain it (see the Concept Overview in Table 9.6 on page 320).

Behavioral Theories

Depression often arises as a reaction to stressful negative events, such as the breakup of a relationship, the death of a loved one, a job loss, or a serious medical illness (Hammen, 2005). Sixty-five percent of people with depression in one study reported a negative life event in the six months prior to the onset of their depression (Frank et al., 1994). People with depression are more likely than nondepressed people to have chronic life stressors, such as financial strain or a bad marriage. People who suffer depression also tend to have a history of traumatic life events, particularly events involving loss (Hammen, 2005).

The Reduction of Positive Reinforcers

Peter Lewinsohn's **behavioral theory of depression** suggests that life stress leads to depression because it reduces the positive reinforcers in a person's life (Lewinsohn & Gotlib, 1995). The person begins to withdraw, which only results in a further reduction in reinforcers, which leads to more withdrawal, and a self-perpetuating chain is created.

For example, imagine that a man is having difficulty in his relationship with his wife. Interactions with her are no longer as positively reinforcing as they formerly were, so he stops initiating these interactions as often. This only worsens the communication between him and his wife, so the relationship becomes even worse. He withdraws further and becomes depressed about this area of his life. Lewinsohn suggests that such a pattern is especially likely in people with poor social skills, because they are more likely to experience rejection by others and to withdraw in response to this rejection, rather than to find ways to overcome the rejection (Lewinsohn, 1974). In addition, once a person begins engaging in

TABLE 9.6	Concept Overview

Psychological Theories of Mood Disorders

The psychological theories of depression have focused on aspects of the environment, of thinking, and of a person's past.

Theory	Description
Behavioral theories	
Lewinsohn's theory	Depressed people experience a reduction in positive reinforcers and an increase in aversive events, which leads to their depression.
Learned helplessness theory	Depressed people lack control, which leads to the belief that they are helpless, which leads to depressive symptoms.
Cognitive theories	
Aaron Beck's theory	Depressed people have a negative cognitive triad of beliefs about the self, the world, and the future, which is maintained by distorted thinking.
Reformulated learned helplessness theory	Depressed people have the tendency to attribute events to internal, stable, and global factors, which contributes to depression.
Ruminative response styles theory	Depressed people tend to ruminate about their symptoms and problems.
Psychodynamic theory	Depressed people are unconsciously punishing themselves because they feel abandoned by another person but cannot punish that person; dependency and perfectionism are risk factors for depression.
Interpersonal theories	Depressed people have poor relationships with others.

depressive behaviors, these behaviors are reinforced by the sympathy and attention they engender in others.

Learned Helplessness Theory

Another behavioral theory—the **learned helplessness theory**—suggests that the type of stressful event most likely to lead to depression is uncontrollable negative events (Seligman, 1975). Such events, especially if frequent or chronic, can lead people to believe that they are helpless to control important outcomes in their environment. In turn, this belief in helplessness leads people to lose their motivation, to reduce actions that might control the environment, and to be unable to learn how to control situations that are controllable. These deficits, known as **learned helplessness deficits,** are similar to the symptoms of depression: low motivation, passivity, and indecisiveness (Seligman, 1975).

The initial evidence for the learned helplessness theory came from studies with animals, as described in Chapter 2. A group of researchers conducted a series of studies in which dogs were given controllable shock, uncontrollable shock, or no shock (Overmier & Seligman, 1967; Seligman & Maier, 1967). The dogs in the controllable shock group could turn off the shock by jumping a short barrier, and they quickly learned how to do so (as did the dogs that had previously received no shock). The dogs in the uncontrollable shock group could not turn off or otherwise escape the shock. The dogs in the controllable and uncontrollable shock conditions received the same total amount of shock. However, when the dogs in the uncontrollable shock group were put into a situation in which they could control the shock, they seemed unable to learn how to do so. They just sat in the box, passive and whimpering, until the shock went off. Even when the experimenter dragged these dogs across the barrier in an attempt to teach them how to turn off the shock, the dogs did not learn the response. The researchers argued that the dogs in the uncontrollable shock group had learned they were helpless to control the shock, and their passivity and inability to learn to control the shock were the result of this learned helplessness.

In turn, the researchers argued that many human depressions are *helplessness depressions*, result-

Children who lose a parent may come to believe that important areas of their lives are not under their control and, thus, develop a helplessness depression.

ing when people come to believe they are helpless to control important outcomes in their environment. For example, children who lose their mothers may come to believe that important areas of their lives are not under their control. The loss of a mother may mean not only the loss of the person to whom the child is most closely attached but also years of disruption and instability as the child is moved from one set of relatives to another, if the father is not able to care for the child. Such chronic instability might persuade the child that life truly is uncontrollable, and this may be why childhood bereavement is a predisposing factor for depression. Similarly, women who are frequently battered by their husbands may develop the belief that there is nothing they can do to control their beatings or other parts of their lives, and this may explain the high rates of depression among battered women (Koss & Kilpatrick, 2001).

Cognitive Theories

"Good morning, Eeyore," shouted Piglet.
"Good morning, Little Piglet," said Eeyore.

"If it *is* a good morning," he said.
"Which I doubt," said he.
"Not that it matters," he said.
(Milne, 1961, p. 54)

Like poor Eeyore, some people have a chronically gloomy way of interpreting the things that happen to them. According to the cognitive theories of depression, these gloomy ways of thinking are a cause of depression.

Aaron Beck's Theory

One of the first cognitive theories of depression was developed by psychiatrist Aaron Beck. Beck (1967) argued that people with depression look at the world through a **negative cognitive triad:** They have negative views of themselves, of the world, and of the future. People with depression then commit many types of errors in thinking—such as jumping to negative conclusions on the basis of little evidence, ignoring good events, focusing only on negative events, and exaggerating negative events—that support their negative cognitive triad (see Table 9.7 on page 322).

People with depression may not be aware that they hold these negative views or that they make these errors in thinking. Often, these negative thoughts are so automatic that people with depression do not realize how they are interpreting situations. A wide range of studies have supported the hypothesis that people with depression show these negative ways of thinking, and some longitudinal studies have shown that these thinking styles predict depression over time (Abramson et al., 2002). Beck's theory led to one of the most widely used and successful therapies for depression, cognitive-behavioral therapy.

Reformulated Learned Helplessness Theory

Another influential cognitive theory of depression, the **reformulated learned helplessness theory,** was proposed to explain how cognitive factors might influence whether a person becomes helpless and depressed following a negative event (Abramson, et al., 1978; Peterson & Seligman, 1984). This theory focuses on people's causal attributions for events. A **causal attribution** is an explanation of why an event happened. According to this theory, people who habitually explain negative events by causes that are internal, stable, and global blame themselves for these negative events, expect negative events to recur in the future, and expect to experience negative events in many areas of their lives. In turn, these expectations lead them to experience long-term learned helplessness deficits plus self-esteem loss in many areas of their lives.

TABLE 9.7   Errors or Distortions in Thinking in Depression

Error	Description
All-or-nothing thinking	You see things in black-and-white categories. If your performance falls short of perfect, you see yourself as a total failure.
Overgeneralization	You see a single negative event as a never-ending pattern of defeat.
Mental filter	You pick out a single negative detail and dwell on it exclusively, so that your vision of all reality becomes darkened, like a drop of ink that discolors an entire beaker of water.
Disqualifying the positive	You reject positive experiences by insisting they "don't count" for some reason. In this way, you can maintain a negative belief that is contradicted by your everyday experiences.
Jumping to conclusions	You make a negative interpretation, even though there are no definite facts that convincingly support your conclusion: (a) *Mind Reading*. You arbitrarily conclude that someone is reacting negatively to you, and you don't bother to check this out. (b) *The Fortune Teller Error*. You anticipate that things will turn out badly, and you feel convinced that your prediction is an already established fact.
Magnification (catastrophizing) or minimization	You exaggerate the importance of things (such as your goof-up or someone else's achievement), or you inappropriately shrink things until they appear tiny (your own desirable qualities or another's imperfections). This is also called the "binocular trick."
Emotional reasoning	You assume that your negative emotions necessarily reflect the way things really are: "I feel it; therefore, it must be true."
"Should" statements	You try to motivate yourself with "shoulds" and "shouldn'ts", as if you had to be whipped and punished before you could be expected to do anything. "Must" and "oughts" are also offenders. The emotional consequence is guilt. When you direct "should" statements toward others, you feel anger, frustration, and resentment.
Labeling and mislabeling	This is an extreme form of overgeneralization. Instead of describing your error, you attach a negative label to yourself: "I'm a *loser*." When someone else's behavior rubs you the wrong way, you attach a negative label to that person. Mislabeling involves describing an event with language that is highly colored and emotionally loaded.
Personalization	You see yourself as the cause of a negative external event, which, in fact, you were not primarily responsible for.

Source: Burns, 1980.

For example, consider a student who becomes depressed after failing a psychology exam. The reformulated learned helplessness theory would suggest that she has blamed her failure on internal causes—she didn't study hard enough—rather than external causes—the exam was too hard. Further, she has assumed that the failure was due to stable causes, such as a lack of aptitude in psychology, rather than unstable causes, such as the instructor's not allowing enough time, and she can expect to fail again. Finally, she has attributed her failure to a global cause, such as her difficulty in learning the material for this particular test. This global attribution would lead to failure in other academic areas.

Again, researchers equate learned helplessness deficits with depression and argue that an internal-stable-global attributional style for negative events puts people at risk for depression. Abramson et al. (1989) argued that hopelessness depression develops when people make pessimistic attributions for the most important events in their lives and perceive that they have no way of coping with the consequences of these events. The reformulated learned helplessness theory and the hopelessness theory have motivated a great deal of research (Abramson et al., 2002).

One of the most definitive studies of this theory of depression was a long-term study of college students (Alloy, Abramson, & Francis, 1999). Researchers interviewed first-year students at two universities and identified those with hopeless attributional styles and those with optimistic attributional styles. They then tracked these students for the next 2½ years, interviewing them every 6 weeks. Among the students with no history of depression, those with a hopeless cognitive style were much more likely to develop a first onset of major depression than were those with an optimistic attributional style (17 percent versus 1 percent). In addition, among those who had a history of depression, students with a hopeless style were more likely to have a relapse of depression than those with an optimistic style (27 percent versus 6 percent). Thus, a pessimistic attributional style predicted both first onsets of depression and relapses of depression.

Is it possible that people with depression are not distorted in their negative views of the world but actually are seeing the world realistically for the terrible place that it is? Researchers began investigating this possibility when they stumbled on a phenomenon now referred to as **depressive realism:** When asked to make judgments about how much control they have over situations that are actually uncontrollable, people with depression are quite accurate. In contrast, nondepressed people greatly overestimate the amount of control they have, especially over positive events. For example, in one study (Alloy & Abramson, 1979), depressed and nondepressed people were asked to judge to what degree they could control the onset of a green light by pushing a button on a display panel. In truth, none of the subjects had control over the onset of the light. In conditions in which the subjects were rewarded whenever the green light came on, the nondepressed people grossly overestimated their control over the onset

of the light. In contrast, the depressed subjects accurately judged that they had no control over the onset of the light.

Subsequently, a long line of research has shown that nondepressed people have a robust illusion that they can control all sorts of situations that truly are out of their control and that they have superior skills, compared with most people (Taylor & Brown, 1988). For example, nondepressed people believe they can control games of chance, such as the lottery; that they are more likely than the average person to succeed in life; that they are more immune to car accidents than other people; and that their social skills are better than most people's. In contrast, people with depression do not seem to hold these illusions of control and superiority. Indeed, people with depression seem amazingly accurate in judging the amount of control they have over situations and their skills at various tasks. This research on illusion of control calls into question the notion that depression results from unrealistic beliefs that one cannot control one's environment or from negative errors in thinking about oneself and the world. Perhaps it is not accurate, realistic thinking that prevents people from becoming depressed but, rather, hope and optimism.

Ruminative Response Styles Theory

Another cognitive theory, the **ruminative response styles theory,** focuses more on the process of thinking, rather than the content of thinking, as a contributor to depression (Nolen-Hoeksema, 2003). Some people, when sad and upset, focus intently on how they feel—their symptoms of fatigue and poor concentration and their sadness and hopelessness—and can identify many possible causes of these symptoms. They do not attempt to do anything about these causes, however, and continue to engage in **rumination** about their depression.

Several studies have shown that people with this more ruminative coping style are more likely to develop major depression and may remain depressed longer than people with a more action-oriented coping style (Nolen-Hoeksema, 2000; Nolen-Hoeksema, Larson, & Grayson, 1999; Nolen-Hoeksema & Morrow, 1991; Nolen-Hoeksema, Parker, & Larson, 1994). Rumination is not just another symptom of depression, although people who are more depressed have more to ruminate about. People with depression differ in the extent to which they ruminate, and those who ruminate more become more severely depressed over time and remain depressed longer than those who do not.

Women are more likely than men to ruminate when they are depressed (Nolen-Hoeksema, 2002; Nolen-Hoeksema et al., 1999). This may be because women are exposed to more circumstances that make them ruminate—more negative events and circumstances over which they feel they have no control. Regardless of the reasons for this gender difference in rumination, women's tendency to ruminate appears to contribute to their higher rates of depression, compared with men (Nolen-Hoeksema et al., 1999).

Psychodynamic Theories

Some people seem to find themselves in unhealthy, destructive relationships over and over again. Each time these relationships end, they vow never to get into similar relationships again. However, they do and then find themselves depressed over the problems in the new relationships or when the relationships inevitably end.

Psychodynamic theorists suggest that such patterns of unhealthy relationships stem from people's childhood experiences that prevented them from developing a strong and positive sense of self reasonably independent of others' evaluations (Arieti & Bemporad, 1980; Bibring, 1953; Blatt & Zuroff, 1992; Freud, 1917). As adults, these people are constantly searching for approval and security in their relationships with others. They are anxious about separation and abandonment and may allow others to take advantage and even abuse them, rather than risk losing the relationship by complaining. They are constantly striving to be "perfect," so that they will be loved. Even when they accomplish great things, they do not feel secure or positive about themselves. Eventually, a problem in a close relationship or a failure to achieve perfection occurs, and they plunge into depression.

Many modern psychodynamic theorists still rely on the groundbreaking work Freud published in his paper *Mourning and Melancholia* to describe just how depression develops when a person perceives he or she has been abandoned or has failed. Freud pointed out that people who are depressed have many of the symptoms of people who are grieving the death of a loved one: They feel sad, alone, unmotivated, and lethargic. Unlike grieving people, people with depression display severe self-hate and self-blame. Indeed, said Freud, people with depression appear to want to punish themselves, even to the point of killing themselves.

Freud argued that people with depression are not actually blaming or punishing themselves. Instead, they are blaming or punishing those who they perceive have abandoned them. People with depression are so dependent on the approval and love of others that much of their ego or sense of self is made up of their images of these others—what Freud called the "love objects." When they believe others have rejected them, people with depression are too frightened to express their rage outwardly. Instead, they turn their anger inward on the parts of their own egos that have incorporated the love objects. Their self-blame and punishment is actually blame and punishment of the others who have abandoned them. This is Freud's **introjected hostility theory** of depression. The case of Giselle illustrates the processes described by the psychodynamic theories of depression.

CASE STUDY

Giselle was raised by two well-meaning but emotionally inhibited parents. The parents had emigrated to the United States from Eastern Europe in the 1970s, fleeing persecution for their anticommunist beliefs. Even after settling in the United States, Giselle's parents remained paranoid about the family's security and constantly told Giselle she had to be "good" or the family would be in danger. Thus, from an early age, Giselle suppressed any childhood willfulness or exuberance. She was not allowed to play with other children; she spent most of her time with the family maid, who had followed them to the United States. Her parents were preoccupied with their uncertain circumstances and unnecessarily belittled Giselle's childhood concerns. For example, when there was an epidemic of flu at Giselle's school, her mother told her not to worry, because only the smart and pretty girls were getting sick. The mother doted on the father when he was in the house, ignoring Giselle.

(continued)

The father paid attention to Giselle only when she was deferential or complimentary.

As an adult, Giselle chose to become a nurse, because she felt it would gain her acceptance and love by patients. Giselle married a man who was somewhat solitary and hypercritical. He was prone to periods of depression and always preoccupied with his own concerns. Giselle became the major source of financial support during her marriage, often taking on extra shifts to earn more money. She had done remarkably well in her career because of her hard work and her repeated efforts to please others. She was also the emotional mainstay in her family, being responsible for taking care of the children and for fulfilling the usual responsibilities of running a household. Giselle rarely complained, however. She needed to be certain that everyone liked her and thought well of her, and she went to extremes of self-sacrifice to ensure the high regard of others.

After several years, her husband left her, telling her that he did not love her any longer and that she no longer gave him any pleasure in his life. In the first few days after her husband announced he was going to leave, Giselle desperately tried to win back his love by indulging his every whim. Eventually, however, they had a violent confrontation, during which he walked out. Later that evening, Giselle emptied her medicine cabinet of all drugs, drove to a secluded area, and ingested the drugs in an effort to kill herself. (Adapted from Bemporad, 1995)

Some research has supported elements of the psychodynamic perspective on depression. For example, people with depression tend to display many of Giselle's personality traits: They are dependent on others, believe that they must be perfect, have poor self-esteem, and are unable to express anger openly (Klein et al., 2002). In addition, many people with depression describe their parents as having characteristics similar to those of Giselle's parents: They are cold and neglectful, excessively moralistic and demanding of perfection, or requiring of complete devotion and dependency from their children in exchange for their love (Blatt & Zuroff, 1992). Most of these studies are cross-

sectional, however, so it is not known whether these characteristics and views are symptoms of the depression or actual causes of it. A few longitudinal studies support elements of psychodynamic theories. For example, one study of middle-aged women found that those who tended to inhibit any expression of anger and who were unassertive in interpersonal interactions were more likely to become depressed over a three-year period (Bromberger & Matthews, 1996).

Traditional psychodynamic perspectives on depression have been adapted by modern theorists to develop the interpersonal theories of depression and therapies based on these theories. We turn now to the interpersonal theories.

Interpersonal Theories

Like psychodynamic theories, **interpersonal theories of depression** are concerned with people's close relationships and their roles in those relationships (Klerman et al., 1984). Disturbances in these roles are thought to be the main source of depression. These disturbances may be recent, as when a woman who believes that her marriage has been successful for years suddenly finds that her husband is having an affair. Often, the disturbances are rooted in long-standing patterns of interactions the people with depression typically have with important others. Drawing from attachment theory (Bowlby, 1982), interpersonal theorists argue that children who do not experience their caregivers as reliable, responsive, and warm develop an insecure attachment to their caregivers, which sets the stage for all future relationships (see Chapter 2). These problematic relationships become represented mentally as negative working models of others and of the self in relation to others. These models are essentially operating rules and expectations about the availability of support from others and the implications of others' lack of support for one's self-worth.

Children with insecure attachments develop expectations that they must be or do certain things in order to win the approval of others, which have been called **contingencies of self-worth** (Kuiper & Olinger, 1986; Kuiper, Olinger, & MacDonald, 1988). These are "if-then" rules concerning self-worth, such as "I'm nothing if a person I care about doesn't love me." If these contingencies of self-worth sound like the dysfunctional beliefs that Beck and other cognitive theories describe, they are—the interpersonal theorists argue that dysfunctional beliefs are the result of insecure attachments in childhood. As long as an individual meets the contingencies of self-worth set up in his or her working model, then he or she will maintain positive self-esteem and remain nondepressed. Failures to meet these contingencies are inevitable, however, and plunge the person into depression.

According to the interpersonal theories, people who are so insecure in their relationships with others engage in **excessive reassurance seeking—**constantly looking for assurances from others that they are accepted and loved (Joiner, 2002). They never quite believe the affirmations other people give, however, and anxiously keep going back for more. After a while, their family members and friends can become weary of this behavior and become frustrated or hostile. The insecure person picks up on these cues of annoyance and becomes panicked over them, leading him or her to feel even more insecure and to engage in even more excessive reassurance seeking. Eventually, the person's social support may withdraw altogether, leading him or her to develop even more depression, as is illustrated in the following case study (from Nolen-Hoeksema, 2006).

CASE STUDY

Rachel was a 48-year-old homemaker from the Bronx, married to her husband, Phil, for 15 years. Phil never really gave Rachel good cause to doubt that he loved her. He was attentive and loving. He was at her side when she had medical problems a few years ago and when her mother died last year. He supported her decision to stay home to raise their two children and was sincerely interested in what she and the kids did during the day while he was working at his law firm.

But still Rachel doubted, and these doubts had grown stronger in the last few months as another one of her depressive periods had set in. How could he love her, when she was so boring? Surely he was just being nice when he asked about her day—he couldn't really be interested, given how exciting his own work was. She had gained weight over the years and felt she was no longer attractive to him. She wondered what he would do if one of the young women lawyers in his firm expressed interest in him.

Rachel tried to keep these concerns to herself, but they leaked out, in little comments to Phil. When he came home in the evening and said, "How was your day?" she sometimes responded, "Oh, boring as usual; you wouldn't be interested." Then, she waited to see what his response was. Phil would usu-ally say something like, "Sure, I'm interested; tell me what you did." Then Rachel would tell him a few incidents from the day but label each one as "nothing" and "silly" as she went along. She listened intently for his response, wanting him to deny that her activities were nothing or silly and becoming anxious and disappointed if he didn't explicitly do so.

When Rachel mentioned that she felt fat or unattractive, Phil would usually respond that she was still his beautiful bride. She responded, "Oh, you have to say that; you're stuck with me." Phil felt frustrated and put off by this but tried to stay calm. "I don't have to say that; I mean it. I love you and I love how you look." But Rachel would not be satisfied: "You love me now, but will you always love me no matter what happens?"

Rachel set up all sorts of other tests of Phil's love for her and ploys to gain assurance of his devotion. If they disagreed with each other about something in the morning, Rachel would ruminate about it after Phil left for work. In her mind, she implicitly believed that, if he hadn't called to talk with her about the disagreement by 10 A.M. this meant he was really angry and their relationship was in trouble. Sometimes, if he hadn't called or e-mailed her by 11 A.M. she'd call or e-mail him with a neutral message, just to see whether he'd mention the morning's disagreement. If he didn't respond almost immediately, Rachel took this as further evidence that he was angry with her, even though she knew he was probably just very busy. If he did respond to her message, but didn't mention the disagreement and how sorry he was for it, Rachel would ruminate about this for the rest of the afternoon. By the time Phil got home in the evening, she was ripe with fear and anger, when he hadn't thought about the disagreement all day because it had been so minor.

A number of influential theories have suggested that women are socialized to base most of their self-concept and self-worth on their relationships with others, and this is what makes them more prone than men to depression. Jack (1991) and Helgeson (1994) both argue that females are

Difficulties in close relationships are often tied to depression.

more likely than males to silence their own wants and needs in a relationship in favor of maintaining a positive emotional tone in the relationship and to feel too responsible for the quality of the relationship. This leads females to have less power and to obtain less benefit from relationships. Some support has been found for this perspective on the gender difference in depression (Baron & Peixoto, 1991; Nolen-Hoeksema & Jackson, 2001).

The interpersonal theories of depression have been supported in several studies (Joiner, 2002). For example, one longitudinal study of college students found that those with an anxious, insecure attachment style had more dysfunctional negative beliefs and subsequently developed lower self-esteem and more depressive symptoms (Roberts, Gotlib, & Kassel, 1996). Most of the research on the interpersonal models of depression has focused on evaluating the therapy that was developed based on this model.

SUMMING UP

- The behavioral theories of depression suggest that stress can induce depression by reducing the number of reinforcers available to people.

- The learned helplessness theory of depression says that uncontrollable events can lead people to believe that important outcomes are outside of their control and thus can lead them to develop depression.

- The cognitive theories of depression argue that people with depression think in distorted and negative ways, and this leads them to become depressed, particularly in the face of negative events. In addition, people who ruminate about their depressive symptoms and the causes and consequences of those symptoms appear more prone to develop severe levels of depression.

- Psychodynamic theories posit that people with depression are overly dependent on the evaluations and approval of others for their self-esteem, as a result of poor nurturing by parents.

- The interpersonal theories of depression suggest that poor attachment relationships early in life can lead children to develop expectations that they must be or do certain things in order to win the approval of others, which puts them at risk for depression. They may also engage in excessive reassurance seeking, which drives away their social support.

SOCIAL PERSPECTIVES ON MOOD DISORDERS

Sociologists have focused on the large age, gender, and cross-cultural differences in rates of depression, and they have tried to understand these disorders in light of those differences.

The Cohort Effect in Depression

Recall that the rates of depression appear to be lower in people over the age of 65 than in younger people and that there are several explanations for this age difference. One further explanation highlights sociocultural changes over history that may have resulted in more recent generations' being at higher risk for depression than people who were born a few generations ago (Klerman & Weissman, 1989). This type of explanation is called a **cohort effect:** People born in one historical period are at different risk for a disorder than are people born in another historical period. For example, fewer than 15 percent of people born before 1940 have experienced episodes of major depression at some time in their lives, whereas over 25 percent of people born after 1970 have already experienced major depression by the age of 30 (see Figure 9.6 on page 328). Proponents of the cohort explanation suggest that more recent generations are more at risk for depression because of the rapid changes in social values that began in the 1960s and the disintegration of the family unit (Klerman & Weissman, 1989).

This decrease in social support and in identification with common social values may have put younger generations at higher risk for depression than older generations were. Another possible explanation is that younger generations have higher expectations for themselves than did older generations, but these expectations are too high to be met.

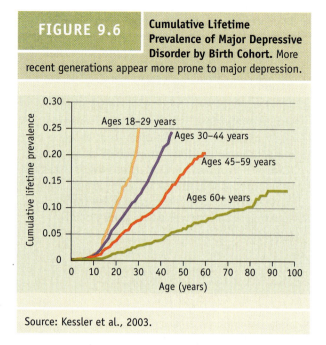

FIGURE 9.6 **Cumulative Lifetime Prevalence of Major Depressive Disorder by Birth Cohort.** More recent generations appear more prone to major depression.

Source: Kessler et al., 2003.

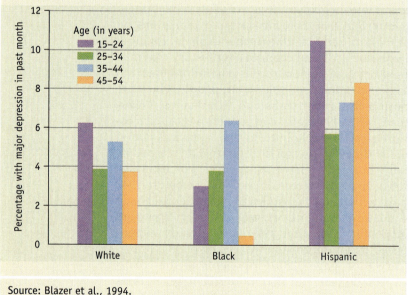

FIGURE 9.7 **Ethnic Differences in Major Depression.** These are the percentages of people in each age group and by ethnicity diagnosed with major depression in the previous month in one study. Hispanic Americans showed the highest rates across all age groups.

Source: Blazer et al., 1994.

Social Status

People who have lower status in society generally tend to show more depression. For example, in one large study done in the United States, people of Hispanic origin had a higher prevalence of major depression in the previous year than European Americans (Blazer et al., 1994) (see Figure 9.7).

This may reflect the higher rate of poverty, unemployment, and discrimination that Hispanics suffer, compared with European Americans.

Figure 9.7 also suggests, however, that African Americans of most ages have even lower rates of major depression than European Americans. This may seem puzzling, given the disadvantaged status of African Americans in U.S. society. However, African Americans have high rates of anxiety disorders, suggesting that the stress of their social status may make them especially prone to anxiety disorders rather than depression. Other studies have found extremely high rates of depression among Native Americans, especially the young (Saluja et al., 2004). Depression among these Native American youth is tied to poverty, hopelessness, and alcoholism.

One of the most compelling social explanations for women's higher rates of depression is that women's lower social status puts them at high risk for physical and sexual abuse, and these experiences often lead to depression. Women are much more likely than men to be the victims of rape, incest, battering, and sexual harassment (Koss & Kilpatrick, 2001). The rates of these types of violence against women are staggering. Most studies of rape estimate that between 14 and 25 percent of women are raped in their lives, most often before the age of 30 (Koss, 1993). One in eight women reports that she has been physically assaulted by her husband in the past year, and 1.8 million women report having been severely assaulted (punched, kicked, choked, or threatened with a gun or knife) (Straus & Gelles, 1990). Survivors of physical and sexual assault show high rates of major depression, anxiety disorders, and substance abuse. Thus, it seems likely that at least some of the difference between women's and men's rates of depression may be tied to the higher rates of abuse of women than of men and the resulting depression in female abuse survivors (Nolen-Hoeksema, 2002).

Cross-Cultural Differences

One cultural group within the United States that has an especially low prevalence of unipolar depression is the Old Order Amish of central Pennsylvania. As noted in Chapter 3, the Amish are a religious community of people who maintain a very simple lifestyle oriented around farming and the church and who reject modern conveniences, such as automobiles, electricity, and telephones. Essentially, the Amish live as people did in nineteenth-century rural America. Extensive research on the mood disorders among the Amish has suggested that their prevalence of major depression is only one-tenth of that of mainstream groups in the

United States (Egeland et al., 1987). Perhaps the simple, agrarian lifestyle of the Amish, with its emphasis on family and community, helps protect its members against depression.

Similarly, cross-national studies have suggested that the prevalence of major depression is lower among less industrialized and less modern countries than among more industrialized and more modern countries (Cross-National Collaborative Group, 1992; Lepine, 2001). Again, it may be that the fast-paced lifestyles of people in modern, industrialized societies, with their lack of stable social support and community values, are toxic to mental health. In contrast, the community- and family-oriented lifestyles of less modern societies may be beneficial to mental health, despite the physical hardships that many people in these societies face because of their lack of modern conveniences.

Alternately, some researchers have suggested that people in less modern cultures may tend to manifest depression with physical complaints, rather than psychological symptoms of depression, such as sadness, loss of motivation, and hopelessness about the future (Tsai & Chentsova-Dutton, 2002). For example, a study of refugees in Somalia found that they had a concept similar to the concept of sadness, which they called *murug* (Carroll, 2004). *Murug* arises when an individual has lost a loved one or another major negative life event has occurred. The symptoms of *murug*, however, are headaches and social withdrawal.

Similarly, in China, people facing severe stress often complain of *neurasthenia*, a collection of physical symptoms such as chronic headaches, pain in the joints, nausea, lack of energy, and palpitations, as illustrated in the following case study (adapted from Kleinman & Kleinman, 1985, pp. 454–455).

CASE STUDY

Lin Hung is a 24-year-old worker in a machine factory in China who complains of headaches, dizziness, weakness, lack of energy, insomnia, bad dreams, poor memory, and a stiff neck. Pain, weakness, and dizziness, along with bouts of palpitations are his chief symptoms. His symptoms began 6 months ago, and they are gradually worsening. His factory doctors believe he has a heart problem, but repeated electrocardiograms have been normal. He believes he has a serious bodily disorder that is worsened by his work and that interferes with his ability to carry out his job responsibilities. Until his father retired from the job Lin now occupies, he was a soldier living not far from home. He didn't want to leave the army, but his father was anxious to retire so he could move to a new apartment owned by his factory in another city. Fearing that his son would not be able to stay in the army and thereafter would not find work, Lin's father pressured him to take over his job, a job the younger Lin never liked or wanted for himself. Lin Hung reluctantly agreed but now finds he cannot adjust to the work. He did not want to be a machinist and cries when he recounts that this is what he must be for the rest of his life. Moreover, he is despondent and lonely living so far away from his parents. He has no friends at work and feels lonely living in the dormitory. He has a girlfriend, but he cannot see her regularly anymore, owing to the change in work sites. They wish to marry, but his parents, who have a serious financial problem because of a very low pension, cannot provide the expected furniture, room, or any financial help. The leaders of his work unit are against the marriage because he is too young. They also criticize him for his poor work performance and frequent days missed from work owing to sickness.

On questioning Lin Hung, psychiatrists trained in Western medicine diagnosed major depression. Like many Chinese, Lin rejected the psychological diagnosis, believing firmly that he was suffering solely from a physical disorder. A psychological diagnosis would not have garnered any sympathy from Lin's coworkers or family, but a physical diagnosis could provide him with an acceptable reason to leave his job and return to his family.

Indeed, the very concept of depression may be unique to Western cultures (Tsai & Chentsova-Dutton, 2002). Symptoms such as decreases in self-esteem and lack of interest in pleasurable activities are only abnormal in cultures that expect people to have high self-esteem and to seek out positive emotions. These are expectations in Western culture, but not in many other cultures of the world.

SUMMING UP

- More recent generations appear to be at higher risk for depression than earlier generations, perhaps because of historical changes in values and social structures related to depression.

- People of lower social status tend to have higher rates of depression. Women's greater vulnerability to depression may be tied to their lower social status and the risks of abuse that accompany this social status.

- Less industrialized cultures may have lower rates of depression than more industrialized cultures. Some studies suggest that the manifestation of depression and mania may be different across cultures.

MOOD DISORDERS TREATMENTS

The mood disorders have a tremendous impact on individuals and on society. In the United States alone, between $3 billion and $6 billion per year is spent on the treatment of depression, and over $40 billion per year goes to cover losses in productivity plus the health care costs of people with mood disorders (Rost et al., 1998). By the year 2020, depression is expected to be the fourth leading cause of disability in the world (Murray & Lopez, 1996).

In any given year, about 60 percent of people suffering from bipolar disorder and about half of people suffering from major depression will seek out treatment for their disorder (Regier et al., 1993; Rost et al., 1998). The rest will suffer through their symptoms without any care. People who do seek treatment tend to be more severely impaired by their symptoms than those who do not seek treatment (Angst, 1998). Most often, the people who eventually seek treatment wait a number of years after their symptoms begin to obtain any help (Kessler et al., 1998).

Fortunately, many forms of treatment are now available for mood disorders, particularly depression. Most of these types of treatment have been shown to work for the majority of people. Thus, although there are many pathways into a mood disorder, there now are many pathways by which people can overcome or control mood disorders as well.

Biological Treatments for Mood Disorders

Most of the biological treatments for depression and mania are drug treatments (see the Concept Overview in Table 9.8). Several classes of antidepressant drugs are used to treat depression. In addition to being treated with drugs, some people with depression are treated with electroconvulsive therapy (ECT). Two new treatments for mood disorders, repetitive transcranial magnetic stimulation (rTMS) and vagus nerve stimulation, hold hope for many people. People with seasonal affective disorder (SAD) seem to benefit from a unique type of therapy: exposure to bright lights. Lithium is the treatment of choice for bipolar disorder, but anti-

TABLE 9.8 Concept Overview

Biological Treatments for Mood Disorders

Type of Treatment	Description and Mode of Action
Medication: antidepressants (tricyclics, monoamine oxidase inhibitors, selective serotonin reuptake inhibitors), lithium, anticonvulsants, calcium channel blockers, antipsychotics	Alter the levels of neurotransmitters or sensitivity of receptors for them
Electroconvulsive therapy	Apply electrical current to the brain; may increase permeability of the blood-brain barrier, cause release of neurotransmitters, stimulate the hypothalamus, increase sensitivity of receptors
Repetitive transcranial magnetic stimulation	Expose patients to repeated, high-intensity magnetic pulses focused on particular brain structures; may change the functioning of neurotransmitters
Vagus nerve stimulation	Stimulate by a small electronic device much like a cardiac pacemaker, which is surgically implanted under a patient's skin in the left chest wall; may increase activity in the hypothalamus and amygdala
Light therapy	Expose the individual to bright light; may "reset" circadian rhythms

convulsants, antipsychotics, and calcium channel blockers are also used.

Drug Treatments for Depression

Effective drug treatments for depression have been around since the 1960s. The late twentieth century, however, saw a rapid growth in the number of drugs available for depression and in the use of these drugs by large numbers of people.

Tricyclic Antidepressants The **tricyclic antidepressants** help reduce the symptoms of depression apparently by preventing the reuptake of norepinephrine and serotonin in the synapses or by changing the responsiveness of the receptors for these neurotransmitters. These drugs are reasonably effective, leading to the relief of acute symptoms of depression in about 60 percent of people with depression (Gijsman et al., 2004; Nemeroff, 2000). Some of the most commonly prescribed tricyclic antidepressants are imipramine, amitriptylene, and desipramine.

Unfortunately, however, the tricyclic antidepressants have a number of side effects. The most common ones are dry mouth, excessive perspiration, blurring of vision, constipation, urinary retention, and sexual dysfunction. Another problem with the tricyclic antidepressants is that they can take four to eight weeks to show an effect (Fava & Rosenbaum, 1995). This is an excruciatingly long time to wait for relief from depression. Finally, the tricyclics can be fatal in overdose, which is only three to four times the average daily prescription for the drug. For this reason, physicians are wary of prescribing these drugs, particularly for people with depression who might be suicidal.

Monoamine Oxidase Inhibitors A second class of drugs used to treat depression is the **monoamine oxidase inhibitors (MAOIs).** MAO is an enzyme that causes the breakdown of the monoamine neurotransmitters in the synapse (Stahl, 1998). MAO inhibitors decrease the action of MAO and thus bring about increases in the levels of the neurotransmitters in the synapses.

The MAOIs are as effective as the tricyclic antidepressants, but physicians are more cautious in prescribing MAOIs, because their side effects are potentially more dangerous (Gitlin, 2002). When people taking MAOIs ingest food rich in an amino acid called *tyramine*, they can experience a rise in blood pressure that can be fatal. The foods that can interact with MAOIs include aged or ripened cheeses, red wine, beer, and chocolate. The MAOIs can also interact with several drugs, including antihypertension medications and over-the-counter drugs such as antihistamines. Finally, MAOIs can cause liver damage, weight gain, severe lowering of blood pressure, several of the same side effects of the tricyclic antidepressants.

Selective Serotonin Reuptake Inhibitors and Related Drugs A newer class of antidepressant drugs consists of the **selective serotonin reuptake inhibitors,** or **SSRIs.** These drugs are similar in structure to the tricyclic antidepressants, but they work more directly to affect serotonin than do the tricyclics. These drugs have become extremely popular in the treatment of depression. The SSRIs are not more effective in the treatment of depression than the antidepressants we have already discussed—about the same percentage of people respond to an SSRI as respond to a tricyclic or an MAOI (Gitlin, 2002; Montgomery et al., 2004).

These drugs have several advantages over the other antidepressants, however, which have made them extremely popular. First, many people begin experiencing relief from their depression after a couple of weeks of using these drugs, whereas it often takes four weeks or more for the other drugs to show significant effects. Second, the side effects of the SSRIs tend to be less severe than the side effects of the other antidepressants. Third, these drugs do not tend to be fatal in overdose and thus are safer than the other antidepressants (Nemeroff & Schatzberg, 1998). Fourth, the SSRIs appear to be helpful in a wide range of symptoms in addition to depression, or those often associated with depression, such as anxiety symptoms, binge eating, and premenstrual symptoms. The SSRIs may be useful in the treatment of the most chronic and persistent types of depression (Frank, Grochocinski, et al., 2000; Keller et al., 1998).

The SSRIs do have side effects, however (Gitlin, 2002). One of the most common is increased agitation or nervousness. People on SSRIs often report

The selective serotonin reuptake inhibitors have become the widest selling antidepressant drugs.

feeling "jittery" or "hyper" and that they cannot sit still. They may have mild tremors and increased perspiration and feel weak. Some find themselves becoming angry or hostile more often. Nausea and stomach cramps or gas are common side effects, as is a decrease in appetite. Sexual dysfunction and decreased sexual drive are reported by some. Finally, there appears to be an increase in risk for suicide among people on SSRIs.

A number of other drugs that have been introduced for the treatment of depression in the past decade share some similarities with the SSRIs or the older antidepressants but cannot be classified in the same categories. Some of these antidepressants were designed to affect the levels of norepinephrine as well as serotonin and thus are referred to as selective serotonin and norepinephrine reuptake inhibitors (SSNRIs). Some examples are mirtazapine (Remeron), nefazodone (Serzone), venlafaxine (Effexor), and duloxetine (Cymbalata).

Bupropion (which goes by the trade names Wellbutrin and Zyban) affects the norepinephrine and dopamine systems. It may be especially useful in people suffering from psychomotor retardation, anhedonia, hypersomnia, cognitive slowing, inattention, and craving; for example, bupropion can help people stop craving cigarettes. In addition, bupropion appears to overcome the sexual side effects of the SSRIs and thus is sometimes used in conjunction with them. The side effects of bupropion include agitation, insomnia, nausea, and seizures.

Although a large selection of drug therapies is now available for the treatment of depression, there are no consistent rules for determining which of the antidepressant drugs to try first with a person with depression. Many clinicians begin with the selective serotonin reuptake inhibitors because their side effects tend to be less significant. As we discuss in *Taking Psychology Personally: Primary Care Physicians Treating Depression*, most people with depression in treatment are being treated by their primary care physicians. People with depression often must try several drugs before finding one that works well for them and has tolerable side effects. When they find the drug that works for them, it is often as if they have regained their lives (Wurtzel, 1995, p. 329):

And then something just kind of changed in me. Over the next few days, I became all right, safe in my own skin. It happened just like that. One morning I woke up, and I really did want to live, really looked forward to greeting the day, imagined errands to run, phone calls to return, and it was not with a feeling of great dread, not with the sense that the first person who stepped on my toe as I walked through the square may well have driven me to suicide. It was as if the miasma of depression had lifted off me, gone smoothly about its business, in the same way that the fog in San Francisco rises as the day wears on.

VOICES

Electroconvulsive Therapy for Depression

Perhaps the most controversial of the biological treatments for depression is **electroconvulsive therapy (ECT).** ECT was introduced in the early twentieth century, originally as a treatment for schizophrenia. Italian physicians Ugo Cerlettii and Lucio Bini decided to experiment with the use of ECT to treat people with schizophrenia, reasoning that ECT could calm them much as experiencing an epileptic seizure would calm and sedate epileptics. Eventually, clinicians found that ECT is not effective for schizophrenia, but it is effective for depression.

ECT consists of a series of treatments in which a brain seizure is induced by passing electrical current through the brain. Patients are first anesthetized and given muscle relaxants, so that they are not conscious when they have the seizure and so that their muscles do not jerk violently during the seizure. Metal electrodes are taped to the head, and a current of 70 to 130 volts is passed through one side of the brain for about one-half of a second. Patients typically go into a convulsion, which lasts about one minute. The full ECT treatment consists of 6 to 12 sessions. ECT is most often given to people with depression who have not responded to drug therapies, and it relieves depression in 50 to 60 percent of these people (Fink, 2001).

Neuroimaging studies show that ECT results in decreases in metabolic activity in several regions of the brain, including the frontal cortex, and the anterior cingulate (Henry et al., 2001; Oquendo et al., 2001) It is not entirely clear, however, how ECT lifts depression.

ECT is controversial for several reasons. First, there were reports in the past of ECT being used as a punishment for patients who were unruly, as was depicted in the movie *One Flew over the Cuckoo's Nest*. Second, ECT can lead to memory loss and difficulties in learning new information. When ECT was first developed, it was administered to both sides of the brain, and the effects on memory and learning were sometimes severe and permanent.

Taking Psychology Personally

Primary Care Physicians Treating Depression

In most of the research on the efficacy of treatments for depression that we've discussed in this chapter, the treatment was administered by a trained clinical psychologist or psychiatrist. The majority of people treated for depression, however, never see a psychologist or psychiatrist (Rost et al., 1998). Instead, most consult their primary care physician (e.g., their "family doctor," internist, or gynecologist).

Actually, patients rarely state that they are depressed. They are more likely to report physical symptoms, such as fatigue, loss of appetite, problems sleeping, or general aches and pains. This is one reason that depression is never detected by primary care physicians in 40 to 50 percent of patients who would qualify for a diagnosis of major depression (Katon et al., 2001). Other reasons include the rushed nature of interactions between physicians and patients in today's world of managed care and the competing demands for that time—if the patient has other, more pressing or obvious medical problems, the physician is likely to attend to those instead of to complaints of malaise (Rost et al., 2000). Many physicians also report that they feel uncomfortable asking patients about depressive symptoms or other mental-health problems, and they worry about offending a patient with such questions.

When a physician does detect depression in a patient, about three-quarters of the time he or she prescribes an antidepressant medication (Williams et al., 1999). At best, only about one-third of patients are given a referral to a mental-health specialist. This may be because many patients do not have insurance benefits that cover mental-health care, and many patients refuse to see a mental-health specialist because of stigmas.

Unfortunately, the care that many primary care physicians provide for patients with depression is inadequate (Simon et al., 2001). The dosages of antidepressants prescribed often are less than what research suggests is necessary for an effective response. Side effects are not monitored systematically. Over 20 percent of patients never fill their prescriptions for antidepressant medications, and as many as 50 percent stop taking the medication without consulting their doctor (Greden, 2001).

Fortunately, studies in primary care settings have shown that the quality of care given to patients with depression can be increased significantly by collaborative care programs, in which primary care physicians work with psychiatrists and psychologists (Katon et al., 2001; Simon et al., 2001). In these programs, the primary care physician continues to be responsible for the care of the patient, but the patient is given educational materials about depression, referrals to psychotherapy or community social services if necessary, and a relatively small number of visits (two to four) with a psychiatrist specializing in depression care. Patients receiving this collaborative care are more likely to take prescribed antidepressant medications, show greater reductions in depression in the short term, and are less likely to relapse over the long term.

If you or someone you know seeks care from a primary care physician for depression, what can you do to ensure that you receive adequate care? First, be honest with your doctor. Talk about your symptoms, even if it makes you uncomfortable. In particular, if you have been having suicidal thoughts, tell your doctor explicitly. If your doctor seems to ignore your reports of depressive symptoms, find another doctor.

Second, ask for a referral to a mental-health specialist if your health insurance covers this. If you don't have insurance for mental-health care, ask your doctor for recommendations for community services that are low-cost or free.

Third, if your doctor prescribes antidepressant medications for you, make sure he or she knows about any medications you are taking, including herbal remedies, such as St. John's wort, to prevent possible interactions between medications. (See Chapter 5 for a discussion of the dangers of mixing herbal remedies with prescription medications.)

Fourth, if you have no intention of taking the antidepressants prescribed for you, tell your doctor—don't just accept the prescription, then ignore it. Ask your doctor about alternative treatments.

Finally, if you begin taking an antidepressant and it doesn't give you serious side effects, continue taking it for a few weeks before you judge whether it's effective. Many antidepressants take awhile to begin to work. If after a few weeks you still are not experiencing any benefits from the antidepressant, or if your symptoms of depression get worse, tell your doctor, so that he or she can change or adjust the prescription or suggest an alternative treatment.

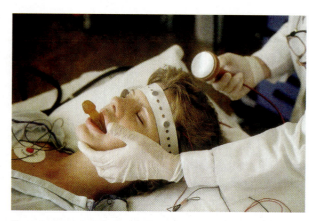

Electroconvulsive therapy is a controversial but effective treatment for depression.

These days, ECT is usually delivered to only one side of the brain, usually the right side, because it is less involved in learning and memory. As a result, patients undergoing modern ECT do not tend to experience significant or long-term memory or learning difficulties (Glass, 2001). Because this unilateral administration is sometimes not as effective as bilateral administration, some people are still given bilateral ECT. Third, although ECT can be extremely effective in eliminating the symptoms of depression, the relapse rate among people who have undergone ECT is as high as 85 percent (Fink, 2001). Fourth, perhaps the strongest reason ECT is controversial is that the idea of having electrical current passed through a person's brain is very frightening and seems like a primitive form of treatment.

Still, ECT is sometimes the only form of treatment that works for people with severe depression. One survey found that about 10 percent of people admitted to the psychiatric wards of general hospitals in the United States with diagnoses of recurrent major depression received ECT (Olfson et al., 1998). The people most likely to receive ECT were older, White, privately insured, and more affluent. It may be that people of color and poor people do not have access to ECT in the hospitals in their neighborhoods. In addition, ECT is used more frequently in eastern and midwestern states than in western states. This may be because ECT is regulated more closely, and frowned upon more, in western states, such as California. Those people who did receive ECT early in their hospital stays had shorter stays than those who did not, suggesting they recovered more quickly from their depression.

Repetitive Transcranial Magnetic Stimulation

In recent years, researchers have been investigating new methods for stimulating the brain without the application of electric current (Sackheim &

Lisanby, 2001). Scientists are using powerful magnets, such as those used in magnetic resonance imaging, to stimulate targeted areas of the brain. The procedure known as **repetitive transcranial magnetic stimulation (rTMS)** exposes patients to repeated, high-intensity magnetic pulses focused on particular brain structures, such as the left prefrontal cortex, which tends to show abnormally low metabolic activity in some people with depression. Studies have suggested that patients with depression given rTMS daily for at least a week tend to experience relief from their symptoms (Chae et al., 2001; George et al., 2003).

How does rTMS work? The electrical stimulation of neurons can result in long-term changes in neurotransmission across synapses (George et al., 2003). Neurotransmission can be enhanced or blunted, depending on the frequency of the stimulation. By stimulating the left prefrontal cortex of people with depression at particular frequencies, researchers have been able to increase neuronal activity, which in turn has had an antidepressant effect. Patients who receive rTMS report few side effects, usually only minor headaches treatable by aspirin. Patients can remain awake, rather than having to be anesthetized, as in electroconvulsive therapy (ECT), thereby avoiding the possible complications of anesthesia. There is a great deal of hope that rTMS will be an effective and safe alternative therapy, particularly for people who do not respond to drug therapies and cannot tolerate ECT.

Vagus Nerve Stimulation

Another new method that holds considerable promise in the treatment of serious depression is **vagus nerve stimulation (VNS)** (Marangell, Martinez, & Niazi, 2004). The vagus nerve is part of the autonomic nervous system; it carries information from the head, neck, thorax, and abdomen to several areas of the brain, including the hypothalamus and amygdala, which are involved in depression. In VNS, the vagus nerve is stimulated by a small electronic device much like a cardiac pacemaker, which is surgically implanted under a patient's skin in the left chest wall. Vagus nerve stimulation was originally used to control seizures in epileptic patients, and some investigators noticed that the therapy also improved mood in these patients (George et al., 2000). The mood effects of VNS occurred even in epileptic patients who were still having seizures, so researchers began studying the mood effects of VNS in patients with depression.

In one study of 38 patients with depressions that had not responded to other forms of treatment, 40 percent got substantial relief from their depression with VNS (George et al., 2000). Another 30 percent of the patients got minimal relief through

VNS. Four patients had negative side effects, including agitation, and 3 patients' surgical wounds did not heal promptly. In another study, of 59 depressed patients, 31 percent obtained significant relief from their depression with VNS; among those who had previously responded to antidepressant medications, 40 percent responded to VNS (Sackheim et al., 2001). About half of all the patients reported mild voice alteration or hoarseness as a side effect of VNS.

How does VNS work when it relieves depression? That is unknown currently, but positron-emission studies show that VNS increases activity in the hypothalamus and amygdala, which may have antidepressant effects (George et al., 2000). Additional research is currently being done on VNS in hopes that it will provide a relatively safe alternative treatment for some people with depression.

Light Therapy

Recall that seasonal affective disorder (SAD) is a form of mood disorder in which people become depressed during the winter months, when there are the fewest hours of daylight. Their moods then brighten in the summer months, when there is more daylight each day. It turns out that many people with SAD who are exposed to bright lights for a few hours each day during the winter months experience complete relief from their depression within a couple of days (Koorengevel et al., 2001; Wileman et al., 2001).

Light therapy may help reduce seasonal affective disorder by resetting *circadian rhythms,* natural cycles of biological activities that occur every 24 hours. The production of several hormones and neurotransmitters varies over the course of the day,

Light therapy can be helpful to people with seasonal affective disorder.

according to circadian rhythms. These rhythms are regulated by internal clocks but can be affected by environmental stimuli, including light. People with depression sometimes show dysregulation of their circadian rhythms. Light therapy may work by resetting circadian rhythms and thereby normalizing the production of hormones and neurotransmitters (Koorengevel et al., 2001).

Another theory is that light therapy works by decreasing levels of the hormone melatonin, secreted by the pineal gland (Wehr et al., 2001). Decreasing melatonin levels can increase levels of norepinephrine and serotonin, thereby reducing the symptoms of depression. Finally, studies suggest that exposure to bright lights may directly increase serotonin levels, thereby decreasing depression (Rosenthal, 1995).

Drug Treatments for Bipolar Disorder

Many fewer drugs are available to treat bipolar disorder than to treat unipolar depression, because this disorder is understood less well than depression and because it is more rare. Fortunately, however, recent years have seen an increase in the number of drugs designed to treat bipolar disorder.

Lithium **Lithium** is the most common treatment for bipolar disorder. A number of controlled trials show that lithium is effective in preventing relapses of bipolar disorder (Geddes et al., 2004; Ghaemi, Pardo, & Hsu, 2004).

Lithium seems to stabilize a number of neurotransmitter systems, including serotonin, dopamine, and glutamate (Dixon & Hokin, 1998; Lenox & Manji, 1995). It appears to be more effective in reducing the symptoms of mania than the symptoms of depression. People with bipolar disorder are often prescribed lithium to help curb their mania and an antidepressant drug to curb their depression (Nemeroff, 2000).

Most people with bipolar disorder take lithium even when they have no symptoms of mania or depression, in order to prevent relapses. People maintained on adequate doses of lithium have significantly fewer relapses than those not maintained on lithium (Maj et al., 1998; Tondo, Jamison, & Baldessarini, 1997). Up to 55 percent of patients develop a resistance to lithium within three years, however, and only about one-third remain symptom-free on lithium (Nemeroff, 2000).

Although lithium has been a lifesaver for many people with bipolar disorder, it poses some problems. First, there are enormous differences among people in their rates of lithium absorption, so the proper dosage varies greatly from one person to the next. Second, the difference between an effective dose of lithium and a toxic dose is small, leaving a very narrow window of therapeutic effectiveness. People who take lithium must be monitored carefully by physicians, who can determine whether the dosage of lithium is adequate to relieve the symptoms of bipolar disorder but not too large to induce toxic side effects. The side effects of lithium range from annoying to life-threatening. Many patients experience abdominal pain, nausea, vomiting, diarrhea, tremors, and twitches (Jamison, 1995, p. 93):

VOICES

I found myself beholden to a medication that also caused severe nausea and vomiting many times a month—I often slept on my bathroom floor with a pillow under my head and my warm, woolen St. Andrews gown tucked over me. I have been violently ill more places than I choose to remember, and quite embarrassingly so in public places.

People on lithium complain of blurred vision and problems in concentration and attention that interfere with their ability to work. Lithium can cause diabetes, hypothyroidism, and kidney dysfunction. It can also contribute to birth defects if taken during the first trimester of a woman's pregnancy.

It is not surprising that many people with bipolar disorder will not take lithium or will go on and off of it, against their physicians' advice. In addition to experiencing side effects, many patients complain that they miss the positive symptoms of their mania—the elated moods, flowing ideas, and heightened self-esteem—and feel washed-out on lithium. Especially during periods of calm, they feel they can manage their illness without lithium and that they can detect when a new episode is coming and go back on the medication then. Usually, however, as a new episode of mania becomes more and more severe, their judgment becomes more impaired, and they do not go back on the lithium.

Anticonvulsants, Antipsychotics, and Calcium Channel Blockers Sometimes, lithium does not overcome mania and, even if it is effective, some people cannot tolerate its side effects. Three other classes of drugs, **anticonvulsants, antipsychotic drugs,** and **calcium channel blockers,** are alternatives to lithium for the treatment of mania.

The most commonly prescribed anticonvulsants are carbamazepine (trade name Tegretol), valproic acid (trade names Depakene and Valproate), and divalproex sodium (trade name Depakote). These drugs can be effective in reducing the symptoms of severe and acute mania, although it is not clear if they are as effective as lithium in

the long-term treatment of bipolar disorder. For this reason, lithium is still usually used first, before trying the anticonvulsants (Ghaemi et al., 2004; Grunze & Walden, 2002). The side effects of carbamazepine include blurred vision, fatigue, vertigo, dizziness, rash, nausea, drowsiness, and liver disease (Nemeroff, 2000). Valproic acid and divalproex sodium seem to induce many fewer side effects and are now used more often than carbamazepine (Frances et al., 1998). But the anticonvulsants can cause birth defects if women take them while pregnant. The anticonvulsants have effects on a multitude of neurotransmitters, but the way in which the anticonvulsants reduce mania is not yet clear (Nemeroff, 2000).

The antipsychotic drugs, which are described in more detail in Chapter 11, are also used to quell the symptoms of severe mania (Nemeroff, 2000). These drugs reduce functional levels of dopamine and seem especially useful in the treatment of psychotic manic symptoms. They have many neurological side effects, however, the most severe of which is an irreversible condition known as *tardive dyskinesia.* People with tardive dyskinesia have uncontrollable tics and movements of their face and limbs. Newer drugs, such as clozapine, olanzapine, and risperidone, do not induce these neurological side effects and are being investigated for use in bipolar disorder (Post, Frye, et al., 2000).

Most recently, drugs known as calcium channel blockers, such as verapamil and nimodipine, have been shown to be effective in treating mania in some, but not all, studies (Keck et al., 2000). The calcium channel blockers are safe for women to take during pregnancy. They seem to induce fewer side effects than lithium and perhaps the anticonvulsants, but they can create dizziness, headache, nausea, and changes in heart rate. It is not currently known how these drugs work to lower mania.

Psychological Treatments for Depression

Each of the psychological theories of depression has led to a treatment designed to overcome the factors that the theory asserts causes depression. Behavior therapy focuses on changing the depressed person's schedule of reinforcements and punishments. Cognitive-behavioral therapy focuses on changing both negative cognitions and maladaptive behaviors. Interpersonal therapy works on dysfunctional relationship patterns, and psychodynamic therapy focus on uncovering the unconscious hostility toward others that is the source of the person's self-punishment (see the Concept Overview in Table 9.9).

TABLE 9.9	Concept Overview

Psychological Treatments for Depression

Each of the psychological treatments for depression aims to reverse the processes contributing to depression.

Type of Treatment	Proposed Mechanism of Action
Behavior therapies	Increase positive reinforcers and decrease aversive events by teaching the person new skills for managing interpersonal situations and the environment and engaging in pleasant activities
Cognitive-behavioral therapy	Challenges distorted thinking and helps the person learn more adaptive ways of thinking and new behavioral skills
Interpersonal therapy	Helps the person change dysfunctional relationship patterns
Psychodynamic therapies	Help the person gain insight into unconscious hostility and fears of abandonment to facilitate change in self-concept and behaviors

Behavior Therapies

Behavior therapies for depression focus on increasing the number of positive reinforcers and decreasing the number of aversive experiences in an individual's life by helping the depressed person change his or her ways of interacting with the environment and other people (Hollon, Haman, & Brown, 2002). Behavior therapies are designed to be short-term, about 12 weeks long.

The first phase of behavior therapies requires a *functional analysis* of the connections between specific circumstances and the depressed person's symptoms. When does the depressed person feel the worst? Are there any situations in which he or she feels better? The therapist may visit the depressed client's home to observe his or her interactions with family members. The client may fill out questionnaires to assess what events he or she finds pleasant or unpleasant. This analysis helps the therapist pinpoint the behaviors and interaction patterns that need to be the focus of therapy. It also helps the client understand the intimate connections between his or her symptoms and daily activities or interactions. This understanding challenges the client's belief that he or she is the helpless victim of uncontrollable forces and sets the stage for the therapist's suggestions for changes in behavior.

Once the therapist and client identify the circumstances that precipitate the client's depressive symptoms, a variety of strategies can be used to make the necessary changes in the client's life. These generally fall into three categories (Thorpe & Olson, 1997):

1. *Change the aspects of the environment that are related to the depressive symptoms.* The depressed person may be encouraged to engage in specific rewarding activities and to avoid depressing activities. For example, a depressed man who typically spends all evening in front of the television, being bored and depressed, might be encouraged to take a half-hour walk around his neighborhood every evening and to limit his television watching to one hour.

2. *Teach the depressed person skills to change his or her negative circumstances, particularly negative social interactions.* For example, a depressed woman who feels her relationship with her child is out of control might be taught parenting skills, so that she is able to interact more effectively and pleasantly with her child.

3. *Teach the client mood-management skills that can be used in unpleasant situations.* It is inevitable that people with depression will find themselves in unpleasant situations some of the time. The therapist may teach the person to use strategies, such as relaxation techniques (see Chapter 7), to reduce negative symptoms even while an unpleasant event is happening. These strategies must be woven together to meet the specific needs of an individual client. For example, consider the following case (adapted from Yapko, 1997).

> Mark worked constantly. When he was not actually at work, he was working at home. He had a position of considerable responsibility and was convinced that, if he didn't stay focused on his job, he'd miss something that

(continued)

would result in his being fired or kicked off the career ladder. Mark had not taken a vacation in several years. Although he wanted to continue to get pay raises and promotions, as he has each year, he was also painfully aware that life was passing him by. He felt stressed, depressed, and hopeless about ever having a "normal" life.

Mark clearly felt rewarded for his one-dimensional life with praise, pay raises, promotions, and the absence of mistakes for which he might get punished. Mark's behavior was governed by his work focus. He engaged in no social activities, lived alone, and did not organize his time to include anything but his work. The behavior therapist suggested that, if he wanted to improve his quality of life, and his outlook on life, he must learn some very specific new behaviors. Mark was encouraged to organize his schedule so that he'd have time for social and recreational opportunities. He learned he needed to actively and deliberately do things that are fun and pleasurable. The therapist practiced with him new ways to meet people and form social relationships (friendships, dating). The therapist also taught him relaxation skills to reduce his stress. Eventually, Mark felt a new sense of control over his life and his depression lifted.

Cognitive-Behavioral Therapy

Cognitive-behavioral therapy represents a blending of cognitive and behavioral theories of depression (Beck et al., 1974; Ellis & Harper, 1961; Lewinsohn et al., 1986; Rehm, 1977). There are two general goals in this therapy. First, it aims to change the negative, hopeless patterns of thinking described by the cognitive models of depression. Second, it aims to help people with depression solve concrete problems in their lives and develop skills for being more effective in their worlds, so that they no longer have the deficits in reinforcers described by behavioral theories of depression.

Like behavior therapy, cognitive-behavioral therapy is designed to be brief. The therapist and client usually agree on a set of goals they wish to accomplish in 6 to 12 weeks. These goals focus on specific problems that clients believe are connected

to their depression, such as problems in their marriage or dissatisfaction with their job. From the very beginning of therapy, the therapist urges clients to take charge of the therapy as much as possible, setting goals and making decisions themselves, rather than relying on the therapist to give them all the answers.

Cognitive Techniques The first step in cognitive-behavioral therapy is to help clients discover the negative, automatic thoughts they habitually have and to understand the link between those thoughts and their depression. Often, the therapist will assign clients the homework of keeping track of times when they feel sad or depressed and writing down on sheets, such as the one in Figure 9.8, what is going through their minds at such times. Clients often report that they did not realize the types of thoughts that went through their heads when certain types of events happened. For example, the client whose automatic thought record is shown in Figure 9.8 did not realize that she had catastrophic thoughts about losing her job every time her boss was a little cross with her.

The second step in cognitive-behavioral therapy is to help clients challenge their negative thoughts. People with depression often believe that there is only one way to interpret a situation—their negative way. Therapists will use a series of questions to help clients consider alternative ways of thinking about a situation and the pros and cons of these alternatives, such as "What is the evidence that you are right in the way you are interpreting this situation?" "Are there other ways of looking at this situation?" and "What can you do if the worst-case scenario comes true?" Of course, these questions don't always move the client toward more positive ways of thinking about the situation. It is important for the therapist to be flexible in pursuing a line of questions or comments, dropping approaches that are not helpful and trying new approaches to which the client might respond better.

The third step in cognitive-behavioral therapy is to help clients recognize the deeper, basic beliefs or assumptions they hold that are feeding their depression. These basic beliefs might be ones such as "If I'm not loved by everyone, I'm a failure" or "If I'm not a complete success at everything, my life is worthless." The therapist will help clients question these beliefs and decide if they truly want to live their lives according to these beliefs. The case of Susan illustrates some of the cognitive components of cognitive-behavioral therapy (adapted from Thorpe & Olson, 1997, pp. 225–227):

FIGURE 9.8	**An Automatic Thoughts Record Used in Cognitive-Behavioral Therapy.** In cognitive-behavioral therapy, patients keep records of the negative thoughts that arise when they feel negative emotions. These records are then used in therapy to challenge the patients' depressive thinking.		

Date	Event	Emotion	Automatic thoughts
April 4	Boss seemed annoyed.	Sad, anxious, worried	Oh, what have I done now? If I keep making him mad, I'm going to get fired.
April 5	Husband didn't want to make love.	Sad	I'm so fat and ugly.
April 7	Boss yelled at another employee.	Anxious	I'm next.
April 9	Husband said he's taking a long business trip next month.	Sad, defeated	He's probably got a mistress somewhere. My marriage is falling apart.
April 10	Neighbor brought over some cookies.	A little happy, mostly sad	She probably thinks I can't cook. I look like such a mess all the time. And my house was a disaster when she came in!

CASE STUDY

Susan was seen for 14 sessions of psychotherapy. She was a young, single, 24-year-old woman. Her goals for therapy were to learn how to overcome chronic feelings of depression and to learn how to deal with temptations to overeat. Susan was unemployed and living with her aunt and uncle in a rural area. She had no means of personal transportation. Hypersensitivity to the reactions of significant others and the belief that they could control her feelings seemed to be central to her low self-concept and feelings of helplessness. Susan described her mother as knowing which "buttons to push." This metaphor was examined and challenged. She was questioned as to how her mother controlled her emotions: Where were these buttons? Did they have a physical reality? Once again, the principle was asserted that it is not the actions of others that cause emotions, but one's cognitions about them.

Then the cognitions she had concerning certain looks or critical statements were examined. When her aunt was looking "sickly and silent," Susan believed that it was because she was displeased with her for not helping enough. The evidence for this belief was examined, and there was none. Alternative explanations were explored, such as the aunt might be truly ill, having a bad day, or upset with her spouse. Susan admitted that all explanations were equally plausible. Furthermore, it was noted that, in ambiguous social situations, she tended to draw the most negative and personalized conclusions.

Her consistent tendency to evaluate her self-worth in terms of her family's approval

(continued)

was examined. Susan still had fantasies of her family becoming like the "Walton" family (e.g., a "normal" family that was loving and accepting of one another; instead, her own family was distant and argumentative with one another). Susan began to let go of this fantasy and grieved over this loss. Once this had been done, she began to gain a better understanding of how her current cognitive distortions could be related to overconcern with familial approval. As she began to let go of her desire to live up to imagined expectations, she stopped seeing herself as a failure.

During the last stage of therapy, Susan's mother visited. This provided a real test of the gains she had made, as it was her mother's criticism that Susan feared the most. At first, she reported feeling easily wounded by her mother's criticism. These examples were used as opportunities to identify and challenge self-defeating thoughts. Soon, Susan was able to see her mother's critical statements as her mother's problem, not her own. She also discovered that, as she became better at ignoring her mother's critical remarks and not taking them to heart, her mother began to be more relaxed and open around her and criticized her less.

Behavioral Techniques Cognitive-behavioral therapists also use behavioral techniques to train clients in new skills they might need to cope better in their life. Often, people with depression are unassertive in making requests of other people or in standing up for their rights and needs. This unassertiveness can be the result of their negative automatic thoughts. For example, a person who often thinks, "I can't ask for what I need, because the other person might get mad and that would be horrible," is not likely to make even reasonable requests of other people. The therapist will first help clients recognize the thoughts behind their actions (or lack of action). Then, the therapist may work with clients to devise exercises or homework assignments in which they practice new skills, such as assertiveness, between therapy sessions.

The Effectiveness of Cognitive-Behavioral Therapy Cognitive-behavioral therapy has proven quite effective in treating depression, including major depression. About 60 to 70 percent of people with depression experience full relief from their symptoms with 12 weeks of cognitive therapy (Hollon et al., 2002; Lewinsohn & Clarke, 1999). Cognitive-behavioral therapy has been successfully adapted for the treatment of depressed children, adolescents, and older persons (Futterman et al., 1995; Garber & Horowitz, 2002; Lewinsohn & Clarke, 1999; Treatment for Adolescents with Depression Study [TADS] Team, 2004).

Interpersonal Therapy

In **interpersonal therapy (IPT),** therapists look for four types of problems in depressed patients (see the Concept Overview in Table 9.10). First, many depressed patients truly are grieving the loss of loved ones, perhaps not from death but from the breakup of important relationships. Interpersonal therapists help clients face such losses and explore their feelings about the losses. Often, clients idealize the people they have lost, feeling as if they will never have relationships as good. Therapists help clients reconstruct their relationships with the lost loved ones, recognizing both the good and bad aspects of the relationships and developing more balanced views of the relationships. Therapists also help clients let go of the past relationships and begin to invest in new relationships.

The second type of problem interpersonal therapy focuses on is interpersonal role disputes. Such disputes arise when people do not agree on their roles in a relationship. For example, a husband and wife may disagree on the proper roles each should play in relation to their children. Or a college student and a parent may disagree on the extent to which the student should follow the parent's wishes in choosing a career. Interpersonal therapists first help the clients recognize the disputes and then guide clients in making choices about concessions they are or are not willing to make to the other people in the relationships.

Therapists may also need to help clients modify and improve their patterns of communicating with others in relationships. For example, a student who resents his parents' intrusions into his private life may tend to withdraw and sulk rather than directly confront his parents about their intrusions. He would be helped in developing more effective ways of communicating his distress over his parents' intrusions.

The third type of problem addressed in interpersonal therapy is role transitions, such as the transition from college to work or from work to full-time motherhood. Sometimes, people become depressed out of grief over the roles they must leave behind. Therapists help clients develop more realistic perspectives toward roles that are lost and help clients regard new roles in a more positive manner. If clients feel unsure about their capabili-

TABLE 9.10	Concept Overview

Interpersonal Therapy

Interpersonal therapists focus on four types of interpersonal problems as sources of depression.

Type of Problem	Therapeutic Approach
Grief, loss	Help the client accept feelings and evaluate a relationship with a lost person; help the client invest in new relationships
Interpersonal role disputes	Help the client make decisions about concessions willing to be made and learn better ways of communicating
Role transitions	Help the client develop more realistic perspectives toward roles that are lost and regard new roles in a more positive manner
Interpersonal skills deficits	Review the client's past relationships, helping the client understand these relationships and how they might be affecting current relationships; directly teach the client social skills, such as assertiveness

ties in new roles, therapists help them develop a sense of mastery in the new roles. Sometimes, clients need help in developing new networks of social support within their new roles, to replace the support systems they left behind in old roles.

The fourth type of problem people with depression take to interpersonal therapy involves deficits in interpersonal skills. Such skill deficits can be the reason that people with depression have inadequate social support networks. Therapists review with clients past relationships, especially important childhood relationships, helping clients understand these relationships and how they might be affecting current relationships. Therapists might also directly teach clients social skills, such as assertiveness.

Interpersonal therapy has been shown to be highly effective in the treatment of depression, with 60 to 80 percent of people with depression recovering during this form of therapy (Weissman & Markowitz, 2002). Like cognitive-behavioral therapy, interpersonal therapy has been successfully adapted for the treatment of children and older adults with depression. It can be used both in individual therapy and in group therapy settings.

An interesting application of interpersonal therapy in a group setting occurred in a study conducted in rural Uganda (Bolton et al., 2003). The people of Uganda have suffered terrible trauma over the decades, and the rate of depression in this country is high. A group of researchers conducted a randomized clinical trial to test the effectiveness of group interpersonal psychotherapy in treating villagers in rural Uganda who were depressed. Their intervention resulted in significant decreases in depression in the villagers who received it, compared with villagers in the control group.

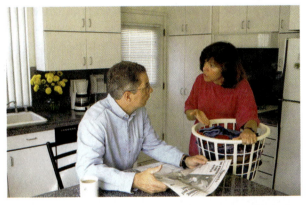

Interpersonal therapy for depression focuses on problems in interpersonal relationships that lead to depression.

Psychodynamic Therapies

In **psychodynamic therapies,** the therapist will closely observe a depressed client's behavior to analyze the sources of his or her depression, just as a behavior or cognitive therapist will. The types of behavior the psychodynamic therapist examines, and the therapist's assumptions about the potential causes of that behavior, are very different from those that concern the behavior or cognitive therapist.

The psychodynamic therapist will closely observe the client's *transference* to the therapist—the ways in which the client treats the therapist as though the therapist were someone else, such as a parent—with the assumption that the client's transference represents unconscious conflicts and concerns with important people in his or her life. The therapist will also observe the client's recollections of both recent events and distant events, searching for themes of abandonment, hostility, and disappointment. The therapist may listen to the client's recounting of dreams for further clues as to the unconscious concerns behind the depression. The therapist will acknowledge and interpret the themes he or she observes in the client's behaviors and recollections, to help the client gain insight, accept these unconscious concerns, and move beyond them.

Although it may seem necessary to have insight to fully gain control over one's depression, long-term psychodynamic therapies have not proven very effective in the treatment of depression (Robinson, Berman, & Neimeyer, 1990). The nature of depression may make it particularly unsuitable for long-term psychodynamic therapies. Many people with depression are too overcome by symptoms of lethargy, poor attention and concentration, and a sense of hopelessness to participate in these therapies. They may not have the energy or motivation to engage in the long process of uncovering and exploring old psychological wounds. They may be so acutely depressed that they need more immediate relief, particularly if they are suicidal.

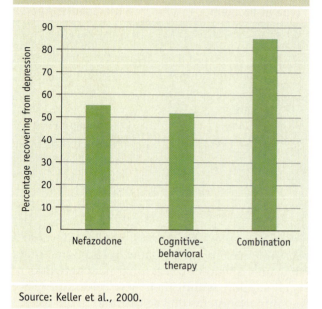

FIGURE 9.9   **Comparison of Drug Therapy and Psychotherapy.** In one study, people with chronic major depression responded equally well to a drug therapy (nefazodone) and cognitive-behavioral therapy but responded best to the combination of the two therapies.

Source: Keller et al., 2000.

Comparisons of Cognitive-Behavioral, Interpersonal, and Drug Therapies

Which of the many treatments for mood disorders is the best? In the past few decades, several studies have compared cognitive-behavioral therapy, interpersonal therapy, and drug therapies with each other. Perhaps surprisingly, these three therapies, despite their vast differences, appear equally effective for the treatment of most people with depression (see DeRubeis et al., 1999; Hollon et al., 2002; Weissman & Markowitz, 2002). A growing number of studies suggest that the combination of psychotherapy and drug therapy is more effective in treating people with chronic depression than is either type of therapy alone (e.g., Hollon et al., 1992; Frank, Grochocinski, 2000; Thase et al., 1997; TADS Team, 2004).

For example, in one study, 681 patients with chronic major depression were randomly assigned to receive nefazodone (trade name Serzone), cognitive-behavioral therapy, or both for 12 weeks (Keller et al., 2000). About half of the people receiving nefazodone or cognitive-behavioral therapy alone experienced relief from their depression (see Figure 9.9). Eighty-five percent of the patients receiving both nefazodone and cognitive-behavioral therapy experienced relief from their depression.

The relapse rates in depression are quite high, even among people whose depression completely disappears in treatment. For this reason, many psychiatrists and psychologists argue that people with a history of recurrent depression should be kept on a maintenance dose of therapy even after their depression has been relieved (Hirschfeld, 1994). Usually, the maintenance therapy is a drug therapy, and many people remain on antidepressant drugs for years after their initial episodes of depression have passed. Studies of interpersonal therapy and cognitive-behavioral therapy show that maintenance doses of these therapies, usually consisting of once-a-month meetings with therapists, can also reduce relapse just as well as drugs (Hollon et al., 2002; Jarrett et al., 1998; Weissman & Markowitz, 2002).

Studies suggest that similar changes in the brain occur whether people with depression undergo psychotherapy or drug therapy. For example, Brody and colleagues (2001) put people with major depression through a PET scan to assess their brain functioning. Compared with control participants, the depressed participants showed abnormal activity in the prefrontal cortex and the temporal lobe. The depressed participants were then given either interpersonal therapy or a selective serotonin reuptake inhibitor for 12 weeks, and their brain functioning was reevaluated at the end of the therapies. The interpersonal therapy group and drug therapy group both showed normalization of their brain functioning over the course of therapy, to similar levels.

In bipolar disorder, combining drug treatment with the psychological therapies may reduce the rate at which patients stop taking their medications and may lead more patients to achieve full remission of their symptoms, compared with lithium treatment alone (Miklowitz et al., 2000; Swarz & Frank, 2001). Psychotherapy can help people with bipolar disorder understand and accept their need for lithium treatment. It also can help them cope with the impact of the disorder on their lives (Jamison, 1995, pp. 88–89):

VOICES

At this point in my existence, I cannot imagine leading a normal life without both taking lithium and having had the benefits of psychotherapy. Lithium prevents my seductive but disastrous highs, diminishes my depressions, clears out the wool and webbing from my disordered thinking, slows me down, gentles me out, keeps me from ruining my career and relationships, keeps me out of a hospital, alive, and makes psychotherapy possible. But, ineffably, psychotherapy *heals*. It makes some sense of the confusion, reins in the terrifying thoughts and feelings, returns some control and hope and possibility of learning from it all. Pills cannot, do not, ease one back into reality; they only bring one back headlong, careening, and faster than can be endured at times. Psychotherapy is a sanctuary; it is a battleground; it is a place I have been psychotic, neurotic, elated, confused, and despairing beyond belief. But, always, it is where I have believed—or have learned to believe—that I might someday be able to contend with all of this.

Depression Prevention

Given the devastating effects depression can have on people's lives, an important goal for the future is to prevent depression in vulnerable people before it ever begins. Several studies using cognitive-behavioral and interpersonal therapy techniques have shown that community-based interventions can prevent first onsets of depression in people at high risk (Munoz et al., 2002). For example, cognitive-behavioral techniques can be used to prevent de-

pression in low-income, minority people who are faced with chronic and overwhelming stressors (Munoz, 1997; Munoz et al., 1995).

Evidence that depression first arises in adolescence has led several researchers to focus on preventing depression in high-risk adolescents. In one study, adolescents at high risk to develop major depression because they already had mild to moderate symptoms of depression were randomly assigned to a cognitive-behavioral intervention or to a no-intervention control group. The students receiving the cognitive-behavioral intervention met for 15 sessions in small groups after school. They received therapy designed to help them overcome negative ways of thinking and to learn more effective coping strategies. Following the therapy, both the intervention group and the no-treatment control group were followed for up to 18 months. The children in the prevention group got some immediate benefit from this intervention; their levels of depressive symptoms declined over the course of the 15 sessions. The remarkable finding of this study was that the intervention seemed to reduce the risk for future depression in these children (Clarke et al., 1995) (see Figure 9.10). Over the year after the intervention ended, a relatively low percentage of the children who received it developed

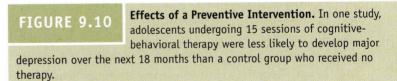

FIGURE 9.10   **Effects of a Preventive Intervention.** In one study, adolescents undergoing 15 sessions of cognitive-behavioral therapy were less likely to develop major depression over the next 18 months than a control group who received no therapy.

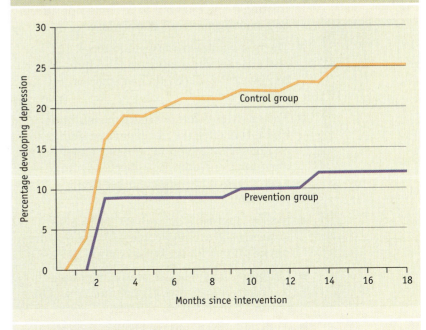

Source: Clarke et al., 1995.

Studies have shown that group therapy for teenagers can prevent or reduce depression.

depression. In contrast, many of the children in the control group developed depression (for similar results, see Gillham et al., 1995; Jaycox et al., 1994). This study gives us hope that many vulnerable children can be spared from the debilitating effects of depressive episodes.

SUMMING UP

- Tricyclic antidepressants are effective in treating depression but have some side effects and can be dangerous in overdose.

- The monoamine oxidase inhibitors (MAOIs) also are effective treatments for depression but can interact with certain medications and foods.

- The selective serotonin reuptake inhibitors (SSRIs) are effective treatments for depression and have become popular because they are less dangerous and their side effects are more tolerable than are those of other drug treatments.

- Electroconvulsive therapy (ECT) involves inducing seizures in people with depression. It can be quite effective but is controversial.

- Lithium is useful in the treatment of mood disorders but requires careful monitoring to prevent dangerous side effects.

- Anticonvulsants, antipsychotics, and calcium channel blockers can help relieve mania.

- Behavioral treatment focuses on increasing positive reinforcers and decreasing aversive events by helping clients change their environments, learn social skills, and learn mood-management skills.

- Cognitive-behavioral treatment combines the techniques of behavior therapies with techniques to identify and challenge depressive thinking patterns.

- Psychodynamic therapies focus on uncovering unconscious hostility and fears of abandonment through the interpretation of transference, memories, and dreams.

- Interpersonal therapy seeks to identify and overcome problems with grief, role transitions, interpersonal role disputes, and deficits in interpersonal skills that contribute to depression.

- Cognitive-behavioral therapy, interpersonal therapy, and drug treatments seem to work equally well with most people with depression, and the combination of drug therapy and one of the psychotherapies may be the most effective.

- Some research suggests that interventions targeting high-risk groups can help prevent or delay first onsets of depression.

CHAPTER INTEGRATION

The mood disorders affect the whole person. Depression and mania involve changes in every aspect of functioning, including biology, cognitions, personality, social skills, and relationships. Some of these changes may be causes of the depression or mania, and some of them may be consequences of the depression or mania.

The fact that the mood disorders are phenomena of the whole person illustrates the intricate connections among the various aspects of functioning: biology, cognitions, personality, and social interactions. These areas of functioning are so intertwined that major changes in any one area will almost necessarily provoke changes in other areas. Many recent models of the mood disorders, particularly depression, suggest that most people who become depressed carry a vulnerability to depression for much of their lives. This may be a biological vulnerability, such as dysfunctions in neurotransmitter systems, or a psychological vulnerability, such as overdependence on others. It is not until these vulnerabilities interact with certain stressors that a full-blown depression is triggered, however.

Kendler and colleagues (Kendler, 1998; Kendler & Karkowski-Shuman, 1997) have suggested that, in major depression, genetic factors may influence vulnerability to depression by altering the individual's relationship to the environment, in addition to inducing biological abnormalities that directly cause depression (see Figure 9.11). First, genetic factors may increase the individual's biological sensitivity to stressors in the environment, by altering the neurotransmitter and neuroendocrine systems involved in the stress response. This makes it more likely that these individuals will react to a stressor with depression. In their large study of twins, they found statistical evidence that being at genetic risk for depression made twins more prone to depression in the face of negative life events. In twins with a low genetic risk for depression (e.g., a monozygotic twin whose cotwin had no history of depression), the probability of a depression, given exposure to a severe life event, was 6.2 percent. In twins with a high genetic risk for depression (a monozygotic twin whose cotwin had a history of depression), the probability of depression, given exposure to a severe life event, was 14.6 percent (Kendler & Karkowski-Shuman, 1997).

Second, genetic factors may influence the probability that individuals will select high- versus low-risk environments for the production of depression. People actively help create their environments by choosing which people they spend time with, where they live, the type of occupation they pursue, and so on. In their twin studies, Kendler

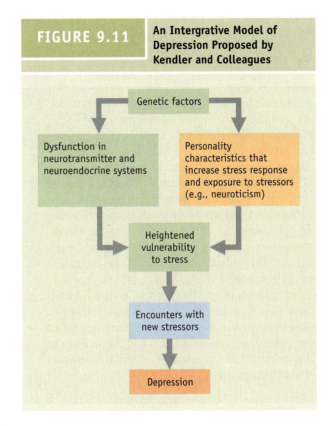

FIGURE 9.11   An Intergrative Model of Depression Proposed by Kendler and Colleagues

and colleagues (1993) found, not surprisingly, that cotwins often shared the same life events, such as the death of a family member. This seems mostly likely due to environmental factors—specifically, having the same family members. But certain other stressors, including being robbed or assaulted or experiencing a major financial stressor, appeared to be influenced primarily by genetic factors. That is, similarities in the twins' environments could not account for their common risk of experiencing these events. In addition, these events did not seem to be solely the result of both twins' being depressed. Kendler and Karkowski-Shuman (1997) suggest that genetic factors may contribute to broad personality characteristics, such as neuroticism or impulsivity, which then lead to greater risk both for negative life events and for depression.

Fortunately, the interconnections among these areas of functioning may mean that improving functioning in one area can improve functioning in other areas. Improving people's biological functioning can improve their cognitive and social functioning and their personalities. Improving people's cognitive and social functioning can improve their biological functioning, and so on. Thus, although there may be many pathways into mood disorders (biological, psychological, and social), there may also be many pathways out of the mood disorders, particularly depression.

Extraordinary People: Follow-Up

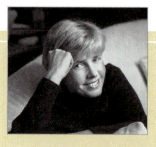

We began this chapter noting the courage of one prominent theorist and researcher of abnormality, Kay Redfield Jamison, in publishing her autobiography describing her experiences with a serious mental disorder. Although many psychiatrists and psychologists have personal histories of mental disorder, they are often reluctant to let it be known, because they fear that it will bias others' attitudes toward their ideas or will affect their professional licenses or their privileges to admit patients to hospitals. They are also concerned, as was Jamison, that their revelation of mental illness would have repercussions for their families.

Why did Jamison feel the need to go public with her illness? Jamison's explanation of her decision to reveal her disorder indicates her personal triumph over fears of others' opinions and her dedication to changing cultural attitudes toward mental disorders (Jamison, 1995, pp. 7–8):

I have no idea what the long-term effects of discussing such issues so openly will be on my personal and professional life, but whatever the consequences, they are bound to be better than continuing to be silent. I am tired of hiding, tired of misspent and knotted energies, tired of the hypocrisy, and tired of acting as though I have something to hide. One is what one is, and the dishon-

esty of hiding behind a degree, or a title, or any manner and collection of words, is still exactly that: dishonest. Necessary, perhaps, but dishonest. I continue to have concerns about my decision to be public about my illness, but one of the advantages of having had manic-depressive illness for more than thirty years is that very little seems insurmountably difficult. Much like crossing the Bay Bridge when there is a storm over the Chesapeake, one may be terrified to go forward, but there is no question of going back. I find myself somewhat inevitably taking a certain solace in Robert Lowell's essential question, *Yet why not say what happened?*

We can only hope that, as the public understands more about the causes of mental disorders, fewer people with these disorders will have to fear the consequences of letting it be known that they suffer. Kay Redfield Jamison, through her courageous decision to talk about her disorder and her eloquent and thoughtful writing and speaking on mental disorders, has moved us a bit closer to the fulfillment of that hope.

Chapter Summary

- There are two general categories of mood disorder: unipolar depression and bipolar disorder. People with unipolar depression experience only the symptoms of depression (sad mood, loss of interest, disruption in sleep and appetite, motor retardation or agitation, loss of energy, worthlessness and guilt, suicidality). (Review Table 9.1.) People with bipolar disorder experience both depression and mania (elated or agitated mood, grandiosity, little need for sleep, racing thoughts and speech, increase in goals and dangerous behavior). (Review Table 9.3.)

- Within unipolar depression, the two major diagnostic categories are major depression and dysthymic disorder. In addition, there are several subtypes of major depression: with melancholic

features, with psychotic features, with catatonic features, with atypical features, with postpartum onset, and with seasonal pattern. (Review Table 9.2.)

- Depression is one of the most common disorders, but there are substantial age, gender, and cross-cultural differences in depression. Bipolar disorder is much less common than the depressive disorders. It tends to be a lifelong problem. The length of individual episodes of bipolar disorder varies dramatically from one person to the next and over the life course, as in depression. The expression of mania may depend on cultural norms.

- Genetic factors probably play a role in determining vulnerability to the mood disorders, especially bipolar disorder. (Review Table 9.5.) Disordered genes may lead to dysfunction in the monoamine neurotransmitter systems. The neurotransmitters norepinephrine, serotonin, and dopamine have been implicated in the mood disorders. In addition, neuroimaging studies show abnormal structure or activity in several areas of the brain, including the prefrontal cortex, hippocampus, anterior cingulate cortex, and amygdala. There is evidence that people with depression have chronic hyperactivity in the hypothalamic-pituitary-adrenal axis, which may make them more susceptible to stress.

- Behavioral theories of depression suggest that people with much stress in their lives may have too low a rate of reinforcement and too high a rate of punishment, which then leads to depression. (Review Table 9.6.) Stressful events can also lead to learned helplessness—the belief that nothing one does can control one's environment—which is linked to depression. Most people who are faced with stressful events do not become depressed, however.

- The cognitive theories of depression argue that the ways people interpret the events in their lives determine whether they become depressed. (Review Table 9.7.) Some evidence suggests that people with depression are actually quite realistic in their negative views of life and that nondepressed people are unrealistically optimistic about life. People who ruminate in response to distress are more prone to depression.

- Interpersonal theories of depression suggest that poor attachment relationships early in life can lead children to develop expectations that they must be or do certain things in order to win the approval of others, which puts them at risk for depression. (Review Table 9.6.)

- Psychodynamic theories of depression suggest that people with depression have chronic patterns of negative relationships and tend to internalize their hostility against others.

- Social theories attribute depression to the effects of low social status, as well as changes in the social conditions that different generations face. In addition, there appear to be differences across cultures in how depression is manifested.

- Most of the biological therapies for the mood disorders are drug therapies. (Review Table 9.8.) Three classes of drugs are commonly used to treat depression: tricyclic antidepressants, monoamine oxidase inhibitors, and selective serotonin reuptake

inhibitors. Each of these is highly effective in treating depression, but each has significant side effects. Electroconvulsive therapy is used to treat severe depressions, particularly those that do not respond to drugs.

- Lithium is the most effective drug for the treatment of bipolar disorder. It has a number of side effects, including nausea, vomiting, diarrhea, tremors, twitches, kidney dysfunction, and birth defects. Alternatives to lithium include anticonvulsant drugs, antipsychotic drugs, and calcium channel blockers.

- Behavior therapies focus on increasing positive reinforcers and decreasing negative events by building social skills and teaching clients how to engage in pleasant activities and cope with their moods. Cognitive-behavioral therapies focus on helping people with depression develop more adaptive ways of thinking and are very effective in treating depression. Interpersonal therapy helps people with depression identify and change their patterns in relationships and is highly effective in treating depression. Psychodynamic therapy helps people with depression uncover unconscious hostility and fears of abandonment. (Review Table 9.9.)

- Direct comparisons of drug therapies with cognitive-behavioral and interpersonal therapies show that they tend to be equally effective in the treatment of depression. The combination of drug therapy and psychotherapy may be more effective than either treatment alone for people with chronic depression.

- Effective prevention programs have been designed to reduce the risk for onset of major depression in high-risk groups.

MindMap CD-ROM

The following resources on the MindMap CD-ROM that came with this text will help you to master the content of this chapter and prepare for tests:

- Videos: Major Depression; Dysthymia; Bipolar Disorder
- Chapter Timeline
- Chapter Quiz

Key Terms

bipolar disorder 303

mania 303

depression 303

unipolar depression 303

delusions 304

hallucinations 304

major depression 304

dysthymic disorder 304

double depression 304

seasonal affective disorder (SAD) 305

bipolar I disorder 310

bipolar II disorder 310

hypomania 310

cyclothymic disorder 310

rapid cycling bipolar disorder 311

monoamines 315

norepinephrine 315

serotonin 315

dopamine 315

monoamine theories 315

hypothalamic-pituitary-adrenal axis (HPA axis) 317

cortisol 317

premenstrual dysphoric disorder 318

behavioral theory of depression 319

learned helplessness theory 320

learned helplessness deficits 320

negative cognitive triad 321

reformulated learned helplessness theory 321

causal attribution 321

depressive realism 323

ruminative response styles theory 323

rumination 323

introjected hostility theory 324

interpersonal theories of depression 325

contingencies of self-worth 325

excessive reasurrance seeking 326

cohort effect 327

tricyclic antidepressants 331

monoamine oxidase inhibitors (MAOIs) 331

selective serotonin reuptake inhibitors (SSRIs) 331

electroconvulsive therapy (ECT) 332

repetitive transcranial magnetic stimulation (rTMS) 334

vagus nerve stimulation (VNS) 334

light therapy 335

lithium 335

anticonvulsants 336

antipsychotic drugs 336

calcium channel blockers 336

behavior therapies 337

cognitive-behavioral therapy 338

interpersonal therapy (IPT) 340

psychodynamic therapies 341

Chapter 10

Florista
by Bernadita Zegers

Razors pain you;
Rivers are damp;
Acids stain you;
And drugs cause cramp.
Guns aren't lawful;
Nooses give;
Gas smells awful;
You might as well live.

—Dorothy Parker, "Resume,"
Dorothy Parker: Complete Poems (1999)

Suicide <

Extraordinary People

■ **William Styron:** *Darkness Visible*

Defining and Measuring Suicide

Suicide is the intentional taking of one's own life. Suicidal thoughts and behaviors are on a continuum from those representing a clear intention to die to those representing ambivalence about dying. Suicide is the eighth leading cause of death in the United States, and internationally an estimated 1 million people die by suicide and 2 million other people make suicide attempts each year. Women are more likely than men to attempt suicide, but men are more likely than women to complete suicide. There are substantial cross-cultural and age differences in suicide.

Understanding Suicide

Generally, suicide notes are brief and concrete and leave few clues. Social approaches to suicide have identified several negative life events or circumstances that increase the risk for suicide. Influential theorist Emil Durkheim described several types of suicide that result from individuals' relationships to society. Sometimes, suicides occur in groups of people, a phenomenon known as suicide clusters or suicide contagion. Psychodynamic theorists attribute suicide to repressed rage, which leads to self-destruction. Several mental disorders increase the risk for suicide, including depression, bipolar disorder, substance abuse, schizophrenia, and anxiety disorders. Cognitive-behavioral theorists argue that hopelessness and dichotomous thinking contribute to suicide. Impulsivity is a behavioral characteristic common to people who commit suicide. Finally, biological theories attribute suicidality to genetic vulnerabilities and to low serotonin levels.

Treating and Preventing Suicidal Tendencies

Drug treatments for suicidality most often consist of lithium or antidepressant medications to reduce impulsive and violent behavior, depression, and mania. Antipsychotic medications and other medications that treat the symptoms of an existing mental disorder may also be used. The psychotherapies for suicide are similar to those used for depression. Dialectical behavior therapy has been designed specifically to address skills deficits and thinking patterns in people who are suicidal. Suicide hot lines and crisis intervention programs provide immediate help to people who are suicidal. Community prevention programs aim to educate the public about suicide and encourage suicidal people to enter treatment. Guns are involved in the majority of suicides, and some research suggests that restricting access to guns can reduce the number of suicide attempts. Society is debating whether people have a right to choose to commit suicide.

Taking Psychology Personally

■ **What to Do If a Friend Is Suicidal**

Chapter Integration

Suicide seems to fit a vulnerability-stress model. Several factors determine an individual's vulnerability to suicide, and various events or circumstances can serve as a trigger. Psychological treatments for suicidality help people recognize suicidal feelings and their personal triggers and develop more effective ways of coping.

Extraordinary People

William Styron: *Darkness Visible*

You may have read some of William Styron's books in your courses on great American literature. This Pulitzer Prize–winning author of such classics as *Sophie's Choice* and *The Confessions of Nat Turner* was at the top of his profession in late October 1985. Styron was in Paris to receive the Prix Mondial Cino del Duca, given yearly to an artist or a scientist whose work reflects certain principles of humanism. This prize was a high honor, and Styron knew he should be feeling full of joy and pride. Instead, as Styron writes, "I was feeling in my mind a sensation close to, but indescribably different from, actual pain. . . . For myself, the pain is most closely connected to drowning or suffocation" (1990, pp. 16–17).

In June 1985, Styron had begun drifting into a deep, severe depression, which overtook his life. He could not sleep at night or during the day. As each day wore on, his mood became worse and his thinking more clouded. He began to loathe his work and himself. On the day he received the Prix Mondial Cino del Duca, he found himself sitting at a dinner in his honor, unable to speak, to eat, or to respond in any way to his hosts. He reached into his coat pocket and realized he had lost the check for $25,000 that was the cash prize for the del Duca award. He thought it was fitting that this had happened, because he did not believe he deserved the award. Later that night, on the way back to his hotel, Styron thought of his many friends and heroes who had committed suicide and realized he would be facing the same decision very soon.

Styron was 60 when depression first cast a shadow over his mind in June 1985. He had been addicted to alcohol for 20 years, but, suddenly that June, his body began to reject alcohol. Even a mouthful of wine made him woozy and dizzy, and he quickly became unable to drink at all. As his alcohol intake stopped, his depression began. At first, it was mild:

> It was not really alarming at first, since the change was subtle, but I did notice that my surroundings took on a different tone at certain times: the shadows of nightfall seemed more somber, my mornings were less buoyant, walks in the woods became less zestful, and there was a moment during my working hours in the late afternoon when a kind of panic and anxiety overtook me, just for a

few minutes, accompanied by a visceral queasiness. (Styron, 1990, p. 42)

By December, though, Styron had become so deeply mired in his depression that he began taking steps to commit suicide. He consulted his lawyer to ensure that his will and estate were in good order. He destroyed his diary in which he had written about his despair. He wrote a few words of parting but tore up all his efforts in disgust. Late one night, after his wife had gone to bed, Styron sat watching the tape of a movie in his living room. A passage from the Brahms *Alto Rhapsody* was played in the movie. Styron writes:

> This sound, which like all music—indeed, like all pleasure—I had been numbly unresponsive to for months, pierced my heart like a dagger, and in a flood of swift recollection I thought of all the joys the house had known: the children who had rushed through its rooms, the festivals, the love and work, the honestly earned slumber, the voices and the nimble commotion, the perennial tribe of cats and dogs and birds, "laughter and ability and Sighing, / And Frocks and Curls." All this I realized was more than I could ever abandon, even as what I had set out so deliberately to do was more than I could inflict on those memories, and upon those, so close to me, with whom the memories were bound. And just as powerfully I realized I could not commit this desecration on myself. I drew upon some last gleam of sanity to perceive the terrifying dimensions of the mortal predicament I had fallen into. I woke up my wife and soon telephone calls were made. The next day I was admitted to the hospital. (1990, pp. 66–67)

Suicide is both an unusual act and a surprisingly familiar one. We can all name movie stars, political leaders, and other people of prominence who killed themselves. Most of us also have come into personal contact with suicide. Nearly half of all teenagers in the United States say that they know someone who has tried to commit suicide (*New York Times/CBS News Poll*, 1999) (see Figure 10.1). One in four teenagers admits to attempting or seriously contemplating suicide (van Heeringen, 2001). Suicide is among the three leading causes of death worldwide among people 15 to 44 years of age (World Health Organization [WHO], 2005). Across the world, more people die from suicide than from homicide.

The impact of suicide on surviving family members and friends can be huge. There is guilt—over not having prevented the suicide, over things that were said to the person who committed suicide, over things that may have contributed to the suicide. There is the shame and stigma of suicide. And there is anger at the person who committed suicide.

In this chapter, we try to understand suicide. With the help of biographies and autobiographies, we peer into the minds of people who have attempted or completed suicide to get a glimpse of what they were feeling and thinking. We examine statistics that reveal substantial differences among age groups, between the genders, and among cultural groups in the rates of suicide. We review explanations of why some people commit suicide. Finally, we discuss programs designed to prevent suicide in high-risk groups and those designed to help survivors of suicide.

Although many people who commit suicide are depressed, as was William Styron, suicidal thoughts and behaviors occur in the context of several disorders in this book. This is why we are discussing suicide in a separate chapter. You'll see that there are several explanations for why some people become suicidal. Most researchers and clinicians view suicide as the result of an intersection of several biological, psychological, and social factors.

DEFINING AND MEASURING SUICIDE

We need to define **suicide**. This may seem simple—it is the purposeful taking of one's own life. This definition is close to that used by the Centers for Disease Control and Prevention (CDC), one of the federal agencies in the United States that track suicide rates. The CDC says that suicide is death from injury, poisoning, or suffocation where there is evidence that the damage was self-inflicted and

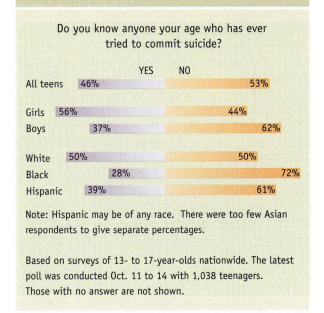

FIGURE 10.1   **Teenagers' Experience with Suicide.** These are the percentages of teenagers in a national poll who answered yes or no to the question "Do you know anyone your age who has ever tried to commit suicide?"

Do you know anyone your age who has ever tried to commit suicide?

	YES	NO
All teens	46%	53%
Girls	56%	44%
Boys	37%	62%
White	50%	50%
Black	28%	72%
Hispanic	39%	61%

Note: Hispanic may be of any race. There were too few Asian respondents to give separate percentages.

Based on surveys of 13- to 17-year-olds nationwide. The latest poll was conducted Oct. 11 to 14 with 1,038 teenagers. Those with no answer are not shown.

Source: *New York Times/CBS News Poll* 1999, p. 1.

that the individual intended to kill himself or herself.

As crisp and clear as this definition seems, there is great variability in the form that suicide takes, and there can be debate over whether to call particular types of death suicide. We may easily agree that a young man who is despondent and shoots himself in the head has committed suicide. It is harder to agree whether a despondent young man who goes on a drinking binge and then crashes his car into a tree has committed suicide. Is an Indian woman who throws herself on her husband's funeral fire committing suicide? Is an elderly person who refuses life support when dying from a painful disease committing suicide? Is a middle-aged person with severe heart disease who continues to smoke cigarettes, eat fatty foods, and drink excessive amounts of alcohol committing suicide? Clearly, suicide-like behaviors fall on a continuum.

Types of Suicide

Influential suicide theorist Edwin Shneidman (1963, 1981, 1993) described four types of people who commit suicide: death seekers, death initiators, death ignorers, and death darers. **Death seekers** clearly and explicitly seek to end their lives. Their intentions to commit suicide may be present for a long period of time, during which they prepare for their death by giving away possessions, writing a will, buying a gun, and so on, as did William Styron. Most often, their intentions are fleeting, and, if they are prevented from committing suicide, they may become ambivalent about their desire to die.

Death initiators also have a clear intention to die but believe that they are simply hastening an inevitable death. Many people with serious illnesses who commit suicide fall into this category. For example, particularly before effective drug treatments for human immunodeficiency virus (HIV) were available, some people infected with HIV committed suicide rather than face the severe illnesses, mental decline, and wasting away that can accompany advanced stages of acquired immune deficiency syndrome (AIDS).

Death ignorers intend to end their lives but do not believe that this means the end of their existence. They see their death as the beginning of a new and better life. Mass suicides by members of religious groups, such as the 1997 suicides of 39 members of the Heaven's Gate religious cult, fall into this category. Similarly, suicide bombers who believe they will receive tremendous rewards from God for their acts are considered death ignorers.

Death darers are ambivalent about dying, and they take actions that greatly increase their chances of death but that do not guarantee they will die. A person who swallows a handful of pills from the medicine cabinet without knowing how lethal they are, then calls a friend, is a death

Suicide bombers have wreaked havoc in many areas of the world, including the Middle East. Those who believe they will receive tremendous rewards from God for their acts are considered death ignorers.

darer. A youngster who randomly loads a gun with one bullet, then points the barrel at his head and pulls the trigger, is a death darer. Death darers may want attention or may want to make someone else feel guilty, more than they want to die (Brent et al., 1988).

What about the people who chronically make lifestyle choices that increase their risk for early death, such as a heart patient who continues to smoke cigarettes? Shneidman (1981, 1993, 2001) describes acts in which people indirectly contribute to their own death, perhaps unconsciously, as **subintentional deaths.** Most researchers and theorists, however, reserve the label *suicide* for deaths that are intentionally caused by the individual.

Suicide Rates

Not surprisingly, it is difficult to obtain accurate suicide rates. The stigma against suicide is a great incentive for labeling a death as anything but a suicide. Sometimes, it is absolutely clear that a death was a suicide—a note is left, the person had been threatening suicide, or a revolver is still in the victim's hand, with powder stains that could mean only a self-inflicted wound. Many deaths are more ambiguous, however, particularly when there are no notes left behind and no clues as to the victim's mental state before the death. Local officials, such as police and coroners, may conspire with family members to label ambiguous deaths as accidents, rather than have the family face the questions that come with suicide (Madge & Harvey, 1999). Accurate data on nonlethal suicide attempts are even more difficult to obtain, particularly since over half of all people who attempt, but do not complete, suicide never seek professional help and thus may not be diagnosed (Crosby, Cheltenham, & Sacks, 1999).

As a result, the statistics on the rates of suicide in various groups are probably gross underestimates. Even so, the statistics indicate that suicide is more common than we would like to believe. It is the eighth leading cause of death in the United States. About 31,000 people kill themselves each year in the United States, which averages to nearly 85 people per day (Centers for Disease Control and Prevention [CDC], 2004). In addition, as many as 3 percent of the population contemplate suicide at sometime in their lives, and between 5 and 16 percent report having had suicidal thoughts at sometime (Crosby et al., 1999; Statham et al., 1998). Suicide is not just an American phenomenon, however. Internationally, an estimated 1 million people die by suicide each year, or one person every 40 seconds (WHO, 2005).

There are large differences in suicide rates between men and women, among age groups, and among cultural groups. We now turn to a description of some of these differences.

Gender Differences

We might expect that, since women are more prone to depression than men and depression is often associated with suicide, rates of suicide in women are much higher than in men. Indeed, three times more women than men *attempt* suicide (Brockington, 2001; Canetto & Sakinofsky, 1998; Welch, 2001). And a study of high school students found that the girls were much more likely than the boys to have considered or planned a suicide attempt (Lewinsohn, Rohde, & Seeley, 1996a). However, men and boys are four times more likely than women and girls to complete suicide (CDC, 2004). This gender difference in suicide completion rate is true in many nations of the world, and across all age ranges, as can be seen in Figure 10.2 (WHO, 2004).

The gender difference in rates of completed suicides may be due in part to gender differences in the means of attempting suicide. Men tend to choose more lethal means of suicide than do women (Canetto & Sakinofsky, 1998; Crosby et al., 1999; Denning et al., 2000). In the United States, men are more likely than women to shoot, stab, or hang themselves. Although guns are still the most common way women commit suicide, women are more likely than men to choose less lethal means, such as drug overdoses. Even if men are often ambivalent about dying, the means they choose to attempt suicide are more likely to be lethal than the means women tend to choose. Some theorists argue, however, that men tend to be more sure in their intent to die when they attempt suicide than women and this is why they choose more lethal means (Jack, 1992; Linehan, 1973). Men may feel that it is not masculine to be ambivalent about their intent to die or to communicate this intent to others in hopes that they will be prevented from succeeding (Canetto & Sakinofsky, 1998). Women, on the other hand, may be more comfortable in using suicide attempts as cries for help.

Finally, guns and alcohol play a role in many suicides. Alcohol lowers inhibitions and increases impulsive behavior, and guns provide a means for carrying out suicidal thoughts. Men are more likely than women to drink alcohol when they are highly distressed and may have more ready access to guns. This may contribute to men's higher rates of completed suicides.

In some countries, women are at least as likely as men to commit suicide. For example, in China, women account for 55 percent of all suicide deaths

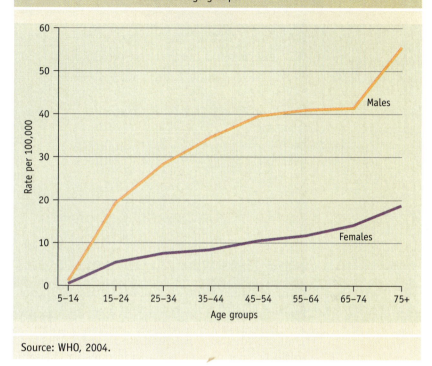

FIGURE 10.2   **Gender and Suicide.** In many nations of the world, men are more likely to commit suicide than women across almost all age groups.

Source: WHO, 2004.

(Ji, Kleinman, & Becker, 2001). The reasons are unclear, but gender roles probably interact with cultural beliefs about suicide to influence rates in both women and men.

Ethnic and Cross-Cultural Differences

Within the United States, there are substantial differences among ethnic groups in rates of suicide (CDC, 2004; Oquendo et al., 2001). European Americans have higher suicide rates than all other groups, at approximately 12 people per 100,000 in the population, and Native Americans are close behind at approximately 11 per 100,000 people. Suicide among Native Americans is tied to poverty, lack of education and hope, discrimination, substance abuse, and the easy availability of firearms (Berman & Jobes, 1995).

Several studies have compared the suicide rates of African Americans and European Americans (Burr, Hartman, & Matteson, 1999; Joe & Kaplan, 2001; O'Donnell et al., 2004). European Americans have higher rates of completed suicide than African Americans, but the rates among African American males have increased greatly in recent decades (Joe & Kaplan, 2001). Other studies show that Hispanic youth in the United States are more likely to contemplate and attempt suicide than African American youth or European American

TABLE 10.1 Reports of Suicidal Thoughts and Attempts over the Past Year Among Urban Ethnic Minority Youth

Item	Black (%)	Hispanic (%)	Black-Hispanic (%)	Other (%)
Seriously considered suicide	14.8	20.2	11.7	9.9
Told someone they have thought about killing themselves	14.8	20.7	15.0	9.9
Thought killing themselves a solution	15.1	17.2	15.0	11.3
Made a suicide plan	12.3	15.2	11.7	11.3
Attempted suicide at least once	8.1	17.9	10.0	16.9
Made multiple suicide attempts	3.8	4.1	8.3	5.6

Source: O'Donnell et al., 2004.

youth, as illustrated by a study of urban youth shown in Table 10.1 (O'Donnell et al., 2004). The rate of completed suicide is not higher for Hispanic youth than for youth in other ethnic groups in the United States, however, and studies of adults tend to find lower completed suicide rates in Hispanic groups than in other groups (Oquendo et al., 2001).

There are cross-national differences in suicide rates, with higher rates in much of Europe, the former Soviet Union, and Australia, and lower rates in Latin America and South America (WHO, 2004) (see Figure 10.3). The suicide rates in the United States, Canada, and England fall between these two extremes. These differences may have to do with cultural and religious norms against suicide. People who belong to religions that expressly forbid suicide are less likely to attempt it (O'Donnell et al., 2004; Statham et al., 1998).

Suicide in Children and Adolescents
Unfortunately, most adults often do not believe children when they voice their suicidal thoughts. Even clinicians formerly thought that young children could not have a concept of suicide and thus were not vulnerable. Now it is understood that, although suicide is relatively rare in young children, it is not impossible. One 10-year-old girl had no history of suicide attempts or mental disorder yet spoke explicitly of her suicidal thoughts (Pfeffer, 1985, p. 80):

VOICES

I often think of killing myself. It started when I was almost hit by a car. Now I want to kill myself. I think of stabbing myself with a knife. When Mom yells at me, I think she does not love me. I worry a lot about my family. Mom is always depressed and sometimes she says she will die soon. My brother becomes very angry, often for no reason. He tried to kill himself last year and had to go to the hospital. Mom was in the hospital once also. I worry a lot about my family. I worry that if something happens to them, no one will take care of me. I feel sad about this.

Another child, a 10-year-old boy, described how anger so often drives suicidal thoughts and actions (Pfeffer, 1985, p. 80):

VOICES

I want to hurt myself when I get upset and angry. I bang my head against the wall or punch the wall with my fist. I wish I were dead. I often think about how to kill myself. I think I will go to France to have myself guillotined. It would be quick and painless. Guns are too painful, so is stabbing myself. Once, I put my head into a sink of water and I got scared. My grandmother found me. I told her I was washing my face. Mom was shocked when she heard about this. She began to cry. She worries a lot and always seems sad.

Girls are much more likely to attempt suicide, but boys are more likely to complete suicide. The gender ratio for completed suicide is even greater

FIGURE 10.3 | Map of Suicide Rates.
Map of Suicide Rates. There are significant differences across countries in suicide rates. This map shows the rate per 100,000 people in different regions.

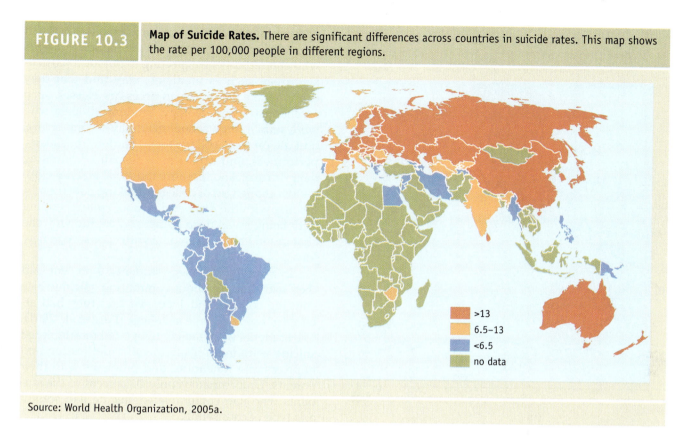

> \>13
> 6.5–13
> <6.5
> no data

Source: World Health Organization, 2005a.

among adolescents and young adults than among older adults: Males are six times more likely than females in this age range to commit suicide (CDC, 2004).

The rate of suicide increases substantially in early adolescence. Each year, one in five teenagers in the United States seriously considers suicide; 15 percent make a specific plan to attempt suicide; nearly 9 percent of adolescents attempt suicide; and about 3 percent make a serious suicide attempt that requires medical attention (Gould, Greenberg, Velting & Shaffer, 2003). Suicide may be more common in adolescence than in childhood because the rate of several types of psychopathology tied to suicide, including depression, anxiety disorders, and substance abuse, increase in adolescence. Suicide rates may also rise at this age because adolescents are more sophisticated in their thinking than are children and can contemplate suicide more clearly. Finally, adolescents may simply have the means to commit suicide (such as access to drugs and guns) more than do children.

There are interesting historical trends in suicide rates among adolescents, particularly among males. Between 1964 and 1988, there was nearly a threefold increase in adolescent male suicides (Gould, Greenberg et al., 2003; Spirito & Esposito-

Smythers, 2006) (see Figure 10.4 on page 358). This increase continued among white males until the mid 1990s, then started to decline. Rates among African American males, although still lower than among European Americans, showed no sign of decline until 1995. The increase in earlier decades has been attributed to increases in adolescents' access to alcohol and other drugs, whereas the relatively recent decrease in suicide rates may be due to the tremendous increase in the prescription of antidepressants for adolescents (Gould, Greensberg et al., 2003). African American youth typically have greater difficulty accessing treatments for mental-health problems, and this may account for the fact that their decline in suicide rates came a bit later than that of European American youth.

The risk factors for suicide in adolescents include current depression, interpersonal problems, insecure relationships with parents, negative thinking and hopelessness, appetite problems, increased substance abuse, aggression, and a suicide attempt by a friend (King et al., 2001; Lewinsohn et al., 1996a, Lewinsohn et al., 2001; Spirito & Esposito-Smythers, 2006; Wagner et al., 2003). In addition, several studies suggest that gay and bisexual youth are at significantly greater risk for suicidal behavior, although the vast majority report no suicidal

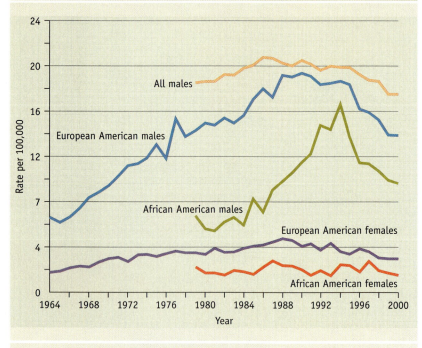

FIGURE 10.4

Teen Suicide Rates, 1964–2000: United States, Ages 15–19 Years. There have been historical trends in suicide rates among teens, with substantial increases among males.

Source: Gould, Greenberg, et al., 2003.

posed in high school. Academic material is much more difficult and standards are higher. Students who entered college expecting to pursue a particular career, such as medicine, may find that they cannot make the grades in necessary classes, such as chemistry and biology. Student athletes who were stars in high school may play second-string, if at all, on their college team. Student musicians, performers, and artists may despair of pursuing their dreams. And there are the social and developmental challenges of college—making new friends, dealing with the drug and alcohol culture, coping with being away from home, and coping with the changes in values that come with exposure to new ideas.

In a survey of college students, 9 percent said they had thought about committing suicide since entering college, and 1 percent said they had attempted suicide while at college (Furr et al., 2001). The students who had contemplated or attempted suicide were more likely to suffer depression and hopelessness, loneliness, and problems with their parents. Unfortunately, only 20 percent of the students who had contemplated suicide had sought any type of counseling.

Suicide in Older Adults

Although there has been a 50 percent decline in suicide rates among older adults over the past few decades, older adults, particularly older men, still remain at relatively high risk for suicide. The highest risk is among European American men over the age of 85 (CDC, 2004). When they attempt suicide, older people are much more likely than younger people to be successful. It seems that most older people who attempt suicide fully intend to die (McIntosh, 1995). In contrast, most young people who attempt suicide are highly ambivalent about it.

Some older people who commit suicide do so because they cannot tolerate the loss of their spouse or other loved ones. For example, an elderly woman who had recently lost her husband to prostate cancer said the following (Nolen-Hoeksema & Larson, 1999, p. 43):

thoughts or behaviors at all (see Gould, Greenberg, et al., 2003; Russell, 2003; Spirito & Esposito-Smythers, 2006). Many adolescents contemplating suicide write letters to friends to say good-bye and give away their possessions. Almost all have thought about committing suicide for sometime before actually attempting it.

Many more adolescents attempt suicide than die by suicide. Adolescents may be especially prone to use suicide attempts as a way of getting attention and help for problems. This does not mean that adolescent suicide attempts are unimportant, however. A history of a suicide attempt is the single best predictor of future suicide attempts and completions (King et al., 2001; Lewinsohn et al., 1996a; Spirito & Esposito-Smythers, 2006). As Kay Redfield Jamison says, referring to suicide in her book *Night Falls Fast: Understanding Suicide*, "If it has ever been taken up as an option, however, the black knight has a tendency to remain in play." (1999, p. 4). Thus, adolescents who attempt suicide once are at high risk for future attempts, which might be successful.

College Students

The college years are full of pressures and changes. Students may face challenges far beyond those

VOICES

I think when you live with someone for a long time, that when they go, you should be able to go, too. I think people should be able to go together. I think it's useless for one person of a pair to stick around. I just think that it should be a natural order of things that if you're together with somebody a long

(continued)

time, you should just go with them when they go. It doesn't make any sense. . . . We grew up together, really. All those years and all the things we did. I don't want to do anything by myself. I don't want to be alone. It was great with him. It's sure a big zero without him.

Suicide rates are highest in the first year after a loss but remain relatively high for several years after the loss (McIntosh, 1995).

Some older persons who commit suicide suffer from debilitating illnesses and wish to escape their pain and suffering. Escape from illness and disabilities may be a particularly strong motive for suicide among men (Canetto & Hollenshead, 2000). An older man may have been strong and healthy his entire life; then, when stricken with a serious disease in old age, he may become confined to a wheelchair or his bed or be forced to enter a nursing home. One study of older people who had committed suicide found that 44 percent had said they could not bear being placed in a nursing home and would rather be dead (Loebel et al., 1991).

Some researchers argue that intentional life-threatening behavior, such as refusing food or medication, is a common form of suicidal behavior in older people (see Harwood et al., 2000). These behaviors range from clearly self-destructive behaviors, such as refusing food with the intent of starving to death, to behaviors with less obvious intent, such as failing to follow a prescribed treatment for an illness or continuing to smoke with emphysema.

Most older persons who lose a spouse or become ill do not commit suicide. Again, those who enter older age with a history of depression or other psychological problems are at greatest risk of responding to the challenges of old age with suicide (Harwood et al., 2000).

SUMMING UP

- Suicide is defined as death from injury, poisoning, or suffocation when there is evidence (either explicit or implicit) that the injury was self-inflicted and that the decedent intended to kill him- or herself.

- Death seekers clearly and explicitly seek to end their lives. Death initiators also have a clear intention to die but believe that they are simply hastening an inevitable death. Death ignorers intend to end their lives but do not believe this

Illness is often a precursor to suicide among older adults.

means the end of their existence. Death darers are ambivalent about dying and take actions that greatly increase their chances of death but that do not guarantee they will die.

- Suicide is the eighth leading cause of death in the United States, and internationally at least 160,000 people die by suicide and 2 million other people make suicide attempts each year.

- Women are more likely than men to attempt suicide, but men are more likely than women to complete suicide.

- Cross-cultural differences in suicide rates may have to do with religious doctrines, stressors, and cultural norms about suicide.

- Young people are less likely than adults to commit suicide, but suicide rates have been rising dramatically for young people in recent decades. The elderly, particularly elderly men, are at high risk for suicide.

UNDERSTANDING SUICIDE

Our ability to understand the causes of suicide is hampered by many factors. First, although it is more common than we would hope, it is still rare enough that it is difficult to study scientifically. Second, in the wake of a suicide, family members and friends may selectively remember certain information about the victim (such as evidence that he or she was depressed) and forget other information. Third, the majority of people who contemplate suicide never actually commit suicide, so it is difficult to determine what causes some people to go through with the act.

Suicide Notes

It would be very helpful if we could get some clues as to the reasons for suicide from the notes left behind by those who commit suicide. Only about one in four people leave a suicide note, however, and often these notes provide only a glimpse into their motives (Jamison, 1999). These notes are often brief and vague and may simply say, "I could not bear it any longer," or "I am tired of living." On the other hand, some suicide notes are very concrete, with explicit instructions or requests, such as how to handle the body, what to tell others about the suicide, and how to distribute assets. Occasionally, the mental anguish that leads to suicide is expressed more fully in the suicide note (Leenaars, 1988, pp. 247–248):

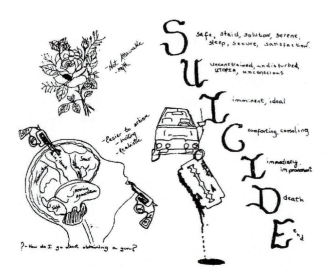

Drawings by a 19-year-old college sophomore.

VOICES

I wish I could explain it so someone could understand it. I'm afraid it's something I can't put into words. There's just this heavy, overwhelming despair—dreading everything. Dreading life. Empty inside, to the point of numbness. It's like there's something already dead inside. My whole being has been pulling back into that void for months. . . . But there's some core-level spark of life that just isn't there. Despite what's been said about my having "gotten better" lately—the voice in my head that's driving me crazy is louder than ever. It's way beyond being reached by anyone or anything, it seems. I can't bear it anymore. I think there's something psychologically twisted—reversed—that has taken over; that I can't fight anymore. I wish that I could disappear without hurting anyone. I'm sorry.

This writer mentions that family members and friends believe she is "getting better." Suicides often happen when people are not in the deepest depths of depression and despair but, rather, when they seem to be getting better, having more energy and engagement in life. This energy, however, can simply give them the energy and freedom to commit suicide, as Elizabeth Wurtzel explains in her autobiography, *Prozac Nation* (1995, p. 315):

The suicide attempt startled even me. It seemed to happen out of context, like something that should have taken place months and months ago. It should never have happened

VOICES

within a few days of returning to Cambridge, at a point when, even I had to admit, the fluoxetine (Prozac) was starting to kick in. After all, I was able to get out of bed in the morning, which may not seem like much, but in my life it was up there with Moses parting the Red Sea. Anybody would have thought that these were signs that my mood was on the upswing, and I guess it was. But just as a little bit of knowledge is a dangerous thing, a little bit of energy, in the hands of someone hell-bent on suicide, is a very dangerous thing.

My improved affect did not in any way sway me from the philosophical conviction that life, at its height and depth, basically sucks.

For people with long-term mental disorders, the prospect of sinking once again into despair leads them to take "preventive action"—to kill themselves before it happens again. Virginia Woolf suffered psychotic depressions and manias and committed suicide when she sensed a new episode coming (1975–1980a, pp. 486–487):

Dearest,
I want to tell you that you have given me complete happiness. No one could have done more than you have done. Please believe that.

(continued)

But I know that I shall never get over this: and I am wasting your life. It is this madness. Nothing anyone says can persuade me. You can work, and you will be much better without me. You see I can't write this even, which shows I am right. All I want to say is that until this disease came on we were perfectly happy. It was all due to you. No one could have been so good as you have been, from the very first day till now. Everyone knows that.

Most suicide notes are positive in their remarks about remaining family members, expressing love and thanks. Sometimes, the note is meant to relieve family members of guilt (Leenaars, 1988, p. 249):

Everyone has been so good to me—has tried so hard. I truly wish that I could be different, for the sake of my family. Hurting my family is the worst of it, and that guilt has been wrestling with the part of me that wanted only to disappear.

Thus, suicide notes often reveal only the obvious—that suicide tends to be driven by mental anguish and a sense of futility about going on.

Social Perspectives on Suicide

Social theorists have been at the forefront of research and theorizing about suicide. They have identified a number of events, and characteristics of societies, that may contribute to a vulnerability to suicide (see the Concept Overview in Table 10.2 on page 362).

Economic Hardship

A variety of stressful life events appear to contribute to an increased risk for suicide (Statham et al., 1998). One type of stressful event consistently linked to increased suicide vulnerability is economic hardship (Fanous, Prescott, & Kendler, 2004; Welch, 2001). For example, the loss of a job can precipitate suicidal thoughts and attempts (Crosby et al., 1999; Platt & Hawton, 2000); as the farm economy has collapsed in the United States in recent decades, the rate of suicide among farmers has increased considerably

(Ragland & Berman, 1990–1991). Men and women who have spent their entire lives trying to make a living from land that may have been in their families for generations can find their dreams shattered and their farms lost forever.

Chronic economic hardship also contributes to suicidality. One nationwide study found that 8.5 percent of people living below the poverty level had thought about committing suicide in the previous year, compared with 5.4 percent of people living above the poverty level (Crosby et al., 1999). The high suicide rate among African American males in recent years may also be tied to perceptions that their economic futures are uncertain at best, as well as comparisons of their economic status with the status of the majority culture. One study found that suicide rates among African American males in the United States were highest in communities where the occupational and income inequalities between African Americans and European Americans were the greatest (Burr et al., 1999).

Serious Illness

Some people who commit suicide, especially older people, suffer from serious illnesses that bring them constant pain and debilitation (Canetto & Hollenshead, 2000). Some illnesses especially likely to increase the risk for suicide are HIV/AIDS, cancers of the brain, and some neurological conditions, including multiple sclerosis (Hughes & Kleespies, 2001). Although people who are seriously ill may always have been at increased risk for suicide, increases in the ability of medical practices to keep people alive long after they have been diagnosed with a serious illness have contributed to the number of seriously ill people wishing they could die. Interestingly, physical illness is a risk factor for suicidal thoughts and attempts in adolescents as well as in older adults (Lewinsohn et al., 1996a). The pain and burden of chronic physical illness are clearly not being well managed by the medical professions, leaving some people feeling incapable of bearing them on their own.

Loss and Abuse

Loss of a loved one through death, divorce, or separation often immediately precedes suicide attempts or completions (Spirito & Esposito-Smythers, 2006). People feel they cannot go on without the lost relationship and wish to end their pain. In addition, people who have experienced certain traumas in childhood, especially sexual abuse or the loss of a parent also appear at increased risk for suicide (Fanous et al., 2004; Spirito & Esposito-Smythers, 2006). For example, a nationwide study

TABLE 10.2 Concept Overview

Social Perspectives on Suicide

Social theorists have attributed suicide to larger events happening in a culture or to major traumas in an individual's life.

Theory	Description
Economic hardship	People who are chronically impoverished or who recently have lost a job are at increased risk for suicide.
Serious illness	People with serious illnesses are at increased risk for suicide.
Loss and abuse	People who have experienced loss or abuse in the distant or recent past are at increased risk for suicide.
Durkheim's theory	Egoistic suicide is committed by people who feel alienated from others, empty of social contacts, and alone in an unsupportive world. Anomic suicide is committed by people who experience severe disorientation because of a major change in their relationships to society. Altruistic suicide is committed by people who believe that taking their own lives will benefit society in some way.
Suicide contagion	When one member of group commits suicide, other members are at increased risk for suicide, perhaps because of "contagion" effects, modeling, increased acceptability of suicide, or the impact of the traumatic event on already vulnerable people.

in the United States found that a history of childhood sexual abuse increases the odds of a suicide attempt by 2 to 4 times for women and 4 to 11 times for men (Molnar, Berkman, & Buka, 2001; see also Brent et al., 2002). Studies focusing on women have found that physical abuse by a partner is a potent predictor of suicide attempts (Kaslow et al., 2000; Ragin et al., 2002). The loss of a parent during childhood may create a lifetime of instability and feelings of abandonment, which can contribute to suicidal intentions. Sexual abuse during childhood may shatter people's trust in others and prevent the development of a strong self-concept, which can protect against suicide.

Durkheim's Theory

In his classic work on suicide, sociologist Emil Durkheim (1897) focused not on specific events that precipitate suicide but, rather, on the mindsets that certain societal conditions can create that increase the risk for suicide. He proposed that there are three types of suicide, based on his analysis of records of suicide for various countries and across historical periods.

Egoistic suicide is committed by people who feel alienated from others, empty of social contacts, and alone in an unsupportive world. A person with schizophrenia who kills herself because she is completely isolated from society may be committing egoistic suicide. **Anomic suicide** is committed by people who experience severe disorientation because of a major change in their relationships to society. A man who loses his job after 20 years of service may feel *anomie*, a complete confusion of his role and worth in society, and may commit anomic suicide. Finally, **altruistic suicide** is committed by people who believe that taking their own lives will benefit society in some way. For instance, during the Vietnam War, Buddhist monks burned themselves to death in public suicides to protest the war.

Durkheim's theory suggests that social ties and integration into a society help prevent suicide if the society discourages suicide and supports individuals in overcoming negative situations in ways other than suicide. However, if a society supports suicide as an act that benefits the society in some situations, then ties with such a society may actually promote suicide. For example, some terrorist groups promote suicide as an honorable, even glorious, act in the service of striking at enemies. William Styron saw suicide as an acceptable act in part because so many of his friends and heroes had committed suicide.

Suicide Contagion

When a well-known member of a society commits suicide, people who closely identify with that person may see suicide as more acceptable (Gould,

Jamieson, & Romer, 2003). When two or more suicides or attempted suicides are nonrandomly bunched in space or time, such as a series of suicide attempts in the same high school or a series of completed suicides in response to the suicide of a celebrity, scientists refer to this as a **suicide cluster** (Joiner, 1999).

Suicide clusters appear most likely to occur among people who knew the person who committed suicide. One well-documented example occurred in a high school of about 1,500 students. Two students committed suicide within 4 days. Then, over an 18-day span, 7 other students attempted suicide, and an additional 23 reported having suicidal thoughts (Brent et al., 1989). Many of those who attempted suicide or had active suicidal thoughts were friends of each other and of the two students who had completed suicide.

Other suicide clusters occur not among close friends but among people who are linked only by media exposure to the suicide of a stranger, often a celebrity. Some studies have suggested that suicide rates, at least among adolescents, increase after a publicized suicide (for a review, see Gould, Jamieson, & Romer, 2003). For example, in the week after Marilyn Monroe committed suicide in 1963, the national suicide rate rose 12 percent. More recently, after the suicide of the popular lead singer of the band Nirvana, Kurt Cobain, there were concerns that young people who identified with Cobain and the message in his music would view suicide as an appropriate way of dealing with the social anomie expressed in that music. At least one fan, a 28-year-old man, went home after a candlelight vigil honoring Cobain and killed himself with a shotgun, just as Cobain had.

What is the reason for suicide clustering? Some theorists have argued these clusters are due to **suicide contagion,** meaning that people somehow "catch" suicidal intentions and behaviors from those who commit suicide (Stack, 1991). Survivors who become suicidal may be modeling the behavior of the friend or admired celebrity who committed suicide. The suicide may also make the idea of suicide more acceptable and thus lower inhibitions for suicidal behavior in survivors. In addition, the local and media attention given to a suicide can be attractive to some people who are feeling alienated and abandoned. After the murder/suicide rampage of two teenagers at Columbine High School in Littleton, Colorado, in 1999, some teenagers said that having the media attention given to the shooters would be an attractive way to "go out."

Thomas Joiner (1999) argues that suicide clusters are best understood as the result of several sets of factors coming together in the same time and place. First, people form relationships with others who possess similar qualities or problems—known as *assortative relationships*. People who are at risk for suicide, because of psychopathology, life problems, or lack of social support from families, may be more likely to gravitate together. For example, teenagers who are outcasts from the popular groups at their high school may hang out together, with social alienation as the primary bond between them.

Second, severe negative events can be triggers for suicide, and these negative events often happen to groups of people as well as to individuals. The suicide of a close friend qualifies as a severe negative event and, thus, may increase the risk for suicide among others, as would any other severe negative event. But when the close friends of the person who committed suicide also carry other risk factors for suicide, then the suicide may be especially likely to trigger suicidality in the survivors.

Psychological Theories of Suicide

Psychological theorists have focused on what goes through the mind of a person who commits suicide. Psychodynamic theorists attribute suicide to repressed rage. Cognitive theorists have identified patterns of thinking that appear to increase the risk for suicide, and a great deal of evidence shows that certain mental disorders increase the risk for suicide (see the Concept Overview in Table 10.3).

TABLE 10.3   Concept Overview

Psychological Theories of Suicide

Psychological theories of suicide focus on the thoughts and motivations of people who attempt suicide.

Theory	Description
Psychodynamic theories	Suicide is the extreme expression of anger at the love object who has abandoned the person.
Mental disorders	Several mental disorders increase the risk for suicide, including depression, bipolar disorder, schizophrenia, substance abuse, and anxiety disorders.
Impulsivity	People who commit suicide have a general tendency toward impulsive acts.
Cognitive theories	Hopelessness and dichotomous thinking increase the risk for suicide.

Psychodynamic Theories

Recall that Freud (1917) argued that depression is anger turned inward on the self. Instead of expressing anger at people they feel have betrayed or abandoned them, depressed people express that anger at themselves, specifically at the part of their ego that represents the lost person. Sometimes, that anger is so great that the depressed person wishes to annihilate that image of the lost person. This means annihilating the self—suicide.

This line of reasoning suggests that suicidal people tend to be filled with rage against others. For example, teenagers who are enraged at their parents but cannot express it may attempt suicide as a means of punishing their parents. As noted in the section "Suicide Notes," however, anger and rage are not the most common emotions that suicidal people express (Shneidman, 1979). Instead, guilt and emotional despair are more common. A psychodynamic theorist might argue that suicidal people don't express anger in suicide notes or in other ways precisely because they cannot express these emotions and are turning the feelings in on themselves. Unfortunately, this argument makes the theory difficult to test.

Near the end of his career, Freud was dissatisfied with his own theory of suicide and believed it a more complex phenomenon than anger turned inward. Although newer psychodynamic theories of suicide have emerged, most still focus on self-directed anger as the core problem in suicidality (Maltsberger, 1999).

Mental Disorders

Over 90 percent of people who commit suicide have probably been suffering from a diagnosable mental disorder (Joiner, Brown, & Wingate, 2005; Spirito & Esposito-Smythers, 2006). The most common disorder among people who commit suicide is a mood disorder—for example, William Styron's suicidal thoughts were part of a debilitating depression. Suicide is associated with several other disorders as well, including borderline personality disorder, disruptive behavior disorders (such as conduct disorder), alcohol and other drug use disorders, anxiety disorders, anorexia nervosa, and schizophrenia (Joiner, Brown, & Wingate, 2005; Spirito & Esposito-Smythers, 2006). Often, psychiatric diagnoses have not been made before an individual commits suicide. Instead, researchers conduct a *psychological autopsy*—an analysis of the person's moods, thoughts, and behaviors based on the reports of family and friends and the individual's writings—after the suicide has occurred.

One group of researchers was able to conduct a prospective study of people who attempted suicide during a year-long study of 13,673 adults randomly chosen from a community sample. All these adults were interviewed twice, one year apart. A structured clinical interview was used to determine whether each adult qualified for the diagnosis of a psychological disorder. Over the year between the two interviews, 40 people in the sample attempted suicide. The researchers randomly chose 40 other people from the rest of the sample who had not attempted suicide to make comparisons with the 40 suicide attempters. When the researchers examined the data from the first interview, they found that 53 percent of those who had attempted suicide had been diagnosed with major depression, compared with 6 percent of those who had not made an attempt (Petronis et al., 1990). Similarly, a prospective study of suicide attempts in adolescents found that major depression greatly increases the risk for suicide (Lewinsohn et al., 1996a).

In the longitudinal study by Petronis and colleagues (1990), 8 percent of the people who attempted suicide had been diagnosed with mania at the first interview, compared with 0.6 percent of the nonattempters. As many as half of people with bipolar disorder attempt suicide, and perhaps one in five will complete suicide (Dunner, 2004; Goodwin & Jamison, 1990). It might seem strange that a manic person would attempt suicide, because the symptoms of mania include elation and heightened self-esteem. However, often the predominant feelings of mania are agitation and irritation mixed with despair over having the illness or in contemplating falling into a debilitating depression. Kay Redfield Jamison, who was featured in the *Extraordinary People* segment of Chapter 9, described one of her suicide attempts, which occurred when she was in a mixed manic and depressive state and was highly agitated (Jamison, 1995, pp. 113–114):

VOICES

In a rage I pulled the bathroom lamp off the wall and felt the violence go through me but not yet out of me. "For Christ's sake," he said, rushing in—and then stopping very quietly. Jesus, I must be crazy, I can see it in his eyes a dreadful mix of concern, terror, irritation, resignation, and why me, Lord? "Are you hurt?" he asks. Turning my head with its fast-scanning eyes I see in the mirror blood running down my arms. I bang my head over and over against the door. God, make it stop, I can't stand it, I know I'm insane again. He really cares, I think, but within ten minutes he too is screaming, and his eyes have a wild

(continued)

look from contagious madness, from the lightning adrenaline between the two of us. "I can't leave you like this," but I say a few truly awful things and then go for his throat in a more literal way, and he does leave me, provoked beyond endurance and unable to see the devastation and despair inside. I can't convey it and he can't see it; there's nothing to be done. I can't think, I can't calm this murderous cauldron, my grand ideas of an hour ago seem absurd and pathetic, my life is in ruins, and worse still—ruinous; my body is uninhabitable. It is raging and weeping and full of destruction and wild energy gone amok. In the mirror I see a creature I don't know but must live and share my mind with.

I understand why Jekyll killed himself before Hyde had taken over completely. I took a massive overdose of lithium with no regrets.

Another psychological disorder that greatly increases the risk for suicide attempts is substance abuse (Fanous et al., 2004; Welch, 2001; Yen et al., 2003). Recall that William Styron had been abusing alcohol for years before he became suicidal. In the prospective study of suicide attempts we have been discussing (Petronis et al., 1990), 33.0 percent of the individuals who attempted suicide were identified as heavy drinkers, compared with 2.5 percent of those who did not make an attempt. The lifetime risk for suicide among people who are dependent on alcohol is seven times greater than the lifetime risk among people who are not alcohol dependent (Joiner et al., 2005). When alcoholism co-occurs with depression, as in Styron's case, the risk for suicide is especially high (Waller, Lyons, & Costantini-Ferrando, 1999). Alcohol lowers people's inhibitions to engage in impulsive acts, even self-destructive ones, such as suicide attempts. Also, people with chronic alcohol problems may have a general tendency toward self-destructive acts and may wreck many of their relationships and their careers, making them feel they do not have much reason to live.

Between 10 and 15 percent of people with schizophrenia commit suicide, a rate 20 times higher than in the general population (Joiner et al., 2005; Tsuang, Fleming, & Simpson, 1999). They may kill themselves to end the torment of accusatory hallucinations telling them they are evil or to end the excruciating social isolation they feel. Most suicide attempts among people with schizophrenia happen not when the people are psychotic but when they are lucid but depressed. Those who are most likely

Alcohol is involved in many suicides.

to commit suicide are young males who have frequent relapses into psychosis but who had a good education and high expectations for themselves before they developed schizophrenia. It seems that these young men cannot face a future that is likely to be so much less than what they had envisioned for themselves (Joiner et al., 2005).

Whatever mental disorder a suicidal individual is suffering from, the most common reason expressed for attempting suicide is to escape intolerable distress (Brown, Comtois, & Linehan, 2002). In addition, people say they want to relieve their loved ones of the burdens of their existence and of caring for them.

Impulsivity

The behavioral characteristic that seems to predict suicide best is **impulsivity,** the general tendency to act on one's impulses rather than to inhibit them when it is appropriate to do so (Joiner et al., 2005). For example, a study of incarcerated men found that those with a history of suicide attempts were more likely to score high on scales measuring impulsivity and sensation seeking (Verona, Patrick, & Joiner, 2001). When impulsivity is overlaid on other psychological problems—such as depression, substance abuse, or life in a chronically stressful environment—it can be a potent contributor to suicide. One family history study showed that the children of parents with a mood disorder who also scored high on measures of impulsivity were at a much greater risk of attempting suicide (Brent et al., 2002). As we discuss in the section "Biological Theories of Suicides," there also is increasing evidence that impulsivity has biological roots (Oquendo & Mann, 2000).

Cognitive Theories

Cognitive theorists have examined the beliefs and attitudes that may contribute to suicide. The cognitive variable that has most consistently predicted

TABLE 10.4 Concept Overview

Biological Theories of Suicide

Biological theories of suicide focus on genetic and biochemical factors that may increase the risk for suicide.

Theory	Description
Genetic theory	Disordered genes increase the risk for suicide.
Neurotransmitter theory	Deficiencies in serotonin lead to impulsive, violent, and suicidal behavior.

suicide is **hopelessness**—the sense that the future is bleak and there is no way of making it more positive (Beck et al., 1985). One group of researchers examined 207 patients who had been hospitalized while contemplating suicide and found that 89 of them expressed utter hopelessness about their futures. Over the next five years, 13 of these 89 hopeless patients committed suicide, compared with only 1 patient who had not expressed hopelessness (Beck et al., 1985). Joiner and colleagues (2005) suggest that hopeless feelings about being a burden on others and about never belonging with others are especially linked to suicidality. Hopelessness may also be one reason people who are suicidal often do not seek treatment.

In addition, some research suggests that people who attempt or commit suicide tend to be rigid in their thinking (Linehan et al., 1987). They engage in **dichotomous thinking,** seeing everything in either/or terms. This inflexibility makes it more difficult for them to consider alternative solutions to their situations or simply to hold out until the suicidal feelings pass.

Biological Theories of Suicide

Genetics and neurotransmitters have been the focus of biological theories of suicide risk (see the Concept Overview in Table 10.4).

Genetic Theory

Suicide runs in families. For example, one study found that the children of parents who had attempted suicide were six times more likely to attempt suicide than were the children of parents who had a mood disorder but had not attempted suicide (Brent et al., 2002, 2003). The study of the Old Order Amish mentioned in Chapters 3 and 9 found that almost three-quarters of the suicides occurring in this culture come from just four large families, all of which have high rates of mood disorders (Egeland & Sussex, 1985).

One extraordinary family that has been plagued by suicide is the Hemingways. Five members of this family, spread across four generations, have committed suicide. Acclaimed novelist Ernest Hemingway killed himself with a shotgun after two treatments with electroconvulsive therapy failed to heal his severe depression. His granddaughter Margaux killed herself with an overdose of barbiturates on the thirty-fifth anniversary of her grandfather's suicide. Margaux had suffered from bulimia and alcoholism. She had had a successful modeling career but, after a series of failed movie appearances, her career had begun to decline. Just before her death, Margaux was reduced to taking parts in low-budget pictures and making guest appearances at European conventions. She allowed the BBC to tape a therapy session in which she said, "There's so much inside, and . . . sometimes I'm afraid that it's so full that it might kill me" (Masters, 1996, p. 148).

Although some of this clustering of suicide within families may be due to environmental factors, such as family members' modeling each other or having common stressors, twin and adoption studies suggest that genetics are involved as well (Joiner et al., 2005). Twin studies estimate that the risk for suicide attempts increase by 5.6 times if one's monozygotic twin has attempted suicide, 4.0 times if one's dizygotic twin has attempted suicide (Glowinski et al., 2001; Joiner et al., 2005). Strong evidence of a genetic component of suicidality remains when researchers control for histories of psychiatric problems in the twins and their families, recent and past negative life events, the twins' closeness to each other socially, and personality factors.

Neurotransmitter Theory

Many studies have found a link between suicide and low levels of the neurotransmitter serotonin in the brain (Asberg & Forslund, 2000; Mann, Brent, & Arango, 2001). For example, postmortem studies of the brains of people who committed suicide find lower than average levels of serotonin (Gross-Isseroff et al., 1998). People with a family history of suicide or who have attempted suicide are more likely to have abnormalities on genes that regulate serotonin (Courtet et al., 2004; Joiner et al., 2005; Joiner, Johnson, & Soderstrom, 2002). People who attempt suicide who have low serotonin levels are 10 times more likely to make another suicide attempt than those with higher serotonin levels (Roy,

1992). Low serotonin levels are linked with suicidality even among people who are not depressed, suggesting that the connection between serotonin and suicidality is not due entirely to a common connection to depression.

Serotonin may generally be linked to impulsive and aggressive behavior (Courtet et al., 2004; Mann et al., 2001). Low serotonin levels are most strongly associated with impulsive and violent suicides. Although these pieces of evidence do not prove that low serotonin levels cause suicidal behavior, they suggest that people with low serotonin levels may be at high risk for impulsive and violent behavior that sometimes results in suicide.

SUMMING UP

- Suicide notes suggest that mental anguish and escape from pain are behind many suicides.
- Several negative life events or circumstances increase the risk for suicide, including economic hardship, serious illness, loss, and abuse.
- Durkheim distinguished among egoistic suicide, which is committed by people who feel alienated from others, empty of social contacts, and alone in an unsupportive world; anomic suicide, which is committed by people who experience severe disorientation because of a major change in their relationships to society; and altruistic suicide, which is committed by people who believe that taking their own lives will benefit society in some way.
- Suicide clusters occur when two or more suicides or attempted suicides are nonrandomly bunched in space or time. This phenomenon is also sometimes called suicide contagion.
- Psychodynamic theorists attribute suicide to repressed rage, which leads to self-destruction.
- Several mental disorders increase the risk for suicide, including depression, bipolar disorder, substance abuse, schizophrenia, and anxiety disorders.
- Cognitive theorists argue that hopelessness and dichotomous thinking contribute to suicide.
- Impulsivity is a behavioral characteristic common to many people who commit suicide.
- Family history, twin, and adoption studies all suggest there is a genetic vulnerability to suicide.
- Many studies have found a link between low serotonin levels and suicide.

The Hemingway family has experienced the suicides of five of its members, including Ernest and Margaux.

TREATING AND PREVENTING SUICIDAL TENDENCIES

A person who is gravely suicidal needs immediate care. In *Taking Psychology Personally: What to Do If a Friend Is Suicidal* on page 368, we discuss useful tips. Sometimes, people require hospitalization to prevent an imminent suicide attempt. They may voluntarily agree to be hospitalized, but, if they do not agree, they can be hospitalized involuntarily for a short period of time (usually about three days). We discuss the pros and cons of involuntary hospitalization in Chapter 18.

Community-based **crisis intervention** programs are available to help people who are highly suicidal deal in the short term with their feelings and then refer them for longer care to mental-health specialists. Some crisis intervention is done over the phone, on **suicide hot lines.** Some communities have suicide prevention centers, which may be part of a larger mental-health system, or stand-alone clinics, where suicidal people can walk in and receive immediate care.

Crisis intervention aims to reduce the risk for an imminent suicide attempt by providing suicidal persons someone to talk with, someone who understands their feelings and problems. The counselor can help them mobilize support from family members and friends and can make a plan to deal with specific problem situations in the short term. The crisis intervention counselor may make a contract with the suicidal person that he or she will not attempt suicide, or at least will recontact the counselor as soon as the suicidal feelings return. The counselor will help the person identify other people he or she can turn to when panicked or overwhelmed. And the counselor will make follow-up appointments with the suicidal person or refer the person to another counselor for long-term treatment.

Taking Psychology Personally

What to Do If a Friend Is Suicidal

What should you do if you suspect that a friend or family member is suicidal? The National Depressive and Manic-Depressive Association (1996), a patient-run advocacy group, makes the following suggestions in *Suicide and Depressive Illness*:

- *Take the person seriously*. Although most people who express suicidal thoughts do not go on to attempt suicide, most people who do commit suicide communicate their suicidal intentions to friends or family members beforehand. Stay calm, but don't ignore the situation.

- *Get help*. Call the person's therapist, a suicide hot line, 911, or any other source of professional mental-health care.

- *Express concern*. Tell the person concretely why you think he or she is suicidal.

- *Pay attention*. Listen closely, maintain eye contact, and use body language to indicate that you are attending to everything the person says.

- *Ask direct questions about whether the person has a plan for suicide and, if so, what that plan is*. Many people fear that asking a person if he or she is thinking about suicide will give him or her the idea, but this is not the case.

- *Acknowledge the person's feelings in a nonjudgmental way*. For example, you might say something like "I know you're feeling really horrible right now, but I want to help you get through this" or "I can't begin to understand completely how you feel, but I want to help you."

- *Reassure the person that things can be better*. Emphasize that suicide is a permanent solution to a temporary problem.

- *Don't promise confidentiality*. You need the freedom to contact mental-health professionals and tell them precisely what is going on.

- *If possible, don't leave the person alone until he or she is in the hands of professionals*. Go with him or her to the emergency room, if need be. Then, once he or she has been hospitalized or has received other treatment, follow up to show you care.

- *Take care of yourself*. Interacting with a person who is suicidal can be an extremely stressful and disturbing experience. Talk with someone you trust about it—perhaps a friend, family member, or counselor—particularly if you worry about how you handled the situation or about finding yourself in that situation again.

People who receive longer-term treatment for suicidality typically receive psychotherapies and medications similar to those used to treat mood disorders. Preventive measures are taken with high-risk people who have not yet attempted suicide to try to reduce the risk for future attempts.

What is most clear from the literature on the treatment of suicidal people is that they are woefully undertreated. Most people who are suicidal never seek treatment (Crosby et al., 1999). Even when their families know they are suicidal, they may not be taken for treatment because of denial and a fear of the stigma of suicide. The people who do receive treatment typically receive inadequate care. One study of depressed people on an inpatient psychiatric ward found that less than a third of those with a history of suicide attempts were being adequately treated (Oquendo et al., 1999).

Drug Treatments

The medication most consistently shown to reduce the risk for suicide is *lithium*. Baldessarini, Tondo, and Hennen (2001) reviewed 33 published treatment studies of people with major depression or bipolar disorder and found that those *not* treated with lithium were 13 times more likely to commit or attempt suicide than those who had been treated with lithium.

As noted in Chapter 9, however, many people have difficulty taking lithium, because of its side effects and toxicity. Most recently, studies have focused on the *selective serotonin reuptake inhibitors (SSRIs)*, such as Celexa, Prozac, Luvox, Zoloft, and Paxil, in the treatment of suicide risk. Some studies suggest that these drugs can reduce impulsive and violent behaviors in general, and suicidal behaviors specifically (see Gould, Greensberg, et al., 2003). Paradoxically, however, some studies suggest that the SSRIs can increase the risk for suicide in some people. It is not clear who is at most risk for this "side effect" of the SSRIs or when it is most likely to happen. This risk is just one of many reasons it is crucial for people taking psychotherapeutic drugs to be closely monitored by physicians with expertise in these drugs.

Antipsychotic medications can be used to treat psychotic symptoms in people with psychotic mood disorders or schizophrenia. Reducing psychotic symptoms may also reduce the risk for suicidality.

Psychological Treatments

The psychological therapies designed for depression, and described in Chapter 9, are most frequently used in the treatment of suicidality. Psychodynamic therapists focus more on exploring unexpressed anger at others, whereas cognitive therapists focus more on the client's hopelessness and dichotomous thinking, as well as on the environmental triggers for suicidal behavior (Henriques, Beck, & Brown, 2003).

Psychologist Marcia Linehan (1999) has developed a cognitive-behavioral intervention designed specifically to address suicidal behaviors and thoughts, which she calls **dialectical behavior therapy.** This therapy was originally developed to treat people with borderline personality disorder, whose moods and self-images have a tendency to swing between extremes (see Chapter 12). (The term *dialectical* in *dialectical behavior therapy* refers to this constant tension between conflicting images or emotions in people with borderline personality disorder.) Dialectical behavior therapy is somewhat like cognitive-behavioral therapy, but it focuses on difficulties in managing negative emotions and in controlling impulsive behaviors. The therapy involves a number of techniques aimed at increasing problem-solving skills, interpersonal skills, and skills in managing negative emotions. Studies comparing this therapy with control conditions suggest that it can reduce suicidal thoughts and behaviors, as well as improve interpersonal skills (Linehan, 1999; Linehan et al., 1991; Shearin & Linehan, 1989).

Therapists often include spouses, partners, and family members in the treatment of people who are suicidal. Some of the problems behind a suicide attempt may reside in troubled relationships and family environments. Even if this is not the case, family members can play a role in preventing future attempts by helping suicidal members recognize when they are vulnerable and actively seek professional help. Finally, suicidality in one member can devastate a family, and often the entire family is in need of psychological help.

Social Approaches and Prevention

Suicide hot lines and crisis intervention centers are forms of suicide prevention programs. They provide help to suicidal people in times of greatest

Psychotherapies for people at high risk for suicide help them identify times when they are vulnerable and develop more adaptive coping skills during these times.

need, hoping to prevent a suicidal act until suicidal feelings have passed.

In addition, many prevention programs aim to educate entire communities about suicide. Many of these programs are based in schools and colleges. Students are given information about the suicide rates in their age group, the risk factors for suicide, and what to do if they or a friend is suicidal.

Unfortunately, studies of the effects of broadly based prevention/education programs have suggested that they are not very helpful and, indeed, might cause harm (Gould, Greenberg, et al., 2003). One major problem with these programs is that they often simultaneously target both the general population of students and students who are at high risk for suicide. The programs may attempt to destigmatize suicide by making it appear quite common and by not mentioning that most suicidal people are suffering from a psychological disorder, in hopes that suicidal students will feel more free to seek help. But such messages can backfire among students who are not suicidal, making suicide seem to be an understandable response to stress. In addition, studies of school-based suicide prevention programs have found that adolescents who had made prior suicide attempts generally reacted negatively to the programs, saying they were less inclined to seek help after seeing the program than before they had seen the program (Gould, Greenberg, et al., 2003).

Recently, researchers have begun tailoring suicide prevention messages to specific populations, particularly high-risk populations, in hopes that the right kind of help will get to the most needy people. David Shaffer and colleagues at Columbia University have designed a program that involves screening adolescents for suicidality, doing a diagnostic interview with the adolescents with the help of a laptop computer, and then interviewing the adolescents to determine the most appropriate referral to a mental-health specialist (Shaffer & Gould, 2000). This program has shown success in identifying high-risk youth and getting them into effective treatment. A similar program for college students has been implemented at Emory University (Haas, Hendin, & Mann, 2003).

Guns and Suicide

In the United States, the majority of suicides, particularly those by men, involve guns (National Institute of Mental Health [NIMH], 2002). Most people who commit suicide by gun do not buy guns expressly to commit suicide. Instead, they use guns that have been in their households for sometime. Often, suicide with guns is an impulsive act committed by people under the influence of alcohol: They may be depressed, get drunk, and retrieve family handguns and shoot themselves. The risk for a suicide attempt with a gun is increased if there is a loaded, unlocked gun in the household (Conwell et al., 2002). Unfortunately, a gunshot to the head is highly likely to end in death, whether or not the person truly intended to commit suicide.

Can we reduce the number of such suicides by restricting people's access to guns? The answer may be yes. Several studies have found that suicide rates decrease when cities and states enact strict antigun legislation that limits people's access to guns (Lambert & Silva, 1998). For example, one study compared two similar metropolitan areas with different degrees of firearms restrictions and found that the urban area with less strict handgun laws had almost six times more suicides involving firearms than the urban area with stricter handgun laws (Sloan et al., 1990). Although people who are intent on committing suicide can find other means to do so if guns are not available, restricting ready access to guns appears to reduce impulsive suicides with guns, particularly among males. In addition, several studies suggest that there is no increase in suicides by means other than guns (e.g., by jumping off buildings or inhaling carbon monoxide) when access to guns is restricted, suggesting that people do not simply substitute different means of committing suicide when guns are not available (Lambert & Silva, 1998). Instead, the lack of availability of guns gives them a cooling off period, during which suicidal impulses can wane.

Opponents of gun control argue that restricting access to guns only makes people more vulnerable to intruders in their homes or to others wishing to do them harm. One study strongly suggests that

this is not the case, however. Researchers examined 398 consecutive deaths by gun in the homes of families who owned guns (usually handguns). Of these deaths, only 0.5 percent were intruders shot by families protecting themselves. In contrast, 83 percent of these deaths were suicides of adolescent or adult family members. Another 12 percent were homicides of one adult in the home by another family member, usually in the midst of quarrels. The final 3 percent of deaths were due to accidental gunshots of one of the family members (Kellermann et al., 1992). The mere presence of a firearm in the home appears to be a risk factor for suicide when other risk factors are taken into account, especially when handguns are improperly secured or are kept loaded (Brent et al., 1991). These data strongly suggest that removing guns from the home is an important preventive measure against suicide.

The "Right" to Commit Suicide

Many societies, including the United States, are currently debating whether people have a right to commit suicide. Some people, such as psychiatrist Thomas Szasz and physician Jack Kevorkian, argue that the right to die as one chooses and when one

Restricting access to guns appears to lower suicide rates.

chooses is a fundamental human right that cannot be regulated by the state. Others note that most people who attempt suicide but do not complete it do not later commit suicide, suggesting that they do not truly wish to die (Harwood et al., 2000). More generally, most people who contemplate suicide, particularly if they are depressed and not suffering from terminal medical illness, are ambivalent about it, and their suicidal wishes pass after relatively short periods of time. This information suggests that preventing suicide is appropriate, at least for people who have serious mental disorders, because many people who attempt suicide are not making rational or permanent choices.

Gender and Assisted Suicide

In most cases of suicide by the seriously ill, ill people kill themselves, but, in a substantial number of cases, they are killed by a medical professional or a family member or friend, an act sometimes referred to as "mercy killing." Although mercy killing, or **euthanasia,** is not legal in the United States, it is not uncommon. Surveys of medical professionals in the United States show that perhaps 20 percent or more have assisted in a patient's suicide or have hastened the death of a seriously ill patient, even without that patient's consent (Canetto & Hollenshead, 2000).

Studies conducted in the United States and Australia show that most mercy killings involve older married couples, with the husband killing his ill wife (Canetto & Hollenshead, 2000). This gender balance stands in stark contrast to the data showing that many more men than women commit suicide, especially among older people. Men may be more willing than women to kill, whether it be themselves or an ill family member. Men may also find it more intolerable to be caught in the caregiver role to an ill spouse than do women (Canetto & Hollenshead, 2000). Ill women are not only killed by their husbands but are also more likely than ill men to be the recipients of physician-assisted death (Canetto & Hollenshead, 1999).

It is not known why women are more likely than men to be assisted in suicide. Some researchers suggest that women's lives are less valued than men's, particularly once they are seriously, chronically ill. For this reason, family members and physicians may agree to assist women in killing themselves (Canetto & Hollenshead, 1999, 2000).

SUMMING UP

- Drug treatments for suicidality most often include lithium or antidepressant medications to reduce impulsive and violent behavior, depression, and mania. Antipsychotic

medications and other medications that treat the symptoms of an existing mental disorder may also be used.

- The psychotherapies for suicide are similar to those used for depression. Dialectical behavior therapy has been specifically designed to address skill deficits and thinking patterns in people who are suicidal.

- Suicide hot lines and crisis intervention programs provide immediate help to people who are highly suicidal.

- Community prevention programs aim to educate the public about suicide and encourage suicidal people to enter treatment.

- Guns are involved in the majority of suicides, and some research suggests that restricting access to guns can reduce the number of suicide attempts.

- Society is debating whether people have a right to choose to commit suicide.

- Women are more likely than men to be assisted in suicide by a spouse or a physician.

CHAPTER INTEGRATION

Suicide seems to fit a diathesis-stress model (see Figure 10.5). Several factors seem to determine an individual's vulnerability to suicide, including a genetic vulnerability to suicide and possibly deficient serotonin levels. Other factors are early life experiences with loss and abuse and later life experiences with traumatic events. Hopeless and dichotomous thinking styles and impulsivity also can lower the threshold for suicidal behavior. And several psychological disorders clearly increase the

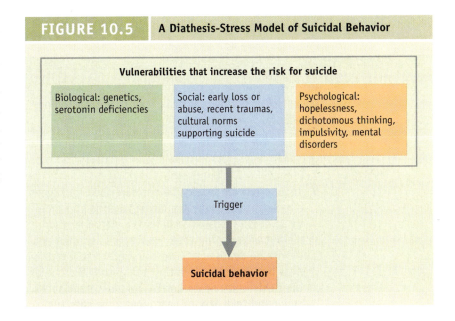

FIGURE 10.5   **A Diathesis-Stress Model of Suicidal Behavior**

Vulnerabilities that increase the risk for suicide

Biological: genetics, serotonin deficiencies

Social: early loss or abuse, recent traumas, cultural norms supporting suicide

Psychological: hopelessness, dichotomous thinking, impulsivity, mental disorders

Trigger

Suicidal behavior

risk for suicide. Many people carry these risk factors, however, and never become suicidal.

Something must trigger active suicidal behavior. These triggers also appear to be legion—the suicide of a close friend or relative, a recent traumatic event, and alcohol or other drug abuse. The difficulty in predicting suicidal behavior is that the specific trigger for one individual may be very different from the trigger for another. This is one reason that psychological treatments for suicidality have focused a great deal on helping people recognize when suicidal feelings are rising, learn what their personal triggers are, and develop more effective ways of coping with mood swings and transient suicidality, so that the trigger never gets fully pulled.

Extraordinary People: Follow-Up

What happened to William Styron, the author we met at the beginning of this chapter, who was seriously depressed and suicidal? Styron was hospitalized and, after seven weeks of antidepressant drugs and psychotherapy, overcame his depression.

What was the cause of Styron's depression? Styron speculates that he has always had a propensity for depression and anxiety. His father apparently suffered from depression, although it was never called depression back then. Styron's mother died when he was 13, and he believes this loss created a psychological vulnerability in him that compounded the genetic vulnerability to depression he may have inherited from his father. Forty years of alcohol abuse may have altered the workings of his neurotransmitter systems, but Styron also believes that he used alcohol to dampen his feelings of anxiety and depression all those years.

A few years after he emerged from his depression, Styron wrote *Darkness Visible*, a memoir of his descent into depression and suicide and his triumph over it. This book became a national best-seller, but not only because Styron was able to describe with great skill and poetry the deepest horrors of depression and suicidality. *Darkness Visible* also gives hope to those who suffer:

For those who have dwelt on depression's dark wood, and known its inexplicable agony, their return from the abyss is not unlike the ascent of the poet, trudging upward and upward out of hell's black depths and at last emerging into what he saw as "the shining world." There, whoever has been restored to health has almost always been restored to the capacity for serenity and joy, and this may be indemnity enough for having endured the despair beyond despair. (Styron, 1990, p. 84)

Chapter Summary

- Suicide is defined as death from injury, poisoning, or suffocation when there is evidence (either explicit or implicit) that the injury was self-inflicted and that the decedent intended to kill him- or herself.

- Theorist Edwin Shneidman has described four types of suicide: Death seekers clearly seek to end their lives; death initiators also have a clear intention to die but believe that they are simply hastening an inevitable death; death ignorers intend to end their lives but do not believe that this means the end of their existence; death darers are ambivalent about dying and take actions that greatly increase their

chances of death but that do not guarantee they will die.

- Suicide is the eighth leading cause of death in the United States. There are substantial differences across ethnic groups within the United States, and across countries worldwide, in rates of suicide.

- Women are more likely than men to attempt suicide, but men are more likely than women to complete suicide. Cross-cultural differences in suicide rates may have to do with religious doctrines, stressors, and cultural norms about suicide. Young people are less likely than adults to commit suicide, but suicide rates have been rising dramatically for young people in recent decades. The elderly, particularly elderly men, are at high risk for suicide.

■ Suicide notes suggest that mental anguish and escape from pain are behind many suicides. Generally, suicide notes are brief and concrete, however, and leave few clues.

■ Several negative life events or circumstances increase the risk for suicide, including economic hardship, serious illness, loss, and abuse. (Review Table 10.2.)

■ Durkheim distinguished among egoistic suicide, which is committed by people who feel alienated from others, empty of social contacts, and alone in an unsupportive world; anomic suicide, which is committed by people who experience severe disorientation because of a major change in their relationships to society; and altruistic suicide, which is committed by people who believe that taking their own lives will benefit society in some way.

■ Suicide clusters (thought to be due to suicide contagion) occur when two or more suicides or attempted suicides are nonrandomly bunched in space or time.

■ Psychodynamic theorists attribute suicide to repressed rage, which leads to self-destruction. Several mental disorders increase the risk for suicide, including depression, bipolar disorder, substance abuse, schizophrenia, and anxiety disorders. Cognitive theorists argue that hopelessness and dichotomous thinking contribute to suicide. Impulsivity is a behavioral characteristic common to people who commit suicide. (Review Table 10.3.)

■ Family history, twin, and adoption studies all suggest there is a genetic vulnerability to suicide. Many studies have found a link between low serotonin levels and suicide. (Review Table 10.4.)

■ Drug treatments for suicidality most often include lithium or antidepressant medications to reduce impulsive and violent behavior, depression, and mania. Antipsychotic medications and other medications that treat the symptoms of an existing mental disorder may also be used.

■ The psychotherapies for suicide are similar to those used for depression. Dialectical behavior therapy has been specifically designed to address skill deficits and thinking patterns in people who are suicidal.

■ Suicide hot lines and crisis intervention programs provide immediate help to people who are highly suicidal. Community prevention programs aim to educate the public about suicide and encourage suicidal people to enter treatment.

■ Guns are involved in the majority of suicides, and some research suggests that restricting access to guns can reduce the number of suicide attempts. Society is debating whether people have a right to choose to commit suicide. Women are more likely than men to be assisted in suicide by a spouse or a physician.

■ Suicide seems to fit a diathesis-stress model. Various biological, psychological, and social factors can contribute to a person's vulnerability to suicide, and events or circumstances can trigger suicidal behavior. (Review Figure 10.5.)

MindMap CD-ROM

The following resources on the MindMap CD-ROM that came with this text will help you to master the content of this chapter and prepare for tests:

■ Chapter Quiz

Key Terms

suicide 353

death seekers 353

death initiators 354

death ignorers 354

death darers 354

subintentional deaths 354

egoistic suicide 362

anomic suicide 362

altruistic suicide 362

suicide cluster 363

suicide contagion 363

impulsivity 365

hopelessness 366

dichotomous thinking 366

crisis intervention 367

suicide hot lines 367

dialectical behavior therapy 369

euthanasia 371

Chapter 11

My Dog and I Are One
by Patricia Schwimmer

Whom Fortune wishes to destroy she first makes mad.

—Publilius Syrus, *Moral Sayings*
(first century B.C.; translated by Darius Lyman)

Schizophrenia <

CHAPTER OVERVIEW

Extraordinary People

■ John Nash: *A Beautiful Mind*

Taking Psychology Personally

■ Helping Families Cope with Schizophrenia

Symptoms, Diagnosis, and Prognosis of Schizophrenia

People with schizophrenia have delusions (beliefs with little grounding in reality), hallucinations (unreal perceptual experiences, such as hearing voices), and disorganized thought, speech, and behavior. Their motivation, affective responses, and quality of communication can also be unusual. Four types of schizophrenia have been identified: paranoid, disorganized, catatonic, and undifferentiated.

Biological Theories of Schizophrenia

There is strong evidence that schizophrenia is transmitted genetically. People with schizophrenia show abnormalities in several areas of the brain, including the prefrontal cortex, ventricles, and hippocampus. A number of prenatal difficulties and obstetrical problems at birth are implicated in the development of schizophrenia, including prenatal hypoxia and exposure to the influenza virus during the second trimester of gestation. Imbalances in the neurotransmitters dopamine, serotonin, glutamate, and GABA are also implicated in schizophrenia.

Psychosocial Perspectives on Schizophrenia

A variety of stressors may worsen the course of schizophrenia. Early psychodynamic theorists suggested that schizophrenia resulted from overwhelmingly negative experiences in early childhood with primary caregivers. More recent theories have focused on the aspects of family life that may increase stress and relapse in schizophrenia. Behavioral theories suggest that the symptoms of schizophrenia can develop through operant conditioning. Cognitive theories accept that there is a biological vulnerability to schizophrenia but see many symptoms as attempts to understand and cope with basic perceptual and attentional problems.

Treatments for Schizophrenia

Drugs called neuroleptics have proven useful in the treatment of schizophrenia; however, they have significant neurological side effects. Newer drugs, known as atypical antipsychotics, appear to be effective without inducing as many side effects as previous drugs. Psychosocial therapies focus on teaching communication and living skills and reducing isolation in people with schizophrenia.

Chapter Integration

There is compelling evidence that the fundamental vulnerability to schizophrenia is a biological one, yet there is also a growing consensus that psychosocial factors contribute to the risk for schizophrenia among people with the biological vulnerability. Theorists are increasingly developing models that integrate the biological and psychosocial factors. The most effective therapies for schizophrenia address both the biological and the psychosocial contributors to the disorder.

Extraordinary People

John Nash: *A Beautiful Mind*

In 1959, at the age of 30, John Nash was widely regarded as one of the premier mathematical minds of his generation. As a young professor at the Massachusetts Institute of Technology, he was tackling mathematical problems others thought were impossible to solve, and solving them with unconventional but highly successful approaches. While still a graduate student at Princeton, he had introduced the notion of equilibrium to game theory, which would eventually revolutionize the field of economics and win him the Nobel Prize.

As writer Sylvia Nasar details in her biography of John Nash, called *A Beautiful Mind*, Nash had always been flamboyant and eccentric, with few social skills and little emotional connection to other people. In 1959, however, Nash's wife noticed a change in his behavior. He became increasingly distant and cold to her, and his behavior grew more and more bizarre:

> Several times, Nash had cornered her with odd questions when they were alone, either at home or driving in the car. "Why don't you tell me about it?" he asked in an angry, agitated tone, apropos of nothing. "Tell me what you know," he demanded. (Nasar, 1998, p. 248)

Nash began writing letters to the United Nations, the FBI, and other government agencies, complaining of conspiracies to take over the world. He also began talking openly about his beliefs that powers from outer space, or perhaps from foreign governments, were communicating with him through the front page of the *New York Times*. Nash gave a series of lectures at Columbia and Yale Universities that were totally incoherent. Nash states,

> I got the impression that other people at MIT were wearing red neckties so I would notice them. As I became more and more delusional, not only persons at MIT but people in Boston wearing red neckties [would seem significant to me]. . . . [There was some relation to] a crypto-communist part. (Nasar, 1998, p. 242)

Nash's wife, Alicia, had him committed to McLean Hospital in April 1959 after his threats to harm her became more severe and as his behavior became increasingly unpredictable. There, Nash was diagnosed as having paranoid schizophrenia and was given medication and daily psychoanalytic therapy.

His behavior calmed. Nash spent much of his time with poet Robert Lowell, who suffered from manic-depression and was hospitalized for the fifth time in 10 years with severe mania. Nash learned to hide his delusions and hallucinations and to behave completely rationally, although his inner world remained much the same as it had been before the hospitalization. After 50 days of confinement, a week after the birth of his first son, Nash was released. On his release, Nash resigned from MIT, furious that the institution had "conspired" in his commitment to McLean Hospital. He withdrew his pension fund and sailed to Europe, vowing never to return.

In Geneva, Nash tried to renounce his American citizenship and eventually destroyed his passport. After being deported from Geneva and Paris, Nash ended up in Princeton two years later, still suffering from the acute symptoms of his schizophrenia. He walked up and down the streets of Princeton with a fixed expression and dead gaze, wearing Russian peasant garments and going into restaurants with bare feet. He talked in lofty terms of world peace and made it clear that he was intimately involved in the development of a world government. He wrote endless letters and made many phone calls to friends and eminaries around the world, talking of numerology and world affairs.

Various people—university officials, psychiatrists, friends—began to urge Alicia to have him committed again. This time, Alicia could not afford a private hospital, and Nash ended up in Trenton State Hospital. Nash was assigned a serial number, as if he were a prison inmate, and shared a room with 30 or 40 other patients. The nearly 600 patients in Nash's section of Trenton State were cared for by just 6 psychiatrists. At Trenton State, Nash was given insulin shock therapy, which was a popular treatment for schizophrenia in the early 1960s but is now discredited. Nonetheless, after six weeks, Nash was considered much improved and was moved to another ward of the hospital. There, he began to work on a paper on fluid dynamics. After six months of hospitalization, a month after his thirty-third birthday, he was discharged. Nash appeared to be well for sometime, but then his thinking, speech, and behavior began to slip again. Eventually, he ended up living with his mother in Roanoke, Virginia.

His daily rounds extended no farther than the library or the shops at the end of Grandin Road in Roanoke, but, in his own mind, he traveled to the remotest reaches of the globe: Cairo, Zebak, Kabul, Bangui, Thebes, Guyana, Mongolia. In these far-away places, he lived in refugee camps, foreign embassies, prisons, and bomb shelters. At other times, he felt that he was inhabiting an Inferno, a purgatory, or a polluted heaven ("a decayed rotting house infested by rats and termites and other vermin"). His identities were like the skins of an onion. Underneath each one lurked another: He was C.O.R.P.S.E. (a Palestinian refugee), a great Japanese shogun, C1423, Esau, L'homme d'Or, Chin Hsiang, Job, Jorap Castro, Janos Norses, and even at times a mouse (Nasar, 1998).

After his mother died, Nash returned to Princeton and lived with Alicia, who had long since divorced him. Nonetheless, she felt some responsibility for him and provided him with as much support as she could muster. There, Nash finally came to know his son. Nash also slowly reintegrated into the world of mathematics at Princeton.

Most of us walk around so secure in our perceptions of the world that we would never think to ask whether those perceptions were real or not. We look at a chair, recognize it as an object for sitting in, and use it accordingly. We hear a friend call our name and look for that friend, confident that he or she is somewhere nearby. We have an idea, realize that if others are going to appreciate that idea we have to communicate it to them, and articulate the idea clearly enough for them to understand it.

What must it be like to walk around not knowing whether your perceptions map onto reality, as did John Nash during the acute phases of his illness? You might question whether the things you see before you really exist. You might wonder if the voices you are hearing come from other people or are only in your head. You might believe that the ideas you are having are being broadcast over the television, so that others already know what you are thinking. If you are unable to tell the difference between what is real and what is unreal, you are suffering from **psychosis.**

Psychosis can take many forms and has many causes. In Chapter 9, we noted that people who suffer mood disorders can become psychotic and have hallucinations and delusions that are horribly depressing or wildly grandiose in content. In addition, the DSM-IV-TR recognizes a number of disorders in which psychosis is the primary feature (see the DSM-IV-TR information in Table 11.1 on page 378).

One of the most common psychotic disorders is **schizophrenia,** a truly puzzling disorder. At times, people with schizophrenia think and communicate clearly, have an accurate view of reality, and function well in daily life. At other times, their thinking and speech are garbled, they lose touch with reality, and they are not able to care for themselves in even the most basic ways.

Schizophrenia exacts heavy costs. There are medical costs: Over 90 percent of people with schizophrenia seek treatment in a mental-health facility or general medicine facility in any given year (Narrow et al., 1993). Studies have estimated that direct medical care alone for people with schizophrenia costs almost $20 billion per year in the United States (Torrey, 1995). Tens of billions of dollars more are lost in productivity. Most people who develop schizophrenia do so in the late teenage or early adult years. By then, they have been educated and are ready to assume their place in society, contributing their unique talents. Then the disorder strikes, often preventing them from making their contributions. Instead, people with schizophrenia may need continual services, including placement in halfway houses and other residential care facilities, rehabilitative therapy, subsidized income, and the help of social workers to obtain needed resources. And they need these

TABLE 11.1   DSM-IV-TR

Psychotic Disorders in the DSM-IV-TR

The DSM-IV-TR recognizes a number of psychotic disorders as well as schizophrenia. In addition, depression and bipolar disorder can include psychotic symptoms, as discussed in Chapter 9.

Disorder	Description
Schizophrenia	At least one month of acute symptoms of delusions, hallucinations, disorganized thought and speech, disorganized behavior, and negative symptoms and at least six months of some symptoms of disorder
Schizophreniform disorder	Same symptoms as schizophrenia, lasting more than one month but less than six months
Schizoaffective disorder	Symptoms of schizophrenia coinciding with symptoms of depression or mania, but at least a two-week period when only symptoms of schizophrenia present
Delusional disorder	Evidence only of nonbizarre delusions (e.g., that one is being followed or deceived) of at least one month's duration; functioning at relatively high level
Brief psychotic disorder	Presence of delusions, hallucinations, disorganized speech or behavior for at least one day but less than one month
Shared psychotic disorder	The individual in a close relationship with someone who is delusional with similar delusions (also known as *folie à deux*)
Substance-induced psychotic disorder	Hallucinations or delusions caused by the direct physiological effects of a substance (such as cocaine)

Source: Reprinted with permission from the *Diagnostic and Statistical Manual of Mental Disorders,* Fourth Edition, Text Revision. Copyright © 2000 American Psychiatric Association.

services for the rest of their lives, because schizophrenia tends to be a lifelong disorder. Author Greg Bottoms (2000, pp. 63–64) describes his brother Michael's descent into schizophrenia:

VOICES

Michael's decline, both mentally and physically, was astonishingly fast. He had gone from being a decent student and an amazing athlete to failing everything in the space of four years; he had gone from being a black belt in karate—lithe, aggressive, handsome—to being a disheveled, Bible-toting one-man show in less than one year. The rapidity of his decline once he hit twenty—particularly the physical decline—caught us all off guard. His poor marks in school had nothing to do with aptitude, but rather with his shifting of focus. He had a mission in life and little time to pursue other things, even if people insisted these things—school, a job, friends—were important.

His body softened dramatically, his hygiene could produce a gag reflex. Where he had once been inordinately handsome, he now had smears of blackheads across his nose, a double chin, greasy hair. . . . He started smoking three packs of Camels a day, sometimes rocked back and forth uncontrollably in the school smoking section during lunch, looking up through his long bangs at the other dopers to tell them that Jesus loved them. . . . He never slept—or if he did, it was maybe an hour or two at a time. . . . Sometimes he'd scream in the middle of the night.

In the United States, 1 to 2 percent of the population will develop schizophrenia at sometime in their lives (Walker et al., 2004). Similarly, studies across the globe find that between 0.5 and 2 percent of the general population suffers with schizophrenia (Gottesman, 1991; Jablensky, 2000). Unfortunately, schizophrenia is one of the most stigmatized psychological disorders, and people have become experts at hiding away loved ones with this disorder. As E. Fuller Torrey, a schizophrenia expert, has said, "People with schizophrenia are the lepers of the twentieth century" (Torrey, 1995, p. 8).

Torrey compiled data from several sources to estimate where people with schizophrenia are being kept, and his estimates are given in Figure 11.1. Note that the majority of people with schizophrenia are living independently or in their family's home. *Taking Psychology Personally: Helping Families Cope with Schizophrenia* highlights the challenges that families of people with schizophrenia face in coping with their loved one's disorder, particularly when that loved one lives at home. Note also in Figure 11.1 that almost as many people with schizophrenia are in jails, prisons, and homeless shelters and on the street as are in hospitals and nursing homes. The criminal system and the shelters are often the repositories for people with schizophrenia who do not have families to support them or the resources to get psychiatric help.

There are differences across groups within the United States in rates of schizophrenia. One large epidemiological study found the highest rates of schizophrenia in African Americans, somewhat lower rates in European Americans, and the lowest rates in Hispanic Americans, although these ethnic differences diminished when socioeconomic status was taken into account (Escobar, 1993). Studies of persons hospitalized for serious mental disorders have found that African Americans are more likely than other groups to be misdiagnosed with schizophrenia, when they are actually suffering from a severe mood disorder (Arnold et al., 2004; Neighbors et al., 2003).

Schizophrenia may be more common in men than in women, although the gender difference in rates of schizophrenia varies among studies and with the criteria used to diagnose schizophrenia (Cannon et al., 1998; Goldstein et al., 2002). Women with schizophrenia tend to have better premorbid (predisorder) histories than men (Goldstein & Lewine, 2000; Jablensky, 2000). They are more likely to have graduated from high school or college, to have married and had children, and to have developed good social skills. This may be, in part, because the onset of schizophrenia in women tends to be later in life, often in the late twenties or early thirties, than for men, who more often develop schizophrenia in their late teens or early twenties (Goldstein & Lewine, 2000). Women also show fewer cognitive deficits than men, particularly in verbal processing (Goldstein et al., 2002).

The reasons for these gender differences in the age of onset, course, and cognitive deficits in

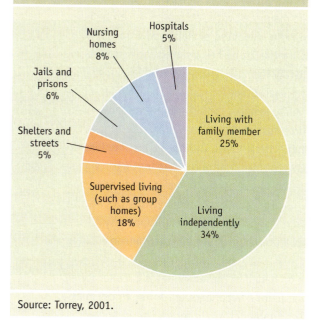

FIGURE 11.1 **Distribution of People with Schizophrenia.** Most people with schizophrenia live with family members or independently, but a number are in hospitals, in nursing homes, in group homes, in jail, or on the street.

Hospitals 5%
Nursing homes 8%
Jails and prisons 6%
Shelters and streets 5%
Supervised living (such as group homes) 18%
Living with family member 25%
Living independently 34%

Source: Torrey, 2001.

schizophrenia are not well understood yet. Estrogen may affect the regulation of dopamine, a neurotransmitter implicated in schizophrenia, in ways that are protective for women. Some of the sex differences, particularly in cognitive deficits, may also be due to normal sexual differences in the brain (Goldstein et al., 2002). The pace of prenatal brain development, which is hormonally regulated, is slower in males than in females and may place males at higher risk than females for brain insults. Exposure to a wide variety of toxins and illnesses in utero increases the risk for abnormal brain development and the development of schizophrenia. Several studies suggest that males with schizophrenia show greater abnormalities in brain structure and functioning than females with schizophrenia (Goldstein & Lewine, 2000).

In this chapter, we first consider the symptoms of schizophrenia and the various forms that schizophrenia can take. After reviewing the prognosis of schizophrenia, we examine its causes. Most theorists view schizophrenia primarily as a biological disorder, but psychological and social factors can influence how severe this disorder becomes and how often an individual has relapses. Effective biological treatments for schizophrenia have been developed in the past 50 years, as we will learn. These biological treatments are often supplemented

Taking Psychology Personally

Helping Families Cope with Schizophrenia

The anguish and confusion of family members who learn that a loved one has been diagnosed with schizophrenia can be huge. Before their eyes, a son, daughter, or sibling who once was full of hope and plans for the future has disintegrated into a being whom they may hardly recognize. The opportunities for blame are many—blaming each other for causing the disorder, blaming the afflicted family member for his or her symptoms, blaming mental-health professionals for not being able to cure the disorder, and blaming themselves. On top of this, families are now being asked to bear the brunt of the care for their members with schizophrenia, acting as psychotherapist, medication specialist, caretaker, rehabilitator, intermediary with the mental-health system, and unconditional emotional support system. It is no wonder that burnout and despair are common among these families.

One advocate on behalf of these families is E. Fuller Torrey. A very personal and painful experience led Torrey to psychiatry and the study of schizophrenia. While Torrey was an undergraduate, his sister, then 17, was diagnosed with schizophrenia. Torrey accompanied his mother and sister to a treatment facility and was appalled at the explanations and treatments offered for her illness. As he pursued a career in medicine, Torrey dedicated himself to finding better explanations and treatments for schizophrenia than those that had been offered to his sister, as well as to improving the treatment of people with serious mental disorders.

One of Torrey's books, *Surviving Schizophrenia* (1995), helps the families of people with schizophrenia understand the disorder and find appropriate treatment for their afflicted family members. This book educates family members on what schizophrenia is and is not, and it includes many specific tips on how to live with the schizophrenic family member and cope with the disorder. The key to surviving schizophrenia, according to Torrey, is having a "SAFE" attitude: a Sense of humor, an Acceptance of the illness, Family balance, and Expectations that are realistic.

Sense of Humor

It may seem strange to think that family members can approach schizophrenia with a sense of humor, but Torrey argues that the families most successful at managing schizophrenia maintain a sense of humor and an appreciation for the absurd. Family members cannot laugh *at* the person with schizophrenia, but they can laugh *with* him or her. For example, one family in which the son typically relapsed in the autumn and required hospitalization had a standing family joke that the son always carved his pumpkins in the hospital.

Acceptance of the Illness

Acceptance of the illness does not mean giving up but, rather, accepting the reality that the disorder will not go away, is likely to place limitations on the family member, and will need active management by the family. Unfortunately, it is more

by psychological and social therapies that help people with schizophrenia cope with the impact of the disorder on their lives, and we discuss those as well. We end this chapter considering theoretical perspectives and treatments that integrate knowledge of the biological and psychosocial contributors to schizophrenia.

SYMPTOMS, DIAGNOSIS, AND PROGNOSIS OF SCHIZOPHRENIA

Schizophrenia is a complex disorder that can take many forms. Indeed, many researchers and clinicians talk about "the schizophrenias," reflecting their belief that several types of schizophrenia are currently captured by the diagnostic criteria for schizophrenia.

Symptoms

There are two categories of symptoms. **Positive symptoms,** also called *Type I symptoms,* are characterized by the presence of unusual perceptions, thoughts, or behaviors. *Positive* refers to the fact that these symptoms represent very salient experiences. In contrast, **negative symptoms,** or *Type II symptoms,* represent losses or deficits in certain domains. They involve the absence of behaviors, rather than the presence of behaviors. People with schizophrenia may also suffer with depression, anxiety, substance abuse, inappropriate affect, anhedonia, and impaired social skills.

Positive Symptoms

The positive, or Type I, symptoms of schizophrenia include delusions, hallucinations, disorganized thought and speech, and disorganized or catatonic

Taking Psychology Personally (*continued*)

common for families to be angry at themselves, at the afflicted family member, at God, and so on. Their anger can be overtly expressed, or it can seethe quietly until a trigger causes a family member to explode. Educating family members about the illness and what they can reasonably expect is one of the most important jobs of mental-health professionals, because it can be the foundation of acceptance.

Family Balance

Caring for a family member with schizophrenia can be overwhelming. Some families put the needs of their member with schizophrenia before those of all the rest. Such families are prone to burnout, and neglected family members can become resentful and hostile. Families must achieve a balance of concern for the afflicted member and appreciation for the needs of the other family members. Caregivers may need to get away occasionally and to find resources, so that they are not providing round-the-clock care and ignoring their own needs.

Expectations That Are Realistic

It can be especially difficult for families to have realistic expectations of their family member with schizophrenia if that person had a particularly promising future before the illness struck. Pressure put on that family member may help trigger new episodes of acute symptoms. Lowering expectations can help family members appreciate the member with schizophre-

nia for who he or she is now, rather than focusing on what they wish were true:

> Several relatives mentioned that giving up hope had paradoxically been the turning point for them in coming to terms with their unhappiness. "Once you give up hope," one mother said, "you start to perk up." "Once you realise he'll never be cured you start to relax." These relatives had lowered their expectations and aspirations for the patient, and had found that doing this had been the first step in cutting the problem down to manageable size. (Creer & Wing, 1974, p. 33)

Clearly, family members should not abandon all expectations of the person with schizophrenia. What is important is having realistic expectations. Again, educating the family about the disease is critical to creating such expectations.

Some family members find that becoming politically active on behalf of people with schizophrenia helps them cope. The National Alliance for the Mentally Ill (NAMI) is the largest national organization focusing on serious mental disorders, including schizophrenia. NAMI was created and is run by consumers (people with disorders) and their families to advocate for more research, better health care and access to health care, and public education. It also runs support groups and educational courses for people with schizophrenia and their families. Many communities have local chapters of NAMI, which can usually be found in the phone book and at **www.nami.org.**

---

behavior (see the Concept Overview in Table 11.2 on page 382). These symptoms can occur in other disorders, particularly in depression and bipolar disorder (see Chapter 9). On the other hand, many people with schizophrenia are also depressed or show tremendous mood swings. This can make the differentiation between schizophrenia and a mood disorder with psychotic features very tricky. If psychotic symptoms occur only during periods of clear depression or mania, then the most appropriate diagnosis is mood disorder with psychotic features. If psychotic symptoms occur substantially in the absence of depression or mania, or if the depression or mania does not meet the criteria for a diagnosis of a mood disorder, then the appropriate diagnosis is schizophrenia or schizoaffective disorder (review Table 11.1).

Delusions Delusions are ideas that an individual believes are true but are highly unlikely and often simply impossible. Of course, most people occasionally hold beliefs that are likely to be wrong, such as the belief that they will win the lottery. These kinds of *self-deceptions* differ from delusions in at least three ways (Strauss, 1969). First, self-deceptions are not completely implausible, whereas delusions often are. It is possible, if highly unlikely, to win the lottery, but it is not possible that one's body is dissolving and floating into space. Second, people harboring self-deceptions may think about these beliefs occasionally, but people harboring delusions tend to be preoccupied with them. Delusional people look for evidence in support of their beliefs, attempt to convince others of these beliefs, and take actions based on them, such as filing

TABLE 11.2   Concept Overview

Positive Symptoms of Schizophrenia

The positive symptoms of schizophrenia represent the presence of unusual perceptions, thoughts, or behaviors.

Symptom	Definition and Example
Delusions	Beliefs with little grounding in reality (e.g., beliefs that one is being persecuted or that one is the Messiah)
Hallucinations	Unreal perceptual or sensory experiences (e.g., hearing, seeing, and feeling things that are not there)
Disorganized thought and speech	Grossly disorganized patterns of speech (e.g., complete incoherence, linking together of words based on sounds instead of meaning)
Disorganized or catatonic behavior	Behavior that is highly unpredictable, is bizarre, and/or shows a complete lack of responsiveness to the outside world (e.g., complete motionlessness for long periods; sudden, untriggered outbursts)

Source: Reprinted with permission from the *Diagnostic and Statistical Manual of Mental Disorders,* Fourth Edition, Text Revision. Copyright © 2000 American Psychiatric Association.

lawsuits against the people they believe are trying to control their minds. Third, people holding self-deceptions typically acknowledge that their beliefs may be wrong, but people holding delusions are often highly resistant to arguments or compelling facts contradicting their delusions. They may view others' arguments against their beliefs as a conspiracy to silence them and as evidence for the truth of their beliefs.

Table 11.3 lists some of the most common types of delusions. A **persecutory delusion** is the type of delusion we hear about most often in media depictions of people with schizophrenia and, indeed, is the most common form. People with persecutory delusions may believe they are being watched or tormented by people they know, such as their professors, or by agencies or persons in authority with whom they have never had direct contact, such as the FBI or a particular congressperson.

Another common type of delusion, the **delusion of reference,** in which people believe that random events or comments by others are directed at them, is related to persecutory delusion. People with delusions of reference may believe that the newscaster on the local television news is reporting on their movements or that the comments of a local politician at a rally are directed at them. John Nash believed that people in Boston were wearing red neckties so he would notice them as part of a crypto-communist plot. Sometimes, delusions of reference are part of a grandiose belief system in which all events are meaningful to the believer. For example, one person with schizophre-

nia was lying in bed, feeling cold and shivering, when a small earthquake occurred near his house. He believed that he had caused the earthquake with his shivering.

Grandiose delusions are beliefs that one is a special person or being or possesses special powers. A person may believe that she is a deity incarnated. She may believe she is the most intelligent, insightful, and creative person on earth or that she has discovered the cure for a disease.

Another common type of delusion is a **delusion of thought insertion,** the belief that one's thoughts are being controlled by outside forces, as the following person with schizophrenia describes:

VOICES

"Suggestions" or "commands" are being transmitted (by a parapsychologist) straight into an unknowing victim's hearing-center, becoming strong impressions on his mind. Those "voices" (which are sometimes accompanied by melodious tones and sounds that either please or irritate the mind) will subliminally change his personality by controlling what kinds of suggestions go into his "subconscious memory" to govern how he feels, or mind-boggle him (trick his mind into believing that they are its own thoughts) during these brainwash and thought-control techniques. Psy-

(continued)

TABLE 11.3   Types of Delusions

These are some types of delusions that are often woven together in a complex and frightening system of beliefs.

Delusion	Definition	Example
Persecutory delusion	False belief that oneself or one's loved ones are being persecuted, watched, or conspired against by others	Belief that the CIA, FBI, and local police are conspiring to catch you in a "sting" operation
Delusion of reference	Belief that random events are directed at oneself	Belief that a newscaster is reporting on your movements
Grandiose delusion	False belief that one has great power, knowledge, or talent or that one is a famous and powerful person	Belief that you are Martin Luther King, Jr., reincarnated
Delusions of being controlled	Beliefs that one's thoughts, feelings, or behaviors are being imposed or controlled by an external force	Belief that an alien has taken over your body and is controlling your behavior
Thought broadcasting	Belief that one's thoughts are being broadcast from one's mind for others to hear	Belief that your thoughts are being transmitted via the Internet against your will
Thought insertion	Belief that another person or object is inserting thoughts into one's head	Belief that your spouse is inserting blasphemous thoughts into your mind through the microwave
Thought withdrawal	Belief that thoughts are being removed from one's head by another person or an object	Belief that your roommate is stealing all your thoughts while you sleep
Delusion of guilt or sin	False belief that one has committed a terrible act or is responsible for a terrible event	Belief that you have killed someone
Somatic delusion	False belief that one's appearance or part of one's body is diseased or altered	Belief that your intestines have been replaced by snakes

chotropic medications are given to the victims who can "discern the voices" over other sounds in order to keep them ignorant to the real truth about their dilemma, and to enhance the chemical-reaction in the brain to the stimulation as their souls: (minds): are enslaved by computers programmed to "think" for them here in George Orwell's America.

Delusional beliefs can be simple and transient, such as when a person with schizophrenia believes the pain he just experienced in his stomach is the result of someone across the room shooting a laser beam at him. Delusional beliefs are often complex and elaborate, however, and the person clings to these beliefs for long periods. The following account illustrates how several types of delusions—grandiose delusions, persecutory delusions, delusions of reference, and delusions of thought control—can co-occur and work together in one person's belief system. Note that, although the following passage is written by a person with schizo-phrenia about his own experience, he speaks of himself in the third person (Zelt, 1981, pp. 527–531).

VOICES

A drama that profoundly transformed David Zelt began at a conference on human psychology. David respected the speakers as scholars and wanted their approval of a paper he had written about telepathy. A week before the conference, David had sent his paper "On the Origins of Telepathy" to one speaker, and the other speakers had all read it. He proposed the novel scientific idea that telepathy could only be optimally studied during the process of birth. . . .

David's paper was viewed as a monumental contribution to the conference and potentially to psychology in general. If scientifically verified, his concept of telepathy, universally present at birth and measurable, might have

(continued)

as much influence as the basic ideas of Darwin and Freud. Each speaker focused on David. By using allusions and nonverbal communications that included pointing and glancing, each illuminated different aspects of David's contribution. Although his name was never mentioned, the speakers enticed David into feeling that he had accomplished something supernatural in writing the paper. . . . David was described as having a halo around his head, and the Second Coming was announced as forthcoming. Messianic feelings took hold of him. His mission would be to aid the poor and needy, especially in underdeveloped countries. . . .

David's sensitivity to nonverbal communication was extreme; he was adept at reading people's minds. His perceptual powers were so developed that he could not discriminate between telepathic reception and spoken language by others. He was distracted by others in a way that he had never been before. It was as if the nonverbal behavior of people interacting with him was a kind of code. Facial expressions, gestures, and postures of others often determined what he felt and thought.

Several hundred people at the conference were talking about David. He was the subject of enormous mystery, profound in his silence. Criticism, though, was often expressed by skeptics of the anticipated Second Coming. David felt the intense communication about him as torturous. He wished the talking, nonverbal behavior, and pervasive train of thoughts about him would stop.

David's *grandiose delusions* were that he had discovered the source of telepathy, that all the scientists thought highly of him, and that he might be the Messiah. As is often the case, these grandiose delusions were accompanied by *persecutory delusions*—that the scientists were criticizing him because they were jealous. David's delusions of reference were that all the scientists were talking about him, directly and indirectly. David believed that he could read others' minds. Finally, he had *delusions of being controlled,* that the scientists were determining what he felt with their facial expressions, gestures, and postures.

Although the types of delusions we have discussed probably occur in all cultures, the specific content of delusions may differ across cultures (Suhail & Cochrane, 2002; Tateyama et al., 1998). For example, persecutory delusions often focus on intelligence agencies or persons of authority in the person's culture. Urban European Americans might fear that the Central Intelligence Agency is after them; Afro Caribbeans may believe that people are killing them with curses (Westermeyer, 1993; for similar results comparing British and Pakistani patients, see Suhail & Cochrane, 2002). Studies comparing Japanese people who have schizophrenia with people in Western Europe who have schizophrenia have found that, among the Japanese, delusions of being slandered by others and delusions that others know something terrible about them are relatively common, perhaps due to the emphasis in Japanese culture on how one is thought of by others. In contrast, among German and Austrian people with schizophrenia, religious delusions of having committed a sin (e.g., "Satan orders me to pray to him; I will be punished") are relatively common, perhaps due to the influence of Christianity in Western Europe (Tateyama et al., 1993).

Some theorists argue that odd or impossible beliefs that are part of a culture's shared belief system cannot be considered delusions when these beliefs are held by individuals in that culture (Fabrega, 1993). For example, if the people of a culture believe that the spirits of dead relatives watch over the living, then individuals in that culture who hold that belief are not considered delusional, although people in other cultures might consider such a belief untrue and impossible. However, even theorists who hold cultural relativist positions on delusions tend to view people who hold extreme manifestations of their culture's shared belief systems as delusional. For example, a person who believed that her dead relatives were tor-

The specific content of hallucinations and delusions may be influenced by culture.

menting her by causing her heart and lungs to rot would be considered delusional, even if she were part of a culture that holds the belief that dead relatives watch over the living.

Hallucinations Have you ever had a strange perceptual experience, such as thinking you saw someone when no one was near, thinking you heard a voice talking to you, or feeling as though your body were floating through the air? If so, you are not alone. One study found that 15 percent of mentally healthy college students report sometimes hearing voices, such as the voice of God telling them to do something, their "conscience" giving them advice, or two voices (usually both their own) debating a topic (Chapman, Edell, & Chapman, 1980). Six percent of students believe they have transmitted thoughts into other people's heads. Most of these students probably would not be diagnosed with schizophrenia because their "hallucinations" were occasional and brief; often occurred when they were tired, stressed, or under the influence of alcohol or other drugs; and did not impair their daily functioning in any way.

The **hallucinations**—unreal perceptual experiences—of people with schizophrenia tend to be much more bizarre and troubling than college students' hallucinations and are precipitated not only by sleep deprivation, stress, or drugs, as this person describes (Long, 1996):

VOICES At one point, I would look at my coworkers and their faces would become distorted. Their teeth looked like fangs ready to devour me. Most of the time I couldn't trust myself to look at anyone for fear of being swallowed. I had no respite from the illness. Even when I tried to sleep, the demons would keep me awake, and at times I would roam the house searching for them. I was being consumed on all sides whether I was awake or asleep. I felt I was being consumed by demons.

An **auditory hallucination** (hearing voices, music, and so on) is the most common type of hallucination, and it is even more common in women than in men. Often, people hear voices accusing them of evil deeds or threatening them. The voices may also tell them to harm themselves. People with schizophrenia may talk back to the voices, even as they are trying to talk to people who are actually in the room with them. The second most common hallucination is the **visual hallucination,** often accompanied by auditory hallucinations. For

example, a person may see Satan standing at her bedside, telling her she is damned and must die.

Hallucinations can involve any sensory modality. **Tactile hallucinations** involve the perception that something is happening to the outside of one's body—for example, that bugs are crawling up one's back. **Somatic hallucinations** involve the perception that something is happening inside one's body—for example, that worms are eating one's intestines. These hallucinations are often frightening, even terrifying.

As with delusions, the types of hallucinations people have in different cultures appear similar, but the specific content of hallucinations may be culturally specific. For example, a person from Asia may see the ghosts of ancestors haunting him or her, but this is not a common experience for Europeans (Browne, 2001; Westermeyer, 1993). As with delusions, clinicians must interpret hallucinations in a cultural context. For example, a Puerto Rican woman might be diagnosed with schizophrenia by a European American interviewer because she believes she has special powers to anticipate events and because she describes what sound like hallucinations, such as "I see images of saints and virgins in the house. I also see the image of Jesus Christ, with the crown of thorns and bleeding." Interviewers who know Puerto Rican culture, however, might recognize this woman's beliefs and experiences as consistent with a spiritual group common in Latin America, which believes in clairvoyance and religious visions (Guarnaccia et al., 1992).

Disorganized Thought and Speech The disorganized thinking of people with schizophrenia is often referred to as a **formal thought disorder.** One of the most common forms of disorganization in schizophrenia is a tendency to slip from one topic to a seemingly unrelated topic with little coherent transition, often referred to as the *loosening of associations,* or *derailment.* For example, one person with schizophrenia posted the following "announcement":

VOICES Things that relate, the town of Antelope, Oregon, Jonestown, Charlie Manson, the Hillside Strangler, the Zodiac Killer, Watergate, King's trial in L.A., and many more. In the last 7 years alone, over 23 Starwars scientists committed suicide for no apparent reason. The AIDS coverup, the conference in South America in 87 had over 1,000 doctors claim that insects can transmit it. To be able to read *(continued)*

> one's thoughts and place thoughts in one's mind without the person knowing it's being done. Realization is a reality of bioelectromagnetic control, which is thought transfer and emotional control, recording individual brain-wave frequencies of thought, sensation, and emotions.

The person who wrote this announcement saw clear connections among the events he listed in the first half of the paragraph and between these events and his concerns about mind reading and bioelectromagnetic control. However, it is hard for us to see these connections.

A person with schizophrenia may answer questions with comments that are barely related to the questions or are completely unrelated to the questions. For example, when asked why he is in the hospital, a man with schizophrenia might answer, "Spaghetti looks like worms. I really think it's worms. Gophers dig tunnels but rats build nests." At times, the person's speech is so disorganized as to be totally *incoherent* to the listener, when it is often referred to as **word salad.** The person may make up words that mean something only to him or her, which are known as *neologisms.* The person with schizophrenia may make associations between words that are based on the sounds of the words, rather than on the content, and these are known as *clangs.* For example, in response to the question "Is that your dog?" a person with schizophrenia might say, "Dog. Dog is Spog. Frog. Leap. Heap, steep, creep, deep, gotta go beep." Or the person may *perseverate* on the same word or statement, saying it over and over again.

The disorganized thought and speech in schizophrenia may be tied to fundamental deficits in cognition and attention (Barch, 2005). People with schizophrenia have difficulty on a wide range of cognitive tasks. For example, they show deficits in **smooth pursuit eye movement** (sometimes referred to as eye tracking). When they are asked to keep their head still and track a moving object, people with schizophrenia have greater difficulty doing this than people without schizophrenia. This suggests they have deficiencies in fundamental attention processes.

In addition, people with schizophrenia show deficits in **working memory,** that is, deficits in the capacity to hold information in memory and manipulate it (Barch, 2005). In turn, these deficits in working memory make it difficult for people with schizophrenia to suppress unwanted or irrelevant information or to pay attention to relevant information. In other words, they find it difficult to identify their thoughts that are relevant to an ongoing conversation or to the situation at hand and to ignore the environmental stimuli that are not relevant to what they are doing or thinking. Working memory deficits also impair their ability to learn and retrieve new information. These deficits together may contribute to the difficulties in reasoning, communication, and problem solving in people with schizophrenia.

Men with schizophrenia tend to show more severe deficits in language, compared with women who have schizophrenia (Goldstein et al., 2002). Some researchers have speculated that this is because language is controlled more bilaterally—by both sides of the brain—in women than in men. Thus, the brain abnormalities associated with schizophrenia may not impact women's language and thought as much as men's because women can use both sides of their brains to compensate for problems. In contrast, language is more localized in men, so that, when these areas of the brain are affected by schizophrenia, men may not be as able to compensate for these deficits.

Disorganized or Catatonic Behavior The disorganized behavior of people with schizophrenia is often what leads others to be afraid of them. People with schizophrenia may display unpredictable and apparently untriggered agitation, suddenly shouting, swearing, or pacing rapidly up and down the street. They may engage in socially unacceptable behavior, such as public masturbation. Many are disheveled and dirty, sometimes wearing few clothes on a cold day or heavy clothes on a very hot day. Short of these more bizarre behaviors, persons with schizophrenia often have trouble organizing their daily routines to ensure that they bathe, dress properly, and eat regularly. It is as if all their concentration must be used to accomplish even one simple task, such as brushing their teeth, and other tasks just do not get done.

In Chapter 9, we discussed **catatonia,** a group of disorganized behaviors that reflect an extreme lack of responsiveness to the outside world. One form of catatonia in schizophrenia is **catatonic excitement,** in which the person becomes wildly agitated for no apparent reason and is difficult to subdue. During a period of catatonic excitement, the individual may articulate a number of delusions or hallucinations or may be largely incoherent. In 1905, German psychiatrist Emil Kraepelin gave the following account of a patient showing signs of catatonic excitement (Laing, 1971, pp. 29–30).

The patient I will show you today has almost to be carried into the rooms, as he walks in a straddling fashion on the outside of his feet. On coming in, he throws off his slippers, sings a hymn loudly, and then cries twice (in English), "My father, my real father!" He is eighteen years old, and a pupil . . . , tall and rather strongly built, but with a pale complexion, on which there is very often a transient flush. The patient sits with his eyes shut, and pays no attention to his surroundings. He does not look up even when he is spoken to, but answers beginning in a low voice, and gradually screaming louder and louder. When asked where he is, he says, "You want to know that too. I tell you who is being measured and is measured and shall be measured. I know all that, and could tell you, but I do not want to." When asked his name, he screams, "What is your name? What does he shut? He shuts his eyes. What does he hear? He does not understand; he understands not. How? Who? Where? When? What does he mean? When I tell him to look he does not look properly. You there, just look. What is it? What is the matter? Attend; he attends not. I say, what is it, then? Why do you give me no answer? Are you getting impudent again? How can you be so impudent? I'm coming! I'll show you! You don't whore for me. You mustn't be smart either; you're an impudent, lousy fellow, such an impudent, lousy fellow I've never met with. Is he beginning again? You understand nothing at all, nothing at all; nothing at all does he understand. If you follow now, he won't follow, will not follow. Are you getting still more impudent? Are you getting impudent still more? How they attend, they do attend," and so on. At the end, he scolds in quite inarticulate sounds.

This patient's catatonic excitement is infused with angry and agitated outbursts, which also have the characteristic disorganization of schizophrenic thought.

Negative Symptoms

The negative, or Type II, symptoms of schizophrenia involve losses, or deficits, in certain domains.

Three types of negative symptoms are recognized by the DSM-IV-TR as core symptoms of schizophrenia: affective flattening, alogia, and avolition (see the Concept Overview in Table 11.4) on page 388.

Affective Flattening **Affective flattening** is a severe reduction in, or even the complete absence of, affective (emotional) responses to the environment. Often, this symptom is also referred to as *blunted affect*. The person's face may remain immobile most of the time, no matter what happens, and his or her body language may be unresponsive to what is going on in the environment. One man set fire to his house, then sat down to watch TV. When it was called to his attention that his house was on fire, he calmly got up and walked outside (Torrey, 1995). People with blunted affect may speak in a monotone voice, without any emotional expression, and may not make eye contact with others.

Affective flattening is a person's lack of overt expression of emotion. We must be cautious, however, in assuming that people demonstrating affective flattening are actually experiencing no emotion. In one study, people with schizophrenia and people without the disorder were shown emotionally charged films while their facial expressions were observed and their physiological arousal was recorded (Kring & Neale, 1996). The

People with catatonia strike strange poses and maintain them for long periods of time without moving.

TABLE 11.4   Concept Overview

Negative Symptoms of Schizophrenia

The negative symptoms of schizophrenia represent the absence of usual emotional and behavioral responses.

Symptom	Description	Examples
Affective flattening (blunted affect)	Severe reduction or complete absence of affective (emotional) responses to the environment	No facial expressions in response to emotionally charged stimuli; no emotional expression in voice
Alogia	Severe reduction or complete absence of speech	Complete mutism for weeks
Avolition	Inability to persist at common, goal-oriented tasks	Inability to get dressed, brush teeth, eat breakfast in morning

Source: Reprinted with permission from the *Diagnostic and Statistical Manual of Mental Disorders,* Fourth Edition, Text Revision. Copyright © 2000 American Psychiatric Association.

people with schizophrenia showed less facial responsiveness to the films than the normal group but reported experiencing just as much emotion and showed even more physiological arousal. Thus, people with schizophrenia who are showing no emotion may be experiencing intense emotion, which they cannot express.

Alogia   Alogia, or poverty of speech, is a reduction in speaking. The person may not initiate speech with others and, when asked direct questions, may give brief, empty replies. The person's lack of speech presumably reflects a lack of thinking, although it may be caused in part by a lack of motivation to speak.

People with schizophrenia may have trouble caring for their own daily needs and may end up on the streets.

Avolition   Avolition is an inability to persist at common, goal-directed activities, including those at work, school, and home. The person has great trouble completing tasks and is disorganized and careless, apparently completely unmotivated. She may sit around all day, doing almost nothing. She may withdraw and become socially isolated.

The negative symptoms of schizophrenia can be difficult to diagnose reliably. First, they involve the absence of behaviors, rather than the presence of behaviors, making them more difficult to detect. Second, they lie on a continuum between normal and abnormal, rather than being clearly bizarre behaviors, as are the positive symptoms. Third, they can be caused by a host of factors other than schizophrenia, such as depression or social isolation, or they may be side effects of medications.

Other Symptoms of Schizophrenia

People with schizophrenia often also suffer significant symptoms of depression and anxiety, and many abuse alcohol and other drugs. A number of other symptoms, or features, of schizophrenia are not part of the formal diagnostic criteria for the disorder but occur frequently. Among these are inappropriate affect, anhedonia, and impaired social skills.

Inappropriate Affect Instead of showing flattened, or blunted, affect, a person with schizophrenia may show *inappropriate affect,* such as laughing at sad things and crying at happy things. This may happen because he or she is thinking about and responding to something other than what is going on in the environment (McGhie & Chapman, 1961, p. 104):

It must look queer to people when I laugh about something that has got nothing to do with what I am talking about, but they don't know what's going on inside and how much of it is running round in my head. You see I might be talking about something quite serious to you and other things come into my head at the same time that are funny and this makes me laugh. If only I could concentrate on the one thing at the one time and I wouldn't look half so silly.

Inappropriate displays of affect may also occur because the brain processes that match stimuli with the proper emotions and emotional responses to those stimuli are not working properly. Unhappy stimuli somehow trigger laughter and happy stimuli trigger sadness. Whatever the cause, inappropriate affect is one of the most striking symptoms of schizophrenia. Often, the person switches from one extreme emotional expression to another for no apparent reason.

Anhedonia Recall that many people who display flattened, or blunted, affect are actually experiencing emotions, although they are not showing them. Some people with schizophrenia, however, experience severe *anhedonia* (a loss of interest in everything in life), similar to the anhedonia that characterizes depression (see Chapter 9). They lose the ability to experience emotion and, no matter what happens, do not feel happy or sad. This emotional void itself can be miserable.

Impaired Social Skills Not surprisingly, the symptoms of schizophrenia make it difficult to have normal interactions with other people. People with schizophrenia show a wide range of *impaired social skills,* including difficulty in holding conversations, in maintaining relationships, and in holding a job. You may be surprised to learn, however, that the difficulties in social skills in schizophrenia may be due more to the negative symptoms than to the positive symptoms of the disorder.

Although the negative symptoms of schizophrenia are less bizarre than the positive symptoms, they are major causes of the problems people with schizophrenia have in functioning in society. People with schizophrenia with many negative symptoms have lower educational attainments and less success in holding jobs, poorer performance on cognitive tasks, and a poorer prognosis than do those with few negative symptoms and predominantly positive symptoms (Andreasen et al., 1990;

Eaton et al., 1998). In addition, the negative symptoms are less responsive to medication than are the positive symptoms: A person with schizophrenia may be able to overcome the hallucinations, delusions, and thought disturbances with medication but may not be able to overcome the affective flattening, alogia, and avolition. Thus, the person may remain chronically unresponsive, unmotivated, and socially isolated, even when he or she is not acutely psychotic (Fenton & McGlashan, 1994).

Diagnosis

Schizophrenia has been recognized as a psychological disorder since the early 1800s (Gottesman, 1991). German psychiatrist Emil Kraepelin is credited with the most comprehensive and accurate description of schizophrenia. In 1883, Kraepelin labeled the disorder **dementia praecox** (precocious dementia), because he believed that the disorder resulted from premature deterioration of the brain. He viewed the disorder as progressive, irreversible, and chronic. Kraepelin's definition of this disorder was a narrow one, which resulted in only a small percentage of people receiving this diagnosis.

The other major figure in the early history of schizophrenia research was Eugen Bleuler. Bleuler disagreed with Kraepelin's view that this disorder always developed at an early age and always led to severe deterioration of the brain. Bleuler introduced the label *schizophrenia* for the disorder, from the Greek words *schizein,* meaning "to split," and *phren,* meaning "mind." Bleuler believed that this disorder involved the splitting of usually integrated psychic functions of mental associations, thoughts, and emotions. (Bleuler did not view schizophrenia as the splitting of distinct personalities, as in dissociative identity disorder, nor do modern psychiatrists and psychologists.)

Bleuler argued that the primary problem underlying the many different symptoms of schizophrenia was the "breaking of associative threads," referring to a breaking of associations among thought, language, memory, and problem solving. He argued that the attentional problems seen in schizophrenia were due to a lack of the necessary links between aspects of the mind. In turn, the behavioral symptoms of schizophrenia (such as alogia) were similarly due to an inability to maintain a train of thought.

Bleuler's view of schizophrenia was much broader than Kraepelin's and led to a broader range of people being given this diagnosis. Bleuler's definition of schizophrenia was adopted by clinicians in the United States in the early twentieth century, whereas the Europeans stuck with Kraepelin's narrower definition. Over the first few decades of the

TABLE 11.5 DSM-IV-TR

Diagnostic Criteria for Schizophrenia

The DSM-IV-TR criteria for schizophrenia require the presence of severe symptoms for at least one month and the presence of some symptoms for at least six months.

A. Core symptoms: two or more of the following present for at least a one-month period:
   1. Delusions
   2. Hallucinations
   3. Disorganized speech
   4. Grossly disorganized or catatonic behavior
   5. Negative symptoms

B. Social/occupational functioning: significant impairment in work, academic performance, interpersonal relationships, and/or self-care

C. Duration: continuous signs of the disturbance for at least six months; at least one month of this period must include symptoms that meet Criterion A above

Source: Reprinted with permission from the *Diagnostic and Statistical Manual of Mental Disorders,* Fourth Edition, Text Revision. Copyright © 2000 American Psychiatric Association.

twentieth century, U.S. clinicians further broadened their definition of schizophrenia, so that eventually anyone experiencing delusions and hallucinations was given the diagnosis (even though delusions and hallucinations can also occur in mood disorders).

Beginning in 1980 with the third edition of the DSM, the pendulum began to swing back toward a narrower definition of schizophrenia in the United States. Now, the DSM-IV-TR states that, in order to be diagnosed with schizophrenia, an individual must show some symptoms of the disorder for at least six months. During this six months, there must be at least one month of acute symptoms, during which two or more of the broad groups of symptoms (e.g., delusions, hallucinations, disorganized speech, disorganized or catatonic behavior, negative symptoms) are present and severe enough to impair the individual's social or occupational functioning (see the DSM-IV-TR diagnostic criteria in Table 11.5). Some people seek treatment shortly after the onset of their symptoms, but most do not and have experienced significant symptoms for many months, even years, before being treated.

Prodromal symptoms are present before people go into the acute phase of schizophrenia, and **residual symptoms** are present after they come out of the acute phase. During the prodromal and residual phases, people with schizophrenia may express beliefs that are not delusional but are unusual. They may have strange perceptual experiences, such as sensing another person in the room, without reporting full-blown hallucinations. They may speak in a somewhat disorganized and tangential way but remain coherent. Their behavior may be peculiar—for example, collecting scraps of paper—but not grossly disorganized. The negative symptoms are especially prominent in the prodromal and residual phases of the disorder. The person may be withdrawn and uninterested in others or in work or school. During the prodromal phase, family members and friends may experience the person with schizophrenia as "gradually slipping away."

Recall from Chapter 9 some of the difficulties in distinguishing schizophrenia from *mood disorders with psychotic features.* Another differential diagnosis that is difficult to make is between schizophrenia and schizoaffective disorder (see the DSM-IV-TR criteria in Table 11.6). *Schizoaffective disorder* is a mix of schizophrenia and mood disorders, with evidence that the schizophrenic symptoms are present even when the mood symptoms are absent. People with schizoaffective disorder simultaneously experience symptoms that meet Criterion A for the diagnosis of schizophrenia (review Table 11.5) and mood symptoms meeting the criteria for a major depressive episode, a manic episode, or an episode of mixed mania/depression. Their mood symptoms must be present for a substantial duration of the time that their schizophrenic symptoms are present. But the main difference between schizoaffective disorder and mood disorders with psychotic features is that, in schizoaffective disorder, people experience schizophrenic symptoms, specifically delusions and hallucinations, in the absence of mood symptoms for at least two weeks.

This all may sound a bit confusing to you, and it is confusing to mental-health professionals as well. The diagnosis of schizoaffective disorder is a controversial one, because many clinicians believe that it is used as a default when clinicians can't decide whether an individual has schizophrenia or a mood disorder. The reliability of the diagnosis of schizoaffective disorder is low, meaning that clinicians don't often agree that an individual warrants this diagnosis.

Within the diagnosis of schizophrenia, many subtypes have been described. In *Type I schizophrenia,* the positive symptoms are much more promi-

TABLE 11.6 DSM-IV-TR

Diagnostic Criteria for Schizoaffective Disorder

The major distinction between schizoaffective disorder and schizophrenia is the presence of severe mood symptoms in schizoaffective disorder.

A. An uninterrupted period of illness during which, at some time, there is either a major depressive episode, a manic episode, or a mixed episode concurrent with symptoms that meet Criterion A for schizophrenia.

B. During the same period of illness, there have been delusions or hallucinations for at least two weeks in the absence of prominent mood symptoms.

C. Symptoms that meet criteria for a mood episode are present for a substantial portion of the total duration of the active and residual periods of the illness.

Source: Reprinted with permission from the *Diagnostic and Statistical Manual of Mental Disorders,* Fourth Edition, Text Revision. Copyright © 2000 American Psychiatric Association.

TABLE 11.7 DSM-IV-TR

Types of Schizophrenia

The DSM-IV-TR recognizes five subtypes of schizophrenia.

Type	Major Features
Paranoid schizophrenia	Delusions and hallucinations with themes of persecution and grandiosity
Disorganized schizophrenia	Incoherence in cognition, speech, and behavior and flat or inappropriate affect
Catatonic schizophrenia	Nearly total unresponsiveness to the environment, as well as motor and verbal abnormalities
Undifferentiated schizophrenia	Diagnosed when a person experiences schizophrenic symptoms but does not meet the criteria for paranoid, disorganized, or catatonic schizophrenia
Residual schizophrenia	History of at least one episode of acute positive symptoms but currently no prominent positive symptoms

Source: Reprinted with permission from the *Diagnostic and Statistical Manual of Mental Disorders,* Fourth Edition, Text Revision. Copyright © 2000 American Psychiatric Association.

nent than the negative symptoms. In *Type II schizophrenia*, the negative symptoms are more prominent than the positive symptoms. This distinction between Type I and Type II schizophrenia is not part of the official DSM-IV-TR diagnostic framework, but it has turned out to be a useful distinction in research on schizophrenia.

The DSM-IV-TR officially divides schizophrenia into five subtypes (see the DSM-IV-TR information in Table 11.7). Three of these types, the *paranoid, disorganized,* and *catatonic* types, have specific symptoms that differentiate them from each other. The other two types, *undifferentiated* and *residual schizophrenia,* are not characterized by specific differentiating symptoms but, rather, by a mix of symptoms that are either acute (in the undifferentiated type) or attenuated (in the residual type).

Paranoid Schizophrenia

The best-known, and most researched, type of schizophrenia is the paranoid type. This is the type that John Nash appeared to suffer from. People with **paranoid schizophrenia** have prominent delusions and hallucinations that involve themes of persecution and grandiosity. Many do not show the grossly disorganized speech or behavior that people with other types of schizophrenia show. They may be lu-

cid and articulate, with elaborate stories of how someone is plotting against them. They may also be able to articulate the deep pain and anguish of believing that they are being persecuted (Torrey, 1995, pp. 53–54):

> Anxiety:
> like metal on metal in my brain
> Paranoia: it is
> making me run away, away, away
> and back again quickly
> to see if I've been caught
> Or lied to
> Or laughed at
> Ha ha ha. The ferris wheel
> in Looney Land is not so funny.

People with paranoid schizophrenia are highly resistant to any arguments against their delusions and may become very irritated with anyone who argues with them. They may act arrogantly and as if they were superior to others or may remain aloof and suspicious. The combination of persecutory and grandiose delusions can lead people with this type of schizophrenia to be suicidal or violent toward others.

The prognosis for people with paranoid schizophrenia is actually better than the prognosis for people with other types of schizophrenia (Hwu et al., 2002). They are more likely to be able to live independently and hold down a job and, thus, show better cognitive and social functioning (Kendler et al., 1994). The onset of paranoid schizophrenia tends to occur later in life than does the onset of other forms of schizophrenia, and episodes of psychosis are often triggered by stress. In general, paranoid schizophrenia is considered a milder, less insidious form of schizophrenia.

Disorganized Schizophrenia

Unlike people with the paranoid type of schizophrenia, people with **disorganized schizophrenia** do not have well-formed delusions or hallucinations. Instead, their thoughts and behaviors are severely disorganized. People with this type of schizophrenia may speak in word salads, completely incoherent to others. They are prone to odd, stereotyped behaviors, such as frequent grimacing or mannerisms such as flapping their hands. They may be so disorganized that they do not bathe, dress, or eat if left on their own.

The emotional experiences and expressions of people with disorganized schizophrenia are also quite disturbed. They may not show any emotional reactions to anything, or they may have unusual and inappropriate emotional reactions to events, such as laughing uncontrollably at a funeral. When they talk, they may display emotions that are apparently unrelated to what they are saying or to what is going on in the environment. For example, a young woman with disorganized schizophrenia responded in the following manner when asked about her mother, who had been recently hospitalized for a serious illness: "Mama's sick. [Giggle.] Sicky, sicky, sicky. [Giggle.] I flipped off a doctor once, did you know that? Flip. I wanta wear my blue dress tomorrow. Dress mess. [Giggle.]"

This type of schizophrenia tends to have an early onset and a continuous course, which is often unresponsive to treatment. People with this type of schizophrenia are among the most disabled by the disorder.

Catatonic Schizophrenia

Catatonic schizophrenia has some of the most distinct features of all the types of schizophrenia. It is very rare, however, and thus has not been well researched. People with catatonic schizophrenia show a variety of motor behaviors and ways of speaking that suggest almost complete unresponsiveness to their environment. The diagnostic criteria for catatonic schizophrenia require two of the following symptoms: (1) catatonic stupor (remaining motionless for long periods of time); (2) catatonic excitement (excessive and purposeless motor activity); (3) the maintenance of rigid postures or complete mutism for long periods of time; (4) odd mannerisms, such as grimacing or hand flapping; and (5) **echolalia** (the senseless repetition of words just spoken by others) or **echopraxia** (repetitive imitation of the movements of another person).

Undifferentiated Schizophrenia and Residual Schizophrenia

People with **undifferentiated schizophrenia** have symptoms that meet the criteria for schizophrenia (delusions, hallucinations, disorganized speech, disorganized behavior, negative symptoms) but do not meet the criteria for paranoid, disorganized, or catatonic schizophrenia. This type of schizophrenia tends to have an onset relatively early in life and to be chronic and difficult to treat.

People with **residual schizophrenia** have had at least one acute episode of acute positive symptoms of schizophrenia but do not currently have any prominent positive symptoms of schizophrenia. They continue to have signs of the disorder, however, including the negative symptoms and mild versions of the positive symptoms. People may have these residual symptoms chronically for several years.

Prognosis

Schizophrenia is more chronic and debilitating than most other mental disorders. Between 50 and 80 percent of people who are hospitalized for one schizophrenic episode will be rehospitalized for another episode at sometime in their lives (Eaton et al., 1992). The life expectancy of people with schizophrenia is as much as 10 years shorter than that of people without schizophrenia (McGlashan, 1988; Mortensen, 2003). People with schizophrenia suffer from infectious and circulatory diseases at a higher rate than do people without the disorder, for reasons that are unclear. As many as 10 to 15 percent of people with schizophrenia commit suicide (Joiner et al., 2005). The following account of a woman about her suicidal thoughts gives a sense of the pain that many people with schizophrenia live with and wish to end through suicide (Anonymous, 1992, p. 334).

I had major fantasies of suicide by decapitation and was reading up on the construction of guillotines. I had written several essays on the problem of the complete destruction of myself; I thought my inner being to be a deeply poisonous substance. The problem, as I saw it, was to kill myself, but then to get rid of my essence in such a way that it did not harm creation.

Despite the pain that many people with schizophrenia suffer for years, most people with schizophrenia do not show a progressive deterioration in functioning across the life span. Instead, most stabilize within 5 to 10 years of their first episode, and the duration of episodes and number of rehospitalizations decline as the person grows older (Eaton et al., 1992, 1998). Studies suggest that between 20 and 30 percent of treated people with schizophrenia recover substantially or completely from their illness within 10 to 20 years of its onset (Breier et al., 1991; Jablensky, 2000). One very long-term study that followed people with schizophrenia for an average of 32 years found that 62 percent had completely recovered or showed only minor impairment in functioning at follow-up (Harding, Zubin, & Strauss, 1987).

Age and Gender Factors

Women who develop schizophrenia have a more favorable course of the disorder than do men who develop it (Goldstein & Lewine, 2000). Women are hospitalized less often and for briefer periods of time than are men, show milder negative symptoms between periods of acute positive symptoms, and have better social adjustment when they are not psychotic. This more favorable course may occur in part because women tend to develop schizophrenia at a later age than do men, and, the later the age of onset of schizophrenia, the more favorable the course of the disorder tends to be.

Why does the functioning of people with schizophrenia often improve with age? Perhaps it is because they find treatments that help them stabilize, or they and their families learn to recognize the early symptoms of a relapse and seek aggressive treatment before their symptoms become acute. Alternatively, the aging of the brain might somehow reduce the likelihood of new episodes of schizophrenia. It has been speculated that the improvement of people with schizophrenia with age might be related to a reduction of dopamine in the brain with age; excess levels of dopamine

have been implicated in schizophrenia (Breier et al., 1991).

Sociocultural Factors

Culture appears to play a strong role in the course of schizophrenia. Schizophrenia tends to have a more benign course in developing countries than in developed countries (Anders, 2003; Jablensky, 2000). Cross-national studies conducted in 10 countries by the World Health Organization and other studies conducted by individual investigators have found that persons who develop schizophrenia in countries such as India, Nigeria, and Colombia are less likely to remain incapacitated by the disorder in the long term than are persons who develop schizophrenia in countries such as Great Britain, Denmark, and the United States (Jablensky, 2000) (see Figure 11.2).

The social environments of people with schizophrenia in developing countries may facilitate adaptation and recovery better than do the social environments of people with schizophrenia in developed countries (Anders, 2003; Karno & Jenkins, 1993). In developing countries, there are broader and closer family networks around the person

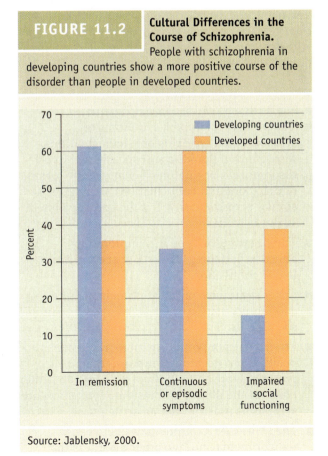

FIGURE 11.2 **Cultural Differences in the Course of Schizophrenia.** People with schizophrenia in developing countries show a more positive course of the disorder than people in developed countries.

Source: Jablensky, 2000.

with schizophrenia, providing more people to care for the person with schizophrenia. This ensures that no one person is solely responsible for the care of someone with schizophrenia, which is risky for both the person with schizophrenia and the caregiver. Families in some developing countries also score lower on measures of hostility, criticism, and overinvolvement than do families in some developed countries. This may help lower relapse rates for their family members with schizophrenia.

Social factors likely contribute to the gender differences in the course of schizophrenia (Mueser et al., 1990). Deviant behavior may be more socially acceptable in women than in men, so women who develop schizophrenia may experience less loss of social support than do men, which helps them cope better with their disorder. Also, women with schizophrenia may have better social skills than do men with schizophrenia. These social skills may help women maintain and make use of their social support networks and reduce stress in their lives, thereby reducing their risk for a relapse of symptoms.

Whatever the reasons for variations among cultures and between men and women in the course of schizophrenia, the conventional wisdom that schizophrenia is inevitably a progressive disorder, marked by more deterioration with time, has been replaced by new evidence that many people with schizophrenia achieve a level of good functioning over time.

SUMMING UP

- The positive, or Type I, symptoms of schizophrenia are delusions, hallucinations, disorganized thinking and speech, and disorganized or catatonic behavior. The forms of delusions and hallucinations are relatively similar across cultures, but the specific content varies by culture.

- The negative, or Type II, symptoms are affective flattening, poverty of speech, and loss of motivation.

- Other symptoms of schizophrenia include anhedonia, inappropriate affect, and impaired social skills.

- Prodromal symptoms are more moderate positive and negative symptoms that are present before an individual goes into an acute phase of the illness, and residual symptoms are symptoms present after an acute phase.

- The DSM-IV-TR differentiates between schizophrenia and two other disorders that include severe mood symptoms. In mood

disorders with psychotic features, the mood symptoms occur in the absence of the schizophrenic symptoms at least some of the time. In schizoaffective disorder, the schizophrenic symptoms occur in the absence of the mood symptoms.

- The DSM-IV-TR further differentiates among paranoid, disorganized, catatonic, undifferentiated, and residual schizophrenia.

BIOLOGICAL THEORIES OF SCHIZOPHRENIA

Given the similarity in the symptoms and prevalence of schizophrenia across cultures and across time, it is not surprising that biological factors have long been thought to play a strong role in the development of schizophrenia. There are several biological theories of schizophrenia (see Concept Overview in Table 11.8). First, there is good evidence for a genetic transmission of schizophrenia, although genetics do not fully explain who gets this disorder. Second, some people with schizophrenia show structural and functional abnormalities in specific areas of the brain, which may contribute to the disorder. Third, many people with schizophrenia have a history of birth complications or prenatal exposure to viruses, which may have affected the development of their brains. Fourth, the neurotransmitter theories of schizophrenia hold that excess levels of the neurotransmitter dopamine play a causal role in schizophrenia. New research is also focusing on the neurotransmitters serotonin, GABA, and glutamate.

Genetic Contributors to Schizophrenia

Family, twin, and adoption studies have all provided evidence that genes are involved in the transmission of schizophrenia (Gottesman & Reilly, 2003; Lichtermann, Karbe, & Maier, 2000). So far, however, the gene for schizophrenia has not been found, and many scientists believe that no single genetic abnormality accounts for this complex disorder (or set of disorders). Some researchers have argued for a polygenic, additive model, in which it takes a certain number and configuration of abnormal genes to create schizophrenia (Gottesman, 1991; Gottesman & Erlenmeyer-Kimling, 2001). Having more disordered genes increases both the likelihood of developing schizophrenia and the severity of the disorder. Individuals born with some of these genes but not enough to reach the threshold for creating full-blown schizophrenia may still show mild symp-

TABLE 11.8 Concept Overview

Biological Theories of Schizophrenia

Biological theories of schizophrenia have attributed the disorder to genetics, structural brain abnormalities, birth complications, prenatal exposure to viruses, and deficits in dopamine and other neurotransmitters.

Theory	Description
Genetic theories	Disordered genes cause schizophrenia, or at least a vulnerability to schizophrenia.
Structural brain abnormalities	Enlarged ventricles may indicate deterioration of a number of brain areas, leading to cognitive and emotional deficits. Reduced volume and neuron density in the frontal cortex and the temporal and limbic areas cause widespread cognitive and emotional deficits.
Birth complications	Delivery complications, particularly those causing loss of oxygen, might damage the brain.
Prenatal viral exposure	Exposure to viruses during the prenatal period might damage the brain.
Neurotransmitter theories	Imbalances in levels of or receptors for dopamine cause symptoms; serotonin, GABA, and glutamate may also play roles.
Integrated theory	Abnormal dopamine levels in prefrontal cortex lead to deficits in working memory, which make it difficult to attend to relevant information, leading to difficulties in reasoning, communication, and problem-solving.

toms of schizophrenia, such as oddities in their speech patterns or thought processes and strange beliefs.

Family Studies

Psychologist Irving Gottesman (1991) compiled more than 40 studies to determine the lifetime risk of developing schizophrenia for people with various familial relationships to a person with schizophrenia. His conclusions are summarized in Figure 11.3 on page 396. Children of two parents with schizophrenia and monozygotic (identical) twins of people with schizophrenia share the greatest number of genes with people with schizophrenia. As the top bars of the graph in Figure 11.3 show, these individuals have the greatest risk of developing schizophrenia sometime in their lives.

As the genetic similarity to a person with schizophrenia decreases, an individual's risk of developing schizophrenia also decreases. Thus, a first-degree relative of a person with schizophrenia, such as a nontwin sibling, who shares about 50 percent of genes with the person with schizophrenia, has about a 10 percent chance of developing schizophrenia. In contrast, a niece or nephew of a person with schizophrenia, who shares about 25 percent of genes with the person with schizophrenia, has only a 3 percent chance of developing schizophrenia.

This is not much different from the general population, in which the risk is about 1 to 2 percent. This relationship between an individual's degree of genetic similarity to a relative with schizophrenia and the individual's own risk of developing schizophrenia strongly suggests that genes play a role in the development of the disorder.

It's important to understand that having a biological relative with schizophrenia increases an individual's risk for schizophrenia but does not mean that an individual will develop schizophrenia. For example, of all children who have one parent with schizophrenia, 87 percent will *not* develop the disorder. On the other hand, 63 percent of people with schizophrenia have *no* first- or second-degree relatives with the disorder (Gottesman & Erlenmeyer-Kimling, 2001).

Even when the child of a person with schizophrenia develops the disorder, this doesn't necessarily mean it is transmitted genetically. Growing up with a parent with schizophrenia, and particularly with two parents with the disorder, is likely to mean growing up in a stressful atmosphere. When a parent is psychotic, the child may be exposed to illogical thought, mood swings, and chaotic behavior. Even when the parent is not acutely psychotic, the residual negative symptoms of schizophrenia—the flattening of affect, lack of

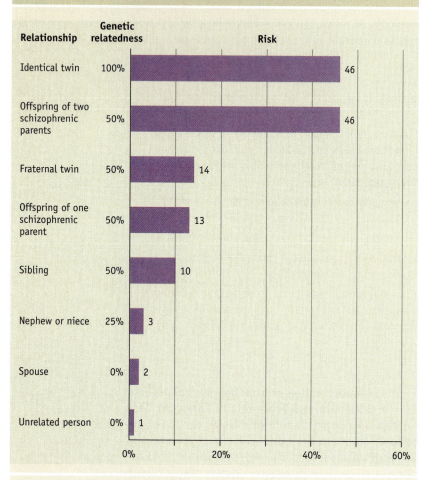

Source: Gottesman, 1991.

FIGURE 11.3   **Risk for Schizophrenia and Genetic Relatedness.** One's risk of developing schizophrenia decreases substantially as one's genetic relationship to a person with schizophrenia becomes more distant.

motivation, and disorganization—may impair the parent's child-care skills.

Is it possible that the high risk of developing schizophrenia seen in the children of people with schizophrenia is due, at least in part, to the stress of living with parents who have schizophrenia? This question has been addressed to some extent in adoption studies.

Adoption Studies

Several adoption studies have found evidence that genetics play an important role in schizophrenia. An early and classic adoption study was conducted by Leonard Heston (1966) in the United States and Canada. He interviewed the adult children of 47 women who had been diagnosed with schizophrenia in the Oregon state mental hospitals in the 1930s. All of these children had been placed in orphanages or with nonmaternal relatives within

three days of their birth. He also interviewed a group of 50 adults who had been adopted shortly after birth but whose mothers had no record of mental illness. If living with a parent with schizophrenia contributes significantly to a child's vulnerability to schizophrenia, then the children of people with schizophrenia who were adopted away from their mothers should have had a lower rate of developing schizophrenia than the 13 percent rate for children who grow up with one parent with schizophrenia (review Figure 11.3).

Heston found, however, that about 17 percent of the adopted-away children of the people with schizophrenia developed schizophrenia as adults, a rate even higher than the average rate of 13 percent for children of one parent with schizophrenia, providing strong evidence that these adoptees carry a genetic risk for schizophrenia. The rate may have been higher for the adopted-away children in the Heston study because the mothers of these children were probably experiencing particularly severe forms of schizophrenia. They had all been hospitalized and had been deemed unfit to be mothers. In contrast, none of the 50 control-group children in the Heston study whose mothers had no mental illness developed schizophrenia as adults.

Other adoption studies have examined the rates of schizophrenia in the biological versus the adoptive relatives of adoptees with schizophrenia, and these studies also support a role for genetics in schizophrenia. For example, Kety and colleagues (1994) found that the biological relatives of adoptees with schizophrenia were 10 times more likely to have a diagnosis of schizophrenia than the biological relatives of adoptees who did not have schizophrenia. In contrast, the adoptive relatives of adoptees with schizophrenia showed no increased risk for schizophrenia.

In one of the largest adoption studies, Tienari (1991) has tracked 155 offspring of mothers with schizophrenia and 185 children of mothers without schizophrenia; all of the children were given up for adoption early in life. To date, approximately 10 percent of the children whose biological mothers had schizophrenia have developed schizophrenia or another psychotic disorder, compared with about 1 percent of the children whose biological mothers did not have schizophrenia.

Twin Studies

In Figure 11.3 are the compiled results of several twin studies of schizophrenia that suggest that the concordance rate for monozygotic (identical) twins is 46 percent, whereas the concordance rate for dizygotic (fraternal) twins is 14 percent. A study that assessed all twins born in Finland between

The Genain quadruplets all have schizophrenia, but the specific forms of schizophrenia differ among the sisters.

1940 and 1957 used statistical modeling to estimate that 83 percent of the variation in schizophrenia is due to genetic factors (Cannon et al., 1998).

Genetic factors may play an even greater role in the more severe forms of schizophrenia than in the mild forms. Gottesman and Shields (1982) found concordance rates for monozygotic (MZ) twins of between 75 and 91 percent when they restricted their sample to persons with only the most severe forms of schizophrenia. In comparison, the concordance rates for MZ twins with mild forms of schizophrenia ranged from 17 to 33 percent.

Even when a person carries a genetic risk for schizophrenia, many other biological and environmental factors may influence whether and how he or she manifests the disorder. The classic illustration of this point is found in the Genain quadruplets, who are now in their sixties. These four women, who shared exactly the same genes and grew up in the same family environment, all developed schizophrenia, but the specific symptoms, onset, course, and outcomes of the disorder varied substantially among them (Mirsky et al., 2000). It's likely that other factors, such as birth complications, contributed to the variation in their risk for schizophrenia, although the specific causes of each twin's disorder have not been pinpointed. Their experiences are evidence that, even if the genes for schizophrenia could be cloned, there would still be a great deal to learn about how this disorder, or group of disorders, emerges out of a genetic predisposition.

Structural Brain Abnormalities

Clinicians and researchers have long believed that there is something fundamentally different about the brains of people with schizophrenia, compared with the brains of people without schizophrenia. Only in the past 20 years, with the development of technologies such as positron-emission tomography (PET scans), computerized axial tomography (CAT scans), and magnetic resonance imaging (MRI), have scientists been able to examine in detail the structure and functioning of the brain. The picture emerging from the use of these technologies is not entirely clear, again probably because there are many different types of schizophrenia, which are often grouped together in studies.

There is increasing evidence, however, for major structural and functional deficits in the brains of some people with schizophrenia (Andreasen, 2001; Barch, 2005). Most theorists of schizophrenia think of it as a *neurodevelopmental disorder*, in which a variety of factors lead to abnormal development of the brain in utero and early in life.

Enlarged Ventricles

The major structural brain abnormality found most consistently in schizophrenia is **enlarged ventricles** (Andreasen et al., 1990; Lieberman et al., 2001) (see Figure 11.4 on page 398). *Ventricles* are fluid-filled spaces in the brain. Enlarged ventricles suggest atrophy, or deterioration, in other brain tissue. People with schizophrenia with ventricular enlargement also show reductions in the prefrontal areas of the brain and an abnormal connection between the prefrontal cortex and the amygdala and hippocampus. Ventricular enlargement might indicate structural deficits in many other areas of the brain, however. Indeed, the different areas of the brain that can deteriorate to create ventricular enlargement might lead to different manifestations of schizophrenia.

People with schizophrenia with ventricular enlargement tend to show social, emotional, and behavioral deficits long before they develop the core symptoms of schizophrenia. They also tend to have more severe symptoms than others with schizophrenia and are less responsive to medication. These characteristics suggest gross alterations in the functioning of the brain, which are difficult to alleviate with treatment.

The gender differences in schizophrenia may be tied, in part, to gender differences in ventricular size. Some studies find that men with schizophrenia have more severely enlarged ventricles than women with schizophrenia (Nopoulos, Flaum, & Andreasen, 1997). This difference may be because men generally show greater loss of tissue volume and increase in ventricle size with age than do women. The normal effects of aging on men's brains may exacerbate the neuroanatomical abnormalities of schizophrenia, causing more severe symptoms and, thus, a worse course.

Enlarged Ventricles in People with Schizophrenia. The left panel shows the enlarged, fluid-filled ventricles (in gray) of a person with schizophrenia, compared with those of a normal person (right panel). This image was taken by Nancy Andreasen.

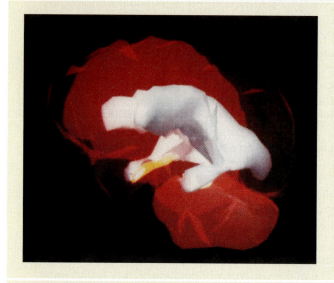
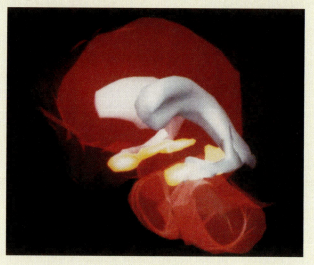

Source: Gershon & Rieder, 1992, p. 128.

Prefrontal Cortex and Other Key Areas

Studies have shown abnormalities in volume, neuron density, and metabolic rate in a number of areas of the brain in people with schizophrenia. These areas include the frontal cortex, temporal lobe, basal ganglia, and limbic area, including the hippocampus, thalamus, and amygdala (Andreasen, 2001; Barch, 2005; Suhara et al., 2002). Some of the most consistent findings are in the **prefrontal cortex.** The prefrontal cortex of the brain is smaller and shows less activity in some areas in people with schizophrenia than in people without schizophrenia (Barch, 2005) (see Figure 11.5). In addition, people at risk for schizophrenia because of a family history, but who have not yet developed the disorder, have been shown to have abnormalities of prefrontal activity (Lawrie et al., 2001).

The prefrontal cortex has connections to all other cortical regions, as well as to the *limbic system,* which is involved in emotion and cognition, and the *basal ganglia,* which are involved in motor movement. The prefrontal cortex is important in language, emotional expression, the planning and producing of new ideas, and the mediation of social interactions. Thus, it seems logical that a person with a prefrontal cortex that is unusually small or inactive would show a wide range of deficits in cognition, emotion, and social interactions, as people with schizophrenia do.

Evidence of this lower level of activity is not found in all people with schizophrenia, however. It is more common in people who predominantly exhibit negative symptoms of schizophrenia (e.g., low motivation, poor social interactions, blunted affect) than in those who predominantly exhibit positive symptoms (e.g., hallucinations and delusions) or mixed symptoms (Fitzgerald et al., 2004).

The *hippocampus* is another area of the brain where differences are being found between people with schizophrenia and people without the disorder (Barch, 2005). The hippocampus plays a critical role in the formation of long-term memories. People with schizophrenia show abnormal hippocampal activation when they are doing tasks that require them to encode information for storage in memory or to retrieve information from memory (Barch et al., 2002; Schacter et al., 2003). Other studies show that people with schizophrenia have abnormalities in the volume and shape of their hippocampus at the cellular level (Knable et al., 2004; Shenton et al., 2001). Similar abnormalities in the hippocampus are found in first-degree relatives of people with schizophrenia (Seidman et al., 2002). These abnormalities in the structure and functioning of the hippocampus might make it difficult for people with schizophrenia to recall information and to use it in

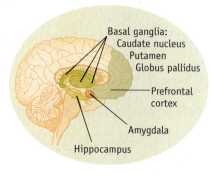

Basal ganglia:
Caudate nucleus
Putamen
Globus pallidus

Prefrontal cortex

Amygdala

Hippocampus

The prefrontal cortex has connections to the basal ganglia and the limbic area, including the hippocampus, thalamus, and amygdala.

ongoing conversations or in understanding current situations. These problems, in turn, may contribute to difficulties in maintaining coherent conversations and accurately interpreting ongoing situations.

Causes of Abnormalities

What causes the neuroanatomical abnormalities in schizophrenia? There might be a number of causes, including specific genetic abnormalities, brain injury due to birth injury, head injury, viral infections, deficiencies in nutrition, and deficiencies in cognitive stimulation (Barch, 2005; Conklin & Iacono, 2002). Recall that some studies have shown that family members of people with schizophrenia also exhibit several of these neuroanatomical abnormalities (Barch, 2005). Similarities between family members might be due either to genetic causes or to other biological or environmental factors shared by family members. In some studies of MZ twins in which one twin has schizophrenia but the other does not, the twin with schizophrenia tends to show neuroanatomical abnormalities, but the other twin does not, even though both twins have identical genetic makeups (Suddath et al., 1990; Thermenos et al., 2004). These studies argue against a solely genetic contribution to family similarities in neuroanatomical abnormalities.

Birth Complications

Serious prenatal and birth difficulties are more frequent in the histories of people with schizophrenia than in those of people without schizophrenia and may play a role in the development of neurological difficulties (Cannon, in press). Delivery complications have been found to combine with a familial risk for schizophrenia to predict the degree of enlargement of the ventricles and abnormalities in the hippocampus in people with schizophrenia.

One type of birth complication that may be especially important in neurological development is oxygen deprivation during labor and delivery, known as **perinatal hypoxia** (Goldstein et al., 2000). As many as 30 percent of people with schizophrenia have a history of perinatal hypoxia. A prospective study of 9,236 people born in Philadelphia between 1959 and 1966 found that the odds of an adult diagnosis of schizophrenia increased in direct proportion to the degree of perinatal hypoxia (Cannon et al., 1999). The authors of this study suggest that the effects of oxygen deprivation interact with a genetic vulnerability for schizophrenia to result in a person's developing this disorder, because the majority of people suffering oxygen deprivation prenatally or at birth do not develop schizophrenia.

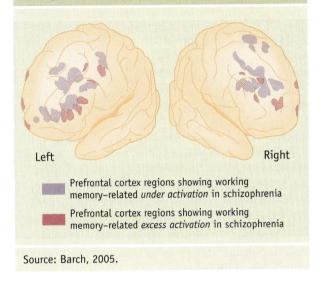

FIGURE 11.5

Areas of the Prefrontal Cortex Showing Abnormal Activity in People with Schizophrenia.

Several areas of the prefrontal cortex show abnormally high or low levels of activity when people with schizophrenia do tasks requiring working memory.

Left   Right

Prefrontal cortex regions showing working memory–related *under activation* in schizophrenia

Prefrontal cortex regions showing working memory–related *excess activation* in schizophrenia

Source: Barch, 2005.

Prenatal Viral Exposure

Epidemiological studies have shown high rates of schizophrenia among persons whose mothers were exposed to the influenza virus while pregnant (Cannon, in press). For example, persons whose mothers were exposed to the influenza epidemic that swept Helsinki, Finland, in 1957 were significantly more likely to develop schizophrenia than people in control groups, particularly if their mothers were exposed during the second trimester of pregnancy (Mednick et al., 1988, 1998). The second trimester is a crucial period for the development of the central nervous system of the fetus. Disruption in this phase of brain development could cause the major structural deficits found in the brains of some people with schizophrenia.

Neurotransmitters

The neurotransmitter **dopamine** has been thought to play a role in schizophrenia for many years (Burt, Creese, & Snyder, 1977). The original dopamine theory was that the symptoms of schizophrenia were caused by excess levels of dopamine in the brain, particularly in the frontal lobe and limbic system. This theory was supported by several lines of evidence.

On one hand, drugs that tend to reduce the symptoms of schizophrenia—the **phenothiazines**—reduce the functional level of dopamine in the brain. Some people who take phenothiazines to reduce their psychotic symptoms develop motor movement disorders similar to those of Parkinson's disease. It is well established that Parkinson's disease is caused by a deficiency of dopamine in the brain. Thus, the movement disorders that people with schizophrenia develop as a result of taking phenothiazines are likely to be caused by these drugs' reducing the levels of dopamine in the brain.

On the other hand, drugs that increase the functional level of dopamine in the brain, such as amphetamines, tend to increase the psychotic symptoms of schizophrenia. Finally, neuroimaging studies suggest that there are more receptors for dopamine and sometimes higher levels of dopamine in some areas of the brain in people with schizophrenia than in people without the disorder. The opposite effects of the phenothiazines and amphetamines on dopamine levels, and subsequently on symptoms of schizophrenia, suggested that excess dopamine led to schizophrenia, according to the original theory.

Now, however, research suggests that the original dopamine theory of schizophrenia was too simple (Conklin & Iacono, 2002; Davis et al., 1991). Many people with schizophrenia do not respond to the phenothiazines, indicating that neurotransmitter systems other than the dopamine system may be involved in the disorder. Even people with schizophrenia who do respond to phenothiazines tend to experience relief only from their positive symptoms (e.g., hallucinations and delusions), not from their negative symptoms. This pattern of relief suggests that simple dopamine depletion does not explain these negative symptoms.

Although the original version of the dopamine theory of schizophrenia (that there are generally higher levels of dopamine in the brains of people with schizophrenia) is not holding up, it is clear that dopamine is involved in schizophrenia. Let's consider a more complex version of the dopamine theory, which can explain both the positive and the negative symptoms of schizophrenia (Conklin & Iacono, 2002; Davis et al., 1991).

First, there may be *excess* dopamine activity in the **mesolimbic pathway,** a subcortical part of the brain involved in cognition and emotion (see Figure 11.6). The mesolimbic pathway is rich with certain types of receptors for dopamine. High dopamine activity in the mesolimbic system may lead to the positive symptoms of schizophrenia: hallucinations, delusions, and thought disorder. In turn, new drugs in the treatment of schizophrenia, known as the **atypical antipsychotics,** may work to reduce the symptoms of schizophrenia by binding to D4 receptors in the mesolimbic pathway, blocking the action of dopamine in this system.

Second, there may be *unusually low* dopamine activity in the prefrontal area of the brain, which is

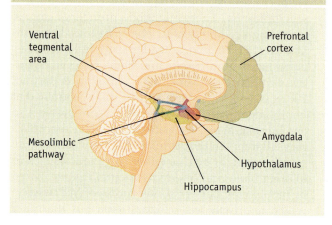

FIGURE 11.6

Areas of Abnormal Dopamine Activity in the Brain in Schizophrenia. There may be excess dopamine activity in the mesolimbic pathway, which begins in the ventral tegmental area and projects to the hypothalamus, amygdala, and hippocampus. But there may be unusually low dopamine activity in the prefrontal cortex.

Ventral tegmental area
Prefrontal cortex
Mesolimbic pathway
Amygdala
Hypothalamus
Hippocampus

involved in attention, motivation, and the organization of behavior. Low dopamine activity here may lead to the negative symptoms of schizophrenia: lack of motivation, an inability to care for oneself in daily activities, and the blunting of affect. This idea fits well with the evidence that structural and functional abnormalities in this part of the brain are associated with the negative symptoms. This idea also helps explain why the phenothiazines, which reduce dopamine activity, do not alleviate the negative symptoms of schizophrenia.

This more complex dopamine theory of schizophrenia seems to integrate research and clinical findings that, at first glance, seem to contradict one another. Another theory posits that, whereas the positive symptoms of schizophrenia are caused by excess dopamine activity in the brain, the negative symptoms are not the result of dopamine imbalances. Instead, the negative symptoms result from structural abnormalities in the frontal lobes of the brain (see Barch, 2005).

Finally, other research suggests that dopamine is not the only neurotransmitter to play an important role in schizophrenia. Serotonin neurons regulate dopamine neurons in the mesolimbic pathway, and some of the newest drugs that treat schizophrenia bind to serotonin receptors (Bondolfi et al., 1998). It may be that the interaction between serotonin and dopamine is critical in schizophrenia (Breier, 1995).

Other research has found abnormal levels of the neurotransmitters glutamate and gamma-aminobutyric acid (GABA) in people with schizophrenia (Goff & Coyle, 2001; Tsai & Coyle, 2002).

FIGURE 11.7 **An Integrated Model of the Links Between Cognitive Deficits and the Symptoms of Schizophrenia.** Theorists have argued that abnormalities in the function of the dopamine system, particularly in the prefrontal cortex, lead to deficits in the working memory, which then make it difficult for people with schizophrenia to attend only to relevant information. This difficulty impairs their ability to reason, communicate, and solve problems.

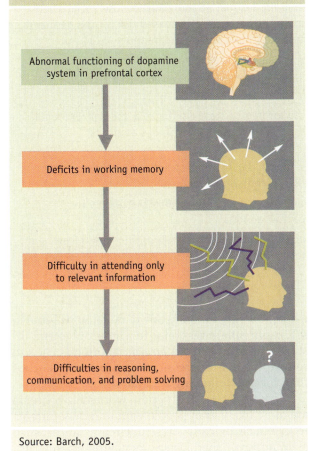

Source: Barch, 2005.

Glutamate and GABA are widespread in the human brain, and deficiencies in these neurotransmitters might contribute to a host of cognitive and emotional symptoms. Glutamate neurons are the major excitatory pathways linking the cortex, limbic system, and thalamus, regions of the brain shown to behave abnormally in people with schizophrenia.

An Integrative Model

Barch (2003, 2005) and others (Docherty et al., 1996; Fitzgerald et al., 2004) have argued that many of the core symptoms of schizophrenia are due to fundamental problems in basic cognitive processes resulting from functional and structural abnormalities in the brain (see Figure 11.7). These core symptoms include disorganized speech and difficulties in communication, logical reasoning, and the tasks of daily

life (such as getting oneself out of bed, dressed, fed, and to work).

Specifically, abnormalities in the dopamine system, particularly in the prefrontal cortex, lead to deficits in working memory. These deficits make it difficult to inhibit irrelevant information from intruding into one's attention and interfere with communication with others, as the following woman with schizophrenia describes (McGhie & Chapman, 1961, p. 104).

VOICES

Everything seems to grip my attention although I am not particularly interested in anything. I am speaking to you just now, but I can hear noises going on next door and in the corridor. I find it difficult to shut these out, and it makes it more difficult for me to concentrate on what I am saying to you.

Working memory deficits also impair the ability to learn new information and to retrieve it when needed. Together, these deficits contribute to the difficulties in reasoning, communication, and problem solving experienced by people with schizophrenia.

This model has been supported by a wide range of studies showing deficits in working memory and related cognitive functions in people with schizophrenia, as well as in the first-degree relatives of people with schizophrenia (Barch, 2005). In addition, these cognitive deficits are linked to abnormalities in the functioning of the prefrontal cortex and in the dopamine system. This model does not explain all the symptoms of schizophrenia (such as the delusions and hallucinations), but it does explain how basic cognitive deficits, tied to brain functioning, can lead to problems in communication, reasoning, and functioning in daily life, which are some of the most damaging symptoms of schizophrenia.

SUMMING UP

- There is strong evidence for a genetic contribution to schizophrenia, although genetics do not fully explain who has the disorder.

- Many people with schizophrenia show significant structural and functional abnormalities in the brain, including low frontal activity and enlarged ventricles.

- A number of prenatal and birth difficulties are implicated in the development of

TABLE 11.9 Concept Overview

Psychosocial Perspectives on Schizophrenia

A number of psychosocial factors may increase the risk of relapse in schizophrenia, even if they do not directly cause the onset of schizophrenia.

Perspective	Description
Social drift and urban birth	Schizophrenia impairs functioning, leading an individual to lose social status; also, people born in poor urban settings are at increased risk for the perinatal diseases and injuries that may contribute to schizophrenia.
Stress and relapse	A variety of stressful events increase risk for relapse.
Psychodynamic theories	Overwhelming rejection by an infant's mother causes the child to lose the ability to distinguish reality from unreality.
Communication patterns	Oddities in communication by a caregiver to a child at risk for schizophrenia increase stress and impair the development of the child's ability to communicate with others.
Expressed emotion	Families that are overinvolved with and hostile toward their member with schizophrenia increase stress, which leads to relapse.
Cognitive theories	The symptoms of schizophrenia arise from an individual's attempts to understand and manage cognitive deficits.
Behavioral theories	People with schizophrenia attend to irrelevant stimuli in the environment and don't know socially acceptable responses to others.

schizophrenia, including prenatal hypoxia and exposure to the influenza virus during the second trimester of gestation.

■ Difficulties in deploying attention may be at the core of many symptoms of schizophrenia.

■ Excess dopamine activity in the mesolimbic pathway and unusually low dopamine activity in the prefrontal area of the brain may work together to create the symptoms of schizophrenia.

■ New research suggests that serotonin, glutamate, and GABA may also play a role in schizophrenia.

PSYCHOSOCIAL PERSPECTIVES ON SCHIZOPHRENIA

Although schizophrenia is strongly linked to biological factors, there is a history of psychological theories of schizophrenia, and contemporary research shows that social factors can clearly influence the course of schizophrenia (see the Concept Overview in Table 11.9).

Social Drift and Urban Birth

Although you may have heard of someone having a "nervous breakdown" following a traumatic

event, it is rare for someone to develop full-blown schizophrenia in response to a stressful event. Instead, the term *nervous breakdown* often is used to refer to severe depressions or anxiety disorders that develop following trauma.

Still, it is true that people with schizophrenia are more likely than people without schizophrenia to live in chronically stressful circumstances, such as in impoverished inner-city neighborhoods and in low-status occupations or unemployment (Dohrenwend, 2000). Most research supports a **social selection** explanation of this link. According to this explanation, the symptoms of schizophrenia interfere with a person's ability to complete an education and hold a job. For these reasons, people with schizophrenia tend to drift downward in social class, compared with their families of origin.

One of the classic studies showing the process of social selection in schizophrenia tracked the socioeconomic status of men with schizophrenia and compared it with the status of their brothers and fathers (Goldberg & Morrison, 1963). The men with schizophrenia tended to end up in socioeconomic classes that were well below those of their fathers. For example, if their fathers were in the middle class, the men with schizophrenia were likely to be in the lower classes. In contrast, the healthy brothers of the people with schizophrenia tended to end up in socioeconomic classes that were equal to or higher than those of their fathers. More recent data also support the social selection theory (Dohrenwend, 2000).

Several studies have shown that people with schizophrenia and other forms of psychosis (such as bipolar disorder with psychotic features) are more likely to have been born in a large city than in a small town (Kendler et al., 1996; Lewis et al., 1992; Takei et al., 1992, 1995; Torrey, Bowler, & Clark, 1997; van Os et al., 2001). For example, studies in the United States find that people with psychotic disorders are as many as five times more likely to have been born and raised in a large metropolitan area than a rural area. Is it the stress of the city that leads to psychosis? Torrey and Yolken (1998) argue that the link between urban living and psychosis is due not to stress but to overcrowding, which increases the risk that a pregnant woman or newborn will be exposed to infectious agents. Many studies have shown that the rates of many infectious diseases, including influenza, tuberculosis, respiratory infections, herpes, and measles, are higher in crowded urban areas than in less crowded areas. As noted earlier, there is a link between prenatal or perinatal exposure to infectious disease and schizophrenia.

Stress and Relapse

Stressful circumstances may not cause someone to develop schizophrenia, but they may trigger new episodes in people who are vulnerable to schizophrenia. When researchers looked at the timing of stressful events relative to the onset of new episodes of psychosis, they found higher levels of stress occurring shortly before the onset of a new episode of psychosis, as compared with other times in the lives of people with schizophrenia (Norman & Malla, 1993).

For example, in one study, researchers followed 30 people with schizophrenia for one year, interviewing them every two weeks to determine if they had experienced any stressful events and/or any increase in their symptoms. They found that the people who had experienced relapses of symptoms were more likely to have experienced negative life events in the month before their relapse (Ventura et al., 1989). It is important not to overstate the link between stressful life events and new episodes of schizophrenia. Over half the people in this study who had had a relapse of their schizophrenia in the year they were followed had *not* experienced negative life events just before their relapse (Ventura et al., 1989). In addition, other studies suggest that many of the life events that people with schizophrenia experience in the weeks before they relapse may actually be caused by the prodromal symptoms that occur just

Poverty is often related to schizophrenia, perhaps as both a contributor and a consequence.

before a relapse into psychosis (Dohrenwend et al., 1987). For example, one of the prodromal symptoms of a schizophrenic relapse is social withdrawal. In turn, the negative life events most often preceding a relapse, such as the breakup of a relationship or the loss of a job, might be caused partially by the person's social withdrawal.

Psychodynamic Theories

Early psychodynamic theorists suggested that schizophrenia resulted from overwhelmingly negative experiences in early childhood with primary caregivers (usually the mother). Freud (1924) argued that, when mothers are extremely harsh and withhold their love from a child, the child regresses to infantile levels of functioning, and the ego loses its ability to distinguish reality from unreality. Later, psychoanalysts Freida Fromm-Reichmann (1948) and Silvano Arieti (1955) elaborated on Freud's theory and more fully described parenting styles in mothers that might cause their children to become schizophrenic. These *schizophrenogenic (schizophrenia-causing) mothers* are at the same time overprotective and rejecting of their children. They dominate their children, not letting them develop an autonomous sense of self and simultaneously making the children feel worthless and unlovable.

These theories did not hold up to scientific scrutiny. Research comparing the parenting styles of mothers of people with schizophrenia and the styles of mothers of people without the disorder did not confirm this theory. Later psychodynamic theorists generally see schizophrenia as the result of biological forces that prevent these individuals from developing an integrated sense of self (Kohut & Wolf, 1978).

Communication Patterns

Another early family theory of schizophrenia, proposed by Gregory Bateson and colleagues (Bateson et al., 1956), was that parents (particularly mothers) of children who become schizophrenic put their children in *double binds* by constantly communicating conflicting messages to the children. Such a mother might physically comfort her child when he falls down and is hurt but, at the same time, be verbally hostile to and critical of the child. Children chronically exposed to such mixed messages supposedly cannot trust their own feelings or their perceptions of the world and, thus, develop distorted views of themselves, of others, and of the environment, which contribute to schizophrenia. Again, however, empirical research has not supported the specific predictions of this double-bind theory of schizophrenia.

Although the double-bind theory of schizophrenia has not been supported, investigations of the *communication patterns* in families of people with schizophrenia have revealed oddities. Most investigators do not believe that these oddities alone cause schizophrenia in children. Rather, the oddities create a stressful environment, which makes it more likely that a child with a biological vulnerability to schizophrenia will develop the full syndrome of schizophrenia or that a person with schizophrenia will have more frequent relapses of psychosis.

Margaret Singer and Lyman Wynne (1965) described *communication deviance* within schizophrenic families as involving vague communications; misperceptions and misinterpretations; odd or inappropriate word usage; and fragmented, disrupted, and poorly integrated communication. Controlled comparisons of interactions in families with a person with schizophrenia and in families without a person with schizophrenia have found significantly higher levels of communication deviance in the families of people with schizophrenia. Some examples of this are statements such as "But the thing is as I said, there's got . . . you can't drive in the alley" and "It's gonna be up and downwards along the process all the while to go through something like this" (Miklowitz et al., 1991).

Such deviant patterns of communication do not appear to have serious, long-lasting effects on children who do not have family histories of schizophrenia (Gottesman, 1991). However, among children at risk for schizophrenia because they have family histories of the disorder, those whose families show high levels of communication deviance are more likely to develop schizophrenia than are those whose families have low levels of communication deviance (Goldstein, 1987).

Expressed Emotion

The family interaction style that has received the most attention by researchers of schizophrenia is **expressed emotion.** Families high in expressed emotion are overinvolved with each other, are overprotective of the disturbed family member, and voice self-sacrificing attitudes toward the disturbed family member, while being critical, hostile, and resentful of the disturbed family member (Brown, Birley, & Wing, 1972; Vaughn & Leff, 1976). Although high expressed-emotion family members do not doubt the legitimacy of their schizophrenic family member's illness, they talk as if the ill family member can exert quite a bit of control over the symptoms (Hooley & Campbell, 2002). They often have many ideas about what the family member can do to improve his or her symptoms, as is illustrated in the following comments from two high expressed-emotion mothers of people with schizophrenia (Hooley, 1998, p. 636):

> I tell him, "Sit down, you're driving me crazy!" Back and forth, back and forth [pacing]. I say, "Why don't you take some good deep breaths and just relax!"

> She was reading in the hospital. I don't know why she stopped. I've been trying to get her to start again. I said, "Read—even if it's only for 15 minutes, Lori. Try!"

Expressed emotion has been assessed through lengthy interviews with people with schizophrenia and their families, through projective tests, and through direct observation of family interactions. A number of studies have shown that people with schizophrenia whose families are high in expressed emotion are much more likely to suffer relapses of psychosis than are those whose families are low in expressed emotion (e.g., Butzlaff & Hooley, 1998; Hooley & Hiller, 1998). An analysis of 27 studies of expressed emotion and schizophrenia showed that 70 percent of patients in high expressed-emotion families relapsed within a follow-up year, compared with 31 percent of patients in low expressed-emotion families (Butzlaff & Hooley, 1998). Being in a high expressed-emotion family may create stresses for a person with schizophrenia, which overwhelm his or her ability to cope and trigger new episodes of psychosis.

The link between high levels of family expressed emotion and higher relapse rates has been found in several cultures, including European countries, the United States, Mexico, and India. In

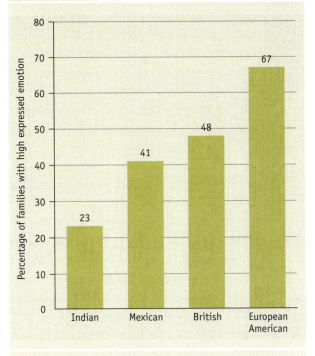

FIGURE 11.8 **Cultural Differences in the Prevalence of Expressed Emotion in Families of People with Schizophrenia.** Families of people with schizophrenia from developing countries tend to show lower levels of expressed emotion than do families of people with schizophrenia from developed countries. This may be one reason that people with schizophrenia from developing countries have fewer relapses than do those from developed countries.

Source: Karno & Jenkins, 1993.

families. They may also be especially prone to relapse, but for reasons other than their exposure to expressed emotion.

Another alternative explanation for the link between family expressed emotion and relapse in people with schizophrenia comes from evidence that family members who are particularly high on expressed emotion are themselves more likely to have some form of psychopathology (Goldstein et al., 1992). Thus, it may be that people with schizophrenia in these families have high rates of relapse because they have a greater genetic loading for psychopathology, as evidenced by the presence of psychopathology in their family members, rather than because their family members are high in expressed emotion. Perhaps the best evidence that family expressed emotion actually influences relapse in schizophrenic patients is that interventions that reduce family expressed emotion tend to reduce the relapse rate in schizophrenic family members.

Cognitive and Behavioral Perspectives

Aaron Beck, a founder of cognitive therapy, and Neil Rector have recently formulated a cognitive model of schizophrenia (Beck & Rector, 2005). They suggest that the neurological abnormalities of schizophrenia create fundamental difficulties in attention, inhibition, and the adherence to rules of communication, which lead people with schizophrenia to try to conserve their limited cognitive resources. One way they do so is to use, to an excessive degree, certain biases or schemas for understanding the overwhelming information streaming through their brains. Delusions arise as a person with schizophrenia tries to explain strange perceptual experiences. Hallucinations result from a hypersensitivity to perceptual input, coupled with a tendency to attribute experiences to external sources. For example, rather than thinking, "I'm hearing things," a person with schizophrenia tends to think, "Someone is trying to talk to me." The negative symptoms of schizophrenia arise from exaggerations of personality characteristics, expectations that social interactions will be aversive, and the need to withdraw and conserve scarce cognitive resources.

This cognitive conceptualization has led to cognitive strategies for treating people with schizophrenia. These strategies help patients identify stressful circumstances associated with the development and worsening of symptoms and learn better ways of coping with that stress. They also teach patients ways of disputing their delusional beliefs and hallucinatory experiences. Negative

Mexico and India, however, the families of people with schizophrenia tend to score lower on measures of expressed emotion than do their counterparts in Europe and the United States (Karno & Jenkins, 1993; Karno et al., 1987) (see Figure 11.8).

Critics of the literature on expressed emotion argue that the hostility and intrusiveness observed in some families of people with schizophrenia might be the result of the symptoms exhibited by the person with schizophrenia, rather than contributors to relapse (Parker, Johnston, & Hayward, 1988). Although families are often forgiving of the positive symptoms of schizophrenia (e.g., hallucinations, delusions, thought disturbances) because they view them as uncontrollable, they can be unforgiving of the negative symptoms (e.g., lack of motivation, blunted affect), viewing them as under the control of the person with schizophrenia (Hooley & Campbell, 2002). People with schizophrenia who have more of these symptoms may elicit more negative expressed emotion from their

symptoms are treated by helping patients develop expectations that being more active and interacting more with other people will have positive benefits. Studies testing this cognitive intervention have shown it to be more effective in reducing symptoms than simply providing support to patients (Beck & Rector, 2005).

Some behaviorists have tried to explain schizophrenic symptoms as having developed through operant conditioning (see Belcher, 1988). They suggest that most people learn what stimuli to attend to in the social environment—such as another person's face or what that person is saying—through experiences in which they attend to these stimuli and are rewarded for doing so. People with schizophrenia do not receive this basic training in what social stimuli to attend to, and how to respond, because of inadequate parenting or extremely unusual circumstances. As a result, they attend to irrelevant stimuli in the environment and do not know the socially acceptable responses to other people.

This behavioral theory of how schizophrenia develops has not been well tested or accepted. But it is clear that behavioral techniques can help people with schizophrenia learn more socially acceptable ways of interacting with others (Belcher, 1988; Braginsky, Braginsky, & Ring, 1969). For example, if family members begin to ignore bizarre comments or behaviors by the person with schizophrenia, and provide reinforcement for socially acceptable behavior, the person with schizophrenia gradually reduces the bizarre behaviors and increases the socially acceptable behaviors.

Cross-Cultural Perspectives

Cultures vary greatly in their explanations for schizophrenia (Anders, 2003; Karno & Jenkins, 1993). Most cultures have a biological explanation for the disorder, including the general idea that it runs in families. Intermingled with biological explanations are theories that attribute the disorder to stress, lack of spiritual piety, and family dynamics. Browne (2001) offers a case study of a woman from Java, whose understanding of her own schizophrenic symptoms included all these factors:

Anik is a 29 year old Javanese woman who was born in a rural area but has lived in the city of Yogyakarta for the last four years. She has been married 1½ years, but is very unhappy in her marriage, feeling her husband was lacking in openness and compassion. Anik has an 8 month-old daughter, but has been unable to care for her for the last several

CASE STUDY

months, so the daughter was living with Anik's aunt in Jakarta. When her illness began, Anik first became withdrawn and didn't sleep or eat. She developed hallucinations of accusatory voices criticizing her husband, his family, and their landlady. Anik also suffered from jealous delusions that her husband was having an affair. She was taken to the hospital by her brother, where her symptoms included *mondar-mandir* ("wandering without purpose"), *nga-muk*, being easily offended and suspicious, talking to herself, crying, insomnia, *malmun* ("daydreaming"), and quickly changing emotions. Her sister-in-law reported that she had been chronically fearful and irritable for some time and would frequently slam doors and yell. In Javanese culture, the control of emotions in social situations is of great importance, so Anik's outbursts were seen as clear signs of some sort of pathology.

Anik had several explanations for her behavior. First and foremost, she believed that she was in a bad marriage, and this stress was a contributing factor. Shortly before her symptoms began, her landlady said something harsh to her, and Anik believed that her startle reaction to this (*goncangan*) led to *sajit hati*, literally "liver sickness." In addition, Anik's mother had a brief period during Anik's childhood when she "went crazy," becoming loud and violent, and Anik believes she may have inherited this tendency from her mother. Anik initially sought to overcome her symptoms by increasing the frequency with which she repeated Muslim prayers and asking to be taken to a Muslim boarding house. Once she was taken to the hospital, she agreed to take antipsychotic medications, which helped her symptoms somewhat. She was discharged from the hospital after a short time, but was rehospitalized multiple times over the next year.

Anik's experience illustrates the interweaving of traditional beliefs and practices concerning people with schizophrenic symptoms and modern biological treatments. Although she agreed to take antipsychotic medicines, the understanding she and her family had of her symptoms was not primarily a biological one but, rather, one rooted in concerns about stress and, to some extent, religion.

SUMMING UP

- People with schizophrenia tend to live in highly stressful circumstances. Most theorists see this as a consequence, rather than as a cause, of schizophrenia.

- Early psychodynamic theories viewed schizophrenia as the result of harsh and inconsistent parenting, which causes an individual to regress to infantile forms of coping. According to other theories, families put schizophrenic members in double binds or have deviant patterns of communication. These theories have not been supported.

- Families high in expressed emotion are overinvolved and overprotective while being critical and resentful. People with schizophrenia who live in families high in expressed emotion may be at increased risk for relapse.

- Cognitive theorists see some schizophrenic symptoms as attempts to understand perceptual and attentional disturbances.

- Behavioral theorists view schizophrenic behaviors as the result of operant conditioning.

- Different cultures have different native theories of schizophrenia.

TREATMENTS FOR SCHIZOPHRENIA

Comprehensive treatment for people with schizophrenia means providing them with medications to help quell symptoms, therapy to help them cope with the consequences of the disorder, and social services to aid in their reintegration into society and to ensure that they have access to all the resources they need for daily life.

Biological Treatments: Drug Therapy

Over the centuries, many treatments for schizophrenia have been developed, based on the scientific theories of the time. Physicians have performed brain surgery on people with schizophrenia in an attempt to "fix" or eliminate the part of the brain causing hallucinations or delusions. These patients were sometimes calmer after their surgeries but often also experienced significant cognitive and emotional deficits as a result of the surgery. *Insulin coma therapy* was used in the 1930s to treat schizophrenia. People with schizophrenia were given massive doses of insulin—the drug used to treat diabetes—until they went into a coma. When they emerged from this coma, however, patients were rarely much better, and the procedure was a highly dangerous one. *Electroconvulsive therapy,* or *ECT,* was also used to treat schizophrenia for a time, until it was clear that it had little effect on the symptoms of schizophrenia (although it is effective in treating serious depression, as we discussed in Chapters 5 and 9).

Mostly, however, people with schizophrenia were simply warehoused. In 1955, one out of every two people in psychiatric hospitals had been diagnosed with schizophrenia, although, by today's standards of diagnosis, they may have suffered from disorders other than schizophrenia (Rosenstein, Milazzo-Sayre, & Manderscheid, 1989). These patients received custodial care—they were bathed, fed, and prevented from hurting themselves physically, often with the use of physical restraints—but few received any treatment that actually reduced their symptoms of schizophrenia. It wasn't until the 1950s that an effective drug treatment for schizophrenia was introduced. Since then, several other antipsychotic drugs have been added to the arsenal of treatments for schizophrenia. Most recently, new types of antipsychotics, the atypical antipsychotics, hold the promise of relieving psychotic symptoms without inducing as many side effects as the traditional antipsychotics.

As we discussed in Chapter 5, in the early 1950s, French researchers Jean Delay and Pierre Deniker found that **chlorpromazine** (Thorazine), one of a class of drugs called the *phenothiazines,* calms agitation and reduces hallucinations and delusions in patients with schizophrenia. Other phenothiazines that became widely used include trifluoperazine (Stelazine), thioridazine (Mellaril), and fluphenazine (Prolixin). They appear to work by blocking receptors for dopamine, thereby reducing dopamine's action in the brain. Many people with schizophrenia can control the positive symptoms of schizophrenia (hallucinations, delusions, thought disturbances) by taking this drug prophylactically—that is, even when they are not experiencing acute symptoms.

The need for the long-term custodial hospitalization of people with schizophrenia was greatly reduced over the next 20 years, so that, by 1971, the number of people with schizophrenia who were hospitalized had decreased to half of what would have been expected if these drugs had not been available. Other classes of antipsychotic drugs were introduced after the phenothiazines, including the *butyrophenones* (such as Haldol) and the *thioxanthenes* (such as Navane). Collectively, these drugs are known as the *neuroleptics.*

Effectiveness and Side Effects of Neuroleptics

Although the neuroleptic drugs revolutionized the treatment of schizophrenia, they do not work for everyone with the disorder. About 25 percent of people with schizophrenia do not respond to the neuroleptics (Spaulding, Johnson, & Coursey, 2001). Even among people who do respond, the neuroleptics are more effective in treating the positive symptoms of schizophrenia than the negative symptoms (e.g., lack of motivation and interpersonal deficits). Many people with schizophrenia who take neuroleptics are not actively psychotic but are still unable to lead normal lives, holding a job and building positive social relationships. People with schizophrenia typically must take neuroleptic drugs prophylactically—that is, all the time to prevent new episodes of acute symptoms. If the drug is discontinued, about 78 percent of people with schizophrenia relapse within one year, and 98 percent within two years, compared with about a third of people who continue on their medications (Gitlin et al., 2001; Sampath et al., 1992).

Unfortunately, however, the neuroleptics have significant side effects, which cause many people to want to discontinue their use. The side effects include grogginess, dry mouth, blurred vision, drooling, sexual dysfunction, visual disturbances, weight gain or loss, constipation, menstrual disturbances in women, and depression. Another common side effect, **akinesia,** is characterized by slowed motor activity, monotonous speech, and an expressionless face (Blanchard & Neale, 1992). Patients taking the phenothiazines often show symptoms similar to those seen in Parkinson's disease, including muscle stiffness, freezing of the facial muscles, tremors and spasms in the extremities, and **akathesis,** an agitation that causes people to pace and be unable to sit still. The fact that Parkinson's disease is caused by a lack of dopamine in the brain suggests that these side effects occur because the drugs reduce the functional levels of dopamine in the brain.

One of the most serious side effects of the neuroleptics is a neurological disorder known as **tardive dyskinesia,** which involves involuntary movements of the tongue, face, mouth, or jaw. People with this disorder may involuntarily smack their lips, make sucking sounds, stick out their tongues, puff their cheeks, or make other bizarre movements over and over again. Tardive dyskinesia is often irreversible and may occur in over 20 percent of persons with long-term use of the phenothiazines (Spaulding et al., 2001).

The side effects of the neuroleptics can be reduced by reducing dosages. For this reason, many clinicians maintain people with schizophrenia on the lowest possible dosage that still keeps acute symptoms at bay, known as a *maintenance dose.* Unfortunately, maintenance doses are often not enough to restore an individual to full functioning. The negative symptoms of schizophrenia may still be present in strong form, and the individual may experience mild versions of the positive symptoms. This clearly makes it hard to function in daily life. Some people with schizophrenia live a revolving-door life of frequent hospitalizations and a marginal life outside the hospital.

Physicians prescribing neuroleptics also have to take cultural differences into consideration. There is some evidence that persons of Asian descent need less neuroleptic medication than do persons of European descent to reach desired blood levels of the drug and to show symptom relief (Lin & Shen, 1991). Asians may also experience the side effects of neuroleptics at lower dosages. It is currently unclear whether these differences in response are due to biological differences or to differences in diet or another environmental variable.

Atypical Antipsychotics

Fortunately, newer drugs, referred to as the *atypical antipsychotics,* seem to be even more effective in treating schizophrenia than the neuroleptics, without inducing the neurological side effects of the neuroleptics (Dossenbach et al., 2004). One of the most common of these drugs, *clozapine,* binds to the D4 dopamine receptor, but it also influences several other neurotransmitters, including serotonin. Clozapine has been effective with many people with schizophrenia who have never responded to the phenothiazines, and it appears to reduce the negative as well as the positive symptoms in many patients (Dossenbach et al., 2004; Spaulding et al., 2001).

Clozapine does not induce tardive dyskinesia, but it does have some side effects. These include dizziness, nausea, sedation, seizures, hypersalivation, weight gain, and irregular heartbeat. In addition, in 1 to 2 percent of the people who take clozapine, a disease called **agranulocytosis** develops. This is a deficiency of granulocytes, which are substances produced by bone marrow to fight infection. This condition can be fatal, so patients taking clozapine must be carefully monitored for the development of this disease.

Physicians often begin treatment with atypical antipsychotics developed in more recent years, such as risperidone. This drug affects serotonin receptors and is a weak blocker of dopamine receptors (Ananth et al., 2001). Risperidone is as effective as clozapine and may work more quickly than clozapine (Bondolfi et al., 1998). It has also been shown to be more effective at preventing relapse than the typical antipsychotic medications, such as haloperidol (Csernansky, Mahmoud, & Brenner, 2002). Risperidone also does not induce tardive dyskinesia, but it can cause sexual dysfunction, sedation, low blood pressure, weight gain, seizures, and problems with concentration.

Other atypical antipsychotic drugs are designed to stabilize dopamine levels across the brain, increasing dopamine where it is deficient and decreasing it where it is excessive (Stahl, 2001). Some of these drugs, including olanzapine, have been shown to decrease the symptoms of schizophrenia while inducing significantly fewer neurological side effects than either the typical antipsychotics or clozapine (Dossenbach et al., 2004; Lieberman et al., 2003).

Despite the potentially serious side effects of the drugs used to treat schizophrenia, many people with schizophrenia and their families regard these drugs as true lifesavers. These drugs have released many people with schizophrenia from lives of psychosis and isolation and have made it possible for them to pursue the everyday activities and goals that most of us take for granted.

Psychological and Social Treatments

With the availability of drugs that control the symptoms of schizophrenia, why would anyone need psychological or social interventions? As the following essay illustrates, drugs cannot completely restore the life of a person with schizophrenia (Anonymous, 1992, p. 335).

VOICES

A note about becoming "sane": Medicine did not cause sanity; it only made it possible. Sanity came through a minute-by-minute choice of outer reality, which was often without meaning, over inside reality, which was full of meaning. Sanity meant choosing reality that was not real and having faith that someday the choice would be worth the fear involved and that it would someday hold meaning.

Many individuals who are able to control the acute psychotic symptoms of schizophrenia with drugs still experience many of the negative symptoms, particularly problems in motivation and in social interactions. Psychological interventions can help them increase their social skills and reduce their isolation and immobility (Bustillo et al., 2001). These interventions can help people with schizophrenia and their families learn to reduce the stress and conflict in their lives, thereby reducing the risk for relapse into psychosis. Psychological interventions can help people with schizophrenia understand their disorder, appreciate the need to remain on their medications, and cope more effectively with the side effects of the medications. Finally, because of the severity of their disorder, many people with schizophrenia have trouble finding or holding jobs, finding enough money to feed and shelter themselves, and obtaining necessary medical or psychiatric care. Psychologists, social workers, and other mental-health professionals can assist people with schizophrenia in meeting these basic needs.

Behavioral, Cognitive, and Social Interventions

Most experts in the treatment of schizophrenia argue for a comprehensive approach that addresses the wide array of behavioral, cognitive, and social deficits in schizophrenia and is tailored to the specific deficits of each individual with schizophrenia (Liberman et al., 2002) (see Table 11.10 on page 410). These treatments are given in addition to medication and can increase everyday functioning and can significantly reduce the risk for relapse (Gumley et al., 2003; Spaulding et al., 2001).

Cognitive interventions include helping people with schizophrenia recognize demoralizing attitudes they may have toward their illness and then change those attitudes, so that they will seek help when they need it and will participate in society to the extent that they can. Behavioral interventions, based on social learning theory (see Chapter 5), include the use of operant conditioning and modeling to teach persons with schizophrenia skills such as initiating and maintaining conversations with others, asking for help or information from physicians, and persisting in an activity, such as cooking or cleaning. These interventions may be administered by the family. A therapist might teach a client's family members to ignore schizophrenic symptoms, such as bizarre comments, but to reinforce socially appropriate behavior by giving attention and positive emotional responses. In psychiatric hospitals and residential treatment centers, *token economies* are sometimes established, based on the principles of operant conditioning. Patients earn tokens, which they can exchange for privileges, such as time watching television or walks on the hospital grounds, by completing assigned duties (such as making their beds) or even just by engaging in appropriate conversations with others.

Social interventions include increasing contact between people with schizophrenia and supportive others, often through self-help support groups. These groups meet to discuss the impact of the

TABLE 11.10   Skill Areas Targeted in Comprehensive Community Treatments

These skill areas are the focus of comprehensive community interventions.

Medication Management

Obtaining information about antipsychotic medication
Knowing the correct self-administration and evaluation of medications
Identifying side effects of medication
Negotiating medication issues with health care providers
Taking long-acting medication by injection

Symptom Management

Identifying and managing warning signs of relapse
Coping with persistent symptoms
Avoiding alcohol and street drugs

Conversation Skills

Starting and maintaining a friendly conversation
Ending a conversation pleasantly

Interpersonal Problem-Solving Skills

Paying attention
Describing problems
Thinking of ideas for solutions
Evaluating solutions
Putting solutions into action

Recreation for Leisure

Identifying the benefits of recreation
Getting information about recreational activities
Evaluating and maintaining a recreational activity

Community Re-entry

Planning community re-entry
Connecting with the community
Coping with stress in the community
Planning a daily schedule
Making and keeping appointments
Solving medication problems
Identifying warning signs of relapse
Developing an emergency relapse prevention program

Source: Liberman et al., 2002.

disorder on their lives, the frustrations of trying to make people understand their disorder, their fears of relapse, their experiences with various medications, and other concerns they must live with day to day. Group members can also help each other learn social skills and problem-solving skills, such as those described in Table 11.10, by giving each other feedback on problem areas and by providing a forum in which individual members can role-play new skills. People with schizophrenia are also often directly taught problem-solving skills for common social situations (Liberman, Eckman, & Marder, 2001). For example, they may practice generating and role-playing solutions when a receptionist tells them there is no one available at a company to interview them for a potential job.

Family Therapy

Recall that communication deviance and high levels of expressed emotion within the family of a person with schizophrenia can substantially increase the risk for and frequency of relapse. This increased risk has led many researchers to examine the effectiveness of family-oriented therapies for people with schizophrenia. The successful therapies tend to combine basic education on schizophrenia with the training of family members in coping with their loved one's inappropriate behaviors and with the disorder's impact on their lives (Bustillo et al., 2001; Falloon, Brooker, & Graham-Hole, 1992; Halford & Hayes, 1991; Hogarty et al., 1991; McFarlane et al., 1995).

In the educational portion of these therapies, families are given information about the biological causes of the disorder, the symptoms of the disorder, and the medications and their side effects. The hope is that this information will reduce self-blame in the family members, increase their tolerance for the uncontrollable symptoms of the disorder, and allow them to monitor their loved one's use of medication and possible side effects. Family members are also taught good communication skills, so as to reduce harsh, conflictual interactions with their member with schizophrenia. Family members learn problem-solving skills to manage problems in the family, such as lack of money, so as to reduce the overall level of stress. They also learn specific behavioral techniques for encouraging appropriate behavior and discouraging inappropriate behavior.

These family-oriented interventions, when combined with drug therapy, appear to be more effective at reducing relapse rates than drug therapy alone. On average, approximately 24 percent of people who receive family-oriented therapy in addition to drug therapy relapse into schizophrenia, compared with 64 percent of people who receive routine drug therapy alone (Bustillo et al., 2001; Pitschel-Walz et al., 2001).

For example, Hogarty and colleagues (1986, 1991) compared the effectiveness of four types of intervention for persons with schizophrenia. The first group received medication only. The other three groups received medication plus one of the following types of psychosocial intervention: social skills training for the person with schizophrenia only, family-oriented treatment, or a combination of social skills training for the person with schizophrenia and family-oriented treatment for his or her family members. In the first year following these treatments, 40 percent of the people in the medication-only group relapsed, compared with only 20 percent in the two psychosocial intervention groups and no one in the group that received both individual social skills training and family-oriented therapy (see Figure 11.9). In the second year of follow-up, the groups that received family-oriented therapy continued to fare better than did those who received medication alone. In this study and others, however, the effects of psychosocial interventions diminished with time if the interventions were not continued. Thus, as with the medications for schizophrenia, psychosocial interventions must be ongoing to continue to reduce the chances of relapse in people with schizophrenia.

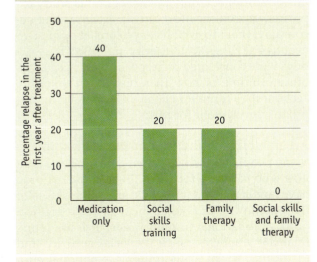

FIGURE 11.9 **Effects of Psychosocial Intervention (with Medication) on Relapse Rates.** In one study, patients with schizophrenia who received social skills training, family therapy, or both in addition to medication had much lower relapse rates in the first year after treatment than did patients who received only medication.

Source: Hogarty et al., 1986.

Some modern treatment facilities provide people with schizophrenia with comprehensive services in a positive, pleasant setting.

In some cultures, people with schizophrenia are more likely to be cared for and deeply embedded in their families than in other cultures. Lopez, Kopelowicz, and Canive (2002) argue that this makes family-oriented interventions even more critical for people from these cultures, but these interventions must be culturally sensitive. One study found that behavior therapies to increase communication actually backfired in some Hispanic families, perhaps because these families already had low levels of expressed emotion and found that the techniques suggested by therapists violated their cultural norms for how family members should interact (Telles et al., 1995). For example, some of the most traditional family members in this study expressed great discomfort during exercises that encouraged them to establish eye contact or express negative feelings to authority figures. These actions were considered disrespectful. This is just another example of how therapists must take into account the culture of clients in designing appropriate interventions for them.

Assertive Community Treatment Programs

Many people with schizophrenia do not have families who can care for them. Even those who do have families have such a wide array of needs—for the monitoring and adjustment of their medications, occupational training, assistance in getting financial resources (such as social security and Medicaid), social skills training, emotional support, and sometimes basic housing—that comprehensive community-based treatment programs are

necessary. **Assertive community treatment programs** provide comprehensive services to people with schizophrenia, using the expertise of medical professionals, social workers, and psychologists to meet the variety of patients' needs 24 hours a day.

In Chapter 5, we discussed the community mental-health movement, which was initiated by President Kennedy in the 1960s to transfer the care of people with serious mental disorders from primarily psychiatric hospitals to comprehensive community-based programs. The idea was that people with schizophrenia and other serious disorders would spend time in the hospital when their symptoms were so severe that hospitalization was necessary; however, when discharged from the hospital, they would go to community-based programs, which would help them reintegrate into society, maintain their medications, gain needed skills, and function at their highest possible levels. Hundreds of halfway houses, group homes, and therapeutic communities were established for people with serious mental disorders who needed a supportive place to live.

One classic example of this was The Lodge, a residential treatment center for people with schizophrenia established by George Fairweather and colleagues (1969). At the Lodge, mental-health professionals were available for support and assistance, but the residents were responsible for running the household and working with other residents to establish healthy behaviors and discourage inappropriate behaviors. The residents also established their own employment agency to find jobs. Follow-up studies showed that Lodge residents fared much better than people with schizophrenia who were simply discharged from the hospital into the care of their families or less intensive treatment programs (Fairweather et al., 1969). For example, Lodge residents were less likely to be rehospitalized and much more likely to hold jobs than were those in a comparison group, even after The Lodge closed.

Other comprehensive treatment programs provide skills training, vocational rehabilitation, and social support to people with schizophrenia who are living at home. Studies of these programs find that they reduce the amount of time spent in the hospital and, as a result, can be cost-effective (Bustillo et al., 2001).

In a model program established in Madison, Wisconsin, by founders of the assertive community treatment program movement (Test & Stein, 1980), mental-health professionals worked with people with schizophrenia who were also chronically disabled. These interventions were provided in the homes or communities of patients for 14 months, and then the patients were followed for another 28 months. Their progress was compared with that of another group of patients, who received standard hospital treatment for their psychotic symptoms. Both groups were treated with antipsychotic medications. The patients who received the home-based intensive skills interventions were less likely than the control-group patients to be hospitalized and more likely to be employed both during the treatment and in the 28 months of follow-up (see Figure 11.10). The home-based intervention group also showed lower levels of emotional distress and psychotic symptoms during the intervention than did the control group.

The differences in symptoms between the two groups diminished after the intervention period ended. In general, the gains that people in skills-based interventions make tend to decline once the interventions end, suggesting that these interventions need to be ongoing (Liberman, 1994). However, the benefits of these interventions can be great.

Despite the proven effectiveness of intensive treatment programs such as these, they have been few and far between. About 800 community mental-health centers are now operating in the United States, but this is only one-third of the number needed. Those that do exist tend to be understaffed, underfunded, and thus unable to provide adequate care to the people they serve.

From its beginning, the community mental-health movement was never funded to a level that could support its lofty goals. With the changes in medical insurance in recent years, funding for mental-health care for the seriously mentally ill has been even tighter. Although billions of dollars are spent on mental-health care per year in the United States, much of that money goes not to direct services to people with schizophrenia but, rather, to subsistence programs, such as social security disability income, and to community services for people with less serious mental disorders (Torrey, 1997). Much of the financial burden of caring for people with schizophrenia falls to state and local governments, which do not have the necessary financial resources, or to families, who are too often bankrupted by the cost of care.

As a result, nearly half of all people with schizophrenia receive little or no care in a given year (Regier et al., 1993; Torrey, 1997; Von Korff et al., 1985). Those who do receive care often are hospitalized only when their symptoms are acute, and then they remain in the hospital for inadequate periods of time for their symptoms to stabilize. They may be discharged with little or no follow-up. Some return to their families, but many end up in nursing homes, where they receive only custodial care, or in single-room-occupancy hotels or rooming houses, often in run-down inner-city neighbor-

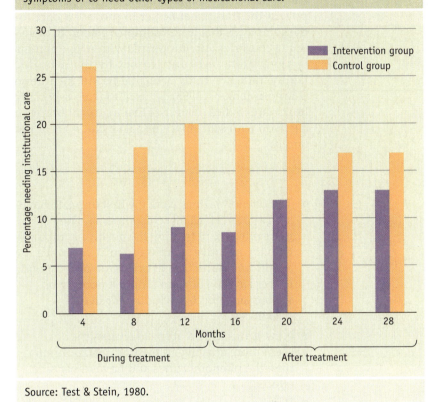

FIGURE 11.10 **Effects of Home-Based Treatment on Need for Institutional Care.** In one study, patients with schizophrenia who received intensive home-based skills training and care were much less likely to be hospitalized for psychotic symptoms or to need other types of institutional care.

Source: Test & Stein, 1980.

hoods. Many are homeless or end up in prison (Torrey, 1995).

Cross-Cultural Treatments: Traditional Healers

In developing countries and in parts of industrialized countries, the symptoms of schizophrenia are sometimes treated by folk or religious healers, according to the cultural beliefs about the meaning and causes of these symptoms. Anthropologists and cultural psychiatrists have described four models that traditional healers tend to follow in treating schizophrenic symptoms (Karno & Jenkins, 1993). According to the *structural model*, there are interrelated levels of experience, such as the body, emotion, and cognition, or the person, society, and culture, and symptoms arise when the integration of these levels is lost. Healing, thus, involves reintegrating these levels, through a change of diet or environment, the prescription of herbal medicines, or rituals.

The *social support model* holds that symptoms arise from conflictual social relationships and that healing involves mobilizing a patient's kin to support him or her through this crisis and reintegrating the patient into a positive social support network. The *persuasive model* suggests that rituals can transform the meaning of symptoms for the patient, diminishing the pain of the symptoms. Finally, in the *clinical model,* it is simply the faith that the patient puts in the traditional healer to provide a cure for the symptoms that leads to improvement. In developing countries, care for people with schizophrenia is more likely to be carried out by the extended family, rather than by a mental-health institution (Karno & Jenkins, 1993). Thus, it may be especially important in these countries that interventions with a person with schizophrenia also include his or her family.

SUMMING UP

- The phenothiazines were the first drugs to have a significant effect on schizophrenia. They are more effective in treating the positive symptoms than the negative symptoms, however, and a significant percentage of people do not respond to them at all. They can induce a number of serious side effects, including tardive dyskinesia.

- New drugs, called atypical antipsychotics, seem more effective in treating schizophrenia than the phenothiazines and have fewer side effects.

- Psychosocial therapies focus on helping people with schizophrenia and their families understand and cope with the consequences of the disorder. They also help the person with schizophrenia gain resources and integrate into the community as much as possible.

- Studies show that providing psychosocial therapy along with medication can significantly reduce the rate of relapse in schizophrenia.

- Community-based comprehensive treatment programs for people with schizophrenia have been underfunded. As a result, many people with this disorder receive little or no useful treatment.

- Traditional healers treat people with schizophrenia within the context of their cultural beliefs.

CHAPTER INTEGRATION

There is probably more consensus among mental-health professionals about the biological roots of schizophrenia than of any other psychopathology we discuss in this book. The evidence that the fundamental vulnerability to schizophrenia is a biological one is compelling, yet there is a growing consensus that psychosocial factors contribute to the risk for schizophrenia among people with the biological vulnerability. Theorists are increasingly developing models that integrate the biological and psychosocial contributors to schizophrenia to provide comprehensive explanations of the development of this disorder (see Figure 11.11).

FIGURE 11.11   **The Interaction of Biological and Psychosocial Factors in Schizophrenia**

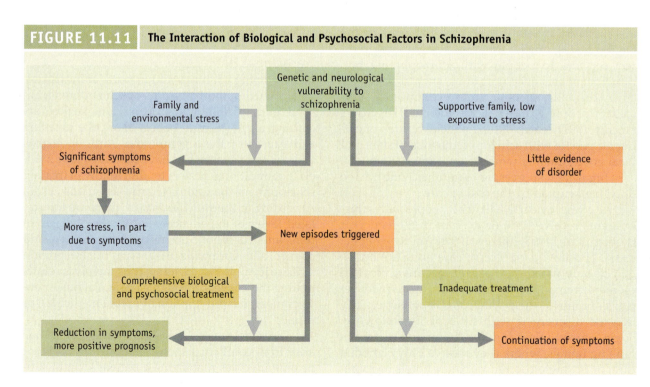

A person with a biological vulnerability to schizophrenia who is raised in a supportive, low-conflict family and who escapes exposure to major stressors may never develop the full syndrome of schizophrenia. He or she may still have mild symptoms, however, because the biological underpinnings of this disorder play such a strong role. On the other hand, a person who has a biological vulnerability and grows up in a stressful atmosphere is more likely to develop the full syndrome of the disorder. Psychosocial stress also clearly contributes to new episodes of psychosis in people with schizophrenia.

Finally, there is a widespread consensus among mental-health professionals that the most effective therapies for schizophrenia are those that address both the biological contributors and the psychosocial contributors to the disorder.

Extraordinary People: Follow-Up

When we left the story of John Nash at the beginning of this chapter, he was slowly reintegrating into the mathematics community at Princeton University. During the 1970s and 1980s, John Nash's illness gradually seemed to subside, although he was not taking any medications or receiving any other treatment. One of his colleagues, Hale Trotter, said,

> My impression was of a very gradual sort of improvement. In the early stages he was making up numbers out of names and being worried by what he found. Gradually, that went away. Then it was more mathematical numerology. Playing with formulas and factoring. It wasn't coherent math research, but it had lost its bizarre quality. Later it was real research. (Nasar, 1998, p. 350)

What accounted for the remission of his illness? Some, including the movie based on the book *A Beautiful Mind*, attribute it to the calm support of Alicia, Nash's wife. Some attribute it to the continued support of his mathematics colleagues. Nash believes he willed himself well, to some extent.

Whatever the reason, Nash was one of those lucky people with schizophrenia whose illness seems to diminish, or even subside altogether, with age. In 1994 John Nash was awarded the Nobel Prize in economics for his contributions to game theory. He and Alicia have remarried and now live in Princeton, where Nash works on his mathematical theories. Nash also helps care for their son, Johnny, who obtained his Ph.D. in mathematics several years ago and has developed paranoid schizophrenia. Although Johnny is receiving the newest treatments for schizophrenia, they help only a little, and he is frequently hospitalized.

As biographer Sylvia Nasar concludes,

The extraordinary journey of this American genius, this man who surprises people, continues. The self-deprecating humor suggests greater self-awareness. The straight-from-the-heart talk with friends about sadness, pleasure, and attachment suggests a wider range of emotional experiences. The daily effort to give others their due, and to recognize their right to ask this of him, bespeaks a very different man from the often cold and arrogant youth. And the disjunction of thought and emotion that characterized Nash's personality, not just when he was ill, but even before are much less evident today. In deed, if not always in word, Nash has come to a life in which thought and emotion are more closely entwined, where getting and giving are central, and relationships are more symmetrical. He may be less than he was intellectually, he may never achieve another breakthrough, but he has become a great deal more than he ever was—"a very fine person," as Alicia put it once. (Nasar, 1998, p. 388)

Even if you have seen the movie *A Beautiful Mind*, it's worth reading the book. Nasar's research into Nash's life is exemplary, and her account is more comprehensive than that in the movie.

Chapter Summary

- The positive (Type I) symptoms of schizophrenia include delusions (ideas the individual believes are true but are certainly false), hallucinations (unreal perceptual experiences), thought disturbances (incoherence of thought and speech), and grossly disorganized or catatonic behavior. (Review Table 11.2.)

- The negative (Type II) symptoms include affective flattening, alogia (poverty of speech), and avolition (the inability to initiate and persist in goal-directed activities). (Review Table 11.4.) Prodromal and residual symptoms are mild versions of the positive and negative symptoms that occur before and after episodes of acute symptoms.

- There are five subtypes of schizophrenia. (Review Table 11.7.) People with the paranoid subtype of schizophrenia have delusions and hallucinations with themes of persecution and grandiosity. This type of schizophrenia tends to begin later in life, and its episodes are often triggered by stress. People with this type of schizophrenia have a better prognosis than do people with other types of schizophrenia.

- The disorganized subtype of schizophrenia shows especially marked disorganization in thought and behavior and either a flattening of affect or frequent inappropriate affect. People with this subtype of schizophrenia are prone to odd, stereotyped behaviors, and their speech is often incoherent. This type of schizophrenia tends to have an early onset and a continuous course, which is often unresponsive to treatment.

- The catatonic subtype of schizophrenia is characterized by motor behaviors and ways of speaking that suggest that the person is completely unresponsive to the environment. The symptoms include motoric immobility, excessive and purposeless motor activity, extreme negativism, peculiar movements, and echolalia or echopraxia.

- People with the undifferentiated subtype of schizophrenia have symptoms that meet the criteria for schizophrenia but do not meet the criteria for paranoid, disorganized, or catatonic schizophrenia.

- People with the residual subtype of schizophrenia have had at least one episode of active symptoms but do not currently have prominent positive symptoms of schizophrenia. They continue to have mild positive symptoms and significant negative symptoms.

- Estimates of the prevalence of schizophrenia in various countries range from about 0.1 percent to 2.0 percent, but most estimates are between 0.5 and 1.0 percent. There are some slight ethnic differences in the rates of schizophrenia, but these may be due to differences in socioeconomic status.

- The content of delusions and hallucinations changes somewhat across cultures, but the form of these symptoms remains similar across cultures, and many clinicians and researchers believe that schizophrenia can be diagnosed reliably across cultures.

- Men may be more prone to schizophrenia than are women, and there are some differences in symptoms between the genders.

- Biological theories of schizophrenia have focused on genetics, structural abnormalities in the brain, and neurotransmitters. (Review Table 11.8.) There is clear evidence for a genetic transmission of schizophrenia, although genetics do not fully account for the disorder. People with schizophrenia show abnormal functioning in the prefrontal areas of the brain and the hippocampus and enlarged ventricles, suggesting atrophy in parts of the brain. Many people with schizophrenia have a history of prenatal difficulties, such as exposure to the influenza virus during the second trimester of gestation, or birth complications, including prenatal hypoxia. Dysfunction in the dopamine systems of the brain may contribute to schizophrenia.

- Stressful events probably cannot cause schizophrenia in people who do not have a vulnerability to the disorder, but they may trigger new episodes of psychosis in people with the disorder.

- Early psychodynamic theories argued that caregivers who are demanding and excessively harsh toward their children, so-called schizophrenogenic mothers, might cause the children to regress to infantile stages, resulting in schizophrenia. These theories have not been supported.

- Several theories have suggested that family communication patterns play a role in schizophrenia. The double-bind theory says that parents put their schizophrenic children in double binds by communicating mutually contradictory demands. The communication deviance theory says that parents create thought disorders in their children by communicating with them in deviant ways. Expressed-emotion theorists argue that some families of people with schizophrenia are simultaneously overprotective and hostile and that this increases the risk for relapse. Only the expressed-emotion theories have received strong empirical support.

■ Cognitive theories suggest that some schizophrenic symptoms are attempts by the individual to understand and manage cognitive deficits. Behavioral theories suggest that schizophrenic behaviors are operantly conditioned. (Review Table 11.9.)

■ Drugs known as the phenothiazines, introduced in the 1950s, bring relief to many people with schizophrenia. The phenothiazines reduce the positive symptoms of schizophrenia but often are not effective with the negative symptoms. Major side effects include tardive dyskinesia, an irreversible neurological disorder characterized by involuntary movements of the tongue, face, mouth, or jaw.

■ Newer drugs, called atypical antipsychotics, seem to induce fewer side effects and are effective in treating both the positive and the negative symptoms of schizophrenia for many people.

■ Psychological and social therapies focus on helping people with schizophrenia reduce stress, improve family interactions, learn social skills, and cope with the impact of the disorder on their lives. Comprehensive treatment programs combining drug therapy with an array of psychological and social therapies have been shown to reduce relapse significantly. These programs tend to be few and underfunded, however. (Review Table 11.10.)

■ People in developing countries tend to show a more positive course of schizophrenia than do people in developed countries. Women tend to have a more positive course than do men.

MindMap CD-ROM

The following resources on the MindMap CD-ROM that came with this text will help you to master the content of this chapter and prepare for tests:

■ Videos: Beautiful Mind: Interview with John Nash and Son; Paranoid Schizophrenia; Schizophrenia—Disorganized Type

■ Chapter Timeline

■ Chapter Quiz

Key Terms

psychosis 377

schizophrenia 377

positive symptoms 380

negative symptoms 380

delusions 381

persecutory delusion 382

delusion of reference 382

grandiose delusions 382

delusion of thought insertion 382

hallucinations 385

auditory hallucination 385

visual hallucination 385

tactile hallucinations 385

somatic hallucinations 385

formal thought disorder 385

word salad 386

smooth pursuit eye movement 386

working memory 386

catatonia 386

catatonic excitement 386

affective flattening 387

alogia 388

avolition 388

dementia praecox 389

prodromal symptoms 390

residual symptoms 390

paranoid schizophrenia 391

disorganized schizophrenia 392

catatonic schizophrenia 392

echolalia 392

echopraxia 392

undifferentiated schizophrenia 392

residual schizophrenia 392

enlarged ventricles 397

prefrontal cortex 398

perinatal hypoxia 399

dopamine 399

phenothiazines 399

mesolimbic pathway 400

atypical antipsychotics 400

social selection 402

expressed emotion 404

chlorpromazine 407

akinesia 408

akathesis 408

tardive dyskinesia 408

agranulocytosis 408

assertive community treatment programs 412

Chapter 12

The Armour
by Gayle Ray

No man can climb out beyond the limitations of his own character.

—John Morley, "Robespierre," *Critical Miscellanies* (1871–1908)

Personality Disorders <

CHAPTER OVERVIEW

Extraordinary People

■ Susanna Kaysen, *Girl, Interrupted*

Defining and Diagnosing Personality Disorders

Personality disorders are long-standing patterns of maladaptive thought, behavior, and emotions. The DSM-IV-TR organizes personality disorders into three groups based on similarities in symptoms. A number of criticisms of the DSM-IV-TR categories have been raised.

Taking Psychology Personally

■ Seeing Yourself in the Personality Disorders

Odd-Eccentric Personality Disorders

People diagnosed with the odd-eccentric personality disorders—paranoid, schizoid, and schizotypal personality disorders—have odd or eccentric patterns of behavior and thought, including paranoia, extreme social withdrawal or inappropriate social interactions, and magical or illusory thinking. This group of disorders, particularly schizotypal personality disorder, may be linked genetically to schizophrenia and may represent mild variations of schizophrenia.

Dramatic-Emotional Personality Disorders

The dramatic-emotional personality disorders include four disorders characterized by dramatic, erratic, and emotional behavior and interpersonal relationships: antisocial personality disorder, histrionic personality disorder, borderline personality disorder, and narcissistic personality disorder.

Anxious-Fearful Personality Disorders

People diagnosed with anxious-fearful personality disorders—avoidant, dependent, and obsessive-compulsive personality disorders—become extremely concerned about being criticized or abandoned by others and thus have dysfunctional relationships with others.

Alternative Conceptualizations of Personality Disorders

Several alternative conceptualizations of personality disorders have been suggested, based on theories of normal personality. One alternative views personality disorders as extreme versions of five basic personality traits.

Chapter Integration

Although empirical research is lacking for many of the personality disorders, some theorists view them as the result of the interaction between a biologically determined temperament and parenting that enhances a child's biological vulnerabilities.

Extraordinary People

Susanna Kaysen: *Girl, Interrupted*

Susanna Kaysen was 18 and depressed, drifting through life and endlessly oppositional toward her parents and teachers. She tried to commit suicide. She began having strange perceptions:

> I was having a problem with patterns. Oriental rugs, tile floors, printed curtains, things like that. Supermarkets were especially bad, because of the long, hypnotic checkerboard aisles. When I looked at these things, I saw other things within them. That sounds as though I was hallucinating, and I wasn't. I knew I was looking at a floor or a curtain. But all patterns seemed to contain potential representations, which in a dizzying array would flicker briefly to life. That could be . . . a forest, a flock of birds, my second grade class picture. Well, it wasn't—it was a rug, or whatever it was, but my glimpses of the other things it might be were exhausting. Reality was getting too dense. (Kaysen, 1993, pp. 40–41)

Kaysen went to see a psychiatrist for a routine evaluation. At the end of one session, he put her in a taxi and sent her to McLean Hospital outside Boston. When she signed herself in, she was told that her stay would be about two weeks. Instead, Kaysen was not released for nearly two years.

Years after she was released from the hospital, Kaysen discovered that her diagnosis had been borderline personality disorder. In her autobiography, *Girl, Interrupted,* she raises many questions about this disorder:

> . . . I had to locate a copy of the *Diagnostic and Statistical Manual of Mental Disorders* and look up Borderline Personality to see what they really thought about me.
>
> It's a fairly accurate picture of me at eighteen, minus a few quirks like reckless driving and eating binges. . . . I'm tempted to try refuting it, but then I would be open to the further charges of "defensiveness" and "resistance."
>
> All I can do is give the particulars: an annotated diagnosis.
>
> . . . "Instability of self-image, interpersonal relationships, and mood . . . uncertainty about . . . long-term goals or career choice. . . ." Isn't this a good description of adolescence? Moody, fickle, faddish, insecure: in short, impossible.
>
> "Self-mutilating behavior (e.g., wrist-scratching). . . ." I've skipped forward a bit. This is the one that caught me by surprise as I sat on the floor of the bookstore reading my diagnosis. Wrist-scratching! I thought I'd invented it. Wrist-banging, to be precise. . . .
>
> I had a butterfly chair. In the sixties, everyone in Cambridge had a butterfly chair. The metal edge of its upturned seat was perfectly placed for wrist-banging. I had tried breaking ashtrays and walking on the shards, but I didn't have the nerve to tread firmly. Wrist-banging—slow, steady, mindless—was a better solution. It was cumulative injury, so each bang was tolerable. . . .
>
> I spent hours in my butterfly chair banging my wrist. I did it in the evenings, like homework. I'd do some homework, then I'd spend half an hour wrist-banging, then finish my homework, then back in the chair for some more banging before brushing my teeth and going to bed.
>
> I was trying to explain my situation to myself. My situation was that I was in pain and nobody knew it; even I had trouble knowing it. So I told myself, over and over, You are in pain. It was the only way I could get through to myself ("counteract feelings of 'numbness'"). I was demonstrating, externally and irrefutably, an inward condition. . . .

"The person often experiences this instability of self-image as chronic feelings of emptiness or boredom." My chronic feelings of emptiness and boredom came from the fact that I was living a life based on my incapacities, which were numerous. A partial list follows. I could not and did not want to: ski, play tennis, or go to gym class; attend to any subject in school other than English and biology; write papers on any assigned topics (I wrote poems instead of papers for English; I got Fs); plan to go or apply to college; give any reasonable explanation for these refusals.

My self-image was not unstable. I saw myself, quite correctly, as unfit for the educational and social systems. But my parents and teachers did not share my self-image. Their image of me was unstable, since it was out of kilter with reality and based on their needs and wishes. They did not put much value on my capacities, which were admittedly few, but genuine. I read everything, I wrote constantly, and I had boyfriends by the barrelful. . . .

I often ask myself if I'm crazy. I ask other people too. "Is this a crazy thing to say?" I'll ask before saying something that probably isn't crazy.

I start a lot of sentences with "Maybe I'm totally nuts," or "Maybe I've gone 'round the bend." If I do something out of the ordinary—take two baths in one day, for example—I say to myself: "Are you crazy?" (Kaysen, 1993, pp. 150–159)

Was Susanna Kaysen just a mixed-up adolescent, with parents who expected too much of her and locked her away when she didn't comply? Or was she a deeply troubled young woman, whose stay in the hospital prevented her complete psychological deterioration? Is the diagnosis of borderline personality disorder a valid psychological disorder, or is it a label we give to people who don't conform? Kaysen's *Girl, Interrupted* (which was made into a motion picture starring Winona Ryder) brings life to the enduring debates about the validity and ethics of the diagnosis of borderline personality disorder.

Personality is all the ways we have of acting, thinking, believing, and feeling that make each of us unique. A *personality trait* is a complex pattern of behavior, thought, and feeling that is stable across time and across many situations.

DEFINING AND DIAGNOSING PERSONALITY DISORDERS

A **personality disorder** is a long-standing pattern of maladaptive behaviors, thoughts, and feelings. To be diagnosed with a personality disorder, an adult must have shown these symptoms since adolescence or early adulthood. The personality disorders are highly controversial in modern clinical psychology because of problems theorists see in the current conceptualization of these disorders and their assessment.

The DSM-IV-TR calls special attention to personality disorders and treats them as different from the acute disorders, such as major depres-

sion and schizophrenia, by placing the personality disorders on Axis II of the diagnostic system, instead of on Axis I with the acute disorders (see Chapter 4). People diagnosed with a personality disorder often experience one of the acute disorders, such as major depression or substance abuse, at sometime in their lives (Grant et al., 2004). Indeed, these acute disorders are often what bring them to the attention of clinicians. People diagnosed with personality disorders tend not to seek therapy until they experience a bout of major depression or until their substance abuse lands them in jail or the hospital, because they often do not see the behaviors that constitute their personality disorder as maladaptive. In addition, they often have serious problems relating to other people, and these relationship problems may bring them into therapy.

The DSM-IV-TR groups personality disorders into three clusters (see the DSM-IV-TR information in Table 12.1 on page 424). *Cluster A* includes three

TABLE 12.1 DSM-IV-TR

Personality Disorders

The DSM-IV-TR groups personality disorders into three clusters.

Cluster A: Odd-Eccentric Personality Disorders

People with these disorders have symptoms similar to those of people with schizophrenia, including inappropriate or flat affect, odd thought and speech patterns, and paranoia. People with these disorders maintain their grasp on reality, however.

Cluster B: Dramatic-Emotional Personality Disorders

People with these disorders tend to be manipulative, volatile, and uncaring in social relationships. They are prone to impulsive, sometimes violent behaviors that show little regard for their own safety or the safety or needs of others.

Cluster C: Anxious-Fearful Personality Disorders

People with these disorders are extremely concerned about being criticized or abandoned by others and, thus, have dysfunctional relationships with others.

Source: Reprinted with permission from the *Diagnostic and Statistical Manual of Mental Disorders,* Fourth Edition, Text Revision. Copyright © 2000 American Psychiatric Association.

disorders characterized by *odd or eccentric behaviors and thinking:* paranoid personality disorder, schizoid personality disorder, and schizotypal personality disorder. Each of these disorders has some of the features of schizophrenia, but people diagnosed with these personality disorders are not psychotic. Their behaviors are simply odd and often inappropriate. For example, they may be chronically suspicious of others or speak in odd ways that are difficult to understand.

Cluster B includes four disorders characterized by *dramatic, erratic, and emotional behavior and interpersonal relationships:* antisocial personality disorder, histrionic personality disorder, borderline personality disorder, and narcissistic personality disorder. People diagnosed with these disorders tend to be manipulative, volatile, and uncaring in social relationships and prone to impulsive behaviors. They may behave in wild and exaggerated ways or even engage in suicidal attempts to try to gain attention.

Cluster C includes three disorders characterized by *anxious and fearful emotions and chronic self-doubt:* dependent personality disorder, avoidant personality disorder, and obsessive-compulsive personality disorder. People diagnosed with these disorders have little self-confidence and difficult relationships with others.

Some of the symptoms just described may sound very familiar. Indeed, the personality disor-

ders are some of the easiest to see in yourself and your family members. The criteria for diagnosing personality disorders are more vague than the criteria for many of the other, more acute disorders and thus leave more room for misapplication (Costa & Widiger, 2002). For example, one of the symptoms of dependent personality disorder is "difficulty expressing disagreement with others because of fear of loss of support or approval." Most of us can probably see signs of this tendency in ourselves or in someone close to us. In *Taking Psychology Personally: Seeing Yourself in the Personality Disorders,* we discuss the problems with diagnosing oneself with the personality disorders.

Problems with the DSM Categories

Many theorists have raised objections to the DSM-IV-TR conceptualization and organization of the personality disorders (see Trull & Durrett, 2005). First, the DSM-IV-TR treats these disorders as categories. That is, each disorder is described as if it represents something qualitatively different from a "normal" personality, yet there is substantial evidence that several of the disorders recognized by the DSM-IV-TR represent the extreme versions of normal personality traits (Widiger, Costa, & McCrae, 2002). Later, we will

Taking Psychology Personally

Seeing Yourself in the Personality Disorders

In Chapter 1, we discussed the tendency for students reading an abnormal psychology textbook to see signs of many mental disorders in themselves or in the people in their lives. Students may be especially prone to see personality disorders in themselves or in others. Indeed, people are considerably more likely to diagnose themselves on self-report questionnaires as having a personality disorder than are clinicians to diagnose them in the context of psychiatric interviews (Weissman, 1993).

Why might this be so? It may occur because people tend to attribute behaviors to personality traits and to ignore the influence of situations on those behaviors (see Ross & Nisbett, 1991). This tendency is often referred to as *fundamental attribution error.*

A classic study demonstrating how strongly people discount situational influences over personality influences was conducted by Jones and Harris (1967). They asked participants to read essays presumably written by other participants. The participants were told that the persons writing the essays had been assigned to present a particular viewpoint on the topic of the essay. For example, they were told that a political science student had been assigned to write an essay defending communism in Cuba or that a debate student had been assigned to attack the proposition that marijuana should be legalized. Despite the fact that the participants were told that the essay writers had been assigned to take a particular viewpoint (and had not chosen that viewpoint), they tended to believe that the essay writers actually held the viewpoint they presented in their essays.

If you think you see signs of one or more personality disorders in yourself or someone close to you, stop and ask yourself the following questions:

■ *What are the situational influences that might be driving my behavior or my friend's or relative's behavior?* For example, let's say that you are concerned that your brother has developed an obsessive-compulsive personality disorder (see pp. 451–452) since he has taken on two jobs to try to help your family with finances. He is preoccupied with schedules and always has lists of things to do; he has become a workaholic; he has become a perfectionist to the point of not being able to get things done; and he has become even more moralistic than he was in high school.

It is true that certain situations can exaggerate the already dysfunctional behaviors of people with obsessive-

compulsive personality disorder. However, consider the possibility that your brother's behaviors, particularly the ones that he has developed since taking these two jobs, are largely driven by the demands of his life rather than by enduring personality traits. Your brother's preoccupation with lists and schedules and his working 20 hours a day are probably behaviors that he believes are necessary, given the demands of the situation. This kind of pressure can cause many people to try to be perfectionists but to become so anxious about the possibility of failing that they cannot do their work. When you find yourself wondering if you or someone you care about has developed a personality disorder, stop to consider the aspects of the situation that might really be responsible for the behaviors you observe.

■ *Am I selectively remembering behaviors that are signs of a personality disorder and selectively forgetting behaviors that contradict the diagnosis of a personality disorder?* One of the strongest reasons people overestimate the influence of personality traits on behaviors is that they selectively pay attention to and remember behaviors that are consistent with personality traits and ignore or forget behaviors that are inconsistent with the traits. For example, if you fear that you are an overly dependent person, you will probably find it quite easy to remember times in the past when you have had trouble making decisions without much advice from others, have felt uncomfortable and helpless when alone, or have been passive in voicing your opinions or needs to others. You will probably forget the many more times when you made decisions with no help from others, actually enjoyed being alone, or spoke up to express your opinions or needs.

It can be helpful to write down all the times in the recent or distant past when you behaved in ways that contradicted the troubling personality trait you think you have. Or you might want to ask a trusted friend to help you sort out whether your behaviors are always consistent with a negative personality trait.

■ *Are the behaviors I am observing part of a longtime pattern of behavior, or do they occur only occasionally?* Most of us occasionally act in dysfunctional or plainly stupid ways. Sometimes, these actions are driven by the situations in which we find ourselves, but sometimes we act in stupid ways even when there is no apparent situational excuse for doing so. A personality disorder is a pattern of behavior that has existed most of a person's life and that the person demonstrates across a range of situations.

(continued)

Taking Psychology Personally (*continued*)

Occasional lapses into dysfunctional behavior do not constitute a personality disorder.

■ *Are the behaviors I am observing significantly impairing or causing distress in my life or the lives of other people?* In order to qualify as a personality disorder, a set of behaviors has to cause significant distress or impairment in a person's life. We all have our quirks, our tendencies to act in ways we wish we would not. It can be helpful to examine these behaviors and make attempts to change them if they are not in line with our values or if they

occasionally get us into trouble. However, most quirks are relatively benign.

As always, if you are quite concerned about whether you or someone you care about has a significant psychological problem, it can be helpful to talk it out with a professional mental-health specialist who is trained to differentiate between psychological disorders and variations in people's behaviors that are not dangerous or unhealthy.

discuss proposals to replace the categorical organization of the personality disorders with one that characterizes them as extreme versions of normal personality traits.

Second, there is a great deal of overlap in the diagnostic criteria for the various personality disorders in the DSM-IV-TR. The majority of people who are diagnosed with one disorder tend to meet the diagnostic criteria for at least one more personality disorder. This overlap suggests that there actually may be fewer personality disorders that adequately account for the variation in personality disorder symptoms. The overlap also makes it very difficult to obtain reliable diagnoses of the personality disorders.

Third, diagnosing a personality disorder often requires information that is hard for a clinician to obtain. For example, the clinician may need accurate information about how an individual treats other people, information about how an individual behaves in a wide variety of situations, or information about how stable an individual's behaviors have been since childhood or adolescence. Again, this difficulty makes it hard to obtain reliable diagnoses of the personality disorders.

Fourth, the personality disorders are conceptualized as stable characteristics of an individual. Longitudinal studies have found, however, that people diagnosed with these disorders vary over time in how many symptoms they exhibit and the severity of these symptoms, so that they go in and out of the diagnosis over time (Shea et al., 2002). In particular, people often look as if they have a personality disorder when they are suffering from an acute Axis I disorder, such as major depression, but then their personality disorder symptoms seem to diminish when their Axis I disorder symptoms subside.

These problems make it difficult for clinicians to be confident of diagnoses of personality disorders. Indeed, the diagnostic reliability of the personality disorders is only fair (Trull & Durrett, 2005; Zanarini et al., 2000). The problems also make it difficult to do research on personality disorders. There is much less research on the epidemiology, causes, and treatment of the personality disorders than there is on most of the other disorders described in this book.

Gender and Ethnic Biases in Construction and Application

We will see throughout this chapter that there are differences in the frequency with which men and women are diagnosed with certain personality disorders, as well as some differences in the frequency with which different ethnic groups are diagnosed. One of the greatest controversies in the literature on personality disorders concerns claims that these apparent differences actually result from biases in the construction of these disorders in the DSM-IV-TR or in clinicians' applications of the diagnostic criteria (Cale & Lilienfeld, 2002; Hartung & Widiger, 1998; Widiger, 1998).

First, some theorists have argued that the diagnoses of histrionic, dependent, and borderline personality disorders, which are characterized by flamboyant behavior, emotionality, and dependence on others, are simply extreme versions of negative stereotypes of women's personalities (Kaplan, 1983; Sprock, 2000; Walker, 1994). For this reason, clinicians may sometimes be too quick to see these characteristics in women clients and to apply these diagnoses. It has also been argued that the diagnostic criteria for antisocial, paranoid, and obsessive-compulsive personality disorders, which are characterized by violent, hostile, and controlling behaviors, represent extremes of negative stereotypes of men. Clinicians may be biased to overapply these diagnoses to men but not to women (Sprock, Blashfield, & Smith, 1990). Similarly, clinicians may be biased to overapply diagnoses of antisocial and paranoid personality disorder to African Americans because they selectively perceive violence and hostility in African American clients (Iwamasa, Larrabee, & Merritt, 2000).

Another way that the DSM-IV-TR constructions of personality disorders may be biased is in not recognizing that the expressions of the symptoms of a disorder may naturally vary between groups. For example, the diagnostic criteria for antisocial personality disorder emphasize overt signs of callous and cruel antisocial behavior, including committing crimes against property and people. Women with antisocial personality disorder may be less likely than men with the disorder to engage in such overt antisocial behaviors, because of greater social sanc-

tions against women for doing so. Instead, women with antisocial personality disorder may find more subtle or covert ways of being antisocial, such as acting cruelly toward their children or covertly sabotaging people at work (Cale & Lilienfeld, 2002). As we will see when we discuss childhood disorders in Chapter 13, the same argument has been made about possible gender differences in the expression of a childhood precursor to antisocial personality disorder, conduct disorder. It may also be that certain ethnic groups, such as European Americans, are better able to hide their symptoms of callous and cruel behavior, because they hold more social power and can exercise these tendencies in ways that are deemed acceptable in the majority culture (e.g., being ruthless in business deals).

Similarly, some theorists have argued that the DSM-IV-TR ignores or downplays possible masculine ways of expressing dependent, histrionic, and borderline personality disorders, and this bias contributes to an underdiagnosis of these disorders in men (see Widiger et al., 1995). For example, one of the criteria for histrionic personality disorder is

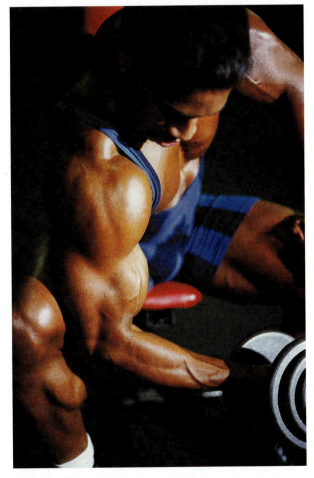

Women and men may exhibit flamboyant and self-aggrandizing behavior in different ways.

"consistently uses physical appearance to draw attention to the self" (APA, 2000). Although the DSM-IV-TR notes that men may express this characteristic by acting "macho" and bragging about their athletic skills, the wording of the criterion brings to mind everyday behaviors more common among women, such as wearing makeup.

Even if the DSM-IV-TR criteria for personality disorders are not biased in their construction, they may be biased in their application. Clinicians may be too quick to see histrionic, dependent, and borderline personality disorders in women or antisocial personality disorder in men. Several studies have shown that, when clinicians are presented with the description of a person who exhibits many of the symptoms of one of these disorders—say, a histrionic personality disorder—they are more likely to make that diagnosis if the person is described as a female than if the person is described as a male (Widiger, 1998). It is important to note that these studies did not suggest that the DSM-IV-TR criteria are themselves gender-biased—only that clinicians seem to be misapplying the DSM-IV-TR according to gender stereotypes.

In response to these concerns about the biased application of the criteria for personality disorders, Widiger (1998) argues that structured interviews, rather than unstructured interviews, should be used in assessing personality disorders. The idea is that the use of structured interviews would increase the chances that the DSM-IV-TR criteria would be applied systematically and fairly to men and women and to people of different ethnic groups. Studies that have used structured interviews tend to show less gender bias in clinicians' applications of the DSM-IV-TR personality disorder criteria than do studies that have used unstructured interviews. However, the structured interviews still yield greater numbers of women than men being diagnosed with histrionic, dependent, and borderline personality disorder and more men than women being diagnosed with antisocial personality disorder (e.g., Kessler et al., 1994). Studies that have compared the impact of structured clinical interviews with that of self-report instruments on the distribution of personality disorder diagnoses among ethnic groups have found that the two methods of assessment produce similar results (Chavira et al., 2003). These results suggest that it is not just clinicians' bias in applying the DSM-IV-TR criteria that leads to gender and ethnic differences in the apparent prevalence of the disorder.

Other theorists have argued that the DSM-IV-TR criteria should be balanced to include equal numbers of symptoms and diagnoses that are pathological variants of masculine and feminine personality traits (Frances, First, & Pincus, 1995; Kaplan, 1983; Walker, 1994). Indeed, the authors of the DSM-IV-TR attempted to include more masculine variations of symptoms thought to be more common in women (e.g., masculine forms of dependency) and more feminine versions of stereotypical masculine symptoms (e.g., feminine forms of antisocial behavior). Some theorists argue the DSM-IV-TR did not go far enough and that the next edition of the DSM should strive for even greater balance in pathologizing men and women. However, others argue that, just because it would be possible to construct a set of diagnostic criteria that yields equal numbers of men and women with each personality disorder, or equal numbers of people in different ethnic groups with each disorder, it does not mean that these criteria reflect the true structure and distribution of personality disorders in people.

ODD-ECCENTRIC PERSONALITY DISORDERS

People diagnosed with the **odd-eccentric personality disorders** (see the Concept Overview in Table 12.2) behave in ways that are similar to the behaviors of people with schizophrenia or paranoid psychotic disorder, but they retain their grasp on reality to a greater degree than do people who are psychotic. That is, they may be paranoid, speak in odd and eccentric ways that make them difficult to understand, have difficulty relating to other people, and have unusual beliefs or perceptual experiences that fall short of delusions and hallucinations. Some researchers consider this group of personality disorders to be part of the "schizophrenia spectrum" (see Nigg & Goldsmith, 1994). That is, these disorders may be precursors to schizophrenia in some people or may be milder versions of schizophrenia. These disorders often occur in people who have first-degree relatives with schizophrenia.

Paranoid Personality Disorder

The defining feature of **paranoid personality disorder** is a pervasive and unwarranted mistrust of others. People diagnosed with this disorder deeply believe that other people are chronically trying to deceive them or to exploit them and are preoccupied with concerns about the loyalty and trustworthiness of others. They are hypervigilant for confirming evidence of their suspicions. They are often penetrating observers of situations, noting details that most other people miss. For example, they notice a slight grimace on the face of their boss or an apparently trivial slip of the tongue by

TABLE 12.2 Concept Overview

Odd-Eccentric Personality Disorders

People with an odd-eccentric personality disorder may exhibit mild signs of schizophrenia.

Label	Key Features	Relationship to Schizophrenia
Paranoid personality disorder	Chronic and pervasive mistrust and suspicion of other people that is unwarranted and maladaptive	Weak relationship
Schizoid personality disorder	Chronic lack of interest in and avoidance of interpersonal relationships, emotional coldness toward others	Unclear relationship
Schizotypal personality disorder	Chronic pattern of inhibited or inappropriate emotion and social behavior, aberrant cognitions, disorganized speech	Strong relationship—considered a mild version of schizophrenia

Source: Reprinted with permission from the *Diagnostic and Statistical Manual of Mental Disorders*, Fourth Edition, Text Revision. Copyright © 2000 American Psychiatric Association.

their spouse, when these would have gone unnoticed by everyone else. Moreover, people diagnosed with paranoid personality disorder consider these events highly meaningful and spend a great deal of time trying to decipher these clues about other people's true intentions. They are also overly sensitive to criticism or potential criticism.

People with paranoid personality disorder tend to misinterpret or overinterpret situations in line with their suspicions. For example, a husband might interpret his wife's cheerfulness one evening as evidence that she is having an affair with a man at work. They are resistant to rational arguments against their suspicions and may take the fact that another person is arguing with them as evidence that this person is part of the conspiracy against them. Some become withdrawn from others in an attempt to protect themselves, but others are aggressive and arrogant, sure that their way of looking at the world is right and superior and that the best defense against the conspiring of others is a good offense. In the following case study, Felix is diagnosed with paranoid personality disorder.

CASE STUDY

Felix is a 59-year-old construction worker who worries that his coworkers might hurt him. Last week, while he was using a table saw, Felix's hand slipped and his fingers came very close to being cut badly. Felix wonders if someone sabotaged the saw, so that somehow the piece of wood he was working with slipped and drew his hand into the saw blade. Since this incident, Felix has observed his coworkers looking at him and whispering to each other. He mentioned his suspicion that the saw had been tampered with to his boss, but the boss told him that was a crazy idea and that Felix obviously had just been careless.

Felix does not have any close friends. Even his brothers and sisters avoid him, because he frequently misinterprets things they say to be criticisms of him. Felix was married for a few years, but his wife left him when he began to demand that she not see any of her friends or go out without him, because he suspected she was having affairs with other men. Felix lives in a middle-class neighborhood in a small town that has very little crime. Still, he owns three handguns and a shotgun, which are always loaded, in expectation of someone breaking into his house.

Prevalence and Prognosis of Paranoid Personality Disorder

Epidemiological studies suggest that between 0.5 and 5.6 percent of people in the general population can be diagnosed with paranoid personality disorder (Bernstein, Useda, & Siever, 1995; Ekselius et al., 2001). Among people treated for the disorder, males outnumber females three to one (Fabrega et al.,

Garfield® by Jim Davis

1991). People diagnosed with paranoid personality disorder appear to be at increased risk for a number of acute psychological problems, including major depression, anxiety disorders, substance abuse, and psychotic episodes (Bernstein et al., 1995; Grant et al., 2004). Not surprisingly, their interpersonal relationships, including intimate ones, tend to be unstable. Retrospective studies suggest that their prognosis is generally poor, with their symptoms intensifying under stress.

Theories and Treatment of Paranoid Personality Disorder

Some family history studies have shown that paranoid personality disorder is somewhat more common in the families of people with schizophrenia than in the families of healthy control subjects. This finding suggests that paranoid personality disorder may be part of the schizophrenic spectrum of disorders (Chang et al., 2002; Kendler et al., 1994; Nigg & Goldsmith, 1994). Twin and adoption studies have not been done to tease apart genetic influences and environmental influences on the development of this disorder.

Cognitive theorists see paranoid personality disorder as the result of an underlying belief that other people are malevolent and deceptive, combined with a lack of self-confidence about being able to defend oneself against others (Beck & Freeman, 1990; Colby, 1981). Thus, the person must always be vigilant for signs of others' deceit or criticism and must be quick to act against others. A study of 17 patients diagnosed with paranoid personality disorder found that they endorsed beliefs as predicted by this cognitive theory more than did patients diagnosed with other personality disorders (Beck et al., 2001).

People diagnosed with paranoid personality disorder usually come into contact with clinicians only when they are in crisis. They may seek treatment for severe symptoms of depression or anxiety but often do not feel a need for treatment of their paranoia. In addition, therapists' attempts to challenge their paranoid thinking are likely to be misinterpreted in line with their paranoid belief systems. For example, a man with paranoid personality disorder may believe his wife paid his therapist to convince him that the wife is not having an affair. For this reason, it can be quite difficult to treat paranoid personality disorder (Millon et al., 2000).

In order to gain the trust of a person diagnosed with a paranoid personality disorder, the therapist must be calm, respectful, and extremely straightforward (Siever & Kendler, 1985). The therapist must behave in a highly professional manner at all times, not attempting to engender a warm, personal relationship with the client that might be misinterpreted. The therapist cannot directly confront the client's paranoid thinking but must rely on more indirect means of raising questions in the client's mind about his or her typical way of interpreting situations. Although many therapists do not expect paranoid clients to achieve full insight into their problems, they hope that, by developing at least some degree of trust in the therapist, the client can learn to trust others a bit more and thereby develop somewhat improved interpersonal relationships.

Cognitive therapy for people diagnosed with this disorder focuses on increasing their sense of self-efficacy for dealing with difficult situations, thus decreasing their fear and hostility toward others. As an example, consider the following interchange between a cognitive therapist and a woman named Ann, who believed that her coworkers were intentionally trying to annoy her and to turn her supervisor against her (Beck & Freeman, 1990, pp. 111–112):

VOICES

Therapist: You're reacting as though this is a very dangerous situation. What are the risks you see?

Ann: They'll keep dropping things and making noise to annoy me.

Therapist: Are you sure nothing worse is at risk?

Ann: Yeah.

Therapist: So you don't think there's much chance of them attacking you or anything?

Ann: Nah, they wouldn't do that.

Therapist: If they do keep dropping things and making noises, how bad will that be?

Ann: Like I told you, it's real aggravating. It really bugs me.

Therapist: So it would continue pretty much as it's been going for years now.

Ann: Yeah. It bugs me, but I can take it.

Therapist: And you know that if it keeps happening, at the very least you can keep handling it the way you have been—holding the aggravation in, then taking it out on your husband when you get home. Suppose we could come up with some ways to handle the aggravation even better or to have them get to you less. Is that something you'd be interested in?

Ann: Yeah, that sounds good.

Therapist: Another risk you mentioned earlier is that they might talk to your supervisor and turn her against you. As you see it, how long have they been trying to do this?

Ann: Ever since I've been there.

Therapist: How much luck have they had so far in doing that?

Ann: Not much.

Therapist: Do you see any indications that they're going to have any more success now than they have so far?

Ann: No, I don't guess so.

Therapist: So your gut reaction is as though the situation at work is really dangerous. But when you stop and think it through, you conclude that the worst they're going to do is to be really aggravating, and that even if we don't come up with anything new, you can handle it well enough to get by. Does that sound right?

Ann: [Smiling] Yeah, I guess so.

Therapist: And if we can come up with some ways to handle the stress better or handle them better, there will be even less they can do to you.

In this interchange, the therapist did not directly challenge Ann's beliefs about her coworkers' intentions but did try to reduce the sense of danger Ann felt about her workplace by helping her redefine the situation as aggravating rather than threatening. The therapist also enlisted Ann in an effort to develop new coping skills that might further reduce her aggravation.

Schizoid Personality Disorder

People diagnosed with **schizoid personality disorder** lack the desire to form interpersonal relationships and are emotionally cold in interactions with others. Other people describe them as aloof, reclusive, and detached or as dull, uninteresting, and humorless. People diagnosed with this disorder show little emotion in interpersonal interactions. They view relationships with others as unrewarding, messy, and intrusive. The man described next shows several of these symptoms (adapted from Spitzer et al., 1981, p. 209):

CASE STUDY

The patient is a 50-year-old retired police officer who is seeking treatment a few weeks after his dog was run over and died. Since that time he has felt sad, tired, and has had trouble sleeping and concentrating. The patient lives alone and has for many years had virtually no conversational contacts with other human beings beyond a "Hello" or "How are you?" He prefers to be by himself, finds talk a waste of time, and feels awkward when other people try to initiate a relationship. He occasionally spends some time in a bar but always off by himself and not really following the general

(continued)

conversation. He reads newspapers avidly and is well informed in many areas but takes no particular interest in the people around him. He is employed as a security guard but is known by his fellow workers as a "cold fish" and a "loner." They no longer even notice or tease him, especially since he never seems to notice or care about their teasing anyway.

The patient floats through life without relationships. His only companion was his dog, whom he dearly loved. At Christmas he bought the dog elaborate gifts and gave himself a wrapped bottle of scotch as if it were a gift from the dog. He believes that dogs are more sensitive and loving than people, and he can express toward them a tenderness and emotion not possible in his relationships with people. The loss of his pets are the only events in his life that have caused him sadness. He experienced the death of his parents without emotion and feels no regret at being completely out of contact with the rest of his family. He considers himself different from other people and regards emotionality in others with bewilderment.

This man would be diagnosed with schizoid personality disorder because of his long-standing avoidance of relationships with other people and his lack of emotions or emotional understanding. As is often the case with people diagnosed with

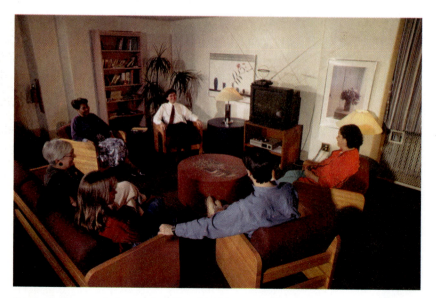

Group therapy can help people with schizoid personality disorder increase their social skills.

personality disorders, he seeks the help of a clinician only when a crisis occurs.

Prevalence of Schizoid Personality Disorder

Schizoid personality disorder is quite rare, with about 0.4 to 1.7 percent of adults manifesting the disorder at sometime in their lives (Ekselius et al., 2001; Weissman, 1993). Among people seeking treatment for this disorder, males outnumber females about three to one (Fabrega et al., 1991). They can function in society, particularly in occupations that do not require interpersonal interactions.

Theories and Treatment of Schizoid Personality Disorder

There is a slightly increased rate of schizoid personality disorder in the relatives of persons with schizophrenia, but the link between the two disorders is not clear (Kendler, Neale, Kessler, Heath, & Eaves, 1993; Nigg & Goldsmith, 1994). Twin studies of the personality traits associated with schizoid personality disorder, such as low sociability and low warmth, strongly suggest that these personality traits may be partially inherited (Costa & Widiger, 2002). This evidence for the heritability of schizoid personality disorder is only indirect, however.

Psychosocial treatments for schizoid personality disorder focus on increasing the person's social skills, social contacts, and awareness of his or her own feelings (Beck & Freeman, 1990; Quality Assurance Project, 1990). The therapist may model the expression of feelings for the client and help the client identify and express his or her own feelings. Social skills training, done through role-plays with the therapist and through homework assignments in which the client tries out new social skills with other people, is an important component of cognitive therapies. Some therapists recommend group therapy for people with schizoid personality disorder. In the context of group sessions, the group members can model interpersonal relationships and the person with schizoid personality disorder can practice new social skills directly with others.

Schizotypal Personality Disorder

Like people diagnosed with schizoid personality disorder, people diagnosed with **schizotypal personality disorder** tend to be socially isolated, to have a restricted range of emotions, and to be uncomfortable in interpersonal interactions. As children, people who develop schizotypal personality disorder are passive, socially unengaged, and hypersensitive to criticism (Olin et al., 1999).

The distinguishing characteristics of schizotypal personality disorder are its oddities in cognition, which generally fall into four categories (Beck & Freeman, 1990). The first is *paranoia or suspiciousness.* People diagnosed with schizotypal personality disorder perceive other people as deceitful and hostile, and much of their social anxiety emerges from this paranoia. The second category is *ideas of reference.* People diagnosed with schizotypal personality disorder tend to believe that random events or circumstances are related to them. For example, they may think it is highly significant that a fire has occurred in a store in which they shopped only yesterday. The third type of odd cognition is *odd beliefs* and *magical thinking.* For example, they may believe that others know what they are thinking. The fourth category of odd thought consists of *illusions* that are just short of hallucinations. For example, they may think they see people in the patterns of wallpaper.

In addition to having these oddities of thought, people diagnosed with schizotypal personality disorder tend to have speech that is tangential, circumstantial, vague, or overelaborate. In interactions with others, they may have inappropriate or no emotional responses to what other people say or do. Their behaviors are also odd, sometimes reflecting their odd thoughts. They may be easily distracted or fixate on an object for long periods of time, lost in thought or fantasy. On neuropsychological tests (see Chapter 4), people with schizotypal personality disorder show deficits in working memory, learning, and recall that are similar to those shown by people with schizophrenia (Barch, 2005).

Although the quality of these oddities of thought, speech, and behavior is similar to that in schizophrenia, it is not as severe as in schizophrenia, and people diagnosed with schizotypal personality disorder maintain basic contact with reality. The woman in the following case study shows many of the oddities of schizotypal personality disorder (adapted from Spitzer et al., 1981, pp. 95–96).

The patient is a 32-year-old unmarried, unemployed woman on welfare who complains that she feels "spacey." Her feelings of detachment have gradually become stronger and more uncomfortable. For many hours each day she feels as if she were watching herself move through life, and the world around her seems unreal. She feels especially strange when she looks into a mirror. For many years she has felt able to read people's minds by a "kind of clairvoyance I don't understand." According to her, several people in her family apparently also have this ability. She is preoccupied by the thought that she has some special mission in life but is not sure what it is; she is not particularly religious. She is very self-conscious in public, often feels that people are paying special attention to her, and sometimes thinks that strangers cross the street to avoid her. She is lonely and isolated and spends much of each day lost in fantasies or watching TV soap operas. She speaks in a vague, abstract, digressive manner, generally just missing the point, but she is never incoherent. She seems shy, suspicious, and afraid she will be criticized. She has no gross loss of contact with reality, such as hallucinations or delusions, and she has never been treated for emotional problems. She has had occasional jobs but drifts away from them because of lack of interest.

Prevalence of Schizotypal Personality Disorder

Between 0.6 and 5.2 percent of people will be diagnosed with schizotypal personality disorder at sometime in their lives (Ekselius et al., 2001; Weissman, 1993). Among people seeking treatment, it is over twice as commonly diagnosed in males as in females (Fabrega et al., 1991). As with the other odd-eccentric personality disorders, people diagnosed with schizotypal personality disorder are at an increased risk for depression and for schizophrenia or isolated psychotic episodes (Siever, Bernstein, & Silverman, 1995).

For a person to be given a diagnosis of schizotypal personality disorder, his or her odd or eccentric thoughts cannot be part of cultural beliefs, such as a cultural belief in magic or specific superstitions. Still, some psychologists have argued that people of color are more often diagnosed with schizophrenic-like disorders, such as schizotypal personality disorder, than are Whites, because White clinicians often misinterpret culturally bound beliefs as evidence of schizotypal thinking (Snowden & Cheung, 1990).

One large study of people in treatment found that the African American patients were more likely than the Caucasian or Hispanic patients to be diagnosed with schizotypal personality disorder on both self-report and standardized diagnostic interviews (Chavira et al., 2003). This finding suggests that African Americans may be diagnosed with this disorder relatively frequently, even when steps are taken to avoid clinician bias. It is possible that African Americans are more likely to be exposed to conditions that enhance a biological vulnerability to schizophrenia-like disorders. Such conditions include perinatal brain damage, urban living, and low socioeconomic status (see Chapter 11 for a discussion of these conditions in schizophrenia).

Theories and Treatment of Schizotypal Personality Disorder

Many more studies of the genetics of schizotypal personality disorder have been conducted than studies of the other odd-eccentric personality disorders. Family history, adoption, and twin studies all suggest that schizotypal personality disorder is transmitted genetically, at least to some degree (see Nigg & Goldsmith, 1994; Siever et al., 1998). In addition, schizotypal personality disorder is much more common in the first-degree relatives of people with schizophrenia than in the relatives of either psychiatric patients or healthy control groups (Gilvarry et al., 2001; Kendler, Neale, Kessler, Heath, & Eaves, 1993). This finding supports the view that schizotypal personality disorder is a mild form of schizophrenia, which is transmitted through genes in ways similar to those of schizophrenia.

Similarly, some of the nongenetic biological factors implicated in schizophrenia are also present in people with schizotypal personality disorder (Barch, 2005). In particular, people diagnosed with this disorder show problems in the ability to sustain attention on cognitive tasks, as well as deficits in memory similar to those seen in people with schizophrenia (e.g., Mitropoulou et al., 2003). People with schizotypal personality disorder also tend to show a dysregulation of the neurotransmitter dopamine in the brain, as do people with schizophrenia (Abi-Dargham et al., 2004). Thus, like people with schizophrenia, people with schizotypal personality disorder may have abnormally high levels of dopamine in some areas of their brains. Finally, people with schizotypal personality disorder show abnormalities in the structure of their brains that are similar to those seen in people with schizophrenia (Barch, 2005).

Schizotypal personality disorder is most often treated with the same drugs that are used to treat schizophrenia, including traditional neuroleptics, such as haloperidol and thiothixene, and the atypical antipsychotics, such as olanzapine (Keshavan et al., 2004; Siever et al., 1998). As in schizophrenia, these drugs appear to relieve psychotic-like symptoms, including ideas of reference, magical thinking, and illusions. Antidepressants are sometimes used to help people with schizotypal personality disorder who are experiencing significant distress.

Although there are few psychological theories of schizotypal personality disorder, psychological therapies have been developed to help these people overcome some of their symptoms. In psychotherapy, it is especially important for therapists to establish good relationships with clients, because these clients typically have few close relationships and tend to be paranoid (Beck & Freeman, 1990). The next step in therapy is to help clients increase social contacts and learn socially appropriate behaviors through social skills training. Group therapy may be especially helpful in increasing clients' social skills. The crucial component of cognitive therapy with clients diagnosed with schizotypal personality disorder is teaching them to look for objective evidence in the environment for their thoughts and to disregard bizarre thoughts. For example, a client who often thinks that he or she is not real can be taught to identify that thought as bizarre and to discount the thought when it occurs, rather than taking it seriously and acting on it.

SUMMING UP

- People diagnosed with the odd-eccentric personality disorders—paranoid, schizoid, and schizotypal personality disorders—have odd thought processes, emotional reactions, and behaviors similar to those of people with schizophrenia, but they retain their grasp on reality.
- People diagnosed with paranoid personality disorder are chronically suspicious of others but maintain their grasp on reality.
- People diagnosed with schizoid personality disorder are emotionally cold and distant from others and have great trouble forming interpersonal relationships.
- People diagnosed with schizotypal personality disorder have a variety of odd beliefs and perceptual experiences but maintain their grasp on reality.
- These personality disorders, especially schizotypal personality disorder, have been linked to familial histories of schizophrenia and some of the biological abnormalities of schizophrenia.
- People diagnosed with these disorders tend not to seek treatment, but, when they do, therapists pay close attention to the therapeutic relationship and help the clients learn to reality-test their unusual thinking.
- Antipsychotics may help people with schizotypal personality disorder reduce their odd thinking.

TABLE 12.3 Concept Overview

Dramatic-Emotional Personality Disorders

People with dramatic-emotional personality disorders tend to have unstable emotions and to engage in dramatic and impulsive behavior.

Label	Key Features	Similar Disorders on Axis I
Antisocial personality disorder	Pervasive pattern of criminal, impulsive, callous, or ruthless behavior; disregard for the rights of others; no respect for social norms	Conduct disorder (diagnosed in children)
Borderline personality disorder	Rapidly shifting and unstable mood, self-concept, and interpersonal relationships; impulsive behavior; transient dissociative states; self-effacement	Mood disorders
Histrionic personality disorder	Rapidly shifting moods, unstable relationships, and intense need for attention and approval; dramatic, seductive behavior	Somatoform disorders, mood disorders
Narcissistic personality disorder	Grandiose thoughts and feelings of one's own worth; obliviousness to others' needs; exploitative, arrogant demeanor	Manic symptoms

Source: Reprinted with permission from the *Diagnostic and Statistical Manual of Mental Disorders*, Fourth Edition, Text Revision. Copyright © 2000 American Psychiatric Association.

DRAMATIC-EMOTIONAL PERSONALITY DISORDERS

People diagnosed with the **dramatic-emotional personality disorders** engage in behaviors that are dramatic and impulsive, and they often show little regard for their own safety or the safety of others (see the Concept Overview in Table 12.3). For example, they may engage in suicidal behaviors or self-damaging acts, such as self-cutting. They may also act in hostile, even violent ways against others. One of the core features of this group of disorders is a lack of concern for others. Two of the disorders in this cluster, antisocial personality disorder and borderline personality disorder, have been the focus of a great deal of research, whereas the other two, narcissistic personality disorder and histrionic personality disorder, have not.

Antisocial Personality Disorder

Severe antisocial tendencies have been recognized under various names as a serious disorder for over two centuries (Sher & Trull, 1994). Pritchard (1837) used the term *moral insanity* to describe people with little self-control and no concern for the rights of others. Later, in 1891, Koch applied the term *psychopathic* to the same individuals. Subsequent writers in the late nineteenth and early twentieth centuries often applied the term *psychopath* to anyone who had a severely maladaptive personality. Today, the label *psychopath* is not part of the official DSM-IV-TR nomenclature. Instead, the DSM-IV-TR diagnoses people with chronic antisocial behaviors as having **antisocial personality disorder (ASPD)**.

The key features of antisocial personality disorder, as defined by the DSM-IV-TR, are an impairment in the ability to form positive relationships with others and a tendency to engage in behaviors that violate basic social norms and values. People with this disorder are deceitful, as indicated by the repeated lying to or conning of others for personal profit or pleasure. They commit violent criminal offenses against others, including assault, murder, and rape, much more frequently than do people without the disorder (Hart & Hare, 1997). When caught, they tend to have little remorse, seeming indifferent to the pain and suffering they have caused others.

A prominent characteristic of antisocial personality disorder is poor control of one's impulses.

People with this disorder have a low tolerance for frustration and often act impetuously, with no apparent concern for the consequences of their behavior. They often take chances and seek thrills with no concern for danger. They are easily bored and restless, unable to endure the tedium of routine or to persist at the day-to-day responsibilities of marriage or a job (Millon et al., 2000). As a result, they tend to drift from one relationship to another and often are in lower-status jobs. They may engage in criminal activity impulsively, and 50 to 80 percent of men in jail may be diagnosable with antisocial personality disorder (Cale & Lilienfeld, 2002).

Antisocial personality disorder (ASPD), as defined by the DSM-IV-TR, differs in some important ways from the characterization of **psychopathy.** Whereas the DSM-IV-TR emphasizes observable antisocial behaviors in the diagnosis of ASPD, a pioneer in the study of psychopathy, Hervey Cleckley (1941), emphasized certain broad personality traits in psychopathy. More recently, Robert Hare (1991) has built on Cleckley's work to develop criteria for the diagnosis of psychopathy, which have been supported in research. These criteria include a superficial charm, a grandiose sense of self-worth, a tendency toward boredom and need for stimulation, pathological lying, an ability to be conning and manipulative, and a lack of remorse. People with psychopathy are cold and callous, gaining pleasure by competing with and humiliating others. They can be cruel and malicious, and they often insist on being seen as faultless. They are dogmatic in their opinions. However, when they need to be, people with psychopathy can be gracious and cheerful, until they get what they want. They then may revert to being brash and arrogant. Cleckley (1941) noted that, although psychopaths often end up in prisons or dead, many of them become successful businesspeople and professionals (see Cleckley, 1941). He suggested that the difference between psychopaths who become successful people and psychopaths who end up in jail is that the successful ones are better able to maintain an outward appearance of being normal. They may be able to do so because they have superior intelligence and can put on a "mask of sanity" and superficial social charm in order to achieve their goals.

Research on people with antisocial tendencies is mixed as to whether people are defined in terms of the Cleckley/Hare criteria for psychopathy, the DSM-IV-TR criteria for antisocial personality disorder, or simply in terms of having a record of severe criminal conduct. For example, several of the genetic studies we will review used prison inmates as their "antisocial" group. Although most inmates

may be diagnosable with antisocial personality disorder, formal assessments of this diagnosis are often not done. These ambiguities in the research literature are important to keep in mind as we discuss the possible causes of and treatments for this disorder.

Prevalence of Antisocial Personality Disorder

Epidemiological studies doing formal assessments of antisocial personality disorder, as defined by the DSM-IV-TR, suggest it is one of the most common personality disorders, with approximately 3 percent of the general population being diagnosed with the disorder at sometime in their lives (Cale & Lilienfeld, 2002; Ekselius et al., 2001). Men are substantially more likely than women to be diagnosed with this disorder. Although some theorists have argued that clinicians are more likely to see antisociality in African Americans than in Caucasians (Iwamasa et al., 2000), epidemiological studies have not found ethnic differences in rates of diagnosis (Cale & Lilienfeld, 2002; Chavira et al., 2003; Cloninger, Bayon, & Przybeck, 1997). People diag-

Over half of men in jail may be diagnosable with antisocial personality disorder.

nosed with this personality disorder are somewhat more likely than people diagnosed with the other personality disorders to have low levels of education (Fabrega et al., 1991).

As many as 80 percent of people with antisocial personality disorder abuse substances, such as alcohol and illicit drugs (Kraus & Reynolds, 2001; Trull, Waudby, & Sher, 2004). Substance abuse, such as binge drinking, may be just one form of the impulsive behavior that is part of antisocial personality disorder. Substance abuse probably feeds impulsive and antisocial behavior among people with this personality disorder. Alcohol and other substances may reduce any inhibitions they do have, making it more likely they will lash out violently at others. People with this disorder are also at a somewhat increased risk for suicide attempts (particularly females) and for violent death (Cale & Lilienfeld, 2002).

The tendency to engage in antisocial behaviors is one of the most stable personality characteristics in this disorder (Loeber & Farrington, 1997; Moffitt, 1993; Perry, 1993). Many adults with antisocial personality disorder show a disregard for societal norms and a tendency for antisocial behavior beginning in childhood, and most would have been diagnosed with conduct disorder as children. For some people with this disorder, however, the antisocial behavior diminishes as they age. This is particularly true of people who were not antisocial as children but became antisocial as adolescents or young adults (Moffitt, 1993). This tendency may be due to a psychological or biological maturation process, or many people with this disorder may simply be jailed or otherwise constrained by society from acting out their antisocial tendencies.

Theories of Antisocial Personality Disorder

A variety of biological and psychosocial theories of antisocial personality disorder have received some empirical support. These theories are summarized in the Concept Overview in Table 12.4 on page 438.

There is substantial support for a genetic influence on antisocial behaviors, particularly criminal behaviors (Eley, Lichenstein, & Stevenson, 1999; Taylor, Iacono, et al., 2000). Twin studies find that the concordance rate for such behaviors is near 50 percent in MZ twins, compared with 20 percent or lower in DZ twins (Carey & Goldman, 1997; Rutter, MacDonald, et al., 1990). Adoption studies find that the criminal records of adopted sons are more similar to the records of their biological fathers than to those of their adoptive fathers (Cloninger & Gottesman, 1987; Mednick et al., 1987). Family history studies show that the family members of people with antisocial personality disorder have

increased rates of this disorder, as well as increased rates of alcoholism and criminal activity (Perry, 1993).

Most theorists suggest that antisocial behavior is not the result of one gene or even a small number of genes. Instead, some people appear to be born with a number of genetically influenced deficits that make them ill-equipped to manage ordinary life, putting them at risk for antisocial behavior (Dodge & Pettit, 2003).

One long-standing theory is that aggressiveness, such as that shown by people with antisocial personality disorder, is linked to the hormone testosterone. Although some studies have found that highly aggressive males have higher levels of testosterone than nonaggressive males, the evidence for a role for testosterone in most forms of aggression is weak (Brain & Susman, 1997). Hormones such as testosterone may play a more important role during prenatal development in organizing the fetal brain in ways that promote or inhibit aggressiveness, rather than having a direct influence on behavior in adolescence or adulthood.

Anthony Hopkins played a terrifying antisocial personality in the film *Silence of the Lambs*.

TABLE 12.4   Concept Overview

Contributors to Antisocial Personality Disorder

There may be many contributors to antisocial personality disorder.

Contributor	Description
Genetic predisposition	Genetic factors contribute to antisocial behavior.
Testosterone	Aggressiveness is associated with high levels of testosterone; alternatively, high levels of testosterone present in utero affect the development of the fetal brain in ways that promote aggressiveness.
Serotonin	Low levels of serotonin contribute to impulsive and aggressive behaviors.
Attention-deficit/hyperactivity disorder	Children with attention-deficit/hyperactivity disorder develop antisocial behavior in response to social rejection and punishment.
Executive functions	People with antisocial personality disorder have deficits in the parts of the brain that are involved in executive functions (planful behavior and self-monitoring).
Arousability	Low levels of arousability lead to fearlessness in dangerous situations and/or stimulation-seeking behavior, which contributes to antisocial personality disorder.
Social cognitive factors	Children with antisocial tendencies have parents who are harsh and neglectful, and the children interpret interpersonal situations in ways that promote aggression.

Recall that a prominent characteristic of antisocial personality disorder is a difficulty in inhibiting impulsive behaviors (Morey, 1993; Rutter, 1997; Sher & Trull, 1994). Some researchers argue that poor impulse control is at the heart of antisocial personality disorder (Rutter, 1997). What might be the biological causes of poor impulse control? Many animal studies have shown that impulsive and aggressive behaviors are linked to low levels of the neurotransmitter **serotonin,** leading to the suggestion that people with antisocial personality disorder may also have low levels of serotonin (Krakowski, 2003). Several studies of humans also suggest that impulsiveness and aggressiveness are correlated with low levels of serotonin (Mann et al., 2001).

Research with children who show antisocial tendencies indicates that a significant percentage, perhaps the majority, have *attention-deficit/hyperactivity disorder (ADHD)*, which involves significant problems with inhibiting impulsive behaviors and main-

taining attention (see Chapter 13). The disruptive behavior of these children leads to frequent punishment and to rejection by peers, teachers, and other adults. These children then become even more disruptive, and some become overtly aggressive and antisocial in their behaviors and attitudes. Thus, at least some adults with antisocial personality disorder may have lifelong problems with attentional deficits and hyperactivity, which then contribute to lifelong problems with controlling their behaviors.

People with antisocial personalities also show deficits in verbal skills and in the **executive functions** of the brain. These functions include the ability to sustain concentration, abstract reasoning, concept and goal formation, the ability to anticipate and plan, the capacity to program and initiate purposive sequences of behavior, self-monitoring and self-awareness, and the ability to shift from maladaptive patterns of behavior to more adaptive ones (see Henry & Moffitt, 1997). In turn, some, but not all, studies have found differences between antisocial adults (usually prison inmates) and the general population in the structure or functioning of the temporal and frontal lobes of the brain (Morgan & Lilienfeld, 2000). These deficits in brain func-

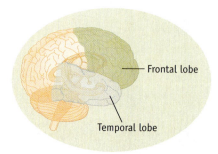

The temporal and frontal lobes of the brain may be implicated in deficits in executive functions in antisocial personality disorder.

tioning and structure might be tied to medical illnesses and exposure to toxins during infancy and childhood, both of which are more common among people who develop criminal records than among those who do not (see Chapter 13). On the other hand, these deficits might be tied to genetic abnormalities. Whatever their causes, low verbal intelligence and deficits in executive functions might contribute to poor impulse control and difficulty in anticipating the consequences of one's actions.

Many studies have suggested that persons with antisocial personality disorder show low levels of arousability, measured by relatively low resting heart rates, low skin conductance activity, and excessive slow-wave electroencephalogram readings (Herpertz et al., 2001; Raine, 1997). One interpretation of these data is that low levels of arousal indicate low levels of fear in response to threatening situations (Raine, 1997). Fearlessness can be put to good use—for instance, bomb disposal experts and British paratroopers also show low levels of arousal (McMillan & Rachman, 1987; O'Connor, Hallam, & Rachman, 1985). However, fearlessness may also predispose some people to antisocial and violent behaviors, such as fighting and robbery, which require fearlessness to execute. In addition, low-arousal children may not fear punishment and may not be deterred from antisocial behavior by the threat of punishment.

A second theory of how low arousability contributes to antisocial personality is that chronically low arousal is an uncomfortable state and leads to stimulation seeking (Eysenck, 1994). Again, if an individual seeks stimulation through prosocial or neutral acts, such as skydiving, stimulation seeking may not lead to antisocial behavior. But some individuals may seek stimulation through antisocial acts that are dangerous or impulsive, such as robbery or fights. The direction that stimulation seeking takes—toward antisocial activities or toward more neutral activities— may depend on the reinforcement that individuals receive for their behaviors. Those who are rewarded for antisocial behavior by family and peers may develop antisocial personalities, whereas those who are consistently punished for such behaviors and given alternative, more neutral behaviors may not (Dishion & Patterson, 1997).

Intelligence may also influence the direction that stimulation seeking takes (Henry & Moffitt, 1997). Children who are intelligent experience more rewards from school and, thus, may be more influenced by the norms of adults and positive peer groups in the choices they make for seeking stimulation. In contrast, children who are less intelligent may find school punishing and may turn to deviant peer groups for gratification and stimulating activities.

Much of the empirical research on the social and cognitive factors that contribute to antisocial behavior has been conducted with children. Many children with antisocial tendencies come from homes in which they have experienced harsh and inconsistent parenting and physical abuse (Dishion & Patterson, 1997; Dodge & Pettit, 2003). The parents of these children alternate between being neglectful and being hostile and violent toward their children. These children learn ways of thinking about the world that promote antisocial behavior (Crick & Dodge, 1994). They enter social interactions with the assumption that other children will be aggressive toward them, and they interpret the actions of their peers in line with this assumption. As a result, they are quick to engage in aggressive behaviors toward others. These social and cognitive factors alone may be enough to lead to antisocial personalities in some children and adults.

Dodge and Pettit (2003) integrated the myriad biological, social, and cognitive factors associated with antisociality into a comprehensive model (see Figure 12.1 on page 440). According to this model, some people are born with neural, endocrine, and psychophysiological dispositions, or are born into sociocultural contexts, that put them at risk for antisocial behavior throughout their lifetimes. Early symptoms of aggression and oppositional behavior in a child lead to, and interact with, harsh discipline and a lack of warmth from parents, as well as conflicts with aggressive peers. These children are at risk for academic and social problems in school, which can motivate them to turn to deviant peer groups, where they are encouraged in antisocial behavior. All along, such children learn that the world is hostile and that they must defend themselves rapidly and often aggressively, and they are prone to impulsive behaviors or reactions to others. These children enter adulthood with a long history of negative interactions with others, violent and impulsive outbursts, and alienation from mainstream society. All these factors feed back on each other, perpetuating the cycle of antisocial behavior into adulthood.

Treatments for Antisocial Personality Disorder

People with antisocial personality disorder tend to believe they do not need treatment. They may submit to therapy when forced to because of marital discord, work conflicts, or incarceration, but they are prone to blaming others for their current situations, rather than accepting responsibility for their actions. As a result, many clinicians do not hold much hope for effectively treating persons with

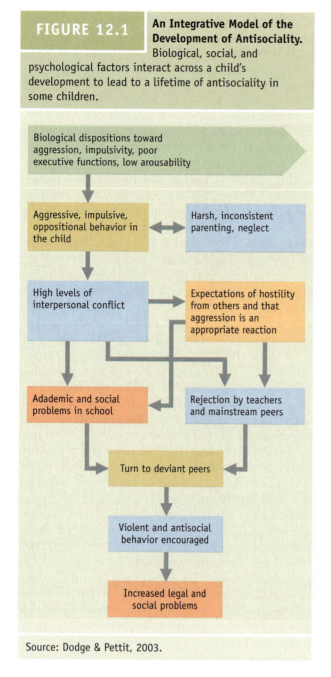

FIGURE 12.1 **An Integrative Model of the Development of Antisociality.** Biological, social, and psychological factors interact across a child's development to lead to a lifetime of antisociality in some children.

Biological dispositions toward aggression, impulsivity, poor executive functions, low arousability

Aggressive, impulsive, oppositional behavior in the child

Harsh, inconsistent parenting, neglect

High levels of interpersonal conflict

Expectations of hostility from others and that aggression is an appropriate reaction

Adademic and social problems in school

Rejection by teachers and mainstream peers

Turn to deviant peers

Violent and antisocial behavior encouraged

Increased legal and social problems

Source: Dodge & Pettit, 2003.

this disorder through psychotherapy (Kraus & Reynolds, 2001; Millon et al., 2000).

When clinicians attempt psychotherapy, they tend to focus on helping the person with antisocial personality disorder gain control over his or her anger and impulsive behaviors by recognizing triggers and developing alternative coping strategies (Kraus & Reynolds, 2001). Some clinicians also try to increase the individual's empathy for the effects of his or her behaviors on others (Hare & Hart, 1993).

Lithium and the atypical antipsychotics have been used successfully to control impulsive/aggres-

sive behaviors in people with antisocial personality disorder (Karper & Krystal, 1997; Markovitz, 2004). More recently, based on the evidence for low levels of serotonin in some animals prone to impulsive and aggressive behavior, researchers have been suggesting the use of drugs that inhibit the reuptake of serotonin into the synapses, such as the selective serotonin reuptake inhibitors (Karper & Krystal, 1997; Kraus & Reynolds, 2001). The efficacy of these drugs in treating antisocial personality disorder is not clear yet.

Borderline Personality Disorder

Recall that Susanna Kaysen, whom we met in the opener to this chapter, suffered a variety of disturbing symptoms and was given a diagnosis of **borderline personality disorder,** which she strongly questioned later in her life. In the following passage, a clinician describes another woman who was later diagnosed with borderline personality disorder (adapted from Linehan, Cochran, & Kehrer, 2001, pp. 502–504).

CASE STUDY

At the initial meeting, Cindy was a 30-year-old, white, married woman with no children who was living in a middle-class suburban area with her husband. She had a college education and had successfully completed almost 2 years of medical school. Cindy was referred by her psychiatrist of 1½ years, who was no longer willing to provide more than pharmacotherapy following a recent hospitalization for a near-lethal suicide attempt. In the 2 years prior to referral, Cindy had been hospitalized at least 10 times (one lasting 6 months) for psychiatric treatment of suicidal ideation; had engaged in numerous instances of parasuicidal behavior, including at least 10 instances of drinking Clorox bleach, multiple deep cuts, and burns; and had had three medically severe or nearly lethal suicide attempts, including cutting an artery in her neck.

Until age 27 Cindy was able to function well in work and school settings, and her marriage was reasonably satisfactory to both partners, although the husband complained of Cindy's excessive anger. When Cindy was in the second year of medical school, a classmate she

(continued)

knew only slightly committed suicide. Cindy stated that when she heard about the suicide, she immediately decided to kill herself also, but had very little insight into what about the situation actually elicited the inclination to kill herself. Within weeks she left medical school and became severely depressed and actively suicidal. Although Cindy presented herself as a person with few psychological problems before the classmate's suicide, further questioning revealed a history of severe anorexia nervosa, bulimia nervosa, and alcohol and prescription medication abuse, originating at the age of 14 years.

Over the course of therapy, a consistent pattern associated with self-harm became apparent. The chain of events would often begin with an interpersonal encounter (almost always with her husband), which culminated in her feeling threatened, criticized, or unloved. These feelings would often be followed by urges either to self-mutilate or to kill herself, depending somewhat on her levels of hopelessness, anger, and sadness. Decisions to self-mutilate and/or to attempt suicide were often accompanied by the thought "I'll show you." At other times, hopelessness and a desire to end the pain permanently seemed predominant. Following the conscious decision to self-mutilate or attempt suicide, Cindy would then immediately dissociate and at some later point cut or burn herself, usually while in a state of "automatic pilot." Consequently, Cindy often had difficulty remembering specifics of the actual acts. At one point, Cindy burned her leg so badly (and then injected it with dirt to convince the doctor that he should give her more attention) that reconstructive surgery was required.

Cindy's symptoms represent some of the benchmarks of borderline personality disorder: out-of-control emotions that cannot be smoothed, a hypersensitivity to abandonment, a tendency to cling too tightly to other people, and a history of hurting oneself.

Instability is a key feature of borderline personality disorder. The *mood* of people with borderline personality disorder is unstable, with bouts of severe depression, anxiety, or anger seeming to

Glenn Close portrayed a woman with borderline personality disorder in *Fatal Attraction*.

arise frequently and often without good reason. Their *self-concept* is unstable, with periods of extreme self-doubt and periods of grandiose self-importance. Their *interpersonal relationships* are extremely unstable, and they can switch from idealizing others to despising them without provocation. People with borderline personality disorder often describe a desperate emptiness, which leads them to cling to new acquaintances or therapists in hopes that they will fill the tremendous void they experience in themselves. They are greatly concerned about abandonment and misinterpret other people's innocent actions as abandonment or rejection. For example, if a therapist has to cancel an appointment because she is ill, a client with borderline personality disorder might interpret this as a rejection by the therapist and become extremely depressed or angry.

Along with the instability of mood, self-concept, and interpersonal relationships comes a tendency toward impulsive, self-damaging behaviors, including self-mutilating behaviors and suicidal behavior. Cindy's self-mutilating behavior was to cut and burn herself. Finally, like Cindy, people with borderline personality disorder are prone to transient dissociative states, in which they feel unreal, lose track of time, and may even forget who they are. Glenn Close's depiction of a woman with borderline personality disorder in the movie *Fatal Attraction* aptly captured this diagnosis.

The variety of symptoms that make up the criteria for a diagnosis of borderline personality disorder reflects, to some extent, the complexity of this disorder. The manifestation of this disorder can be quite different from one person to the next and from one day to the next within any one person. Indeed, Trull and Durrett (2005) note that there are 126 ways an individual can meet the criteria for borderline personality disorder. The varied list of symptoms also reflects the difficulty that clinicians have had in agreeing on a conceptualization of this disorder (Gunderson, Zanarini, & Kisiel, 1995).

The term *borderline* has been used loosely for many years to refer to people who could not be fit easily into existing diagnoses of emotional disorders or psychotic disorders and who were extremely difficult to treat (Millon et al., 2000). One result of the variety of symptoms listed in the diagnostic criteria for the disorder is that there is a great deal of overlap between the borderline diagnosis and several of the other personality disorders, including paranoid, antisocial, narcissistic, histrionic, and schizotypal personality disorders (Grilo, Sanislow, & McGlashan, 2002). Indeed, most people diagnosed with borderline personality disorder also meet the diagnostic criteria for at least one other personality disorder.

People with borderline personality disorder also tend to receive diagnoses of one of the acute disorders, including substance abuse, depression, and generalized anxiety disorder; simple phobias; agoraphobia; posttraumatic stress disorder; panic disorder; or somatization disorder (Fabrega et al., 1991; Kraus & Reynolds, 2001; Weissman, 1993). About 75 percent of people with this disorder attempt suicide and about 10 percent die by suicide (Kraus & Reynolds, 2001; Linehan et al., 2001). The greatest risk for suicide appears to be in the first year or two after people diagnosis. This may be because people are often not diagnosed with this disorder until a crisis brings them to the attention of the mental-health system.

The symptoms of borderline personality disorder create a number of severe and debilitating problems for people with this disorder and for people in their environment. A longitudinal study that followed 351 young adults diagnosed with the disorder found that their impulsivity and emotional instability led to difficulties in relating with other people, in meeting their social role obligations (for example, as a parent), and in achieving their academic and work goals (Bagge et al., 2004).

Prevalence of Borderline Personality Disorder

Epidemiological studies suggest that between 1 and 2 percent of the population will develop borderline personality disorder in their lives (Kraus & Reynolds, 2001; Weissman, 1993). In clinical settings, borderline personality disorder is much more often diagnosed in women than in men. It is somewhat more commonly diagnosed in people of color than in Whites and in people in lower socioeconomic classes (Chavira et al., 2003; Grilo et al., 2002). A large study of people in treatment for personality disorders found that Hispanics were more likely than Caucasians or African Americans to be diagnosed with borderline personality disorder (Chavira et al., 2003). This difference might occur because factors that contribute to this disorder, such as extreme stress, are more common among Hispanics. On the other hand, clinicians may overdiagnose this disorder in Hispanic people because they do not take into account the Hispanic cultural norms that permit a greater expression of strong emotions, such as anger, aggressiveness, and sexual attraction (Chavira et al., 2003).

People with this disorder are high users of outpatient mental-health services (Bender et al., 2001). One community study found that 50 percent had used some form of mental-health service in the past six months (Swartz et al., 1990). Follow-up studies of people treated as inpatients for borderline personality disorder suggest that about 50 percent continue to meet the diagnostic criteria for the disorder seven years later (Links, Heslegrave, & van Reekum, 1998). The more severe the symptoms at the time of treatment, the more likely the disorder is to be chronic.

Theories of Borderline Personality Disorder

Several family history studies of borderline personality disorder have been conducted, and the evidence that this disorder is transmitted genetically is mixed (Dahl, 1993; Nigg & Goldsmith, 1994). There are high rates of mood disorders in the families of persons diagnosed with borderline personality disorder, however (Kendler, Meale, Kessler, Heath, & Eaves, 1993). Functional magnetic resonance imaging (fMRI) studies show that people with borderline personality disorder have greater activation of the amygdala in response to pictures of emotional faces, as do people with mood and anxiety disorders, which may contribute to their difficulties in regulating their moods (Donegan et al., 2003) (see Figure 12.2). Recall that the amygdala is a part of the brain that is important in the processing of emotion. Similarly, positron-emission tomography studies have found decreased metabolism in the prefrontal cortex of patients with borderline personality disorder, as is also found in patients with mood disorders (Soloff et al., 2000). Most researchers do not suggest that borderline personality disorder is simply a type of affective disorder, but there clearly are links between the two disorders.

Impulsive behaviors in people with borderline personality disorder are correlated with low levels of serotonin (see Weston & Siever, 1993). Recall

The amygdala and the prefrontal cortex have been implicated in borderline personality disorder.

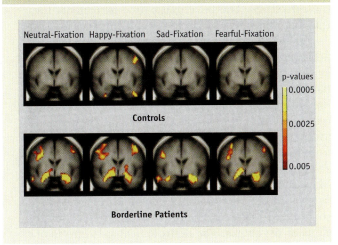

FIGURE 12.2 **Map Showing Activated Regions in the Amygdala for Normal Control and Borderline Personality Disorder Groups for Four Facial Expressions.** People with borderline personality disorder showed more activity in the amygdala in response to all emotional faces.

that impulsive behaviors in people with antisocial personality disorder have also been linked to low serotonin levels. This link suggests that low serotonin levels are not associated with one diagnostic category but, rather, with impulsive behaviors in general.

Psychoanalytic theorists, particularly those in the object relations school (see Chapter 2), have been extremely interested in borderline personality disorder (see Kernberg, 1979; Klein, 1952). They suggest that people with this disorder have very poorly developed views of themselves and others, stemming from poor early relationships with caregivers. These early caregivers may have encouraged the children's dependence on them. They may have punished the children's attempts at individuation and separation, so the children never learned to fully differentiate their views of themselves from their views of others. This makes them extremely reactive to others' opinions of them and to the possibility of being abandoned by others. When they perceive others as rejecting them, they reject themselves and may engage in self-punishment or self-mutilation.

They also have never been able to integrate the positive and negative qualities of either their self-concept or their concept of others, because their early caregivers were comforting and rewarding when they remained dependent and compliant toward them but hostile and rejecting when they tried to individuate from them. They tend to see themselves and other people as either all good or all bad and vacillate between these two views, a process known as **splitting.** The instability in emo-

tions and interpersonal relationships is due to splitting: Their emotions and their perspectives on their interpersonal relationships reflect their vacillation between the all-good and the all-bad self and the all-good and all-bad other.

Empirical studies have found that people with borderline personality disorder are more likely than people without the disorder to report childhoods marked by instability, abuse, neglect, and parental psychopathology (Helgeland & Torgersen, 2004). Of course, this is true of the childhoods of people with many different types of psychopathology and does not directly address the object relations theory of the development of this disorder.

One influential theorist, Marcia Linehan (Linehan et al., 2001), focuses on deficits in the ability to regulate emotions, which are probably physiologically based. Extreme emotional reactions to situations lead to impulsive actions. In addition, Linehan argues that people with borderline personality disorder have histories of significant others' discounting and criticizing their emotional experiences. Such histories make it even harder for them to learn appropriate emotion-regulation skills and to understand and accept their emotional reactions to events. People with this disorder come to rely on others to help them cope with difficult situations but do not have enough self-confidence to ask for help from others in mature ways. They become manipulative and indirect in trying to gain support from others.

Finally, research suggests that a number of people with borderline personality disorder have histories of physical and sexual abuse during childhood (Zanarini, 1997). Some theorists believe that the severe problems in self-concept seen in people with borderline personality disorder frequently are the result of childhood abuse (Kraus & Reynolds, 2001). Recently, researchers have found a variety of abnormalities in the structure and functioning of brain regions in people with both a history of sexual abuse and borderline personality disorder, including reductions in the volume of the hippocampus and amygdala and an abnormal change in blood flow in the prefrontal cortex with exposure to trauma-related memories (Schmahl et al., 2004; Tebartz van Elst et al., 2003). Although the implications of these findings are not yet known, they may suggest that early trauma alters the functioning of the brain in ways that contribute to the symptoms of borderline personality disorder.

Treatments for Borderline Personality Disorder

Over the past two decades, Linehan and colleagues have developed a therapy blending cognitive-behavioral techniques with interpersonal and psychodynamic techniques for the treatment of people with borderline personality disorder, which they call **dialectical behavior therapy** (Linehan et al., 2001). This therapy focuses on helping clients gain a more realistic and positive sense of self, learn adaptive skills for solving problems and regulating emotions, and correct their dichotomous thinking. Therapists teach clients to monitor their self-disparaging thoughts and black-or-white evaluations of people and situations and to challenge these thoughts and evaluations. Therapists also help clients learn appropriate assertiveness skills for close relationships, so that they can express their needs and feelings in a mature manner. Clients may learn how to control impulsive behavior by monitoring the situations most likely to lead to such behaviors and learn alternative ways to handle such situations. Controlled clinical trials testing dialectical behavior therapy have found that the therapy reduces depression, anxiety, and self-mutilating behavior while increasing interpersonal functioning (Bohus et al., 2004; Linehan, Heard, & Armstrong, 1993).

Psychodynamic treatments for people with borderline personality disorder involve helping clients clarify feelings, confronting them with their tendency to split images of the self and other, and interpreting clients' transference relationships with therapists (Kernberg, 1989). Many people with borderline personality disorder at times become extremely angry toward their therapists, as they move from idealizing to devaluing them. Therapists can use such times to help clients understand their splitting defenses and to set clear limits on the clients'

behaviors. Clients may also be taught more adaptive means of solving everyday problems, so that the world does not appear so overwhelming. Self-destructive tendencies are addressed, with therapists helping clients identify the feelings leading to these acts and develop healthy ways of coping with these feelings. The psychodynamic treatments for this disorder have not been studied empirically.

The drug treatments for people with borderline personality disorder have focused on reducing the symptoms of anxiety and depression through antianxiety drugs and antidepressants and on controlling impulsive behaviors with selective serotonin reuptake inhibitors. The antidepressants have been found to have some positive effects on the symptoms of this disorder and may help reduce aggressiveness and impulsivity (Hollander et al., 2001; Markovitz, 2004). Antipsychotics are sometimes used with people who have severe borderline personality disorder, particularly when they exhibit signs of psychosis. The neurological side effects of the phenothiazines (see Chapter 11) lead many people to discontinue taking these drugs (Soloff et al., 1993). Studies of the atypical antipsychotics clozapine and olanzapine have suggested that these drugs may relieve psychotic-like symptoms and other symptoms of borderline personality disorder in many people (Benedetti et al., 1998; Hough, 2001; Markovitz, 2004). Overall, however, the results of drug treatment studies have been mixed, and adding a drug treatment to an effective psychotherapy, such as dialectical behavior therapy, does not appear to improve recovery rates (Linehan et al., 2001; Simpson et al., 2004).

Histrionic Personality Disorder

Histrionic personality disorder shares features with borderline personality disorder, including rapidly shifting emotions and intense, unstable relationships. Whereas people with borderline personality disorder are often self-effacing in an attempt to win favor from others, people with histrionic personality disorder usually want to be the center of attention. People with borderline personality disorder may desperately cling to others in self-doubt and need, but people with histrionic personality disorder simply want the attention of others. These individuals pursue others' attention by being highly dramatic, being overtly seductive, and emphasizing the positive qualities of their physical appearance. They tend to speak in global terms. Others see them as self-centered and shallow, unable to delay gratification, demanding, and overly dependent. In the following case study, Debbie was diagnosed with

Suicidal behavior is common among people with borderline personality disorder.

histrionic personality disorder (Beck & Freeman, 1990, pp. 211–212).

> Debbie was a 26-year-old woman who worked as a salesclerk in a trendy clothing store and who sought therapy for panic disorder with agoraphobia. She dressed flamboyantly, with an elaborate and dramatic hairdo. Her appearance was especially striking, since she was quite short (under 5 feet tall) and at least 75 pounds overweight. She wore sunglasses indoors throughout the evaluation and constantly fiddled with them, taking them on and off nervously and waving them to emphasize a point. She cried loudly and dramatically at various points in the interview, going through large numbers of tissue. She continually asked for reassurance. ("Will I be OK?" "Can I get over this?") She talked nonstop throughout the evaluation. When gently interrupted by the evaluator, she was very apologetic, laughing and saying, "I know I talk too much"; yet she continued to do so throughout the session.

Prevalence of Histrionic Personality Disorder

Between 1.3 and 2.2 percent of the population will develop this disorder at sometime in their lives, and the vast majority of persons diagnosed with this disorder are women (Ekselius et al., 2001; Weissman, 1993). People with this disorder are more likely to be separated or divorced than married. They tend to exaggerate medical problems and make more medical visits than the average person, as do people with somatoform disorders, and there is an increased rate of suicidal behavior and threats in this group (Kraus & Reynolds, 2001; Nestadt et al., 1990). People with this disorder most often seek treatment for depression or anxiety (Fabrega et al., 1991).

Theories and Treatment of Histrionic Personality Disorder

Although discussions of histrionic personalities date back to the ancient Greek philosophers, little is known about its causes or effective treatments. Family history studies indicate that histrionic personality disorder clusters in families, along with borderline personality disorder, antisocial personality disorder, and somatization disorder (Dahl,

1993). It is unclear whether this disorder is genetically related or results from processes within the family or environment.

Psychodynamic treatments focus on uncovering repressed emotions and needs and helping people with histrionic personality disorder express these emotions and needs in more socially appropriate ways. Cognitive therapy focuses on identifying these patients' assumptions that they cannot function on their own and helping them formulate goals and plans for their lives that do not rely on the approval of others (Beck & Freeman, 1990). Therapists attempt to help clients tone down their dramatic evaluations of situations by challenging these evaluations and suggesting more reasonable evaluations. None of the therapies for this disorder have been tested empirically.

Narcissistic Personality Disorder

The characteristics of **narcissistic personality disorder** are similar to those of histrionic personality disorder. In both disorders, individuals act in a dramatic and grandiose manner, seek admiration from others, and are shallow in their emotional expressions and relationships with others. Whereas people with histrionic personality disorder look to others for approval, however, people with narcissistic personality disorder rely on their own self-evaluations and see dependency on others as weak and dangerous. They are preoccupied with thoughts of their self-importance and with fantasies of power and success and view themselves as superior to most others. In interpersonal relationships, they make unreasonable demands for others to follow their wishes, ignore the needs and wants of others, exploit others to gain power, and are arrogant and demeaning. David, in the

Flamboyance is one symptom of histrionic personality disorder.

following case study, has been diagnosed with narcissistic personality disorder (adapted from Beck & Freeman, 1990, pp. 245–247).

David was an attorney in his early 40s when he sought treatment for depressed mood. He cited business and marital problems as the source of his distress and wondered if he was having a midlife crisis. David had grown up in a comfortable suburb of a large city, the oldest of three children and the only son of a successful businessman and a former secretary. Always known to have a bit of a temper, David usually provoked his parents and his sisters into giving in to his wishes. Even if they didn't give in to his demands, he reported that he usually went ahead and did what he wanted, anyway. David spoke of being an "ace" student and a "super" athlete but could not provide any details that would validate a superior performance in these areas. He also recollected that he had his pick of girlfriends, as most women were "thrilled" to have a date with him.

David went to college, fantasizing about being famous in a high-profile career. He majored in communications, planning to go on to law school and eventually into politics. He met his first wife during college, the year she was the university homecoming queen. They married shortly after their joint graduation. He then went on to law school, and she went to work to support the couple.

During law school, David became a workaholic, fueled by fantasies of brilliant work and international recognition. He spent minimal time with his wife and, after their son was born, even less time with either of them. At the same time, he continued a string of extramarital affairs, mostly brief sexual encounters. He spoke of his wife in an annoyed, devaluing way, complaining about how she just did not live up to his expectations. He waited until he felt reasonably secure in his first job so that he could let go of her financial support and then he sought a divorce. He continued to see his son occasionally, but he rarely paid his child support.

After his divorce, David decided that he was totally free to just please himself. He loved spending all his money on himself, and he lavishly decorated his condominium and bought an attention-getting wardrobe. He constantly sought the companionship of attractive women. He was very successful at making initial contacts and getting dates, but he rarely found anyone good enough to date more than once or twice. Sometimes he played sexual games to amuse himself, such as seeing how fast he could make sexual contact or how many women would agree to have sex with him. He eventually married Susan, the daughter of a well-known politician, and was presently unhappy with her and what she expected of him. He thought that she was lucky to have him and therefore did not really have the right to make demands. He knew that there would be plenty of other, prettier women who would be glad to cater to his needs.

At work, David believed that, because he was "different" from other people, they had no right to criticize him. But he had every right to criticize others. He also believed that other people were weak and needed contact with someone like him in order to bring direction or pleasure into their lives. He saw no problem in taking advantage of other people if they were "stupid" enough to allow him to do so.

David felt better when someone flattered him; when he was in a group social situation where he could easily grab the center of attention; and when he could fantasize about obtaining a high-level position, being honored for his great talent, or just being fabulously wealthy.

People with narcissistic personality disorder can be extremely successful in societies that reward self-confidence and assertiveness, such as the United States (Millon et al., 2000). When they grossly overestimate their abilities, however, they can make poor choices in their careers and may experience many failures. In addition, they annoy other people and can alienate the important people in their lives. People with this disorder seek treatment most often for depression and for trouble adjusting to life stressors (Fabrega et al., 1991).

Prevalence of Narcissistic Personality Disorder

Most epidemiological studies suggest that narcissistic personality disorder is rare, with a lifetime prevalence of less than 1 percent (Gunderson, Ronningstam, & Smith, 1995; Weissman, 1993), although one community study found a prevalence of 2.9 percent (Ekselius et al., 2001). It is more frequently diagnosed in men.

Theories and Treatment of Narcissistic Personality Disorder

Sigmund Freud (1914) viewed narcissism as a phase that all children pass through before transferring their love for themselves to significant others. Children can become fixated in this narcissistic phase, however, if they experience caregivers as untrustworthy and decide that they can rely only on themselves or if they have parents who indulge them and instill in them a grandiose sense of their abilities and worth (see also Horney, 1939). Later psychodynamic writers (Kernberg, 1998; Kohut, 1971) argued that narcissistic people actually suffer from low self-esteem and feelings of emptiness and pain as a result of rejection from parents and that narcissistic behaviors are reaction formations against these problems with self-worth.

Cognitive theorists Beck and Freeman (1990) argued that some narcissistic people develop assumptions about their self-worth that are unrealistically positive as the result of indulgence and overvaluation by significant others during childhood. Other narcissists develop the belief that they are unique or exceptional in reaction to being singled out as different from others due to ethnic or economic status or as a defense against rejection by important people in their lives. One study found that people diagnosed with narcissistic personality disorder were significantly more likely to endorse beliefs such as "I don't have to be bound by rules that apply to other people" than were people diagnosed with other disorders (Beck et al., 2001).

People with narcissistic personality disorder do not tend to seek treatment, except when they develop depression or are confronted with severe interpersonal problems (Beck & Freeman, 1990). They generally see any problems they encounter as due to the weaknesses of others, rather than their own weaknesses. Cognitive techniques can help these clients develop more sensitivity to the needs of others and more realistic expectations of their own abilities by learning to challenge their initially self-aggrandizing ways of interpreting situations (Millon et al., 2000). Such self-challenging doesn't come easily for these people, however, and they of-

ten do not remain in therapy once their acute symptoms or interpersonal problems decrease.

SUMMING UP

- People with dramatic-emotional personality disorders—antisocial, borderline, histrionic, and narcissistic personality disorders—have histories of unstable relationships and emotional experiences and of dramatic, erratic behavior.

- People with antisocial personality disorder regularly violate the basic rights of others and many engage in criminal acts.

- Antisocial personality disorder may have strong biological roots but is also associated with harsh and nonsupportive parenting.

- People with borderline personality disorder vacillate between all-good and all-bad evaluations of themselves and others.

- People with histrionic and narcissistic personality disorder act in flamboyant manners. People with histrionic personality disorder are overly dependent and solicitous of others, whereas people with narcissistic personality disorder are dismissive of others.

- None of these personality disorders responds consistently well to current treatments.

ANXIOUS-FEARFUL PERSONALITY DISORDERS

The **anxious-fearful personality disorders**—avoidant personality disorder, dependent personality disorder, and obsessive-compulsive personality disorder—are all characterized by a chronic sense of anxiety or fearfulness and behaviors intended to ward off feared situations (see the Concept Overview in Table 12.5 on page 448). In each of the three disorders, people fear something different, but they are all nervous and not very happy.

Avoidant Personality Disorder

Avoidant personality disorder has been studied more than the other two anxious-fearful personality disorders. People with avoidant personality disorder are extremely anxious about being criticized by others, so they avoid interactions with others in which there is any possibility of being criticized. They might choose occupations that are socially isolated, such as park rangers in the wilderness. When they must interact with others, people with avoidant personality disorder are restrained, nervous, and hypersensitive to signs of

TABLE 12.5 Concept Overview

Anxious-Fearful Personality Disorders

People with the anxious-fearful personality disorders are chronically anxious.

Label	Key Features	Similar Disorders on Axis I
Avoidant personality disorder	Pervasive anxiety, a sense of inadequacy, and a fear of being criticized, which lead to the avoidance of social interactions and nervousness	Social phobia
Dependent personality disorder	Pervasive selflessness, a need to be cared for, and a fear of rejection, leading to total dependence on and submission to others	Separation anxiety disorder, dysthymic disorder
Obsessive-compulsive personality disorder	Pervasive rigidity in one's activities and interpersonal relationships, including emotional constriction, extreme perfectionism, and anxiety about even minor disruptions in one's routine	Obsessive-compulsive disorder

Source: Reprinted with permission from the *Diagnostic and Statistical Manual of Mental Disorders,* Fourth Edition, Text Revision. Copyright © 2000 American Psychiatric Association.

being evaluated or criticized. They are terrified of saying something silly or doing something that will embarrass themselves. They tend to be depressed and lonely. They may crave relationships with others, but they feel unworthy of these relationships and isolate themselves, as the following case study illustrates (Spitzer et al., 1981, p. 59).

> **CASE STUDY**
>
> A 27-year-old, single, male bookkeeper was referred to a consulting psychologist because of a recent upsurge in anxiety that seemed to begin when a group of new employees was assigned to his office section. He feared that he was going to be fired, though his work was always highly commended. A clique had recently formed in the office, and, though very much wanting to be accepted into this "in group," the patient hesitated to join the clique unless explicitly asked to do so. Moreover, he "knew he had nothing to offer them" and thought that he would ultimately be rejected anyway.
>
> The patient spoke of himself as having always been a shy, fearful, quiet boy. Although he had two "good friends" whom he continued to see occasionally, he was characterized by fellow workers as a loner, a nice young man who usually did his work efficiently but on his own. They noted that he always ate by himself in the company cafeteria and never joined in the "horsing around."

Prevalence of Avoidant Personality Disorder

Studies suggest that from 1 to 7 percent of people can be diagnosed with avoidant personality disorder. There are no strong gender differences in its prevalence (Ekselius et al., 2001; Fabrega et al., 1991; Weissman, 1993). People with this disorder are prone to chronic dysthymic disorder and to bouts of major depression and severe anxiety (Grant et al., 2004).

There is overlap between the characteristics of avoidant personality disorder and those of social phobia (van Velzen, Emmelkamp, & Scholing, 2000) (see Chapter 7). People with avoidant personality disorder have a general sense of inadequacy and a pervasive, general fear of being criticized, which leads them to avoid most types of social interaction. People with social phobia tend to fear specific social situations in which they will be expected to perform (such as giving a talk in class) and tend not to have a general sense of inadequacy. People with social phobia tend to want to connect with others, whereas people with avoidant personality disorder do not. People with schizoid personality disorder also withdraw from social situations; however, unlike people with avoidant personality disorder, they do not view themselves as inadequate and incompetent.

Theories and Treatment of Avoidant Personality Disorder

Family history studies show that avoidant personality disorder is more common in the first-degree relatives of people with the disorder than in the relatives of normal control groups (Dahl, 1993). Studies have not been done to determine whether this is due to a genetic transmission of the disorder or to certain family environments. What may be transmitted is a particular type of *temperament*, or level of emotional arousal and reactivity. Studies of temperamental differences among very young children suggest that some children may be born with a shy, fearful temperament, which causes them to avoid most people (Pilkonis, 1995).

Cognitive theorists suggest that people with avoidant personality disorder develop dysfunctional beliefs about being worthless as a result of rejection by important others early in life (Beck & Freeman, 1990). Cognitive theorists contend that the children whose parents reject them conclude, "I must be a bad person for my mother to treat me so badly," "I must be different or defective," and "If my parents don't like me, how could anyone?" (Beck & Freeman, 1990, p. 261). They assume that they will be rejected by others, as they were rejected by their parents, and thus avoid interactions with others. Their thoughts are of this sort: "Once people get to know me, they see I'm really inferior." When they must interact with others, they are unassertive and nervous, because they think, "I must please this person in every way or she will criticize me." They also tend to discount any positive feedback they receive from others, believing that others are just being nice or do not see how incompetent they really are. A study of 130 patients with avoidant personality disorder found that they endorsed beliefs such as this more often than patients with other personality disorders (Beck et al., 2001).

Cognitive and behavior therapies have proven helpful for people with avoidant personality disorder (Shea, 1993). These therapies have included graduated exposure to social settings, social skills training, and challenges to negative automatic thoughts about social situations. People receiving these therapies show increases in the frequency and range of social contacts, decreases in avoidance behaviors, and increases in comfort and satisfaction in social activities (Pretzer, 2004).

People with avoidant personality disorder may choose professions that allow them to avoid other people.

Dependent Personality Disorder

People with **dependent personality disorder** are anxious about interpersonal interactions, but their anxiety stems from a deep need to be cared for by others, rather than a concern that they will be criticized. Their desire to be loved and taken care of by others leads persons with dependent personality disorder to deny any of their own thoughts and feelings that might displease others, to submit to even the most unreasonable demands, and to cling frantically to others. People with this personality disorder cannot make decisions for themselves and do not initiate new activities, except in an effort to please others. In contrast to people with avoidant personality disorder, who avoid relationships, people with dependent personality disorder can function only within a relationship. They deeply fear rejection and abandonment and may allow themselves to be exploited and abused rather than lose relationships, as in the case of Francesca:

> Francesca was in a panic, because her husband seemed to be getting increasingly annoyed with her. Last night, he became very angry when Francesca asked him to cancel an upcoming business trip, because she was terrified of being left at home alone. In a rage, her husband shouted, "You can't ever be alone! You can't do anything by yourself! You can't even decide what to have for dinner by yourself! I'm sick of it. Grow up and act like an adult!"

(continued)

C A S E   S T U D Y

It was true that Francesca had a very difficult time making decisions for herself. While she was in high school, she couldn't decide which courses to take and talked with her parents and friends for hours about what she should do, finally doing whatever her best friend or her mother told her to do. When she graduated from high school, she didn't feel smart enough to go to college, even though she had gotten good grades in high school. She drifted into a job because her best friend had a job with the same company, and she wanted to remain close to that friend. The friend eventually dumped Francesca, however, because she was tired of Francesca's incessant demands for reassurance. Francesca frequently bought gifts for the friend and offered to do the friend's laundry or cooking, in obvious attempts to win the friend's favor. But Francesca also talked to the friend for hours in the evening, asking her whether she thought Francesca had made the right decision about some trivial issue, such as what to buy her mother for Christmas and how she thought Francesca was performing on the job.

Soon after her friend dumped her, Francesca met her future husband, and, when he showed some interest in her, she quickly tried to form a close relationship with him. She liked the fact that he seemed strong and confident, and, when he asked her to marry him, Francesca thought that perhaps finally she would feel safe and secure. However, especially since he has begun to get angry with her frequently, Francesca has been worrying constantly that he is going to leave her.

Prevalence of Dependent Personality Disorder

Between 1.6 percent and 6.7 percent of people will develop dependent personality disorder at sometime in their lives (Ekselius et al., 2001; Weissman, 1993). Higher rates of the disorder are found when self-report research methods are used than when structured clinical interviews are used, suggesting that many people feel they have this disorder, when clinicians would not diagnose it in them. More women than men are diagnosed with this

disorder in clinical settings (Fabrega et al., 1991). Periods of dysthymia, major depression, and chronic anxiety over being separated from important others are common in people with the disorder (Grant et al., 2004).

Theories and Treatment of Dependent Personality Disorder

Dependent personality disorder runs in families, but it is unclear whether this is due to genetics or to family environments (Dahl, 1993). Children with histories of anxiety about separation from their parents or of chronic physical illness appear more prone to develop dependent personality disorder.

Cognitive theories argue that people with dependent personality disorder have beliefs such as "I am needy and weak," which drive their dependent behaviors. A study of 38 patients with dependent personality disorder found that they endorsed such beliefs more often than patients with other personality disorders (Beck et al., 2001).

Unlike people with many of the other personality disorders, persons with dependent personality disorder frequently seek treatment (Millon et al., 2000). Although many psychosocial therapies are used in the treatment of this disorder, none have been systematically tested for their effectiveness. Psychodynamic treatment focuses on helping clients gain insight into the early experiences with caregivers that led to their dependent behaviors through the use of free association, dream interpretation, and interpretation of the transference process. Nondirective and humanistic therapies may be helpful in fostering autonomy and self-confidence in persons with dependent personality disorder (Millon et al., 2000).

Cognitive-behavioral therapy for dependent personality disorder includes behavioral techniques designed to increase assertive behaviors and to decrease anxiety, as well as cognitive techniques designed to challenge assumptions about the need to rely on others (Beck & Freeman, 1990). Clients might be given graded exposure to anxiety-provoking situations, such as requesting help from a salesperson. Clients might also be taught relaxation skills, so that they can overcome anxiety enough to engage in homework assignments. They and their therapists might develop a hierarchy of increasingly difficult independent actions that the clients gradually attempt on their own—for example, beginning with deciding what to have for lunch and ending with deciding what job to take. After making each decision, clients are encouraged to recognize their competence and challenge the negative thoughts they had about making the decision.

"RONALD IS EXTREMELY COMPULSIVE."

© Sidney Harris, courtesy ScienceCartoonsPlus.com

Obsessive-Compulsive Personality Disorder

The characteristics of self-control, attention to detail, perseverance, and reliability are highly valued in many societies, including U.S. society. Some people, however, carry these traits to an extreme and become rigid, perfectionistic, dogmatic, ruminative, and emotionally blocked. These people are said to have **obsessive-compulsive personality disorder.** The obsessive-compulsive personality disorder shares features with obsessive-compulsive disorder (see Chapter 7), but obsessive-compulsive personality disorder represents a more generalized way of interacting with the world than does obsessive-compulsive disorder, which often involves only specific and constrained obsessional thoughts and compulsive behaviors.

People with obsessive-compulsive personality disorder seem grim and austere, tensely in control of their emotions, and lacking in spontaneity (Millon et al., 2000). They are workaholics and see little need for leisure activities or friendships. Other people experience them as stubborn, stingy, possessive, moralistic, and officious. They tend to relate to others in terms of rank or status and are ingratiating and deferential to "superiors" but dis-

missive, demeaning, or authoritarian toward "inferiors." Although they are extremely concerned with efficiency, their perfectionism and obsessions about following rules often interfere with their completion of tasks, as in the following case study (Spitzer et al., 1983, pp. 63–64).

CASE STUDY

Ronald Lewis is a 32-year-old accountant who is "having trouble holding on to a woman." He does not understand why, but the reasons become very clear as he tells his story. Mr. Lewis is a remarkably neat and well-organized man who tends to regard others as an interference to the otherwise mechanically perfect progression of his life. For many years he has maintained an almost inviolate schedule. On weekdays he arises at 6:47, has two eggs soft-boiled for 2 minutes, 45 seconds, and is at his desk at 8:15. Lunch is at 12:00, dinner at 6:00, bedtime at 11:00. He has separate Saturday and Sunday schedules, the latter characterized by a methodical and thorough trip through *The New York Times*. Any change in schedule causes him to feel varying degrees of anxiety, annoyance, and a sense that he is doing something wrong and wasting time.

Orderliness pervades Mr. Lewis's life. His apartment is immaculately clean and meticulously arranged. His extensive collections of books, records, and stamps are all carefully catalogued, and each item is reassuringly always in the right and familiar place. Mr. Lewis is highly valued at his work because his attention to detail has, at times, saved the company considerable embarrassment. . . . His perfectionism also presents something of a problem, however. He is the slowest worker in the office and probably the least productive. He gets the details right but may fail to put them in perspective. His relationships to coworkers are cordial but formal. He is on a "Mr. and Ms." basis with people he has known for years in an office that generally favors first names. Mr. Lewis's major problems are with women and follow the same repetitive pattern. At first, things go well.

(continued)

Soon, however, he begins to resent the intrusion upon his schedule a woman inevitably causes. This is most strongly illustrated in the bedtime arrangements. Mr. Lewis is a light and nervous sleeper with a rather elaborate routine preceding his going to bed. He must spray his sinuses, take two aspirin, straighten up the apartment, do 35 sit-ups and read two pages of the dictionary. The sheets must be of just the right crispness and temperature and the room must be noiseless. Obviously, a woman sleeping over interferes with his inner sanctum and, after sex, Mr. Lewis tries either to have the woman go home or sleep in the living room. No woman has put up with this for very long.

Prevalence of Obsessive-Compulsive Personality Disorder

Between 1.7 and 7.7 percent of the population can be diagnosed with obsessive-compulsive personality disorder, and it is more common in men than women (Ekselius et al., 2001; Fabrega et al., 1991; Weissman, 1993). People with this disorder are prone to depression and anxiety, but not to the same extent as people with avoidant or dependent personality disorder (Grant et al., 2004).

Theories and Treatment of Obsessive-Compulsive Personality Disorder

There are no family history, twin, or adoption studies specifically focusing on obsessive-compulsive personality disorder.

Early psychodynamic theorists attributed this personality disorder to fixation at the anal stage of development because the patient's parents were overly strict and punitive during toilet training (Freud, 1923). Harry Stack Sullivan (1953) argued that obsessive-compulsive personalities arise when children grow up in homes where there is much anger and hate that is hidden behind superficial love and niceness. The children do not develop interpersonal skills and, instead, avoid intimacy and follow rigid rules to gain a sense of self-esteem and self-control. These theories have not been empirically tested.

Cognitive theories suggest that people with this disorder harbor beliefs such as "Flaws, defects or mistakes are intolerable." One study found that people diagnosed with obsessive-compulsive personality disorder endorsed such beliefs significantly more often than people diagnosed with other personality disorders (Beck et al., 2001).

Supportive therapies may assist people with this disorder in overcoming the crises that send them for treatment, and behavior therapies can be used to decrease their compulsive behaviors (Beck & Freeman, 1990; Millon et al., 2000). For example, a client may be given the assignment to alter her usual rigid schedule for the day, first by simply getting up 15 minutes later than she usually does and then gradually changing additional elements of her schedule. The client may be taught to use relaxation techniques to overcome the anxiety created by alterations in the schedule. She might also write down the automatic negative thoughts she has about changes in the schedule ("Getting up 15 minutes later is going to put my entire day off"). In the next therapy session, she and the therapist might discuss the evidence for and against these automatic thoughts.

SUMMING UP

- People with the anxious-fearful personality disorders—avoidant, dependent, and obsessive-compulsive personality disorders—are chronically fearful or concerned.
- People with avoidant personality disorder worry about being criticized.
- People with dependent personality disorder worry about being abandoned.
- People with obsessive-compulsive personality disorder are locked into rigid routines of behavior and become anxious when their routines are violated.
- Some children may be born with temperamental predispositions toward shy and avoidant behaviors, or childhood anxiety may contribute to dependent personalities.
- These disorders may arise from a lack of nurturing parenting and basic fears about one's ability to function competently.

ALTERNATIVE CONCEPTUALIZATIONS OF PERSONALITY DISORDERS

The DSM-IV-TR scheme for conceptualizing and categorizing personality disorders is intentionally atheoretical. In other words, the authors of the DSM-IV-TR sought to describe the personality disorders that had been observed in clinical practice and research, independent of any theoretical conceptualization of personality that suggests which personality disorders should exist in humans. Many theorists have criticized this lack of theory, however, saying that it impedes the progress of research on personality disorders, because a good theory of personality disorders suggests which specific hypotheses about these disorders researchers should be tested.

Several theoretical schemes for the personality disorders have been suggested (see Trull & Durrett, 2005). Many of these schemes view the personality disorders as extreme variants of normal personality traits.

Five-Factor Model

One of the leading theories of "normal" personality is the **five-factor model,** which posits that any individual's personality is organized along five broad dimensions, or factors, of personality. These factors are often referred to as the Big 5: *neuroticism, extraversion, openness to experience, agreeableness, and conscientiousness* (McCrae & Costa, 1999) (see the Concept Overview in Table 12.6). Considerable research suggests that these five dimensions capture a great deal of the variation in people's personalities, and that the personality traits these dimensions describe are strongly influenced by genetics (Jang, McCrae, et al., 1998). These traits have

also been replicated in cultures very different from that of the United States, where they have been studied most (Benet-Martinez & John, 1998; Yang et al., 2002).

In turn, the DSM-IV-TR personality disorders can be conceptualized along these five dimensions (Costa & Widiger, 2002; Lynam & Widiger, 2001). For example, people with antisocial personality disorder can be characterized as high in antagonism and low in conscientiousness. People with dependent personality disorder can be characterized as high in agreeableness and high in neuroticism.

Several studies have found that people diagnosed with a personality disorder score higher on the traits that the five-factor model suggests they should score higher on (see Trull & Durrett, 2005). In addition, a longitudinal study of people in treatment for borderline, avoidant, or schizotypal personality disorder found that the degree to which they changed over time in the manifestation of their personality disorder was predicted by the degree to which they had previously changed in their scores on relevant Big 5 dimensions (Warner et al., 2004).

One advantage of translating the personality disorders into the Big 5 personality traits is that

---

| TABLE 12.6 | Concept Overview |

Big 5 Personality Factors

The five-factor model of personality posits that all personalities can be characterized by combinations of the five personality factors described in this table.

Factor	Key Characteristics
Neuroticism	Individuals high on neuroticism scales are chronically anxious, hostile, depressed, self-conscious, and impulsive and have poor coping skills; people low on neuroticism scales lack these problems.
Extraversion	Individuals high on extraversion scales are sociable, active, talkative, interpersonally oriented, optimistic, fun-loving, and affectionate; people low on extraversion scales (referred to as introverts) are reserved, sober, aloof, independent, and quiet.
Openness to experience	Individuals high in this factor actively seek and appreciate experiences for their own sake and are curious, imaginative, and willing to entertain new and unconventional ideas; people low in this factor are conventional in their beliefs and attitudes, conservative in their tastes, dogmatic, rigid in their beliefs, set in their ways, and emotionally unresponsive.
Agreeableness	Individuals high in this factor are softhearted, good-natured, trusting, helpful, forgiving, and altruistic; people low in this factor are cynical, rude, suspicious, uncooperative, and irritable and can be manipulative, vengeful, and ruthless.
Conscientiousness	Individuals high in this factor are organized, reliable, hardworking, self-directed, punctual, scrupulous, ambitious, and persevering; people low in this factor are aimless, unreliable, lazy, careless, lax, negligent, and hedonistic.

Source: Costa & McCrae, 1992.

research on gender differences in the Big 5 can be used to make hypotheses about what kinds of gender differences are likely to occur in the personality disorders (Corbitt & Widiger, 1995). For example, women tend to score higher than men on both neuroticism and agreeableness. If dependent personality disorder is an extreme version of this personality constellation, then we would expect women to be diagnosed with this personality disorder more than men, as they are (Widiger et al., 1994). On the other hand, the five-factor model suggests that there should be a personality disorder characterized by antagonistic closed-mindedness, and, because men tend to score higher on both antagonism and closed-mindedness, this personality disorder should be more frequently diagnosed in men than in women (Widiger, 1998). There is, however, no personality disorder in the DSM-IV-TR for antagonistic closed-mindedness. Thus, the five-factor model suggests a new personality disorder, which could be the focus of new research, and it suggests some hypotheses about the distribution of this disorder in males versus females. It is this guiding of research, provided by a theory such as the five-factor model, that leads many researchers to argue that the DSM-IV-TR should not be so atheoretical.

Evaluations of Dimensional Models

Critics of dimensional models note that redefining personality disorders in light of theories of normal personality does not avoid the difficult questions of where cutoffs should be drawn between what is normal and what is pathological. In addition, just because dimensional models, such as the five-factor model, describe normal personality well, this does not mean that they describe personality disorders well (Davis & Millon, 1993). Dimensional models are usually based on extensive empirical research on people in the general population, and they may be unlikely to capture the personality characteristics of the small portion of the population that has extreme personality disturbances. However, studies have replicated the five-factor model in psychiatric samples (Bagby et al., 1999). In addition, the empirical evidence that dimensional models capture the DSM-IV-TR personality disorders well is growing rapidly (Trull & Durrett, 2005).

These debates about the appropriate conceptualization and categorization of personality disorders are likely to continue for many years. They are difficult to resolve in part because it is inherently difficult to determine where normality ends and abnormality begins and to derive accurate ways of describing personality and its variants.

These debates are also difficult to resolve because the personality disorders do not represent discrete and acute sets of symptoms, as do many of the Axis I disorders. Instead, they appear to be naturally chronic, pervasive, and amorphous.

SUMMING UP

- Some critics of the definitions of personality disorders in the DSM-IV-TR have suggested that the personality disorders represent extremes of normal personality traits. These critics argue for dimensional models of these disorders.
- One scheme suggests organizing the personality disorders along dimensions of the Big 5 personality traits: neuroticism, extraversion, openness to experience, agreeableness, and conscientiousness.

CHAPTER INTEGRATION

Although the empirical research on the personality disorders is too lacking to allow a clear integration

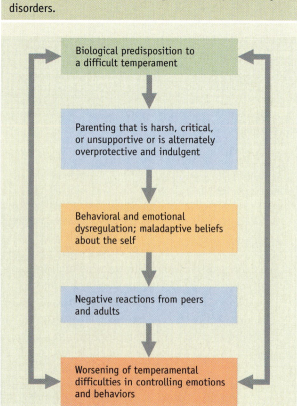

FIGURE 12.3   **An Integrated Model of the Personality Disorders.** A difficult temperament may combine with difficult parenting to lead to personality disorders.

of the biological, psychological, and social factors impinging on these disorders, some theoretical models have attempted this integration. They serve as the basis for current research (Millon et al., 2000; Siever & Davis, 1991; Trull & Durrett, 2005). According to these models, at the root of many of the personality disorders may be a biological predisposition to a certain kind of difficult temperament (see Figure 12.3).

For example, in the case of avoidant, dependent, and obsessive-compulsive personality disorders, an anxious and fearful temperament may be involved. In narcissistic and antisocial personality disorders, an impulsive and aggressive temperament may contribute. In borderline and histrionic personality disorders, a unstable, overly emotional temperament may be involved.

Children born with any of these temperaments are difficult to parent effectively. If parents can be supportive of these children yet set appropriate limits on their behavior, the children may never develop severe enough behavior or emotional problems to be diagnosed with a personality disorder. If parents are unable to counteract children's temperamental vulnerabilities or if they exacerbate these vulnerabilities with harsh, critical, unsupportive parenting or overprotective, indulgent parenting, then the children's temperamental vulnerabilities may grow into severe behavior and emotional problems, as well as maladaptive beliefs about the self. These problems will influence how others—teachers, peers, and eventually employers and mates—interact with the individuals, perhaps in ways that further exacerbate their temperamental vulnerabilities.

In this way, a lifelong pattern of dysfunction, called a personality disorder, may emerge out of the interaction between a child's biologically based temperament and others' reactions to that temperament.

Extraordinary People: Follow-Up

One of the fascinating aspects of Susanna Kaysen's autobiography, *Girl, Interrupted*, is that it provides a rare look inside an inpatient psychiatric ward from the perspective of a patient. The snippets of daily life on the ward are simultaneously touching and disturbing—friends who hurt themselves and attempt suicide, patients given powerful drugs and electroconvulsive therapy, young women wandering through life.

Kaysen's evaluation of the hospital is as complex as her own symptoms of distress:

> For many of us, the hospital was as much a refuge as it was a prison. Though we were cut off from the world and all the trouble we enjoyed stirring up out there, we were also cut off from the demands and expectations that had driven us crazy. What could be expected of us now that we were stowed away in a loony bin?
>
> The hospital shielded us from all sorts of things. We'd tell the staff to refuse phone calls or visits from anyone we didn't want to talk to, including our parents.
>
> "I'm too upset!" we'd wail, and we wouldn't have to talk to whoever it was.
>
> As long as we were willing to be upset, we didn't have to get jobs or go to school. We could weasel out of anything except eating and taking our medication.
>
> In a strange way we were free. We'd reached the end of the line. We had nothing more to lose. Our privacy, our liberty, our dignity: All of this was gone and we were stripped down to the bare bones of our selves.
>
> Naked, we needed protection, and the hospital protected us. Of course, the hospital had stripped us naked in the first place—but that just underscored its obligation to shelter us. (Kaysen, 1993, p. 94)

If you read *Girl, Interrupted*, or see the movie by the same name, you will get a flavor of the controversies surrounding the personality disorders, particularly borderline personality disorder. Are they just extreme versions of normal personalities? Are they vehicles for pathologizing people who don't "fit in"? Or are they legitimate diagnoses for people suffering from significant mental-health problems?

- The DSM-IV-TR divides the personality disorders into three clusters: the odd-eccentric disorders, the dramatic-emotional disorders, and the anxious-fearful disorders (Table 12.1). This organization is based on symptom clusters. It assumes that there is a dividing line between normal personality and pathological personality.

- The odd-eccentric disorders are characterized by odd or eccentric patterns of behavior and thought, including paranoia, extreme social withdrawal or inappropriate social interactions, and magical or illusory thinking. (Review Table 12.2.) This group of disorders, particularly schizotypal personality disorder, may be genetically linked to schizophrenia and may represent mild variations of schizophrenia. People with these disorders tend to have poor social relationships and are at increased risk for some acute psychiatric disorders, especially depression and schizophrenia.

- Psychoanalytic and cognitive therapies have been devised for these disorders, but they have not been empirically tested for their efficacy. Neuroleptic and atypical antipsychotic drugs appear to reduce the odd thinking of people with schizotypal personality disorder.

- The dramatic-emotional personality disorders include four disorders characterized by dramatic, erratic, and emotional behavior and interpersonal relationships: antisocial personality disorder, borderline personality disorder, histrionic personality disorder, and narcissistic personality disorder. (Review Table 12.3.) Persons with these disorders tend to be manipulative, volatile, uncaring in social relationships, and prone to impulsive behaviors.

- Antisocial personality disorder (ASPD) is one of the most common personality disorders and is more common in men than in women. There are several possible contributors to antisocial personality disorder. (Review Table 12.4.) These contributors include a genetic predisposition; the effects of testosterone on fetal brain development; low levels of serotonin; low arousability; attention-deficit-hyperactivity disorder; harsh, inconsistent parenting; and assumptions about the world that promote aggressive responses. (Review Figure 12.1.)

- Psychotherapy is not considered extremely effective for people with antisocial personality disorder.

- Lithium, the selective serotonin reuptake inhibitors, and antipsychotics may help control impulsive behaviors.

- People with borderline personality disorder show instability in their moods, self-concept, and interpersonal relationships. This disorder is more common in women than in men. People with the disorder may suffer from low levels of serotonin, which lead to impulsive behaviors. There is little evidence that borderline personality disorder is transmitted genetically, but the family members of people with this disorder show high rates of mood disorders.

- Psychoanalytic theorists argue that borderline personality disorder is the result of poorly developed and integrated views of the self, which are due to poor early relationships with caregivers. Cognitive theorists see this disorder as stemming from deficits in self-concept. Many people with this disorder were the victims of physical and sexual abuse in childhood.

- Drug treatments have not proven very effective for borderline personality disorder. Psychoanalytic and cognitive therapies focus on establishing a stronger self-identity in people with this disorder.

- Histrionic and narcissistic personality disorders are both characterized by dramatic self-presentations and unstable personal relationships. A person with histrionic personality disorder looks to others for approval, whereas a person with narcissistic personality disorder relies on self-evaluations.

- The anxious-fearful personality disorders include three disorders characterized by anxious and fearful emotions and chronic self-doubt, leading to maladaptive behaviors: dependent personality disorder, avoidant personality disorder, and obsessive-compulsive personality disorder. (Review Table 12.5.)

- Dependent personality disorder is more common in women, obsessive-compulsive personality disorder is more common in men, and avoidant personality disorder is equally common in men and women. Dependent and avoidant personality disorders tend to run in families, but it is not clear whether this is due to genetics or to family environments.

- Several alternative models of the personality disorders have been developed. One prominent model is based on theories of normal personality. The five-factor model of personality suggests that five basic factors describe most of personality: neuroticism, extraversion, openness to experience, agreeableness, and conscientiousness. (Review Table 12.6.) Personality disorders may be extreme variants of these factors.

MindMap CD-ROM

The following resources on the MindMap CD-ROM that came with this text will help you to master the content of this chapter and prepare for tests:

- Video: Borderline Personality Disorder
- Chapter Timeline
- Chapter Quiz

Key Terms

personality 423

personality disorder 423

odd-eccentric personality disorders 428

paranoid personality disorder 428

schizoid personality disorder 431

schizotypal personality disorder 432

dramatic-emotional personality disorders 435

antisocial personality disorder (ASPD) 435

psychopathy 436

serotonin 438

executive functions 438

borderline personality disorder 440

splitting 443

dialectical behavior therapy 444

histrionic personality disorder 444

narcissistic personality disorder 445

anxious-fearful personality disorders 447

avoidant personality disorder 447

dependent personality disorder 449

obsessive-compulsive personality disorder 451

five-factor model 453

> Chapter 13

In the Fields
by Daniel Nevins

*Youth, even in its sorrows, always has a brilliancy of
its own.*

—Victor Hugo, "Saint Denis," *Les Miserables*
(1962; translated by Charles E. Wilbour)

Childhood Disorders <

Extraordinary People

■ Temple Grandin: *Thinking in Pictures*

Behavior Disorders

The behavior disorders include attention-deficit/ hyperactivity disorder (ADHD), conduct disorder, and oppositional defiant disorder. Children with attention-deficit/hyperactivity disorder have trouble maintaining attention and controlling impulsive behavior and are hyperactive. Children with conduct or oppositional defiant disorder engage in frequent antisocial or defiant behavior.

Separation Anxiety Disorder

One of the most common emotional disorders of childhood is separation anxiety disorder, in which children are extremely anxious about any separation from their primary caregivers. Behavioral and cognitive therapies are often used to treat this disorder.

Elimination Disorders

The two elimination disorders are enuresis—uncontrolled wetting—and encopresis—uncontrolled bowel movements. The most effective treatment is a behavioral technique that teaches children to awaken at night when they need to go to the bathroom.

Disorders of Cognitive, Motor, and Communication Skills

Disorders of cognitive, motor, and communication skills involve deficits and delays in the development of fundamental skills. These include learning disorders, a motor skills disorder, and the communication disorders.

Taking Psychology Personally

■ College Students with Mental Disorders

Mental Retardation

Children diagnosed with mental retardation have deficits in cognitive skills that range from mild to severe. A number of genetic factors and biological traumas in the early years of life can contribute to mental retardation. Social factors, such as poverty or lack of a good education, can also contribute to mental retardation.

Pervasive Developmental Disorders

The pervasive developmental disorders include autism, Asperger's disorder, Rett's disorder, and childhood disintegrative disorder. These disorders are characterized by severe and lasting impairment in several areas of development, including social interaction, communication with others, everyday behaviors, interests, and activities. Autism, the most researched of these disorders, has biological roots but often responds well to behavioral interventions.

Chapter Integration

The study of psychological disorders in children is often referred to as developmental psychopathology. Researchers in this field are concerned with the interdependence of biological, psychological, and social development in children, recognizing that disruptions in any one of these three systems are likely to affect the other systems.

Extraordinary People

Temple Grandin: *Thinking in Pictures*

Dr. Temple Grandin, professor of animal sciences at Colorado State University, has designed one-third of all the livestock-handling facilities in the United States. She has published dozens of scientific papers and gives lectures throughout the world. Sometimes, those lectures describe the new equipment and procedures she has designed for safer and more humane handling of animals. Sometimes, however, those lectures describe her life with autism.

As a young child, Grandin had all the classic symptoms of autism. When she was a baby, she had no desire to be held by her mother and struggled to get away, but she was calm if left alone in a baby carriage. She seldom made eye contact with others, seemed to have no interest in people, and was constantly staring off into space. She frequently threw wild tantrums and smeared her feces around. If left alone, she rocked back and forth or spun around indefinitely. She could sit for hours on the beach, watching sand dribbling through her fingers, in a trancelike state. She still had not begun talking at age 2½. She was labeled as "brain-damaged," because 40 years ago doctors did not know about autism.

Fortunately, Grandin's mother was dogged about finding good teachers, learning ways to calm her daughter, and encouraging her daughter to speak and engage in the social world. Grandin had learned to speak by the time she entered elementary school, although most of her deficits in social interactions remained. When she was 12 years old, Grandin scored 137 on an IQ test but still was thrown out of a regular school because she didn't fit in. She persisted, however, and eventually went to college, earning a degree in psychology, and then to graduate school, where she earned a Ph.D. in animal sciences.

Grandin's autobiography *Thinking in Pictures* (1995), and her most recent book, *Animals in Translation* (Grandin & Johnson, 2005), provide remarkable insights into the motivations and experiences behind some of the strange symptoms of autism. She describes how she, like many people with autism, thinks visually instead of verbally:

Today, everyone is excited about the new virtual reality computer systems in which the user wears special goggles and is fully immersed in video game action. To me, these systems are like crude cartoons. My imagination works like the computer graphics programs that created the lifelike dinosaurs in Jurassic Park. When I do an equipment simulation in my imagination or work on an engineering problem, it is like seeing it on a videotape in my mind. I can view it from any angle, placing myself above or below the equipment and rotating it at the same time. I don't need any fancy graphics program that can produce three-dimensional design simulations. I can do it better and faster in my head. (Grandin, 1995, p. 21)

This ability to visualize has been of tremendous value in Grandin's career as a facilities designer. She can literally take a "cow's-eye view" of holding facilities and equipment, seeing what a cow sees as it is shuttled down a shoot, even before the equipment is built. This has led her to develop revolutionary new designs for this equipment that prevent animals from panicking and, thus, either hurting themselves, possibly fatally, or being exposed to cruel tactics, such as electric cattle prods.

Thinking in pictures instead of words is part of what made it difficult for her to learn language, however. She was able to learn nouns relatively easily, because she could visualize the objects to which these words refer. Other components of language were more difficult, until she developed a means for visualizing them, too:

I also visualize verbs. The word "jumping" triggers a memory of jumping hurdles at the mock Olympics held at my elementary school. Adverbs often trigger inappropriate images—"quickly" reminds me of Nestle's

Quick—unless they are paired with a verb, which modifies my visual image. For example, "he ran quickly" triggers an animated image of Dick from the first grade reading book running fast, and "he walked slowly" slows the image down. As a child, I left out words such as "is," "the," and "it," because they had no meaning by themselves. Similarly, words like "of" and "an" made no sense. Eventually, I learned how to use them properly, because my parents always spoke correct English and I mimicked their speech patterns. To this day certain verb conjugations, such as "to be," are absolutely meaningless to me. (Grandin, 1995, pp. 30–31)

Still, Grandin has been able to thrive in her career and her personal life, channeling some of her symptoms of autism into good use and overcoming other symptoms with intellect and good humor. Not all people with autism are able to do this, but Grandin's autobiography is a testimony to the importance of early detection and intervention for children with serious mental-health problems.

We like to think of childhood as a time relatively free from stress, when boys and girls can enjoy the simple pleasures of everyday life and are immune from major psychological problems. Yet this was not the case for Temple Grandin, nor is it the case for many children. Large-scale epidemiological studies suggest that more than a third of all children suffer from a significant emotional or behavior disorder by the time they are 16 (Costello et al., 2003). As you can see in Table 13.1 on page 462, boys are more vulnerable to mental-health problems than are girls prior to age 16. Overall, a substantial minority of children and adolescents do not live a carefree existence. Instead, they experience distressing symptoms severe enough to warrant attention from mental-health professionals.

For some children, psychological symptoms and disorders are linked to major stressors in their environment. A large and growing number of children in the United States and other countries are faced with severe circumstances that would overwhelm the coping capacities of many adults. In the United States, about 18 percent of children live below the poverty line (*Washington Post,* 2004). Children living in the inner cities—particularly in housing projects, where many poor families reside—are often exposed to violence. For example, in one study of 9- to 12-year-old children in an urban area in the United States, 97 percent reported witnessing or being the victim of some sort of violence in the past year; 37 percent of the children had been beaten up; 19 percent had been chased or

threatened (Purugganan et al., 2003). Those who had been exposed to violence had significantly more negative mental-health symptoms than those who had not been exposed.

Most children who face one such stressor are beset by multiple stressors. For example, children in poverty are more likely than other children to witness or be the victims of violence, to use illicit drugs, to engage in unprotected sexual intercourse, and to face racial and ethnic discrimination and harassment. These stressors appear to have a cumulative effect on children's risk for psychological problems. The more stressors a child encounters, the more likely he or she is to experience severe psychological symptoms (Cicchetti & Toth, 2005).

What is remarkable is that many, perhaps most, children who face major stressors do *not* develop severe psychological symptoms or disorders. These children have been referred to as *resilient* children (Garmezy, 1991; Luthar, 2003). It is not known exactly what makes these children so resilient in the face of stress, but having at least one healthy, competent adult to rely on seems to help. Temple Grandin's mother, for example, played a key role in her daughter's early life. In addition, studies of homeless children suggest that those who have high-quality interactions with a parent are no more likely to develop psychological problems than are children who are not homeless (Masten & Powell, 2003).

Conversely, many children who develop psychological disorders do not have any major stressors in their lives to which the development of the

TABLE 13.1   Prevalence of Mental Disorders in Children.

Estimated percentages of children who suffer psychological disorders by age 16 years (note that children can be diagnosed with more than one disorder).

Diagnosis	Total	Girls	Boys
Any disorder	36.7	31.0	42.3
Any anxiety disorder	9.9	12.1	7.7
Any depressive disorder	9.5	11.7	7.3
Any behavior disorder	23.0	16.1	29.9
Conduct disorder	9.0	3.8	14.1
Oppositional defiant disorder	11.3	9.1	13.4
ADHD*	4.1	1.1	7.0
Substance use disorder (e.g., alcohol abuse)	12.2	10.1	14.3

Source: Costello, Mustillo, et al., 2003.
*ADHD = attention-deficit/hyperactivity disorder.

disorders can be linked. These children may come from privileged backgrounds, in which they have not been exposed to any traumas or chronic problems. However, they still develop psychological disorders or symptoms.

It seems that among children, as among adults, most psychological disorders are the result of multiple factors, such as biological predispositions plus environmental stressors. One biological factor that has been implicated in the development of many psychological disorders in children is temperament. As noted in Chapter 12, *temperament* is a child's arousability and general mood. Children with "difficult" temperaments are highly sensitive to stimulation, become upset easily, and have trouble calming themselves when upset. They also tend to have generally negative moods and trouble adapting to new situations, particularly social situations (Thomas & Chess, 1984). Children with difficult temperaments are more likely than other children to have both minor and major psychological problems during childhood and later in life (Caspi et al., 2003).

Temperament probably has strong biological roots, including genetic roots (Rothbart & Bates, 1998). The link between temperament and the development of psychological problems is not exclusively biological, however. Children with difficult temperaments elicit more negative interactions from others, including their parents. Adults act less affectionately toward children with difficult temperaments, and other children are more likely

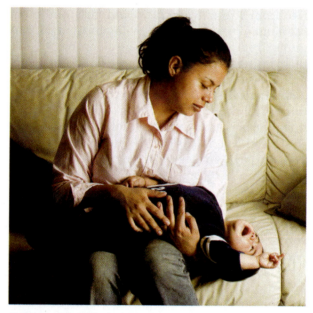

Children with difficult temperaments can make parenting stressful.

to be hostile toward these children. The negative environments that children with difficult temperaments create for themselves may contribute to their psychological problems, rather than the actual difficult temperaments. Conversely, children with difficult temperaments who receive high-quality parenting are not at high risk for psychological problems, whereas children with difficult

TABLE 13.2 Concept Overview

Disorders of Childhood

These disorders have their first onset in childhood.

Category	Specific Disorders
Behavior disorders	Attention-deficit/hyperactivity disorder
	Conduct disorder
	Oppositional defiant disorder
Separation/anxiety disorder	
Elimination disorders	Enuresis
	Encopresis
Disorders in cognitive, motor, and communication skills	Learning disorders
	Reading disorder (dyslexia)
	Mathematics disorder
	Disorder of written expression
	Motor skills disorder
	Developmental coordination disorder
	Communication disorders
	Expressive language disorder
	Mixed receptive-expressive language disorder
	Phonological disorder
	Stuttering
Mental retardation	Mild, moderate, severe, and profound mental retardation
Pervasive developmental disorders	Autism
	Rett's disorder
	Childhood disintegrative disorder
	Asperger's disorder
Tic disorders	Tourette's disorder
	Chronic motor or focal tic disorder
	Transient tic disorder
Feeding and eating disorders	Pica
	Rumination disorder
	Feeding disorder of infancy or early childhood
Other disorders	Selective mutism
	Reactive attachment disorder
	Stereotypic movement disorder

temperaments who are part of dysfunctional families are at high risk (Plomin, 1994).

In this chapter, we examine the roles that biology and psychosocial factors play in the development of specific psychological disorders in children. A large number of disorders can be diagnosed in children. The Concept Overview in Table 13.2 lists several disorders that are usually first diagnosed in childhood or infancy. In addition, several disorders we have already discussed can also occur for the first time during childhood or adolescence. We reviewed information on childhood depression in Chapter 9 and on the anxiety disorders in childhood in Chapters 6 and 7.

We focus on some of the most common and severe of the disorders that usually begin in infancy or childhood. First, we discuss the behavior disorders, specifically attention-deficit/hyperactivity disorder, conduct disorder, and oppositional defiant disorder. Children with these disorders have trouble paying attention and controlling socially inappropriate behaviors. Then we turn to an anxiety disorder that is prevalent in children, separation anxiety disorder.

The third group of disorders we discuss is the elimination disorders, enuresis and encopresis. Children with these disorders have trouble controlling bladder and bowel movements far beyond the age at which most children learn to control them. The fourth group is disorders of cognitive, motor, and communication skills, and the fifth is mental retardation. Finally, the sixth group is pervasive developmental disorders. Within this sixth group, we focus on autism, the disorder that Temple Grandin has had since infancy, because it has been the focus of more research.

The study of childhood disorders has expanded greatly in the past two decades and has grown into a field known as *developmental psychopathology*. Developmental psychopathologists try to understand when children's behaviors cross the line from the normal difficulties of childhood into unusual or abnormal problems that warrant concern (Cicchetti & Toth, 2005). Most children have transient emotional or behavior problems sometime during childhood. That is, most children go through periods in which they are unusually fearful or easily distressed or engage in behaviors such as lying or stealing, but these periods pass relatively quickly and are often specific to certain situations. Differentiating these normal periods of distress from signs of a developing psychological disorder is not easy. Developmental psychopathologists also try to understand the impact of normal development on the form that abnormal behaviors take. That is, children's levels of cognitive, social, and emotional development can affect the types of symptoms they show. These developmental considerations make the assessment, diagnosis, and treatment of childhood disorders quite challenging, but helping children overcome their problems and get back on the path to healthy development can be highly rewarding.

BEHAVIOR DISORDERS

The *behavior disorders* have been the focus of a great deal of research, probably because children with these disorders can be quite difficult to deal with, and their behaviors can exact a heavy toll on society. The three behavior disorders we discuss are *attention-deficit/hyperactivity disorder, conduct disorder*, and *oppositional defiant disorder*. These are distinct disorders, but they often co-occur in the same child (see the Concept Overview in Table 13.3).

Attention-Deficit/ Hyperactivity Disorder

"Pay attention! Slow down! You're so hyper today!" These are phrases that most children hear their parents saying to them at least occasionally. A major focus of socialization is helping children learn to pay attention, control their impulses, and organize their behaviors, so that they can accomplish long-term goals. Some children have tremendous trouble learning these skills, however, and may be diagnosed with **attention-deficit/ hyperactivity disorder,** or **ADHD.** Eddie is a young boy with ADHD (adapted from Spitzer et al., 1994, pp. 351–352):

CASE STUDY

Eddie, age 9, was referred to a child psychiatrist at the request of his school because of the difficulties he creates in class. His teacher complains that he is so restless that his classmates are unable to concentrate. He is hardly ever in his seat and mostly roams around the class, talking to other children while they are working. When the teacher is able to get him to stay in his seat, he fidgets with his hands and feet and drops things on the floor. He never seems to know what he is going to do next and may suddenly do something quite outrageous. His most recent suspension from school was for swinging from the fluorescent light fixture over the blackboard. Because he was unable to climb down again, the class was in an uproar.

His mother says that Eddie's behavior has been difficult since he was a toddler and that, as a 3-year-old, he was unbearably restless and demanding. He has always required little sleep and been awake before anyone else.

(continued)

TABLE 13.3   Concept Overview

Behavior Disorders

The behavior disorders involve extreme inattention, hyperactivity, and socially inappropriate behavior.

Disorder	Symptoms	Proposed Etiologies	Treatments
Attention-deficit/ hyperactivity disorder (ADHD)	Inattention, hyperactivity, impulsivity	1. Immaturity of the brain, particularly frontal lobes, caudate nucleus, and corpus callosum 2. Genetic predisposition 3. Prenatal and birth complications 4. Disrupted families	1. Stimulant drugs (e.g., Ritalin) 2. Behavior therapy focused on reinforcing attentive, goal-directed behaviors and extinguishing impulsive, hyperactive behaviors
Conduct disorder	Behaviors that violate the basic rights of others and the norms for social behavior	1. Genetic predisposition 2. Deficits in brain regions involved in planning and controlling behavior 3. Difficult temperament 4. Lower physiological arousal to punishment 5. Serotonin imbalances 6. Higher testosterone level 7. Poor parental supervision, parental uninvolvement, parental violence 8. Delinquent peer groups 9. Cognitions that promote aggression	1. Antidepressants, neuroleptics, stimulants, lithium 2. Cognitive-behavioral therapy focused on changing hostile cognitions, teaching children to take others' perspectives, and teaching problem-solving skills
Oppositional defiant disorder	Argumentativeness, negativity, irritability, defiance, but behaviors not as severe as in conduct disorder	Same as conduct disorder	Same as conduct disorder

When he was small, "he got into everything," particularly in the early morning, when he would awaken at 4:30 A.M. or 5:00 A.M. and go downstairs by himself. His parents would awaken to find the living room or kitchen "demolished." When he was 4 years old, he managed to unlock the door of the apartment and wander off into a busy main street but, fortunately, was rescued from oncoming traffic by a passerby.

Eddie has no interest in TV and dislikes games or toys that require any concentration or patience. He is not popular with other children and at home prefers to be outdoors, playing with his dog or riding his bike. If he does play with toys, his games are messy and destructive, and his mother cannot get him to keep his things in any order.

Eddie's difficulties in paying attention and his impulsivity go far beyond what is normal for a child his age. Most elementary school age children can sit still for a period of time and like to engage in at least some games that require patience and concentration. They can inhibit their impulses to jump up in class and talk to other children or to walk out into busy traffic. Eddie cannot do any of these things. His behavior has a character of being driven and disorganized, following one whim and then the next, as is common in children with ADHD (see Table 13.4 for DSM-IV-TR symptoms).

There are three subtypes of ADHD. Most children and adolescents with ADHD have the *Combined Type,* which is defined by the presence of six or more of the symptoms of inattention and six or more of the symptoms of hyperactivity-impulsivity listed in Table 13.4. The *Predominantly Inattentive Type* is diagnosed if six or more symptoms of inattention but fewer than six symptoms of hyperactivity-impulsivity are present. Some researchers argue that certain symptoms indicating a *sluggish cognitive tempo* are also important parts of the Predominantly Inattentive Type. These symptoms include the slow retrieval of information from memory and slow processing of infor-

---

TABLE 13.4   DSM-IV-TR

Symptoms of Attention-Deficit/Hyperactivity Disorder (ADHD)

The symptoms of attention-deficit/hyperactivity disorder fall into three clusters: inattention, hyperactivity, and impulsivity.

Inattention

Does not pay attention to details and makes careless mistakes

Has difficulty sustaining attention

Does not seem to be listening when others are talking

Does not follow through on instructions or finish tasks

Has difficulty organizing behaviors

Avoids activities that require sustained effort and attention

Loses things frequently

Is easily distracted

Is forgetful

Hyperactivity

Fidgets with hands or feet and squirms in seat

Leaves his or her seat when it is inappropriate

Runs around or climbs excessively

Has difficulty engaging in quiet activities

Often acts as if "driven by a motor"

Often talks excessively

Impulsivity

Blurts out responses while others are talking

Has difficulty waiting his or her turn

Often interrupts or intrudes on others

Source: Reprinted with permission from the *Diagnostic and Statistical Manual of Mental Disorders,* Fourth Edition, Text Revision. Copyright © 2000 American Psychiatric Association.

mation, low levels of alertness, drowsiness, and daydreaming (McBurnett, Pfiffner, & Frick, 2001). The *Predominantly Hyperactive-Impulsive Type* is diagnosed if six or more symptoms of hyperactivity-impulsivity but fewer than six symptoms of inattention are present. Eddie appears to have this type. Jason, however, in the following case study, appears to have the Predominantly Inattentive Type:

CASE STUDY

Jason, a second-grade student, was known by his classmates as "The Space Cadet." He often spent classtime drawing pictures of space ships and aliens instead of paying attention to what was going on. When the teacher tried to get his attention, she often had to nearly shout at him, and then he would raise his head slowly, as if he'd been in another world.

On the playground, Jason was not popular. He was seldom chosen for baseball teams because he tended to ignore what was happening in the field and, instead, gazed at the vehicles passing by on the road or the children playing in an adjacent playground. Jason also had a temper, and he sometimes exploded at another child if he felt he was being insulted. Most days on the playground, Jason just flitted from one group of children to another, intrusively inserting himself into ongoing games, getting angry when something didn't go his way, and stalking off to the next group of children.

At home, Jason's parents had to watch over him closely. He was constantly losing things, particularly books and materials related to school, so every morning was a panic as he and his parents searched far and wide for books and homework sheets, which Jason usually had forgotten to complete the night before.

Many children like Eddie and Jason do poorly in school. Because they cannot pay attention or quell their hyperactivity, they do not learn the material they are being taught and perform below their intellectual capabilities (Whalen & Henker, 1998). In addition, 20 to 25 percent of children with ADHD have serious learning disabilities that make it doubly hard for them to concentrate in school and to learn (Wilens, Biederman, & Spencer, 2002).

Some children with ADHD have extremely poor relationships with other children and, like Eddie and Jason, are rejected outright by other children (Hinshaw & Melnick, 1995). When interacting with their peers, children with ADHD are disorganized and never finish anything. They are intrusive, irritable, and demanding. They want to play by their own rules and have explosive tempers, so that, when things do not go their way, they may become physically violent (Whalen & Henker, 1998).

The behavior problems of some children with ADHD are so severe that they may also be diagnosed with a *conduct disorder*. Children with conduct disorders grossly violate the norms for appropriate behavior toward others by acting in uncaring and even violent ways. Between 45 and 60 percent of children with ADHD develop conduct disorders, abuse drugs, or become juvenile delinquents (Waschbusch, 2002; Wilens et al., 2002). The conduct problems that some children with ADHD have persist into adulthood (Abramowitz, Kosson, & Seidenberg, 2004).

ADHD has become a popular diagnosis to give to children who are disruptive in school or at home, and the media attention on ADHD over the past decade has made it seem that there is an epidemic of this disorder. However, various epidemiological studies indicate that only 1 to 7 percent of children develop ADHD (Angold et al., 2002; Wilens et al., 2002). Boys are about three times more likely than girls to develop ADHD in childhood and early adolescence (Angold et al., 2002). Boys with ADHD tend to have more disruptive behavior than girls with ADHD, and this may lead to an underidentification of ADHD in girls (Biederman et al., 2002). ADHD is found across most cultures and ethnic groups.

The long-term outcomes for children with ADHD vary considerably. The symptoms of ADHD persist from childhood into young adulthood for about three-quarters of these children (Wilens et al., 2002). Adults who were diagnosed with ADHD as children are at increased risk for antisocial personality disorder, substance abuse, mood and anxiety disorders, marital problems, traffic accidents, legal infractions, and frequent job changes (Barkley et al., 2004; Wilens et al., 2002). Adults who have ADHD are at high risk for depression, anxiety disorders, substance abuse, and antisocial personality disorder (Biederman et al., 2004). However, many children grow out of ADHD. By early adulthood, their ADHD

Children normally have high energy levels but only a minority of children can be labeled hyperactive.

symptoms have passed, and they go on to lead normal, healthy lives (Mannuza et al., 1998).

Biological Contributors to ADHD

ADHD was formerly referred to as *minimal brain damage,* under the assumption that the attentional deficits and hyperactivity were due to mild brain damage. Most children who develop ADHD, however, have no history of brain injury, and most children with some brain injury do not develop ADHD.

Modern studies have shown that children with ADHD differ from children with no psychological disorders on a variety of measures of neurological functioning and cerebral blood flow (Barkley, 1996; Wilens et al., 2002). The areas of the brain most likely involved in ADHD include the frontal lobes; the caudate nucleus within the basal ganglia; the corpus callosum, which connects the two lobes of the brain; and the pathways between these structures (Bradley & Golden, 2001). Each of these brain areas and pathways plays an important role in the deployment of attention, the regulation of impulses, and the planning of complex behavior. One hypothesis is that children with ADHD are neurologically immature—their brains are slower in developing than are other children's—and this is why they

Corpus callosum

Caudate nucleus

Frontal lobe

These areas of the brain are most likely involved in ADHD.

are unable to maintain attention and control their behavior at a level that is appropriate for their age. This *immaturity hypothesis* helps explain why the symptoms of ADHD decline with age in many children.

The neurotransmitter that is most consistently implicated in ADHD is dopamine (Dougherty et al., 1999; Krause et al., 2000). Although serotonin seems to play a role in aggressive behavior, it does not appear to be central to ADHD (Wilens et al., 2002).

ADHD runs in families. Between 10 and 35 percent of the immediate family members of children with ADHD are also likely to have the disorder (Barkley, 1996; Biederman et al., 1986, 1990). Several other disorders also tend to run in the families of children with ADHD, including antisocial personality disorder, alcoholism, and depression (Barkley, 1991; Faraone et al., 1991). Twin studies and adoption studies also suggest that genetic factors play a role in vulnerability to ADHD (Eaves et al., 1997; Gilger, Pennington, & DeFries, 1992; Nadder et al., 1998; Rhee et al., 1999). It is not clear exactly what aspects of the ADHD syndrome are inherited, whether they are problems with attention, hyperactivity, impulsivity, or aggressivity. Molecular genetics studies suggest that the dopamine transporter genes may be abnormal in ADHD (Wilens et al., 2002).

Many children with ADHD have histories of prenatal and birth complications, including maternal ingestion of large amounts of nicotine or barbiturates during pregnancy, low birthweight, premature delivery, and difficult delivery, leading to oxygen deprivation (Bradley & Golden, 2001). Some investigators suspect that moderate to severe drinking by mothers during pregnancy can lead to the kinds of problems in inhibiting behaviors seen in children with ADHD. As preschoolers, some of these children were exposed to high concentrations of lead, when they ingested lead-based paint (Fergusson, Horwood, & Lynskey, 1993).

The popular notion that hyperactivity in children is caused by dietary factors, such as consuming large amounts of sugar, has not been supported in controlled studies (Whalen & Henker, 1998). A few studies do suggest, however, that a subset of children with ADHD have severe allergies to food additives and that removing these additives from these children's diets can reduce hyperactivity (Bradley & Golden, 2001).

Psychological and Social Contributors to ADHD

Children with ADHD are more likely than children without psychological disturbances to belong to families in which there are frequent disruptions, such as changes in residence or parental divorce (Barkley et al., 1990). Their fathers are more prone to antisocial and criminal behavior, and the children's interactions with their mothers are often marked with hostility and conflict (Barkley et al., 1990). Some investigators argue that there is a nongenetic form of ADHD that is caused by environmental adversity (Bauermeister et al., 1992). Others argue, however, that both ADHD and difficult family environments are the result of genetic predispositions to problems with lack of control (see Barkley, 1996).

Certainly, having a child with ADHD can impose significant stress on parents and a family. The explosive temper; the impulsive, dangerous activities; the school difficulties; and the rejection by peers can lead to constant conflict between children and the parents and siblings. Family members may not understand that a child with ADHD cannot voluntarily control his or her behavior simply when told to and, thus, may blame the child. Much of the treatment of ADHD in a child involves the parents, and sometimes siblings, in reshaping the family's interactions to reduce the symptoms of ADHD in the target child and to improve overall family functioning.

Treatments for ADHD

The most common treatment for ADHD in children is the use of stimulant drugs, such as Ritalin, Dexedrine, and Adderall. It may seem odd to give a stimulant drug to a hyperactive child, but between 70 and 85 percent of ADHD children respond to these drugs with *decreases* in demanding, disruptive, and noncompliant behavior (Joshi, 2004). They also show increases in positive mood, in the ability to be goal-directed, and in the quality of their interactions with others. The stimulants may work because they increase dopamine levels in the synapses of the brain by enhancing the release and inhibiting the reuptake of this neurotransmitter (Joshi, 2004).

The side effects of stimulants include reduced appetite, insomnia, edginess, and gastrointestinal upset. They can also increase the frequency of tics in children with ADHD. Some youth abuse stimulants, and recent reports have focused on college students who "fake" ADHD in order to get a prescription for stimulants, which they use to help them stay awake and work long hours in college (Joshi, 2004; Wilens et al., 2002).

Nationwide, the number of children prescribed stimulant medications increased by 200 to 300 percent in the past two decades (Joshi, 2004). Some researchers have argued that this greater use

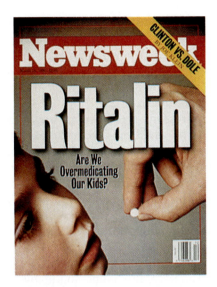

Some people think that attention-deficit/hyperactivity disorder is being overdiagnosed and that too many children are being prescribed Ritalin and other stimulant drugs.

is due to an increase in recognition of the disorder and treatment-seeking for children with ADHD. Others argue that it represents an inappropriate overuse of drugs, particularly for children who are difficult to control (see Angold et al., 2000). However, there is scant empirical evidence on which to judge these competing claims.

In one cross-sectional study of four U.S. communities, only 12 percent of the children meeting the diagnostic criteria for ADHD had received stimulants in the preceding year, suggesting that most children with the disorder are going untreated (Jensen et al., 1999). On the other hand, in a longitudinal study of children in a predominantly rural area, 72 percent of those with ADHD received stimulants at some point during the four years they were followed, suggesting that most children with ADHD are being treated (Angold et al., 2000). In this study, most of the children who were taking stimulants, however, did *not* have symptoms meeting the diagnostic criteria for ADHD. The boys and younger children in this study were especially likely to be prescribed stimulants in the absence of symptoms meeting the criteria for ADHD. More research is needed to determine how appropriately stimulants are being used.

Other drugs that are used to treat ADHD include clonidine and guanfacine, which affect levels of norepinephrine. These drugs can help reduce tics, which are common in children with ADHD, and increase cognitive performance (Joshi, 2004). The side effects of these drugs include dry mouth, fatigue, dizziness, constipation, and sedation. More recently, atomoxetine, which inhibits the re-uptake of norepinephrine, has been approved for use in the treatment of ADHD.

Antidepressant medications are sometimes prescribed to children and adolescents with ADHD, particularly if they also have depression. These drugs have some positive effects on cognitive performance but are not as effective against ADHD as the stimulants (Wilens et al., 2002). Bupropion is an antidepressant with particularly strong effects on dopamine levels, and it appears to be more effective against ADHD than some of the other antidepressants.

Unfortunately, the gains made by children with ADHD when treated with medications alone are short-term (Joshi, 2004). Longer-term gains can be had by combining stimulant therapy with behavior therapy that focuses on reinforcing attentive, goal-directed, and prosocial behaviors and extinguishing impulsive and hyperactive behaviors (DuPaul & Barkley, 1993). Parents can be taught behavioral methods for promoting positive behaviors and extinguishing maladaptive behaviors in their children (Anastopoulos & Farley, 2003). In addition, parents' own psychological problems and the impairments in parenting skills that these problems create may be the focus of psychosocial interventions for children with ADHD.

Behavioral training programs for children with ADHD and their parents have been shown to improve functioning significantly in the children and their families (Anastopoulos & Farley, 2003; Chronis et al., 2004). For example, the child and his parents might design a contract that says that, every time the child complies with a request from his parents to wash his hands, to set the dinner table, and to put away his toys, he earns a chip. At the end of each week, he can exchange his chips for toys or fun activities. Each time the child refuses to comply, however, he loses a chip. If the child throws a tantrum or becomes aggressive, he must go to his room for a time-out. Such techniques can help parents break the cycle of arguments with their children that leads to escalations in the children's behaviors, which in turn lead to more arguments and perhaps physical violence. These techniques also help children learn to anticipate the consequences of their behaviors and to make less impulsive choices about their behaviors.

Several studies suggest that the combination of stimulant therapy and psychosocial therapy is more likely to lead to both short-term and long-term improvements than either type of therapy

alone. For example, in one multisite study, 579 children with ADHD, average age about 8 years, were randomly assigned to receive the combination of Ritalin and behavior therapy, one of these therapies alone, or routine community care (Jensen et al., 2001). After 14 months of treatment, 68 percent of the children in the combined treatment group showed a reduction in or complete discontinuation of their ADHD behaviors, such as aggression and lack of concentration. In the medication-alone group, 56 percent showed a reduction in or discontinuation of symptoms. Behavior therapy alone led to a reduction of symptoms in only 34 percent of the group members, and only 25 percent of the children given routine community care showed reductions in symptoms over that time period.

Conduct Disorder and Oppositional Defiant Disorder

Have you ever lied? Have you ever stolen something? Have you ever hit someone? Most of us would have to answer yes to some and probably all of these questions. Fewer of us would answer yes to the following questions:

- Have you ever pulled a knife or a gun on another person?
- Have you ever forced someone into sexual activity?
- Have you ever deliberately set a fire, with the hope of doing serious damage to someone else's property?
- Have you ever broken into someone else's car or house with the intention of stealing?

Many children who have **conduct disorder** answer yes to these questions and engage in other serious transgressions of societal norms for behavior (see the DSM-IV-TR symptoms in Table 13.5). These children have chronic patterns of unconcern for the basic rights of others. Consider the following case of a boy named Phillip (Jenkins, 1973, pp. 60–64):

> Phillip, age 12, was suspended from a small-town Iowa school and referred for psychiatric treatment by his principal, who sent along the following note with Phillip:
>
> > This child has been a continual problem since coming to our school. He does not get along on the playground because he is mean to other children.

(continued)

He disobeys school rules, teases the patrol children, steals from the other children, and defies all authority. Phillip keeps getting into fights with other children on the bus.

He has been suspended from cafeteria privileges several times for fighting, pushing, and shoving. After he misbehaved one day at the cafeteria, the teacher told him to come up to my office to see me. He flatly refused, lay on the floor, and threw a temper tantrum, kicking and screaming.

The truth is not in Phillip. When caught in actual misdeeds, he denies everything and takes upon himself an air of injured innocence. He believes we are picking on him. His attitude is sullen when he is refused anything. He pouts, and when asked why he does these things, he points to his head and says, "Because I'm not right up here." This boy needs help badly. He does not seem to have any friends. His aggressive behavior prevents the children from liking him. Our school psychologist tested Phillip, and the results indicated average intelligence, but his school achievement is only at the third- and low fourth-grade level.

TABLE 13.5 DSM-IV-TR

Symptoms of Conduct Disorder

The symptoms of conduct disorder include behaviors that violate the basic rights of others and the norms for appropriate social behavior.

Bullies, threatens, or intimidates others

Initiates physical fights

Uses weapons in fights

Engages in theft and burglary

Is physically abusive to people and animals

Forces others into sexual activity

Lies and breaks promises often

Violates parents' rules about staying out at night

Runs away from home

Sets fires deliberately

Vandalizes and destroys others' property deliberately

Often skips school

Source: Reprinted with permission from the *Diagnostic and Statistical Manual of Mental Disorders,* Fourth Edition, Text Revision. Copyright © 2000 American Psychiatric Association.

We all have known bullies and children who often get into trouble. Only 3 to 7 percent of children exhibit behaviors serious enough to qualify for a diagnosis of conduct disorder, however (Costello, Compton, et al., 2003; Maughan et al., 2004). Still, the behaviors of children with conduct disorder exact a high cost to society. For example, the cost of vandalism to schools by juveniles in the United States is estimated to be over $600 million per year. Juveniles account for almost 20 percent of all violent-crime arrests (*Newsweek*, 1993). About half of all adolescent boys and 25 percent of adolescent girls report being attacked by someone at school (Offord, 1997).

Unfortunately, many children with conduct disorder continue to have serious difficulty conforming to societal norms in adolescence and adulthood (Maughan et al., 2000; Offord et al., 1992). As adolescents, about half engage in criminal behavior and drug abuse. As adults, about 75 to 85 percent are chronically unemployed, have histories of unstable personal relationships, fre-

quently engage in impulsive physical aggression, or abuse their spouses (Lahey & Loeber, 1997). Between 35 and 40 percent will be diagnosed with antisocial personality disorder as adults. Youth who develop conduct disorder as children are more likely than those whose conduct problems begin in adolescence to show a wide range of psychological problems and violent behavior as adults (Loeber & Farrington, 2000; Moffitt, Caspi, Rutter, et al., 2001). For example, one study that followed children in three countries found that boys who exhibited physical aggression early in life were especially likely to show chronic conduct problems into adulthood (Broidy et al., 2003).

The DSM-IV-TR also recognizes a less severe pattern of chronic misbehavior than is seen in conduct disorder, known as **oppositional defiant disorder.** Children with oppositional defiant disorder frequently lose their temper or have temper tantrums, argue with adults, actively defy requests or rules, deliberately do things to annoy other people, blame others for their own mistakes, are easily annoyed by others, are angry and resentful, and are spiteful or vindictive (see the DSM-IV-TR symptoms in Table 13.6). Unlike children with conduct disorder, however, children with oppositional defiant disorder are not aggressive toward people or animals, do not destroy property, and do not show a pattern of theft and deceit. Several of the symptoms of oppositional defiant disorder can be seen in the case of 9-year-old Jeremy (adapted from Spitzer et al., 1994, p. 343):

CASE STUDY

Jeremy has been difficult to manage since nursery school. The problems have slowly escalated. Whenever he is without close supervision, he gets into trouble. At school, he teases and kicks other children, trips them, and calls them names. He is described as bad-tempered and irritable, even though at times he seems to enjoy school. Often he appears to be deliberately trying to annoy other children, though he always claims that others have started the arguments. He does not become involved in serious fights but does occasionally exchange a few blows with another child.

Jeremy sometimes refuses to do what his two teachers tell him to do, and this year has been particularly difficult with one who takes him in the afternoon for arithmetic, art, and science lessons. He gives many reasons why he should not have to do his work and argues when told to do it. At home, Jeremy's behavior is quite variable. On some days he is defiant and rude to his mother, needing to be told to do everything several times before he will do it, though eventually he usually complies. On other days he is charming and volunteers to help, but his unhelpful days predominate. His mother says, "The least little thing upsets him, and then he shouts and screams." Jeremy is described as spiteful and mean with his younger brother, Rickie. His mother also comments that he tells many minor lies, though, when pressed, is truthful about important things.

The symptoms of oppositional defiant disorder often begin very early in life, during the toddler and preschool years. Some children with oppositional defiant disorder, however, seem to outgrow their behaviors by late childhood or early

TABLE 13.6 DSM-IV-TR

Symptoms of Oppositional Defiant Disorder

The symptoms of oppositional defiant disorder are not as severe as the symptoms of conduct disorder but have their onset at an earlier age, and oppositional defiant disorder often develops into conduct disorder.

Often loses temper

Often argues with adults

Often refuses to comply with requests or rules

Deliberately tries to annoy others

Blames others for his or her mistakes or misbehaviors

Is touchy or easily annoyed

Is angry and resentful

Is spiteful or vindictive

Source: Reprinted with permission from the *Diagnostic and Statistical Manual of Mental Disorders,* Fourth Edition, Text Revision. Copyright © 2000 American Psychiatric Association.

adolescence. A subset of children with oppositional defiant disorder, particularly those who tend to be aggressive, go on to develop conduct disorder in childhood and adolescence. Indeed, it seems that almost all children who develop conduct disorder during elementary school had symptoms of oppositional defiant disorder in the earlier years of their lives.

Boys are about three times more likely than girls to be diagnosed with conduct disorder or oppositional defiant disorder (Angold et al., 2002; Maughan et al., 2004). This pattern may exist because the causes of these disorders are more frequently present in boys than in girls. Also, boys with conduct disorder tend to be more physically aggressive than girls with conduct disorder and, thus, may be more likely to draw attention to themselves (Maughan et al., 2000; Tiet et al., 2001).

Some researchers have suggested that antisocial aggressive behavior is not rarer in girls than in boys—it just looks different (Crick & Grotpeter, 1995; Zoccolillo, 1993). Girls' aggression is more likely to be indirect and verbal, rather than physical, and to involve the alienation, ostracism, and character defamation of others. Girls exclude their peers, gossip about them, and collude with others to damage the social status of their targets.

It is clear, however, that girls with conduct and oppositional defiant disorders, like boys with these disorders, are at risk for severe problems throughout their lives. Girls with conduct disorder are just as likely as boys with conduct disorders to engage in stealing, lying, and substance abuse (Tiet et al., 2001). Long-term studies of girls diagnosed with conduct disorder find that, as adolescents and adults, they show high rates of depression and anxiety disorders, severe marital problems, criminal activity, and early, unplanned pregnancies (Moffitt et al., 2001).

Biological Contributors to Conduct Disorder and Oppositional Defiant Disorder

Antisocial behavior clearly runs in families. Children with conduct disorder are much more likely than children without this disorder to have parents with antisocial personalities (Smith & Farrington, 2004). Their fathers are also highly likely to have histories of criminal arrest and alcohol abuse, and their mothers tend to have histories of depression.

Twin and adoption studies indicate that both conduct disorder and oppositional defiant disorder are heritable. For example, one study examined 1,116 pairs of 5-year-old twins and found that 82 percent of the variability in conduct disorder was due to genetic factors (Arseneault et al., 2003).

Some researchers have suggested that children with conduct disorder have fundamental neurological deficits in the frontal lobes, brain systems involved in planning and controlling behavior (Seguin et al., 1995). One piece of evidence that neurological deficits play a role in the development of conduct disorder is the fact that many children with conduct disorder also have attention-deficit/hyperactivity disorder (Moffitt & Silva, 1988). Recall that children with ADHD have trouble maintaining attention and tend to be irritable and impulsive in their actions. These problems can lead to the development of conduct disorder when they bring about failure in school and, thus, to a rejection of school, to poor peer relationships, and to rejection by their peers.

One source of the neurological deficits these children suffer may be exposure to neurotoxins and drugs while in the womb or during the preschool years (Loeber, 1990). These neurological deficits then lead to oppositional behavior in early childhood, followed by increasingly more aggressive and severe antisocial behavior as the child ages.

Another clue that biological factors are involved in conduct disorder is that there are often signs of trouble in diagnosed children, even in infancy. Children who develop conduct disorder tend to have been difficult babies and toddlers, at least by their parents' reports (Henry et al., 1996; Shaw, Keenan, & Vondra, 1994; Shaw & Winslow, 1997). They were irritable and demanding and did not comply with their parents' requests. They were impulsive, seemed to have little control over their behaviors, and responded to frustration with aggression. This correlation suggests that diagnosed children are born with a particular kind of difficult temperament that portends the antisocial behaviors they will engage in as older children (Frick & Morris, 2004).

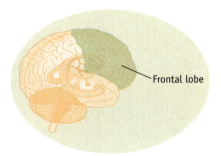

The frontal lobes, which are involved in planning and controlling behavior, may be implicated in conduct disorder.

One way that children learn to control their behavior is by associating punishment with misbehavior and rewards with good behavior. Children with conduct disorder may have more difficulty learning from punishments and rewards, because they tend to become less physiologically aroused than other children by the reinforcements and punishments they receive (Quay, 1993; Raine, Venables, & Williams, 1996). Some studies have found that boys with aggressive conduct disorder have unusually low levels of cortisol. This hormone is secreted by the hypothalamus-pituitary-adrenal axis of the neuroendocrine system and is an indicator of the body's responsiveness to stress (McBurnett et al., 2000).

The role of serotonin in violent behavior has been the focus of many studies (Berman, Kavoussi, & Coccaro, 1997). One study of a large, community-based sample found that young men whose blood serotonin levels were high relative to other men their age were much more likely to have committed a violent crime (Moffitt et al., 1998). Serotonin levels were not correlated with propensity to violence in women, however.

Finally, a popular theory of aggressive behavior is that it is linked to the hormone testosterone. A meta-analysis (see Chapter 3) of studies of testosterone and aggression in humans found a small but statistically significant correlation of .14 (Book, Starzyk, & Quinsey, 2001). Rowe and colleagues (2004) found that the association between testosterone and aggression depends on the social context of the individuals being tested. In a study of 9- to 15-year-old boys, they found that higher levels of testosterone were associated with more conduct disorder symptoms in boys whose peers were prone to engage in socially deviant behaviors. In boys whose peers were not deviant, testosterone was associated with leadership rather than conduct disorder symptoms.

Social Contributors to Conduct and Oppositional Defiant Disorders

Conduct disorder and oppositional defiant disorder are found more frequently in children in lower socioeconomic classes and in urban areas than in children in higher socioeconomic classes and rural areas (Costello, Keeler, & Angold, 2001). This may be because a tendency toward antisocial behavior runs in families, and families with members who engage in antisocial behavior may experience "downward social drift": The adults in these families cannot maintain good jobs, and the families tend to decline in socioeconomic status. Alternatively, this tendency may be due to differences between socioeconomic groups in some of the environmental causes of antisocial behavior, such as poverty and poor parenting.

A recent "experiment of nature" provided more evidence for a causal role of poverty on antisocial behavior than for a "downward drift" hypothesis. Costello, Compton, et al. (2003) had been following 1,420 children in rural North Carolina for several years. About one-quarter of these children were Native American. During their study, a casino operated by Native Americans opened, providing a sudden and substantial increase in income for some of the Native American children. The rates of conduct and oppositional defiant disorders went down among Native American children whose families benefited from the casino money, but not among the Native American children whose families did not benefit from the money.

The quality of parenting children receive, particularly children with a vulnerability to hyperactivity and conduct disturbances, is strongly related to whether they develop the full syndrome of conduct disorder (Bird et al., 2001; Smith & Farrington, 2004). Children who are physically maltreated by their parents or severely neglected are more likely to develop disruptive and delinquent behavior (Stouthamer-Loeber et al., 2001). A related variable is parental uninvolvement: Children whose parents are not involved in their everyday lives—for example, children whose parents do not know who their friends are or what they are doing in school—are more likely to develop conduct disturbances. When the parents of children with conduct disturbances do interact with their children, these

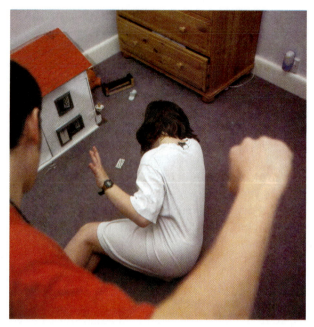

Children who are physically maltreated by their parents are more likely to develop symptoms of conduct disorders.

interactions often are characterized by hostility, physical violence, and ridicule (Dishion & Patterson, 1997). The picture of these families is one in which parents frequently ignore the children or are absent from home but when the children transgress in some way, the parents lash out violently at them (Lochman, White, & Wayland, 1991; Smith & Farrington, 2004). Also, these parents are more likely to give severe physical punishments to boys than to girls, which may partially account for the higher rate of conduct disturbances in boys (Lytton & Romney, 1991).

Children living in such families may turn to their peers to receive validation and to escape their parents. Unfortunately, these peer groups may consist of other children with conduct disturbances. Deviant peer groups tend to encourage delinquent acts, even providing opportunities for such acts (Dishion & Patterson, 1997). For example, the members of a peer group of adolescents may dare a new member to commit a robbery to "show he is a man" and provide him with a weapon and a getaway car. Children who become part of deviant peer groups are especially likely to begin abusing alcohol and illicit drugs, which in turn leads to increases in deviant acts (McBride, Joe, & Simpson, 1991).

Individuals with antisocial tendencies tend to choose mates with similar tendencies (Smith & Farrington, 2004). Conversely, adolescents and young adults with conduct disturbances who form close relationships with others who do not have such problems are much more likely to grow out of their conduct disturbances. For example, delinquent young men who marry young women with no histories of conduct problems tend to cease their delinquent acts and never engage in such acts again (Sampson & Laub, 1992).

The biological factors and family factors that contribute to conduct disorder may coincide, sending a child on a trajectory toward antisocial behaviors that is difficult to stop (Loeber, 1990; Reid & Eddy, 1997) (see Figure 13.1 on page 476). The neuropsychological problems associated with antisocial behaviors are linked to maternal drug use, poor prenatal nutrition, pre- and postnatal exposure to toxic agents, child abuse, birth complications, and low birthweight (Moffitt, 1993; Silberg et al., 2003). Infants and toddlers with these neuropsychological problems are more irritable, impulsive, awkward, overreactive, and inattentive than their peers and are slower learners. This makes them difficult for parents to care for, and they are at increased risk for maltreatment and neglect. Added to this, the parents of these children are likely to be teenagers and to have psychological problems of their own that contribute to ineffective, harsh, or inconsistent parenting. Thus, children may carry a biological predisposition to disruptive, antisocial behaviors and may experience parenting that contributes to these behaviors.

In a longitudinal study following children from age 3 into adulthood, Moffitt, Caspi, and colleagues (Moffitt & Caspi, 2001; Moffitt et al., 2001) gathered information on a particularly pernicious form of conduct disorder that begins early in childhood and persists into a violent adulthood. They found that this disorder is the outcome of an interaction between a biological disposition to a difficult temperament and cognitive deficits and a risky environment characterized by inadequate parenting and disrupted family bonds. In contrast, youth who are antisocial only in adolescence are much less likely to carry this combination of biological and environmental risk factors. Similarly, another study found that impulsivity in boys is linked to a greater risk for delinquency in late adolescence only among those who grow up in violent, poor neighborhoods (Lynam et al., 2000).

Cognitive Contributors to Conduct Disorder

Children with conduct disorder tend to process information about social interactions in ways that promote aggressive reactions to these interactions (Crick & Dodge, 1994). They enter social interactions with assumptions that other children will be aggressive toward them, and they use these assumptions, rather than cues from specific situations, to interpret the actions of their peers (Dodge & Schwartz, 1997). For example, when another child accidentally bumps into him or her, a child with a conduct disorder assumes that the bumping was intentional and meant to provoke a fight. In addition, children with conduct disorder tend to believe that any negative actions that peers take against them, such as taking their favorite pencils, are intentional rather than accidental. When deciding on what action to take in response to a perceived provocation by a peer, children with conduct disorder tend to think of a narrow range of responses, usually including aggression (Pettit, Dodge, & Brown, 1988; Rubin, Daniels-Bierness, & Hayvren, 1982; Spivack & Shure, 1974). When pressed to consider responses other than aggression, these children generate ineffective or vague responses. They often consider responses other than aggression to be useless or unattractive (Crick & Ladd, 1990).

Children who think about their social interactions in these ways are likely to act aggressively toward others. Then others may retaliate: Other children will hit them, parents and teachers will punish them, and others will perceive them negatively. In turn, these actions by others may feed the children's assumptions that the world is against them, causing them to misinterpret future actions by others. A cycle of interactions can be built that maintains and encourages aggressive, antisocial behaviors.

Again, the best evidence that thinking patterns are causes, rather than just correlates, of antisocial behavior in children comes from studies showing that changing aggressive children's thinking patterns can change their tendencies to act aggressively. Let's turn to these interventions and others for children with conduct disorder.

Drug Therapies for Conduct Disorder

Children with severely aggressive behavior have been prescribed a variety of drugs, although medications have not proven consistently helpful for them (Chang, 2004). Antidepressant drugs, particularly the selective serotonin reuptake inhibitors, may help reduce irritable and agitated behavior in children (Emslie et al., 2004). Children with conduct disorder are sometimes prescribed neuroleptic drugs, and controlled studies suggest that these drugs suppress aggressive behavior in these children (Gadow, 1992). It is unclear whether the drugs have any effect on the other symptoms of conduct

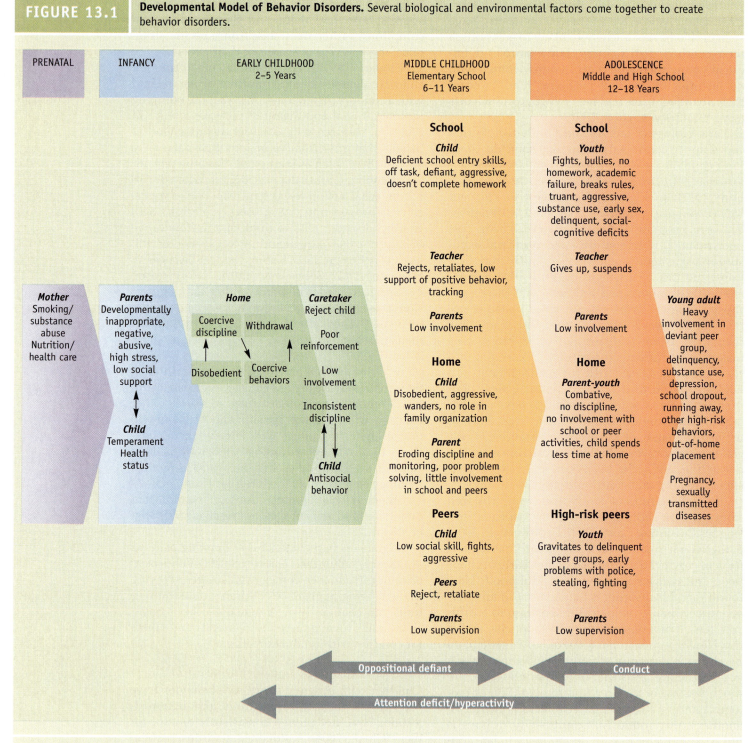

FIGURE 13.1 | **Developmental Model of Behavior Disorders.** Several biological and environmental factors come together to create behavior disorders.

Source: From J. B. Reid and J. M. Eddy, "The Prevention of Antisocial Behavior: Some Considerations in the Search for Effective Interventions" in D. M. Stoff et al. (Eds.), *Handbook of Antisocial Personality Disorder.* Copyright © 1997 John Wiley & Sons, Inc.

disorder, such as lying and stealing. Children with conduct disorder are frequently prescribed stimulant drugs, and these drugs also suppress aggressive behaviors (Joshi, 2004). Finally, controlled studies suggest that mood stabilizers, including lithium and anticonvulsant drugs, may be an effective treatment for children with aggressive conduct disorder (Chang & Simeonova, 2004).

Psychological and Social Therapies for Conduct and Oppositional Defiant Disorders

Most psychotherapies for conduct disorder are derived from social learning theory (see Chapter 2). They focus on changing the children's ways of interpreting interpersonal interactions, teaching them to take the perspectives of others and to care about those perspectives, to use self-talk as a way of controlling impulsive behaviors, and to use more adaptive ways of solving conflicts than aggression (Kazdin, 2003a; Lochman, Barry, & Pardini, 2003). Many therapies try to involve parents as well as children and to change the interaction patterns in the family that help maintain children's antisocial behavior (Webster-Stratton & Reid, 2003).

Cognitive-Behavioral Therapy The first step in cognitive-behavioral therapy is to teach children to recognize situations that trigger anger or aggressive behaviors or in which they tend to be impulsive. This is done through observing children in their natural settings and then pointing out to them situations in which they misbehave or seem angry, discussing hypothetical situations and how the children would react to them and having children keep diaries of their feelings and behaviors. The children also are taught to analyze their thoughts in these situations and to consider alternative ways of interpreting situations. Their assumptions that other children or adults act meanly toward them intentionally are challenged, and they are helped to take other people's perspectives on situations.

Next, the children may be taught to use self-talk to help them avoid negative reactions to situations: They learn to talk to themselves in difficult situations, repeating phrases that help them calm themselves, and to consider adaptive ways of coping with situations. For example, a child who tends to respond to provocation by others by immediately beginning to hit and kick might learn to think,

Slow down, slow down, slow down. Breathe deeply. Count to five. Slow down, slow down, slow down—think about what to do. Don't want to get mad. Slow down, slow down.

Therapists teach adaptive problem-solving skills by discussing real and hypothetical problem situations with children and by helping them generate a variety of positive solutions to the problems. These solutions might be modeled by the therapists and then practiced by the children in role-plays. For example, if a therapist and child are discussing how to respond to another child who has cut in line in the school lunchroom, the therapist might initially model an assertive (rather than aggressive) response, such as saying, "I would like you to move to the back of the line," to the cutting child. Then, the child in therapy might practice the assertive response and pretend to be the child cutting in line in order to gain some perspective on why the child is doing this.

Some psychosocial therapies for children with conduct disorder also include parents, particularly if the family dynamics are supporting the children's conduct disorder (Kazdin, 2003b; Reid & Eddy, 1997; Webster-Stratton & Reid, 2003). Parents are taught to reinforce positive behaviors in their children and to discourage aggressive or antisocial behaviors. Parents are also taught strategies similar to the ones already described for controlling their own angry outbursts and discipline techniques that are not violent.

Unfortunately, it can be difficult to get the parents who need the most improvement in parenting skills to participate in therapy (Kazdin, 2003a). In addition, to be effective, therapists need to be sensitive to cultural differences in the norms for the behavior of children and parents. For example, in families of color, it is often useful to engage the extended family (grandparents, aunts, uncles) in family therapy, as well as the parents of a child with conduct disorder (Dudley-Grant, 2001).

Studies of the therapies based on social learning theory suggest that they can be very effective in reducing aggressive and impulsive behavior in children, particularly interventions made in the home, in the classroom, and in peer groups (August et al., 2001; Kazdin, 2003a; Webster-Stratton & Reid, 2003). Unfortunately, many children relapse into conduct disorder after a while, particularly if their parents have poor parenting skills, alcoholism or other drug abuse, or other psychopathology. Interventions are most likely to have long-term, positive effects if they begin early in a disturbed child's life (Estrada & Pinsof, 1995). Booster sessions of additional therapy after a course of initial therapy also help a child avoid relapsing into conduct disorder (Lochman et al., 1991).

Ethnic Differences in Interventions for Antisocial Behavior A recent study of youth growing up in a largely rural area of North Carolina found no differences between African American and European American youth in rates of conduct disorder, but the European American youth had higher rates of oppositional defiant disorder (Angold et al.,

2002). The European American youth were more likely to obtain treatment from mental-health specialists than the African American youth, who tended to receive what treatment they got in the context of the school system.

The criminal justice system may deal differently with African American and European American adolescents who behave in antisocial ways (Tolan & Gorman-Smith, 1997). Researchers examined the case records of all adolescents who were sent to correctional schools or to state psychiatric hospitals in one area of Connecticut over a year (Lewis, Balla, & Shanok, 1979). The adolescents sent to psychiatric hospitals and those sent to jail were just as likely to have histories of violence and had equal levels of emotional problems. However, the adolescents sent to jail were much more likely to be African American than European American, whereas those sent to psychiatric hospitals were much more likely to be European American than African American. It appears that disturbed African American adolescents are incarcerated, whereas disturbed European Americans are hospitalized.

SUMMING UP

- The behavior disorders include attention-deficit/hyperactivity disorder, conduct disorder, and oppositional defiant disorder.

- Children with attention-deficit/hyperactivity disorder are inattentive, impulsive, and overactive. Many do not do well in school, and their relationships with their peers are extremely impaired.

- Some children with attention-deficit/hyperactivity disorder grow out of this disorder, but some continue to show the symptoms into adulthood, and they are at high risk for conduct problems and emotional problems throughout their lives.

- The two therapies that are effective in treating ADHD are stimulant drugs and behavior therapies that teach children how to control their behaviors. The combination of medications and behavior therapies appears to lead to the most long-lasting improvement.

- Children with conduct disorder engage in behaviors that severely violate societal norms, including chronic lying, stealing, and violence toward others.

- Children with oppositional defiant disorder engage in antisocial behaviors that are less severe than those of conduct disorder but that indicate a negative, irritable approach to others.

- Some children outgrow oppositional defiant disorder, but a subset develop full conduct disorder.

- Children who develop conduct disorder often continue to engage in antisocial behaviors into adulthood and have high rates of criminal activity and drug abuse.

- Neurological deficits may be involved in conduct disorder. These deficits may make it more difficult for children with this disorder to learn from reinforcements and punishments and to control their behaviors.

- Children with conduct disorder tend to have parents who are neglectful much of the time and violent when annoyed with them.

- Children with conduct disorder tend to think about interactions with others in ways that contribute to their aggressive reactions.

- Drug therapies are sometimes used to help children with conduct disorder control their behavior, and cognitive-behavioral therapies help them learn to interpret and respond to situations differently.

SEPARATION ANXIETY DISORDER

Children can suffer from depression, panic attacks, obsessive-compulsive disorder, generalized anxiety disorder, posttraumatic stress disorder, and phobias. The childhood versions of most of these disorders are discussed in the chapters on the individual disorders. One emotional disorder that is specific to childhood is **separation anxiety disorder** (see the DSM-IV-TR symptoms in Table 13.7).

Many infants become anxious and upset if separated from their primary caregivers. They cry loudly and cannot be consoled by anyone but their primary caregivers. This is a normal consequence of an infant's development of the understanding that objects (including mothers and fathers) continue to exist even when they are not in direct sight, as well as a consequence of the infant's attachment to caregivers. With development, however, most infants come to understand that their caregivers will return, and they find ways to comfort themselves while their caregivers are away, so that they are not excessively anxious.

Some children continue to be extremely anxious when separated from their caregivers, even into childhood and adolescence. They may refuse to go to school, because they fear the separation from their caregivers. They cannot sleep at night unless they are with their caregivers. They have nightmares with themes of separation. They follow their caregivers around the house. If they are sepa-

TABLE 13.7	DSM-IV-TR

Symptoms of Separation Anxiety Disorder

Children who show much more than the usual anxiety when separated from caregivers may be diagnosed with separation anxiety disorder.

Excessive distress when separated from home or caregivers or when anticipating separation

Persistent and excessive worry about losing, or harm coming to, caregivers

Persistent reluctance or refusal to go to school or elsewhere because of fear of separation

Excessive fear about being alone

Reluctance to go to sleep without caregivers nearby

Repeated nightmares involving themes of separation

Repeated complaints of physical symptoms when separation from caregivers occurs or is anticipated

Source: Reprinted with permission from the *Diagnostic and Statistical Manual of Mental Disorders,* Fourth Edition, Text Revision. Copyright © 2000 American Psychiatric Association.

Children with separation anxiety disorder often cling desperately to their parents.

rated from their caregivers, they worry tremendously that something bad will happen to the caregivers. They have exaggerated fears of natural disasters (e.g., tornadoes, earthquakes) and of robbers, kidnappers, and accidents. They may have stomachaches and headaches and become nauseated if forced to separate from their caregivers. Younger children may cry unconsolably. Older children may avoid activities, such as being on a baseball team, that might take them away from their caregivers, preferring to spend all the time possible with their caregivers.

Many children go through short episodes of a few days of these symptoms after traumatic events, such as getting lost in a shopping mall. Separation anxiety disorder is not diagnosed unless a child shows symptoms for at least four weeks and the symptoms significantly impair the child's ability to function in everyday life. Children with this disorder may be very shy, sensitive, and demanding of adults.

About 3 percent of children under 11 years of age experience separation anxiety disorder (Angold et al., 2002; Bowen, Offord, & Boyle, 1990). It is more common in girls than in boys. Left untreated, this disorder can recur frequently throughout childhood and adolescence, significantly interfering with the child's academic progress and peer relationships. One study examined the adult outcomes of children with separation anxiety who had refused to go to school because of their anxiety, comparing them with people who had had no psychiatric disorders as children. The investigators found that those who had had separation anxiety disorder had more psychiatric problems as adults than the comparison group, were more likely to continue to live with their parents even though they were adults, and were less likely to have married and had children (Flakierska-Praquin, Lindstrom, & Gilberg, 1997).

Biological Contributors to Separation Anxiety Disorder

Biological factors may be involved in the development of separation anxiety disorder (see the Concept Overview in Table 13.8 on page 480). Children with this disorder tend to have family histories of anxiety and depressive disorders (Biederman et al., 2001; Manicavasagar et al., 2001). Twin studies suggest that separation anxiety disorder is heritable, but more so in girls than in boys (Eaves et al., 1997; Feigon et al., 2001).

Earlier, we discussed the role of difficult temperament in the development of conduct disorder. A different kind of temperament is implicated in the development of anxiety disorders in children. Kagan, Reznick, and Snidman (1987) suggest that some children are born high in **behavioral inhibition**—they are shy, fearful, and irritable as toddlers and cautious, quiet, and introverted as

TABLE 13.8 Concept Overview	
Proposed Causes of and Treatments for Separation Anxiety Disorder	
Biological and environmental factors may contribute to separation anxiety disorder, which is often treated with cognitive-behavioral therapy.	
Proposed Causes	**Description**
Biological predisposition	There may be a genetic predisposition to anxiety disorders, including separation anxiety and panic attacks.
Behavioral inhibition	Children are born with an inhibited, fearful temperament.
Traumatic and uncontrollable events	Some children develop separation anxiety after a traumatic event; studies of nonhuman primates show that chronic uncontrollability can contribute to anxiety.
Parenting experiences	Parents may encourage fearful behavior and not encourage appropriate independence.
Treatment	**Description**
Cognitive-behavioral therapy	Children are taught self-talk to challenge negative thoughts and relaxation to quell anxiety; periods of separation from parents are increased gradually; parents are taught to model and reinforce nonanxious behavior.

school-age children. These children tend to avoid or withdraw from novel situations, are clingy with parents, and become excessively aroused when exposed to unfamiliar situations.

Some studies suggest that children high in behavioral inhibition as infants are at increased risk to develop anxiety disorders in childhood (Biederman et al., 1990, 1993; Caspi et al., 2003). These children's parents also are prone to anxiety disorders, particularly panic disorder, and many have a history of anxiety disorders that dates back to their own childhood. One study found that children who were behaviorally inhibited had abnormalities on the gene that regulates corticotropin-releasing hormone (CRH), which plays an important role in stress responses (Smoller et al., 2003). This association between the abnormal gene and behavioral inhibition was particularly strong in children whose parents also had an anxiety disorder.

Psychological and Sociocultural Contributors to Separation Anxiety Disorder

Children may learn to be anxious from their parents or as an understandable response to their environments. In some cases, separation anxiety disorder develops following traumatic events:

CASE STUDY

In the early morning hours, 7-year-old Maria was abruptly awakened by a loud rumbling and violent shaking. She sat upright in bed and called out to her 10-year-old sister, Rosemary, who was leaping out of her own bed 3 feet away. The two girls ran for their mother's bedroom as their toys and books plummeted from shelves and dresser tops. The china hutch in the hallway teetered in front of them and then fell forward with a crash, blocking their path to their mother's room. Mrs. Marshall called out to them to go back and stay in their doorway. They knew the doorway was a place you were supposed to go during an earthquake, so they huddled there together until the shaking finally stopped. Mrs. Marshall climbed over the hutch and broken china to her daughters. Although they were all very shaken and scared, they were unhurt.

Two weeks later, Maria began to complain every morning of stomachaches, headaches, and dizziness, asking to stay home from

(continued)

school with her mother. After four days, when a medical examination revealed no physical problems, Maria was told she must return to school. She protested tearfully, but her mother insisted, and Rosemary promised to hold her hand all the way to school. In the classroom, Maria could not concentrate on her schoolwork and was often out of her seat, looking out the window in the direction of home. She told her teacher she needed to go home to see if her mother was okay. When she was told she couldn't go home, she began to cry and shake so violently that the school nurse called Mrs. Marshall, who picked up Maria and took her home. The next morning, Maria's protests grew stronger and she refused to go to school until her mother promised to go with her and sit in her classroom for the first hour. When Mrs. Marshall began to leave, Maria clung to her, crying, pleading for her not to leave, and following her into the hallway. The next day, Maria refused to leave the house for her Brownie meeting and her dancing lessons or even to play in the front yard. She followed her mother around the house and insisted on sleeping with her at night. "I need to be with you, Mommy, in case something happens," she declared.

Parents may contribute to the development of a separation anxiety disorder in their children by being overprotective and by modeling anxious reactions to separations from their children (Kendall, 1992). The families of children with separation anxiety disorder tend to be especially close-knit, not encouraging developmentally appropriate levels of independence in the children.

Some of the best evidence that environmental and parenting factors can influence the development of anxiety disorders in youngsters comes from studies of nonhuman primates. Mineka and colleagues (1986) found that rhesus monkeys who were given adequate food and water from ages 2 to 6 months, but could not control their access to food and water, developed a fearfulness and became generally inhibited in their behavior. Other monkeys given the same amount of food and water, but under conditions that they could exert some control over, did not become fearful. This re-

sult suggests that some human children who are raised in conditions over which they have little control may develop anxiety symptoms.

Moreover, Suomi (1999) found that, although some rhesus monkeys seem to be born behaviorally inhibited, the extent to which they develop serious signs of fearfulness and anxiety later in life depends on the parenting they receive. Those who are raised by anxious mothers, which also are inhibited and inappropriately responsive to the infants, are prone to develop monkey versions of anxiety disorders. Those that are raised by calm, responsive mothers that model appropriate reactions to stressful situations typically are not any more likely to develop anxiety problems as adolescents or adults than are those that are not born behaviorally inhibited.

Treatments for Separation Anxiety Disorder

Cognitive-behavioral therapies are most often used to treat separation anxiety disorder (Kendall, Aschenbrand, & Hudson, 2003). Children are taught to manage their anxiety better by developing new skills at coping and at challenging cognitions that feed their anxiety. They might be taught relaxation exercises to practice during periods of separation from their parents. Their fears about separation are challenged, and they are taught to use self-talk to calm themselves when they become anxious.

As therapy progresses, periods of separation from their parents are increased in number and duration. Parents must be willing to participate in the therapy and to cope with their children's (and their own) reactions to attempts to increase periods of separation. Parents may need to be taught to model nonanxious reactions to separations from their children and to reinforce nonanxious behavior in their children.

Controlled clinical trials of this type of therapy show that it can be effective in the short term and maintain its effects in the long term (Shortt, Barrett, & Fox, 2001; Velting, Setzer, & Albano, 2004). For example, Mark Dadds and colleagues (1999) provided a 10-week school-based intervention for anxiety-ridden children and their parents. They found that these children were much less likely than a control group who received no intervention to be diagnosed with separation anxiety or another anxiety disorder over the 2 years following the intervention (see Figure 13.2 on page 482).

Here is how Maria was treated for her separation anxiety:

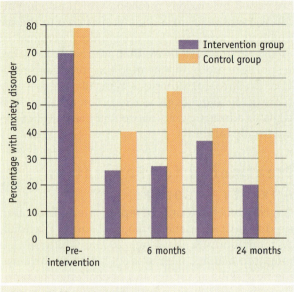

FIGURE 13.2   Effects of Cognitive-Behavioral Therapy for Separation Anxiety Disorder.

Schoolchildren with separation anxiety and other anxiety disorders and their parents were given a 10-week cognitive-behavioral intervention. These children were less likely than a control group of children over the next 2 years to be diagnosed with an anxiety disorder.

Source: Dadds et al., 1999.

and praise each morning for sleeping in her own bed.

The first few times Mrs. Marshall left the classroom, Maria followed her out. Soon, however, she began to stay in her chair and received stickers. At home, she remained in her own bed the first night, even though she was told she had to stay only two hours to earn her sticker. At her own request, she returned to Brownie meetings and attended summer camp.

Many kinds of drugs are used in the treatment of childhood anxiety disorders, including antidepressants; antianxiety drugs, such as the benzodiazepines; stimulants; and antihistamines. The selective serotonin reuptake inhibitors, such as fluoxetine, are most frequently used and have been most consistently shown to be effective in reducing anxiety symptoms in children (Birmaher et al., 2003; Thienemann, 2004). There is greater support for the efficacy of cognitive-behavioral therapy than for drug therapies in the treatment of separation anxiety disorder, however.

SUMMING UP

- Children can suffer from all the emotional disorders, including depression and all the anxiety disorders. Separation anxiety disorder is one disorder specific to children.
- Children with separation anxiety disorder are excessively fearful about separation from primary caregivers. They may become extremely agitated or ill when they anticipate separation, and they may curtail usual activities to avoid separation.
- Separation anxiety disorder appears to be associated with a family history of anxiety disorders.
- Children who are behaviorally inhibited as infants appear at risk for separation anxiety disorder as adults.
- Parents may enhance a vulnerability to separation anxiety disorder by their reactions to children's distress.
- Cognitive-behavioral therapies can help children with separation anxiety disorder quiet their anxieties and resume everyday activities.

CASE STUDY

Mrs. Marshall was instructed to take Maria to school and leave four times during the period she was there. Initially, Mrs. Marshall left for 30 seconds each time. Over time, she gradually increased the amount of time and distance she was away while Maria remained in the classroom. Maria was given a sticker at the end of the school day for each time she remained in her seat while her mother was out of the room. In addition, she was praised by her teacher and her mother, and positive self-statements (e.g., "My mommy will be okay; I'm a big girl and I can stay at school") were encouraged. No response was made when Maria failed to stay in her chair. Maria could exchange her stickers for prizes at the end of each week.

At home, Mrs. Marshall gave minimal attention to Maria's inquiries about her well-being and ignored excessive, inappropriate crying. Eventually, Maria was given a sticker

ELIMINATION DISORDERS

CASE STUDY

On the morning of her third birthday, Gretchen walked into the kitchen and announced to her mother, "I'm a big girl now, and I'm going to wear big girl underpants. No more diapers." She, indeed, did wear "big girl underpants" that day, and, although she had a couple of accidents during the day, at bedtime Gretchen was extremely proud of herself for being such a big girl. Within a few weeks, she was able to wear big girl underpants all day without any accidents.

Most children gain sufficient control over their bladder and bowel movements by about age 4 that they no longer need to wear diapers during the day or night. Like Gretchen, many children view the ability to control their bladder and bowel movements as a marker of their passage into being "big boys or girls." It is understandable, then, that children who lose this control, particularly when they are far past the preschool years and into middle childhood, can experience shame and distress. These children might be diagnosed with one of the two **elimination disorders,** enuresis or encopresis (see the Concept Overview in Table 13.9 on page 484).

Enuresis

Occasional wetting of the bed at night is common among elementary school children, particularly during times of stress. Children over age 5 are diagnosed with **enuresis** when they have wet the bed or their clothes at least twice a week for three months (APA, 2000). Most children with enuresis wet only at night. A subset of children with enuresis wet during the daytime only, most often at school. These children may be socially anxious about using the public toilets at school or prone to becoming preoccupied with other things they are doing. They do not use the toilet as they need to and tend to have wetting accidents.

Bed-wetting is relatively common, as disorders go, among young children, but the prevalence decreases with age. About 15 to 20 percent of 5-year-olds wet the bed at least once per month. By adolescence, the prevalence of bed-wetting de-creases to 1 to 2 percent (Angold et al., 2002; Houts, 2003).

Enuresis runs in families, and approximately 75 percent of children with enuresis have biological relatives who had the disorder. Some of these children may have inherited a biological vulnerability to the disorder in the form of unusually small bladders or lower bladder threshold for involuntary voiding. About 5 to 10 percent of children with enuresis have urinary tract infections (Mellon & McGrath, 2000). A variety of other biological causes for enuresis have been suggested, but none have received consistent empirical support (Ondersma & Walker, 1998).

Psychodynamic and family systems theorists suggest that enuresis is due to conflicts and anxiety caused by disruptions or dysfunction in the family (Olmos de Paz, 1990). For example, some children develop enuresis when new babies are born into the family, perhaps because they feel threatened by the attention their parents are giving to the new baby and resentful toward the new baby but cannot express their feelings freely. Behaviorists suggest that enuresis may be due to lax or inappropriate toilet training, that enuretic children never learned appropriate bladder control and, thus, have recurrent problems during childhood (Erickson, 1992).

Children with enuresis are usually taken to their pediatricians rather than mental-health specialists, and physicians often prescribe antidepressants to treat enuresis (Ondersma & Walker, 1998). Tricyclic antidepressants, particularly imipramine, are commonly used. It is not clear how these drugs affect wetting, but increases in norepinephrine may help in bladder control. About half the children treated with imipramine show reductions in wetting, but up to 95 percent relapse once the medication is discontinued (Ondersma & Walker, 1998). In addition, the tricyclic antidepressants have dangerous side effects in children, including sleep disturbances, tiredness, gastrointestinal distress, and cardiac irregularities. Overdoses can be fatal.

Synthetic antidiuretic hormone (ADH) has emerged as the drug of choice for nighttime enuresis (Houts, 2003; Ondersma & Walker, 1998). This drug concentrates urine, thereby reducing urine output from the kidney to the bladder. It reliably reduces nighttime wetting; however, children typically relapse into wetting once the medication is discontinued.

A behavioral method referred to as the **bell and pad method** is a reliable, long-term solution to enuresis (Houts, 2003). A pad is placed under the

TABLE 13.9	Concept Overview

Elimination Disorders

The elimination disorders involve uncontrolled wetting and defecation far beyond the age at which children usually gain control over these functions.

Disorder	Symptoms	Proposed Causes	Treatments
Enuresis	Unintended urination at least two times per week for 3 months; child over 5 years of age	1. Genetic vulnerability 2. Conflicts or anxiety 3. Lax or inappropriate toilet training	1. Antidepressant drugs, synthetic antidiuretic hormone 2. Bell and pad behavioral method
Encopresis	Unintended defecation at least one time per month for 3 months; child over 4 years of age	Usually begins after episodes of severe constipation; changes in colon reduce ability to know when to use toilet, leading to accidents	1. Medication to clear out colon, laxatives or mineral oil to soften stools, increase in dietary fiber 2. Behavioral contracting to increase appropriate toilet use and diet change, relaxation methods

child while she sleeps. This pad has a sensory device to detect even small amounts of urine. If the child wets during her sleep, a bell connected to the pad rings and awakens the child. Through classical conditioning, the child learns to wake up when she has a full bladder and needs to urinate. Reviews of dozens of studies of the bell and pad method and related methods conclude that they are highly effective, with over 70 percent of chil-

Children are very proud of themselves when they learn to control their bowel and bladder movements; thus, loss of control can be very distressing.

dren completely cured of bed-wetting, often within four weeks (Houts, 2003; Mellon & Mc-Grath, 2000).

Encopresis

Encopresis is repeated defecation into clothing or onto the floor and is rarer than enuresis. To be diagnosed with encopresis, children must have at least one such event a month for at least 3 months and must be at least 4 years of age. Fewer than 1 percent of children can be diagnosed with encopresis, and it is more common in boys than in girls (Angold et al., 2002).

Encopresis usually begins after one or more episodes of severe constipation, which may result from environmental factors, such as the withholding of bowel movements during toilet training or a refusal to use the toilet during school; a genetic predisposition toward decreased bowel motility; food intolerance; or certain medications (Stark et al., 1997). Constipation can cause distention of the colon, decreasing the child's ability to detect the urge to have a bowel movement, fecal hardening and buildup in the colon, and subsequent leakage of fecal material. The child may then increase the problem by avoiding using the toilet because of large or painful bowel movements, which in turn makes him or her more insensitive to fecal matter in the colon and, thus, less able to know when it is time to use the toilet.

Encopresis is typically treated by a combination of medications to clear out the colon, laxatives or mineral oil to soften stools, recommendations to increase dietary fiber, and encouragement to the child to sit on the toilet a certain amount of time each day. This medical management strategy works for 60 to 80 percent of children with encopresis.

Stark and colleagues (1997) used a behavioral treatment program for a group of children with encopresis who did not respond to medical management. This behavioral program included contracting around toileting behaviors and diet, the use of rewards for appropriate toilet usage, and relaxation techniques. In addition, all the children received standard medical management. Eighty-six percent of the children had stopped soiling by the end of the treatment and did not require further treatment.

SUMMING UP

- Enuresis—persistent, uncontrolled wetting by children who have attained bladder control—runs in families and has been attributed to a variety of biological causes. Psychodynamic theories attribute it to emotional distress. Behavioral theories attribute it to poor toilet training.

- Antidepressants help reduce enuresis in the short term, but not in the long term, and carry significant side effects.

- Behavioral methods that help children learn to awaken and go to the bathroom can help reduce nighttime enuresis.

- Encopresis—persistent, uncontrolled soiling by children who have attained control of defecation—typically begins after one or more episodes of constipation, which creates distention in the colon and decreases a child's ability to detect needed bowel movements.

- Medical management and behavioral techniques can help reduce encopresis.

DISORDERS OF COGNITIVE, MOTOR, AND COMMUNICATION SKILLS

Beginning from the first day home from the hospital with a new baby, parents eagerly track their child's development, watching for the emergence of cognitive skills, motor skills, and communication skills. The first responsive smile from a child, the first tentative steps, and the first babbling words are occasions for major celebrations. Although most parents become anxious when it

seems their children are not developing a skill "on time" (or perhaps even ahead of other children), their fears usually are allayed as their children's skills eventually emerge.

Sometimes, though, important skills do not emerge or develop fully in a child. A child might not learn to crawl or walk until many months after most children do. A child might have severe trouble with reading or arithmetic, despite having good teachers. Approximately 20 percent of children have significant impairment in important cognitive, motor, or communication skills (APA, 2000). These problems are more common in boys than in girls. They can greatly affect a child's achievement in school and can lower self-esteem and well-being. When deficits in fundamental skills are severe enough to interfere with a child's progress, the child may be diagnosed with a learning disorder, a motor skills disorder, or a communication disorder (see the Concept Overview in Table 13.10).

Learning Disorders

The DSM-IV-TR describes three *learning disorders*. These disorders are diagnosed only when a child's performance on standardized tests is significantly below that expected for his or her age, schooling, and overall level of intelligence. **Reading disorder,** also known as *dyslexia*, involves deficits in the ability to read. This disorder is usually apparent by the fourth grade. About 4 percent of children have a reading disorder, and they are more common in boys than girls (Rutter et al., 2004).

Mathematics disorder involves deficits in the ability to learn math. It includes problems in understanding mathematical terms, in recognizing numerical symbols, in clustering objects into groups, in counting, and in following mathematical principles. Although many of us feel that we are not great at math, deficits in math skills severe enough to warrant this diagnosis occur in only about 1 percent of children (APA, 2000). The disorder is usually apparent at about second or third grade.

A **disorder of written expression** involves deficits in the ability to write. Children with this disorder have severe trouble spelling, constructing a sentence or paragraph, or writing legibly. This disorder is rare.

Children with learning disorders can become demoralized and disruptive in class. If their learning disorder is never treated, they are at high risk of dropping out of school, with as many as 40 percent never finishing high school (APA, 2000). As adults, they may have problems getting and keeping good jobs. The emotional side effects of

TABLE 13.10	Concept Overview

Disorders of Cognitive, Motor, and Communication Skills

These disorders involve deficits in specific skills.

Disorder	Description
Learning Disorders	
Reading disorder (dyslexia)	Deficits in ability to read
Mathematics disorder	Deficits in mathematics skills
Disorder of written expression	Deficits in the ability to write
Motor Skills Disorder	
Developmental coordination disorder	Deficits in the ability to walk, run, hold on to objects
Communication Disorders	
Expressive language disorder	Deficits in the ability to express oneself through language
Mixed receptive-expressive language disorder	Deficits in the ability both to express oneself through language and to understand the language of others
Phonological disorder	Use of speech sounds inappropriate for age or dialect
Stuttering	Severe problems in word fluency

Actor Tom Cruise has struggled with dyslexia

learning disorders may also affect their social relationships.

On the other hand, many children overcome learning disorders. For example, actor Tom Cruise suffers from dyslexia.

Motor Skills Disorder

The one *motor skills disorder*, called **developmental coordination disorder,** involves deficits in fundamental motor skills, such as walking, running, or holding on to objects. This disorder is not diagnosed if a child's motor skills deficits are due to a medical condition, such as cerebral palsy or muscular dystrophy, or to a serious mental disorder, such as autism. A young child with developmental coordination disorder may be clumsy and very slow in achieving major milestones, such as walking, crawling, sitting, tying shoelaces, or zipping pants. Older children may be unable to assemble puzzles, build models, play ball, or write their names. This disorder is relatively common, with as many as 6 percent of children between 5 and 11 years of age suffering from it (APA, 2000).

Communication Disorders

The *communication disorders* involve deficits in the ability to communicate verbally, because of a severely limited vocabulary, severe stuttering, or an inability to articulate words correctly. Children with **expressive language disorder** have a limited vocabulary, difficulty in learning new words, difficulty in retrieving words or the right word, and poor grammar. They may use a limited variety of sentence types (such as only questions or declarations), omit critical parts of sentences, or use words in an unusual order. Some children with this disorder show signs of it from a very early age, whereas others develop language normally for a while but then begin to show signs of the disorder. Between 3 and 7 percent of children may be affected by this disorder (APA, 2000). Some children also have problems in understanding the language produced by others, as well as in expressing their own thoughts. These children are said to have a **mixed receptive-expressive language disorder.**

Children with **phonological disorder** do not use speech sounds that are appropriate for their age or dialect. They may substitute one sound for another (e.g., use a *t* for a *k* sound) or omit certain sounds (such as final consonants on words). Their words come out sounding like baby talk. They may say *wabbit* for *rabbit,* or *bu* for *blue.* Approximately 2 to 3 percent of 6- to 7-year-olds have moderate to severe phonological disorder. The prevalence falls to 0.5 percent by age 17 (APA, 2000).

Finally, children who suffer from **stuttering** have significant problems in speech fluency, often including frequent repetitions of sounds or syllables (such as "I-I-I-I see him"). The severity of their speech problems varies from situation to situation but is usually worse when they are under pressure to speak well, as when giving a verbal report. Stuttering often begins gradually and almost always before the age of 10 (APA, 2000). As many as 80 percent of children who stutter recover on their own by age 16. Others, however, go on to stutter as adults. Stuttering can reduce a child's self-esteem and cause him or her to limit goals and activities. The more aware the child is of stuttering, the more nervous he or she may become, which just increases the stuttering.

Causes and Treatment of Disorders of Cognitive, Motor, and Communication Skills

The causes of the disorders of cognitive, motor, and communication skills are not well understood. Genetic factors are implicated in several of the disorders, especially reading disorder and stuttering.

Learning disorders can lead to frustration and low self-esteem.

These disorders may also be linked to lead poisoning, birth defects, sensory dysfunction, or impoverished environments. The treatment of these disorders usually involves therapies designed to build and correct missing skills, such as reading therapy for dyslexia, physical therapy for developmental coordination disorder, and speech therapy for the communication disorders. The use of computerized exercises has proven helpful to children with learning and communication disorders (Merzenich et al., 1996). Studies suggest that the atypical antipsychotic medication risperidone can reduce stuttering (Maguire et al., 2000).

SUMMING UP

- Learning disorders include reading disorder (an inability to read, also known as dyslexia), mathematics disorder (an inability to learn math), and disorder of written expression (an inability to write).

- Developmental coordination disorder involves deficits in fundamental motor skills.

- Communication disorders include expressive language disorder (an inability to express

Taking Psychology Personally

College Students with Mental Disorders

We've noted throughout this chapter that many of the disorders that first arise in childhood persist at least into the young adult years. In addition, as you've read other chapters in this book, you've probably noticed that many other disorders have their first onset during the young adult years, including depression, bipolar disorder, anxiety disorders, and schizophrenia. That means that a significant proportion of young adults are suffering from significant emotional problems, or disorders of cognitive, motor, or communication skills, that they either have had since childhood or are just beginning to experience.

Several years ago, young adults with mental disorders or learning problems often did not attend college or dropped out before completing their degree, because the stresses of college so exacerbated their symptoms that they could not control their symptoms. These days, however, the treatments for many mental disorders and learning disabilities are effective enough that many more young people with mental disorders are attending college (Megivern, 2002). This group includes students with severe mental disorders, such as schizophrenia.

For many of these students, attending and completing college is a critical and positive experience, building their self-esteem and launching them into a productive and happy adult life.

For some students, however, the stress of college is very difficult to cope with. They may feel cut off from their usual sources of support in their family, their friends, and the psychologist or psychiatrist they have developed a relationship with. They may find it difficult to obtain high-quality, consistent care at their college. Many students report experiences of stigmatization and discrimination against them when professors or other students find out about their diagnoses (Megivern, 2002).

If you or someone you know is coping with the combined stress of college life and a significant mental disorder, what can you, or someone you know, do? Here are a few ideas:

■ *Develop a relationship with a mental-health professional.* Some students prefer to maintain a relationship with a therapist or physician with whom they were working before they came to college, because they feel that this person knows their history and what treatments have

oneself through language), mixed receptive-expressive language disorder (an inability to express oneself through language or to understand the language of others), phonological disorder (the use of speech sounds inappropriate for the age and dialect), and stuttering (deficits in word fluency).

■ Some of these disorders, particularly reading disorder and stuttering, may have genetic roots. Many other factors have been implicated in these disorders, but they are not well understood.

■ Treatment usually focuses on building skills in problem areas through specialized training and computerized exercises.

MENTAL RETARDATION

Mental retardation involves deficits in a wide range of skills. It is defined as significantly subaverage intellectual functioning. A child's level of intellectual functioning can be assessed by standardized tests, usually referred to as *IQ tests* (see Chapter 4

for a discussion of these tests). Low scores on an IQ test do not, by themselves, warrant a diagnosis of mental retardation. This diagnosis requires that a child also show significant problems in performing the tasks of daily life. Specifically, in order to be diagnosed with mental retardation, a child must show deficits, relative to other children that age, in at least two of the following skill areas: communication, self-care, home living, social or interpersonal skills, use of community resources (such as riding a bus), self-direction, academic skills, work, leisure, health, and personal safety (see the DSM-IV-TR criteria in Table 13.11 on page 486).

The severity of mental retardation varies greatly. Children with *mild mental retardation* can feed and dress themselves with minimal help, may or may not have average motor skills, and can learn to talk and write in simple terms. They can get around their own neighborhoods well, although they may not be able to venture beyond their neighborhoods without help. If they are put in special education classes that address their specific deficits, they can achieve a high school education and become self-sufficient. As adults, they can

Taking Psychology Personally (*continued*)

worked or not worked in the past. Other students feel the need to have a mental-health provider near their college, so that they can interact with this person face to face on a regular basis. In addition, a mental-health specialist who practices near the college may be able to intervene for a student with college administrators or professionals if the need arises. What is important is to establish a relationship with a specialist whom you trust and who is available as your symptoms wax and wane. You can consult *Taking Psychology Personally* in Chapter 5 for tips on how to find a mental-health professional in your area.

■ *Investigate support services for students with mental disorders at your college*. Services are often available for students with mental-health problems through the student disabilities office in a college. For example, if you sometimes require longer periods to take tests or complete assignments because of your disorder, your student disabilities office may be able to help you negotiate this issue with your professor.

■ *Investigate peer support groups for students with mental disorders*. Many colleges have support groups or outreach groups for students with mental disorders. These groups

may be run by students, and they may have a mental-health specialist as a consultant or an advisor. Such groups can provide peers who understand what it is like to have a mental disorder and who can help other students obtain treatment and other resources. Some groups have community education or action programs to inform students about mental disorders and increase resources for students with mental disorders.

■ *Take college at your own pace*. Just as students with chronic and severe medical disorders, such as diabetes or cystic fibrosis, sometimes need to take extra time to complete their college courses and degrees, students with serious mental disorders sometimes need some extra time. Pressuring yourself to take a full load of classes and press on at a high speed when your symptoms are quite severe can be risky. Work with your mental-health provider and your college to design a course of study that fits your needs and maximizes your chances of completing your goals.

---

shop for specific items and cook simple meals for themselves. They may be employed in unskilled or semiskilled jobs. Their scores on IQ tests tend to be between about 50 and 70.

Children with *moderate mental retardation* typically have significant delays in language development, such as using only 4 to 10 words by the age of 3. They may be physically clumsy and, thus, have some trouble dressing and feeding themselves. They typically do not achieve beyond the second-grade level in academic skills but, with special education, can acquire simple vocational skills. As adults, they may not be able to travel alone or shop or cook for themselves. Their scores on IQ tests tend to be between about 35 and 50.

Children with *severe mental retardation* have very limited vocabularies and speak in two- or three-word sentences. They may have significant deficits in motor development and may play with toys inappropriately (e.g., banging two dolls together, rather than having them interact symbolically). As adults, they can feed themselves with spoons and dress themselves if the clothing is not complicated with many buttons or zippers. They

cannot travel alone for any distance and cannot shop or cook for themselves. They may be able to learn some unskilled manual labor, but many do not. Their IQ scores tend to run between 20 and 35.

Children and adults with *profound mental retardation* are severely impaired and require full-time custodial care. They cannot dress themselves completely. They may be able to use spoons, but not knives and forks. They tend not to interact with others socially, although they may respond to simple commands. They may achieve vocabularies of 300 to 400 words as adults. Many persons with profound mental retardation suffer from frequent illnesses, and their life expectancy is shorter than normal. Their IQ scores tend to be under 20.

Experts on mental retardation divide this disorder into two types: *organic retardation* and *cultural-familial retardation* (Hodapp, Burack, & Zigler, 1998). In cases of organic retardation, there is clear evidence of a biological cause for the disorder, and the level of retardation tends to be more severe. In cases of cultural-familial retardation, there is less evidence for the role of biology and more evidence for the role of environment in the development of the

TABLE 13.11 DSM-IV-TR

Criteria for Diagnosing Mental Retardation

The diagnosis of mental retardation requires that a child show both poor intellectual functioning and significant defects in everyday skills.

A. Significantly subaverage intellectual functioning, indicated by an IQ of approximately 70 or below

B. Significant deficits in at least two of the following areas:

1. communication
2. self-care
3. home living
4. social or interpersonal skills
5. use of community resources
6. self-direction
7. academic skills
8. work
9. leisure
10. health
11. personal safety

C. Onset before age 18

Source: Reprinted with permission from the *Diagnostic and Statistical Manual of Mental Disorders,* Fourth Edition, Text Revision. Copyright © 2000 American Psychiatric Association.

disorder. The retardation tends to be less severe, and there is a good chance that, with the right intervention, the child will eventually develop normal abilities.

Biological Causes of Mental Retardation

A large number of biological factors can cause mental retardation, including chromosomal and gestational disorders, exposure to toxins prenatally and in early childhood, infections, physical trauma, metabolism and nutrition problems, and gross brain disease (see the Concept Overview in Table 13.12). We examine these factors first and then turn to the sociocultural factors implicated in mental retardation.

Genetic Contributors to Mental Retardation

Intellectual skills are at least partially inherited. The IQs of adopted children correlate much more strongly with those of their biological parents than with those of their adoptive parents. Similarly, the IQs of monozygotic twins are much more strongly correlated than are the IQs of dizygotic twins, even when the twins are reared apart (Scarr, Weinberg, & Waldman, 1993; Simonoff, Bolton, & Rutter, 1998). Families of children with mental retardation tend to have high incidences of a variety of intellectual problems, including the different levels of mental retardation and autism (Camp et al., 1998).

Two metabolic disorders that are genetically transmitted and that cause mental retardation are *phenylketonuria (PKU)* and *Tay-Sachs disease.* PKU is carried by a recessive gene and occurs in about 1 in 20,000 births. Children with PKU are unable to metabolize phenylalanine, an amino acid. As a result, phenylalanine and its derivative, phenyl pyruvic acid, build up in the body and cause permanent brain damage. Fortunately, an effective treatment is available, and children who receive this treatment from an early age can develop an average level of intelligence. Most states mandate testing for PKU in newborns. If untreated, children with PKU typically have IQs below 50.

Tay-Sachs disease also is carried by a recessive gene and occurs primarily in Jewish populations. It usually does not appear until a child is between 3 and 6 months old. At this point, a progressive degeneration of the nervous system begins, leading to mental and physical deterioration. These children usually die before the age of 6 years, and there is no effective treatment.

Several types of chromosomal disorders can lead to mental retardation. Recall from Chapter 2 that children are born with 23 pairs of chromosomes. Twenty-two of these pairs are known as *autosomes,* and the 23rd pair contains the *sex chromosomes.* One of the best-known causes of mental retardation is *Down syndrome*, which occurs when chromosome 21 is present in triplicate rather than in duplicate. (For this reason, Down syndrome is also referred to as *Trisomy 21*). Down syndrome occurs in about 1 in every 800 children born in the United States.

From childhood, almost all people with Down syndrome have mental retardation, although the level of their retardation varies from mild to profound. Children with Down syndrome have round, flat faces and almond-shaped eyes; small noses; slightly protruding lips and tongues; and short, square hands. They tend to be short in stature and somewhat obese. Many of these chil-

TABLE 13.12 Concept Overview

Factors Associated with Mental Retardation

A large number of factors contribute to mental retardation.

Predisposing Factor	Examples of Specific Disorders or Conditions
Genetic disorders	Down syndrome, Tay-Sachs disease, Fragile X syndrome, phenylketonuria, Trisomy 13 and 18
Early alterations of embryonic development	Down syndrome, prenatal exposure to toxins (e.g., maternal alcohol consumption or other substance abuse)
Later pregnancy and perinatal problems	Fetal malnutrition, placental insufficiency, prematurity, hypoxia, low birthweight, intracranial hemorrhage
Acquired childhood diseases/accidents	Infections (e.g., meningitis, encephalitis), malnutrition, head trauma (e.g., car or household accident, child abuse), poisoning (e.g., lead, mercury), environmental deprivation (psychosocial disadvantage, neglect)
Environmental influences and other mental disorders	Deprivation, child abuse, severe mental disorders
Unknown	

dren have congenital heart defects and gastrointestinal difficulties. As adults, they seem to age more rapidly than normal, and their life expectancy is shorter than average. People with Down syndrome have abnormalities in the neurons in their brains that resemble those found in Alzheimer's disease. About 25 to 40 percent of them lose their memories and the ability to care for themselves in adulthood.

Fragile X syndrome, which is the second most common cause of mental retardation in males after Down syndrome, is caused when a tip of the X chromosome breaks off. This syndrome is characterized by severe to profound mental retardation, speech defects, and severe deficits in interpersonal interaction. Males with Fragile X syndrome have large ears, long faces, and enlarged testes. Two other chromosomal abnormalities that cause mental retardation are *Trisomy 13* (chromosome 13 is present in triplicate) and *Trisomy 18* (chromosome 18 is present in triplicate). Both of these disorders lead to severe retardation and shortened life expectancy.

The risk of having a child with Down syndrome or any other chromosomal abnormalities increases the older the mother or father is when they conceive the child. This may be because, the older a parent is, the more likely his or her chro-

mosomes are to have degenerated or to have been damaged by toxins.

The Prenatal Environment: Alcohol and Other Drugs

The intellectual development of a fetus can be profoundly affected by the quality of its prenatal environment. When a pregnant woman contracts the rubella (German measles) virus, the herpes virus, or syphilis, there is a risk of physical damage to the fetus that can cause mental retardation. Chronic maternal disorders, such as high blood pressure and diabetes, can interfere with fetal nutrition and brain development and, therefore, can affect the intellectual capacities of the fetus. If these disorders are treated effectively throughout the pregnancy, the risk of damage to the fetus is low.

Most drugs that a pregnant woman takes can pass through the placenta to the fetus. It is estimated that 325,000 babies born in the United States each year are exposed prenatally to illicit drugs (Gonzalez & Campbell, 1994). Much media attention has been focused on "crack babies," infants born to women who smoked crack cocaine while pregnant. Any form of cocaine constricts the mother's blood vessels, reducing oxygen and blood flow to the fetus and possibly resulting in brain damage and retardation. Crack babies tend to be less alert than other babies and not as responsive, either emotionally or cognitively. They are more excitable and less able to regulate their sleep-wake patterns. They tend to be irritable and distractible (Napiorkowski et al., 1996; Tronick et al., 1996). Studies suggest that mothers who take cocaine during pregnancy differ in many ways from mothers who do not: They are older, more socially disadvantaged, and more likely to use tobacco, alcohol, marijuana, and other illicit drugs (Tronick et al., 1996). These other risk factors, in addition to exposure to cocaine, may severely impair the intellectual growth of their children.

Fetuses whose mothers abuse alcohol during pregnancy are at increased risk for mental retardation and a collection of physical defects known as **fetal alcohol syndrome (FAS)** (Fried & Watkinson, 1990). Children with fetal alcohol syndrome have an average IQ of only 68, along with poor judgment, distractibility, difficulty in perceiving social cues, and the inability to learn from experience. As adolescents, their academic functioning is only at the second- to fourth-grade level, and they have great trouble following directions. It is estimated that about 1 in 700 children in the United States is born with fetal alcohol syndrome (Streissguth, Randels, & Smith, 1991). Abel Dorris was one such child (adapted from Dorris, 1989; Lyman, 1997):

CASE STUDY

Abel Dorris was adopted when he was 3 years old by Michael Dorris. Abel's mother had been a heavy drinker throughout the pregnancy and after Abel was born, and she later died at age 35 of alcohol poisoning. Abel had been born almost seven weeks premature, with low birthweight. He had been abused and malnourished before being removed to a foster home. At age 3, Abel was small for his age, was not yet toilet-trained, and could speak only about 20 words. He had been diagnosed as mildly retarded. His adoptive father hoped that, in a positive environment, Abel could catch up.

At age 4, Abel was still in diapers and weighed only 27 pounds. He had trouble remembering the names of other children and his activity level was unusually high. When alone, he would rock back and forth rhythmically. At age 4, he suffered the first of several severe seizures, which caused him to lose consciousness for days. No drug treatments seemed to help.

When he entered school, Abel had trouble learning to count, to identify colors, and to tie his shoes. He had a short attention span and difficulty following simple instructions. Despite devoted teachers, when he finished elementary school, Abel still could not add, subtract, or identify his place of residence. His IQ was measured in the mid-60s.

Eventually, at age 20, Abel entered a vocational training program and moved into a supervised home. His main preoccupations were his collections of stuffed animals, paper dolls, newspaper cartoons, family photographs, and old birthday cards. At age 23, he was hit by a car and killed.

Is it safe for a woman to drink alcohol at all during pregnancy? The answer may be no. Studies of the effects of moderate maternal drinking on reproductive outcomes such as birthweight, gestational age, rate of miscarriage or stillbirth, congenital abnormalities, and social and cognitive development suggest that even low to moderate levels of drinking during pregnancy are associated with subtle alcohol-related birth defects (Jacobson & Jacobson, 2000; Kelly, Day, & Streissguth, 2000; Olson et al., 1998). For example, longitudinal studies of children exposed prenatally to alcohol show negative effects on growth at 6 years of age and on learning and memory skills at 10 years of age, even if they do not evidence the full syndrome of FAS (Cornelius et al., 2002).

The First Years of Life

Severe head traumas that damage children's brains can lead to mental retardation. *Shaken baby syndrome* is caused when a baby is shaken violently, leading to intracranial injury and retinal hemorrhage (Caffey, 1972). Babies' heads are relatively large and heavy, compared with the rest of their bodies, and their neck muscles are too weak to control their heads when they are shaken back and forth in whiplash fashion. The rapid movement of their heads when shaken can lead to their brains' being bruised from being banged against the skull wall. Bleeding can also occur in and around the brain and behind the eyes. This bleeding can lead to seizures, partial or total blindness, paralysis, mental retardation, or death. Although the violent shaking of a baby sometimes is part of a pattern of physical abuse by a parent, it often happens innocently. A frustrated parent may not know that shaking a baby can lead to permanent brain damage, as in the following case of a father of a young infant.

Jill's mother was very ill, so she left me with the baby for the day while she went to her mother's house to help her. About 2 o'clock, the baby started crying for some reason. I changed him, I fed him, I rocked him, I sang to him. Nothing would quiet him down. He kept crying and crying, for hours. Finally, around 6 P.M., I got so overwhelmed with his crying that I just shook him, hard, but only for a few seconds. He immediately quieted down, so I thought I had done the right thing. I put him to bed and he seemed to sleep peacefully. But then we had trouble waking him for his feeding. The next day, he was listless, just like a rag doll. Jill rushed him to the doctor. They did a series of tests and said that he might have brain damage! That was four years ago. Since then, he has been delayed in many areas of his development. The doctors say he will never be normal. I just wish I had known that you aren't supposed to shake a baby.

Young children face a number of other hazards in addition to shaken baby syndrome. Exposure to toxic substances, such as lead, arsenic, and mercury, during early childhood can lead to mental retardation by damaging specific areas of the brain. The importance of protecting children from accidental ingestion of these substances cannot be overemphasized. Children can also incur brain damage, leading to mental retardation, through accidents, including traffic accidents in cars in which they are not properly buckled.

Social Contributors to Mental Retardation

Children who have either organic or cultural-familial mental retardation are more likely to come from low socioeconomic groups (Brooks-Gunn, Klebanov, & Duncan, 1996; Camp et al., 1998). This may be because their parents also have mental retardation and have not been able to acquire well-paying jobs. The social disadvantages of being poor may also contribute to lower than average intellectual development. Poor mothers are less likely to receive good prenatal care, increasing the risk of their children being born prematurely. Chil-

dren living in lower socioeconomic areas are at increased risk for exposure to lead, because many old, run-down buildings have lead paint, which chips off and is ingested by the children. Poor children are concentrated in the inner cities in poorly funded schools, and this is especially true for poor minority children. Poor children who have lower IQs receive less favorable attention from teachers and fewer learning opportunities, especially if they are also members of minorities (Alexander, Entwisle, & Thompson, 1987). Poor children are less likely to have parents who read to them, who encourage academic success, and who are involved in their schooling. These factors may directly affect a child's intellectual development and may exacerbate the biological conditions that interfere with a child's cognitive development (Camp et al., 1998).

Treatments for Mental Retardation

Interventions for mentally retarded children must be comprehensive, intensive, and probably long-term to show benefits (Singh, Oswald, & Ellis, 1998). The Concept Overview in Table 13.13 on page 494 summarizes these treatments.

Behavioral Strategies

Typically, a child's parents or caregivers are enlisted in treatment and are taught new skills for enhancing the child's positive behaviors and reducing negative behaviors. Behavioral strategies are often used to help children and adults learn new skills, from identifying colors correctly to using vocational skills. The desired behavior may be modeled in incremental steps and rewards given to the child or adult as he or she comes closer and closer to mastering the skill. Behavioral strategies can also help to reduce self-injurious and other maladaptive behaviors. Behavioral methods do not simply focus on isolated skills but, rather, are typically integrated into a comprehensive program designed to maximize the individual's ability to integrate into the community.

Drug Therapies

Medications are used to reduce seizures, which are common among people with mental retardation; to help control aggressive or self-injurious behavior; and to help improve mood (Singh et al., 1998). Neuroleptic medications (see Chapter 11) can reduce aggressive, destructive, and antisocial behavior. The potential for neurological side effects has made these medications controversial, however. The atypical antipsychotics, such as risperidone, have been shown to reduce aggression and self-injurious behavior in adults with mental retardation without

TABLE 13.13 Concept Overview

Treatments for Mental Retardation

Comprehensive treatment programs for mental retardation involve behavioral, biological, and sociocultural interventions.

Behavioral Strategies

Caregivers are taught skills for enhancing the child's positive behaviors and reducing negative behaviors.

Desired behaviors are modeled in incremental steps; rewards are given to the child as he or she masters the skill.

Self-injurious behavior is extinguished.

Drug Therapies

Neuroleptic medications reduce aggressive and antisocial behavior.

Atypical antipsychotics reduce aggression and self-injury.

Antidepressant medications reduce depression, improve sleep, and reduce self-injury.

Social Programs

Early intervention programs are provided, including comprehensive services addressing physical, developmental, and educational needs and the training of parents.

Children are mainstreamed into regular classrooms.

Group homes provide comprehensive services to adults.

Children or adults with severe physical disabilities or behavior problems are institutionalized.

inducing serious neurological side effects (Cohen et al., 1998). Antidepressant medications can reduce depressive symptoms, improve sleep patterns, and help control self-injurious behavior in mentally retarded individuals (Singh et al., 1998).

Social Programs

Social programs have focused on early intervention—integration of the child into the mainstream of other children where possible, group homes that provide comprehensive care, and institutionalization when necessary.

Early Intervention Programs Many experts recommend beginning comprehensive interventions with children at risk for mental retardation from the first days of life. These measures include intensive one-on-one interventions with children to enhance their development of basic skills; efforts to reduce the social conditions that might interfere with the children's development, such as child abuse, malnutrition, or exposure to toxins; and adequate medical care.

One such program was the Infant Health and Development Program (Gross, Brooks-Gunn, & Spiker, 1992). This program focused on children with a birthweight of 2,500 grams or less and a gestational age of 37 completed weeks or less. The program enrolled a total of 985 infants across eight sites in the United States. Two-thirds of these infants were randomly assigned to receive high-quality pediatric care for high-risk infants. The other third received the same pediatric care plus an early educational intervention program.

The intervention had three components. First, specially trained counselors visited each child's home during the first three years of the child's life, providing support to the mothers and fostering parent-child activities that would enhance the children's development. The mothers were given training in good parenting practices and in ways of facilitating their children's cognitive development. For example, the mothers were taught ways to calm their babies (who tended to be irritable), ways to provide appropriate levels of stimulation and opportunities for self-motivated actions and explorations, and ways to reduce stress in their environments. Second, the children in the intervention program went daily to a child development center with specially trained teachers, who worked to overcome the children's intellectual and physical deficits. Third, parent support groups were started to help the parents cope with the stresses of parenting.

At 36 months of age, the children in the intervention group were significantly less likely to have IQ scores in the low range than were those in the control group, who received only medical care (Infant Health and Development Program, 1990). Among the infants with birthweights between 2,001 and 2,500 grams, the effects of the program were especially strong: At age 36 months, they had IQ scores an average of 13 points higher than the infants in the control group with similar birthweights. The infants with birthweights under 2,000 grams also benefited from the program, but to a lesser degree: Their 36-month IQ scores were an average of 6.6 points higher than the control-group infants with similar birthweights. Both the "heavier" and "lighter" birthweight groups who received the intervention condition also showed fewer behavior and emotional problems at 36 months than did the children in the control groups.

The "heavier" birthweight children continued to show benefits in cognitive development from the intervention at 60 months and 96 months of age, compared with the control groups (Brooks-Gunn, Klebanov, & Liaw, 1995). Differences between the intervention groups and the control groups in behavior and emotional problems had disappeared by this age, however. Thus, as has been the case with many early intervention programs, benefits were seen in the short term; however, without continuation of the intervention, such benefits often diminish with time.

What accounted for the positive effects of the intervention? The home environments of the children in the intervention improved significantly (Berlin et al., 1998; McCormick et al., 1998). There were more learning materials available, and their mothers more actively stimulated the children's learning. The mothers of the children in the intervention program were better at assisting their children in problem solving, remaining more responsive and persistent with their children. In turn, these children showed more enthusiasm and involvement in learning tasks. In addition, the mothers in the intervention program reported better mental health than the mothers in the control group. The mothers in the intervention group were also less likely to use harsh disciplinary strategies with their children than the mothers in the control group. All of these factors were associated with the better outcomes of the children in the intervention groups.

Mainstreaming Controversy exists over whether children with mental retardation should be placed in special education classes or *mainstreamed*—that is, put into regular classrooms. On one hand, special education classes can concentrate on the children's needs, providing them with extra training in skills they lack. On the other hand, some critics argue that these classes stigmatize children and provide them with an education that asks less of them than they are capable of achieving. Critics also have charged that minority children often are placed inappropriately in special education classes because they score lower on culturally biased achievement tests and IQ tests.

Placing children with mental retardation in a classroom with children of average intelligence, however, can put them at certain disadvantages.

When interventions with children with learning difficulties involve parents, they tend to be more effective.

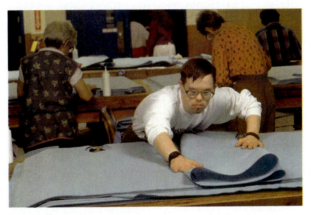
Adults with Down syndrome are often mainstreamed into jobs in the public sector.

One study found that children with mental retardation were viewed negatively by the other children in their classrooms. Zigler and Hodapp (1991) argue that children with mental retardation who are mainstreamed may often not receive the special training they need. Studies of the academic progress of children with mental retardation in special education programs and in regular classrooms, however, tend to find little difference in the performance of these two groups. Many children today spend some time in special education and some time in regular classrooms over the course of the week.

Group Homes Many adults with mental retardation live in group homes, where they receive assistance in the tasks of daily living (e.g., cooking, cleaning) and training in vocational and social skills. They may work in sheltered workshops during the day, doing unskilled or semiskilled labor. Increasingly, they are being mainstreamed into the general workforce, often in service-related jobs (e.g., in fast-food restaurants or as baggers in grocery stores). Community-based programs for adults with mental retardartion have been shown to be effective in enhancing their social and vocational skills in some studies of specific programs.

Institutionalization In the past, most children with mental retardation were institutionalized for life. Institutionalization is less common these days, but children with severe physical disabilities or with significant behavior problems, such as problems controlling aggression, may still be institutionalized (Blacher, Hanneman, & Rousey, 1992). African American and Latino families are less likely to institutionalize their children with mental retardation than are European American families (Blacher et al., 1992). This may be because African American and Latino families are less likely than European American families to have the financial resources to place their children in high-quality institutions. It may also be because African American and Latino cultures place a stronger emphasis on caring for ill or disabled family members within the family.

SUMMING UP

- Mental retardation is defined as subaverage intellectual functioning, indexed by an IQ score of under 70 and deficits in adaptive behavioral functioning. There are four levels of mental retardation, ranging from mild to profound.
- A number of biological factors are implicated in mental retardation, including metabolic disorders (PKU, Tay-Sachs disease); chromosomal disorders (Down syndrome, Fragile X, Trisomy 13, and Trisomy 18); prenatal exposure to rubella, herpes, syphilis, or drugs (especially alcohol); premature delivery; and head traumas (such as those arising from being violently shaken).
- There is some evidence that intensive and comprehensive educational interventions, administered very early in life, can help decrease the level of mental retardation.
- Controversy exists over whether children with mental retardation should be put in special education classes or mainstreamed into normal classrooms.

PERVASIVE DEVELOPMENTAL DISORDERS

The **pervasive developmental disorders** are characterized by severe and lasting impairment in several areas of development, including social interactions, communication with others, everyday behaviors, interests, and activities. The pervasive developmental disorder that is probably most familiar is **autism**—a disorder in which children show deficits in social interaction, communication, activities, and interests. Many children with autism also show at least mild levels of mental retardation, although this was not true of Temple Grandin, whose life with autism is described in the chapter opener.

Autism affects many aspects of a child's development: communication skills, social interactions, cognitive skills, and motor development (see the DSM-IV-TR symptoms in Table 13.14). The most salient features of autism, however, are the impairments in social interaction (Kanner, 1943). Some autistic children seem to live in worlds of their own, uninterested in other children or in their own caregivers. Richard is a child with autism (adapted from Spitzer et al., 1994, pp. 336–337):

CASE STUDY

Richard, age 3½, appeared to be self-sufficient and aloof from others. He did not greet his mother in the mornings or his father when he returned from work, though, if left with a baby-sitter, he tended to scream much of the time. He had no interest in other children and ignored his younger brother. His babbling had no conversational intonation. At age 3 he could understand simple practical instructions. His speech consisted of echoing some words and phrases he had heard in the past, with the original speaker's accent and intonation; he could use one or two such phrases to indicate his simple needs. For example, if he said, "Do you want a drink?" he meant he was thirsty. He did not communicate by facial expression or use gesture or mime, except for pulling someone along with him and placing his or her hand on an object he wanted. He was fascinated by bright lights and spinning objects and would stare at them while laughing, flapping his hands, and dancing on tiptoe. He also

(continued)

TABLE 13.14 DSM-IV-TR

Symptoms of Autism

The symptoms of autism include a range of deficits in social interaction, communication, and activities and interests. To be diagnosed with autism, children must show these deficits before the age of 3.

Deficits in Social Interaction

Little use of nonverbal behaviors that indicate a social "connection," such as eye-to-eye gazes, facial reactions to others (smiling or frowning at others' remarks as appropriate), body postures that indicate interest in others (leaning toward a person who is speaking), or gestures (waving good-bye to a parent)

Failure to develop peer relationships as other children do

Little expression of pleasure when others are happy

Little reciprocity in social interactions

Deficits in Communication

Delay in, or total absence of, spoken language

In children who do speak, significant trouble in initiating and maintaining conversations

Unusual language, including repetition of certain phrases and pronoun reversal

Lack of make-believe play or imitation of others at a level appropriate for the child's age

Deficits in Activities and Interests

Preoccupation with certain activities or toys and compulsive adherence to routines and rituals

Stereotyped and repetitive movements, such as hand flapping and head banging

Preoccupation with parts of objects (such as the arm of a doll instead of the whole doll) and unusual uses of objects (lining up toys in rows instead of playing "pretend" with them)

Source: Reprinted with permission from the *Diagnostic and Statistical Manual of Mental Disorders,* Fourth Edition, Text Revision. Copyright © 2000 American Psychiatric Association.

displayed the same movements while listening to music, which he liked from infancy. He was intensely attached to a miniature car, which he held in his hand, day and night, but he never played imaginatively with this or any other toy. He could assemble jigsaw puzzles rapidly (with one hand because of the car held in the other), whether the picture side was exposed or hidden. From age 2 he had collected kitchen utensils and arranged them in repetitive patterns all over the floors of the house. These pursuits, together with occasional periods of aimless running around, constituted his whole repertoire of spontaneous activities.

The major management problem was Richard's intense resistance to any attempt to change or extend his interests. Removing his toy car, disturbing his puzzles or patterns, even retrieving, for example, an egg whisk or a spoon for its legitimate use in cooking, or trying to make him look at a picture book precipitated temper tantrums that could last an hour or more, with screaming, kicking, and the biting of himself or others. These tantrums could be cut short by restoring the status quo. Otherwise, playing his favorite music or going for a long car ride were sometimes effective.

(continued)

His parents had wondered if Richard might be deaf, but his love of music, his accurate echoing, and his sensitivity to some very soft sounds, such as those made by unwrapping chocolate in the next room, convinced them that this was not the cause of his abnormal behavior. Psychological testing gave Richard a mental age of 3 years in non-language-dependent skills (such as assembling objects) but only 18 months in language comprehension.

The Diagnosis of Autism

Autism involves three types of deficits. The first type includes deficits in *social interaction,* such as a lack of interaction with family members. Even as infants, children with autism seem not to connect with other people, including their parents, as Temple Grandin did not. They may not smile and coo in response to their caregivers or initiate play with their caregivers, the way most young infants do. They may not want to cuddle with their parents, even when they are frightened. Whereas most infants love to gaze on their caregivers as the caregivers gaze adoringly at them, autistic infants may hardly ever make eye-to-eye contact. When they are a bit older, children with autism may not be interested in playing with other children, preferring to remain in solitary play. They also do not seem to react to other people's emotions. In the chapter opener, Temple Grandin described how she had to work hard to overcome her lack of understanding of social interactions.

It was formerly thought that children with autism were preoccupied with internal thoughts and fantasies, much as people with schizophrenia might be preoccupied with hallucinations and delusions. Indeed, autism in children formerly was considered a precursor to adult schizophrenia. Studies have shown, however, that these children do not develop the classic symptoms of schizophrenia as adults (for example, they show no evidence of hallucinations and delusions) and that adults with schizophrenia do not have histories of full autistic disorder as young children (Gillberg, 1991). In addition, autism and schizophrenia do not co-occur in families at a high rate, suggesting that they have different genetic causes.

The second type of deficit in autism has to do with *communication.* Approximately 50 percent of children with autism do not develop useful speech (Gillberg, 1991). Those who do develop language may not use it as other children do. In the previous case study, Richard showed several of the communication problems of children with autism. Rather than generating his own words, he simply echoed what he had just heard, in a phenomenon called *echolalia.* He reversed pronouns, using *you* when he meant *I.* When he did try to generate his own words or sentences, he did not modulate his voice for expressiveness, sounding almost like a voice-generating machine.

The third type of deficit concerns the *activities and interests* of children with autism. Rather than engaging in symbolic play with toys, they are preoccupied with one part of a toy or an object, as Richard was preoccupied with his miniature car, or as Temple Grandin was interested only in watching sand drip through her fingers. Children with autism may engage in bizarre, repetitive behaviors with toys. For example, rather than using two dolls to play "dollies have tea," a child with autism might take the arm off one doll and simply pass it back and forth between her two hands. Routines and rituals are often extremely important to children with autism: When any aspect of their daily routine is changed—for example, if a child's mother stops at the bank on the way to school—they may fly into a rage. Some children perform stereotyped and repetitive behaviors using parts of their own bodies, such as incessantly flapping their hands or banging their heads against walls. These behaviors are sometimes referred to as *self-stimulatory behaviors,* under the assumption that these children engage in these behaviors for self-stimulation. It is not clear, however, that this is their true purpose.

Children with autism often do poorly on measures of intellectual ability, such as IQ tests, with 29 percent having mild to moderate intellectual impairments and 42 percent having severe intellectual impairments (Fombonne, 1999). The deficits of some children with autism, however, are confined to skills that require language and perspective-taking skills, and they may score in the average range on subtests that do not require language skills. Temple Grandin is one person with autism who is clearly of above-average intelligence. Much has been made in the popular press about the special talents that some children with autism have, such as the ability to play music without having been taught or to draw extremely well, or exceptional memory and mathematical calculation abilities, as was depicted in the movie *Rain Man.* These persons are sometimes referred to as *savants.* These cases are quite rare, however (Poutska & Bolte, 2004).

Dustin Hoffman played a man with autism who had some extraordinary abilities.

By definition, the symptoms of autism have their onset before the age of 3. However, children with autism are not simply delayed in their development of important skills. When they do develop language or social interaction patterns, there is a deviancy in the nature of these that is striking. It is important to note, though, that there is a wide variation in the severity and outcome of this disorder. Howlin and colleagues (2004) followed 68 individuals who had been diagnosed with autism as children and who had a performance IQ of at least 50. As adults, one-fifth of them had been able to obtain some sort of academic degree, five had gone on to college, and two had obtained postgraduate degrees. Almost a third were employed and about a quarter had close friendships. The majority, however, remained very dependent on their parents or required some form of residential care. Fifty-eight percent had overall outcomes that were rated as "poor" or "very

poor." They were unable to live alone or hold a job and had persistent problems in communication and social interactions.

By far, the best predictor of the outcome of autism is a child's IQ and amount of language development before the age of 6 (Howlin et al., 2004; Nordin & Gillberg, 1998). Children who have IQs above 50 and communicative speech before age 6 have a much better prognosis than do those with IQs below 50 and no communicative speech before age 6. In the study by Howlin and colleagues (2004), people with an IQ of 70 or above were especially likely to achieve a "good" or "very good" outcome.

The prevalence of autism has been rising in recent years, probably because of the increased attention to and recognition of the disorder (Tager-Flusberg, Joseph, & Folstein, 2001). A review of epidemiological studies estimated that the prevalence of autism is about 5 per 10,000 children, and the prevalence of all forms of pervasive developmental disorder is 14 per 10,000 children (Fombonne, 1999). Boys outnumber girls about three to one. The prevalence of autism does not appear to vary by national origin, ethnicity, socioeconomic status, or parental education.

Pervasive Developmental Disorders Other Than Autism

Other pervasive developmental disorders include *Rett's disorder, childhood disintegrative disorder,* and *Asperger's disorder* (see the Concept Overview in Table 13.15 on page 500). In both **Rett's disorder** and **childhood disintegrative disorder**, children appear to develop normally for a while and then show apparently permanent loss of basic skills in social interaction, language, and/or movement.

Asperger's disorder is characterized by deficits in social interaction and in activities and interests that are similar to those of autism (review these deficits in Table 13.14). Asperger's disorder differs from autism in that there are no significant delays or deviance in language, and, in the first three years of life, children show normal levels of curiosity about the environment and acquire most normal cognitive skills. Children with Asperger's syndrome tend to have IQ scores within the average range.

Children with Asperger's disorder tend to have difficulty in relationships with others and to engage in unusual behaviors (such as memorizing ZIP codes) to the point of being obsessed with arcane facts and issues. They can be rather formal in their speech, and the disorder has sometimes been referred to as the "little professor syndrome."

TABLE 13.15 Concept Overview

Pervasive Developmental Disorders

The pervasive developmental disorders are characterized by severe and lasting deficits in several areas of development.

Disorder	Description
Autism	Deficits in social interaction; in communication, including significant language deficits; and in activities and interests
Rett's disorder	Apparently normal development through the first 5 months of life and normal head circumference at birth but then deceleration of head growth between 5 and 48 months, loss of motor and social skills already learned, and poor development of motor skills and language
Childhood disintegrative disorder	Apparently normal development for the first 2 years, followed by significant loss of previously acquired skills between ages 2 and 10 and abnormalities of functioning in social interaction, communication, and activities
Asperger's disorder	Deficits in social interaction and in activities and interests, but not in language or basic cognitive skills

The prevalence of Asperger's disorder is not clear, and many individuals are able to function well enough in life that they go undiagnosed. Current estimates suggest that the prevalence is between 1 and 36 people per 10,000 (Volkmar et al., 2004). It is an increasingly popular diagnosis, so its apparent prevalence may increase in future years.

Controversy currently exists over whether Asperger's disorder is simply a mild variant of autism or a disorder distinct from autism (Macintosh & Dissanayake, 2004). The amount of research on Asperger's disorder is increasing, however, and it should be better understood in the years to come. For now, most of what is known about pervasive developmental disorders comes from studies of autism.

Contributors to Autism

Over the years, a wide variety of theories of autism have been proposed (see the Concept Overview in Table 13.16). The psychiatrist who first described autism, Leo Kanner (1943), thought that it was caused partly by biological factors and partly by poor parenting. He and later psychoanalytic theorists (Bettelheim, 1967) described the parents of children with autism as cold, distant, and uncaring (hence the description "refrigerator mothers"). The child's symptoms were seen as a retreat inward to a secret world of fantasies in response to unavailable parents. Research over the decades has clearly

shown, though, that parenting practices play little or no role in the development of autism.

Deficits in Theory of Mind

One of the leading theories of autism is that these children have deficits in *theory of mind*, which is the ability both to understand that people—including oneself—have mental states and to use this understanding to interact and communicate with others (Baron-Cohen & Swettenham, 1997). Having a theory of mind is essential to comprehending, explaining, predicting, and manipulating the behavior of others.

Most young children show signs of developing a theory of mind by 18 months, by engaging in symbolic play, using objects to represent something other than what they really are (Lillard, 1993, 1996). By about age 3, children are able to understand the difference between their own mental states and those of others. They seem to understand what others can perceive, and they know that people may differ in what they see, know, expect, like, and want (Yirmiya et al., 1998). By age 4 to 5, children understand false beliefs (for example, that Mommy thinks they are hiding in the closet when they are really hiding in the bedroom), realize the distinction between appearance and reality, understand the concepts of desire and intention, and understand that people's actions are guided by their thoughts, beliefs, and desires (Wellman, 1994).

TABLE 13.16 Concept Overview

Contributors to Autism

The modern theories of autism view it as the result of biological factors.

Contributor	Description
Deficits in theory of mind	Deficits in the ability to understand that people have mental states and to use this understanding to interact and communicate with others
Genetic predisposition	Predisposition to a broad range of cognitive impairments
Chromosomal abnormalities	Possible aberrations on the long arm of chromosome 15 or in the number and structure of the sex chromosomes
Neurological deficits	Broad array of neurological problems, including seizure disorders
Prenatal and birth complications	Neurological deficits that could be caused by a number of complications
Neurotransmitter imbalances	Possible imbalances in serotonin and norepinephrine levels

Children with autism often fail tasks assessing theory of mind, even when they perform appropriately on other cognitive tasks for their age group (Yirmiya et al., 1998). Temple Grandin describes how the interests and perspectives of other people often strike her as odd and incomprehensible. The absence of a theory of mind may make it impossible for these children to understand and operate in the social world and to communicate appropriately with others. Their strange play behavior—specifically, the absence of symbolic play—may also represent an inability to understand anything but the concrete realities before them.

Biological Factors

Biological factors have been implicated in the development of autism. Family and twin studies strongly suggest that genetics play a role in the development of the disorder. The siblings of children with autism are 50 times more likely to have the disorder than are the siblings of children without autism (Szatmari et al., 1998; Tager-Flusberg et al., 2001). Twin studies show concordance rates for autism to be about 60 to 80 percent for monozygotic twins and 0 to 10 percent for dizygotic twins (Bailey et al., 1995). In addition, about 90 percent of the MZ twins of children with autism have a significant cognitive impairment, compared with 10 percent of DZ twins. Finally, children with autism have a higher than average rate of other genetic disorders associated with cognitive impairment, including Fragile X syndrome and PKU (Szatmari et al., 1998). These data

suggest that a general vulnerability to several types of cognitive impairment, only one of which is manifested as autism, runs in families.

Aberrations in almost all of the chromosomes have been found in studies comparing individuals with and without autism (Gillberg, 1998). The most frequently and consistently reported chromosomal abnormalities found in autism are aberrations on the long arm of chromosome 15 and in the sex chromosomes.

It seems likely that neurological factors are involved in autism. The broad array of deficits seen in autism suggests disruption in the normal development and organization of the brain (Minshew, Sweeney, & Bauman, 1997). In addition, approximately 30 percent of children with autism develop seizure disorders by adolescence, suggesting a severe neurological dysfunction (Fombonne, 1999).

Neuroimaging studies have suggested a variety of structural and functional deficits in the brains of individuals with autism. A consistent finding is a greater head and brain size in children with the disorder than in those without the disorder (Lotspeich et al., 2004). Functional MRI studies suggest that, when doing tasks tapping theory of mind, people with autism show less activity in the medial frontal cortex and medial temporal cortex than

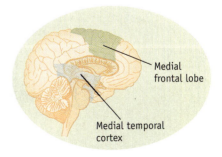

These areas of the brain have been implicated in autism.

people without autism (Frith & Frith, 2000). At a more fundamental level, people with autism do not show the same pattern of brain activation as people without autism when doing face perception and recognition tasks (Schultz et al., 2000).

Neuorological dysfunctions could be the result of genetic factors. Alternately, there is a higher than average rate of prenatal and birth complications among children with autism. These complications might have created neurological damage (Dykens & Volkmar, 1997). Finally, studies have found differences between children with and without the disorder in levels of the neurotransmitters serotonin and dopamine, although the meaning of these differences is not entirely clear (Anderson & Hoshino, 1997).

The variety of biological factors implicated in autism may indicate that there are several subtypes of autism, each with its own biological cause. With a disorder as rare as autism, it is difficult to study enough children to discover subtypes. Ideally, recent advances in the technology of biomedical research, such as the use of magnetic resonance imagery and genetic mapping, will provide more detailed data on the biology of autism.

Treatments for Autism

A number of drugs have been shown to improve some of the symptoms of autism, such as overactivity, stereotyped behaviors (e.g., head-banging, hand-flapping), sleep disturbances, and tension (Kerbeshian, Burd, & Avery, 2001; Volkmar, 2001). The selective serotonin reuptake inhibitors appear to reduce repetitive behavior and aggression, and they improve social interactions in some people

Intensive behavior therapy can help children with autism learn communication and social skills.

with autism. The antipsychotic medications are used to reduce obsessive and repetitive behavior and to improve self-control. Naltrexone, a drug that blocks receptors for opiates, has been shown to be useful in reducing hyperactivity in some children with autism. Finally, stimulants are used to improve attention. These drugs do not alter the basic autistic disorder, but they may make it easier for people with the disorder to participate in school and in interventions.

Psychosocial therapies for autism combine behavioral techniques and structured educational services (Koegel, Koegel, & Brookman, 2003; Lovaas & Smith, 2003). Operant conditioning strategies are used to reduce excessive behaviors, such as repetitive or ritualistic behaviors, tantrums, and aggression, and to alleviate deficits or delays, such as deficits in communication, and deficits in interactions with caregivers and peers. These techniques may be implemented in highly structured schools designed especially for children with autism or in regular classrooms if the child is mainstreamed. The specific deficits a child has in cognitive, motor, or communication skills are targeted, and materials that reduce possible distractions (such as reading books that do not have words printed in bright colors) are used. Parents may be taught to implement the techniques continually when the children are at home.

One pioneering study showed that 47 percent of children with autism given this intensive behavioral treatment for at least 40 hours per week for at least 2 years achieved normal intellectual and educational functioning by age 7, compared with 2 percent of children who received only institutional care (Lovaas, 1987). Several other studies have shown remarkable improvements in cognitive skills and behavioral control in children with autism when they were treated with a comprehensive behavior therapy administered both by their parents and in their school setting (Bregman & Gerdtz, 1997; Koegel et al., 2003; Lovaas & Smith, 2003; Ozonoff & Cathcart, 1998; Schreibman & Charlop-Christy, 1998).

SUMMING UP

■ The pervasive developmental disorders are characterized by severe and lasting impairment in several areas of development, including social interaction, communication, everyday behaviors, interests, and activities. They include Asperger's disorder, Rett's disorder, childhood disintegrative disorder, and autism.

■ Autism is characterized by significant interpersonal, communication, and behavioral deficits. Two-thirds of children with autism score in the mentally retarded range on IQ tests.

- There is wide variation in the outcome of autism, although the majority of autistic children must have continual care as adults. The best predictors of a good outcome in autism are an IQ above 50 and language development before the age of 6.

- The biological causes of autism may include a genetic predisposition to cognitive impairment, central nervous system damage, prenatal complications, and neurotransmitter imbalances.

- Drugs reduce some behaviors in autism but do not eliminate the core of the disorder.

- Behavior therapy is used to reduce inappropriate and self-injurious behaviors and to encourage prosocial behaviors in children with autism.

CHAPTER INTEGRATION

As noted earlier, the study of psychological disorders in children is often referred to as developmental psychopathology. This label explicitly recognizes that, in order to understand psychopathology in children, researchers must understand normal biological, psychological, and social development. Moreover, developmental psychopathologists are concerned with the interdependence of biological, psychological, and social development in children, recognizing that disruptions in any one of these three systems send perturbations through the other systems. The interdependence of these systems is probably even greater in children than in adults, because children are not mature enough to compartmentalize their troubles and are highly dependent on their caregivers and environment for even their most basic needs.

One example of the interplay among biology, psychology, and the social environment comes from a study of adopted children (Ge et al., 1996) (see Figure 13.3). Some of the adopted children in this study had biological parents who had antisocial personalities or histories of substance abuse. The other adopted children had biological parents with no histories of psychological problems. The children whose biological parents had histories of psychopathology were more likely than the other children to be hostile and antisocial themselves. Most researchers who do not take a biopsychosocial approach to childhood disorders would stop with these results and declare them clear evidence

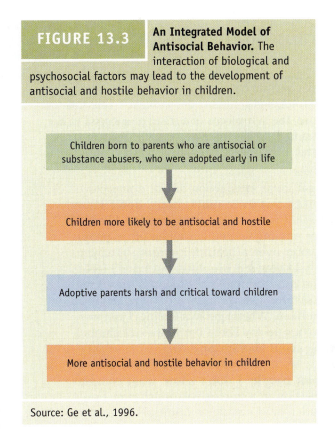

FIGURE 13.3   **An Integrated Model of Antisocial Behavior.** The interaction of biological and psychosocial factors may lead to the development of antisocial and hostile behavior in children.

Children born to parents who are antisocial or substance abusers, who were adopted early in life

Children more likely to be antisocial and hostile

Adoptive parents harsh and critical toward children

More antisocial and hostile behavior in children

Source: Ge et al., 1996.

for the genetic inheritance of antisocial and hostile tendencies.

The researchers in this study, however, went further and looked at the parenting behaviors of the children's adoptive parents. They found that the adoptive parents of the antisocial/hostile children were more harsh and critical in their parenting than were the adoptive parents of the children who were not antisocial and hostile. It appeared that the antisocial/hostile children drew out harsh and critical behaviors from their adoptive parents. The harsh and critical parenting these children received only exacerbated the children's antisocial behaviors. Thus, the children with biological parents who were antisocial or were substance abusers appeared to have a genetic predisposition to being antisocial and hostile. Then, in effect, their genes also created an environment of parenting practices by their adoptive parents that contributed to more antisocial behavior by the children.

These children were on a developmental trajectory in which their biology and social environment were acting in synergy to lead them toward serious conduct disturbances. This kind of synergy among biology, psychology, and the social environment is the rule, rather than the exception, in the development of psychopathology, particularly in children.

Extraordinary People: Follow-Up

Temple Grandin, whom we met at the beginning of this chapter, has generally been able to overcome, or even use, the symptoms of autism to succeed in her profession, but she still finds it very difficult to understand emotions and social relationships. She explains,

> I get great satisfaction out of doing clever things with my mind, but I don't know what it is like to feel rapturous joy. I know I am missing something when other people swoon over a beautiful sunset. Intellectually I know it is beautiful, but I don't feel it. The closest thing I have to joy is the excited pleasure I feel when I have solved a design problem. When I get this feeling, I just want to kick up my heels. I'm like a calf gamboling about on a spring day.
>
> My emotions are simpler than those of most people. I don't know what complex emotion in a human relationship is. I only understand simple emotions, such as fear, anger, happiness, and sadness. I cry during sad movies, and sometimes I cry when I see something that really moves me. But complex emotional relationships are beyond my comprehension. (Grandin, 1995, p. 89)

Grandin often finds it difficult to operate in the social world. She does not "read" other people well, and she often finds herself offending people or being stared at for her social awkwardness:

> Social interactions that come naturally to most people can be daunting for people

with autism. As a child, I was like an animal that had no instincts to guide me; I just had to learn by trial and error. I was always observing, trying to work out the best way to behave, but I never fit in. I had to think about every social interaction. When other students swooned over the Beatles, I called their reaction an ISP—interesting sociological phenomenon. I was a scientist trying to figure out the ways of the natives. I wanted to participate, but did not know how. . . .

> All my life I have been an observer, and I have always felt like someone who watches from the outside. I could not participate in the social interactions of high school life. . . . My peers spent hours standing around talking about jewelry or some other topic with no real substance. What did they get out of this? I just did not fit in. I never fit in with the crowd, but I had a few friends who were interested in the same things, such as skiing and riding horses. Friendship always revolved around what I did rather than who I was. (p. 132)

Still, Grandin does not regret that she has autism. She says,

> If I could snap my fingers and be a nonautistic person, I would not. Autism is part of what I am. (p. 60)

Chapter Summary

- More than a third of children suffer from a significant emotional or behavior disorder by the time they are 16. (Review Table 13.1.)

- The behavior disorders include attention-deficit/hyperactivity disorder (ADHD), conduct disorder, and oppositional defiant disorder. (Review Table 13.3.)

- ADHD is characterized by inattentiveness, impulsivity, and hyperactivity. (Review Table 13.4.) Children with ADHD do poorly in school and in peer relationships and are at increased risk of

developing conduct disorder. ADHD is more common in boys than in girls.

- Biological factors that have been implicated in the development of ADHD include genetics, exposure to toxins prenatally and early in childhood, and abnormalities in neurological functioning. In addition, many children with ADHD come from families in which there are many disruptions, although it is not clear if this is a cause or just a correlate of ADHD.

- Treatments for ADHD usually involve stimulant drugs and behavior therapy designed to decrease children's impulsivity and hyperactivity and to help them control aggression.

- Conduct disorder is characterized by extreme antisocial behavior and the violation of other people's rights and of social norms. (Review Table 13.5.) Conduct disorder is more common in boys than in girls and is highly stable across childhood and adolescence. Adults who had conduct disorder as children are at increased risk for criminal behavior and a host of problems in fitting into society.

- Children with oppositional defiant disorder are easily angered and tend to violate rules and requests. (Review Table 13.6.) Unlike children with conduct disorder, they do not tend to be aggressive toward other people or animals, to steal, or to destroy property.

- Genetics and neurological problems leading to attention deficits are implicated in the development of conduct disorder. In addition, children with conduct disorder tend to have parents who are harsh and inconsistent in their discipline practices and who model aggressive, antisocial behavior. Psychologically, children with conduct disorder tend to process information in ways that are likely to lead to aggressive reactions to others' behaviors.

- The treatment for conduct disorder is most often cognitive-behavioral, focusing on changing children's ways of interpreting interpersonal situations and helping them control their angry impulses. Neuroleptic drugs and stimulant drugs are also sometimes used to treat conduct disorder.

- Children can develop all the major emotional disorders (such as mood disorders and anxiety disorders), but separation anxiety disorder, by definition, begins in childhood. Its symptoms include chronic worry about separation from parents or about parents' well-being, dreams and fantasies about separation from parents, refusal to go to school, and somatic complaints. (Review Table 13.7.) This disorder is more common in girls.

- Separation anxiety disorder runs in families, which may suggest either that genetics plays a role in its development or that parents model anxious behavior for their children. Separation anxiety often arises following major traumas, particularly if parents are anxious and overprotective of their children. (Review Table 13.8.)

- The therapy for separation anxiety follows behaviorist principles and involves relaxation training and increasing periods of separation from parents.

- The elimination disorders are enuresis, the repeated wetting of clothes or bed linens in children over the age of 5, and encopresis, repeated defecation in the clothes or on the floor in children over the age of 4. (Review Table 13.9.) Enuresis is more common and has been studied more extensively than encopresis and has been linked to psychological stress, inappropriate or lax toilet training, and genetics.

- Enuresis is often treated with the bell and pad method, which helps children learn to awaken when their bladders are full, so that they can go to the bathroom. Antidepressants are also used to treat enuresis, but their effects disappear when the children stop taking them.

- Encopresis most often begins after episodes of constipation. It is treated by medical management and regular toilet sitting.

- The disorders of cognitive, motor, and communication skills involve deficits and delays in the development of fundamental skills. (Review Table 13.10.)

- The learning disorders include reading disorder (an inability to read, also known as dyslexia), mathematics disorder (an inability to learn math), and disorder of written expression (an inability to write).

- Developmental coordination disorder involves deficits in fundamental motor skills.

- The communication disorders include expressive language disorder (an inability to express oneself through language), mixed receptive-expressive language disorder (an inability to express oneself through language or to understand the language of others), phonological disorder (the use of speech sounds inappropriate for one's age and dialect), and stuttering (deficits in word fluency).

- Some of these disorders, particularly reading disorder and stuttering, may have genetic roots. Many other factors have been implicated in these disorders, but they are not well understood.

- Treatment usually focuses on building skills in problem areas through specialized training, as well as the use of computerized exercises.

- Mental retardation is defined as subaverage intellectual functioning, indexed by an IQ score below 70 and deficits in adaptive behavioral functioning. (Review Table 13.11.) There are four levels of mental retardation, ranging from mild to profound.

- A number of biological factors are implicated in mental retardation, including metabolic disorders (PKU, Tay-Sachs disease); chromosomal disorders

(Down syndrome, Fragile X syndrome, Trisomy 13, and Trisomy 18); prenatal exposure to rubella, herpes, syphilis, or drugs (especially alcohol, as in fetal alcohol syndrome); premature delivery; and head traumas (such as those arising from being violently shaken as an infant). (Review Table 13.12.)

■ There is some evidence that intensive and comprehensive educational interventions, administered very early in an affected child's life, can help decrease the level of mental retardation.

■ Controversy exists over whether children with mental retardation should be put in special education classes or mainstreamed into normal classrooms.

■ The pervasive developmental disorders are characterized by severe and lasting impairment in several areas of development, including social interaction, communication with others, everyday behaviors, interests, and activities. They include Asperger's disorder, Rett's disorder, childhood disintegrative disorder, and autism. (Review Table 13.15.)

■ Autism is characterized by significant interpersonal, communication, and behavioral deficits. (Review Table 13.14.) Many children with autism score in the range for mental retardation on IQ tests. The outcomes of autism vary widely, although the majority of people with autism must have continual care, even as adults. The best predictors of a good outcome in autism are an IQ above 50 and language development before the age of 6.

■ The possible biological causes of autism include a genetic predisposition to cognitive impairment, chromosomal abnormalities, central nervous system damage, prenatal and birth complications, and neurotransmitter imbalances. (Review Table 13.16.)

■ Drugs reduce some behaviors in autism but do not eliminate the core of the disorder. Behavior therapy is used to reduce inappropriate and self-injurious behaviors and to encourage prosocial behaviors.

MindMap CD-ROM

The following resources on the MindMap CD-ROM that came with this text will help you to master the content of this chapter and prepare for tests:

■ Videos: ADHD; Asperger's Disorder
■ Chapter Timeline
■ Chapter Quiz

Key Terms

attention-deficit/hyperactivity disorder (ADHD) 464

conduct disorder 470

oppositional defiant disorder 471

separation anxiety disorder 478

behavioral inhibition 479

elimination disorders 483

enuresis 483

bell and pad method 483

encopresis 484

reading disorder 485

mathematics disorder 485

disorder of written expression 485

developmental coordination disorder 486

expressive language disorder 487

mixed receptive-expressive language disorder 487

phonological disorder 487

stuttering 487

mental retardation 488

fetal alcohol syndrome (FAS) 492

pervasive developmental disorders 496

autism 496

Rett's disorder 499

childhood disintegrative disorder 499

Asperger's disorder 499

> Chapter 14

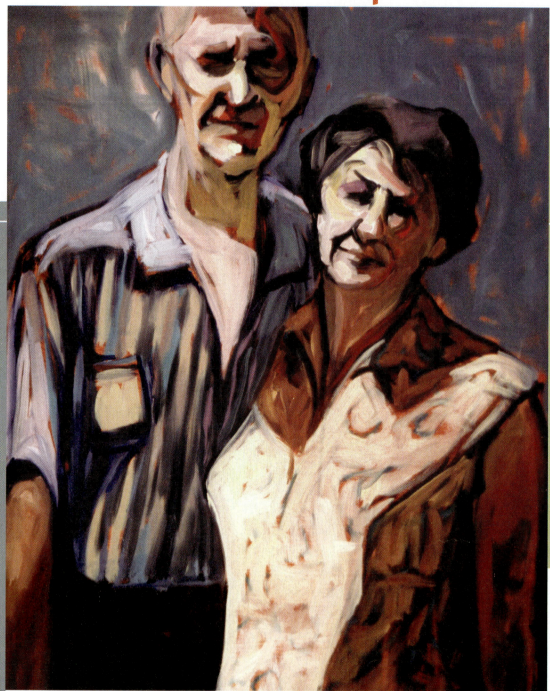

Untitled #4
by Deborah Schneider

Men are not prisoners of fate, but only prisoners of their own minds.

—Franklin D. Roosevelt,
Pan American Day address (1939)

Cognitive Disorders and Life-Span Issues <

CHAPTER OVERVIEW

Extraordinary People

■ **Iris Murdoch: *Elegy for Iris***

Dementia

Dementia is characterized by memory loss, deterioration in language skills and the ability to engage in voluntary behaviors, and the failure to recognize objects or people. The most common cause of dementia is Alzheimer's disease, but several other medical conditions can also cause it. Dementia is also an effect of chronic intoxication with alcohol and other toxic substances. There is no effective treatment for dementia, but memory aids and drugs to increase cognitive functioning and reduce distress can help.

Taking Psychology Personally

■ **How Does Dementia Affect Caregivers?**

Delirium

The symptoms of delirium are disorientation, recent memory loss, and the clouding of consciousness. Medical conditions, surgery, many different drugs, high fever, and infections increase the risk for delirium.

Amnesia

The amnesic disorders can involve retrograde amnesia, which is a loss of memory for past events, and anterograde amnesia, which is the inability to learn new information. Amnesia can result from some medical illnesses, brain damage due to injury, and long-term substance abuse.

Mental Disorders in Later Life

All of the disorders discussed in previous chapters can occur in later life. The characteristics, prevalence, and treatment of these disorders can be different for the elderly, however.

Chapter Integration

Many changes take place in the brain and the rest of the body with aging, and these are influenced by genetic and other biological vulnerabilities. The impact of these changes on the everyday behavior of older people varies tremendously, however, in part due to differences in personality and the social environment.

Extraordinary People

Iris Murdoch: *Elegy for Iris*

When she was a young woman teaching philosophy at Oxford University, Iris Murdoch met John Bayley, a recent graduate in English. They fell in love, married two years later, and settled in Oxford, where John eventually taught and became an eminent literary critic. Iris went on to write a total of 26 novels and several textbooks on philosophy and to be considered one of the greatest writers of the twentieth century. She received honorary doctorates from many major universities and was named a Dame of the British Empire. These two intellectual giants shared a life and love that was extraordinary for its passion, its intimacy, and its fun.

John Bayley writes,

> The more I got to know Iris during the early days of our relationship, the less I understood her. Indeed, I soon began not to want to understand her. I was far too preoccupied at the time to think of such parallels, but it was like living in a fairy story—the kind with sinister overtones and not always a happy ending— in which a young man loves a beautiful maiden who returns his love but is always disappearing into some unknown and mysterious world, about which she will reveal nothing. (Bayley, 1999, pp. 45–46)

Tragedy eventually did befall the couple, although not until John and Iris had been married nearly 40 years. In 1994, Iris developed Alzheimer's disease. This brilliant novelist and philosopher was reduced to grunts, squeaks, and murmurs, asking the same questions over and over and not being able to care for her own basic needs.

John's account of his life with Iris after she developed Alzheimer's disease, published in *Elegy for Iris* (1999), is a story of the triumph of love over the great stresses of caring for a person with severe dementia. Following are some passages from this wonderful love story:

> Alzheimer's is, in fact, like an insidious fog, barely noticeable until everything around has disappeared. After that, it is no longer possible to believe that a world outside the fog exists. (p. 281)

> The sense of someone's mind. Only now an awareness of it; other minds are usually taken for granted. I wonder sometimes if Iris is secretly thinking: How can I escape? What am I to do? Has nothing replaced the play of her mind when she was writing, cogitating, living in her mind? I find myself devoutly hoping not. (p. 228)

> Our mode of communication seems like underwater sonar, each bouncing pulsations off the other, then listening for an echo. The baffling moments at which I cannot understand what Iris is saying, or about whom or what—moments which can produce tears and anxieties, though never, thank goodness, the raging frustration typical of many Alzheimer's sufferers—can sometimes be dispelled by embarking on a jokey parody of helplessness, and trying to make it mutual, both of us at a loss of words. (pp. 51–52)

> The face of an Alzheimer's patient has been clinically described as the "lion face." An apparently odd comparison, but in fact a very apt one. The features settle into a leonine impassivity which does remind one of the king of beasts, and the way his broad expressionless mask is represented in painting and sculpture. . . .

> The face of the Alzheimer's sufferer indicates only an absence: It is a mask in the most literal sense. That is why the sudden appearance of a smile is so extraordinary. The lion face becomes the face of the Virgin Mary, tranquil in sculpture and painting,

with a gravity that gives such a smile its deepest meaning. (pp. 53–54)

This terror of being alone, of being cut off for even a few seconds from the familiar object, is a feature of Alzheimer's. If Iris could climb inside my skin now, or enter me as if I had a pouch like a kangaroo, she would do so. She has no awareness of what I am doing, only an awareness of what I am. The worlds and gestures of love still come naturally, but they cannot be accompanied by that wordless communication which depends on the ability to use words. (p. 127)

I make a savage comment today about the grimness of our outlook. Iris looks relieved and intelligent. She says, "But I love you." (p. 233)

"When are we going?"

"I'll tell you when we go."

Iris always responds to a jokey tone. But it is sometimes hard to maintain. Violent irritation possesses me and I shout out before I can stop myself, "Don't keep asking me when we are going!" . . .

Her face just crumples into tears. I hasten to comfort her, and she always responds

to comfort. We kiss and embrace now much more than we used to. (p. 235)

[A lady] told me in her own deliberately jolly way that living with an Alzheimer's victim was like being chained to a corpse [and] went on to an even greater access of desperate facetiousness, saying, "And, as you and I know, it's a corpse that complains all the time."

I don't know it. In spite of her anxious and perpetual queries, Iris seems not to know how to complain. She never has. Alzheimer's, which can accentuate personality traits to the point of demonic parody, has only been able to exaggerate a natural goodness in her.

On a good day, her need for a loving presence, mutual pattings and murmurs, has something angelic about it; she seems herself in the presence found in an ikon. It is more important for her still on days of silent tears, a grief seemingly unaware of that mysterious world of creation she has lost, and yet aware that something is missing. (pp. 76–77)

Our modern culture tends to equate aging with disease and decline. Stories such as that of Iris Murdoch paint a picture of deterioration and emotional turmoil, which many young people think are inevitable in old age. Some diseases are more likely to occur late in life, and normal aging involves some decline in cognitive and physical abilities. Most older people, however, are physically and mentally healthy, living happy and productive lives. Indeed, the rate of most psychological disorders is lower among older people than among younger people (Whitbourne, 2000).

However, between 10 and 20 percent of people over the age of 65 have psychological problems severe enough to qualify for a diagnosis and to warrant treatment (Gatz, Kasl-Godley, & Karel, 1996). The rate of psychological problems is even higher among the "old-old," those over 85 years of age. The subfield of psychology concerned with psy-

chological disorders in late life is known as *geropsychology.* Just as developmental psychopathologists try to understand children's psychological problems in the context of normal development during childhood and adolescence, geropsychologists try to understand psychological problems in older people in the context of the many biological, psychological, and social changes people undergo in later life.

All of the disorders we have discussed so far in this book can occur among older people. Near the end of this chapter, we will discuss the prevalence, characteristics, and treatment of depression, anxiety, and substance use disorders in older people. First, however, we focus on disorders that most often arise for the first time in old age—the **cognitive disorders**—dementia, delirium, and amnesia. These disorders are characterized by impairments in cognition caused by a medical condition

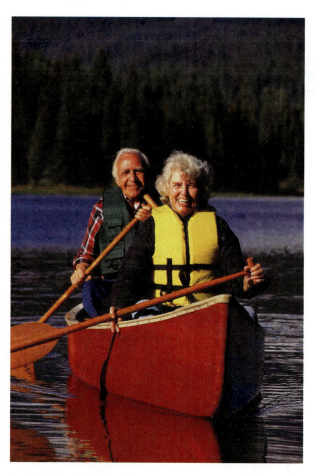

Most older people are physically and mentally healthy, leading productive lives.

(such as Alzheimer's disease, which Iris Murdoch suffered) or by substance intoxication or withdrawal. The impairments in cognition include memory deficits, language disturbances, perceptual disturbances, impairment in the capacity to plan and organize, and the failure to recognize or identify objects. These disorders were formerly called *organic brain disorders*. This label was discontinued in the DSM-IV-TR, however, because it implies that other disorders are *not* caused by biological factors, when it is clear that many disorders recognized by the DSM-IV-TR have biological causes.

The cognitive impairments seen in dementia, delirium, and amnesia can also occur in other psychological disorders. For example, people with schizophrenia have language impairments and perceptual disturbances. People with depression may have problems with concentration and memory. Dementia, delirium, and amnesia are diagnosed when cognitive impairments appear to be the result of nonpsychiatric medical diseases, sub-

stance intoxication, or substance withdrawal, but not when the cognitive impairments appear only to be symptoms of other psychiatric disorders, such as schizophrenia or depression.

DEMENTIA

CASE STUDY

Aside from sustaining a head injury of uncertain significance while a young man in the service, Mr. Abbot B. Carrington had no medical or psychiatric problems until the age of 56. At that time, employed as an officer of a bank, he began to be forgetful. For example, he would forget to bring his briefcase to work or he would misplace his eyeglasses. His efficiency at work declined. He failed to follow through with assignments. Reports that he prepared were incomplete. Although still friendly and sociable, Mr. Carrington began to lose interest in many of his usual activities. He ignored his coin collection. He no longer thoroughly perused *The Wall Street Journal* each day. When he discussed economics, it was without his previous grasp of the subject. After about a year of these difficulties, he was gradually eased out of his responsible position at the bank and eventually retired permanently. At home, he tended to withdraw into himself. He would arise early each morning and go for a long walk, occasionally losing his way if he reached an unfamiliar neighborhood. He needed to be reminded constantly of the time of day, of upcoming events, and of his son's progress in college. He tried to use electric appliances without first plugging them into the socket. He shaved with the wrong side of the razor. Mostly, he remained a quiet, pleasant, and tractable person, but sometimes, particularly at night, he became exceptionally confused, and at these times he might be somewhat irritable, loud, and difficult to control.

Approximately 2 years following the onset of these symptoms, he was seen by a neurologist, who conducted a detailed examination of his mental status. The examiner noted that Mr. Carrington was neatly dressed, polite, and cooperative. He sat passively in the office as his

(continued)

wife described his problems to the doctor. He himself offered very little information. In fact, at one point, apparently bored by the proceedings, he unceremoniously got up from his chair and left the room to wander in the corridor. He did not know the correct date or the name and location of the hospital in which he was being examined. Mr. Carrington was then told the date and place, but 10 minutes later he had forgotten this information. Although a presidential election campaign was then in progress, he did not know the names of the candidates. Despite his background in banking and economics, he could not give any relevant information concerning inflation, unemployment, or the prime lending rate. When questioned about the events of his own life, Mr. Carrington was also frequently in error. He confused recent and remote events. For example, he thought his father had recently died, but in fact this had occurred many years earlier. He could not provide a good description of his occupation.

Mr. Carrington's speech was fluent and well articulated, but vague and imprecise. He used long, roundabout, cliché-filled phrases to express rather simple ideas. Sometimes he would use the wrong word, as when he substituted *prescribe* for *subscribe*. Despite his past facility with figures, he was unable to do simple calculations. With a pencil and paper, he could not copy two-dimensional figures or a cube. When instructed to draw a house, he drew a succession of attached squares. Asked to give a single word that would define the similarity between an apple and an orange, he replied, "Round." He interpreted the proverb "People who live in glass houses shouldn't throw stones" to mean that "People don't want their windows broken." He seemed to have little insight into his problem. He appeared apathetic rather than anxious or depressed. (Adapted from Spitzer et al., 1981, pp. 243–244)

Mr. Carrington was slowly losing his ability to remember the most fundamental facts of his life, to express himself through language, and to carry out the basic activities of everyday life. This is the pic-

ture of **dementia,** the most common cognitive disorder.

Dementia most commonly occurs in later life. The estimated prevalence of the most common type of dementia—that due to Alzheimer's disease—is 5 to 10 percent in people over 65 years of age (Aguero-Torres, Fratiglioni, & Winblad, 1998; Epple, 2002). The prevalence of most types of dementia increases with age, with an estimated prevalence of 20 to 50 percent in people over 85 years of age.

News coverage on dementia has increased substantially in recent years, and at times it seems that there is an epidemic of this disorder. Three factors have probably contributed to the increased public attention to dementia. First, there have been substantial advances in the understanding of some types of dementia in the past decade, which have made the news. Second, in previous generations, people died of heart disease, cancer, and infectious diseases at younger ages and, therefore, did not reach the age at which dementia often has its onset. These days, however, people are living long enough for dementia to develop and affect their functioning. Third, as the baby-boom generation ages, the number of people who reach the age at which dementia typically emerges is increasing. Indeed, the number of people with dementia is expected to double in the next 50 years, due to the aging of the general population (Max, 1993). The cost to society in health care and to individuals in time spent caring for family members with dementia is likely to be staggering.

Symptoms of Dementia

There are five types of cognitive deficits in dementia (see the DSM-IV-TR symptoms in Table 14.1 on page 514). The most prominent is a *memory deficit*, which is required for the diagnosis of dementia. In the early stages of dementia, the memory lapses may be similar to those that we all experience from time to time—forgetting the name of someone we know casually, our own phone number, or what we went into the next room to get. Most of us eventually remember what we temporarily forget, either spontaneously or by tricks that jog our memories. The difference with dementia is that memory does not return spontaneously and may not respond to reminders or other memory cues.

People in the early stages of dementia may repeat questions because they do not remember asking them moments ago, or they do not remember getting answers. They frequently misplace items, such as keys or wallets. They may try to compensate for the memory loss. For example, they may

TABLE 14.1	DSM-IV-TR

Major Symptoms of Dementia

Dementia is characterized by the permanent loss of basic cognitive functions.

Memory impairment, including impaired ability to learn new information or to recall previously learned information

Aphasia (language disturbance)

Apraxia (inability to carry out motor activities despite intact motor function)

Agnosia (failure to recognize or identify objects despite intact sensory functioning)

Disturbance in executive functioning (such as planning, organizing, sequencing, and abstracting information)

Source: Reprinted with permission from the *Diagnostic and Statistical Manual of Mental Disorders*, Fourth Edition, Text Revision. Copyright © 2000 American Psychiatric Association.

carefully write down their appointments or things they need to do. Eventually, however, they forget to look at their calendars or lists. As the memory problems become more apparent, they may become angry when asked questions or make up answers in an attempt to hide memory loss. Later, as dementia progresses, they may become lost in familiar surroundings and be unable to find their way unaccompanied.

Eventually, long-term memory also becomes impaired. People with dementia forget the order of major events in their lives, such as graduation from college, marriage, and the birth of their children. After a time, they unable to recall the events at all and may not even know their own names.

The second type of cognitive impairment is a *deterioration of language*, known as **aphasia.** People with dementia have tremendous difficulty producing the names of objects or people and may often use terms such as *thing* or vague references to *them* to hide their inability to produce names. If asked to identify a cup, for example, they may say that it is a *thing for drinking* but be unable to name it as a cup. They may be unable to understand what another person is saying and to follow simple requests, such as "Turn on the lights and shut the door." In advanced stages of dementia, people

may exhibit **echolalia**—the repetition of what they hear—or **palialia**—the repetition of sounds or words.

The third cognitive deficit is **apraxia,** impairment in the ability to execute common actions, such as waving good-bye or putting on a shirt. This deficit is not caused by problems in motor functioning (such as moving the arm), in sensory functioning, or in the comprehension of what action is required. People with dementia simply are unable to carry out actions that are requested of them or that they wish to carry out.

The fourth cognitive deficit is **agnosia,** the failure to recognize objects or people. People with dementia may not be able to identify common objects, such as chairs or tables. At first, they fail to recognize casual friends or distant family members. With time, they may not recognize their spouses or children or even their own reflections in a mirror.

The fifth cognitive deficit is a loss of **executive functions.** Executive functions are the functions of the brain that involve the ability to plan, initiate, monitor, and stop complex behaviors. Cooking Thanksgiving dinner requires executive functioning. Each menu item (e.g., the turkey, the stuffing, the pumpkin pie) requires different ingredients and preparation. The cooking of various menu items must be coordinated, so that all the items are ready at the same time. People in the early stages of dementia may attempt to cook Thanksgiving dinner but forget important components (such as the turkey) or fail to coordinate the dinner, burning certain items while undercooking others. People in later stages of dementia are unable even to plan or initiate a complex task such as this.

Deficits in executive functions also involve problems in the kind of abstract thinking required to evaluate new situations and respond appropriately to these situations. For example, in the previous case study, when Mr. Carrington was presented with the proverb "People who live in glass houses shouldn't throw stones," he was unable to interpret the abstract meaning of the proverb. Instead, he interpreted it concretely to mean "People don't want their windows broken."

In addition to having these cognitive deficits, people with dementia often show changes in emotional and personality functioning. Shoplifting and exhibitionism are common occurrences caused by declines in judgment and the ability to control impulses. People with dementia may become depressed when they recognize their cognitive deterioration. Often, however, they do not recognize or admit to their cognitive deficits. This can lead them to take unrealistic or dangerous actions, such as driving a car when they are too impaired to do so safely. People with dementia may become paranoid and angry with family members and friends, whom they see as thwarting their desires and freedoms. They may accuse others of stealing the belongings they have misplaced. They may believe that others are conspiring against them—the only conclusion left for them when they simply do not remember conversations in which they agreed to some action, such as starting a new medication or moving into a treatment facility for people with dementia. Violent outbursts are not unusual.

Types of Dementia

Dementia has several causes (see Figure 14.1). The most common is Alzheimer's disease, and great strides are being made in the understanding of Alzheimer's dementia. Dementia can also be caused by vascular disease (a blockage of blood to the brain, commonly referred to as a stroke); by head injury; by progressive diseases, such as Parkinson's disease and HIV disease; and by chronic drug abuse (see the Concept Overview in Table 14.2).

Dementia of the Alzheimer's Type

In 1995, the family of former President Ronald Reagan announced that he had been diagnosed with Alzheimer's disease. Although the family decided to maintain their privacy concerning the specific manifestations of the disease, their announcement of Reagan's diagnosis helped bring attention to this disease, which affects nearly 4 million Americans (Max, 1993).

Dementia due to **Alzheimer's disease** is the most common type of dementia and accounts for over 50 percent of all dementias (Torti et al., 2004). Alzheimer's dementias typically begin with mild memory loss, but as the disease progresses, the memory loss and disorientation quickly become profound, as did Iris Murdoch's. About two-thirds of Alzheimer's patients show psychiatric symptoms, including agitation, irritability, apathy, and dysphoria. John Bayley writes in *Elegy for Iris* that these emotional symptoms were as difficult as the cognitive symptoms for him to deal with. As the disease worsens, people may become violent and experience hallucinations and delusions. The disease usually begins after the age

Former President Ronald Reagan, who died in 2004 at the age of 93, was diagnosed with Alzheimer's disease.

FIGURE 14.1 | **Leading Causes of Dementia.** Alzheimer's disease causes over half of all cases of dementia. "Other causes" of dementia are chronic alcoholism, nutritional deficiencies, and metabolic imbalances.

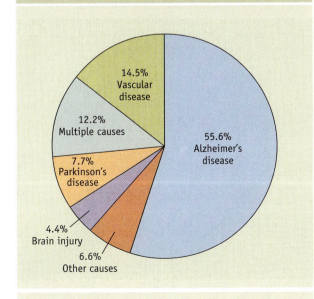

Source: Max, 1993.

TABLE 14.2 Concept Overview

Types of Dementia

Dementia can be caused by a number of progressive diseases, as well as by repeated head injury.

Alzheimer's type
Vascular dementia
Dementia due to head injury
Dementia associated with other medical conditions
  Parkinson's disease
  HIV disease
  Huntington's disease
  Pick's disease
  Creutzfeldt-Jakob disease
  Chronic heavy use of alcohol, inhalants, and sedative drugs

of 65, but there is an early-onset type of Alzheimer's disease that tends to progress more quickly than the late-onset type. On average, people with this disease die within 8 to 10 years of its diagnosis, usually as a result of physical decline or independent diseases common in old age, such as heart disease. Iris Murdoch was diagnosed with Alzheimer's disease in 1994 and died in 1999.

Brain Abnormalities in Alzheimer's Disease
This type of dementia was first described in 1906 by Alois Alzheimer. He observed severe memory loss and disorientation in a 51-year-old female patient. Following her death at age 55, an autopsy revealed that filaments within nerve cells in her brain were twisted and tangled. These **neurofibrillary tangles** are common in the brains of Alzheimer's patients but rare in people without cognitive disorders (Beatty, 1995). They appear to interfere with the basic functioning of neurons in many areas of the brain. Another brain abnormality seen in Alzheimer's disease is **plaques.** These plaques are deposits of a class of protein, called **amyloid,** that accumulate in the spaces between the cells of the cerebral cortex, hippocampus, amyg-

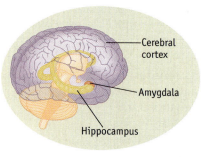

Plaques that accumulate between cells in these and other areas of the brain are seen in Alzheimer's disease.

dala, and other areas of the brain structures critical to memory and cognitive functioning (Atiya et al., 2003; Du et al., 2001).

There is extensive cell death in the cortex of Alzheimer's patients, resulting in the shrinkage, or atrophy, of the cortex and enlargement of the ventricles of the brain (see Figure 14.2). The remaining cells lose much of their dendrites—the branches that link one cell to other cells (see Figure 14.3). The results of all these brain abnormalities are profound memory loss and an inability to coordinate one's activities.

Causes of Alzheimer's Disease What causes the brain deterioration of Alzheimer's disease? This is an area of tremendous research activity, and new answers to this question emerge each day. Alzheimer's disease has been attributed to viral infections, immune system dysfunction, exposure to toxic levels of aluminum, deficiencies of the vitamin folate, and head traumas.

Much of the current research, however, has focused on genes that might transmit a vulnerability to this disorder and on the amyloid proteins that form the plaques found in the brains of almost all Alzheimer's patients. Family history studies suggest that 25 to 50 percent of relatives of patients with Alzheimer's disease eventually develop the disease, compared with only about 10 percent of family members of elderly people without Alzheimer's disease (Plassman & Breitner, 1996).

FIGURE 14.2 **Cortical Atrophy in Alzheimer's Disease.** Alzheimer's patients show widespread atrophy, or shrinkage, in the cortex and enlargement in the ventricular areas of the brain (butterfly-shaped spaces in the center).

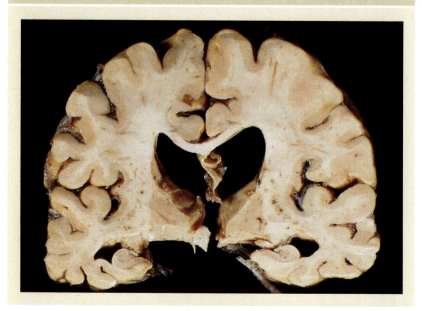

FIGURE 14.3 **Loss of Neuronal Dendrites in Alzheimer's Disease.** (a) Dendrites in the brain of a healthy person. (b) Shrunken and deteriorated dendrites in the brain of an Alzheimer's patient.

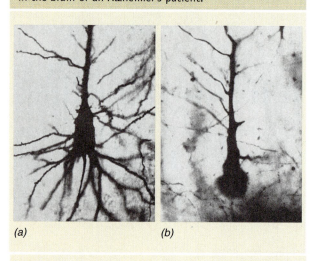

(a)   (b)

Source: Beatty, 1995.

Several genes have been linked to Alzheimer's disease. A defective gene on chromosome 19 is associated with an increased risk for the late-onset form of Alzheimer's disease, which is the most common form. This gene appears to be responsible for a rare protein, known as ApoE4. ApoE4 is one of a group of proteins that transport cholesterol through the blood. ApoE4 binds to the amyloid protein and may play a role in the regulation of amyloid protein. The ApoE4 gene has been estimated to account for 45 to 60 percent of all cases of Alzheimer's disease (Atiya et al., 2003; Petegnief et al., 2001). One study found that people with two copies of the ApoE4 gene (one on both of their chromosome 19s) were eight times more likely to have Alzheimer's disease than were people with no copies of the ApoE4 gene on either of their chromosome 19s (Corder, Saunders, & Strittmatter, 1993).

One of the most fascinating studies to show a link between ApoE4 and Alzheimer's disease is the Nun Study, a longitudinal study of several hundred elderly nuns in the School Sisters of Notre Dame. Research David Snowdon and colleagues confirmed that the nuns without the ApoE4 gene were much more likely to maintain high levels of intellectual functioning into advanced age (Riley et al., 2000). Even more remarkable was evidence that the nuns who entered old age with greater intellectual strengths were less likely to develop severe dementia, even when their brains showed evidence of significant neurofibrillary tangles and senile plaques (Snowdon, 1997). For example, the level of linguistic skills that the nuns showed in journal writings when they were in their twenties significantly predicted their risk of developing dementia in later life (Snowdon et al., 1996). The best example was Sister Mary, who had high cognitive test scores right up until her death at 101 years of age. An evaluation of Sister Mary's brain revealed that Alzheimer's disease had spread widely through her brain, but her cognitive test scores had slipped only from the "superior" range to the "very good" range as she aged. Other results from this study showed that tiny strokes may lead a mildly deteriorating brain to develop full-fledged dementia (Snowdon et al., 1997).

Other genes are implicated in the development of less common forms of Alzheimer's disease, which begin in middle age and are more strongly familial. The first of these genes is on chromosome 21 (Bird et al., 1998). The first clue that a defective gene on chromosome 21 may be linked with Alzheimer's disease came from the fact that people with Down syndrome are more

The Sisters of Notre Dame have participated in a fascinating study of the effects of early experiences on mental and physical health in old age.

likely than people in the general population to develop Alzheimer's disease in later life. Down syndrome is caused by an extra chromosome 21. Researchers hypothesized that the gene responsible for some forms of Alzheimer's disease may be on chromosome 21 and that people with Down syndrome are more prone to Alzheimer's disease because they have an extra chromosome 21 (Mayeux, 1996).

This hypothesis has been supported by linkage studies of families with high rates of Alzheimer's disease. These studies have found links between the presence of the disease and the presence of an abnormal gene on chromosome 21 (see Goate et al., 1991; St. George-Hyslop et al., 1987). In turn, this abnormal gene on chromosome 21 is near the gene responsible for producing a precursor of the amyloid protein known as the amyloid precursor protein gene, or APP gene. It may be that defects along this section of chromosome 21 cause an abnormal production and buildup of amyloid proteins in the brain, resulting in Alzheimer's disease.

A defective gene on chromosome 14 has been linked to early-onset Alzheimer's disease (Sherrington, Rogaev, & Liang, 1995). This discovery is especially exciting because this defective chromosome 14 gene may be implicated in almost 80 percent of early-onset Alzheimer's disease. This gene appears to be responsible for a protein, on the membranes of cells, known as S182. The link between S182 and the amyloid protein or other processes responsible for Alzheimer's disease is not yet known. Finally, another gene, E5-1, on chromosome 1, has been linked to Alzheimer's disease (Lendon, Ashall, & Goate, 1997).

People with Alzheimer's disease also show deficits in a number of neurotransmitters, including acetylcholine, norepinephrine, serotonin, somatostatin (a corticotropin-releasing factor), and peptide Y (Small, 1998). The deficits in acetylcholine are particularly noteworthy, because this neurotransmitter is thought to be critical in memory function. The degree of cognitive decline seen in patients with Alzheimer's disease is significantly correlated with the degree of deficits in acetylcholine (Knopman, 2003). In turn, drugs that enhance acetylcholine levels can slow the rate of cognitive decline in some Alzheimer's sufferers.

It is likely that much more about the causes of Alzheimer's disease will be learned in the next few years, because the technologies to study the genetic and neurological processes of the disease are advancing rapidly and because many researchers are investigating this disorder. Four and a half million people in the United States and 18 million people worldwide have been diagnosed with Alzheimer's disease, and this number is expected to increase by at least 300 percent by the year 2050 (Tariot, 2003). We can hope that, by then, this disorder will be understood well enough to be treated effectively.

Vascular Dementia

The second most common type of dementia, after Alzheimer's dementia, is **vascular dementia** (formerly called *multi-infarct dementia*). To be diagnosed with vascular dementia, a person must have symptoms or laboratory evidence of **cerebrovascular disease.** Cerebrovascular disease occurs when the blood supply to areas of the brain is blocked, causing tissue damage in the brain. Neuroimaging techniques, such as PET and MRI, can detect areas of tissue damage and reduced blood flow in the brain, confirming cerebrovascular disease (see Figure 14.4).

Sudden damage to an area of the brain due to the blockage of blood flow or to hemorrhaging (bleeding) is called a **stroke.** Vascular dementia

FIGURE 14.4	MRI Showing Tissue Damage Following a Stroke (Dark Blue Areas)

Source: Beatty, 1995.

can occur after one large stroke or an accumulation of small strokes. Cerebrovascular disease can be caused by high blood pressure and the accumulation of fatty deposits in the arteries, which block blood flow to the brain. It can also be a complication of head injuries and diseases that inflame the brain. The specific cognitive deficits and emotional changes a person experiences depend on the extent and location of the brain tissue damage (Desmond & Tatemichi, 1998).

About 25 percent of stroke patients develop cognitive deficits severe enough to qualify for a diagnosis of dementia (Stephens et al., 2004). A greater risk of developing dementia is seen in stroke patients who are older (over 80 years of age), who have less education, who have a history of strokes, and who have diabetes. The finding that greater education protects against the development of vascular dementia corresponds the with findings of studies of Alzheimer's disease.

Even stroke patients who do not immediately develop dementia are at increased risk of developing dementia, compared with people the same age who do not suffer a stroke. Follow-ups of stroke victims who remained free of dementia in the 3 months after their stroke found that about one-third of them developed dementia within the next 52 months, compared with 10 percent of a control group (Desmond & Tatemichi, 1998). The patients most likely to develop dementia eventually tended to have additional strokes over this time, some of which were obvious and others of which were "silent" and only detected later. In addition, patients who had medical events or conditions that caused widespread oxygen or blood deficiency, such as seizures, cardiac arrhythmias, congestive heart failure, and pneumonia, were more likely to develop dementia.

Dementia Due to Head Injury

A 41-year-old factory worker named Leland was returning home along a rural road one night after work. A drunk driver ran a stop sign and collided at a high rate of speed with the driver's side of Leland's car. Leland was not wearing a seat belt. The collision sent Leland through the windshield and onto the pavement. He lived but sustained substantial head injuries, as well as many broken bones and cuts. Leland was unconscious for over two weeks and then spent another two months in the hospital, recovering from his injuries.

When he returned home to his family, Leland was not himself. Before the accident, he was a quiet man who doted on his family and frequently displayed a wry sense of humor. After the accident, Leland was sullen and chronically irritable. He screamed at his wife or children for the slightest annoyance. He even slapped his wife once when she confronted him about his verbal abuse of the children.

Leland did not fare much better at work. He found he now had great trouble concentrating on his job, and he could not follow his boss's instructions. When his boss approached Leland about his inability to perform his job, Leland could not express much about the trouble he was having. He became angry at his boss and accused him of wanting to fire him. Leland had always been much liked by his coworkers, and they welcomed him back after the accident with sincere joy, but soon he began to lash out at them, as he was at his wife and children. He accused a close friend of stealing from him.

These symptoms continued acutely for about 3 months. Gradually, they declined. Finally, about 18 months after the accident, Leland's emotional and personality functioning appear to be back to normal. His cognitive functioning has also improved greatly, but he still finds it more difficult to pay attention and to complete tasks than he did before the accident.

Leland's symptoms were characteristic of people with traumatic brain injury (see the symptoms in Table 14.3). He showed changes in both his cognitive abilities and his usual emotional and personality functioning. Fortunately, Leland's symptoms subsided after several months. Many victims of brain injury never fully recover (Beatty, 1995).

Brain damage can be caused by penetrating injuries, such as those caused by gunshots, or closed head injuries, typically caused by blows to the head. The most common causes of closed head injuries are motor vehicle accidents, followed by falls, blows to the head during violent assault, and sports injuries. Dementia that follows a single closed head injury is more likely to dissipate with time than is dementia that follows repeated closed head injuries, such as experienced by boxers. Young men are most likely to suffer dementia due to head injury, because they take more risks associated with head injuries than do other groups.

Dementia pugilistica is a type of dementia due to repetitive head injuries (Jordan, 1998). It was first described in boxers but has been seen frequently in professional football, soccer, and ice hockey players. Dementia pugilistica is characterized by the cognitive symptoms of dementia described thus far;

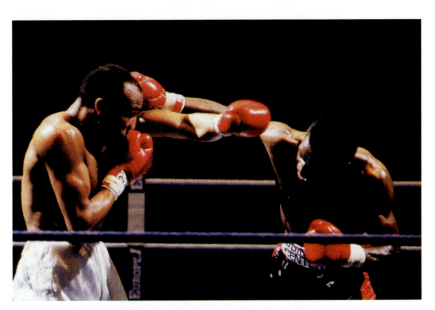

People engaged in sports such as boxing are at risk for brain injuries that can lead to severe cognitive deficits.

TABLE 14.3	Symptoms of Frontal Lobe Injuries

Social and Behavioral Changes

Disorderliness, suspiciousness, argumentativeness, disruptiveness, anxiousness

Apathy, lack of concern for others

Uncharacteristic lewdness, inattention to personal appearance or hygiene

Intrusiveness, boisterousness, pervasive profanity, loud talking

Risk taking, poor impulse control, increased alcohol use

Affective Changes

Apathy, indifference, shallowness

Lability of affect, irritability, mania

Inability to control rage and violent behavior

Intellectual Changes

Reduced capacity to use language, symbols, logic

Reduced ability to use mathematics, to calculate, to process abstract information, to reason

Diminished ability to focus, to concentrate, to be oriented in time and place

Source: Beatty, 1995.

---

various personality changes, such as excessive jealousy and rage; and shaking and loss of motor functioning, such as in Parkinson's disease. In one study of exprofessional boxers, 17 percent had clinical evidence of central nervous system damage attributable to boxing (Roberts, 1969). About half of these men showed some signs of impairment in intellectual functioning, and about 30 percent showed severe cognitive impairment.

Dementia Associated with Other Medical Conditions

A variety of serious medical conditions can produce dementia. The most common ones are Parkinson's disease, HIV disease, and Huntington's disease, and these will be discussed here. Other types of dementia we won't be discussing include those caused by two rare diseases, Pick's disease and Creutzfeldt-Jakob disease; brain tumors; endocrine conditions (such as hypothyroidism); nutritional conditions (such as deficiencies of thiamine, niacin, and vitamin B-12), infectious conditions (such as syphilis), and other neurological diseases (such as multiple sclerosis). In addition, the chronic, heavy use of alcohol, inhalants, and the sedative drugs, especially in combination with nu-

tritional deficiencies, can cause brain damage and dementia. As many as 10 percent of chronic alcohol abusers may develop dementia (Winger, Hofmann, & Woods, 1992). Alcohol-related dementia usually has a slow, insidious onset. It can be slowed with nutritional supplements but is often irreversible.

Parkinson's Disease *Parkinson's disease* is a degenerative brain disorder that affects about 1 of every 100,000 people (Mayeux et al., 1992). The primary symptoms of Parkinson's disease are tremors, muscle rigidity, and the inability to initiate movement. In a longitudinal community-based study of patients with Parkinson's disease, 78 percent developed dementia over the eight years they were followed (Aarsland et al., 2003). Parkinson's disease results from the death of the brain cells that produce the neurotransmitter dopamine. The death of these cells can be caused by certain drugs or by inflammation of the brain, but the cause of Parkinson's disease is often unclear. Muhammed Ali and Michael J. Fox (see Chapter 4) are just two well-known people with Parkinson's disease.

HIV Disease The *human immunodeficiency virus (HIV)*, the virus that causes AIDS, can cause dementia, as Mariel's story illustrates.

Mariel is a 29-year-old single Puerto Rican woman. She has no children and currently lives with her mother and aunt in the Bronx. Since June 1993, she has been unemployed and supported by her family. Mariel was found to be HIV-positive eight years ago, when she was donating blood. She had contracted the virus when raped at age 17 by a family friend. The offender later died of AIDS. For two years, Mariel lived and worked as a store clerk in Puerto Rico. When she developed *Pneumocystis carinii* pneumonia, her mother insisted that she return to New York City to obtain better medical care.

In the hospital, Mariel was referred for a psychiatric consultation, because she was found wandering in a corridor distant from her room. When the psychiatrist arrived in her room, he found her lying on her bed, with half her body outside the covers, rocking back and forth while clutching a pink teddy bear, appearing to stare at the television expressionlessly. When asked a series of questions about where she was, what day it was, and so on, she answered correctly, indicating she was oriented to the time and place, but her responses were greatly delayed, and it was almost impossible to engage her in conversation. She said she wanted to leave the hospital to find a place to think. Her mother reported that Mariel had told her she wanted to die.

Over the next few days in the hospital, Mariel became increasingly withdrawn. She sat motionless for hours, not eating voluntarily, and did not recognize her mother when she visited. At times, Mariel became agitated and appeared to be responding to visual hallucinations. When asked to state where she was and her own birthdate, Mariel did not answer and either turned away or became angry and agitated.

As the pneumonia subsided, these acute psychological symptoms dissipated, but Mariel continued to be inattentive, apathetic, and withdrawn and to take a long time to answer simple questions. Suspecting depression, the psychiatrist prescribed an antidepressant medication, but it had little effect on Mariel's symptoms. After being discharged from the hospital, Mariel showed increasing trouble in expressing herself to her mother and in remembering things her mother had told her. She spent all day in her room, staring out the window, with little interest in the activities her mother suggested to her.

HIV probably enters the brain in the early stages of infection (Price, 1998). Memory and concentration become impaired. Infected persons' mental processes slow—they may have difficulty following conversations or plots in movies or may take much longer to organize their thoughts and to complete simple, familiar tasks. Their behaviors may change—they may withdraw socially, become indifferent to familiar people and responsibilities, and lose their spontaneity. They may complain of fatigue, depression, irritability, agitation, emotional instability, and reduced sex drive. Sometimes, although rarely, they experience hallucinations or delusions. Weakness in the legs or hands, clumsiness, loss of balance, and lack of coordination are common complaints. People may trip more frequently, drop things, or have difficulty writing or eating. If the dementia progresses, the deficits become more global and more severe. Speech becomes increasingly impaired, as does the understanding of language. The ability to walk is lost, and people are confined to bed, often with indifference to their surroundings and their illness.

HIV-associated dementia is diagnosed when the deficits and symptoms become severe and global, with a significant disruption of daily activities and functioning. Epidemiological studies estimate that from 20 to 50 percent of HIV-infected persons will develop dementia, although the incidence and severity of HIV-associated dementia have decreased as antiretroviral drugs have become widely used in treating people with HIV (Sperber & Shao, 2003). These drugs have had greater success in treating the opportunistic infections of HIV than in treating HIV's effects on the brain, however.

Huntington's Disease Huntington's disease is a rare genetic disorder that afflicts people early in life, usually between the ages of 25 and 55. People with this disease develop severe dementia and chorea—irregular jerks, grimaces, and twitches. Huntington's disease is transmitted by a single dominant gene on chromosome 4 (Gusella et al., 1993). If one parent has the gene, his or her children have a 50 percent chance of inheriting the gene and developing the disease. There are many neurotransmitter changes in the brains of people with Huntington's disease. It is not yet clear which of these changes is responsible for the dementia and chorea.

Treatments for Dementia

There are two classes of drugs approved to treat the cognitive symptoms of dementia. The first includes the cholinesterase inhibitors, such as donepezil (Aricept), rivastigmine (Exelon), and galantamine (Reminyl). These drugs help prevent the breakdown of the neurotransmitter acetylcholine, and randomized trials show they have a modest positive effect on the symptoms of dementia (Knopman, 2003; Trinh et al., 2003). The side effects of these drugs include nausea, diarrhea, and anorexia.

A drug called memantine (Namenda) was approved in 2003 for the treatment of moderate to severe Alzheimer's disease. It appears to work by regulating the activity of the neurotransmitter glutamate, which plays an essential role in learning and memory. Because Parkinson's disease is also associated with too little of the neurotransmitter dopamine in the brain, some Parkinson's patients are given other drugs that increase dopamine levels and, thus, provide some relief from their symptoms.

A great deal of media attention has been given to the role of antioxidants in slowing cognitive decline in Alzheimer's disease. Antioxidants include natural products, such as vitamin E, and manufactured products, such as a selective monoamine oxidase-B inhibitor known as selegiline. A few controlled trials have shown that Alzheimer's patients given antioxidants show slower rates of decline than those given placebo treatment, although they do not show improvement in cognitive functioning (Knopman, 2003; Sano et al., 1997). Ginkgo biloba, a plant extract sold without prescription, has been shown to stabilize and improve cognitive functioning in some Alzheimer's patients (see Le Bars et al., 1997). Antioxidants may work by reducing levels of monoamine oxidase-B in the brain, which normally increase with aging but increase at excessive rates among people with Alzheimer's disease—particularly in the hippocampus, which plays an important role in memory—causing cell damage (Thal, 1998).

Many of the other drugs used to treat people with dementia are meant to treat the secondary symptoms of the disorder, rather than the primary cognitive symptoms. Antidepressant and antianxiety drugs are used to help control the emotional symptoms of people with dementia. Antipsychotic drugs help control hallucinations, delusions, and agitation (Trinh et al., 2003).

Behavior therapies can be helpful in controlling patients' angry outbursts and emotional instability (Rovner et al., 1996). Often, family members are given training in behavioral techniques to help them manage patients at home. These techniques not only reduce stress and emotional distress among caregiving family members but also may result in fewer behavior problems in the family member with dementia (Teri et al., 2003). For more information about the effects of a patient's dementia on caregiving family members, see *Taking Psychology Personally: How Does Dementia Affect Caregivers?* on pages 524–525.

The Impact of Gender and Culture on Dementia

There are more elderly women than men with dementia, particularly Alzheimer's dementia (Gao et al., 1998). This simply may be because women tend to live longer than men and, thus, live long enough to develop age-related dementias. Among people with dementia, women tend to show greater decline in language skills than do men—even though, among people without dementia, women tend to score better on tests of language skills than do men (Buckwalter et al., 1993). The reason for the greater impact of dementia on language in women compared with men is unknown. Some researchers have speculated that language skills are distributed across both sides of the brain in women but are more localized in the left side of the brain in men, and this somehow makes women's language skills more vulnerable to the effects of dementia.

In general, African Americans are more frequently diagnosed with dementia than are European Americans. The types of dementias that African Americans and European Americans develop differ, however (Chun et al., 1998). African Americans are more likely than European Americans to be diagnosed with vascular dementia. The reason may be that African Americans have higher rates of hypertension and cardiovascular disease, which contribute to vascular dementia. In contrast, European Americans may be more likely than African Americans to have dementias due to Alzheimer's disease and Parkinson's disease. The genetic factors leading to these diseases may be more prevalent in European Americans than in African Americans.

The likelihood that a person with dementia will be institutionalized instead of being cared for in the family is greater for European Americans than for Asians and Latinos (Mausbach et al., 2004; Torti et al., 2004). The reason may be that Asian and Latino cultures have a more positive view of caring for sick and elderly family members than does the European American culture. There is also greater societal pressure in Asian and Latino cultures to care for ill family members in the home.

Perhaps the greatest cross-cultural issue in dementia is the impact of culture and education on the validity of the instruments used to assess cognitive impairment. One of the most common paper-and-pencil assessment tools is the *Mini-Mental State Examination* (Folstein, Folstein, & McHugh, 1975). Selected items from this questionnaire are presented in Figure 14.5. People with low levels of education tend to perform more poorly on this questionnaire than do people with more education, whether or not they have dementia (Murden et al., 1991). This performance may lead to some poorly educated elderly people being misdiagnosed as having dementia.

Indeed, studies in the United States, Europe, Israel, and China show that people with low levels of education are more likely to be diagnosed with dementia than are people with more education (Katzman, 1993; Stern et al., 1994). The relationship between lower education and dementia is not just a factor of the measures used to assess dementia, however. Neuroimaging studies of people with dementia find that those with less education show more of the brain deterioration associated with dementia than do those with more education. It may be that people with more education have a higher socioeconomic status, which in turn provides them with better nutrition and health care, which protect them against the conditions contributing to Alzheimer's disease. Education and, more generally, cognitive activity throughout one's life may actually increase brain resources in ways that forestall the development of dementia in people prone to the disorder (Snowdon et al., 1996).

SUMMING UP

- Dementia is typically a permanent deterioration in cognitive functioning, often accompanied by emotional changes.

- The five types of cognitive impairments in dementia are memory impairment, aphasia, apraxia, agnosia, and loss of executive functions.

- The most common type of dementia is due to Alzheimer's disease.

- The brains of Alzheimer's patients show neurofibrillary tangles, plaques made up of amyloid protein, and cortical atrophy.

- Recent theories of Alzheimer's disease focus on three genes that might contribute to the buildup of amyloid in the brains of Alzheimer's disease patients.

- Dementia can also be caused by cerebrovascular disorder, head injury, and progressive disorders, such as Parkinson's disease, HIV disease, Huntington's disease, and, more rarely, Pick's disease, Creutzfeldt-Jakob disease, and a number of other medical conditions. Finally, chronic drug abuse and the

FIGURE 14.5   **Mini-Mental State Examination.** The Mini-Mental State Examination is one of the most commonly used tests to assess patients' cognitive functioning and orientation.

Mini-Mental State Examination
(Add points for each correct response.)

			Score	Points
Orientation				
1. What is the	Year?		___	1
	Season?		___	1
	Date?		___	1
	Day?		___	1
	Month?		___	1
2. Where are we?	State?		___	1
	County?		___	1
	Town or city?		___	1
	Hospital?		___	1
	Floor?		___	1

Registration

3. Name three objects, taking one second to say each. Then ask the patient all three after you have said them. Give one point for each correct answer. Repeat the answers until patient learns all three. ___ **3**

Attention and calculation

4. Serial sevens. Give one point for each correct answer. Stop after five answers. Alternate: Spell WORLD backwards. ___ **5**

Recall

5. Ask for names of three objects learned in Q.3. Give one point for each correct answer. ___ **3**

Language

6. Point to a pencil and a watch. Have the patient name them as you point. ___ **2**

7. Have the patient repeat 'No ifs, ands, or buts.' ___ **1**

8. Have the patient follow a three-stage command: 'Take a paper in your right hand. Fold the paper in half. Put the paper on the floor.' ___ **3**

9. Have the patient read and obey the following: 'CLOSE YOUR EYES.' (Write it in large letters.) ___ **1**

10. Have the patient write a sentence of his or her choice. (The sentence should contain a subject and an object, and should make sense. Ignore spelling errors when scoring.) ___ **1**

11. Enlarge the design printed below to 1.5 cm per side, and have the patient copy it. (Give one point if all sides and angles are preserved and if the intersecting sides form a quadrangle.) ___ **1**

_____ = Total 30

Taking Psychology Personally

How Does Dementia Affect Caregivers?

Dementia exacts a heavy toll on the family members of patients, as well as on the patients themselves, as is depicted in the book *Elegy for Iris*. From the first onset of symptoms, patients with dementia live an average of 8 years, and as many as 20 years, with the lifetime cost for treatment averaging $175,000 per patient in the United States (Tariot, 2003). In the United States, the societal cost of Alzheimer's disease alone is estimated at $100 billion per year in medical care, loss of productivity, and personal caregiving expenses (DeKosky & Orgogozo, 2001).

If a person with dementia is cared for in the home, the caregivers must deal with a wide range of troubling symptoms. The patient's confusion and memory loss may cause him or her to lose important items, to wander away from home into dangerous situations, or to engage in dangerous behaviors, such as putting clothes in the oven and turning it on. The emotional and behavioral symptoms of dementia—paranoia, agitation, anxiety, and depression—can be very stressful for family members to deal with, as John Bayley describes in *Elegy for Iris*.

The primary caregiver to a person with dementia is most often a woman—the daughter, daughter-in-law, or wife of the patient (Dunkin & Anderson-Hanley, 1998; Torti et al., 2004). Often, this primary caregiver is also raising her own children and trying to hold down a job. This is the *sandwich generation* of women, caught in the middle of caring for young children and for elderly parents or parents-in-law. These primary caregivers show higher rates of depression, anxiety, and physical illness than do noncaregivers, particularly when they do not have the financial resources to pay for assistance (Dunkin & Anderson-Hanley, 1998; Torti et al., 2004). Some caregivers become so frustrated with their family members with dementia that they resort to violence and abuse (adapted from Gallagher-Thompson, Lovett, & Rose, 1991, pp. 68–69):

Mr. E was a 60-year-old caregiver of a rather frail younger brother (Robert) who had been diagnosed with dementia. Robert had been an alcoholic earlier in life and was the type of person who settled disagreements with verbal and/or physical abuse. Mr. E and his brother had begun sharing a household following the

CASE STUDY

deaths of both their wives about 5 years before. Shortly thereafter, Robert was diagnosed with Alzheimer's disease and eventually developed substantial cognitive and physical deficits. Mr. E felt guilty about doing anything other than keeping his brother in the home with him, although Robert's disabilities were very distressing to him and Robert's increasing hostility and angry verbal outbursts were hard to handle. At the same time, Mr. E was developing a romantic interest and resented not being able to follow through with that as he pleased; instead, he felt quite inhibited by his brother's presence in his home. The situation gradually worsened to the point where the two brothers were given to frequent angry outbursts, leading, at times, to Mr. E hitting Robert. Afterwards, he would feel extremely guilty about this and concerned that he might lose control during one of these episodes and actually hurt his brother.

A number of communities provide support groups for caregivers and therapy focused on developing problem-solving skills for managing the person with dementia at home. For example, the man in the case study, Mr. E, joined an anger-management class and learned new ways of interpreting and reacting to his brother's behaviors. He read about Alzheimer's disease and learned to challenge his beliefs that his brother was intentionally acting in ways to annoy him. He learned to walk away from his brother's angry outbursts. He found other resources in the community to help him care for his brother, so that he could pursue his own interests more fully. These programs have proven effective in reducing caregivers' emotional problems and feelings of burden in some studies, although not in all studies (Miller, Newcomer, & Fox, 1999).

Medications can help control some of the patients' behaviors. Antipsychotic medications may decrease agitation and psychosis. The cholinesterase inhibitors help reduce the symptoms of dementia. The changes brought about by these medications appear to reduce the burden on caregivers as well (Torti et al., 2004).

If you become a caregiver to someone with dementia, how can you manage the stress? The following are some tips from the Alzheimer's Association (www.alz.org).

■ *Investigate the resources in your community.* There may be support groups for you, financial resources for medical and custodial care for your family member, or groups that will provide respite care (for example, sitting with your family member when you need to be away from the house). You can find out about these resources through your family physician, your religious institution, or local chapters of the Alzheimer's Association or other groups focused on people with dementia.

■ *Become educated about dementia and caregiving techniques.* It can be helpful to know what to expect from your family member, as well as how to interpret and cope with his or her symptoms.

■ *Engage in legal and financial planning.* You may need to consult a financial advisor or an attorney to plan for the day when you may need to place your family member in a

care facility or to ensure that his or her finances are appropriately managed. The Alzheimer's Association Web site has lots of good information about the legal and financial issues you may need to deal with.

■ *Take care of yourself by watching your diet, exercising, and getting plenty of rest.* Caregivers often neglect their own well-being, but this doesn't help their ill family member any more than it helps them. Consult your physician if you develop health problems, and consider getting help from a support group or a counselor to deal with the emotional issues you are facing.

■ *Be realistic about what you can do.* There may come a time when you cannot manage your family member physically because of his or her symptoms, or the stress of caregiving becomes too much for you or your family. Give yourself credit for what you have done, and don't blame yourself if you can't do it all on your own. Ask for help from other family members, friends, and anyone else who may be able to relieve your stress.

nutritional deficiencies that often accompany it can lead to dementia.

■ Some drugs help reduce the cognitive symptoms and accompanying depression, anxiety, and psychotic symptoms in some patients with dementia.

■ Gender, culture, and education all play roles in vulnerability to dementia.

DELIRIUM

Delirium is characterized by disorientation, recent memory loss, and a clouding of consciousness (see the DSM-IV-TR criteria in Table 14.4 on page 526). A delirious person has difficulty focusing, sustaining, or shifting attention. These signs arise suddenly, within several hours or days. They fluctuate over the course of a day and often become worse at night, a condition known as *sundowning*. The duration of these signs is short—rarely more than a month. Delirious patients are often agitated or frightened. They may also experience disrupted sleep-wake cycles, incoherent speech, illusions, and hallucinations.

The signs of delirium usually follow a common progression (Cole, 2004). In the early phase, patients report mild symptoms, such as fatigue, decreased

concentration, irritability, restlessness, or depression. They may experience mild cognitive impairments or perceptual disturbances. As the delirium worsens, the person's orientation becomes disrupted. For example, the patient may think she is in her childhood home, when she is actually in the hospital. If undetected, the delirium progresses, and the person's orientation to familiar people becomes distorted. For example, a delirious patient misidentifies his wife or fails to recognize his child. Immediate memory is the first to be affected, followed by intermediate memory (memories of events occurring in the past 10 minutes), and finally remote, or distant, memory. When intervals of these symptoms alternate with intervals of lucid functioning and the symptoms become worse at night, a diagnosis of delirium is likely. If the person is not disoriented (to time, place, or person) or recent memory loss is absent, a diagnosis of delirium is unlikely.

The onset of delirium may be very dramatic, as when a normally quiet person suddenly becomes loud, verbally abusive, and combative or when a compliant hospital patient tries to pull out his IVs and will not be calmed by family or medical staff. Sometimes, though, the onset of delirium is subtle and manifests as an exaggerated form of an individual's normal personality

---

TABLE 14.4 DSM-IV-TR

Diagnostic Criteria for Delirium

Delirium is characterized by disorientation, recent memory loss, and a clouding of consciousness.

Disturbance of consciousness, such as reduced clarity of awareness of the environment, with reduced ability to focus, sustain, or shift attention

Change in cognition (such as memory deficit, disorientation, language disturbance) or development of a perceptual disturbance that is not accounted for by a dementia

Disturbance that develops over a short period of time, usually hours to days, and tends to fluctutate during the course of the day

Evidence that the disturbance is caused by the direct physiological consequences of a medical condition

Source: Reprinted with permission from the *Diagnostic and Statistical Manual of Mental Disorders*, Fourth Edition, Text Revision. Copyright © 2000 American Psychiatric Association.

---

traits. For example, a perfectionistic nurse recovering from surgery may complain loudly and harshly about the "inadequate" care she is receiving from the attending nurses. It would be easy for attending staff to regard her irritability as consistent with her personality style and her recovery: "She must be feeling better; she's beginning to complain." In this type of case, the delirium may go unrecognized until severe symptoms of delirium emerge.

Sometimes, delirious patients just appear confused. People who know them well say, "He just doesn't seem like himself." These delirious patients may call acquaintances by the wrong names or forget how to get to familiar locations. For example, they may not remember where their rooms are. In such cases, often the first indication of delirium comes from the observations of family or medical staff. They notice that the person seems calm during the day but agitated at night. It is important to monitor such a patient around the clock. Detecting delirium may require the frequent testing of the person's orientation. Close monitoring is also important because, with delirium, accidents, such as falling out of bed or stepping into traffic, are common.

Delirium typically is a signal of a serious medical condition. When it is detected and the underlying medical condition treated, delirium is temporary and reversible. The longer delirium continues, however, the more likely it is that the person will suffer permanent brain damage, because the causes of delirium, if left untreated, can induce permanent changes in the functioning of the brain.

Causes of Delirium

The specific causes of delirium are not known (Cole, 2004). Patients with delirium often show abnormal EEG activity. There is evidence that delirium may be mediated by abnormal activity in the neurotransmitter acetylcholine, and drugs affecting acetylcholine activity can reduce the symptoms of delirium (Cole, 2004).

Dementia is the strongest predictor of delirium, increasing the risk fivefold. A wide range of medical disorders, including stroke, congestive heart failure, HIV infection and other infectious diseases, and high fever, are associated with a risk for delirium. Intoxication with illicit drugs and withdrawal from these drugs or prescription medications can lead to delirium. Other possible causes include fluid and electrolyte imbalances, and toxic substances (see Table 14.5).

Delirium is probably the most common psychiatric syndrome found in the general hospital, particularly in older people. About 15 to 20 percent of older people are delirious on admission to the hospital for a serious illness, and another 10 to 15 percent develop delirium while in the hospital. Older people often experience delirium following surgery (Brown & Boyle, 2002; Cole, 2004). The delirium may be the result of the patient's medical disorder or the effects of medications. It may also result from sensory isolation. A syndrome known as *ICU/CCU psychosis* occurs in intensive care and cardiac care units (Maxmen & Ward, 1995): When patients are kept in unfamiliar surroundings that are monotonous, they may hear noises from machines as human voices, see the walls quiver, or hallucinate that someone is tapping them on the shoulder.

TABLE 14.5 Substances That Can Induce Delirium		
A wide range of substances can cause delirium.		
Alcohol	Antimicrobials	Inhalants
Amphetamines	Antiparkinsonian drugs	Muscle relaxants
Anesthetics	Cannabis	Opioids
Analgesics	Carbon dioxide	Organophosphate insecticides
Antiasthmatic agents	Carbon monoxide	Phencyclidine
Anticholinesterase	Cocaine	Psychotropic medications with anticholinergic side effects
Anticonvulsants	Corticosteroids	
Antihistamines	Gastrointestinal medications	Sedatives, hypnotics, and anxiolytics
Antihypertensive and cardiovascular medications	Hallucinogens	Volatile substances, such as fuel or paint

Source: Reprinted with permission from the *Diagnostic and Statistical Manual of Mental Disorders,* Fourth Edition, Text Revision. Copyright © 2000 American Psychiatric Association.

Among the elderly, a high mortality rate is associated with delirium (Byrne, 1994; Cole, 2004). Typically, the reason is that the underlying condition or the cause of the delirium is very serious. Between 15 and 40 percent of delirious hospital patients die within one month, as compared with half that rate in nondelirious patients.

Some people are at increased risk for delirium. The risk factors include age (the older the person, the higher the risk), gender (males are more at risk than females), and preexisting brain damage or dementia (Brown & Boyle, 2002). African Americans have higher rates of delirium than European Americans. This higher rate may occur because African Americans are less likely to have health insurance, so many do not receive early medical care for serious illnesses. As a result, their illnesses may be more likely to become severe enough to cause delirium.

Treatments for Delirium

It is extremely important that delirium be recognized and treated quickly. If a delirious person is not already hospitalized, an immediate referral to a physician should be made. If another medical condition is associated with the delirium (such as stroke or congestive heart failure), the first priority is to treat that condition (Cole, 2004). Drugs that may be contributing to the delirium must be discontinued. Antipsychotic medications are sometimes used to treat the patient's confusion. It may also be necessary to prevent people with delirium from harming themselves (Maxmen & Ward, 1995). Often, nursing care is required to monitor people's states and to prevent them from wandering off, tripping, or ripping out intravenous tubes and to manage their behavior if they should become noncompliant or violent. In some instances, restraints are necessary.

SUMMING UP

- Delirium is characterized by disorientation, recent memory loss, and a clouding of consciousness.
- The onset of delirium can be either sudden or slow.
- The many causes of delirium include medical diseases, the trauma of surgery, illicit drugs, medications, high fever, and infections.
- Delirium must be treated immediately by treating its underlying causes, to prevent brain damage and to prevent people from hurting themselves.

AMNESIA

A 46-year-old divorced housepainter is admitted to the hospital with a history of 30 years of heavy drinking. He has had two previous admissions for detoxification, but his family states that he has not had a drink in several weeks, and he shows no signs of alcohol withdrawal. He looks malnourished, however, and

(continued)

appears confused and mistakes one of his physicians for a dead uncle.

Within a week, the patient seems less confused and can find his way to the bathroom without direction. He remembers the names and birthdays of his siblings but has difficulty naming the past five presidents. More strikingly, he has great difficulty in retaining information for longer than a few minutes. He can repeat a list of numbers immediately after he has heard them but a few minutes later does not recall being asked to perform the task. Shown three objects (keys, comb, ring), he cannot recall them 3 minutes later. He does not seem worried about this. Asked if he can recall the name of his doctor, he replies, "Certainly," and proceeds to call the doctor "Dr. Masters" (not his name), and he claims to have met him in the Korean War. He tells a long, untrue story about how he and Dr. Masters served as fellow soldiers. (Adapted from Spitzer et al., 1981, pp. 41–42)

In dementia and delirium, people show multiple cognitive deficits, including memory deficits, language deficits, disorientation, an inability to recognize objects or people, and an inability to think abstractly or plan and carry through with an activity. In **amnesia,** only memory is affected. A person with amnesia is impaired in the ability to learn new information (**anterograde amnesia**) or to recall previously learned information or past events (**retrograde amnesia**). Amnesic disorders often follow periods of confusion and disorientation and delirium.

The patterns of amnesia represented in soap operas and other television shows—with people suddenly losing their memories for everything they previously knew—are unrealistic. Commonly, people with amnesia can remember events from the distant past but not from the recent past. For example, a 60-year-old patient may be able to tell where he went to high school and college but be unable to remember that he was admitted to the hospital yesterday. He will also forget meeting his doctor from one day to the next. In profound amnesia, a person may be completely disoriented about place or time, but rarely does a person with amnesia forget his or her own identity.

Often, people with amnesia do not realize they have profound memory deficits and deny evidence of these deficits. They may seem unconcerned with obvious lapses in memory or may make up stories to cover their lapses in memory. They may become agitated with others who point out their memory lapses. They may even accuse others of conspiring against them.

Amnesia can be caused by brain damage due to strokes, head injuries, chronic nutritional deficiencies, exposure to toxins (such as through carbon monoxide poisoning), or chronic substance abuse. *Korsakoff's syndrome* is a form of amnesia caused by damage to the thalamus, a part of the brain that acts as a relay station to other parts of the brain. Chronic, heavy alcohol use is associated with Korsakoff's syndrome, probably because the alcoholic neglects nutrition and thus develops thiamine deficiencies (see Chapter 17).

The course of amnesia depends on the cause. If, for example, a stroke occurs in the hippocampus, the memory loss that results will include events after the date of the stroke. Memories prior to the stroke will remain intact. If the memory loss is caused by alcohol or other toxins, it is often broader and the onset can be insidious. For some people, remote memory may also become impaired.

The first step in the treatment of amnesia is to remove, if possible, any conditions contributing to the amnesia, such as alcohol use or exposure to toxins. In addition, attention to nutrition and the treatment of any accompanying health condition (such as hypertension) can help prevent further deterioration. Finally, because new surroundings and routines may prove too difficult or impossible for the person with amnesia to learn, the environment should be kept as familiar as possible. Often, as with dementia, it can be helpful to have clocks, calendars, photographs, labels, and other kinds of reminders prominent.

SUMMING UP

- Amnesia is characterized only by memory loss.
- Retrograde amnesia is a loss of memory for past events. Anterograde amnesia is an inability to remember new information.
- Amnesia can be caused by brain damage due to strokes, head injuries, chronic nutritional deficiencies, exposure to toxins (such as through carbon monoxide poisoning), or chronic substance abuse.

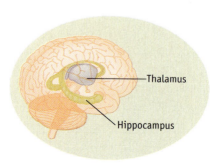

Damage to the thalamus causes Korsakoff's syndrome, and stroke damage to the hippocampus causes memory loss for events after the stroke.

- The treatment of amnesia can involve removing the agents contributing to the amnesia and helping the person develop memory aids.

MENTAL DISORDERS IN LATER LIFE

All of the disorders we have considered in previous chapters of this book also can occur in later life, and in several chapters we have discussed the characteristics of disorders as people move into old age. For the remainder of this chapter, we focus on three of the most common mental disorders among older adults—the anxiety disorders, depression, and the substance use disorders.

Assessing psychopathology in older people can be difficult, in part because psychological problems very often co-occur with medical problems (Zarit & Haynie, 2000). Sometimes, the symptoms of depression, anxiety, or confusion, for example, can be the consequences of medical problems. Other times, they are independent of medical problems but contribute to them, as when a depressed person is not motivated to take the medications needed to overcome a medical problem. Still other times, emotional symptoms arise in response to the disability, pain, or loss that occurs because of a medical problem. Finally, some psychological symptoms are side effects of the many medications an ill older person is taking. Teasing apart psychological symptoms from medical problems is critical to an accurate assessment, but it can be very difficult.

Assessment is also complicated by the fact that older people may not present the same symptoms of a disorder as do younger people. In the mood and anxiety disorders, older people often complain of physical problems, rather than the psychological concerns associated with these disorders. This can lead to misdiagnosis, or to people ignoring the elderly person's somatic complaints as "normal for old age." Older people may be more reluctant to admit to psychological problems as well, because they grew up in a period in which these problems were heavily stigmatized.

Anxiety Disorders

Anxiety is one of the most common problems among older adults, with up to 15 percent of people over the age of 65 experiencing an anxiety disorder (Scogin, Floyd, & Forde, 2000). Some anxiety disorders among older people are continuations of persistent disorders they have had all their lives. Other times, anxiety first arises in old age. It often takes the form of worry about loved ones or about the older person's own health or safety, and it frequently exists along with medical illnesses and depression, as with Mrs. Johnson (adapted from Scogin et al., 2000, pp. 117–118):

CASE STUDY

Mrs. Johnson is a 71-year-old female who was referred by a family practice physician who works in a nearby town. Mrs. Johnson had become extremely anxious and moderately depressed following a major orthopedic surgery, a total hip replacement. She was a retired office worker.

I was immediately struck by her general level of anxiety. For example, she expressed fears about her ability to get her husband to take her to an appointment and was concerned that she might not be the right type of person for psychological treatment. Her anxiety seemed to interfere with her ability to adequately attend to and process information. For example, she seemed to have difficulty getting down the directions to my office. She stated that she was concerned about being able to find the building and that she would leave her house early in case she got lost. Mrs. Johnson was early to her appointment. She looked distraught throughout the session. She wrung her hands, cried on a couple of occasions, and repeatedly stated, "I don't want to be a burden." Her main concern was that, due to her recent surgery, she might not be able to continue living in the home she and her husband had lived in most of her adult life. She was extremely afraid of having a fall and not being found for hours.

Mrs. Johnson stated that, when she was raising her children, she worried about their education and about money. Her children were living various distances away from her, so that their involvement, at least physically, was not an option. Mrs. Johnson indicated that she loved all her children but that she worried about two of them. Both had been divorced and she was concerned about their well-being and that of her three grandchildren. She reported not having the desire to eat because her stomach was "fluttery." I asked, "Do you

(continued)

find yourself worrying about things?" to which she responded, "Yes, a lot. I worry that I've begun to be a burden for my husband. I worry about my hip and I worry about not being able to get around. I guess I'm crazy because I worry about being worried so much." I assured her that she was not crazy, just anxious, which can oftentimes make you feel like you are crazy.

Mrs. Johnson was diagnosed with generalized anxiety disorder, or GAD (see Chapter 7). One study estimated that 1.9 percent of older adults suffer from GAD in any given six-month period (Blazer, George, & Hughes, 1991). This rate is lower than the rate among young adults, but, as in young adults, older women are about twice as likely as older men to suffer from the disorder. Older adults may worry more about health and family issues than do younger adults (Scogin et al., 2000). Too often, their worries about health are dismissed as understandable, when they are part of the larger picture of GAD.

Panic disorder is relatively rare in older age. One epidemiological study estimated that only 0.1 percent of people over 65 can be diagnosed with this disorder (Regier et al., 1988). Obsessive-compulsive disorder is also quite rare. It was diagnosed in only 0.8 percent of the older people in this study.

The symptoms of posttraumatic stress disorder (PTSD) and acute stress disorder are relatively common among older people, often occurring in response to the loss of a loved one (Bonanno & Kaltman, 1999). PTSD is also common among combat veterans. Some of these veterans have experienced the flashbacks and other symptoms of PTSD their entire lives, but late-onset PTSD can occur in older veterans (Schnurr, Spiro, & Paris, 2000). Vietnam veterans are just beginning to reach the period known as old age. Given the high rates of PTSD in these veterans (see Chapter 6), the rates of PTSD among the elderly may increase in the next couple of decades.

Very few older adults seek treatment for anxiety disorders, and those who do tend to consult their family physicians, rather than mental-health professionals (Scogin et al., 2000). For the older people who do seek help, cognitive-behavioral therapy and supportive therapy based on a more humanistic model have both been shown to be effective in the treatment of anxiety symptoms (Stanley & Novy, 2000). Simple relaxation training is also effective in reducing tension and anxiety (Scogin et al., 1992).

Physicians frequently prescribe an antianxiety drug, such as a benzodiazepine, when an older patient complains of anxiety. With age, there are changes in drug absorption, distribution, metabolism, and sensitivity to side effects. Side effects, such as unsteadiness, can lead to falls and bone fractures in frail elderly people. With the benzodiazepines, tolerance can develop with prolonged use, leading to severe withdrawal effects, as well as the rebound of anxiety symptoms, once the person discontinues use. Antidepressant drugs, including buspirone and the selective serotonin reuptake inhibitors, are increasingly being used to treat anxiety symptoms, with fewer side effects and withdrawal effects than occur with the benzodiazepines. Older adults often are taking several prescription and over-the-counter medications that can interact with psychotropic drugs. All of these factors make the management of drug therapy in older adults more complex than in younger adults (Scogin et al., 2000).

Depression

CASE STUDY

Mrs. Scott was a 76-year-old widowed mother of three children who came to the Clinic for Older Adults, an ambulatory psychiatric clinic for seniors, at the behest of her oldest son, Roger. When first greeted in the waiting room, Mrs. Scott was sitting on the edge of her seat, wringing her hands, looking anxiously from one corner of the room to another. Roger was sitting next to his mother, slumped in his chair and visibly irritated. Once she was alone with the interviewer, Mrs. Scott explained that she was terribly upset because her bowel was no longer working. She had been constipated for five days and took this as evidence that her bowel had "died" and that she would likely be dead within a matter of days. She further stated that she had been to see her primary care physician repeatedly for the problem and got only false reassurances that she was basically healthy but needed to adjust her diet and take a daily fiber supplement. She then tearfully related how "fed up" her children were with her and her bowel problems and fervently asked the interviewer not to tell

(continued)

Roger that she had been talking about her problems again. She hinted that her children would be better off without her because "they just don't understand what I'm going through and are too busy with their own lives to worry about me." When asked if she had other difficulties, Mrs. Scott stated only that she was quite lonely and wished her children would visit her more often. In response to specific questions about depressive symptoms, Mrs. Scott stated that her sleep had been quite interrupted for the past several months and that she woke typically around 5 A.M. with abdominal cramping and fears about dying. She estimated that in the past six months she had lost about 20 pounds, in part because she had lost her appetite and in part because she was afraid to eat and "clog up" her body. Although she had been an avid reader in the past, she now found it difficult to focus or concentrate on anything other than her bowel. When asked if her problems had gotten so bad that she thought about dying or hurting herself, her eyes welled with tears and she admitted that she asked the Lord each night to take her and put her out of her misery.

Later when asked about her sister, who had died unexpectedly from a stroke 6 months previously, Mrs. Scott initially turned away and then wept bitterly. She began to describe how her sister had been her close companion throughout life and especially since Mrs. Scott's husband died 10 years earlier. After this brief release of sorrow, she then abruptly asked that the interview be terminated because she could not imagine how any of this could help her with her "real" problem. (Adapted from King & Markus, 2000, pp. 141–142)

Among older people living in the community, only about 1 to 3 percent can be diagnosed with major depression (Gatz et al., 1996). Depression is much more common among those in acute care or chronic care settings, where the prevalence reaches 12 to 20 percent. Symptoms not quite meeting the criteria for major depression occur in approximately 15 percent of the community-dwelling elderly and up to 30 percent of the institutionalized

Depression can be a life threatening disorder in elderly people.

elderly (King & Marcus, 2000). As we discussed in Chapter 9, women outnumber men among depressed people, but this age gap narrows, and in some studies disappears, among people over 65 (Gatz et al., 1996). Bipolar disorder is quite rare among the elderly and is even more rarely diagnosed for the first time in old age (King & Markus, 2000). Thus, we will focus our discussion on unipolar depression.

Depression greatly reduces the quality of life for older people. One study estimated that depression ranks with arthritis and heart disease as the diseases inflicting the greatest burden on quality of life in the elderly (Unützer et al., 2000). In fact, depression can be lethal for older people. The suicide rate among older White males is the highest of any group in the United States, and 60 to 75 percent of older suicide victims are depressed (Conwell, 1996) (see the discussion of suicide among the elderly in Chapter 10). In addition, depression may hasten the progression of several medical diseases. Among people who have had a heart attack, depression increases the risk of dying from the heart attack by five times (Frasure-Smith, Lesperance, & Talajic, 1995). In nursing home patients, major depression hastens mortality, regardless of what physical ailment the person suffers from (Rovner, 1993).

About half of older people who are depressed were depressed as younger adults, and about half have symptoms that initially arose in older age (King & Marcus, 2000). Older people are less likely than younger people to report the psychological symptoms of depression, such as depressed mood, guilt, low self-esteem, and suicidal ideation. They are more likely to complain of somatic problems (such as the case study's Mrs. Scott's abdominal cramps), psychomotor abnormalities (such as agitation or extreme slowing), and cognitive impairments (King & Markus, 2000). Many depressed elders show a **depletion syndrome**, consisting of loss of interest, loss of energy, hopelessness, helplessness, and psychomotor retardation (Newmann, Engel, & Jensen, 1991). Depression is less likely to lead to impairment in functioning in older people, perhaps because they are less likely to be in the workforce or in the process of raising children. As a result, depression is often misdiagnosed, or missed altogether, by family members and physicians.

Differentiating a primary depression from one caused by medical illness or medications can be quite difficult. Several medical illnesses can cause depression-like symptoms, including multiple sclerosis, Cushing's disease, Parkinson's disease, Huntington's disease, Addison's disease, cerebrovascular disease, hypothyroidism, chronic obstructive pulmonary disease, and vitamin deficiency (King & Markus, 2000). It is important for an older adult who appears to be depressed to have a thorough medical examination in an attempt to rule out any medical disorders that may be causing his or her symptoms.

One of the most difficult differential diagnoses to make is between depression and dementia, particularly because the two disorders often occur together. Dementia can cause depression, and depression can cause changes in brain functioning that increase the risk for future irreversible dementia (King & Markus, 2000). Some rules of thumb can help differentiate depression from dementia, although they are not foolproof.

First, although depressed people often complain about memory problems, their cognitive deficits tend to be less severe than those found in people with dementia, and they tend to be more aware of their cognitive problems than are people with dementia. Second, the noncognitive symptoms of depression tend to be more severe in people with primary depression than in people with dementia. Third, depressed people often have trouble doing "free recall" memory tasks but can recognize things they know if shown them, whereas people with dementia have difficulty in both free recall and recognition memory tasks. Finally, depressed people are more likely to have a rapid onset of symptoms, whereas the onset of dementia is much more gradual.

Depression that occurs first in old age is very often associated with the disability and pain due to medical illness (King & Marcus, 2000). In addition,

older people are often caring for spouses or other loved ones who are seriously ill, and caregiving is a risk factor for depression. The loss of a spouse or another loved one to death leads to depressive symptoms in most people. These grief-related symptoms are normal and are not diagnosed as depression unless they persist for several months beyond the loss. "Complicated grief," or grief that eventually is diagnosed as major depression, also tends to be characterized by profound guilt, thoughts that one would be better off dead, profound inactivity, persistent impairment in functioning, and hallucinations that go beyond the common experience of hearing or seeing a dead loved one (APA, 2000).

There is a substantial amount of research on the treatment of depression in the elderly, and it is clear that several treatments can be successful (see Lyness, 2004). Antidepressant medications are frequently used, and they are effective in 50 to 70 percent of older depressed people (King & Markus, 2000). The tricyclic antidepressants and monoamine oxidase inhibitors can have cardiac side effects that are dangerous for older people, however, so the selective serotonin reuptake inhibitors are used more often. Physicians must still monitor older patients to ensure that dosage levels are not too high and serious side effects do not emerge. Electroconvulsive therapy is disproportionately used with older depressed people than with younger ones, particularly among those who have not responded to medication therapy or whose medical conditions (e.g., cardiac problems) preclude the use of antidepressant medications.

Gallagher-Thompson, Thompson, and colleagues have conducted a number of studies comparing cognitive, behavior, and interpersonal therapies for depressed elders and have found all of these treatments to be effective (Powers et al., 2002). Thompson and colleagues (2001) compared cognitive-behavioral therapy (CBT) alone, a tricyclic antidepressant alone, and combined CBT and a tricyclic and found that the CBT alone and the combined treatment were both superior to the drug treatment alone. There was no difference between the combined treatment and CBT alone. Reynolds and colleagues (2000) have used the combination of interpersonal therapy with drug therapy (a tricyclic or a selective sertonin reuptake inhibitor) to treat older people with recurrent or chronic depression with consistent success.

Substance Use Disorders

We tend to think of substance use disorders as problems of the young. Indeed, the use of "hard" drugs, such as cocaine or heroin, is quite rare

Some elderly people abuse prescription drugs.

(and other drugs and medications) more slowly, so it can more readily cause toxic effects in the body, including changes in brain chemistry and cognitive deficits. In addition, women tend to metabolize alcohol and some other drugs less efficiently than men, so the same doses can lead to greater toxic effects, especially if usage occurs over many years.

The abuse of and dependence on prescription drugs is a much greater problem among the elderly. Although only 13 percent of the U.S. population is over the age of 65, they account for a third of all prescription drug expenditures (Lisansky-Gomberg, 2000). The most commonly prescribed drugs are diuretics, cardiovascular drugs, and sedatives. Older people are also more likely than younger people to purchase over-the-counter drugs, including analgesics, vitamins, and laxatives.

The abuse of drugs, such as benzodiazepines, may begin innocently. Physicians tend to be liberal in their prescription of these drugs to older patients, and as many as a third of older people take these drugs at least occasionally—for insomnia or after a loss, for example (Wetherell et al., 2005). As tolerance for the drug develops, and an older person learns of the withdrawal effects of discontinuing the drug, he or she may seek out ways to get more of it, by copying prescriptions or seeing multiple physicians. The slurred speech and memory problems that can be caused by drugs may be overlooked in the elderly as normal symptoms of old age. They can often hide their drug abuse for long periods of time. Eventually, the side effects of the drugs, the withdrawal symptoms they experience when they try to go "cold turkey" off the drugs, or interaction effects with other medications may land them in a hospital emergency room, as with Eleanor (Lisansky-Gomberg, 2000, p. 277):

among the elderly. Many chronic users of illicit substances die before they reach old age, and others grow out of their use. Adults currently above the age of 65 probably never did use illicit substances as frequently as people in younger generations, because the use of these drugs was less acceptable and the drugs were less available when they were adolescents and young adults. Certain types of substance abuse and dependence are a frequent problem among older people, however, including alcohol-related problems and the misuse of prescription drugs (Lisansky-Gomberg, 2000).

Approximately 2 percent of people over 65 can be diagnosed with alcohol abuse or dependence, and about 8 percent can be considered heavy drinkers (Helzer, Burnam, & McEvoy, 1991; Molgaard et al., 1990). You might assume that most older people with alcohol problems have been alcoholics most of their lives, but one-third to one-half first develop problems after the age of 65 (Liberto, Oslin, & Ruskin, 1996). Tolerance for alcohol decreases with age, so it takes fewer drinks for an older person to have a high blood-alcohol concentration. Older people also metabolize alcohol

CASE STUDY

Eleanor is a widow of 72; she keeps reasonably busy by volunteering in a few community organizations. Since her husband died 10 years ago, she has had difficulty sleeping. Her physician, who perceives the sleep difficulties as based on depression and grieving, prescribed antidepressants. Because her insomnia continued, he also prescribed sedatives. She is now a regular user of sedatives and has appeared in the emergency department of the local hospital recently complaining of logginess and fatigue.

The treatment for older substance abusers is similar to that for younger abusers (see Chapter 17), although withdrawal symptoms may be more dangerous for older abusers and, thus, must be monitored more carefully (Lisansky-Gomberg, 2000). Psychotherapies that have been shown to be useful tend to have the following characteristics (Schonfeld & Dupree, 1997):

- Elders are treated along with people their age in a supportive, nonconfrontational approach.
- Negative emotional states (such as depression and loneliness) and their relationship to the substance abuse are a focus of the intervention.
- Social skills and social networks are rebuilt.
- Staff members are respectful and interested in working with older adults.
- Linkages are made with medical facilities and community resources (such as housing services).

Due to increasing longevity and the size of the baby-boom generation, the proportion of the population that is above the age of 65 will increase dramatically over the next few decades (King & Marcus, 2000). In addition, the older adult population will become much more ethnically diverse: Although 85 percent of Americans over 65 in 1995 were non-Hispanic White, this proportion is expected to decrease to 66 percent by 2030 (Whitbourne, 2000). In turn, the proportion of older people who are of Hispanic and Asian descent will increase. Much more research is needed on the psychological health needs of older people, particularly older people of color.

SUMMING UP

- Mental disorders are less common among older adults than younger adults, but 10 to 20 percent of older people suffer significant psychopathology.
- Psychological problems can be difficult to differentiate from medical problems. In addition, older people may complain of different symptoms than younger people do or may be less likely to seek help.
- Anxiety disorders are fairly common among older people, particularly generalized anxiety disorder and posttraumatic stress disorder.
- Anxiety disorders can be treated with antianxiety drugs, antidepressants, or psychotherapy.

- Depression is a common problem among the elderly, and suicide rates are extremely high among elderly White males.
- Some older people show a depletion syndrome, consisting of loss of interest, loss of energy, hopelessness, helplessness, and psychomotor retardation.
- Differentiating depression from dementia can be particularly difficult, but certain patterns of memory loss can help in the differentiation.
- Antidepressant medications and ECT are commonly used to treat severe depression in older people. Cognitive-behavioral and interpersonal therapies have been shown to work very well.
- Alcohol use problems can begin in older age, particularly since the metabolism of and tolerance for alcohol change with age.
- The abuse of and dependence on prescription drugs are significant problems among older people.
- The treatment of substance use disorders for older people is similar to that for younger people.

CHAPTER INTEGRATION

Geropsychologists have emphasized the importance of understanding the cognitive disorders and psychological problems experienced by older people in the context of normal aging. Aging is not just a biological process—it is the interaction of biological, psychological, and social processes, as depicted in Figure 14.6.

Certain changes take place in the brain and the rest of the body with aging, and these are influenced by our genetic and other biological vulnerabilities. The impact of these changes on the everyday behavior of older people varies tremendously, however, in part due to differences in personality and the social environment. Some people become sedentary when their bodies lose some of the strength and endurance they had as younger adults, whereas others institute exercise programs that help them maintain much of their youthful fitness. Similarly, the likelihood of developing many diseases in old age is substantially influenced by a person's behaviors as a younger adult. For example, people who keep mentally active into middle and old age may be less likely to develop Alzheimer's disease.

Much of what we attribute to biological aging—for example, memory loss—is not the result of aging per se but, rather, of diseases such as those discussed in this chapter. But even the pro-

FIGURE 14.6   Integrating Biological and Psychosocial Factors in Aging

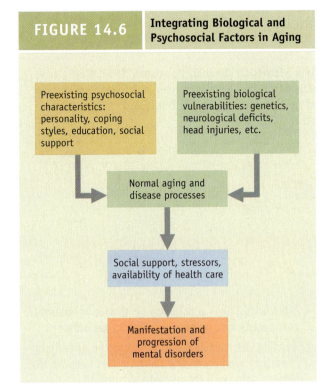

Preexisting psychosocial characteristics: personality, coping styles, education, social support

Preexisting biological vulnerabilities: genetics, neurological deficits, head injuries, etc.

Normal aging and disease processes

Social support, stressors, availability of health care

Manifestation and progression of mental disorders

gression of these biological diseases is substantially affected by psychological and social variables. For example, many people in the early stages of dementia become paranoid, irritable, and impulsive. These symptoms may be especially pronounced in people who were somewhat paranoid, irritable, or impulsive even before they developed dementia.

The social environment can greatly affect the severity of cognitive deficits. If a person who is easily confused or forgetful is further stressed by family members who frequently become annoyed with the person or expect too much of him or her, the cognitive deficits can become even more severe. Thus, even though the cognitive disorders are rooted in medical disease or in chronic intoxication with substances such as alcohol, there are several ways in which psychosocial factors can influence the severity and manifestation of these disorders.

Extraordinary People: Follow-Up

John Bayley's depiction of his life with Iris Murdoch after she developed Alzheimer's disease is remarkable for his elegant and engaging description of her symptoms and the impact of those symptoms on their life together. It is even more remarkable, however, for the fact that it is first and foremost a love story.

> There are so many doubts and illusions and concealments in any close relationship. Even in our present situation, they can come as an unexpected shock. Iris's tears sometimes seem to signify a whole inner world which she is determined to keep from me and shield me from. There is something ghastly in the feeling of relief that this can't be so; and yet the illusion of such an inner world still there—if it is an illusion—can't help haunting me from time to time. There are moments when I almost welcome it. Iris has always had—must have had—so vast and rich and complex an inner world, which it used to give me immense pleasure not to know anything about. Like looking at a map of South Africa as a child and wondering about the sources of the Amazon, and what unknown cities might be hidden there in the jungle. Have any of those hidden places survived in her? (Bayley, 1999, pp. 258–259)
>
> Life is no longer bringing the pair of us "closer and closer apart," in the poet's tenderly ambiguous words. Every day we move closer and closer together. We could not do otherwise. There is a certain comic irony—happily, not darkly comic—that after more than forty years of taking marriage for granted, marriage has decided it is tired of this, and is taking a hand in the game. Purposefully, persistently, involuntarily, our marriage is now getting somewhere. It is giving us no choice—and I am glad of that.
>
> Every day, we are physically closer; and Iris's little "mouse cry," as I think of it,

(continued)

Extraordinary People: Follow-Up (*continued*)

signifying loneliness in the next room, the wish to be back beside me, seems less and less forlorn, more simple, more natural. She is not sailing into the dark: The voyage is over, and under the dark escort of Alzheimer's she has arrived somewhere. So have I. (pp. 265–266)

Iris Murdoch died in February 1999, just a few months after *Elegy for Iris* was published. A movie based on this extraordinary book and couple was released in 2001.

Chapter Summary

■ Aging is not simpy a biological process. Rather, it involves the interaction of biological, psychological, and social processes. (Review Figure 14.6.) Most older people are physically and mentally healthy.

■ Dementia is typically a permanent deterioration in cognitive functioning, often accompanied by emotional changes. The five types of cognitive impairment in dementia are memory impairment, aphasia, apraxia, agnosia, and loss of executive functions. (Review Table 14.1.)

■ The most common type of dementia is due to Alzheimer's disease. The brains of Alzheimer's patients show neurofibrillary tangles, plaques made up of amyloid protein, and cortical atrophy. (Review Figures 14.2 and 14.3.) Recent theories of Alzheimer's disease focus on three genes that might contribute to the buildup of amyloid protein in the brains of Alzheimer's patients.

■ Dementia can also be caused by cerebrovascular disorder, head injury, and progressive disorders, such as Parkinson's disease, HIV disease, Huntington's disease, Pick's disease, and Creutzfeldt-Jakob disease. Chronic drug abuse and the nutritional deficiencies that often accompany it can lead to dementia.

■ Drugs help reduce the cognitive symptoms of dementia and the accompanying depression, anxiety, and psychotic symptoms in some patients.

■ Delirium is characterized by disorientation, recent memory loss, and a clouding of consciousness. (Review Table 14.4.) Delirium typically is a signal of a serious medical condition, such as a stroke, congestive heart failure, an infectious disease, high fever, or drug intoxication or withdrawal. (Review

Table 14.5.) It is a common syndrome in hospitals, particularly among elderly surgical patients.

■ Treating delirium involves treating the underlying condition leading to the delirium and keeping the patient safe until the symptoms subside.

■ In amnesia, only patients' memories are affected. Anterograde amnesia is the most common form of amnesia and is characterized by the inability to learn or retain new information. Retrograde amnesia is the inability to recall previously learned information or past events.

■ Amnesic disorders can be caused by strokes, head injuries, chronic nutritional deficiencies, exposure to toxins, and chronic substance abuse. The course and treatment of amnesia depend on the cause.

■ Mental disorders are less common among older adults than younger adults, but 10 to 20 percent of older people suffer significant psychopathology.

■ Anxiety disorders are fairly common among older people, particularly generalized anxiety disorder and posttraumatic stress disorder. Anxiety disorders can be treated with antianxiety drugs, antidepressants, or psychotherapy.

■ Depression is a common problem among the elderly, and suicide rates are extremely high among elderly White males. Some older people show a depletion syndrome, consisting of loss of interest, loss of energy, hopelessness, helplessness, and psychomotor retardation. Differentiating depression from dementia can be particularly difficult, but certain patterns of memory loss can help in the differentiation.

■ Antidepressant medications and ECT are commonly used to treat severe depression in older people. Cognitive-behavioral and interpersonal therapies have been shown to work very well.

■ Alcohol use problems can begin in older age, particularly since the metabolism of and tolerance for alcohol change with age. The abuse of and dependence on prescription drugs are significant problems among older people. The treatment of substance use disorders for older people is similar to that for younger people.

MindMap CD-ROM

The following resources on the MindMap CD-ROM that came with this text will help you to master the content of this chapter and prepare for tests:

■ Video: Alzheimer's Disease
■ Chapter Timeline
■ Chapter Quiz

Key Terms

cognitive disorders 511

dementia 513

aphasia 514

echolalia 514

palialia 514

apraxia 514

agnosia 514

executive functions 514

Alzheimer's disease 515

neurofibrillary tangles 516

plaques 516

amyloid 516

vascular dementia 518

cerebrovascular disease 518

stroke 518

delirium 525

amnesia 528

anterograde amnesia 528

retrograde amnesia 528

depletion syndrome 532

Chapter 15

Wednesday's Child
by John S. Bunker

We love good looks rather than what is practical,
Though good looks may prove destructive.

—La Fontaine, "The Stag and His Reflection," *Fables*
(1668–1694; translated by Marianne Moore)

Eating Disorders <

Extraordinary People

■ **Diana, Princess of Wales**

Anorexia Nervosa

Anorexia nervosa is a disorder in which people refuse to maintain a body weight that is healthy and normal for their age and height. They have distorted body images and intense fears of becoming fat, and women with anorexia lose their menstrual periods. People with the restricting type of anorexia nervosa refuse to eat in order to prevent weight gain. People with the binge/purge type periodically engage in bingeing and then purge to prevent weight gain.

Bulimia Nervosa

Bulimia nervosa is characterized by uncontrolled binge eating, followed by behaviors designed to prevent weight gain, such as purging, fasting, and excessive exercising. People with the purging type of bulimia nervosa use self-induced vomiting, diuretics, or laxatives to prevent weight gain. People with the nonpurging type use fasting and exercise to prevent weight gain.

Binge-Eating Disorder

Binge-eating disorder is a provisional diagnosis in the DSM-IV-TR, and it is characterized by binge eating without behaviors designed to prevent weight gain. Many people with binge-eating disorder are overweight. The disorder is more common in women, and binge eating may be more prevalent in African Americans than in European Americans. There currently are debates as to whether binge eating is a serious public health concern or if we should be concerned primarily about the obesity that often accompanies binge eating.

Understanding Eating Disorders

Societal pressures to be thin may play a role in the development of the eating disorders. Eating disorders may sometimes develop as a way of coping with negative emotions or as the result of rigid, dichotomous thinking. Adolescent females who develop eating disorders often appear to come from families that are overcontrolling, require "perfection," and do not allow the expression of negative feelings. Although some women who develop eating disorders have histories of sexual abuse, sexual abuse seems to be a general risk factor for psychological problems, rather than a specific risk factor for eating disorders. Eating disorders may be, in part, heritable. The families of people with eating disorders also tend to have high rates of depression. People with eating disorders may have disruptions in the hypothalamus, a part of the brain involved in the regulation of eating and emotions, as well as in levels of neurotransmitters, including serotonin.

Treatments for Eating Disorders

People with anorexia nervosa must often be hospitalized and forced to gain weight. Then, behavior therapy and family therapy are used to try to help them overcome their disordered eating behaviors and attitudes. Cognitive-behavioral therapy, interpersonal therapy, and supportive-expressive therapy have proven useful in the treatment of bulimia nervosa. Antidepressants are helpful in reducing bingeing and purging and in enhancing a sense of control in people with bulimia nervosa. Antidepressants may also prove useful in treating anorexia nervosa, although there are only a few studies of their effectiveness to date. Prevention programs for eating disorders are popular, but their effects are unclear.

Taking Psychology Personally

■ **Is There Such a Thing as a Healthy Diet?**

Chapter Integration

Interacting social, psychological, and biological factors may lead a person to develop an eating disorder.

There may be more than one pathway into an eating disorder. Once disordered behaviors begin, they tend to be maintained.

Extraordinary People

Diana, Princess of Wales

Perhaps the most famous person to suffer from bulimia nervosa, Diana, Princess of Wales, shocked the world when she made her suffering public. Never before had a member of the British royal family been so open, particularly about symptoms that could be diagnosed as a psychological disorder. After the birth of her first son, William, Diana suffered a postpartum depression (see Chapter 9). She attributed this depression to an accumulation of great changes in her life—her marriage at 19 to the Prince of Wales; her difficult pregnancy, which came early in that marriage; the tremendous media attention given her; and the early signs that her marriage was falling apart. Diana felt she had little support from her husband or family, however, in fighting this depression and, thus, began to cope with her pain in maladaptive ways. The following is her story of how her bulimia developed, as told to a British Broadcasting Corporation (BBC) interviewer in November 1995.

Diana: When no one listens to you, or you feel no one's listening to you, all sorts of things start to happen. For instance, you have so much pain inside yourself that you try and hurt yourself on the outside because you want help, but it's the wrong help you're asking for. People see it as crying wolf or attention-seeking, and they think because you're in the media all the time you've got enough attention. But I was actually crying out because I wanted to get better in order to go forward and continue my duty and my role as wife, mother, Princess of Wales. So yes, I did inflict it upon myself. I didn't like myself, I was ashamed because I couldn't cope with the pressures.

Question: Were you able to admit that you were in fact unwell, or did you feel compelled simply to carry on performing as the Princess of Wales?

Diana: I felt compelled to perform. Well, when I say perform, I was compelled to go out and do my engagements and not let people down and support them and love them. And in a way by being out in public they supported me, although they weren't aware just how much healing they were giving me, and it carried me through.

Question: But did you feel that you had to maintain the public image of a successful Princess of Wales?

Diana: Yes I did, yes I did.

Question: The depression was resolved, as you say, but it was subsequently reported that you suffered bulimia. Is that true?

Diana: Yes, I did. I had bulimia for a number of years. And that's like a secret disease. You inflict it upon yourself because your self-esteem is at a low ebb, and you don't think you're worthy or valuable. You fill your stomach up four or five times a day—some do it more—and it gives you a feeling of comfort. It's like having a pair of arms around you, but it's temporarily, temporary. Then you're disgusted at the bloatedness of your stomach, and then you bring it all up again. And it's a repetitive pattern which is very destructive to yourself.

Question: How often would you do that on a daily basis?

Diana: Depends on the pressures going on. If I'd been on what I call an awayday, or I'd been up part of the country all day, I'd come home feeling pretty empty, because my engagements at that time would be to do with people dying, people very sick, people's marriage problems, and I'd come home and it would be very difficult to know how to comfort myself having been comforting lots of other people, so it would be a regular pattern to jump into the fridge. It was a symptom of what was going on in my marriage. I was crying out for help, but giving the wrong signals, and people were using my bulimia as a coat on a hanger: they decided that was the problem—Diana was unstable.

Princess Diana certainly led an unusual life, and some of the pressures that may have contributed to her eating disorder were ones very few of us can expect to encounter. Still, the kind of love-hate relationship she had with food is familiar to many of us, as this excerpt from a college student's diary shows:

VOICES

Dear Diary: This morning I had a half of a grapefruit for breakfast, and some coffee—no sugar or cream. For lunch, I had an apple and a diet soda. For dinner, I had some plain white rice and a salad with just some lemon squeezed over it. So I was feeling really good about myself, really virtuous. That is, until Jackie came over, and completely messed up my day. She brought over a movie to watch, which was fine. But then she insisted on ordering a pizza. I told her I didn't want any, that I wasn't hungry (which was a lie, because I was starving). But she ordered it anyway. The pizza arrived, and I thought I could be good and not have any. But it was just sitting there on the table, and I couldn't think of anything except having some. I couldn't concentrate on the movie. I kept smelling the pizza and feeling the emptiness in my stomach. Like a weakling, I reached out and got one piece, a small piece. It was ice cold by then, and kind of greasy, but I didn't care. I ate that piece in about 5 seconds flat. Then I had another piece. And another. I stopped after four pieces. But I still couldn't pay attention to the movie. All I could think about was what a pig I was for eating that pizza, and how I'll never lose the 10 pounds I need to lose to fit into a smaller size dress. Jackie's gone now, and I still keep thinking about how ugly and fat I am, and how I have no willpower. I didn't deserve to have that pizza tonight, because I haven't lost enough weight this month. I'm going to have to skip breakfast and lunch tomorrow, and exercise for a couple of hours, to make up for being a complete pig tonight.

Our culture is obsessed with weight and with how much food we eat. A nationwide study in the United States found that 38 percent of normal-weight women thought they were overweight (Chang & Christakis, 2003). Weight concerns are even greater among college women; a study of 2,200 college students in six universities across the United States found that two-thirds of the women were unhappy with their weight (Rozin, Bauer, & Catanese, 2003). Dissatisfaction with the shape and size of the body is greater among women than men (Lewinsohn et al., 2002; Rozin et al., 2003) (see Figure 15.1 on page 542).

Dieting is the most common way people try to overcome their body dissatisfaction. Only one-third

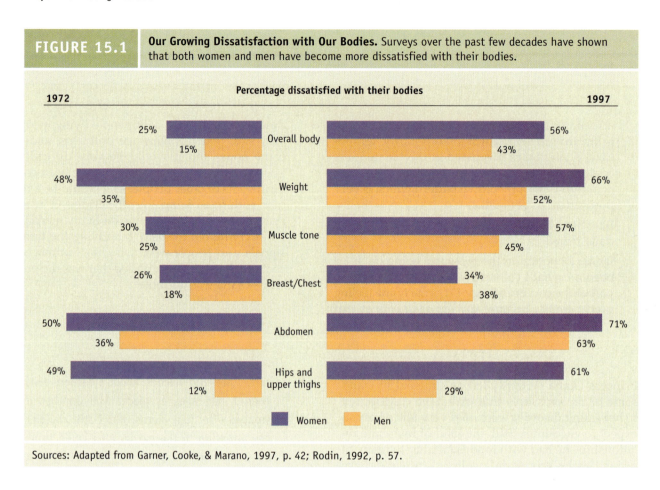

FIGURE 15.1   **Our Growing Dissatisfaction with Our Bodies.** Surveys over the past few decades have shown that both women and men have become more dissatisfied with their bodies.

Sources: Adapted from Garner, Cooke, & Marano, 1997, p. 42; Rodin, 1992, p. 57.

of college women say they "never" diet, compared with 58 percent of college men (Rozin et al., 2003). Dieting is hard, however, and almost everyone who loses weight through dieting gains it all back and often more (Byrne, Cooper, & Fairburn, 2003). Many people spend their lives losing and gaining back tens of pounds in a cycle of "yo-yo" dieting.

Some people turn to more extreme means to make themselves look "better." The popularity of cosmetic surgery to improve appearance has exploded in recent years, with procedures such as liposuction and breast augmentation doubling in popularity in four years (Sarwer, Magee, & Crerand, 2004). The most popular procedure these days is injections of *Botulinum* toxin (e.g., Botox) to reduce wrinkles, with 1.6 million people receiving this procedure per year. In all, Americans spend over $30 billion per year on weight-loss products, including $8 billion per year on spas and exercise clubs, $382 million on diet books, $10 billion on diet soft drinks, and billions of dollars on low-calorie foods and artificial sweeteners. To put this into perspective, consider that the federal government spends about $30 billion per year on all education, training, employment, and social services programs.

Why do people care so much about their weight? There are health concerns that drive the attempt to lose weight. Being overweight can contribute to serious diseases, such as high blood pressure, heart disease, and diabetes. Overweight people have shorter life spans than do people who are not overweight.

The driving force behind most people's attempts to eat less and lose weight, however, is the desire to be more attractive and increase self-esteem (Gruber et al., 2001). Food has become more than something we eat to maintain healthy bodies or because it tastes good, and exercise is not just something we do to improve our health. What we eat and how much we exercise have become linked to feelings of worth, merit, guilt, sin, rebelliousness, and defiance. Weight and how attractive we feel are integral parts of our self-esteem.

For some people, concerns about eating and weight become so overwhelming and behaviors oriented toward eating or avoiding eating get so out of control that they are said to have eating disorders. There are three specific types of eating disorders: anorexia nervosa, bulimia nervosa, and binge-eating disorder. **Anorexia nervosa** is characterized by a pursuit of thinness that leads peo-

FIGURE 15.2   **Women's and Men's Body Images.** Female and male undergraduates were shown figures of their own sex and asked to indicate figures that looked most like their current shape, their ideal figure, and the figure they felt would be most attractive to the opposite sex. Men selected very similar figures for all three choices, but women selected very different figures for their current figure and either their ideal figure or the figure they thought would be most attractive.

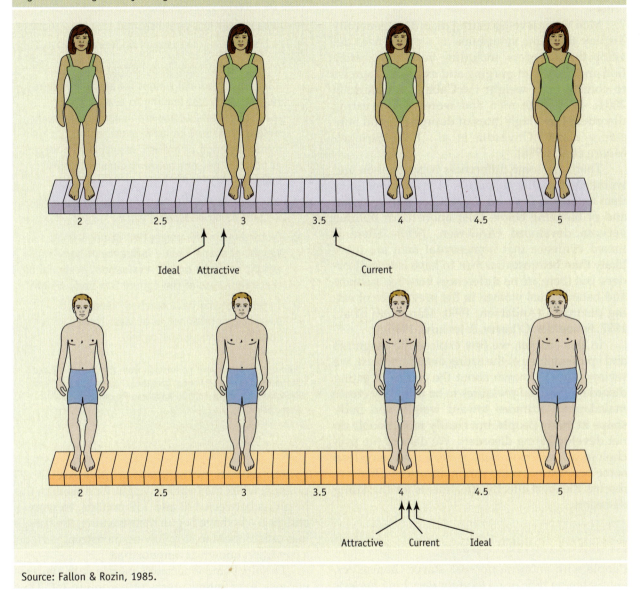

Source: Fallon & Rozin, 1985.

ple to starve themselves. As Princess Diana described, **bulimia nervosa** is characterized by a cycle of bingeing followed by extreme behaviors to prevent weight gain, such as self-induced vomiting. People with **binge-eating disorder** regularly binge but do not engage in behaviors to purge what they eat. The eating disorders are the focus of this chapter.

Traditionally, women have felt more pressure than men to be very thin (see Figure 15.2), and we will see that the eating disorders are much more common among women than men. In recent years,

however, there has been an increased emphasis on men attaining a superfit look, having lean lower bodies and strong, toned upper bodies. A study of boys' action toys found that they have grown more muscular over time, with many contemporary action figures far exceeding the muscularity of even the largest human bodybuilders (Pope et al., 1999b). The number of articles in men's magazines on achieving such a look has risen dramatically, and television stars reach stardom in part because they have this look (Nemeroff et al., 1994). The male centerfolds in *Playgirl* magazine have become increasingly muscular over the past two decades (Leit, Pope, & Gray, 2001). One study found that, on average, men want to be much more muscular than they actually are (Pope et al., 2000). This look is more difficult for some men to attain than for others.

Men who develop eating disorders generally display the same symptoms as women who develop the disorders, including body dissatisfaction and the use of purging and excessive exercise to control their weight (McCabe & Ricciardelli, 2004). Also, both men and women with eating disorders have high rates of depression and substance abuse (Olivardia et al., 1995; Striegel-Moore et al., 1998).

There are some differences between men and women with eating disorders. Men are more likely than women to have histories of being overweight and of bingeing before their anorexia or bulimia nervosa developed (Andersen, 1990). There is mixed evidence that homosexual men are more likely than heterosexual men to have eating disorders, but there are no differences between lesbians and heterosexual women in the prevalence of eating disorders (Andersen, 1990; Mangweth et al., 1997; Schneider, O'Leary, & Jenkins, 1995).

In this chapter, we first explore the diagnosis and epidemiology of the eating disorders. Next, we review what is known about the causes of eating disorders. Societal pressures to be thin may create maladaptive attitudes toward weight and body shape in many people, but clearly most people do not develop eating disorders. We discuss the psychological and biological factors that may lead some people to develop eating disorders. Then, we discuss the most effective treatments for the eating disorders.

ANOREXIA NERVOSA

People with anorexia nervosa starve themselves, subsisting on little or no food for very long periods of time, yet they remain sure that they still need to lose more weight.

Diagnosis, Prevalence, and Prognosis of Anorexia Nervosa

The diagnosis of anorexia nervosa requires that a person refuse to maintain a body weight that is healthy and normal for his or her age and height (see the DSM-IV-TR criteria in Table 15.1). The DSM-IV-TR criteria for anorexia nervosa require that a person's weight be at least 15 percent below the minimum healthy weight for his or her age and height (APA, 2000). Often, the person's weight is much below this. For example, a 5-foot 6-inch

---

TABLE 15.1   DSM-IV-TR

Diagnostic Criteria for Anorexia Nervosa

The DSM-IV-TR specifies that both intentional extreme weight loss and distorted thoughts about one's body are key features of anorexia nervosa.

A. Refusal to maintain body weight at or above a minimally normal weight for age and height (e.g., weight loss leading to a weight at least 15 percent below minimum healthy body weight, or failure to make expected weight gain during a period of growth, resulting in a weight at least 15 percent below minimum healthy body weight)

B. Intense fear of gaining weight or becoming fat, despite being underweight

C. Distortions in the perception of one's body weight or shape, undue influence of body weight or shape on self-evaluation, or denial of the seriousness of the current low body weight

D. In females who have reached menarche, amenorrhea (absence of at least three consecutive menstrual cycles)

Source: Reprinted with permission from the *Diagnostic and Statistical Manual of Mental Disorders,* Fourth Edition, Text Revision. Copyright © 2000 American Psychiatric Association.

---

young woman with anorexia may weigh 95 pounds, when the healthy weight for a woman this height is between 120 and 159 pounds. In women and girls who have begun menstruating, the weight loss causes them to stop having menstrual periods, a condition known as **amenorrhea.**

Despite being emaciated, people with anorexia nervosa have intense fears of becoming fat. They have very distorted images of their bodies, often believing they are fat and needing to lose more weight. The self-evaluations of anorexics hinge entirely on their weight and their control over their eating. They believe they are good and worthwhile only when they have complete control over their eating and when they are losing weight. The weight loss causes people with anorexia to be chronically fatigued, yet they drive themselves to exercise excessively and to keep up a grueling schedule at work or school.

People with anorexia often develop elaborate rituals around food, as writer Marya Hornbacher describes in her autobiography, *Wasted* (Hornbacher, 1998, pp. 254–255):

VOICES

I would spread my paper out in front of me, set the yogurt aside, check my watch. I'd read the same sentence over and over, to prove that I could sit in front of food without snarfing it up, to prove it was no big deal. When five minutes had passed, I would start to skim my yogurt. . . . You take the edge of your spoon and run it over the top of the yogurt, being careful to get only the melted part. Then let the yogurt drip off until there's only a sheen of it on the spoon. Lick it—wait, be careful, you have to only lick a teeny bit at a time, the sheen should last at least four or five licks, and you have to lick the back of the spoon first, then turn the spoon over and lick the front, with the tip of your tongue. Then set the yogurt aside again. Read a full page, but don't look at the yogurt to check the melt progression. Repeat. Repeat. Do not take a mouthful, do not eat any of the yogurt unless it's melted. Do not fantasize about toppings, crumbled Oreos, or chocolate sauce. Do not fantasize about a sandwich. A sandwich would be so *complicated*.

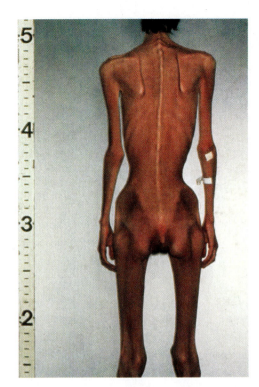

People with anorexia nervosa weigh significantly less than what they should for their height and weight.

About 1 percent of people will develop anorexia nervosa at sometime in their lives, and between 90 and 95 percent of people diagnosed with anorexia nervosa are female (Hoek & van Hoeken, 2003; Striegel-Moore, Dohm, et al., 2003). White women are somewhat more likely than Black women to develop the disorder. Anorexia nervosa usually begins in adolescence, between the ages of 15 and 19 (Striegel-Moore, 1995). The course of the disorder varies greatly from person to person. Long-term studies done in Europe suggest that as many as half of the women who develop anorexia nervosa are fully recovered 10 years after treatment, but the remainder continue to suffer from eating-related problems or other psychopathology, particularly depression (Herpertz-Dahlmann, Muller, et al., 2001; Lowe et al., 2001; Wentz et al., 2001).

Anorexia nervosa is a very dangerous disorder physiologically. The death rate among people with anorexia is 5 to 8 percent (Polivy & Herman, 2002). Some of the most serious consequences of anorexia are the cardiovascular complications, including bradycardia (extreme slowing of heart rate), arrhythmia (irregular heart beat), and heart failure. Another potentially serious complication of anorexia is acute expansion of the stomach, to the point of rupturing. Bone strength is an issue for women with anorexia who have amenorrhea, presumably because low es-

trogen levels affect bone strength. Kidney damage has been seen in some patients with anorexia, and impaired immune system functioning may make people with anorexia more vulnerable to severe illnesses.

Types of Anorexia Nervosa

In the previous Voices excerpt, Hornbacher describes one of the two types of anorexia, the restricting type (see the Concept Overview in Table 15.2 on page 546). People with the **restricting type of anorexia nervosa** simply refuse to eat as a way of preventing weight gain. Some people with anorexia who are restrictors attempt to go for days without eating anything. Most eat very small amounts of food each day, in part simply to stay alive and in part because of pressures from others to eat. Hornbacher survived for months on one cup of yogurt and one fat-free muffin per day. Daphne, in the following case study, also has the restricting type of anorexia nervosa.

Daphne is 5 feet 11 inches tall and weighs 102 pounds. She has felt "large" since her height soared above her schoolmates in the fifth grade. She has been on a diet ever since. During her junior year in high school, Daphne *(continued)*

TABLE 15.2 Concept Overview

Comparisons of Eating Disorders

The eating disorders vary on these characteristics.

Symptom	AN*— Restricting Type	AN*— Binge/Purge Type	BN*— Purging Type	BN*— Nonpurging Type	Binge-Eating Disorder
Body weight	Must be underweight by more than 15 percent	Must be underweight by more than 15 percent	Often normal or somewhat overweight	Often normal or somewhat overweight	Often significantly overweight
Body image	Severely disturbed	Severely disturbed	Overconcerned with weight	Overconcerned with weight	Often disgusted with overweight
Binges	No	Yes	Yes	Yes	Yes
Purges or other compensatory behaviors	No	Yes	Yes	No	No
Sense of lack of control over eating	No	During binges	Yes	Yes	Yes
Amenorrhea in females	Yes	Yes	Not usually	Not usually	No

*AN refers to anorexia nervosa, BN to bulimia nervosa.

CASE STUDY

decided that she had to take drastic measures to lose more weight. She began by cutting her calorie intake to about 1,000 calories per day. She lost several pounds, but not fast enough for her liking, so she cut her intake to 500 calories per day. She also began a vigorous exercise program of cross-country running. Each day, Daphne would not let herself eat until she had run at least 10 miles. Then she would have just a few vegetables and a handful of cereal. Later in the day, she might have some more vegetables and some fruit, but she would wait until she was so hungry that she was faint. Daphne dropped to 110 pounds and she stopped menstruating. Her mother expressed some concern about how little Daphne was eating, but since her mother tended to be overweight, she did not discourage Daphne from dieting.

When it came time to go to college, Daphne was excited but also frightened, because she had always been a star student in high school and wasn't sure she could maintain her straight As in college. In the first examination period in college, Daphne got mostly As

but one B. She felt very vulnerable, like a failure, and as if she was losing control. She also was unhappy with her social life, which, by the middle of the first semester, was going nowhere. Daphne decided that things might be better if she lost more weight, so she cut her food intake to two apples and a handful of cereal each day. She also ran at least 15 miles each day. By the end of fall semester, she was down to 102 pounds. She was also chronically tired, had trouble concentrating, and occasionally fainted. Still, when Daphne looked in the mirror, she saw a fat, homely young woman who needed to lose more weight.

The other type is the **binge/purge type of anorexia nervosa,** in which people periodically engage in bingeing or purging behaviors (e.g., self-induced vomiting or the misuse of laxatives or diuretics). This disorder is different from bulimia nervosa in at least two ways. First, people with the binge/purge type of anorexia continue to be at least 15 percent below a healthy body weight, whereas people with bulimia nervosa are typically at normal weight or somewhat overweight. Second, women with binge/purge anorexia often develop amenorrhea, whereas women with bulimia nervosa usually do not. Often, a person with the binge/purge type of anorexia nervosa does not engage in binges in which she eats large amounts of food; however, if she eats even a small amount of food, she feels as if she has binged and will purge this food.

People with the restricting type of anorexia are more likely than those with the binge/purge type to have deep feelings of mistrust of others and a tendency to deny they have a problem. People with binge/purge anorexia are more likely to have problems with unstable moods and impulse control, with alcohol and other drug abuse, and with self-mutilation (Garner, Garfinkel, & O'Shaughnessy, 1985). They also tend to have more chronic courses of the disorder.

SUMMING UP

- Anorexia nervosa is characterized by self-starvation, a distorted body image, intense fears of becoming fat, and amenorrhea.

- The lifetime prevalence of anorexia is about 1 percent, with 90 to 95 percent of cases being female.

- Anorexia usually begins in adolescence, and the course is variable from one person to another.

- People with the restricting type refuse to eat in order to prevent weight gain.

- People with the binge/purge type periodically engage in bingeing and then purge to prevent weight gain.

BULIMIA NERVOSA

The core characteristics of bulimia nervosa, from which Princess Diana suffered, are uncontrolled eating, or **bingeing,** followed by behaviors designed to prevent weight gain from the binges (see the DSM-IV-TR criteria in Table 15.3). The DSM-IV-TR defines a binge as occurring in a discrete period of time, such as an hour or two, and involving eating an amount of food that is definitely larger than most people would eat during a similar period of time and in similar circumstances. There are tremendous variations among people with eating disorders in the sizes of their binges, however. The average binge is about 1,500 calories. Less than a third of binge episodes contain more than 2,000 calories. One-third of the binge episodes contain only 600 calories, and many people will say that they consider eating just one piece of cake a binge. What makes that a binge for people with an eating disorder is the sense that they have no control over their

TABLE 15.3 DSM-IV-TR
Diagnostic Criteria for Bulimia Nervosa

People with bulimia nervosa regularly binge eat and then attempt to avoid gaining weight from their binge.

A. Recurrent episodes of binge eating, characterized by both of the following:

   1. eating, in a discrete period of time (such as within a two-hour period), an amount of food that is definitely larger than most people would eat during a similar period of time and under similar circumstances

   2. a sense of lack of control over eating during the episode

B. Recurrent inappropriate behaviors to prevent weight gain, such as self-induced vomiting; misuse of laxatives, diuretics, enemas, or other medications; fasting; or excessive exercise

C. The binge eating and inappropriate purging behaviors both occur, on average, at least twice a week for three months.

D. Self-evaluation is unduly influenced by body shape and weight.

Source: Reprinted with permission from the *Diagnostic and Statisical Manual of Mental Disorders,* Fourth Edition, Text Revision. Copyright © 2000 American Psychiatric Association.

eating, that they feel compelled to eat, even though they are not hungry. The DSM-IV-TR recognizes this aspect of binges, and the criteria for a binge include a sense of lack of control over eating.

The behaviors people with bulimia use to control their weight include self-induced vomiting; the abuse of laxatives, diuretics, or other purging medications; fasting; and excessive exercise. As with people with anorexia nervosa, the self-evaluations of people with bulimia nervosa are heavily influenced by their body shapes and weights. When they are thin, they feel like a "good person." People with bulimia nervosa do not tend to show gross distortions in their body images, as people with anorexia nervosa do. Whereas a woman with anorexia nervosa who is emaciated and sees herself as obese, a woman with bulimia nervosa has more realistic perceptions of her actual body shape. Still, people with bulimia are constantly dissatisfied with their shapes and weights and concerned about losing weight.

People with bulimia nervosa are distinguished from people with the binge/purge type of anorexia nervosa primarily by their body weight: The criteria for binge/purge anorexia require that a person be at least 15 percent below normal body weight, whereas there are no weight criteria for bulimia nervosa. People with the restricting type of anorexia nervosa also differ from people with bulimia nervosa in that they do not engage in binges—restrictors severely limit their food intake all of the time (review Table 15.2).

Self-induced vomiting is the behavior people associate most often with bulimia. Bulimia is often discovered by family members, roommates, and friends when people with the disorder are caught vomiting or when they leave messes after they vomit. In one sorority, the frequent purging behavior of the members was discovered in a particularly odd way (Hubbard et al., 1999, p. 52):

> At first it seemed like a minor, if mystifying, problem: In the spring of 1996, plastic sandwich bags began disappearing by the hundreds from the kitchen of a sorority house at a large northeastern university. When the sorority's president investigated, she found a disturbing explanation: The bags, filled with vomit, were hidden in a basement bathroom. "I was shocked," says the president (who later learned that the building's pipes, eroded by gallons of stomach acid, would have to be replaced). "Yet in a way it made sense." Most of her 45 housemates, she recalls, worried about

weight. "It was like a competition to see who could eat the least. At dinner they would say, 'All I had today was an apple,' or 'I haven't had anything.' It was surreal."

Dentists recognize people with bulimia, because frequent vomiting can rot teeth from exposure to stomach acid. People who use self-induced vomiting or purging medications are said to have the **purging type of bulimia nervosa.** The cycle of bingeing and then purging or other compensatory behaviors to control weight becomes a way of life, as in the case of Alice (Spitzer et al., 1981, p. 146):

> Alice is a single 17-year-old who lives with her parents, who insisted that she be seen because of binge eating and vomiting. She achieved her greatest weight of 180 pounds at 16 years of age. Her lowest weight since she reached her present height of 5 feet 9 inches has been 150 pounds, and her present weight is about 160 pounds. Alice states she has been dieting since age ten and says she has always been . . . slightly chubby. At age 12 she started binge eating and vomiting. She was a serious competitive swimmer at that time, and it was necessary for her to keep her weight down. She would deprive herself of all food for a few days and then get an urge to eat. She could not control this urge, and would raid the refrigerator and cupboards for ice cream, pastries, and other desserts. She would often do this at night, when nobody was looking, and would eat, for example, a quart of ice cream, an entire pie, and any other desserts she could find. She would eat until she felt physical discomfort and then she would become depressed and fearful of gaining weight, following which she would self-induce vomiting. When she was 15 she was having eating binges and vomiting four days a week. Since age 13 she has gone through only one period of six weeks without gaining weight or eating binges and vomiting.

Some social settings, such as being part of a cheerleading team, may increase the risk for eating disorders.

People who use excessive exercise or fasting to control their weight but do not engage in purging are said to have the **nonpurging type of bulimia nervosa.** People who use excessive exercise to control their weight can easily hide their bulimia if they are part of a group that values exercise, such as students on a college campus. The following passage was written by a male psychologist who developed the nonpurging type of bulimia nervosa over a period of years. This man grew up viewing food as a source of comfort and bingeing as a way of escaping from overbearing and disapproving parents. He fasted for a day or more after a binge to control his weight. As the pressures of his job and a failed marriage increased, his bulimic pattern of bingeing and then fasting grew more serious (Wilps, 1990, pp. 19–21).

VOICES

I would sigh with relief when Sunday evening came, since I had no work responsibilities until the next morning, and I would have just returned my son to his mother's custody. I would then carefully shop at convenience stores for "just right" combinations of cheese, lunch meats, snack chips, and sweets such as chocolate bars. I would also make a stop at a neighborhood newsstand to buy escapist paperback novels (an essential part of the binge) and then settle down for a three-hour session of reading and slow eating until I could barely keep my eyes open. My binges took the place of Sunday dinner, averaging approximately 6,000 kilocalories in size. Following the binge, my stomach aching with distension, I would carefully clean my teeth, wash all the dishes, and fall into a drugged slumber. I would typically schedule the following day as a heavy working day with evening meetings in order to distract myself from increasing hunger as I fasted. I began running. . . . I would typically run for one hour, four to five days per week, and walked to work as a further weight control measure. . . . As time went on, I increased the frequency of these binges, probably because of the decreasing structured demands for my time. They went from weekly to twice per week, then I was either bingeing or fasting with no normal days in my week at all. My sleep patterns were either near-comatose or restless, with either sweating after a binge or shivering after a fast. I became increasingly irritable and withdrawn . . . prompting increased guilt on my part that I resented the intrusion of my friends, my patients, and even my son into my cycle. . . . The nadir of my life as a bulimic occurred when I found myself calling patients whom I had scheduled for evening appointments, explaining to them that I was ill, then using the freed evening for bingeing. . . . I was physically exhausted most of the time, and my hands, feet, and abdomen were frequently puffy and edematous, which I, of course, interpreted as gain in body fat and which contributed to my obsession with weight and food. I weighed myself several times per day in various locations, attending to half pound variations as though my life depended on them.

The prevalence of bulimia nervosa is estimated to be between 0.5 and 3 percent in the general population (Wilson, 2005; Striegel-Moore & Franko, 2003). It is much more common in women than in men, and in European Americans than in African Americans (Striegel-Moore, Dohm, et al., 2003).

Symptoms of bulimia nervosa are quite common, particularly among adolescent and young adult women, and Figure 15.3 on page 550 lists questions from one of the surveys commonly used to measure maladaptive eating attitudes. One study of 2,200 students in six colleges around the United States found that 15 percent of the women admitted to having engaged in some purging behavior, and 28 percent classified themselves as obsessed with their weight (rates for men on the two questions were 4 percent and 11 percent, respectively) (Rozin et al., 2003).

Researchers in Oregon followed a large group of adolescents for several years, examining the ebb and flow of what they called *partial-syndrome eating disorders*—behaviors that smack of anorexia or bulimia nervosa but don't meet the full criteria for the disorders (Lewinsohn, Striegel-Moore, & Seeley, 2000; Striegel-Moore, Seeley, & Lewinsohn, 2003). Adolescents with partial-syndrome eating disorders may binge at least once a week, but not multiple times per week. They may be underweight, but not a full 15 percent underweight. They tend to be highly concerned with their weight and judge themselves on the basis of their weight. However, their symptoms don't add up to a full-blown eating disorder.

The researchers found that the adolescents with partial-syndrome eating disorders, the vast majority of whom were girls, were just as likely as those with full-blown eating disorders to have several psychological problems, both as adolescents and later in their twenties. These problems included anxiety disorders, substance abuse, depression,

FIGURE 15.3   **Check Your Own Attitudes Toward Eating.** Psychologist David Garner and colleagues (Garner, Olmstead, & Polivy, 1984) developed the Eating Disorder Inventory to assess people's attitudes and behaviors toward eating and their bodies. People who score higher on this questionnaire are more prone to eating disorders. As you read through these items, think about whether you would say each one is true of you always, usually, often, sometimes, rarely, or never. If you find you have answered "usually" or "always" to many of these items, you might want to reconsider your attitudes toward food and your body and perhaps talk to someone you trust about them.

Eating Disorder Inventory

I think my stomach is too big.

I eat when I am upset.

I stuff myself with food.

I think about dieting.

I think that my thighs are too large.

I feel ineffective as a person.

I feel extremely guilty after overeating.

I am terrified of gaining weight.

I get confused as to whether or not I am hungry.

If I gain a pound, I worry that I will keep gaining.

I have the thought of trying to vomit in order to lose weight.

I eat or drink in secrecy.

Source: From D. Garner, A. K. Cooke, and H. E. Marano, "The 1997 Body Image Survey" in *Psychology Today*, 30–44, 1997. Reprinted with permission from *Psychology Today Magazine*, Copyright © 1997 Sussex Publishers, Inc.

and attempted suicide. Almost 90 percent had a full-blown psychiatric disorder when they were in their early twenties. Those with partial-syndrome eating disorders also had lower self-esteem, poorer social relationships, poorer physical health, and lower life satisfaction than those with no signs of an eating disorder. They were less likely to have earned a bachelor's degree and more likely to be unemployed.

The onset of bulimia nervosa most often occurs between the ages of 15 and 29 (Striegel-Moore, 1995). Many people with bulimia nervosa are of normal weight or are slightly overweight. You might conclude, then, that bulimia is not as physically dangerous as anorexia. Although the death rate among people with bulimia is not as high as among people with anorexia, bulimia also has serious medical complications. One of the most serious is an imbalance in the body's electrolytes, which results from fluid loss following excessive and chronic vomiting, laxative abuse, and diuretic abuse. Electrolytes are biochemicals that help regulate the heart, and imbalances in electrolytes can lead to heart failure.

Bulimia nervosa tends to be a chronic condition. People seeking treatment for this disorder typically report years of unremitting symptoms. A study of the natural course of bulimia nervosa in 102 women, most of whom did not receive treatment, found that, over a five-year period, half to two-thirds had some form of eating disorder of clinical severity at each of several assessment points over that period (Fairburn et al., 2000, 2003). One-third still had a diagnosable eating disorder at the end of five years. The factors associated with a more persistent course include obesity as a child, an excessive valuation of shape and low weight, increasing dietary restraint, and a high level of social maladjustment.

Cultural and Historical Trends

Several theorists have argued that the eating disorders are culture-bound syndromes, occurring primarily in wealthy, developed countries in which food is abundant and thinness is highly valued (Garner & Garfinkel, 1980; McCarthy, 1990; Sobal & Stunkard, 1989). In addition, the prevalence of eating disorders may have increased over recent decades, as the availability of food has increased but cultural norms (at least in the United States and Europe) have increasingly prized thinness for women (Striegel-Moore, 1995; Stunkard, 1997).

Keel and Klump (2003) did a meta-analysis of existing studies to test these ideas. As we discussed in Chapter 3, in a meta-analysis, all studies relevant to a hypothesis—in this case, that the prevalence of the eating disorders varies across cultures and over time—are analyzed together and the trends across the studies are summarized statistically. Keel and Klump found that the evidence for cultural and historical differences in the prevalence of eating disorders was different for anorexia and bulimia nervosa.

There was only modest evidence of cultural or historical differences in the prevalence of anorexia nervosa. Cases of self-starvation have been described since the medieval times and in most re-

Standards of beauty vary greatly across cultures.

gions of the world. The motivations given for self-starvation do seem to vary across culture and time. In "non-Westernized" countries and in centuries past, the stated motivations for excessive fasting have had less to do with weight concerns and more to do with stomach discomfort, or with religious reasons (Keel & Klump, 2003). Patients with anorexia in Asian countries also do not have the distorted body images that are characteristic of anorexia in the United States and Europe and readily admit that they are very thin. Nonetheless, they stubbornly refuse to eat, as is illustrated by the case of one Chinese woman (adapted from Sing, 1995, pp. 27–29):

Miss Y, aged 31, was 5 foot 3 inches. She had formerly weighed 110 pounds but now weighed 48 pounds. Her anorexia began four years previously, when she was suddenly deserted by her boyfriend, who came from a neighboring village. Greatly saddened by his departure for England, Miss Y started to complain of abdominal discomfort and reduced her food intake. She became socially withdrawn and unemployed. At her psychiatric examination, she wore long hair and was shockingly emaciated—virtually a skeleton. She had sunken eyes, hollow cheeks, and pale, cold skin. She recognized her striking wasting readily but claimed a complete lack of hunger and blamed the weight loss on an unidentifiable abdominal problem. Her concern over the seriousness of her physical condition was perfunctory. When asked whether she consciously tried to restrict the amount she ate, she said, "No." When questioned why she had gone for periods of eight or more waking hours without eating anything, she said it was because she had no hunger and felt distended, pointing to the lower left side of her abdomen. All physical examinations revealed no biological source for her feelings of distension, however. Miss Y was often in a low mood and became

(continued)

transiently tearful when her grief over the broken relationship was acknowledged. However, she resisted all attempts to discuss this loss in detail and all other psychological and medical treatments. Miss Y later died of cardiac arrest. Postmortem examination revealed no specific pathology other than multiple organ atrophy due to starvation.

One question that can be raised is whether self-starvation in the absence of weight concerns can be called anorexia nervosa, since weight concerns are a defining feature of the disorder in the DSM-IV-TR. On the other hand, the DSM-IV-TR itself is a culture-bound document, representing Western views of mental disorders.

In contrast to the prevalence data for anorexia nervosa, the prevalence of bulimia nervosa does seem to vary substantially across cultures and across historical time. It is considerably more common in the past 50 years than previously, and in Westernized cultures than in non-Westernized cultures. Keel and Klump (2003) suggest that bulimia nervosa may vary more by culture and historical period because the bingeing that is part of this disorder requires the availability of abundant food, whereas people can starve themselves, as in anorexia nervosa, whether or not food is abundant.

SUMMING UP

- Bulimia nervosa is characterized by uncontrolled bingeing, followed by behaviors designed to prevent weight gain from the binges.
- People with the purging type use self-induced vomiting, diuretics, or laxatives to prevent weight gain.
- People with the nonpurging type use fasting and exercise to prevent weight gain.
- The definition of a binge has been controversial, but the DSM-IV-TR specifies that it must involve the consumption of an unusually large amount of food in a short time, as well as a sense of lack of control.
- The prevalence of the full syndrome of bulimia nervosa is estimated to be between 0.5 and 3 percent. It is much more common in women than in men.
- The onset of bulimia nervosa is most often in adolescence, and its course, if left untreated, is unclear.
- Although people with bulimia nervosa do not tend to be severely underweight, there are a variety of possible medical complications of the disorder.

BINGE-EATING DISORDER

The DSM-IV-TR mentions one further eating disorder, called binge-eating disorder. This disorder resembles bulimia nervosa in many ways, except that a person with binge-eating disorder does not regularly engage in purging, fasting, or excessive exercise to compensate for binges. Binge-eating disorder is not one of the officially recognized forms of eating disorders in the DSM-IV-TR largely because its authors felt that there has been too little research on this disorder to sanction the diagnosis. Rather, the diagnostic criteria for binge-eating disorder were placed in the appendix of the DSM-IV-TR for further study.

People with binge-eating disorder may eat continuously throughout the day, with no planned mealtimes. Others engage in discrete binges on large amounts of food, often in response to stress and feelings of anxiety or depression. They may eat very rapidly and be almost in a daze as they eat, as the man in the following case study describes.

CASE STUDY

"The day after New Year's Day I got my check cashed. I usually eat to celebrate the occasion, so I knew it might happen. On the way to the bank I steeled myself against it. I kept reminding myself of the treatment and about my New Year's resolution about dieting. . . .

"Then I got the check cashed. And I kept out a hundred. And everything just seemed to go blank. I don't know what it was. All of my good intentions just seemed to fade away. They just didn't seem to mean anything anymore. I just said, 'What the hell,' and started eating, and what I did then was an absolute sin."

He described starting in a grocery store where he bought a cake, several pieces of pie, and boxes of cookies. Then he drove through heavy midtown traffic with one hand, pulling food out of the bag with the other hand and eating as fast as he could. After consuming all of his groceries, he set out on a furtive round of restaurants, staying only a short time in each and eating only small amounts. Although in constant dread of discovery, he had no idea what "sin" he felt he was committing. He knew only that it was not pleasurable. "I didn't en-

(continued)

joy it at all. It just happened. It's like a part of me just blacked out. And when that happened there was nothing there except the food and me, all alone." Finally he went into a delicatessen, bought another $20 worth of food and drove home, eating all the way, "until my gut ached." (Stunkard, 1993, pp. 20–21)

People with binge-eating disorder are often significantly overweight and say they are disgusted with their bodies and ashamed of their bingeing. They typically have histories of frequent dieting, memberships in weight-control programs, and family obesity (Fairburn et al., 1997). As many as 30 percent of people currently in weight-loss programs may have binge-eating disorder. In contrast, approximately 1 to 3 percent of the general population has the disorder (Striegel-Moore et al., 2003; Striegel-Moore & Franko, 2003).

As with anorexia and bulimia nervosa, binge-eating disorder is more common in women than in men, in both the general community and among people in weight-loss programs. The symptom of binge-eating is more common in African American women than European American women, but at least one study found that European American women are more likely than African American women to be diagnosed with the full syndrome of binge-eating disorder (Striegel-Moore, Dohm, et al., 2003; Striegel-Moore & Franko, 2003). People with binge-eating disorder have high rates of depression and anxiety and possibly more alcohol abuse and personality disorders than those without binge-eating disorder (Castonguay, Eldredge, & Agras, 1995; Telch & Stice, 1998). One study found that 18 percent of a group of 48 women with binge-eating disorder, most of whom had sought no treatment, still had an eating disorder five years later, usually binge-eating disorder (Fairburn et al., 2000). This suggests that the course of this disorder is more favorable than that of anorexia nervosa or bulimia nervosa, but a subset of people with this disorder do have it chronically.

SUMMING UP

- Binge-eating disorder is a provisional diagnosis in the DSM-IV-TR. It is characterized by binge eating in the absence of behaviors designed to prevent weight gain.
- Binge eating is common, perhaps more so among African Americans than among European Americans, but binge-eating disorder affects only about 2 percent of the population.

- Women are more likely than men to develop binge-eating disorder.

UNDERSTANDING EATING DISORDERS

A number of biological, sociocultural, and psychological factors have been implicated in the development of the eating disorders (see the Concept Overview in Table 15.4). It is likely that it takes an accumulation of several of these factors for any individual to develop an eating disorder. In this section, we consider each of these factors, as well as the evidence regarding each factor.

Biological Theories

As is the case with most psychological disorders, anorexia and bulimia nervosa tend to run in families (Bulik, 2004). There are a few large, population-based twin studies of anorexia nervosa, and they have found that 48 to 74 percent of the variability in the disorder is due to genetic factors (Klump et al., 2001; Kortegaard et al., 2001; Wade et al., 2000). Twin studies of bulimia nervosa put the heritability

TABLE 15.4 Concept Overview

Contributors to the Eating Disorders

A number of biological, sociocultural, and psychological factors have been said to contribute to the eating disorders.

Biological Factors

Genetic predisposition to eating disorders
Predisposition to depression
Dysregulation of hypothalamus
Serotonin imbalances

Sociocultural and Psychological Factors

Pressures to be thin
Cultural norms of attractiveness
Food used as a way of coping with negative emotions
Overconcern with others' opinions
Rigid, dichotomous thinking style, perfectionism
Family dynamics characterized by overcontrolling parents who do not allow the expression of emotion
History of sexual abuse

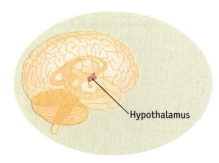

The hypothalamus plays a central role in regulating eating and is implicated in disordered eating behavior in bulimia and anorexia.

of this disorder at 59 to 83 percent (Bulik, Sullivan, & Kendler, 1998; Wade et al., 1999).

Much of the current research on the biological causes of bulimia and anorexia focuses on the bodily systems that regulate appetite, hunger, satiety, the initiation of eating, and the cessation of eating. The *hypothalamus* plays a central role in regulating eating. It receives messages about the body's recent food consumption and nutrient level and sends messages to cease eating when the body's nutritional needs have been met. These messages are carried by a variety of neurotransmitters, including norepinephrine, serotonin, and dopamine, and a number of hormones, such as cortisol and insulin. Disordered eating behavior might be caused by imbalances in or the dysregulation of any of the neurochemicals involved in this system or by structural or functional problems in the hypothalamus. For example, if this system were disrupted, it could cause the individual to have trouble detecting hunger accurately or to stop eating when full, which are both characteristics of people with eating disorders.

There is evidence that people with eating disorders have disruptions in the hypothalamus (Study Group on Anorexia Nervosa, 1995). People with anorexia nervosa show lowered functioning of the hypothalamus and abnormalities in the levels or regulation of several hormones important to the functioning of the hypothalamus, including serotonin and dopamine (Brambilla et al., 2001; Frank et al., 2001). It is unclear whether these disruptions are causes or consequences of the self-starvation of anorexia. Some studies find that people with anorexia continue to show abnormalities in hypothalamic and hormonal functioning and in neurotransmitter levels after they gain some weight, whereas other studies show that these abnormalities disappear with weight gain (Polivy & Herman, 2002).

Many people with bulimia show abnormalities in the neurotransmitter serotonin (Franko et al., 2004; Wurtman, 1987; Wurtman & Wurtman, 1984). Deficiencies in serotonin might lead the body to crave carbohydrates, and people with bulimia often binge on high-carbohydrate foods. They may then take up self-induced vomiting or other types of purges in order to avoid gaining weight from eating carbohydrates.

Thus, a number of biological abnormalities are associated with anorexia nervosa and bulimia nervosa. These abnormalities could contribute to disordered eating behavior by causing the body to crave certain foods or by making it difficult for a person to read the body's signals of hunger and fullness. Just why people with eating disorders also develop the distorted body images and other cognitive and emotional problems seen in the eating disorders is not clear. In addition, many of the biological abnormalities seen in the eating disorders might be the consequences, rather than the causes, of the disorders.

Sociocultural and Psychological Factors

Societal pressures to be thin and attractive probably play a role in the eating disorders, although many people who are exposed to these pressures do not develop eating disorders. Certain psychological factors may also need to come into play for an eating disorder to develop.

Societal Pressures and Cultural Norms

Psychologists have linked the historical and cross-cultural differences in the prevalence of eating disorders to differences in the standards of beauty for women at different historical times and in different cultures (Garner & Garfinkel, 1980; McCarthy, 1990; Sobal & Stunkard, 1989). In addition, certain groups within a culture, such as athletes, may have standards for appearance that put them at greater risk for eating disorders.

Standards of Beauty The ideal shape for women in the United States and Europe has become thinner over the past 45 years. Models in fashion magazines, winners of the Miss America and Miss Universe pageants, and Barbie dolls—all icons of beauty for women—have been getting thinner (Garner & Garfinkel, 1980; Keel & Klump, 2003; Wiseman et al., 1992) (see Figure 15.4). Indeed, the average model in a fashion magazine these days is pencil thin, with a figure that is physically unattainable by most adult women.

Both anorexia nervosa and bulimia nervosa are much more common in females than in males. This gender difference has largely been attributed to the fact that thinness is more valued and encouraged in females than in males. For example, studies of popular women's and men's magazines find 10 times more diet articles in women's magazines than in men's magazines (Andersen & DiDomenico, 1992; Nemeroff et al., 1994). Half of all women report frequent dissatisfaction with their appearance, whereas fewer than one-third of men report the same (Thompson & Stice, 2001). In recent years, women's magazines have moved somewhat away

| FIGURE 15.4 | **Our Changing Beauty Standards.** In the period from 1959 to 1978, the average weight of women who were *Playboy* centerfolds or who won the Miss America contest became lower and lower, relative to what would be expected for women of their height. |

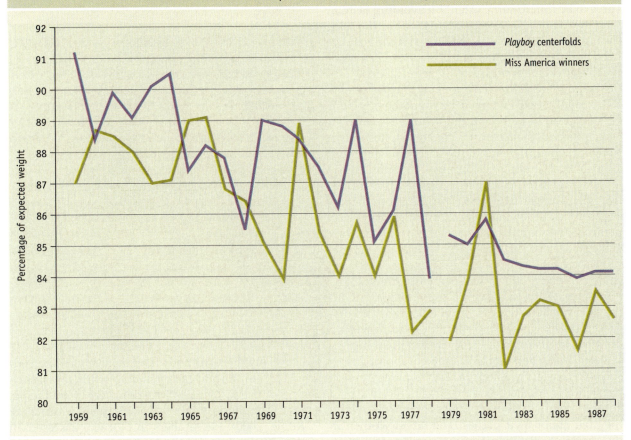

Source: From C. V. Wiseman, et al., "Cultural Expectations of Thinness in Women: An Update" in *International Journal of Eating Disorders*, 11. Copyright © 1992 John Wiley & Sons, Inc.

from articles solely on dieting toward articles on fitness and exercise (Nemeroff et al., 1994). Unfortunately, however, women's motivations for exercise are still more likely to be for weight control than are men's motivations, and exercising for weight control is more likely to contribute to eating-disordered behavior than is exercising for health (McDonald & Thompson, 1992).

The thin-ideal promoted in women's magazines seems to have an effect on women's attitudes toward themselves. Stice and Shaw (1994) showed young women images from fashion magazines of ultra-thin models, or images from magazines that didn't portray thin models, for a three-minute period (Stice & Shaw, 1994). These women who saw the fashion magazine images experienced increases in depression, shame, guilt, stress, insecurity, and body dissatisfaction, compared with the women exposed to the other images. In turn, those women who had the most increases in negative mood and body dissatisfaction, and who most strongly sub-

scribed to the thin-ideal for women, showed increases in the symptoms of bulimia. If just three minutes of exposure to these fashion models can have such effects, think what the constant exposure that young women experience does to their self-image and well-being.

Stice and colleagues looked at what chronic exposure to the thin-ideal in fashion magazines actually does to adolescent girls' mental health (Stice, Spangler, & Agras, 2001). They randomly gave 219 girls, ages 13 to 17, a 15-month subscription to a leading fashion magazine or no subscription, then followed them over time. They found that the girls who already felt pressured to be thin and dissatisfied with their bodies became more depressed over time if they had been given the subscription to the fashion magazine than if they had not. In addition, the girls who started the study with little social support from family members and friends became more dissatisfied with their bodies, dieted more, and showed more bulimic symptoms if they were given the fashion magazine subscription than if they were not.

Adolescent girls and women can avoid pressures to be thin to some extent by avoiding fashion magazines and other media depictions of the thin-ideal. We can't completely avoid our friends, however, and they are sometimes the worst carriers of the thin-ideal message. In another study, Stice, Maxfield, and Wells (2003) had women college students talk to another college woman whom they thought was just another student, but who was really an accomplice in their study. This accomplice was a thin, attractive 19-year-old woman who was 5 foot 10 inches tall and weighed only 127 pounds (they also had a second accomplice who was 20 years old, 5 foot 9 inches, and 126 pounds). First, both the target woman student and the accomplice watched a neutral film about a seascape, supposedly so they could rate how they felt about the film. But, after the film, the accomplice launched into a prescripted conversation with the target woman student. In the *pressure condition,* the accomplice complained about how dissatisfied she was with her weight and discussed the extreme exercise routine and restrictive diet she was using to reduce her weight. In the *neutral condition,* the accomplice talked about classes she was currently taking and her plans for the weekend. Then, the experimenter entered the room and both women filled out questionnaires on how they felt about their bodies. The target women in the pressure condition became significantly more dissatisfied with their own bodies after talking with the thin accomplice about her own weight concerns. In contrast, the women in the neutral condition did not become more dissatisfied with their bodies after talking with the same woman about matters unrelated to weight or dieting.

Of course, not all women accept the thin-ideal for themselves. Table 15.5 lists some items from questionnaires designed to assess the internalization of the thin-ideal. Longitudinal studies have shown that women who internalize the thin-ideal are more likely to develop bulimic symptoms, as well as to show increases in dieting and body dissatisfaction over time (Stice, 2003; Thompson & Stice, 2001). Experimental studies have shown that interventions designed to get women to argue against the thin-ideal and recognize pressures from the media to subscribe to this ideal result in reductions in women's acceptance of this ideal and decreases in body dissatisfaction, dieting, and bulimic pathology (Stice et al., 2000; Stice, Chase, Stormer, et al., 2001; Stormer & Thompson, 1998).

Athletes and Eating Disorders One group that appears to be at increased risk for unhealthy eating habits and full-blown eating disorders is athletes,

TABLE 15.5 Items from Questionnaires Measuring Internalization of the Thin-Ideal

These are some items assessing women's internalization of the thin-ideal promoted in today's media.

I would like my body to look like the women that appear in TV shows and movies.

I wish I looked like the women pictured in magazines that model underwear.

Music videos that show women who are in good physical shape make me wish that I were in better physical shape.

Slender women are more attractive.

Women with toned bodies are more attractive.

Women with long legs are more attractive.

Sources: Stice & Agras, 1998; Thompson et al., 1999.

especially those in sports in which weight is considered an important factor in competitiveness, such as gymnastics, ice skating, dancing, horse racing, wrestling, and bodybuilding (Smolak, Murnen, & Ruble, 2000). Researchers in Norway assessed all the 522 elite female athletes between the ages of 12 and 35 in that country for the presence of eating disorders. They found that those in sports classified as "aesthetic" or "weight-dependent," including diving, figure skating, gymnastics, dance, judo, karate, and wrestling, were most likely to have anorexia or bulimia nervosa (Sundgot-Borgen, 1994) (see Table 15.6). When the women athletes with eating disorders were asked about the triggers for their eating disorders, many said they felt that the physical changes of puberty came too early for them and decreased their competitive edge. They had started dieting severely to try to maintain their prepubescent figures. The case of Heidi, described by her therapist, illustrates several of these triggers (adapted from Pipher, 1994, pp. 165–168):

Heidi arrived in my office after gymnastics practice. Blond and pretty, she was dressed in a shiny red and white warm-up suit. We talked about gymnastics, which Heidi had been involved in since she was six. At that time, she was selected to train with the university coaches. Now she trained four hours a day, six
(continued)

TABLE 15.6 Rates of Eating Disorders in Elite Women Athletes

Sports that emphasize weight are especially likely to encourage eating disorders.

Sport	Percentage with an Eating Disorder
Aesthetic sports (e.g., figure skating, gymnastics)	35
Weight-dependent sports (e.g., judo, wrestling)	29
Endurance sports (e.g., cycling, running, swimming)	20
Technical sports (e.g., golf, high jumping)	14
Ball game sports (e.g., volleyball, soccer)	12

Source: Data from Sundgot-Borgen, 1994.

CASE STUDY

days a week. She didn't expect to make an Olympic team, but she anticipated a scholarship to a Big-8 school.

Heidi glowed when she talked about gymnastics, but I noticed her eyes were red and she had a small scar on the index finger of her right hand. (When a hand is repeatedly stuck down the throat, it can be scarred by the acids in the mouth.) I wasn't surprised when she said she was coming in for help with bulimia.

Heidi said, "I've had this problem for two years, but lately it's affecting my gymnastics. I am too weak, particularly on the vault, which requires strength. It's hard to concentrate."

"I blame my training for my eating disorder," Heidi continued. "Our coach has weekly weigh-ins where we count each others' ribs. If they are hard to count we're in trouble."

I clucked in disapproval. Heidi explained that since puberty she had had trouble keeping her weight down. After meals, she was nervous that she'd eaten too much. She counted calories; she was hungry but afraid to eat. In class she pinched the fat on her side and freaked out. The first time she vomited after a gymnastics meet. Coach took her and the

other gymnasts to a steak house. Heidi ordered a double cheeseburger and onion rings. After she ate, she obsessed about the weigh-in the next day, so she decided, just this once, to get rid of her meal. She slipped into the restaurant bathroom and threw up.

She blushed. "It was harder than you would think. My body resisted, but I was able to do it. It was so gross that I thought, 'I'll never do that again,' but a week later I did. At first it was weekly, then twice a week. Now it's almost every day. My dentist said that acid is eating away the enamel of my teeth."

Bodybuilding is an increasingly popular sport, but bodybuilders routinely have substantial weight fluctuations as they try to shape their bodies for competition and then binge in the off-seasons. For example, one study compared male bodybuilders with men with diagnosed eating disorders. This study found that the bodybuilders had a pattern of eating and exercising as obsessive as that of the men with eating disorders, but with a focus on gaining muscle, rather than losing fat (Mangweth et al., 2001). In another study of male bodybuilders, 46 percent reported bingeing after most competitions, and 85 percent reported gaining significant weight (an average of 15 pounds) in the off-season. Then, they dieted to prepare for competition, losing an average of 14 pounds (Anderson et al., 1995). In a parallel study of female bodybuilders and weight lifters, 42 percent

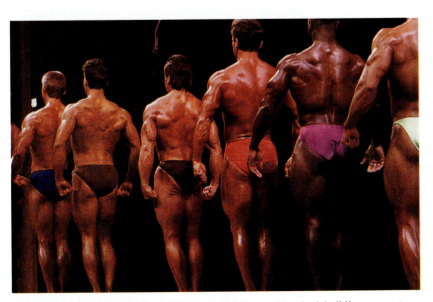

Sports that require certain body shapes or weights, such as bodybuilding, seem to breed eating disorders.

reported having been anorexic at sometime in their lives, 67 percent were terrified of being fat, and 58 percent were obsessed with food (Anderson et al., 1995). A study of female weightlifters found that they often abused ephedrine, a stimulant that helps reduce body fat, particularly if they had symptoms of an eating disorder (Gruber & Pope, 1998).

Amateur athletics may actually protect some young women against eating disorders. Smolak et al. (2000) reviewed studies of the relationship between athletics and eating problems in women. They concluded that, although elite athletes do show increased rates of eating disorders, nonelite athletes, particularly those participating in high school sports in which thinness is not emphasized, show lower rates of eating problems than nonathletes.

Socioeconomics and Ethnicity In the United States and Europe, there may be differences among socioeconomic and ethnic groups in the prevalence of eating disorders. Some studies find that anorexia and bulimia nervosa are more prevalent among the upper and middle classes than among lower socioeconomic classes. This association between socioeconomic status and these eating disorders is found among Caucasians, African Americans, and Hispanics. Perhaps because African Americans and Hispanics are more likely than Caucasians to be in lower socioeconomic groups, the overall rates of anorexia and bulimia are lower in African Americans and Hispanics than in Caucasians (Mulholland & Mintz, 2001; Pate et al., 1992). Other researchers have argued that the rate of these eating disorders is lower in African Americans and Hispanics because they are less likely to accept the thin-ideal promoted in Caucasian culture (Osvold & Sodowsky, 1993).

Bingeing and Emotion Regulation

The bingeing of eating disorders sometimes serves as a maladaptive strategy for dealing with painful emotions, as Princess Diana described her own binge eating (Fairburn et al., 1995; McCarthy, 1990). Depressive symptoms and negative affect have been found to predict the future onset or exacerbation of bulimic symptoms (Cooley & Toray, 2001; Field et al., 1999; Killen et al., 1996; Stice, Burton, & Shaw, 2004; Stice, Presnell, & Spangler, 2002), as well as relapse into binge eating among obese people (Byrne et al., 2003). For example, Stice and colleagues (2002) followed a group of adolescent girls over two years. They found that the girls who engaged in emotional eating—eating when they felt distressed in an attempt to feel bet-

ter—were significantly more likely to develop chronic binge eating over the two years.

In addition, Stice and colleagues (2002) have identified two subtypes of disordered eating patterns involving binge eating. One subtype is connected to excessive attempts at losing weight. Women with this *dieting subtype* are greatly concerned about their body shapes and sizes, and they try their best to maintain a strict, low-calorie diet but frequently fall off the wagon and engage in binge eating. They then use vomiting or exercise to try to purge themselves of the food or the weight it puts on their bodies. The other subtype is the *depressive subtype*. These women are also concerned about weight and body size but are plagued by feelings of depression and low self-esteem; they often eat to quell these feelings.

Women with the depressive subtype of disordered eating patterns suffer even greater social and psychological consequences over time than women with the dieting subtype of disordered eating (Stice et al., 2002). They have more difficulties in their relationships with family and friends; are more likely to suffer significant psychiatric disorders, such as anxiety disorders; and are less likely to respond well to treatment. One long-term study found that, over a period of five years, women with the depressive subtype were more likely to be diagnosed with major depression or an anxiety disorder and were more likely to continue to engage in severe binge eating, compared with women who had the dieting subtype (Stice & Fairburn, 2003). Indeed, 80 percent of the women with the depressive subtype developed a full-blown major depression over that five years.

Cognitive Models of Eating Disorders

Several types of negative cognitions are associated with an increased risk for eating disorders, particularly bulimia nervosa in women. Fairburn (1997) proposed a cognitive model of bulimia nervosa that suggests that the overvaluation of appearance is of primary importance in the development of the disorder. According to Fairburn (1997), people who consider their body shape one of the most important aspects of their self-evaluation, and who believe that achieving thinness will bring social and psychological benefits, will engage in excessive dieting and purging behaviors to reduce their weight. In line with Fairburn's model, a meta-analysis of relevant studies found that women who internalize the thin-ideal for women and are dissatisfied with their own bodies show greater eating pathology (Stice, 2002).

Vohs and colleagues (1999, 2001) have suggested that disordered eating is especially likely to result when body dissatisfaction is combined with perfectionism and low self-esteem. Women who are dissatisfied with their bodies and have a deep need to be perfect, including to have a perfect body, but who have low self-esteem will engage in maladaptive strategies to control their weight, including excessive dieting and purging. Vohs and colleagues found that young women with all three of these cognitive characteristics were more likely to develop bulimic symptoms than women with just one or two of these characteristics.

Other research confirms that people with eating disorders are more concerned with the opinions of others, are more conforming to others' wishes, and are more rigid in their evaluations of themselves and others than are other people (Polivy & Herman, 2002; Striegel-Moore, Silberstein, & Rodin, 1993). Studies of the cognitions of people with eating disorders show that they have a dichotomous thinking style, in which everything is either all good or all bad. For example, if they eat one cookie, they may think that they have blown their diets and might as well eat the whole box of cookies. They will say they cannot break their rigid eating routines or they will completely lose control over their eating. They obsess over their eating routines and plan their days down to the smallest detail around these routines.

The cognitions of women with eating disorders may be organized around issues of body size and control even at a nonconscious level. Women with and without significant symptoms of bulimia were shown a variety of pictures of other women. The women in these pictures varied in terms of both their body size and the emotions shown on their faces, although the participants were not told that these were the critical dimensions along which the photos varied. Women with bulimic symptoms were more likely than women without bulimic symptoms to attend to information about body size than information about facial emotion, as well as to classify the photos on the basis of body size rather than facial emotion (Viken et al., 2002). These results suggest that women who have bulimic symptoms organize their perceptions of the world around body size, even at an implicit level, more than women who do not have significant bulimic symptoms.

Family Dynamics

Hilde Bruch (1973, 1982) is a pioneer in the psychoanalytic study of eating disorders. Her theory is most concerned with girls who develop anorexia nervosa, although it has also been used to understand the development of bulimia nervosa and binge-eating disorder. Bruch noted that anorexia nervosa often occurs in girls who have been unusually "good girls," high achievers, dutiful and compliant daughters who are always trying to please their parents and others by being "perfect." These girls tend to have parents who are overinvested in their daughters' compliance and achievements, who are overcontrolling, and who will not allow the expression of feelings, especially negative feelings.

Another pioneer in theorizing about anorexia, Salvador Minuchin, describes the families of people with anorexia as **enmeshed families** (Minuchin et al., 1978). There is extreme interdependence and intensity in the family interactions, so that the boundaries between the identities of individual family members are weak and easily crossed. This might describe the family life of Princess Diana when she was part of the Royal Family.

Bruch argues that, throughout their daughters' lives, these parents are ineffective and inappropriate in their parenting, responding primarily to the parents' own schedules and needs, rather than to their daughters' needs for food or comfort (Bruch, 1973). As a result, the daughters do not learn to identify and accept their own feelings and desires. Instead, they learn to monitor closely the needs and desires of others and to comply with others' demands, as we can see in the case of Rachel and her family:

CASE STUDY

Rachel is a 16-year-old with anorexia nervosa. Her parents are highly educated and very successful, having spent most of their careers in the diplomatic corps. Rachel, her two brothers, and her parents are "very close, as are many families in the diplomatic corps, because we move so much," although the daily care of the children has always been left to nannies. The children had to follow strict rules for appropriate conduct, both in the home and outside. These rules were partly driven by the requirements of the families of diplomats to "be on their best behavior" in their host country and partly driven by Rachel's parents' very conservative religious beliefs. Rachel, as the only daughter in the family, always had to behave as "a proper lady" to counteract the stereotype of American girls as brash and sexually promiscuous. All the children were required to act mature beyond their years, controlling any emotional outbursts, taking defeats and disappointments without complaint, and happily picking up and moving every couple of years when their parents were reassigned to another country.

Rachel's anorexic behaviors began when her parents announced they were leaving the diplomatic corps to return to the United States. Rachel had grown very fond of their last post in Europe, because she had finally found a group of friends that she liked *and* whom her parents approved of, and she liked her school. She had always done well in school but often had hated the harshly strict schoolteachers. In her present school, she felt accepted by her teachers as well as challenged by the work. When Rachel told her parents she would like to finish her last year of high school in this school rather than go to the United States with them, they flatly refused to even consider it. Rachel tried to talk with her parents, suggesting she stay with the family of one of her friends, who was willing to have her, but her parents cut her off and told her they would not discuss the idea further. Rachel became sullen and withdrawn and stopped eating shortly after the family arrived in the United States.

As a result of such family dynamics, girls with anorexia have fundamental deficits in their senses of self and identities. They experience themselves as always acting in response to others, rather than in response to their own wishes and needs. They do not accurately identify their own feelings or desires and, thus, do not cope appropriately with distress. They do not even accurately identify bodily sensations, such as hunger, and this may contribute greatly to their ability to starve themselves for long periods of time.

Why do eating disorders often develop in adolescence? One of the important tasks of adolescence is separation and individuation from one's family. Girls from these families deeply fear separation, because they have not developed the ability to act and think independently of their families. They also fear involvement with peers, especially sexual involvement, because they do not understand their feelings or trust their judgment, yet they recognize at some level their need to separate from their families and take their place among their peers. They harbor rage against their parents for their overcontrol. They become angry, negativistic, defiant, and distrustful. They also discover that controlling their food intake both gives them a sense of control over their lives and elicits concern from their parents. The rigid control of their bodies provides a sense of power over the self and the family that the girls have never had before. It also provides a way of avoiding peer relationships—the girl dons the persona of someone with anorexia—sickly, distant, untouchable, and superior in her self-control. Other psychoanalytic theorists have taken this argument further to suggest that a girl with anorexia is primarily avoiding sexual maturity and relationships by stopping pubertal maturation by self-starvation (Lerner, 1986).

Why would girls, but not boys, in such families develop eating disorders? It may be because, in general, parents tend to appreciate the need for boys to separate from the family in adolescence and give them the freedom to separate. Especially in these enmeshed families, parents are terrified of their girls' independence. The mothers of these girls may need their daughters to remain dependent because their own identities are tied too closely to their daughters (Bruch, 1973; Palazzoli, 1974). Thus, there are tremendous pressures on girls to remain enmeshed with their families, but boys have more opportunity to break free and build their own identities.

Research has confirmed that the families of girls with eating disorders have high levels of conflict, that the expression of negative emotions is discouraged in the families, and that control and perfectionism are key family themes (Polivy & Herman, 2002). These negative characteristics are not specific to the families of girls with eating disorders, however. They are also prevalent in the families of children with depression, anxiety disorders, and several other forms of psychopathology. What may distinguish families in which eating disorders develop is that the mothers in these families believe their daughters should lose more weight, are critical of overweight in their daughters, and are themselves more likely to have disordered eating patterns (Hill & Franklin, 1998). In addition, a lack of awareness of their own bodily sensations may allow some girls in these families to ignore even the most severe hunger pangs (Leon et al., 1995). Girls who come from these troubled families but are not able to ignore their hunger completely may fall into a binge/purge form of anorexia nervosa or into bulimia nervosa.

Unfortunately, the majority of studies of the families and personality characteristics of people with anorexia or bulimia have compared people who already have eating disorders with those who do not (Polivy & Herman, 2002). As a result, it is not known to what extent these family and personality characteristics are causes of anorexia or bulimia. The controlling nature of parents' behaviors toward their children may be a consequence as well as a cause of the disorder—parents are exerting control to try to save their children's lives.

Similarly, many of the personality characteristics of people with eating disorders may be consequences as well as causes of the disorder. Studies of healthy people who engage in self-starvation as part of an experiment show that depression, anxiety, rigidity, obsessiveness, irritability, concrete thinking, and social withdrawal appear after a few weeks of self-starvation (Keys et al., 1950). The success of psychological therapies for eating disorders provides more evidence that psychological factors are implicated in the development or at least the maintenance of these disorders.

A controversial theory that has gained much attention is that the eating disorders often result from experiences of sexual abuse. One reason that this theory has been controversial is that it stems from clinical reports of high rates of sexual abuse among persons seeking therapy for eating disorders rather than from controlled studies. Another reason is that it has led some therapists to urge their clients with eating disorders to search through their pasts for memories of childhood sexual abuse and then take action against their abusers as part of their therapy. Proponents of this theory argue that survivors of sexual abuse develop eating disorders as a symbol of self-loathing and a way of making themselves unattractive in an attempt to prevent further sexual abuse.

Several careful studies have been done to examine the rates of sexual abuse among women and men with eating disorders and to compare these rates with those of people with other psychological disorders and people with no disorders (see the review by Polivy & Herman, 2002; also Bulik et al., 1997; Kinzl et al., 1994; Pope & Hudson, 1992; Rorty, Yager, & Rossotto, 1994; Welch & Fairburn, 1994). These studies have found that, although people with eating disorders tend to have higher rates of sexual abuse than people with no psychological disorders, they do not tend to have higher rates of sexual abuse than do people with other psychological disorders, such as depression or anxiety. In other words, sexual abuse seems to be a general risk factor for psychological problems, including eating disorders, depression, and anxiety, rather than a specific risk factor for eating disorders.

SUMMING UP

- There is evidence that tendencies toward both anorexia nervosa and bulimia nervosa are heritable.

- Eating disorders may be tied to dysfunction in the hypothalamus, a part of the brain that helps regulate eating behavior.

- Some studies show abnormalities in levels of the neurotransmitters serotonin and norepinephrine in people with eating disorders.

- Cultural and societal norms regarding beauty may play a role in the eating disorders. Eating disorders are more common in groups that consider extreme thinness attractive than in groups that consider a heavier weight attractive.

- Eating disorders develop as a means of gaining some control over or of coping with negative emotions. In addition, people with eating disorders tend to show rigid, dichotomous thinking.

- People who develop eating disorders tend to come from families that are overcontrolling and perfectionistic but that discourage the expression of negative emotions.

- People who are so unaware of their own bodily sensations that they can starve themselves may develop anorexia nervosa. People who remain aware of their bodily sensations and cannot starve themselves but who are prone to anxiety and impulsivity may develop binge-eating disorder or bulimia nervosa.

- Girls may be more likely than boys to develop eating disorders in adolescence because girls are not given as much freedom as boys to develop independence and their own identities.

- People with eating disorders are more likely than people without eating disorders to have a history of sexual abuse, but a history of sexual abuse is also common among people with several other disorders.

TREATMENTS FOR EATING DISORDERS

In this section, we discuss several psychotherapies and biological treatments that have proven successful in the treatment of anorexia, of bulimia, or both (see the Concept Overview in Table 15.7). There are several empirical studies of the effectiveness of treatments for bulimia nervosa and an increasing number for binge-eating disorder. The number of studies for anorexia nervosa is low, and many of these studies are plagued by small sample sizes and other methodological problems (Wilson, 2005).

Psychotherapy for Anorexia Nervosa

It can be very difficult to engage people who have anorexia nervosa in psychotherapy. Because they often feel that others try to control them and that they must maintain absolute control over their own behaviors, they can be extremely resistant to

---

TABLE 15.7　Concept Overview

Treatments for Eating Disorders

A number of treatments for the eating disorders have been developed.

Treatment	Description
Anorexia Nervosa	
1. Hospitalization and refeeding	1. Hospitalize the patient and force him or her to ingest food to prevent death from starvation.
2. Behavior therapy	2. Make rewards contingent upon eating. Teach relaxation techniques.
3. Techniques to help the patient accept and value his or her emotions	3. Use cognitive or supportive-expressive techniques to help the patient explore the emotions and issues underlying behavior.
4. Family therapy	4. Raise the family's concern about anorexic behavior. Confront the family's tendency to be overcontrolling and to have excessive expectations.
Bulimia Nervosa	
1. Cognitive-behavioral therapy	1. Teach the client to recognize the cognitions around eating and to confront the maladaptive cognitions. Introduce "forbidden foods" and regular diet and help the client confront irrational cognitions about these.
2. Interpersonal therapy	2. Help the client identify interpersonal problems associated with bulimic behaviors, such as problems in a marriage, and deal with these problems more effectively.
3. Supportive-expressive psychodynamic therapy	3. Provide support and encouragement for the client's expression of feelings about problems associated with bulimia in a nondirective manner.
4. Tricyclic antidepressants and selective serotonin reuptake inhibitors.	4. Help reduce impulsive eating and negative emotions that drive bulimic behaviors.

therapists' attempts to change their behaviors and attitudes. Regardless of the type of psychotherapy a therapist uses with client with anorexia, much work must be done to win the client's trust and participation in the therapy and to maintain this trust and participation as the client begins to regain that dreaded weight.

Winning the trust of someone with anorexia can be especially difficult if the therapist is forced to hospitalize her because she has lost so much weight that her life is in danger, yet hospitalization and forced refeeding are often necessary to save her life. Because people with anorexia nervosa typically do not seek treatment themselves, they often do not come to the attention of therapists until they are so emaciated and malnourished that they have a medical crisis, such as cardiac problems, or their families fear for their lives. The first job of the therapist is to help save the individual's life. Because a person with anorexia will not eat voluntarily, this may mean hospitalizing her and feeding her intravenously. During the hospitalization, the therapist begins the work of engaging the client in facing and solving the psychological issues causing her to starve herself.

Individual Therapy

Individual therapy with people with anorexia often focuses on their inability to recognize and trust their own feelings, with the goal of building their self-awareness and independence from others (Bruch, 1973). This can be very difficult, because many clients with anorexia are resistant to therapy and suspicious of therapists, whom they think are just other people trying to control their lives. Others may be engaged in therapy but look to therapists to define their feelings for them, just as their parents have done for years. Therapists must convey to clients that their feelings are their own, valuable and legitimate, and the proper focus of attention in therapy. Only when clients can learn to read their feelings accurately will they also read their sensations of hunger and fullness accurately and be able to respond to them.

Behavior therapies are often used in the treatment of anorexia. Rewards are made contingent upon the person's gaining weight. If the client is hospitalized, certain privileges in the hospital are used as rewards, such as watching television, going outside the hospital, or receiving visitors. The client may also be taught relaxation techniques, which she can use as she becomes extremely anxious about ingesting food. Some studies suggest that the majority of patients benefit from behavior therapies, gaining weight to within 15 percent of normal body weight (Agras, 1987; Fairburn, 2005).

The relapse rate with behavior therapies alone is very high, however. Most patients return to their anorexic eating patterns soon after therapy ends or they are released from the hospital, unless they are engaged in other therapies that confront some of the emotional issues accompanying their anorexia.

Family Therapy

In *family systems therapy*, the person with anorexia and her family are treated as a unit (Minuchin et al., 1978). With some families, therapists must first raise the parents' level of anxiety about their children's eating disorders, because the parents have been implicitly or explicitly supporting the children's avoidance of food. Therapists will identify the patterns in the families' interactions that are contributing to their children's sense of being controlled, such as being overprotective while not allowing their children the right to express their own needs and feelings. Parents' unreasonable expectations for their children are confronted, and families are helped to develop healthy ways of expressing and resolving conflict between the members.

One study of 50 girls with anorexia and their families found that family therapy was successful with 86 percent of the cases (Minuchin et al., 1978). These successful girls had normal eating patterns and good relations at home and at school even 2½ years after treatment. This study focused on young girls (an average age of 14 years) who had shown anorexic symptoms for only a short time. Other studies suggest that girls with anorexia who have shown symptoms for much longer and who are older when they enter treatment are not as likely to benefit from family therapy (Dare et al., 1990).

Psychotherapy can help many people with anorexia, but it typically is a long process, often taking years for full recovery. Along the way, many people with anorexia who have an initial period of recovery, with a restoration of their weight to normal levels and their eating to healthy patterns, relapse into bulimic or anorexic behaviors. They often continue to have self-esteem deficits, family problems, and periods of depression and anxiety (Eckert et al., 1995). Most therapists combine techniques from different modes of therapy to meet the individual needs of people with anorexia. Even multimethod inpatient treatment programs do not consistently overcome anorexia, however, and graduates of these programs often continue to show severely restrained eating, perfectionism, and low body weight (Sullivan et al., 1998). The difficulty in helping people with anorexia recover fully may indicate the depth of the psychological issues driving self-starvation.

Taking Psychology Personally

Is There Such a Thing as a Healthy Diet?

There are negative health effects of being overweight, as well as some radical public health policies to reduce the amount of high-calorie food people consume. But why not simply propose that overweight people go on a diet?

One big problem with diets is that many people who develop eating disorders begin their dysfunctional patterns simply by going on diets (Abbott et al., 1998; Fairburn et al., 1997). Their diets may be innocuous at first, the type of diets most people think are safe and healthy, such as diets that are low in fats and high in fruits and vegetables. The diets may then become more and more extreme, perhaps because the simple and healthy diets do not achieve the desired weight loss.

Even moderate dieting can create a set of psychological and physiological conditions that make it difficult for an individual to maintain healthy eating patterns. Dieting creates chronic frustration, irritability, and emotional reactivity, which can make people more impulsive in their eating patterns (Federoff, Polivy, & Herman, 1997; Polivy & Herman, 2002). Dieting also changes people's ability to read their bodies' cues about hunger and satiety and people's attitudes toward food.

In a classic study, researchers compared the eating patterns of chronic dieters with the patterns of people not dieting. These people were taken into a laboratory and first asked to drink two milkshakes, one milkshake, or no milkshake. Then they were asked to try three flavors of ice cream and to rate the ice cream. The people who were not dieting decreased the amount of ice cream they ate as a function of how many milk-

shakes they had consumed before the rating task: The more milkshakes they had consumed during the "preload," the less ice cream they ate during the rating task. The chronic dieters, however, ate more ice cream during the rating task if they had consumed milkshakes during the preload. Those who had consumed two milkshakes during the preload ate even more ice cream during the rating task than did those who had consumed only one milkshake (Herman & Mack, 1975). Dieters develop beliefs that, if they violate their diets in any way, they might as well violate them totally and binge. In addition, dieting may enhance the physiological appeal of forbidden foods, making it difficult to resist them, especially after a taste or smell of them. People actually prefer sweet-tasting foods more when they are on diets than when they are not (Rodin, Slochower, & Fleming, 1977).

Another physiological explanation is that each person has a "natural" weight, which the body will fight to maintain, even if the person attempts to lose weight (Keesey, 1986). This natural weight is often referred to as a **set point.** The set point is determined in part by a person's metabolic rate, which is known to be heavily influenced by genetics (Wadden, Brownell, & Foster, 2002). When a person diets, his metabolic rate actually slows down, reducing his body's need for food. Unfortunately, the slowing of the metabolic rate also means that the body is not using up the food he consumes as quickly, making it more likely that this food will turn to fat, even though he may be eating much less food than usual. The implication of this *set*

In *Taking Psychology Personally: Is There Such a Thing as a Healthy Diet?*, we explore whether people who do need to diet can do so healthily.

Psychotherapy for Bulimia Nervosa

Treatment for bulimia nervosa is different from treatment for anorexia nervosa in many ways. First, by the time a person with anorexia nervosa obtains treatment, she may be near death, so extreme measures may need to be taken to save her life, such as hospitalization and forced refeeding. This is less likely to be the case for a person with bulimia nervosa. Second, the psychological issues of anorexia and bulimia can be different. For people with anorexia, these issues often have to do

with family dynamics, concerns about losing control, and a greatly distorted body image. For people with bulimia, psychological issues may involve learning to cope more effectively with emotions, learning to control binge and purge behaviors, and learning more adaptive ways to think about food and one's body.

Cognitive-behavioral therapy (CBT) has received the most empirical support for the effective treatment of bulimia nervosa (Whittal, Agras, & Gould, 1999; Wilson 2005). This therapy is based on the view that the extreme concerns about shape and weight are the central features of the disorder (Fairburn, 1997). The therapist teaches the client to monitor the cognitions that accompany her eating, particularly her binge episodes and her purging episodes (Wilson, Fairburn, & Agras, 1997). Then,

Taking Psychology Personally (*continued*)

point theory is that permanently changing weight may require some people to be on highly restrictive diets permanently.

People rarely stay on restrictive diets or keep their weight off after diets, however. In 1992, *Consumer Reports* did a survey of 95,000 of its readers who had tried to lose weight in the previous three years (*Consumer Reports,* 1993). One in five of these readers had joined commercial weight-loss programs, such as Weight Watchers. Interestingly, 25 percent of these people who had joined commercial weight-loss programs were not even moderately overweight at the start. On average, the people who had joined commercial weight-loss programs lost 10 to 20 percent of their starting weight, but they gained back half that weight in six months and two-thirds of the weight in two years. Only 25 percent of them kept the weight off for more than two years.

What's an overweight person to do, then? Exercise is one thing. Exercise may be the one way people can overcome the effects of dieting on metabolic rates and keep their weight off (Jeffery et al., 1998). People who exercise regularly increase their basal metabolic rate, so the body burns more calories, even when at rest. Thus, people who exercise may be able to maintain lower weights, even without continuing to restrict the amount of food they eat. In addition, several studies show that moderate exercise (the equivalent of 30 to 60 minutes per day of brisk walking, either in small spurts or all at once) is associated with substantial decreases in health risks and mortality, even among people with genetic predispositions to major diseases, people who smoke, and people who are overweight (Blair, Lewis, & Booth, 1989; Paffenberger et al., 1986). Thus, even if people do not lose weight through exercise, they may be improving their health and increasing their longevity.

Obesity experts also agree that decreasing the intake of fats and salt and increasing the intake of complex carbohydrates have positive health effects, even if they do not lead to weight loss. Most of us can reduce fats in our diet by switching from whole milk to skim milk and from high-fat meats to lower-fat meats and fish and by using low-fat dressings and spreads. We can increase complex carbohydrates by snacking on fruits, vegetables, and whole grains, rather than on fatty foods, such as potato chips and cookies.

Overweight people who want to lose weight might consider trying to achieve "reasonable" weight loss, rather than "ideal" weights (Wadden et al., 2002). The effects of biological factors, such as genetics, on weight may be strong enough that overweight people can never achieve the ideal weights they wish to chieve, at least not without chronic self-starvation. Many overweight people find themselves bingeing out of hunger or frustration or yo-yo dieting, both of which harm their self-esteem and possibly their health. If overweight people can adopt healthier diets, exercise regularly, and stabilize at weights that are reasonable, given their family backgrounds and their histories of weight loss and gain, both their physical and psychological health may improve.

---

the therapist helps the client confront these cognitions and develop more adaptive attitudes toward her weight and body shape. An interchange between a therapist and client might go like this:

VOICES

Therapist: What were you thinking just before you began to binge?

Client: I was thinking that I felt really upset and sad about having no social life. I wanted to eat just to feel better.

Therapist: And, as you were eating, what were you thinking?

Client: I was thinking that the ice cream tasted really good, that it was making me feel good. But I was also thinking that I shouldn't be eating this, that I'm bingeing again. But then I thought that my life is such a wreck that I deserve to eat what I want to make me feel better.

Therapist: And what were you thinking after you finished the binge?

Client: That I was a failure, a blimp, that I have no control, that this therapy isn't working.

Therapist: Okay, let's go back to the beginning. You said you wanted to eat because you thought it would make you feel better. Did it?

(continued)

Client: Well, as I said, the ice cream tasted good and it felt good to indulge myself.

Therapist: But, in the long run, did bingeing make you feel better?

Client: Of course not. I felt terrible afterward.

Therapist: Can you think of anything you might say to yourself the next time you get into such a state, when you want to eat in order to make yourself feel better?

Client: I could remind myself that I'll feel better only for a little while, but then I'll feel terrible.

Therapist: How likely do you think it is that you'll remember to say this to yourself?

Client: Not very likely.

Therapist: Is there any way to increase the likelihood?

Client: Well, I guess I could write it on a card or something and put the card near my refrigerator.

Therapist: That's a pretty good idea. What else could you do to prevent yourself from eating when you feel upset? What other things could you do to relieve your upset, other than eat?

Client: I could call my friend Keisha and talk about how I feel. Or I could go for a walk—someplace away from food—like up in the hills, where it's so pretty. Walking up there always makes me feel better.

Therapist: Those are really good ideas. It's important to have a variety of things you can do, other than eat, to relieve bad moods.

The behavioral components of this therapy involve introducing forbidden foods (such as bread) back into the client's diet and helping her confront her irrational thoughts about these foods, such as "If I have just one doughnut, I'm inevitably going to binge." Similarly, the client is taught to eat three healthy meals a day and to challenge the thoughts she has about these meals and the possibility of gaining weight. Cognitive-behavioral therapy for bulimia usually lasts about three to six months and involves 10 to 20 sessions.

Controlled studies of the efficacy of cognitive-behavioral therapy for bulimia find that about one-half of clients completely stop the binge/purge cycle (Wilson, 2005; Wilson et al., 2002). Clients undergoing this therapy also show a decrease in depression and anxiety, an increase in social functioning, and a lessening of concern about dieting and weight. Comparisons with drug therapies show that cognitive-behavioral therapy is more effective than drug therapies in producing the complete cessation of binge eating and purging and in preventing relapse in the long term (Wilson, 2005).

Other studies of the treatment of bulimia have compared cognitive-behavioral therapy (CBT) with three other types of therapy—*interpersonal therapy (IPT), supportive-expressive psychodynamic therapy,* and behavior therapy without a focus on cognitions (Agras et al., 2000; Fairburn, Jones, et al., 1991; Fairburn et al., 1995; Garner et al., 1993; Wilson et al., 1999, 2002). In interpersonal therapy, client and therapist discuss interpersonal problems that are related to the client's eating disorder, and the therapist works actively with the client to develop strategies to solve these interpersonal problems. In supportive-expressive therapy, the therapist encourages the client to talk about problems related to the eating disorder, especially interpersonal problems, but in a highly nondirective manner. In behavior therapy, the client is taught how to monitor her food intake, is reinforced for introducing avoided foods into her diet, and is taught coping techniques for avoiding bingeing. In the studies, all the therapies resulted in significant improvement in the clients' eating behaviors and emotional well-being, but the cognitive-behavioral and interpersonal therapy clients showed the greatest and most enduring improvements. Comparisons of CBT and IPT suggest that CBT is significantly more effective than IPT and works more quickly, with substantial improvement being shown in CBT by three to six weeks into treatment (Agras et al., 2000; Fairburn, Jones, et al., 2001; Wilson et al., 1999, 2002).

For binge-eating disorder, cognitive-behavioral therapy has been shown to be more effective than no treatment and than antidepressant medications (Grilo et al., 2002; Ricca et al., 2001). Interpersonal therapy has proven equally effective as CBT for binge-eating disorder (Wilfley et al., 1993, 2002). In addition, *dialectical behavior therapy (DBT),* which was originally developed to treat borderline personality disorder (Linehan, Kanter, & Comtois, 1999), has proven effective in the treatment of binge-eating disorder. Dialectical behavior therapy has many of the components of cognitive-behavioral therapy, but it focuses on deficits of emotion regulation as key to disordered eating behavior. In one study, 44 women with binge-eating disorder were randomly assigned to group DBT or to no treatment (Telch, Agras, & Linehan, 2001). After 20 weeks of treatment, 89 percent of the women in the DBT group had stopped binge eating, compared with 12.5 percent of the women in the no treatment group. Six months following treatment, 56 percent of the women were still abstaining from binge eating. (The women in the control group received treatment during this time, so follow-up data were not available for them.)

In general, psychotherapies have had more success in reducing binge eating than in reducing weight in obese people with binge-eating disorder (Wonderlich et al., 2003).

Biological Therapies

Recall that many people with eating disorders are also depressed or have histories of depression in their families. This connection to depression has led many psychiatrists to use antidepressant drugs to treat the eating disorders, particularly bulimia nervosa (de Zwann, Roerig, & Mitchell, 2004). *Tricyclic antidepressants* are superior to placebos in reducing bingeing and vomiting and in enhancing a sense of control in people with bulimia (e.g., McCann & Agras, 1990). Patients with bulimia often continue to engage in severe dieting, however, and relapse into the binge/purge cycle shortly after stopping the drugs. The *monoamine oxidase (MAO) inhibitors* also have proven more effective than placebos in the treatment of bulimia but are not typically prescribed, because they require severe dietary restrictions to prevent dangerous side effects.

The *selective serotonin reuptake inhibitors (SSRIs)*, such as fluoxetine (trade name Prozac), have been the focus of much research on biological treatments for bulimia nervosa. These drugs appear to reduce binge-eating and purging behaviors, but they often do not restore the individual to normal eating habits (deZwann et al., 2004). Adding cognitive-behavioral therapy to antidepressant treatment increases the rate of recovery from the disorder (Wilson, 2005).

Tricyclic antidepressants and MAO inhibitors have not been proven effective in the treatment of anorexia in controlled clinical trials (deZwann et al., 2004). Fluoxetine may be helpful in treating anorexia, once patients have been restored to a normal weight (Kaye et al., 2001).

For people with binge-eating disorder, antidepressants do not appear to be as consistently effective in reducing binge eating as do cognitive-behavioral treatments (Wonderlich et al., 2003).

SUMMING UP

- People with anorexia nervosa often must be hospitalized, because they are so emaciated

and malnourished that they are in a medical crisis.

- Behavior therapy for anorexia nervosa involves making rewards contingent upon the client's eating. Clients may be taught relaxation techniques to handle their anxiety about eating.

- Family therapy focuses on understanding the role of anorexic behaviors in the family unit. Therapists challenge parents' attitudes toward their children's behaviors and try to help the family find more adaptive ways of interacting with each other.

- Individual therapy for anorexia may focus on helping clients identify and accept their feelings and confront their distorted cognitions about their bodies.

- Psychotherapy can be helpful for anorexia but is usually a long process, and the risk for relapse is high.

- Several studies show that cognitive-behavioral therapy, which focuses on distorted cognitions about eating, is effective in the treatment of bulimia.

- Interpersonal therapy, which focuses on the quality of a client's relationships, and supportive-expressive therapy, can be effective in the treatment of bulimia.

- Tricyclic antidepressants and selective serotonin reuptake inhibitors have been shown to be helpful in the treatment of bulimia. The MAO inhibitors can also be helpful but are not usually prescribed, because they require dietary restrictions to avoid side effects.

- Antidepressants have not proven as useful in the treatment of anorexia nervosa, but some studies suggest that the selective serotonin reuptake inhibitors may be helpful.

CHAPTER INTEGRATION

Several experts have suggested that a group of biological, psychological, and social factors interact to create the eating disorders (Agras & Kirkley, 1986; Polivy & Herman, 2002; Striegel-Moore, 1993). Any one of these factors alone may not be enough to push someone to develop anorexia or bulimia nervosa but may do so when combined (see Figure 15.5 on page 568).

First, societal pressures for thinness clearly provide a potent impetus for the development of unhealthy attitudes toward eating, especially for women. If these pressures were simply toward

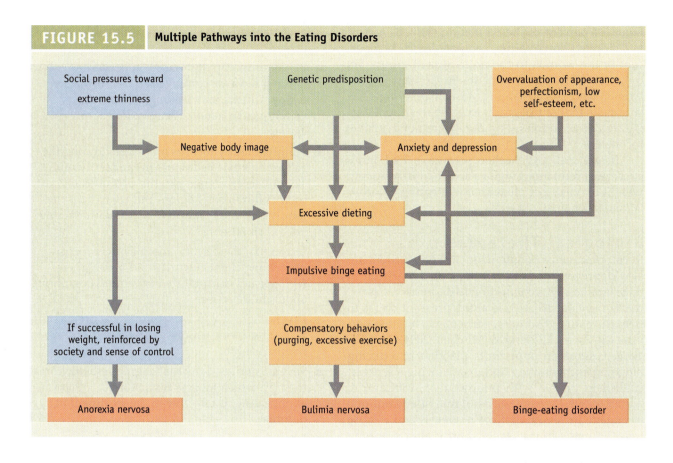

FIGURE 15.5   Multiple Pathways into the Eating Disorders

achieving a healthy weight and the maintenance of fitness, they would not be so dangerous. However, the ideal weight for women promoted by beauty symbols in developed countries is much lower than that considered healthy and normal for the average woman; thus, she develops a negative body image. This leads her to engage in excessive dieting. Unfortunately, excessive dieting sets up the conditions for impulsive binge eating, which then makes her have negative emotions and even lower self-esteem.

Second, biological factors may interact with these societal pressures to make some people more likely than others to develop eating disorders. People who develop eating disorders may have genetic predispositions to these disorders or to the dysregulation of their hormones or neurotransmitters. It is unclear just how their genetic vulnerabilities lead to the symptoms of eating disorders, but they may contribute to an ability to diet excessively. Another biological factor that may predispose some people to acquiesce to the pressures to diet and be thin is a tendency toward anxiety or mild depression. Many people with eating disorders, especially people with bulimia, are easily distressed and emotionally labile and tend to eat impulsively in response to their moods. Although problems in mood in people with eating disorders

may be the result of environmental circumstances or of the stresses of having eating disorders, they may also be biologically caused in at least some people who develop eating disorders.

Personality factors may also interact with societal pressures to be thin and/or with the biological predispositions described to lead some people to develop eating disorders. Perfectionism, all-or-nothing thinking, and low self-esteem may make people more likely to engage in extreme measures to control their weight in response to unwelcome weight gains or in an attempt to achieve an ideal of attractiveness and therefore increase their self-esteem. These personality characteristics are more likely to develop in children whose parents are lacking in affection and nurturance and, at the same time, are controlling and demanding of perfection.

Whatever pathway an individual takes into the eating disorders, these behaviors tend to be maintained once they begin. The excessive concern over weight among people with anorexia or bulimia nervosa is constantly reinforced by societal images, and any weight loss they achieve is reinforced by peers and family. People with anorexia may also be reinforced by the sense of control they gain over their lives by dieting. People with bulimia nervosa and binge-eating disorder may greatly desire control but are unable to maintain it and, so, fall into binge eating as an escape from negative emotions and thoughts about the self. The compensatory behaviors of bulimia nervosa help the individual regain some sense of control, however fragile, and thus are reinforced.

Thus, it may take a mixture of these factors, rather than any single one, to lead someone to de-velop a full eating disorder. Once the disorder sets in, however, it tends to be reinforced and perpetu-ated. Note also that many of the same factors con-tribute to each of the eating disorders.

Extraordinary People: Follow-Up

Although Diana, Princess of Wales led an extra-ordinary life, the triggers for her eating disorders were very common, as she explained in her BBC interview:

Question: What was the cause?

Diana: The cause was the situation where my husband and I had to keep everything together because we didn't want to disappoint the pub-lic, and yet obviously there was a lot of anxiety going on within our four walls.

Question: Do you mean between the two of you?

Diana: Uh, uh.

Question: And so you subjected yourself to this phase of bingeing and vomiting?

Diana: You could say the word subjected, but it was my escape mechanism, and it worked, for me, at that time.

Question: Did you seek help from any other members of the Royal Family?

Diana: No. You, you have to know that when you have bulimia you're very ashamed of your-self and you hate yourself, so—and people think you're wasting food—so you don't dis-cuss it with people. And the thing about bulimia is your weight always stays the same, whereas with anorexia you visibly shrink. So you can pre-tend the whole way through. There's no proof. . . .

Question: How long did this bulimia go on for?

Diana: A long time, a long time. But I'm free of it now.

Question: Two years, three years?

Diana: Mmm. A little bit more than that.

Diana suffered symptoms of depression, but she felt she had to be "perfect" at all times and show no weakness, even to her immediate family. The bu-limia became a release valve for her negative emo-tions, but it further damaged her self-esteem and sense of control. Diana perceived her family as un-supportive and overcontrolling and felt unable to reach out to them directly, so she used the bulimic behaviors as cries for help. As most of the world knows, Diana and her husband, Charles, divorced in 1996. She continued to live a glamorous life with the elite of Europe—and to be a devoted mother to her sons, William and Harry—until her death in a car crash in 1997.

Chapter Summary

- The eating disorders include anorexia nervosa, bulimia nervosa, and binge-eating disorder. (Review Table 15.2.)

- Anorexia nervosa is characterized by self-starvation, a distorted body image, intense fears of becoming fat, and amenorrhea. (Review Table 15.1.) People with the restricting type of anorexia nervosa refuse to eat in order to prevent weight gain. People with the binge/purge type periodically engage in bingeing and then purge to prevent weight gain.

- The lifetime prevalence of anorexia is about 1 percent, with 90 to 95 percent of cases being female. Anorexia nervosa usually begins in adolescence, and the course is variable from one person to another. It is a very dangerous disorder, and the death rate among people with anorexia is between 5 and 8 percent.

■ Bulimia nervosa is characterized by uncontrolled bingeing, followed by behaviors designed to prevent weight gain from the binges. (Review Table 15.3.) People with the purging type use self-induced vomiting, diuretics, or laxatives to prevent weight gain. People with the nonpurging type use fasting and exercise to prevent weight gain.

■ The prevalence of bulimia nervosa is between 0.5 and 3 percent. The onset of bulimia nervosa is most often in adolescence. Although people with bulimia do not tend to be underweight, there are several dangerous medical complications in bulimia nervosa.

■ People with binge-eating disorder engage in bingeing, but not in purging or behaviors designed to compensate for the binges. It is more common in women than in men, and people with the disorder tend to be significantly overweight. Binge-eating disorder is not officially recognized by the DSM-IV-TR, but the diagnostic criteria were placed in an appendix for further study.

■ The biological factors implicated in the development of the eating disorders include genetics, the dysregulation of hormonal and neurotransmitter systems, and generally lower functioning in the hypothalamus. (Review Table 15.4.)

■ Sociocultural theorists have attributed the eating disorders to pressures toward thinness in Western cultures and in the media. (Review Table 15.4.)

■ Eating disorders may develop in some people as maladaptive strategies for coping with negative emotions. Also, certain cognitive factors, including the overvaluation of appearance, perfectionism, low self-esteem, excessive concern about others' opinions, and a rigid, dichotomous thinking style may contribute to the development of the eating disorders. (Review Table 15.4.)

■ The families of girls with eating disorders may be overcontrolling, overprotective, and hostile and may not allow the expression of feelings. In adolescence, these girls may develop eating disorders as a way of exerting control. (Review Table 15.4.)

■ Sexual abuse is a risk factor for eating disorders, as well as for several other psychological problems. (Review Table 15.4.)

■ There are few treatments for anorexia shown to be successful in empirical studies. Cognitive-behavioral therapy has proven the most effective therapy for reducing the symptoms of bulimia and preventing relapse. Interpersonal therapy, supportive-expressive therapy, and behavior therapy also appear to be effective for bulimia nervosa. Antidepressants are effective in treating bulimia, but the relapse rate is high. (Review Table 15.7.)

■ Biological, psychological, and social factors may interact to create eating disorders. Any one factor alone may not be enough to push someone to develop an eating disorder, but combinations of these factors may do so. (Review Figure 15.5.) Whatever pathway an individual takes into the eating disorders, these behaviors tend to be maintained once they begin.

MindMap CD-ROM

The following resources on the MindMap CD-ROM that came with this text will help you to master the content of this chapter and prepare for tests:

■ Videos: Anorexia Nervosa; Bulimia Nervosa

■ Interactive Segment: Perception of Body Shape

■ Chapter Timeline

■ Chapter Quiz

Key Terms

anorexia nervosa 542

bulimia nervosa 543

binge-eating disorder 543

amenorrhea 544

restricting type of anorexia nervosa 545

binge/purge type of anorexia nervosa 546

bingeing 547

purging type of bulimia nervosa 548

nonpurging type of bulimia nervosa 548

enmeshed families 559

set point 564

> # Chapter 16

Shadow of Her Former Self
by Diana Ong

I don't know whether it's normal or not, but sex has always been something that I take seriously. I would put it higher than tennis on my list of constructive things to do.

—Art Buchwald, *Leaving Home: A Memoir* (1993)

Sexual Disorders <

CHAPTER OVERVIEW

Extraordinary People

■ **David Reimer:** *The Boy Who Was Raised as a Girl*

Sexual Dysfunctions

The most common sexual disorders are sexual dysfunctions. The sexual dysfunctions include sexual desire, sexual arousal, orgasm, and sexual pain disorders. Occasional problems in all of these areas are very common. These problems are given a diagnosis when they are persistent, cause significant distress, and interfere with intimate relationships. The sexual dysfunctions can have a host of biological causes, including undiagnosed diabetes, drug use, and hormonal and vascular abnormalities. Possible psychological causes include relationship concerns, traumatic experiences, maladaptive attitudes and cognitions, and an upbringing or a cultural environment that devalues or degrades sex. A number of drugs are now available that treat some of the sexual dysfunctions. Psychotherapy can decrease people's inhibitions about sex and teach them new techniques for optimal sexual enjoyment.

Taking Psychology Personally

■ **Practicing Safe Sex**

Paraphilias

People with paraphilias engage in sexual activities that involve nonhuman objects, nonconsenting adults, the suffering or humiliation of themselves or their partner, or children. The paraphilias include fetishism, transvestism, sexual sadism and masochism, voyeurism, exhibitionism, frotteurism, and pedophilia.

Gender Identity Disorder

Gender identity is one's perception of oneself as male or female. A person with gender identity disorder believes he or she was born with the wrong sex's genitals and is fundamentally a person of the opposite sex. Some people with gender identity disorder undergo surgery and hormonal treatments to change their sex.

Chapter Integration

The interplay of biological, psychological, and social factors is especially apparent in matters of sexuality. Biological factors can be greatly moderated by psychological and social factors.

Extraordinary People

David Reimer: *The Boy Who Was Raised as a Girl*

In April 1966, 8-month-old Bruce Reimer was to undergo a routine circumcision to alleviate a painful medical condition on his penis. The operation went terribly wrong, however, and Bruce's penis was accidentally severed. None of the doctors whom Bruce's anguished parents consulted could offer any hope of restoring the penis and suggested that Bruce would never be able to function as a normal male. Dr. John Money of Johns Hopkins University offered them a solution, however—raise Bruce as a girl and have him undergo sex reassignment therapy. Money firmly believed that one's gender identity depends on the environment in which one is raised, not on the genes or genitals with which one is born. He had published several papers on his work with hermaphrodites—children born with a variety of anomalies of the internal and external sex organs that made them neither obviously male nor female. His research showed that the sex the children were assigned by their parents was the sex they later identified themselves as, regardless of their chromosomal makeup.

Money's theories were at the center of raging controversies in psychology and psychiatry in the 1950s and 1960s about the origins of gender identity. As writer John Colapinto (2001) chronicles in *As Nature Made Him: The Boy Who Was Raised as a Girl*, Money was the leader of a group of sex researchers who argued that gender identity is entirely determined by environment, not biology. On the opposite side were researchers such as Milton Diamond, who argued that the research clearly shows that chromosomal sex and exposure to hormones in utero heavily determine gender identity.

When Bruce's parents contacted Money, they presented him with the perfect opportunity to prove his points. Not only had Bruce been born a normal male, but he had an identical twin brother as well. If reassigning Bruce's sex to a girl with surgery, and raising him as a girl resulted in Bruce's fully accepting himself as a girl, when his identical twin brother identified himself as a boy, Money's theories of gender identity would be soundly supported.

Bruce's parents renamed him Brenda Lee and began dressing him in feminine clothes. They took the child to Johns Hopkins to undergo a bilateral orchidectomy—the removal of both testicles—at the age of 22 months. When Brenda's parents returned

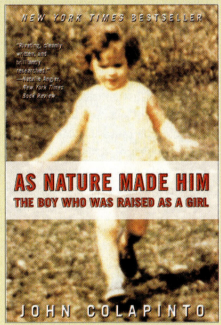

home with the child, they furnished her with dolls and tried to reinforce in every way her identity as a girl. Brenda, however, resisted. She ripped at the frilly dresses her mother gave her to wear. As her brother, Brian, recalled, "When I say there was nothing feminine about Brenda . . . I mean there was *nothing* feminine. She walked like a guy. Sat with her legs apart. She talked about guy things, didn't give a crap about cleaning house, getting married, wearing makeup. We both wanted to play with guys, build forts and have snowball fights and play army. She'd get a skipping rope for a gift, and the only thing we'd use that for was to tie people up, whip people with it" (Colapinto, 2001, p. 57).

As Brenda grew up, she became more convinced that she was not a girl. Her parents kept reinforcing her femininity, but Brenda would have nothing of it. She was defiant and difficult in school. Other children teased her and rejected her for her "tomboyishness." She flatly refused further surgery to create a vagina for her and insisted on urinating standing up. Still, her parents persisted at treating Brenda as a girl, at Money's insistence. At the age of 12, Brenda began to take estrogen; as a result, she began to develop breasts. Her voice also began to crack, however, just like her brother Brian's. John Money and a host of psychiatrists kept trying to convince Brenda to submit to the vaginal surgery, but she steadfastly refused. Finally, when Brenda was 14, her father told her the entire truth about the botched circumcision and the surgery she underwent at age 22 months, as well as her parents' decision to raise her as a girl. She was amazed, but another emotion was even stronger: "I was *relieved*. . . . Suddenly it all made sense why I felt the way I did. I wasn't some sort of weirdo. I wasn't crazy" (Colapinto, 2001, p. 180).

Brenda immediately decided to revert to her biological sex. She renamed herself David, after the biblical king and giant-slayer. David began to take injections of testosterone and in 1980 underwent a double mastectomy to remove the breasts he had grown. Then, a month before his sixteenth birthday, he underwent surgery to create a rudimentary penis. David's reentry into life as a boy was rough, however. He was sexually attracted to girls but terrified at the thought of initiating sex with a girl because she would find out the truth about him. The artificial genitals that had been fashioned for him frequently became blocked, and he underwent several additional surgeries and treatments. Over the next few years, David attempted suicide and secluded himself in a mountain cabin for months at a time.

Finally, shortly after his 22nd birthday, David underwent a new kind of surgery to create a more acceptable and functional penis. In 1990, David married a young woman named Jane, who knew everything about his past and loved him completely.

Although any individual case study is limited in its generalizability, David Reimer's story raises many questions about the biological and social contributors to our self-concept as male and female, our sexual preferences, and the role of sexuality and gender in psychological well-being. In this chapter, we consider how biology interacts with social norms and psychological factors in producing both sexual health and sexual disorders.

Sexual disorders fall into three distinct categories. First, *sexual dysfunctions* involve problems in experiencing sexual arousal or in carrying through with a sexual act to the point of sexual satisfaction. Second, *paraphilias* involve sexual activities that are focused on nonhuman objects, children or nonconsenting adults, or suffering or humiliation. There are several types of paraphilias, and they vary in the severity of their impact on other people. Third, *gender identity disorder* involves the belief that one has been born with the body of the wrong gender. People with this disorder feel trapped in the wrong body, wish to be rid of their genitals, and want to live as a member of the other gender.

In this chapter, we discuss specific sexual disorders within each of these three categories. We begin with some of the most common disorders that both men and women suffer: sexual dysfunctions. Then we move to the paraphilias, which are less common and primarily experienced by men. Finally, we discuss the most uncommon sexual disorder, gender identity disorder.

SEXUAL DYSFUNCTIONS

The **sexual dysfunctions** are a set of disorders in which people have trouble engaging in and enjoying sexual relationships with other people. Occasional problems with sexual functioning are extremely common. In a representative sample of more than 3,000 adults in the United States, Laumann, Paik, and Rosen (1999) found that 43 percent of the women and 31 percent of the men reported occasional dysfunctions.

In order to understand the sexual dysfunctions, it is important to understand something about the human sexual response—what happens in our bodies when we feel sexually aroused, when we engage in sexual intercourse or other forms of sexual stimulation, and when we reach orgasm.

The Sexual Response Cycle

Before the work of William Masters and Virginia Johnson in the 1950s and 1960s, little was known about what happened in the human body during sexual arousal and activity. Masters and Johnson (1970) observed people engaging in a variety of sexual practices in a laboratory setting and recorded the physiological changes that occurred during sexual activity.

Masters and Johnson and later researchers argued that the sexual response cycle can be divided into five phases: desire, excitement or arousal, plateau, orgasm, and resolution (see Figures 16.1 and 16.2). **Sexual desire** is the urge to engage in any type of sexual activity. The **arousal phase,** or *excitement phase*, consists of a psychological experience of arousal and pleasure and the physiological changes known as *vasocongestion* and *myotonia*. **Vasocongestion** is the filling of blood vessels and tissues with blood, also known as *engorgement*. In males, erection of the penis is caused by an increased flow of blood into the arteries of the penis, accompanied by a decrease in the outflow of blood from the penis through the veins. In females, vasocongestion causes the clitoris to enlarge, the labia to swell, and the vagina to moisten. **Myotonia** is muscular tension. Dur-

| FIGURE 16.1 | **Male Sexual Response Cycle.** Males experience characteristic changes in physiology during each phase of their sexual response cycle. |

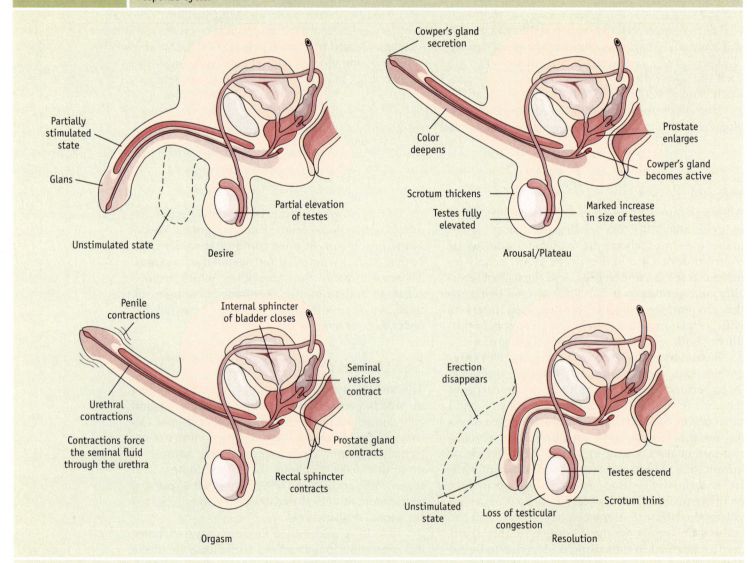

Source: Adapted from Hyde, 1990, p. 199.

ing the arousal phase, many muscles in the body may become more tense, culminating in the muscular contractions known as **orgasm.**

Following the arousal phase is the **plateau phase.** During this period, excitement remains at a high but stable level. This period is pleasurable in itself, and some people try to extend this period as long as possible before reaching orgasm. During both the arousal and the plateau phases, the person may feel tense all over, the skin is flushed, salivation increases, the nostrils flare, the heart pounds, breathing is heavy, and the person may be oblivious to external stimuli or events.

The arousal and plateau phases are followed by orgasm. Physiologically, orgasm is the discharge of the neuromuscular tension built up during the excitement and plateau phases. Both males and fe-

males experience a sense of the inevitability of orgasm just before it happens.

In males, orgasm involves rhythmic contractions of the prostate, the seminal vesicles, the vas deferens, and the entire length of the penis and urethra, accompanied by the ejaculation of semen (see Figure 16.1). In males, a *refractory period* follows ejaculation. During this period, the male cannot achieve full erection and another orgasm, regardless of the type or intensity of sexual stimulation. The refractory period lasts from a few minutes to several hours.

In females, orgasm generally involves rhythmic contractions of the orgasmic platform (see Figure 16.2) and more irregular contractions of the uterus, which are not always felt. Because females do not have a refractory period, they are capable of

FIGURE 16.2 **Female Sexual Response Cycle.** At each phase of the sexual response cycle in females, there are characteristic changes in physiology.

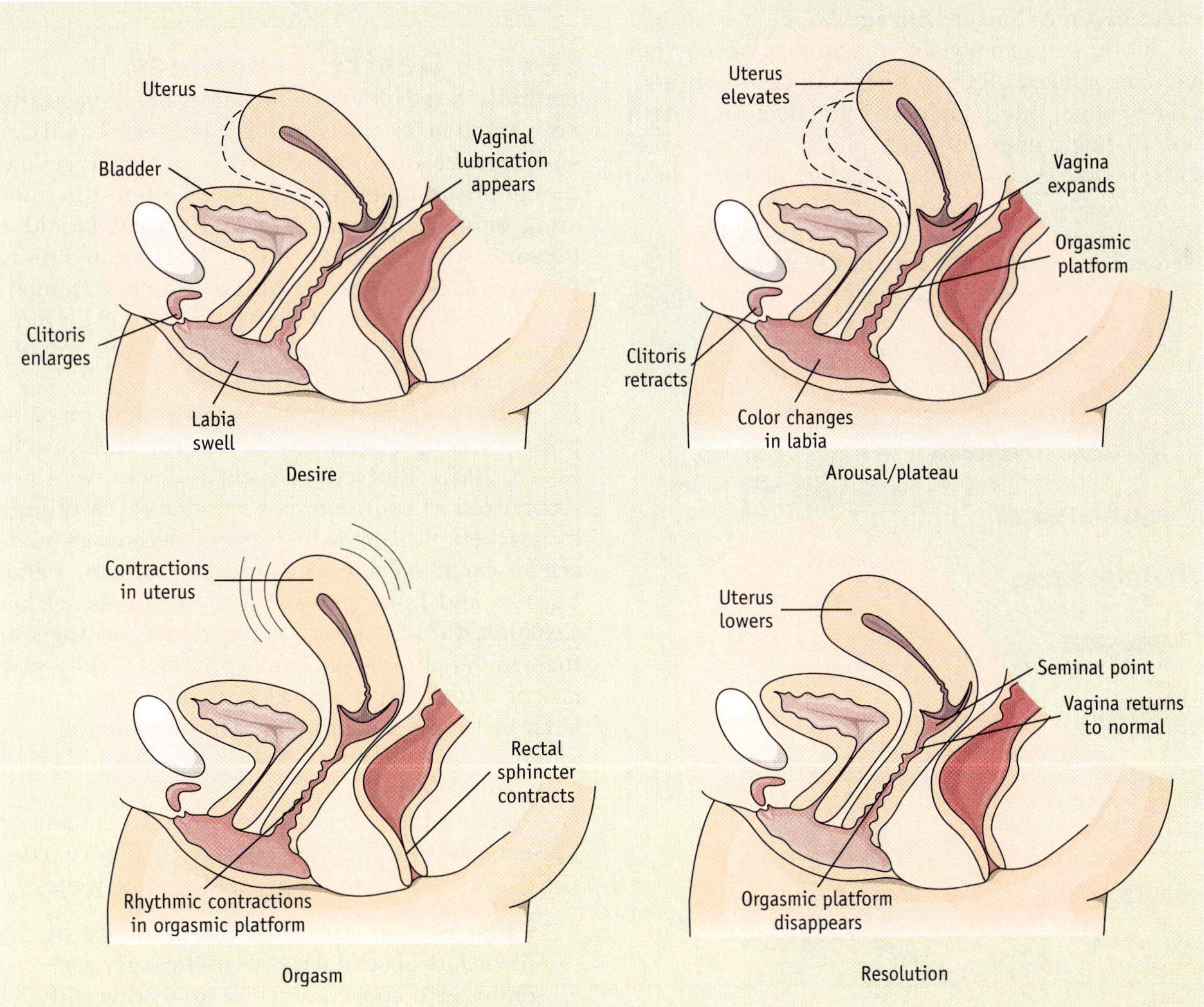

Source: Adapted from Hyde, 1990, p. 200.

experiencing additional orgasms immediately following one. However, not all women want to have multiple orgasms or find it easy to be aroused to multiple orgasms.

Following orgasm, the entire musculature of the body relaxes, and men and women tend to experience a state of deep relaxation, the stage known as **resolution.** A man loses his erection, and a woman's orgasmic platform subsides.

Both males and females experience the same five phases. There are some differences between the male and female sexual responses, however (Masters, Johnson, & Kolodny, 1993). First, there is greater variability in the female response pattern than in the male response pattern. Sometimes, the excitement and plateau phases are short for a female and she reaches a discernible orgasm quickly. At other times, the excitement and plateau phases are longer, and she may or may not experience a full orgasm. Second, as we have noted, there typically is a refractory period following orgasm for males but not for females. This refractory period in males becomes longer with age.

If you are sexually active, you may or may not have recognized all these phases in your own sexual response cycle. People vary greatly in the length and distinctiveness of each phase. For example, some people do not notice a distinct plateau phase

and feel they go straight from arousal to orgasm. Being aware of how your body reacts to sexual stimulation can help you recognize what helps you get the most pleasure from sexual activity and what interferes with that pleasure.

Occasional, transient problems in sexual functioning are extremely common (see Figure 16.3). To qualify for a diagnosis of a sexual dysfunction, the difficulty must be more than occasional, and it must cause significant distress or interpersonal difficulty. The DSM-IV-TR divides sexual dysfunctions into four categories: sexual desire disorders, sexual arousal disorders, orgasmic disorders, and sexual pain disorders (see the Concept Overview in Table 16.1). (There are two other diagnoses in addition to those listed in Table 16.1: sexual dysfunction due to a medical condition and substance-induced sexual dysfunction, which we discuss in the section "Causes of Sexual Dysfunctions.") In reality, these dysfunctions overlap greatly, and many people who seek treatment for a sexual problem have more than one of these dysfunctions.

Sexual Desire Disorders

An individual's level of sexual desire is basically how much he or she wants to have sex. Sexual desire can be manifested in a person's sexual thoughts and fantasies, a person's interest in initiating or participating in sexual activities, and a person's awareness of sexual cues from others (Schiavi & Segraves, 1995). People vary tremendously in their levels of sexual desire, and an individual's level of sexual desire can vary greatly across time (see Tables 16.2 and 16.3).

Lack of sexual desire is the most common complaint of people seeking sex therapy (Leiblum & Rosen, 2000). Problems of sexual desire were not recognized as common, nor as separate disorders, by sex therapists in the first several decades of modern research on sexual disorders (Kaplan, 1995). Masters and Johnson, the pioneers of research on sexuality, did not include sexual desire disorders in their initial studies of sexual problems. They saw lack of sexual desire as a consequence of other problems in sexual functioning. The expectation was that treating these sexual dysfunctions would bring back sexual desire.

Another pioneer in sex research, Helen Singer Kaplan, was one of the first to recognize sexual desire disorders as a separate problem. She writes,

> I first became aware of the existence of disorders of sexual desire in the early seventies as a consequence of analyzing our treatment failures. As I reviewed the charts, it became clear that we had failed

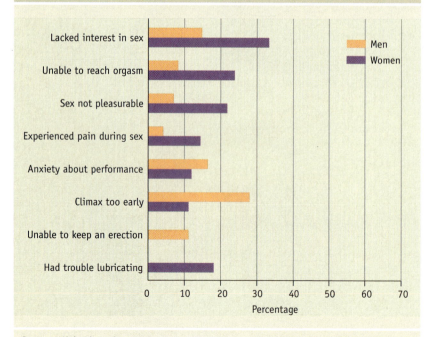

FIGURE 16.3

Percentage of People Who Have Had a Sexual Difficulty in the Past Year. A national survey found that many people report having had one or more sexual difficulties in the past year.

Source: Michael et al., 1994, p. 126.

TABLE 16.1	Concept Overview

Sexual Dysfunction Disorders

The DSM-IV-TR defines a number of sexual dysfunction disorders.

Sexual Desire Disorders	Description
Hypoactive sexual desire disorder	Persistent lack of sexual fantasies and desire for sexual activity
Sexual aversion disorder	Persistent and extreme aversion to genital sexual contact with a sexual partner

Sexual Arousal Disorders	Description
Female sexual arousal disorder	In women, recurrent inability to attain or maintain the swelling-lubrication response of sexual excitement
Male erectile disorder	In men, recurrent inability to attain or maintain an erection until the completion of sexual activity

Orgasmic Disorders	Description
Female orgasmic disorder	In women, recurrent delay in or absence of orgasm following sexual excitement
Premature ejaculation	In men, inability to delay ejaculation as desired
Male orgasmic disorder	In men, recurrent delay in or absence of orgasm following sexual excitement

Sexual Pain Disorders	Description
Dyspareunia	Genital pain associated with intercourse
Vaginismus	In women, involuntary contractions of the muscles surrounding the vagina, which interferes with sexual functioning

Source: Reprinted with permission from the *Diagnostic and Statistical Manual of Mental Disorders,* Fourth Edition, Text Revision. Copyright © 2000 American Psychiatric Association.

TABLE 16.2	Responses to the Question "How Often Do You Think About Sex?"

A national survey found a large variation in how often people think about sex and great differences between men and women.

	"Every Day" or "Several Times a Day"	"A Few Times a Month" or "A Few Times a Week"	"Less Than Once a Month" or "Never"
Men	54%	43%	4%
Women	19	67	14

Source: From R. T. Michael et al., *Sex in America.* Copyright © 1994 by CSG Enterprises, Inc. By permission of Little, Brown and Company.

TABLE 16.3 How Often Do People Have Sex?		
A national survey of adults in the United States found a great deal of variation in how frequently people had sex.		
	Percentage Reporting	
Frequency	**Men**	**Women**
Two to three times per week	30	26
A few times per month	36	37
A few times per year or not at all	27	30

Source: From E. O. Laumann et al., *The Social Organization of Sexuality: Sexual Practices in the United States.* Copyright © 1994 University of Chicago Press, Chicago, IL.

to recognize a considerable subgroup of patients who had little or no desire for sex or for sex with their partners. These patients had developed impotence or orgasmic disorders mainly because they had tried to make love without feeling lust or desire, and we had been trying to treat these secondary genital dysfunctions without being aware of the underlying desire disorders. This meant that some of our so-called "resistant" patients were not resistant to sex therapy at all. We had simply been treating them for the wrong thing! (Kaplan, 1995, p. 2)

Kaplan and other influential theorists (Kaplan, 1977; Masters, Johnson, & Kolodny, 1979) published their research on problems of sexual desire in the late 1970s. By the publication of the third edition of the DSM in 1980, these disorders had earned their own diagnostic category in the official nomenclature.

The percentage of people seeking therapy who report problems of sexual desire has increased sharply in the past 20 to 30 years (Bach, Wincze, & Barlow, 2001; Kaplan, 1995). Although the reasons for this increase are not clear, media attention to sexual desire disorders leads people to recognize that they have a problem that therapists can treat and, thus, to seek treatment. People who lack sexual desire can be diagnosed with one of two sexual desire disorders: hypoactive sexual desire disorder and sexual aversion disorder.

Hypoactive Sexual Desire Disorder

People with **hypoactive sexual desire disorder** have little desire for sex—they do not fantasize about sex or initiate sexual activity—and this lack of sexual desire causes them marked distress or interpersonal difficulty. In some rare cases, people report never having had much interest in sex, either with other people or privately, as in the viewing of erotic films, masturbation, or fantasy. In most cases of hypoactive sexual desire, the individual used to enjoy sex but has lost interest in it, despite the presence of a willing and desirable partner. A diagnosis of hypoactive sexual desire is not given if the individual's lack of desire is the result of transient circumstances in his or her life, such as being too busy or fatigued from overwork to care about sex. Also, a diagnosis of sexual desire disorder is not given if the lack of desire is actually caused by one of the other problems in sexual functioning, such as pain during intercourse or an inability to achieve orgasm. In such cases, the diagnosis a person receives focuses on the primary dysfunction, rather than on the lack of desire that is the result of the primary dysfunction.

Inhibited desire can be either generalized to all partners or situations or specific to certain partners or types of stimulation. A person who has had little desire for sexual activity most of his or her life has a *generalized sexual desire disorder.* A person who lacks the desire to have sex with his or her partner, but has sexual fantasies about other people, may be diagnosed with a *situational sexual desire disorder.* Obviously, the judgment about when a person's sexual desire has been too low for too long is a subjective one. Often, people seek treatment for a lack of sexual desire primarily because their partner's sexual desire appears to be considerably greater than their own and the difference is causing conflict in the relationship (Masters et al., 1993). Low sexual desire is one of the most common problems for which people seek treatment (Bach et al., 2001).

In the study of more than 3,000 adults done by Laumann and colleagues, 22 percent of the women and 5 percent of the men reported low sexual desire (Laumann et al., 1999). Men with this disorder tend to be older (average age 50) than women with the disorder (average age 33). Women with hypoactive sexual desire are more likely than men to report anxiety, depression, and life stress. Hypoactive sexual desire is more often connected to problems in relationships for women than for men.

Sexual Aversion Disorder

The other type of sexual desire disorder is **sexual aversion disorder.** People with this disorder do not simply have a passive lack of interest in sex; they actively avoid sexual activities. When they do engage in sex, they may feel sickened by it or experience acute anxiety. Some people experience a generalized aversion to all sexual activities, including kissing and touching.

Sexual aversion disorder in women is frequently tied to sexual assault experiences, as in the case of Norma (adapted from Spitzer et al., 1994, p. 213):

CASE STUDY

Norma and Gary were having sex approximately once every 1 to 2 months, and only at Gary's insistence. Their sexual activity consisted primarily of Gary stimulating Norma to orgasm by manually caressing her genitals while he masturbated himself to orgasm.

Norma had always had a strong aversion to looking at or touching her husband's penis. During an interview she explained that she had had no idea of the origin of this aversion until her uncle's recent funeral. At the funeral she was surprised to find herself becoming angry as the eulogy was read. Her uncle had been a world-famous concert musician and was widely respected and admired. She believes she suddenly recalled having been sexually molested by him when she was a child. From the ages of 9 to 12, her uncle had been her music teacher. The lessons included "teaching [her] rhythm" by having her caress his penis in time with the beating of the metronome. This repelled her, but she was frightened to tell her parents about it. She finally refused to continue lessons at age 12 without ever telling her parents why. At some point during her adolescence, she said, she "forgot what he did to me."

Sexual Arousal Disorders

People with *sexual arousal disorders* do not experience the physiological changes that make up the excitement or arousal phase of the sexual response cycle. **Female sexual arousal disorder** involves a recurrent inability to attain or maintain the swelling-lubrication response of sexual excitement. **Male erectile disorder** involves the recurrent inability to attain or maintain an erection until the completion of sexual activity. Much less is known about female sexual arousal disorder than about male erectile disorder (which is commonly referred to as *impo-*

tence). Female sexual arousal disorder is common, however. About 20 percent of women report difficulties with lubrication or arousal during sexual activity (Laumann et al., 1999; Michael et al., 1994). Men with the *lifelong* form of male erectile disorder have never been able to sustain erections for a desired period of time. Men with the *acquired* form of the disorder were able to sustain erections in the past but no longer can. Occasional problems in gaining or sustaining erections are very common, with as many as 30 million men in the United States having erectile problems at sometime in their lives. Such problems do not constitute a disorder until they become persistent and significantly interfere with a man's interpersonal relationships or cause him distress. Only 4 to 9 percent of men have problems sufficient to warrant a diagnosis of male erectile disorder (Laumann et al., 1999; Spector & Carey, 1990). Paul Petersen is one of these men (adapted from Spitzer et al., 1994, pp. 198–199):

CASE STUDY

Paul and Geraldine Petersen have been living together for the last 6 months and are contemplating marriage. Geraldine describes the problem that has brought them to the sex therapy clinic.

"For the last 2 months he hasn't been able to keep his erection after he enters me."

The psychiatrist learns that Paul, age 26, is a recently graduated lawyer, and that Geraldine, age 24, is a successful buyer for a large department store. They both grew up in educated, middle-class, suburban families. They met through mutual friends and started to have sexual intercourse a few months after they met and had no problems at that time.

Two months later, Paul moved from his family home into Geraldine's apartment. This was her idea, and Paul was unsure that he was ready for such an important step. Within a few weeks, Paul noticed that, although he continued to be sexually aroused and wanted intercourse, as soon as he entered his partner, he began to lose his erection and could not stay inside. They would try again, but by then his desire had waned and he was unable to achieve another erection. Geraldine would become extremely angry with Paul, but he would just walk away from her.

(continued)

The psychiatrist learned that sex was not the only area of contention in the relationship. Geraldine complained that Paul did not spend enough time with her and preferred to go to baseball games with his male friends. Even when he was home, he would watch all the sports events that were available on TV and was not interested in going to foreign movies, museums, or the theater with her. Despite these differences, Geraldine was eager to marry Paul and was pressuring him to set a date.

Male erectile disorder is sometimes, although not always, part of a constellation of problems in a couples relationship, as we will discuss later.

Orgasmic Disorders

Women with **female orgasmic disorder,** or *anorgasmia,* experience a recurrent delay in or the complete absence of orgasm after having reached the excitement phase of the sexual response cycle. The DSM-IV-TR specifies that this diagnosis should be made only when a woman is unable to achieve orgasm despite receiving adequate stimulation. About one in four women report difficulties reaching orgasm (Laumann et al., 1999). The problem is greater among postmenopausal women, with about one in three reporting some problems reaching orgasm during sexual stimulation (Rosen & Leiblum, 1995; Spector & Carey, 1990).

The most common form of orgasmic disorder in males is **premature ejaculation.** Men who have this disorder persistently ejaculate with minimal sexual stimulation before they wish to ejaculate. Laumann and colleagues (1999) found that 21 percent of men reported problems with premature ejaculation. Spector and Carey (1990) estimate that between 30 and 40 percent of men have significant trouble delaying ejaculation at will. Again, it is a judgment call about when premature ejaculation becomes a sexual dysfunction. Premature ejaculation must cause significant distress or interpersonal problems before it is considered a disorder. Some men seeking treatment for this problem simply cannot prevent ejaculation before their partner reaches orgasm. Others ejaculate after very little stimulation, long before their partner is fully aroused. One problem with the definition of premature ejaculation is that whether the ejaculation is premature depends in part on how quickly the man's partner becomes aroused to orgasm. Because of the inherent difficulty in defining "premature," this disorder is often referred to as *rapid* ejaculation.

Men with premature ejaculation resort to applying desensitizing creams to their penises before sex, wearing multiple condoms, distracting themselves by doing complex mathematical problems while making love, not allowing their partners to touch them, and masturbating multiple times shortly before having sex in an attempt to delay their ejaculations (Althof, 1995). These tactics are generally unsuccessful and can make their partner feel shut out of the sexual encounter, as in the following account (McCarthy, 1989, pp. 151–152).

CASE STUDY

Bill and Margaret were a couple in their late 20s who had been married for 2 years. Margaret was 27 and the owner of a hair-styling studio. Bill was 29 and a legislative lobbyist for a financial institution. This was a first marriage for both. They had had a rather tumultuous dating relationship before marriage. Margaret had been in individual and group therapy for 1½ years at a university counseling center before dropping out of school to enroll in a hair-styling program. During their dating period, Margaret reentered individual therapy, and Bill, who had never participated in therapy, attended five conjoint sessions. That therapist helped Bill and Margaret deal with issues in their relationship and increased their commitment to marrying. However, the therapist made an incorrect assumption in stating that with increased intimacy and the commitment of marriage, the ejaculatory control problem would disappear. . . .

Margaret saw the early ejaculation as a symbol of lack of love and caring on Bill's part. As the problem continued over the next 2 years, Margaret became increasingly frustrated and withdrawn. She demonstrated her displeasure by resisting his sexual advances, and their intercourse frequency decreased from three or four times per week to once every 10 days. A sexual and marital crisis was precipitated by Margaret's belief that Bill was acting more isolated and distant when they did have intercourse. When they talked about their sexual relationship, it was usually in bed after intercourse, and the communication quickly broke down into tears, anger, and ac-

(continued)

cusations. Bill was on the defensive and handled the sexual issue by avoiding talking to Margaret, which frustrated her even more.

Unbeknownst to Margaret, Bill had attempted a do-it-yourself technique to gain better control. He had bought a desensitizing cream he'd read about in a men's magazine and applied it to the glans of his penis (the caplike structure at the end of the penis) 20 minutes before initiating sex. He also masturbated the day before couple sex. During intercourse he tried to keep his leg muscles tense and think about sports as a way of keeping his arousal in check. Bill was unaware that Margaret felt emotionally shut out during sex. Bill was becoming more sensitized to his arousal cycle and was worrying about erection. He was not achieving better ejaculatory control, and he was enjoying sex less. The sexual relationship was heading downhill, and miscommunication and frustration were growing.

Men with **male orgasmic disorder** experience a recurrent delay in or the absence of orgasm following the excitement phase of the sexual response cycle. In most cases of this disorder, a man cannot ejaculate during intercourse but can ejaculate with manual or oral stimulation. Eight percent of men report problems in reaching orgasm (Laumann et al., 1999).

Sexual Pain Disorders

The final two sexual dysfunctions are sexual pain disorders, *dyspareunia* and *vaginismus*. **Dyspareunia** is genital pain associated with intercourse. It is rare in men but, in community surveys, 10 to 15 percent of women report frequent pain during intercourse (Laumann et al., 1994). In women, the pain may be shallow during intromission (insertion of the penis into the vagina) or deep during penile thrusting. Dyspareunia in women can be the result of dryness of the vagina, caused by antihistamines or other drugs; infection of the clitoris or vulval area; injury or irritation to the vagina; or tumors of the internal reproductive organs. In men, dyspareunia involves painful erections or pain during thrusting.

Vaginismus occurs only in women and involves the involuntary contraction of the muscles surrounding the outer third of the vagina when vaginal penetration with a penis, finger, tampon, or speculum is attempted. Women with vaginismus may experience sexual arousal and have orgasms when their clitoris is stimulated. However, when a penis or another object is inserted into the vagina, the muscles surrounding its opening contract involuntarily. In other women with this disorder, even the anticipation of vaginal insertion may result in this muscle spasm. It is estimated that 5 to 17 percent of women experience vaginismus (Reissing, Binik, & Khalife, 1999).

Causes of Sexual Dysfunctions

How do sexual dysfunctions arise? Most sexual dysfunctions probably have multiple causes, including biological causes and psychosocial causes (see the Concept Overview in Table 16.4 on page 584). Perhaps the most common cause of one sexual dysfunction is another sexual dysfunction. For example, one study found that about 40 percent of people with hypoactive sexual desire disorder also had a diagnosis of an arousal or orgasmic disorder (Segraves & Segraves, 1991). That is, even when they do engage in sex, these people have difficulty becoming aroused or reaching orgasm. This, in turn, greatly reduces their desire to engage in sexual activity. Similarly, many people who experience pain during sexual activity lose all desire for sex.

When people seek help for sexual dysfunctions, clinicians conduct thorough assessments of their medical conditions, the drugs they are taking, the characteristics of their relationships, their attitudes toward their sexuality, and their sexual practices. Even when one of these factors can be identified as the primary cause of a sexual dysfunction, usually several areas of a person's life have been affected by the dysfunction, including his or her self-concept and relationships. All these areas need to be addressed in treatment.

Biological Causes

The DSM-IV-TR sets apart sexual dysfunctions that are caused by medical conditions by giving them a separate diagnosis. Many medical illnesses can cause problems in sexual functioning in both men and women. One of the most common contributors to sexual dysfunction is diabetes, which can result in reduced circulation, leading to reduced erectile tissue, and thus to reduced arousal (Bach et al., 2001; Schiavi et al., 1995). Diabetes often goes undiagnosed, so people may believe that psychological factors are causing their sexual dysfunction, when the cause is really undiagnosed diabetes. Other diseases that are common causes of sexual dysfunction, particularly in men, are cardiovascular disease, multiple sclerosis, renal failure, vascular disease, spinal cord injury, and injury of the autonomic nervous system by surgery or radiation (APA, 2000; Bach et al., 2001; Kelly, 1998).

TABLE 16.4   Concept Overview

Causes of Sexual Dysfunctions

A host of biological, psychological, and sociocultural factors can contribute to sexual dysfunctions.

Biological Causes	Psychological Causes	Sociocultural Causes
Medical conditions	Psychological disorders	Relationship problems
Diabetes	Depression	Lack of communication
Cardiovascular disease	Anxiety disorders	Differences in sexual expectations
Multiple sclerosis	Schizophrenia	Conflicts unrelated to sex
Renal failure	Attitudes and cognitions	Trauma
Vascular disease	Belief that sex is "dirty" or "disgusting"	Cultural taboos against sex
Spinal cord injury	Performance anxiety	
Autonomic nervous system injury		
Prescription drugs		
Antihypertensive medications		
Antipsychotic medications		
Antidepressant medications		
Lithium		
Tranquilizers		
Recreational drugs		
Marijuana		
Cocaine		
Amphetamines		
Nicotine		
Alcohol		
In men		
Low levels of androgen hormones or high levels of estrogen and prolactin		
Genital or urinary tract infections		
In women		
Low levels of estrogen		
Vaginal dryness or irritation		
Injuries during childbirth		

As many as 40 percent of cases of male erectile disorder are caused by one of these medical conditions. In men with cardiovascular disease, sexual dysfunction can be caused directly by the disease, which can, for example, reduce the functioning of the vascular system. Sexual dysfunction may be a psychological response to the presence of the disease. For example, a man who recently had a heart attack may fear he will have another if he has sex and, thus, loses his desire for sex.

In men, abnormally low levels of the androgen hormones, especially testosterone, or high levels of the hormones estrogen and prolactin can cause sexual dysfunction (Bach et al., 2001). In women, hormones do not seem to have a consistent, direct effect on sexual desire. For example, levels of most reproductive hormones change in women over the menstrual cycle, but there is no consistent effect of these hormones on sexual desire—simply, there is variance among women in what parts of their menstrual cycles they feel the most sexual desire (Beck, 1995; Schiavi & Segraves, 1995). Hormones may have an indirect effect on sexual desire by affecting sexual arousal, however. Low levels of estrogen can cause decreases in vasocongestion and vaginal lubrication, leading to diminished sexual arousal, pain during sexual activity, and therefore lowered sexual desire (Sherwin, 1991). Levels of estrogen drop greatly at menopause. Thus, postmenopausal women often complain of lowered sexual desire and arousal. Similarly, women who have had radical hysterectomies, which remove the main source of estrogen, the ovaries, can experience reductions in both sexual desire and arousal.

Vaginal dryness or irritation, which causes pain during sex and therefore lowers sexual desire and arousal, can be caused by radiation therapy, endometriosis, antihistamines, douches, tampons, vaginal contraceptives, and infections, such as vaginitis or pelvic inflammatory disease. Injuries during childbirth that have healed poorly, such as a poorly repaired episiotomy, can cause coital pain in women (Masters et al., 1993). The biological causes of pain during sex in men include genital or urinary tract infections, especially prostatitis, and a rare condition called *Peyronie's disease,* which causes deposits of fibrous tissue in the penis. Women who have had gynecological cancers sometimes report pain, changes in the vaginal anatomy, and problems with their body image or sexual self-concept (Lagana et al., 2001).

Several prescription drugs can diminish sexual drive and arousal and interfere with orgasm. These include antihypertensive drugs taken by people with high blood pressure, antipsychotic drugs, antidepressants, lithium, and tranquilizers. Indeed, one of the most common side effects of the widely used selective serotonin reuptake inhibitors is sexual dysfunction (Bach et al., 2001).

Many recreational drugs, including marijuana, cocaine, amphetamines, and nicotine, can impair sexual functioning (Schiavi & Segraves, 1995). Even though people often drink alcohol to make them feel more sexy and uninhibited, even small amounts of alcohol can significantly impair sexual functioning. Chronic alcoholics often have diagnosable sexual dysfunctions (Bach et al., 2001; Schiavi, 1990). When a sexual dysfunction is caused by substance use, it is given the diagnosis of **substance-induced sexual dysfunction.**

For a man with erectile disorder, one of the best ways to know if the dysfunction has biological causes is to determine whether he has erections during sleep, as healthy men do. If he is having nocturnal erections, then chances are that his erectile problems have psychological origins, at least in part. If he is not having nocturnal erections, then

Although many people drink alcohol to decrease their sexual inhibitions, alcohol can also decrease sexual performance.

chances are the erectile problems have biological causes (Ackerman & Carey, 1995). A thorough assessment of nocturnal erections can be done with devices that directly measure men's erections. In a sleep laboratory, strain gauges are attached to the base and glans (end structure) of the penis to record the magnitude, duration, and pattern of erections, while electroencephalographs record the sleep pattern.

Women also experience cyclic episodes of vasocongestion during sleep, which can be monitored to determine if a woman experiencing arousal problems has a biological disorder. Vasocongestion in women can be measured with a vaginal photoplethysmograph, a tampon-shaped device inserted into a woman's vagina, which records the changes that accompany vasocongestion.

In sum, a number of medical conditions and drugs can affect sexual desire, arousal, and orgasm. It is critical at the outset of any treatment program to determine if any of these factors are contributing to a sexual dysfunction.

Psychological Causes

Our emotional well-being and our beliefs and attitudes about sex greatly influence our sexuality.

Psychological Disorders A number of psychological disorders can cause sexual dysfunction (Bach et al., 2001). Loss of sexual functioning is a common symptom in depression. A person with depression may have no desire for sex or may experience any of the problems in sexual arousal and functioning we have discussed. Unfortunately, the medications used to treat depression often induce problems in sexual functioning. Similarly, people with an anxiety disorder, such as generalized anxiety disorder, panic disorder, or obsessive-compulsive disorder, may find their sexual desire and functioning waning. Loss of sexual desire and functioning is very common among people with schizophrenia.

Attitudes and Cognitions People who have been taught that sex is dirty, disgusting, or sinful or is a "necessary evil" may understandably lack the desire to have sex. They may also know so little about their own bodies and sexual responses that they do not know how to make sex pleasurable. Such is the case with Mrs. Booth (adapted from Spitzer et al., 1994, pp. 251–252):

> CASE STUDY
>
> Mr. and Mrs. Booth have been married for 14 years and have three children, ages 8 through 12. They are both bright and well-educated. Both are from Scotland, from which they moved 10 years ago because of Mr. Booth's work as an industrial consultant. They present with the complaint that Mrs. Booth has been able to participate passively in sex "as a duty" but has never enjoyed it since they have been married.
>
> Before their marriage, although they had had intercourse only twice, Mrs. Booth had been highly aroused by kissing and petting and felt she used her attractiveness to "seduce" her husband into marriage. She did, however, feel intense guilt about their two episodes of premarital intercourse; during their honeymoon, she began to think of sex as a chore that could not be pleasing. Although she periodically passively complied with intercourse, she had almost no spontaneous desire for sex. She never masturbated, had never reached orgasm, thought of all variations such as oral sex as completely repulsive, and was preoccupied with a fantasy of how disapproving her family would be if she ever engaged in any of these activities.
>
> Mrs. Booth is almost totally certain that no woman she respects in any older generation has enjoyed sex and that despite the "new vogue" of sexuality, only sleazy, crude women let themselves act like "animals." These beliefs have led to a pattern of regular but infrequent sex that at best is accommodating and gives little or no pleasure to her or her husband.
>
> Whenever Mrs. Booth comes close to having a feeling of sexual arousal, numerous negative thoughts come into her mind such as, "What am I, a tramp?"; "If I like this, he'll just want it more often"; and "How could I look at myself in the mirror after something like this?" These thoughts almost inevitably are accompanied by a cold feeling and an insensitivity to sensual pleasure. As a result, sex is invariably an unhappy experience. Almost any excuse, such as fatigue or being busy, is sufficient for her to rationalize avoiding intercourse.

Women with severely negative attitudes toward sex, like Mrs. Booth's, also tend to experience dyspareunia and vaginismus, because they have been taught that sex is painful and frightening (Rosen & Leiblum, 1995). Although such attitudes toward sex may be declining among younger people, many younger and older women still report a fear of "letting go," which interferes with orgasm (Heiman & Grafton-Becker, 1989; Tugrul & Kabakci, 1997). They say they fear losing control or acting in a way that will embarrass them. This fear of loss of control may result from a distrust of one's partner, a sense of shame about sex, a poor body image, or a host of other factors.

Another set of attitudes that interfere with sexual functioning appear to be rampant among middle-aged and younger adults. These attitudes are often referred to as *performance concerns* or **performance anxiety** (LoPiccolo, 1992; Masters & Johnson, 1970). People worry so much about whether they are going to be aroused and have orgasms that this worry interferes with sexual functioning: "What if I can't get an erection? I'll die of embarrassment!" "I've got to have an orgasm, or he'll think I'm frigid!" "Oh, my God, I just can't get aroused tonight!" These worried thoughts are so distracting that people cannot focus on the pleasure that sexual stimulation is giving them and, thus, do not become as aroused as they want to or need to in order to reach orgasm (Barlow, Sakheim, & Beck, 1983; Cranston-Cuebas & Barlow, 1990) (see Figure 16.4).

In addition, many people engage in spectatoring: They anxiously attend to reactions and performance during sex as if they were spectators (Masters & Johnson, 1970). Spectatoring distracts from sexual pleasure and interferes with sexual functioning. Unfortunately, people who have had some problems in sexual functioning only develop more performance concerns, which then further interfere with their functioning. By the time they

FIGURE 16.4 **A Model Showing How Anxiety and Cognitive Interference Can Produce Erectile Dysfunction and Other Sexual Disorders**

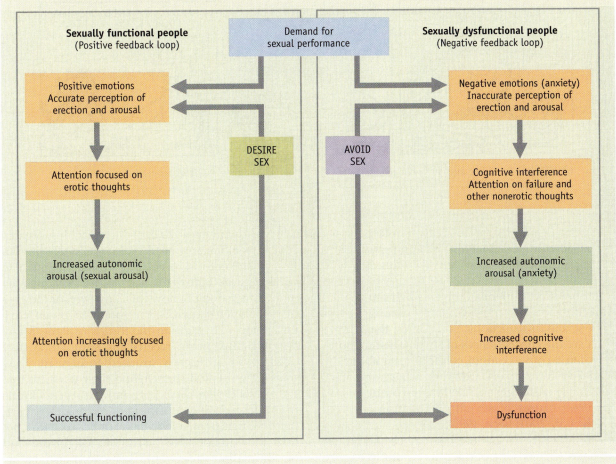

FIGURE 16.4 **A Model Showing How Anxiety and Cognitive Interference Can Produce Erectile Dysfunction and Other Sexual Disorders**

Source: Barlow, 1986.

seek treatment for sexual dysfunction, they may be so anxious about performing sexually that they avoid all sexual activity.

More chronic problems can develop from the way young men learn about their own sexual responses during adolescence. Most males, perhaps 90 percent, have their first orgasmic experience during masturbation as adolescents (McCarthy, 1989). Masturbation is usually practiced in an intense, rapid manner, where the only focus is on ejaculation. Many young men do not view masturbation as a positive, healthy exercise in which they are learning about their bodies. Rather, they feel guilty or embarrassed and anxious about being caught masturbating, so they hurry through it, not paying attention to their bodies' levels of arousal and not learning anything about ejaculatory control. In partner sex, they can become aroused without much stimulation from their partners and may fear ejaculating before their partners become aroused. Thus, they avoid allowing partners to stimulate them and focus, instead, on stimulating

their partners as quickly as possible, so that they can have intercourse. As a result, they come to associate high levels of arousal with anxiety over premature ejaculation, and this anxiety only increases the chance of premature ejaculation.

With experience and maturity, most males gain ejaculatory control through a number of processes, as described by Barry McCarthy (1989, p. 146): "(1) a regular rhythm of being sexual; (2) increased comfort with practice; (3) a more give-and-take 'pleasuring process' rather than goal-oriented foreplay; (4) allowance of more time for the variety of sensations in the sexual experience; (5) greater intimacy and security resulting in increased sexual comfort; (6) partner encouragement for a slower, more tender, rhythmic sexual interchange; and (7) shift of intercourse positions and/or thrusting movements."

Interpersonal and Sociocultural Factors

Although our internal psychological states and beliefs play important roles in our sexuality, sex is largely an interpersonal activity—one that societies

Garfield ®   by Jim Davis

attempt to control. For this reason, interpersonal and sociocultural factors also play important roles in people's sexual interests and activities.

Relationship Problems Problems in intimate relationships are extremely common among people with sexual dysfunctions. Sometimes, these problems are the consequences of sexual dysfunctions, as when a couple cannot communicate about the sexual dysfunction of one of the partners and grow distant from each other. Relationship problems can be direct causes of sexual dysfunctions as well (Bach et al., 2001; Beck, 1995).

Conflicts between partners may be about their sexual activities. One partner may want to engage in a type of sexual activity that the other partner is not comfortable with, or one partner may want to engage in sexual activity much more often than the other partner. People with inhibited desire, arousal, or orgasm often have sexual partners who do not know how to arouse them or are not concerned with their arousal and focus on only themselves. Partners often do not communicate with each other about what is arousing, so that, even if each partner intends to please the other, neither knows what the other wants him or her to do (Ackerman & Carey, 1995; Speckens et al., 1995).

Anorgasmia (lack of orgasm) in women may be tied to lack of communication between a woman and a male partner about what the woman needs to reach orgasm (Hurlbert, 1991). In sexual encounters between men and women, men are still more likely to be the ones who decide when to initiate sex, how long to engage in foreplay, when to penetrate, and what position to use during intercourse. A man's pattern of arousal is often not the same as a woman's pattern of arousal, and he may be making these decisions on the basis of his level of arousal and needs for stimulation, not understanding that hers may be different.

Most women have difficulty reaching orgasm by coitus alone and need oral or manual stimulation of the clitoris to become aroused enough to reach orgasm (Hite, 1976; Kaplan, 1974). Many men and women do not know this, however, or they believe that men should be able to bring women to orgasm by penile insertion and thrusting alone. Many women, thus, never receive the stimulation they need to be sufficiently aroused to orgasm. They may feel inhibited from telling their partners that they would like them to stimulate their clitoris more, because they are afraid of hurting their partners' feelings or angering them, or because they believe they do not have the right to ask for the kind of stimulation they want. Some women fake orgasms to protect their partners' egos. Often, their partners know that they are not fully satisfied, however. Communication between partners may break down further, and sex may become a forum for hostility rather than pleasure.

Conflicts between partners that are not directly about their sexual activity can affect their sexual relationship as well, as we saw in the case of Paul and Geraldine Peterson (Beck, 1995; Rosen & Leiblum, 1995). Anger, distrust, and lack of respect for one's partner can greatly interfere with sexual desire and functioning. When one partner suspects that the other partner has been unfaithful or is losing interest in the relationship, all sexual interest may disappear. Often, there is an imbalance of power in relationships, and people feel exploited, subjugated, and underappreciated by their partners, leading to problems in their sexual relationships (Rosen & Leiblum, 1995).

One study of men and women seeking treatment for hypoactive sexual desire disorder found that women are more likely than men to report problems in their marital relationships, other stressful events in their lives, and higher levels of psychological distress (Donahey & Carroll, 1993). Men seeking treatment are more likely than women to be experiencing other types of sexual dysfunction in addition to low sexual desire, such as erectile dysfunction. Thus, for men, it appears that issues of sexual functioning precipitate their entry into treatment, whereas, for women, lack of sexual desire is linked to a broader array of psychosocial problems.

Trauma Reductions in sexual desire and functioning often follow personal traumas, such as the loss of a loved one, the loss of a job, or the diagnosis of severe illness in one's child. Unemployment in men may contribute to declines in sexual desire and functioning (Morokoff & Gillilland, 1993). Traumas such as unemployment can challenge a person's self-esteem and self-concept, interfering with his or her sexual self-concept. Traumas can also cause a person to experience a depression that includes a loss of interest in most pleasurable activities, including sex. In such cases, clinicians typically focus on treating the depression, with the expectation that sexual desire will resume once the depression has lifted.

One type of personal trauma that is often associated with sexual desire disorders in women is sexual assault (DiLillo, 2001). A woman who has been raped may lose all interest in sex and be disgusted or extremely anxious when anyone, particularly a man, touches her. Her sexual aversion may be tied to a sense of vulnerability and loss of control or to a conditioned aversion to all forms of sexual contact (Leiblum & Rosen, 1988). In addition, male partners of women who have been raped sometimes cannot cope with the rapes and withdraw from sexual encounters with them. This withdrawal may be more common among men who accept rape myths, such as "Women who get raped were asking for it" and "Women enjoy being raped." Women rape survivors may then feel victimized yet again, and their interest in sex may decline even further.

Cross-Cultural Differences Other cultures recognize types of sexual dysfunction not described in the DSM-IV-TR. For example, both the traditional Chinese medical system and the Ayurvedic medical system, which is native to India, teach that loss of semen is detrimental to a man's health (Dewaraja & Sasaki, 1991). Masturbation is strongly discouraged, because it results in semen loss without the possibility of conception. A study of 1,000 consecutive patients seeking treatment in a sexual clinic in India found that 77 percent of the male patients reported difficulties with premature ejaculation and 71 percent were concerned about nocturnal emissions associated with erotic dreams (Verma, Khaitan, & Singh, 1998).

A depersonalization syndrome, known as *Koro*, thought to result from semen loss, has been reported among Malaysians, Southeast Asians, and southern Chinese. This syndrome involves an acute anxiety state, with a feeling of panic and impending death, and a delusion that the penis is shrinking into the body and disappearing. The patient or his relatives may grab and hold the penis until the attack of Koro is ended to stop the penis from disappearing into the body.

In Polynesian culture, there is no word for erection problems in men (Mannino, 1999). If a man does not have an erection, it is assumed that he does not want sex. In some African cultures, the preference is for women's vaginas to be dry and tight for sexual intercourse (Brown, Ayowa, & Brown, 1993). Several herbal treatments are used to achieve this dryness.

In surveys in the United States, less educated and poorer men and women tend to experience more sexual dysfunctions. These problems include having pain during sex, not finding sex pleasurable, being unable to reach orgasm, lacking interest in sex, climaxing too early, and, for men, having trouble maintaining erections (Laumann et al., 1994). People in lower educational and income groups may have more sexual dysfunctions because they are under more psychological stress, their physical health is worse, or they have not had the benefit of educational programs that teach people about their bodies and healthy social relationships.

Trends Across the Life Span

Our stereotypes tell us that young adults, particularly men, can't get enough sex but that sexual activity declines steadily with age, and older adults (i.e., over about 65 years old) hardly ever have sex.

Many older adults remain sexually active and experience little decline in sexual functioning.

It is true that sexual activity is greater among younger adults than older adults, but many older adults remain sexually active well into old age (Bartlik & Goldstein, 2001a, 2001b).

Age-related biological changes can affect sexual functioning. Adequate levels of testosterone are necessary for sexual desire in both men and women. Testosterone levels begin to decline in one's fifties for men and continue to decline steadily through life (Meston, 1997). It becomes more difficult for many men to achieve and maintain erections as they grow old, and the incidence of erectile dysfunction increases with age (Rosen, 1996). Diminished estrogen in postmenopausal women can lead to vaginal dryness and lack of lubrication and, thus, to a reduction in sexual responsivity (Bartlik & Goldstein, 2001a). In many cases of sexual dysfunction in men and women, the cause is not age per se but medical conditions, which are more common in older men and women than in younger people.

For both older men and women, the loss of a lifelong spouse, losses of other family members and friends, health concerns, and discomfort with one's own aging can contribute to sexual problems (Bartlik & Goldberg, 2000, Bartlik & Goldstein, 2001a, 2001b). Conflicts and dissatisfactions in a couple's relationship can become worse as they spend more time together because one or both retire and their children move out of the house. Older couples may need to learn to be more flexible and patient with each other as their bodies change and to try new techniques for stimulating each other. There are a number of biological and psychosocial treatments for sexual dysfunctions in both older and younger people.

Treatments for Sexual Dysfunctions

Because most sexual dysfunctions have multiple causes, treatments often involve a combination of approaches, often including biological interventions, psychosocial therapy focusing on problems in a relationship or the concerns of an individual client, and behavior therapies to help clients learn new skills for increasing sexual arousal and pleasure.

Biological Therapies

If a sexual dysfunction is the direct result of another medical condition, such as diabetes, treating the medical condition often reduces the sexual dysfunction. Similarly, if medications are contributing to a sexual dysfunction, adjusting the dosage or switching to a different type of medication that does not have the sexual side effects can relieve sexual difficulties. Also, getting a person to stop using recreational drugs, such as marijuana, that are causing a sexual dysfunction can often cure the dysfunction (Rosen & Ashton, 1993).

A number of biological treatments are available for men with male erectile disorder (see Table 16.5). A number of drugs have proven useful for the treatment of this disorder (Segraves, 2003). The one that has received the most media attention in recent years is sildenafil (trade name Viagra). Sildenafil is a selective inhibitor of cyclic guanosine monophosphate-specific phosphodiesterase type 5, which plays a critical role in erections. This drug has proven effective both in men whose erectile dysfunction has no known organic cause and in men whose erectile dysfunction is caused by medical conditions, such as hypertension, diabetes, or spinal cord injury (Segraves, 2003; Seidman et al., 2001). Sildenafil does have side effects, though, including headaches, flushing, and stomach irritation, and it does not work in up to 44 percent of men (Bach et al., 2001).

Yohimbine comes from the bark of the yohimbe tree, which Africans have chewed for centuries to increase their sexual desire and functioning. Yohimbine has been shown in some studies to improve erectile functioning in men (Segraves, 2003). Some people can have a severe allergic reaction to yohimbine, including difficulty swallowing and swelling in lips, tongue, and face. Other side effects can include fast or irregular heartbeat, dizziness, and tremors. The antidepressant trazadone, and apomorphine, which affects dopamine levels, can also help men with erectile dysfunction increase their ability to have erections (Segraves, 2003).

Some antidepressants, particularly the selective serotonin reuptake inhibitors (SSRIs), can cause sexual dysfunction. Other drugs can be used, in conjunction with these antidepressants, to reduce the sexual side effects of the antidepressants. One drug that has proven helpful in this regard is bupropion, which goes by the trade names Wellbutrin and Zyban (Ashton & Rosen, 1998). Bupropion appears to reduce the sexual side effects of the SSRIs and can be effective as an antidepressant on its own (Coleman et al., 2001). Sildenafil may also help men whose erectile dysfunction is caused by taking antidepressants, thereby allowing them to continue taking the antidepressants without losing sexual functioning (Balon, 1998).

For men suffering from premature ejaculation, antidepressants can be helpful, including fluoxetine (Prozac), clomipramine (Anafranil), and sertraline (Zoloft). Several studies suggest these drugs significantly reduce the frequency of premature ejaculation (Segraves, 2003).

Several studies have examined the effects of hormone therapy—specifically, the use of testos-

TABLE 16.5 Medical and Surgical Treatments for Male Erectile Disorder

A number of interventions can overcome male erectile disorder.

Treatments	How They Work	Effectiveness
Medications		
Oral medications		
Such as Viagra, Vasomax	Relax muscles that surround small blood vessels in the penis, allowing dilation, so that blood can flow more freely	Effective
Yohimbine, trazadone, apomorphine	Possible involvement of neurotransmitters	Modest improvement in some men
Injections	Injections of smooth muscle relaxants into penis	Moderately effective in most cases but high attrition rate
Topical creams	Topical cream or ointment with vasoactive properties	Uncertain efficacy
Surgery		
Vascular surgery	Unblocks blood vessels that supply the penis	May have limited, short-term benefit
Semirigid surgical prosthesis	Surgical implantation of silicone rods into the penis	Moderately effective, low partner satisfaction ratings
Inflatable prosthesis	Surgical implantation of an inflatable device	Highly effective, high patient and partner satisfaction ratings
Other		
Vacuum pump	Vacuum constriction device that creates a vacuum when held over the penis	Effective in producing erections but not sexual arousal

Sources: Kelly, 1998; Rosen, 1996.

terone—to increase sexual desire in men and women with hypoactive sexual desire disorder. Hormone replacement therapy can be very effective for men whose low levels of sexual desire or arousal are linked to low levels of testosterone, although not for men whose low sexual desire or arousal are not linked to low levels of testosterone (Segraves, 2003). For women, the effects of testosterone therapy are mixed. Some studies find that high levels of testosterone increase sexual desire and arousal in women but also run the risk of significant side effects, including masculinizing effects (e.g., chest hair and voice changes) (Shifren et al., 2000). More moderate levels of testosterone do not have consistent effects on libido for women. The antidepressant bupropion has proven helpful in treating some women with hypoactive sexual desire (Segraves et al., 2004).

A large multinational, double-blind, placebo-controlled study investigated the effects of sildenafil for women with sexual arousal disorder (Basson et al., 2001, 2002). In both premenopausal and postmenopausal women, sildenafil had no demonstrable effect in reversing sexual problems. Other studies have also failed to find that this drug helps women with arousal disorders (Segraves, 2003). Interestingly, the drug does increase vasocongestion and lubrication in women; however, these physiological changes do not consistently lead to greater subjective arousal in women. It seems that, particularly for women, sexual arousal and pleasure take more than physiological arousal.

Women with vaginal dryness may find that using vaginal lubricants significantly increases their ability to become sexually aroused. Hormone replacement therapy can be effective for men whose low levels of sexual desire or arousal are linked to low levels of testosterone or for women whose low sexual desire or arousal, or dyspareunia, are linked to low levels of estrogen (Schiavi & Segraves, 1995; Schiavi et al., 1997).

Psychotherapy

The introduction of drugs, such as sildenfil, that can overcome sexual dysfunctions, at least in men, has dramatically changed the nature of the treatments for these disorders. With the financial and time constraints imposed by managed care, many people seeking treatment for a sexual dysfunction are only offered a medication, not psychotherapy (Leiblum & Rosen, 2000). Many people want only a medication and do not want to engage in psychotherapy to address the possible psychological and interpersonal contributors to their sexual problems.

A variety of psychotherapeutic techniques have been developed, however, and have been shown to help people with sexual dysfunctions (Leiblum & Rosen, 2000). These techniques include individual psychotherapy, in which the person explores the thoughts and previous experiences that impede them from enjoying a positive sexual life. Couples therapy is often used to help couples develop more satisfying sexual relationships. And, as part of both individual and couples therapy, behavioral techniques are used to teach people skills to enhance their sexual experiences and to improve their communication and interactions with their sexual partners.

One psychosocial source of difficulties in sexual functioning can be a fear of contracting a sexually transmitted disease or of becoming pregnant. In *Taking Psychology Personally: Practicing Safe Sex,* we discuss strategies to enhance your safety in sexual encounters.

Individual and Couples Therapy A therapist begins treatment by assessing the attitudes, beliefs, and personal history of an individual client or both members of a couple, to discover the experiences, thoughts, and feelings that are contributing to sexual problems. Cognitive-behavioral interventions are often used to address the attitudes and beliefs that interfere with sexual functioning (McCarthy, 2001; Pridal & LoPiccolo, 2000; Rosen & Leiblum, 1995). For example, a man who fears that he will embarrass himself by not sustaining an erection in a sexual encounter may be challenged to examine the evidence for this having happened to him in the past. If this were a common occurrence for this man, his therapist would explore the cognitions surrounding the experience and help the man challenge these cognitions and practice more positive cognitions. Similarly, a woman who has low sexual desire or difficulties reaching orgasm because she was taught by her parents that sex is dirty would learn to challenge this belief and to adopt a more accepting attitude toward sex.

When one member of a couple has a sexual dysfunction, it may be the result of problems in the couple's relationship, and it may contribute to problems in the relationship. Many therapists prefer to treat sexual dysfunctions in the context of the couple's relationship, if possible, rather than focusing only on the individual suffering the sexual dysfunction. The therapist may use role plays during therapy sessions to observe how the couple talk about sex with each other and perceive each other's role in sexual encounters (e.g., Pridal & LoPiccolo, 2000).

Some couples in long-standing relationships have abandoned the *seduction rituals*—the activities that arouse sexual interest in both partners—they followed when they were first together (McCarthy, 2001; Verhulst & Heiman, 1988). Couples in which both partners work may be particularly prone to try to squeeze in sexual encounters late at night, when both partners are very tired and not very interested in sex. These encounters may be rushed or not fully satisfying and lead to a gradual decline in interest for any sexual intimacy. A therapist may encourage a couple to set aside enough time so that they can engage in seduction rituals and satisfying sexual encounters (McCarthy, 1997). For example, partners may decide to hire a baby-sitter for their children, have a romantic dinner out, and then go to a hotel, where they can have sex without rushing or being interrupted by their children.

Partners often differ in their *scripts* for sexual encounters—their expectations about what will take place during a sexual encounter and about what each partner's responsibilities are (Pridal & LoPiccolo, 2000). Resolving these differences in scripts may be a useful goal in therapy. For example, if a woman lacks desire for sex because she feels her partner is too rough during sex, a therapist may encourage the partner to slow down and show the woman the kind of gentle intimacy she needs to enjoy sex. In general, therapists help partners understand what each other wants and needs from sexual interactions and negotiate mutually acceptable and satisfying repertoires of sexual exchange.

When the conflicts between partners involve matters other than their sexual practices, the therapist focuses on these conflicts primarily and the sexual dysfunction only secondarily. Such conflicts may involve an imbalance of power in the relationship, distrust or hostility, or disagreements over important values or decisions. Cognitive-behavioral therapies are most commonly used, although some therapists use psychodynamic interventions, and some use interventions based on family systems therapy. Cognitive-behavioral therapies have been researched more than other types of therapy and have been shown to be effective for several types of sexual dysfunctions (see Leiblum & Rosen, 2000).

Whether a therapist uses a cognitive-behavioral or another therapeutic approach to addressing the psychological issues involved in a sexual dysfunc-

Taking Psychology Personally

Practicing Safe Sex

One of the most common causes of low sexual desire or problems in sexual functioning is fear—fear of being hurt, of getting pregnant or causing someone else to become pregnant, or of getting a sexually transmitted disease (STD). Practicing safe sex cannot protect you from violence by a partner or from a sexual dysfunction, but it can decrease your risk for pregnancy and sexually transmitted diseases, which can improve your sexual satisfaction and protect your health.

Sexually transmitted diseases, such as acquired immune deficiency syndrome (AIDS), chlamydia, herpes, genital warts, gonorrhea, and syphilis, often have no obvious signs or symptoms. You cannot know if a potential sexual partner has an STD by just looking at him or her. Thus, it is essential to practice safe sex if you are going to be sexually active.

What does practicing safe sex mean? The following are some general tips:

- *Have monogamous sexual relationships.* Have sex with only one person, who in turn is having sex only with you. If you or your partner change sexual partners frequently, your risk of contracting a sexually transmitted disease is increased.

- *Know your partner's sexual history before you engage in sexual activity.* It can be very difficult to talk about your partner's history or your own. Volunteer information about your own history and then ask your partner about his or hers. Persist if your partner tries to brush aside your concerns and be prepared to postpone or refuse sexual contact if your partner will not answer your questions. Consider having both of you tested for HIV.

- *Avoid sexual activity if you or your partner might have been exposed to any sexually transmitted disease.* Most of the sexually transmitted diseases can be treated medically, and sex can be resumed when the disease is cured or under control.

- *Wash your genitals after sexual contact.* Washing helps reduce the risk but does not eliminate it.

- *Urinate immediately after intercourse.* Doing so helps flush out some germs.

- *Do not have sex under the influence of alcohol or other drugs.* Alcohol and other drugs can lead you to practice unsafe sex, can lead to misunderstandings between partners about what sexual activities are acceptable, and can impair your ability to resist unwanted sexual activities.

- *Use condoms for vaginal and anal intercourse.*

  Use a condom *every* time you have sex.

  Put condoms on during foreplay, before there is any pre-ejaculatory fluid.

  After ejaculation and before the penis relaxes, remove the condom by holding it around the base and withdrawing it from the penis.

  Use another condom if sex is repeated.

  Store condoms in a cool, dry place (not a wallet or the glove compartment of a car).

  Never test condoms by inflating them or stretching them.

  Never use oil-based lubricants, such as petroleum jelly (Vaseline), on condoms.

  Never reuse condoms.

- *Know that oral sex can also spread STDs.* Males should wear condoms during oral sex. Partners performing oral sex on women should use dental dams or other latex barriers to protect their mouths from direct exposure to vaginal fluids.*

Many people do not practice safe sex because they feel it reduces spontaneity and excitement in sexual encounters. However, condom use can be eroticized so that it becomes a part of foreplay. Also, knowing that you are practicing safe sex can reduce fear and, therefore, increase your ability to enjoy sexual encounters. Most important, protecting yourself from sexually transmitted diseases, particularly AIDS, should always be a higher priority than having a little more spontaneity in any sexual encounter.

*Adapted from "Breaking the STD Chain," distributed by Cowell Student Health Center and the Office of Residential Education, Stanford University.

---

tion, direct sex therapy using behavioral techniques often is also a part of therapy. When a sexual dysfunction seems to be due, at least in part, to inadequate sexual skills of the client and his or her partner, sex therapy focusing on these practices can be useful. Some people have never learned what practices give them or their partners pleasure or have fallen out of the habit of engaging in these practices. Sex therapy teaches these practices and helps partners develop a regular pattern of satisfying sexual encounters (see the Concept Overview in Table 16.6 on page 594).

TABLE 16.6 Concept Overview

Sex Therapy

Sex therapy is designed to help individuals learn what their bodies need for sexual satisfaction.

Sensate Focus Therapy

Phase one: gentle nongenital touching, focusing on pleasurable sensations and communication

Phase two: stimulation of partner's breasts and genitals without intercourse

Phase three: intercourse with a focus on enhancing and sustaining pleasure, not orgasm and performance

Stop-Start Technique (for Premature Ejaculation)

Phase one: stimulation of the man's penis stops just before he ejaculates; he relaxes and concentrates on bodily sensations until arousal passes

Phase two (if female partner involved): the woman inserts the man's penis into her vagina but remains quiet

Phase three: the female partner creates some thrusting motion with slow, long strokes

Squeeze Technique (for Premature Ejaculation)

The man's partner stimulates him to erection but then applies a firm squeeze to his penis to reduce erection. Exercise continues until the man learns to control ejaculation.

Relaxation Technique (for Vaginismus)

The woman is taught to relax the muscles at the opening of her vagina; gradually, she inserts larger dilators while practicing relaxation exercises and becoming accustomed to the feel of the object in her vagina.

Sex therapy often includes teaching or encouraging clients to masturbate (Heiman, 2000). The goals of masturbation are for the people to explore their own bodies to discover what is arousing and to become less inhibited about their own sexuality. Then, individuals are taught to communicate what they have learned to their partners. This technique can be especially helpful for anorgasmic women, many of whom have never masturbated and have little knowledge of what they need to become aroused. Studies show that more than 80 percent of anorgasmic women are able to have an orgasm when they learn to masturbate, and 20 to 60 percent are able to have an orgasm with their partner after learning to masturbate (Heiman, 2000). Women also report increased enjoyment and satisfaction from sex, a more relaxed attitude toward sex and life, and increased acceptance of their bodies.

The client's cognitions while engaging in new sexual exercises can be evaluated and used as a focus of therapy sessions (McCarthy, 1997). For example, a woman who is learning how to masturbate for the first time may realize that she has thoughts such as "I'm going to get caught and I'll be so embarrassed," "I shouldn't be doing this—this is sinful," and "Only pathetic people do this" while masturbating. A cognitive-behavioral therapist can then help the woman address the accuracy of these thoughts and decide whether she wants to maintain this attitude toward masturbation. If the woman is in psychodynamic therapy, the therapist might explore the origins of the woman's attitudes about masturbation in her early relationships. Thus, the behavioral techniques of sex therapy not only directly teach the client new sexual skills but also provide material for discussion in therapy sessions.

Sensate Focus Therapy   One of the mainstays of sex therapy is **sensate focus therapy** (Althof, 2000; Masters & Johnson, 1970). In this therapy, one partner is active, carrying out a set of exercises to stimulate the other partner, while the other partner is the passive recipient, focusing on the pleasure that the exercises bring. Then, the partners switch roles, so that each spends time being both the giver and the recipient of the stimulation. The exercises should be carried out at quiet, unhurried times, which the partners plan.

In the early phases of this therapy, partners are instructed *not* to be concerned about or even to attempt intercourse. Rather, they are told to focus intently on the pleasure created by the exercises.

These instructions are meant to reduce performance anxiety and concern about achieving orgasm.

In the first phase of sensate focus therapy, partners spend time gently touching each other, but not around the genitals. They are instructed to focus on the sensations and to communicate with each other about what does and does not feel good. The goal is to have the partners spend intimate time together, communicating, without pressure for intercourse. This first phase may continue for several weeks, until the partners feel comfortable with the exercise and have learned what gives each of them pleasure.

In the second phase of sensate focus therapy, the partners spend time directly stimulating each other's breasts and genitals but still without attempting to have intercourse and instead focusing on intimacy and communication. If the problem is a female arousal disorder, the woman guides her partner to stimulate her in arousing ways. It is acceptable for a woman to be aroused to orgasm during these exercises, but the partners are instructed not to attempt intercourse until she regularly becomes fully aroused by her partner during sensate focus exercises. If the problem is a male erectile disorder, the man guides his partner in touching him in ways that feel arousing. If he has an erection, he is to let it come and go naturally. Intercourse is forbidden until he is able to have erections easily and frequently during the sensate focus exercises.

Throughout these exercises, the partner with the problem is instructed to be selfish and to focus only on the arousing sensations and on communicating with his or her partner about what feels good. The touching should proceed in a relaxed and nondemanding atmosphere. Once the partner with the problem regularly experiences arousal with genital stimulation, the partners may begin having intercourse, but the focus remains on enhancing and sustaining pleasure, rather than on orgasm or performance.

The following case study indicates how the behavioral techniques of sensate focus therapy can help a couple recognize and confront the complex personal and interpersonal issues that may be interfering with their enjoyment of sex (Althof, 2000, p. 270).

In sensate focus therapy, people are encouraged to spend time exploring what sexually arouses each other without feeling pressured to reach orgasm.

CASE STUDY

Murray, a 53-year-old successful insurance agent, and his wife, a 50-year-old nutritional counselor, had been married for 28 years. With the exception of time spent on vacation, Murray had a 7-year history of erectile dysfunction. The frequency of their love making had gradually declined to its current level of once every 4 months. Murray reported considerable performance anxiety, enhanced by his competitive personality style. He summed up his dilemma: "When you have a life full of successes, you don't get much practice at how to deal with inadequacy."

During the first hour [of therapy], sensate focus exercises were suggested, and instructions given to engage in sensual nongenital touching. They returned in a week, noting how difficult it had been to find time to pleasure one another. Their mutual avoidance was discussed and understood as a means of warding off feelings of inadequacy. Working through the resistance allowed the couple to engage in the exercises three times over the course of

(continued)

the next week. With the pleasuring, Murray began to achieve good, long-lasting erections.

Therapy then progressed to include genital touching. After the first week, they talked about their problem of "silliness." They realized that humor had been used to cope with the dysfunction. Now, however, joking in bed seemed to inhibit sexual closeness. Murray's good erections were maintained, although he was having trouble concentrating on his sensations. Further exploration revealed that he was focusing his attention in a driven, intense manner. To counter this, [the therapist] redirected him to maintain a relaxed awareness akin to meditation. Murray found this analogy helpful, and the couple felt ready to proceed with vaginal containment. During the following week, they "disobeyed" and moved on to have mutually satisfying intercourse. They feared the recurrence of the old problem, but it did not return, and the remaining two sessions were spent talking about their sexual life. Despite otherwise good communication, they had never been able before to broach this topic with one another.

Techniques for Treating Premature Ejaculation
Two techniques are useful in helping a man with premature ejaculation gain control over his ejaculations: the stop-start technique (Semans, 1956) and the squeeze technique (Masters & Johnson, 1970). The **stop-start technique** can be carried out either through masturbation or with a partner. In the first phase, the man is told to stop stimulating himself or to tell his partner to stop stimulation just before he is about to ejaculate. He then relaxes and concentrates on the sensations in his body until his level of arousal declines. At that point, he or his partner can resume stimulation, again stopping before the point of ejaculatory inevitability. If stimulation stops too late and the man ejaculates, he is encouraged not to feel angry or disappointed but to enjoy the ejaculation and reflect on what he has learned about his body and then resume the exercise. If a man is engaging in this exercise with a female partner, they are instructed not to engage in intercourse until he has sufficient control over his ejaculations during her manual stimulation of him.

In the second phase of this process, when a female partner is involved, the man lies on his back, with his female partner on top of him, and she

inserts his penis into her vagina but then remains quiet. Most men with premature ejaculation have intercourse only in the man-on-top position, with quick and short thrusting during intercourse, which makes it very difficult for them to exert control over their ejaculations. The goal is for the man to enjoy the sensation of being in the woman's vagina without ejaculating. During the exercise, he is encouraged to touch or massage his partner and to communicate with her about what each is experiencing. If he feels he is reaching ejaculatory inevitability, he can request that she dismount and lie next to him until his arousal subsides. The partners are encouraged to engage in this exercise for at least 10 to 15 minutes, even if they must interrupt it several times to prevent him from ejaculating.

In the third phase of the stop-start technique, she creates some thrusting motion while still on top of him, but using slow, long strokes. The partners typically reach orgasm and experience the entire encounter as highly intimate and pleasurable. Female partners of men with premature ejaculation often have trouble reaching orgasm themselves, because the men lose their erections after ejaculating long before the women are highly aroused, and tension is high between the partners during sex. The stop-start technique can create encounters in which female partners receive the stimulation they need to reach orgasm as well.

The **squeeze technique** is used somewhat less often, because it is harder to teach to partners (McCarthy, 2001). The man's partner stimulates him to an erection; then, when he signals that ejaculation is imminent, the partner applies a firm but gentle squeeze to his penis, either at the glans or at the base, for three or four seconds. This results in a partial loss of erection. The partner can then stimulate him again to the point of ejaculation and use the squeeze technique to stop the ejaculation. The goal of this technique, as with the stop-start technique, is for the man with a premature ejaculation disorder to learn to identify the point of ejaculatory inevitability and to control his arousal level at that point.

Techniques for Treating Vaginismus Vaginismus is often treated by deconditioning the woman's automatic tightening of the muscles of her vagina (Leiblum, 2000). She is taught about the muscular tension at the opening of her vagina and the need to learn to relax those muscles. In a safe setting, she is instructed to insert her own fingers into her vagina. She examines her vagina in a mirror and practices relaxation exercises. She may also use silicon or metal vaginal dilators made for this exercise. Gradually, she inserts larger and larger dilators, as she practices relaxation exercises and becomes accustomed to the feel of the dilator in her vagina. If she has a partner, his or her fingers may be used instead of the dilator. If the woman has a male partner, eventually she guides his penis into her vagina, while remaining in control.

Gay, Lesbian, and Bisexual People

Most of the treatments for sexual dysfunctions assume that the client is in a heterosexual relationship, but sexual dysfunctions can arise in gay, lesbian, and bisexual relationships as well. Often, the causes of their sexual dysfunctions are the same as the causes of sexual dysfunctions in heterosexual people, such as medical disorders or medications, biological aging, or conflicts with partners. Many of the problems in sexual functioning experienced by gay, lesbian, and bisexual people, however, may have to do with society's attitudes toward them and the particular stressors they face (Gilman et al., 2001). They may have lost partners and friends to AIDS, and grief and depression can impair sexual functioning. The fear of contracting the human immunodeficiency virus (HIV) can also heighten sexual anxiety and dampen sexual desire.

Gay, lesbian, and bisexual people must constantly deal with homophobia. They may face frequent discrimination and harassment. They have strong fear of homophobic violence against them. Gay, lesbian, and bisexual parents face chronic challenges to their legitimacy as parents. All of these pressures can interfere with normal sexual functioning.

Therapists treating gay, lesbian, or bisexual clients must be sensitive to the psychological conflicts and stresses these clients face as a result of society's rejection of their lifestyle, as well as to the contributions of these stresses to their sexual functioning (APA, 2000). Most of the sex therapy treatments can readily be adapted for gay, lesbian, or bisexual couples. It can be important to take into account the special social context in which any psychological problem reported by a gay, lesbian, or bisexual client occurs, however.

We should note that the attitude of clinical psychology as a profession toward homosexuality has changed over the past several decades. Early versions of the DSM listed homosexuality, particularly "ego-dystonic homosexuality" (which meant that the person did not want to be homosexual), as a mental disorder. Gay men, lesbians, and bisexual people argued that their sexual orientation is a natural part of themselves and a characteristic that causes them no discomfort and that they don't wish to alter or eliminate. In addition, there was little evidence that psychotherapy could lead a ho-

Sexual dysfunctions can also arise in the context of gay, lesbian, and bisexual relationships.

mosexual person to become heterosexual. In 1973, the American Psychiatric Association removed homosexuality from its list of recognized psychological disorders (Spitzer, 1981).

Large, epidemiological studies find that gay and bisexual men show a higher prevalence of depression and panic attacks than heterosexual men, however, and lesbian and bisexual women show a greater prevalence of generalized anxiety disorder than heterosexual women (Cochran, Sullivan, & Mays, 2003). These higher rates of mental-health problems seem to be due to the greater levels of stress in the lives of gay, lesbian, and bisexual individuals because of homophobia and discrimination.

Cultural Issues

The treatments for the sexual dysfunctions must also take into account the religious, moral, and cultural values that clients have concerning sex. The treatments described so far in this chapter tend to be based on the assumption that men and women should have sex when they wish and should enjoy it each time they have it. This assumption is not shared by persons of all backgrounds. Inhibitions about sex based on religious or cultural teachings are often seen as the causes of sexual dysfunctions by sex therapists. At the very least, cultural inhibitions against talking about sex can get in the way of therapy. The experienced therapist works within the values framework of the sexual partners, first finding out what is in their current repertoire of sexual activity and then building on that, according to their comfort.

Finally, many cultures have their own folk remedies for sexual dysfunctions (Kelly, 1998; Mannino, 1999). In Africa, impotent men drink potions and engage in ritual ceremonies to overcome their dysfunction. Hashish is the cure for sexual dysfunction in males in Morocco, whereas women who are anorgasmic are encouraged to take a younger lover or have a lesbian relationship. In Thailand, men drink a tonic made of the bile of a cobra, the blood of a monkey, and local liquor. In India, they apply an herb to the penis that is a potent irritant. In other parts of the world, the testes and penises of seals and tigers are consumed to overcome erectile problems in men. Traditional Chinese healers use a number of herbal preparations and acupuncture to treat sexual dysfunctions.

SUMMING UP

- The sexual response cycle includes five phases: desire, excitement or arousal, plateau, orgasm, and resolution.

- People with disorders of sexual desire have little or no desire to engage in sex. These disorders include hypoactive sexual desire disorder and sexual aversion disorder.

- People with sexual arousal disorders do not experience the physiological changes that make up the excitement or arousal phase of the sexual response cycle. These disorders include female sexual arousal disorder and male erectile disorder.

- Women with female orgasmic disorder do not experience orgasm or have greatly delayed orgasm after reaching the excitement phase. Men with premature ejaculation reach ejaculation before they wish. Men with male orgasmic disorder have a recurrent delay in or an absence of orgasm following sexual excitement.

- The two sexual pain disorders are dyspareunia, genital pain associated with intercourse, and vaginismus, involuntary contraction of the vaginal muscles in women.

- The biological causes of sexual dysfunctions include undiagnosed diabetes or other medical conditions, prescription or recreational drug use (including alcohol), and hormonal or vascular abnormalities.

- The psychological causes include psychological disorders and maladaptive attitudes and cognitions (especially performance concerns).

- The sociocultural and interpersonal causes include problems in intimate relationships, traumatic experiences, and an upbringing or a cultural environment that devalues or degrades sex.

- When the cause of a sexual dysfunction is biological, treatments that eradicate the cause can cure the sexual dysfunction. Alternately, drug therapies or prostheses can be used.

- Sex therapy corrects the inadequate sexual practices of a client and his or her partner. The techniques of sex therapy include sensate focus therapy, instruction in masturbation, the stop-start and squeeze techniques, and the deconditioning of vaginal contractions.

- Couples therapy focuses on decreasing conflicts between couples over their sexual practices or over other areas of their relationship.

- Individual psychotherapy helps people recognize conflicts or the negative attitudes behind their sexual dysfunctions and resolve these.

PARAPHILIAS

People find all sorts of creative ways to fulfill their sexual needs and desires while remaining within the limits set on sexual behavior by their society. Some examples in Western culture include the use of erotic fantasies, pictures or stories, or sex toys to enhance arousal while engaging in masturbation or sexual encounters with others. People vary greatly in what they do and do not find arousing (see Table 16.7). One person may find oral sex the most stimulating form of activity, whereas another person may be repulsed by oral sex. One man may become extremely aroused while watching a wet T-shirt contest, but another man may experience such a contest as silly. One woman may find men with beards extremely sexy, whereas another woman may dislike facial hair on men. Most of the time, these variations in preferences about sexually arousing stimuli simply provide spice to life.

Societies have always drawn lines between the types of sexual activities they allow and the types they do not allow. Judgments about what are acceptable sexual activities vary by culture and across historical periods. In Western cultures prior to the twentieth century and in some Islamic nations today, men are prohibited from seeing most of women's bodies, except their faces and hands, for fear that viewing women's legs and perhaps even their arms or their hair could sexually arouse men.

TABLE 16.7 What Kinds of Sexual Practices Do People Find Appealing?

A national survey of 18- to 44-year-olds found that many different sexual practices appeal to people, with men finding more activities appealing than women do.

Practice	Percentage Saying "Very Appealing"	
	Men	Women
Vaginal intercourse	83	78
Watching partner undress	50	30
Receiving oral sex	50	33
Giving oral sex	37	19
Group sex	14	1
Anus stimulated by partner's fingers	6	4
Using dildos/vibrators	5	3
Watching others do sexual things	6	2
Having a same-gender sex partner	4	3
Having sex with a stranger	5	1

Source: Michael et al., 1994.

Although we may like to think that, in our modern culture, we disallow only the sexual behaviors that are truly "abnormal," our judgments about what are normal and abnormal sexual behaviors are still subjective and culturally specific. Consider the following series of behaviors exhibited by three men. The first man goes to a public beach to watch women in skimpy bikinis. The second man pays to see a female topless dancer in a nightclub. The third man stands outside a woman's bedroom window at night, secretly watching her undress. The behavior of the first man is not only allowed but also is promoted in many movies, television shows, and commercials. The behavior of the second man is a form of allowed sexual commerce. Only the behavior of the third man is prohibited both by modern cultural norms and by laws. All three men, however, intend to view women's partially or fully nude bodies because they find such activity sexually arousing.

Atypical sexual behaviors that the DSM-IV-TR considers to be disorders are the **paraphilias** (Greek for "besides" and "love"). When people with paraphilias violate laws, they are referred to as *sex offenders*. The paraphilias are sexual activities that involve (1) nonhuman objects, (2) nonconsenting adults, (3) suffering or the humiliation of the person or the person's partner, or (4) children (see the Concept Overview in Table 16.8 on page 600). Paraphilias are sometimes divided into those that involve the consent of others (such as some sadomasochistic practices) and those that involve nonconsenting others (as in pedophilia). They can also be divided into those that involve contact with others (such as frotteurism) and those that do not necessarily involve contact with others (such as some fetishes).

Many people have occasional paraphilic fantasies. For example, one study of men's sexual fantasies found that 62 percent fantasized having sex with a young girl, 33 percent fantasized raping a woman, 12 percent fantasized being humiliated during sex, 5 percent fantasized having sexual activity with an animal, and 3 percent fantasized having sexual activity with a young boy (Crepault & Couture, 1980). In a study of male college undergraduates, 21 percent reported being sexually attracted to children, 9 percent fantasized having sex with children, 5 percent masturbated to fantasies of having sex with children, and 7 percent indicated they would become sexually involved with children if they could be assured they would never be discovered (Briere & Runtz, 1989). Most of these men would not be diagnosed with paraphilias because their fantasies were not the primary focus of their sexual arousal and they reported making no attempts to act out these fantasies.

For persons diagnosed with paraphilias, atypical sexual acts are their primary forms of sexual arousal. They often feel compelled to engage in their paraphilias, even though they know they could be punished by law or when they are distressed about feeling so compelled. Some people with paraphilia pay prostitutes to help them act out their fantasies, because it is difficult to find willing partners. Others with paraphilias force their fantasies on unwilling victims.

The paraphilias differ greatly in how severely they affect people other than the person with the paraphilia. We begin our discussion of the paraphilias with the one that is most benign: fetishism. People with *fetishism* do not typically impose their atypical sexual practices on other people. Indeed, the focus of their sexual activities are nonhuman objects. The second set of paraphilias we discuss,

TABLE 16.8   Concept Overview

The Paraphilias

The paraphilias are sexual activities that involve nonhuman objects, nonconsenting adults, suffering or the humiliation of oneself or one's partner, or children.

Diagnosis	Description
Fetishism	A person uses inanimate objects as the preferred or exclusive source of sexual arousal.
Transvestism	In this fetish, a heterosexual man dresses in women's clothing as his primary means of becoming sexually aroused.
Sexual sadism	Sexual gratification is obtained through inflicting pain and humiliation on one's partner.
Sexual masochism	Sexual gratification is obtained through experiencing pain and humiliation at the hands of one's partner.
Voyeurism	Sexual arousal is obtained by compulsively and secretly watching another person undressing, bathing, engaging in sex, or being naked.
Exhibitionism	Sexual gratification is obtained by exposing one's genitals to involuntary observers.
Frotteurism	Sexual gratification is obtained by rubbing one's genitals against or fondling the body parts of a nonconsenting person.
Pedophilia	Adults obtain sexual gratification by engaging in sexual activities with young children.

Source: Reprinted with permission from Diagnostic and Statistical Manual of Mental Disorders, Fourth Edition, Text Revision. Copyright © 2000 American Psychiatric Association.

sadism and *masochism*, are less benign, because they hold the potential for physical harm, even if both partners are engaging in the sexual activity willingly. The third set of paraphilias—*voyeurism, exhibitionism*, and *frotteurism*—are not benign, because, by definition, they require victims. Finally, the most severe paraphilia is *pedophilia*, because the victims of pedophiles are the most powerless victims: children.

Fetishism

Fetishism involves the use of inanimate objects (fetishes) as the preferred or exclusive source of sexual arousal or gratification. Soft fetishes are objects that are soft, furry, or lacy, such as frilly women's panties, stockings, and garters. Hard fetishes are objects that are smooth, harsh, or black, such as spike-heeled shoes, black gloves, and garments made of leather or rubber. These soft and hard objects are somewhat arousing to many people and, indeed, are promoted as arousing by their manufacturers. For most people, however, the objects simply add to the sexiness of the people wearing them, and their desire is for sex with those people. For the person with fetishism, the desire is linked to the object itself (adapted from Spitzer et al., 1994, p. 247):

CASE STUDY

A 32-year-old, single, male, freelance photographer presented with the chief complaint of "abnormal sex drive." The patient related that although he was somewhat sexually attracted by women, he was far more attracted by "their panties."

To the best of the patient's memory, sexual excitement began at about age 7, when he came upon a pornographic magazine and felt stimulated by pictures of partially nude women wearing panties. His first ejaculation occurred at 13 via masturbation to fantasies of women wearing panties. He masturbated into his older sister's panties, which he had stolen without her knowledge. Subsequently, he stole panties from her friends and from other women he met socially. He found pretexts to "wander" into the bedrooms of women during social occasions and would quickly rummage through their possessions until he found a pair of panties to his satis-

(continued)

faction. He later used these to masturbate into and then "saved them" in a "private cache." The pattern of masturbating into women's underwear had been his method of achieving sexual excitement and orgasm from adolescence until the present consultation.

The patient first had sexual intercourse at 18. Since then he had had intercourse on many occasions, and his preferred partner was a prostitute paid to wear panties, with the crotch area cut away, during the act. On less common occasions when sexual activity was attempted with a partner who did not wear panties, his sexual excitement was sometimes weak.

The patient felt uncomfortable dating "nice women" as he felt that friendliness might lead to sexual intimacy and that they would not understand his sexual needs. He avoided socializing with friends who might introduce him to such women. He recognized that his appearance, social style, and profession all resulted in his being perceived as a highly desirable bachelor. He felt anxious and depressed because his social life was limited by his sexual preference.

People with transvestism gain sexual pleasure by dressing in the clothes of the opposite sex.

One elaborate form of fetishism is **transvestism,** also referred to as *cross-dressing,* in which heterosexual men dress in women's clothing as their primary means of becoming sexually aroused. They may surreptitiously wear only one women's garment, such as a pair of women's panties, under their business suits. The complete cross-dresser fully clothes himself in women's garments and applies makeup and a wig. Some men engage in cross-dressing alone. Others participate in transvestite subcultures, in which groups of men gather for drinks, meals, and dancing while elaborately dressed as women (adapted from Spitzer et al., 1994, pp. 257–258):

CASE STUDY

Mr. A., a 65-year-old security guard, is distressed about his wife's objections to his wearing a nightgown at home in the evening, now that his youngest child has left home. His appearance and demeanor, except when he is dressing in women's clothes, are always masculine, and he is exclusively heterosexual. Occasionally, over the past 5 years, he has worn an inconspicuous item of female clothing even when dressed as a man, sometimes a pair of panties, sometimes an ambiguous pinkie ring. He always carries a photograph of himself dressed as a woman.

His first recollection of an interest in female clothing was putting on his sister's underpants at age 12, an act accompanied by sexual excitement. He continued periodically to put on women's underpants—an activity that invariably resulted in an erection, sometimes a spontaneous emission, and sometimes masturbation but never accompanied by fantasy. Although he occasionally wished to be a girl, he never fantasized himself as one. During his single years he was always attracted to women but was shy about sex. Following his marriage at age 22, he had his first heterosexual intercourse.

His involvement with female clothes was of the same intensity even after his marriage. Beginning at age 45, after a chance exposure to a magazine called *Transvestia,* he began to increase his cross-dressing activity. He learned there were other men like himself, and he became more and more preoccupied with

(continued)

female clothing in fantasy and progressed to periodically dressing completely as a woman. More recently he has become involved in a transvestite network, writing to other transvestites contacted through the magazine and occasionally attending transvestite parties. These parties have been the only times that he has cross-dressed outside his home.

Although still committed to his marriage, sex with his wife has dwindled over the past 20 years as his waking thoughts and activities have become increasingly centered on cross-dressing. Over time this activity has become less eroticized and more an end in itself, but it still is a source of some sexual excitement. He always has an increased urge to dress as a woman when under stress; it has a tranquilizing effect. If particular circumstances prevent him from cross-dressing, he feels extremely frustrated.

Some clinicians question whether fetishism should qualify as a psychiatric diagnosis or should be considered a variation in human sexual activity. Many, perhaps most, people with fetishism do not seek therapy or feel particularly disturbed about their behavior. In most cases, the behavior is socially harmless because it is done in private and does not involve the infliction of harm on others. Fetishism is one of the most common secondary diagnoses of persons with other types of paraphilias, however (Abel & Osborn, 1992). That is, many people who have fetishes also engage in other atypical sexual practices, including pedophilia, exhibitionism, and voyeurism. Thus, for some people, fetishes are part of a larger pattern of atypical sexual behaviors, including behaviors that have victims.

Sexual Sadism and Sexual Masochism

Sexual sadism and **sexual masochism** are two separate diagnoses, although sadistic and masochistic sexual practices often are considered together as a pattern referred to as **sadomasochism.** In sexual sadism, a person gains sexual gratification by inflicting pain and humiliation on his or her sex partner. In sexual masochism, a person gains sexual gratification by suffering pain or humiliation during sex. Some people occasionally engage in moderately sadistic or masochistic behaviors during sex or simulate such behaviors without actually carry-

ing through with the infliction of pain or suffering. Persons who are diagnosed with sexual sadism or masochism engage in these behaviors as their primary form of sexual gratification.

The sexual rituals in sadism and masochism fall into four types: physical restriction, which involves the use of bondage, chains, or handcuffs as part of sex; the administration of pain, in which one partner inflicts pain or harm on the other with beatings, whippings, electrical shock, burning, cutting, stabbing, strangulation, torture, mutilation, and even death; hypermasculinity practices, including the aggressive use of enemas, fists, and dildos in the sexual act; and humiliation, in which one partner verbally and physically humiliates the other during sex (Sandnabba et al., 2002). The partner who is the victim in such encounters may be a willing victim or may be a nonconsenting victim on whom the person with sadism carries out his or her wishes. A variety of props may be used in such encounters, including black leather garments, chains, shackles, whips, harnesses, and ropes. Men are much more likely than women to enjoy sadomasochistic sex, in the roles of both sadist and masochist (Sandnabba et al., 2002). Some women find such activities exciting, but others consent to them only to please their partners or because they are paid to do so, and some are unconsenting victims.

Voyeurism, Exhibitionism, and Frotteurism

Voyeurism involves secretly watching another person undressing, bathing, doing things in the nude, or engaging in sex as a primary form of sexual arousal. For a diagnosis to be made, the voyeuristic behavior must be repetitive over six months and be compulsive. The person being observed must be unaware of it and would be upset if he or she knew about it. Almost all people who engage in voyeurism are men who watch women. They typically masturbate while watching or shortly after watching women.

Exhibitionism is, in some ways, the mirror image of voyeurism. The person who engages in exhibitionism obtains sexual gratification by exposing his or her genitals to involuntary observers, who are usually complete strangers. In the vast majority of cases, the person who engages in exhibitionism is a man who bares all to surprised women. He typically confronts women in a public place, such as a park, bus, or subway, either with his genitals already exposed or by flashing open his coat to expose his bare genitals. His arousal comes from observing the victim's surprise, fear, or disgust or from a fantasy that his victim is becoming sexually aroused. His behavior is often compulsive and impulsive: He feels a sense of excitement, fear, restlessness, and sexual arousal and then feels compelled to find relief by exhibiting himself. Some people with exhibitionism masturbate while exhibiting themselves. Others experience little or no arousal during the act, however, and instead they store these exhibitionist episodes in memory and use them during later masturbatory session (Becker, 2000), as in the following case study (adapted from Spitzer et al., 1994, pp. 117–118):

CASE STUDY

A 27-year-old engineer requested consultation at a psychiatric clinic because of irresistible urges to exhibit his penis to female strangers. At age 18, for reasons unknown to himself, he first experienced an overwhelming desire to engage in exhibitionism. He sought situations in which he was alone with a woman he did not know. As he approached her, he would become sexually excited. He would then walk up to her and display his erect penis. He found that her shock and fear further stimulated him, and usually he would then ejaculate. He also fantasized past encounters while masturbating. He feels guilty and ashamed after exhibiting himself and vows never to repeat it. Nevertheless, the desire often overwhelms him, and the behavior recurs frequently, usually at periods of tension.

People who engage in exhibitionism are more likely than most sex offenders to get caught, in part because of the public nature of their behavior but also because some of them seem to invite arrest by doing things such as repeatedly returning to places where they have already exhibited themselves. People who engage in exhibitionism are also likely to continue their behavior after having been caught.

Frotteurism is another paraphilia that often co-occurs with voyeurism and exhibitionism. The person who engages in frotteurism gains sexual gratification by rubbing against and fondling parts of the body of a nonconsenting person. Often, the person engages in this behavior in crowded places where his target may not realize that the contact has anything to do with sexuality, such as a crowded elevator. Most people with frotteurism are young men between 15 and 25 years of age, but little else is known about this disorder.

Pedophilia

The most troubling and most common paraphilia is **pedophilia.** People with pedophilia are sexually attracted to children and prefer to engage in sex with children rather than with other adults. The diagnosis of pedophilia generally requires that the sexual encounters be with children under the age of 13 and initiated by persons 16 years old or older and at least 5 years older than the children. Laws in most of the United States, however, define *child molesting* or *statutory rape* to include adults having sex with persons under the age of 18 (Green, 1993).

Sexual encounters between people with pedophilia and their child victims are often brief, although they may recur frequently. The contact most often consists of the person with pedophilia exposing and touching the child's genitals (Abel & Osborn, 1992). Other people with pedophilia perform fellatio (oral stimulation of the penis) or cunnilingus (oral stimulation of the female genitals) on children or penetrate children's vaginas, mouths, or anuses with their fingers, foreign objects, or their penises. People with pedophilia may threaten children with harm, physically restrain them, or tell them that they will punish them or their loved ones if the children do not comply with the pedophiles' wishes. Other people with pedophilia are loving, caring, and gentle to the child, using emotional closeness to gain sexual access to the child. This is especially true in incestuous relationships, in which people with pedophilia see themselves as simply being good, loving parents and believe that what they do to the child is not sexual but loving.

Defrocked priest Paul Shanley was convicted of pedophilia.

Most people with pedophilia are heterosexual men abusing young girls (Fagan et al., 2002). Homosexual men with pedophilia typically abuse young boys. Women can have pedophilia, but this is more rare.

Dr. Crone, a 35-year-old, single child psychiatrist, has been arrested and convicted of fondling several neighborhood girls, ages 6 to 12. Friends and colleagues were shocked and dismayed, as he had been considered by all to be particularly caring and supportive of children.

Dr. Crone's first sexual experience was at age 6, when a 15-year-old female camp counselor performed fellatio on him several times over the course of the summer—an experience that he had always kept to himself. As he grew older, he was surprised to notice that the age range of girls who attracted him sexually did not change, and he continued to have recurrent erotic urges and fantasies about girls between the ages of 6 and 12. Whenever he masturbated, he would fantasize about a girl in that age range, and on a couple of occasions over the years, he had felt himself to be in love with such a youngster.

Intellectually, Dr. Crone knew that others would disapprove of his many sexual involvements with young girls. He never believed, however, that he had caused any of these youngsters harm, feeling instead that they were simply sharing pleasurable feelings together. He frequently prayed for help and that his actions would go undetected. He kept promising himself that he would stop, but the temptations were such that he could not. (Adapted from Spitzer et al., 1994, pp. 187–188)

Mental-health experts are divided over whether people with pedophilia should be viewed primarily as persons with a psychiatric disorder that needs treating or as criminals who should be incarcerated (McConaghy, 1998). Even those who view pedophilia primarily as a disorder to be treated tend to agree that people with pedophilia should be prevented from engaging in their behaviors, often through incarceration.

Causes of Paraphilias

Many of the paraphilias may have similar causes, which may account for the fact that many people with paraphilia engage in a number of different paraphilic behaviors. Over 90 percent of people with paraphilias are men (McConaghy, 1998).

Attempts to link paraphilic behavior, particularly sexually aggressive paraphilias, to testosterone abnormalities have met with limited success (Langevin, 1992). Similarly, although some studies have found links between other hormones or endocrine abnormalities and paraphilias, no consistent biological cause of the paraphilias has been found (Maletzky, 1998).

Behavioral theories of the paraphilias explain them as due to an initial classical pairing of intense early sexual arousal with a particular stimulus (see Figure 16.5). For example, a youngster may become aroused when spying on the baby-sitter's lovemaking or when being held down and tickled erotically. This is followed by intensive operant conditioning in which the stimulus is present during masturbation. For example, the individual may repeatedly fantasize a particular scenario, such as watching the baby-sitter's lovemaking, while masturbating. This reinforces the association between the stimulus and sexual arousal. The individual may attempt to inhibit the undesired arousal or his behaviors, but, paradoxically, these attempts at inhibition increase the frequency and intensity of these fantasies. Eventually, the sexual arousal may generalize to other stimuli similar to the initial fantasy, such as actually watching other people's lovemaking or being naked, leading to paraphilic behavior (e.g., voyeurism). Often, the person with paraphilia also lacks adequate alternative sexual reinforcement opportunities and skills for relating appropriate to other adults.

These classic behavioral theories have been supplemented with principles of social learning theory (see Chapter 2), which suggest that the larger environment of a child's home and culture influence his or her tendency to develop deviant sexual behavior. Children whose parents frequently use physical punishment on them and who engage in aggressive, often sexual, contact with each other are more likely to engage in impulsive, aggressive, perhaps sexualized acts toward others as they grow older. Many people with pedophilia have poor interpersonal skills and feel intimidated when interacting sexually with adults.

A study of 64 convicted sex offenders with various types of paraphilias found that, compared with offenders who had committed property crimes and did not have paraphilias, the sex offenders had higher rates of childhood emotional abuse and family dysfunction and childhood sex-

FIGURE 16.5 | A Behavioral Account of the Development of Paraphilias

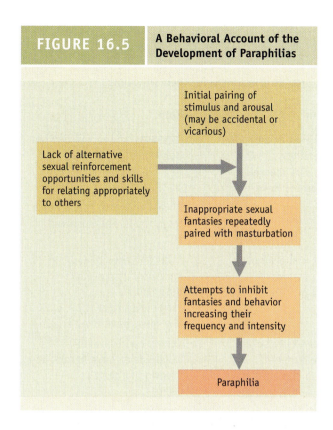

Lack of alternative sexual reinforcement opportunities and skills for relating appropriately to others

Initial pairing of stimulus and arousal (may be accidental or vicarious)

Inappropriate sexual fantasies repeatedly paired with masturbation

Attempts to inhibit fantasies and behavior increasing their frequency and intensity

Paraphilia

ual abuse (Lee et al., 2002). Childhood sexual abuse was a particularly strong predictor of pedophilia. Similarly, studies of juvenile sex offenders, most of whom had assaulted a younger child, find that many are likely to have suffered sexual abuse earlier in childhood (Gerardin & Thibaut, 2004).

Cognitive theorists have also identified a number of distortions and assumptions that people with paraphilias have about their behaviors and the behaviors of their victims, as shown in Table 16.9 on page 606 (Gerardin & Thibaut, 2004; Maletzky, 1998). These distortions may have been learned from their parents' deviant messages about sexual behavior. They justify the person's victimization of others.

Treatments for Paraphilias

Most people with paraphilia do not seek treatment for their behaviors. Treatment is often forced on those who engage in illegal acts (voyeurism, exhibitionism, frotteurism, pedophilia) after they are arrested for breaking the law by engaging in their behaviors. Simple incarceration does little to change these behaviors, and the recidivism rate among convicted sex offenders is very high.

Biological interventions have been tried, primarily with people with pedophilia and men who commit rape. These interventions formerly included surgery on the centers of the brain thought to control sexual behavior and surgery to stop the production of the hormones influencing sexual arousal. Ceasing the production of these hormones lowers recidivism rates among people with paraphilia who have committed sexual crimes (Maletsky & Field, 2003). Ethical concerns over the irreversibility of this treatment and the ability of offenders to freely consent to it have led to it being rarely used.

These days, sex offenders might be offered antiandrogen drugs that suppress the functioning of the testes, such as depo-Provera, thereby reducing the production of testosterone and possibly reducing the sex drive. These drugs are typically used in conjunction with psychotherapy and can be useful for hypersexual men who are motivated to change their behavior (Maletzky & Field, 2003). Follow-up studies have shown that people with paraphilia treated with antiandrogen drugs do show great reductions in their paraphilic behavior (Bradford, 1995; Gerardin & Thibaut, 2004; Maletzky & Field, 2003). These drugs can have significant side effects, however, and reduce overall sexual drive for the individual. Difficult ethical questions arise when the use of these drugs is part of a deal struck with a sex offender for a lighter sentence or parole.

Most recently, the selective serotonin reuptake inhibitors (SSRIs) have been used to reduce sexual drive and paraphilic behavior. Some studies find positive effects of these drugs on sexual drive and impulse control (e.g., Greenberg et al., 1996), although the effects are not totally consistent across studies (see Maletzky & Field, 2003).

Insight-oriented therapies alone have not proven extremely successful in changing behavior in people with paraphilia. Behavior modification therapies are commonly used to treat paraphilia and can be successful if people with paraphilia are willing to change their behavior. **Aversion therapy** is used to extinguish sexual responses to objects or situations that a person with paraphilia finds arousing. During such therapy, a person with paraphilia might receive painful but harmless electric shocks or loud bursts of noise while viewing photographs of what arouse him or her (such as children) or while actually touching objects that arouse him or her (such as women's panties). **Desensitization** procedures may be used to reduce the person's anxiety about engaging in normal sexual encounters with other adults. For example, people with paraphilia might be taught relaxation exercises, which they then use to control their anxiety as they gradually build up fantasies of interacting sexually with other adults in ways that are fulfilling to them and their partners (Maletzky, 1998).

Cognitive therapy is sometimes used to help people with a predatory paraphilia (i.e., pedophilia, exhibitionism, voyeurism) identify and challenge thoughts and situations that trigger their behaviors

TABLE 16.9 Distortions, Assumptions, and Justifications

People with paraphilia or who engage in rape may engage in cognitions that provide a rationale for their behaviors.

Category	Pedophilia	Exhibitionism	Rape
Misattributing blame	"She started it by being too cuddly." "She would always run around half dressed."	"She kept looking at me like she was expecting it." "The way she was dressed, she was asking for it."	"She was saying 'no' but her body said 'yes.'"
Minimizing or denying sexual intent	"I was teaching her about sex . . . better from her father than someone else."	"I was just looking for a place to pee." "My pants just slipped down."	"I was trying to teach her a lesson. . . . She deserved it."
Debasing the victim	"She'd had sex before with her boyfriend." "She always lies."	"She was just a slut anyway."	"The way she came on to me at the party, she deserved it." "She never fought back. . . . She must have liked it."
Minimizing consequences	"She's always been real friendly to me, even afterward." "She was messed up even before it happened."	"I never touched her so I couldn't have hurt her." "She smiled so she must have liked it."	"She'd had sex with hundreds of guys before. It was no big deal."
Deflecting censure	"This happened years ago. . . . Why can't everyone forget about it?"	"It's not like I raped anyone."	"I only did it once."
Justifying the cause	"If I wasn't molested as a kid, I'd never have done this."	"If I knew how to get dates, I wouldn't have to expose."	"If my girlfriend gave me what I want, I wouldn't be forced to rape."

Source: From "The Paraphilias: Research and Treatment" by Barry M. Maletsky, from *A Guide to Treatments That Work*, edited by Peter Nathan and Jack Gorman, copyright © 1998 by Peter E. Nathan and Jack M. Gorman. Used by permission of Oxford University Press, Inc.

and serve as justifications of their behaviors, such as those in Table 16.9 (Maletzky, 1998; McConaghy, 1998). Part of the work with people with a predatory paraphilia involves empathy training—getting the offender to understand the impact of his behavior on his victims and to care about it. Five components of empathy training include (1) encouraging identification with the victim, (2) getting the client to take responsibility for his acts, (3) encouraging his acceptance of the harm created by the acts, (4) encouraging the client to reverse roles with the victim, and (5) encouraging the client to empathize with the victim (Maletzky, 1998).

With nonpredatory paraphilias (e.g., fetishism), cognitive interventions may be combined with behavioral interventions designed to help people learn more appropriate ways of approaching and interacting with people they find attractive, in socially acceptable ways (Cole, 1992). Role-plays might be used to give the person with a paraphilia practice in initiating contact and eventually negotiating a positive sexual encounter with another person. Finally, group therapy in which people with paraphilias come together to support each other through changes in their behavior can be helpful.

Outcome studies comparing these treatments with control groups that receive no treatment have not been done for most types of therapy because of ethical concerns. Several studies, however, that have followed people with paraphilias after they have received treatment, usually consisting of a comprehensive program of various psychosocial interventions, suggest that these treatments are useful (Alexander, 1999). Table 16.10 summarizes the outcomes of more than 7,000 sex offenders with paraphilia treated in a clinic that emphasized cognitive and behavioral interventions (Maletzky, 1998). Successful treatment was defined as the completion of all treatment sessions, the reporting of no deviant sexual behavior at any follow-up ses-

TABLE 16.10 Treatment Outcomes for Sex Offenders with Paraphilias (*n* = 7,156)

These data suggest that cognitive-behavioral treatment may help reduce paraphilic behavior.

Category	*n*	Percentage Meeting Criteria For Success*
Situational pedophilia, heterosexual	3,012	96.6
Predatory pedophilia, heterosexual	864	88.3
Situational pedophilia, homosexual	717	91.8
Predatory pedophilia, homosexual	596	80.1
Exhibitionism	1,130	95.4
Voyeurism	83	93.9
Public masturbation	77	94.8
Frotteurism	65	89.3
Fetishism	33	94.0
Transvestic fetishism	14	78.6

Source: From "The Paraphilias: Research and Treatment" by Barry M. Maletsky, from *A Guide to Treatments That Work*, edited by Peter Nathan and Jack Gorman, copyright © 1998 by Peter E. Nathan and Jack M. Gorman. Used by permission of Oxford University Press, Inc.

*Treatment success was defined as (1) completing all treatment sessions, (2) reporting no deviant sexual behavior at any follow-up sessions, (3) demonstrating no deviant sexual arousal at any follow-up session, (4) having no repeat legal charges for a sexual crime at any follow-up session. Follow-up sessions occurred at 6, 12, 24, 36, 48, and 60 months after the end of active treatment.

sions up to five years after treatment, and no legal charges for sexual offenses during the follow-up period. A follow-up of these patients 25 years after treatment found that approximately 90 percent still met these criteria for successful treatment. The child molesters and exhibitionists achieved better overall success than the pedophiles and rapists (Maletzky & Steinhauser, 2002).

SUMMING UP

- The paraphilias are a group of disorders in which people's sexual activity is focused on (1) nonhuman objects, (2) nonconsenting adults, (3) suffering or the humiliation of oneself or one's partner, or (4) children.
- Fetishism involves the use of inanimate objects (such as panties or shoes) as the preferred or exclusive source of sexual arousal or gratification. Transvestism is when a man dresses in the clothes of a woman to sexually arouse himself.
- Voyeurism involves observing another person nude or engaging in sexual acts, without that person's knowledge or consent, in order to become sexually aroused.

- Exhibitionism involves exposing oneself to another without that person's consent, in order to become sexually aroused.
- Frotteurism involves rubbing up against another without his or her consent, in order to become sexually aroused.
- Sadism and masochism involve physically harming another or allowing oneself to be harmed for sexual arousal.
- Pedophilia involves engaging in sexual acts with a child.
- Behavioral theories suggest that the sexual behaviors of people with paraphilia result from classical and operant conditioning.
- Treatments for the paraphilias include biological interventions to reduce sexual drive, behavioral interventions to decondition arousal to paraphilic objects, and training in interpersonal and social skills.

GENDER IDENTITY DISORDER

For most people, their perception of themselves as male or female, referred to as **gender identity,** is a fundamental component of their self-concept, as is illustrated in the story of David Reimer that began this chapter. Gender identity differs from **gender role,** which is a person's belief about how he or she should behave as a male or female in society. Many females choose to engage in behaviors considered part of the masculine gender role, such as playing aggressive sports or pursuing competitive careers, but still have a fundamental sense of themselves as female. Similarly, many males choose to engage in behaviors considered part of the feminine gender role, such as caring for children, cooking, or sewing, but still have a fundamental sense of themselves as male. David Reimer was forced to behave as a girl in his early childhood, but he still had a fundamental sense of himself as male.

Gender identity and gender roles differ from **sexual orientation,** which is a person's preference for sexual partners either of the opposite sex or of the same sex. Most gay men have a fundamental sense of themselves as male and, therefore, have male gender identities. Most lesbians have a fundamental sense of themselves as female and, therefore, have female gender identities. Although gay men and lesbians are often portrayed as violating stereotypic gender roles, many adhere to traditional roles for their genders, except in their choices of sexual partners.

Gender identity disorder (GID) is diagnosed when individuals believe that they were born with the wrong sex's genitals and are fundamentally persons of the opposite sex (see the DSM-IV-TR criteria in Table 16.11). Stephanie, in the following case study, would be diagnosed with this disorder (adapted from Dickey & Stephens, 1995, pp. 442–443):

CASE STUDY

Stephanie was 30 when she first attended our clinic. She gave a history of conviction that she was, in fact, male and wished to rid herself of identifiably female attributes and acquire male traits and features. She said she had been cross-living and employed as a male for about 1 year, following the breakdown of a 10-year marriage. She was taking testosterone prescribed by her family physician. She presented at our clinic with a request for removal of her uterus and ovaries.

She did not give a childhood history of tomboy attitudes, thoughts, or behavior. She said social interaction with other children, boys or girls, was minimal. Desperate for a friend, she fantasized "an articulate and strong" boy, exactly her own age, named Ronan. They were always together and they talked over everything: thoughts and feelings and the events of her life. Cross-dressing in her father's clothing also began during childhood. There was no history of sexual arousal associated with or erotic fantasy involving cross-dressing.

Puberty at age 12 and the accompanying bodily changes apparently did not overly distress Stephanie. Sexual and romantic feelings focused on "slender, feminine-appearing men." At 16, Stephanie met such a man and they were together for 2 years. Her next romantic involvement was with a "male bisexual transvestite." Sexual interaction according to Stephanie, included experimentation with drugs and "role reversals." She and her partner cross-dressed, and Stephanie took the dominant and active role. During vaginal sex, she imagined herself as a male with another male.

At 19, she met a slender, good-looking man. They were compatible and married soon after. The marriage was a success. Stephanie's preferred position for intercourse was with both kneeling, she behind her husband, rubbing her pubic area against him while masturbating him. She would imagine she had a penis and was penetrating him. Stephanie's marriage broke down after the couple's business failed. She decided to live full-time in the male role as Jacob. While on the West Coast, she started treatment with male hormones. She moved back east and presented at our clinic for assessment. She saw herself as a male, primarily attracted to gay or gay-appearing males. She was uninterested in relationships with women, except perhaps as purely sexual encounters of short duration.

Gender identity disorder of childhood is a rare condition in which a child persistently rejects his or her anatomic sex and desires to be or insists he or she is a member of the opposite sex. Girls with this disorder seek masculine-type activities and male peer groups to a degree far beyond that of a "tomboy." Sometimes, these girls express the belief that they will eventually grow penises. Boys with the disorder seek feminine-type activities and female peer groups and tend to begin cross-dressing

TABLE 16.11 DSM-IV-TR

Criteria for a Diagnosis of Gender Identity Disorder

People with gender identity disorder believe they were born with the wrong sex's body and are truly members of the other sex.

A. Strong and persistent identification with the other sex. In children, this is manifested by four or more of the following:

   1. repeatedly stated desire to be, or insistence that he or she is, the other sex.

   2. in boys, preference for cross-dressing or simulating female attire; in girls, insistence on wearing only stereotypic masculine clothing.

   3. strong and persistent preferences for cross-sex roles in play and in fantasies.

   4. intense desire to participate in the stereotypic games and pastimes of the other sex.

   5. strong preference for playmates of the other sex.

   In adolescents or adults, identification with the other sex may be manifested with symptoms such as the stated desire to be the other sex, frequently passing as the other sex, desire to live or be treated as the other sex, or the conviction that he or she has the typical feelings or reactions of the other sex.

B. Persistent discomfort with his or her sex and sense of inappropriateness in the gender role of that sex.

C. Disturbance is not concurrent with a physical intersex condition and causes significant distress or problems in functioning.

Source: Reprinted with permission from the *Diagnostic and Statistical Manual of Mental Disorders*, Fourth Edition, Text Revision. Copyright © 2000 American Psychiatric Association.

in girls' clothes at a very early age (Zucker, 2005). They express disgust with their penises and wish they would disappear. Boys with gender identity disturbances are more likely to be taken by their parents for counseling than are girls with the disturbance, probably because parents are more concerned about violations of gender roles in boys than in girls.

Adults who might be diagnosed with gender identity disorder are also referred to as **transsexuals.** Transsexual people may dress in the clothes of the opposite sex but, unlike transvestites, do not do this to gain sexual arousal. They simply believe they are putting on the clothes of the gender they really belong to. Some transsexual people who can afford it seek sex-change operations. The sexual preferences of transsexual people vary. Some are asexual, having little interest in either sex; some are heterosexual; and some are homosexual. Transsexualism is rare, with an estimated prevalence of 1 per 30,000 males and 1 per 100,000 females (Bradley & Zucker, 1997; Katchadourian, 1989).

Some transsexual people are so disturbed by their misassignment of gender that they develop alcohol and other drug abuse problems and other psychological disorders, but these problems seem to be consequences rather than causes of their transsexualism (Lombardi, 2001). Low self-esteem and psychological distress also result from their rejection by others. High rates of HIV infection

among transsexual people have been reported in some studies (Lombardi, 2001). HIV may be contracted through risky sexual behaviors or through the sharing of needles during drug use or the injection of hormones. Many avoid seeking medical care because of negative interactions with physicians. Indeed, some physicians refuse to treat transsexual people. Leslie Feinberg, an activist and author, described her harrowing experiences in trying to receive medical care (Feinberg, 2001, pp. 897–898):

VOICES

Five years ago, while battling an undiagnosed case of bacterial endocarditis, I was refused care at a Jersey City emergency room. After the physician who examined me discovered that I am female-bodied, he ordered me out of the emergency room despite the fact that my temperature was above 104 degrees. He said I had a fever "because you are a very troubled person." Weeks later I was hospitalized with the same illness in New York City in a Catholic hospital where management insists patients be put in wards on the basis of birth sex. They place transsexual women who have completed sex-reassignment surgery in male wards. Putting me in a female ward created a furor. I awoke in

(continued)

the night to find staff standing around my bed ridiculing my body and referring to me as a "Martian." The next day the staff refused to work unless "it" was removed from the floor. These and other expressions of hatred forced me to leave.

In recent years, critics of the diagnosis of gender identity disorder have argued that it pathologizes a normal variant on human sexuality and gender roles (see Zucker, 2005). If you examine the criteria for "strong and persistent identification with the other sex," point A in the DSM-IV-TR criteria (review Table 16.11), you will notice that a child might be diagnosable with GID for having persistent cross-sex behavior without the stated desire that he or she is actually of the opposite sex. Thus, a child might be diagnosed with GID only for consistently refusing to conform with his or her stereotypic gender role. In addition, the dysphoria some children and adults who engage in cross-gender behavior experience might be due to social reactions to them, rather than to an inherent dysphoria about their own identity.

Zucker (2005) argues that the desire of people diagnosed with GID to undergo sex reassignment through surgery and hormonal treatment is evidence that people with this disorder are not just choosing an alternative lifestyle but truly have a psychological impairment. The debate over the legitimacy of GID as a diagnosis will continue for some time to come.

Contributors to Gender Identity Disorder

The genetic sex of an individual is determined at conception by the chromosomes received from the mother and father, but sexual development from that point on is influenced by many factors. For the first few weeks of gestation, the gonads and internal and external genital structures are neither male nor female. If the Y chromosome is present, the gonads of the embryo differentiate into testes. Then they secrete testosterone, and male genitalia develop in the fetus. If the Y chromosome is not present, the gonads develop into ovaries, which do not secrete androgen, and female genitalia develop.

Parts of the hypothalamus, such as the anterior hypothalamus and the bed nucleus of stria terminalis, may be involved in gender identity disorder.

Bed nucleus of stria terminalis

Anterior hypothalamus

Biological theories of gender identity disorder have focused on the effects of prenatal hormones on brain development (Bradley, 1995; Bradley & Zucker, 1997). Although several specific mechanisms have been implicated, in general these theories suggest that people who develop gender identity disorder have been exposed to unusual levels of hormones, which influence later gender identity and sexual orientation by influencing the development of the hypothalamus and other brain structures involved in sexuality. These brain/hormone theories were bolstered when reports were published in the early 1990s of differences between homosexual and heterosexual men in the anterior hypothalamus (LeVay, 1993). To date, these reports have not been well replicated by other investigators, however. The relevance of studies of biological factors in homosexuality to gender identity disorder is not always clear, as well.

One of the few studies directly focusing on transsexual people found significant differences between male transsexuals and a group of nontranssexual men in a cluster of cells in the hypothalamus called the bed nucleus of stria terminalis (Zhou, Hofman, & Swaab, 1995). This cluster of cells was half as large in the transsexuals as in the nontranssexual men. Typically, this cluster of cells is smaller

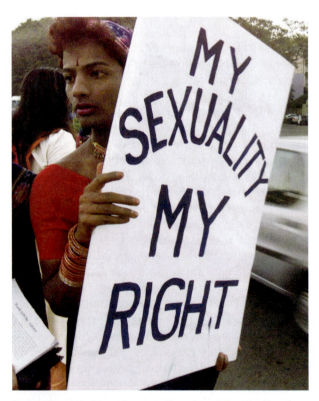

Some transsexual people argue they do not have a disorder but do have a right to live their life as they wish.

in women's brains than in men's, and the male transsexuals' cluster of cells was close to the size usually found in women's brains. This cluster of cells is known to play a role in sexual behavior, at least in male rats. Thus, it may be that the size of this cell cluster in the hypothalamus plays a role in gender identity disorder, at least in men.

Another group of studies that suggested that prenatal hormones play a role in gender identity disorder focused on girls who were exposed to elevated levels of testosterone in utero due to an illness in the mother or medications the mother took while pregnant (see Hines, 2004). Most of these girls were born with some degree of masculinization of their genitalia, which is treated early in infancy through surgical correction and hormone replacement; then they are raised as girls. Studies have suggested that these girls tend to have more masculine behavior than other girls (Berenbaum & Hines, 1992; Slijper et al., 1998). In addition, more of these girls have a homosexual or bisexual sexual orientation than girls not exposed to testosterone in utero (Dittman, Kappes, & Kappes, 1992; Money & Schwartz, 1976). Most of these girls do identify themselves as female, but they are at increased risk for gender identity disorder (Slijper et al., 1998). These findings lend some support to a prenatal hormone theory of gender identity disorder, although in general the evidence has been somewhat weak (Zucker, 2005).

Most of the psychosocial theories of gender identity disorder focus on the role parents play in shaping their children's gender identity. Parents encourage children to identify with one sex or the other, by reinforcing "gender-appropriate" behavior and punishing "gender-inappropriate" behavior. From early infancy, they buy male or female clothes for their children and sex-stereotyped toys (dolls or trucks). They encourage or discourage playing rough-and-tumble games or playing with dolls. In a long-term study of a large sample of boys with gender identity disorder, Green (1986) found that their parents were less likely than the parents of boys without gender identity disorder to discourage cross-gender behaviors. That is, these boys were not punished, subtly or overtly, for engaging in feminine behavior, such as playing with dolls or wearing dresses, as much as boys who did not have gender identity disorder. Further, boys who were highly feminine (although did not necessarily have gender identity disorder) tended to have mothers who had wanted a girl rather than a boy, saw their baby sons as girls, and dressed their baby sons as girls. When the boys were older, their mothers tended to prohibit rough-and-tumble play, and the boys had few opportunities to have male playmates. About one-third of these boys had no father in the home, and those who did have a father in the home tended to be very close to their mothers.

Other studies suggest that another factor in gender identity disorder, in addition to the reinforcements parents give for gender identification in their children, is parental psychopathology (Bradley, 1995; Marantz & Coates, 1991). Significant percentages of the parents of children with gender identity disorder suffer from depression, severe anxiety, or personality disorders. It may be that these parents create a difficult emotional atmosphere in the home, which makes the child anxious and unsure of him- or herself. Then, if the parent reinforces the child for cross-gendered behavior, the child may be especially likely to adopt a cross-gendered identity as a way of pleasing the parent and reducing his or her own anxiety.

In general, however, the evidence for various theories of gender identity disorder is weak. Most theorists believe that gender identity is the result of a number of biological and social factors, including chromosomes, hormones, and socialization. Gender identity disorder might result from variations in the development of any of these factors.

Treatments for Gender Identity Disorder

Therapists who work with people with gender identity disorder tend not to try to "cure" them by convincing them to accept the body with which they were born and the gender associated with that body (Bradley, 1995). This tactic simply does not work with most people with gender identity disorder. Instead, therapists help these individuals clarify their gender identity and sexual orientation. Some people with gender identity disorder choose to undergo gender reassignment treatment, which provides them with the genitalia and secondary sex characteristics (e.g., breasts) of the gender with which they identify. Sex reassignment cannot change their chromosomes, nor can it enable people born male to bear children or people born female to impregnate a woman.

Sex reassignment requires a series of surgeries and hormone treatments, often taking two or more years. Before undertaking any of these medical procedures, patients are usually asked to dress and live in their new gender for a year or two, to ensure that they are confident about their decisions before proceeding. Then, a lifetime of hormone treatments is begun. Male-to-female transsexuals take estrogen, which fosters the development of female secondary sex characteristics. This drug causes fatty deposits to develop in the breasts and hips, softens the skin, and inhibits the growth of a beard. Female-to-male transsexuals take androgens, which promote male secondary sex characteristics. This drug causes the voice to deepen, hair to become distributed in a male pattern, fatty tissue in the breast to recede, and muscles to enlarge. The clitoris may grow larger.

Sex reassignment surgery is primarily cosmetic. In male-to-female surgery, the penis and testicles are removed, and tissue from the penis is used to create an artificial vagina. The construction of male genitals for a female-to-male reassignment is technically more difficult. First, the internal sex organs (ovaries, fallopian tubes, uterus) and any fatty tissue remaining in the breasts are removed. The urethra is rerouted through the enlarged clitoris, or an artificial penis and scrotum are constructed from tissue taken from other parts of the body. This penis allows for urination while standing but cannot achieve a natural erection. Other procedures, such as artificial implants, may be used to create an erection

Sex reassignment surgery has always been controversial. Some follow-up studies suggest that the outcome tends to be positive when patients are carefully selected for such sex reassignment procedures based on their motivation for change and their overall psychological health and are given psychological counseling to assist them through the change (Bradley & Zucker, 1997; Lindemalm, Korlin, & Uddenberg, 1986; Smith, van Goozen, & Cohen-Kettenis, 2001). Although many of these patients are unable to experience orgasm during sex, most are satisfied with their sex lives and are psychologically well adjusted to their new genders.

SUMMING UP

- Gender identity disorder (GID) is diagnosed when individuals believe they were born with the wrong sex's genitals and are fundamentally persons of the opposite sex. This disorder in adults is also called transsexualism.

- Biological theories suggest that unusual exposure to prenatal hormones affects the development of the hypothalamus and other brain structures involved in sexuality, leading to gender identity disorder.

- Socialization theories suggest that the parents of children (primarily boys) with gender identity disorder do not socialize gender-appropriate behaviors. Other theories suggest that the parents of children who develop this disorder have high rates of psychopathology.

- Some people with this disorder undergo sex reassignment treatment to change their genitalia and live as a member of the sex they believe they are.

CHAPTER INTEGRATION

Nowhere is the interplay of biological, psychological, and social forces more apparent than in matters of sexuality (see Figure 16.6). Biological factors influence gender identity, sexual orientation, and sexual functioning. These biological factors can be greatly moderated, however, by psychological and social factors. The meaning to people of a sexual dysfunction, an unusual sexual practice, or an atypical gender identity is heavily influenced by their attitudes toward their sexuality and by the reactions they get from people around them. In addition, as we saw with sexual dysfunctions, purely psychological and social conditions can cause a person's body to stop functioning as it normally would.

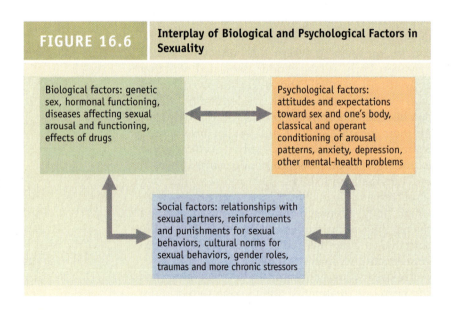

FIGURE 16.6 Interplay of Biological and Psychological Factors in Sexuality

Biological factors: genetic sex, hormonal functioning, diseases affecting sexual arousal and functioning, effects of drugs

Psychological factors: attitudes and expectations toward sex and one's body, classical and operant conditioning of arousal patterns, anxiety, depression, other mental-health problems

Social factors: relationships with sexual partners, reinforcements and punishments for sexual behaviors, cultural norms for sexual behaviors, gender roles, traumas and more chronic stressors

Extraordinary People: Follow-Up

What became of David Reimer, the boy who was raised as a girl, and the research that suggested this was an appropriate treatment for him? In 1997, researcher Milton Diamond and psychiatrist Keith Sigmundson, who had treated David when he was the child Brenda and had become convinced that the "experiment" to turn the child into a girl was a failure, published a paper revealing the outcome of this experiment. The paper hit the medical and psychological communities like a bombshell. Until that point, the academic community had assumed that the little boy raised as a girl had grown successfully into a woman. Diamond and Sigmundson's paper presented clear evidence from David's case and the cases of other children who had undergone sex reassignment that simply deciding which sex a child would be does not determine the child's gender identity. The cases of children who had been born with both male and female gonads or with ambiguous genitals also made it clear that gender identity is complex and often not binary—male or female.

Years later, David reflected on the assumptions that drove the decision to turn him into a girl after his penis was severed:

> You know, if I had lost my arms and my legs and wound up in a wheelchair where you're moving everything with a little rod in your mouth—would that make me less of a person? It just seems that they implied that you're nothing if your penis is gone. The second you lose that, you're nothing and they've got to do surgery and hormones to turn you into something. Like you're a zero. It's like your whole personality, everything about you is all directed—all pinpointed—toward what's between the legs. And to me, that's ignorant. (Colapinto, 2001, p. 262)

David's story, and Colapinto's book, *As Nature Made Him,* appear to argue that gender identity is completely determined by biological sex. The stories of many other children who eventually reject their biological sex or who live somewhere in between male and female argue against a purely biological origin of gender identity. Colapinto (2001, p. 280) writes,

> Despite [its] medical-scientific context, I've always believed that [David's] story transcends the incessant quibbling over the nature/nurture debate. David's is a story about identity in its largest sense—not simply *sexual* identity. His story, for all its uniqueness, is a universal one, and reminds us how it is every person's individual responsibility to define for himself who he is, and to assert that against a world that often opposes, ridicules, oppresses, or undermines him.

David Reimer committed suicide in 2004. He had lost his job, had financial difficulties, and been separated from his wife. His mother said he was still grieving the death of his brother two years before. In a newspaper story after David's death, however, John Colapinto, his biographer, noted, "David's blighted childhood was never far from his mind. Just before he died, he talked to his wife about his sexual 'inadequacy,' his inability to be a true husband. Jane tried to reassure him. But David was already heading for the door" (*Slate Magazine*, 2004).

Chapter Summary

- The interplay of biological, psychological, and social forces is nowhere more apparent than in matters of sexuality. (Review Figure 16.6.)

- The sexual response cycle can be divided into the desire, arousal, plateau, orgasm, and resolution phases. (Review Figures 16.1 and 16.2.)

- Sexual desire is manifested in sexual thoughts and fantasies, an awareness of sexual cues from others, and the initiation of or participation in sexual activities.

- The arousal phase consists of a psychological experience of arousal and pleasure and the physiological changes known as vasocongestion (the filling of blood vessels and tissues with blood) and myotonia (muscle tension).

■ During the plateau phase, excitement remains at a high but stable level.

■ Orgasm involves the discharge of built-up neuromuscular tension. In males, orgasm involves rhythmic contractions of the prostate, the seminal vesicles, the vas deferens, and the entire length of the penis and urethra, accompanied by the ejaculation of semen. In females, orgasm involves rhythmic contractions of the orgasmic platform and more irregular contractions of the uterus.

■ Following orgasm, the entire musculature of the body relaxes, and men and women tend to experience a state of deep relaxation, the stage known as resolution. Males experience a refractory period following orgasm, during which they cannot be aroused to another orgasm. Females do not have a refractory period.

■ Occasional problems with sexual functioning are extremely common. To qualify for a diagnosis of a sexual dysfunction, a person must be experiencing a problem that causes significant distress or interpersonal difficulty, that is not the result of another Axis I disorder, and that is not due exclusively to the direct effects of substance use or medical illness. (Review Table 16.1.)

■ The psychological factors leading to sexual dysfunction most commonly involve negative attitudes toward sex, traumatic or stressful experiences, and conflicts with sexual partners. A variety of biological factors, including medical illnesses, the side effects of drugs, nervous system injury, and hormonal deficiencies, can cause sexual dysfunctions. (Review Table 16.4.)

■ Sexual desire disorders (hypoactive sexual desire disorder and sexual aversion disorder) are among the most common sexual dysfunctions. Persons with these disorders experience a chronically lowered or absent desire for sex.

■ The sexual arousal disorders include female sexual arousal disorder and male erectile disorder (formerly called impotence).

■ Women with female orgasmic disorder experience a persistent or recurrent delay in or the complete absence of orgasm, after having reached the excitement phase of the sexual response cycle. Men with premature ejaculation persistently experience ejaculation (after minimal sexual stimulation) before, on, or shortly after penetration and before they wish it.

■ Men with male orgasmic disorder experience a persistent or recurrent delay in or the absence of orgasm following the excitement phase of the sexual response cycle.

■ The sexual pain disorders include dyspareunia, which is genital pain associated with intercourse, and vaginismus, in which a woman experiences involuntary contraction of the muscles surrounding the outer third of the vagina when the vagina is penetrated.

■ Fortunately, most of the sexual dysfunctions can be treated successfully. Biological treatments include drugs that increase sexual functioning, such as Viagra, and the alleviation of medical conditions that might be contributing to sexual dysfunction. (Review Table 16.5.)

■ The psychological treatments combine (1) psychotherapy focused on the personal concerns of the individual with the dysfunction and on the conflicts between the individual and his or her partner and (2) sex therapy designed to decrease inhibitions about sex and to teach new techniques for optimal sexual enjoyment. (Review Table 16.6.)

■ One important set of techniques in sex therapy is sensate focus exercises. The exercises lead partners through three stages, from gentle nongenital touching, to direct genital stimulation, and finally to intercourse focused on enhancing and sustaining pleasure, rather than on orgasm and performance.

■ Men with premature ejaculation can be helped with the stop-start technique or the squeeze technique.

■ The paraphilias are a group of disorders in which the focus of the individual's sexual urges and activities are (1) nonhuman objects, (2) nonconsenting adults, (3) suffering or humiliation of oneself or one's partner, or (4) children. (Review Table 16.8.)

■ People with pedophilia seek sexual gratification with young children. Most are heterosexual men seeking sex with young girls. Many people with pedophilia have poor interpersonal skills, feel intimidated when interacting sexually with adults, and are victims of childhood sexual abuse.

■ Voyeurism involves secretly watching another person undressing, bathing, doing things in the nude, or engaging in sex as a preferred or exclusive form of sexual arousal. Almost all people who engage in voyeurism are men who watch women.

■ Exhibitionism involves sexual gratification by exposing the genitals to involuntary observers, who are usually complete strangers. In the vast majority of cases, a person who engages in exhibitionism is a man who bares all to surprised women, typically in public places.

■ Frotteurism is another paraphilia, which often co-occurs with voyeurism and exhibitionism. A person who engages in frotteurism gains sexual gratification by rubbing against and fondling parts of the body of a nonconsenting person.

■ A person who engages in sexual sadism gains sexual gratification by inflicting pain and humiliation on his or her sex partner. A person who engages in sexual masochism gains sexual gratification by suffering pain or humiliation during sex. Some people occasionally engage in moderately sadistic or masochistic behaviors during sex or simulate such behaviors without actually inflicting pain or suffering. Persons who are diagnosed with sexual sadism or masochism engage in these behaviors as their preferred or exclusive forms of sexual gratification.

■ Fetishism is a paraphilia that involves the use of isolated body parts or inanimate objects as the preferred or exclusive sources of sexual arousal or gratification. A particular form of fetish is transvestism, in which an individual dresses in clothes of the opposite sex in order to become sexually aroused. Usually, transvestism involves a man dressing in women's clothes.

■ Gender identity disorder (GID) is diagnosed when an individual believes that he or she was born with the wrong genitals and is fundamentally a person of the opposite sex. Gender identity disorder of childhood is a rare condition in which a child persistently rejects his or her anatomic sex and desires to be or insists he or she is a member of the opposite sex. (Review Table 16.11.)

■ Gender identity disorder in adulthood is often referred to as transsexualism. Transsexual persons experience a chronic discomfort and sense of inappropriateness with their gender and genitals, wish to be rid of them, and want to live as members of the opposite sex. Transsexual individuals often dress in the clothes of the opposite sex but, unlike transvestites, do not do so to gain sexual arousal.

MindMap CD-ROM

The following resources on the MindMap CD-ROM that came with this text will help you to master the content of this chapter and prepare for tests:

■ Videos: Taking a Sexual History; Changing Genders
■ Interactive Segment: Androgeny
■ Chapter Timeline
■ Chapter Quiz

Key Terms

sexual dysfunctions 575

sexual desire 576

arousal phase 576

vasocongestion 576

myotonia 576

orgasm 577

plateau phase 577

resolution 578

hypoactive sexual desire disorder 580

sexual aversion disorder 580

female sexual arousal disorder 581

male erectile disorder 581

female orgasmic disorder 582

premature ejaculation 582

male orgasmic disorder 583

dyspareunia 583

vaginismus 583

substance-induced sexual dysfunction 585

performance anxiety 586

sensate focus therapy 594

stop-start technique 596

squeeze technique 596

paraphilias 599

fetishism 600

transvestism 601

sexual sadism 602

sexual masochism 602

sadomasochism 602

voyeurism 602

exhibitionism 602

frotteurism 603

pedophilia 603

aversion therapy 605

desensitization 605

gender identity 607

gender role 608

sexual orientation 608

gender identity disorder (GID) 608

transsexuals 609

> Chapter 17

The Ferryman's
by George E. Dunne

*Refrain to-night, And that shall lend a kind of easiness
To the next abstinence; the next more easy; For use
almost can change the stamp of nature.*

—William Shakespeare, *Hamlet* (3:4:165; 1600)

Substance-Related Disorders <

CHAPTER OVERVIEW

Extraordinary People

■ **Celebrity Drug Users**

Society and Substance Use

Societies around the world and across time have had very different attitudes about substance use, leading to different responses to substance users.

Definitions of Substance-Related Disorders

Substance intoxication and withdrawal are characteristic behavioral and physical symptoms resulting from substance use. Substance abuse and dependence are diagnosed when substance use significantly interferes with an individual's functioning. Dependence also may involve the development of tolerance to substances.

Depressants

The depressants include alcohol, benzodiazepines, barbiturates, and inhalants. They produce the symptoms of depression and cognitive impairment.

Stimulants

The stimulants—cocaine, amphetamines, nicotine, and caffeine—activate the central nervous system and the parts of the brain that register pleasure.

Opioids

The opioids cause euphoria, lethargy, unconsciousness, and seizures and can be highly addictive.

Hallucinogens and PCP

The hallucinogens and PCP produce perceptual illusions and distortions and symptoms ranging from a sense of peace and tranquillity to feelings of unreality and violence.

Cannabis

Cannabis creates a high feeling, cognitive and motor impairments, and in some people, hallucinogenic effects.

Club Drugs

Some common club drugs, in addition to LSD, are ecstasy, GHB, ketamine, and rohypnol. They have a variety of euphoric and sedative effects and can be extremely dangerous.

Theories of Substance Use, Abuse, and Dependence

Biological theories attribute vulnerability to substance disorders largely to genetic predispositions. Psychosocial theories focus on environmental reinforcements and beliefs that support substance use.

Treatments for Substance-Related Disorders

Detoxification is the first step in treatment. Drugs may aid in withdrawal and abstinence. Alcoholics Anonymous is a widely used treatment. Behavioral and cognitive treatments extinguish substance use behaviors and change thoughts that motivate substance use.

Taking Psychology Personally

■ **Tips for Responsible Drinking**

Chapter Integration

The substances involved in substance use disorders are powerful biological agents that directly affect the brain. Some people may have biological predispositions that make substance use either more or less rewarding, but environmental influences can also affect the choices that they make. Both biological and psychosocial factors play a role in the familial transmission of substance use and dependence.

Extraordinary People

Celebrity Drug Users

Comedian Chris Farley was at the height of his career. This veteran of Chicago's famed Second City was catapulted to stardom when he landed a slot on *Saturday Night Live*. There, his slapstick and baudy routines made him an instant favorite and drew comparisons to one of his heroes, John Belushi. Like Belushi, Farley was overweight (weighing nearly 300 pounds) and had an "in your face" style of comedy. Also like Belushi, Farley lived hard and fast, abusing alcohol, cocaine, heroin, and other drugs. After *Saturday Night Live*, Farley moved on to star in movies such as *Tommy Boy*, *Black Sheep*, and *Beverly Hills Ninja*.

On December 18, 1997, Chris Farley was found dead at the age of 33 in his condominium on the sixtieth floor of the John Hancock Building in Chicago. He had spent the night drinking, drugging, and debauching with friends. An autopsy later showed that he had overdosed on morphine and cocaine. There were also traces of marijuana in his urine. The coroner noted that heart disease, possibly due to Farley's excessive weight, also contributed to his death and that his liver showed clear evidence of damage from chronic heavy alcohol use.

Chris Farley is just one of many celebrities who have suffered, and even died, from substance abuse. For our purposes, a **substance** is any natural or synthesized product that has psychoactive effects—it changes perceptions, thoughts, emotions, and behaviors. Some of the substances we discuss in this chapter are cocaine, heroin, and amphetamines. These are popularly referred to as *drugs*, and people who have problems as a result of taking these drugs are often referred to as **drug addicts.** We use the more neutral term *substance*, however, because some of the disorders we discuss in this chapter involve substances that you might not normally think of as drugs, such as nicotine and alcohol. Also, as we see, a person need not be physically dependent on a substance, as is implied by the term *addict*, in order to have problems resulting from taking the substance.

Nearly half of the U.S. population admits to having tried an illegal substance at sometime in their lives, and approximately 15 percent have used one in the past year (Substance Abuse and Mental Health Services Administration [SAMHSA], 2005). Illicit drug use is highest among young adults (SAMHSA, 2005) (see Figure 17.1). Men are much more likely than women to have used an illicit substance in their lives. Once women begin to use a substance, however, they are at least as likely to become dependent on it and may suffer greater physiological damage from some substances than men (Van Etten & Anthony, 2001). Substance use also varies quite substantially by ethnic group in the United States, as you can see in Figure 17.1.

The occasional use of illegal drugs peaked in the 1970s and has declined since then (Johnston et al., 2004). Most illegal drugs are now used by a minority of college students, although there is a recent increase in the use of ecstasy, and alcohol use has remained stable over time (see Figure 17.2 on page 622). One study surveyed seniors at a college in the eastern United States each decade since the 1960s and compared users and nonusers of illegal drugs on grades and extracurricular activities (Pope, Ionescu-Pioggia, & Pope, 2001). In the earlier decades, the users and nonusers did not differ, but, in 1999, the drug users had significantly lower grades and spent less time in extracurricular activities than the nonusers. Thus, college drug users appear to have become a more distinct group, whose lifestyle has diverged more from the rest of the student body in recent years.

SOCIETY AND SUBSTANCE USE

Societies differ in their attitudes about substances with psychoactive effects, some seeing their use as a matter of individual choice and others seeing it as a grave public health and security concern. These attitudes are reflected in different laws and approaches to treatment (Goldstein, 1994; Mac-Coun, 1998). Many Muslim countries following Islamic law strictly prohibit alcohol and enforce penalties against people caught using this or any other substance. When the Communists took over China in the late 1940s, they made it a major goal to eradicate the widespread use of opium. Traffickers were executed, and users were sent to the countryside for rehabilitation and reeducation. Today, antidrug laws are still strictly enforced, and punishments for the use or sale of illicit substances remain severe.

In Great Britain, substance addiction is considered a medical disease, and people who abuse or are dependent on substances are treated by physicians. Although traffickers in illegal substances are aggressively prosecuted by the British government, the users of illegal substances are more often referred for treatment than arrested for possession of substances. Heroin use is as prevalent as it is in the United States, but physicians in Great Britain are more comfortable with long-term methadone maintenance than are physicians in the United States. The Dutch make a distinction in their law enforcement between "soft" drugs (such as cannabis) and "hard" drugs (such as cocaine and heroin). Although both types of substances are illegal, the possession, use, and sale of cannabis are rarely prosecuted, whereas the importing, manufacture, and sale of the hard substances are subject to heavy penalties, which are enforced.

The Dutch system is based on the belief that enforcing a strict prohibition of softer drugs would drive users underground, where they would come into contact with persons trafficking in harder drugs and would be more likely to begin using these drugs.

In the mid-twentieth century, Zurich, Switzerland, became famous for its "needle park," where the sale and use of substances, including heroin and cocaine, were carried out in the open and allowed by authorities, while a doctor employed by the government stood by in a small kiosk to handle any emergencies and to distribute clean needles for the injection of substances. Opponents of the park argued that it made it extremely easy for troubled young people to become part of the drug scene and generally legitimized illicit drug use. In 1992, the park was closed because of evidence that

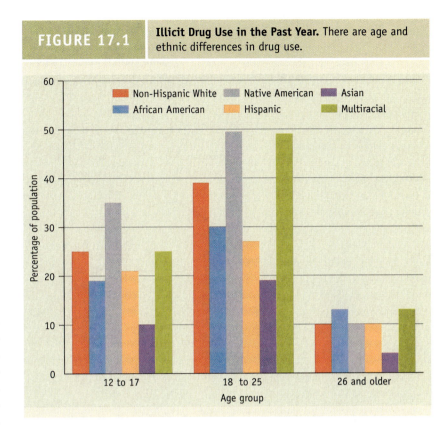

FIGURE 17.1   **Illicit Drug Use in the Past Year.** There are age and ethnic differences in drug use.

addicts from around Europe had poured into the city and crime had soared.

Within the United States, attitudes toward substance use have varied greatly over time and across subgroups. The American ambivalence toward alcohol use is nicely illustrated in a letter written in the mid-twentieth century by a U.S. Congressman in response to a question from one of his constituents: "Dear Congressman, how do you stand on whiskey?" Because the congressman did not know how the constituent stood on alcohol, he fashioned the following safe response:

> My dear friend, I had not intended to discuss this controversial subject at this particular time. However, I want you to know that I do not shun a controversy. On the contrary, I will take a stand on any issue at any time, regardless of how fraught with controversy it may be. You have asked me how I feel about whiskey. Here is how I stand on the issue.
>
> If when you say whiskey, you mean the Devil's brew; the poison scourge; the bloody monster that defiles innocence, dethrones reason, destroys the home, creates misery, poverty, fear; literally takes the bread from the mouths of little children; if you mean the evil drink that topples the

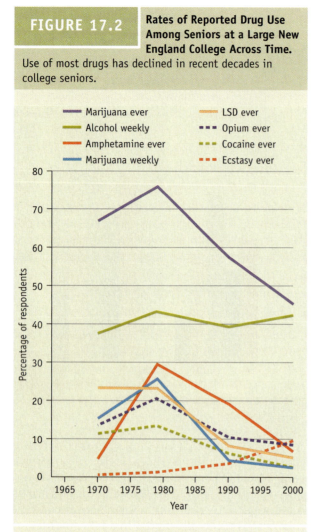

FIGURE 17.2 Rates of Reported Drug Use Among Seniors at a Large New England College Across Time.

Use of most drugs has declined in recent decades in college seniors.

Source: From Pope, H. G., Jr., Ionescu-Pioggia, M. & Pope, K. W., 2001, "Drug Use and Lifestyle Among College Undergraduates: A 30-Year Longitudinal Study." Reprinted with permission from American Journal of Psychiatry, 158. Copyright © 2001 American Psychiatric Association.

Christian man and woman from the pinnacles of righteous, gracious living into the bottomless pit of degradation and despair, shame and helplessness and hopelessness; then certainly, I am against it with all of my power.

But, if when you say whiskey, you mean the oil of conversation, the philosophic wine, the ale that is assumed when great fellows get together, that puts a song in their hearts and laughter on their lips, and the warm glow of contentment in their eyes; if you mean Christmas cheer; if you mean that stimulating drink that puts the spring in the old gentlemen's step on a frosty morning; if you mean the drink that enables the man to magnify his joy and his happiness and to forget, if only for a little while, life's great tragedies and heartbreaks and sorrows; if you mean that drink, the sale of which pours into our Treasury untold millions of dollars which are used to provide tender care for little crippled children, our blind, our deaf, our pitiful aged and infirm; to build highways, hospitals, and schools; then certainly, I am in favor of it. This is my stand, and I will not compromise. Your congressman. (Quoted in Marlatt et al., 1993, p. 462)

Many substances come from plants and have been used for medicinal purposes for centuries. As long ago as 1500 B.C., natives in the Andes highlands chewed coca leaves to increase their endurance (Cocores, Pottash, & Gold, 1991). Coca leaves can be manufactured into cocaine. Cocaine was used legally throughout Europe and then America into the twentieth century to relieve fatigue and was an ingredient in the original Coca-Cola drink and more than 50 other widely available drinks and elixirs.

Opium, a milky juice produced from the poppy plant, has been used for hundreds of years to relieve pain, particularly in Asian and European countries. The leaves of a plant called *khat* have been chewed in parts of eastern Africa, the Middle East, and South America for hundreds of years to produce a sense of well-being and relief from fatigue. Today, modern derivatives of khat are used

Coca-Cola originally contained cocaine.

to make amphetamines, a class of drugs used to treat attention-deficit/hyperactivity disorder, narcolepsy, and obesity and included in over-the-counter cold remedies and appetite suppressants for weight control.

Substances have also been used for religious ceremonies to produce psychological changes important for the ceremonies. For example, the peyote cactus contains a substance that, when chewed, causes people to experience visual hallucinations, in the form of brightly colored lights, or vivid, kaleidoscopic visions of geometric forms, animals, and people. The Aztecs and other native groups in Mexico and the Kiowa, Comanche, and other native groups in the United States and Canada have used peyote as part of religious rituals for hundreds of years.

When substances are used not as part of medical treatments or religious or ceremonial rituals but, rather, by individuals to change their moods, thoughts, and perceptions, other members of society begin to get nervous. This is because some individuals have great difficulty in using substances in moderation and begin to build their lives around using the substances. Their use of substances may lead to significant problems in their abilities to function in their daily lives—they may shirk their job and family responsibilities, they may act impulsively or bizarrely, and they may endanger their own lives and the lives of others. Such a person is said to have a **substance-related disorder.**

Societies have strong motivations for regulating the use of psychoactive substances. In the United States alone, the use of psychoactive substances for nonmedicinal and nonreligious purposes costs society over $240 billion a year in accidents, crime, health care costs, and lost productivity. Illnesses and accidents associated with alcohol alone result in about $6 billion in inpatient hospital costs and nearly $2 billion in outpatient medical costs. Alcohol is associated with over half of the deaths due to traffic accidents and homicides and with 30 percent of all suicides (Hunt, 1998).

DEFINITIONS OF SUBSTANCE-RELATED DISORDERS

There are four substance-related conditions recognized by the DSM-IV-TR: *substance intoxication, substance withdrawal, substance abuse,* and *substance dependence* (see the Concept Overview in Table 17.1). In the first part of this chapter, we discuss the criteria for each of these conditions. In the remainder of this chapter, we discuss how these conditions are manifested in the context of the substances most commonly linked to them.

These substances can be grouped into five categories: (1) central nervous system depressants, including alcohol, barbiturates, benzodiazepines, and inhalants; (2) central nervous system stimulants, including cocaine, amphetamines, nicotine, and caffeine; (3) opioids, including heroin and morphine; (4) hallucinogens and phencyclidine (PCP); and (5) cannabis. Intoxication, withdrawal, abuse, and dependence can occur with most, although not all, of these substances (see the DSM-IV-TR information in Table 17.2 on page 624). In addition, we will consider a mixed group of drugs referred to as club drugs, including ecstasy, GHB, ketamine, and rohypnol, which have become very popular among youth in recent years.

TABLE 17.1	Concept Overview

Definitions of Substance Intoxication, Withdrawal, Abuse, and Dependence

These definitions of substance intoxication, withdrawal, abuse, and dependence apply across a variety of substances, but the specific symptoms depend on the substance used.

Substance intoxication	Experience of significant maladaptive behavioral and psychological symptoms due to the effect of a substance on the central nervous system
Substance withdrawal	Experience of clinically significant distress in social, occupational, or other areas of functioning due to the cessation or reduction of substance use
Substance abuse	Diagnosis given when recurrent substance use leads to significant harmful consequences
Substance dependence	Diagnosis given when substance use leads to physiological dependence or significant impairment or distress

Source: Reprinted with permission from the *Diagnostic and Statistical Manual of Mental Disorders,* Fourth Edition, Text Revision. Copyright © 2000 American Psychiatric Association.

TABLE 17.2   DSM-IV-TR

Diagnosis for Each Class of Substances

The "X's" indicate which diagnoses are recognized for each substance in the DSM-IV-TR.

	Intoxication	Withdrawal	Abuse	Dependence
Alcohol	X	X	X	X
Barbiturates	X	X	X	X
Benzodiazepines	X	X	X	X
Inhalants	X		X	X
Cocaine	X	X	X	X
Amphetamines	X	X	X	X
Caffeine	X			
Opioids	X	X	X	X
Hallucinogens	X		X	X
Phencyclidine	X		X	X
Cannabis	X		X	X
Nicotine		X		X

Source: Reprinted with permission from the *Diagnostic and Statistical Manual of Mental Disorders,* Fourth Edition, Text Revision. Copyright © 2000 American Psychiatric Association.

TABLE 17.3   DSM-IV-TR

Other Substances That Can Lead to Substance Use Disorders

Anesthetics and analgesics	Muscle relaxants
Anticholinergic agents	Nonsteroidal anti-inflammatory medications
Anticonvulsants	Antidepressant medications
Antihistamines	Lead
Blood pressure medications	Rat poisons with strychnine
Antimicrobial medications	Pesticides
Antiparkinsonian medications	Nerve gas
Corticosteroids	Antifreeze
Gastrointestinal medications	Carbon monoxide or dioxide

Source: Reprinted with permission from the *Diagnostic and Statistical Manual of Mental Disorders,* Fourth Edition, Text Revision. Copyright © 2000 American Psychiatric Association.

There are many other substances used for in-toxicating effects that more rarely lead to substance-related disorders (see the DSM-IV-TR information in Table 17.3). Although most people exposed to the substances listed in Table 17.3 experience either no psychoactive effects or only mild and transient effects, some people experience significant problems in cognition and mood, anxiety, hallucinations, delusions, and seizures when exposed. These people may be given the diagnosis of *other substance-related disorder.*

After we discuss specific substances and the disorders associated with them, we discuss the theories of why some people are more prone than others to develop substance-related disorders, examining gender and cultural differences. Then, we discuss the treatments available for people with substance-related disorders. Most of these theories and treatments focus on people with alcohol-related disorders but have been adapted for people with other disorders.

Intoxication

Substance intoxication is a set of behavioral and psychological changes that occur as a direct result of the physiological effects of a substance on the central nervous system. When people are intoxicated, their perceptions change and they may see or hear strange things. Their attention is often diminished or they are easily distracted. Their good judgment is gone and they may be unable to "think straight." They cannot control their bodies as well as they normally can, and they may stumble or be too slow or awkward in their reactions. They often want to sleep either a lot or not at all. Their interpersonal interactions change—they may become more gregarious than usual, more withdrawn, or more aggressive and impulsive. People begin to be intoxicated soon after they begin ingesting a substance, and, the more they ingest, the more intoxicated they become. Intoxication begins to decline as the amount of a substance in people's blood or tissue declines, but the symptoms of intoxication may last for hours or days after the substance is no longer detectable in the body.

The specific symptoms of intoxication depend on what substance is taken, how much is taken, how long the substance has been ingested, and the user's tolerance for the substance. Short-term, or acute, intoxication can produce different symptoms than chronic intoxication. For example, the first time people take a moderate dose of cocaine, they may be outgoing, friendly, and very upbeat. With chronic use over days or weeks, they may begin to withdraw socially and become less gregarious. People's expectations about a substance's effects can also influence the types of symptoms shown. People who expect marijuana to make them relaxed may experience relaxation, whereas people who are frightened of the disinhibition that marijuana creates may experience anxiety, as happened with the woman in the following case study (adapted from Spitzer et al., 1994, pp. 204–205):

> In the middle of a rainy October night, a family doctor in a Chicago suburb was awakened by an old friend who begged him to get out of bed and come quickly to a neighbor's house, where he and his wife had been visiting. The caller, Lou Wolff, was very upset because his

CASE STUDY

> wife, Sybil, had smoked some marijuana and was "freaking out."
>
> The doctor arrived at the neighbor's house to find Sybil lying on the couch looking quite frantic, unable to get up. She said she was too weak to stand, that she was dizzy, was having palpitations, and could feel her blood "rushing through [her] veins." She kept asking for water because her mouth was so dry she could not swallow. She was sure there was some poison in the marijuana.
>
> Sybil, age 42, was the mother of three teenage boys. She worked as a librarian at a university. She was a very controlled, well-organized woman who prided herself on her rationality. It was she who had asked the neighbors to share some of their high-quality homegrown marijuana with her, because marijuana was a big thing with the students and she "wanted to see what all the fuss was about."
>
> Her husband said that she took four or five puffs on a joint and then wailed, "There's something wrong with me. I can't stand up." Lou and the neighbors tried to calm her, telling her she should just lie down and she would soon feel better; but the more they reassured her, the more convinced she became that something was really wrong with her.
>
> The doctor examined her. The only positive findings were that her heart rate was increased and her pupils dilated. He said to her, "For heaven's sake, Sybil, you're just a little stoned. Go home to bed." Sybil did go home to bed, where she stayed for 2 days, feeling "spacey" and weak but no longer terribly anxious. She recovered completely and vowed never to smoke marijuana again.

The setting in which a substance is taken can influence the types of symptoms people develop. For example, when people consume a few alcoholic drinks at a party, they may become uninhibited and loud, but, when they consume the same amount at home alone, they may simply become tired and depressed. The environment in which people become intoxicated can also influence how maladaptive the intoxication is: People who drink alcohol only at home may be at less risk of causing harm to themselves or others than are people who typically drink at bars and drive home under the influence of alcohol.

Most people have been intoxicated, usually with alcohol, at sometime in their lives. The diagnosis of substance intoxication is given only when the behavioral and psychological changes the person experiences are significantly maladaptive in that they substantially disrupt the person's social and family relationships, cause occupational or financial problems, or place the individual at significant risk for adverse effects, such as traffic accidents, severe medical complications, or legal problems.

Withdrawal

Substance withdrawal involves a set of physiological and behavioral symptoms that result when people who have been using substances heavily for prolonged periods of time stop using the substances or greatly reduce their use. The symptoms of withdrawal from a given substance are typically the opposite of the symptoms of intoxication with the same substance. The diagnosis of substance withdrawal is not made unless the withdrawal symptoms cause significant distress or impairment in a person's everyday functioning. For example, although the symptoms of caffeine withdrawal (nervousness, headaches) are annoying to many people, they do not typically cause significant impairment in people's functioning or great distress. For this reason, caffeine withdrawal is not included as a diagnostic category in the DSM-IV-TR.

The symptoms of withdrawal can begin a few hours after a person stops ingesting substances that break down quickly in the body, such as alcohol or heroin. The more intense symptoms of withdrawal usually end within a few days to a few weeks. However, withdrawal symptoms, including seizures, may develop several weeks after a person stops taking high doses of substances that take a long time to leave the body completely, such as some antianxiety substances. In addition, subtle physiological signs of withdrawal, such as problems in attention, perception, or motor skills, may be present for many weeks or months after a person stops using a substance.

Abuse

The diagnosis of **substance abuse** is given when a person's recurrent use of a substance results in significant harmful consequences. Thus, people may use substances, including illegal substances, without having a psychiatric diagnosis, but, when their use causes chronic harmful consequences, they are considered to have a substance use disorder. There are four categories of harmful consequences that suggest substance abuse (APA, 2000) (see the DSM-IV-TR criteria in Table 17.4) First, the individual *fails*

TABLE 17.4 **DSM-IV-TR**

Criteria for Diagnosing Substance Abuse

The criteria for diagnosing substance abuse require repeated problems as a result of the use of a substance.

One or more of the following occurs during a 12-month period, leading to significant impairment or distress:

1. failure to fulfill important obligations at work, home, or school as a result of substance use
2. repeated use of the substance in situations in which it is physically hazardous to do so
3. repeated legal problems as a result of substance use
4. continued use of the substance despite repeated social or legal problems as a result of use

Source: Reprinted with permission from the *Diagnostic and Statistical Manual of Mental Disorders*, Fourth Edition, Text Revision. Copyright © 2000 American Psychiatric Association.

---

to fulfill important obligations at work, school, or home. He or she may fail to show up at work or for classes, be unable to concentrate and therefore perform poorly, and perhaps even take the substance at work or at school. Second, the individual *repeatedly uses the substance in situations in which it is physically hazardous to do so*, such as while driving a car or a boat. Third, the individual *repeatedly has legal problems as a result of substance use*, such as arrests for the possession of illegal substances or for drunk driving. Fourth, the individual *continues to use the substance, even though he or she has repeatedly had social or legal problems as a result of the use*. A person has to show repeated problems in at least one of these categories within a 12-month period to qualify for a diagnosis of substance abuse.

For some people, the abuse of a particular group of substances evolves into dependence on those substances. In such cases, the diagnosis of substance dependence preempts the diagnosis of substance abuse, since dependence is considered a more advanced condition than abuse. Some individuals abuse substances for years without ever becoming dependent on them, however.

Dependence

The diagnosis of **substance dependence** is closest to what people often refer to as *drug addiction* (see the DSM-IV-TR criteria in Table 17.5). A person is

TABLE 17.5	**DSM-IV-TR**

Criteria for Diagnosing Substance Dependence

Substance dependence often involves evidence of physiological dependence plus repeated problems due to the use of the substance.

Maladaptive pattern of substance use, leading to three or more of the following:

1. tolerance, as defined by either
   a. the need for markedly increased amounts of the substance to achieve intoxication or desired effect
   b. markedly diminished effect with continued use of the same amount of the substance
2. withdrawal, as manifested by either
   a. the characteristic withdrawal syndrome for the substance
   b. the same or a closely related substance is taken to relieve or avoid withdrawal symptoms
3. the substance is often taken in larger amounts or over a longer period than was intended
4. there is a persistent desire or unsuccessful effort to cut down or control substance use
5. a great deal of time is spent in activities necessary to obtain the substance, use the substance, or recover from its effects
6. important social, occupational, or recreational activities are given up or reduced because of substance use
7. the substance use is continued despite knowledge of having a persistent or recurrent physical or psychological problem caused by or exacerbated by the substance.

Source: Reprinted with permission from the *Diagnostic and Statistical Manual of Mental Disorders*, Fourth Edition, Text Revision. Copyright © 2000 American Psychiatric Association.

physiologically dependent on a substance when he or she shows either tolerance or withdrawal from the substance. **Tolerance** is present when a person experiences less and less effect from the same dose of a substance and needs greater and greater doses of a substance in order to achieve intoxication. People who have smoked cigarettes for years often smoke more than 20 cigarettes a day, when the same amount would have made them violently ill when they first began smoking. A person who is highly tolerant to a substance may have a very high blood level of the substance without being aware of any effects of the substance. For example, people who are highly tolerant to alcohol may have blood-alcohol levels far above those used in the legal definition of intoxication but show few signs of alcohol intoxication. The risk for tolerance varies greatly from one substance to the next. Alcohol, opioids, stimulants, and nicotine have high risks for tolerance, whereas cannabis and PCP appear to have lower risks for tolerance.

People who are physiologically dependent on substances often show severe withdrawal symptoms when they stop using the substances. The symptoms may be so severe that the substances must be withdrawn gradually in order to prevent the symptoms from becoming overwhelming or dangerous. These people may take the substances to relieve or avoid withdrawal symptoms. For example, a person dependent on alcohol may have a drink first thing in the morning to relieve withdrawal symptoms.

Physiological dependence (i.e., evidence of tolerance or withdrawal) is not required for a diagnosis of substance dependence, however. The diagnosis can be given when a person compulsively uses a substance, despite experiencing significant social, occupational, psychological, or medical problems as a result of that use.

Most people who are dependent on a substance crave the substance and will do almost anything to get it (e.g., steal, lie, prostitute themselves) when the craving is strong. Their entire lives may revolve around obtaining and ingesting the substance. They may have attempted repeatedly to cut back on or quit using the substance, only to find themselves compulsively taking the substance again. In the following case study, Lucy is physically and psychologically dependent on both heroin and crack cocaine (adapted from Inciardi, Lockwood, & Pottieger, 1993, pp. 160–161):

By the time Lucy was 18, she was heavily addicted to heroin. Her mother took her to a detoxification program. After the 21-day regimen, Lucy was released but immediately relapsed to heroin use. By age 24, Lucy was mainlining heroin and turning tricks regularly to support both her and a boyfriend's drug habits. Lucy's boyfriend admitted himself to a drug rehabilitation program. When he completed his treatment stay, they both stopped their heroin use. However, they began snorting cocaine. Lucy left this boyfriend not too long afterwards. She went to work in a massage parlor, and the other women there introduced her to crack. This was 1984 and Lucy was 30 years old, a veteran drug addict and prostitute.

Lucy left the massage parlor and began working on the streets. Her crack use increased continually until 1986, when she tried to stop. In her opinion, crack was worse than heroin, so she started injecting narcotics again. But she never stopped using crack.

Because of her crack use, Lucy began doing things she had never even contemplated before, even while on heroin. For instance, she had anal sex and she sold herself for less money than ever before. She even began trading sex for drugs rather than money. Lucy also regularly worked in crack houses. She described them as "disgusting" and crowded. People would smoke and have sex in the same room in front of other people. Lucy insisted that her crack-house tricks rent rooms for sex, refusing to have sex in front of others. After having sex, Lucy would return to the stroll. Lucy would have five to seven customers a night, and most of the sex was oral. During this time, Lucy either stayed with her sister or slept in cars.

The way a substance is administered can be an important factor in determining how rapidly a person will become intoxicated and the likelihood that it will produce withdrawal symptoms or lead to abuse or dependence. The routes of administration that produce rapid and efficient absorption of the substance into the bloodstream lead to more intense intoxication and a greater likelihood of dependence. These routes include injecting, smoking,

Smoking, snorting, or injecting a substance can lead to more intense intoxication and a greater chance of dependence than eating or drinking it.

and snorting the substance. These routes of administration are also more likely to lead to overdose.

Some substances act more rapidly on the central nervous system and, thus, lead to faster intoxication. They are more likely to lead to dependence or abuse. Finally, substances whose effects wear off quickly are more likely to lead to dependence or abuse than are substances with longer-lasting effects.

Let's turn now to discussing what intoxication, withdrawal, abuse, and dependence look like for the substances associated with substance disorders in the DSM-IV-TR. We begin with the depressants, which include alcohol, benzodiazepines, barbiturates, and the inhalants.

DEPRESSANTS

The depressants slow the activity of the central nervous system. In moderate doses, they make people relaxed and somewhat sleepy, reduce concentration, and impair thinking and motor skills. In heavy doses, they can induce stupor (see the Concept Overview in Table 17.6).

Alcohol

Alcohol is a classic central nervous system depressant, but its effects on the brain occur in two distinct phases. In low doses, alcohol causes many people to feel more self-confident, more relaxed, and perhaps slightly euphoric. They may be less inhibited, and it may be this disinhibitory effect that many people find attractive. At increasing doses, however, alcohol induces many of the symptoms of depression, including fatigue and lethargy, decreased motivation, sleep disturbances, depressed mood, and confusion. Also, although many people take alcohol to feel more sexy (mainly by reducing

TABLE 17.6 Concept Overview

Intoxication with and Withdrawal from Depressants

The depressants are among the most widely used substances.

Drug	Intoxication Symptoms	Withdrawal Symptoms
Alcohol, benzodiazepines, and barbiturates	Behavioral changes (e.g., inappropriate sexual or aggressive behavior, mood lability, impaired judgment)	Autonomic hyperactivity (e.g., sweating or a pulse rate greater than 100)
	Slurred speech	Hand tremor
	Incoordination	Insomnia
	Unsteady gait	Nausea or vomiting
	Rapid eye movement	Transient hallucinations or illusions
	Attention and memory problems	Psychomotor agitation
	Stupor or coma	Anxiety
		Grand mal seizures
Inhalants	Behavioral changes (e.g., belligerence, assaultiveness, apathy, impaired judgment)	Not a diagnosis in DSM-IV-TR
	Dizziness	
	Involuntary rapid eyeball movements	
	Incoordination	
	Slurred speech	
	Unsteady gait	
	Lethargy	
	Depressed reflexes	
	Psychomotor retardation	
	Tremor	
	Muscle weakness	
	Blurred vision	
	Stupor or coma	
	Euphoria	

Source: Reprinted with permission from the *Diagnostic and Statistical Manual of Mental Disorders*, Fourth Edition, Text Revision. Copyright © 2000 American Psychiatric Association.

their sexual inhibitions), even low doses of alcohol can severely impair sexual functioning.

People who are intoxicated with alcohol slur their words, walk with unsteady gaits, have trouble paying attention or remembering things, and are slow and awkward in their physical reactions. They may act inappropriately, becoming aggressive or saying rude things. Their moods may swing from exuberance to despair. With extreme intoxication, they may fall into a stupor or coma. Often, they do not recognize they are intoxicated or may flatly deny it, even though it is obvious. Once sober, they

may have amnesia, known as a **blackout,** for the events that occurred while they were intoxicated.

One critical determinant of how quickly people become intoxicated with alcohol is whether their stomachs are full or empty. When the stomach is empty, alcohol is more quickly delivered from the stomach to the small intestine, where it is rapidly absorbed into the body. The person with a full stomach may drink significantly more drinks before reaching a dangerous blood-alcohol level or showing clear signs of intoxication. People in countries where alcohol is almost always consumed with

Drinking alcohol with food leads to slower absorption of the alcohol.

meals, such as in France, show lower rates of alcohol-related substance disorders than do people in countries where alcohol is often consumed on an empty stomach.

The *legal definition* of alcohol intoxication is much narrower than the criteria for a diagnosis of alcohol intoxication. Most states in the United States consider a person to be under the influence of alcohol if his or her blood-alcohol level is above 0.05, 0.08, or 0.10. As Table 17.7 indicates, it does not take very many drinks for most people to reach this blood-alcohol level. Deficits in attention, reaction time, and coordination arise even with the first drink and can interfere with the ability to operate a car or machinery safely and to perform other tasks requiring a steady hand, coordination, clear thinking, and clear vision. These deficits are not always readily observable, even to trained observers (Winger et al., 1992). People often leave parties or bars with blood-alcohol levels well above the legal limit and dangerous deficits in their ability to drive, without appearing drunk.

Drinking large quantities of alcohol can result in death, even in people who are not chronic abusers of alcohol. About one-third of these deaths occur as a result of respiratory paralysis, usually as a result of a final, large dose of alcohol in people who are already intoxicated. Alcohol can also interact fatally with a number of substances—for example, antidepressant drugs (Winger et al., 1992).

Most deaths due to alcohol, however, come from automobile accidents, private plane and boat accidents, and drownings. Nearly half of all fatal automobile accidents and deaths due to falls or fires and over a third of all drownings are alcohol-related (Flemming & Manwell, 2000; Hunt, 1998). More than half of all murderers and their victims are believed to be intoxicated with alcohol at the time of the murders, and people who commit suicide often do so under the influence of alcohol.

Alcohol Abuse and Dependence

People given the diagnosis of **alcohol abuse** use alcohol in dangerous situations (such as when driving), fail to meet important obligations at work or at home as a result of their alcohol use, and have recurrent legal or social problems as a result of their alcohol use. People given the diagnosis of **alcohol dependence** typically have all the problems of an alcohol abuser; plus they may show physiological tolerance to alcohol, they spend a great deal of time intoxicated or withdrawing from alcohol, they often organize their lives around drinking, or they continue to drink despite having significant social, occupational, medical, or legal problems that result from drinking. The characteristics of alcohol dependence match what most people associate with the label *alcoholism*. Table 17.8 on page 632 lists a variety of problems experienced by people who abuse or are dependent on alcohol.

There are at least three distinct patterns of alcohol use by alcohol abusers and dependents. Some people drink large amounts of alcohol every day and plan their days around their drinking. Others abstain from drinking for long periods of time and then go on binges, which last days or weeks. They may stop drinking when faced with crises they must deal with, such as their children's illnesses, or with threats of sanctions for drinking, such as threats of being fired. When they begin drinking again, they may be able to control their drinking for a while, but it may soon escalate until severe problems develop. Still others are sober during the weekdays but drink heavily during the evenings or perhaps only on weekends. Nick and his buddies fit into the third group:

> Nick began drinking in high school, but his drinking escalated when he moved away from his parents' home to go to college. After just a couple of weeks at college, Nick became friends with a group of guys who liked to party really hard on the weekends. On Thursday nights, they would begin to drink beer, often getting quite drunk. They would get a little loud and obnoxious, and sometimes their neighbors in the dormitory would complain to the resident

(continued)

TABLE 17.7 Relationships Among Sex, Weight, Oral Alcohol Consumption, and Blood-Alcohol Level

It doesn't take very many drinks for most people to reach the blood-alcohol level of 0.05 or 0.10, which are the legal definitions of intoxication in most states.

Total Alcohol Content (Ounces)	Beverage Intake*	Blood-Alcohol Level (Percent)					
		Female (100 lb)	Male (100 lb)	Female (150 lb)	Male (150 lb)	Female (200 lb)	Male (200 lb)
1/2	1 oz spirits[†] 1 glass wine 1 can beer	0.045	0.037	0.03	0.025	0.022	0.019
1	2 oz spirits 2 glasses wine 2 cans beer	0.090	0.075	0.06	0.050	0.045	0.037
2	4 oz spirits 4 glasses wine 4 cans beer	0.180	0.150	0.12	0.100	0.090	0.070
3	6 oz spirits 6 glasses wine 6 cans beer	0.270	0.220	0.18	0.150	0.130	0.110
4	8 oz spirits 8 glasses wine 8 cans beer	0.360	0.300	0.24	0.200	0.180	0.150
5	10 oz spirits 10 glasses wine 10 cans beer	0.450	0.370	0.30	0.250	0.220	0.180

Source: Data from Ray & Ksir, 1993, p. 194.

*In one hour.

[†]100-proof spirits (50 percent alcohol).

CASE STUDY

assistant of the dorm about them. They would typically sleep off their hangovers on Friday, missing classes, and then begin drinking again Friday afternoon. They would continue to drink through Saturday, finally stopping on Sunday to sleep and recover. Nick was able to keep a decent grade average through his first year in college, despite missing many classes. In his sophomore year, however, the classes in his major were getting harder. Nick's drinking was also getting more out of hand. He still would abstain from drinking from about Sunday afternoon until noon on Thursday. But, when he would go get the keg of beer for his group of buddies on Thursday afternoon, he'd also pick up a few fifths of vodka or whatever hard liquor was the cheapest. His buddies would stick to the beer, but Nick would mix the beer with shots of hard liquor and was usually extremely drunk by dinner on Thursday. He started getting really mean and stupid when he was drunk. He punched a hole in the wall of his dorm room one night; when the resident assistant came up to investigate what was going on, he threatened her, saying he would "smack her across the room" if she didn't shut up and leave. That got him kicked out of his dormitory and off campus. Nick didn't mind being away from the "geeks" who studied all the time and liked

(continued)

having his own apartment, where his buddies could come to drink. Nick remained intoxicated from Thursday afternoon until Sunday morning, drinking all day and evening, except when he was passed out. He usually slept through most of his classes on Monday; when he did go, he was so hungover that he couldn't pay attention. His grades were falling, and even his drinking buddies were getting disgusted with Nick's behavior.

Binge drinking is defined as consuming five or more drinks within a couple of hours of each other (although some researchers define a binge for women as consuming four or more drinks within a

TABLE 17.8   Problems Experienced by People Who Are Diagnosed with Alcohol Abuse or Dependence

People with alcohol abuse or dependence typically have many problems due to their alcohol use.

Symptom	Percentage Saying Yes
Family objected to respondent's drinking	62
Thought him- or herself an excessive drinker	59
Consumed a fifth of liquor in one day	70
Engaged in daily or weekly heavy drinking	80
Told physician about drinking	22
Friends or professionals said drinking too much	39
Wanted to stop drinking but couldn't	21
Made efforts to control drinking	19
Engaged in morning drinking	21
Had job troubles due to drinking	15
Lost job	7
Had trouble driving	35
Was arrested while drinking	31
Had physical fights while drinking	50
Had two or more binges	29
Had blackouts while drinking	57
Had any withdrawal symptom	28
Had any medical complication	22
Continued to drink with serious illness	14
Couldn't do ordinary work without drinking	12

Source: Data from Helzer, Bucholz, & Robins, 1992.

short time). In a nationwide survey, 23 percent of Americans reported binge drinking in the previous month (SAMHSA, 2005). Binge drinking on college campuses is common. Nationwide, 44 percent of college students report binge drinking in the past month, compared with 39 percent of 18- to 22-year-olds not in college (SAMHSA, 2005). Binge drinking is especially common among members of fraternities and sororities, with 76 percent of members saying they binge drink and 15 percent having engaged in binge drinking at least six times in the previous two weeks (Wahlberg, 1999).

Family members, friends, and business associates often recognize when an individual is abusing or is dependent on alcohol, and they confront the individual. Sometimes, this leads the individual to seek help, but denial is strong. One confrontation or even a series of confrontations often does not motivate someone who is abusing alcohol to change his or her behavior or to seek help.

There is increasing evidence that alcohol dependence is a heterogeneous disorder and that different subtypes of alcohol dependence have different causes and prognoses. One reliable distinction is between alcoholics who also have antisocial personalities and alcoholics who do not have antisocial personalities (Zucker et al., 1996). Antisocial alcoholics have more severe symptoms of alcoholism, tend to remain alcoholic for longer, have poorer social functioning, have more marital failures, and have heavier drug involvement, compared with nonantisocial alcoholics (Zucker et al., 1996). Antisocial alcoholics are more likely to come from families with alcoholism and to have begun drinking earlier than nonantisocial alcoholics. In turn, the children of antisocial alco-

Heavy drinking can be part of the culture of a peer group, but it still can lead to alcohol abuse and dependence in some members.

holics are more likely to have behavior problems than are the children of nonantisocial alcoholics (Puttler et al., 1998).

Another distinction that has been made is between negative affect alcoholism and other alcoholisms (Sher, Grekin, & Williams, 2005). People with negative affect alcoholism tend to have had depressive and anxiety symptoms in childhood and adolescence and to have only begun severe alcohol use and abuse in adulthood. This pattern appears to be more common in women than in men (Nolen-Hoeksema, 2004).

Alcohol Withdrawal

People who are dependent on alcohol can experience severe alcohol withdrawal symptoms, which can be divided into three stages (Winger et al., 1992). The first stage, which usually begins within a few hours after drinking has been stopped or sharply curtailed, includes tremulousness (the "shakes"), weakness, and profuse perspiration. A person may complain of anxiety (the "jitters"), headache, nausea, and abdominal cramps. He or she may begin to retch and vomit. The person's face is flushed, and he or she is restless and easily startled but alert. The person's EEG pattern may be mildly abnormal. He or she may begin to see or hear things, at first only with eyes shut but with time also with eyes open. People whose dependence on alcohol is relatively moderate may experience only this first stage of withdrawal, and the symptoms may disappear within a few days.

The second stage of withdrawal involves convulsive seizures, which may begin as early as 12 hours after stopping drinking but more often appear during the second or third day. The third stage of withdrawal is characterized by **delirium tremens,** or **DTs.** Auditory, visual, and tactile hallucinations occur. The person may also develop bizarre, terrifying delusions, such as a belief that monsters are attacking. He or she may sleep little and become severely agitated, continuously active, and completely disoriented. Fever, profuse perspiration, and an irregular heartbeat may develop. Delirium tremens is a fatal condition in approximately 10 percent of cases. Death may occur from hyperthermia (greatly increased body temperature) or the collapse of the peripheral vascular system. Fortunately, only about 11 percent of individuals with alcohol dependence ever experience seizures or DTs (Schuckit et al., 1995). Seizures and DTs are more common among people who drink large amounts in single sittings and who have additional medical illnesses.

People who make it through the entire withdrawal syndrome can show complete recovery from withdrawal symptoms. The following is a case study presented by groundbreaking psychiatrist Emil Kraepelin to medical students in the nineteenth century. It is about a man going through delirium tremens after prolonged alcohol dependence (Spitzer et al., 1981, pp. 304–305).

CASE STUDY

The innkeeper, aged thirty-four, whom I am bringing before you to-day was admitted to the hospital only an hour ago. He understands the questions put to him, but cannot quite hear some of them, and gives a rather absent-minded impression. He states his name and age correctly. . . . Yet he does not know the doctors, calls them by the names of his acquaintances, and thinks he has been here for two or three days. It must be the Crown Hotel, or, rather, the "mad hospital." He does not know the date exactly. . . .

He moves about in his chair, looks round him a great deal, starts slightly several times, and keeps on playing with his hands. Suddenly he gets up, and begs to be allowed to play on the piano for a little at once. He sits down again immediately, on persuasion, but then wants to go away "to tell them something else that he has forgotten." He gradually gets more and more excited, saying that his fate is sealed; he must leave the world now; they might telegraph to his wife that her husband is lying at the point of death. We learn, by questioning him, that he is going to be executed by electricity, and also that he will be shot. "The picture is not clearly painted," he says; "every moment someone stands now here, now there, waiting for me with a revolver. When I open my eyes, they vanish." He says that a stinking fluid has been injected into his head and both his toes, which causes the pictures one takes for reality; that is the work of an international society, which makes away with those "who fell into misfortune innocently through false steps." With this he looks eagerly at the window, where he sees houses and trees vanishing and reappearing. With slight pressure on his eyes, he sees first sparks, then a hare, a picture, a head, a washstand-set, a half-moon, and a human head, first dully and then in colours. If you show him a speck on the floor,

(continued)

he tries to pick it up, saying that it is a piece of money. If you shut his hand and ask him what you have given him, he keeps his fingers carefully closed, and guesses that it is a leadpencil or a piece of indiarubber. The patient's mood is half apprehensive and half amused. His head is much flushed, and his pulse is small, weak, and rather hurried. His face is bloated and his eyes are watery. His breath smells strongly of alcohol and acetone. His tongue is thickly furred, and trembles when he puts it out, and his outspread fingers show strong, jerky tremors.

Long-Term Effects of Alcohol Abuse

Heavy, prolonged use of alcohol can have toxic effects on several systems of the body, including the stomach, esophagus, pancreas, and liver (for a review, see Nolen-Hoeksema, 2004). Comedian Chris Farley showed evidence of liver damage from chronic alcohol abuse. One of the most common medical conditions associated with alcohol abuse and dependence is low-grade hypertension. This factor, combined with increases in triglycerides and low-density lipoprotein (or "bad") cholesterol, puts alcohol abusers at increased risk for heart disease. Alcohol abusers and dependents are often malnourished, in part because chronic alcohol ingestion decreases the absorption of critical nutrients from the gastrointestinal system and in part because they tend to "drink their meals." Some alcohol abusers show chronic thiamine deficiencies, which can lead to several disorders of the central nervous system, including numbness and pain in the extremities, deterioration in the muscles, and the loss of visual acuity for both near and far objects (Martin & Bates, 1998)

Alcohol-induced persisting amnesic disorder, a permanent cognitive disorder caused by damage to the central nervous system, consists of two syndromes. **Wernicke's encephalopathy** involves mental confusion and disorientation and, in severe states, coma. **Korsakoff's psychosis** involves a loss of memory for recent events and problems in recalling distant events. The person may confabulate, telling implausible stories in an attempt to hide his or her inability to remember. **Alcohol-induced dementia** is the loss of intellectual abilities, including memory, abstract thinking, judgment, or problem solving, often accompanied by personality changes, such as increases in paranoia. This syndrome is found in approximately 9 percent of people who chronically abuse alcohol or are dependent and is a common cause of adult dementia (Winger et al.,

1992). More subtle deficits due to central nervous system damage are observed in many chronic abusers of alcohol, even after they have stopped using alcohol (Martin & Bates, 1998).

Children of mothers who chronically ingest large amounts of alcohol while pregnant may be born with **fetal alcohol syndrome (FAS)** (Streissguth et al., 1999). This syndrome is characterized by retarded growth, facial abnormalities, central nervous system damage, mental retardation, motor abnormalities, tremors, hyperactivity, heart defects, and skeletal anomalies (see also Chapter 13). The risk for fetal alcohol syndrome is highest among women who are chronic, heavy alcohol users while pregnant, particularly those who drink heavily early in pregnancy.

However, even low to moderate levels of drinking during pregnancy are associated with subtle alcohol-related birth defects (Jacobson & Jacobson, 2000; Kelly et al., 2000; Olson et al., 1998). For example, children exposed to alcohol in the womb are slower to grow physically by 6 years of age, and have deficits in learning and memory skills at 10 years of age (Cornelius et al., 2002). These results hold even after controlling for correlates of prenatal alcohol use, including income, and tobacco and marijuana use. Thus, experts believe that there is no level of drinking during pregnancy that is safe for the fetus.

Cultural Differences in Alcohol Disorders

There are marked differences across cultures in the use of alcohol and in rates of alcohol-related problems (see Figure 17.3). Low rates of alcohol consumption in Eastern Mediterranean and some African countries are tied to the influence of Islam and its prohibitions against alcohol. Low rates of alcohol consumption in Southeast Asia may be due in part to the absence, in 50 percent of people of Asian descent, of an enzyme that eliminates the first breakdown product of alcohol, acetaldehyde. When these individuals consume alcohol, they experience a flushed face and heart palpitations, and the discomfort of this effect often leads them to avoid alcohol altogether. Figure 17.3 shows moderate rates in the Western Pacific countries, which include Japan and China, where consumption is relatively low, but also include Australia, where consumption is relatively high.

Alcohol dependence and abuse are the most common disorders in the United States, with 8 to 24 percent of the population reporting symptoms that qualify them for a diagnosis of dependence or abuse at sometime in their lives, depending on which nationwide survey you look at (Sher, Grekin, & Williams, 2005). Within the United States, there are substantial differences among ethnic groups in alcohol use (see Figure 17.4 on page 636). One group in the United States that appears at high risk for alcohol abuse and dependence is Native Americans. For example, a study of adult members of a Pacific Northwest reservation community found that 27 percent qualified for a diagnosis of alcohol dependence. Deaths related to alcohol are as much as five times more common among Native Americans than in the general U.S. population (Manson et al., 1992). Hospital records indicate that alcohol-related illnesses are three times higher among Native Americans than among all people in the United States and twice the rates for other ethnic minority groups in the United States. The higher rates of alcohol-related problems among Native Americans have been tied to their excessive rates of poverty and unemployment, lower education, and greater sense of helplessness and hopelessness.

Gender and Alcohol Use

In a community survey done in the United States, about 62 percent of men over age 12 said they had consumed at least one alcoholic beverage in the past month, compared with 46 percent of women (SAMHSA, 2005) (see Figure 17.5 on page 636). Men are also more likely than women to binge drink, to drink heavily, and to have alcohol use disorders. About 13 percent of American men and 6 percent of American women will meet the criteria for alcohol abuse at sometime in their lives, and about 20 percent of men and 8 percent of women will meet the criteria for alcohol dependence at sometime in their lives (Kessler et al., 1994). The gender gap in alcohol use is much greater among men and women who subscribe to traditional gender roles, which condone drinking for men but not for women (Huselid & Cooper, 1992). Similarly, in ethnic minority groups of the United States in which traditional gender roles are more widely accepted, such as Hispanics and recent Asian immigrants, the gender gap in drinking is greater than it is among Whites, due largely to high percentages of women in the minority groups who completely abstain from alcohol.

Trends Across the Life Span

Studies of adolescents and young adults find a widespread abuse of alcohol (Lewinsohn et al., 1996b; Nelson & Wittchen, 1998), particularly among males. One nationwide sample found that the proportions of eighth-, tenth-, and twelfth-graders who reported drinking an alcoholic beverage in the 30-day period prior to the survey were 20 percent, 35 percent, and 48 percent, respectively (Johnston et al., 2004). One study of more than 3,000 14- to 24-year-olds found that 15 percent of

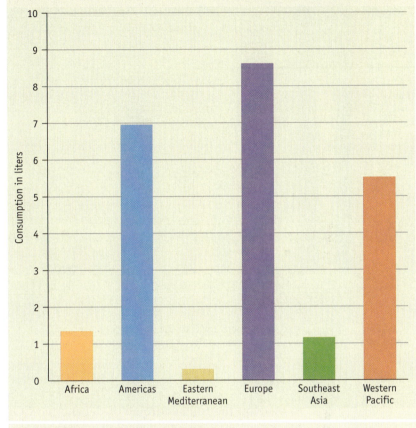

FIGURE 17.3 **Consumption of Pure Alcohol in Various Regions of the World.** Cultures vary greatly in their consumption of alcohol. (Southeast Asia includes India and neighboring countries. Western Pacific includes Australia, China, Japan, and the Pacific Rim Countries.)

Source: World Health Organization, 2005b.

the males and about 5 percent of the females could be diagnosed with alcohol abuse, according to the DSM-IV (Nelson & Wittchen, 1998). Alcohol dependence was lower, with about 10 percent of the males and 3 percent of the females qualifying for the diagnosis. Over time, about half of the adolescents and young adults who abused alcohol stopped abusing alcohol, but the alcohol abusers were much more likely than the nonabusers to become dependent on alcohol eventually.

Young and middle-aged adults who are diagnosed with alcohol dependence tend to show a chronic course, at least over a five-year period. One study, which followed 1,346 people, found that two-thirds of those diagnosed with alcohol dependence still had the diagnosis five years later (Schuckit, Smith, Danko, et al., 2001). Of those initially diagnosed with alcohol abuse, 55 percent continued to show some signs of abuse or dependence five years later, but only 3.5 percent went on

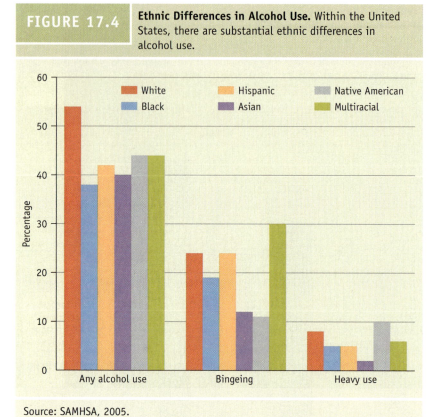

FIGURE 17.4 | **Ethnic Differences in Alcohol Use.** Within the United States, there are substantial ethnic differences in alcohol use.

Source: SAMHSA, 2005.
Note: Bingeing is defined as five or more drinks on the same occasion at least once in the past 30 days. Heavy use is defined as five or more drinks on the same occasion on at least 5 different days in the past 30 days.

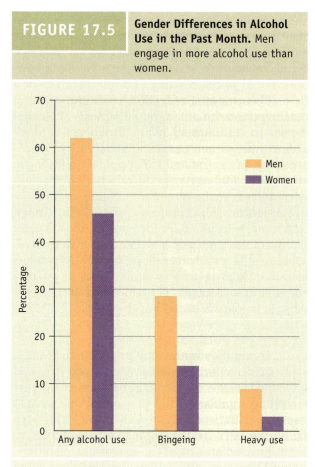

FIGURE 17.5 | **Gender Differences in Alcohol Use in the Past Month.** Men engage in more alcohol use than women.

Source: SAMHSA, 2005.
Note: Bingeing is defined as five or more drinks on the same occasion at least once in the past 30 days. Heavy use is defined as five or more drinks on the same occasion on at least 5 different days in the past 30 days.

to develop the full syndrome of dependence. Of the participants with no alcohol diagnosis at baseline, only 2.5 percent met the criteria for alcohol dependence five years later, but 12.8 percent met the criteria for alcohol abuse at follow-up. Those who were more likely to have a diagnosis at follow-up included men, people with marital instability, and those who had also used illegal drugs.

As we saw in Figure 17.1, the use of illegal substances in general declines as adults get older, and this is true for alcohol as well (Sher, Grekin, & Williams, 2005). Elderly people are less likely than younger adults to abuse or be dependent on alcohol, probably for several reasons. First, with age, the liver metabolizes alcohol at a slower rate, and the lower percentage of body water increases the absorption of alcohol. As a result, older people can become intoxicated faster and experience the negative effects of alcohol more severely and quickly. Second, as people grow older, they may become more mature in their choices, including the choice about drinking alcohol to excess. Third, older people have grown up under stronger prohibitions against alcohol use and abuse and in a society in which there was more stigma associated with alcoholism, leading them to curtail their use of alcohol

more than younger people do. Finally, people who have used alcohol excessively for many years may die from alcohol-related diseases before they reach old age.

Benzodiazepines, Barbiturates, and Inhalants

Three other groups of substances that, like alcohol, depress the central nervous system are benzodiazepines, barbiturates, and inhalants. Intoxication with and withdrawal from these substances are quite similar to alcohol intoxication and withdrawal. Users initially may feel euphoric and become disinhibited but then experience depressed moods, lethargy, perceptual distortions, loss of coordination, and other signs of central nervous system depression.

Benzodiazepines (such as Xanax, Valium, Halcion, Librium, and Klonopin) and **barbiturates** (such as Quaalude) are legally manufactured and sold by prescription, usually for the treatment of anxiety and insomnia. In the United States, approximately 90 percent of people hospitalized for medical care or surgery are prescribed sedatives. Large quantities of these substances end up on the illegal black market, however. These substances are especially likely to be taken in combination with other psychoactive substances to produce greater feelings of euphoria or to relieve the agitation created by other substances (Schuckit, 1995).

There are two common patterns in the development of benzodiazapine or barbiturate abuse and dependence (Schuckit, 1995; Sowers, 1998). The most common pattern is followed by a teenager or young adult who begins using these substances recreationally, often at "bring your own drug" parties, to produce a sense of well-being or euphoria. Their use then escalates to chronic use and physiological dependence. This pattern is especially likely among persons who already have other substance abuse problems with alcohol, opioids, cocaine, amphetamines, or other substances.

A second pattern is seen in people, particularly women and older people, who initially use sedatives under physicians' care for anxiety or insomnia but then gradually increase their use as tolerance develops, without the knowledge of their physicians. They obtain prescriptions from several physicians or even photocopy their prescriptions. When confronted about their sedative use and dependency, they may deny that they use the drugs to produce euphoria or that they are dependent on the sedatives. Barbiturates and benzodiazepines cause decreases in blood pressure, respiratory rate, and heart rate. In overdose, they can be extremely dangerous and even fatal. Death can occur from respiratory arrest or cardiovascular collapse. Overdose is especially likely to occur when people take these substances (particularly the benzodiazepines) in combination with alcohol. Nationwide surveys find that, from 1995 to 2002, emergency room visits involving benzodiazepines increased 41 percent (SAMHSA, 2005).

Inhalants are volatile substances that produce chemical vapors, which can be inhaled and which depress the central nervous system. A recent user of an inhalant may appear drunk or disoriented, have slurred speech, be nauseated and lack appetite, and be inattentive, irritable, or depressed. One group of inhalants is solvents, such as gasoline, glue, paint thinners, and spray paints. Users may inhale vapors directly from the cans or bottles containing the substances, soak rags with the substances and then hold the rags to their mouths and noses, or place the substances in paper or plastic bags and then inhale the gases from the bags. The chemicals reach the lungs, bloodstream, and brain very rapidly. Others are

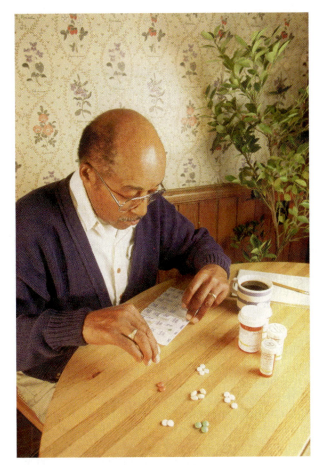

Older people may become addicted to sedatives after using them under a doctor's care.

medical anesthetic gases, such as nitrous oxide ("laughing gas"), which can also be found in whipped cream dispensers and products that boost octane levels. Nitrites are a special class of inhalants that dilate blood vessels and relax muscles and are used as sexual enhancers. Illegally packaged nitrites are called "poppers" or "snappers" on the street.

The greatest users of inhalants are young people. National surveys find that about 6 percent of U.S. children have tried inhalants by the time they have reached fourth grade, and inhalant abuse peaks between the seventh and ninth grades (National Institute on Drug Abuse [NIDA], 2002d). Seventeen percent of eighth-graders report having used inhalants at sometime in their lives (NIDA, 2002a). One group that appears especially prone to using inhalants is Native American teenagers. Some studies have found that nearly all the children on some Native American reservations have experimented with gasoline inhaling. Hispanic American teenagers also appear to have higher rates of inhalant use than other groups of teenagers in the United States, and it is estimated that 500,000

Brain Damage in an Inhalant Abuser. The right panel shows extensive shrinkage in the brain of an inhalant abuser, compared with the brain of a nonabuser (left panel).

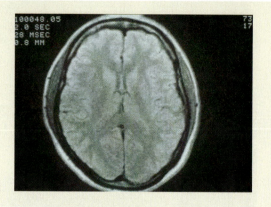 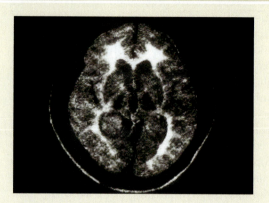

Source: http://www.drugabuse.gov/ResearchReports/

children in Mexico City are addicted to inhalants (Hartman, 1998). Males are more likely than females to use inhalants.

Chronic users of inhalants may have a variety of respiratory irritations and rashes due to the inhalants. Inhalants can cause permanent damage to the central nervous system, including degeneration and lesions of the brain, leading to cognitive deficits, including severe dementia (NIDA, 2002d) (see Figure 17.6). Recurrent use can also cause hepatitis and liver and kidney disease.

Death can occur from depression of the respiratory or cardiovascular systems. *Sudden sniffing death* is due to acute irregularities in the heartbeat or loss of oxygen. Sometimes, users suffocate themselves when they go unconscious with plastic bags filled with inhalants firmly placed over their noses and mouths. Users can also die or become seriously injured when the inhalants cause them to have delusions that they can do fantastic things, such as fly, and they jump off cliffs or tall buildings to try it.

SUMMING UP

- At low doses, alcohol produces relaxation and a mild euphoria. At higher doses, it produces the classic signs of depression and cognitive and motor impairment.

- A large proportion of deaths due to accidents, murders, and suicides are alcohol-related.

- Alcohol withdrawal symptoms can be mild or so severe as to be life threatening.

- People who abuse or are dependent on alcohol experience a wide range of social and interpersonal problems and are at risk for many serious health problems.

- Women drink less alcohol than do men in most cultures and are less likely to have alcohol-related disorders than are men.

- Benzodiazepines and barbiturates are sold legally by prescription for the treatment of anxiety and insomnia.

- Benzodiazepines and barbiturates can cause an initial rush plus a loss of inhibitions. These pleasurable sensations are then followed by depressed mood, lethargy, and physical signs of central nervous system depression.

- Benzodiazepines and barbiturates are dangerous in overdose and when mixed with other substances.

- Inhalants are substances that produce chemical vapors, such as gasoline or paint thinner. Inhalants can cause permanent organ and brain damage and accidental deaths due to suffocation or dangerous delusional behavior.

STIMULANTS

The stimulants are drugs that activate the central nervous system, causing feelings of energy, happiness, and power, a decreased desire for sleep, and a diminished appetite (see the Concept Overview in Table 17.9). Cocaine and amphetamines are the two types of stimulants associated with severe substance-related disorders. Both substances are used by people to get a psychological lift, or rush. Both substances cause dangerous increases in blood pressure and heart rate, changes in the rhythm and electrical activity of the heart, and constriction of the blood vessels, which can lead to heart attacks, respiratory arrest, and seizures. In the United States, toxic reactions to cocaine and amphetamines

TABLE 17.9	Concept Overview

Intoxication with and Withdrawal from Stimulants

The stimulants activate the central nervous system.

Drug	Intoxication Symptoms	Withdrawal Symptoms
Cocaine and amphetamines	Behavioral changes (e.g., euphoria or affective blunting; changes in sociability; hypervigilance; interpersonal sensitivity; anxiety, tension, or anger; impaired judgment) Rapid heartbeat Dilation of pupils Elevated or lowered blood pressure Perspiration or chills Nausea or vomiting Weight loss Psychomotor agitation or retardation Muscular weakness Slowed breathing Chest pain Confusion, seizures, coma	Dysphoric mood Fatigue Vivid, unpleasant dreams Insomnia or hypersomnia Increased appetite Psychomotor retardation or agitation
Nicotine	Not a diagnosis in DSM-IV-TR	Dysphoria or depressed mood Insomnia Irritability, frustration, or anger Anxiety Difficulty concentrating Restlessness Decreased heart rate Increased appetite or weight gain
Caffeine	Restlessness Nervousness Excitement Insomnia Flushed face Frequent urination Stomach upset Muscle twitching Rambling flow of thought or speech Rapid heartbeat Periods of inexhaustibility Psychomotor agitation	Marked fatigue or drowsiness Marked anxiety or depression Nausea or vomiting

Source: Reprinted with permission from the *Diagnostic and Statistical Manual of Mental Disorders,* Fourth Edition, Text Revision. Copyright © 2000 American Psychiatric Association.

account for 40 percent of all substance-related cases seen in hospital emergency rooms and for 50 percent of sudden deaths in which substances are involved (Goldstein, 1994). These substances are costly, both to users and to society.

Caffeine and nicotine are also stimulants and can result in diagnosable substance-related disorders. Although the psychological effects of caffeine and nicotine are not as severe as those of cocaine and amphetamines, these drugs, particularly nicotine, can have long-term negative effects, so we discuss them as well.

Prescription stimulants, including Dexedrine and Ritalin, are used to treat asthma and other respiratory problems, obesity, neurological disorders, and a variety of other diseases. Since 1990, the abuse

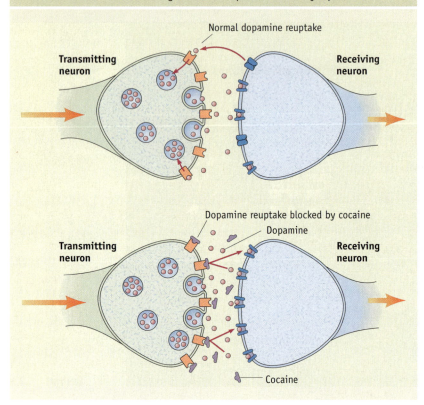

FIGURE 17.7 **Effects of Cocaine on Dopamine Systems.** Cocaine blocks transporters for the reuptake of dopamine, resulting in excess dopamine in the synapses.

of these drugs has increased 165 percent (NIDA, 2002f), and about a million people in the United States use stimulants for nonmedical reasons.

Cocaine

Cocaine is a white powder extracted from the coca plant and one of the most highly addictive substances known. People can snort the powder, which causes its effects on the brain to be felt quickly, or dissolve the powder in water and inject it intravenously. In the 1970s, freebase cocaine appeared when users developed a method for separating the most potent chemicals in cocaine by heating it with ether. This process produced a cocaine base, or freebase, that is even more powerful. It is usually smoked in a water pipe or mixed in a tobacco or marijuana cigarette. Crack is a form of freebase cocaine that is boiled down into tiny chunks, or rocks, which are usually smoked.

Cocaine activates the ventral tegmental area and the nucleus accumbens, the areas of the brain that register reward and

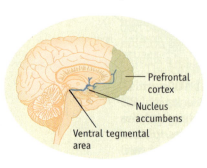

Cocaine activates the ventral tegmental area and the nucleus accumbens, the areas of the brain that register reward and pleasure.

pleasure (Gatley et al., 1998). Normally, when a pleasurable event occurs, dopamine is released into the synapses in these areas of the brain and then binds to receptors on neighboring synapses (see Figure 17.7). Cocaine blocks the reuptake of dopamine into the transmitting neuron, causing dopamine to accumulate in the synapse, maintaining the pleasurable feeling.

Initially, cocaine produces a sudden rush of intense euphoria, followed by great self-esteem, alertness, energy, and a general feeling of competence, creativity, and social acceptability. Users often do not feel drugged. Instead, they feel they have become the people they always wanted to be. When taken at high doses or chronically, however, cocaine leads to grandiosity, impulsiveness, hypersexuality, compulsive behavior, agitation, and anxiety, reaching the point of panic and paranoia. After stopping use of the substance, users may feel exhausted and depressed and sleep a great deal. Users also feel an intense craving for more of the substance, for both its physiological and its psychological effects.

Many current cocaine abusers and dependents started with heavy alcohol or marijuana use and then graduated to harder substances, including cocaine (Denison et al., 1998; Miller, 1991). The extraordinarily rapid and strong effects of cocaine on the brain's reward centers, however, seem to make this substance more likely than most illicit substances to result in patterns of abuse and dependence, even among people who have never been heavy users of any other substances, such as the dentist in the following case study.

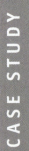

CASE STUDY

Dr. Arnie Rosenthal is a 31-year-old white male dentist, married for 10 years with two children. His wife insisted he see a psychiatrist because of uncontrolled use of cocaine, which over the past year had made it increasingly difficult for him to function as a dentist. During the previous 5 years he used cocaine virtually every day, with only occasional periods of abstinence of 1 or 2 weeks. For the past 4 years he wanted to stop cocaine use, but his desire was overridden by a "compulsion" to take the drug. He estimates having spent $12,000 to $15,000 on cocaine during the past year.

The patient's wife, who accompanied him to the interview, complained primarily about her husband's lack of energy and motivation, which started with his drug use 5 years ago.

(continued)

She complained that "he isn't working; he has no interests outside of me and the kids—not even his music—and he spends all of his time alone watching TV." She is also bothered by his occasional temper outbursts, but that is less troubling to her. . . . During his second year in dental school he got married, while being supported comfortably by his inlaws. After having been married 1 year he began using marijuana, smoking a joint each day upon coming home from school, and spent the evenings "staring" at TV. When he graduated from dental school his wife was pregnant, and he was "scared to death" at the prospect of being a father. His deepening depression was characterized by social isolation, increased loss of interests, and frequent temper outbursts. He needed to be intoxicated with marijuana, or occasionally sedatives, for sex, relaxation, and socialization. Following the birth of the child he "never felt so crazy," and his marijuana and sedative use escalated. Two years later, a second child was born. Dr. Rosenthal was financially successful, had moved to an expensive suburban home with a swimming pool, and had two cars and "everything my parents wanted for me." He was 27 years old, felt he had nothing to look forward to, felt painfully isolated, and the drugs were no longer providing relief.

He tried cocaine for the first time and immediately felt good. "I was no longer depressed. I used cocaine as often as possible because all my problems seemed to vanish, but I had to keep doing it. The effects were brief and it was very expensive, but I didn't care. When the immediate effects wore off, I'd feel even more miserable and depressed so that I did as much cocaine as I was able to obtain." He is now continuously nervous and irritable. Practicing dentistry has become increasingly difficult. (Adapted from Spitzer et al., 1983, pp. 81–83)

Because cocaine has a short half-life (the time needed for half of the drug to disappear from the body), its effects wear off quickly. As a result, the person dependent on cocaine must take frequent doses of the substance to maintain a high. In addition, a tolerance to cocaine can develop, so that the individual must obtain larger and larger amounts of cocaine to experience any high. Cocaine dependents spend huge amounts of money on the substance and may become involved in theft, prostitution, or drug dealing to obtain enough money to purchase cocaine. The desperation to obtain cocaine seen in many frequent users also can lead them to engage in extremely dangerous behaviors. Many cocaine users contract HIV, the virus that causes AIDS, by sharing needles with infected users or by having unprotected sex in exchange for money or more cocaine.

Some other frequent medical complications of cocaine use are disturbances in heart rhythm and heart attacks; chest pain and respiratory failure; neurological effects, including strokes, seizure, and headaches; and gastrointestinal complications, including abdominal pain and nausea. The physical symptoms include chest pain, blurred vision, fever, muscle spasms, convulsions, and coma. Recall that, when comedian Chris Farley died, he had cocaine in his bloodstream, as well as morphine and heroin.

Although cocaine began as a wealthy person's substance because of its high cost, a sharp reduction in the cost of cocaine in the 1970s led to its widespread use at all socioeconomic levels. Fourteen percent of people in the United States have tried cocaine at least once in their lives (SAMHSA, 2005). Fortunately, the use of cocaine has fallen since the mid-1980s. In 1986, 13 percent of adolescents said they had used cocaine in the past year, but, in 2003, a survey of twelfth-graders in U.S. high schools found that 5 percent had used it in the past year (Johnston et al., 2004). This decline may have to do, in part, with antidrug campaigns in schools and in the media and with the highly publicized deaths of rock stars and athletes due to cocaine overdose. The decline has occurred primarily among casual users of cocaine. Chronic abusers and dependents have continued to use cocaine. There is also some evidence that the use of crack has not fallen off in recent years.

Amphetamines

The U.S. pharmaceutical industry annually manufactures 8 to 10 billion doses of the stimulants known as **amphetamines,** under names such as Dexedrine and Benzedrine (Miller, 1991). The drugs are most often swallowed as pills but can be injected intravenously, and methamphetamine can be snorted or smoked. These drugs were initially introduced as antihistamines, but people soon recognized their stimulant effects. These days, many people use them to combat depression or chronic fatigue from overwork or simply to boost their self-confidence and energy (Miller, 1991). They are also a component of diet drugs. Many of these drugs are used appropriately under the supervision of physicians, but a great many doses are diverted from prescription use to illegal use and abuse. On the street, amphetamines are known as "speed," "meth," and "chalk."

Amphetamines have their effects by causing the release of the neurotransmitters dopamine and norepinephrine and by blocking the reuptake of these neurotransmitters. The symptoms of intoxication with amphetamines are similar to the symptoms of cocaine intoxication: euphoria, self-confidence, alertness, agitation, and paranoia (Wyatt & Ziedonis, 1998).

Like cocaine, amphetamines can produce perceptual illusions that are frightening. The movement of other people and objects may seem distorted or exaggerated. Users may hear frightening voices making derogatory statements about them, see sores all over their bodies, or feel snakes crawling on their arms. They may have delusions that they are being stalked. They may act out violently against others as a result of their paranoid delusions. Some amphetamine users are aware that these experiences are not real, but some lose their reality testing and develop *amphetamine-induced psychotic disorders* (adapted from Spitzer et al., 1994, pp. 139–140):

People in fast-paced, highly demanding jobs, such as these commodities traders, sometimes use amphetamines to keep going.

CASE STUDY

An agitated 42-year-old businessman was admitted to the psychiatric service after a period of 2½ months in which he found himself becoming increasingly distrustful of others and suspicious of his business associates. He was taking their statements out of context, "twisting" their words, and making inappropriately hostile and accusatory comments; he had, in fact, lost several business deals that had been "virtually sealed." Finally, he fired a shotgun into the backyard late one night when he heard noises that convinced him that intruders were about to break into his house and kill him.

One and one-half years previously, he had been diagnosed as having narcolepsy because of daily irresistible sleep attacks and episodes of sudden loss of muscle tone, and he had been placed on an amphetaminelike stimulant, methylphenidate. His narcolepsy declined and he was able to work quite effectively as the sales manager of a small office-machine company and to participate in an active social life with his family and a small circle of friends.

In the 4 months before this admission, he had been using increasingly large doses of methylphenidate to maintain alertness late at night because of an increasing amount of work that could not be handled during the day. He reported that during this time he could often feel his heart race and he had trouble sitting still.

Legal problems for amphetamine abusers typically arise because of aggressive or inappropriate behavior while intoxicated or as a result of buying the drug illegally. Tolerance to amphetamines develops quickly, so frequent users can become physically dependent on the drug in a short period. They may switch from swallowing pills to injecting amphetamines intravenously. Some go on a speed run, in which they inject amphetamines frequently over several days, without eating or sleeping. When a speed run ends, they crash into a physical and emotional depression, which can be so severe that they may become suicidal. Acute withdrawal symptoms typically subside within a few days, but chronic users may experience mood instability, memory loss, confusion, paranoid thinking, and perceptual abnormalities for weeks, months, and perhaps even years. Most often, they battle the withdrawal symptoms with another speed run.

Abuse of amphetamines can cause a number of medical problems, particularly cardiovascular problems. These include rapid or irregular heartbeat, increased blood pressure, and irreversible, stroke-producing damage to the small blood vessels in the brain. Elevated body temperature and convulsions can occur during overdoses, leading to death. Sharing needles to inject amphetamines can lead to the contraction of HIV or hepatitis.

Nationwide surveys find that about 4 percent of the population has tried amphetamines in their lifetimes (SAMHSA, 2002b). Amphetamines are increasingly used in the workplace by people trying to keep up with the rapid pace of today's work world. Employers may even provide amphetamines to employees to keep them working and increase their productivity. When the employees finally go home, they may use depressants, such as alcohol, to come down off the speed. Although amphetamines may have the desired effects on employee morale and productivity in the short run, over time people become irritable and hostile and need more and more amphetamines to avoid withdrawal effects. Their health declines, as well as their personal relationships. Between 1995 and 2002, emergency room visits involving amphetamines increased 54 percent in the nation (SAMHSA, 2005).

Nicotine

All of the substances we have discussed thus far, except alcohol and the inhalants, are illegal for nonprescription use, and there are many laws regulating the use of alcohol. One of the most addictive substances, however, is fully legal for use by adults and readily available for use by adolescents.

Nicotine is an alkaloid found in tobacco. Cigarettes are the most popular nicotine delivery device. Cigarettes deliver nicotine to the brain within a few seconds after a person begins smoking. In the United States, 70 percent of people over age 12 have smoked cigarettes at sometime in their lives, and 30 percent currently smoke (SAMHSA, 2005). Smoking usually begins in the early teens. A survey of twelfth-graders done in 2001 found that 61 percent had smoked a cigarette at sometime in their lives, 30 percent had smoked in the past month, and 10 percent were smoking at least a half a pack a day (Monitoring the Future, 2002). Among people who continue to smoke through age 20, 95 percent become regular, daily smokers. In general, the use of tobacco has declined in the United States and other industrialized countries over the past few decades. In contrast, its use is increasing in developing countries (Giovini et al., 1994).

In the United States, the decrease in smoking rates over time has been greater for men than for women, so that today men are only slightly more likely than women to smoke (NIDA, 2002e; SAMHSA, 2005). In addition, female adolescents have been initiating smoking more frequently than male adolescents, and, once they are addicted to tobacco, women are less likely than men to quit. The ad campaigns by cigarette companies aimed specifically at women are also credited with increasing smoking among women.

Nicotine operates on both the central and peripheral nervous systems. It results in the release of several biochemicals that may have direct reinforcing effects on the brain, including dopamine, norepinephrine, serotonin, and the endogenous opioids. Although people often say they smoke to reduce stress, the physiological effects of nicotine actually resemble the fight-or-flight response—several systems in the body are aroused in preparation to fight or flee a stressor, including the cardiovascular and respiratory systems (see Chapter 6 for a discussion of the fight-or-flight response). The subjective sense that smoking reduces stress may actually reflect the

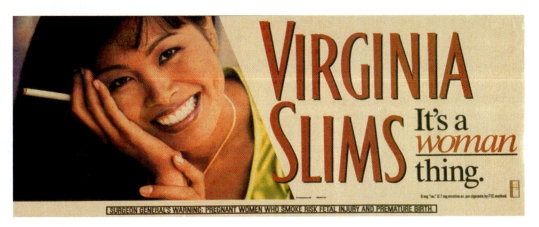

Cigarette companies often target women in their ad campaigns.

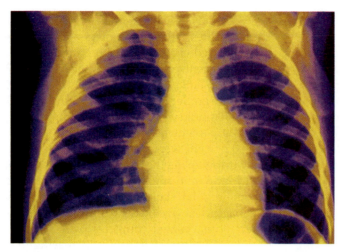 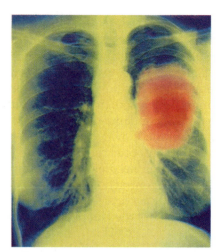

Smoking is the leading cause of lung cancer. The lungs on the left are healthy. The lungs on the right are from a smoker and show cancer in the red area.

reversal of tension and irritability that build in smokers between cigarettes because they are addicted to the nicotine (Parrott, 1998). In other words, nicotine addicts need nicotine to remain feeling normal because of nicotine's effects on the body and brain.

In 1964, on the basis of a review of 6,000 empirical studies, the surgeon general of the United States concluded that smoking, particularly cigarette smoking, causes lung cancer, bronchitis, and probably coronary heart disease. An estimated $80 billion of annual U.S. health care costs is attributable to smoking (NIDA, 2002e). Mortality rates for smokers are 70 percent greater than for nonsmokers. This means that a person between 30 and 35 years of age who smokes two packs of cigarettes a day will die eight to nine years earlier than will a nonsmoker. The chief causes of increased mortality rates among smokers are coronary heart disease, lung cancer, emphysema, and chronic bronchitis. Tobacco use accounts for 19 percent of all deaths in the United States (Goldstein, 1998). The babies of women who smoke while pregnant are smaller at birth. The longer a person smokes and the more he or she smokes per day, the greater the health risks.

Increasing attention is being paid to the effects of passive smoking—unintentionally inhaling the smoke from nearby smokers' cigarettes. This smoke contains more toxins than does the smoke that the smoker actively inhales, although the passive smoker does not inhale the smoke in concentrations as high as the smoker does. Children of parents who smoke have 30 to 80 percent more chronic respiratory problems than do nonsmokers and nearly 30 percent more hospitalizations for bronchitis and pneumonia (Winger et al., 1992).

Tobacco manufacturers have tried to claim that nicotine is not an addictive drug, but it causes most of the core symptoms of physiological and psychological dependence. The best evidence of nicotine dependence is the presence of tolerance to the substance and withdrawal symptoms after quitting. Chronic, heavy smokers become so tolerant to nicotine that they show no adverse physiological reactions to a dosage of nicotine that would have made them violently nauseated when they first began smoking. When they try to stop smoking or are prohibited from smoking for an extended period (such as at work or on an airplane), they show severe withdrawal symptoms: They are depressed, irritable, angry, anxious, frustrated, restless, and hungry; they have trouble concentrating; and they desperately crave another cigarette. These symptoms are immediately relieved by smoking another cigarette, another sign of physiological dependence.

Because nicotine is relatively cheap and available, people who are nicotine dependent do not tend to spend large amounts of time trying to obtain nicotine. They may, however, become panicked if they run out of cigarettes and replacements are not available. They may also spend large amounts of their day engaged in smoking or chewing tobacco and continue to use nicotine even though it is damaging their health, such as after they have been diagnosed with emphysema. They may skip social or recreational activities as a result of their habit. For example, people may turn down dinner invitations at the homes of friends who do not allow smoking. Or they may stop playing tennis because they have trouble breathing. With the increasing restrictions on smoking in the workplace, nicotine

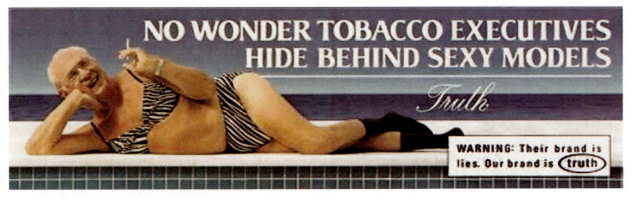

NO WONDER TOBACCO EXECUTIVES HIDE BEHIND SEXY MODELS

Truth

WARNING: Their brand is lies. Our brand is (truth)

Programs to prevent and reduce smoking have become quite creative.

dependents may even begin to turn down or switch jobs to avoid these restrictions.

Over 70 percent of people who smoke say they wish they could quit (Goldstein, 1998). Quitting is difficult, however, in part because the withdrawal syndrome is so difficult to withstand. Only about 7 percent of smokers who attempt to quit smoking are still abstinent after one year, and most relapse within a few days of quitting (NIDA, 2002e). The craving for cigarettes can remain long after smokers have stopped smoking: 50 percent of people who quit smoking report they have desired cigarettes in the past 24 hours (Goldstein, 1994). Fortunately, the antidepressant bupropion (trade names Wellbutrin and Zyban) can significantly reduce the craving for nicotine and help smokers stop smoking permanently (Goldstein, 1998).

There are increasing calls for the U.S. government to declare nicotine a drug, much like marijuana and other substances that produce psychological changes and physiological dependence and are detrimental to health. Such a declaration would then lead to strict governmental regulation of the sale and use of tobacco. Antismoking advocates argue that nicotine dependence is a negative psychological and physiological condition just as bad as other substance dependencies. Moreover, between the effects of secondary smoke and the health care dollars spent treating diseases due to smoking, nicotine dependence exacts a much bigger toll on people who are not nicotine dependent than do most other substance dependencies.

Opponents of the antismoking movement argue that nicotine is not truly a psychoactive substance—nicotine does not cause great changes in mood, thought, or perceptions, as do cannabis, cocaine, heroin, and alcohol. They argue that the negative health effects of smoking are the smoker's business only and that people do many things that are not good for their health—they eat high-

cholesterol foods, they sit in the sun without sunscreen—but these activities are not regulated by the government. This debate is likely to rage for some time to come, particularly given the issues of personal freedom and the massive amounts of money involved.

Caffeine

Caffeine is by far the most heavily used stimulant drug. Seventy-five percent of caffeine is ingested through coffee (Chou, 1992). The average American drinks about two cups of coffee per day, and a cup of brewed coffee has about 100 milligrams of caffeine. Other sources of caffeine include tea (about 40 milligrams of caffeine per 6 ounces), caffeinated soda (45 milligrams per 12 ounces), over-the-counter analgesics and cold remedies (25 to 50 milligrams per tablet), weight-loss drugs (75 to 200 milligrams per tablet), and chocolate and cocoa (5 milligrams per chocolate bar).

Caffeine stimulates the central nervous system, increasing levels of dopamine, norepinephrine, and serotonin. It causes metabolism, body temperature, and blood pressure to increase. Our appetite wanes and we feel more alert; however, in doses equivalent to just two to three cups of coffee, caffeine can cause a number of unpleasant symptoms, including restlessness, nervousness, and hand tremors. We may experience an upset stomach and feel our heart beating rapidly or irregularly. We may have trouble going to sleep later on and need to urinate frequently. These are the symptoms of *caffeine intoxication*. Extremely large doses of caffeine can cause extreme agitation, seizures, respiratory failure, and cardiac problems.

The DSM-IV-TR specifies that a diagnosis of caffeine intoxication should be given only if an individual experiences significant distress or impairment in functioning as a result of the symptoms. For example, someone drinking too much coffee

Garfield ®   by Jim Davis

GARFIELD © *Paws, Inc. Reprinted with permission of Universal Press Syndicate. All Rights Reserved.*

for several days in a row during exam week might be so agitated that she cannot sit through exams and so shaky she cannot drive a car.

Some heavy coffee drinkers joke that they are "caffeine addicts." Actually, they cannot be diagnosed with caffeine dependence disorder, according to the DSM-IV-TR, because to date there is little evidence that dependence on the drug causes significant social and occupational problems. Still, caffeine users can develop tolerance to caffeine and undergo withdrawal symptoms if they stop ingesting caffeine. They may find that they have to have several cups of coffee in the morning to feel "normal," and, if they do not get their coffee, they experience significant headaches, fatigue, and anxiety.

SUMMING UP

- Cocaine and amphetamines produce a rush of euphoria, followed by increases in self-esteem, alertness, and energy. With chronic use, however, they can lead to grandiosity, impulsiveness, hypersexuality, agitation, and paranoia.
- Withdrawal from cocaine and amphetamines causes the symptoms of depression, exhaustion, and an intense craving for more of the substance.
- Cocaine seems particularly prone to lead to dependence, because it has extraordinarily rapid, strong effects on the brain and its effects wear off quickly.
- The intense activation of the central nervous system caused by cocaine and amphetamines can lead to a number of cardiac, respiratory, and neurological problems, and these substances are responsible for a large percentage of substance-related medical emergencies and deaths.

- Nicotine is an alkaloid found in tobacco. It affects the release of several neurochemicals in the body. Nicotine subjectively reduces stress but causes physiological arousal similar to that seen in the fight-or-flight response.
- Smoking is associated with a higher rate of heart disease, lung cancer, emphysema, and chronic bronchitis, and it substantially increases mortality rates.
- The majority of people who smoke wish they could quit but have trouble doing so, in part because tolerance develops to nicotine and withdrawal symptoms are difficult to tolerate.
- Caffeine is the most commonly used stimulant drug. Caffeine intoxication can cause agitation, tremors, heart irregularities, and insomnia. People can develop a tolerance for and withdrawal from caffeine.

OPIOIDS

Morphine, heroin, codeine, and methadone are all known as **opioids.** They derive from the sap of the opium poppy, which has been used for thousands of years to relieve pain. Our bodies actually produce natural opioids, some of which are called *endorphins* and *enkaphalins*, to cope with pain. For example, a sports injury induces the body to produce endorphins to reduce the pain of the injury to avoid shock. Doctors may also prescribe synthetic opioids, such as hydrocodone (trade names Lorcet, Lortab, Vicodin) or oxycodone (Percodan, Percocet, Oxycontin) to help with pain.

Morphine was widely used as a pain reliever in the nineteenth century, until it was discovered that it is highly addictive. Heroin was developed from morphine in the late nineteenth century and used for a time for medicinal purposes. By 1917, however, it was clear that heroin and all opioids

TABLE 17.10   Intoxication with and Withdrawal from Opioids

The opioids include morphine, heroin, codeine, and methadone.

Drug	Intoxication Symptoms	Withdrawal Symptoms
Opioids	Behavioral changes (e.g., initial euphoria followed by apathy, dysphoria, psychomotor agitation or retardation, impaired judgment)	Dysphoric mood
	Constriction of pupils	Nausea or vomiting
	Drowsiness or coma	Muscle aches
	Slurred speech	Tearing or nasal mucus discharge
	Attention and memory problems	Dilation of pupils
	Hallucinations or illusions	Goose bumps
		Sweating
		Diarrhea
		Yawning
		Fever
		Insomnia

Source: Reprinted with permission from the *Diagnostic and Statistical Manual of Mental Disorders,* Fourth Edition, Text Revision. Copyright © 2000 American Psychiatric Association.

have dangerous addictive properties, and the U.S. Congress passed a law to make heroin illegal and to ban the other opioids except for specific medical needs. Heroin remained widely available on the street, however.

There was an explosion of heroin use during the Vietnam War, when young soldiers facing horrific circumstances found heroin cheap and easy to obtain in Vietnam. Fortunately, most of these soldiers stopped using heroin once they returned to the United States. But those who had experience with IV drugs or opioids before going to Vietnam tended to come back physically dependent on the drugs, which they continued to use when they returned to the United States. Current use of heroin expands and contracts with the drug's price and availability on the street. When the drug is cheap and highly available, "epidemics" of use occur.

When used illegally, opioids are often injected directly into the veins (*mainlining*), snorted, or smoked. The initial symptom of opioid intoxication is often euphoria (see Table 17.10). People describe a sensation in the abdomen like a sexual orgasm, referring to it as a *thrill, kick,* or *flash* (Winger et al., 1992). They may have a tingling sensation and a pervasive sense of warmth. Their pupils dilate, and they pass into a state of drowsiness, during which they are lethargic, their speech is slurred, and their mind may be clouded. They may experience periods of light sleep, with vivid dreams. Pain is reduced. A person in this state is referred to as being *on the nod.*

Severe intoxication with opioids can lead to unconsciousness, coma, and seizures. These substances can suppress the part of the brain stem controlling the respiratory and cardiovascular systems to the point of death. Basically, people stop breathing and their hearts stop pumping. The drugs are especially dangerous when used in combination with depressants, such as alcohol and sedatives. Withdrawal symptoms include dysphoria, anxiety, and agitation; an achy feeling in the back and legs; increased sensitivity to pain; and craving for more opioids. The person may be nauseated, vomit, and have profuse sweating and goose bumps, diarrhea, and fever. These symptoms usually come on within 8 to 16 hours of the last use of morphine or heroin and peak within 36 to 72 hours. In chronic or heavy users, the symptoms may continue strongly for 5 to 8 days and in a milder form for weeks to months.

Many people who develop opioid abuse or dependence begin using these drugs after having used alcohol, marijuana, and related drugs and perhaps some of the depressants and stimulants. The first use of heroin is typically in the late teen years, after people have experimented with several of these other drugs (Schuckit, 1995). About 1 percent of teenagers admit to having used heroin at sometime in the past year (Johnston et al., 2004). They may become psychologically dependent on the effects of the drugs first, then later become physiologically dependent. Once they are physiologically dependent, IV heroin users need to shoot up every four to six hours to avoid physical withdrawal. This is enormously expensive but makes it almost impossible to hold a regular job. As a result, many people dependent on opioids turn to stealing, prostitution, and other crimes to get money for the drug. Heavy users often have a police record by their early twenties.

Most street heroin is cut with other drugs or substances, so that users do not know the actual strength of the drug or its true contents. As a result, they are at high risk for overdose or death. One of the greatest dangers to opioid abusers and dependents is the risk of contracting HIV through contaminated needles or unprotected sex, in which many opioid abusers engage in exchange for more of the substance. In some areas of the United States, up to 60 percent of chronic heroin users are infected with HIV. Intravenous users also can contract hepatitis, tuberculosis, serious skin abscesses, and deep infections. Women who use heroin during pregnancy are at risk for miscarriage and premature delivery, and children born to addicted mothers are at increased risk for sudden infant death syndrome.

The abuse of, and dependence on, opioid pain relievers has increased significantly in recent years (SAMHSA, 2005). Emergency room visits involving pain relievers increased 153 percent from 1995 to 2002. The most frequently abused drug is *oxycodone,* and emergency room visits involving this drug increased 512 percent between 1995 and 2002. An estimated 11 million Americans age 12 and older have used oxycodone nonmedically at least once in their lifetime. In 2003, conservative commentator Rush Limbaugh admitted to being addicted to the prescription painkillers, creating a media sensation, given his previous arguments that drug abusers should be convicted and "sent up the river" (*Newsweek*, 2003).

SUMMING UP

- The opioids include heroin, morphine, codeine, and methadone, and the synthetic opioids include hydrocodone (Lorcet, Lortab, Vicodin) and oxycodone (Percodan, Percocet, Oxycontin).

- The opioids cause an initial rush, or euphoria, followed by a drowsy, dreamlike state. Severe intoxication can cause respiratory and cardiovascular failure.

- Withdrawal symptoms include dysphoria, anxiety, and agitation; an achy feeling in the back and legs; increased sensitivity to pain; and craving for more opioids.

- Opioid users who inject drugs can contract HIV and a number of other disorders by sharing needles.

HALLUCINOGENS AND PCP

Most of the substances we have discussed so far can produce perceptual illusions and distortions when taken in large doses. The hallucinogens and phenylcyclidine (PCP) produce perceptual changes even in small doses (see the Concept Overview in Table 17.11). A clear withdrawal syndrome from the hallucinogens and PCP has not been documented, so the DSM-IV-TR does not currently recognize withdrawal from these drugs as a diagnosis.

The **hallucinogens** are a mixed group of substances, including lysergic acid diethylamide (LSD) and peyote. Perhaps the best-known hallucinogen is LSD, which was first synthesized in 1938 by Swiss chemists. It was not until 1943 that the substance's psychoactive effects were discovered, when Dr. Albert Hoffman accidentally swallowed a minute amount of LSD and experienced visual hallucinations similar to those in schizophrenia. He later purposefully swallowed a small amount of LSD and reported the effects (Hoffman, 1968, pp. 185–186).

VOICES

As far as I remember, the following were the most outstanding symptoms: vertigo, visual disturbances; the faces of those around me appeared as grotesque, colored masks; marked motor unrest, alternating with paresis; an intermittent heavy feeling in the head, limbs, and the entire body, as if they were filled with metal; cramps in the legs, coldness, and loss of feeling in the hands; a metallic taste on the tongue; dry constricted sensation in the throat; feeling of choking; confusion alternating between clear recognition of my condition, in which state I sometimes observed, in the manner of an independent, neutral observer, that I shouted half insanely or babbled incoherent words. Occasionally, I felt as if I were out of my body. The doctor found a rather weak pulse but an otherwise normal circulation. Six hours after ingestion of the LSD my condition had already improved considerably. Only the visual disturbances were still pronounced. Everything seemed to sway and the proportions were distorted like the reflections in the surface of moving water. Moreover, all objects appeared in unpleasant, constantly changing colors, the predominant shades being sickly green and blue. When I

(continued)

closed my eyes, an unending series of colorful, very realistic and fantastic images surged in upon me. A remarkable feature was the manner in which all acoustic perceptions (e.g., the noise of a passing car) were transformed into optical effects, every sound causing a corresponding colored hallucination constantly changing in shape and color like pictures in a kaleidoscope.

As Hoffman describes, one of the symptoms of intoxication from LSD and other hallucinogens is synesthesia, the overflow from one sensory modality to another. People say they hear colors and see sounds. Time seems to pass very slowly. The boundaries between oneself and the environment seem gone. Moods may shift from depression to elation to fear. Some people become anxious, even panicked. Others feel a sense of detachment and a great sensitivity for art, music, and feelings. These experiences led to these drugs' being labeled psychedelic, from the Greek words for "soul" and "to make manifest." LSD was used in the 1960s as part of the consciousness-expanding movement. More recently, the hallucinogen known as ecstasy is used by people who believe that it enhances insight, relationships, and mood.

The hallucinogens are dangerous drugs, however. Although LSD was legal for use in the early 1960s, by 1967, reports of "bad acid trips," or "bummers," had become common, particularly in the Haight-Ashbury district of San Francisco, where many LSD enthusiasts from around the United States congregated (Smith & Seymour, 1994). The symptoms included severe anxiety, paranoia, and loss of control. Some people on bad trips would walk off roofs or jump out windows, believing they could fly, or walk into the sea, believing they were "one with the universe." For some people, the anxiety and hallucinations caused by hallucinogens are so severe that they become psychotic and require hospitalization and long-term treatment. Some people experience flashbacks to their psychedelic experiences long after the drug has worn off. These flashbacks can be extremely distressing. The most recent pattern of use for hallucinogens has been as part of the club scene and "raves" (Morrison, 1998).

Phenylcyclidine (PCP), also known as *angel dust, PeaCePill, Hog,* and *Tranq,* is manufactured as a powder to be snorted or smoked. Although PCP is not classified as a hallucinogen, it has many of the same effects. At lower doses, it produces a sense of intoxication, euphoria or affective dulling, talkativeness, lack of concern, slowed reaction time, vertigo, eye twitching, mild hypertension, abnormal invol-

TABLE 17.11   Concept Overview

Intoxication with Hallucinogens and PCP

The hallucinogens and PCP cause a variety of perceptual and behavioral changes.

Drug	Intoxication Symptoms
Hallucinogens	Behavioral changes (e.g., marked anxiety or depression, the feeling that others are talking about you, fear of losing your mind, paranoia, impaired judgment)
	Perceptual changes while awake (e.g., intensification of senses, depersonalization, illusions, hallucinations)
	Dilation of pupils
	Rapid heartbeat
	Sweating
	Palpitations
	Blurring of vision
	Tremors
	Incoordination
PCP	Behavioral changes (e.g., belligerence, assaultiveness, impulsiveness, unpredictability, psychomotor agitation, impaired judgment)
	Involuntary rapid eyeball movement
	Hypertension
	Numbness
	Loss of muscle coordination
	Problems speaking due to poor muscle control
	Muscle rigidity
	Seizures or coma
	Exceptionally acute hearing
	Perceptual disturbances

Source: Reprinted with permission from the *Diagnostic and Statistical Manual of Mental Disorders,* Fourth Edition, Text Revision. Copyright © 2000 American Psychiatric Association.

untary movements, and weakness. At intermediate doses, it leads to disorganized thinking, distortions of body image (such as feeling that one's arms do not belong to the rest of one's body), depersonalization, and feelings of unreality. A user may become hostile, belligerent, and even violent (Morrison, 1998). At higher doses, it produces amnesia and coma, analgesia sufficient to allow surgery, seizures, severe respiratory problems, hypothermia, and hyperthermia. The effects of PCP begin immediately after injecting, snorting, or smoking it, reaching a peak within minutes. The symptoms of severe intoxication can persist for several days. As a result, people with PCP intoxication are often misdiagnosed as having psychotic disorders not related to substance use.

As with the substances we have discussed so far, hallucinogen or PCP abuse is diagnosed when individuals repeatedly fail to fulfill major role obligations at school, work, or home due to intoxication with these drugs. They may use the drugs in dangerous situations, such as while driving a car, and may have legal troubles due to their possession of the drugs. Particularly because these drugs can cause paranoia or aggressive behavior, people who use them frequently may find their work and social relationships being affected. About 11 percent of the U.S. population reports ever having tried a hallucinogen or PCP, but only 0.4 percent report using it in the past month (SAMHSA, 2002a). Use is higher among teenagers, however, with 2 to 3 percent reporting using LSD, ecstasy, or a hallucinogen in the past month (Monitoring the Future, 2002).

SUMMING UP

- The hallucinogens create perceptual illusions and distortions—sometimes fantastic, sometimes frightening. Some people feel more sensitive to art, music, and other people. The hallucinogens also create mood swings and paranoia. Some people experience frightening flashbacks to experiences under the hallucinogens.

- PCP causes euphoria or affective dulling, abnormal involuntary movements, and weakness at low doses. At intermediate doses, it leads to disorganized thinking, depersonalization, feelings of unreality, and aggression. At higher doses, it produces amnesia and coma, analgesia sufficient to allow surgery, seizures, severe respiratory problems, hypothermia, and hyperthermia.

CANNABIS

The leaves of the **cannabis** (or hemp) plant can be cut, dried, and rolled into cigarettes or inserted into food and beverages. In North America, the product is known as *marijuana, weed, pot, grass, reefer,* and *Mary Jane.* It is called *ganja* in Jamaica, *kif* in North Africa, *dagga* in South Africa, *bhang* in In-

dia and the Middle East, and *macohna* in South America (Winger et al., 1992). It is the most widely used illicit substance in the world. Hashish is a dried resin extract from the cannabis plant, sold in cubes in America.

Cannabis is the most commonly used illegal drug in the United States, with about one-third of the population reporting they have used this drug at sometime in their lives, and 5 percent use it monthly (SAMHSA, 2002a). Teenagers are especially heavy users of marijuana, with about 50 percent of twelfth-graders saying they have used it at sometime in their lives and about 22 percent reporting using it in the past month (Johnston et al., 2004). The use of cannabis has increased in the past decade or so, and the potency of cannabis has become greater as well. About 7 percent of the population would qualify for a diagnosis of cannabis abuse, and 2 to 3 percent of the population would qualify for a diagnosis of cannabis dependence (Kendler & Prescott, 1998a).

The symptoms of cannabis intoxication may develop within minutes if the cannabis is smoked but may take a few hours to develop if taken orally (see the Concept Overview in Table 17.12). The acute symptoms last 3 to 4 hours, but some symptoms may linger or recur for 12 to 24 hours. Intoxication with cannabis usually begins with a "high" feeling of well-being, relaxation, and tranquillity. Users may feel dizzy, sleepy, or "dreamy." They may become more aware of their environments, and everything may seem funny. They may be-

TABLE 17.12 Concept Overview

Intoxication with Cannabis

Cannabis is the most commonly used illegal drug in the United States.

Drug	Intoxication Symptoms
Cannabis	Behavioral changes (e.g., impaired motor coordination, euphoria, anxiety, sensation of slowed time, impaired judgment)
	Red eyes
	Increased appetite
	Dry mouth
	Rapid heartbeat

Source: Reprinted with permission from the *Diagnostic and Statistical Manual of Mental Disorders,* Fourth Edition, Text Revision. Copyright © 2000 American Psychiatric Association.

come grandiose or lethargic. People who are very anxious, depressed, or angry may become more so under the influence of cannabis.

The cognitive symptoms of cannabis intoxication are negative. People may believe they are thinking profound thoughts, but their short-term memories are impaired to the point that they cannot remember thoughts long enough to express them in sentences (de Wit, Kirk, & Justice, 1998). Thus, they perform poorly on a wide range of tests and may not be able to hold a conversation. Motor performance is also impaired. People's reaction times are slower, and their concentration and judgment are deficient; as a result, they are at risk for accidents. The cognitive impairments caused by cannabis can last for up to a week after a person stops heavy use (Pope, Gruber, et al., 2001). These effects appear to be even greater for women than for men (Pope et al., 1997).

Cannabis has hallucinogenic effects at moderate to large doses. Users experience perceptual distortions, feelings of depersonalization, and paranoid thinking. The changes in perceptions may be experienced as pleasant by some but as very frightening by others. Some users may have severe anxiety episodes resembling panic attacks (Phariss, Millman, & Beeder, 1998).

The physiological symptoms of cannabis intoxication include increases in heart rate, an irregular heartbeat, increases in appetite, and dry mouth. Cannabis smoke is irritating and, thus, increases the risk for chronic cough, sinusitis, bronchitis, and emphysema. It contains even larger amounts of known carcinogens than does tobacco, so it creates a high risk for cancer. The chronic use of cannabis lowers sperm count in men and may cause irregular ovulation in women.

In part because of the increased potency of cannabis, many people who formerly might have been casual users of cannabis, including high school students, have developed problems with abuse and dependence. They may smoke marijuana often enough that their school performance suffers, their lives revolve around smoking, and they have frequent accidents as a result of intoxication. Physical tolerance to cannabis can develop, so users need greater amounts to avoid withdrawal symptoms. The symptoms of withdrawal include a loss of appetite, hot flashes, a runny nose, sweating, diarrhea, and hiccups (Kouri & Pope, 2000).

In recent years, several groups have advocated the legalization of marijuana cigarettes for medical uses (Grinspoon & Bakalar, 1995). THC, the active compound in cannabis, can help relieve nausea in cancer patients undergoing chemotherapy and increase appetite in AIDS patients. It also helps in the treatment of asthma and glaucoma. THC can be given in pill form, but some people argue that the level of THC that enters the body is more controllable when it is taken in a marijuana cigarette. People who ingest THC in pill form do not risk the respiratory damage caused by the smoke from marijuana cigarettes, however.

SUMMING UP

- Cannabis creates a high feeling, cognitive and motor impairments, and in some people hallucinogenic effects.
- Cannabis use is high. Significant numbers of people, especially teenagers, have impaired performance at school, on the job, and in relationships as a result of chronic use. Marijuana use can also lead to a number of physical problems, especially respiratory problems.

CLUB DRUGS

One of the most alarming developments in the world of illicit drug use in recent years is the increase in the use of drugs as part of the club scene among young adults, including at raves. Raves began in Europe in the 1980s. These events, which are often sponsored by club owners or businesspeople, are held in warehouses, basements, tenements, and other large spaces. Participants often ingest drugs with stimulant and hallucinogenic properties, then spend the night listening and dancing to "techno music." After the drug effects disappear, people are usually exhausted and may spend several hours sleeping. One of the greatest health concerns during

There has been an increase in recent years in the use of drugs as part of the club scene.

raves is dehydration, so some rave organizers encourage participants to drink fluids and take breaks from the dancing. Agitation and paranoia can set into the crowd, creating the possibility of a chaotic scene, which can result in injury.

Emergency room visits involving club drugs doubled from 1994 to 1999, although they have decreased somewhat in more recent years (SAMHSA, 2005). Some common club drugs, in addition to LSD, are *ecstasy* (3-4 methylenedioxymethamphetamine, or MDMA), *GHB* (gamma-hydroxybutyrate), *ketamine*, and *rohypnol* (flunitrazepam).

Ecstasy has the stimulant effects of an amphetamine along with occasional hallucinogenic properties. Users experience heightened energy and restlessness, and they claim that their social inhibitions decrease and their affection for others increases. These disinihibiting and "social" effects of ecstasy led a small number of unscrupulous therapists to use the drug as part of therapy for a short time.

Even the short-term use of ecstasy can have long-term negative effects on cognition and health, however. Studies of monkeys given ecstasy for just four days found that they had brain damage lasting six to seven years (SAMHSA, 2002b). Humans who use ecstasy score lower on tests related to attention, memory, learning, and general intelligence than people who do not use the drug. The euphoric effects of ecstasy, and some of the brain damage, may be due to alterations in the functioning of serotonin in the brain—serotonin levels in ecstasy users are half that of people who do not use ecstasy. One of the more bizarre effects of ecstasy is teeth-grinding; some users suck a baby pacifier at raves to relieve the grinding. One study showed that 60 percent of ecstasy users had worn their teeth through the enamel (Peroutka, Newman, & Harris, 1988). Long-term users of ecstasy are at risk for several cardiac problems and liver failure, and they show increased rates of anxiety, depression, psychotic symptoms, and paranoia (Gold, Tabrah, & Frost-Pineda, 2001).

GHB is an anabolic steroid (a synthetic derivative of the hormone testosterone) and a central nervous system depressant. At low doses, it can relieve anxiety and promote relaxation. At higher doses, it can result in sleep, coma, or death. In the 1980s, GHB was widely used by bodybuilders and athletes to lose fat and build muscle, and it was widely available over the counter in health food stores. In 1990, GHB was banned except under the supervision of a physician because of reports of severe side effects, including high blood pressure, wide mood swings, liver tumors, and violent behavior. Other side effects include sweating,

headache, decreased heart rate, nausea, vomiting, impaired breathing, loss of reflexes, and tremors. GHB is considered one of the date rape drugs, because it has been associated with several sexual assaults. It goes by the street names Grievous Bodily Harm, G., Liquid Ecstasy, and Georgia Home Boy.

Ketamine (which goes by the street names Vitamin K, Kit Kat, Keller, Super Acid, and Super C) is a rapid-acting anesthetic that produces hallucinogenic effects in users ranging from rapture to paranoia to boredom. Ketamine can elicit an out-of-body or near-death experience. It can also render the user comatose. It has effects similar to those of PCP, including numbness, loss of coordination, a sense of invulnerability, muscle rigidity, aggressive or violent behavior, slurred or blocked speech, an exaggerated sense of strength, and a blank stare. Because ketamine is an anesthetic, users feel no pain, which can lead them to injure themselves.

A ketamine "high" usually lasts an hour, but it can last 4 to 6 hours, and it takes 24 to 48 hours for users to feel completely normal again. Large doses can produce vomiting and convulsions and may lead to oxygen starvation of the brain and muscles. One gram can cause death. Ketamine is also a date rape drug, because it is used by sexual assault perpetrators to anesthetize victims.

A final club drug, and another date rape drug, is rohypnol, which goes by the slang names Roofies, Rophiees, Roche, and the Forget-Me-Not Pill. It is a member of the benzodiazepine family and has sedative and hypnotic effects. Users may experience a high, as well as muscle relaxation, drowsiness, impaired judgment, blackouts, hallucinations, dizziness, and confusion. Rohypnol is manufactured in tablet form, which can easily be crushed and slipped into someone's drink. It is odorless, colorless, and tasteless, so victims often don't notice that their drink has been altered. Some people take it willingly. The side effects of the drug include headaches, muscle pain, and seizures. When used in combination with alcohol or other depressants, rohypnol can be fatal.

SUMMING UP

- Some common club drugs, in addition to LSD, are ecstasy (3-4 methylenedioxymethamphetamine, or MDMA), GHB (gamma-hydroxybutyrate), ketamine, and rohypnol (flunitrazepam).

- Ecstasy has the stimulant effects of an amphetamine along with occasional hallucinogenic properties. Even the short-term use of ecstasy can have long-term negative effects on cognition and health. Long-term users of ecstasy are at risk for several cardiac problems and liver failure, and they show increased rates of anxiety, depression, psychotic symptoms, and paranoia.

- GHB is an anabolic steroid and a central nervous system depressant. At low doses, it can relieve anxiety and promote relaxation. At higher doses, it can result in sleep, coma, or death.

- Ketamine is an anesthetic that produces hallucinogenic effects. Large doses can produce vomiting and convulsions, even death.

- Rohypnol has sedative and hypnotic effects. It is one of the date rape drugs, along with GHB and ketamine. When used in combination with alcohol or other depressants, it can be fatal.

THEORIES OF SUBSTANCE USE, ABUSE, AND DEPENDENCE

All the substances we have discussed in this chapter affect several biochemicals in the brain, and these chemicals can have direct reinforcing effects on the brain. The brain appears to have its own "pleasure pathway" which affects our experience of reward. This pathway begins in the midbrain ventral tegmental area, then goes forward through the nucleus accumbens and on to the frontal cortex (Korenman & Barchas, 1993). This pathway is rich in neurons sensitive to the neurotransmitter dopamine.

Some drugs, such as amphetamines and cocaine, act directly to increase the availability of dopamine in this pathway, leading to the strong sense of reward or "high" that these drugs produce. Other drugs increase the availability of dopamine in more indirect ways. For example, the neurons in the ventral tegmental area are kept from continuous firing by GABA neurons, so the firing of GABA neurons reduces the "high" caused by activity in the dopamine neurons. The opiate drugs inhibit GABA, which in turn stops the GABA neurons from inhibiting dopamine, which makes dopamine available in the reward center.

The chronic use of psychoactive substances may produce permanent changes in the reward centers, causing a craving for these substances even after withdrawal symptoms pass. The repeated use of substances such as cocaine, heroin, and amphetamines causes dopamine neurons to become hyperactive, or sensitized. This sensitization can be permanent, so that these neurons will be activated more highly by subsequent exposure to the psychoactive substance or by stimuli that are associated with the substance (such as the pipe that a cocaine user formerly used to smoke crack). Subjectively, this sensitization creates a chronic, strong craving for the substance, which is made worse every time a former user comes into contact with stimuli that remind him or her of the substance. This craving can create a powerful physiological motivation for relapsing back into substance abuse and dependence (Robinson & Berridge, 1993). Susan, who was dependent on cocaine and alcohol but has been abstinent for three months, described this phenomenon (Engel, 1989, p. 40):

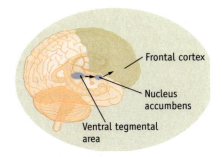

The brain's "pleasure pathway" begins in the ventral tegmental area, then goes through the nucleus accumbens and on to the frontal cortex. It is rich in neurons sensitive to dopamine.

VOICES

Right now, I mean, I wanna go out and—I mean I want a line so bad, you know, I can taste it. Right now. I know I'm not supposed to. I just want it, though. Coke.

The substances we have discussed in this chapter have powerful effects on the brain, in both the short term and the long term, which can make these substances hard for people to resist once they have used them. Substances such as cocaine that have especially rapid and powerful effects on the brain but that also wear off very quickly create great risk for dependency. Even people trying a substance casually can find the rapid, intense, but short-lived high so compelling that they crave more and soon increase their use.

Psychoactive drugs affect a number of other biochemical and brain systems. For example, alcohol has its sedative and anti-anxiety effects largely by enhancing the activity of the neurotransmitter GABA in the septal/hippocampal system. Alcohol also affects serotonin systems, which in turn are associated with changes in mood.

Most people never even try most of the substances discussed in this chapter, and, of those who do try them, most do not abuse them or become dependent on them. Why not? We turn now to other theories of substance abuse and dependence that have tried to explain the differences between people in terms of their vulnerability to substance-related

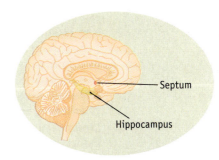

Alcohol has it sedative and anti-anxiety effects largely by enhancing the activity of the neurotransmitter GABA in the septal/hippocampal system. It also affects serotonin systems, which influence mood.

disorders. Most theories of substance-related disorders have focused on alcohol abuse and dependence, probably because alcohol-related disorders are more widespread than the other disorders. For this reason, much of our discussion of theories concerns the development of alcohol abuse and dependence. Several of these theories have been applied to explain the development of abuse and dependence on disorders other than alcohol, however, and we note these as we go along.

For years, alcoholism and other drug addictions were considered the result of a moral deficiency. Alcoholics and other drug addicts were simply perceived as weak, bad people who would not exert control over their impulses. Since the 1960s, that view has largely been replaced by the **disease model** of alcoholism and other drug addictions, which views these disorders as incurable physical diseases, like epilepsy or diabetes (Jellinek, 1960). This model has been supported somewhat by research on the genetics and biology of alcoholism and other drug addiction, but there clearly are social and psychological forces that make some people more prone to these disorders than are others. In the following sections, we discuss the biological, social, and psychological factors that increase people's vulnerability to substance abuse and dependence.

Biological Theories

As is the case with most disorders we have discussed in this book, many of the biological theories of substance use disorders focus on the role of genetics and neurotransmitters. In addition, research suggests that people who become substance dependent or abusive may react differently physiologically to substances than do those who do not become dependent or abusive. Third, some theorists have argued that alcoholism, and perhaps other forms of substance dependence, really represents an underlying biological depression.

Genetic Factors

Family history, adoption, and twin studies all suggest that genetics may play a substantial role in determining who is at risk for substance use disorders (Bierut et al., 1998; Crabbe, 2002; Kendler, Davis, & Kessler, 1997; McGue, 1999; Merikangas, Dierker, & Szatmari, 1998). For example, family studies show that the relatives of people with substance-related disorders are eight times more likely to also have a substance disorder than are the relatives of people with no substance-related disorder (Merikangas et al., 1998). There seems to be a common underlying genetic vulnerability to substance abuse and dependence in general (Tsuang et al., 1998), perhaps accounting for the fact that individuals who use one substance are likely to use multiple substances.

Similarly, twin studies have clearly shown that a substantial portion of the family transmission of substance abuse and dependence is due to genetics (Crabbe, 2002; Kendler & Prescott, 1998b; Lerman et al., 1999; Pomerleau & Kardia, 1999; Prescott & Kendler, 1999). For example, in a study of more than 3,000 male twins, Prescott and Kendler (1999) found concordance rates for alcohol dependence among monozygotic twins of .48, compared with .32 among dizygotic twins. The evidence for heritability was strong only for early-onset alcoholism (first symptoms before age 20), but not for late-onset alcoholism.

Until recently, studies often used all-male samples, or, if they had a female subsample, it tended to be small, and gender differences were not analyzed. In the past few years, however, data from mixed-sex samples have been reanalyzed and large-scale genetic studies have been reported. Some studies suggest that genetics play a stronger role in alcohol use disorders among men than women (Bierut et al., 1998; Jang, Livesley, & Vernon, 1997). For example, some twin studies find no evidence for a genetic contribution to alcohol dependence in women, or they find that the genetic contribution for women is less than that for men (Caldwell & Gottesman, 1991; McGue, 1999; McGue, Pickens, & Svikis, 1992). In contrast, one large twin study found similar heritability for alcohol dependence in women and men (Heath, Bucholz, Madden et al., 1997), whereas another study found modestly higher heritability for women than for men (Prescott & Kendler, 1999). Environmental circumstances, such as sexual abuse, are stronger predictors of alcoholism in women than in men, however (McGue, 1999). Researchers are currently debating whether the contributors to alcoholism and other drug dependencies are different, at least in magnitude, for women and men.

The first reports suggesting that genes play a role in smoking were published over 40 years ago by Fisher (1958), who found that the concordance rate for smoking is significantly higher in monozygotic twins than in dizygotic twins. Several subsequent publications confirmed this finding (Carmelli et al., 1992; Hannah, Hopper, & Mathews, 1983; Heath & Martin, 1993; Hughes, 1986). Hughes (1986) summarized the data from 18 twin studies of smoking and concluded that 53 percent of the variation in smoking behavior was attributable to genetic causes.

Genes affect vulnerability to substance use disorders in part by influencing the functioning of neurotransmitter systems involved in the metabolism and biosynthesis of substances. Research on alcoholism has shown that a variation in two genes (called ADH2 and ADH3) that control the enzymes that break down alcohol into its metabolite, acetaldehyde, is related to low alcohol risk in Asian populations (Reich et al., 1998). In addition, a variation in one of the genes for aldehyde dehydrogenase, the enzyme that breaks down acetaldehyde, the toxic metabolite of alcohol, into acetic acid, is associated with a very low risk for alcoholism in Asians. Persons with this genetic variant experience a buildup of acetaldehyde when they drink alcohol, leading to an aversive flushing response, which discourages alcohol use.

Other genes involved in drug abuse are related to central nervous system functioning, including genes associated with the GABA/benzodiazepine receptor complex, the NMDA receptor (a glutamate receptor that is sensitive to alcohol), calcium channels, cyclic AMP, and G proteins (see Sher, Grekin, & Williams, 2005). There also has been interest in the genes associated with the transport and metabolism of serotonin, because some substances, particularly alcohol, affect the functioning of serotonin systems in animals.

Much research has focused on the genes controlling the dopamine system, given its importance in the reinforcing properties of substances. Genetic variation in the dopamine receptor gene (labeled DRD2) and the dopamine transporter gene (labeled SLC6A3) may influence dopamine concentrations at the synapses and responses to dopamine, thereby influencing how reinforcing a person finds substances such as nicotine (Pomerleau & Kardia, 1999). People who have certain abnormalities in these genes that result in more dopamine at the synapses appear less likely to become smokers than people without these abnormalities (Lerman et al., 1999). In addition, smokers with the SLC6A3 abnormality are more likely to quit smoking than those without it (Sabol et al., 1999).

Alcohol Reactivity

When given moderate doses of alcohol, the sons of alcoholics, who are presumably at increased risk for alcoholism, experience less impairment, subjectively, in their cognitive and motor performance and on some physiological indicators than do the sons of nonalcoholics (Schuckit & Smith, 1996, 1997). At high doses of alcohol, however, the sons of alcoholics are just as intoxicated, by both subjective and objective measures, as are the sons of nonalcoholics. This lower reactivity to moderate doses of alcohol among the sons of alcoholics may lead them to drink substantially more before they begin to feel drunk. As a result, they may not learn to recognize subtle, early signs of intoxication and

may not learn to quit drinking before they become highly intoxicated. They may also develop a high physiological tolerance for alcohol, which leads them to ingest more and more alcohol to achieve any level of subjective intoxication.

Long-term studies of men with low reactivity to moderate doses of alcohol show that they are significantly more likely to become alcoholics over time than are men with greater reactivity to moderate doses of alcohol (Schuckit, 1998; Schuckit & Smith, 1997). The low-reactivity men are especially likely to develop alcohol problems if they encounter significant stress or if they have a tendency toward poor behavioral control. There is some evidence that low reactivity is genetically transmitted (Schuckit, Edenberg, et al., 2001).

Women may be less prone than men to alcoholism because they are much *more* sensitive than men to the intoxicating effects of alcohol (Lex, 1995). At a given dose of alcohol, about 30 percent more of the alcohol enters a woman's bloodstream than enters a man's, because women have less of an enzyme that neutralizes and breaks down alcohol. For these reasons, a woman experiences the subjective and overt symptoms of alcohol intoxication at lower doses than a man and may experience more severe withdrawal symptoms if she drinks too much. These factors may lead many women to drink less than men do. Women who do abuse alcohol, however, may be at more risk for the negative health effects of alcohol than are men, because their blood concentrations of alcohol are higher than those of men who abuse (see Nolen-Hoeksema, 2004).

Alcoholism as a Form of Depression

As many as 70 percent of people with alcohol dependency have depressive symptoms severe enough to interfere with daily living (Schuckit, 1991). In addition, early family history studies suggested that alcohol-related disorders and unipolar depression run together in families, with alcoholism more prevalent in male relatives and unipolar depression more prevalent in female relatives (Winokur & Clayton, 1967). These trends led some researchers to argue that alcoholism and depression are genetically related, or perhaps one disorder, and that many male alcoholics are actually depressed and denying their depression or self-medicating with alcohol (see Williams & Spitzer, 1983).

Although many people with alcohol-related problems appear to use alcohol to cope with daily stresses and emotional distress, it is probably not wise to consider alcoholism simply another form of depression for several reasons. First, although the children of alcoholics do have higher rates of depression than do the children of nonalcoholics, these depressions might result more from the stresses of having alcoholic parents than from genetics (Schuckit, 1995). Second, several family history studies have failed to find higher rates of alcoholism among the offspring of depressed people than among the offspring of nondepressed people, as one would suspect if depression and alcoholism were genetically related (Merikangas, Weissman, & Pauls, 1985).

Third, because alcohol is a central nervous system depressant, it can cause the classic symptoms of depression. In addition, the social consequences of alcohol abuse and dependency (e.g., loss of relationships, loss of job) can cause depression. Thus, when depression and alcohol dependency co-occur in individuals, the depression is just as likely to be a consequence as a cause of the alcohol dependency. Indeed, large epidemiological studies find that the odds of depression preceding alcoholism are equal to the odds that alcoholism will precede depression (Swendsen et al., 1998).

Fourth, studies show that adolescents who are depressed are not more likely to become alcoholics than are adolescents who are not depressed, as we might expect if alcoholism is often a response to depression (Schuckit, 1995). Fifth, simply prescribing antidepressant medications to a person with alcohol abuse or dependency is not enough to help him or her overcome the alcohol-related problems in the long run (Volpicelli, 2001). The risk of relapse is high unless he or she also undergoes treatment directly targeted at the drinking.

Sixth, depression among alcoholics usually disappears once they become abstinent, even without any antidepressant treatment, again suggesting that the depression is secondary to the alcoholism, rather than its cause (Brown et al., 1995). Finally, alcoholism and other drug addictions co-occur with a wide range of other psychological disorders in addition to depression—including bipolar disorder, the personality disorders, the anxiety disorders, and schizophrenia—as well as with histories of physical or sexual abuse (Schuckit et al., 1998).

Psychological Theories

Behavioral theories suggest that children and adolescents may learn substance use behaviors from the modeling of their parents and important others in their culture. Studies of the children of alcoholics find that, even as preschoolers, they are more likely than other children to be able to identify alcoholic drinks and to view alcohol use as a normal part of daily life (Zucker et al., 1995). The children of parents who abuse alcohol by frequently getting drunk or driving while intoxicated learn that these are acceptable behaviors and, thus, are more likely to engage in them as well (Chassin et al., 1999).

Because alcohol-related problems are more common among males than females, most of the adults modeling the inappropriate use of alcohol are male. In turn, because children are more likely to learn from adults who are similar to themselves, male children and male adolescents may be more likely to learn these behaviors from the adults in their world than are female children and female adolescents. Thus, maladaptive patterns of alcohol use may be passed down through the males in a family through modeling.

The cognitive theories of alcohol abuse have focused on people's expectations of the effects of alcohol and their beliefs about the appropriateness of using alcohol to cope with stress (Marlatt et al., 1988). People who expect alcohol to reduce their distress and who do not have other, more adaptive means of coping available to them (such as problem solving or supportive friends or family) are more likely than others to drink alcohol when they are upset and to have social problems related to drinking. For example, one study found that both men and women who believed that alcohol helped them relax and handle stress better and who tended to cope with stressful situations with avoidance rather than problem solving drank more often and had more drinking-related problems (Cooper et al., 1992). In long-term studies of the sons of alcoholics, men who used alcohol to cope and who expected alcohol to relax them were more likely to develop alcohol abuse or dependence, whether or not they had low reactivity to low doses of alcohol

Children may learn substance-related behaviors from their parents.

(Schuckit, 1998). In the section "Treatments for Substance-Related Disorders," we review therapies that try to change people's beliefs about alcohol as a coping tool and to give people more appropriate strategies for coping with their problems.

One personality characteristic that is consistently related to an increased risk for substance abuse and dependence is known as *behavioral undercontrol,* the tendency to be impulsive, sensation-seeking, and prone to antisocial behavior. People with high levels of behavioral undercontrol take psychoactive drugs at an earlier age, ingest more psychoactive drugs, and are more likely to be diagnosed with substance abuse or dependence (e.g., Mason & Windle, 2002; McGue et al., 2001; White, Xie, & Thompson, 2001). In turn, behavioral undercontrol runs strongly in families, and twin studies suggest that this may be due in part to genes (Rutter et al., 1999). Thus, it may be that genetics influence the presence of behavioral undercontrol, which in turn influences the risk of individuals to substance use disorders.

Sociocultural Approaches

VOICES

It was great being stoned. It was, you know, it was great. I just could evade all the bull—and just be stoned, do anything stoned. I just wanted to block everything out, is basically what it was. (Engel, 1989, p. 27)

The reinforcing effects of substances—the highs that stimulants produce, the calming and "zoning out" effects of the depressants and opioids—may be more attractive to people under great psychological stress, particularly those under chronic stress. Thus, there are higher rates of substance abuse and dependence among people facing chronic, severe stress—people living in poverty and with few hopes, women in abusive relationships, and adolescents whose parents fight frequently and violently (Stewart, 1996; Zucker, Chermack, & Curran, 1999). For these people, the effects of substances may be especially reinforcing. Plus, they may see few costs to becoming dependent on substances, because they feel they have little to lose.

Chronic stress combined with an environment that supports and even promotes the use of substances as an escape is a recipe for widespread substance abuse and dependence. Such was the situation for soldiers fighting in the Vietnam War.

The conditions under which they fought and lived created chronic stress. Illegal drugs, especially heroin and marijuana, were readily available, and the culture of the 1960s supported drug experimentation.

Only 1 percent of the soldiers who served in Vietnam had been dependent on heroin or other hard substances before the war. During the war, half the soldiers used these substances at least occasionally, and 20 percent were dependent on them. Fortunately, once these soldiers left that environment and returned home, their substance use dropped to the same level it was before they went to Vietnam (Robins, Helzer, & Davis, 1975).

Some people cannot leave their stress behind, because the stress is present where they live. Indeed, many people dependent on substances were introduced to these substances by their family members and grew up in horrible conditions, from which everyone around them was using substances to escape (Zucker et al., 1995), as is the case with LaTisha:

CASE STUDY

LaTisha, 35 years old when interviewed, was born and raised in Miami. Her mother was a barmaid and she never knew her father. She grew up with two brothers and four sisters, all of whom have different fathers. Her mother used pills during LaTisha's childhood, particularly Valium.

LaTisha took her first alcoholic drink when she was 12, introduced to her by her mother. However, she didn't drink regularly until she was 17, although she started sniffing glue at age 13. LaTisha's mother often brought men home from the bar to have sex with them for money. At 14, LaTisha's mother "turned her out" (introduced her to prostitution) by setting her up with "dates" from the bar. LaTisha was not aware until years later that the men had been paying her mother. LaTisha also recalls having been sexually abused by one of her mother's male friends when she was about 8.

When LaTisha was 16, her older brother returned home from the army. He and his friends would smoke marijuana. In an attempt to "be with the crowd," LaTisha also began smoking marijuana. At a party, her brother introduced her to "downers"—prescription sedatives and

(continued)

tranquilizers. LaTisha began taking pills regularly, eventually taking as many as 15 a day for about a year and a half. She was most often using both Valium and Quaalude.

By 17, LaTisha's brother had introduced her to heroin. Almost immediately, she began speedballing—injecting as well as snorting heroin, cocaine, and various amphetamines. During all the phases of LaTisha's injection-substance use, sharing needles was common. By age 24, LaTisha was mainlining heroin and turning tricks every day. (Adapted from Inciardi et al., 1993, pp. 160–161)

It does not take conditions as extreme as LaTisha's to create an atmosphere that promotes substance use and abuse. More subtle environmental reinforcements and punishments for substance use and abuse clearly influence people's substance use habits. Some societies discourage any use of alcohol, often as part of religious beliefs, and alcohol abuse and dependence in these societies are rare. Other societies, including many European cultures, allow the drinking of alcohol but strongly discourage excessive drinking and irresponsible behavior while intoxicated. Alcohol-related disorders are less common in these societies than in those with few restrictions, either legal or cultural, on alcohol use (Winger et al., 1992).

Most of the theories about the gender differences in substance use disorders have focused on alcohol use disorders, as well as on differences in the reinforcements and punishments for substance use between men and women and their resulting attitudes toward their own use (Nolen-Hoeksema, 2004). Substance use, particularly alcohol use, is much more acceptable for men than for women in many societies. Heavy drinking is part of what "masculine" men do, and it is modeled by heroes and cultural icons. In contrast, until quite recently, heavy drinking was a sign that a woman was "not a lady." Societal acceptance of heavy drinking by women has increased in recent generations, and so has the rate of alcohol use by young women.

Women tend to be less likely than men to carry several other risk factors for drug and alcohol abuse and dependence (see Nolen-Hoeksema, 2004). Women appear less likely than men to have undesirable personality traits associated with substance use disorder (aggressiveness, behavioral undercontrol, sensation-seeking). They also appear to be less motivated to drink to reduce distress (at least among social drinkers) and less likely to expect

drug consumption to have positive outcomes. On the other hand, women may carry certain protective factors against the development of substance-related problems, such as being more nurturant toward others.

The evidence regarding gender differences in the consequences of alcohol consumption suggests that women suffer alcohol-related physical illnesses at lower levels of exposure to alcohol than men. In addition, heavy alcohol use is associated with several reproductive problems in women. Women may be more likely than men to suffer more cognitive and motor impairment due to alcohol. Women may also be more likely than men to suffer physical harm and sexual assault when they are using alcohol.

Taken together, this pattern of results suggests that women's lower rates of alcohol-related disorders may be due both to the absence of risk factors for alcohol use and abuse in women and to women's sensitivity to the negative consequences of alcohol consumption. Women appear less likely to carry many of the risk factors for the initiation of heavy alcohol use. When they do use alcohol, women may notice they feel intoxicated at a much earlier stage of intoxication than men, and they may be more likely to find these effects aversive or frightening, leading them to inhibit their alcohol consumption. This lower consumption, in turn, protects women from developing a tolerance to high doses of alcohol, as well as alcohol-related social and occupational problems.

When women do become substance abusers, their patterns of use and reasons for use tend to differ from men's. Whereas men tend to begin using substances in the context of socializing with male friends, women are most often initiated into substance use by family members, partners, or lovers (Boyd & Guthrie, 1996; Gomberg, 1994; Inciardi et al., 1993; Sterk, 1999). One study found that 70 percent of female crack users were living with men who were also substance users, and many were living with multiple abusers (Inciardi et al., 1993).

SUMMING UP

- Psychoactive substances have powerful effects on the parts of the brain that register reward and pleasure. The repeated use of a substance may sensitize this system, causing a craving for more of the substance.

- Substance use disorders appear to be influenced by genetics. The genes involved in these disorders influence the neurotransmitters that regulate the metabolism and biosynthesis of substances.

- Some theorists view alcoholism as a form of depression, although the prevailing evidence suggests that alcoholism and depression are distinct disorders.

- Behavioral theories of alcoholism note that people are reinforced or punished by other people for their alcohol-related behaviors and model alcohol-related behaviors from parents and important others.

- Cognitive theories argue that people who develop alcohol-related problems have strong expectations that alcohol will help them feel better and cope better when they face stressful times.

- One personality trait associated with increased risk for substance use disorders is behavioral undercontrol, which in turn appears to be influenced by genetics.

- Sociocultural theorists note that alcohol and other drug use increases among people under severe stress.

- The gender differences in substance-related disorders may be due to men having more risk factors for substance use and women being more sensitive to the negative consequences of substance use.

Men tend to begin using substances in the context of socializing with friends, whereas women are often introduced to substance use by their male partners.

TREATMENTS FOR SUBSTANCE-RELATED DISORDERS

Historically, the treatments for substance-related disorders have been based on the disease model, which views these disorders as medical diseases (MacCoun, 1998). The disease model suggests that biological treatments are most appropriate. It also suggests that people with these disorders have no control over their use of substances because of their disease and, thus, must avoid all use of the substances. Alcoholics Anonymous, a self-help group that focuses on helping alcoholics accept that they have a disease and abstain completely from drinking, is based on a disease model. It is the most widely prescribed intervention by the proponents of biological perspectives on alcoholism.

Psychological interventions have been based on a **harm-reduction model** of treatment (Marlatt, 1998). Proponents of this approach focus on the psychological and sociocultural factors that lead people to use substances inappropriately and on helping people gain control over their use of substances through behavioral and cognitive interventions. The harm-reduction model does not presume that people must avoid all use of substances—for example, that alcoholics must never take another drink—although it is strongly recommended that people with substance use disorders restrict their exposure to substances.

Whether a clinician follows the disease model or the harm-reduction model of intervention, he or she will most often recommend **detoxification** as the first step in any treatment program. Basically, individuals are assisted in stopping their use of the substance, and then the substance is allowed to be eliminated from the body. Many detoxification programs are in hospitals and clinics, so that physicians can monitor individuals through their withdrawal from the drug, making them more comfortable and intervening if their life is in danger. Detoxification is especially important when the substance being used can cause permanent organ or brain damage or is frequently lethal, such as cocaine, amphetamines, and inhalants.

Once people stop using the substance and are through the withdrawal process, a variety of biological and psychosocial therapies are used to help them prevent relapse. These therapies are often combined in comprehensive substance treatment programs. People check themselves into these programs, where they remain for a few weeks or months until they feel they have gained control over their substance use and dependence.

Biological Treatments

Medications can be used to help wean individuals off a substance, to reduce their desire for a substance, and to maintain their use of substances at a controlled level.

Antianxiety Drugs, Antidepressants, and Antagonists

Although many substance-dependent people can withstand withdrawal symptoms with emotional support, for other people the symptoms are so severe that medications may be prescribed to reduce these symptoms (Carroll, 2001; O'Brien & McKay, 1998). For people who are alcohol dependent, a benzodiazepine, which has depressant effects similar to those of alcohol, can be prescribed to reduce the symptoms of tremor and anxiety, to decrease pulse and respiration rates, and to stabilize blood pressure. The dosage of the drug is decreased each day, so that a patient withdraws from the alcohol slowly but does not become dependent on the benzodiazepine. Antidepressants are also used to help people weather the withdrawal syndrome so as to continue abstaining from substance use (O'Brien & McKay, 1998; Schuckit, 1996). The selective serotonin reuptake inhibitors can help reduce the impulsive consumption of and craving for alcohol.

Antidepressant drugs are sometimes used to treat alcoholics or other drug addicts who are depressed, but the efficacy of these drugs in treating either the alcohol or other drug problems or the depression in the absence of psychotherapy has not been consistently supported (Nunes & Levin, 2004). There are wide differences between people with substance use disorders in response to the SSRIs, which are not currently well understood (Naranjo & Knoke, 2001).

Antagonist drugs block or change the effects of the addictive drug, reducing the desire of the addict for the drug. **Naltrexone** and **naloxone** are opioid antagonists—they block the effects of opioids, such as heroin. Heroin dependents are also given other drugs that reduce the reinforcing effects of heroin and thus reduce their desire for it. If a person takes heroin while on naltrexone or naloxone, he or she will not experience the positive effects of the heroin. This, theoretically, can reduce the desire for the drug and, therefore, use of the drug. The opioid antagonists must be administered very carefully, however, because they can cause severe withdrawal reactions in people addicted to opioids.

Naltrexone has also proven useful in blocking the high that can be caused by alcohol. (Naltrexone may block the effects of alcohol as well as opioids, because it blocks the effects of the release of endorphins during drinking.) Alcoholics on naltrexone report that their craving for alcohol is diminished and they drink less (Anton, 2001). In one study, researchers administered naltrexone or a placebo to male and female alcoholics for 12 weeks (Volpicelli et al., 1997). The participants were also given individual therapy once per week to address their ad-

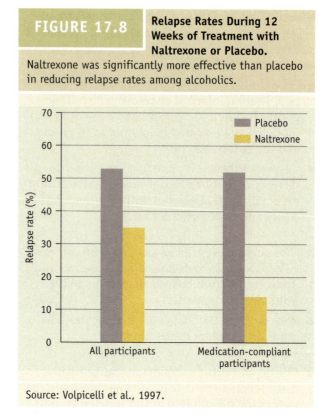

FIGURE 17.8   **Relapse Rates During 12 Weeks of Treatment with Naltrexone or Placebo.** Naltrexone was significantly more effective than placebo in reducing relapse rates among alcoholics.

Source: Volpicelli et al., 1997.

diction. As Figure 17.8 shows, participants who took naltrexone were significantly less likely than those who took placebo to relapse during the 12 weeks of treatment. Moreover, participants who were more medication-compliant—who took 80 percent or more of their prescribed naltrexone—had a relapse rate of only 14 percent, compared with a relapse rate of 52 percent for the placebo group.

The drug acamprosate affects glutamate and GABA receptors in the brain, which in turn are involved in the craving for alcohol. Preliminary studies have suggested that alcoholics who are prescribed acamprosate stay abstinent longer and may crave alcohol less than alcoholics given placebo (Anton, 2001).

One drug that can make alcohol actually punishing is **disulfiram,** commonly referred to as *Antabuse* (Carroll, 2001). Just having one drink can make a person taking disulfiram feel sick and dizzy and can make him or her vomit, blush, and even faint. People must be very motivated to agree to remain on disulfiram, and it works to reduce alcohol consumption only as long as they take it.

In the pharmacological treatment of nicotine dependence, there are two general approaches (Mooney & Hatsukami, 2001). The first and most common is nicotine replacement therapy—the use of nicotine gum, the nicotine patch, nicotine nasal spray, or the nicotine inhaler to prevent withdrawal effects for a user who wishes to stop smoking. It is hoped that the individual will gradually reduce his or her use of the nicotine replacements, weaning off of the physiological effects of nicotine slowly.

The other approach is to prescribe a medication that reduces the craving for nicotine. The only medication currently approved for this use is bupropion (marketed for smoking cessation as Zyban), which is an antidepressant. The ways in which bupropion helps people stop smoking are not currently clear but may involve changes in the neurotransmitter dopamine (Mooney & Hatsukami, 2001).

Methadone Maintenance Programs

Gradual withdrawal from heroin can be achieved with the help of the synthetic drug **methadone.** This drug itself is an opioid, but it has less potent and longer-lasting effects than heroin when taken orally. The person dependent on heroin takes methadone while discontinuing the use of heroin. The methadone helps reduce the extreme, negative symptoms of withdrawal from heroin. Individuals who take heroin while on methadone do not experience the intense psychological effects of heroin, because methadone blocks receptors for heroin.

Although the goal of treatment is eventually to withdraw individuals from methadone, some patients continue to use methadone for years, under physicians' care, rather than taper off their use. These **methadone maintenance programs** are controversial. Some people believe that they allow the heroin dependent simply to transfer dependency to another substance that is legal and provided by a physician. Other people believe that methadone maintenance is the only way to keep some heroin dependents from going back on the street and becoming readdicted. Studies following patients in methadone maintenance programs do find that they are much more likely than patients who try to withdraw from heroin without methadone to remain in psychological treatment, and they are less likely to relapse into heroin use or to become reinvolved in criminal activity (Carroll, 2001; O'Brien & McKay, 1998).

Behavioral and Cognitive Treatments

Several behavioral and cognitive techniques are used in the treatment of substance use disorders, and several studies have shown these treatments to be quite effective (Volpicelli, 2001). These techniques have certain goals in common. The first is to motivate the individual to stop using the drug. People who enter treatment are often ambivalent about stopping use, and they may have been forced into treatment against their desires. The second goal is to teach new coping skills to replace the use of substances to cope with stress and negative feelings. The third is to change the reinforcements a person has for using substances—for example, an individual may need to disengage from social circles in which drug use is "part of the scene." The fourth is to enhance the individual's supports from nonusing friends and family. The final goal is often to foster adherence to pharmacotherapies the person is using in conjunction with psychotherapy.

Behavioral Treatments

Behavioral treatments based on **aversive classical conditioning** are sometimes used to treat alcohol dependency and abuse, either alone or in combination with biological or other psychosocial therapies (Finney & Moos, 1998; Schuckit, 1995). Drugs, such as disulfiram (Antabuse), that make the ingestion of alcohol unpleasant or toxic, are given to people who are alcohol dependent. If they take drinks of alcohol, the drug interacts with the alcohol to cause nausea and vomiting. Eventually, through classical conditioning, they develop conditioned responses to the alcohol—namely, nausea and vomiting. They then learn to avoid the alcohol, through operant conditioning, in order to avoid the aversive response to it. Studies have shown such aversive conditioning to be effective in reducing alcohol consumption, at least in the short term (Schuckit, 1995). "Booster" sessions are often needed to reinforce the aversive conditioning, however, because it tends to weaken with time.

An alternative is **covert sensitization therapy,** in which people who are alcohol dependent use imagery to create associations between thoughts of alcohol use and thoughts of highly unpleasant consequences of alcohol use. An example of a sensitization scene that a therapist might take a client through begins as follows (Rimmele, Miller, & Dougher, 1989, p. 135):

VOICES

You finish the first sip of beer, and you . . . notice a funny feeling in your stomach. . . . Maybe another drink will help. . . . As you tip back . . . that funny feeling in your stomach is stronger, and you feel like you have to burp. . . . You swallow again, trying to force it down, but it doesn't work. You can feel the gas coming up. . . . You swallow more, but suddenly your mouth is filled with a sour liquid that burns the back of your throat and goes up your nose. . . . [You] spew the liquid all over the counter and sink. . . .

The imagery gets even more graphic from there. Covert sensitization techniques seem effective in creating conditioned aversive responses to the sight and smell of alcohol and in reducing alcohol consumption.

Finally, some people who are alcohol dependent develop classically conditioned responses to the environmental cues often present when they drink. For example, when they see or smell their favorite alcoholic beverages, they begin to salivate and report cravings to drink. These conditioned responses increase the risk for relapse among people who are abstinent or trying to quit drinking. A behavior therapy known as **cue exposure and response prevention** is used to extinguish this conditioned response to cues associated with alcohol intake (Rankin, Hodgson, & Stockwell, 1983). Clients are exposed to their favorite types of alcohol, are encouraged to hold glasses to their lips, and are urged to smell the alcohol, but they are prohibited from or strongly encouraged not to drink any of the alcohol. Eventually, this procedure reduces the desire to drink and increases the ability to avoid drinking when the opportunity arises (Rankin et al., 1983). The procedure probably should be coupled with strategies for coping with and removing oneself from tempting situations.

Cognitive Treatments

Interventions based on the cognitive models of alcohol abuse and dependency help clients identify the situations in which they are most likely to drink and to lose control over their drinking and their expectations that alcohol will help them cope better with those situations (Marlatt et al., 1998). Therapists then work with clients to challenge these expectations by reviewing the negative effects of alcohol on their behavior. For example, a therapist may focus on a recent party at which a client was feeling anxious and, thus, began to drink heavily. The therapist might have the client recount the embarrassing and socially inappropriate behaviors he engaged in while intoxicated, to challenge the notion that the alcohol helped him cope effectively with his party anxiety. Therapists also help clients learn to anticipate and reduce stress in their lives and to develop more adaptive ways of coping with stressful situations, such as seeking the help of others or engaging in active problem solving. Finally, therapists help clients learn to say, "No, thanks," when offered drinks and to deal effectively with social pressure to drink by using assertiveness skills.

The following is an excerpt from a discussion between a therapist and a client with alcohol-related problems in which the therapist is helping the client generate strategies for coping with the stress of a possible job promotion. The therapist encourages the client to brainstorm coping strategies, without evaluating them for the moment, so that the client feels free to generate as many possible strategies as he can (adapted from Sobell & Sobell, 1978, pp. 97–98).

VOICES

Client: I really want this job, and it'll mean a lot more money for me, not only now but also at retirement. Besides, if I refused the promotion, what would I tell my wife or my boss?

Therapist: Rather than worrying about that for the moment, why don't we explore what kinds of possible behavioral options you have regarding this job promotion? Remember, don't evaluate the options now. Alternatives, at this point, can include anything even remotely possible; what we want you to do is come up with a range of possible alternatives. You don't have to carry out an alternative just because you consider it.

Client: You know, I could do what I usually do in these kinds of situations. In fact, being as nervous as I've been these past couple of months, I've done that quite often.

Therapist: You mean drinking?

Client: Yeah, I've been drinking quite heavily some nights when I get home, and my wife is really complaining.

Therapist: Well, OK, drinking is one option. What other ways could you deal with this problem?

Client: Well, I could take the job, and on the side I could take some night courses in business at a local college. That way I could learn how to be a supervisor. But, gee, that would be a lot of work. I don't even know if I have the time. Besides, I don't know if they offer the kind of training I need.

Therapist: At this point, it's really not necessary to worry about how to carry out the options but simply to identify them. You're doing fine. What are some other ways you might handle the situation?

(continued)

Client: Well, another thing I could do is to simply tell the boss that I'm not sure I'm qualified and either tell him that I don't want the job or ask him if he could give me some time to learn my new role.

Therapist: OK. Go on, you're doing fine.

Client: But what if the boss tells me that I have to take the job, I don't have any choice?

Therapist: Well, what general kinds of things might happen in that case?

Client: Oh, I could take the job and fail. That's one option. I could take the job and learn how to be a supervisor. I could refuse the job, risk being fired, and maybe end up having to look for another job. You know, I could just go and talk to my supervisor right now and explain the problem to him and see what comes of that.

Therapist: Well, you've delineated a lot of options. Let's take some time to evaluate them before you reach any decision.

The therapist then helps the client evaluate the potential effectiveness of each option and anticipate any potential negative consequences of each action. The client decides to accept the promotion but to take some courses at the local college to increase his business background. The therapist discusses with the client the stresses of managing a new job and classes, and they generate ways the client can manage these stresses other than by drinking.

In most cases, therapists using these cognitive-behavioral approaches encourage clients to abstain from alcohol, especially when clients have histories of frequent relapses into alcohol abuse. When clients' goals are to learn to drink socially and therapists believe that clients have the capability to achieve these goals, therapists may focus on teaching clients to engage in social, or controlled, drinking.

A wide range of studies have shown that cognitive-behavioral approaches are effective in the treatment of abuse and dependence on alcohol, cannabis, nicotine, heroin, amphetamines, and cocaine (Dennis et al., 2000; McCrady, 2001; Mooney & Hatsukami, 2001; NIDA, 2002b, 2002c, 2002d; Waldron et al., 2001)

The Controlled Drinking Controversy

The notion that some alcoholics can learn to engage in controlled, social drinking directly clashes with the idea that alcoholism is a biological disease and that, if an alcoholic takes even one sip of alcohol, he or she will lose all control and plunge back into full alcoholism. In 1973, researchers Mark and Linda Sobell published one of the first studies showing that a cognitive-behaviorally oriented controlled drinking program can work for alcoholics, perhaps even better than a traditional abstinence program. They found that the alcoholics who had had their controlled drinking intervention were significantly less likely than alcoholics in the abstinence program to relapse into severe drinking, and they were significantly more likely to be functioning well over the two years following treatment.

These findings were assailed by proponents of the alcohol-as-a-disease model. For example, Pendery, Maltzman, and West (1982) published a 10-year follow-up of the alcoholics in the Sobells' controlled drinking group in the journal *Science*, based on interviews with these alcoholics, and their family members, as well as investigations of public records. Pendery and colleagues reported that, 10 years after the Sobells' study, 40 percent of the men in the controlled drinking treatment group were drinking excessively, 20 percent were dead from alcohol-related causes, 30 percent had given up attempts at controlled drinking in favor of becoming abstinent, and only 5 percent were engaging in controlled drinking. Subsequently, the TV program *60 Minutes* did a segment on the evils of controlled drinking treatments, which was introduced with Harry Reasoner standing at the graveside of one of the people from the Sobells' study. The Sobells were publicly charged with fraud, and multiple investigations of the Sobells' work followed, including one by the U.S. Congress, interrupting their research for years. They were eventually cleared of any wrongdoing.

Behavioral interventions help alcoholics learn new ways to cope with depression and anxiety.

In a response to the Pendery and colleagues article titled "Aftermath of a Heresy," Mark and Linda Sobell (Sobell & Sobell, 1984) detailed the many flaws in the Pendery article, the greatest of which was the lack of any information on the outcomes of the alcoholics who had been in the abstinence program in the Sobells' original study. They noted that claims that 30 percent of the men in their controlled drinking group were abstinent and 5 percent were engaging in controlled drinking suggest a much better long-term outcome for these men than other studies have suggested is true of alcoholics who are treated by abstinence programs. The Sobells were able to track down the mortality rates of the men in the abstinence treatment group in their study. Whereas Pendery and colleagues had reported that 20 percent of the men in the controlled drinking treatment group had died over the 10 years after the study, the Sobells found that 30 percent of the men in the abstinence treatment groups had died in the same 10 years, with all but one of these deaths directly attributable to alcohol.

Subsequent research by the Sobells and many others has shown that controlled drinking programs can work, at least for people with mild to moderate alcohol problems or dependence (see Marlatt, 1998, and Sobell & Sobell, 1995, for reviews). People who have had many alcohol-related problems generally have trouble with controlled drinking and must remain abstinent in order to avoid relapse into alcohol dependency.

Relapse Prevention

Unfortunately, the relapse rate for people undergoing any kind of treatment for alcohol abuse and dependency is high. The **abstinence violation effect** is a powerful contributor to relapse. There are two components to the abstinence violation effect. The first is a sense of conflict and guilt when an alcoholic who has been abstinent violates the abstinence and has a drink. He or she may then continue to drink to try to suppress the conflict and guilt. The second is a tendency to attribute the violation of abstinence to a lack of willpower and self-control, rather than to situational factors. Thus, the person may think, "I'm an alcoholic and there's no way I can control my drinking. The fact I had a drink proves this." This type of thinking may pave the way to continued, uncontrolled drinking.

Relapse prevention programs teach alcoholics to view slips as temporary and situationally caused. Therapists work with clients to identify high-risk situations for relapse and to avoid those situations or to exercise effective coping strategies for the situations. For example, a client may identify parties as high-risk situations for relapse. If she decides to go to a party, she may first practice with her therapist some assertiveness skills for resisting pressure from friends to drink and write down other coping strategies she can use if she feels tempted to drink, such as starting a conversation with a supportive friend or practicing deep breathing exercises. She may also decide that, if the temptation to drink becomes too great, she will ask a supportive friend to leave the party with her and go somewhere for coffee, until the temptation to drink passes.

Only about 10 percent of people who are alcohol dependents or abusers ever seek treatment. Another 40 percent may recover on their own, often as the result of maturation or positive changes in their environment (such as getting a good job or getting married to a supportive person) that help them and motivate them to get control of their drinking (Sobell & Sobell, 1995). The remainder of people with significant alcohol problems continue to have these problems throughout their lives. Some of these people become physically ill or completely unable to hold jobs or maintain their relationships. Others are able to hide or control their alcohol abuse and dependency enough to keep their jobs and may be in relationships with people who facilitate their alcohol dependency. Often, they have periods, sometimes long periods, of abstinence, but then, perhaps when facing stressful events, they begin drinking again. This is why preventing the development of alcohol abuse and dependency and other substance-related problems is so important.

Alcoholics Anonymous

Alcoholics Anonymous (AA) is an organization created by and for people with alcohol-related problems. Its philosophy is based on the disease model of alcoholism, which views alcoholism as a disease that causes alcoholics to lose all control over their drinking once they have the first drink. The implication of this model is that the only way to control alcoholism is to abstain completely from any alcohol. AA prescribes 12 steps that people dependent on alcohol must take toward recovery. The first step is to admit they are alcoholics and powerless to control the effects of alcohol. AA encourages members to seek help from a higher power, to admit to their weaknesses, and to ask for forgiveness. The goal for all members is complete abstinence.

Group members provide moral and social support for each other and make themselves available to each other in times of crisis. Once they are able, group members are expected to devote themselves to helping other alcoholics. AA members believe that people are never completely cured of alcoholism—they are always "recovering alcoholics," with the potential of falling back into alcohol dependency with one drink. AA meetings include testimonials from recovering alcoholics about their paths into alcoholism, such as the one that follows, which are meant to motivate others to abstain from alcohol (Spitzer et al., 1983, pp. 87–89).

VOICES

I am Duncan. I am an alcoholic. . . . I know that I will always be an alcoholic, that I can never again touch alcohol in any form. It'll kill me if I don't keep away from it. In fact, it almost did. . . . I must have been just past my 15th birthday when I had that first drink that everybody talks about. And like so many of them—and you—it was like a miracle. With a little beer in my gut, the world was transformed. I wasn't a weakling anymore, I could lick almost anybody on the block. And girls? Well, you can imagine how a couple of beers made me feel, like I could have any girl I wanted. So, like so many of you, my friends in the Fellowship, alcohol became the royal road to love, respect, and self-esteem. If I couldn't feel good about myself when I wasn't drinking, if I felt stupid or lazy or ugly or misunderstood, all I had to do was belt down a few and everything got better. Of course, I was fooling myself, wasn't I, because I was as ugly and dumb and lazy when I was drunk as when I was sober. But I didn't know it. . . .

Though it's obvious to me now that my drinking even then, in high school, and after I got to college, was a problem, I didn't think so at the time. After all, everybody was drinking and getting drunk and acting stupid, and I didn't really think I was different. A couple of minor auto accidents, one conviction for drunken driving, a few fights—nothing out of the ordinary, it seemed to me at the time. True, I was drinking quite a lot, even then, but my friends seemed to be able to down as much beer as I did. I guess the fact that I hadn't really had any blackouts and that I could go for days without having to drink reassured me that things hadn't gotten out of control. And that's the way it went, until I found myself drinking even more—and more often—and suffering

more from my drinking, along about my third year of college. . . . [Eventually] I did cut down on my drinking by half or more. I only drank on weekends—and then only at night. And I set more-or-less arbitrary limits on how much I would drink, as well as where and when I would drink. And that got me through the rest of college and, actually, through law school as well. I'd drink enough to get very drunk once or twice a week, but only on weekends, and then I'd tough it out through the rest of the week.

[Later] on, the drinking began to affect both my marriage and my career. With enough booze in me and under the pressures of guilt over my failure to carry out my responsibilities to my wife and children, I sometimes got kind of rough physically with them. I would break furniture, throw things around, then rush out and drive off in the car. I had a couple of wrecks, lost my license for two years because of one of them. Worst of all was when I tried to stop. By then I was totally hooked, so every time I tried to stop drinking, I'd experience withdrawal in all its horrors. I never had DTs, but I came awfully close many times, with the vomiting and the "shakes" and being unable to sit still or to lie down. And that would go on for days at a time. . . . Then, about four years ago, with my life in ruins, my wife given up on me and the kids with her, out of a job, and way down on my luck, the Fellowship and I found each other. Jim, over there, bless his heart, decided to sponsor me—we'd been friends for a long time, and I knew he'd found sobriety through this group. I've been dry now for a little over two years, and with luck and support, I may stay sober. I've begun to make amends for my transgressions, I've faced my faults squarely again instead of hiding them with booze, and I think I may make it.

The practices and philosophies of AA do not appeal to everyone. The emphases on one's powerlessness, need for a higher power, and complete abstinence turn many people away. In addition, many people who subscribe to AA's philosophy still find it difficult to maintain complete abstinence and "fall off the wagon" at various times throughout their lives. However, many people have found AA

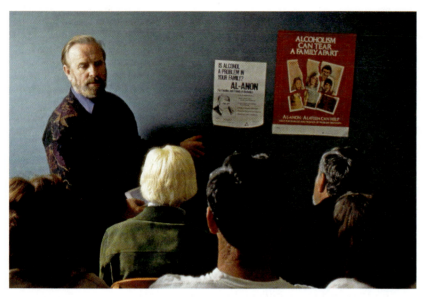

Many abstinence programs for substance abuse are based on Alcoholics Anonymous.

very helpful in their recovery from alcohol abuse and dependency, and AA remains the most common source of treatment for people with alcohol-related problems. There are about 23,000 chapters of AA across 90 countries, and it is estimated that 800,000 people attend meetings (Goodwin, 1988). Evaluations of 12-step programs, such as AA, have found that they are as effective as the behavioral and cognitive programs in the treatment of alcoholism (Finney & Moos, 1998; Project MATCH Research Group, 1998). Self-help groups modeled on Alcoholics Anonymous have also been formed to assist people with dependencies on other drugs, including Narcotics Anonymous, Cocaine Anonymous, and Potsmokers Anonymous.

Other self-help organizations have been developed that do not have the spiritual focus of AA and, instead, often apply cognitive-behavioral principles in a self-help format. These include Self-Management and Recovery Training (SMART), Secular Organizations for Sobriety/Save Ourselves (SOS), and Moderation Management (MM).

Prevention Programs for College Students

In the United States, young adults between 18 and 24 years of age have the highest rates of alcohol consumption and make up the largest proportion of problem drinkers of any age group. College students are even more likely to drink than are their peers who are not in college. Among college students, 73 to 98 percent drink alcohol, in response to easy access to alcohol, social activities that focus on drinking, and peer pressure to drink. As much as 20 to 25 percent of college students report having experienced alcohol-related problems, such as an inability to complete schoolwork or an alcohol-related accident. Alcohol-related accidents are the leading cause of death in college students (Marlatt et al., 1993). Heavy drinking is also associated with acute alcohol toxicity (which can be lethal), date rape, unsafe sexual activity, vandalism, and impaired academic performance.

The pattern of drinking among college students has shifted over time. A greater percentage of students abstain completely from alcohol, but those who do drink are more likely to be heavy drinkers (Marlatt et al., 1993). These heavy drinkers are most likely to be binge drinkers, who drink large quantities of alcohol on weekends, typically at social events, often with the intention of getting drunk.

Many colleges are developing programs to reduce drinking and drinking-related problems among students. Most of these programs emphasize the health-related consequences of drinking, but such long-term concerns do not tend to impress young people, who are more likely to be focused on the short-term gains of alcohol use. Simply providing information about the dangers of alcohol abuse and trying to invoke a fear of these dangers have little effect. Some college counselors refer students with drinking problems to abstinence programs, such as Alcoholics Anonymous, but college students often find the focus on admitting one's powerlessness and the principle of lifelong abstinence so unattractive that they will not attend these programs. Finally, many colleges try to provide alternative recreational activities that do not focus on alcohol. In general, however, such prevention programs designed to stop drinking altogether have had limited success.

Psychologist Alan Marlatt and colleagues at the University of Washington (Marlatt, Blume, & Parks, 2001; Parks, Anderson, & Marlatt, 2001) have argued that a more credible approach to college drinking is to recognize alcohol use as normative behavior among young adults and to focus education on the immediate risks of the excessive use of alcohol (such as alcohol-related accidents) and on the payoffs of moderation (such as the avoidance of hangovers). They view young drinkers as relatively inexperienced in regulating their use of alcohol and as in need of skills training to prevent their abuse of alcohol. Learning to drink safely is compared to learning to drive safely, and people must learn to anticipate hazards and avoid "unnecessary accidents."

Based on this harm-reduction model, the Alcohol Skills Training Program (ASTP) targets heavy-drinking college students for intervention. In eight weekly sessions of 90 minutes, participants are first taught to be aware of their drinking habits, including when, where, and with whom they are most likely to overdrink, by keeping daily records of their alcohol consumption and the situations in which they drink. They are also taught to calculate their own blood-alcohol levels. It often comes as a surprise to people how few drinks it takes to be legally intoxicated.

Next, participants' beliefs about the "magical" effects of drinking on social skills and sexual prowess are challenged. They discuss the negative effects of alcohol on social behaviors, on the ability to drive, and on weight gain, and they discuss hangovers. Participants are encouraged to set personal goals for limiting alcohol consumption, based on their maximum blood-alcohol levels and their desires to avoid the negative effects of alcohol. They learn skills for limiting consumption, such as alternating alcoholic and nonalcoholic beverages and selecting drinks based on quality rather than quantity, such as buying two good beers rather than a six-pack of generic beer. In later sessions, members are taught to consider alternatives to drinking alcohol to reduce negative emotional states, such as using relaxation exercises or reducing sources of stress in their lives. Finally, in role-plays, participants are taught skills for avoiding high-risk situations in which they are likely to overdrink and skills for resisting peer pressure to drink. Some ideas from the ASTP program are described in *Taking Psychology Personally*: *Tips for Responsible Drinking.*

Evaluations of ASTP have shown that participants do decrease their alcohol consumption and problems and increase their social skills in resisting alcohol abuse (Fromme et al., 1994; Marlatt, Baer, & Larimer, 1995). ASTP was designed for a group format, and the use of group pressure to encourage change in individuals and as a forum for role playing has many advantages. Adaptations of this program delivered to individuals either in person or in written form as a self-help manual also have shown positive effects on drinking habits (Baer et al., 1992, 2001).

In one study, Marlatt and colleagues (Marlatt et al., 1998) attempted to intervene with high-risk drinkers when they might be most open to intervention, in their first year of college. They identified a group of high school students who were about to matriculate into the University of Washington and who were already drinking at least monthly and consuming at least five to six drinks in one sitting or who reported frequent alcohol-related problems. These high-risk students were then randomly assigned to receive either a one-session intervention based on the Alcohol Skills Training Program or no intervention, sometime in January through March of their first year of college. Both groups of students were followed for the next two years. Over that two years, the intervention group showed less drinking overall and fewer harmful consequences of drinking (such as getting into alcohol-related accidents) over the subsequent two years than did the comparison group. In addition, approximately 90 percent of those receiving the intervention said it was helpful and that they would recommend it to friends. The work of Marlatt and colleagues suggests that problem drinkers of college age can learn to reduce their intake of alcohol and to avoid the harmful consequences of alcohol consumption if they receive nonconfrontational training on the skills necessary for harm reduction.

Gender-Sensitive Treatment Programs

The differences in the contexts for men's and women's substance abuse suggest the need for different approaches to treating men and women (Beckman, 1994). For men, treatment may need to focus on challenging the societal supports for their substance use and their view that substance use is an appropriate way to cope. It may also need to focus on men's tendency to act in aggressive and impulsive ways, particularly when intoxicated. For women, treatment may need to focus more on issues of self-esteem and powerlessness and on helping them remove themselves from abusive environments.

Women who violate social norms so greatly as to become substance abusers may have more severe underlying emotional problems than do men who become substance abusers (Beckman, 1994). In addition, because women substance abusers typically are living with partners and other family members who are also substance abusers, they may not have the necessary support from their environment to stop their substance use (Riehman, Hser, & Zeller, 2000). Rarely do husbands or boyfriends participate in the treatment of women substance users, and they may even oppose the woman's seeking treatment. In contrast, women partners often participate in male substance abusers' treatment (Higgins et al., 1994). One recent study found that, when male partners can be brought into treatment for women substance abusers, the women show greater remission of their substance abuse problems than if they receive only individual therapy (Winters et al., 2002). As substance use among women increases, however, treatment programs will need to become more sensitive to the differences in the patterns and motives of substance use in women and men and must design their programs to meet the needs of both genders.

SUMMING UP

- Detoxification is the first step in treating substance-related disorders.

- Antianxiety and antidepressant drugs can help ease withdrawal symptoms. Antagonist drugs can block the effects of substances, reduce desire for the drug, or make the ingestion of the drug aversive.

- Methadone maintenance programs substitute methadone for heroin in the treatment of heroin addicts. These programs are controversial but may be the only way some heroin addicts will get off the streets.

- Behavior therapies based on aversive classical conditioning are sometimes used to treat substance use disorders.

- Treatments based on social learning and cognitive theories focus on training people with substance use disorders in more adaptive coping skills and challenging their positive expectations about the effects of substances.

- The most common treatment for alcoholism is Alcoholics Anonymous, a self-help group that encourages alcoholics to admit their weaknesses and to call on a higher power and other group members to help them remain completely abstinent from alcohol. Related groups are available for people dependent on other substances.

- Prevention programs for college students aim to teach them the responsible use of alcohol.

- Different treatments may be needed for men and women that take into account the different contexts for their substance use.

CHAPTER INTEGRATION

The substances we have discussed in this chapter are powerful biological agents. They affect the brain directly, producing changes in mood, thoughts, and perceptions. Some people may find these changes more positive or rewarding than other people do, because they are genetically or biochemically predisposed to do so (see Figure 17.9). The rewards and punishments in the environment can clearly affect an individual's choice to pursue the effects of substances, however. Even many long-term, chronic substance abusers can abstain from use if they receive strong environmental support for abstention.

People who find substances more rewarding, for biological or environmental reasons, will develop expectations that substances will be rewarding, which in turn will enhance how rewarding they actually are. In turn, heavy substance users choose friends and environments that support their substance use. They also tend to find partners who are also heavy substance users, creating a biological and psychosocial environment for their children that promotes substance abuse and dependence. Thus, the cycle of familial transmission of substance abuse and dependence has intersecting biological and psychosocial components.

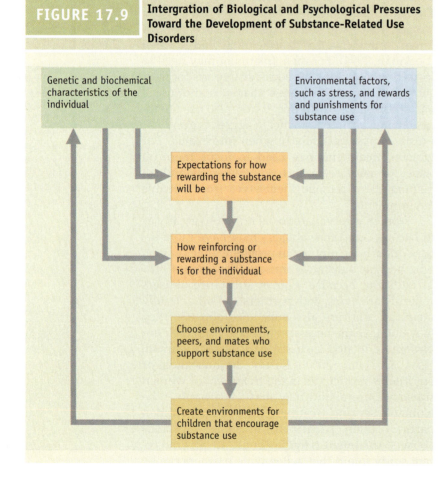

| FIGURE 17.9 | **Intergration of Biological and Psychological Pressures Toward the Development of Substance-Related Use Disorders** |

Genetic and biochemical characteristics of the individual

Environmental factors, such as stress, and rewards and punishments for substance use

Expectations for how rewarding the substance will be

How reinforcing or rewarding a substance is for the individual

Choose environments, peers, and mates who support substance use

Create environments for children that encourage substance use

Taking Psychology Personally

Tips for Responsible Drinking

The following are some tips for reducing your own drinking and for preventing problems due to drinking at social events, from the work of Alan Marlatt and colleagues (1998):

- *Set a limit on how much you will drink* before you go to a party or another social function. You might want to use Table 17.7 to set your drink limit, so that you do not exceed a low to moderate blood-alcohol level. Tell a friend what your limit is and get a commitment from that friend to help you stick to that limit.

- *Alternate between alcoholic and nonalcoholic beverages* at the party.

- *Eat foods high in protein and carbohydrates* before and at the party.

- *Designate someone in your group to drive*. That person should drink *no* alcoholic beverages at the party.

- *If you are throwing the party, serve plenty of nonalcoholic beverages and attractive food and try to focus the party on something other than alcohol consumption*, such as music.

- *If someone at the party appears to be very intoxicated, encourage him or her to stop drinking. Do not let him or her drive* away from the party. Instead, call a taxi or have someone who has not been drinking drive him or her home.

- *If a person passes out after drinking heavily, lay the person on his or her side*, rather than on his or her back, in case of vomiting. Call medical personnel.

- *If you get drunk at a party, after you have recovered, review the reasons for your overdrinking*. Were you trying to get rid of a bad mood? Were you nervous and trying to relax? Did certain people push you to drink? Did you tell yourself that you were not drinking that much? Try to develop concrete, realistic plans for avoiding, in future situations, the reasons you overdrank.

Extraordinary People: Follow-Up

Without much trouble, many of us could name a number of other celebrities besides Chris Farley who abuse or abused illicit drugs or have died from drug overdoses: rapper Ol' Dirty Bastard, Dee Dee Ramone of the punk band The Ramones, River Phoenix, Jimmy Hendrix, Charlie Parker, Janis Joplin, Jim Morrison, and, years ago, Marilyn Monroe and Elvis Presley. Comedian Richard Prior was permanently disfigured in an explosion while he was freebasing cocaine. As guitarist Keith Richards of the Rolling Stones said, "I used to know a few guys that did drugs all the time, but they're not alive anymore. . . . And you get the message after you've been to a few funerals."

But what message do fans, especially young fans, get from celebrities who use, and die from, drugs? It's easy to dismiss the celebrity drug deaths as the result of out-of-control excess by spoiled rich people who can't manage their drug use. The drug-related antics of people such as Chris Farley seem so outrageous that we can easily believe we'd never fall into such behavior.

At the same time, celebrity drug users—the ones who are alive—also can serve as models for cool and hip behavior. Many openly admit their drug use on talk shows and say little about the harm drugs are doing to their minds, bodies, and careers. They make snide jokes about their attempts to "get on the wagon." Alcohol and even illicit drug use is a staple of popular movies, where the star characters use these substances to cope with stress, to increase their sex appeal, and to live their lives each day.

Certainly, there are celebrities who have quit using drugs and who use their fame to campaign against drug use, especially by youth. But the overwhelming message that comes from the popular media is one that promotes alcohol and other drug use. What is extraordinary about celebrity drug users is their power to shape popular opinion about drug use and abuse.

- A substance is any natural or synthesized product that has psychoactive effects. The five groups of substances most often leading to substance disorders are (1) central nervous system depressants, including alcohol, barbiturates and benzodiazepines, and inhalants; (2) central nervous system stimulants, including cocaine, amphetamines, nicotine, and caffeine; (3) opioids; (4) hallucinogens and PCP; and (5) cannabis.

- Substance intoxication is indicated by a set of behavioral and psychological changes that occur as a direct result of the physiological effects of a substance on the central nervous system. Substance withdrawal involves a set of physiological and behavioral symptoms that result from the cessation of or reduction in heavy and prolonged use of a substance. The specific symptoms of intoxication and withdrawal depend on the substance being used, the amount of the substance ingested, and the method of ingestion. (Review Table 17.1.)

- Substance abuse is indicated when an individual shows persistent problems in one of four categories: (1) failure to fulfill major role obligations at work, school, or home; (2) substance use in situations in which such use is physically hazardous; (3) substance-related legal problems; and (4) continued substance use despite social or interpersonal problems. (Review Table 17.4.)

- Substance dependence is characterized by a maladaptive pattern of substance use, leading to significant problems in a person's life and usually leading to tolerance to the substance, withdrawal symptoms if the substance is discontinued, and compulsive substance-taking behavior. (Review Table 17.5.)

- The routes of administration that produce rapid and efficient absorption of a substance into the bloodstream (intravenous injection, smoking, snorting) lead to a more intense intoxication, a greater likelihood of dependence, and a greater risk for overdose. Substances that act more rapidly on the central nervous system and whose effects wear off more quickly (such as cocaine) and that lead to faster intoxication are more likely to lead to dependence or abuse.

- At low doses, alcohol produces relaxation and a mild euphoria. At higher doses, it produces the classic signs of depression and cognitive and motor impairment. A large proportion of deaths due to accidents, murders, and suicides are alcohol-related. Alcohol withdrawal symptoms can be mild or so severe as to be life threatening. Alcohol abusers

and dependents experience a wide range of social and interpersonal problems and are at risk for many serious health problems. (Review Table 17.8.)

- Women drink less alcohol than men do in most cultures and are less likely to have alcohol-related problems. Persons of Asian descent typically drink less and thus are less prone to alcohol-related problems. (Review Figures 17.4, 17.5.)

- Benzodiazepines and barbiturates are sold by prescription for the treatment of anxiety and insomnia. One pattern of the development of abuse of or dependence on these substances is reflected by the teenager or young adult who begins using the substances recreationally to produce a sense of well-being or euphoria but then escalates to chronic use and physiological dependence. A second pattern is shown by individuals who begin to use substances under physicians' care for insomnia or anxiety but then escalate their usage without the knowledge of their physicians.

- The inhalants are volatile agents that people sniff to produce a sense of euphoria, disinhibition, and increased aggressiveness or sexual performance. The biggest users and abusers of inhalants are young boys, particularly Native American teenagers and Hispanic teenagers. Inhalants are extremely dangerous, because they can cause permanent brain damage even with casual use, several major diseases, and suffocation when the user goes unconscious with the plastic bag used for inhaling still over his or her head. (Review Table 17.6.)

- Cocaine activates the parts of the brain that register reward and pleasure and produces a sudden rush of euphoria, followed by increased self-esteem, alertness, and energy and a greater sense of competence, creativity, and social acceptability. The user may also experience frightening perceptual changes. The withdrawal symptoms of cocaine include exhaustion, a need for sleep, and depression. The extraordinarily rapid, strong effects of cocaine on the brain's reward centers seem to make this substance more likely than most illicit substances to result in patterns of abuse and dependence. (Review Table 17.9.)

- The amphetamines are readily available by prescription for the treatment of certain disorders but often end up in the black market and used by people to help them keep going through the day or to counteract the effects of depressants or heroin. They can make people feel euphoric, invigorated, self-confident, and gregarious, but they also can make people restless, hypervigilant, anxious, and aggressive and can result in several dangerous physiological symptoms and changes.

- The opioids are a group of substances developed from the juice of the poppy plant. The most commonly used illegal opioid is heroin. The initial symptom of opioid intoxication is euphoria. It is followed by a sense of drowsiness, lethargy, and periods of light sleep. Severe intoxication can lead to respiratory difficulties, unconsciousness, coma, and seizures. The withdrawal symptoms include dysphoria, anxiety, agitation, sensitivity to pain, and craving for more substance. (Review Table 17.10.)

- The hallucinogens, PCP, and cannabis all produce perceptual changes, which include sensory distortions and hallucinations. For some people, these are pleasant experiences, but, for others, they are extremely frightening. Similarly, some people experience a sense of euphoria or relaxation while on these substances, and others become anxious and agitated. (Review Tables 17.11, 17.12.)

- Some common club drugs, in addition to LSD, are ecstasy (3-4 methylenedioxymethamphetamine, or MDMA), GHB (gamma-hydroxybutyrate), ketamine, and rohypnol (flunitrazepam). They have several euphoric and sedative effects and are used by perpetrators of date rape.

- Nicotine is another widely available substance. Smoking tobacco is legal but causes cancer, bronchitis, and coronary heart disease in users and a range of birth defects in the children of women who smoke when pregnant. People can become physiologically dependent on nicotine and undergo difficult withdrawal symptoms when they stop smoking.

- The disease model of alcoholism views alcoholism as a biological disorder in which the individual has no control over his or her drinking and, therefore, must remain abstinent. Other theorists see alcoholism along a continuum of drinking habits, as modifiable through therapy.

- There is evidence that genes play a role in vulnerability to substance-related disorders, through their effects on the synthesis and metabolism of substances. Men genetically predisposed to alcoholism are less sensitive to the effects of low doses of alcohol.

- Some theorists view alcoholism as a form of depression, but the prevailing evidence suggests that alcoholism and depression are distinct disorders.

- Behavioral theories of alcoholism note that people are also reinforced or punished by other people for their alcohol-related behaviors and model the alcohol-related behaviors of important others.

Cognitive theories argue that people who develop alcohol-related problems have strong expectations that alcohol will help them feel better and cope better when they face stressful times. One personality characteristic aassociated with substance use disorders is behavioral undercontrol.

- Gender differences in substance-related disorders may be due to men having more risk factors for substance use and women being more sensitive to the negative consequences of substance use.

- Medications can be used to ease the symptoms of withdrawal from many substances and to reduce cravings for substances. The symptoms of withdrawal from opioids can be so severe that dependents are given the drug methadone to curtail the symptoms as they try to discontinue their heroin use. Methadone also blocks the effects of subsequent doses of heroin, reducing people's desire to obtain heroin. Methadone maintenance programs, which continue to administer methadone to former heroin dependents, are controversial.

- The most common treatment for alcoholism is Alcoholics Anonymous, a self-help group that encourages alcoholics to admit their weaknesses and to call on a higher power and other group members to help them remain completely abstinent from alcohol.

- Behavior therapies based on aversive classical conditioning are sometimes used to treat alcoholism. Alcoholics in these therapies use a drug that makes them ill if they ingest alcohol or use imagery to develop a conditioned aversive response to the sight and smell of alcohol.

- Treatments based on social learning and cognitive theories focus on training alcoholics in more adaptive coping skills and challenging their positive expectations about the effects of alcohol. Many therapists in the cognitive-behavioral tradition reject the disease model of alcoholism and suggest that some alcoholics may learn to engage in controlled social drinking.

MindMap CD-ROM

The following resources on the MindMap CD-ROM that came with this text will help you to master the content of this chapter and prepare for tests:

- Videos: Substance Abuse; Alcohol Addiction; Chemical Basis of Addiction
- Chapter Timelime
- Chapter Quiz

Key Terms

substance 620

drug addicts 620

substance-related disorder 623

substance intoxication 625

substance withdrawal 626

substance abuse 626

substance dependence 626

tolerance 627

blackout 629

alcohol abuse 630

alcohol dependence 630

delirium tremens (DTs) 633

alcohol-induced persisting amnesic disorder 634

Wernicke's encephalopathy 634

Korsakoff's psychosis 634

alcohol-induced dementia 634

fetal alcohol syndrome (FAS) 634

benzodiazepines 636

barbiturates 636

inhalants 637

cocaine 640

amphetamines 641

nicotine 643

caffeine 645

opioids 646

hallucinogens 648

phenylcyclidine (PCP) 649

cannabis 650

disease model 654

harm-reduction model 659

detoxification 659

antagonist drugs 660

naltrexone 660

naloxone 660

disulfiram 660

methadone 661

methadone maintenance programs 661

aversive classical conditioning 661

covert sensitization therapy 661

cue exposure and response prevention 662

abstinence violation effect 664

relapse prevention programs 664

> Chapter 18

Sun and Moon (Subtitled *Starker Traum*) by Paul Klee

All, too, will bear in mind this sacred principle, that though the will of the majority is in all cases to prevail, that will to be rightful must be reasonable; that the minority possess their equal rights, which equal law must protect, and to violate would be oppression.

—Thomas Jefferson, first inaugural address (1801)

Mental Health and the Law <

CHAPTER OVERVIEW

Extraordinary People

- **One Family's Struggle with Schizophrenia and the "System"**

Judgments About People Accused of Crimes

Mental-health professionals are called upon to help determine if accused people are competent to stand trial and if accused people were "sane" at the time the crimes were committed. The insanity defense has undergone many changes in recent history, often in response to its use in high-profile crimes. It is based on the notion that a person who was mentally incapacitated at the time of a crime should not be held responsible for the crime.

Involuntary Commitment and Civil Rights

People can be committed involuntarily to psychiatric facilities if they are gravely disabled by psychological disorders or are imminent dangers to themselves or others. These criteria are difficult to apply accurately and consistently.

Clinicians' Duties to Clients and Society

Some specific duties clinicians have are the duties to provide competent and appropriate treatment; to avoid multiple relationships, especially sexual relationships, with clients; and to protect clients' confidentiality. Client confidentiality can be broken, however, when clients are threatening others or abusing children or elderly people. Clinicians also have a duty to provide ethical service to diverse populations.

Taking Psychology Personally

- **Guidelines for Ethical Service to Culturally Diverse Populations**

Chapter Integration

The law takes a largely biological view of psychological disorders, seeing them as similar to medical diseases. Mental-health professionals, on the other hand, tend to view psychological disorders in a more integrated way, considering the biological, psychological, and social vulnerabilities and circumstances that interact to influence an individual's behavior or mental health.

Extraordinary People

One Family's Struggle with Schizophrenia and the "System"

Greg Bottoms (shown at right), in his disturbing book *Angelhead* (2000), recalls his older brother Michael's descent into severe paranoid schizophrenia and the range of responses he and his family had to Michael's symptoms. This is a story of a family that had no idea what was happening to its eldest son, tried to cope with it on its own, finally got a diagnosis for Michael's symptoms, and then found the mental-health and judicial systems tragically inadequate in helping them cope.

The Bottoms family was newly moved to the suburbs, and the parents worked hard to afford their middle-class existence. The increasingly bizarre and violent behavior of their eldest son was met with restrictions on his freedoms (which he blatantly violated), screaming criticism, and beatings. Nothing would stop his disease, however, and his younger brother, Greg, watched him deteriorate with a mix of horror and fascination (Bottoms, 2000):

> Michael's world started breaking into tiny pieces. He laughed for no reason, nowhere near a punch-line. He said off-color things about death and dying and torture, about corpses and axes and Satan. He would look at a clock to tell the time, but then he'd see the round frame, the glass, the hands red and black, one sweeping, one still, and the actual calculation of time suddenly escaped him, moved just out of reach of his thoughts. (p. 22)
>
> He felt confused these days, once he knew he was outside of his dreams. People—teachers, my mother, his last few remaining friends—would talk to him but then their words would get lost before they reached his mind; it was as if the words would sometimes get caught up in the air, as if the air were heavy, almost solid, and the words, like hard objects, fell to the ground before they reached him. Other times, when the words did reach him, each word was wearing a disguise, each word actually contained the meanings of many words and

how was he to know, how the ——— was he to know, if he could trust the legitimacy, the honesty of this word . . . ? Whenever I encountered him, he would stare at me until I walked out of a room, my heart pounding, a permanent frown on his face. Michael kept to himself—hunched, lonely, looking over his shoulder always. I thought of him as dangerous, someone to lock the door against. (pp. 38–40)

Michael's parents clearly felt completely overwhelmed with him. His father eventually gave up responding to him with violence, in part because he feared violent retribution from Michael, and took to throwing him out of the house on a regular basis. His mother tried to comfort and shield him, which Michael sometimes received with gratitude, but sometimes with derision and psychotic threats on her life:

> My mother, years later when I was badgering her with questions about Michael, told me that he used to hold a lighter up to her face while she drove him to the mall, saying that he would burn her if she didn't give him money, asking her if she knew what God did to stingy cunts. (p. 119)

Michael regularly beat up his younger brothers, Greg and Ron, and threatened the lives of everyone in the family. As much as he feared his brother's violence, however, Greg also suffered from the embarrassment of having a "crazy" brother. Avoidance and denial became a way of life:

Ours was a small Southern town—white colonial homes, churches. Community mattered. Everyone was friendly, even if only for appearances' sake. My mother and father knew the principal, the guidance counselor. These people began to feel sorry for them, concerned, in that administrative way, about Michael's tenuous—and dwindling—ability to function in the world. They would call my parents for conferences. My parents would often cancel, make up some excuse, their shame over their son having become nearly crippling. My own embarrassment over my brother's odd religion was at first debilitating, then simply numbing. . . .

He became the talk of the town, the bad boy who'd lost his mind, because of the Bible toting and random quoting of scripture. He would stop kids on the street, in the school parking lot, in hallways to remind them of their sins and quote scripture. He was a kind of village idiot, our small, all-white, suburban school's one truly great spectacle. (pp. 62–63)

Michael was not diagnosed with schizophrenia until he was in his early twenties. Instead of feeling some sort of relief that they finally had a label and a way of understanding Michael's behavior, his family felt tremendous guilt:

I have an image of my mother staring at the dark world of our kitchen table, saying, I don't know what we're going to do, saying this with no inflection, like the undead talking in a late-night movie. It was February. There was cold, sharp light in the room. A pitiful midday sun made geometric shapes in the color of stained teeth on the kitchen floor. My mother, after hearing the news, barely spoke for days. My father sat in his favorite chair, the TV droning on in front of him, but he wasn't even looking at the screen; he seemed to be looking at the blank wall behind it. It seemed so obvious once I knew—not that he was schizophrenic but that he was definitely severely mentally ill. I had known many "burnouts" or "heads" at school of one degree or another—I was, in a way, one myself—but no one came close to my brother's strangeness. . . .

I knew he was sick. And, most important, I realized for the first time it wasn't his fault. I had blamed Michael, hated Michael, for his behavior. So finding out suddenly, nearly a decade after his first psychotic break, that none of the behavior was entirely his fault, was nearly unbearable, making us all—particularly my father and I—feel immoral and ruthless to such a degree that shame is not a strong enough word. (pp. 92–93)

Unfortunately, Michael's diagnosis did not bring effective treatment. His parents spent all the money they had on doctors and occasional stints in institutions. Michael's symptoms did not respond to the antipsychotic drugs very well, at least when he actually took the medications. He came to believe they were part of a conspiracy to control his mind and usually refused them. He was increasingly violent toward his family members, so, when he lived at home, which was most of the time, his parents and brothers spent much of their time avoiding him. They locked their bedroom doors at night to protect themselves. One day, Michael went after his father and youngest brother with a bat, believing they had been talking about him and deserved to die. They tried everything they could to have him institutionalized but were constantly told that this was not possible unless they could prove he was a danger to himself or others. The stories of Michael's violent behaviors toward the family apparently weren't convincing enough.

Mental-health professionals are regularly asked to help families, such as the Bottoms family, battle the laws guiding the treatment of people with psychological disorders. Following are two other scenarios that raise legal and ethical issues for mental-health practitioners:

> A 60-year-old man wanders the streets as the temperature plummets below freezing, talking to imaginary creatures and stripping off his warm clothes. When asked if he wants shelter or food, he curses and turns away. The police apprehend the man and take him to court. A psychologist is asked to determine whether the man is such a danger to himself that he should be held against his will.

> A middle-aged man kills three people in a shooting rampage. When arrested, he says that he was obeying voices telling him to shoot "sinners." A psychiatrist is asked to evaluate whether this man is telling the truth.

Situations such as these raise fundamental questions about society's values: Do people have the right to conduct their lives as they wish, even if their behaviors pose a risk to their own health and well-being? Under what conditions should people be absolved of responsibility for behaviors that harm others? Should the diagnosis of a psychological disorder entitle a person to special services and protection against discrimination? Questions such as these are concerned with the values of personal freedom, society's obligation to protect its vulnerable members, and society's right to protect itself against the actions of individuals.

Mental-health professionals are increasingly being brought into such situations to help individuals and society make judgments about the appropriate actions to take. It would be nice if mental-health professionals could simply turn to the research literature for objective information that indicates which judgment is best in each situation. Frequently, however, there is no research literature relevant to a situation, or the research holds conflicting messages. Moreover, at its best, research can tell us only what is *likely* to be right or true in a given situation but not what is *definitely* right or true. That is, the predictions

we can make from the research literature are *probabilistic*—they tell us how likely people are to do something but not that they definitely will do something. Also, we are limited in our ability to generalize from the research literature to individual cases. Finally, because most of such judgments involve conflicts between different values, ethical principles, or moral principles, research and clinical judgment can tell us only so much about the right resolution.

This chapter is about the interface between psychology and the law. Because the law has tended to regard at least some psychological disorders as medical illnesses or diseases, the phrase **mentally ill** is used throughout this chapter. Most previous chapters did not use this term because it connotes a medical view of psychological problems, which is only one of several ways to view psychological problems. We will see, however, that the law is inconsistent in its view of psychological disorders, and this view has changed quite frequently.

We first examine how the law regards people charged with crimes who might have psychological disorders. Mental-health professionals help legal authorities decide when people's psychological disorders make them incompetent to stand trial and when they should be considered not guilty by reason of insanity. Then, we discuss when a person can be held in a mental-health facility against his or her will. Over the past 50 years, the criteria for commitment and the rights of committed patients have changed greatly. Finally, we discuss certain duties that courts and professional organizations have argued clinicians have toward clients and society: the duty to provide competent treatment, the duty to avoid multiple relationships with clients, the duty to maintain clients' confidentiality, the duty to protect persons their clients are threatening to harm, the duty to report suspected child or elder abuse, and the duty to provide ethical service to diverse populations.

JUDGMENTS ABOUT PEOPLE ACCUSED OF CRIMES

Two critical judgments that mental-health professionals are asked to make about people accused of crimes are *whether they are competent to stand trial* and *whether they were sane at the time the crimes were committed*. Mental-health professionals actually do not make the final judgments about the dispensation of people accused of crimes. Instead, they only make recommendations to the court. Their recommendations can be influential in judges' or juries' decisions, however.

Competence to Stand Trial

One of the fundamental principles of law is that, in order to stand trial, accused individuals must have a rational understanding of the charges against them and the proceedings of the trial and must be able to participate in their defense. People who do not have an understanding of what is happening to them in a courtroom and who cannot participate in their own defense are said to be **incompetent to stand trial.** Incompetence may involve impairment in several capacities, including the capacity to understand information, to think rationally about alternative courses of action, to make good choices, and to appreciate one's situation as a criminal defendant (Hoge, Bonnie, et al., 1997).

Impaired competence may be a common problem: Defense attorneys suspect impaired competence in their clients in up to 10 percent of cases. Although only a handful of these clients are referred for formal evaluation, between 24,000 and 60,000 evaluations of criminal defendants for competence to stand trial are performed every year in the United States (MacArthur Research Network on Mental Health and the Law, 1998). Competence judgments are, thus, some of the most frequent types of judgments that mental-health professionals are asked to make for courts. Judges appear to value the testimony of mental-health experts concerning defendants' competence and rarely rule against the experts' recommendations.

As a result, the consequences of competence judgments for defendants are great. If they are judged incompetent, trials are postponed as long as there is reason to believe that they will become competent in the foreseeable future, and defendants

Competence to stand trial is one of the most common judgments psychologists are asked to help courts make.

may be forced to receive treatment. Incompetent defendants who are wrongly judged competent may not contribute adequately to their defense and may be wrongly convicted and incarcerated. Defendants who are suspected to be incompetent are described by their attorneys as much less helpful in establishing the facts of their case and much less actively involved in making decisions about their defense (MacArthur Research Network on Mental Health and the Law, 1998).

Not surprisingly, defendants with long histories of psychiatric problems, particularly schizophrenia or psychotic symptoms, are more likely to be referred for competence evaluations (Nicholson & Kugler, 1991). Defendants referred for competence evaluations also tend to have lower levels of education and to be poor, unemployed, and unmarried. Over half have been accused of violent offenses. Women are more likely than men, and members of ethnic minority groups are more likely than European Americans, to be judged incompetent (Nicholson & Kugler, 1991). This may be because women and ethnic minority persons who commit crimes are more likely to have severe psychological problems that make them incompetent to stand trial. On the other hand, evaluators may have lower thresholds for judging women and ethnic minorities incompetent. In addition, when evaluators do not speak the same languages as ethnic minority defendants, the defendants may not understand the evaluators' questions, and evaluators may not understand the defendants' answers. In these instances, evaluators may tend to interpret this lack of communication as an indication of defendants' incompetence to stand trial.

Psychologists have developed tests of cognitive abilities important to following legal proceedings, and people who perform poorly on these tests are more likely to be judged incompetent to stand trial. These tests have not been widely used, however. Instead, judgments of incompetence are usually given to people who have existing diagnoses of psychotic disorders or who have symptoms indicating severe psychopathology, such as gross disorientation, delusions, hallucinations, and thought disorder (Cochrane, et al., 2001).

Insanity Defense

Insanity is a legal term, rather than a psychological or medical term, and it has been defined in various ways. All of these definitions reflect the fundamental doctrine that people cannot be held fully responsible for their acts if they were so mentally incapacitated at the time of the acts that they could not conform to the rules of society. Note that people do not have to be chronically insane for the insanity defense to apply. They only have to be judged to have been insane at the time they committed the acts. This judgment can be difficult to make.

The **insanity defense** has been one of the most controversial applications of psychology to the law. The lay public often thinks of the insanity defense as a means by which guilty people "get off." When the insanity defense has been used successfully in celebrated cases, as when John Hinckley successfully used this defense after shooting for-

John Hinckley was judged not guilty by reason of insanity for shooting President Ronald Reagan. This judgment inspired a reappraisal of the insanity defense.

mer President Ronald Reagan and the president's press secretary, Jim Brady, in 1981, there have been calls to eliminate the insanity defense altogether (Steadman et al., 1993). Indeed, these celebrated cases have often led to reappraisals of the insanity defense and redefinitions of the legal meaning of insanity.

The insanity defense is used much less often than the public tends to think. As is shown in Table 18.1, fewer than 1 in 100 defendants in felony cases file an insanity plea, and of these, only 26 percent result in acquittal (Silver, Cirincione, & Steadman, 1994). Thus, only about 1 in 400 people charged with a felony are judged not guilty by reason of insanity. About two-thirds of these people have diagnoses of schizophrenia, and most have histories of psychiatric hospitalizations and previous crimes (McGreevy, Steadman, & Callahan, 1991).

Almost 90 percent of the people who are acquitted after pleading the insanity defense are male, and two-thirds of them are White (McGreevy et al., 1991; Warren et al., 2004). The reasons men and Whites are more likely to plead the insanity defense successfully are unclear but may have to do with their greater access to competent attorneys who can effectively argue the insanity defense. In the past decade or two, as society has become more aware of the plight of abused and battered women, increasing numbers of women are pleading the insanity defense after injuring or killing partners who had been abusing them for years.

TABLE 18.1 Comparison of Public Perceptions of the Insanity Defense with Actual Use and Results

The public perceives that many more accused persons use the insanity defense successfully than is actually the case.

	Public Perception	Reality
Percentage of felony indictments for which an insanity plea is made	37%	1%
Percentage of insanity pleas resulting in "not guilty by reason of insanity"	44%	26%
Percentage of persons "not guilty by reason of insanity" sent to mental hospitals	51%	85%
Percentage of persons "not guilty by reason of insanity" set free	26%	15%
Conditional release		12%
Outpatient treatment		3%
Unconditional release		1%
Length of confinement of persons "not guilty by reason of insanity" (in months)		
All crimes	21.8	32.5
Murder		76.4

Source: Data from Silver et al., 1994.

Christopher Pittman argued that Zoloft led him to kill his grandparents, but a jury rejected this defense.

Andrea Yates argued that severe psychosis and postpartum depression led her to drown her five young children in 2001. Her argument was denied and she was convicted of murder.

One case is that of Lorena and John Bobbitt. According to Lorena Bobbitt, her husband, John, had sexually and emotionally abused her for years. One night in 1994, John returned home drunk and raped Lorena. In what her attorneys described as a brief psychotic episode, Lorena cut off her husband's penis and threw it away. She was acquitted of charges of malicious injury by reason of temporary insanity. She was referred to a mental institution for further evaluation and released a few months later.

Another controversial application of the insanity defense by women has been its use by women who have committed infanticide, supposedly as the result of psychotic postpartum depression (Williamson, 1993). Severe postpartum depression with psychotic symptoms is very rare, and violence by these women against their newborns is even more rare (Nolen-Hoeksema, 1990). When such violence does occur, some courts have accepted that the mothers' behaviors were the result of the postpartum psychosis and have judged these women not guilty by reason of insanity. Often, however, the public cannot accept any excuse for a woman killing her own children and rejects the insanity defense in cases of postpartum depression.

Most recently, a version of the insanity defense referred to as the "Zoloft defense" has been used to argue that the antidepressant Zoloft can cause people to suddenly commit violent acts that are out of their control. In one case, 12-year-old Christopher Pittman shot both his grandparents, then burned their house down. His defense was that Zoloft had caused him to become violent and lose control. In February 2005, however, jurors rejected this defense and convicted Pittman of the crime.

Even when a defendant is judged not guilty by reason of insanity, it usually is not the case that he or she "gets off." Of those people acquitted because of insanity, about 85 percent are sent to mental hospitals, and all but 1 percent are put under some type of supervision and care. Of those who are sent to mental hospitals, the average length of stay (or incarceration) in the hospital is almost three years when all types of crimes are considered, and over six years for those who had been accused (and acquitted by reason of insanity) of murder. John Hinckley, who shot former President Reagan in 1981, has been incarcerated in St. Elizabeth's Hospital ever since he was found not guilty by reason of insanity. Some states require that people judged not guilty by reason of insanity cannot be incarcerated in mental institutions for longer than they would have served prison sentences if they had been judged guilty of their crimes, but not all states have this rule. In short, there is little evidence that the insanity defense is widely used to help people avoid incarceration for their crimes.

TABLE 18.2	Concept Overview

Insanity Defense Rules

Five rules have been used for determining whether an individual was insane at the time he or she committed the crime and therefore whether he or she should not be held responsible for the crime.

Rule	The Individual Is Not Held Responsible for a Crime If . . .
M'Naghten rule	At the time of the crime, the individual was so affected by a disease of the mind that he or she did not know the nature of the act he or she was committing or did not know it was wrong.
Irresistible impulse rule	At the time of the crime, the individual was driven by an irresistible impulse to perform the act or had a diminished capacity to resist performing the act.
Durham rule	The crime was a product of a mental disease or defect.
ALI rule	At the time of the crime, as a result of a mental disease or defect, the person lacked substantial capacity either to appreciate the criminality (wrongfulness) of the act or to conform his or her conduct to the law.
American Psychiatric Association definition of insanity	At the time of the crime, as a result of mental disease or mental retardation, the person was unable to appreciate the wrongfulness of his or her conduct.

Insanity Defense Rules

Five rules have been used in modern history to evaluate defendants' pleas that they should be judged not guilty by reason of insanity (see the Concept Overview in Table 18.2).

M'Naghten Rule The first insanity defense rule is the **M'Naghten rule.** Daniel M'Naghten lived in England in the mid-1800s and had the delusion that the English Tory party was persecuting him. He set out to kill the Tory prime minister but mistakenly shot the prime minister's secretary. At his trial, the jury judged M'Naghten not guilty by reason of insanity. There was a public outcry at this verdict, leading the House of Lords to formalize a rule for when a person could be absolved from responsibility for his or her acts because of a mental disorder. This rule became known as the M'Naghten rule, and it still is used in many jurisdictions today:

> To establish a defense on the ground of insanity, it must be clearly proved that at the time of committing the act, the party accused was labouring under such a defect of reason, from disease of the mind, as not to know the nature and quality of the act he was doing, or if he did know it, that he did not know he was doing what was wrong.

The M'Naghten rule reflects the doctrine that a person must have a "guilty mind"—in Latin, *mens rea*—or the intention to commit the illegal act in order to be held responsible for the act.

It might seem that applying the M'Naghten rule is a straightforward matter—one simply determines whether a person suffers from a disease of the mind and whether during the crime he or she understood that his or her actions were wrong. Unfortunately, it is not that simple. A major problem in applying the M'Naghten rule emerges in determining what is meant by a "disease of the mind." The law has been unclear and inconsistent in what disorders it recognizes as diseases of the mind. The most consistently recognized diseases are psychoses. It has been relatively easy for the courts and the public to accept that someone experiencing severe delusions and hallucinations is suffering from a disease and, at times, may not know right from wrong. However, defendants have argued that several other disorders, such as alcoholism, severe depression, and posttraumatic stress disorder, are diseases of the mind that impair judgments of right and wrong. It is much more difficult for courts, the lay public, and mental-health professionals to agree on these claims.

A second major problem is that the M'Naghten rule requires that a person did not know right from wrong at the time of the crime in order to be judged not guilty by reason of insanity. This is a difficult judgment to make, because it is a retrospective judgment. Even when everyone agrees that a defendant suffers from a severe psychological disorder, this does not necessarily mean that, at the time of the crime, he or she was incapable of knowing "right from wrong" as the M'Naghten rule requires. For example, serial killer Jeffrey Dahmer, who tortured, killed, dismembered, and ate his victims, clearly seemed to have a psychological disorder. Nevertheless, the jury denied his insanity defense in part because he took great care to hide his crimes from the local police, suggesting that he knew what he was doing was wrong or against the law.

Irresistible Impulse Rule The second rule used to judge the acceptability of the insanity defense is the **irresistible impulse rule.** First applied in Ohio in 1934, the irresistible impulse rule broadened the conditions under which a criminal act could be considered the product of insanity to include "acts of passion." Even if a person knew the act he or she was committing was wrong, if the person was driven by an irresistible impulse to perform the act or had a diminished capacity to resist performing the act, then he or she might be absolved of responsibility for performing the act.

One of the most celebrated applications of the notion of diminished capacity was the "Twinkie Defense" of Dan White. In 1979, Dan White assassinated San Francisco mayor George Moscone and a city council member named Harvey Milk. White argued that he had had diminished capacity to resist the impulse to shoot Moscone and Milk due to the psychological effects of extreme stress and the consumption of large amounts of junk food. Using a particularly broad definition of diminished capacity in force in California law at the time, the jury convicted White of manslaughter instead of first-degree murder. Variations of the Twinkie Defense have rarely been attempted since White's trial.

Durham Rule In 1954, Judge David Bazelon further broadened the criteria for the legal definition of insanity in his ruling on the case *Durham v. United States*, which produced the third rule for defining insanity, the **Durham rule.** According to the Durham rule, the insanity defense could be accepted for any crimes that were the "product of mental disease or mental defect." This rule allowed defendants to claim that the presence of any disorder recognized by mental-health professionals could be the "cause" of their crimes. The Durham rule did not require that defendants show they were incapacitated by their disorders or that they

did not understand that their acts were illegal. The Durham rule had been dropped by almost all jurisdictions by the early 1970s.

ALI Rule The fourth rule for deciding the acceptability of the insanity defense comes from the American Law Institute's Model Penal Code. Motivated by dissatisfaction with the existing legal definitions of insanity, a group of lawyers, judges, and scholars associated with the American Law Institute (ALI) worked to formulate a better definition, which eventually resulted in what is known as the **ALI rule:**

> A person is not responsible for criminal conduct if at the time of such conduct as the result of mental disease or defect he lacks substantial capacity either to appreciate the criminality (wrongfulness) of his conduct or to conform his conduct to the requirements of the law.

This rule is broader than the M'Naghten rule, because it requires only that the defendant have a lack of appreciation of the criminality of his or her act, not an absence of understanding of the criminality of the act. The defendant's inability to conform his or her conduct to the requirements of the law can come from the emotional symptoms of a psychological disorder, as well as from the cognitive deficits caused by the disorder. This expanded understanding incorporates some of the crimes recognized by the irresistible impulse rule. The ALI rule is clearly more restrictive than the Durham rule, however, because it requires some lack of appreciation of the criminality of one's act, rather than merely the presence of a mental disorder. The ALI rule further restricts the types of mental disorders that can contribute to a successful insanity defense:

> As used in this Article, the term "mental disease or defect" does not include an abnormality manifested only by repeated criminal or otherwise antisocial conduct.

This further restriction prohibits defense attorneys from arguing that a defendant's long history of antisocial acts is itself evidence of the presence of a mental disease or defect. Further, in 1977, in the case *Barrett v. United States*, it was ruled that "temporary insanity created by voluntary use of alcohol or drugs" also does not qualify a defendant for acquittal by reason of insanity.

The ALI rule was widely adopted in the United States, including in the jurisdiction in which John Hinckley was tried for shooting Ronald Reagan. Hinckley had a long-standing diagnosis of schizophrenia and an obsession with actress Jodi Foster. Letters he wrote to Foster before shooting Reagan indicated that he committed the act under the delusion that this would impress Foster and cause her to return his love. Hinckley's defense attorneys successfully argued that he had had a diminished capacity to understand the wrongfulness of shooting Reagan or to conform his behaviors to the requirements of the law. The public outcry over the judgment that Hinckley was "not guilty by reason of insanity" initiated another reappraisal of the legal definition of insanity and the use of the insanity defense (Steadman et al., 1993).

American Pyschiatric Association Definition
The reappraisal led to the fifth legal redefinition of insanity in the **Insanity Defense Reform Act,** put into law by Congress in 1984. The Insanity Defense Reform Act adopted the **American Psychiatric Association definition of insanity** in 1983. This definition dropped the provision in the ALI rule that absolved people of responsibility for criminal acts if they were unable to conform their behavior to the law and retained the wrongfulness criterion initially proposed in the M'Naghten rule. This definition reads as follows:

> A person charged with a criminal offense should be found not guilty by reason of insanity if it is shown that, as a result of mental disease or mental retardation, he was unable to appreciate the wrongfulness of his conduct at the time of his offense.

This definition now applies in all cases tried in federal courts and in about half the states. Also, as a result of the Hinckley verdict, most states now require that a defendant pleading not guilty by reason of insanity prove he or she was insane at the time of the crime. Previously, the burden of proof had been on the prosecution to prove that the defendant was sane at the time the crime was committed (Steadman et al., 1993).

Problems with the Insanity Defense
Mental-health professionals tend to be strong proponents of the notion that psychological disorders can impair people's ability to follow the law. They believe that this should be taken into consideration when judging an individual's responsibility for his or her actions. Cases that are built on the insanity defense often use mental-health professionals to provide expert opinions in such cases. Despite their expertise, mental-health professionals often disagree about the nature and causes of psychological disorders, the presence or absence of psycho-

logical disorders, and the evaluation of defendants' states of mind at the time crimes were committed (Warren et al., 2004). Usually, lawyers on both sides of the case find mental-health professionals who support their point of view, and the two professionals are inevitably in disagreement with each other. This disagreement leads to confusion for judges, juries, and the public.

Mental-health professionals have also raised concerns about the rules used to determine the acceptability of the insanity defense. Behind these rules is the assumption that most people, including most people with psychological disorders, have free will and can usually choose how they will act in any given situation. Many current models of both normal and abnormal behavior suggest that people are not that much in control of their behaviors. Because of biological predispositions, early life experiences, or disordered patterns of thinking, people often act in irrational and perhaps uncontrolled ways. This view makes it more difficult to say when a person should or should not be held responsible for his or her behaviors.

Guilty but Mentally Ill
In a sixth, and most recent, reform of the insanity defense, some states have adopted as an alternative to the verdict "not guilty by reason of insanity" the verdict **guilty but mentally ill (GBMI).** Defendants convicted as guilty but mentally ill are incarcerated for the normal terms designated for their crimes, with the expectation that they will also receive treatment for their mental illness. Proponents of the GBMI verdict argue that it recognizes the mental illness of defendants while still holding them responsible for their actions. Critics argue that the GBMI verdict is essentially a guilty verdict and a means of eliminating the insanity defense (Tanay, 1992). In addition, juries may believe they are ensuring that a person gets treatment by judging him or her guilty but mentally ill, but there are no guarantees that a person convicted under GBMI will receive treatment. In most states, it is left up to legal authorities to decide whether to incarcerate these people in mental institutions or prisons and, if they are sent to prisons, whether to provide them with treatment for their mental illness.

SUMMING UP
- One judgment mental-health professionals are asked to make is about an accused person's competence to stand trial.
- Another judgment is whether the accused person was "sane" at the time he or she committed a crime.

- The insanity defense has undergone many changes over recent history, often in response to its use in high-profile crimes.

- Five rules have been used to evaluate the acceptability of a plea of not guilty by reason of insanity: the M'Naghten rule, the irresistible impulse rule, the Durham rule, the ALI rule, and the American Psychiatric Association definition of insanity.

- All of these rules require that a defendant be diagnosed with a "mental disease" but do not clearly define the term *mental disease.*

- Most of these rules also require that the defendant is unable to understand the criminality of his or her actions or conform his or her actions to the law in order to be judged not guilty by reason of insanity.

- Many states have introduced the alternative verdict of guilty but mentally ill.

INVOLUNTARY COMMITMENT AND CIVIL RIGHTS

In the best circumstances, people who need treatment for psychological disorders seek it themselves. They work with mental-health professionals to find the medication and/or psychotherapy that helps reduce their symptoms and keeps their disorder under control; however, many people who have serious psychological problems do not recognize their need for treatment or may refuse treatment for a variety of reasons. For example, a woman with persecutory delusions and hallucinations may fear treatment, believing that doctors are part of the conspiracy against her. A man in a manic episode may like many of the symptoms he is experiencing—the high energy, inflated self-esteem, and grandiose thoughts—and not want to take medication that would reduce these symptoms. A teenager who is abusing illegal drugs may believe that it is her right to do so and that there is nothing wrong with her. Can these people be forced into mental institutions and to undergo treatment against their will? These are the questions we address in this section.

Civil Commitment

Prior to 1969, in the United States the **need for treatment** was sufficient cause to hospitalize people against their will and force them to undergo treatment. Such involuntary hospitalization is called **civil commitment.** All that was needed for civil commitment was a certificate signed by two physicians, stating that a person needed treatment and was not agreeing to it voluntarily. The person could then be confined, often indefinitely, without

the advice of an attorney, a hearing, or an appeal. In Great Britain and several other countries around the world, need for treatment still is one criterion for civil commitment.

Since 1969, however, the need for treatment alone is no longer sufficient legal cause for civil commitment in most states in the United States. This change came about as part of the patients' rights movement of the 1960s, in which concerns were raised about the personal freedom and civil liberties of mental patients (see Chapter 5). Opponents of the civil commitment process argued that it allowed people to be incarcerated simply for having "alternative lifestyles" or different political or moral values (Szasz, 1963a, 1977). Certainly, there were many cases in the former Soviet Union and other countries of political dissidents being labeled mentally ill and in need of treatment and then being incarcerated in prisons for years. In the United States, there also were disturbing cases of the misuse of civil commitment proceedings. For example, Mrs. E. P. W. Packard was one of several women involuntarily hospitalized by their husbands for holding "unacceptable" and "sick" political or moral views (Weiner & Wettstein, 1993). Mrs. Packard remained hospitalized for three years until she won her release and then began crusading against civil commitment.

Criteria for Involuntary Commitment

The three criteria currently used in the United States and in many other countries to commit someone to a psychiatric facility against his or her will are (1) grave disability, (2) dangerousness to self, and (3) dangerousness to others (see the Concept Overview in Table 18.3 on page 686). In addition, most states require that the danger people pose to themselves or to others be *imminent*—if they are not immediately incarcerated, they or someone else will likely be harmed in the very near future. Finally, all persons committed to psychiatric facilities must be diagnosed with mental disorders.

Grave Disability The **grave disability** criterion requires that people be so incapacitated by mental disorders that they cannot care for their basic needs for food, clothing, and shelter. This criterion is, in theory, much more severe than the need for treatment criterion, because it requires that the person's survival be in immediate danger due to illness. At least 30 states in the United States use the grave disability criterion in civil commitment hearings, and, in those states, about 80 percent of persons involuntarily committed are committed on the basis of grave disability (Turkheimer & Parry, 1992).

TABLE 18.3	Concept Overview

Criteria for Involuntary Commitment

Three criteria are currently used to determine if an individual can be involuntarily committed to a mental-health facility.

Criteria	Description
Grave disability	The individual is so incapacitated by a mental disorder that he or she cannot care for the basic needs for food, clothing, and shelter.
Dangerousness to self	The individual is an imminent danger to him- or herself.
Dangerousness to others	The individual presents an imminent danger to others.

One might think that the grave disability criterion could be used to hospitalize homeless people on the streets who appear to be psychotic and do not seem able to take care of their basic needs. This is what former New York mayor Ed Koch thought in the bitter winter of 1988, when he invoked the legal principle of *parens patriae* (sovereign as parent) to have mentally ill homeless people picked up from the streets of New York and taken to mental-health facilities. Mayor Koch argued that it was the city's duty to protect these mentally ill homeless people from the ravages of the winter weather, because they were unable to do it for themselves. One of the homeless people who was involuntarily taken to a psychiatric facility was 40-year-old Joyce Brown, who was subsequently given a diagnosis of paranoid schizophrenia. Brown had been living on the streets on and off for years, despite efforts by her family to get her into psychiatric treatment. She refused treatment of any kind. When Brown was involuntarily hospitalized in the winter of 1988 as part of Koch's campaign, she and the American Civil Liberties Union contested her commitment and won her release on the grounds that the city had no right to incarcerate Brown if she had no intention of being treated.

One of the legal precedents of Joyce Brown's release was *Donaldson v. O'Connor* (1975). Kenneth Donaldson had been committed to a Florida state hospital for 14 years. Donaldson's father had originally had him committed, believing that Donaldson was delusional and therefore a danger to himself. At the time, Florida law allowed people to be committed if their mental disorders might impair their ability to manage their finances or to protect themselves against being cheated by others. Throughout his hospitalization, Donaldson refused medication, because it violated his Christian Science beliefs. The superintendent, O'Connor, considered this refusal

to be a symptom of Donaldson's mental disorder. Even though Donaldson had been caring for himself adequately before his hospitalization and had friends who offered to help care for him if he was released from the hospital, O'Connor and the hospital continually refused Donaldson's requests for release. Donaldson sued, on the grounds that he had received only custodial care during his hospitalization and that he was not a danger to himself. He requested to be released to the care of his friends and family. The Supreme Court agreed and ruled that "a State cannot constitutionally confine . . . a nondangerous individual, who is capable of surviving safely in freedom by himself or with the help of willing and responsible family and friends."

In practice, however, most persons involuntarily committed because of grave disability do not have the American Civil Liberties Union championing their rights or the personal wherewithal to file suit. Often, these are people with few financial resources, friends, or families who have long histories of serious mental illness. The elderly mentally ill are especially likely to be committed because of grave disability (Turkheimer & Parry, 1992). Often, these people are committed to psychiatric facilities because there are not enough less restrictive treatment facilities available in their communities, and their families do not have the ability to care for them.

Dangerousness to Self The criterion of **dangerousness to self** is most often invoked when it is believed that a person is imminently suicidal. In such cases, the person is often held in an inpatient psychiatric facility for a few days while undergoing further evaluation and possibly treatment. Most states allow short-term commitments without a court hearing in emergency situations such as this. All that is needed is a certification by the attending mental-health professionals that the individual is in imminent danger to him- or herself. If the mental-health professionals judge that the person needs further treatment but the person does not voluntarily agree to treatment, they can go to court to ask that the person be committed for a longer period of time.

Dangerousness to Others The third criterion under which people can be committed involuntarily is **dangerousness to others**. If a mentally ill person is going to hurt another if set free, society has claimed the right to protect itself against this person by holding the person against his or her will. This action may seem completely justified, yet the appropriateness of this criterion rests on predictions of who will be dangerous and who will not. Some research has suggested that predictions of dangerousness tend to be wrong more often than they are correct (McNiel & Binder, 1991; Monahan & Walker, 1990). As a tragic example, serial killer Jeffrey Dahmer was arrested and jailed in 1988 for sexually molesting a 13-year-old boy. He was released in 1990 with only a limited follow-up by mental-health professionals, despite concerns raised by his family about his mental health. Dahmer proceeded to drug, molest, kill, and dismember at least 17 additional victims over the next few years before being apprehended.

Several states have adopted special laws concerning sex offenders, such as Dahmer (Winick, 2003). Under these laws, repeat offenders can be labeled "sexually violent predators" and can be kept in confinement even after their prison terms have been served. In 1997, the U.S. Supreme Court upheld the Kansas version of the sexual predator law, finding that the defendant in this case, who had committed sexual crimes against children, had a sufficient mental condition to authorize involuntary psychiatric hospitalization. All 50 states have some form of registration and community notification laws, in which sex offenders must register with the police and the communities where they live must be notified of their existence. Thus, our laws and society see sex offenders as especially dangerous and impose more constraints on their freedoms.

Violence Among People with Mental Disorders

Are people with psychological disorders more likely to be violent than people without disorders? Research suggests that there is some increased risk, particularly among people with substance abuse disorders, personality disorders, or schizophrenic disorders (Arseneault et al., 2000; Banks et al., 2004; Monahan & Steadman, 2001).

One ethical question facing society is whether it has an obligation to provide mental-health services to people who cannot take care of themselves.

Serial killer Jeffrey Dahmer clearly had psychological problems, but mental-health professionals did not foresee the terrible crimes he would commit.

In one major study, researchers followed 1,136 men and women with mental disorders for one year after being discharged from a psychiatric hospital, monitoring their own self-reports of violent behaviors, reports in police and hospital records, and reports by other informants, such as family members (Steadman et al., 1998). Their records of violent activity were compared with those of 519 people living in the same neighborhoods in which the former patients resided after their hospital discharge. The community group was interviewed only once, at the end of the year-long study, and asked about violent behavior in the past 10 weeks. Serious violent acts were defined as battery that resulted in physical injury, sexual assaults, assaultive acts that involved the use of a weapon, and threats made with a weapon in hand.

The likelihood that the former patients would commit a violent act was strongly related to their diagnosis and whether they had a substance abuse problem. About 18 percent of the former patients who had a diagnosis of a major mental disorder (e.g., schizophrenia, major depression, other psychotic disorder) *without* a history of substance abuse committed a serious violent act in the year following discharge, compared with 31 percent of those with a major mental disorder *and* a history of substance abuse, and 43 percent of those with a diagnosis of an "other" mental disorder (i.e., a personality or adjustment disorder) *and* a co-occurring substance abuse problem. The researchers were somewhat surprised to find that the former patients were most likely to commit a violent act in the first couple of months following their discharge and were less likely to do so as the year wore on (see Figure 18.1). They suggested that patients may still be in crisis shortly after their hospitalization, and it takes some months for social support systems and treatment to begin to affect their behavior.

The rate of violence in the community sample was also strongly related to whether individuals had a history of substance abuse: 11 percent of those with a substance abuse problem committed a violent act during the year of the study, compared with 3 percent of those with no substance abuse problem. Although the overall rate of violence in the community sample was lower than in the patient sample, this difference was statistically significant only when the researchers considered violence by the former patients shortly after their discharge. At the end of that year, the former patients were no more likely to commit a violent act than the community comparison group.

The targets of violence by both the former patients and the community comparisons were most often family members, followed by friends and acquaintances. The former patients were actually somewhat less likely than the comparison group to commit a violent act against a stranger (13.8 percent of the acts committed by former patients versus 22.2 percent of acts committed by the comparison group).

The rates of violence committed in this study may seem high, for both the patient group and the comparison group. The patient group probably represented people with more serious psychological disorders, who were facing acute crises in their lives. The comparison group was largely from low socioeconomic backgrounds and in impoverished neighborhoods. These contextual factors may account for the relatively high rate of violence.

The researchers who conducted this study emphasized that their data show how inappropriate it is to consider "former mental patients" a homogeneous group of people who are all prone to violence. The presence of substance abuse problems was a strong predictor of violent behavior both in this group and in a group of people who had not been mental patients. Moreover, the majority of people with serious mental disorders did not commit any violent acts in the year after their discharge, particularly against random strangers, as media depictions of "former mental patients" often suggest.

Other research has suggested that violence by mentally ill women tends to be *underestimated* by clinicians (Coontz, Lidz, & Mulvey, 1994; Robbins, Monahan, & Silver, 2003). Clinicians do not expect mentally ill women to be violent to the same degree that they expect mentally ill men to be violent. As a result, they do not probe mentally ill women for evidence regarding violence as much as they probe mentally ill men. In reality, however, mentally ill women are as likely to commit violent acts toward others as are mentally ill men (Robbins et al., 2003).

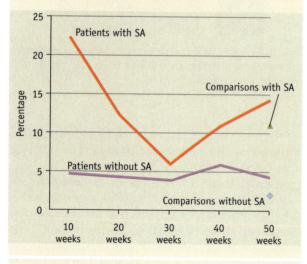

FIGURE 18.1   **Likelihood of Violence.** The lines represent the percentage of patients with or without a substance abuse problem, and the points represent community comparisons with or without a substance abuse problem, who committed a violent act in the previous 10 weeks, in this study.

Source: Steadman et al., 1998.

The victims of mentally ill women's violent acts are most likely to be family members; mentally ill men also are most often violent toward family members, but they commit violent acts against strangers more often than do mentally ill women (Newhill, Mulvey, & Lidz, 1995). Mentally ill men who commit violence are more likely to have been drinking before the violence, and to be arrested, compared with mentally ill women who commit violence (Robbins et al., 2003).

Racial stereotypes lead people to expect that mentally ill persons from ethnic minority groups are more likely to commit acts of violence than are White mentally ill people. There are, however, no differences among the ethnic groups in rates of violence among mentally ill people (Mulvey, 1995). Thus, new research is clarifying the true rates of violence among the mentally ill and some predictors of violence in this group.

Prevalence of Involuntary Commitment

How often are people involuntarily committed to a psychiatric facility? There are sparse data to answer this question, but the available studies suggest that about one in four admissions to inpatient psychiatric facilities in the United States are involuntary, and about 15 to 20 percent of inpatient admissions in European countries are involuntary (Monahan et al., 1999). Admissions to state and county mental hospitals are much more likely to be involuntary than admissions to other types of hospitals (see Table 18.4).

These numbers probably underestimate the number of people coerced into mental-health care, because parents and legal guardians often "volunteer" a protesting child or an incompetent adult for admission (Monahan et al., 1999). One study found that nearly half of the adults admitted voluntarily to inpatient psychiatric facilities said that someone other than they had initiated their going to the hospital, and 14 percent of the patients were under the custody of someone else at the time they were admitted (Hoge, Poythress et al., 1997; see also Segal, Laurie, & Fanskoviak, 2004). Nearly 40 percent of the legally voluntary patients believed they would have been involuntarily committed if they had not "volunteered" to be hospitalized. Some of the patients felt they had been coerced by their own therapists, who did not include them in the admissions process (Monahan et al., 1999):

I talked to him this morning. I said, "You . . . didn't even listen to me. You . . . call yourself a counselor. . . . Why did you decide to do this instead of . . . try to listen to me and under-

VOICES

stand . . . what I was going through." And he said, "Well, it doesn't matter, you know, you're going anyway." . . . He didn't listen to what I had to say. . . . He didn't listen to the situation. . . . He had decided before he ever got to the house . . . that I was coming up here. Either I come freely or the officers would have to subdue me and bring me in.

Patients involuntarily committed often may need treatment that they cannot acknowledge they need. About half of patients who feel coerced into treatment eventually acknowledge that they needed treatment, but about half continue to believe they did not need treatment (Gardner et al., 1999).

Procedurally, most states mandate that persons being considered for involuntary commitment have the right to a public hearing, the right to counsel, the right to call and confront witnesses, the right to appeal decisions, and the right to be placed in the least restrictive treatment setting. In practice, however, attorneys and judges typically defer to the judgment of mental-health professionals about a person's mental illness and meeting of the criteria for commitment (Turkheimer & Parry, 1992). Thus, even the attorneys who are supposed to be upholding an individual's rights tend to acquiesce to the judgment of mental-health professionals, particularly if the attorney is court-appointed, as is often the case. Again, it appears that many attorneys who

TABLE 18.4	Frequency of Involuntary Admissions to Psychiatric Facilities

These data reveal the percentage of all admissions to various types of psychiatric facilities that involve involuntary commitments. Data are from the United States in 1986.

Type of Facility	Percentage of All Admissions That Are Involuntary
State and county hospitals	61.6
Multiservice mental-health organizations (e.g., community mental-health centers)	46.1
Private psychiatric hospitals	15.6
Nonfederal general hospitals	14.8
Veterans Administration hospitals	5.6

Source: Monahan et al., 2001.

are going along with the commitment of their clients are doing so because they believe the clients need treatment and that there are not enough facilities in the community to provide this treatment (Turkheimer & Parry, 1992).

Civil Rights

People who have been committed to a mental institution often feel that they have given up all their civil rights. But numerous court cases over the years have established that these people retain most of their civil rights and have certain additional rights, due to their committed status.

Right to Treatment

One fundamental right of people who have been committed is the **right to treatment.** In the past, mental patients, including those involuntarily committed and those who sought treatment voluntarily, were often warehoused. The conditions in which they lived were appalling, with little stimulation or pleasantries, let alone treatment for their disorders. In *Wyatt v. Stickney* (1972), patient Ricky Wyatt and others filed a class action suit against a custodial facility in Alabama, charging that they received no useful treatment and lived in minimally acceptable living conditions. They won their case. A federal court ruled that the state could not simply shelter patients who had been civilly committed but had to provide them with active treatment.

Many prison inmates have severe mental disorders (Lamb, Weinberger, & Gross, 2004). For example, one study of all 805 women felons entering prison in North Carolina in 1991 and 1992 found that 64 percent had a lifetime history of a major psychiatric disorder, including major depression, an anxiety disorder, a substance use disorder, or a personality disorder, and 46 percent had suffered

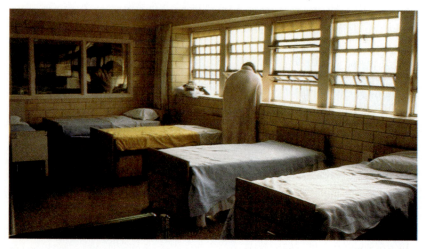

One fundamental right of people committed to a mental-health facility is the right to be treated rather than just warehoused.

such a disorder in the previous six months (Jordan et al., 1996). In addition, nearly 80 percent of these women had been exposed to an extreme trauma, such as sexual abuse, at sometime in their lives. Another study of 1,272 women jail detainees awaiting trial in Chicago found that over 80 percent had a lifetime history of a psychiatric disorder, and 70 percent were symptomatic within the previous six months (Teplin, Abram, & McClelland, 1996). In both studies, the most common diagnosis the women received was substance abuse or dependence, but substantial percentages of the women also had major depression and/or borderline or antisocial personality disorder. Studies of male prison inmates also find that over 50 percent can be diagnosed with a mental disorder, most often a substance-related disorder or antisocial personality disorder (Collins & Schlenger, 1983; Hodgins & Cote, 1990; Neighbors et al., 1987).

Numerous court decisions have mandated that prison inmates receive necessary mental-health services, just as they should receive necessary medical services. Most inmates with mental disorders do not receive services, however. A study of male inmates found that only 37 percent of those with schizophrenia or a major mood disorder received services while in jail (Teplin, 1990), and a study of female inmates found that only 23.5 percent suffering schizophrenia or a major mood disorder received services in jail (Teplin, Abram, & McClelland, 1997). Depression in inmates is particularly likely to go unnoticed and untreated, yet suicide is the second most frequent cause of death among jail detainees, accounting for 39 percent of all inmate deaths (Patterson, 1994).

The services inmates do receive are often minimal. Drug treatments may involve only the provision of information about drugs and perhaps Alcoholics Anonymous or Narcotics Anonymous meetings in the prison. Treatment for schizophrenia or depression may involve only occasional visits with a prison physician, who prescribes a standard drug treatment but does not have the time or expertise to follow individuals closely.

Comprehensive treatment programs focusing on the special needs of prison inmates with mental disorders have been proven successful at reducing their symptoms of mental disorder, substance abuse, and recidivism. Many of these treatment programs are focused on male inmates, because they outnumber female inmates greatly. The female inmate population has grown more rapidly than the male inmate population in the past decade, however, more than tripling in that time frame (Teplin et al., 1997).

Female inmates may have different needs for services, compared with male inmates, for several reasons. Female inmates may be more likely than male inmates to have a history of sexual and physical abuse, which needs to be addressed in treatment. Female inmates are more likely than male inmates to be suffering from depression or anxiety. And female inmates are more likely than male inmates to have children for whom they will become caregivers once they are released from prison (Teplin et al., 1997).

Right to Refuse Treatment

Another basic right is the **right to refuse treatment.** One of the greatest fears of people committed against their will is that they will be given drugs or other treatments that rob them of their consciousness, personality, and free will. Many states do not allow mental institutions and prisons to administer treatments without the informed consent of patients. **Informed consent** means that a patient accepts treatment after receiving a full and understandable explanation of the treatment being offered and making a decision based on his or her own judgment of the risks and benefits of the treatment. The right to refuse treatment is not recognized in some states, however, and in most states this right can be overruled in many circumstances (Monahan et al., 2001). Particularly if a patient is psychotic or manic, it may be judged that he or she cannot make a reasonable decision about treatment; thus, the decision must be made by others. The simple fact that patients have a psychiatric diagnosis, particularly if it is a diagnosis of schizophrenia, is enough to declare them incompetent to make decisions about their treatment in some jurisdictions (Grisso & Appelbaum, 1998). However, studies using reliable measures of patients' abilities to make rational decisions suggest that as much as 75 percent of those with schizophrenia and 90 percent of those with depression have adequate decision-making capacity (Grisso & Appelbaum, 1995).

Patients' psychiatrists and perhaps families may seek court rulings allowing them to administer treatment even if patients refuse treatment. Judges most often agree with the psychiatrists' or families' requests to force treatment on patients. Most cases in which patients refuse treatment never get to court, however. Clinicians and family members pressure and persuade patients to accept treatment, and eventually most patients agree to treatment after initially refusing it (Griffin, Steadman, & Petrila, 2002; Monahan et al., 2001).

SUMMING UP

- People can be held in mental-health facilities involuntarily if they are judged to have grave disabilities that make it difficult for them to meet their own basic needs or that pose imminent danger to themselves or to others. Each of the criteria used to make such judgments has its flaws, however, creating concerns about the appropriateness of civil commitment.

- Short-term commitments can occur without court hearings on the certification of mental-health professionals that individuals are in emergency situations. Such commitments are most likely to happen for individuals who are actively suicidal.

- Longer-term commitments require court hearings. Patients have the rights to have attorneys and to appeal rulings.

- Other basic rights of patients are the right to be treated while being hospitalized and the right to refuse treatment (at least in some states).

- Research shows higher rates of violence by people with mental disorders, particularly those who also have a history of substance abuse, but the rates are not as high as some stereotypes would suggest.

CLINICIANS' DUTIES TO CLIENTS AND SOCIETY

A clinician's primary responsibility to the client is a *duty to provide competent and appropriate treatment* for the client's problems. A number of other duties also deserve mention.

First, according to the ethical guidelines that clinicians are expected to follow, there is a *duty to not become involved in multiple relationships* with clients. Thus, therapists should avoid becoming involved in business or social relationships with clients, and therapists should not treat members of their own families. Such multiple relationships can cloud therapists' judgments about the best treatment for their clients. Of great concern is the potential sexual involvement of therapists with clients. No matter how egalitarian a therapist is, the relationship between a therapist and client is always a relationship of power. The client goes to the therapist, vulnerable and seeking answers. The therapist is in a position to exploit the client's vulnerability. Current professional guidelines for psychologists and psychiatrists assert that it is not acceptable for a therapist to become sexually involved with a client, even if the client seems to be consenting voluntarily to such a liaison. Further, a therapist must not become intimately involved with a client for at least two years after the therapeutic relationship has ended. Sexual contact between a therapist and client is not just unethical—it is a felony in some states.

The vast majority of cases of sexual liaisons between therapists and clients involve male therapists and female clients. Older studies asking therapists (anonymously) if they had ever had sexual contact with their clients suggested that as much as 12 percent of male therapists and 3 percent of female therapists had, at sometime in their careers, had such relationships with clients (Holroyd & Brodsky, 1977). Fortunately, the rates of such abuse have decreased dramatically in more recent surveys, which suggest that about 1 to 4 percent of male therapists and less than 1 percent of female therapists have had sexual liaisons with clients (Borys & Pope, 1989; Pope, Tabachnick, & Keith-Spiegel, 1987). The decrease in rates of such liaisons is probably due to a number of factors, including the criminalization of the act, malpractice suits brought against therapists who have become sexually involved with clients, and increased sensitivity to the wrongness of such relationships among professionals and the organizations that govern them. On the other hand, therapists may be simply less willing to admit to having sexual relationships with their clients now than they were in previous years due to the increased sanctions against such relationships.

Second, therapists have a *duty to protect client confidentiality*. Therapists must not reveal information about their clients, including clients' identities, to anyone except with the clients' permission or under special circumstances. One of those special circumstances occurs when a therapist believes a client needs to be committed involuntarily and must convince a court of this.

Another condition under which therapists can violate their clients' confidentiality happens when they believe clients may harm other people. Based on the decision in *Tarasoff v. Regents of the University of California* (1974), in many jurisdictions clinicians now have a *duty to protect persons who might be in danger because of their clients*. Tatiana Tarasoff was a student at the University of California at Berkeley in the late 1960s. A graduate student named Prosenjit Poddar was infatuated with Tarasoff, who had rejected him. Poddar told his therapist in the student counseling service that he planned to kill Tarasoff when she returned from vacation. The therapist informed the campus police, who picked up Poddar for questioning. Poddar agreed to leave Tarasoff alone, and the campus police released him. Two months later, Poddar killed Tarasoff. Tarasoff's parents sued the university, arguing that the therapist should have protected Tarasoff from Poddar. The California courts agreed and established that therapists have a duty to warn persons who are threatened by their clients during therapy sessions and to take actions to protect these persons.

In addition, in most states, therapists have a *duty to report suspected child abuse* to the proper authorities, even when such reports violate their clients' confidentiality. These authorities then are required to investigate these reports and determine whether to file charges and to remove children from potentially abusive situations. In some states, therapists also have a *duty to report suspected abuse of elderly persons*. Therapists consider confidentiality to be one of the most fundamental rights of clients, but, in these cases, the courts have ruled that confidentiality must be broken to protect innocent people whom clients might harm or are harming.

Finally, in recent years, a new duty has been added to the clinicians' obligations: *to provide ethical service to culturally diverse populations*. We examine this duty in the *Taking Psychology Personally: Guidelines for Ethical Service to Culturally Diverse Populations*.

SUMMING UP

- First and foremost, clinicians have a duty to provide competent care to their clients.
- Clinicians must also avoid multiple relationships with their clients, particularly sexual relationships.
- They must protect their clients' confidentiality, except under special circumstances. One of these special circumstances occurs when therapists believe clients need to be committed involuntarily.
- Two other duties therapists have to society require them to break clients' confidentiality: the duty to protect people whom clients are threatening to harm and the duty to report suspected child or elder abuse.
- Recently, clinicians have been charged to provide ethical service to diverse populations.

CHAPTER INTEGRATION

There has been perhaps less integration of biological, social, and psychological viewpoints in the law's approach to issues of mental health than in the mental-health field itself. The rules governing the insanity defense suggest that the law takes a biological perspective on psychological disorders, conforming to the belief that a mental disease is like a medical disease (see Figure 18.2 on page 694). Similarly, civil commitment rules require certification that a person has a mental disorder or disease before he or she can be committed, further legitimizing psychiatric diagnostic systems that are based on medical models.

Taking Psychology Personally

Guidelines for Ethical Service to Culturally Diverse Populations

What can psychologists do to provide the best possible service and treatment to people who are of ethnicities or cultures different from their own? The following are some guidelines from the American Psychological Association for ethical conduct by psychologists treating culturally diverse populations (Office of Ethnic Minority Affairs, 1993). If you are hoping to become a psychologist, these guidelines provide a sense of the competencies you will be expected to gain in your training. If you are being treated by a psychologist, the guidelines provide some expectations you may have of your therapist, particularly if he or she is from a culture different from your own.

- *Psychologists educate their clients to the processes of psychological intervention,* such as goals and expectations; the scope and, where appropriate, legal limits of confidentiality; and the psychologists' orientations.

- *Psychologists are cognizant of relevant research and practice issues as related to the population being served.*

   Psychologists acknowledge that ethnicity and culture impact behavior and take those factors into account when working with various ethnic groups.

   Psychologists seek out educational and training experiences to enhance their understanding and thereby address the needs of these populations more appropriately and effectively. These experiences include cultural, social, psychological, political, economic, and historical material specific to the ethnic group being served.

   Psychologists recognize the limits of their competencies and expertise. Psychologists who do not possess knowledge and training about an ethnic group seek consultation with, and/or make referrals to, appropriate experts as necessary.

   Psychologists consider the validity of a given instrument or procedure and interpret resulting data, keeping in mind the cultural and linguistic characteristics of the person being assessed.

- *Psychologists recognize ethnicity and culture as significant parameters in understanding psychological processes.*

   Psychologists, regardless of ethnic background, are aware of how their own cultural background/experiences, attitudes, values, and biases influence psychological processes. They make efforts to correct any prejudices and biases.

   A psychologist's practice incorporates an understanding of the client's ethnic and cultural background. This

includes the client's familiarity and comfort with the majority culture as well as ways in which the client's culture may add to or improve various aspects of the majority culture and/or of society at large.

Psychologists help clients increase their awareness of their own cultural values and norms, and they facilitate the discovery of ways clients can apply this awareness to their own lives and to society at large. For example, psychologists may be able to help parents distinguish between generational conflict and culture gaps when problems arise between them and their children. In the process, psychologists can help both parents and children appreciate their own distinguishing cultural values.

Psychologists seek to help a client determine whether a "problem" stems from racism or bias in others, so that the client does not inappropriately personalize problems. For example, the concept of "healthy paranoia," whereby ethnic minorities develop defensive behaviors in response to discrimination, illustrates this principle.

- *Psychologists respect the roles of family members and community structures, hierarchies, values, and beliefs within the client's culture.*

   Psychologists identify resources in the family and the larger community.

   Clarification of the psychologist's role and the client's expectations precedes intervention. For example, it is not uncommon for an entire Native American family to enter a clinic to provide support to the family member in distress. Many of the healing practices found in Native American communities are centered in the family and the whole community.

- *Psychologists respect clients' religious and/or spiritual beliefs and values,* including attributions and taboos, since they affect clients' worldview, psychosocial functioning, and expressions of distress.

- *Psychologists interact in the language requested by the client* and, if this is not feasible, make an appropriate referral.

- *Psychologists consider the impact of adverse social, environmental, and political factors* in assessing problems and designing interventions.

- *Psychologists attend to, as well as work to eliminate, biases, prejudices, and discriminatory practices.*

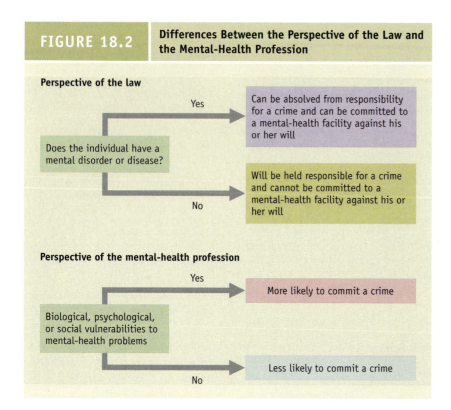

FIGURE 18.2   Differences Between the Perspective of the Law and the Mental-Health Profession

Perspective of the law

Does the individual have a mental disorder or disease?

Yes → Can be absolved from responsibility for a crime and can be committed to a mental-health facility against his or her will

No → Will be held responsible for a crime and cannot be committed to a mental-health facility against his or her will

Perspective of the mental-health profession

Biological, psychological, or social vulnerabilities to mental-health problems

Yes → More likely to commit a crime

No → Less likely to commit a crime

In each of the areas discussed in this chapter, however, there are mental-health professionals advocating a more integrated and complex view of mental disorders than that traditionally held by the law. These professionals are trying to educate judges, juries, and laypeople that some people have biological, psychological, or social predispositions to disorders and that other biological, psychological, or social factors can interact with predispositions to trigger the onset of disorders or certain manifestations of disorders. What is most difficult to explain is the probabilistic nature of the predictions that can be made about mental disorders and the behavior of people with these disorders. That is, a predisposition or certain recent life experiences may make it more likely that a person will develop a disorder or engage in a specific behavior (such as a violent behavior), but they do not determine the disorder or the specific behavior.

We all prefer to have predictions about the future that are definite, especially when we are making decisions that will determine a person's freedom or confinement. That kind of definitiveness is not possible, however, given the present knowledge of the ways biological, psychological, and social forces interact to influence people's behavior.

Extraordinary People: Follow-Up

Unfortunately, the story of Michael Bottoms' descent into schizophrenia, and his family's struggle with the mental-health system to get him treatment, doesn't have a happy ending. Eventually, the family found an institution that would take their insurance and placed Michael there. He hated the place, though, refused his medications, and attempted suicide. This landed him in a state psychiatric hospital for a while. Later, he "confessed" to a murder he had not committed, having been convinced by the voices in his head that this was the sin that he was paying such a high price for. He was jailed, but DNA evidence proved Michael couldn't have committed the murder.

After he was exonerated for this murder, Michael was back home again, on high doses of antipsychotic medications but totally delusional, believing that God spoke directly to him and that his family was evil. Indeed, he decided that his father was the antichrist and that, to save his family's souls, he had to kill them. One night, as his father lay dying of cancer and his family slept behind

locked doors, Michael set the house on fire. He rode to the end of the street on his bicycle, then sat watching, expecting his family's souls to float past him on the way to Heaven. The family escaped. As they stood, watching the firefighters try to extinguish the fire, Mr. Bottoms told the other family members this was the best thing that could happen, because now Michael could really be put away. In the next instant, however, he feared that Michael had been in the house and was dying in the fire. He tried to run into the house to look for Michael but was held back by the firefighters. In the meantime, Michael rode up on his bicycle, completely nonchalant. A police officer asked Michael if he could ask him some questions, and Michael held out his hands for the handcuffs. Then, he turned to his mother and asked her casually what she was going to make for breakfast. Michael confessed to setting the fire with the purpose of killing his family. He was convicted for attempted murder and arson and was sent to prison for 30 years. Michael's father died shortly thereafter, in part from pneumonia contracted the night of the fire. Says Michael's brother, Greg,

> For a long time after Michael went to prison, I never spoke his name. When asked, I said I had only one brother, younger. I couldn't say the name "Michael" without feeling sick and anxious and embarrassed and sad. Acknowledging his existence was admitting his link to me and to all my weaknesses, failures, and humiliations. And it was, it is. Because no matter how I might define success, I am equally formed, if not more so, of human failure, mortal inadequacy, of loss as well as gain, and I am part of my brother just as he—whether he knows it or not, whether either of us want it or not—is part of me. . . .
>
> [In his letters from prison] he said he was sorry and asked for forgiveness, said that he loved our mother and he loved me and he loved my younger brother Ron. He said that he loved us all, always had and always would, and I believed him, because I don't think any of this happened for lack of love; I think, in fact, that the story of my brother, of my family, could be construed as a story of how wrong love might go, when mental illness—when spirits and angels and demons—invade your life. . . .
>
> Last year Michael came up for parole. I slept fitfully during the week before his hear-

ing. I couldn't eat, I was petrified. It all seemed as if it were going to happen again. I called my mother every day that week, to see if she had heard anything, to see how she was doing, which was always better than I was, because she is, deep down, a stronger person. Finally, on a Saturday morning, she called to tell me that he had not been given parole, that the person from the parole board whom she had spoken with had said that he was "not doing well, not at all," that he was violent and uncooperative, and that he would most likely have to serve the full length of his sentence.

> My mother and I felt a sad sort of relief, yet being confronted with all this again rendered us both speechless. So we just stayed on the line, listening to each other breathe. (Bottoms 2000, pp. 201–203)

The story of the Bottoms family's inability to afford long-term care for Michael or to have him institutionalized due to his violence is all too familiar to families of people with serious mental disorders. Insurance coverage for mental-health care is lacking for many people and completely unavailable for others. In many cases, it takes an act as serious as Michael's attempt to kill his family to institutionalize an individual for more than a few weeks. A balance between protecting the rights of people with mental disorders and protecting their families from the consequences of their mental disorders is often difficult to find.

Chapter Summary

- One of the fundamental principles of law is that, in order to stand trial, an accused individual must have a reasonable degree of rational understanding of the charges against him or her and the proceedings of the trial and must be able to participate in his or her defense. People who do not have an understanding of what is happening to them in a courtroom and who cannot participate in their own defense are said to be incompetent to stand trial. Defendants who have histories of psychotic disorders, who have current symptoms of

psychosis, or who perform poorly on tests of important cognitive skills may be judged incompetent to stand trial.

- Five rules for judging the acceptability of the insanity defense have been used in recent history: the M'Naghten rule, the irresistible impulse rule, the Durham rule, the ALI rule, and the American Psychiatric Association definition of insanity. Each of these rules requires that the defendant be diagnosed with a mental disorder, and most of the rules require it be shown that the defendant did not appreciate the criminality of his or her act or could not control his or her behaviors at the time of the crime. (Review Table 18.2.)

■ The verdict of guilty but mentally ill was introduced following public uproar over recent uses of the insanity defense in high-profile cases. Persons judged guilty but mentally ill are confined for the duration of a regular prison term but with the presumption that they will be given psychiatric treatment.

■ Mental-health professionals have raised a number of concerns about the insanity defense. It requires after-the-fact judgments of a defendant's state of mind at the time of the crime. In addition, the rules governing the insanity defense presume that people have free will and usually can control their actions. These presumptions contradict some models of normal and abnormal behavior that suggest that behavior is strongly influenced by biological, psychological, and social forces.

■ Civil commitment is the procedure through which a person may be committed for treatment in a mental institution against his or her will. In most jurisdictions, three criteria are used to determine whether individuals may be committed: if they suffer from grave disability that impairs their ability to care for their own basic needs, if they are imminent dangers to themselves, and if they are imminent dangers to others. Each of these criteria requires a subjective judgment on the part of clinicians and often predictions about the future clinicians may not be good at making. In particular, the prediction of who will pose a danger to others in the future is a difficult one to make, and it is often incorrect. (Review Table 18.3.)

■ Once committed, patients have the right to be treated and the right to refuse treatment.

■ People with mental disorders, particularly those who also have a history of substance abuse, are somewhat more likely to commit violent acts, especially against family members and friends, than people without mental disorders.

■ Mental-health professionals have a number of duties to their clients and to society. They have a duty to provide competent care, to avoid multiple relationships with clients, and to uphold clients' confidentiality, except in unusual circumstances. They have a duty to warn people whom their client is threatening and to report suspected child or elder abuse. They also have a duty to provide ethical service to diverse populations.

■ In the areas of law discussed in this chapter, there are mental-health professionals advocating a more integrated and complex view of mental disorders than that traditionally held by the law, which takes a primarily biological view. (Review Figure 18.2.)

MindMap CD-ROM

The following resources on the MindMap CD-ROM that came with this text will help you to master the content of this chapter and prepare for tests:

■ Chapter Timeline
■ Chapter Quiz

Key Terms

mentally ill 678
incompetent to stand trial 679
insanity 679
insanity defense 680
M'Naghten rule 682
irresistible impulse rule 683
Durham rule 683
ALI rule 683
Insanity Defense Reform Act 684
American Psychiatric Association definition of insanity 684

guilty but mentally ill (GBMI) 684
need for treatment 685
civil commitment 685
grave disability 685
dangerousness to self 686
dangerousness to others 687
right to treatment 690
right to refuse treatment 691
informed consent 691

GLOSSARY

A

ABAB (reversal) design type of experimental design in which an intervention is introduced, withdrawn, and then reinstated, and the behavior of a participant is examined on and off the treatment

abstinence violation effect what happens when a person attempting to abstain from alcohol use ingests alcohol and then endures conflict and guilt by making an internal attribution to explain why he or she drank, thereby making him or her more likely to continue drinking in order to cope with the self-blame and guilt

acculturation extent to which a person identifies with his or her group of origin and its culture or with the mainstream dominant culture

acute stress disorder disorder similar to posttraumatic stress disorder but occurs within one month of exposure to the stressor and does not last more than four weeks; often involves dissociative symptoms

adjustment disorder stress-related disorder that involves emotional and behavioral symptoms (depressive symptoms, anxiety symptoms, and/or antisocial behaviors) that arise within three months of the onset of a stressor

adoption study study of the heritability of a disorder by finding adopted people with a disorder and then determining the prevalence of the disorder among their biological and adoptive relatives, in order to separate out contributing genetic and environmental factors

affective flattening negative symptom of schizophrenia that consists of a severe reduction or the complete absence of affective responses to the environment

agnosia impaired ability to recognize objects or people

agoraphobia anxiety disorder characterized by fear of places and situations in which it would be difficult to escape, such as enclosed places, open spaces, and crowds

agranulocytosis condition characterized by a deficiency of granulocytes, which are substances produced by the bone marrow and fight infection; 1 to 2 percent of people who take clozapine develop this condition

akathesis agitation caused by neuroleptic drugs

akinesia condition marked by slowed motor activity, a monotonous voice, and an expressionless face, resulting from taking neuroleptic drugs

alcohol abuse diagnosis given to someone who uses alcohol in dangerous situations, fails to meet obligations at work or at home due to alcohol use, and has recurrent legal or social problems as a result of alcohol use

alcohol dependence diagnosis given to someone who has a physiological tolerance to alcohol, spends a lot of time intoxicated or in withdrawal, or continues to drink despite significant legal, social, medical, or occupational problems that result from alcohol (often referred to as alcoholism)

alcohol-induced dementia loss of intellectual abilities due to prolonged alcohol abuse, including memory, abstract thinking, judgment, and problem solving, often accompanied by changes in personality, such as increases in paranoia

alcohol-induced persisting amnesic disorder permanent cognitive disorder caused by damage to the central nervous system due to prolonged alcohol abuse, consisting of Wernicke's encephalopathy and Korsakoff's psychosis

ALI rule legal principle stating that a person is not responsible for criminal conduct if he or she lacks the capacity to appreciate the criminality (wrongfulness) of the act or to conform his or her conduct to the requirements of the law as a result of mental disease

alogia deficit in both the quantity of speech and the quality of its expression

alternate form reliability extent to which a measure yields consistent results when presented in different forms

altruistic suicide suicide committed by people who believe that taking their own lives will benefit society

Alzheimer's disease progressive neurological disease that is the most common cause of dementia

amenorrhea cessation of the menses

American Psychiatric Association definition of insanity definition of insanity stating that people cannot be held responsible for their conduct if, at the time they commit crimes, as the result of mental disease or mental retardation they are unable to appreciate the wrongfulness of their conduct

amnesia impairment in the ability to learn new information or to recall previously learned information or past events

amphetamines stimulant drugs that can produce symptoms of euphoria, self-confidence, alertness, agitation, paranoia, perceptual illusions, and depression

amyloid class of proteins that can accumulate between cells in areas of the brain critical to memory and cognitive functioning

anal stage according to Freud, psycho-sexual stage that occurs between the ages of 18 months and 3 years; the focus of gratification is the anus, and children are interested in toilet activities; parents can cause children to be fixated in this stage by being too harsh and critical during toilet training

analogue study study that creates conditions in the laboratory meant to represent conditions in the real world

animal studies studies that attempt to test theories of psychopathology using animals

animal type phobias extreme fears of specific animals that may induce immediate and intense panic attacks and cause the individual to go to great lengths to avoid the animals

anomic suicide suicide committed by people who experience a severe disorientation and role confusion because of a large change in their relationship to society

anorexia nervosa eating disorder in which people fail to maintain body weights that are normal for their ages and heights and suffer from fears of becoming fat, distorted body images, and amenorrhea

antagonist drugs drugs that block or change the effects of an addictive drug, reducing desire for the drug

anterograde amnesia deficit in the ability to learn new information

antianxiety drugs drugs used to treat anxiety, insomnia, and other psychological symptoms

anticonvulsants drugs used to treat mania and depression

antidepressants drugs used to treat the symptoms of depression, such as sad mood, negative thinking, and disturbances of sleep and appetite; three common types are monoamine oxidase inhibitors, tricyclics, and selective serotonin reuptake inhibitors

antipsychotic drugs drugs used to treat psychotic symptoms, such as delusions, hallucinations, and disorganized thinking

antisocial personality disorder (ASPD) pervasive pattern of criminal, impulsive, callous, and/or ruthless behavior, predicated upon disregard for the rights of others and an absence of respect for social norms

anxiety state of apprehension, tension, and worry

anxiety sensitivity belief that bodily symptoms have harmful consequences

anxious-fearful personality disorders category including avoidant, dependent, and obsessive-compulsive personality disorders, which are characterized by a chronic sense of anxiety or fearfulness and behaviors intended to ward off feared situations

aphasia impaired ability to produce and comprehend language

applied tension technique technique used to treat blood-injection-injury type phobias in which the therapist teaches the client to increase his or her blood pressure and heart rate, thus preventing the client from fainting

apraxia impaired ability to initiate common voluntary behaviors

arousal phase in the sexual response cycle, psychological experience of arousal and pleasure as well as physiological changes, such as the tensing of muscles and enlargement of blood vessels and tissues (also called the excitement phase)

Asperger's disorder pervasive developmental disorder characterized by deficits in social skills and activities; similar to autism but does not include deficits in language or cognitive skills

assertive community treatment programs system of treatment that provides comprehensive services to people with schizophrenia, employing the expertise of medical professionals, social workers, and psychologists to meet the variety of patients' needs 24 hours per day

assessment process of gathering information about a person's symptoms and their possible causes

attention-deficit/hyperactivity disorder (ADHD) syndrome marked by deficits in controlling attention, inhibiting impulses, and organizing behavior to accomplish long-term goals

atypical antipsychotics drugs that seem to be even more effective in treating schizophrenia than phenothiazines without the same neurological side effects; they bind to a different type of dopamine receptor than other neuroleptic drugs

auditory hallucination auditory perception of a phenomenon that is not real, such as hearing a voice when one is alone

autism childhood disorder marked by deficits in social interaction (such as a lack of interest in one's family or other children), communication (such as failing to modulate one's voice to signify emotional expression), and activities and interests (such as engaging in bizarre, repetitive behaviors)

automatic thoughts thoughts that come to mind quickly and without intention, causing emotions such as fear or sadness

aversion therapy treatment that involves the pairing of unpleasant stimuli with deviant or maladaptive sources of pleasure in order to induce an aversive reaction to the formerly pleasurable stimulus

aversive classical conditioning pairing of alcohol with a substance (such as disulfiram) that will interact with it to cause nausea or vomiting in order to make alcohol itself a conditioned stimulus to be avoided

avoidant personality disorder pervasive anxiety, sense of inadequacy, and fear of being criticized that lead to the avoidance of most social interactions with others and to restraint and nervousness in social interactions

avolition inability to persist at common goal-directed activities

B

barbiturates drugs used to treat anxiety and insomnia that work by suppressing the central nervous system and decreasing the activity level of certain neurons

behavior genetics study of the processes by which genes affect behavior and the extent to which personality and abnormality are genetically inherited

behavior therapies therapies that focus on changing a person's specific behaviors by replacing unwanted behaviors with desired behaviors

behavioral assessment in behavior therapies, the therapist's assessment of the clients' adaptive and maladaptive behaviors and the triggers for these behaviors

behavioral assignments "homework" given to clients to practice new behaviors or gather new information between therapy sessions

behavioral inhibition set of behavioral traits including shyness, fearfulness, irritability, cautiousness, and introversion; behaviorally inhibited children tend to avoid or withdraw from novel situations, are clingy with parents, and become excessively aroused when exposed to unfamiliar situations

behavioral observation method for assessing the frequency of a client's behaviors and the specific situations in which they occur

behavioral theories theories that focus on an individual's history of reinforcements and punishments as causes for abnormal behavior

behavioral theory of depression view that depression results from negative life events that represent a reduction in positive reinforcement; sympathetic responses to depressive behavior then serve as positive reinforcement for the depression itself

behaviorism study of the impact of reinforcements and punishments on behavior

bell and pad method treatment for enuresis in which a pad placed under a sleeping child to detect traces of urine sets off a bell when urine is detected, awakening the child to condition him or her to wake up and use the bathroom before urinating

benzodiazepines drugs that reduce anxiety and insomnia

binge-eating disorder eating disorder in which people compulsively overeat either continuously or on discrete binges but do not behave in ways to compensate for the overeating

bingeing eating a large amount of food in one sitting

binge/purge type of anorexia nervosa type of anorexia nervosa in which periodic bingeing or purging behaviors occur along with behaviors that meet the criteria for anorexia nervosa

biofeedback group of techniques designed to help people change bodily processes by learning to identify signs that the processes are going awry and then learning ways of controlling the processes

biological approach view that biological factors cause and should be used to treat abnormality

biological theories theories of abnormality that focus on biological causes of abnormal behaviors

bipolar disorder disorder marked by cycles between manic episodes and depressive episodes; also called manic-depression

bipolar I disorder form of bipolar disorder in which the full symptoms of mania are experienced; depressive aspects may be more infrequent or mild

bipolar II disorder form of bipolar disorder in which only hypomanic episodes are experienced, and the depressive component is more pronounced

blackout amnesia for events that occurred during intoxication

blood-injection-injury type phobias extreme fears of seeing blood or an injury or of receiving an injection or another invasive medical procedure, which cause a drop in heart rate and blood pressure and fainting

body dysmorphic disorder syndrome involving obsessive concern over a part of the body the individual believes is defective

borderline personality disorder syndrome characterized by rapidly shifting and unstable mood, self-concept, and interpersonal relationships, as well as impulsive behavior and transient dissociative states

bulimia nervosa eating disorder in which people engage in bingeing and behave in ways to prevent weight gain from the binges, such as self-induced vomiting, excessive exercise, and abuse of purging drugs (such as laxatives)

buspirone drug that appears to alleviate the symptoms of general anxiety for some, has very few side effects, and is unlikely to lead to physical dependence

butyrophenone class of drug that can reduce psychotic symptoms; includes haloperidol (Haldol)

C

caffeine chemical compound with stimulant effects

calcium channel blockers drugs used to treat mania and depression

cannabis substance that causes feelings of well-being, perceptual distortions, and paranoid thinking

case studies in-depth analyses of individuals

castration anxiety according to Freud, boys' fear that their fathers will retaliate against them by castrating them; this fear serves as motivation for them to put aside their desires for their mothers and to aspire to become like their fathers

cataplexy episodes of sudden loss of muscle tone lasting from a few seconds to minutes

catatonia group of disorganized behaviors that reflect an extreme lack of responsiveness to the outside world

catatonic excitement state of constant agitation and excitability

catatonic schizophrenia type of schizophrenia in which people show a variety of motor behaviors and ways of speaking that suggest almost complete unresponsiveness to their environment

catharsis expression of emotions connected to memories and conflicts, which, according to Freud, leads to the release of energy used to keep these memories in the unconscious

caudate nucleus part of the basal ganglia that is involved in carrying the impulses to the thalamus that direct primitive patterns of primitive behavior, such as aggression, sexuality, and bodily excretion

causal attribution explanation for why an event occurred

cerebral cortex part of the brain that regulates complex activities, such as speech and analytical thinking

cerebrovascular disease disease that occurs when the blood supply to the brain is blocked, causing tissue damage to the brain

childhood disintegrative disorder pervasive developmental disorder in which children develop normally at first but later show permanent loss of basic skills in social interactions, language, and/or movement

chlorpromazine antipsychotic drug

civil commitment forcing of a person into a mental-health facility against his or her will

classical conditioning form of learning in which a neutral stimulus becomes associated with a stimulus that naturally elicits a response, thereby making the neutral stimulus itself sufficient to elicit the same response

classification system set of syndromes and the rules for determining whether an individual's symptoms are part of one of these syndromes

client-centered therapy (CCT) Carl Rogers' form of psychotherapy, which consists of an equal relationship between therapist and client as the client searches for his or her inner self, receiving unconditional positive regard and an empathic understanding from the therapist

cocaine central nervous system stimulant that causes a rush of positive feelings initially but that can lead to impulsiveness, agitation, and anxiety and can cause withdrawal symptoms of exhaustion and depression

cognitions thoughts or beliefs

cognitive-behavioral therapy treatment focused on changing negative patterns of thinking and solving concrete problems through brief sessions in which a therapist helps a client challenge negative thoughts, consider alternative perspectives, and take effective actions

cognitive disorders dementia, delirium, or amnesia characterized by impairments in cognition (such as deficits in memory, language, or planning) and caused by a medical condition or by substance intoxication or withdrawal

cognitive theories theories that focus on belief systems and ways of thinking as the causes of abnormal behavior

cognitive therapies therapeutic approaches that focus on changing people's maladaptive thought patterns

cohort effect effect that occurs when people born in one historical period are at different risk for a disorder than are people born in another historical period

community mental-health centers clinics that provide mental-health care based in the community through teams of social workers, therapists, and physicians who coordinate care

community mental-health movement movement launched in 1963 that attempted to provide coordinated mental-health services to people in community-based treatment centers.

compulsions repetitive behaviors or mental acts that an individual feels he or she must perform

computerized tomography (CT) method of analyzing brain structure by passing narrow X-ray beams through a person's head from several angles to produce measurements from which a computer can construct an image of the brain

concordance rate probability that both twins will develop a disorder if one twin has the disorder

concurrent validity extent to which a test yields the same results as other measures of the same phenomenon

conditioned response (CR) in classical conditioning, response that first followed a natural stimulus but that now follows a conditioned stimulus

conditioned stimulus (CS) in classical conditioning, previously neutral stimulus that, when paired with a natural stimulus, becomes sufficient to elicit a response

conditions of worth external standards some people feel they must meet in order to be acceptable

conduct disorder syndrome marked by chronic disregard for the rights of others, including specific behaviors, such as stealing, lying, and engaging in acts of violence

conscious mental contents and processes of which we are actively aware

construct validity extent to which a test measures only what it is intended to measure

content validity extent to which a measure assesses all the important aspects of a phenomenon that it purports to measure

context environment and circumstances in which a behavior occurs

contingencies of self-worth "if-then" rules concerning self-worth, such as "I'm nothing if a person I care about doesn't love me"

continuous reinforcement schedule system of behavior modification in which certain behaviors are always rewarded or punished, leading to rapid learning of desired responses

continuous variable factor that is measured along a continuum (such as 0–100) rather than falling into a discrete category (such as "diagnosed with depression")

control group in an experimental study, group of subjects whose experience resembles that of the experimental group in all ways, except that they do not receive the key manipulation

control theory cognitive theory that explains people's variance in behavior in certain domains in terms of their beliefs that they can or cannot effectively control situations in that domain

conversion disorder syndrome marked by a sudden loss of functioning in a part of the body, usually following an extreme psychological stressor

coronary heart disease (CHD) chronic illness that is a leading cause of death in the United States, occurring when the blood vessels that supply the heart with oxygen and nutrients are narrowed or closed by plaque, resulting in a myocardial infarction (heart attack) when closed completely

correlation coefficient statistic used to indicate the degree of relationship between two variables

correlational studies method in which researchers assess only the relationship between two variables and do not manipulate one variable to determine its effects on another variable

cortisol hormone that helps the body respond to stressors, inducing the fight-or-flight response

covert sensitization therapy pairing of mental images of alcohol with other images of highly unpleasant consequences resulting from its use in order to create an aversive reaction to the sight and smell of alcohol and reduce drinking

crisis intervention program that helps people who are highly suicidal and refers them to mental-health professionals

cross-sectional type of research examining people at one point in time but not following them over time

cue exposure and response prevention therapy to reduce relapse among alcoholics by tempting them with stimuli that induce cravings to drink while preventing them from actually drinking, allowing them to habituate to the cravings and reduce temptation

cultural relativism view that norms among cultures set the standard for what counts as normal behavior, which implies that abnormal behavior can only be defined relative to these norms; no universal definition of abnormality is therefore possible; only definitions of abnormality relative to a specific culture are possible

cyclothymic disorder milder but more chronic form of bipolar disorder that consists of alternation between hypomanic episodes and mild depressive episodes over a period of at least two years

D

dangerousness to others legal criterion for involuntary commitment that is met when a person would pose a threat or danger to other people if not incarcerated

dangerousness to self legal criterion for involuntary commitment that is met when a person is imminently suicidal or a danger to him- or herself as judged by a mental-health professional

day treatment centers centers where people with mental-health problems can obtain treatment all day, including occupational and rehabilitative therapies, but live at home at night

death darers individuals who are ambivalent about dying and take actions that increase their chances of death but that do not guarantee they will die

death ignorers individuals who intend to end their lives but do not believe this means the end of their existence

death initiators individuals who intend to die but believe that they are simply speeding up an inevitable death

death seekers individuals who clearly and explicitly seek to end their lives

defense mechanisms strategies the ego uses to disguise or transform unconscious wishes

degradation process in which a receiving neuron releases an enzyme into the synapse, breaking down neurotransmitters into other biochemicals

deinstitutionalization movement in which thousands of mental patients were released from mental institutions; a result of the patients' rights movement, which was aimed at stopping the dehumanizing of mental patients and at restoring their basic legal rights

delirium cognitive disorder that is acute and usually transient, including disorientation and memory loss

delirium tremens (DTs) symptoms that result during severe alcohol withdrawal, including hallucinations, delusions, agitation, and disorientation

delusion of reference false belief that external events, such as people's actions or natural disasters, relate somehow to oneself

delusions fixed beliefs with no basis in reality

delusions of thought insertion beliefs that one's thoughts are being controlled by outside forces

demand characteristics factors in an experiment that suggest to participants how the experimenter would like them to behave

dementia cognitive disorder in which a gradual and usually permanent decline of intellectual functioning occurs; can be caused by a medical condition, substance intoxication, or withdrawal

dementia praecox historical name for schizophrenia

dependent personality disorder pervasive selflessness, a need to be cared for, and fear of rejection, which lead to total dependence on and submission to others

dependent variable factor that an experimenter seeks to predict

depersonalization disorder syndrome marked by frequent episodes of feeling detached from one's own body and mental processes, as if one were an outside observer of oneself; symptoms must cause significant distress or interference with one's ability to function

depletion syndrome set of symptoms shown by depressed older people, consisting of loss of interest, loss of energy, hopelessness, helplessness, and psychomotor retardation

depression state marked by either a sad mood or a loss of interest in one's usual activities, as well as feelings of hopelessness, suicidal ideation, psychomotor agitation or retardation, and trouble concentrating

depressive realism phenomenon whereby depressed people make more realistic judgments as to whether they can control actually uncontrollable events than do nondepressed people, who exhibit an illusion of control over the same events

desensitization treatment used to reduce anxiety by rendering a previously threatening stimulus innocuous by repeated and guided exposure to the stimulus under nonthreatening circumstances

detoxification first step in treatment for substance-related disorders, in which a person stops using the substance and allows it to exit the body fully

developmental coordination disorder disorder involving deficits in the ability to walk, run, or hold on to objects

diagnosis label given to a set of symptoms that tend to occur together

Diagnostic and Statistical Manual of Mental Disorders **(DSM)** official manual for diagnosing mental disorders in the United States, containing a list of specific criteria for each disorder, how long a person's symptoms must be present to qualify for a diagnosis, and requirements that the symptoms interfere with daily functioning in order to be called disorders

dialectical behavior therapy cognitive-behavioral intervention aimed at teaching problem-solving skills, interpersonal skills, and skills at managing negative emotions

dichotomous thinking inflexible way of thinking in which everything is viewed in either/or terms

differential diagnosis determination of which of two or more possible diagnoses is most appropriate for a client

discomfort criterion for abnormality that suggests that only behaviors that cause a person great distress should be labeled as abnormal

disease model view that alcoholism (or another drug addiction) is an incurable physical disease, like epilepsy or diabetes, and that only total abstinence can control it

disorder of written expression developmental disorder involving deficits in the ability to write

disorganized schizophrenia syndrome marked by incoherence in cognition, speech, and behavior as well as flat or inappropriate affect (also called hebephrenic schizophrenia)

dissociation process whereby different facets of an individual's sense of self, memories, or consciousness become split off from one another

dissociative amnesia loss of memory for important facts about a person's own life and personal identity, usually including the awareness of this memory loss

dissociative fugue disorder in which a person moves away and assumes a new identity, with amnesia for the previous identity

dissociative identity disorder (DID) syndrome in which a person develops more than one distinct identity or personality, each of which can have distinct facial and verbal expressions, gestures, interpersonal styles, attitudes, and even physiological responses

dissociative symptoms symptoms suggesting that facets of the individual's sense of self, memories, or consciousness have become split off from one another

disulfiram drug that produces an aversive physical reaction to alcohol and is used to encourage abstinence; commonly referred to as Antabuse

dizygotic (DZ) twins twins who average only 50 percent of their genes in common because they developed from two separate fertilized eggs

dopamine neurotransmitter in the brain, excess amounts of which have been thought to cause schizophrenia

double depression disorder involving a cycle between major depression and dysthymic disorder

double-blind experiment study in which both the researchers and the participants are unaware of which experimental condition the participants are in, in order to prevent demand effects

dramatic-emotional personality disorders category including antisocial, borderline, narcissistic, and histrionic personality disorders, which are characterized by dramatic and impulsive behaviors that are maladaptive and dangerous

drug addicts people who are physically dependent on substances and who suffer from withdrawal when not taking the substances

Durham rule legal principle stating that the presence of a mental disorder is sufficient to absolve a criminal of responsibility for a crime

dyspareunia genital pain associated with sexual intercourse

dyssomnias primary sleep disorders that involve abnormalities in the amount, quality, or timing of sleep

dysthymic disorder type of depression that is less severe than major depression but more chronic; diagnosis requires the presence of a sad mood or anhedonia, plus two other symptoms of depression, for at least two years, during which symptoms do not remit for two months or longer

E

echolalia communication abnormality in which an individual simply repeats back what he or she hears rather than generating his or her own speech

echopraxia repetitive imitation of another person's movements

effectiveness in therapy outcome research, how well a therapy works in real-world settings

efficacy in therapy outcome research, how well a therapy works in highly controlled settings with a narrowly defined group of people

ego part of the psyche that channels libido acceptable to the superego and within the constraints of reality

egoistic suicide suicide committed by people who feel alienated from others and lack social support

Electra complex Freud's theory that girls realize during the phallic stage that they don't have a penis and are horrified at the discovery; they realize that their mothers also don't have penises and disdain females for this deficit; an attraction for the father ensues, following the belief that he can provide a penis

electroconvulsive therapy (ECT) treatment for depression that involves the induction of a brain seizure by passing electrical current through the patient's brain while he or she is anesthetized

elimination disorders disorders in which a child shows frequent, uncontrolled urination or defecation far beyond the age at which children usually develop control over these functions

encopresis diagnosis given to children who are at least 4 years old and who defecate inappropriately at least once a month for 3 months

endocrine system system of glands that produces many different hormones

enlarged ventricles fluid-filled spaces in the brain that are larger than normal and suggest atrophy or deterioration in other brain tissue

enmeshed families families in which there is extreme interdependence in family interactions, so that the boundaries between the identities of individual members are weak and easily crossed

enuresis diagnosis given to children over 5 years of age who wet the bed or their clothes at least twice a week for 3 months

epidemiology study of the frequency and distribution of a disorder, or a group of disorders, in a population

euthanasia killing of another person as an act of mercy

excessive reassurance seeking constantly looking for assurances from others that one is accepted and loved

executive functions functions of the brain that involve the ability to sustain concentration; use abstract reasoning and concept formation; anticipate, plan, program; initiate purposeful behavior; self-monitor; and shift from maladaptive patterns of behavior to more adaptive ones

exhibitionism obtainment of sexual gratification by exposing one's genitals to involuntary observers

existential anxiety universal human fear of the limits and responsibilities of one's existence

existential theories views that uphold personal responsibility for discovering one's personal values and meanings in life and then living in accordance with them; people face existential anxiety due to awareness of their life's finitude and must overcome both this anxiety and obstacles to a life governed by the meanings they give to it, in order to achieve mental health and avoid maladaptive behavior

experimental group in an experimental study, group of participants that receives the key manipulation

experimental studies studies in which the independent variables are directly manipulated and the effects on the dependent variable are examined

expressed emotion family interaction style in which families are overinvolved with each other, are overprotective of the disturbed family member, voice self-sacrificing attitudes to the disturbed family member, and simultaneously are critical, hostile, and resentful of this member

expressive language disorder disorder involving deficits in the ability to express oneself through language

external validity extent to which a study's results can be generalized to phenomena in real life

extinction abolition of a learned behavior

eye movement desensitization and reprocessing (EMDR) highly controversial therapy for trauma survivors in which a client attends to the image of the trauma, thoughts about the trauma, and the physical sensations of anxiety aroused by the trauma while the therapist quickly moves a finger back and forth in front of the client's eyes to elicit a series of repeated, rapid, jerky, side-to-side eye movements ("saccades")

F

face validity extent to which a test seems to measure a phenomenon on face value, or intuition

factitious disorder by proxy disorder in which the individual creates an illness in another individual in order to gain attention

factitious disorders disorders marked by deliberately faking physical or mental illness to gain medical attention

family history study study of the heritability of a disorder involving identifying people with the disorder and people without the disorder and then determining the disorder's frequency within each person's family

family systems theories theories that see the family as a complex system that works to maintain the status quo

family systems therapy psychotherapy that focuses on the family, rather than the individual, as the source of problems; family therapists challenge communication styles, disrupt pathological family dynamics, and challenge defensive conceptions in order to harmonize relationships among all members and within each member

female orgasmic disorder in women, recurrent delay in or absence of orgasm after having reached the excitement phase of the sexual response cycle (also called anorgasmia)

female sexual arousal disorder in women, recurrent inability to attain or maintain the swelling-lubrication response of sexual excitement

fetal alcohol syndrome (FAS) syndrome that occurs when a mother abuses alcohol during pregnancy, causing the baby to have lowered IQ, increased risk for mental retardation, distractibility, and difficulties with learning from experience

fetishism paraphilia in which a person uses inanimate objects as the preferred or exclusive source of sexual arousal

fight-or-flight response physiological changes in the human body that occur in response to a perceived threat, including the secretion of glucose, endorphins, and hormones as well as the elevation of heart rate, metabolism, blood pressure, breathing, and muscle tension

five-factor model personality theory that posits that any individual's personality is organized along five broad dimensions of personality: neuroticism, extraversion, openness to experience, agreeableness, and conscientiousness

flooding (implosive therapy) behavioral technique in which a client is intensively exposed to a feared object until the anxiety diminishes

formal thought disorder state of highly disorganized thinking (also known as loosening of associations)

free association method of uncovering unconscious conflicts in which the client is taught to talk about whatever comes to mind, without censoring any thoughts

frotteurism obtainment of sexual gratification by rubbing one's genitals against or fondling the body parts of a nonconsenting person

G

gamma-aminobutyric acid (GABA) neurotransmitter that carries inhibiting messages from one neuron to another

gender identity one's perception of oneself as male or female

gender identity disorder (GID) condition in which a person believes that he or she was born with the wrong sex's genitals and is fundamentally a person of the opposite sex

gender roles according to Freud, what society considers to be the appropriate behaviors for males or females

general adaptation syndrome physiological changes that occur when an organism reacts to stress; includes the stages of alarm, resistance, and exhaustion

general paresis disease that leads to paralysis, insanity, and eventually death; discovery of this disease helped establish a connection between biological diseases and mental disorders

generalizability extent to which the results of a study generalize to, or inform us about, people other than those who were studied

generalized anxiety disorder (GAD) anxiety disorder characterized by chronic anxiety in daily life

genital stage psychosexual stage that occurs around the age of 12, when children's sex drives reemerge; if a child has successfully resolved the phallic stage, interest in sex turns toward heterosexual relationships

global assumptions fundamental beliefs that encompass all types of situations

glove anesthesia state in which people lose all feeling in one hand as if they were wearing a glove that wiped out all physical symptoms

grandiose delusions elevated thinking about the self, ideas of omnipotence, and the taking of credit for occurrences not personally facilitated

grave disability legal criterion for involuntary commitment that is met when a person is so incapacitated by a mental disorder that he or she cannot care for his or her own basic needs, such as for food, clothing, or shelter, and his or her survival is threatened as a result

group comparison study study that compares two or more distinct groups on a variable of interest

group therapy therapy conducted with groups of people rather than one on one between a therapist and client

guided mastery techniques interventions designed to increase health-promoting behaviors by providing explicit information about how to engage in these behaviors as well as opportunities to engage in these behaviors in increasingly challenging situations

guilty but mentally ill (GBMI) verdict that requires a convicted criminal to serve the full sentence designated for his or her crime, with the expectation that he or she will also receive treatment for mental illness

H

halfway houses organizations that offer people with long-term mental-health problems a structured, supportive environment in which to live while they reestablish a job and ties to their friends and family

hallucinations perceptual experiences that are not real

hallucinogens substances, including LSD and MDMA, that produce perceptual illusions and distortions even in small doses

harm-reduction model approach to treating substance use disorders that views alcohol use as normative behavior and focuses education on the immediate risks of the excessive use of alcohol (such as alcohol-related accidents) and on the payoffs of moderation (such as avoidance of hangovers)

health psychology study of the effects of psychological factors on health

histrionic personality disorder syndrome marked by rapidly shifting moods, unstable relationships, and an intense need for attention and approval, which is sought by means of overly dramatic behavior, seductiveness, and dependence

hopelessness sense that the future is bleak and there is no way of making it more positive

hormone chemical that carries messages throughout the body, potentially affecting a person's moods, levels of energy, and reactions to stress

human laboratory study experimental study involving human participants

humanistic theories views that people strive to develop their innate potential for goodness and self-actualization; abnormality arises as a result of societal pressures to conform to unchosen dictates that clash with a person's self-actualization needs and from an inability to satisfy more basic needs, such as hunger

humanistic therapy (person-centered therapy) type of therapy in which the goal is to help the client discover his or her place in the world and to accomplish self-actualization through self-exploration; based on the assumption that the natural tendency for humans is toward growth

hypersomnia type of dyssomnia that involves being chronically sleepy and sleeping for long periods at a time

hypertension condition in which the blood supply through the blood vessels is excessive and can lead to deterioration of the cell tissue and hardening of the arterial walls

hypoactive sexual desire disorder condition in which a person's desire for sex is diminished to the point that it causes him or her significant distress or interpersonal difficulties and is not due to transient life circumstances or another sexual dysfunction

hypochondriasis syndrome marked by chronic worry that one has a physical symptom or disease that one clearly does not have

hypomania state in which an individual shows mild symptoms of mania

hypothalamic-pituitary-adrenal axis (HPA axis) three key components of the neuroendocrine system that work together in a feedback system interconnected with the limbic system and the cerebral cortex

hypothalamus component of the brain that regulates eating, drinking, sex, and basic emotions; abnormal behaviors involving any of these activities may be the result of dysfunction in the hypothalamus

hypothesis testable statement about two or more variables and the relationship between them

I

id according to Freud, most primitive part of the unconscious; consists of drives and impulses seeking immediate gratification

immune system system that protects the body from disease-causing microorganisms and affects our susceptibility to diseases

impulsivity difficulty in controlling behaviors; acting without thinking first

in vivo exposure technique of behavior therapy in which clients are encouraged to experience directly the stimuli that they fear

incidence number of new cases of a specific disorder that develop during a specific period of time

incompetent to stand trial legal status of an individual who lacks a rational understanding of the charges against him or her, an understanding of the proceedings of his or her trial, or the ability to participate in his or her own defense

independent variable factor that is manipulated by an experimenter or used to predict the dependent variable

informed consent procedure (often legally required prior to treatment administration) in which a patient receives a full and understandable explanation of the treatment being offered and makes a decision about whether to accept or refuse the treatment

inhalants solvents, such as gasoline, glue, or paint thinner, that one inhales to produce a high and that can cause permanent central nervous system damage as well as liver and kidney disease

insanity legal term denoting a state of mental incapacitation during the time a crime was committed

insanity defense defense used by people accused of a crime in which they state that they cannot be held responsible for their illegal acts because they were mentally incapacitated at the time of the act

Insanity Defense Reform Act 1984 law, affecting all federal courts and about half of the state courts, that finds a person not guilty by reason of insanity if it is shown that, as a result of mental disease or mental retardation, the accused was unable to appreciate the wrongfulness of his or her conduct at the time of the offense

insomnia type of dyssomnia that involves difficulty in initiating or maintaining sleep; chronically nonrestorative sleep

integrationist approach approach to psychopathology that emphasizes how biological, psychological, and social factors interact and influence each other to produce and maintain mental-health problems

intelligence tests tests that assess a person's intellectual strengths and weaknesses

internal reliability extent to which a measure yields similar results among its different parts as it measures a single phenomenon

internal validity extent to which all factors that could extraneously affect a

study's results are controlled within a laboratory study

interoceptive awareness heightened awareness of bodily cues that a panic attack may soon happen

interpersonal theories theories that attribute abnormal behavior to problems in interpersonal realtionships

interpersonal theories of depression theories that view the causes of depression as rooted in interpersonal relationships

interpersonal therapy (IPT) more structured, short-term version of psychodynamic therapies

interrater reliability extent to which an observational measure yields similar results across different judges (also called interjudge reliability)

introject to internalize moral standards because following them makes one feel good and reduces anxiety

introjected hostility theory Freud's theory explaining how depressive people, being too frightened to express their rage for their rejection outwardly, turn their anger inward on parts of their own egos; their self-blame and punishment is actually blame and punishment intended for others who have abandoned them

irresistible impulse rule legal principle stating that even a person who knowingly performs a wrongful act can be absolved of responsibility if he or she was driven by an irresistible impulse to perform the act or had a diminished capacity to resist performing the act

K

Korsakoff's psychosis alcohol-induced permanent cognitive disorder involving deficiencies in one's ability to recall both recent and distant events

L

la belle indifference feature of conversion disorders involving an odd lack of concern about one's loss of functioning in an area of one's body

latency stage according to Freud, period of psychosexual development, following the phallic stage, in which libidinal drives are quelled and children's energy turns toward the development of skills and interests and toward becoming fully socialized to the world; the opposite sex is avoided

learned helplessness deficits symptoms such as low motivation, passivity, indecisiveness, and an inability to control outcomes that result from exposure to uncontrollable negative events

learned helplessness theory view that exposure to uncontrollable negative events leads to a belief in one's inability to control important outcomes and a subsequent loss of motivation, indecisiveness, and failure of action,

libido according to Freud, psychical energy derived from physiological drives

light therapy treatment for seasonal affective disorder that involves exposure to bright lights during the winter months

limbic system part of the brain that relays information from the primitive brain stem about changes in bodily functions to the cortex, where the information is interpreted

lithium drug used to treat manic and depressive symptoms

locus ceruleus area of the brain stem that plays a part in the emergency response and may be involved in panic attacks

longitudinal type of research evaluating the same group(s) of people for an extended period of time

lymphocytes immune system cells that attack viruses

M

magnetic resonance imaging (MRI) method of measuring both brain structure and brain function through the construction of a magnetic field that affects hydrogen atoms in the brain, emitting signals that a computer then records and uses to produce a three-dimensional image of the brain

major depression disorder involving a sad mood or anhedonia plus four or more of the following symptoms: weight loss or a decrease in appetite, insomnia or hypersomnia, psychomotor agitation or retardation, fatigue, feelings of worthlessness or severe guilt, trouble concentrating, and suicidal ideation; these symptoms must be present for at least two weeks and must produce marked impairments in normal functioning

maladaptive in reference to behaviors, causing people who have the behaviors physical or emotional harm, preventing them from functioning in daily life, and/or indicating that they have lost

touch with reality and/or cannot control their thoughts and behavior (also called dysfunctional)

male erectile disorder in men, recurrent inability to attain or maintain an erection until the completion of sexual activity

male orgasmic disorder in men, recurrent delay in or absence of orgasm following the excitement phase of the sexual response cycle

malingering feigning of a symptom or a disorder for the purpose of avoiding an unwanted situation, such as military service

managed care health care system in which all necessary services for an individual patient are supposed to be coordinated by a primary care provider; the goals are to coordinate services for an existing medical problem and to prevent future medical problems before they arise

mania state of persistently elevated mood, feelings of grandiosity, overenthusiasm, racing thoughts, rapid speech, and impulsive actions

mathematics disorder developmental disorder involving deficits in the ability to learn mathematics

mental hygiene movement movement to treat mental patients more humanely and to view mental disorders as medical diseases

mental illness phrase used to refer to a physical illness that causes severe abnormal thoughts, behaviors, and feelings

mental retardation developmental disorder marked by significantly subaverage intellectual functioning, as well as deficits (relative to other children) in life skill areas, such as communication, self-care, work, and interpersonal relationships

mentally ill legal description of an individual who purportedly suffers from a mental illness, which is analogous (in this view) to suffering from a medical disease

mesmerism treatment for hysterical patients based on the idea that magnetic fluids in the patients' bodies are affected by the magnetic forces of other people and objects; the patients' magnetic forces are thought to be realigned by the practitioner through his or her own magnetic force

mesolimbic pathway subcortical part of the brain involved in cognition and emotion

meta-analysis statistical technique for summarizing the results across several studies

methadone opioid that is less potent and longer-lasting than heroin; taken by heroin users to decrease their cravings and help them cope with negative withdrawal symptoms

methadone maintenance programs treatments for heroin abusers that provide doses of methadone to replace heroin use and that seek eventually to wean addicted people from the methadone itself

mixed receptive-expressive language disorder disorder involving deficits in the ability to express oneself through language and to understand the language of others

M'Naghten rule legal principle stating that, in order to claim a defense of insanity, accused persons must have been burdened by such a defect of reason, from disease of the mind, as not to know the nature and quality of the act they were doing or, if they did know it, that they did not know what they were doing what was wrong

modeling process of learning behaviors by imitating others, especially authority figures or those like oneself

monoamine oxidase inhibitors (MAOIs) class of antidepressant drugs

monoamine theories theories that low levels of monoamines, particularly norepinephrine and serotonin, cause depression, whereas excessive or imbalanced levels of monoamines, particularly dopamine, cause mania

monoamines neurotransmitters, including catecholamines (epinephrine, norepinephrine, and dopamine) and serotonin, that have been implicated in the mood disorders

monozygotic (MZ) twins twins who share 100 percent of their genes, because they developed from a single fertilized egg

moral anxiety anxiety that occurs when one is punished for expressing id impulses and come to associate those with punishment

moral treatment type of treatment delivered in mental hospitals in which patients were treated with respect and dignity and were encouraged to exercise self-control

myotonia in the sexual response cycle, muscular tension in the body, which culminates in contractions during orgasm

N

naloxone drug that blocks the positive effects of heroin and can lead to a decreased desire to use it

naltrexone drug that blocks the positive effects of alcohol and heroin and can lead to a decreased desire to drink or use substances

narcissistic personality disorder syndrome marked by grandiose thoughts and feelings of one's own worth as well as an obliviousness to others' needs and an exploitive, arrogant demeanor

narcolepsy type of dyssomnia that involves irresistible attacks of sleep

natural environment type phobias extreme fears of events or situations in the natural environment that cause impairment in one's ability to function normally

need for treatment legal criterion operationalized as a signed certificate by two physicians stating that a person requires treatment but will not agree to it voluntarily; formerly a sufficient cause to hospitalize the person involuntarily and force him or her to undergo treatment

negative cognitive triad perspective seen in depressed people in which they have negative views of themselves, of the world, and of the future

negative reinforcement process in which people avoid being exposed to feared objects, and this avoidance is reinforced by the subsequent reduction of their anxiety

negative symptoms in schizophrenia, deficits in functioning that indicate the absence of a capacity present in normal people, such as affective flattening (also called Type II symptoms)

neurofibrillary tangles twists or tangles of filaments within nerve cells, especially prominent in the cerebral cortex and hippocampus, common in the brains of Alzheimer's disease patients

neuroleptic drug used to treat psychotic symptoms

neuropsychological tests tests of cognitive, sensory, and/or motor skills that attempt to differentiate people with deficits in these areas from normal subjects

neurosis according to Freud, a set of maladaptive symptoms caused by unconscious anxiety

neurotic anxiety according to Freud, anxiety that occurs when one is repeatedly prevented from expressing one's id impulses

neurotic paradox psychoanalytic term for a condition in which an individual's way of coping with unconscious concerns creates even more problems in that individual's life

neurotransmitters biochemicals, released from a sending neuron, that transmit messages to a receiving neuron in the brain and nervous system

nicotine alkaloid found in tobacco; operates on both the central and peripheral nervous systems, resulting in the release of biochemicals, including dopamine, norepinephrine, serotonin, and the endogenous opioids

nonpurging type of bulimia nervosa type of bulimia nervosa in which bingeing is followed by excessive exercise or fasting to control weight gain

norepinephrine neurotransmitter that is involved in the regulation of mood

null hypothesis alternative to a primary hypothesis, stating that there is no relationship between the independent variable and the dependent variable

O

object relations view held by a group of modern psychodynamic theorists that one develops a self-concept and appraisals of others in a four-stage process during childhood and retains them throughout adulthood; psychopathology consists of an incomplete progression through these stages or an acquisition of poor self and other concepts

observational learning learning that occurs when a person observes the rewards and punishments of another's behavior and then behaves in accordance with the same rewards and punishments

obsessions uncontrollable, persistent thoughts, images, ideas, or impulses that an individual feels intrude upon his or her consciousness and that cause significant anxiety or distress

obsessive-compulsive disorder (OCD) anxiety disorder characterized by obsessions (persistent thoughts) and compulsions (rituals)

obsessive-compulsive personality disorder pervasive rigidity in one's activities and interpersonal relationships; includes qualities such as emotional constriction, extreme perfectionism, and anxiety resulting from even slight disruptions in one's routine ways

odd-eccentric personality disorders disorders, including paranoid, schizotypal, and schizoid personality disorders, marked by chronic odd and/or inappropriate behavior with mild features of psychosis and/or paranoia

Oedipus complex according to Freud, major conflict of male sexual development, during which boys are sexually attracted to their mothers and hate their fathers as rivals

operant conditioning form of learning in which behaviors lead to consequences that either reinforce or punish the organism, leading to an increased or a decreased probability of a future response

operationalization specific manner in which one measures or manipulates variables in a study

opioids substances, including morphine and heroin, that produce euphoria followed by a tranquil state; in severe intoxication, can lead to unconsciousness, coma, and seizures; can cause withdrawal symptoms of emotional distress, severe nausea, sweating, diarrhea, and fever

oppositional defiant disorder syndrome of chronic misbehavior in childhood marked by belligerence, irritability, and defiance, although not to the extent found in a diagnosis of conduct disorder

oral stage according to Freud, earliest psychosexual stage, lasting for the first 18 months of life; libidinal impulses are best satisfied through the stimulation of the mouth area, including actions such as feeding or sucking; major issues of concern are dependence and the reliability of others

organic amnesia loss of memory caused by brain injury resulting from disease, drugs, accidents (blows to head), or surgery

orgasm discharge of neuromuscular tension built up during sexual activity; in men, entails rhythmic contractions of the prostate, seminal vesicles, vas deferens, and penis and seminal discharge; in women, entails contractions of the orgasmic platform and uterus

P

pain disorder syndrome marked by the chronic experience of acute pain that appears to have no physical cause

palialia continuous repetition of sounds and words

panic attacks short, intense periods during which an individual experiences physiological and cognitive symptoms of anxiety, characterized by intense fear and discomfort

panic disorder disorder characterized by recurrent, unexpected panic attacks

paranoid personality disorder chronic and pervasive mistrust and suspicion of other people that are unwarranted and maladaptive

paranoid schizophrenia syndrome marked by delusions and hallucinations that involve themes of persecution and grandiosity

paraphilias atypical sexual activities that involve one of the following: (1) nonhuman objects, (2) nonconsenting adults, (3)the suffering or humiliation of oneself or one's partner, or (4) children

parasomnias primary sleep disorders that involve abnormal behavioral and physiological events occurring during sleep

partial reinforcement schedule form of behavior modification in which a behavior is rewarded or punished only some of the time

patients' rights movement movement to ensure that mental patients retain their basic rights and to remove them from institutions and care for them in the community

pedophilia adult obtainment of sexual gratification by engaging in sexual activities with young children

penis envy according to Freud, wish to have the male sex organ

performance anxiety anxiety over sexual performance that interferes with sexual functioning

perinatal hypoxia oxygen deprivation during labor and delivery; an obstetrical complication that may be especially important in neurological development

persecutory delusion false, persistent belief that one is being pursued by other people

personality habitual and enduring ways of thinking, feeling, and acting that make each person unique

personality disorder chronic pattern of maladaptive cognition, emotion, and behavior that begins in adolescence or early adulthood and continues into later adulthood

personality inventories questionnaires that assess people's typical ways of thinking, feeling, and behaving; used to obtain information about people's well-being, self-concept, attitudes, and beliefs

pervasive developmental disorders disorders characterized by severe and persisting impairment in several areas of development

phallic stage according to Freud, psycho-sexual stage that occurs between the ages of 3 and 6: the focus of pleasure is the genitals; important conflicts of sexual development emerge this time, differing for boys and girls

phenothiazines drugs that reduce the functional level of dopamine in the brain and tend to reduce the symptoms of schizophrenia

phenylcyclidine (PCP) substance that produces euphoria, slowed reaction times, and involuntary movements at low doses; disorganized thinking, feelings of unreality, and hostility at intermediate doses; and amnesia, analgesia, respiratory problems, and changes in body temperature at high doses

phonological disorder disorder involving the use of speech sounds inappropriate for one's age or dialect

pituitary major endocrine gland that lies partly on the outgrowth of the brain and just below the hypothalamus; produces the largest number of different hormones and controls the secretions of other endocrine glands

placebo control group in a therapy outcome study, group of people whose treatment is an inactive substance (to compare with the effects of a drug) or a nontheory-based therapy providing social support (to compare with the effects of psychotherapy)

plaques deposits of amyloid protein that accumulate in the extracellular spaces of the cerebral cortex, hippocampus, and other forebrain structures in people with Alzheimer's disease

plateau phase in the sexual response cycle, period between arousal and orgasm, during which excitement remains high but stable

pleasure principle drive to maximize pleasure and minimize pain as quickly as possible

polygenic combination of many genes, each of which makes a small contribution to an inherited trait

positive symptoms in schizophrenia, hallucinations, delusions, and disorganization in thought and behavior (also called Type I symptoms)

positron-emission tomography (PET) method of localizing and measuring brain activity by detecting photons that result from the metabolization of an injected isotope

posttraumatic stress disorder (PTSD) anxiety disorder characterized by (1) repeated mental images of experiencing a traumatic event, (2) emotional numbing and detachment, and (3) hypervigilance and chronic arousal

preconscious according to Freud, area of the psyche that contains material from the unconscious before it reaches the conscious mind

predictive validity extent to which a measure accurately forecasts how a person will think, act, and feel in the future

predisposition tendency to develop a disorder that must interact with other biological, psychological, or environmental factors for the disorder to develop

prefrontal cortex region at the front of the brain important in language, emotional expression, the planning and producing of new ideas, and the mediation of social interactions

prefrontal lobotomy type of psychosurgery in which the frontal lobes of the brain are severed from the lower centers of the brain in people suffering from psychosis

premature ejaculation man's inability to delay ejaculation after minimal sexual stimulation or until one wishes to ejaculate, causing significant distress or interpersonal problems

premenstrual dysphoric disorder syndrome in which a woman experiences an increase in depressive symptoms during the premenstrual period and relief from these symptoms with the onset of menstruation

prepared classical conditioning theory that evolution has prepared people to be easily conditioned to fear objects or situations that were dangerous in ancient times

prevalence proportion of the population that has a specific disorder at a given point or period in time

primary prevention cessation of the development of psychological disorders before they start

primary process thinking wish fulfillment, or fantasies, humans use to conjure up desired objects or actions; an example is a hungry infant's imagining its mother's breast when she is not present

prodromal symptoms in schizophrenia, milder symptoms prior to an acute phase of the disorder, during which behaviors are unusual and peculiar but not yet psychotic or completely disorganized

projective test presentation of an ambiguous stimulus, such as an inkblot, to a client, who then projects unconscious motives and issues onto the stimulus in his or her interpretation of its content

prototypes images of the self and others in relation to the self formed from experiences with family during childhood

psychic epidemics phenomena in which large numbers of people begin to engage in unusual behaviors that appear to have a psychological origin

psychoanalysis form of treatment for psychopathology involving alleviating unconscious conflicts driving psychological symptoms by helping people gain insight into their conflicts and finding ways of resolving these conflicts

psychodynamic theories theories developed by Freud's followers but usually differing somewhat from Freud's original theories

psychodynamic therapies therapies focused on uncovering and resolving unconscious conflicts that drive psychological symptoms

psychogenic amnesia loss of memory in the absence of any brain injury or disease and thought to have psychological causes

psychological approach approach to abnormality that focuses on personality, behavior, and ways of thinking as possible causes of abnormality

psychological theories theories that view mental disorders as caused by psychological processes, such as beliefs, thinking styles, and coping styles

psychopathology symptoms that cause mental, emotional, and/or physical pain

psychopathy set of broad personality traits including superficial charm, a grandiose sense of self-worth, a tendency toward boredom and need for stimulation, pathological lying, an ability to be conning and manipulative, and a lack of remorse

psychosexual stages according to Freud, tages in the developmental process children pass through; in each stage, sex drives are focused on the stimulation of certain areas of the body and particular psychological issues can arouse anxiety

psychosis state involving a loss of contact with reality as well as an inability to differentiate between reality and one's subjective state

psychosomatic disorders syndromes marked by identifiable physical illness or defect caused at least partly by psychological factors

psychosurgery rare treatment for mental disorders in which a neurosurgeon attempts to destroy small areas of the brain thought to be involved in a patient's symptoms

psychotherapy treatment for abnormality that consists of a therapist and client discussing the client's symptoms and their causes; the therapist's theoretical orientation determines the foci of conversations with the client

purging type of bulimia nervosa type of bulimia nervosa in which bingeing is followed by the use of self-induced vomiting or purging medications to control weight gain

R

random assignment assignment of participants in an experiment to groups based on a random process

rapid cycling bipolar disorder diagnosis given when a person has four or more cycles of mania and depression within a single year

reading disorder developmental disorder involving deficits in reading ability

realistic anxiety anxiety that occurs when one faces a real danger or threat, such as a tornado

reality principle idea that the ego seeks to satisfy one's needs within the realities of society's rules, rather than following the abandon of the pleasure principle

receptors molecules on the membranes of neurons to which neurotransmitters bind

reflection method of responding in which a therapist expresses his or her attempt to understand what the client is experiencing and trying to communicate

reformulated learned helplessness theory view that people who attribute negative events to internal, stable, and global causes are more likely than other people to experience learned helplessness deficits following such events and are thus predisposed to depression

relapse prevention programs treatments that seek to offset continued alcohol use by identifying high-risk situations for those attempting to stop or cut down on drinking and teaching them either to avoid those situations or to use assertiveness skills when in them, while viewing setbacks as temporary

reliability degree of consistency in a measurement—that is, the extent to which it yields accurate measurements of a phenomenon across several trials, across different populations, and in different forms

repetitive transcranial magnetic stimulation (rTMS) biological treatment that exposes patients to repeated, high-intensity magnetic pulses that are focused on particular brain structures in order to stimulate those structures

replication repetition of the same results from study to study

repression defense mechanism in which the ego pushes anxiety-provoking material back into the unconscious

residual schizophrenia diagnosis made when a person has already experienced a single acute phase of schizophrenia but currently has milder and less debilitating symptoms

residual symptoms in schizophrenia, milder symptoms following an acute phase of the disorder, during which behaviors are unusual and peculiar but not psychotic or completely disorganized

resistance in psychodynamic therapy, when a client finds it difficult or impossible to address certain material, the client's resistance signals an unconscious conflict, which the therapist then tries to interpret

resolution in the sexual response cycle, state of deep relaxation following orgasm in which a man loses his erection and a woman's orgasmic platform subsides

response shaping technique used in behavior therapy in which a person's behavior problems are changed to desirable behaviors through operant conditioning

restricting type of anorexia nervosa type of anorexia nervosa in which weight gain is prevented by refusing to eat

retrograde amnesia deficit in the ability to recall previously learned information or past events

Rett's disorder pervasive developmental disorder in which children develop normally at first but later show permanent loss of basic skills in social interactions, language, and/or movement

reuptake process in which a sending neuron reabsorbs some of the neurotransmitter in the synapse, decreasing the amount left in the synapse

right to refuse treatment right, although not recognized by all states, of involuntarily committed people to refuse drugs or other treatment

right to treatment fundamental right of involuntarily committed people to active treatment for their disorders rather than shelter alone

risk factors conditions or variables associated with a higher risk of having a disorder

role-play technique used in behavioral therapy in which the client and the therapist take on the roles of people involved with the client's maladaptive behaviors; the therapist observes the client's behavior in the role-play to assess what aspects of that behavior need to change

rumination focusing on one's personal concerns and feelings of distress repetitively and passively

ruminative response styles theory theory stating that tendencies to focus on one's symptoms of distress and the possible causes and consequences of these symptoms, in a passive and repetitive manner, leads to depression

S

sadomasochism pattern of sexual rituals between a sexually sadistic "giver" and a sexually masochistic "receiver"

sample group of people taken from a population of interest to participate in a study

schizoid personality disorder syndrome marked by a chronic lack of interest in and avoidance of interpersonal relationships as well as emotional coldness in interactions with others

schizophrenia disorder consisting of unreal or disorganized thoughts and perceptions as well as verbal, cognitive, and behavioral deficits

schizotypal personality disorder chronic pattern of inhibited or inappropriate emotion and social behavior as well as aberrant cognitions and disorganized speech

scientific method systematic method of obtaining and evaluating information relevant to a problem

seasonal affective disorder (SAD) disorder identified by a two-year period in which a person experiences major depression during winter months and then recovers fully during the summer; some people with this disorder also experience mild mania during summer months

secondary prevention detection of psychological disorders in their earliest stages and treatment designed to reduce their development

secondary process thinking rational deliberation, as opposed to the irrational thought of primary process thinking

selective serotonin reuptake inhibitors (SSRIs) class of antidepressant drugs

self-actualization fulfillment of one's potential for love, creativity, and meaning

self-efficacy beliefs beliefs that one can engage in the behaviors necessary to overcome a situation

self-help groups groups that form to help the members deal with a common problem

self-monitoring method of assessment in which a client records the number of times per day that he or she engages in a specific behavior and the conditions surrounding the behavior

sensate focus therapy treatment for sexual dysfunction in which partners alternate between giving and receiving stimulation in a relaxed, openly communicative atmosphere, in order to reduce performance anxiety and concern over achieving orgasm by learning each partner's sexual fulfillment needs

separation anxiety disorder syndrome of childhood and adolescence marked by the presence of abnormal fear or worry over becoming separated from one's caregiver(s) as well as clinging behaviors in the presence of the caregiver(s)

serotonin neurotransmitter that is involved in the regulation of mood and impulsive responses

set point natural body weight determined by a person's metabolic rate, diet, and genetics

sexual aversion disorder condition in which a person actively avoids sexual activities and experiences sex as unpleasant or anxiety-provoking

sexual desire in the sexual response cycle, an urge or inclination to engage in sexual activity

sexual dysfunctions problems in experiencing sexual arousal or carrying through with sexual acts to the point of sexual arousal

sexual masochism sexual gratification obtained through experiencing pain and humiliation at the hands of one's partner

sexual orientation one's preference for partners of the same or opposite sex with respect to attraction and sexual desire

sexual sadism sexual gratification obtained through inflicting pain and humiliation on one's partner

single-case experimental design experimental design in which an individual or a small number of individuals is studied intensively; the individual is put through some sort of manipulation or intervention, and his or her behavior is examined before and after this manipulation to determine the effects

situational type phobias extreme fears of situations such as public transportation, tunnels, bridges, elevators, flying, driving, or enclosed spaces

sleep apnea repeated episodes of upper-airway obstruction during sleep; people with sleep apnea typically snore loudly, go silent and do not breathe for several seconds at a time, then gasp for air

sleep restriction therapy treatment for insomnia that involves initially restricting the amount of time that people with insomnia can try to sleep at night

smooth pursuit eye movement task in which individuals are asked to keep their head still and track a moving object (sometimes referred to as eye tracking); some people with schizophrenia show deficits on this task

social approach approach to abnormality that focuses on interpersonal relationships, culture, society, and the environment as possible causes of abnormality

social learning theory theory that people learn behaviors by imitating and observing others and by learning about the rewards and punishments that follow behaviors

social phobia extreme fear of being judged or embarrassed in front of people, causing the individual to avoid social situations

social selection explanation of the effects of the symptoms of schizophrenia on a person's life and the resulting tendency to drift downward in social class, as compared with the person's family of origin

social skills training technique often used in behavior therapy to help people with problems in interacting and communicating with others

social structural theories theories that focus on environmental and societal demands as causes of abnormal behavior

somatic hallucinations perceptions that something is happening inside one's body—for example, that worms are eating one's intestines

somatization disorder syndrome marked by the chronic experience of unpleasant or painful physical symptoms for which no organic cause can be found

somatoform disorders disorders marked by unpleasant or painful physical symptoms that have no apparent organic cause and that are often not physiologically possible, suggesting that psychological factors are involved

specific phobias extreme fears of specific objects or situations that cause an individual to routinely avoid those objects or situations

splitting in object relations theory, phenomenon wherein a person splits conceptions of self and others into either all-good or all-bad categories, neglecting to recognize people's mixed qualities

squeeze technique sex therapy technique used for premature ejaculation; the man's partner stimulates him to an erection, and then when he signals that ejaculation is imminent, the partner applies a firm but gentle squeeze to his

penis, either at the glands or at the base, for three or four seconds, the goal of this technique is for the man to learn to identify the point of ejaculatory inevitability and to control his arousal level at the point

statistical significance likelihood that a study's results have occurred only by chance

stimulus-control therapy behavioral intervention for insomnia that involves a set of instructions designed to reduce behaviors that might interfere with sleep and to regulate sleep wake schedules

stop-start technique sex therapy technique used for premature ejaculation; the man or his partner stimulates his penis until he is about to ejaculate; the man then relaxes and concentrates on the sensations in his body until his level of arousal declines; the goal of this technique is for the man to learn to identify the point of ejaculatory inevitability and to control his arousal level at that point

stress experience of events that we perceive as endangering our physical or psychological well-being

stress-management interventions strategies that teach clients to overcome the problems in their lives that are increasing their stress

stroke sudden damage to the brain due to blockage of blood flow or hemorrhaging

structured interview meeting between a clinician and a client or a client's associate(s) in which the clinician asks questions that are standardized, written in advance, and asked of every client

stuttering significant problem in speech fluency, often including frequent repetitions of sounds or syllables

subintentional deaths acts in which individuals indirectly contribute to their own deaths

substance naturally occurring or synthetically produced product that alters perceptions, thoughts, emotions, and behaviors when ingested, smoked, or injected

substance abuse diagnosis given when a person's recurrent substance use leads to significant harmful consequences, as manifested by a failure to fulfill obligations at work, school, or home, the use of substances in physically hazardous situations, legal problems, and continued use despite social and legal problems

substance dependence diagnosis given when a person's substance use leads to physiological dependence or significant impairment or distress, as manifested by an inability to use the substance in moderation; a decline in social, occupational, or recreational activities; or the spending of large amounts of time obtaining substances or recovering from their effects

substance intoxication experience of significantly maladaptive behavioral and psychological symptoms due to the effect of a substance on the central nervous system that develops during or shortly after use of the substance

substance withdrawal experience of clinically significant distress in social, occupational, or other areas of functioning due to the cessation or reduction of substance use

substance-induced sexual dysfunction problems in sexual functioning caused by substance use

substance-related disorder inability to use a substance in moderation and/or the intentional use of a substance to change one's thoughts, feelings, and/or behaviors, leading to impairment in work, academic, personal, or social endeavors

suicide purposeful taking of one's own life

suicide cluster when two or more suicides or attempted suicides nonrandomly occur closely together in space or time

suicide contagion phenomenon in which the suicide of a well-known person is linked to the acceptance of suicide by people who closely identify with that individual

suicide hot lines organizations in which suicide crisis intervention is done over the phone

superego part of the unconscious that consists of absolute moral standards internalized from one's parents during childhood and from one's culture

supernatural theories theories that see mental disorders as the result of supernatural forces, such as divine intervention, curses, demonic possession, and/or personal sins; mental disorders can be cured through religious rituals, exorcisms, confessions, and/or death

symptom questionnaire questionnaire that assesses what symptoms a person is experiencing

synapse space between a sending neuron and a receiving neuron into which neurotransmitters are first released (also known as the synaptic gap)

syndrome set of symptoms that tend to occur together

systematic desensitization therapy type of behavior therapy that attempts to reduce client anxiety through relaxation techniques and progressive exposure to feared stimuli

T

tactile hallucinations perceptions that something is happening to the outside of one's body—for example, that bugs are crawling up one's back

tardive dyskinesia neurological disorder marked by involuntary movements of the tongue, face, mouth, or jaw, resulting from taking neuroleptic drugs

test-retest reliability index of how consistent the results of a test are over time

theory set of assumptions about the likely causes of abnormality and appropriate treatments

therapeutic alliance during therapy, the therapist is empathetic and supportive of the client in order to create a relationship of trust with the client and to encourage the exploration of difficult issues

therapy outcome study experimental study that assesses the effects of an intervention designed to reduce psychopathology in an experimental group, while performing no intervention or a different type of intervention on another group

third variable problem possibility that variables not measured in a study are the real cause of the relationship between the variables measured in the study

thought-stopping techniques strategies that involve finding ways to stop intrusive thoughts

token economy application of operant conditioning in which patients receive tokens for exhibiting desired behaviors that are exchangeable for privileges and rewards; these tokens are withheld when a patient exhibits unwanted behaviors

tolerance condition of experiencing less and less effect from the same dose of a substance

transference in psychodynamic therapies, the client's reaction to the therapist as if the therapist were an important person in his or her early development; the client's feelings and beliefs about this other person are transferred onto the therapist

transsexuals people who experience chronic discomfort with their gender and genitals as well as a desire to be rid of their genitals and to live as a member of the opposite sex

transvestism paraphilia in which a heterosexual man dresses in women's clothing as his primary means of becoming sexually aroused

trephination procedure in which holes were drilled in the skulls of people displaying abnormal behavior to allow evil spirits to depart their bodies; performed in the Stone Age

tricyclic antidepressants class of antidepressant drugs

twin studies studies of the heritability of a disorder by comparing concordance rates between monozygotic and dizygotic twins

Type A behavior pattern personality pattern characterized by time urgency, hostility, and competitiveness

U

unconditional positive regard essential part of humanistic therapy; the therapist expresses that he or she accepts the client, no matter how unattractive, disturbed, or difficult the client is

unconditioned response (UR) in classical conditioning, response that naturally follows when a certain stimulus appears, such as a dog salivating when it smells food

unconditioned stimulus (US) in classical conditioning, stimulus that naturally elicits a reaction, as food elicits salivation in dogs

unconscious area of the psyche where memories, wishes, and needs are stored and where conflicts among the id, ego, and superego are played out

undifferentiated schizophrenia diagnosis made when a person experiences schizophrenic symptoms, such as delusions and hallucinations, but does not meet criteria for paranoid, disorganized, or catatonic schizophrenia

unipolar depression type of depression consisting of depressive symptoms but without manic episodes

unstructured interview meeting between a clinician and a client or a client's associate(s) that consists of open-ended, general questions that are particular to each person interviewed

unusualness criterion for abnormality that suggests that abnormal behaviors are rare or unexpected

V

vaginismus in women, involuntary contractions of the muscles surrounding the outer third of the vagina that interfere with penetration and sexual functioning

vagus nerve stimulation (VNS) treatment in which the vagus nerve—the part of the autonomic nervous system that carries information from the head, neck, thorax, and abdomen to several areas of the brain, including the hypothalamus and amygdala—is stimulated by a small electronic device much like a cardiac pacemaker, which is surgically implanted under a patient's skin in the left chest wall

validity degree of correspondence between a measurement and the phenomenon under study

variable measurable factor or characteristic that can vary within an individual, between individuals, or both

vascular dementia second most common type of dementia, associated with symptoms of cerebrovascular disease (tissue damage in the brain due to a blockage of blood flow)

vasocongestion in the sexual response cycle, the filling of blood vessels and tissues with blood, leading to erection of the penis in males and enlargement of the clitoris, swelling of the labia, and vaginal moistening in women (also called engorgement)

visual hallucination visual perception of something that is not actually present

voyeurism obtainment of sexual arousal by compulsively and secretly watching another person undressing, bathing, engaging in sex, or being naked

vulnerability-stress models comprehensive models of the many factors that lead some people to develop a given mental disorder

W

wait list control group in a therapy outcome study, group of people that functions as a control group while an experimental group receives an intervention and then receives the intervention itself after a waiting period

Wernicke's encephalopathy alcohol-induced permanent cognitive disorder involving mental disorientation, confusion, and, in severe states, coma

word salad speech that is so disorganized that a listener cannot comprehend it

working memory ability to hold information in memory and manipulate it

working through method used in psychodynamic therapies in which the client repeatedly goes over and over painful memories and difficult issues as a way to understand and accept them

REFERENCES

A

Aarsland, D., Andersen, K., Larsen, J. P., Lolk, A., & Kragh-Sørensen, P. (2003). Prevalence and characteristics of dementia in Parkinson disease. *Archives of Neurology, 60,* 387–392.

Abbott, B. B., Schoen, L. S., & Badia, P. (1984). Predictable and unpredictable shock: Behavioral measures of aversion and physiological measures of stress. *Psychological Bulletin, 96,* 45–71.

Abbott, D. W., de Zwaan, M., Mussell, M. P., Raymond, N. C., Seim, H. C., Crow, S. J., Crosby, R. D., & Mitchell, J. E. (1998). Onset of binge eating and dieting in overweight women: Implications for etiology, associated features and treatment. *Journal of Psychosomatic Research, 44,* 367–374.

Abel, G. G., & Osborn, C. (1992). The paraphilias: The extent and nature of sexually deviant and criminal behavior. *Psychiatric Clinics of North America, 15,* 675–687.

Abi-Dargham, A., Kegeles, L. S., Zea-Ponce, Y., Mawlawi, O., Martinez, D., Mitropoulou, V., O'Flynn, K., Koenigsberg, H. W., van Heertum, R., Cooper, T., Laruelle, M., & Siever, L. J. (2004). Striatal amphetamine-induced dopamine release in patients with schizotypal personality disorder studied with single photon emission computed tomography and [123I]Iodobenzamide. *Biological Psychiatry, 55,* 1001–1006.

Abramowitz, C. S., Kosson, D. S., & Seidenberg, M. (2004). The relationship between childhood attention deficit hyperactivity disorder and conduct problems and adult psychopathy in male inmates. *Personality and Individual Differences, 36,* 1031–1047.

Abramowitz, J. S. (1997). Effectiveness of psychological and pharmacological treatments for obsessive-compulsive disorder: A quantitative review. *Journal of Consulting & Clinical Psychology, 65,* 44–52.

Abramson, L. Y., Alloy, L. B., Hankin, B. L., Haeffel, G. J., MacCoon, D. G., & Gibb, B. E. (2002). Cognitive vulnerability-stress models of depression in a self-regulatory and psychobiological context. In I. H. Gotlib & C. L. Hammen (Eds.), *Handbook of depression* (pp. 268–294). New York: Guilford Press.

Abramson, L. Y., Metalsky, G. I., & Alloy, L. B. (1989). Hopelessness depression: A theory-based subtype of depression. *Psychological Review, 96,* 358–372.

Abramson, L. Y., Seligman, M. E. P., & Teasdale, J. (1978). Learned helplessness in humans: Critique and reformulation. *Journal of Abnormal Psychology, 87,* 49–74.

Ackerman, M. D., & Carey, M. P. (1995). Psychology's role in the assessment of erectile dysfunction: Historical perspectives, current knowledge, and methods. *Journal of Consulting & Clinical Psychology, 63,* 862–876.

Addis, M. E., Hatgis, C., Krasnow, A. D., Jacob, K., Bourne, L., & Mansfield, A. (2004). Effectiveness of cognitive-behavioral treatment for panic disorder versus treatment as usual in a managed care setting. *Journal of Consulting & Clinical Psychology, 72,* 625–635.

Ader, R. (2001). Psychoneuroimmunology. *Current Directions in Psychological Science, 10,* 94–98.

Aderibigbe, Y. A., Bloch, R. M., & Walker, W. R. (2001). Prevalence of depersonalization and derealization experiences in a rural population. *Social Psychiatry & Psychiatric Epidemiology, 36,* 63–69.

Agras, S., Sylvester, D., & Oliveau, D. (1969). The epidemiology of common fears and phobia. *Comprehensive Psychiatry, 10,* 151–156.

Agras, W. S. (1987). *Eating disorders: Management of obesity, bulimia, and anorexia nervosa.* New York: Pergamon Press.

Agras, W. S., & Kirkley, B. G. (1986). Bulimia: Theories of etiology. In K. D. Brownell & J. P. Foreyt (Eds.), *Handbook of eating disorders: Physiology, psychology, and treatment of obesity, anorexia, and bulimia* (pp. 367–378). New York: Basic Books.

Agras, W. S., Walsh, B. T., Fairburn, C. C., Wilson, G. T., & Kraemer, H. C. (2000). A multicenter comparison of cognitive-behavioral therapy and interpersonal psychotherapy for bulimia nervosa. *Archives of General Psychiatry, 57,* 459–466.

Aguero-Torres, H., Fratiglioni, L., & Winblad, B. (1998). Natural history of Alzheimer's disease and other dementias: Review of the literature in the light of the findings from the Kungholmen Project. *International Journal of Geriatric Psychiatry, 13,* 755–766.

Akhtar, S., Wig, N. N., Varma, V. K., Pershad, D., & Verma, S. K. (1975). A phenomenological analysis of symptoms in obsessive-compulsive neurosis. *British Journal of Psychiatry, 127,* 342–348.

Alexander, K. L., Entwisle, D. R., & Thompson, M. S. (1987). School performance, status relations, and the structure of sentiment: Bringing the teacher back in. *American Sociological Review, 52,* 665–682.

Alexander, M. A. (1999). Sexual offender treatment efficacy revisited. *Sexual Abuse: Journal of Research & Treatment, 11,* 101–116.

Allderidge, P. (1979). Hospitals, madhouses and asylums: Cycles in the care of the insane. *British Journal of Psychiatry, 134,* 321–334.

Allen, J. B., & Iacono, W. G. (2001). Assessing the validity of amnesia in dissociative identity disorder: A dilemma for the DSM and the courts. *Psychology, Public Policy, & Law, 7,* 311–344.

Allison, J., Blatt, S. J., & Zimet, C. N. (1968). *The interpretation of psychological tests.* New York: Harper & Row.

Alloy, L. B., & Abramson, L. Y. (1979). Judgment of contingency in depressed and nondepressed students: Sadder but wiser? *Journal of Experimental Psychology: General, 108,* 441–485.

Alloy, L. B., Abramson, L. Y., & Francis, E. L. (1999). Do negative cognitive styles confer vulnerability to depression? *Current Directions in Psychological Science, 8,* 128–132.

Althof, S. E. (1995). Pharmacologic treatment of rapid ejaculation. *Psychiatric Clinics of North America, 18,* 85–94.

Althof, S. E. (2000). Erectile dysfunction: Psychotherapy with men and couples. In S. R. Leiblum & R. C. Rosen (Eds.), *Principles and practice of sex therapy* (3rd ed., pp. 242–275). New York: Guilford Press.

Altshuler, L. L., Bartzokis, G., Grieder, T., Curran, J., & Mintz, J. (1998). Amygdala enlargement in bipolar disorder and hippocampal reduction in schizophrenia: An MRI study demonstrating neuroanatomic specificity. *Archives of General Psychiatry, 55,* 663–664.

American Heart Association. (2002). Diseases and conditions. Available at www.americanheart.org

American Psychiatric Association (APA). (1994). *Diagnostic and statistical manual of mental disorders* (4th ed.). Washington, DC: American Psychiatric Association.

American Psychiatric Association (APA). (2000). *Diagnostic and statistical manual of mental disorders* (4th ed., Text Revision). Washington, DC: American Psychiatric Association.

American Psychological Association. (2000). Guidelines for psychotherapy with lesbian, gay, and bisexual clients. *American Psychologist, 55,* 1440–1451.

Ananth, J., Burgoyne, K. S., Gadasalli, R., & Aquino, S. (2001). How do the atypical antipsychotics work? *Journal of Psychiatry & Neuroscience, 26,* 385–394.

Anastopoulos, A. D., & Farley, S. E. (2003). A cognitive-behavioral training program for parents of children with attention-deficit/hyperactivity disorder. In A. E. Kazdin & J. R. Weisz (Eds.), *Evidence-based psychotherapies for children and adolescents* (pp. 187–203). New York: Guilford Press.

Anders, S. L. (2003). Improving community-based care for the treatment of schizophrenia: Lessons from native Africa. *Psychiatric Rehabilitation Journal, 27*, 51–58.

Andersen, A. E. (Ed.). (1990). *Males with eating disorders.* New York: Brunner/Mazel.

Andersen, A. E., & DiDomenico, L. (1992). Diet vs. shape content of popular male and female magazines: A dose-response relationship to the incidence of eating disorders? *International Journal of Eating Disorders, 11*, 283–287.

Anderson, E. M., & Lambert, M. J. (1995). Short-term dynamically oriented psychotherapy: A review and meta-analysis. *Clinical Psychology Review, 15*, 503–514.

Anderson, G., Yasenik, L., & Ross, C. A. (1993). Dissociative experiences and disorders among women who identify themselves as sexual abuse survivors. *Child Abuse & Neglect, 17*, 677–686.

Anderson, G. M., & Hoshino, Y. (1997). Neurochemical studies of autism. In D. J. Cohen & F. R. Volkmar (Eds.), *Handbook of autism and pervasive developmental disorders* (pp. 325–343). Toronto: Wiley.

Anderson, N. B., Lane, J. D., Taguchi, F., & Williams, R. B. (1989). Patterns of cardiovascular responses to stress as a function of race and parental hypertension in men. *Health Psychology, 8*, 525–540.

Anderson, R. E., Bartlett, S. J., Morgan, G. D., & Brownell, K. D. (1995). Weight loss, psychological, and nutritional patterns in competitive male body builders. *International Journal of Eating Disorders, 18*, 49–57.

Andreasen, N. (2001). Neuroimaging and neurobiology of schizophrenia. In K. Miyoshi, C. M. Shapiro, M. Gaviria, & Y. Morita (Eds.), *Contemporary neuropsychiatry* (pp. 265–271). Tokyo: Springer-Verlag.

Andreasen, N. C., Flaum, M., Swayze, V. W., Tyrrell, G., & Arndt, S. (1990). Positive and negative symptoms in schizophrenia: A critical reappraisal. *Archives of General Psychiatry, 47*, 615–621.

Angold, A., Costello, E. J., & Worthman, C. M. (1998). Puberty and depression: The roles of age, pubertal status, and pubertal timing. *Psychological Medicine, 28*, 51–61.

Angold, A., Erkanli, A., Egger, H. L., & Costello, J. (2000). Stimulant treatment for children: A community perspective. *Journal of the American Academy of Child & Adolescent Psychiatry, 39*, 975–994.

Angold, A., Erkanli, A., Farmer, E. M. Z., Fairbank, J. A., Burns, B. J., Keeler, G., & Costello, J. (2002). Psychiatric disorder, impairment, and service use in rural African American and white youth. *Archives of General Psychiatry, 59*, 893–901.

Angst, J. (1998). Treated versus untreated major depressive episodes. *Psychopathology, 31*, 37–44.

Angst, J., Gamma, A., Endrass, J., Goodwin, R., Ajdacic, V., Eich, D., & Rössler, W. (2004). Obsessive-compulsive severity spectrum in the community: Prevalence, comorbidity, and course. *European Archives of Psychiatry & Clinical Neuroscience, 254*, 156–164.

Angst, J., Vollrath, M., Koch, R., & Dobler-Mikola, A. (1989). The Zurich Study: VII. Insomnia: Symptoms, classification and prevalence. *European Archives of Psychiatry & Clinical Neuroscience, 238*, 285–293.

Anonymous. (1983). First-person account. *Schizophrenia Bulletin, 9*, 152–155.

Anonymous. (1992). First-person account: Portrait of a schizophrenic. *Schizophrenia Bulletin, 18*, 333–334.

Anton, R. F. (2001). Pharmacologic approaches to the management of alcoholism. *Journal of Clinical Psychiatry, 62*(Suppl. 20), 11–17.

Appelbaum, P. S. (2003). The "quiet" crisis in mental health services. *Health Affairs, 22*, 110–116.

Arieti, S. (1955). *Interpretation of schizophrenia.* New York: R. Brunner.

Arieti, S., & Bemporad, J. R. (1980). The psychological organization of depression. *American Journal of Psychiatry, 137*, 1360–1365.

Arnold, L. M., Keck, P. E., Jr., Collins, J., Wilson, R., Fleck, D. E., Corey, K. B., Amicone, J., Adebimpe, V. R., & Strakowski, S. M. (2004). Ethnicity and first-rank symptoms in patients with psychosis. *Schizophrenia Research, 67*, 207–212.

Arseneault, L., Moffitt, T. E., Caspi, A., Taylor, A., Rijsdijk, F. V., Jaffee, S. R., Ablow, J. C., & Measelle, J. R. (2003). Strong genetic effects on cross-situational antisocial behaviour among 5-year-old children according to mothers, teachers, examiner-observers, and twins' self-reports. *Journal of Child Psychology & Psychiatry, 44*, 832–848.

Arseneault, L., Moffitt, T. E., Caspi, A., Taylor, P. J., & Silva, P. A. (2000). Mental disorders and violence in a total birth cohort. *Archives of General Psychiatry, 57*, 979–986.

Asberg, M., & Forslund, K. (2000). Neurobiological aspects of suicidal behavior. *International Review of Psychiatry, 12*, 62–74.

Ashton, A. K., & Rosen, R. C. (1998). Bupropion as an antidote for serotonin reuptake inhibitor–induced sexual dysfunction. *Journal of Clinical Psychiatry, 59*, 112–115.

Astin, J. A. (1998). Why patients use alternative medicine: Results of a national study. *Journal of the American Medical Association, 279*, 1548–1553.

Atiya, M., Hyman, B. T., Albert, M. S., & Killiany, R. (2003). Structural magnetic resonance imaging in established and prodromal Alzheimer's disease: A review. *Alzheimer's Disease & Associated Disorders, 17*, 177–195.

August, G. L., Realmutto, G. M., Hektner, J. M., & Bloomquist, M. L. (2001). An integrated components preventive intervention for aggressive elementary school children: The early risers' program. *Journal of Consulting & Clinical Psychology, 69*, 614–626.

B

Bach, A. K., Wincze, J. P., & Barlow, D. H. (2001). Sexual dysfunction. In D. H. Barlow (Ed.), *Clinical handbook of psychological disorders: A step-by-step treatment manual* (3rd ed., pp. 562–608). New York: Guilford Press.

Bachrach, H. M., Galatzer-Levy, R., Skolnikoff, A., & Waldron, S. (1991). On the efficacy of psychoanalysis. *Journal of the American Psychoanalytic Association, 39*, 871–916.

Baer, J. S., Kivlahan, D. R., Blume, A. W., McKnight, P., & Marlatt, G. A. (2001). Brief intervention for heavy-drinking college students: 4-year follow-up and natural history. *American Journal of Public Health, 91*, 1310–1316.

Baer, J. S., Marlatt, G. A., Kivlahan, D. R., & Fromme, K. (1992). An experimental test of three methods of alcohol risk reduction with young adults. *Journal of Consulting & Clinical Psychology, 60*, 974–979.

Bagby, R. M., Costa, P. T., McCrae, Robert R., Livesley, W. J., Kennedy, S. H., Levitan, R. D., Levitt, A. J., Joffe, R. T., & Young, L. T. (1999). Replicating the five factor model of personality in a psychiatric sample. *Personality & Individual Differences, 27*, 1135–1139.

Bagge, C., Nickell, A., Stepp, S., Durrett, C., Jackson, K., & Trull, T. J. (2004). Borderline personality disorder features predict negative outcomes 2 years later. *Journal of Abnormal Psychology, 113*, 279–288.

Baker, A., & Shalhoub-Kevorkian, N. (1999). Effects of political and military traumas on children: The Palestinian case. *Clinical Psychology Review, 19*, 935–950.

Baker, D., Hunter, E., Lawrence, E., Medford, N., Patel, M., Senior, C., Sierra, M., Lambert, M. V., Phillips, M. L., & David, A. S. (2003). Depersonalisation disorder: Clinical features of 204 cases. *British Journal of Psychiatry, 182*, 428–433.

Baldessarini, R. J., Tondo, L., & Hennen, J. (2001). Treating the suicidal patient with bipolar disorder: Reducing suicide risk with lithium. *Annals of the New York Academy of Sciences, 932*, 24–38.

Ballenger, J. C., Davidson, J. R. T., Lecrubier, Y., Nutt, D. J., Marshall, R. D., Nemeroff, C. B., Shalev, A. Y., & Yehuda, R. (2004). Consensus statement update on posttraumatic stress disorder from the International Consensus Group on Depression and Anxiety. *Journal of Clinical Psychiatry, 65*(Suppl. 1), 55–62.

Balon, R. (1998). Fluoxamine-induced erectile dysfunction responding to sildenafil. *Journal of Sex & Marital Therapy, 24*, 313–317.

Bandura, A. (1969). *Principles of behavior modification.* New York: Holt, Rinehart & Winston.

Bandura, A. (1977). Self-efficacy: Toward a unifying theory of behavioral change. *Psychological Review, 84*, 191–215.

Bandura, A. (1986). *Social foundations of thought and action.* Englewood Cliffs, NJ: Prentice Hall.

Bandura, A. (1995). *Self-efficacy in changing societies.* New York: Cambridge University Press.

Banks, S., Robbins, P. C., Silver, E., Vesselinov, R., Steadman, H. J., Monahan, J., Mulvey, E. P., Appelbaum, P. S., Grisso, T., & Roth, L. H. (2004). A multiple-models approach to violence risk assessment among people with mental disorder. *Criminal Justice & Behavior, 31*, 324–340.

Banse, R. (2004). Adult attachment and marital satisfaction: Evidence for dyadic configuration effects. *Journal of Social & Personal Relationships, 21*, 273–282.

Barch, D. M. (2003). Cognition in schizophrenia: Does working memory work? *Current Directions in Psychological Science, 12,* 146–150.

Barch, D. M. (2005). The cognitive neuroscience of schizophrenia. *Annual Review of Clinical Psychology, 1,* 321–353.

Barch, D. M., Csernansky, J. G., Conturo, T., & Snyder, A. Z. (2002). Working and long-term memory deficits in schizophrenia: Is there a common prefrontal mechanism? *Journal of Abnormal Psychology, 111,* 478–494.

Barefoot, J. C., Dahlstrom, W. G., & Williams, R. B. (1983). Hostility, CHD incidence, and total mortality: A 25-yr follow-up study of 255 physicians. *Psychosomatic Medicine, 45,* 59–63.

Barefoot, J. C., Dodge, K. A., Peterson, B. L., Dahlstrom, W. G., & Williams, R. B., Jr. (1989). The Cook-Medley Hostility Scale: Item content and ability to predict survival. *Psychosomatic Medicine, 51,* 46–57.

Barefoot, J. C., Siegler, I. C., Nowlin, J. B., & Peterson, B. L. (1987). Suspiciousness, health, and mortality: A follow-up study of 500 older adults. *Psychosomatic Medicine, 49,* 450–457.

Barkley, R. A. (1991). Attention deficit hyperactivity disorder. *Psychiatric Annals, 21,* 725–733.

Barkley, R. A. (1996). Attention deficit/ hyperactivity disorder. In E. J. Mash & R. A. Barkley (Eds.), *Child psychopathology* (pp. 63–112). New York: Guilford Press.

Barkley, R. A., Fischer, M., Edelbrock, C. S., & Smallish, L. (1990). The adolescent outcome of hyperactive children diagnosed by research criteria: I. An 8-year prospective follow-up study. *Journal of the American Academy of Child & Adolescent Psychiatry, 29,* 546–557.

Barkley, R. A., Fischer, M., Smallish, L., & Fletcher, K. (2004). Young adult follow-up of hyperactive children: Antisocial activities and drug use. *Journal of Child Psychology & Psychiatry, 45,* 195–211.

Barlow, D. H. (1986). Causes of sexual dysfunction: The role of anxiety and cognitive interference. *Journal of Consulting & Clinical Psychology, 54,* 140–148.

Barlow, D. H. (1988). *Anxiety and its disorders: The nature and treatment of anxiety and panic.* New York: Guilford Press.

Barlow, D. H., & Craske, M. G. (1994). *Mastery of your anxiety and panic (MAP II).* Albany, NY: Graywind.

Barlow, D. H., Craske, M. G., Cerny, J. A., & Klosko, J. S. (1989). Behavioral treatment of panic disorder. *Behavior Therapy, 20,* 261–282.

Barlow, D. H., Gorman, J. M., Shear, M. K., & Woods, S. W. (2000). Cognitive-behavioral therapy, imipramine, or their combination for panic disorder: A randomized controlled trial. *Journal of the American Medical Association, 283,* 2529–2536.

Barlow, D. H., Sakheim, D. K., & Beck, J. G. (1983). Anxiety increases sexual arousal. *Journal of Abnormal Psychology, 92,* 49–54.

Baron, P., & Peixoto, N. (1991). Depressive symptoms in adolescents as a function of personality factors. *Journal of Youth & Adolescence, 20,* 493–500.

Baron-Cohen, S., & Swettenham, J. (1997). Theory of mind in autism: Its relationship to executive function and central coherence. In D. J. Cohen & F. R. Volkmar (Eds.), *Handbook of autism and pervasive developmental disorders* (pp. 880–893). Toronto: Wiley.

Barsky, A. J., Wyshak, G., & Klerman, G. L. (1992). Psychiatric comorbidity in DSM-III-R hypochondriasis. *Archives of General Psychiatry, 49,* 101–108.

Bartlik, B., & Goldberg, J. (2000). Female sexual arousal disorder. In S. R. Leiblum & R. C. Rosen (Eds.), *Principles and practice of sex therapy* (3rd ed., pp. 85–117). New York: Guilford Press.

Bartlik, B., & Goldstein, M. Z. (2001a). Practical geriatrics: Maintaining sexual health after menopause. *Psychiatric Services, 51,* 751–753.

Bartlik, B., & Goldstein, M. Z. (2001b). Practical geriatrics: Men's sexual health after midlife. *Psychiatric Services, 52,* 291–293.

Basoglu, M., Kiliç, C., Salcioglu, E., & Livanou, M. (2004). Prevalence of posttraumatic stress disorder and comorbid depression in earthquake survivors in Turkey: An epidemiological study. *Journal of Traumatic Stress, 17,* 133–141.

Basoglu, M., Mineka, S., Paker, M., Aker, T., Livanou, M., & Gok, S. (1997). Psychological preparedness for trauma as a protective factor in survivors of torture. *Psychological Medicine, 27,* 1421–1433.

Basson, R., Berman, J., Burnett, A., Derogatis, L., Ferguson, D., Fourcroy, J., Goldstein, I., Graziottin, A., Heiman, J., Laan, E., Leiblum, S., Padma-Nathan, H., Rosen, R., Segraves, K., Segraves, R. T., Shabsigh, R., Sipski, M., Wagner, G., & Whippie, B. (2001). Report of the international consensus development conference on female sexual dysfunction: Definitions and classifications. *Journal of Sex & Marital Therapy, 27,* 83–94.

Basson, R., McInnes, R., Smith, M. D., Hodgson, G., & Koppiker, N. (2002). Efficacy and safety of sildenafil citrate in women with sexual dysfunction associated with female sexual arousal disorder. *Journal of Women's Health & Gender-Based Medicine, 11,* 367–377.

Bastien, C. H., Morin, C. M., Ouellet, M.-C., Blais, F. C., & Bouchard, S. (2004). Cognitive-behavioral therapy for insomnia: Comparison of individual therapy, group therapy, and telephone consultations. *Journal of Consulting & Clinical Psychology, 72,* 653–659.

Bateson, G., Jackson, D. D., Haley, J., & Weakland, J. (1956). Toward a theory of schizophrenia. *Behavioral Science, 1,* 251–264.

Bauermeister, J. J., Alegria, M., Bird, H. R., Rubio-Stipec, M., et al. (1992). Are attentional-hyperactivity deficits unidimensional or multidimensional syndromes? Empirical findings from a community survey. *Journal of the American Academy of Child & Adolescent Psychiatry, 31,* 423–431.

Baum, A., & Posluszny, D. M. (2001). Traumatic stress as a target for intervention with cancer patients. In A. Baum (Ed.), *Psychosocial interventions for cancer* (pp. 143–173). Washington, DC: American Psychological Association.

Baum, A. S., & Burnes, D. W. (1993). *A nation in denial: The truth about homelessness.* Boulder, CO: Westview Press.

Baxter, L., Schwartz, J., Bergman, K., & Szuba, M. (1992). Caudate glucose metabolic rate changes with both drug and behavior therapy for obsessive-compulsive disorder. *Archives of General Psychiatry, 49,* 681–689.

Baxter, L. R., Jr., Clark, E. C., Iqbal, M., & Ackermann, R. F. (2001). Cortical-subcortical systems in the mediation of obsessive-compulsive disorder: Modeling the brain's mediation of a classic "neurosis." In D. G. Lichter & J. L. Cummings (Eds.), *Frontal-subcortical circuits in psychiatric and neurological disorders* (pp. 207–230). New York: Guilford Press.

Bayley, J. (1999). *Elegy for Iris.* New York: St. Martin's Press.

Beatty, J. (1995). *Principles of behavioral neuroscience.* Dubuque, IA: Wm. C. Brown.

Beaubrun, G., & Gray, G. E. (2000). A review of herbal medicines for psychiatric disorders. *Psychiatric Services, 51,* 1130–1134.

Beck, A. T. (1967). *Depression: Clinical, experimental, and theoretical aspects.* New York: Harper & Row.

Beck, A. T. (1976). *Cognitive therapy and the emotional disorders.* New York: International Universities Press.

Beck, A. T. (1997). Cognitive therapy: Reflections. In J. K. Zeig (Ed.), *The evolution of psychotherapy: The third conference* (pp. 55–69). New York: Brunner/Mazel.

Beck, A. T., & Beck, R. W. (1972). Screening depressed patients in family practice: A rapid technique. *Postgraduate Medicine, 52,* 81–85.

Beck, A. T., Butler, A. C., Brown, G. K., Dahlsgaard, K. K., Newman, C. F., & Beck, J. S. (2001). Dysfunctional beliefs discriminate personality disorders. *Behaviour Research & Therapy, 39,* 1213–1225.

Beck, A. T., & Emery, G. (1985). *Anxiety disorders and phobias: A cognitive perspective.* New York: Basic Books.

Beck, A. T., & Freeman, A. M. (1990). *Cognitive therapy of personality disorders.* New York: Guilford Press.

Beck, A. T., & Rector, N. A. (2005). Cognitive approaches to schizophrenia: Theory and therapy. *Annual Review of Clinical Psychology, 1,* 577–606.

Beck, A. T., Rush, A. J., Shaw, B. F., & Emery, G. (1979). *Cognitive therapy of depression.* New York: Guilford Press.

Beck, A. T., Steer, R. A., Kovacs, M., & Garrison, B. (1985). Hopelessness and eventual suicide: A 10-year prospective study of patients hospitalized with suicidal ideation. *American Journal of Psychiatry, 142,* 559–563.

Beck, A. T., Ward, C. H., Mendelson, M., Moch, J. E., & Erbaugh, J. (1962). Reliability of psychiatric diagnosis: II. A study of consistency of clinical judgments and ratings. *American Journal of Psychiatry, 119,* 351–357.

Beck, A. T., Weissman, A., Lester, D., & Trexler, L. (1974). The measurement of pessimism: The Hopelessness Scale. *Journal of Consulting & Clinical Psychology, 42,* 861–865.

Beck, J. G. (1995). Hypoactive sexual desire: An overview. *Journal of Consulting & Clinical Psychology, 63,* 919–927.

Becker, J. V. (2000). Exhibitionism. In A. E. Kazdin (Ed.), *Encyclopedia of Psychology, Vol. 3* (pp. 288–290). Washington, DC: American Psychological Association.

Becker, J. V., & Kavoussi, R. J. (1996). Sexual and gender identity disorders. In R. E. Hales & S. C. Yudofsky (Eds.), *The American*

Psychiatric Press synopsis of psychiatry (pp. 605–623). Washington, DC: American Psychiatric Press.

Becker-Blease, K. A., Deater-Deckard, K., Eley, T., Freyd, J. J., Stevenson, J., & Plomin, R. (2004). A genetic analysis of individual differences in dissociative behaviors in childhood and adolescence. *Journal of Child Psychology & Psychiatry, 45*, 522–532.

Beckman, L. J. (1994). Treatment needs of women with alcohol problems. *Alcohol Health & Research World, 18*, 206–211.

Beiser, M. (1988). Influences of time, ethnicity, and attachment on depression in Southeast Asian refugees. *American Journal of Psychiatry, 145*, 46–51.

Belcher, J. R. (1988). The future role of state hospitals. *Psychiatric Hospitals, 19*, 79–83.

Bell, C. J., & Nutt, D. J. (1998). Serotonin and panic. *British Journal of Psychiatry, 172*, 465–471.

Bellack, A. S., Morrison, R. L., & Mueser, K. T. (1992). Behavioral interventions in schizophrenia. In S. M. Turner, K. S. Calhoun, & H. E. Adams (Eds.), *Handbook of clinical behavior therapy* (pp. 135–154). New York: Wiley.

Belle, D., & Doucet, J. (2003). Poverty, inequality, and discrimination as sources of depression among U.S. women. *Psychology of Women Quarterly, 27*, 101–113.

Bemporad, J. (1995). Long-term analytic treatment of depression. In E. E. Beckham & W. R. Leber (Eds.), *Handbook of depression* (2nd ed., pp. 391–403). New York: Guilford Press.

Bender, D. S., Dolan, R. T., Skodol, A. E., Sanislow, C. A., Dyck, I. R., McGlasgan, T. H., Shea, M. T., Zanarini, M. C., Oldham, J. M., & Gunderson, J. G. (2001). Treatment utilization by patients with personality disorders. *American Journal of Psychiatry, 158*, 295–302.

Bender, L. (1938). *A visual motor gestalt test and its clinical use.* New York: The American Orthopsychiatric Association.

Benedetti, F., Sforzini, L., Colombo, C., Maffei, C., & Smeraldi, E. (1998). Low-dose clozapine in acute and continuation treatment of severe borderline personality disorder. *Journal of Clinical Psychology, 59*, 103–107.

Benet-Martinez, V., & John, O. P. (1998). Los Cinco Grandes across cultures and ethnic groups: Multitrait-multimethod analyses of the Big Five in Spanish and English. *Journal of Personality & Social Psychology, 75*, 729–750.

Bennett, A. E. (1947). Mad doctors. *Journal of Nervous & Mental Disorders, 29*, 11–18.

Benotsch, E. G., Christensen, A. J., & McKelvey, L. (1997). Hostility, social support, and ambulatory cardiovascular activity. *Journal of Behavioral Medicine, 20*, 163–176.

Berenbaum, S. A., & Hines, M. (1992). Early androgens are related to childhood sex-typed toy preferences. *Psychological Science, 3*, 203–206.

Bergman, A. J., Harvey, P. D., Roitman, S. L., Mohs, R. C., Marder, D., Silverman, J. M., & Siever, L. J. (1998). Verbal learning and memory in schizotypal disorder. *Schizophrenia Bulletin, 24*, 635–641.

Berlin, L. J., Brooks-Gunn, J., McCartoon, C., & McCormick, M. C. (1998). The effectiveness of early intervention: Examining risk factors and pathways to enhanced development. *Preventive Medicine, 27*, 238–245.

Berman, A. L., & Jobes, D. A. (1995). Suicide prevention in adolescents (age 12–18). *Suicide & Life-Threatening Behavior, 25*, 143–154.

Berman, M. E., Kavoussi, R. J., & Coccaro, E. F. (1997). Neurotransmitter correlates of human aggression. In D. M. Stoff, J. Breiling, & J. D. Maser (Eds.), *Handbook of antisocial personality disorder* (pp. 305–314). New York: Wiley.

Bernstein, D. P., Useda, D., & Siever, L. J. (1995). Paranoid personality disorder. In W. J. Livesley (Ed.), *The DSM-IV personality disorders* (pp. 45–57). New York: Guilford Press.

Bettelheim, B. (1967). *The empty fortress: Infantile autism and the birth of the self.* New York: Free Press.

Beutler, L. E., Daldrup, R., Engle, D., & Guest, P. D. (1988). Family dynamics and emotional expression among patients with chronic pain and depression. *Pain, 32*, 65–72.

Bibring, E. (1953). The mechanism of depression. In P. Greenacre (Ed.), *Affective disorders* (pp. 13–48). New York: International Universities Press.

Biederman, J., Faraone, S. V., Hirschfeld-Becker, D. R., Friedman, D., Robin, J. A., & Rosenbaum, J. F. (2001). Patterns of psychopathology and dysfunction in high-risk children of parents with panic disorder and major depression. *American Journal of Psychiatry, 158*, 49–57.

Biederman, J., Faraone, S. V., Monuteaux, M. C., Bober, M., & Cadogen, E. (2004). Gender effects on attention-deficit/hyperactivity disorder in adults, revisited. *Biological Psychiatry, 55*, 692–700.

Biederman, J., Mick, E., Faraone, S. V., Braaten, E., Doyle, A., Spencer, T., Wilens, T. E., Frazier, E., & Johnson, M. (2002). Influence of gender on attention deficit hyperactivity disorder in children referred to a psychiatric clinic. *American Journal of Psychiatry, 159*, 36–42.

Biederman, J., Munir, K., Knee, D., Habelow, W., et al. (1986). A family study of patients with attention deficit disorder and normal controls. *Journal of Psychiatric Research, 20*, 263–274

Biederman, J., Rosenbaum, J. F., Bolduc-Murphy, E. A., Faraone, S. V., Chaloff, J., Hirshfeld, D. R., & Kagan, J. (1993). Behavioral inhibition as a temperamental risk factor for anxiety disorders. *Child & Adolescent Psychiatric Clinics of North America, 2*, 667–684.

Biederman, J., Rosenbaum, J. F., Hirshfeld, D. R., Faraone, V., Bolduc, E., Gersten, M., Meminger, S., & Reznick, S. (1990). Psychiatric correlates of behavioral inhibition in young children of parents with and without psychiatric disorders. *Archives of General Psychiatry, 47*, 21–26.

Bierut, L. J., Dinwiddie, S. H., Begleiter, H., Crowe, R. R., Hesselbrock, V., Nurnberger, J. I., Porjesz, B., Schuckit, M. A., & Reich, T. (1998). Familial transmission of substance dependence: Alcohol, marijuana, cocaine, and habitual smoking. *Archives of General Psychiatry, 55*, 982–988.

Bird, H. R., Canino, G. J., Davies, M., Zhang, H., Ramirez, R., & Lahey, B. B. (2001). Prevalence and correlates of antisocial behaviors among three ethnic groups. *Journal of Abnormal Child Psychology, 29*, 465–478.

Bird, T. D., Lampe, T. H., Wijsman, E. M., & Schellenberg, G. D. (1998). Familial Alzheimer's: Genetic studies. In M. F. Folstein (Ed.), *Neurobiology of primary dementia* (pp. 27–42). Washington, DC: American Psychiatric Press.

Birmaher, B., Axelson, D. A., Monk, K., Kalas, C., Clark, D. B., Ehmann, M., Bridge, J., Heo, J., & Brent, D. A. (2003). Fluoxetine for the treatment of childhood anxiety disorders. *Journal of the American Academy of Child & Adolescent Psychiatry, 42*, 415–423.

Blacher, J. B., Hanneman, R. A., & Rousey, A. B. (1992). Out-of-home placement of children with severe handicaps: A comparison of approaches. *American Journal on Mental Retardation, 96*, 607–616.

Blair, A. J., Lewis, J., & Booth, D. A. (1989). Behavior therapy for obesity: The role of clinicians in the reduction of overweight. *Counseling Psychology Quarterly, 2*, 289–301.

Blanchard, E. B., Hickling, E. J., Taylor, A. E., Loos, W. R., et al. (1996). Who develops PTSD from motor vehicle accidents. *Behavior Research & Therapy, 34*, 1–10.

Blanchard, J. J., & Neale, J. M. (1992). Medication effects: Conceptual and methodological issues in schizophrenia research. *Clinical Psychology Review, 12*, 345–361.

Blatt, S. J., & Zuroff, D. C. (1992). Interpersonal relatedness and self-definition: Two prototypes for depression. *Clinical Psychology Review, 12*, 527–562.

Blazer, D. G., George, L., & Hughes, D. (1991). The epidemiology of anxiety disorders. In C. Salzman & B. Liebowitz (Eds.), *Anxiety disorders in the elderly* (pp. 17–30). New York: Springer-Verlag.

Blazer, D. G., Kessler, R. C., McGonagle, K. A., & Swartz, M. S. (1994). The prevalence and distribution of major depression in a national community sample: The National Comorbidity Study. *American Journal of Psychiatry, 151*, 979–986.

Blazer, D. G., Kessler, R. C., & Swartz, M. (1998). Epidemiology of recurrent major and minor depression with a seasonal pattern: The National Comorbidity Study. *British Journal of Psychiatry, 172*, 164–167.

Bliss, E. L. (1980). Multiple personalities: A report of 14 cases with implications for schizophrenia and hysteria. *Archives of General Psychiatry, 37*, 1388–1397.

Bliss, E. L. (1986). *Multiple personality, allied disorders, and hypnosis.* New York: Oxford University Press.

Boeschen, L. E., Koss, M. P., Figueredo, J., & Coan, J. A. (2001). Experiential avoidance and post-traumatic stress disorder: A cognitive mediational model of rape recovery. *Journal of Aggression, Maltreatment & Trauma, 4*, 211–245.

Bohart, A. C. (1990). Psychotherapy integration from a client-centered perspective. In G. Lietaer (Ed.), *Client-centered and experiential psychotherapy in the nineties* (pp. 481–500). Leuven, Belgium: Leuven University Press.

Bohart, A. C. (1995). The person-centered psychotherapies. In A. S. Gurman (Ed.), *Essential psychotherapies: Theory and practice* (pp. 55–84). New York: Guilford Press.

Bohus, M., Haaf, B., Simms, T., Limberger, M. F., Schmahl, C., Unckel, C., Lieb, K., & Linehan, M. M. (2004). Effectiveness of inpatient dialectical behavioral therapy for borderline personality disorder: A controlled trial. *Behaviour Research & Therapy, 42,* 487–499.

Boland, R. J., & Keller, M. B. (2002). Course and outcome of depression. In I. H. Gotlib & C. L. Hammen (Eds.), *Handbook of depression* (pp. 43–60). New York: Guilford Press.

Bölte, S., & Poustka, F. (2004). Comparing the intelligence profiles of savant and nonsavant individuals with autistic disorder. *Intelligence, 32,* 121–131.

Bolton, P., Bass, J., Neugebauer, R., Verdeli, H., Clougherty, K. F., Wickramaratne, P., Speelman, L., Ndogoni, L., & Weissman, M. (2003). Group interpersonal psychotherapy for depression in rural Uganda. *Journal of the American Medical Association, 289,* 3117–3124.

Bonanno, G. A., & Kaltman, S. (1999). Toward an integrative perspective on bereavement. *Psychological Bulletin, 125,* 760–776.

Bondolfi, G., Dufour, H., Patris, M., May, J. P., Billeter, U., Eap, C. B., & Bauman, P. (1998). Risperidone versus clozapine in treatment-resistant chronic schizophrenia: A randomized double-blind study. *American Journal of Psychiatry, 155,* 449–504.

Book, A. S., Starzyk, K. B., & Quinsey, V. L. (2001). The relationship between testosterone and aggression: A meta-analysis. *Aggression & Violent Behavior, 6,* 579–599.

Booth-Kewley, S., & Friedman, H. S. (1987). Psychological predictors of heart disease: A quantitative review. *Psychological Bulletin, 101,* 343–362.

Bootzin, R. R., & Perlis, M. L. (1992). Nonpharmacologic treatments of insomnia. *Journal of Clinical Psychiatry, 53,* 37–41.

Borkovec, T. (2002). Life in the future versus life in the present. *Clinical Psychology: Science & Practice, 9,* 76–80.

Borkovec, T. D. (1994). The nature, functions, and origins of worry. In G. C. L. Davey & F. Tallis (Eds.), *Worrying: Perspectives on theory, assessment, and treatment* (pp. 5–34). Sussex, UK: Wiley.

Borkovec, T. D., & Mathews, A. M. (1988). Treatment of nonphobic anxiety disorders: A comparison of nondirective, cognitive, and coping desensitization therapy. *Journal of Consulting & Clinical Psychology, 56,* 877–884.

Borkovec, T. D., Newman, M. G., & Castonguay, L. G. (2003). Cognitive-behavioral therapy for generalized anxiety disorder with integrations from interpersonal and experiential therapies. *CNS Spectrums, 8,* 382–389.

Borkovec, T. D., Newman, M. G., Pincus, A. L., & Lytle, R. (2002). A component analysis of cognitive-behavioral therapy for generalized anxiety disorder and the role of interpersonal problems. *Journal of Consulting & Clinical Psychology, 70,* 288–298.

Borkovec, T. D., & Ruscio, A. M. (2001). Psychotherapy for generalized anxiety disorder. *Journal of Clinical Psychiatry, 62*(Suppl. 11), 37–42.

Borkovec, T. D., & Whisman, M. A. (1996). Psychosocial treatment for generalized anxiety disorder. In M. R. Mavissakalian (Ed.), *Long-term treatments of anxiety disorders* (pp. 171–199). Washington, DC: American Psychiatric Press.

Borys, D. S., & Pope, K. S. (1989). Dual relationships between therapist and client: A national study of psychologists, psychiatrists, and social workers. *Professional Psychology: Research & Practice, 20,* 283–293.

Bottoms, G. (2000). *Angelhead.* New York: Three Rivers Press.

Bouchard, T. J., & Loehlin, J. C. (2001). Genes, evolution, and personality. *Behavior Genetics, 31,* 243–273.

Bourden, K., Boyd, J., Rae, D., & Burns, B. (1988). Gender differences in phobias: Results of the EAC community survey. *Journal of Anxiety Disorders, 2,* 227–241.

Bourin, M., Baker, G. B., & Bradwejn, J. (1998). Neurobiology of panic disorder. *Journal of Psychosomatic Research, 44,* 163–180.

Bouton, M. E., Mineka, S., & Barlow, D. H. (2001). A modern learning theory perspective on the etiology of panic disorder. *Psychological Review, 108,* 4–32.

Bowen, R. C., Offord, D. R., & Boyle, M. H. (1990). The prevalence of overanxious disorder and separation anxiety disorder: Results from the Ontario Child Health Study. *Journal of the American Academy of Child & Adolescent Psychiatry, 29,* 753–758.

Bower, G. H. (1981). Mood and memory. *American Psychologist, 36,* 129–148.

Bowlby, J. (1982). *Attachment and loss* (2nd ed.). New York: Basic Books.

Boyd, C. J., & Guthrie, B. (1996). Women, their significant others, and crack cocaine. *American Journal on Addictions, 5,* 156–166.

Bradley, J. D. D., & Golden, C. J. (2001). Biological contributions to the presentation and understanding of attention-deficit/hyperactivity disorder: A review. *Clinical Psychology Review, 21,* 907–929.

Bradley, S. J. (1995). Psychosexual disorders in adolescence. In J. M. Oldham & M. B. Riba (Eds.), *Review of psychiatry* (Vol. 14, pp. 735–754). Washington, DC: American Psychiatric Press.

Bradley, S. J., & Zucker, K. J. (1997). Gender identity disorder: A review of the past 10 years. *Journal of the American Academy of Child & Adolescent Psychiatry, 36,* 872–880.

Brady, K., Pearlstein, T., Asnis, G. M., Baker, D., Rothbaum, B., Sikes, C. R., & Farfel, G. M. (2000). Efficacy and safety of sertraline treatment of posttraumatic stress disorder: A randomized controlled trial. *Journal of the American Medical Association, 283,* 1837–1844.

Braginsky, B. M., Braginsky, D. D., & Ring, K. (1969). *Methods of madness: The mental hospital as last resort.* New York: Holt.

Brain, P. F., & Susman, E. J. (1997). Hormonal aspects of aggression and violence. In D. M. Stoff, J. Breiling, & J. D. Maser (Eds.), *Handbook of antisocial personality disorder* (pp. 314–323). New York: Wiley.

Brambilla, F., Bellodi, L., Arancio, C., Ronchi, P., & Limonta, D. (2001). Central dopaminergic function in anorexia and bulimia nervosa: A psychoneuroendocrine approach. *Psychoneuroendocrinology, 26,* 393–409.

Braun, B. G. (Ed.). (1986). *Treatment of multiple personality disorder.* Washington, DC: American Psychiatric Press.

Brawman-Mintzer, O., & Yonkers, K. A. (2001). Psychopharmacology in women. In N. L. Stotland (Ed.), *Psychological aspects of women's health care: The interface between psychiatry and obstetrics and gynecology* (2nd ed., pp. 401–420). Washington, DC: American Psychiatric Press.

Breggin, P. R. (1997). *Brain-disabling treatments in psychiatry: Drugs, electroshock, and the role of the FDA.* New York: Springer.

Bregman, J. D., & Gerdtz, J. (1997). Behavioral interventions. In D. J. Cohen & F. R. Volkmar (Eds.), *Handbook of autism and pervasive developmental disorders* (pp. 606–630). Toronto: Wiley.

Breier, A. (1995). Serotonin, schizophrenia and antipsychotic drug action. *Schizophrenia Research, 14,* 187–202.

Breier, A., Schreiber, J. L., Dyer, J., & Pickar, D. (1991). National Institute of Mental Health longitudinal study of chronic schizophrenia: Prognosis and predictors of outcome. *Archives of General Psychiatry, 48,* 239–246.

Bremner, J. D. (1998). Neuroimaging of posttraumatic stress disorder. *Psychiatric Annals, 28,* 445–450.

Bremner, J. D., Narayan, M., Anderson, E. R., Staib, L. H., Miller, H. L., & Charney, D. S. (2000). Hippocampal volume reduction in major depression. *American Journal of Psychiatry, 157,* 115–118.

Bremner, J. D., Vythilingam, M., Anderson, G., Vermetten, E., McGlashan, T., Heninger, G., Rasmusson, A., Southwick, S. M., & Charney, D. S. (2003). Assessment of the hypothalamic-pituitary-adrenal axis over a 24-hour diurnal period and in response to neuroendocrine challenges in women with and without childhood sexual abuse and posttraumatic stress disorder. *Biological Psychiatry, 54,* 710–718.

Brent, D. A., Kerr, M. M., Goldstein, C., Bozigar, J., Wartella, M., & Allan, M. J. (1989). An outbreak of suicide and suicidal behavior in a high school. *Journal of the American Academy of Child & Adolescent Psychiatry, 28,* 918–924.

Brent, D. A., Kupfer, D. J., Bromet, E. J., & Dew, M. A. (1988). The assessment and treatment of patients at risk for suicide. In A. J. Frances & R. E. Hales (Eds.), *American Psychiatric Press review of psychiatry* (Vol. 7). Washington, DC: American Psychiatric Press.

Brent, D. A., Oquendo, M., Birmaher, B., Greenhill, L., Kolko, D., Stanley, B., Zelazny, J., Brodsky, B., Bridge, J., Ellis, S., Salazer, J. O., & Mann, J. J. (2002). Familial pathways to early-onset suicide attempt. *Archives of General Psychiatry, 59,* 801–807.

Brent, D. A., Oquendo, M., Birmaher, B., Greenhill, L., Kolko, D., Stanley, B., Zelazny, J., Brodsky, B., Firinciogullari, S., Ellis, S. P., & Mann, J. J. (2003). Peripubertal suicide attempts in offspring of suicide attempters with siblings concordant for suicidal behavior. *American Journal of Psychiatry, 160,* 1486–1493.

Brent, D. A., Perper, J. A., Allman, C. J., Moritz, G. M., Wartella, M. E., & Zelenak, J. P. (1991). The presence and accessibility of firearms in the homes of adolescent suicide: A case-control study. *Journal of the American Medical Association, 266,* 2989–2995.

Brevoort, P. (1998). The booming U.S. botanical market: A new overview. *HerbalGram, 44,* 33–46.

Briere, J., & Conte, J. R. (1993). Self-reported amnesia for abuse in adults molested as children. *Journal of Traumatic Stress, 6,* 21–31.

Briere, J., & Runtz, M. (1989). University males' sexual interest in children: Predicting potential indices of "pedophilia" in a nonforensic sample. *Child Abuse & Neglect, 13,* 65–75.

Brockington, I. (2001). Suicide in women. *International Clinical Psychopharmacology, 16*(Suppl. 12), 7–19.

Brody, A. L., Saxena, S., Stoessel, P., Gillies, L. A., Fairbanks, L. A., Alborzian, S., Phelps, M. E., Huang, S., Wu, H., Ho, M. L., Ho, M. K., Au, S. C., Maidment, K., & Baxter, L. R. (2001). Regional brain metabolic changes in patients with major depression treated with either paroxetine or interpersonal therapy: Preliminary findings. *Archives of General Psychiatry, 58,* 631–640.

Broidy, L. M., Nagin, D. S., Tremblay, R. E., Bates, J. E., Brame, B., Dodge, K. A., Fergusson, D., Horwood, J. L., Loeber, R., Laird, R., Lynam, D. R., Moffitt, T. E., Pettit, G. S., & Vitaro, F. (2003). Developmental trajectories of childhood disruptive behaviors and adolescent delinquency: A six-site, cross-national study. *Developmental Psychology, 39,* 222–245.

Bromberger, J. T., & Matthews, K. A. (1996). A longitudinal study of the effects of pessimism, trait anxiety, and life stress on depressive symptoms in middle-aged women. *Psychology & Aging, 11,* 207–213.

Brooks-Gunn, J., Klebanov, P. K., & Duncan, G. J. (1996). Ethnic differences in children's intelligence test scores: Role of economic deprivation, home environment, and maternal characteristics. *Child Development, 67,* 396–408.

Brooks-Gunn, J., Klebanov, P. K., & Liaw, F. (1995). The learning, physical, and emotional environment of the home in the context of poverty: The Infant Health and Development Program. *Children & Youth Services Review, 17,* 251–276.

Brown, D., Scheflin, A. W., & Whitfield, C. L. (1999). Recovered memories: The current weight of the evidence in science and in the courts. *Journal of Psychiatry & Law, 27,* 5–156.

Brown, G. W., Birley, J. L., & Wing, J. K. (1972). Influence of family life on the course of schizophrenic disorders: A replication. *British Journal of Psychiatry, 121,* 241–258.

Brown, J. E., Ayowa, O. B., & Brown, R. C. (1993). Dry and tight: Sexual practices and potential risks in Zaire. *Social Science & Medicine, 37,* 989–994.

Brown, M. Z., Comtois, K. A., & Linehan, M. M. (2002). Reasons for suicide attempts and nonsuicidal self-injury in women with borderline personality disorder. *Journal of Abnormal Psychology, 111,* 198–202.

Brown, S. A., Inaba, R. K., Gillin, J. C., & Schuckit, M. A. (1995). Alcoholism and affective disorder: Clinical course of depressive symptoms. *American Journal of Psychiatry, 152,* 45–52.

Brown, T. A., Campbell, L. A., Lehman, C. L., Grisham, J. R., & Mancill, R. B. (2001). Current and lifetime comorbidity of the DSM-IV anxiety and mood disorders in a large clinical sample. *Journal of Abnormal Psychology, 110,* 585–599.

Brown, T. A., Di Nardo, P. A., Lehman, C. L., & Campbell, L. A. (2001). Reliability of DSM-IV anxiety and mood disorders: Implications for the classification of emotional disorders. *Journal of Abnormal Psychology, 110,* 49–58.

Brown, T. A., O'Leary, T. A., & Barlow, D. H. (2001). Generalized anxiety disorder. *Clinical handbook of psychological disorders: A step-by-step treatment manual* (3rd ed., pp. 154–208). New York: Guilford Press.

Brown, T. M., & Boyle, M. F. (2002). The ABC of psychological medicine: Delirium. *British Medical Journal, 325,* 644–647.

Browne, K. O. (2001). Cultural formulation of psychiatric diagnoses. *Culture, Medicine, & Psychiatry, 25,* 411–425.

Brownell, K. D. (2003). Diet, obesity, public policy, and defiance. In R. J. Sternberg (Ed.), *Psychologists defying the crowd: Stories of those who battled the establishment and won* (pp. 47–64). Washington, DC: American Psychological Association.

Brownell, K. D., & Horgen, K. B. (2004). *Food fight: The inside story of the food industry, America's obesity crisis, and what we can do about it.* Chicago: Contemporary Books.

Bruch, H. (1973). *Eating disorders: Obesity, anorexia nervosa, and the person within.* New York: Basic Books.

Bruch, H. (1982). Anorexia nervosa: Therapy and theory. *American Journal of Psychiatry, 139,* 1531–1538.

Bruch, M. A., & Cheek, J. M. (1995). Developmental factors in childhood and adolescent shyness. In R. G. Heimberg, M. R. Liebowitz, D. A. Hope, & F. R. Schneier (Eds.), *Social phobia: Diagnosis, assessment, and treatment.* New York: Guilford Press.

Brugha, T. S., Sharp, H. M., Cooper, S. A., Weisender, C., Britto, D., Shrikwin, R., Sherrif, T., & Kirwan, P. H. (1998). The Leicester 500 Project. Social support and the development of postnatal depressive symptoms, a prospective cohort survey. *Psychological Medicine, 28,* 63–79.

Buchsbaum, M. S., Someya, T., Wu, J. C., Tang, C. Y., & Bunney, W. E. (1997). Neuroimaging bipolar illness with positron emission tomography and magnetic resonance imaging. *Psychiatric Annals, 27,* 489–495.

Buckwalter, J., Sobel, E., Dunn, M. E., & Diz, M. M. (1993). Gender differences on a brief measure of cognitive functioning in Alzheimer's disease. *Archives of Neurology, 50,* 757–760.

Bugental, J. F. T. (1997). There is a fundamental division in how psychotherapy is conceived. In J. K. Zeig (Ed.), *The evolution of psychotherapy: The third conference* (pp. 185–193). New York: Brunner/Mazel.

Bulik, C. M. (2004). Genetic and biological risk factors. In J. K. Thompson (Ed.), *Handbook of eating disorders and obesity* (pp. 3–16). Hoboken, NJ: Wiley.

Bulik, C. M., Sullivan, P. F., Fear, J., & Pickering, A. (1997). Predictors of the development of bulimia nervosa in women with anorexia nervosa. *Journal of Nervous & Mental Disease, 185,* 704–707.

Bulik, C. M., Sullivan, P. F., & Kendler, K. S. (1998). Heritability of binge-eating and broadly defined bulimia nervosa. *Biological Psychiatry, 44,* 1210–1218.

Bulik, C. M., Sullivan, P. F., Wade, T. D., & Kendler, K. S. (1999). Twin studies of eating disorders: A review. *International Journal of Eating Disorders, 27,* 1–20.

Bulman, R. J., & Wortman, C. G. (1977). Attributions of blame and coping in the "real world": Severe accident victims react to their lot. *Journal of Personality & Social Psychology, 35,* 351–363.

Bunney, W. E., & Davis, J. M. (1965). Norepinephrine in depressive reactions: A review. *Archives of General Psychiatry, 13,* 483–493.

Burnam, M. A., Stein, J. A., Golding, J. M., & Siegel, J. M. (1988). Sexual assault and mental disorders in a community population. *Journal of Consulting & Clinical Psychology, 56,* 843–850.

Burnette, E. (1997). Community psychologists help South Africans mend. *APA Monitor, 28.* Retrieved from the World Wide Web: www.apa.org/monitor/sep97/safrica.html

Burns, D. (1980). *Feeling good: The new mood therapy.* New York: Morrow.

Burns, D., & Nolen-Hoeksema, S. (1991). Coping styles, homework assignments and the effectiveness of cognitive-behavioral therapy. *Journal of Consulting & Clinical Psychology, 59,* 305–311.

Burr, J. A., Hartman, J. T., & Matteson, D. W. (1999). Black suicide in U.S. metropolitan areas: An examination of the racial inequality and social integration-regulation hypotheses. *Social Forces, 77,* 1049–1081.

Busfield, J. (1986). *Managing madness: Changing ideas and practice.* London: Hutchinson.

Bustillo, J. R., Lauriello, J., Horan, W. P., & Keith, S. J. (2001). The psychosocial treatment of schizophrenia: An update. *American Journal of Psychiatry, 158,* 163–175.

Butcher, J. N. (1990). *The MMPI-2 in psychological treatment.* New York: Oxford University Press.

Butler, G., Fennell, M., Robson, P., & Gelder, M. (1991). Comparison of behavior therapy and cognitive behavior therapy in the treatment of generalized anxiety disorder. *Journal of Consulting & Clinical Psychology, 59,* 167–175.

Butzel, J. S., Talbot, N. L., Duberstein, P. R., Houghtalen, R. P., Cox, C., & Giles, D. E. (2000). The relationship between traumatic events and dissociation among women with histories of childhood sexual abuse. *Journal of Nervous & Mental Disease, 188,* 547–549.

Butzlaff, R. L., & Hooley, J. M. (1998). Expressed emotion and psychiatric relapse. *Archives of General Psychiatry, 55,* 547–552.

Byrne, E. J. (1994). *Confusional states in older people.* Boston: E. Arnold.

Byrne, S., Cooper, Z., & Fairburn, C. (2003). Weight maintenance and relapse in obesity: A qualitative study. *International Journal of Obesity, 27,* 955–962.

Bystritsky, A., Ackerman, D. L., Rosen, R. M., Vapnik, T., Gorvis, E., Maidment, K. M., & Saxena, S. (2004). Augmentation of serotonin reuptake inhibitors in refractory obsessive-compulsive disorder using adjunctive olanzapine: A placebo-controlled trial. *Journal of Clinical Psychiatry, 65,* 565–568.

C

Cade, J. (1949). Lithium salts in the treatment of psychotic excitement. *Medical Journal of Australia, 36,* 349–352.

Cadoret, R. J., & Cain, C. A. (1980). Sex differences in predictors of antisocial behavior in adoptees. *Archives of General Psychiatry, 37,* 1171–1175.

Caffey, J. (1972). On the theory and practice of shaking infants. *American Journal of Diseases of Children, 124,* 161–172.

Caldwell, C. B., & Gottesman, I. I. (1991). Sex-differences in the risk for alcoholism—A twin study. *Behavior Genetics, 21,* 563.

Cale, E. M., & Lilienfeld, S. O. (2002). Sex differences in psychopathy and antisocial personality disorder: A review and integration. *Clinical Psychology Review, 22,* 1179–1207.

Cameron, N., & Rychlak, J. F. (1985). *Personality development and psychopathology: A dynamic approach.* Boston: Houghton Mifflin.

Camp, B. W., Broman, S. H., Nichols, P. L., & Leff, M. (1998). Maternal and neonatal risk factors for mental retardation: Defining the "at-risk" child. *Early Human Development, 50,* 159–173.

Campbell, M., Adams, P. B., Small, A. M., Kafantaris, V., Silva, R. R., Shell, J., Perry, R., & Overall, J. E. (1995). Lithium in hospitalized aggressive children with conduct disorder: A double-blind and placebo-controlled study. *Journal of the American Academy of Child & Adolescent Psychiatry, 34,* 445–453.

Campo, J. V., & Fritz, G. (2001). A management model for pediatric somatization. *Psychosomatics, 42,* 467–476.

Canetto, S. S., & Hollenshead, J. D. (1999). Gender and physician-assisted suicide: An analysis of the Kevorkian cases. *Omega, 40,* 165–208.

Canetto, S. S., & Hollenshead, J. D. (2000). Older women and mercy killing. *Omega, 42,* 83–99.

Canetto, S. S., & Sakinofsky, I. (1998). The gender paradox in suicide. *Suicide & Life-Threatening Behavior, 28,* 1–23.

Canino, G. J., Rubio-Stipec, M., & Bravo, M. (1988). Psychiatric diagnostic nosology in transcultural epidemiology research. *Acta Psiquiatrica Psicologica de America Latina, 34,* 251–259.

Cannon, T. D., Kapiro, J., Lonnqvist, J., Huttunen, M., & Koskenvuo, M. (1998). The genetic epidemiology of schizophrenia in a Finnish twin cohort. *Archives of General Psychiatry, 55,* 67–74.

Cannon, T. D., Rosso, I. M., Bearden, C. E., Sanchez, L. E., & Hadley, T. (1999). A prospective cohort study of neurodevelopmental processes in the genesis and epigenesis of schizophrenia. *Development & Psychopathology, 11,* 467–485.

Caplan, P. J., & Gans, M. (1991). Is there empirical justification for the category of "self-defeating personality disorder"? *Feminism & Psychology, 1,* 263–278.

Cardozo, B. L., Kaiser, R., Gotway, C. A., & Agani, F. (2003). Mental health, social functioning, and feelings of hatred and revenge in Kosovar Albanians one year after the war in Kosovo. *Journal of Traumatic Stress, 16,* 351–360.

Cardozo, B. L., Vergara, A., Agani, F., & Gotway, C. A. (2000). Mental health, social functioning, and attitudes of Kosovar Albanians following the war in Kosovo. *Journal of the American Medical Association, 284,* 569–577.

Carey, G., & Goldman, D. (1997). The genetics of antisocial behavior. In D. M. Stoff, J. Breiling, & J. D. Maser (Eds.), *Handbook of antisocial personality disorder* (pp. 243–254). New York: Wiley.

Carmelli, D. S., Swan, G. E., Robinette, D., & Fabsitz, R. (1992). Genetic influence on smoking: A study of male twins. *New England Journal of Medicine, 327,* 829–833.

Carroll, J. K. (2004). *Murug, waali,* and *gini:* Expressions of distress in refugees from Somolia. *Primary Care Companion to the Journal of Clinical Psychiatry, 6,* 119–125.

Carroll, K. M. (2001). Combined treatments for substance dependence. In M. T. Sammons & N. B. Schmidt (Eds.), *Combined treatments for mental disorders.* Washington, DC: American Psychological Association.

Carter, J. C., & Fairburn, C. G. (1998). Cognitive-behavioral self-help for binge eating disorder: A controlled effectiveness study. *Journal of Consulting & Clinical Psychology, 66,* 616–623.

Carter, M. M., Hollon, S. D., Carson, R. S., & Shelton, R. C. (1995). Effects of a safe person on induced distress following a biological challenge in panic disorder with agoraphobia. *Journal of Abnormal Psychology, 104,* 156–163.

Caspi, A. (1993). Why maladaptive behaviors persist: Sources of continuity and change across the life course. In D. C. Funder (Ed.), *Studying lives through time: Personality and development* (pp. 343–376). Washington, DC: American Psychological Association.

Caspi, A., Harrington, H., Milne, B., Amell, J. W., Theodore, R. F., & Moffitt, T. E. (2003). Children's behavioral styles at age 3 are linked to their adult personality traits at age 26. *Journal of Personality, 71,* 495–513.

Castiglioni, A. (1946). *Adventures of the mind* (1st American ed.). New York: Knopf.

Castonguay, L. G., Eldredge, K. L., & Agras, W. S. (1995). Binge eating disorder: Current state and future directions. *Clinical Psychology Review, 15,* 865–890.

Cauce, A. M., Domenech-Rodriguez, M., Pardise, M., Cochran, B. N., Shea, J. M., Srebnik, D., & Baydar, N. (2002). Cultural and contextual influences in mental health help seeking: A focus on ethnic minority youth. *Journal of Consulting and Clinical Psychology, 70,* 44–55.

Ceci, S. J., & Bruck, M. (1995). *Jeopardy in the courtroom.* Washington, DC: American Psychological Association.

Centers for Disease Control and Prevention (CDC), National Center for Injury Prevention and Control. (2004). Web-based injury statistics query and reporting system. Retrieved from http://www.cdc.gov/ncipc/wisqars/default.htm

Cervantes, R. C., Salgado de Snyder, V. N., & Padilla, A. M. (1989). Posttraumatic stress in immigrants from Central America and Mexico. *Hospital & Community Psychiatry, 40,* 615–619.

Chae, J.-H., Nahas, Z., Li, X., & George, M. S. (2001). Transcranial magnetic stimulation in psychiatry: Research and therapeutic applications. *International Review of Psychiatry, 13,* 18–23.

Chambless, D. C., Cherney, J., Caputo, G. C., & Rheinstein, B. J. (1987). Anxiety disorders and alcoholism: A study with inpatient alcoholics. *Journal of Anxiety Disorders, 1,* 29–40.

Chang, C.-J., Chen, W. J., Liu, S. K., Cheng, J. J., Yang, W.-C. O., Chang, H.-J., Lane, H.-Y., Lin, S.-K., Yang, T.-W., & Hwu, H.-G. (2002). Morbidity risk of psychiatric disorders among the first degree relatives of schizophrenia patients in Taiwan. *Schizophrenia Bulletin, 28,* 379–392.

Chang, K. D. (2004). Pediatric psychopharmacology: An overview. In H. Steiner (Ed.), *Handbook of mental health intervention in children and adolescents: an integrated developmental approach* (pp. 245–257). San Francisco: Jossey-Bass.

Chang, K. D., & Simeonova, D. I. (2004). Mood stabilizers: Use in pediatric psychopharmacology. In H. Steiner (Ed.), *Handbook of mental health intervention in children and adolescents: An integrated developmental approach* (pp. 363–412). San Francisco: Jossey-Bass.

Chang, V. W., & Christakis, N. A. (2003). Self-perception of weight appropriateness in the United States. *American Journal of Preventative Medicine, 24,* 332–339.

Chapman, L. J., Edell, W. S., & Chapman, J. P. (1980). Physical anhedonia, perceptual aberration, and psychosis proneness. *Schizophrenia Bulletin, 6,* 639–653.

Chapman, T. F., Manuzza, S., & Fyer, A. J. (1995). Epidemiology and family studies of social phobia. In R. G. Heimberg, M. R. Liebowitz, D. A. Hope, & F. R. Schneier (Eds.), *Social phobia: Diagnosis, assessment, and treatment* (pp. 21–40). New York: Guilford Press.

Charney, D. S. (2004). Psychobiological mechanisms of resilience and vulnerability: Implications for successful adaptation to extreme stress. *American Journal of Psychiatry, 161,* 195–216.

Charney, D. S., Nagy, L. M., Bremner, J. D., Goddard, A. W., Yehuda, R., & Southwick, S. M. (2000). Neurobiologic mechanisms of human anxiety. In B. S. Fogel (Ed.), *Synopsis of neuropsychiatry* (pp. 273–288). Philadelphia: Lippincott Williams & Wilkins.

Chassin, L., Pitts, S. C., DeLucia, C., & Todd, M. (1999). A longitudinal study of children of alcoholics: Predicting young adult substance use disorders, anxiety, and depression. *Journal of Abnormal Psychology, 108,* 106–119.

Chavira, D. A., Grilo, C. M., Shea, M. T., Yen, S., Gunderson, J. G., Morey, L. C., Skodol, A. E., Stout, R. L., Zanarini, M. C., & Mcglashan, T. H. (2003). Ethnicity and four personality disorders. *Comprehensive Psychiatry, 44,* 483–491.

Chemtob, C. M., Bauer, G. B., Neller, G., Hamada, R., Glisson, C., & Stevens, V. (1990). Posttraumatic stress disorder among

Special Forces Vietnam veterans. *Military Medicine, 155*, 16–20.

Chodorow, N. (1978). *The reproduction of mothering.* Berkeley: University of California Press.

Chou, T. (1992). Wake up and smell the coffee: Caffeine, coffee, and the medical consequences. *Western Journal of Medicine, 157*, 544–553.

Chouinard, G. (2004). Issues in the clinical use of benzodiazepines: Potency, withdrawal, and rebound. *Journal of Clinical Psychiatry, 65*(Suppl. 5), 7–12.

Christophersen, E. R., & Mortweet, S. L. (2001). *Treatments that work with children: Empirically supported strategies for managing childhood problems.* Washington, DC: American Psychological Association.

Chronis, A. M., Chacko, A., Fabiano, G. A., Wymbs, B. T., & Pelham, W. E., Jr. (2004). Enhancements to the behavioral parent training paradigm for families of children with ADHD: Review and future directions. *Clinical Child & Family Psychology Review, 7*, 1–27.

Chun, M. R., Schofield, P., Stern, Y., Tatemichi, T. K., & Mayeux, R. (1998). The epidemiology of dementia among the elderly: Experience in a community-based registry. In M. F. Folstein (Ed.), *Neurobiology of primary dementia* (pp. 1–26). Washington, DC: American Psychiatric Press.

Cicchetti, D., & Rogosch, F. A. (1996). Equifinality and multifinality in developmental psychopathology. *Development & Psychopathology, 8*, 597–600.

Cicchetti, D., & Rogosch, F. A. (2001a). Diverse patterns of neuroendocrine activity in maltreated children. *Development & Psychopathology, 13*, 677–694.

Cicchetti, D., & Rogosch, F. A. (2001b). The impact of child maltreatment and psychopathology upon neuroendocrine functioning. *Development & Psychopathology, 13*, 783–804.

Cicchetti, D., & Toth, S. L. (2005). Child maltreatment. *Annual Review of Clinical Psychology, 1*, 439–466.

Clancy, S. A., McNally, R. J., Schacter, D. L., Lenzenweger, M. F., & Pitman, R. K. (2002). Memory distortion in people reporting abduction by aliens. *Journal of Abnormal Psychology, 111*, 455–461.

Clancy, S. A., Schacter, D. L., McNally, R. J., & Pitman, R. (2000). False recognition in women reporting recovered memories of sexual abuse. *Psychological Science, 11*, 26–31.

Clark, D. A., & Purdon, C. (1993). New perspectives for a cognitive theory of obsessions. *Australian Psychologist, 28*, 161–167.

Clark, D. M. (1988). A cognitive model of panic attacks. In S. Rachman & J. D. Maser (Eds.), *Panic: Psychological perspectives* (pp. 71–89). Hillsdale, NJ: Erlbaum.

Clark, D. M., Ehlers, A., McManus, F., Hackmann, A., Fennell, M., Campbell, H., Flower, T., Davenport, C., & Louis, B. (2003). Cognitive therapy versus fluoxetine in generalized social phobia: A randomized placebo-controlled trial. *Journal of Consulting & Clinical Psychology, 71*, 1058–1067.

Clark, D. M., Salkovskis, P. M., Hackmann, A., Middleton, H., Anastasiades, P., & Gelder, M. (1994). A comparison of cognitive therapy, applied relaxation, and imipramine in the treatment of panic disorder. *British Journal of Psychiatry, 164*, 759–769.

Clark, D. M., Salkovskis, P. M., Hackmann, A., Wells, A., Ludgate, J., & Gelder, M. (1999). Brief cognitive therapy for panic disorder: A randomized controlled trial. *Journal of Consulting & Clinical Psychology, 67*, 583–589.

Clark, D. M., & Wells, A. (1995). A cognitive model of social phobia. In R. G. Heimberg, M. R. Liebowitz, D. A. Hope, & F. R. Schneier (Eds.), *Social phobia: Diagnosis, assessment and treatment* (pp. 69–93). New York: Guilford Press.

Clarke, G. N., Hawkins, W., Murphy, M., Sheeber, L. B., Lewinsohn, P. M., & Seeley, J. R. (1995). Targeted prevention of unipolar depressive disorder in an at-risk sample of high school adolescents: A randomized trial of a group cognitive intervention. *Journal of the American Academy of Child & Adolescent Psychiatry, 34*, 312–321.

Classen, C., Koopman, C., Hales, R., & Spiegel, D. (1998). Acute stress disorder as a predictor of posttraumatic stress symptoms. *American Journal of Psychiatry, 155*, 620–624.

Cleckley, H. M. (1941). *The mask of sanity: An attempt to reinterpret the so-called psychopathic personality.* St. Louis, MO: C. V. Mosby.

Cloninger, C. R., & Gottesman, I. I. (1987). Genetic and environmental factors in antisocial behavior disorders. In S. A. Mednick, T. E. Moffitt, & S. A. Stack (Eds.), *The causes of crime: New biological approaches* (pp. 92–109). New York: Cambridge University Press.

Cloninger, R., Bayon, C., & Przybeck, T. (1997). Epidemiology and Axis I comorbidity of antisocial personality. In D. M. Stoff, J. Breiling, & J. D. Maser (Eds.), *Handbook of antisocial personality disorder* (pp. 12–21). New York: Wiley.

Cochran, S. D., Sullivan, J. G., & Mays, V. M. (2003). Prevalence of mental disorders, psychological distress, and mental services use among lesbian, gay, and bisexual adults in the United States. *Journal of Consulting & Clinical Psychology, 71*, 53–61.

Cochrane, R. E., Grisso, T., & Frederick, R. I. (2001). The relationship between criminal charges, diagnoses, and psycholegal opinions among federal pretrial defendants. *Behavioral Sciences & the Law, 19*, 565–582.

Cocores, J., Pottash, A. C., & Gold, M. S. (1991). Cocaine. In N. S. Miller (Ed.), *Comprehensive handbook of drug and alcohol addiction* (pp. 341–352). New York: Marcel Dekker.

Cohen, J. A., Deblinger, E., Mannarino, A. P., & Steer, R. A. (2004). A multisite, randomized controlled trial for children with sexual abuse–related PTSD symptoms. *Journal of the American Academy of Child & Adolescent Psychiatry, 43*, 393–402.

Cohen, S. (1996). Psychological stress, immunity, and upper respiratory infections. *Current Directions in Psychological Science, 5*, 86–90.

Cohen, S., Tyrrell, D. A., & Smith, A. P. (1991). Psychological stress and susceptibility to the common cold. *New England Journal of Medicine, 325*, 606–612.

Cohen, S. A., Ohrig, K., Lott, R. S., & Kerrick, J. M. (1998). Risperidone for aggression and self-injurious behavior in adults with mental retardation. *Journal of Autism & Developmental Disorders, 28*, 229–233.

Colapinto, J. (2001). *As nature made him: The boy who was raised as a girl.* New York: HarperCollins.

Colas, E. (1998). *Just checking: Scenes from the life of an obsessive-compulsive.* New York: Pocket Books.

Colby, D. M. (1981). Modeling a paranoid mind. *Behavioral & Brain Sciences, 4*, 515–560.

Colder, C. R., & Chassin, L. (1993). The stress and negative affect model of adolescent alcohol use and the moderating effects of behavioral undercontrol. *Journal of Studies on Alcohol, 54*, 326–333.

Cole, D. A., Martin, J. M., Peeke, L. G., Seroczynski, A. D., & Hoffman, K. (1998). Are cognitive errors of underestimation predictive or reflective of depressive symptoms in children: A longitudinal study. *Journal of Abnormal Psychology, 107*, 481–496.

Cole, M. G. (2004). Delirium in elderly patients. *American Journal of Geriatric Psychiatry, 12*, 7–21.

Cole, W. (1992). Incest perpetrators: Their assessment and treatment. *Psychiatric Clinics of North America, 15*, 689–701.

Coleman, C. C., King, B. R., Bolden-Watson, C., Book, M. J., Segraves, R. T., Richard, N., Ascher, J., Batey, S., Jamerson, B., & Metz, A. (2001). A placebo-controlled comparison of the effects on sexual functioning of bupropion sustained release and fluoxetine. *Clinical Therapeutics: The International Peer-Reviewed Journal of Therapy, 23*, 1040–1058.

Coles, M. E., Hart, T. A., & Heimberg, R. G. (2005). Cognitive-behavioral group treatment for social phobia. In R. Crozier & L. E. Alden (Eds.), *International handbook of social anxiety.* London: Wiley.

Collins, J. J., & Schlenger, W. E. (1983, November 9–13). *The prevalence of psychiatric disorder among admissions to prison.* Paper presented at the American Society of Criminology 35th Annual Meeting, Denver.

Compton, W. M., Helzer, J. E., Hwu, H., Yeh, E., McEvoy, L., Tipp, J. E., & Spitznagel, E. L. (1991). New methods in cross-cultural psychiatry: Psychiatric illness in Taiwan and the United States. *American Journal of Psychiatry, 148*, 1697–1704.

Conklin, H. M., & Iacono, W. G. (2002). Schizophrenia: A neurodevelopmental perspective. *Current Directions in Psychological Science, 11*, 33–37.

Consumer Reports. (1993, June). Diets: What works—What doesn't. *Consumer Reports,* pp. 347–357.

Conwell, Y. (1996). Outcomes of depression. *American Journal of Geriatric Psychiatry, 4*(Suppl. 1), 34–44.

Conwell, Y., Duberstein, P. R., Connor, K., Eberly, S., Cox, C., & Caine, E. D. (2002). Access to firearms and risk for suicide in middle-aged and older adults. *American Journal of Geriatric Psychiatry, 10*, 407–416.

Cooley, E., & Toray, T. (2001). Body image and personality predictors of eating disorder symptoms during the college years. *International Journal of Eating Disorders, 30*, 28–36.

Coons, P. M. (1980). Multiple personality: Diagnostic considerations. *Journal of Clinical Psychiatry, 41,* 330–336.

Coons, P. M. (1984). *Childhood antecedents of multiple personality.* Paper presented at the Meeting of the American Psychiatric Association, Los Angeles.

Coons, P. M. (1986). Treatment progress in 20 patients with multiple personality disorder. *Journal of Nervous & Mental Disease, 174,* 715–721.

Coons, P. M. (1994). Confirmation of childhood abuse in child and adolescent cases of multiple personality disorder and dissociative disorder not otherwise specified. *Journal of Nervous & Mental Disease, 182,* 461–464.

Coons, P. M., & Bowman, E. S. (2001). Ten-year follow-up study of patients with dissociative identity disorder. *Journal of Trauma & Dissociation, 2,* 73–89.

Coons, P. M., Cole, C., Pellow, T. A., & Milstein, V. (1990). Symptoms of posttraumatic stress disorder and dissociation in women victims of abuse. In R. P. Kluft (Ed.), *Incest-related syndromes of adult psychopathology* (pp. 205–226). Washington, DC: American Psychiatric Press.

Coons, P. M., & Milstein, V. (1986). Psychosexual disturbances in multiple personality: Characteristics, etiology, and treatment. *Journal of Clinical Psychiatry, 47,* 106–110.

Coons, P. M., & Milstein, V. (1990). Self-mutilation associated with dissociative disorders. *Dissociation: Progress in the Dissociative Disorders, 3,* 81–87.

Coontz, P. D., Lidz, C. W., & Mulvey, E. P. (1994). Gender and the assessment of dangerousness in the psychiatric emergency room. *International Journal of Law & Psychiatry, 17,* 369–376.

Cooper, M. L., Russell, M., Skinner, J. B., Frone, M. R., & Mudar, P. (1992). Stress and alcohol use: Moderating effects of gender, coping, and alcohol expectancies. *Journal of Abnormal Psychology, 101,* 139–152.

Corbitt, E. M., & Widiger, T. A. (1995). Sex differences among the personality disorders: An exploration of the data. *Clinical Psychology: Science & Practice, 2,* 225–238.

Corder, E. H., Saunders, A. M., & Strittmatter, W. J. (1993). Gene dose of apolipoprotein E type 4 allele and the risk of Alzheimer's disease in late onset families. *Science, 261,* 921–923.

Cornblatt, B., Obuchowski, M., Andreasen, A., & Smith, C. (1998). High-risk research in schizophrenia: New strategies, new designs. In M. F. Lenzenweger & R. H. Dworkin (Eds.), *Origins of the development of schizophrenia* (pp. 349–383). Washington, DC: American Psychological Association.

Cornelius, M. D., Goldschmidt, L., Day, N. L., & Larkby, C. (2002). Alcohol, tobacco and marijuana use among pregnant teenagers: 6-year follow-up of offspring growth effects. *Neurotoxicology & Teratology, 24,* 703–710.

Corove, M. B., & Gleaves, D. H. (2001). Body dysmorphic disorder: A review of conceptualizations, assessments, and treatment strategies. *Clinical Psychology Review, 21,* 949–970.

Costa, P. T., & Widiger, T. A. (Eds.). (2002). *Personality disorders and the five-factor model of personality* (2nd ed., pp. 215–221). Washington, DC: American Psychological Association.

Costello, E. J., Compton, S. N., Keeler, G., & Angold, A. (2003). Relationships between poverty and psychopathology: A natural experiment. *Journal of the American Medical Association, 290,* 2023–2029.

Costello, E. J., Keeler, G. P., & Angold, A. (2001). Poverty, race/ethnicity, and psychiatric disorder: A study of rural children. *American Journal of Public Health, 91,* 1494–1498.

Costello, E. J., Mustillo, S., Erkanli, A., Keeler, G., & Angold, A. (2003). Prevalence and development of psychiatric disorders in children and adolescence. *Archives of General Psychiatry, 60,* 837–844.

Cott, J. (1995). Natural product formulations available in Europe for psychotropic indications. *Psychopharmacology, 31,* 745–751.

Courtet, P., Picot, M.-C., Bellivier, F., Torres, S., Jollant, F., Michelon, C., Castelnau, D., Astruc, B., Buresi, C., & Malafosse, A. (2004). Serotonin transporter gene may be involved in short-term risk of subsequent suicide attempts. *Biological Psychiatry, 55,* 46–51.

Cousins, N. (1976). Anatomy of an illness as perceived by the patient. *New England Journal of Medicine, 295,* 1458–1463.

Cousins, N. (1985). Therapeutic value of laughter. *Integrative Psychiatry, 3,* 112.

Couzin, J. (2004). Volatile chemistry: Children and antidepressants. *Science, 305,* 468–470.

Coyne, J. C., & Gotlib, I. H. (1983). The role of cognition in depression: A critical appraisal. *Psychological Bulletin, 94,* 472–505.

Crabbe, J. C. (2002). Genetic contributions to addiction. *Annual Review of Psychology, 53,* 435–462.

Craig, T. K., Boardman, A. P., Mills, K., & Daly-Jones, O. (1993). The South London Somatisation Study: I. Longitudinal course and the influence of early life experiences. *British Journal of Psychiatry, 163,* 579–588.

Cranston-Cuebas, M. A., & Barlow, D. H. (1990). Cognitive and affective contributions to sexual functioning. *Annual Review of Sex Research, 1,* 119–161.

Craske, M. G., & Barlow, D. H. (2001). Panic disorder and agoraphobia. In D. H. Barlow (Ed.), *Clinical handbook of psychological disorders: A step-by-step treatment manual* (3rd ed., pp. 1–59). New York: Guilford Press.

Craske, M. G., Brown, T. A., & Barlow, D. H. (1991). Behavioral treatment of panic disorder: A two-year follow-up. *Behavior Therapy, 22,* 289–304.

Craske, M. G., & Waters, A. M. (2005). Panic disorder, phobias, and generalized anxiety disorder. *Annual Review of Clinical Psychology, 1,* 197–226.

Creer, C., & Wing, J. K. (1974). *Several relatives mentioned.* London: Institute of Psychiatry.

Crepault, C., & Couture, M. (1980). Men's erotic fantasies. *Archives of Sexual Behavior, 9,* 565–581.

Crick, N. R., & Dodge, K. A. (1994). A review and reformulation of social information-processing mechanisms in children's social adjustment. *Psychological Bulletin, 115,* 74–101.

Crick, N. R., & Grotpeter, J. K. (1995). Relational aggression, gender, and social-psychological adjustment. *Child Development, 66,* 710–722.

Crick, N. R., & Ladd, G. W. (1990). Children's perceptions of the outcomes of social strategies: Do the ends justify being mean? *Developmental Psychology, 26,* 612–620.

Crits-Christoph, P. (1992). The efficacy of brief dynamic psychotherapy: A meta-analysis. *American Journal of Psychiatry, 149,* 151–158.

Crits-Christoph, P. (1997). Limitations of the dodo bird verdict and the role of clinical trials in psychotherapy research: Comment on Wampold et al. (1997). *Psychological Bulletin, 122,* 216–220.

Crits-Christoph, P., & Barber, J. P. (2000). Long-term psychotherapy. In C. R. Snyder & R. E. Ingram (Eds.), *Handbook of psychological change: Psychotherapy processes and practices for the 21st century* (pp. 455–473). New York: Wiley.

Cronbach, L. J., & Meehl, P. E. (1955). Construct validity in psychological tests. *Psychological Bulletin, 52,* 281–302.

Crosby, A. E., Cheltenham, M. P., & Sacks, J. J. (1999). Incidence of suicidal ideation and behavior in the United States, 1994. *Suicide & Life-Threatening Behavior, 29,* 131–140.

Cross, S. E., & Madson, L. (1997). Models of the self: Self-construals and gender. *Psychological Bulletin, 122,* 5–37.

Cross-National Collaborative Group. (1992). The changing rate of major depression. *Journal of the American Medical Association, 268,* 3098–3105.

Crowe, R. R. (1990). Panic disorder: Genetic considerations. *Journal of Psychiatric Research, 24*(Suppl. 2), 129–134.

Cruess, D. G., Antoni, M. H., Gonzalez, J., Fletcher, M. A., Klimas, N., Duran, R., Ironson, G., & Schneiderman, N. (2003). Sleep disturbance mediates and association between psychological distress and immune status among HIV-positive men and women on combination antiretroviral therapy. *Journal of Psychosomatic Research, 54,* 185–189.

Csernansky, J. G., Mahmoud, R., & Brenner, R. (2002). A comparison of risperidone and haloperidol for the prevention of relapse in patients with schizophrenia. *New England Journal of Medicine, 346,* 16–22.

Culpepper, L. (2004). Identifying and treating panic disorder in primary care. *Journal of Clinical Psychiatry, 65*(Suppl. 5), 19–23.

Curtis, J. (1998). *"Do not grieve for me," James Whale: A new world of gods and monsters.* Boston: Faber & Faber.

D

Dadds, M. R., Holland, D. E., Barrett, P. M., & Spence, S. H. (1999). Early intervention and prevention of anxiety disorders in children: Results at 2-year follow-up. *Journal of Consulting & Clinical Psychology, 67,* 145–150.

Dahl, A. A. (1993). The personality disorders: A critical review of family, twin, and adoption studies. *Journal of Personality Disorders* (Spr. Suppl. 1), 86–99.

Dain, N. (1980). *Clifford W. Beers, advocate for the insane.* Pittsburgh, PA: University of Pittsburgh Press.

Damasio, H., Grabowski, T., Frank, R., Galaburda, A. M., & Damasio, A. R. (1994). The return of Phineas Gage: Clues about the brain from the skull of a famous patient. *Science, 264,* 1102–1105.

Dana, R. H. (1998). *Understanding cultural identity in intervention and assessment.* Thousand Oaks, CA: Sage.

Dana, R. H. (2000). *Handbook on cross-cultural and multicultural personality assessment.* Mahwah, NJ: Erlbaum.

Dana, R. H. (2001). Clinical diagnosis of multicultural populations in the United States. In L. A. Suzuki & J. G. Ponterotto (Eds.), *Handbook of multicultural assessment: Clinical, psychological, and educational applications* (2nd ed., pp. 101–131). San Francisco: Jossey-Bass.

D'Andrea, M., & Daniels, J. (1995). Helping students learn to get along: Assessing the effectiveness of a multicultural developmental guidance project. *Elementary School Guidance & Counseling, 30,* 143–154.

Dare, C., Eisler, I., Russell, G. F., & Szmukler, G. I. (1990). The clinical and theoretical impact of a controlled trial of family therapy in anorexia nervosa. *Journal of Marital & Familial Therapy, 16,* 39–57.

Davenport, D. S., & Yurich, J. M. (1991). Multicultural gender issues. *Journal of Counseling & Development, 70,* 64–71.

Davidson, J., Pearlstein, T., Londborg, P., Brady, K. T., Rothbaum, B., Bell, J., Maddock, R., Hegel, M. T., & Farfel, G. (2001). Efficacy of sertraline in preventing relapse of posttraumatic stress disorder: Results of a 28-week double-blind, placebo-controlled study. *American Journal of Psychiatry, 158,* 1974–1981.

Davidson, J. R. T. (2001). Pharmacotherapy of generalized anxiety disorder. *Journal of Clinical Psychiatry, 62*(Suppl. 11), 46–50.

Davidson, J. R. T. (2003). Pharmacotherapy of social phobia. *Acta Psychiatrica Scandinavica, 108*(Suppl. 417), 65–71.

Davidson, J. R. T. (2004). Long-term treatment and prevention of posttraumatic stress disorder. *Journal of Clinical Psychiatry, 65*(Suppl. 1), 44–48.

Davidson, J. R. T., DuPont, R. L., Hedges, D., & Haskins, J. T. (1999). Efficacy, safety, and tolerability of venlafaxine extended release and buspirone in outpatients with generalized anxiety disorder. *Journal of Clinical Psychiatry, 60,* 528–535.

Davidson, J. R. T., Rothbaum, B. O., van der Kolk, B. A., Sikes, C. R., & Farfel, G. M. (2001). Multicenter, double-blind comparison of sertraline and placebo in the treatment of posttraumatic stress disorder. *Archives of General Psychiatry, 58,* 485–492.

Davidson, P. R., & Parker, K. C. H. (2001). Eye movement desensitization and reprocessing (EMDR): A meta-analysis. *Journal of Consulting & Clinical Psychology, 69,* 305–316.

Davidson, R. J., Pizzagalli, D., & Nitschke, J. B. (2002). The representation and regulation of emotion in depression: Perspectives from affective neuroscience. In I. H. Gotlib & C. L. Hammen (Eds.), *Handbook of depression* (pp. 219–244). New York: Guilford Press.

Davidson, R. J., Pizzagalli, D., Nitschke, J. B., & Putnam, K. (2002). Depression: Perspectives from affective neuroscience. *Annual Review of Psychology, 53,* 545–574.

Davis, K. L., Kahn, R. S., Ko, G., & Davidson, M. (1991). Dopamine in schizophrenia: A review and conceptualization. *American Journal of Psychiatry, 148,* 1474–1486.

Davis, R. D., & Millon, T. (1993). The five-factor model for personality disorders: Apt or misguided? *Psychological Inquiry, 4,* 104–109.

DeKosky, S. T., & Orgogozo, J.-M. (2001). Alzheimer disease: Diagnosis, costs, and dimensions of treatment. *Alzheimer Disease & Associated Disorders, 15*(Suppl. 1), 3–7.

Delay, J., Deniker, P., & Harl, J. M. (1952). Traitement des etats d'excitation et d'agitation par une methode medicamenteuse derivee de l'hibernotherapie. *Annuls Medicine Psychologie, 110,* 262–267.

Delizonna, L. L., Wincze, J. P., Litz, B. T., Brown, T. A., & Barlow, D. H. (2001). A comparison of subjective and physiological measures of mechanically produced and erotically produced erections (or, is an erection an erection?). *Journal of Sex & Marital Therapy, 27,* 21–31.

Dell, P. F. (1998). Axis II pathology in outpatients with dissociative identity disorder. *Journal of Nervous & Mental Disease, 186,* 352–356.

Dell, P. F., & Eisenhower, J. W. (1990). Adolescent multiple personality disorder: A preliminary study of eleven cases. *Journal of the American Academy of Child & Adolescent Psychiatry, 29,* 359–366.

Dembroski, T. M., MacDougall, J. M., Williams, J. M., & Haney, T. L. (1985). Components of Type A hostility and anger: Relationship to angiographic findings. *Psychosomatic Medicine, 47,* 219–233.

Denison, M. E., Paredes, A., Bacal, S., & Gawin, F. H. (1998). Psychological and psychiatric consequences of cocaine. In R. E. Tartar (Ed.), *Handbook of substance abuse: Neurobehavioral pharmacology* (pp. 201–213). New York: Plenum Press.

Denning, D. G., Conwell, Y., King, D., & Cox, C. (2000). Method choice, intent, and gender in completed suicide. *Suicide & Life-Threatening Behavior, 30,* 282–288.

Dennis, M. L., Babor, T. F., Diamond, G., Donaldson, J., Godley, S. H., Tims, F., Titus, J. C., Webb, C., Herrell, J., & the CYT Steering Committee. (2000). *The cannabis youth treatment (CYT) experiment: Preliminary findings.* Rockville, MD: Substance Abuse and Mental Health Services Administration, Center for Substance Abuse Treatment. Retrieved from the World Wide Web: http://samhsa.gov/centers/csat/content/recoverymonth/000907rptcover.html

DePrince, A. P., & Freyd, J. J. (1999). Dissociation, attention, and memory. *Psychological Science, 10,* 449–452.

DePrince, A. P., & Freyd, J. J. (2001). Memory and dissociative tendencies: The roles of attentional context and word meaning in a directed forgetting task. *Journal of Trauma & Dissociation, 2,* 67–82.

DeRubeis, R. J., Gelfand, L. A., Tang, T. Z., & Simons, A. D. (1999). Medications versus cognitive behavior therapy for severely depressed outpatients: Mega-analysis of four randomized comparisons. *American Journal of Psychiatry, 156,* 1001–1013.

deSilva, P., Rachman, S., & Seligman, M. (1977). Prepared phobias and obsessions. *Behaviour Research & Therapy, 15,* 65–77.

Desmond, D. W., & Tatemichi, T. K. (1998). Vascular dementia. In M. F. Folstein (Ed.), *Neurobiology of primary dementia* (pp. 167–190). Washington, DC: American Psychiatric Press.

de Snyder, V. N. S., Diaz-Perez, M. D., & Ojeda, V. D. (2000). The prevalence of nervios and associated symptomatology among inhabitants of Mexican rural communities. *Culture, Medicine & Psychiatry, 24,* 453–470.

Deutsch, A. (1937). *The mentally ill in America: A history of their care and treatment from colonial times.* Garden City, NY: Doubleday, Doran & Company.

Dewaraja, R., & Sasaki, Y. (1991). Semen-loss syndrome: A comparison between Sri Lanka and Japan. *American Journal of Psychotherapy, 45,* 14–20.

de Wit, H., Kirk, J. M., & Justice, A. (1998). Behavioral pharmacology of cannabinoids. In R. E. Tarter (Ed.), *Handbook of substance abuse: Neurobehavioral pharmacology* (pp. 131–146). New York: Plenum Press.

de Zwaan, M., Roerig, J. L., & Mitchell, J. E. (2004). Pharmacological treatment of anorexia nervosa, bulimia nervosa, and binge eating disorder. In J. K. Thompson (Ed.), *Handbook of eating disorders and obesity* (pp. 186–217). Hoboken, NJ: Wiley.

de Zwaan, M., Roerig, J. L., & Mitchell, J. E. (2004). Pharmacological treatment of anorexia nervosa, bulimia nervosa and binge-eating disorder. In J. K. Thompson (Ed.), *Handbook of eating disorders and obesity* (pp. 234–266). Hoboken, NJ: Wiley.

Dickinson, E. (1890/1955). *Poems: Including variant readings critically compared with all known manuscripts.* Cambridge, MA: Belknap Press.

DiLillo, D. (2001). Interpersonal functioning among women reporting a history of childhood sexual abuse: Empirical findings and methodological issues. *Clinical Psychology Review, 21,* 553–576.

Dishion, T. J., & Patterson, G. R. (1997). The timing and severity of antisocial behavior: Three hypotheses within an ecological framework. In D. M. Stoff, J. Breiling, & J. D. Maser (Eds.), *Handbook of antisocial personality disorder* (pp. 205–217). New York: Wiley.

Dittman, R. W., Kappes, M. E., & Kappes, M. H. (1992). Sexual behavior in adolescent and adult females with congenital and adrenal hyperplasia. *Psychoneuroendocrinology, 17,* 153–170.

Dixon, D., Cruess, S., Kilbourn, K., Klimas, N., Fletcher, M. A., Ironson, G., Baum, A., Schneiderman, N., & Antoni, M. H. (2001). Social support mediates loneliness and human herpes virus Type 6 (HHV-6) antibody titers. *Journal of Applied Social Psychology, 31,* 1111–1132.

Dixon, J. F., & Hokin, L. E. (1998). Lithium acutely inhibits and chronically up-regulates and stabilizes glutamate uptake by presynaptic nerve endings in mouse cerebral cortex. *Neurobiology, 95,* 8363–8368.

Dobson, K. S. (1989). A meta-analysis of the efficacy of cognitive therapy for depression.

Journal of Consulting & Clinical Psychology, 57, 414–419.

Dobson, K. S., Backs-Dermott, B. J., & Dozois, D. J. A. (2000). Cognitive and cognitive-behavioral therapies. In C. R. Snyder & R. E. Ingram (Eds.), *Handbook of psychological change: Psychotherapy processes and practices for the 21st century* (pp. 409–428). New York: Wiley.

Docherty, N. M., Grosh, E. S., Wexler, B. E. (1996). Affective reactivity of cognitive functioning and family history in schizophrenia. *Psychiatry, 139,* 59–64.

Dodge, K., & Schwartz, D. (1997). Social information processing mechanisms in aggressive behavior. In D. M. Stoff, J. Breiling, & J. D. Maser (Eds.), *Handbook of antisocial personality disorder* (pp. 171–180). New York: Wiley.

Dodge, K. A., & Pettit, G. S. (2003). A biopsychosocial model of the development of chronic conduct problems in adolescence. *Developmental Psychology, 39,* 349–371.

Dohrenwend, B. P. (2000). The role of adversity and stress in psychopathology: Some evidence and its implications for theory and research. *Journal of Health and Social Behavior, 41,* 1–19.

Dohrenwend, B. P., Levav, I., Shrout, P. E., Link, B. G., Skodol, A. E., & Martin, J. L. (1987). Life stress and psychopathology: Progress on research begun with Barbara Snell Dohrenwend. *American Journal of Community Psychology, 15,* 677–715.

Donahey, K. M., & Carroll, R. A. (1993). Gender differences in factors associated with hypoactive sexual desire. *Journal of Sex & Marital Therapy, 19,* 25–40.

Donegan, N. H., Sanislow, C. A., Blumberg, H. P., Fulbright, R. K., Lacadie, C., Skudlarski, P., Gore, J. C., Olson, I. R., McGlashan, T. H., & Wexler, B. E. (2003). Amygdala hyperreactivity in borderline personality disorder: Implications for emotional dysregulation. *Biological Psychiatry, 54,* 1284–1293.

Dorahy, M. J. (2001). Dissociative identity disorder and memory dysfunction: The current state of experimental research and its future directions. *Clinical Psychology Review, 21,* 771–795.

Dorfman, W. I., & Leonard, S. (2001). The Minnesota Multiphasic Personality Inventory-2 (MMPI-2). In W. I. Dorfman & S. M. Freshwater (Eds.), *Understanding psychological assessment* (pp. 145–171). Dordrecht, Netherlands: Kluwer Academic Publishers.

Dornbusch, S. M., Carlsmith, J. M., Duncan, P. D., Gross, R. T., Martin, J. A., Ritter, P. L., & Siegel-Gorelick, B. (1984). Sexual maturation, social class, and the desire to be thin among adolescent females. *Developmental & Behavioral Pediatrics, 5,* 308–314.

Dorris, M. (1989). *The unbroken cord.* New York: Harper & Row.

Dossenbach, M., Erol, A., el Mahfoud Kessaci, M., Shaheen, M. O., Sunbol, M. M., Boland, J., Hodge, A., O'Halloran, R. A., & Bitter, I. (2004). Effectiveness of antipsychotic treatments for schizophrenia: Interim 6-month analysis from a prospective observational study (IC-SOHO) comparing olanzapine, quetiapine, risperidone, and haloperidol. *Journal of Clinical Psychiatry, 65,* 312–321.

Dougherty, D., Donab, A., Spencer, T., et al. (1999). Dopamine transporter density in patients with attention deficit hyperactivity disorder. *The Lancet, 354,* 2132–2133.

Doyle, A., & Pollack, M. H. (2004). Long-term management of panic disorder. *Journal of Clinical Psychiatry, 65*(Suppl. 5), 24–28.

Drake, C. L., Roehrs, T., & Roth, T. (2003). Insomnia causes, consequences, and therapeutics: An overview. *Depression & Anxiety, 18,* 163–176.

Drevets, W. C. (2001). Neuroimaging and neuropathological studies of depression: Implications for the cognitive-emotional features of mood disorders. *Current Opinions in Neurobiology, 11,* 240–249.

Drevets, W. C., Price, J. L., Simpson, J. R. J., Todd, R. D., Reich, T., et al. (1997). Subgenual prefrontal cortex abnormalities in mood disorders. *Nature, 386,* 824–827.

Du, Y., Dodel, R., Hampel, H., Buerger, K., Lin, S., Eastwood, B., Bales, K., Gao, F., Moeller, H. J., Oertel, W., Farlow, M., & Paul, S. (2001). Reduced levels of amyloid B-peptide antibody in Alzheimer disease. *Neurology, 57,* 801–805.

Dudley-Grant, G. R. (2001). Eastern Caribbean family psychology with conduct disordered adolescents from the Virgin Islands. *American Psychologist, 56,* 47–57.

Dündar, Y., Dodd, S., Strobl, J., Boland, A., Dickson, R., & Walley, T. (2004). Comparative efficacy of newer hypnotic drugs for the short-term management of insomnia: A systematic review and meta-analysis. *Human Psychopharmacology: Clinical & Experimental, 19,* 305–322.

Dunkin, J. J., & Anderson-Hanley, C. (1998). Dementia caregiver burden: A review of the literature and guidelines for assessment and intervention. *Neurology, 51,* S53–S60.

Dunner, D. L. (2004). Correlates of suicidal behavior and lithium treatment in bipolar disorder. *Journal of Clinical Psychiatry, 65*(Suppl. 10), 5–10.

DuPaul, G. J., & Barkley, R. A. (1993). Behavioral contributions to pharmacology: The utility of behavioral methodology in medication treatment of children with attention deficit hyperactivity disorder. *Behavior Therapy, 24,* 47–65.

Durkheim, E. (1897). *Le suicide: Etude de sociologie.* Paris: F. Alcan.

Dykens, E. M., & Volkmar, F. R. (1997). Medical condition associated with autism. In D. J. Cohen & F. R. Volkmar (Eds.), *Handbook of autism and pervasive developmental disorders* (pp. 388–410). Toronto: Wiley.

E

Earls, F. (2001). Community factors supporting child mental health. *Child & Adolescent Psychiatric Clinics of North America, 10,* 693–709.

Eaton, W. W., Moortensenk, P. B., Herrman, H., & Freeman, H. (1992). Long-term course of hospitalization for schizophrenia: I. Risk for rehospitalization. *Schizophrenia Bulletin, 18,* 217–228.

Eaton, W. W., Thara, R., Federman, E., & Tien, A. (1998). Remission and relapse in schizophrenia: The Madras longitudinal study. *Journal of Nervous & Mental Disease, 186,* 357–363.

Eaves, L. J., Silberg, J. L., Meyer, J. M., Maes, H. H., Simonoff, E., Pickles, A., Rutter, M., Neale, M. C., Reynolds, C. A., Erikson, M. T., Heath, A. C., Loeber, R., Truett, K. R., & Hewitt, J. K. (1997). Genetics and developmental psychopathology: 2. The main effects of genes and environment on behavior problems in the Virginia Twin Study of Adolescent Behavioral Development. *Journal of Child Psychology & Psychiatry, 38,* 965–980.

Eckert, E. D., Halmi, K. A., Marchi, P., & Grove, W. (1995). Ten-year follow-up of anorexia nervosa: Clinical course and outcome. *Psychological Medicine, 25,* 143–156.

Edelmann, R. J. (1992). *Anxiety: Theory, research, and intervention in clinical and health psychology.* Chichester, NY: Wiley.

Edinger, D. (1963). *Bertha Pappenheim, Leben und Schriften.* Frankfurt, Germany: Ner-Tamid Verlag.

Egeland, J. A. (1986). Cultural factors and social stigma for manic-depression: The Amish Study. *American Journal of Social Psychiatry, 6,* 279–286.

Egeland, J. A. (1994). An epidemiologic and genetic study of affective disorders among the Old Order Amish. In D. F. Papolos & H. M. Lachman (Eds.), *Genetic studies in affective disorders: Overview of basic methods, current directions, and critical research issues* (pp. 70–90). Oxford, UK: Wiley.

Egeland, J. A., Gerhard, D. S., Pauls, D. L., Sussex, J. N., Kidd, K. K., Allen, C. R., Hostetter, A. M., & Housman, D. E. (1987). Bipolar affective disorders linked to DNA markers on Chromosome 11. *Nature, 325,* 783–787.

Egeland, J. A., & Hostetter, A. M. (1983). Amish study: I. Affective disorders among the Amish, 1976–1980. *American Journal of Psychiatry, 140,* 56–61.

Egeland, J. A., Hostetter, A. M., & Eshleman, S. K. (1983). Amish study III: The impact of cultural factors on bipolar diagnosis. *American Journal of Psychiatry, 140,* 67–71.

Egeland, J. A., & Sussex, J. N. (1985). Suicide and family loading for affective disorders. *Journal of the American Medical Association, 254,* 915–918.

Ehlers, A. (1995). A 1-year prospective study of panic attacks: Clinical course and factors associated with maintenance. *Journal of Abnormal Psychology, 104,* 164–172.

Ehlers, A., Clark, D. M., Dunmore, E., Jaycox, L., Meadows, E., & Foa, E. (1998). Predicating response to exposure treatment in PTSD: The role of mental defeat and alienation. *Journal of Traumatic Stress, 11,* 457–471.

Ehlers, A., Mayou, R., & Bryant, B. (1998). Psychological predictors of chronic posttraumatic stress disorder after motor vehicle accidents. *Journal of Abnormal Psychology, 107,* 508–519.

Ehrensaft, M. K., Wasserman, G. A., Verdelli, L., Greenwald, S., Miller, L. S., & Davies, M. (2003). Maternal antisocial behavior, parenting practices, and behavior problems in boys at risk for antisocial behavior. *Journal of Child & Family Studies, 12,* 27–40.

Eisenberg, L. (1958). School phobia: A study in the communication of anxiety. *American Journal of Psychiatry, 114,* 712–718.

Eisenbruch, M., de Jong, J. T. V. M., & van de Put, W. (2004). Bringing order out of chaos: A culturally competent approach to managing the problems of refugees and victims of organized violence. *Journal of Traumatic Stress, 17,* 123–131.

Ekselius, L., Tilfors, M., Furmark, T., & Fredrikson, M. (2001). Personality disorders in the general population: DSM-IV and ICD-10 defined prevalence as related to sociodemographic profile. *Personality & Individual Differences, 30,* 311–320.

Elder, G. H., & Clipp, E. C. (1989). Combat experience and emotional health: Impairment and resilience in later life. *Journal of Personality, 57,* 311–341.

Elder, G. H., Liker, J. K., & Jaworski, B. J. (1984). Hardship in lives: Depression influences. In K. A. McCluskey & H. W. Reese (Eds.), *Lifespan developmental psychology: Historical and generational effects.* Orlando, FL: Academic Press.

Eley, T. C., Bolton, D., O'Connor, T. G., Perrin, S., Smith, P., & Plomin, R. (2003). A twin study of anxiety-related behaviours in pre-school children. *Journal of Child Psychology & Psychiatry, 44,* 945–960.

Eley, T. C., Lichenstein, P., & Stevenson, J. (1999). Sex differences in the etiology of aggressive and nonaggressive antisocial behavior: Results from two twin studies. *Child Development, 70,* 155–168.

Elkin, I., Shea, T., Watkins, J. T., Imber, S. D., Sotsky, S. M., Collins, J. F., Glass, D. R., Pilkonis, P. A., Leber, W. R., Docherty, J. P., Fiester, S. J., & Parloff, M. B. (1989). National Institute of Mental Health treatment of depression collaborative research program: General effectiveness of treatments. *Archives of General Psychiatry, 46,* 971–982.

Ellason, J. W., & Ross, C. A. (1997). Two-year follow-up of inpatients with dissociative identity disorder. *American Journal of Psychiatry, 154,* 832–839.

Ellason, J. W., Ross, C. A., & Fuchs, D. L. (1996). Lifetime Axis I and II comorbidity and childhood trauma history in dissociative identity disorder. *Psychiatry, 59,* 255–266.

Ellis, A. (1997). The evolution of Albert Ellis and emotive behavior therapy. In J. K. Zeig (Ed.), *The rational evolution of psychotherapy: The third conference* (pp. 69–78). New York: Brunner/Mazel.

Ellis, A., & Harper, R. A. (1961). *A guide to rational living.* Englewood Cliffs, NJ: Prentice Hall.

Ellison, L. F., & Morrison, H. I. (2001). Low serum cholesterol concentration and risk of suicide. *Epidemiology, 12,* 168–172.

Emmelkamp, P. M. G. (1994). Behavior therapy with adults. In A. E. Bergin (Ed.), *Handbook of psychotherapy and behavior change* (4th ed., pp. 379–427). New York: Wiley.

Emslie, G. J., Portteus, A. M., Kumar, E. C., & Hume, J. H. (2004). Antidepressants: SSRIs and novel atypical antidepressants—An update on psychopharmacology. In H. Steiner (Ed.), *Handbook of mental health intervention in children and adolescents: An integrated developmental approach* (pp. 318–362). San Francisco: Jossey-Bass.

Eng, W., Heimberg, R. G., Coles, M. E., Schneier, F. R., & Liebowitz, M. R. (2000). An empirical approach to subtype identification in individuals with social phobia. *Psychological Medicine, 30,* 1345–1357.

Engel, J. (1989). *Addicted: Kids talking about drugs in their own words.* New York: T. Doherty.

Engels, G. I., Garnefski, N., & Diekstra, R. F. W. (1993). Efficacy of rational-emotive therapy: A quantitative analysis. *Journal of Consulting & Clinical Psychology, 61,* 1083–1090.

Ensminger, M. E. (1995). Welfare and psychological distress: A longitudinal study of African/American urban mothers. *Journal of Health & Social Behavior, 36,* 346–359.

Ensminger, M. E., & Hee-Soon, J. (2001). The influence of patterns of welfare receipt during the child-rearing years on later physical and psychological health. *Women & Health, 32,* 25–46.

Epple, D. M. (2002). Senile dementia of the Alzheimer type. *Clinical Social Work Journal, 30,* 95–110.

Epstein, J., Saunders, B. E., & Kilpatrick, D. G. (1997). Predicting PTSD in women with a history of childhood rape. *Journal of Traumatic Stress, 10,* 573–588.

Erdelyi, M. H. (1992). Psychodynamics and the unconscious. *American Psychologist, 47,* 784–787.

Erickson, M. T. (1992). *Behavior disorders of children and adolescents.* Englewood Cliffs, NJ: Prentice Hall.

Erlenmeyer-Kimling, L. (2001). Early neurobehavioral deficits as phenotypic indicators of the schizophrenia genotype and predictors of later psychosis. *American Journal of Medical Genetics, 105,* 23–24.

Erlenmeyer-Kimling, L., Rock, D., Squires-Wheeler, E., & Roberts, S. (1991). Early life precursors of psychiatric outcomes in adulthood in subjects at risk for schizophrenia or affective disorders. *Psychiatry Research, 39,* 239–256.

Escobar, J. I. (1993). Psychiatric epidemiology. In A. C. Gaw (Ed.), *Culture, ethnicity, and mental illness* (pp. 43–73). Washington, DC: American Psychiatric Press.

Escobar, J. I., Burnam, M. A., Karno, M., & Forsythe, A. (1987). Somatization in the community. *Archives of General Psychiatry, 44,* 713–718.

Escobar, J. I., Gara, M., Waitzkin, H., Cohen Silver, R., Holman, A., & Compton, W. (1998). DSM-IV hypochondriasis in primary care. *General Hospital Psychiatry, 20,* 155–159.

Estrada, A. U., & Pinsof, W. M. (1995). The effectiveness of family therapies for selected behavioral disorders of childhood. *Journal of Marital & Family Therapy, 21,* 403–440.

Exner, J. E. (1993). *The Rorschach: A comprehensive system: Vol. 1. Basic foundations* (3rd ed.). New York: Wiley.

Eysenck, H. J. (1994). The biology of morality. In B. Puka (Ed.), *Defining perspectives in moral development* (pp. 212–229). New York: Garland.

Eysenck, H. J. (Ed.). (1967). *The biological basis of personality.* Springfield, IL: Charles C Thomas.

F

Fabrega, H. (1993). Toward a social theory of psychiatric phenomena. *Behavioral Science, 38,* 75–100.

Fabrega, H., Ulrich, R., Pilkonis, P., & Mezzich, J. (1991). On the homogeneity of personality disorder clusters. *Comprehensive Psychiatry, 32,* 373–386.

Fagan, P. J., Wise, T. N., Schmidt, C. W., Jr., & Berlin, F. S. (2002). Pedophilia. *Journal of the American Medical Association, 288,* 2458–2465.

Fahy, T. A. (1988). The diagnosis of multiple personality disorder: A critical review. *British Journal of Psychiatry, 153,* 597–606.

Fairbank, J. A., Hansen, D. J., & Fitterling, J. M. (1991). Patterns of appraisal and coping across different stressor conditions among former prisoners of war with and without posttraumatic stress disorder. *Journal of Consulting & Clinical Psychology, 59,* 274–281.

Fairburn, C. G. (1997). Eating disorders. In D. M. Clark & C. G. Fairburn (Eds.), *Science and practice of cognitive behaviour therapy* (pp. 209–241). London: Oxford University Press.

Fairburn, C. G. (2005). Evidence-based treatment of anorexia nervosa. *International Journal of Eating Disorders, 37,* 26–30.

Fairburn, C. G., & Harrison, P. J. (2003). Eating disorders. *Lancet, 361,* 407–416.

Fairburn, C. G., Cooper, Z., Doll, H. A., Norman, P., & O'Connor, M. (2000). The natural course of bulimia nervosa and binge eating disorder in young women. *Archives of General Psychiatry, 57,* 659–665.

Fairburn, C. G., Jones, R., Peveler, R. C., & Carr, S. J. (1991). Three psychological treatments for bulimia nervosa: A comparative trial. *Archives of General Psychiatry, 48,* 463–469.

Fairburn, C. G., Norman, P. A., Welch, S. L., O'Connor, M. E., Doll, H. A., & Peveler, R. C. (1995). A prospective study of outcome in bulimia nervosa and the long-term effects of three psychological treatments. *Archives of General Psychiatry, 52,* 304–312.

Fairburn, C. G., Stice, E., Cooper, Z., Doll, H. A., Norman, P. A., & O'Connor, M. E. (2003). Understanding persistence in bulimia nervosa: A 5-year naturalistic study. *Journal of Consulting & Clinical Psychology, 71,* 103–109.

Fairburn, C. G., Welsh, S. L., Doll, H. A., Davies, B. A., & O'Connor, M. E. (1997). Risk factors for bulimia nervosa. *Archives of General Psychiatry, 54,* 509–517.

Fairweather, G. W., Sanders, D. H., Maynard, H., & Cressler, D. L. (1969). *Community life for the mentally ill: An alternative to institutional care.* Chicago: Aldine.

Fallon, A. E., & Rozin, P. (1985). Sex differences in perceptions of desirable body shape. *Journal of Abnormal Psychology, 94,* 102–105.

Falloon, I. R., Brooker, C., & Graham-Hole, V. (1992). Psychosocial interventions for schizophrenia. *Behavior Change, 9,* 238–245.

Fals-Stewart, W., Marks, A. P., & Schafer, J. (1993). A comparison of behavioral group therapy and individual behavior therapy in treating obsessive-compulsive disorder. *Journal of Nervous & Mental Disease, 181,* 189–193.

Fanous, A. H., Prescott, C. A., & Kendler, K. S. (2004). The prediction of thoughts of death or self-harm in a population-based sample of female twins. *Psychological Medicine, 34*, 301–312.

Faraone, S. V., Biederman, J., Keenan, K., & Tsuang, M. T. (1991). A family-genetic study of girls with DSM-III attention deficit disorder. *American Journal of Psychiatry, 148*, 112–117.

Faravelli, C., Giugni, A., Salvatori, S., & Ricca, V. (2004). Psychopathology after rape. *American Journal of Psychiatry, 161*, 1483–1485.

Fauerbach, J. A., Lawrence, J. W., Schmidt, C. W., Munster, A. M., & Costa, P. T. (2000). Personality predictors of injury-related posttraumatic stress disorder. *Journal of Nervous & Mental Disease, 188*, 510–517.

Fava, G. A., Rafanelli, C., Grandi, S., Conti, S., Ruini, C., Magelli, L., & Belluardo, P. (2001). Long-term outcome of panic disorder with agoraphobia treated by exposure. *Psychological Medicine, 31*, 891–898.

Fava, M., Copeland, P. M., Schweiger, U., & Herzog, D. B. (1989). Neurochemical abnormalities of anorexia nervosa and bulimia nervosa. *American Journal of Psychiatry, 146*, 963–971.

Fava, M., & Rosenbaum, J. F. (1995). Pharmacotherapy and somatic therapies. In E. E. Beckham & W. R. Leber (Eds.), *Handbook of depression* (2nd ed., pp. 280–301). New York: Guilford Press.

Fawzy, F. I., Kemeny, M. E., Fawzy, N. W., Elashoff, R., et al. (1990). A structured psychiatric intervention for cancer patients: II. Changes over time in immunological measures. *Archives of General Psychiatry, 47*, 729–735.

Feder, A., Olfson, M., Fuentes, M., Shea, S., Lantigua, R. A., & Weissman, M. M. (2001). Medically unexplained symptoms in an urban general medicine practice. *Psychosomatics, 42*, 261–268.

Federoff, I. C., Polivy, J., & Herman, C. P. (1997). The effect of preexposure to food cues on the eating behavior of restrained and unrestrained eaters. *Appetite, 28*, 33–47.

Feigon, S. A., Waldman, I. D., Levy, F., & Hay, D. A. (2001). Genetic and environmental influences on separation anxiety disorder symptoms and their moderation by age and sex. *Behavior Genetics, 31*, 403–411.

Feinberg, L. (2001). Trans health crisis: For us it's life or death. *American Journal of Public Health, 91*, 897–900.

Fennell, M. J. V., & Teasdale, J. D. (1987). Cognitive therapy for depression: Individual differences and the process of change. *Cognitive Therapy & Research, 11*, 253–271.

Fenton, W. S., & McGlashan, T. H. (1994). Antecedents, symptom progression, and long-term outcome of the deficit syndrome in schizophrenia. *American Journal of Psychiatry, 151*, 351–356.

Fergusson, D. M., Horwood, J. L., & Lynskey, M. T. (1993). Early dentine lead levels and subsequent cognitive and behavioural development. *Journal of Child Psychology & Psychiatry & Allied Disciplines, 34*, 215–227.

Ferris, C. F., & de Vries, G. J. (1997). Ethological models for examining the neurobiology of aggressive and affiliative behaviors. In D. M. Stoff, J. Breiling, & J. D. Maser (Eds.), *Handbook of antisocial personality disorder* (pp. 255–268). New York: Wiley.

Field, A. E., Camargo, C. A., Jr., Taylor, C. B., Berkey, C. S., Frazier, L., Gillman, M. W., & Colditz, G. A. (1999). Overweight, weight concerns, and bulimic behaviors among girls and boys. *Journal of the American Academy of Child & Adolescent Psychiatry, 38*, 754–760.

Figley, C. R., & Leventman, S. (Eds.). (1980). *Strangers at home: Vietnam veterans since the war.* New York: Brunner/Mazel.

Fink, M. (2001). Convulsive therapy: A review of the first 55 years. *Journal of Affective Disorders, 63*, 1–15.

Fink, P., Hansen, M. S., & Oxhøj, M.-L. (2004). The prevalence of somatoform disorders among internal medical inpatients. *Journal of Psychosomatic Research, 56*, 413–418.

Finkelhor, D. (1984). *Child sexual abuse: New theory and research.* New York: Free Press.

Finkelhor, D., & Dzuiba-Leatherman, J. (1994). Victimization of children. *American Psychologist, 49*, 173–183.

Finney, J. W., & Moos, R. H. (1998). Psychosocial treatments for alcohol use disorders. In P. E. Nathan (Ed.), *A guide to treatments that work* (pp. 156–166). New York: Oxford University Press.

First, M. B., Spitzer, R. L., Gibbon, M., & Williams, J. B. W. (1997). *Structured Clinical Interview for DSM-IV Axis I Disorders—Non-patient edition (version 2.0).* New York: New York State Psychiatric Institute, Biometrics Research Department.

Fishbain, D. A., & Goldberg, M. (1991). The misdiagnosis of conversion disorder in a psychiatric emergency service. *General Hospital Psychiatry, 13*, 177–181.

Fisher, R. A. (1958). *The cancer controversy.* London: Oliver & Boyd.

Fitzgerald, P. B., Brown, T. L., Daskalakis, Z. J., de Castella, A., Kulkarni, J., Marston, N. A. U, & Oxley, T. (2004). Reduced plastic brain responses in schizophrenia: A transcranial magnetic stimulation study. *Schizophrenia Research, 71*, 17–26.

Fitzgerald, T. E., Tennen, H., Affleck, G., & Pransky, G. S. (1993). The relative importance of dispositional optimism and control appraisals in quality of life after coronary artery bypass surgery. *Journal of Behavioral Medicine, 16*, 25–43.

Flakierska-Praquin, N., Lindstrom, M., & Gilberg, C. (1997). School phobia with separation anxiety disorder: A comparative 20- to 29-year follow up study of 35 school refusers. *Comprehensive Psychology, 38*, 17–22.

Flemming, M., & Manwell, L. B. (2000). Epidemiology. In G. Zernig (Ed.), *Handbook of alcoholism* (pp. 271–286). Boca Raton, FL: CRC Press.

Foa, E., & Kozak, M. (1993). Obsessive-compulsive disorder: Long-term outcome of psychological treatment. In M. Mavissakalian & R. Prien (Eds.), *Long-term treatment of anxiety disorders.* Washington, DC: American Psychiatric Press.

Foa, E. B., Dancu, C. V., Hembree, E., Jaycox, L. H., Anonymous, & Street, G. P. (1999). A comparison of exposure therapy, stress inoculation training, and their combination for reducing posttraumatic stress disorder in female assault victims. *Journal of Consulting & Clinical Psychology, 67*, 194–200.

Foa, E. B., Feske, U., Murdock, T. B., & Kozak, M. J. (1991). Processing threat-related information in rape victims. *Journal of Abnormal Psychology, 100*, 156–162.

Foa, E. B., & Franklin, E. (2001). Obsessive-compulsive disorder. In D. H. Barlow (Ed.), *Clinical handbook of psychological disorders: A step-by-step treatment manual* (3rd ed., pp. 209–263). New York: Guilford Press.

Foa, E. B., & Hearst-Ikeda, D. (1996). Emotional dissociation in response to trauma: An information-processing approach. In L. K. Michelson (Ed.), *Handbook of dissociation: Theoretical, empirical, and clinical perspectives* (pp. 207–224). New York: Plenum Press.

Foa, E. B., & Jaycox, L. H. (1999). Cognitive-behavioral theory and treatment of posttraumatic stress disorder. In D. Spiegel (Ed.), *Efficacy and cost-effectiveness of psychotherapy* (pp. 23–61). Washington, DC: American Psychiatric Association.

Foa, E. D., & Riggs, D. S. (1995). Posttraumatic stress disorder following assault: Theoretical considerations and empirical findings. *Current Directions in Psychological Science, 4*, 61–65.

Follette, W. C., & Hayes, S. C. (2000). Contemporary behavior therapy. In C. R. Snyder & R. E. Ingram (Eds.), *Handbook of psychological change: Psychotherapy processes and practices for the 21st century* (pp. 381–408). New York: Wiley.

Folstein, M. F., Folstein, S. E., & McHugh, P. R. (1975). Mini-mental state: A practical method for grading the cognitive state of patients for the clinician. *Journal of Psychiatric Research, 12*, 189–198.

Fombonne, E. (1999). The epidemiology of autism: A review. *Psychological Medicine, 29*, 769–786.

Forsyth, D. R., & Corazzini, J. G. (2000). Groups as change agents. In C. R. Snyder & R. E. Ingram (Eds.), *Handbook of psychological change: Psychotherapy processes and practices for the 21st century* (pp. 309–336). New York: Wiley.

Fox, M. J. (2002). *Lucky man: A memoir.* New York: Hyperion Press.

Fraley, R. C., & Bonanno, G. A. (2004). Attachment and loss: A test of three competing models on the association between attachment-related avoidance and adaptation to bereavement. *Personality & Social Psychology Bulletin, 30*, 878–890.

Frances, A., Kahn, D., Carpenter, D., Docherty, J., & Donovan, S. (1998). The expert consensus guidelines for treating depression in bipolar disorder. *Journal of Clinical Psychiatry, 59*(Suppl. 4), 73–79.

Frances, A. J., First, M. B., & Pincus, H. A. (1995). *DSM-IV guidebook.* Washington, DC: American Psychiatric Press.

Frank, E., Anderson, B., Reynolds, C. F., & Ritenour, A. (1994). Life events and the research diagnostic criteria endogenous subtype: A confirmation of the distinction using the Bedford College methods. *Archives of General Psychiatry, 51*, 519–524.

Frank, E., Grochocinski, V. J., Spanier, C. A., Buysse, D. J., Cherry, C. R., Houck, P. R., Stapf, D. M., & Kupfer, D. J. (2000). Interpersonal psychotherapy and antidepressant medication: Evaluation of a sequential treatment strategy in women with recurrent major depression. *Journal of Clinical Psychiatry, 61*, 51–57.

Frank, E., Swartz, H. A., & Kupfer, D. J. (2000). Interpersonal and social rhythm therapy: Managing the chaos of bipolar disorder. *Biological Psychiatry, 48,* 593–604.

Frank, G. K., Kaye, W. H., Weltzin, T. E., Perel, J., Moss, H., McConaha, C., & Pollice, C. (2001). Altered response to meta-chlorophenylpiperazine in anorexia nervosa: Support for a persistent alteration of serotonin activity after short-term weight restoration. *International Journal of Eating Disorders, 30,* 57–68.

Frank, J. D. (1978). *Effective ingredients of successful psychotherapy.* New York: Brunner/Mazel.

Frankl, V. E. (1963). *Man's search for meaning: An introduction to logotherapy.* Boston: Beacon Press.

Franko, D. L., Wonderlich, S. A., Little, D., & Herzog, D. B. (2004). Diagnosis and classification of eating disorders. In J. K. Thompson (Ed.), *Handbook of eating disorders and obesity* (pp. 58–80). Hoboken, NJ: Wiley.

Frasure-Smith, N., Lesperance, F., & Talajic, M. (1995). Depression and 18-month prognosis after myocardial infarction. *Circulation, 91,* 999–1005.

Fredrickson, B. L., & Joiner, T. (2002). Positive emotions trigger upward spirals toward emotional well-being. *Psychological Science, 13,* 172–175.

Fredrickson, B. L., Tugade, M. M., Waugh, C. E., & Larkin, G. R. (2003). What good are positive emotions in crisis? A prospective study of resilience and emotions following the terrorist attacks on the United States on September 11th, 2001. *Journal of Personality & Social Psychology, 84,* 365–376.

Freeman, A., & Reinecke, M. A. (1995). Cognitive therapy. In A. S. Gurman (Ed.), *Essential psychotherapies: Theory and practice* (pp. 182–225). New York: Guilford Press.

Freeston, M. H., Ladouceur, R., Thibodeau, N., & Gagnon, F. (1992). Cognitive intrusions in a non-clinical population: II. Associations with depressive, anxious, and compulsive symptoms. *Behaviour Research & Therapy, 30,* 263–271.

Fremont, W. P. (2004). Childhood reactions to terrorism-induced trauma: A review of the past 10 years. *Journal of the Academy of Child & Adolescent Psychiatry, 43,* 381–392.

Freud, S. (1905). *Collected works.* London: Hogarth Press.

Freud, S. (1909). *Analysis of a phobia of a five-year-old boy* (Vol. III). New York: Basic Books.

Freud, S. (1914). *Psychopathology of everyday life* (Authorized English ed.). New York: Macmillan.

Freud, S. (1917). *Mourning and melancholia. Collected works.* London: Hogarth Press.

Freud, S. (1920). *A general introduction to psychoanalysis.* New York: Boni & Liveright.

Freud, S. (1923). *The ego and id.* London: Hogarth Press.

Freud, S. (1924). The loss of reality in neurosis and psychosis. In J. Strachey (Ed.), *Sigmund Freud's collected papers* (Vol. 2, pp. 272–282). London: Hogarth Press.

Freyd, J. J. (1996). *Betrayal trauma: The logic of forgetting childhood abuse.* Cambridge, MA: Harvard University Press.

Freyd, J. J., Martorella, S. R., Alvarado, J. S., Hayes, A. E., & Christman, J. C. (1998).

Cognitive environments and dissociative tendencies: Performance on the standard Stroop task for high versus low dissociators. *Applied Cognitive Psychology, 12,* S91–S103.

Frick, P. J., & Morris, A. S. (2004). Temperament and developmental pathways to conduct problems. *Journal of Clinical Child & Adolescent Psychology, 33,* 54–68.

Fried, P. A., & Watkinson, B. (1990). 36- and 48-month neurobehavioral follow-up of children prenatally exposed to marijuana, cigarettes, and alcohol. *Journal of Developmental & Behavioral Pediatrics, 11,* 49–58.

Friedman, M., & Rosenman, R. H. (1974). *Type A behavior and your heart.* New York: Knopf.

Friedman, M., Rosenman, R. H., Straus, R., Wurm, M., & Kositcheck, R. (1968). The relationship of behavior pattern A to the state of coronary vasculature. *American Journal of Medicine, 44,* 525–537.

Frith, C., & Frith, U. (2000). The physiological basis of theory of mind: Functional neuroimaging studies. In S. Baron-Cohen, H. Tager-Flusberg, & D. Cohen (Eds.), *Understanding other minds: Perspectives from autism and developmental cognitive neuroscience* (2nd ed., pp. 334–356). Oxford, UK: Oxford University Press.

Fritz, G. K., Fritsch, S., & Hagino, O. (1997). Somatoform disorders in children and adolescents: A review of the past 10 years. *Journal of the American Academy of Child & Adolescent Psychiatry, 36,* 1329–1338.

Fromme, K., Marlatt, G. A., Baer, J. S., & Kivlahan, D. R. (1994). The Alcohol Skills Training Program: A group intervention for young adult drinkers. *Journal of Substance Abuse Treatment, 11,* 143–154.

Fromm-Reichmann, F. (1948). Notes on the development of treatments of schizophrenia by psychoanalytic psychotherapy. *Psychiatry, 2,* 263–273.

Fugh-Berman, A., & Cott, J. M. (1999). Dietary supplements and natural products as psychotherapeutic agents. *Psychosomatic Medicine, 61,* 712–728.

Furr, S. R., Westefeld, J. S., McConnell, G. N., & Jenkins, J. M. (2001). Suicide and depression among college students: A decade later. *Professional Psychology: Research & Practice, 32,* 97–100.

Futterman, A., Thompson, L., Gallagher-Thompson, D., & Ferris, R. (1995). Depression in later life: Epidemiology, assessment, etiology, and treatment. In E. E. Beckham & W. R. Leber (Eds.), *Handbook of depression* (2nd ed., pp. 494–525). New York: Guilford Press.

Fyer, A. J., Liebowitz, M. R., Gorman, J. M., & Campeas, R. (1987). Discontinuation of alprazolam treatment in panic patients. *American Journal of Psychiatry, 144,* 303–308.

Fyer, A. J., Mannuzza, S., Chapman, T. F., Martin, L. Y., et al. (1995). Specificity in familial aggregation of phobic disorders. *Archives of General Psychiatry, 52,* 564–573.

G

Gadow, K. D. (1991). Clinical issues in child and adolescent psychopharmacology. *Journal of Consulting & Clinical Psychology, 59,* 842–852.

Gadow, K. D. (1992). Pediatric psychopharmacology: A review of recent

research. *Journal of Child Psychology & Psychiatry & Allied Disciplines, 33,* 153–195.

Galea, S., Ahern, J., Resnick, H., Kilpatrick, D., Bucuvalas, M., Gold, J., & Vlahov, D. (2002). Psychological sequelae of the September 11 terrorist attacks in New York City. *New England Journal of Medicine, 346,* 982–987.

Gannon, L. R., Haynes, S. N., Cuevas, J., & Chavez, R. (1987). Psychophysiological correlates of induced headaches. *Journal of Behavioral Medicine, 10,* 411–423.

Gao, S., Hendrie, H., Hall, K., & Hui, S. (1998). The relationship between age, sex, and the incidence of dementia and Alzheimer's disease: A meta-analysis. *Archives of General Psychiatry, 55,* 809–815.

Garb, H. N., Florio, C. M., & Grove, W. M. (1998). The validity of the Rorschach and the Minnesota Multiphasic Personality Inventory. *Psychological Science, 9,* 402–404.

Garber, J., & Horowitz, J. L. (2002). Depression in children. In I. H. Gotlib & C. L. Hammen (Eds.), *Handbook of depression* (pp. 510–540). New York: Guilford Press.

Garber, J., Walker, L. S., & Zeman, J. (1991). Somatization symptoms in a community sample of children and adolescents: Further validation of the Children's Somatization Inventory. *Psychological Assessment, 3,* 588–595.

Gardner, H. (2003). Three distinct meanings of intelligence. In R. J. Sternberg & J. Lautrey (Eds.), *Models of intelligence: International perspectives* (pp. 43–54). Washington, DC: American Psychological Association.

Gardner, W., Lidz, C. W., Hoge, S. K., Monahan, J., Eisenberg, M. M., Bennett, N. S., Mulvey, E. P., & Roth, L. H. (1999). Patients' revisions of their beliefs about the need for hospitalization. *American Journal of Psychiatry, 156,* 1385–1391.

Garfield, S. L. (1994). Research on client variables in psychotherapy. In A. E. Bergin (Ed.), *Handbook of psychotherapy and behavior change* (4th ed., pp. 190–228). New York: Wiley.

Garmezy, N. (1991). Resilience and vulnerability to adverse developmental outcomes associated with poverty. *American Behavioral Scientist, 34,* 416–430.

Garner, D., Cooke, A. K., & Marano, H. E. (1997, January/February). The 1997 body image survey results. *Psychology Today,* pp. 30–44.

Garner, D. M., & Garfinkel, P. E. (1980). Socio-cultural factors in the development of anorexia nervosa. *Psychological Medicine, 10,* 647–656.

Garner, D. M., & Garfinkel, P. E. (Eds.). (1985). *Handbook of psychotherapy for anorexia nervosa and bulimia.* New York: Guilford Press.

Garner, D. M., & Garfinkel, P. E. (Eds.). (1997). *Handbook for treatment for eating disorders* (2nd ed.). New York: Guilford Press.

Garner, D. M., Garfinkel, P. E., & O'Shaughnessy, M. (1985). The validity of the distinction between bulimia with and without anorexia nervosa. *American Journal of Psychiatry, 142,* 581–587.

Garner, D. M., Olmstead, M. P., & Polivy, J. (1984). *The EDI.* Odessa, FL: Psychological Assessment Resources.

Garner, D. M., Rockert, W., Davis, R., & Garner, M. V. (1993). Comparison of cognitive-behavioral and supportive-expressive therapy for bulimia nervosa. *American Journal of Psychiatry, 150*, 37–46.

Garner, D. M., & Wooley, S. C. (1991). Confronting the failure of behavioral and dietary treatments for obesity. *Clinical Psychology Review, 11*, 729–780.

Garrison, C. Z., Bryant, E. S., Addy, C. L., Spurrier, P. G., Freedy, J. R., & Kilpatrick, D. G. (1995). Posttraumatic stress disorder in adolescents after Hurricane Andrew. *Journal of the American Academy of Child & Adolescent Psychiatry, 34*, 1193–1201.

Gatley, S. J., Gifford, A. N., Volkow, N. D., & Fowler, J. S. (1998). Pharmacology of cocaine. In R. E. Tarter (Ed.), *Handbook of substance abuse: Neurobehavioral pharmacology* (pp. 161–185). New York: Plenum Press.

Gatz, M., Kasl-Godley, J. E., & Karel, M. J. (1996). Aging and mental disorders. In J. E. Birren (Ed.), *Handbook of the psychology of aging* (4th ed., pp. 365–382). San Diego, CA: Academic Press.

Ge, X., Conger, R. D., Cadoret, R. J., & Neiderhiser, J. M. (1996). The developmental interface between nature and nurture: A mutual influence model of child antisocial behavior and parent behaviors. *Developmental Psychology, 32*, 574–589.

Geddes, J. R., Burgess, S., Hawton K., Jamison, K., & Goodwin, G. M. (2004). Long-term lithium therapy for bipolar disorder: Systematic review and meta-analysis of randomized controlled trials. *American Journal of Psychiatry, 161*, 217–222.

Geer, J. H., & Maisel, E. (1972). Evaluating the effects of the prediction-control confound. *Journal of Personality & Social Psychology, 23*, 314–319.

Gelenberg, A. J., Lydiard, R. B., Rudolph, R. L., Aguiar, L., Haskins, J. T., & Salinas, E. (2000). Efficacy of venlafaxine extended-release capsules in nondepressed outpatients with generalized anxiety disorder: A 6-month randomized controlled trial. *Journal of the American Medical Association, 283*, 3082–3088.

Geller, B., Tillman, R., Craney, J. L., & Bolhofner, K. (2004). Four-year prospective outcome and natural history of mania in children with a prepubertal and early adolescent bipolar disorder phenotype. *Archives of General Psychiatry, 61*, 459–467.

George, M., Sackeim, H. A., Marangell, L. B., Husain, M. M., Nahas, Z., Lisanby, S. H., Ballenger, J. C., & Rush, A. J. (2000). Vagus nerve stimulation: A potential therapy for resistant depression? *Psychiatric Clinics of North America, 23*, 757–783.

George, M. S., Nahas, Z., Kozel, F. A., Li, X., Yamanaka, K., Mishory, A., & Bohning, D. E. (2003). Mechanisms and current state of transcranial magnetic stimulation. *CNS Spectrums, 8*, 511–514.

Gerardin, P., & Thibaut, F. (2004). Epidemiology and treatment of juvenile sexual offending. *Pediatric Drugs, 6*, 79–91.

Gershon, E. S., & Rieder, R. O. (1992, September). Major disorders of mind and brain. *Scientific American, 267*, 126–133.

Ghaemi, S. N., Pardo, T. B., & Hsu, D. J. (2004). Strategies for preventing the recurrence of bipolar disorder. *Journal of Clinical Psychiatry, 65*(Suppl. 10), 16–23.

Gijsman, H. J., Geddes, J. R., Rendell, J. M., Nolen, W. A., & Goodwin, G. M. (2004). Antidepressants for bipolar depression: A systematic review of randomized, controlled trials. *American Journal of Psychiatry, 161*, 1537–1547.

Giles, J. (1994, April 18). The poet of alienation. *Newsweek*, pp. 46–47.

Gilger, J. W., Pennington, B. F., & DeFries, J. C. (1992). A twin study of the etiology of comorbidity: Attention-deficit hyperactivity disorder and dyslexia. *Journal of the American Academy of Child & Adolescent Psychiatry, 31*, 343–348.

Gillberg, C. (1991). Outcome in autism and autistic-like conditions. *Journal of the American Academy of Child & Adolescent Psychiatry, 30*, 375–382.

Gillberg, C. (1998). Chromosomal disorders and autism. *Journal of Autism & Developmental Disorders, 28*, 415–425.

Gillespie, N. A., Zhu, G., Heath, A. C., Hickie, I. B., & Martin, N. G. (2000). The genetic aetiology of somatic distress. *Psychological Medicine, 30*, 1051–1061.

Gillham, J. E., Reivich, K. J., Jaycox, L. H., & Seligman, M. E. P. (1995). Prevention of depressive symptoms in schoolchildren: Two-year followup. *Psychological Science, 6*, 343–351.

Gillis, L. S., Elk, R., Ben-Arie, O., & Teggin, A. (1982). The Present State Examination: Experiences with Xhosa-speaking psychiatric patients. *British Journal of Psychiatry, 141*, 143–147.

Gilman, S. E., Cochran, S. D., Mays, V. M., Hughes, M., Ostrow, D., & Kessler, R. C. (2001). Risk of psychiatric disorders among individuals reporting same-sex sexual partners in the National Comorbidity Survey. *American Journal of Public Health, 91*, 933–939.

Gilvarry, C. M., Russell, A., Hemsley, D., & Murray, R. M. (2001). Neuropsychological performance and spectrum personality traits in the relatives of patients with schizophrenia and affective psychosis. *Psychiatry Research, 101*, 89–100.

Ginns, E. I., Ott, J., Egeland, J. A., Allen, C. R., Fann, C. S. J., Pauls, D. L., Weissenbach, J., Carulli, J. P., Falls, K. M., Keith, T. P., & Paul, S. (1996). A genome-wide search for chromosomal loci linked to bipolar affective disorder in the Old Order Amish. *Nature Genetics, 12*, 431–435.

Ginns, E. I., St. Jean, P., Philibert, R. A., Galdzicka, M., Damschroder-Williams, P., et al. (1998). A genomewide search for chromosomal loci linked to mental health wellness in relatives at high risk for bipolar affective disorder among the Old Order Amish. *Proceedings of the National Academy of Sciences, USA, 95*, 15531–15536.

Giovini, G. A., Schooley, M. W., Zhu, B., Chrismon, J. H., Tomar, S. L., Peddicord, J. P., Merritt, R. K., Husten, C. G., & Eriksen, M. P. (1994). Surveillance for selected tobacco-use behaviors—United States, 1900–1994. *Morbidity & Mortality Weekly Report, 43*, 1–43.

Gitlin, M. (2002). Pharmacological treatment of depression. In I. H. Gotlib & C. L. Hammen (Eds.), *Handbook of depression* (pp. 360–382). New York: Guilford Press.

Gitlin, M., Nuechterlein, K., Subotnik, K. L., Ventura, J., Mintz, J., Fogelson, D. L., Bartzokis, G., & Aravagiri, M. (2001). Clinical outcome following neuroleptic discontinuation in patients with remitted recent-onset schizophrenia. *American Journal of Psychiatry, 158*, 1835–1842.

Glaser, R., Rice, J., Speicher, C. E., Stout, J. C., & Kiecolt-Glaser, J. C. (1986). Stress depresses interferon production by leukocytes concomitant with a decrease in natural killer cell activity. *Behavioral Neuroscience, 100*, 675–678.

Glasgow, M. S., Engel, B. T., & D'Lugoff, B. C. (1989). A controlled study of a standardized behavioral stepped treatment for hypertension. *Psychosomatic Medicine, 51*, 10–26.

Glasgow, M. S., Gaader, K. R., & Engel, B. T. (1982). Behavioral treatment of high blood pressure: I. Acute and sustained effects of relaxation and systolic blood pressure biofeedback. *Psychosomatic Medicine, 44*, 155–170.

Glass, G. V., & Singer, J. E. (1972). *Urban stress: Experiments on noise and social stressors*. New York: Academic Press.

Glass, R. M. (2001). Electroconvulsive therapy: Time to bring it out of the shadows. *Journal of the American Medical Association, 285*, 1346–1348.

Glassman, A. (1969). Indoleamines and affective disorders. *Psychosomatic Medicine, 31*, 107–114.

Gleaves, D. H., & Freyd, J. J. (1997, September). Questioning additional claims about the false memory syndrome epidemic. *American Psychologist*, pp. 993–994.

Gleaves, D. H., Hernandez, E., & Warner, M. S. (2003). The etiology of dissociative identity disorder: Reply to Gee, Allen, and Powell (2003). *Professional Psychology: Research & Practice, 34*, 116–118.

Gleaves, D. H., May, M. C., & Cardena, E. (2001). An examination of the diagnostic validity of dissociative identity disorder. *Clinical Psychology Review, 21*, 577–608.

Gleaves, D. H., Smith, S. M., Butler, L. D., & Spiegel, D. (2004). False and recovered memories in the laboratory and clinic: A review of experimental and clinical evidence. *Clinical Psychology: Science & Practice, 11*, 3–28.

Glowinski, A. L., Bucholz, K. K., Nelson, E. C., Fu, Q., Madden, P. A. F., Reich, W., & Heath, A. C. (2001). Suicide attempts in an adolescent female twin sample. *Journal of the American Academy of Child & Adolescent Psychiatry, 40*, 1300–1307.

Goate, A., Chartier-Harlin, M.-C., Mullan, M., Brown, J., Crawford, F., Fidani, L., Giuffa, L., Haynes, A., Irving, N., James, L., et al. (1991). Segregation of a missense mutation in the amyloid precursor protein gene with familial Alzheimer's disease. *Nature, 349*, 704–706.

Goff, D. C., & Coyle, J. T. (2001). The emerging role of glutamate in the pathophysiology and treatment of schizophrenia. *American Journal of Psychiatry, 158*, 1367–1377.

Gold, M. S., Tabrah, H., & Frost-Pineda, K. (2001). Psychopharmacology of MDMA (ecstasy). *Psychiatric Annals, 31*, 675–681.

Gold, P. E., Cahill, L., & Wenk, G. L. (2002). Ginko biloba: A cognitive enhancer?

Psychological Science in the Public Interest, 3, 2–11.

Goldberg, E. M., & Morrison, S. L. (1963). Schizophrenia and social class. *British Journal of Psychiatry, 109,* 785–802.

Golden, C. J., & Freshwater, S. M. (2001). Luria-Nebraska Neuropsychological Battery. In W. I. Dorfman & S. M. Freshwater (Eds.), *Understanding psychological assessment* (pp. 59–75). Dordrecht, Netherlands: Kluwer Academic Publishers.

Goldstein, A. (1994). *Addiction: From biology to drug policy.* New York: W. H. Freeman.

Goldstein, G., & Hersen, M. (Eds.). (1990). *Handbook of psychological assessment.* Elmsford, NY: Pergamon Press.

Goldstein, J. M., & Lewine, R. R. J. (2000). Overview of sex differences in schizophrenia: Where have we been and where do we go from here? In D. J. Castle, J. McGrath, & J. Kulkarni (Eds.), *Women and schizophrenia* (pp. 111–141). Cambridge, UK: Cambridge University Press.

Goldstein, J. M., Seidman, L. J., Buka, S. L., Horton, N. J., Donatelli, J. L., Rieder, R. O., & Tsuang, M. T. (2000). Impact of genetic vulnerability and hypoxia on overall intelligence by age 7 in offspring at high risk for schizophrenia compared with affective psychoses. *Schizophrenia Bulletin, 26,* 323–334.

Goldstein, J. M., Seidman, L. J., O'Brien, L. M., Horton, N. J., Kennedy, D. N., Makris, N., Caviness, V. S., Faraone, S. V., & Tsuang, M. T. (2002). Impact of normal sexual dimorphisms on sex differences in structural brain abnormalities in schizophrenia assessed by magnetic resonance imaging. *Archives of General Psychiatry, 59,* 154–164.

Goldstein, M. G. (1998). Bupropion sustained release and smoking cessation. *Journal of Clinical Psychology, 59*(Suppl. 4), 66–72.

Goldstein, M. J. (1987) The UCLA high-risk project. *Schizophrenia Bulletin, 13,* 505–514.

Goldstein, M. J., Talovic, S. A., Nuechterlein, K. H., & Fogelson, D. L. (1992). Family interaction versus individual psychopathology: Do they indicate the same processes in the families of schizophrenia? *British Journal of Psychiatry, 161,* 97–102.

Gomberg, E. S. (1994). Risk factors for drinking over a woman's life span. *Alcohol Health & Research World, 18,* 220–227.

Gonzalez, N. M., & Campbell, M. (1994). Cocaine babies: Does prenatal exposure to cocaine affect development? *Journal of the American Academy of Child & Adolescent Psychiatry, 33,* 16–19.

Goodwin, D. W. (1988). *Alcohol and the writer.* Kansas City, MO: Andrews and McMeel.

Goodwin, F., & Ghaemi, S. (1998). Understanding manic-depressive illness. *Archives of General Psychiatry, 55,* 23–25.

Goodwin, F. K., & Jamison, K. R. (1990). *Manic-depressive illness.* New York: Oxford University Press.

Goodwin, P. J., Leszcz, M., Ennis, M., et al. (2001). The effect of group psychosocial support on survival in metastatic breast cancer. *New England Journal of Medicine, 345,* 1719–1726.

Gorman, J. M. (2003). Treating generalized anxiety disorder. *Journal of Clinical Psychiatry, 64*(Suppl. 2), 24–29.

Gorman, J. M., Liebowitz, M. R., Fyer, A. J., Fyer, M. R., & Klein, D. F. (1986). Possible respiratory abnormalities in panic disorder. *Psychopharmacological Bulletin, 221,* 797–801.

Gorman, J. M., Papp, L. A., & Coplan, J. D. (1995). Neuroanatomy and neurotransmitter function in panic disorder. In S. P. Roose & R. A. Glick (Eds.), *Anxiety as symptom and signal* (pp. 39–56). Hillsdale, NJ: Analytic Press.

Gottesman, I. I. (1991). *Schizophrenia genesis: The origins of madness.* New York: W. H. Freeman.

Gottesman, I. I., & Erlenmeyer-Kimling, L. (2001). Family and twin strategies as a head start in defining prodromes and endophenotypes for hypothetical early-interventions in schizophrenia. *Schizophrenic Research, 51,* 93–102.

Gottesman, I. I., & Reilly, J. L. (2003). Strengthening the evidence for genetic factors in schizophrenia (without abetting genetic discrimination). In M. F. Lenzenweger & J. M. Hooley (Eds.), *Principles of experimental psychopathology: Essays in honor of Brendan A. Maher* (pp. 31–44). Washington, DC: American Psychological Association.

Gottesman, I. I., & Shields, J. (1982). *Schizophrenia, the epigenetic puzzle.* New York: Cambridge University Press.

Gould, M., Jamieson, P., & Romer, D. (2003). Media contagion and suicide among the young. *American Behavioral Scientist, 46,* 1269–1284.

Gould, M. S., Greenberg, T., Velting, D. M., & Shaffer, D. (2003). Youth suicide risk and preventive interventions: A review of the past 10 years. *Journal of the American Academy of Child & Adolescent Psychiatry, 42,* 386–405.

Graeff, F. G., Guimaraes, F. S., Francisco, S., De Andrade, T. G. C. S., & Deakin, J. F. W. (1996). Role of 5-HT in stress, anxiety, and depression. *Pharmacology, Biochemistry, & Behavior, 54,* 129–141.

Grandin, T. (1995). *Thinking in pictures and my other reports from my life with autism.* New York: Vintage Books.

Grandin, T., & Johnson, C. (2005) *Animals in translation: Using the mysteries of autism to decode animal behavior.* New York: Scribner.

Grant, B., Stinson, F., Dawson, D., Chou, P., Dufour, M., Compton, W., Pickering, R., & Kaplan, K. (2004). Prevalence and co-occurrence of substance use disorders and independent mood and anxiety disorders: results from the national epidemiologic survey on alcohol and related conditions. *Archives of General Psychiatry, 61,* 807–816.

Grant, B. F., Hasin, D. S., Stinson, F. S., Dawson, D. A., Chou, S. P., Ruan, W. J., & Huang, B. (2005). Co-occurrence of 12-month mood and anxiety disorders and personality disorders in the US: Results from the national epidemiologic survey on alcohol and related conditions. *Journal of Psychiatric Research, 39,* 1–9.

Grattan-Smith, P., Fairly, M., & Procopis, P. (1988). Clinical features of conversion disorder. *Archives of Disease in Childhood, 63,* 408–414.

Gray, E., & Cosgrove, J. (1985). Ethnocentric perception of childbearing practices in protective services. *Child Abuse & Neglect, 9,* 389–396.

Gray, J. A. (1987). *The psychology of fear and stress* (2nd ed.). Cambridge, UK: Cambridge University Press.

Greaves, G. B. (1980). Multiple personality: 165 years after Mary Reynolds. *Journal of Nervous & Mental Disease, 168,* 577–596.

Greden, J. F. (2001). *Treatment of recurrent depression.* Washington, DC: American Psychiatric Association.

Green, A. H. (1993). Child sexual abuse: Immediate and long-term effects and intervention. *Journal of the American Academy of Child & Adolescent Psychiatry, 32,* 890–902.

Green, R. (1986). Gender identity in childhood and later sexual orientation: Follow-up of 78 males. *Annual Progress in Child Psychiatry & Child Development,* 214–220.

Greenberg, D. M., Bradford, J. M., Curry, S., & O'Rouche, A. (1996, May). *A controlled study of the treatment of paraphilia disorders with selective serotonin inhibitors.* Paper presented at the annual meeting of the Canadian Academy of Psychiatry and the Law, Tremblay, Quebec.

Greenberg, L. S., Elliot, R., & Lietaer, G. (1994). Research on humanistic and experiential psychotherapies. In A. Bergin & S. Garfield (Eds.), *Handbook of psychotherapy and behavior change* (4th ed., pp. 509–542). New York: Wiley.

Griffin, P. A., Steadman, H. J., & Petrila, J. (2002). The use of criminal charges and sanctions in mental health courts. *Psychiatric Services, 53,* 1285–1289.

Grilo, C. M., Sanislow, C. A., & McGlashan, T. H. (2002). Co-occurrence of DSM-IV personality disorders with borderline personality disorder. *Journal of Nervous & Mental Disease, 190,* 552–554.

Grinspoon, L., & Bakalar, J. B. (1995). Marihuana as medicine: A plea for reconsideration. *Journal of the American Medical Association, 273,* 1875–1876.

Grisso, T., & Applebaum, P. S. (1995). The MacArthur Treatment Competence Study: III. Abilities of patients to consent to psychiatric and medical treatments. *Law & Human Behavior, 19,* 149–174.

Grisso, T., & Applebaum, P. S. (1998). *Assessing competence to consent to treatment: A guide for physicians and other health professionals.* New York: Oxford University Press.

Grob, G. N. (1994). *The mad among us: A history of the care of America's mentally ill.* Cambridge, MA: Harvard University Press.

Gross, R. T., Brooks-Gunn, J., & Spiker, D. (1992). Efficacy of educational interventions for low birth weight infants: The Infant Health and Development Program. In S. L. Friedman & M. D. Sigman (Eds.), *The psychological development of low birth weight children: Advances in applied developmental psychology.* Norwood, NJ: Ablex.

Gross-Isseroff, R., Biegon, A., Voet, H., & Weizman, A. (1998). The suicide brain: A review of postmortem receptor/transporter binding studies. *Neuroscience & Biobehavioral Reviews, 22,* 653–661.

Gruber, A. J., & Pope, H. G. (1998). Ephedrine abuse among 36 female weightlifters. *American Journal of Addiction, 7,* 256–261.

Gruber, A. J., Pope, H. G., Lalonde, J. K., & Hudson, J. I. (2001). Why do young women diet? The roles of body fat, body perception, and body ideal. *Journal of Clinical Psychiatry, 62,* 609–611.

Grunze, H., & Walden, J. (2002). Relevance of new and newly rediscovered anticonvulsants for atypical forms of bipolar disorder. *Journal of Affective Disorders, 72*(Suppl. 1), 15–21.

Guarnaccia, P. J., Canino, G., Rubio-Stipec, M., & Bravo, M. (1993). The prevalence of *ataques de nervios* in the Puerto Rico Disaster Study: The role of culture in psychiatric epidemiology. *Journal of Nervous & Mental Disease, 181,* 157–165.

Guarnaccia, P. J., Guevara-Ramos, L. M., Gonzales, G., Canino, G. J., & Bird, H. (1992). Cross-cultural aspects of psychiatric symptoms in Puerto Rico. *Community & Mental Health, 7,* 99–110.

Guarnaccia, P. J., Rivera, M., Franco, F., Neighbors, C., & Allende-Ramos, C. (1996). The experiences of *ataques de nervios:* Toward an anthropology of emotions in Puerto Rico. *Culture, Medicine, & Psychiatry, 15,* 139–165.

Gumley, A., O'Grady, M., McNay, L., Reilly, J., Power, K., & Norrie, J. (2003). Early intervention for relapse in schizophrenia: Results of a 12-month randomized controlled trial of cognitive behavioural therapy. *Psychological Medicine, 33,* 419–431.

Gunderson, J. G., Ronningstam, E., & Smith, L. E. (1995). Narcissistic personality disorder. In W. J. Livesley (Ed.), *The DSM-IV personality disorders* (pp. 201–212). New York: Guilford Press.

Gunderson, J. G., Zanarini, M. C., & Kisiel, C. L. (1995). Borderline personality disorder. In W. J. Livesley (Ed.), *The DSM-IV personality disorders* (pp. 141–157). New York: Guilford Press.

Guo, Y. J., Chen, C.-H., Lu, M.-L., Tan, H. K.-L., Lee, H.-W., & Wang, T.-N. (2004). Posttraumatic stress disorder among professional and non-professional rescuers involved in an earthquake in Taiwan. *Psychiatry Research, 127,* 35–41.

Gusella, J. F., MacDonald, M. E., Ambrose, C. M., & Duyao, M. P. (1993). Molecular genetics of Huntington's disease. *Archives of Neurology, 50,* 1157–1163.

H

Haas, A. P., Hendin, H., & Mann, J. J. (2003). Suicide in college students. *American Behavioral Scientist, 46,* 1224–1240.

Hagengimana, A., Hinton, D., Bird, B., Pollack, M., & Pitman, R. K. (2003). Somatic panic-attack equivalents in a community sample of Rwandan widows who survived the 1994 genocide. *Psychiatry Research, 117,* 1–9.

Halford, W. K., & Hayes, R. (1991). Psychological rehabilitation of chronic schizophrenic patients: Recent findings on social skills training and family psychoeducation. *Clinical Psychology Review, 11,* 23–44.

Hall, G. C. N. (2001). Psychotherapy research with ethnic minorities: Empirical, ethical, and conceptual issues. *Journal of Consulting & Clinical Psychology, 69,* 502–510.

Hammen, C. (1991). Generation of stress in the course of unipolar depression. *Journal of Abnormal Psychology, 100,* 555–561.

Hammen, C. (1992). Cognitive, life stress, and interpersonal approaches to a developmental psychopathology model of depression. *Development & Psychopathology, 4,* 189–206.

Hammen, C. (2005). Stress and depression. *Annual Review of Clinical Psychology, 1,* 293–320.

Harding, C. M., Zubin, J., & Strauss, J. S. (1987). Chronicity in schizophrenia: Fact, partial fact, or artifact? *Hospital & Community Psychiatry, 38,* 477–486.

Hare, R. (1991) *The Hare Psychopathy Checklist—Revised Manual.* Multi-Health Systems, Inc.

Hare, R. D., & Hart, S. D. (1993). Psychopathy, mental disorder, and crime. In S. Hodgins (Ed.), *Mental disorder and crime* (pp. 104–115). Thousand Oaks, CA: Sage.

Harrell, J. P. (1980). Psychological factors and hypertension: A status report. *Psychological Bulletin, 87,* 482–501.

Harris, M. J., Milich, R., Corbitt, E. M., & Hoover, D. W. (1992). Self-fulfilling effects of stigmatizing information on children's social interactions. *Journal of Personality & Social Psychology, 63,* 41–50.

Hart, S. D., & Hare, R. D. (1997). Psychopathy: Assessment and association with criminal conduct. In D. M. Stoff, J. Breiling, & J. D. Maser (Eds.), *Handbook of antisocial personality disorder* (pp. 22–35). New York: Wiley.

Harter, S. (1983). Developmental perspectives on the self-system. In P. H. Mussen (Ed.), *Handbook of child development* (pp. 275–385). New York: Wiley.

Hartman, D. E. (1998). Behavioral pharmacology of inhalants. In R. E. Tarter (Ed.), *Handbook of substance abuse: Neurobehavioral pharmacology* (pp. 263–268). New York: Plenum Press.

Hartung, C. M., & Widiger, T. A. (1998). Gender differences in the diagnosis of mental disorders: Conclusions and controversies of the DSM-IV. *Psychological Bulletin, 123,* 260–278.

Harvey, A. G., & Rapee, R. M. (1995). Cognitive-behavior therapy for generalized anxiety disorder. *Psychiatric Clinics of North America, 4,* 859–870.

Harwood, D. M. J., Hawton, K., Hope, T., & Jacoby, R. (2000). Suicide in older people: Mode of death, demographic factors, and medical contact before death. *International Journal of Geriatric Psychiatry, 15,* 736–743.

Hasler, G., Drevets, W. C., Manji, H. K., & Charney, D. S. (2004). Discovering endophenotypes for major depression. *Neuropsychopharmacology, 29,* 1765–1781.

Hauri, P., & Fisher, J. (1986). Persistent psychophysiologic (learned) insomnia. *Sleep, 9,* 38–53.

Haynes, S. G., Feinleib, M., & Kannel, W. B. (1980). The relationship of psychosocial factors to coronary heart disease in the Framingham study: III. Eight-year incidence of coronary heart disease. *American Journal of Epidemiology, 111,* 37–58.

Hayward, C., Gotlib, I. H., Schraedley, P. K., & Litt, I. F. (1999). Ethnic differences in the association between pubertal status and symptoms of depression in adolescent girls. *Journal of Adolescent Health, 25,* 143–149.

Hayward, C., Killen, J. D., Kraemer, H. C., & Taylor, C. B. (1998). Linking self-reported childhood behavioral inhibition to adolescent social phobia. *Journal of the American Academy of Child & Adolescent Psychiatry, 37,* 1308–1316.

Hayward, C., Killen, J. D., Kraemer, H. C., & Taylor, C. B. (2000). Predictors of panic attacks in adolescents. *Journal of the American Academy of Child & Adolescent Psychiatry, 39,* 207–214.

Heath, A. C., Bucholz, K. K., Madden, P. A. F., Dinwiddie, S. H., Slutske, W. S., Bierut, L. J., Statham, D. J., Dunne, M. P., Whitfield, J. B., & Martin, N. G. (1997). Genetic and environmental contributions to alcohol dependence risk in a national twin sample: Consistency of findings in women and men. *Psychological Medicine, 27,* 1381–1396.

Heath, A. C., & Martin, N. G. (1993). Genetic models for the natural history of smoking: Evidence for a genetic influence on smoking. *Addictive Behaviors, 18,* 19–34.

Hebert, L. E., Scherr, P. A., Bienias, J. L., Bennet, D. A., & Evans, D. A. (2003). Alzheimer disease in the US population: Prevalence estimates using the 2000 census. *Archives of Neurology, 60,* 1119–1122.

Heim, C., Meinlschmidt, G., & Nemeroff, C. B. (2003). Neurobiology of early-life stress. *Psychiatric Annals, 33,* 18–26.

Heim, C., Plotsky, P. M., & Nemeroff, C. B. (2004). Importance of studying the contributions of early adverse experience to neurobiological findings in depression. *Neuropsychopharmacology, 29,* 641–648.

Heiman, J. R. (2000). Orgasmic disorders in women. In S. R. Leiblum & R. C. Rosen (Eds.), *Principles and practice of sex therapy* (3rd ed., pp. 118–153) New York: Guilford Press.

Heiman, J. R., & Grafton-Becker, V. (1989). Orgasmic disorders in women. In S. R. Leiblum & R. C. Rosen (Eds.), *Principles and practice of sex therapy: Update for the 1990s* (pp. 51–88). New York: Guilford Press.

Heimberg, R. G. (2001). Current status of psychotherapeutic interventions for social phobia. *Journal of Clinical Psychiatry, 62*(Suppl. 1), 36–42.

Heimberg, R. G., Liebowitz, M., Hope, D. A., Schneier, F. R., Holt, C. S., Welkowitz, L. A., Juster, H. R., Campeas, R., Bruck, M. A., Cloitre, M., Fallon, B., & Klein, D. F. (1998). Cognitive behavioral group therapy vs. phenelzine therapy for social phobia: 12-week outcome. *Archives of General Psychiatry, 55,* 1113–1141.

Heinrichs, N., & Hofman, S. G. (2001). Information processing in social phobia: A critical review. *Clinical Psychology Review, 21,* 751–770.

Heise, L., Ellsberg, M. & Gottemuller, M. (1999). Ending violence against women. *Population Reports,* Series L, No. 11, December 1-43. Baltimore: Johns Hopkins University School of Public Health, Population Information Program.

Heiser, N. A., Turner, S. M., & Beidel, D. C. (2003). Shyness: Relationship to social phobia and other psychiatric disorders. *Behaviour Research & Therapy, 41,* 209–221.

Helgeland, M. I., & Torgersen, S. (2004). Developmental antecedents of borderline personality disorder. *Comprehensive Psychiatry, 45,* 138–147.

Helgeson, V. S. (1994). Relation of agency and communion to well-being: Evidence and potential explanations. *Psychological Bulletin, 116,* 412–428.

Helzer, J. E., Bucholz, K., & Robins, L. N. (1992). Five communities in the United States: Results of the Epidemiologic Catchment Area Survey. In J. E. Helzer & G. J. Canino (Eds.), *Alcoholism in North America, Europe, and Asia.* New York: Oxford University Press.

Helzer, J. E., Burnam, A., & McEvoy, L. T. (1991). Alcohol abuse and dependence. In L. Robins & D. Reiger (Eds.), *Psychiatric disorders in America: The Epidemiologic Catchment Area Study* (pp. 9–38). New York: Free Press.

Hendrick, V., Altshuler, L., & Suri, R. (1998). Hormonal changes in the postpartum and implications for postpartum depression. *Psychosomatics, 39,* 93–101.

Henriques, G., Beck, A. T., & Brown, G. K. (2003). Cognitive therapy for adolescent and young adult suicide attempters. *American Behavioral Scientist, 46,* 1258–1268.

Henry, B., Caspi, A., Moffitt, T. E., & Silva, P. A. (1996). Temperamental and familial predictors of violent and nonviolent criminal convictions: Age 3 to age 18. *Developmental Psychology, 32,* 614–623.

Henry, B., & Moffitt, T. E. (1997). Neuropsychological and neuroimaging studies of juvenile delinquency and adult criminal behavior. In D. M. Stoff, J. Breiling, & J. D. Maser (Eds.), *Handbook of antisocial personality disorder* (pp. 280–288). New York: Wiley.

Henry, M. E., Schmidt, M. E., Matochik, J. A., Stoddard, E. P., & Potter, W. Z. (2001). The effects of ECT on brain glucose: A pilot FDG PET study. *Journal of ECT, 17,* 33–40.

Herman, C. P., & Mack, D. (1975). Restrained and unrestrained eating. *Journal of Personality, 43,* 647–660.

Herman, J. L., & Harvey, M. R. (1997). Adult memories of childhood trauma: A naturalistic clinical study. *Journal of Traumatic Stress, 10,* 557–571.

Herpertz, S. C., Werth, U., Lucas, G., Qunaibi, M., Schuerkens, A., Kunert, H., Freese, R., Flesch, M., Mueller-Isberner, R., Osterheider, M., & Sass, H. (2001). Emotion in criminal offenders with psychopathy and borderline personality disorders. *Archives of General Psychiatry, 58,* 737–745.

Herpertz-Dahlmann, B., Muller, B., Herpertz, S., & Heussen, N. (2001). Prospective 10-year follow-up in adolescent anorexia nervosa— Course, outcome, psychiatric comorbidity, and psychosocial adaptation. *Journal of Child Psychology & Psychiatry, 42,* 603–612.

Heston, L. L. (1966). Psychiatric disorders in foster home reared children of schizophrenic mothers. *British Journal of Psychiatry, 112,* 819–825.

Hettema, J. M., Neale, M. C., & Kendler, K. S. (2001). A review and meta-analysis of the genetic epidemiology of anxiety disorders. *American Journal of Psychiatry, 158,* 1568–1578.

Hewlett, W. A. (2000). Benzodiazepines in the treatment of obsessive-compulsive disorder. In W. K. Goodman (Ed.), *Obsessive-compulsive disorder: Contemporary issues in treatment* (pp. 405–429). Mahwah, NJ: Erlbaum.

Higgins, S. T., Budney, A. J., Beckel, W. K., & Badger, G. J. (1994). Participation of significant others in outpatient behavioral treatment predicts greater cocaine abstinence.

American Journal of Drug & Alcohol Abuse, 20, 47–56.

Hilgard, E. R. (1977/1986). *Divided consciousness: Multiple controls in human thought and action.* New York: Wiley.

Hilgard, E. R. (1992). Divided consciousness and dissociation. *Consciousness & Cognition: An International Journal, 1,* 16–31.

Hill, A. J., & Franklin, J. A. (1998). Mothers, daughters, and dieting: Investigating the transmission of weight control. *British Journal of Clinical Psychology, 37,* 3–13.

Hines, M. (2004). Psychosexual development in individuals who have female pseu- dohermaphroditism. *Child & Adolescent Psychiatric Clinics of North America, 13,* 641–656.

Hinshaw, S. P., & Melnick, S. M. (1995). Peer relationships in boys with attention-deficit hyperactivity disorder with and without comorbid aggression. *Development & Psychopathology, 7,* 627–647.

Hirschfeld, R. (1994). Guidelines for the long- term treatment of depression. *Journal of Clinical Psychiatry, 55*(Suppl. 12), 59–67.

Hite, S. (1976). *The Hite report: A nationwide study on female sexuality.* New York: Macmillan.

Hlastala, S. A., Frank, E., Kowalski, J., Sherrill, J. T., & Tu, X. M. (2000). Stressful life events, bipolar disorder, and the "kindling model." *Journal of Abnormal Psychology, 109,* 777–787.

Hodapp, R. M., Burack, J. A., & Zigler, E. (1998). Developmental approaches to mental retardation: A short introduction. In J. A. Burack, R. M. Hodapp, & E. Zigler (Eds.), *Handbook of mental retardation and development* (pp. 3–19). New York: Cambridge University Press.

Hodgins, S., & Cote, G. (1990). Prevalence of mental disorders among penitentiary inmates in Quebec. *Canadian Journal of Mental Health, 39,* 1–4.

Hoek, H. W., & van Hoeken, D. (2003). Review of the prevalence and incidence of eating disorders. *International Journal of Eating Disorders, 34,* 383–396.

Hoffman, A. (1968). Psychotomimetic agents. In A. Burger (Ed.), *Drugs affecting the central nervous system* (Vol. 2). New York: Marcel Dekker.

Hoffman, R. E., Boutros, N. N., Hu, S., Berman, R. M., Krystal, J. H., & Charney, D. S. (2000). Transcranial magnetic stimulation and auditory hallucinations in schizophrenia. *The Lancet, 355,* 1073–1075.

Hoffman, R. E., Hawkins, K. A., Gueorguieva, R., Boutros, N. N., Rachid, F., Carroll, K., & Krystal, J. H. (2003). Transcranial magnetic stimulation of left temporoparietal cortex and medication-resistant auditory hallucinations. *Archives of General Psychiatry, 60,* 49–56.

Hofmann, S. G. (2004). Cognitive mediation of treatment change in social phobia. *Journal of Consulting & Clinical Psychology, 72,* 393–399.

Hogarty, G. E., Anderson, C. M., Reiss, D. J., Kornblith, S. J., Greenwald, D. P., Jaund, C. D., & Madonia, M. J. (1986). Family psychoeducation, social skills training, and maintenance chemotherapy in the aftercare treatment of schizophrenia: I. One-year effects of a controlled study on relapse and expressed emotion. *Archives of General Psychiatry, 43,* 633–642.

Hogarty, G. E., Anderson, C. M., Reiss, D. J., Kornblith, S. J., Greenwald, D. P., Ulrich, R. F., & Carter, M. (1991). Family psychoeducation, social skills training, and maintenance chemotherapy in the aftercare treatment of schizophrenia: II. Two-year effects of a controlled study on relapse and adjustment. *Archives of General Psychiatry, 48,* 340–347.

Hogarty, G. E., Greenwald, D., Ulrich, R. F., Kornblith, S. J., DiBarry, A. L., Cooley, S., Carter, M., & Flesher, S. (1997). Three-year trials of personal therapy among schizophrenic patients living with or independent of family: II. Effects of adjustment of patients. *American Journal of Psychiatry, 154,* 1514–1524.

Hogarty, G. E., Kornblith, S. J., Greenwald, D., DiBarry, A. L., Cooley, S., Ulrich, R. F., Carter, M., & Flesher, S. (1997). Three-year trials of personal therapy among schizophrenic patients living with or independent of family: I. Description of study and effects on relapse rates. *American Journal of Psychiatry, 154,* 1504–1513.

Hoge, C. W., Castro, C. A., Messer, S. C., McGurk, D., Cotting, D. I., & Koffman, R. L. (2004). Combat duty in Iraq and Afghanistan, mental health problems, and barriers to care. *New England Journal of Medicine, 351,* 13–22.

Hoge, S. K., Bonnie, R. J., Poythress, N., Monahan, J., Eisenberg, M., & Feucht- Haviar, T. (1997). The MacArthur Adjudicative Competence Study: Development and validation of a research instrument. *Law & Human Behavior, 21,* 141–179.

Hoge, S. K., Poythress, N., Bonnie, R. J., Monahan, J., Eisenberg, M., & Feucht- Haviar, T. (1997). The MacArthur Adjudicative Competence Study: Diagnosis, psychopathology, and competence-related abilities. *Behavioral Sciences & the Law, 15,* 329–345.

Holden, C. (1980). Identical twins reared apart. *Science, 207,* 1323–1328.

Hollander, E., Allen, A., Lopez, R. P., Bienstock, C. A., Grossman, R., Siever, L. J., Merkatz, L., & Stein, D. J. (2001). A preliminary double-blind, placebo-controlled trial of divalproex sodium in borderline personality disorder. *Journal of Clinical Psychiatry, 62,* 199–203.

Hollon, S. D., DeRubeis, R. J., Evans, M. D., Wiemer, M. J., Garvey, M. J., Grove, W. M., & Tuason, V. B. (1992). Cognitive therapy and pharmacotherapy for depression: Singly and in combination. *Archives of General Psychiatry, 49,* 774–781.

Hollon, S. D., Haman, K. L., & Brown, L. L. (2002). Cognitive-behavioral treatment of depression. In I. H. Gotlib & C. L. Hammen (Eds.), *Handbook of depression* (pp. 383–403). New York: Guilford Press.

Holmes, T. H., & Rahe, R. H. (1967). The social readjustment rating scale. *Journal of Psychosomatic Research, 11,* 213–218.

Holroyd, J. C., & Brodsky, A. M. (1977). Psychologists' attitudes and practices regarding erotic and nonerotic physical contact with patients. *American Psychologist, 32,* 843–849.

Holstein, J. A. (1993). *Court-ordered insanity: Interpretive practice and involuntary commitment.* New York: A. de Gruyter.

Hooley, J. M. (1998). Expressed emotion and psychiatric illness: From empirical data to clinical practice. *Behavior Therapy, 29,* 631–646.

Hooley, J. M., & Campbell, C. (2002). Control and controllability: Beliefs and behaviour in high and low expressed emotion relatives. *Psychological Medicine, 32,* 1091–1099.

Hooley, J. M., & Hiller, J. B. (1998). Expressed emotion and the pathogenesis of relapse in schizophrenia. In M. F. Lenzenweger & R. H. Dworkin (Eds.), *Origins of the development of schizophrenia* (pp. 447–468). Washington, DC: American Psychological Association.

Hornbacher, M. (1998). *Wasted.* New York: HarperPerennial.

Horney, K. (1934/1967). The overvaluation of love: A study of present-day feminine type. In H. Kelman (Ed.), *Feminine psychology* (pp. 182–213). New York: W. W. Norton.

Horney, K. (1939). *New ways in psychoanalysis.* New York: W. W. Norton.

Hornig, C. D., & McNally, R. J. (1995). Panic disorder and suicide attempt: A reanalysis of data from the Epidemiologic Catchment Area study. *British Journal of Psychiatry, 167,* 76–79.

Hornstein, N. L., & Putnam, F. W. (1992). Clinical phenomenology of child and adolescent dissociative disorders. *Journal of the American Academy of Child & Adolescent Psychiatry, 31,* 1077–1085.

Horowitz, M. J. (1976). *Stress response syndromes.* New York: Aronson.

Hough, D. W. (2001). Low-dose olanzapine for self-mutilation behavior in patients with borderline personality disorder. *Journal of Clinical Psychiatry, 62,* 296–297.

Hough, R. L., Canino, G. J., Abueg, F. R., & Gusman, F. D. (1996). PTSD and related stress disorders among Hispanics. In A. J. Marsella, M. J. Friedman, E. T. Gerrity, & R. M. Scurfield (Eds.), *Ethnocultural aspects of posttraumatic stress disorder* (pp. 483–504). Washington, DC: American Psychological Association.

Houts, A. C. (2003). Behavioral treatment for enuresis. In A. E. Kazdin & J. R. Weisz (Eds.), *Evidence-based psychotherapies for children and adolescents* (pp. 389–406). New York: Guilford Press.

Howlin, P., Goode, S., Hutton, J., & Rutter, M. (2004). Adult outcome for children with autism. *Journal of Child Psychology & Psychiatry, 45,* 212–229.

Hubbard, K., O'Neill, A.-M., Cheakalos, C., Baker, K., Berenstein, L., Breu, G., Duffy, T., Fowler, J., Greissinger, L. K., Matsumoto, N., Smith, P., Weinstein, F., & York, M. (1999, April 12). Out of control. *People Magazine,* pp. 52–69.

Hudson, J. L., & Rapee, R. M. (2001). Parent-child interactions and anxiety disorders: An observational study. *Behaviour Research & Therapy, 39,* 1411–1427.

Hudziak, J. J., van Beijsterveldt, C. E. M., Althoff, R. R., Stanger, C., Rettew, D. C., Nelson, E. C., Todd, R. D., Bartels, M., & Boomsma, D. I. (2004). Genetic and environmental contributions to the Child Behavior Checklist Obsessive-Compulsive Scale: A cross-cultural twin study. *Archives of General Psychiatry, 61,* 608–616.

Hugdahl, K., & Ohman, A. (1977). Effects of instruction on acquisition and extinction of electrodermal response to fear-relevant stimuli. *Journal of Experimental Psychiatry: Human Learning & Memory, 3,* 608–618.

Hughes, D., & Kleespies, P. (2001). Suicide in the medically ill. Suicidal behavior among Latino youth. *Suicide & Life-Threatening Behavior, 31,* 48–59.

Hughes, J. R. (1986). Genetics of smoking: A review. *Behavior Therapy, 17,* 335–345.

Hunt, W. A. (1998). Pharmacology of alcohol. In R. E. Tarter, R. T. Ammerman, & P. J. Ott (Eds.), *Handbook of substance abuse: Neurobehavioral pharmacology* (pp. 7–21). New York: Plenum Press.

Huppert, J. D., Bufka, L. F., Barlow, D. H., Gorman, J. M., Shea, K. M., & Woods, S. W. (2001). Therapists, therapist variables, and cognitive-behavioral therapy outcome in a multicenter trial for panic disorder. *Journal of Consulting & Clinical Psychology, 69,* 747–755.

Hur, Y., Bouchard, T. J., Jr., & Eckert, E. (1998). Genetic and environmental influences on self-reported diet: A reared-apart twin study. *Physiology & Behavior, 64,* 629–636.

Hurlbert, D. F. (1991). The role of assertiveness in female sexuality: A comparative study between sexually assertive and sexually nonassertive women. *Journal of Sex & Marital Therapy, 17,* 183–190.

Huselid, R. F., & Cooper, M. L. (1992). Gender roles as mediators of sex differences in adolescent alcohol use and abuse. *Journal of Health & Social Behavior, 33,* 348–362.

Hwu, H.-G., Chen, C.-H., Hwang, T.-J., Liu, C.-M., Cheng, J. L., Lin, S.-K., Liu, S.-K., Chen, C.-H., Chi, Y.-Y., Ou-Young, C.-W., Lin, H.-N., & Chen, W. J. (2002). Symptom patterns and subgrouping of schizophrenic patients: Significance of negative symptoms assessed on admission. *Schizophrenic Research, 56,* 105–119.

Hyde, J. S. (1990). *Understanding human sexuality.* New York: McGraw-Hill.

Hyman, I. E., & Billings, F. J. (1998). Individual differences and the creation of false childhood memories. *Memory, 6,* 1–20.

Hypericum Depression Trial Study Group. (2002). Effects of Hypericum perforatum (St. John's wort) in major depressive disorder. *Journal of the American Medical Association, 287,* 1807–1814.

I

Inciardi, J. A., Lockwood, D., & Pottieger, A. E. (1993). *Women and crack cocaine.* New York: Macmillan.

Infant Health and Development Program. (1990). Enhancing the outcome of low-birth-weight, premature infants: A multisite randomized trial. *Journal of the American Medical Association, 263,* 3035–3042.

Ingram, R. E., Hayes, A., & Scott, W. (2000). Empirically supported treatments: A critical analysis. In C. R. Snyder & R. E. Ingram (Eds.), *Handbook of psychological change: Psychotherapy processes and practices for the 21st century* (pp. 40–60). New York: Wiley.

Insel, T. R. (Ed.). (1984). *New findings in obsessive-compulsive disorder.* Washington, DC: American Psychiatric Press.

Insel, T. R., Hoover, C., & Murphy, D. L. (1983). Parents of patients with obsessive-compulsive disorder. *Psychological Medicine, 13,* 807–811.

Ironside, R. N., & Batchelor, I. R. C. (1945). *Aviation neuro-psychiatry.* Baltimore: Williams & Wilkins.

Ironson, G., Wynings, C., Schneiderman, N., Baum, A., Rodriguez, M., Greenwood, D., Benight, C., Antoni, M., LaPerriere, A., Huang, H.-S., Klimas, N., & Fletcher, M. A. (1997). Posttraumatic stress symptoms, intrusive thoughts, loss and immune function after Hurricane Andrew. *Psychosomatic Medicine, 59,* 128–141.

Iwamasa, G. Y., Larrabee, A. L., & Merritt, R. D. (2000). Are personality disorder criteria ethnically biased? A card-sort analysis. *Cultural Diversity and Ethnic Minority Psychology, 6,* 284–296.

J

Jablensky, A. (2000) Epidemiology of schizophrenia: The global burden of disease and disability. *European Archives of Psychiatry & Clinical Neuroscience, 250,* 274–285.

Jack, D. C. (1991). *Silencing the self: Women and depression.* New York: HarperPerennial.

Jack, R. (1992). *Women and attempted suicide.* Hillsdale, NJ: Erlbaum.

Jacobson, E. (1964). *The self and the object world.* New York: International Universities Press.

Jacobson, S. W., & Jacobson, J. L. (2000). Teratogenic insult and neurobehavioral function in infancy and childhood. In C. A. Nelson (Ed.), *The Minnesota symposia on child psychology, Vol. 31: The effects of early adversity on neurobehavioral development* (pp. 61–112). Mahwah, NJ: Erlbaum.

James, W. (1890). *The principles of psychology.* New York: Henry Holt.

James, W. (1948). *Psychology. (Briefer Course).* Cleveland, OH: World.

Jamison, K. R. (1993). *Touched with fire: Manic-depressive illness and the artistic temperament.* New York: Free Press.

Jamison, K. R. (1995). *An unquiet mind: A memoir of moods and madness.* New York: Knopf.

Jamison, K. R. (1999). *Night falls fast: Understanding suicide.* New York: Knopf.

Jang, K. L., Livesley, W. J., & Vernon, P. A. (1997). Gender-specific etiological differences in alcohol and drug problems: A behavioral genetic analysis. *Addiction, 92,* 1265–1276.

Jang, K. L., McCrae, R. R., Angleitner, A., Riemann, R., & Livesley, W. J. (1998). Heritability of facet-level traits in a cross-cultural twin sample: Support for a hierarchical model of personality. *Journal of Personality & Social Psychology, 74,* 1556–1565.

Jang, K. L., Paris, J., Zweig-Frank, H., & Livesley, W. J. (1998). Twin study of dissociative experience. *Journal of Nervous & Mental Disease, 186,* 345–351.

Janoff-Bulman, R. (1992). *Shattered assumptions: Toward a new psychology of trauma.* New York: Maxwell Macmillan International.

Janoff-Bulman, R., & Frieze, I. H. (1983). A theoretical perspective for understanding reactions to victimization. *Journal of Social Issues, 39,* 1–17.

Jarrett, R. B., Basco, M. R., Risser, R., Ramanan, J., Marwill, M., Kraft, D., & Rush, A. J. (1998). Is there a role for continuation phase cognitive therapy for depressed patients? *Journal of Consulting & Clinical Psychology, 66,* 1036–1040.

Jaycox, L. H., Reivich, K. J., Gillham, J., & Seligman, M. E. P. (1994). Preventing depressive symptoms in school children. *Behaviour Research & Therapy, 32,* 801–816.

Jefferson, J. W. (2001). Benzodiazepines and anticonvulsants for social phobia (social anxiety disorder). *Journal of Clinical Psychiatry, 62*(Suppl. 1), 50–53.

Jeffery, R. W., Wing, R. R., Thorson, C., & Burton, L. R. (1998). Use of personal trainers and financial incentives to increase exercise in a behavioral weight-loss program. *Journal of Consulting & Clinical Psychology, 66,* 777–783.

Jellinek, E. (1960). *The disease concept of alcoholism.* Highland Park, NJ: Hillhouse.

Jemmott, J. B., Jemmott, L. S., Spears, H., & Hewitt, N. (1992). Self-efficacy, hedonistic expectancies, and condom-use intentions among inner-city black adolescent women: A social cognitive approach to AIDS risk behavior. *Journal of Adolescent Health, 13,* 512–519.

Jemmott, L. S., & Jemmott, J. B. (1992). Increasing condom-use intentions among sexually active adolescent women. *Nursing Research, 41,* 273–279.

Jenkins, J. H., & Karno, M. (1992). The meaning of expressed emotion: Theoretical issues raised by cross-cultural research. *American Journal of Psychiatry, 149,* 9–21.

Jenkins, J. H., Kleinman, A., & Good, B. J. (1991). Cross-cultural studies of depression. In J. Becker (Ed.), *Psychosocial aspects of depression* (pp. 67–99). Hillsdale, NJ: Erlbaum.

Jenkins, R. L. (1968). The varieties of children's behavioral problems and family dynamics. *American Journal of Psychiatry, 124,* 1440–1445.

Jenkins, R. L. (1973). *Behavior disorders of childhood and adolescence.* Springfield, IL: Charles C Thomas.

Jensen, P. S., Hinshaw, S. P., Swanson, J. M., Greenhill, L. L., Conners, C. K., Arnold, L. E., Abikoff, H. B., Elliott, G., Hechtman, L., Hoza, B., March, J. S., Newcorn, J. H., Severe, J. B., Vitiello, B., Wells, K., & Wigal, T. (2001). Findings from the NIMH Multimodal Treatment Study of ADHD (MTA): Implications and applications for primary care providers. *Journal of Developmental & Behavioral Pediatrics, 22,* 60–73.

Jensen, P. S., Kettle, L., Roper, M. T., Sloan, M. T., Dulcan, M. K., Hoven, C., Bird, H. R., Bauermeister, J. J., & Payne, J. D. (1999). Are stimulants overprescribed? Treatment of ADHD in four U.S. communities. *Journal of the American Academy of Child & Adolescent Psychiatry, 38,* 797–804.

Ji, J., Kleinman, A., & Becker, A. E. (2001). Suicide in contemporary China: A review of China's distinctive suicide demographics in their sociocultural context. *Harvard Review of Psychiatry, 9,* 1–12.

Joe, S., & Kaplan, M. S. (2001). Suicide among African American men. *Suicide & Life-Threatening Behavior, 31*(Suppl.), 106–121.

Johannessen, D. J., Cowley, D. S., Walker, D. R., & Jensen, C. F. (1989). Prevalence, onset and clinical recognition of panic states in hospitalized male alcoholics. *American Journal of Psychiatry, 146,* 1201–1203.

Johnson, W., McGue, M., Krueger, R. F., & Bouchard, T. J. (2004). Marriage and personality: A genetic analysis. *Journal of Personality & Social Psychology, 86,* 285–294.

Johnston, L. D., O'Malley, P. M., Bachman, J. G., & Schulenberg, J. E. (2004). *Monitoring the future national results on adolescent drug use: Overview of key findings, 2003.* Bethesda, MD: National Institute on Drug Abuse.

Joiner, T. E. (1999). The clustering and contagion of suicide. *Current Directions in Psychological Science, 8,* 89–92.

Joiner, T. E., Jr., Brown, J. S., & Wingate, L. R. (2005). The psychology and neurobiology of suicidal behavior. *Annual Review of Psychology, 56,* 287–314.

Joiner, T. E., Jr. (2002). Depression in its interpersonal context. In I. H. Gotlib & C. L. Hammen (Eds.), *Handbook of depression* (pp. 295–313). New York: Guilford Press.

Joiner, T. E., Johnson, F., & Soderstrom, K. (2002). Association between serotonin transporter gene polymorphism and family history of completed and attempted suicide. *Suicide & Life-Threatening Behavior, 32,* 329–332.

Jones, E. E., & Harris, V. A. (1967). The attribution of attitudes. *Journal of Experimental Social Psychology, 3,* 1–24.

Jonnal, A. H., Gardner, C. O., & Prescott, C. A. (2000). Obsessive and compulsive symptoms in a general population sample of female twins. *American Journal of Medical Genetics, 96,* 791–796.

Jordan, B. D. (1998). Dementia pugilistia. In M. F. Folstein (Ed.), *Neurobiology of primary dementia* (pp. 191–204). Washington, DC: American Psychiatric Press.

Jordan, B. K., Schlenger, W. E., Fairbank, J. A., & Caddell, J. M. (1996). Prevalence of psychiatric disorders among incarcerated women: II. Convicted felons entering prison. *Archives of General Psychiatry, 53,* 513–519.

Jorge, R. E., Robinson, R. G., Tateno, A., Narushima, K., Acion, L., Moser, D., Arndt, S., & Chemerinski, E. (2004). Repetitive transcranial magnetic stimulation as treatment of poststroke depression: A preliminary study. *Biological Psychiatry, 55,* 398–405.

Joshi, S. V. (2004). Psychostimulants, atomoxetine, and alpha-agonists. In H. Steiner (Ed.), *Handbook of mental health intervention in children and adolescents: An integrated developmental approach* (pp. 258–287). San Francisco: Jossey-Bass.

Joyce, P. R., Rogers, G. R., Miller, A. L., Mulder, R. T., Luty, S. E., & Kennedy, M. A. (2003). Polymorphisms of DRD4 and DRD3 and risk of avoidant and obsessive personality traits and disorders. *Psychiatry Research, 119,* 1–10.

Judd, L. L., & Akiskal, H. S. (2000). Delineating the longitudinal structure of depressive illness: Beyond clinical subtypes and duration thresholds. *Pharmacopsychiatry, 33,* 3–7.

Judd, L. L., & Akiskal, H. S. (2003). The prevalence and disability of bipolar spectrum

disorders in the US population: Re-analysis of the ECA database taking into account subthreshold cases. *Journal of Affective Disorders, 73,* 123–131.

Judd, L. L., Akiskal, H., Maser, J., Zeller, P. J., Endicott, J., Coryell, W., Paulus, M., Kunovac, J., Leon, A., Mueller, T., Rice, J., & Keller, M. (1998). A prospective 12-year study of subsyndromal and syndromal depressive symptoms in unipolar major depressive disorders. *Archives of General Psychiatry, 55,* 694–700.

Judd, L. L., Akiskal, H. S., Schetteler, P. J., Endicott, J., Maser, J., Solomon, D. A., Leon, A. C., Rice, J. A., & Keller, M. B. (2002). The long-term natural history of the weekly symptomatic status of bipolar I disorder. *Archives of General Psychiatry, 59,* 530–537.

Judd, L. L., Paulus, M. P., Wells, K. B., & Rapaport, M. H. (1996). Socioeconomic burden of subsyndromal depressive symptoms and major depression in a sample of the general population. *American Journal of Psychiatry, 153,* 1411–1417.

Jun-mian, X. (1987). Some issues in the diagnosis of depression in China. *Canadian Journal of Psychiatry, 32,* 368–370.

K

Kagan, J., Reznick, J. S., & Snidman, M. (1987). The physiology and psychology of behavioral inhibition in children. *Child Development, 58,* 1459–1473.

Kamen-Siegel, L., Rodin, J., Seligman, M. E., & Dwyer, J. (1991). Explanatory style and cell-mediated immunity in elderly men and women. *Health Psychology, 10,* 229–235.

Kanner, L. (1943). Autistic disturbances of affective contact. *Nervous Child, 21,* 217–250.

Kaplan, H. S. (1974). *The new sex therapy: Active treatment of sexual dysfunction.* New York: Brunner/Mazel.

Kaplan, H. S. (1977). Hypoactive sexual desire. *Journal of Sex & Marital Therapy, 3,* 3–9.

Kaplan, H. S. (1995). *The sexual desire disorders: Dysfunctional regulation of sexual motivation.* New York: Brunner/Mazel.

Kaplan, M. (1983). The issue of sex bias in DSM-III: Comments on the articles by Spitzer, Williams, and Kass. *American Psychologist, 38,* 802–803.

Karasek, R. A., Russell, R. S., & Theorell, T. (1982). Physiology of stress and regeneration in job related cardiovascular illness. *Journal of Human Stress, 8,* 29–42.

Karno, M., & Golding, J. M. (1991). Obsessive compulsive disorder. In L. R. Robins & D. A. Regier (Eds.), *Psychiatric disorders in America: The Epidemiologic Catchment Area study.* New York: Maxwell Macmillan International.

Karno, M., Hough, R., Burnam, A., Escobar, J. I., Timbers, D. M., Santana, F., & Boyd, J. H. (1987). Lifetime prevalence of specific psychiatric disorders among Mexican Americans and non-Hispanic whites in Los Angeles. *Archives of General Psychiatry, 44,* 695–701.

Karno, M., & Jenkins, J. H. (1993). Cross-cultural issues in the course and treatment of schizophrenia. *Psychiatric Clinics of North America, 16,* 339–350.

Karper, L. P., & Krystal, J. H. (1997). Pharmacotherapy of violent behavior. In D.

M. Stoff, J. Breiling, & J. D. Maser (Eds.), *Handbook of antisocial personality disorder* (pp. 436–444). New York: Wiley.

Kaslow, N., Thompson, M., Meadows, L., Chance, S., Puett, R., Hollins, L., Jessee, S., & Kellermann, A. (2000). Risk factors for suicide attempts among African American women. *Depression & Anxiety, 12,* 13–20.

Katchadourian, H. A. (1989). *Fundamentals of human sexuality* (5th ed.). New York: Holt, Rinehart & Winston.

Katon, W., Rutter, C., Ludman, E. J., Von Korff, M., Lin, E., Simon, G., Bush, T., Walker, E., & Unützer, J. (2001). A randomized trial of relapse prevention of depression in primary care. *Archives of General Psychiatry, 58,* 241–247.

Katon, W., Sullivan, M., & Walker, E. (2001). Medical symptoms without identified pathology: Relationship to psychiatric disorders, childhood and adult trauma, and personality traits. *Annals of International Medicine, 134,* 917–925.

Katon, W., Von Korff, M., Lin, E., Simon, G., Walker, E., Unützer, J., Bush, T., Russo, J., & Ludman, E. (1999). Stepped collaborative care for primary care patients with persistent symptoms of depression: A randomized trial. *Archives of General Psychiatry, 56,* 1109–1115.

Katz, R., & Wykes, T. (1985). The psychological difference between temporally predictable and unpredictable stressful events: Evidence for information control theories. *Journal of Personality & Social Psychology, 48,* 781–790.

Katzman, R. (1993). Education and the prevalence of dementia and Alzheimer's disease. *Neurology, 43,* 13–20.

Kavanagh, D. J. (1992). Recent developments in expressed emotion and schizophrenia. *British Journal of Psychiatry, 160,* 601–620.

Kaye, W. H., Nagata, T., Weltzin, T. E., Hsu, G., Sokol, M. S., McConaha, C., Plotnicov, K. H., Weise, J., & Deep, D. (2001). Double-blind placebo-controlled administration of fluoxetine in restricting- and restricting-purging-type anorexia nervosa. *Biological Psychiatry, 49,* 644–652.

Kaysen, S. (1993). *Girl, interrupted.* New York: Random House.

Kazdin, A. E. (1991). Effectiveness of psychotherapy with children and adolescents. *Journal of Consulting & Clinical Psychology, 59,* 785–798.

Kazdin, A. E. (2003a). Problem-solving skills training and parent management training for conduct disorder. In A. E. Kazdin & J. R. Weisz (Eds.), *Evidence-based psychotherapies for children and adolescents* (pp. 241–262). New York: Guilford Press.

Kazdin, A. E. (2003b). Psychotherapy for children and adolescents. *Annual Review of Psychology, 54,* 253–276.

Kazdin, A. E., & Weisz, J. R. (2003). *Evidence-based psychotherapies for children and adolescents.* New York: Guilford Press.

Keane, T. M., Gerardi, R. J., Quinn, S. J., & Litz, B. T. (1992). Behavioral treatment of post-traumatic stress disorder. In S. M. Turner, K. S. Calhoun, & H. E. Adams (Eds.), *Handbook of clinical behavior therapy* (pp. 87–97). New York: Wiley.

Keck, P. E., McElroy, S. L., Strakowski, S., West, S., Sax, K., Hawkins, J., Bourne, M. L., & Haggard, P. (1998). 12-month outcome of patients with bipolar disorder following hospitalization or a manic or mixed episode. *American Journal of Psychiatry, 155,* 646–652.

Keck, P. E., Jr., Mendlwicz, J., Calabrese, J. R., Fawcett, J., Suppes, T., Vestergaard, P. A., & Carbonell, C. (2000). A review of randomized, controlled clinical trials in acute mania. *Journal of Affective Disorders, 59*(Suppl. 1), 31–37.

Keel, P. K., & Klump, K. L. (2003). Are eating disorders culture-bound syndromes? Implications for conceptualizing their etiology. *Psychological Bulletin, 129,* 747–769.

Keesey, R. E. (1986). A set-point theory of obesity. In K. D. Brownell & J. P. Foreyt (Eds.), *Handbook of eating disorders* (pp. 45–62). New York: Basic Books.

Keller, M. B., Kocsis, J. H., Thase, M. E., Gelenberg, A. J., Rush, A. J., Koran, L., Schatzberg, A., Russell, J., Hirschfeld, R., Klein, D., McCullough, J. P., Fawcett, J. A., Kornstein, S., LaVange, L., & Harrison, W. (1998). Maintenance phase efficacy of sertraline for chronic depression: A randomized controlled trial. *Journal of the American Medical Association, 280,* 1665–1672.

Keller, M. B., McCullough, J. P., Klein, D. N., Arnow, B., Dunner, D. L., Gelenberg, A. J., Markowitz, J. C., Nemeroff, C. B., Russell, J. M., Thase, M. E., Trivedi, M. H., & Zajecka, J. (2000). A comparison of nefazodone, the cognitive behavioral analysis system of psychotherapy, and their combination for the treatment of chronic depression. *New England Journal of Medicine, 342,* 1462–1470.

Kellermann, A. L., Rivara, F. P., Somes, G., & Reay, D. T. (1992). Suicide in the home in relation to gun ownership. *New England Journal of Medicine, 327,* 467–472.

Kelly, G. F. (1998). *Sexuality today: The human perspective.* New York: McGraw-Hill.

Kelly, S. J., Day, N., & Streissguth, A. P. (2000). Effects of prenatal alcohol exposure on social behavior in humans and other species. *Neurotoxicology & Teratology, 22,* 143–149.

Kemeny, M. E. (2003). The psychobiology of stress. *Current Directions in Psychological Science, 12,* 124–129.

Kenardy, J. A., Dow, M. G. T., Johnston, D. W., Newman, M. G., Thomson, A., & Taylor, C. B. (2003). A comparison of delivery methods of cognitive-behavioral therapy for panic disorder: An international multicenter trial. *Journal of Consulting and Clinical Psychology, 71,* 1068–1075.

Kendall, P. C. (1992). *Anxiety disorders in youth: Cognitive-behavioral interventions.* Boston: Allyn & Bacon.

Kendall, P. C., Aschenbrand, S. G., & Hudson, J. L. (2003). Child-focused treatment of anxiety. In A. E. Kazdin & J. R. Weisz (Eds.), *Evidence-based psychotherapies for children and adolescents* (pp. 81–100). New York: Guilford Press.

Kendall, P. C., Hollon, S. D., Beck, A. T., Hammen, C. L., & Ingram, R. E. (1987). Issues and recommendations regarding use of the Beck Depression Inventory. *Cognitive Therapy & Research, 11,* 289–299.

Kendall-Tackett, K. A., Williams, L. M., & Finkelhor, D. (1993). Impact of sexual abuse on children: A review and synthesis of recent empirical studies. *Psychological Bulletin, 113,* 164–180.

Kendler, K. (1998). Major depression and the environment: A psychiatric genetic perspective. *Pharmacopsychiatry, 31,* 5–9.

Kendler, K., & Karkowski-Shuman, L. (1997). Stressful life events and genetic liability to major depression: Genetic control of exposure to the environment? *Psychological Medicine, 27,* 539–547.

Kendler, K. S., Davis, C. G., & Kessler, R. C. (1997). The familial aggregation of common psychiatric and substance use disorders in the National Comorbidity Survey: A family history study. *British Journal of Psychiatry, 170,* 541–548.

Kendler, K. S., Gallagher, T. J., Abelson, J. M., & Kessler, R. C. (1996). Lifetime prevalence, demographic risk factors, and diagnostic validity of nonaffective psychosis as assessed in a U.S. community sample. *Archives of General Psychiatry, 53,* 1022–1031.

Kendler, K. S., McGuire, M., Gruenberg, A. M., & Walsh, D. (1994). Outcome and family study of the subtypes of schizophrenia in the west of Ireland. *American Journal of Psychiatry, 151,* 849–856.

Kendler, K. S., Myers, J., Prescott, C. A., & Neale, M. C. (2001). The genetic epidemiology of irrational fears and phobias in men. *Archives of General Psychiatry, 58,* 257–265.

Kendler, K. S., Neale, M. C., Kessler, R. C., & Heath, A. C. (1992). Major depression and generalized anxiety disorder: Same genes, (partly) different environments? *Archives of General Psychiatry, 49,* 716–722.

Kendler, K. S., Neale, M. C., Kessler, R. C., & Heath, A. C. (1993). Panic disorder in women: A population-based twin study. *Psychological Medicine, 23,* 397–406.

Kendler, K. S., Neale, M. C., Kessler, R. C., Heath, A. C., & Eaves, L. J. (1992). A population-based twin study of major depression in women. *Archives of General Psychiatry, 49,* 257–266.

Kendler, K. S., Neale, M. C., Kessler, R. C., Heath, A. C., & Eaves, L. J. (1993). A test of the equal-environment assumption in twin studies of psychiatric illness. *Behavior Genetics, 23,* 21–28.

Kendler, K. S., & Prescott, C. A. (1998a). Cannabis use, abuse, and dependence in a population-based sample of female twins. *American Journal of Psychiatry, 155,* 1016–1022.

Kendler, K. S., & Prescott, C. A. (1998b). Cocaine use, abuse, and dependence in a population-based sample of female twins. *British Journal of Psychiatry, 173,* 345–350.

Kendler, K. S., & Prescott, C. A. (1999). A population based twin study of lifetime major depression in men and women. *Archives of General Psychiatry, 56,* 39–44.

Kennedy, S. H., Evans, K. R., Kruger, S., Mayberg, H. S., Meyer, J. H., et al. (2001). Changes in regional brain glucose metabolism measured with positron emission tomography after paroxetine treatment of major depression. *American Journal of Psychiatry, 158,* 899–905.

Kerbeshian, J., Burd, L., & Avery, K. (2001). Pharmacotherapy of autism: A review and clinical approach. *Journal of Developmental and Physical Disabilities, 13,* 199–228.

Kernberg, O. F. (1979). Psychoanalytic profile of the borderline adolescent. *Adolescent Psychiatry, 7,* 234–256.

Kernberg, O. F. (1989). *Psychodynamic psychotherapy of borderline patients.* New York: Basic Books.

Kernberg, O. F. (1998). Pathological narcissism and narcissistic personality disorder: Theoretical background and diagnostic classification. In E. F. Ronningstam (Ed.), *Disorders of narcissism* (pp. 29–58). Washington, DC: American Psychiatric Press.

Keshavan, M., Shad, M., Soloff, P., & Schooler, N. (2004). Efficacy and tolerability of olanzapine in the treatment of schizotypal personality disorder. *Schizophrenia Research, 71,* 97–101.

Kessler, R. C. (2003). The impairments caused by social phobia in the general population: Implications for intervention. *Acta Psychiatrica Scandinavica, 108*(Suppl. 417), 19–27.

Kessler, R. C., Andrade, L. H., Bijl, R. V., Offord, D. R., Demler, O. V., & Stein, D. J. (2002). The effects of co-morbidity on the onset and persistence of generalized anxiety disorder in the ICPE surveys. *Psychological Medicine, 32,* 1213–1225.

Kessler, R. C., Berglund, P., Demler, O., Jin, R., Koretz, D., Merikangas, K. R., Rush, A. J., Walters, E. E., & Wang, P. S. (2003). The epidemiology of major depressive disorder: Results from the national comorbidity survey replication (NCS-R). *Journal of the American Medical Association, 289,* 3095–3105.

Kessler, R. C., Berglund, P. A., Bruce, M. L., Koch, J. R., et al. (2001). The prevalence and correlates of untreated serious mental illness. *Health Services Research, 36,* 987–1007.

Kessler, R. C., Davis, C. G., & Kendler, K. S. (1997). Childhood adversity and adult psychiatric disorder in the U.S. National Comorbidity Survey. *Psychological Medicine, 27,* 1101–1119.

Kessler, R. C., Frank, R. G., Edlund, M., Katz, S. J., Lin, E., & Leaf, P. (1997). Differences in the use of psychiatric outpatient services between the United States and Ontario. *New England Journal of Medicine, 336,* 551–557.

Kessler, R. C., McGonagle, K. A., Zhao, S., Nelson, C. B., Hughes, M., Eshleman, S., Wittchen, H., & Kendler, K. S. (1994). Lifetime and 12-month prevalence of DSM-III-R psychiatric disorders in the United States: Results from the National Comorbidity Study. *Archives of General Psychiatry, 51,* 8–19.

Kessler, R. C., Olfson, M., & Berglund, P. A. (1998). Patterns and predictors of treatment contact after first onset of psychiatric disorders. *American Journal of Psychiatry, 155,* 62–69.

Kessler, R. C., Sonnega, A., Bromet, E., Hughes, M., & Nelson, C. B. (1995). Posttraumatic stress disorder in the National Comorbidity Survey. *Archives of General Psychiatry, 52,* 1048–1060.

Kessler, R. C., Stein, M. B., & Berglund, P. (1998). Social phobia subtypes in the National Comorbidity Survey. *American Journal of Psychiatry, 155,* 613–619.

Kety, S. S., Wender, P. H., Jacobsen, B., Ingraham, L. J., Jansson, L., Faber, B., & Kinney, D. K. (1994). Mental illness in the biological and adoptive relative of

schizophrenic adoptees: Replication of the Copenhagen study in the rest of Denmark. *Archives of General Psychiatry, 51,* 442–455.

Keys, A., Brozek, J., Henschel, A., Mickelsen, O., & Taylor, H. L. (1950). *The biology of human starvation.* Minneapolis: University of Minnesota Press.

Kiecolt-Glaser, J. K., Malarkey, W. B., Chee, M., & Newton, T. (1993). Negative behavior during marital conflict is associated with immunological down-regulation. *Psychosomatic Medicine, 55,* 395–409.

Kiecolt-Glaser, J. K., McGuire, L., Robles, T. F., & Glaser, R. (2002). Emotions, morbidity, and mortality: New perspectives from psychoneuroimmunology. *Annual Review of Psychology, 53,* 83–107.

Kiecolt-Glaser, J. K., & Newton, T. L. (2001). Marriage and health: His and hers. *Psychological Bulletin, 127,* 472–503.

Kiesler, C. A., & Sibulkin, A. E. (1983). Proportion of inpatient days for mental disorders: 1969–1978. *Hospital & Community Psychiatry, 34,* 606–611.

Kihlstrom, J. F. (2001). Dissociative disorders. In P. B. Sutker (Ed.), *Comprehensive handbook of psychopathology* (3rd ed., pp. 259–276). New York: Kluwer Academic/Plenum Publishers.

Kihlstrom, J. F. (2005). Dissociative disorders. *Annual Review of Clinical Psychology, 1,* 227–254.

Kihlstrom, J. F., & Couture, L. J. (1992). Awareness and information processing in general anesthesia. *Journal of Psychopharmacology, 6,* 410–417.

Kihlstrom, J. F., Glisky, M. L., & Angiulo, M. J. (1994). Dissociative tendencies and dissociative disorders. *Journal of Abnormal Psychology, 103,* 117–124.

Killen, J. D., Taylor, C. B., Hayward, C., Haydel, K. F., Wilson, D. M., Hammer, L., Kraemer, H., Blair-Greiner, A., & Strachowski, D. (1996). Weight concerns influence the development of eating disorders: A 4-year prospective study. *Journal of Consulting & Clinical Psychology, 64,* 936–940.

Kilpatrick, D. G., Edmunds, C., & Seymour, A. (1992). *Rape in America: A report to the nation.* Charleston: National Victims Center & the Crime Victims Research and Treatment Center, Medical University of South Carolina.

Kilpatrick, D. G., & Saunders, B. E. (1996). *Prevalence and consequences of child victimization: Results from the national survey of adolescents.* U.S. Department of Justice, Office of Justice Programs, National Institute of Justice, Grant No. 93-IJ-CX-0023.

Kilpatrick, D. G., Veronen, L. J., & Resick, P. A. (1979). The aftermath of rape: Recent empirical findings. *American Journal of Orthopsychiatry, 49,* 658–669.

Kim, L. I. C. (1993). Psychiatric care of Korean Americans. In A. C. Gaw (Ed.), *Culture, ethnicity, and mental illness* (pp. 347–375). Washington, DC: American Psychiatric Press.

King, D. A., & Markus, H. E. (2000). Mood disorders in older adults. In S. K. Whitbourne (Ed.), *Psychopathology in later adulthood* (pp. 141–172). New York: Wiley.

King, D. W., King, L. A., Foy, D. W., Keane, T. M., & Fairbank, F. A. (1999). Posttraumatic stress disorder in a national sample of female

and male Vietnam veterans: Risk factors, war-zone stressors, and resilience-recovery variables. *Journal of Abnormal Psychology, 108,* 164–170.

King, N. H., Gullone, E., & Tonge, B. J. (1993). Self-reports of panic attacks and manifest anxiety in adolescents. *Behaviour Research & Therapy, 31,* 111–116.

King, R. A., Schwab-Stone, M., Flisher, A. J., Greenwald, S., Kramer, R. A., Goodman, S. H., Lahey, B. B., Shaffer, D., & Gould, M. S. (2001). Psychosocial and risk behavior correlates of youth suicide attempts and suicidal ideation. *Journal of the American Academy of Child & Adolescent Psychiatry, 40,* 837–846.

Kinzie, J. D. (2001). The Southeast Asian refugee: The legacy of severe trauma. In W.-S. Tseng (Ed.), *Culture and psychotherapy: A guide to clinical practice* (pp. 173–191). Washington, DC: American Psychiatric Press.

Kinzie, J. D., & Leung, P. K. (1993). Psychiatric care of Indochinese Americans. In A. C. Gaw (Ed.), *Culture, ethnicity, and mental illness* (pp. 281–304). Washington, DC: American Psychiatric Press.

Kinzl, J. F., Traweger, C., Guenther, V., & Biebl, W. (1994). Family background and sexual abuse associated with eating disorders. *American Journal of Psychiatry, 151,* 1127–1131.

Kirk, S. A., & Kutchins, H. (1992). *The selling of DSM: The rhetoric of science in psychiatry.* New York: A. de Gruyter.

Kirmayer, L. J. (2001). Cultural variations in the clinical presentation of depression and anxiety: Implications for diagnosis and treatment. *Journal of Clinical Psychiatry, 62*(Suppl. 13), 22–28.

Kirmayer, L. J., & Taillefer, S. (1997). Somatoform disorders. In S. M. Turner & M. Herseen (Eds.), *Adult psychopathology and diagnosis* (3rd ed., pp. 333–383). New York: Wiley.

Kirsch, I., & Lynn, S. J. (1998). Dissociation theories of hypnosis. *Psychological Bulletin, 123,* 100–115.

Kisiel, C. L., & Lyons, J. S. (2001). Dissociation as a mediator of psychopathology among sexually abused children and adolescents. *American Journal of Psychiatry, 158,* 1034–1039.

Klein, D. F. (1964). Delineation of two drug-responsive anxiety syndromes. *Psychopharmacologia, 5,* 397–408.

Klein, D. N., Durbin, C. E., Shankman, S. A., & Santiago, N. J. (2002). Depression and personality. In I. H. Gotlib & C. L. Hammen (Eds.), *Handbook of depression* (pp. 115–140). New York: Guilford Press.

Klein, D. N., Lewinsohn, P. M., & Seeley, J. R. (1996). Hypomanic personality traits in a community sample of adolescents. *Journal of Affective Disorders, 38,* 135–143.

Klein, D. N., Lewinsohn, P. M., Seeley, J. R., & Rohde, P. (2001). A family study of major depressive disorder in a community sample of adolescents. *Archives of General Psychiatry, 58,* 13–20.

Klein, M. (1952). Notes on some schizoid mechanisms. In M. Klein, P. Heimann, S. Isaacs, & J. Riviere (Eds.), *Developments in psychoanalysis.* London: Hogarth Press.

Kleinman, A., & Kleinman, J. (1985). Somatization: The interconnections in Chinese society among culture, depressive experiences, and meanings of pain. In A. Kleinman & B. Good (Eds.), *Culture and depression* (pp. 429–490). Berkeley: University of California Press.

Klerman, G. L., & Weissman, M. M. (1989). Increasing rates of depression. *Journal of the American Medical Association, 261,* 2229–2235.

Klerman, G. L., Weissman, M. M., Rounsaville, B., & Chevron, E. (1984). *Interpersonal psychotherapy of depression.* New York: Basic Books.

Kline, P. (1993). *The handbook of psychological testing.* New York: Routledge.

Klorman, R., Cicchetti, D., Thatcher, J. E., & Ison, J. R. (2003). Acoustic startle in maltreated children. *Journal of Abnormal Child Psychology, 31,* 359–370.

Klosko, J. S., Barlow, D. H., Tassinari, R., & Cerny, J. A. (1990). A comparison of alprazolam and behavior therapy in treatment of panic disorder. *Journal of Consulting & Clinical Psychology, 58,* 77–84.

Kluft, R. P. (1985). The natural history of multiple personality disorder. In R. P. Kluft (Ed.), *Childhood antecedents of multiple personality* (pp. 197–238). Washington, DC: American Psychiatric Press.

Kluft, R. P. (1987). Unsuspected multiple personality disorder: An uncommon source of protracted resistance, interruption, and failure in psychoanalysis. *Hillside Journal of Clinical Psychiatry, 9,* 100–115.

Klump, K. L., Miller, K. B., Keel, P. K., McGue, M., & Iacono, W. G. (2001). Genetics and environmental influences on anorexia nervosa syndromes in a population-based twin sample. *Psychological Medicine, 31,* 737–740.

Knable, M. B., Barci, B. M., Webster, M. J., Meador-Woodruff, J., & Torrey, E. F. (2004). Molecular abnormalities of the hippocampus in severe psychiatric illness: Postmortem findings from the Stanley Neuropathology Consortium. *Molecular Psychiatry, 9,* 609–620.

Knopman, D. (2003). Pharmacotherapy for Alzheimer's disease: 2002. *Clinical Neuropharmacology, 26,* 93–101.

Koegel, R. L., Koegel, L. K., & Brookman, L. I. (2003). Empirically supported pivotal response interventions for children with autism. In A. E. Kazdin & J. R. Weisz (Eds.), *Evidence-based psychotherapies for children and adolescents* (pp. 341–357). New York: Guilford Press.

Kohut, H. (1971). *The analysis of the self: A systematic approach to the treatment of narcissistic personality disorders.* New York: New York International Universities Press.

Kohut, H. (1984). *How does analysis cure?* Chicago: University of Chicago Press.

Kohut, H., & Wolf, E. S. (1978). The disorders of the self and their treatment: An outline. *International Journal of Psychoanalysis, 59,* 413–425.

Koopman, C., Classen, C., & Spiegel, D. A. (1994). Predictors of posttraumatic stress symptoms among survivors of the Oakland/Berkeley, California, firestorm. *American Journal of Psychiatry, 151,* 888–894.

Koopman, C., Drescher, K., Bowles, S., Gusman, F., Blake, D., Dondershine, H., Chang, V., Butler, L. D., & Spiegel, D. (2001). Acute, dissociative reactions in veterans with

PTSD. *Journal of Trauma & Dissociation, 2,* 91–111.

Koorengevel, K. M., Gordijn, M. C. M., Beersma, D. G. M., Meesters, Y., den Boer, J. A., & van der Hoofdakker, R. H. (2001). Extraocular light therapy in winter depression: A double-blind placebo-controlled study. *Biological Psychiatry, 50,* 691–698.

Kopelman, M. D. (1987). Crime and amnesia: A review. *Behavioral Sciences & the Law, 5,* 323–342.

Korenman, S. G., & Barchas, J. D. (1993). *Biological basis of substance abuse.* New York: Oxford University Press.

Kortegaard, L. S., Hoerder, K., Joergensen, J., Gillberg, C., & Kyvik, K. O. (2001). A preliminary population-based twin study of self-reported eating disorder. *Psychological Medicine, 31,* 361–365.

Koss, J. D. (1990). Somatization and somatic complaint syndromes among Hispanics: Overview and ethnopsychological perspectives. *Transcultural Psychiatric Research Review, 27,* 5–29.

Koss, M. P. (1993). Rape: Scope, impact, interventions, and public policy responses. *American Psychologist, 48,* 1062–1069.

Koss, M. P., Figueredo, A. J., & Prince, R. J. (2002). Cognitive mediation of rape's mental, physical, and social health impact: Tests of four models in cross-sectional data. *Journal of Consulting & Clinical Psychology, 70,* 926–941.

Koss, M. P., & Kilpatrick, D. G. (2001). Rape and sexual assault. In E. Gerrity (Ed.), *The mental health consequences of torture* (pp. 177–193). New York: Kluwer Academic/Plenum Publishers.

Koss-Chioino, J. D. (1995). Traditional and folk approaches among ethnic minorities. In J. F. Aponte (Ed.), *Psychological interventions and cultural diversity* (pp. 145–163). Boston: Allyn & Bacon.

Kouri, E. M., & Pope, H. G. (2000). Abstinence symptoms during withdrawal from chronic marijuana use. *Experimental & Clinical Psychopharmacology, 8,* 483–492.

Krakow, B., Hollifield, M., Johnston, L., Koss, M., Schrader, R., Warner, T. D., Tandberg, D., Lauriello, J., McBride, L., Cutchen, L., Cheng, D., Emmons, S., Germain, A., Melendrez, D., Sandoval, D., & Prince, H. (2001). Imagery rehearsal therapy for chronic nightmares in sexual assault survivors with posttraumatic stress disorder: A randomized controlled trial. *Journal of the American Medical Association, 286,* 537–545.

Krakow, B., Hollifield, M., Schrader, R., Koss, M., Tandberg, D., Lauriello, J., McBride, L., Warner, T. D., Cheng, D., Edmond, T., & Kellner, R. (2000). A controlled study of imagery rehearsal for chronic nightmares in sexual assault survivors with PTSD: A preliminary report. *Journal of Traumatic Stress, 13,* 589–609.

Krakowski, M. (2003). Violence and serotonin: Influence of impulse control, affect regulation, and social functioning. *Journal of Neuropsychiatry & Clinical Neurosciences, 15,* 294–305.

Kraus, G., & Reynolds, D. J. (2001). The "A-B-C's" of the Cluster B's: Identifying, understanding, and treating Cluster B

personality disorders. *Clinical Psychology Review, 21,* 345–373.

Krause, K., Dresel, S. H., Krause, J., et al. (2000). Increased striatal dopamine transporter in adult patients with attention deficit hyperactivity disorder: Effects of methylphenidate as measured by single photon emission computed tomography. *Neuroscience & Letters, 285,* 107–110.

Kring, A. M. (2000). Gender and anger. In A. H. Fischer (Ed.), *Gender and emotion: Social psychological perspectives* (pp. 211–231). New York: Cambridge University Press.

Kring, A. M., & Neale, J. M. (1996). Do schizophrenic patients show a disjunctive relationship among expressive, experiential, and psychophysiological components of emotion? *Journal of Abnormal Psychology, 105,* 249–257.

Kroll, J. (1973). A reappraisal of psychiatry in the Middle Ages. *Archives of General Psychiatry, 29,* 276–283.

Krueger, R. F. (2002). Psychometric perspectives on comorbidity. In J. E. Helzer & J. J. Hudziak (Eds.), *Defining psychopathology in the 21st century: DSM-V and beyond* (pp. 41–54). Washington, DC: American Psychiatric Publishing.

Kryger, M. H., Roth, T., & Dement, W. C. (Eds.). (1994). *Principles and practice of sleep medicine.* Philadelphia: Saunders.

Krystal, H. (Ed.). (1968). *Massive psychic trauma.* New York: International Universities Press.

Kubany, E. S., Hill, E. E., Owens, J. A., Iannce-Spencer, C., McCaig, M. A., Tremayne, K. J., & Williams, P. L. (2004). Cognitive trauma therapy for battered women with PTSD (CTT-BW). *Journal of Consulting & Clinical Psychology, 72,* 3–18.

Kuhn, R. (1958). The treatment of depressive states with G22355 (imipramine hydrochloride). *American Journal of Psychiatry, 115,* 459–464.

Kuiper, N. A., & Olinger, L. J. (1986). Dysfunctional attitudes and a self-worth contingency model of depression. *Advances in Cognitive-Behavioral Research & Therapy, 5,* 115–142.

Kuiper, N. A., Olinger, L. J., & MacDonald, M. R. (1988). Vulnerability and episodic cognitions in a self-worth contingency model of depression. In L. B. Alloy (Ed.), *Cognitive processes in depression* (pp. 289–309). New York: Guilford Press.

Kujawa, M. J., & Nemeroff, C. B. (2000). The biology of bipolar disorder. In A. Marneros & J. Angst (Eds.), *Bipolar disorders: 100 years after manic-depressive insanity* (pp. 281–314). London: Kluwer Academic Publishers.

L

LaFromboise, T. D., Trimble, J. E., & Mohatt, G. V. (1998). Counseling intervention and American Indian tradition: An integrative approach. In D. R. Atkinson (Ed.), *Counseling American minorities* (5th ed., pp. 159–182). New York: McGraw-Hill.

Lagana, L., McGarvey, E. L., Classen, C., & Koopman, C. (2001). Psychosexual dysfunction among gynecological cancer survivors. *Journal of Clinical Psychology in Medical Settings, 8,* 73–84.

LaGreca, A. M., Silverman, W. K., Vernberg, E. M., & Prinstein, M. J. (1996). Symptoms of posttraumatic stress in children after Hurricane Andrew: A prospective study. *Journal of Consulting & Clinical Psychology, 64,* 712–723.

LaGreca, A. M., Silverman, W. K., & Wasserstein, S. B. (1998). Children's predisaster functioning as a predictor of posttraumatic stress following Hurricane Andrew. *Journal of Consulting & Clinical Psychology, 66,* 883–892.

Lahey, B. B., & Loeber, R. (1997). Attention-deficit/hyperactivity disorder, oppositional defiant disorder, conduct disorder, and adult antisocial behavior: A life span perspective. In D. M. Stoff, J. Breiling, & J. D. Maser (Eds.), *Handbook of antisocial personality disorder* (pp. 51–59). New York: Wiley.

Lai, T.-J., Chang, C.-M., Connor, K. M., Lee, L.-C., & Davidson, J. R. T. (2004). Full and partial PTSD among earthquake survivors in rural Taiwan. *Journal of Psychiatric Research, 38,* 313–322.

Laing, R. D. (1971). *Self and others.* Oxford, UK: Penguin Books.

Lalonde, J. K., Hudson, J. I., Gigante, R. A., & Pope, H. G. (2001). Canadian and American psychiatrists' attitudes towards dissociative disorders diagnoses. *Canadian Journal of Psychiatry, 46,* 407–412.

Lamb, H. R. (2001). *Best of new directions for mental health services, 1979–2001.* San Francisco: Jossey-Bass.

Lamb, H. R., & Weinberger, L. E. (Eds.). (2001). *Deinstitutionalization: Promise and problems.* San Francisco: Jossey-Bass.

Lamb, H. R., Weinberger, L. E., & Gross, B. H. (2004). Mentally ill persons in the criminal justice system: Some perspectives. *Psychiatric Quarterly, 75,* 107–126.

Lambert, M. C., Knight, F., Overly, K., Weisz, J. R., Desrosiers, M., & Thesiger, C. (1992). Jamaican and American adult perspectives on child psychopathology: Further exploration of the threshold model. *Journal of Consulting & Clinical Psychology, 60,* 146–149.

Lambert, M. J., & Bergen, A. E. (1994). The effectiveness of psychotherapy. In A. E. Bergen & S. L. Garfield (Eds.), *Handbook of psychotherapy and behavior change* (Vol. 4, pp. 143–189). New York: Wiley.

Lambert, M. T., & Silva, P. S. (1998). An update on the impact of gun control legislation on suicide. *Psychiatric Quarterly, 69,* 127–134.

Lang, A. J., & Stein, M. B. (2001). Social phobia: Prevalence and diagnostic threshold. *Journal of Clinical Psychiatry, 62*(Suppl. 1), 5–10.

Langevin, R. (1992). Biological factors contributing to paraphilic behavior. *Psychiatric Annals, 22,* 309–314.

Laudenslager, M. L., Ryan, S. M., Drugan, R. C., Hyson, R. L., & Maier, S. F. (1983). Coping and immunosuppression: Inescapable but not escapable shock suppresses lymphocyte proliferation. *Science, 221,* 569–570.

Laumann, E. O., Gagnon, J. H., Michael, R. T., & Michaels, S. (1994). *The social organization of sexuality: Sexual practices in the United States.* Chicago: University of Chicago Press.

Laumann, E. O., Paik, A., & Rosen, R. C. (1999). Sexual dysfunction in the United States. *Journal of the American Medical Association, 281,* 537–544.

Lavoie, K. L., Miller, S. B., Conway, M., & Fleet, R. P. (2001). Anger, negative emotions, and cardiovascular reactivity during interpersonal conflict in women. *Journal of Psychosomatic Research, 51,* 503–512.

Lawrie, S. M., Whalley, H. C., Abukmeil, S. S., Kestelman, J. N., Donnelly, L., Miller, P., Best, J. J. K., Owens, D. G. C., & Johnstone, E. C. (2001). Brain structure, genetic liability, and psychotic symptoms in subjects at high risk of developing schizophrenia. *Biological Psychiatry, 49,* 811–823.

Leary, T. (1957). *Interpersonal diagnosis of personality.* New York: Ronald.

LeBars, P. L., Katz, M. M., Berman, N., Itil, T. M., Freedman, A. M., & Schatzberg, A. F. (1997). A placebo-controlled, double-blind, randomized trial of an extract of ginkgo biloba for dementia. *Journal of the American Medical Association, 278,* 1327–1332.

Lee, J. K. P., Jackson, H. J., Pattison, P., & Ward, T. (2002). Developmental risk factors for sexual offending. *Child Abuse & Neglect, 26,* 73–92.

Lee, S., Lee, A. M., Ngai, E., Lee, D. T. S., & Wing, Y. K. (2001). Rationales for food refusal in Chinese patients with anorexia nervosa. *International Journal of Eating Disorders, 29,* 224–229.

Lee, Y.-J. (2004). Overview of the therapeutic management of insomnia with zolpidem. *CNS Drugs, 18*(Suppl. 1), 17–23.

Leenaars, A. A. (1988). *"I wish I could explain it," Suicide notes: Predictive clues and patterns.* New York: Human Sciences Press.

Lèger, D., Guilleminault, C., Bader, G., Levy, E., & Paillard, M. (2002). Medical and socio-professional impact of insomnia. *Sleep, 25,* 625–629.

Lehman, D. R., Wortman, C. B., & Williams, A. F. (1987). Long-term effects of losing a spouse or child in a motor vehicle crash. *Journal of Personality & Social Psychology, 52,* 218–231.

Leiblum, S. R. (2000). Vaginismus: A most perplexing problem. In S. R. Leiblum & R. C. Rosen (Eds.), *Principles and practice of sex therapy* (3rd ed., pp. 181–202) New York: Guilford Press.

Leiblum, S. R., & Rosen, R. C. (1988). *Sexual desire disorders.* New York: Guilford Press.

Leiblum, S. R., & Rosen, R. C. (2000). *Principles and practice of sex therapy* (3rd ed.). New York: Guilford Press.

Leit, R. A., Pope, H. G., & Gray, J. J. (2001). Cultural expectations of muscularity in men: The evolution of Playgirl centerfolds. *International Journal of Eating Disorders, 29,* 90–93.

Lemaire, J., & Despret, V. (2001). Collective post-traumatic disorders, residual resources, and an extensive context of trust: Creating a network in a refugee camp in former Yugoslavia. *International Journal of Mental Health, 30,* 22–26.

Lendon, C. L., Ashall, F., & Goate, A. M. (1997). Exploring the etiology of Alzheimer disease using molecular genetics. *Journal of the American Medical Association, 277,* 825–831.

Lenox, R. H., & Manji, H. K. (1995). Lithium. In A. F. Schatzberg & C. B. Nemeroff (Eds.), *The American psychiatric press textbook of psychopharmacology* (pp. 303–350). Washington, DC: American Psychiatric Press.

Leon, G. R., Fulkerson, J. A., Perry, C. L., & Early-Zald, M. B. (1995). Prospective analysis of personality and behavioral vulnerabilities and gender influences in the later development of disordered eating. *Journal of Abnormal Psychology, 104,* 140–149.

Lepine, J.-P. (2001). Epidemiology, burden, and disability in depression and anxiety. *Journal of Clinical Psychiatry, 62*(Suppl. 13), 4–10.

Lepore, S. J. (1995). Cynicism, social support and cardiovascular reactivity. *Health Psychology, 14,* 210–216.

Lerman, C., Caporaso, N. E., Audrain, J., Main, D., Bowman, E. D., Lockshin, B., Boyd, N. R., & Shields, P. G. (1999). Evidence suggesting the role of specific genetic factors in cigarette smoking. *Health Psychology, 18,* 14–20.

Lerner, H. D. (1986). Current developments in the psychoanalytic psychotherapy of anorexia nervosa and bulimia nervosa. *Clinical Psychologist, 39,* 39–43.

Lerner, M. J. (1980). *The belief in a just world: A fundamental delusion.* New York: Plenum Press.

Lester, D. (2003). Adolescent suicide from an international perspective. *American Behavioral Scientist, 46,* 1157–1170.

LeVay, S. (1993). *The sexual brain.* Cambridge, MA: MIT Press.

Leventhal, T., & Brooks-Gunn, J. (2003). Moving to opportunity: An experimental study of neighborhood effects on mental health. *American Journal of Public Health, 93,* 1576–1582.

Leverenz, J. B., Wilkinson, C. W., Wamble, M., Corbin, S., Grabber, J. E., et al. (1999). Effect of chronic high-dose exogenous cortisol on hippocampal neuronal number in aged nonhuman primates. *Journal of Neuroscience, 19,* 2356–2361.

Levy, S. M., & Heiden, L. (1991). Depression, distress, and immunity: Risk factors for infectious disease. *Stress Medicine, 7,* 45–51.

Levy, S. M., Herberman, R. B., Whiteside, T., & Sanzo, K. (1990). Perceived social support and tumor estrogen/progesterone receptor status as predictors of natural killer cell activity in breast cancer patients. *Psychosomatic Medicine, 52,* 73–85.

Lewinsohn, P. M. (1974). A behavioral approach to depression. In R. J. Friedman & M. M. Katz (Eds.), *The psychology of depression: Contemporary theory and research.* Washington, DC: Winston-Wiley.

Lewinsohn, P. M., & Clarke, G. N. (1999). Psychosocial treatments for adolescent depression. *Clinical Psychology Review, 19,* 329–342.

Lewinsohn, P. M., & Essau, C. A. (2002). Depression in adolescents. In I. H. Gotlib & C. L. Hammen (Eds.), *Handbook of depression* (pp. 541–559). New York: Guilford Press.

Lewinsohn, P. M., & Gotlib, I. H. (1995). Behavioral therapy and treatment of depression. In E. E. Beckham & W. R. Leber (Eds.), *Handbook of depression* (2nd ed., pp. 352–375). New York: Guilford Press.

Lewinsohn, P. M., Klein, D. N., & Seeley, J. R. (2000). Bipolar disorder during adolescence and young adulthood in a community sample. *Bipolar Disorders, 2,* 281–293.

Lewinsohn, P. M., Muñoz, R. F., Youngren, M. A., & Zeiss, A. M. (1986). *Control your depression*. Englewood Cliffs, NJ: Prentice Hall.

Lewinsohn, P. M., Rohde, P., & Seeley, J. R. (1996a). Adolescent suicidal ideation and attempts: Prevalence, risk factors, and clinical implications. *Clinical Psychology and Scientific Practice, 3,* 25–46.

Lewinsohn, P. M., Rohde, P., & Seeley, J. R. (1996b). Alcohol consumption in high school adolescents: Frequency of use and dimensional structure of associated problems. *Addiction, 91,* 375–390.

Lewinsohn, P. M., Rohde, P., Seeley, J. R., & Baldwin, C. L. (2001). Gender differences in suicide attempts from adolescence to young adulthood. *Journal of the American Academy of Child & Adolescent Psychiatry, 40,* 427–434.

Lewinsohn, P. M., Seeley, J. R., & Klein, D. N. (2003). Bipolar disorders during adolescence. *Acta Psychiatrica Scandinavica, 108,* 47–50.

Lewinsohn, P. M., Seeley, J. R., Moerk, K. C., & Striegel-Moore, R. H. (2002). Gender difference in eating disorder symptoms in young adults. *International Journal of Eating Disorders, 32,* 426–440.

Lewinsohn, P. M., Steinmetz, J. L., Larson, D. W., & Franklin, J. (1981). Depression-related cognitions: Antecedent or consequence? *Journal of Abnormal Psychology, 90,* 213–219.

Lewinsohn, P. M., Striegel-Moore, R. H., & Seeley, J. R. (2000). Epidemiology and natural course of eating disorders in young women from adolescence to young adulthood. *Journal of the American Academy of Child & Adolescent Psychiatry, 39,* 1284–1292.

Lewinsohn, P. M., Zinbarg, R., Seeley, J. R., Lewinsohn, M., & Sack, W. H. (1997). Lifetime comorbidity among anxiety disorders and between anxiety disorders and other mental disorders in adolescents. *Journal of Anxiety Disorders, 11,* 377–394.

Lewis, D. O., Balla, D. A., & Shanok, S. S. (1979). Some evidence of race bias in the diagnosis and treatment of the juvenile offender. *American Journal of Orthopsychiatry, 49,* 53–61.

Lewis, G., David, A., Andreasson, S., & Allebeck, P. (1992). Schizophrenia and city life. *The Lancet, 340,* 137–140.

Lex, B. W. (1995). Alcohol and other psychoactive substance dependence in women and men. In M. V. Seeman (Ed.), *Gender and psychopathology* (pp. 311–358). Washington, DC: American Psychiatric Association.

Liberman, R. P. (1994). Psychosocial treatments for schizophrenia. *Psychiatry, 57,* 104–114.

Liberman, R. P., Eckman, T. A., & Marder, S. R. (2001). Rehab rounds: Training in social problem solving among persons with schizophrenia. *Psychiatric Services, 52,* 31–33.

Liberman, R. P., Glynn, S., Blair, K. E., Ross, D., & Marder, S. R. (2002). In vivo amplified skills training: Promoting generalization of independent living skills for clients with schizophrenia. *Psychiatry: Interpersonal & Biological Processes, 65,* 137–155.

Liberto, J. G., Oslin, D. W., & Ruskin, P. E. (1996). Alcoholism in the older population. In L. L. Carstensen, B. A. Edelstein, & L. Dornbrand (Eds.), *The practical handbook of clinical gerontology* (pp. 324–348). Thousand Oaks, CA: Sage.

Liberzon, I., & Phan, K. (2003). Brain-imaging studies of posttraumatic stress disorder. *CNS Spectrums, 8,* 641–650.

Liberzon, I., Taylor, S. F., Amdur, R., Jung, T. D., Chamberlain, K. R., Minoshima, S., Koeppe, R. A., & Fig, L. M. (1999). Brain activation in PTSD in response to trauma-related stimuli. *Biological Psychiatry, 45,* 817–826.

Lichtermann, D., Karbe, E., & Maier, W. (2000). The genetic epidemiology of schizophrenia and of schizophrenia spectrum disorders. *European Archives of Psychiatry & Clinical Neuroscience, 250,* 304–310.

Lieberman, J., Chakos, M., Wu, H., Alvir, J., Hoffman, E., Robinson, D., & Bilder, R. (2001). Longitudinal study of brain morphology in first episode schizophrenia. *Biological Psychiatry, 49,* 487–499.

Lieberman, J. A., Tollefson, G., Tohen, M., Green, A. I., Gur, R. E., Kahn, R., McEvoy, J., Perkins, D., Sharma, T., Zipursky, R., Wei, H., & Hamer, R. M. (2003). Comparative efficacy and safety of atypical and conventional antipsychotic drugs in first-episode psychosis: A randomized, double-blind trial of olanzapine versus haloperidol. *American Journal of Psychiatry, 160,* 1396–1404.

Light, K. C., & Sherwood, A. (1989). Race, borderline hypertension, and hemodynamic responses to behavioral stress before and after beta-adrenergic blockade. *Health Psychology, 8,* 577–595.

Lilienfeld, S. O., Lynn, S. J., Kirsch, I., Chaves, J. F., Sarvin, T. R., Ganaway, G. K., & Powell, R. A. (1999). Dissociative identity disorders and the sociocognitive model: Recalling the lessons of the past. *Psychological Bulletin, 125,* 507–523.

Lillard, A. S. (1993). Young children's conceptualization of pretend: Action or mental representational states? *Child Development, 64,* 372–386.

Lillard, A. S. (1996). Body or mind: Children's categorizing of pretense. *Child Development, 67,* 1717–1734.

Lin, K.-M., & Shen, W. W. (1991). Pharmacotherapy for Southeast Asian psychiatric patients. *Journal of Nervous & Mental Disease, 179,* 346–350.

Lindemalm, G., Korlin, D., & Uddenberg, N. (1986). Long-term follow-up of "sex change" in 13 male-to-female transsexuals. *Archives of Sexual Behavior, 15,* 187–210.

Linehan, M. M. (1973). Suicide and attempted suicide: Study of perceived sex differences. *Perceptual & Motor Skills, 37,* 31–34.

Linehan, M. M. (1999). Standard protocol for assessing and treating suicidal behaviors for patients in treatment. In D. G. Jacobs (Ed.), *The Harvard Medical School guide to suicide assessment and intervention* (pp. 146–187). San Francisco: Jossey-Bass.

Linehan, M. M., Armstrong, H. E., Suarez, A., & Allmon, D. (1991). Cognitive-behavioral treatment of chronically parasuicidal borderline patients. *Archives of General Psychiatry, 48,* 1060–1064.

Linehan, M. M., Camper, P., Chiles, J. A., Strosahl, K., & Shearin, E. N. (1987). Interpersonal problem-solving and parasuicide. *Cognitive Therapy & Research, 11,* 1–12.

Linehan, M. M., Cochran, B. N., & Kehrer, C. A. (2001). Dialectical behavior therapy for borderline personality disorder. In D. H. Barlow (Ed.), *Clinical handbook of psychological disorders: A step-by-step treatment manual* (pp. 470–522). New York: Guilford Press.

Linehan, M. M., Heard, H. L., & Armstrong, H. E. (1993). Naturalistic follow-up of a behavioral treatment for chronically parasuicidal borderline patients. *Archives of General Psychiatry, 50,* 971–974.

Linehan, M. M., Kanter, J. W., & Comtois, K. A. (1999). Dialectical behavior therapy for borderline personality disorder: Efficacy, specificity, and cost effectiveness. In D. S. Janowsky (Ed.), *Psychotherapy indications and outcomes* (pp. 93–118). Washington, DC: American Psychiatric Press.

Linehan, M. M., Schmidt, H., Dimeff, L. A., Craft, J. C., Kanter, J., & Comtois, K. A. (1999). Dialectical behavior therapy for patients with borderline personality disorder and drug-dependence. *American Journal on Addiction, 8,* 279–292.

Links, P. S., Heslegrave, R., & van Reekum, R. (1998). Prospective follow-up study of borderline personality disorder: Prognosis, prediction of outcome, and Axis II comorbidity. *Canadian Journal of Psychiatry, 43,* 265–270.

Lipowski, Z. J. (1990). *Delirium: Acute confusional states.* New York: Oxford University Press.

Lisansky-Gomberg, E. S. (2000). Substance abuse disorders, In S. K. Whitbourne (Ed.), *Psychopathology in later adulthood* (pp. 277–298). New York: Wiley.

Lochman, J. E., Barry, T. D., & Pardini, D. A. (2003). Anger control training for aggressive youth. In A. E. Kazdin & J. R. Weisz (Eds.), *Evidence-based psychotherapies for children and adolescents* (pp. 263–281). New York: Guilford Press.

Lochman, J. E., White, K. J., & Wayland, K. K. (1991). Cognitive-behavioral assessment and treatment with aggressive children. In P. Kendall (Ed.), *Therapy with children and adolescents: Cognitive behavioral procedures* (pp. 25–65). New York: Guilford Press.

Loebel, J. P., Loebel, J. S., Dager, S. R., Centerwall, B. S., & Reay, D. T. (1991). Anticipation of nursing home placement may be a precipitant of suicide among the elderly. *Journal of the American Geriatric Society, 39,* 407–408.

Loeber, R. (1990). Development and risk factors of juvenile antisocial behavior and delinquency. *Clinical Psychology Review, 10,* 1–41.

Loeber, R., & Farrington, D. P. (1997). Strategies and yields of longitudinal studies on anti-social behavior. In D. M. Stoff, J. Breiling, & J. D. Maser (Eds.), *Handbook of antisocial personality disorder* (pp. 125–139). New York: Wiley.

Loeber, R., & Farrington, D. P. (2000). Young children who commit crime: Epidemiology, developmental origins, risk factors, early interventions, and policy implications. *Development & Psychopathology, 12,* 737–762.

Loftus, E. F. (1993). The reality of repressed memories. *American Psychologist, 48,* 518–537.

Loftus, E. F. (2003). Make-believe memories. *American Psychologist, 58,* 867–873.

Loftus, E. F., & Ketchum, K. (1994). *The myth of repressed memory.* New York: St. Martin's Press.

Lombardi, E. (2001). Enhancing transgender health care. *American Journal of Public Health, 91,* 869–872.

Long, P. W. (1996). Internet mental health. Retrieved from the World Wide Web: http://www.mentalhealth.com/

Lopez, S. R., & Guarnaccia, P. J. J. (2000). Cultural psychopathology: Uncovering the social world of mental illness. *Annual Review of Psychology, 51,* 571–598.

Lopez, S. R., Kopelowics, A., & Canive, J. M. (2002). Strategies in developing culturally congruent family interventions for schizophrenia: The case of Hispanics. In H. P. Lefley & D. L. Johnson (Eds.), *Family interventions in mental illness: International perspectives* (pp. 61–90). Westport, CT: Praeger.

LoPiccolo, J. (1992). Paraphilias. *Nordisk Sexolgi, 10,* 1–14.

Lotspeich, L. J., Kwon, H., Schumann, C. M., Fryer, S. L., Goodlin-Jones, B. L., Buonocore, M. H., Lammers, C. R., Amaral, D. G., & Reiss, A. L. (2004). Investigation of neuroanatomical differences between autism and Asperger syndrome. *Archives of General Psychiatry, 61,* 291–298.

Lovaas, O. I. (1987). Behavioral treatment and normal educational and intellectual functioning in young autistic children. *Journal of Consulting & Clinical Psychology, 55,* 3–9.

Lovaas, O. I., & Smith, T. (2003). Early and intensive behavioral intervention in autism. In A. E. Kazdin & J. R. Weisz (Eds.), *Evidence-based psychotherapies for children and adolescents* (pp. 325–340). New York: Guilford Press.

Lowe, B., Zipfel, S., Buchholz, C., Dupont, Y., Reas, D. L., & Herzog, W. (2001). Long-term outcome of anorexia nervosa in a prospective 21-year follow-up study. *Psychological Medicine, 31,* 881–890.

Luborsky, L. (1973). Forgetting and remembering (momentary forgetting) during psychotherapy. In M. Mayman (Ed.), *Psychoanalytic research and psychological issues* (pp. 29–55). New York: International Universities Press.

Luborsky, L. (1984). *Principles of psychoanalytic psychotherapy: A manual for supportive-expressive treatment.* New York: Basic Books.

Luborsky, L., & Crits-Cristoph, P. (1990). *Understanding transference: The core conflictual relationship theme method.* New York: Basic Books.

Ludwig, A. M. (1992). Creative achievement and psychopathology: Comparison among professions. *American Journal of Psychotherapy, 46,* 330–356.

Luria, A. (1973). *The working brain.* New York: Basic Books.

Luthar, S. S. (2003). *Resilience and vulnerability: Adaptation in the context of childhood adversities.* Cambridge, UK: Cambridge University Press.

Lyman, R. (1997, April 15). Michael Dorris dies at 52: Wrote of his son's suffering. *The New York Times,* p. 24.

Lynam, D. R., Caspi, A., Moffitt, T. E., Wikstrom, P. H., Loeber, R., & Novak, S. (2000). The interaction between impulsivity and neighborhood context on offending: The effects of impulsivity are stronger in poorer neighborhoods. *Journal of Abnormal Psychology, 109,* 563–574.

Lynam, D. R., & Widiger, T. A. (2001). Using the five factor model to represent the DSM-IV personality disorders: An expert consensus approach. *Journal of Abnormal Psychology, 110,* 401–402.

Lyness, J. M. (2004). Treatment of depressive conditions in later life: Real-world light for dark (or dim) tunnels. *Journal of the American Medical Association, 291,* 1626–1628.

Lytton, H., & Romney, D. M. (1991). Parents' differential socialization of boys and girls: A meta-analysis. *Psychological Bulletin, 109,* 267–296.

M

MacArthur Research Network on Mental Health and the Law. (1998). Executive summary. Retrieved from the World Wide Web: http://ness.sys.Virginia.EDU/macarthur/violence.html

Maccoby, N., & Altman, D. G. (1988). Disease prevention in communities: The Stanford Heart Disease Prevention Program. In R. H. Price (Ed.), *Fourteen ounces of prevention: A casebook for practitioners* (pp. 165–174). Washington, DC: American Psychological Association.

MacCoun, R. J. (1998). Toward a psychology of harm reduction. *American Psychologist, 53,* 1199–1208.

Machover, K. A. (1949). *Personality projection in the drawing of the human figure: A method of personality investigation.* Springfield, IL: Charles C Thomas.

Macintosh, K. E., & Dissanayake, C. (2004). Annotation: The similarities and differences between autistic disorder and Asperger's disorder: A review of the empirical evidence. *Journal of Child Psychology & Psychiatry, 45,* 421–434.

MacKinnon, D., Jamison, K. R., & DePaulo, J. R. (1997). Genetics of manic depressive illness. *Annual Review of Neuroscience, 20,* 355–373.

Madge, N., & Harvey, J. G. (1999). Suicide among the young—The size of the problem. *Journal of Adolescence, 22,* 145–155.

Maguire, G. A., Riley, G. D., Franklin, D. L., & Gottschalk, L. A. (2000). Risperidone for the treatment of stuttering. *Journal of Clinical Psychopharmacology, 20,* 479–482.

Maher, B. A. (1974). Delusional thinking and perceptual disorder. *Journal of Individual Psychology, 30,* 98–113.

Maher, W. B., & Maher, B. A. (1985). Psychopathology: I. From ancient times to eighteenth century. In G. A. Kimble & K. Schlesinger (Eds.), *Topics in the history of psychology* (Vol. 2). Hillsdale, NJ: Erlbaum.

Mahler, M. (1968). *On human symbiosis and the vicissitudes of individuation: Vol. I. Infantile psychosis.* New York: International Universities Press.

Maj, M., Pirozzi, R., Magliano, L., & Bartoli, L. (1998). Long-term outcome of lithium prophylaxis in bipolar disorder: A 5-year prospective study of 402 patients at a lithium clinic. *American Journal of Psychiatry, 155,* 30–35.

Maletzky, B. (1998). The paraphilias: Research and treatment. In P. E. Nathan (Ed.), *A guide to treatments that work* (pp. 472–500). New York: Oxford University Press.

Maletzky, B. M., & Field, G. (2003). The biological treatment of dangerous sexual offenders, a review and preliminary report of the Oregon pilot *depo-Provera* program. *Aggression and Violent Behavior, 8,* 391–412.

Maletzky, B. M., & Steinhauser, C. (2002). A 25-year follow-up of cognitive/behavioral therapy with 7,275 sexual offenders. *Behavior Modification, 26,* 123–147.

Maltsberger, J. T. (1999). The psychodynamic understanding of suicide. In D. G. Jacobs (Ed.), *The Harvard Medical School guide to suicide assessment and intervention* (pp. 72–82). San Francisco: Jossey-Bass.

Mangweth, B., Pope, H. G., Kemmler, G., Ebenbichler, C., Hausmann, A., De Col, C., Kreutner, B., Kinzl, J., & Biebl, W. (2001). Body image and psychopathology in male bodybuilders. *Psychotherapy & Psychosomatics, 70,* 38–43.

Manicavasagar, V., Silove, D., Rapee, R., Waters, F., & Momartin, S. (2001). Parent-child concordance for separation anxiety: A clinical study. *Journal of Affective Disorders, 65,* 81–84.

Mann, J. J., Brent, D. A., & Arango, V. (2001). The neurobiology and genetics of suicide and attempted suicide: A focus on the serotonergic system. *Neuropsychopharmacology, 24,* 467–477.

Mannino, J. D. (1999). *Sexually speaking.* New York: McGraw-Hill.

Mannuza, S., Klein, R. G., Bessler, A., Malloy, P., & LaPadula, M. (1998). Adult psychiatric status of hyperactive boys grown up. *American Journal of Psychiatry, 155,* 493–498.

Manson, S., Beals, J., O'Nell, T., Piasecki, J., Bechtold, D., Keane, E., & Jones, M. (1996). Wounded spirits, ailing hearts: PTSD and related disorders among American Indians. In A. J. Marsella, M. J. Friedman, E. T. Gerrity, & R. M. Scurfield (Eds.), *Ethnocultural aspects of posttraumatic stress disorder* (pp. 255–283). Washington, DC: American Psychiatric Press.

Manson, S. M., Shore, J. H., Baron, A. E., Ackerson, L., & Neligh, G. (1992). Alcohol abuse and dependence among American Indians. In J. E. Helzer & G. J. Canino (Eds.), *Alcoholism in North America, Europe, and Asia* (pp. 113–127). New York: Oxford University Press.

Manu, P., Lane, T. J., & Matthews, D. A. (1989). Somatization disorder in patients with chronic fatigue. *Psychosomatics, 30,* 388–395.

Manu, P., Lane, T. J., & Matthews, D. A. (1992). Chronic fatigue syndromes in clinical practice. *Psychotherapy & Psychosomatics, 58,* 60–68.

Maramba, G. G., & Nagayama Hall, G. C. (2002). Meta-analyses of ethnic match as a predictor of dropout, utilization, and level of functioning. *Cultural Diversity & Ethnic Minority Psychology, 8,* 290–297.

Marangell, L. B. (2004). The importance of subsyndromal symptoms in bipolar disorder. *Journal of Clinical Psychiatry, 65*(Suppl. 10), 24–27.

Marangell, L. B., Martinez, J. M., & Niazi, S. K. (2004). Vagus nerve stimulation as a potential option for treatment-resistant depression. *Clinical Neuroscience Research, 4,* 89–94.

Marantz, S., & Coates, S. (1991). Mothers of boys with gender identity disorder: A comparison of matched controls. *Journal of the American Academy of Child & Adolescent Psychiatry, 30,* 310–315.

Marcantonio, E. R., Simon, S. E., Bergmann, M. A., Jones, R. N., Murphy, J. M., & Morris, J. N. (2003). Delirium symptoms in post-acute care: Prevalent, persistent, and associated with poor functional recovery. *Journal of the American Geriatrics Society, 51,* 4–9.

March, J. S., Biederman, J., Wolkow, R., Safferman, A., Mardekian, J., Cook, E. H., Cutler, N. R., Dominguez, R., Ferguson, J., Muller, B., Riesenberg, R., Rosenthal, M., Sallee, F. E., & Wagner, K. D. (1998). Sertraline in children and adolescents with obsessive-compulsive disorder. *Journal of the American Medical Association, 280,* 1752–1756.

Marcos, L. R. (1979). Effects of interpreters on the evaluation of psychopathology in non-English-speaking patients. *American Journal of Psychiatry, 136,* 171–174.

Marcus, D. K., & Church, S. E. (2003). Are dysfunctional beliefs about illness unique to hypochondriasis? *Journal of Psychosomatic Research, 54,* 543–547.

Margraf, J. (1993). Hyperventilation and panic disorder: A psychophysiological connection. *Advances in Behaviour Research & Therapy, 15,* 49–74.

Margraf, J., Barlow, D. H., Clark, D. M., & Telch, M. J. (1993). Psychological treatment of panic: Work in progress on outcome, active ingredients, and follow-up. *Behaviour Research & Therapy, 31,* 1–8.

Markovitz, P. J. (2004). Recent trends in the pharmacotherapy of personality disorders. *Journal of Personality Disorders, 18,* 99–101.

Marks, I. M., & Swinson, R. (1992). Behavioral and/or drug therapy. In G. D. Burrows, S. M. Roth, & R. Noyes, Jr. (Eds.), *Handbook of anxiety* (Vol. 5). Oxford, UK: Elsevier.

Marlatt, G. A. (Ed.). (1998). *Harm reduction: Pragmatic strategies for managing high-risk behaviors.* New York: Guilford Press.

Marlatt, G. A., Baer, J. S., Donovan, D. M., & Kivlahan, D. R. (1988). Addictive behaviors: Etiology and treatment. *Annual Review of Psychology, 39,* 223–252.

Marlatt, G. A., Baer, J. S., Kivlahan, D. R., Dimeff, L. A., Larimer, M. E., Quigley, L. A., Somers, J. M., & Williams, E. (1998). Screening and brief intervention for high-risk college student drinkers: Results from a 2-year follow-up assessment. *Journal of Consulting & Clinical Psychology, 66,* 604–615.

Marlatt, G. A., Baer, J. S., & Larimer, M. (1995). Preventing alcohol abuse in college students: A harm reduction approach. In G. M. Boyd, J. Howard, & R. A. Zucker (Eds.), *Alcohol problems among adolescents: Current directions in prevention research* (pp. 147–172). Hillsdale, NJ: Erlbaum.

Marlatt, G. A., Blume, A. W., & Parks, G. A. (2001). Integrating harm reduction therapy and traditional substance abuse treatment. *Journal of Psychoactive Drugs, 33,* 13–21.

Marlatt, G. A., Larimer, M. E., Baer, J. S., & Quigley, L. A. (1993). Harm reduction for alcohol problems: Moving beyond the controlled drinking economy. *Behavior Therapy, 24,* 461–503.

Marshall, G. N., & Orlando, M. (2002). Acculturation and peritraumatic dissociation in young adult Latino survivors of community violence. *Journal of Abnormal Psychology, 111,* 166–174.

Marshall, R. D., Beebee, K., Oldham, M., & Zaninelli, R. (2001). Efficacy and safety of paroxetine treatment for chronic PTSD: A fixed-dose, placebo-controlled study. *American Journal of Psychiatry, 158,* 1982–1988.

Marshall, R. D., & Galea, S. (2004). Science for the community: Assessing mental health after 9/11. *Journal of Clinical Psychiatry, 65*(Suppl. 1), 37–43.

Martenyi, F., Brown, E. B., Zhang, H., Koke, S. C., & Prakash, A. (2002). Fluoxetine v. placebo in prevention of relapse in post-traumatic stress disorder. *British Journal of Psychiatry, 181,* 315–320.

Martin, A., Scahill, L., Charney, D. S., & Leckman, J. F. (2002). *Pediatric psychopharmacology: Principles and practice.* New York: Oxford University Press.

Martin, C. S., & Bates, M. E. (1998). Psychological and psychiatric consequences of alcohol. In R. E. Tarter, R. T. Ammerman, & P. J. Ott (Eds.), *Handbook of substance abuse: Neurobehavioral pharmacology* (pp. 33–50). New York: Plenum Press.

Martin, J. L. R., Barbanoj, M. J., Schlaepfer, T. E., Thompson, E., Perez, V., & Kulisevsky, J. (2003). Repetitive transcranial magnetic stimulation for the treatment of depression: Systematic review and meta-analysis. *British Journal of Psychiatry, 182,* 480–491.

Maslow, A. H. (1954). *Motivation and personality.* New York: Harper & Row.

Masten, A. S., & Powell, J. L. (2003). A resilience framework for research, policy, and practice. In S. E. Luthar (Ed.), *Resilience and vulnerability: Adaptation in the context of childhood adversities* (pp. 1–25). New York: Cambridge University Press.

Masters, K. (1996, July 15). It hurts so much. *Time,* p. 148.

Masters, W. H., & Johnson, V. E. (1970). *Human sexual inadequacy.* Boston: Little, Brown.

Masters, W. H., Johnson, V. E., & Kolodny, R. C. (1993). *Biological foundations of human sexuality.* New York: HarperCollins.

Masters, W. H., Johnson, V. E., & Kolodny, R. C. (Eds.). (1979). *Ethical issues in sex therapy & research.* Boston: Little, Brown.

Matarazzo, J. D. (1985). Psychotherapy. In G. A. Kimble & K. Schlesinger (Eds.), *Topics in the history of psychology.* Hillsdale, NJ: Erlbaum.

Mathews, A., & MacLeod, C. (1994). Cognitive approaches to emotion and emotional disorders. *Annual Review of Psychology, 45,* 25–50.

Mathews, A., & MacLeod, C. (2005). *Annual Review of Clinical Psychology, 1,* 167–196.

Mathews, J. (1996, July 30). Pressures of supporting business, family leave widow little time to mourn. *Baltimore Sun,* p. 5B.

Matthews, A., Mogg, K., Kentish, J., & Eysenck, M. (1995). Effect of psychological treatment on cognitive bias in generalized anxiety disorder. *Behavior Research & Therapy, 33,* 293–303.

Matthews, K. A., Wing, R. R., Kuller, L. H., & Meilhan, E. N. (1990). Influences of natural menopause on psychological characteristics and symptoms of middle-aged healthy women. *Journal of Consulting & Clinical Psychology, 58,* 345–351.

Maughan, B., Pickles, A., Rowe, R., Costello, E. J., & Angold, A. (2000). Developmental trajectories of aggressive and non-aggressive conduct problems. *Journal of Quantitative Criminology, 16,* 199–221.

Maughan, B., Rowe, R., Messer, J., Goodman, R., & Meltzer, H. (2004). Conduct disorder and oppositional defiant disorder in a national sample: Developmental epidemiology. *Journal of Child Psychology & Psychiatry, 45,* 609–621.

Mausbach, B. T., Coon, D. W., Depp, C., Rabinowitz, Y. G., Wilson-Arias, E., Kraemer, H. C., Thompson, L. W., Lane, G., & Gallagher-Thompson, D. (2004). Ethnicity and time to institutionalization of dementia patients: A comparison of Latina and Caucasian female family caregivers. *Journal of the American Geriatrics Society, 52,* 1077–1084.

Max, W. (1993). The economic impact of Alzheimer's disease. *Neurology, 43,* S6–S10.

Maxmen, J. S., & Ward, N. G. (1995). *Essential psychopathology and its treatment.* New York: W. W. Norton.

May, R., & Yalom, I. (1995). Existential psychotherapy. In R. J. Corsini & D. Wedding (Eds.), *Current psychotherapies* (5th ed., pp. 363–402). Itasca, IL: Peacock.

Mayberg, H. S., Brannan, S. K., Mahurin, R. K., Jerabek, P. A., Brickman, J. S., et al. (1997). Cingulate function in depression: A potential predictor of treatment response. *NeuroReport, 8,* 1057–1061.

Mayeux, R. (1996). Understanding Alzheimer's disease: Expect more genes and other things. *Annals of Neurology, 39,* 689–690.

Mayeux, R., Denaro, J., Hemenegildo, N., & Marder, K. (1992). A population-based investigation of Parkinson's disease with and without dementia: Relationship to age and gender. *Archives of Neurology, 49,* 492–497.

Mayou, R., Bryant, B., & Ehlers, A. (2001). Prediction of psychological outcomes one year after a motor vehicle accident. *American Journal of Psychiatry, 158,* 1231–1238.

Mazzoni, G., & Loftus, E. F. (1998). Dream interpretations can change beliefs about the past. *Psychotherapy, 35,* 177–187.

McBride, A. A., Joe, G. W., & Simpson, D. D. (1991). Prediction of long-term alcohol use, drug use, and criminality among inhalant users. *Hispanic Journal of Behavioral Sciences, 13,* 315–323.

McBurnett, K., Lahey, B. B., Rathouz, P. L., & Loeber, R. (2000). Low salivary cortisol and persistent aggression in boys referred for disruptive behavior. *Archives of General Psychiatry, 57,* 38–43.

McBurnett, K., Pfiffner, L. J., & Frick, P. J. (2001). Symptom properties as a function of ADHD type: An argument for continued study of sluggish cognitive tempo. *Journal of Abnormal Child Psychology, 29,* 207–213.

McCabe, M. P., & Ricciardelli, L. A. (2004). Weight and shape concerns of boys and men. In J. K. Thompson (Ed.), *Handbook of eating disorders and obesity* (pp. 606–634). Hoboken, NJ: Wiley.

McCann, U. D., & Agras, W. S. (1990). Successful treatment of nonpurging bulimia nervosa with desipramine: A double-blind, placebo-controlled study. *American Journal of Psychiatry, 147,* 1509–1513.

McCarthy, B. W. (1989). Cognitive-behavioral strategies and techniques in the treatment of early ejaculation. In S. R. Leiblum & R. C. Rosen (Eds.), *Principles and practice of sex therapy: Update for the 1990s* (pp. 141–167). New York: Guilford Press.

McCarthy, B. W. (1997). Strategies and techniques for revitalizing a nonsexual marriage. *Journal of Sex & Marital Therapy, 23,* 231–240.

McCarthy, B. W. (2001). Relapse prevention strategies and techniques with erectile dysfunction. *Journal of Sex & Marital Therapy, 27,* 1–8.

McCarthy, M. (1990). The thin ideal, depression and eating disorders in women. *Behaviour Research & Therapy, 28,* 205–215.

McConaghy, N. (1998). Paedophilia: A review of the evidence. *Australian & New Zealand Journal of Psychiatry, 32,* 252–265.

McConnell, C. F., Bretz, K. M., & Dwyer, W. O. (2003). Falling asleep at the wheel: A close look at 1,269 fatal and serious injury-producing crashes. *Behavioral Sleep Medicine, 1,* 171–183.

McCormick, M. C., McCarton, C., Brooks-Gunn, J., Belt, P., & Gross, R. T. (1998). The infant health development program: Interim summary. *Developmental & Behavioral Pediatrics, 19,* 359–370.

McCrady, B. S. (2001). Alcohol use disorders. In D. H. Barlow (Ed.), *Clinical handbook of psychological disorders: A step-by-step treatment manual* (3rd ed., pp. 376–433). New York: Guilford Press.

McCrae, R. R., & Costa, P. T. (1999). A five-factor theory of personality. In L. A. Pervin (Ed.), *Handbook of personality: Theory and research* (2nd ed., pp. 139–153). New York: Guilford Press.

McDonald, K., & Thompson, J. K. (1992). Eating disturbance, body image dissatisfaction, and reasons for exercising: Gender differences and correlational findings. *International Journal of Eating Disorders, 11,* 289–292.

McFarlane, W. R., Lukens, E., Link, B., & Dushay, R. (1995). Multiple-family groups and psychoeducation in the treatment of schizophrenia. *Archives of General Psychiatry, 52,* 679–687.

McGhie, A., & Chapman, J. (1961). Disorders in attention and perception in early schizophrenia. *Schizophrenia Bulletin, 34,* 103–116.

McGlashan, T. H. (1988). A selective review of recent North American long-term followup studies of schizophrenia. *Schizophrenia Bulletin, 14,* 515–542.

McGovern, C. M. (1985). *Masters of madness.* Hanover, NH: University Press of New England.

McGreevy, M. A., Steadman, H. J., & Callahan, L. A. (1991). The negligible effects of California's 1982 reform of the insanity defense test. *American Journal of Psychiatry, 148,* 744–750.

McGue, M. (1999). The behavioral genetics of alcoholism. *Current Directions in Psychological Science, 8,* 109–115.

McGue, M., Iacono, W. G., Legrand, L. N., Malone, S., & Elkins, I. (2001). Origins and consequences of age at first drink: I. Associations with substance-use disorders, disinhibitory behavior and psychopathology, and P3 amplitude. *Alcoholism: Clinical & Experimental Research, 25,* 1156–1165.

McGue, M., Pickens, R. W., & Svikis, D. S. (1992). Sex and age effects on the inheritance of alcohol problems: A twin study. *Journal of Abnormal Psychology, 101,* 3–17.

McGuffin, P., & Katz, R. (1989). The genetics of depression and manic-depressive disorder. *British Journal of Psychiatry, 155,* 294–304.

McGuire, R. J., Carlisle, J. M., & Young, B. G. (1965). Sexual deviation as conditioned behavior. *Behavior Research & Therapy, 2,* 185–190.

McIntosh, D. N., Silver, R. C., & Wortman, C. B. (1993). Religion's role in adjustment to a negative life event: Coping with the loss of a child. *Journal of Personality & Social Psychology, 65,* 812–821.

McIntosh, J. L. (1995). Suicide prevention in the elderly (age 65–99). *Suicide & Life-Threatening Behaviors, 25,* 180–192.

McLean, P. D., Whittal, M. L., Thordarson, D. S., Taylor, S., Soechting, I., Koch, W. J., Paterson, R., & Anderson, K. W. (2001). Cognitive versus behavior therapy in the group treatment of obsessive-compulsive disorder. *Journal of Consulting & Clinical Psychology, 69,* 205–214.

McMillan, T. M., & Rachman, S. J. (1987). Fearlessness and courage: A laboratory study of paratrooper veterans of the Falklands War. *British Journal of Psychology, 78,* 375–383.

McNally, R. J. (1994). *Panic disorder: A critical analysis.* New York: Guilford Press.

McNally, R. J. (1996). Cognitive bias in the anxiety disorders. *Nebraska Symposium on Motivation, 43,* 211–250.

McNally, R. J. (1999a). Anxiety sensitivity and information-processing biases for threat. In S. Taylor (Ed.), *Anxiety sensitivity: Theory, research, and treatment of the fear of anxiety* (pp. 183–197). Mahwah, NJ: Erlbaum.

McNally, R. J. (1999b). On the experimental induction of panic. *Behavior therapy, 30,* 331–339.

McNally, R. J. (2003). Recovering memories of trauma: A view from the laboratory. *Current Directions in Psychological Science, 12,* 32–35.

McNally, R. J., Clancy, S. A., & Schacter, D. L. (2001). Directed forgetting of trauma cues in adults reporting repressed or recovered memories of childhood sexual abuse. *Journal of Abnormal Psychology, 110,* 151–156.

McNally, R. J., Clancy, S. A., Schacter, D. L., & Pitman, R. K. (2000a). Cognitive processing of trauma cues in adults reporting repressed, recovered, or continuous memories of childhood sexual abuse. *Journal of Abnormal Psychology, 109,* 355–359.

McNally, R. J., Clancy, S. A, Schacter, D. L., & Pitman, R. K. (2000b). Personality profiles, dissociation, and absorption in women reporting repressed, recovered, or continuous memories of childhood sexual abuse. *Journal of Consulting Clinical Psychology, 68,* 1033–1037.

McNiel, D. E., & Binder, R. L. (1991). Clinical assessment of the risk of violence among psychiatric inpatients. *American Journal of Psychiatry, 148,* 1317–1321.

McWilliams, N., & Weinberger, J. (2003). Psychodynamic psychotherapy. In G. Stricker & T. A. Widiger (Eds.), *Handbook of psychology: Clinical psychology* (Vol. 8, pp. 253–277). New York: Wiley.

Mechanic, D., & Bilder, S. (2004). Treatment of people with mental illness: A decade-long perspective. *Health Affairs, 23,* 84–95.

Mednick, B., Reznick, C., Hocevar, D., & Baker, R. (1987). Long-term effects of parental divorce on young adult male crime. *Journal of Youth & Adolescence, 16,* 31–45.

Mednick, S. A., Machon, R. A., Huttunen, M. O., & Bonett, D. (1988). Adult schizophrenia following prenatal exposure to an influenza epidemic. *Archives of General Psychiatry, 45,* 189–192.

Mednick, S. A., Watson, J. B., Huttunen, M., Cannon, T. D., Katila, H., Machon, R., Mednick, B., Hollister, M., Parnas, J., Schulsinger, F., Sajaniemi, N., Voldsgaard, P., Pyhala, R., Gutkind, D., & Wang, X. (1998). A two-hit working model of the etiology of schizophrenia. In M. F. Lenzenweger & R. H. Dworkin (Eds.), *Origins of the development of schizophrenia* (pp. 27–66). Washington, DC: American Psychological Association.

Megivern, D. (2002). Disability services and college students with psychiatric disabilities. *Journal of Social Work in Disability and Rehabilitation, 1,* 25–42.

Meichenbaum, D., & Jaremko, M. (Eds.). (1983). *Stress reduction and prevention.* New York: Plenum Press.

Mellon, M. W., & McGrath, M. L. (2000). Empirically supported treatments in pediatric psychology: Nocturnal enuresis. *Journal of Pediatric Psychology, 25,* 193–214.

Menza, M., Lauritano, M., Allen, L., Warman, M., Ostella, F., Hamer, R. M., & Escobar, J. (2001). Treatment of somatization with nefazodone: A prospective, open-label study. *Annals of Clinical Psychiatry, 13,* 153–158.

Merikangas, K. R., Dierker, L. C., & Szatmari, P. (1998). Psychopathology among offspring of parents with substance abuse and/or anxiety disorders: A high-risk study. *Journal of Child Psychology & Psychiatry, 5,* 711–720.

Merikangas, K. R., Lieb, R., Wittchen, H.-U., & Avenevoli, S. (2003). Family and high-risk studies of social anxiety disorder. *Acta Psychiatrica Scandinavica, 108*(Suppl. 417), 28–37.

Merikangas, K. R., Weissman, M. M., & Pauls, D. L. (1985). Genetic factors in the sex ratio of major depression. *Psychological Medicine, 15,* 63–69.

Merrill, L. L., Thomsen, C. J., Sinclair, B. B., Gold, S. R., & Milner, J. S. (2001). Predicting the impact of child sexual abuse on women: The role of abuse severity, parental support, and coping strategies. *Journal of Consulting & Clinical Psychology, 69,* 992–1006.

Mervaala, E., Fohr, J., Kononen, M., Valkonen-Korhonen, M., Vainino, P., et al. (2000). Quantitative MRI of the hippocampus and amygdala in severe depression. *Psychological Medicine, 30,* 117–125.

Merzenich, M. M., Jenkins, W. M., Johnston, P., Schreiner, C., Miller, S. L., & Tallal, P. (1996). Temporal processing deficits of language-learning impaired children ameliorated by training. *Science, 271*, 77–81.

Meston, C. M. (1997). Aging and sexuality: In successful aging. *Western Journal of Medicine, 167*, 285–290.

Mezzich, J. E., Kirmayer, L. J., Kleinman, A., Fabrega, H., Jr., Parron, D. L., Good, B. J., Lin, K.-M., & Manson, S. M. (1999). The place of culture in DSM-IV. *Journal of Nervous & Mental Disease, 187*, 457–464.

Micallef, J., & Blin, O. (2001). Neurobiology and clinical pharmacology of obsessive-compulsive disorder. *Clinical Neuropharmacology, 24*, 191–207.

Michael, R. T., Gagnon, J. H., Laumann, E., & Kolata, G. (1994). *Sex in America: A definitive survey.* Boston: Little, Brown.

Miklowitz, D. J., Simoneau, T. L., George, E. L., Richards, J. A., Kalbag, A., Sachs-Ericsson, N., & Suddath, R. (2000). Family-focused treatment of bipolar disorder: 1-year effects of a psychoeducational program in conjunction with pharmacotherapy. *Biological Psychiatry, 48*, 582–592.

Miklowitz, D. J., Velligan, D. I., Goldstein, M. J., & Nuechterlein, K. H. (1991). Communication deviance in families of schizophrenic and manic patients. *Journal of Abnormal Psychology, 100*, 163–173.

Milam, J. E., Richardson, J. L., Marks, G., Kemper, C. A., & McCutchan, A. J. (2004). The roles of dispositional optimism and pessimism in HIV disease progression. *Psychology & Health, 19*, 167–181.

Miller, J. B. (1976). *Toward a new psychology of women.* Boston: Beacon Press.

Miller, N. S. (Ed.). (1991). *Comprehensive handbook of drug and alcohol addiction.* New York: Dekker.

Miller, R., Newcomer, R., & Fox, P. (1999). Effects of the Medicare Alzheimer's disease demonstration on nursing home entry. *Health Services Research, 34*, 691–714.

Miller, S. D. (1989). Optical differences in cases of multiple personality disorder. *Journal of Nervous & Mental Disease, 177*, 480–486.

Miller, T. Q., Smith, T. W., Turner, C. W., & Guijarro, M. L. (1996). Meta-analytic review of research on hostility and physical health. *Psychological Bulletin, 119*, 322–348.

Millon, T. (1969). *Modern psychopathology: A biosocial approach to maladaptive learning and functioning.* Philadelphia: Saunders.

Millon, T., Davis, R., Millon, C., Escovar, L., & Meagher, S. (2000). *Personality disorders in modern life.* New York: Wiley.

Milne, A. A. (1961). *Winnie-the-Pooh.* New York: E. P. Dutton.

Mineka, S. (1985). Animal models of anxiety based disorders: Their usefulness and limitations. In A. H. Tuma & J. Maser (Eds.), *Anxiety and the anxiety disorders* (pp. 199–244). Hillsdale, NJ: Erlbaum.

Mineka, S., Davidson, M., Cook, M., & Keir, R. (1984). Observational conditioning of snake fear in rhesus monkeys. *Journal of Abnormal Psychology, 93*, 355–372.

Mineka, S., Gunnar, M., & Champoux, M. (1986). Control and early socioemotional development: Infant rhesus monkeys reared in controllable versus uncontrollable environments. *Child Development, 57*, 1241–1256.

Mineka, S., & Kelly, K. A. (1989). The relationship between anxiety, lack of control and loss of control. In A. Steptoe (Ed.), *Stress, personal control and health* (pp. 163–191). Chichester, UK: Wiley.

Mineka, S., & Zinbarg, R. (1998). Experimental approaches to the anxiety and mood disorders. In J. G. Adair (Ed.), *Advances in psychological science: Vol. 1. Social, personal, and cultural aspects* (pp. 429–454). Hove, UK: Psychology Press/Erlbaum Taylor & Francis.

Minshew, N. J., Sweeney, J. A., & Bauman, M. L. (1997). Neurological aspects of autism. In D. J. Cohen & F. R. Volkmar (Eds.), *Handbook of autism and pervasive developmental disorders* (pp. 344–369). Toronto: Wiley.

Minuchin, S. (1981). *Family therapy techniques.* Cambridge, MA: Harvard University Press.

Minuchin, S., Rosman, B. L., & Baker, L. (1978). *Psychosomatic families: Anorexia nervosa in context.* Cambridge, MA: Harvard University Press.

Miranda, J., Bernal, G., Lau, A., Kohn, L., Hwang, W. C., & La Fromboise, T. (2005). *Annual Review of Clinical Psychology, 1*, 113–142.

Mirsalimi, H., Perleberg, S. H., Stovall, E. L., & Kaslow, N. J. (2003). Family psychotherapy. In G. Stricker & T. A. Widiger (Eds.), *Handbook of psychology: Clinical psychology* (Vol. 8, pp. 367–387). New York: Wiley.

Mirsky, A. E., Bieliauskas, L. A., French, L. M., Van Kammen, D. P., Joensson, E., & Sedvall, S. (2000). A 39-year follow-up on the Genain quadruplets. *Schizophrenia Bulletin, 26*, 699–708.

Mitler, M. M., & Miller, J. C. (1995). Some practical considerations and policy implications of studies and sleep patterns. *Behavioral Medicine, 21*, 184–185.

Mitropoulou, V., Barch, D., Harvey, P., Maldari, L., New, B., Cornblatt, B., & Siever, L. (2003). Two studies of attentional processing in schizotypal personality disorder. *Schizophrenia Research, 60*, S148.

Mitropoulou, V., Harvey, P. D., Maldari, L. A., Moriarty, P. J., New, A. S., Silverman, J. M., & Siever, L. J. (2002). Neuropsychological performance in schizotypal personality disorder: Evidence regarding diagnostic specificity. *Biological Psychiatry, 52*, 1175–1182.

Moffitt, T. E. (1990). Juvenile delinquency and attention deficit disorder: Boys' developmental trajectories from age 3 to age 15. *Child Development, 61*, 893–910.

Moffitt, T. E. (1993). The neuropsychology of conduct disorder. *Development & Psychopathology, 5*, 135–151.

Moffitt, T. E., Brammer, G. L., Caspi, A., Fawcet, J. P., Raleigh, M., Yuwiler, A., & Silva, P. A. (1998). Whole blood serotonin relates to violence in an epidemiological study. *Biological Psychiatry, 43*, 446–457.

Moffitt, T. E., & Caspi, A. (2001). Childhood predictors differentiate life-course persistent and adolescence-limited antisocial pathways among males and females. *Development & Psychopathology, 13*, 355–375.

Moffitt, T. E., Caspi, A., Harrington, H., & Milne, B. J. (2001). Males on the life-course persistent and adolescence-limited antisocial pathways: Follow-up at age 26. *Developmental Psychology, 14*, 179–206.

Moffitt, T. E., Caspi, A., Rutter, M., & Silva, P. A. (2001). *Sex differences in antisocial behaviour: Conduct disorder, delinquency, and violence in the Dunedin Longitudinal Study.* Cambridge, UK: Cambridge University Press.

Moffitt, T. E., & Silva, P. A. (1988). Self-reported delinquency, neuropsychological deficit, and history of attention deficit disorder. *Journal of Abnormal Child Psychology, 16*, 553–569.

Molgaard, C. A., Nakamura, C. M., Stanford, E. P., Peddecord, K. M., & Morton, D. J. (1990). Prevalence of alcohol consumption among older persons. *Journal of Community Health, 15*, 239–251.

Molnar, B. E., Berkman, L. F., & Buka, S. L. (2001). Psychopathology, childhood sexual abuse and other childhood adversities: Relative links to subsequent suicidal behavior in the U.S. *Psychological Medicine, 31*, 965–977.

Monahan, J. (2001). Major mental disorder and violence: Epidemiology and risk assessment. In G. Pinard (Ed.), *Clinical assessment of dangerousness: Empirical contributions* (pp. 89–102). New York: Cambridge University Press.

Monahan, J., Bonnie, R. J., Appelbaum, P. S., Hyde, P. S., Steadman, H. J., & Swartz, M. S. (2001). Mandated community treatment: Beyond outpatient commitment. *Psychiatric Services, 52*, 1198–1205.

Monahan, J., Lidz, C. W., Hoge, S. K., Mulvey, E. P., Eisenberg, M. M., Roth, L. H., Gardner, W. P., & Bennett, N. (1999). Coercion in the provision of mental health services: The MacArthur studies. In J. Morrissey & J. Monahan (Eds.), *Research in community and mental health* (Vol. 10, pp. 13–30). Stamford, CT: JAI Press.

Monahan, J., & Steadman, H. J. (2001). Violence risk assessment: A quarter century of research. In L. E. Frost (Ed.), *The evolution of mental health law* (pp. 195–211). Washington, DC: American Psychological Association.

Monahan, J., & Walker, L. (1990). *Social science in law: Cases and materials.* Westbury, NY: Foundation Press.

Money, J., & Schwartz, M. (1976). Fetal androgens in the early treated adrenogenital syndrome of 46 XX hermaphroditism: Influence on assertive and aggressive types of behavior. *Aggressive Behavior, 2*, 19–30.

Monitoring the Future. (2002). 2002 data from in-school surveys of 8th, 10th, and 12th grade students. Retrieved November 1, 2004, from: http://monitoringthefuture.org/data/02data .html

Monroe, S. M., & Hadjiyannakis, K. (2002). The social environment and depression: Focusing on severe life stress. In I. H. Gotlib & C. L. Hammen (Eds.), *Handbook of depression* (pp. 314–340). New York: Guilford Press.

Montgomery, S. A., Entsuah, R., Hackett, D., Kunz, N. R., & Rudolph, R. L. (2004). Venlafaxine versus placebo in the preventive treatment of recurrent major depression. *Journal of Clinical Psychiatry, 65*, 328–336.

Mooney, M. E., & Hatsukami, D. K. (2001). Combined treatments for smoking cessation. In M. T. Sammons & N. B. Schmidt (Eds.), *Combined treatments for mental disorders* (pp. 191–213). Washington, DC: American Psychological Association.

Morey, L. C. (1993). Psychological correlates of personality disorder. *Journal of Personality Disorders* (Suppl.), 149–166.

Morgan, A. B., & Lilienfeld, S. O. (2000). A meta-analytic review of the relation between antisocial behavior and neuropsychological measures of executive function. *Clinical Psychological Review, 20,* 113–136.

Morgan, C. A., Hazlett, G., Wang, S., Richardson, E. G., Jr., Schnurr, P., & Southwick, S. M. (2001). Symptoms of dissociation in humans experiencing acute, uncontrollable stress: A prospective investigation. *American Journal of Psychiatry, 158,* 1239–1247.

Mori, D., Chaiken, S., & Pliner, P. (1987). "Eating lightly" and the self-presentation of femininity. *Journal of Personality & Social Psychology, 53,* 693–702.

Morokoff, P. J., & Gilliland, R. (1993). Stress, sexual functioning, and marital satisfaction. *Journal of Sex Research, 30,* 43–53.

Morrison, N. K. (1998). Behavioral pharmacology of hallucinogens. In R. E. Tarter (Ed.), *Handbook of substance abuse: Neurobehavioral pharmacology* (pp. 229–240). New York: Plenum Press.

Mortensen, P. B. (2003). Mortality and physical illness in schizophrenia. In R. M. Murray & P. B. Jones (Eds.), *The epidemiology of schizophrenia* (pp. 275–287). New York: Cambridge University Press.

Moscicki, E. (1995). Epidemiology of suicidal behavior. *Suicide & Life-Threatening Behavior, 25,* 22–35.

Mowrer, O. H. (1939). A stimulus-response analysis of anxiety and its role as a reinforcing agent. *Psychological Review, 46,* 553–566.

Mueser, K. T., Bellack, A. S., Morrison, R. L., & Wade, J. H. (1990). Gender, social competence, and symptomatology in schizophrenia: A longitudinal analysis. *Journal of Abnormal Psychology, 99,* 138–147.

Mukherjee, S., Shukla, S., Woodle, J., Rosen, A. M., & Olarte, S. (1983). Misdiagnosis of schizophrenia in bipolar patients: A multiethnic comparison. *American Journal of Psychiatry, 140,* 1571–1574.

Mulholland, A. M., & Mintz, L. B. (2001). Prevalence of eating disorders among African American women. *Journal of Consulting & Clinical Psychology, 48,* 111–116.

Mulvey, E. P. (1995). Personal communication.

Mulvey, E. P., Geller, J. L., & Roth, L. H. (1987). The promise and peril of involuntary outpatient commitment. *American Psychologist, 42,* 571–584.

Munoz, R. F. (1997). The San Francisco Depression Prevention Research Project. In G. W. Albee (Ed.), *Primary prevention works* (pp. 380–400). Thousand Oaks, CA: Sage.

Munoz, R. F., Le, H. N., Clarke, G., & Jaycox, L. (2002). Preventing the onset of major depression. In I. H. Gotlib & C. L. Hammen (Eds.), *Handbook of depression* (pp. 343–359). New York: Guilford Press.

Munoz, R. F., Mrazek, P. J., & Haggerty, R. J. (1996). Institute of Medicine report on prevention of mental disorders: Summary and commentary. *American Psychologist, 51,* 1116–1122.

Munoz, R. F., Ying, Y. W., Bernal, G., Perez-Stable, E. J., Sorensen, J. L., Hargreaves, W. A., Miranda, J., & Miller, L. S. (1995). Prevention of depression with primary care patients: A randomized controlled trial. *American Journal of Community Psychology, 23,* 199–222.

Murden, R. A., McRae, T. D., Kaner, S., & Bucknam, M. E. (1991). Minimental state exam scores vary with education in blacks and whites. *Journal of the American Geriatrics Society, 39,* 149–155.

Murphy, J. M. (1976). Psychiatric labeling in cross-cultural perspective. *Science, 191,* 1019–1028.

Murray, C. J., & Lopez, A. D. (1996). *The global burden of disease: A comprehensive assessment of mortality and disabilities from diseases, injuries, and risk factors in 1990 and projected to 2020.* Cambridge, MA: Harvard University School of Public Health.

Murray, H. A. (1943). *Thematic apperception test manual.* Cambridge, MA: Harvard University Press.

N

Nadder, T. S., Silberg, J. L., Eaves, L. J., Maes, H. H., & Meyer, J. M. (1998). Genetic effects on ADHD symptomatology in 7- to 13-year-old twins: Results from a telephone survey. *Behavior Genetics, 28,* 83–99.

Nakao, M., Nomura, S., Shimosawa, T., Yoshiuchi, K., Kumano, H., Kuboki, T., Suematsu, H., & Fujita, T. (1997). Clinical effects of blood pressure biofeedback treatment on hypertension by auto-shaping. *Psychosomatic Medicine, 59,* 331–338.

Napiorkowski, B., Lester, B. M., Freier, C., Brunner, S., Dietz, L., Nadra, A., & Oh, W. (1996). Effects of in utero substance exposure on infant neurobehavior. *Pediatrics, 98,* 71–75.

Naranjo, C. A., & Knoke, D. M. (2001). The role of selective serotonin reuptake inhibitors in reducing alcohol consumption. *Journal of Clinical Psychiatry, 62*(Suppl. 20), 18–25.

Narrow, W. E., Regier, D. A., Rae, D., Manderscheid, R. W., & Locke, B. Z. (1993). Use of services by persons with mental and addictive disorders. *Archives of General Psychiatry, 50,* 95–107.

Nasar, S. (1998). *A beautiful mind.* New York: Simon & Schuster.

National Institute of Mental Health (NIMH). (2002). Suicide facts. Retrieved from the World Wide Web: http://www.nimh.nih.gov/research/suifact.htm

National Institute on Drug Abuse (NIDA). (2002a). Cocaine abuse and addiction. Retrieved from the World Wide Web: http://www.drugabuse.gov/ResearchReports/Cocaine/ cocaine2.html

National Institute on Drug Abuse (NIDA). (2002b). Heroin: Abuse and addiction. Retrieved from the World Wide Web: http://www.drugabuse.gov/ResearchReports/heroin/ heroin2.html

National Institute on Drug Abuse (NIDA). (2002c). Inhalant abuse. Retrieved from the World Wide Web: http://www.drugabuse.gov/ResearchReports/Inhalants/inhalants2.html

National Institute on Drug Abuse (NIDA). (2002d). Methamphetamine: Abuse and addiction. Retrieved from the World Wide Web: http://www.drugabuse.gov/ResearchReports/Methamph/methamph2.html

National Institute on Drug Abuse (NIDA). (2002e). Nicotine addiction. Retrieved from the World Wide Web: http://www.drugabuse.gov/ResearchReports/ Nicotine/nicotine2.html

National Institute on Drug Abuse (NIDA). (2002f). Prescription drugs: Abuse and addiction. Retrieved from the World Wide Web: http://www.drugabuse.gov/ResearchReports/Prescription/prescription2.html

Neal, J. A., & Edelmann, R. J. (2003). The etiology of social phobia: Toward a developmental profile. *Clinical Psychology Review, 23,* 761–786.

Neighbors, H. W. (1984). Professional help use among black Americans: Implications for unmet need. *American Journal of Community Psychology, 12,* 551–566.

Neighbors, H. W., Trierweiler, S. J., Ford, B. C., & Muroff, J. R. (2003). Racial differences in DSM diagnosis using a semi-structured instrument: The importance of clinical judgment in the diagnosis of African Americans. *Journal of Health & Social Behavior, 43,* 237–256.

Neighbors, H. W., Williams, D. H., Gunnings, T. S., Lipscomb, W. D., Broman, C., & Lepkowski, J. (1987). *The prevalence of mental disorder in Michigan prisons: Final report.* Ann Arbor: Michigan Department of Corrections, University of Michigan, School of Public Health, Department of Community Health Programs, Community Mental Health Program.

Nelson, C. B., & Wittchen, H. (1998). DSM-IV alcohol disorders in a general population sample of adolescents and young adults. *Addiction, 93,* 1065–1077.

Nelson, J. C., Mazure, C. M., Jatlow, P. I., Bowers, M. B., Jr., & Price, L. H. (2004). Combining norepinephrine and serotonin reuptake inhibition mechanisms for treatment of depression: A double-blind, randomized study. *Biological Psychiatry, 55,* 296–300.

Nemeroff, C. B. (2000). An ever-increasing pharmacopoeia for the management of patients with bipolar disorder. *Journal of Clinical Psychiatry, 61*(Suppl. 13), 19–25.

Nemeroff, C. B. (2004). Neurobiological consequences of childhood trauma. *Journal of Clinical Psychiatry, 65*(Suppl. 1), 18–28.

Nemeroff, C. B., & Schatzberg, A. F. (1998). Pharmacological treatment of unipolar depression. In P. E. Nathan (Ed.), *A guide to treatments that work* (pp. 212–225). New York: Oxford University Press.

Nemeroff, C. J., Stein, R. I., Diehl, N. S., & Smilack, K. M. (1994). From the Cleavers to the Clintons: Role choices and body orientation as reflected in magazine article content. *International Journal of Eating Disorders, 16,* 167–176.

Nestadt, G., Romanoski, A. J., Chahal, R., & Merchant, A. (1990). An epidemiological study of histrionic personality disorder. *Psychological Medicine, 20,* 413–422.

Nestadt, G., Samuels, J., Riddle, M., Bienvenu, J., Liang, K., LaBuda, M., Walkup, J., Grados, M., & Hoehn-Saric, R. (2000). A family study of obsessive-compulsive disorder. *Archives of General Psychiatry, 57,* 358–363.

Neugebauer, R. (1979). Medieval and early modern theories of mental illness. *Archives of General Psychiatry, 36,* 477–483.

Neuner, F., Schauer, M., Klaschik, C., Karunakara, U., & Elbert, T. (2004). A comparison of narrative exposure therapy, supportive counseling, and psychoeducation for treating posttraumatic stress disorder in an African refugee settlement. *Journal of Consulting & Clinical Psychology, 72,* 579–587.

Newhill, C. E., Mulvey, E. P., & Lidz, C. W. (1995). Characteristics of violence in the community by female patients seen in a psychiatric emergency service. *Psychiatric Services, 46,* 785–789.

Newmann, J. P. (1989). Aging and depression. *Psychology & Aging, 4,* 150–165.

Newmann, J. P., Engel, R. J., & Jensen, J. E. (1991). Age differences in depressive symptom experiences. *Journal of Gerontology, 46,* P224–P235.

Newsweek. (2003, October 20). I am addicted to prescription pain medication. [Electronic version]. *Newsweek.*

New York Times/**CBS News Poll.** (1999, October 20). Teenagers' concerns. *New York Times,* p. A1.

Nicholson, R. A., & Kugler, K. E. (1991). Competent and incompetent criminal defendants: A quantitative review of comparative research. *Psychological Bulletin, 109,* 355–370.

Nicol-Smith, L. (1996). Causality, menopause, and depression: A critical review of the literature. *British Medical Journal, 313,* 1229–1232.

Nigg, J. T., & Goldsmith, H. H. (1994). Genetics of personality disorders: Perspectives from personality and psychopathology research. *Psychological Bulletin, 115,* 346–380.

Nock, M. K., & Kazdin, A. E. (2001). Parent expectancies for child therapy: Assessment and relation to participant in treatment. *Journal of Child & Family Studies, 10,* 155–180.

Noga, J. T., Vladar, K., & Torrey, E. F. (2001). A volumetric magnetic resonance imaging study of monozygotic twins discordant for bipolar disorder. *Psychiatry Research: Neuroimaging, 106,* 25–34.

Nolen-Hoeksema, S. (1990). *Sex differences in depression.* Stanford, CA: Stanford University Press.

Nolen-Hoeksema, S. (2000). The role of rumination in depressive disorders and mixed anxiety/depressive symptoms. *Journal of Abnormal Psychology, 109,* 504–511.

Nolen-Hoeksema, S. (2002). Gender differences in depression. In I. H. Gotlib & C. L. Hammen (Eds.), *Handbook of depression* (pp. 492–509). New York: Guilford Press.

Nolen-Hoeksema, S. (2003). The response styles theory. In C. Papageorgiou & A. Wells (Eds.), *Depressive rumination: Nature, theory, and treatment* (pp. 107–124). New York: Wiley.

Nolen-Hoeksema, S. (2004). Gender differences in risk factors and consequences for alcohol use and problems. *Clinical Psychology Review, 24,* 981–1010.

Nolen-Hoeksema, S. (2006). *Eating, Drinking, Overthinking: The Toxic Triangle of Food, Alcohol, and Depression—And Women Can Break Free.* New York: Henry Holt.

Nolen-Hoeksema, S., & Jackson, B. (2001). Mediators of the gender difference in rumination. *Psychology of Women Quarterly, 25,* 37–47.

Nolen-Hoeksema, S., & Larson, J. (1999). *Coping with loss.* Mahwah, NJ: Erlbaum.

Nolen-Hoeksema, S., Larson, J., & Grayson, C. (1999). Explaining the gender difference in depressive symptoms. *Journal of Personality & Social Psychology, 77,* 1061–1072.

Nolen-Hoeksema, S., & Morrow, J. (1991). A prospective study of depression and distress following a natural disaster: The 1989 Loma Prieta earthquake. *Journal of Personality & Social Psychology, 61,* 105–121.

Nolen-Hoeksema, S., Parker, L. E., & Larson, J. (1994). Ruminative coping with depressed mood following loss. *Journal of Personality & Social Psychology, 67,* 92–104.

Nopoulos, P., Flaum, M., & Andreasen, N. C. (1997). Sex differences in brain morphology in schizophrenia. *American Journal of Psychiatry, 154,* 1648–1654.

Norcross, J. C. (2002). Empirically supported therapy relationships. In J. C. Norcross (Ed.), *Psychotherapy relationships that work: Therapist contributions and responsiveness to patients* (pp. 3–16). London: Oxford University Press.

Norcross, J. C., Beutler, L. E., & Caldwell, R. (2002). Integrative conceptualization and treatment of depression. In M. A. Reinecke & M. R. Davidson (Eds.), *Comparative treatments of depression* (pp. 397–426). New York: Springer.

Nordin, V., & Gillberg, C. (1998). The long-term course of autistic disorders: Update on follow-up studies. *Acta Psychiatrica Scandinavica, 97,* 99–108.

Norman, R. M., & Malla, A. K. (1993). Stressful life events and schizophrenia: II. Conceptual and methodological issues. *British Journal of Psychiatry, 162,* 166–174.

Norris, F. H., Perilla, J. L., Ibanez, G. E., & Murphy, A. D. (2001). Sex differences in symptoms of posttraumatic stress: Does culture play a role? *Journal of Traumatic Stress, 14,* 7–28.

Norris, F. H., & Uhl, G. A. (1993). Chronic stress as a mediator of acute stress: The case of Hurricane Hugo. *Journal of Applied Social Psychology, 23,* 1263–1284.

Northey, W. F., Jr., & Primer, V. (2004). Comprehensive handbook of psychotherapy. *Journal of Marital & Family Therapy, 30,* 108–109.

Nowell, P. D., Buysse, D. J., Morin, C. M., Reynolds, III, C. F., & Kuper, D. J. (1998). Effective treatments for selected sleep disorders. In P. E. Nathan (Ed.), *A guide to treatments that work* (pp. 531–543). New York: Oxford University Press.

Noyes, R., Crowe, R. R., Harris, E. L., Hamra, B. J., McChesney, C. M., & Chaudhry, D. R. (1986). Relationship between panic disorder and agoraphobia: A family study. *Archives of General Psychiatry, 43,* 227–232.

Noyes, R., Langbehn, D. R., Happel, R. L., Stout, L. R., Muller, B. A., & Longley, S. L. (2001). Personality dysfunction among somatizing patients. *Psychosomatics, 42,* 320–329.

Nunes, E. V., & Levin, F. R. (2004). Treatment of depression in patients with alcohol or other drug dependence: A meta-analysis. *Journal of the American Medical Association, 291,* 1887–1896.

Nutt, D. J., & Malizia, A. L. (2004). Structural and functional brain changes in posttraumatic stress disorder. *Journal of Clinical Psychiatry, 65*(Suppl. 1), 11–17.

O

O'Brien, C. P., & McKay, J. R. (1998). Psychopharmacological treatments of substance use disorders. In P. E. Nathan (Ed.), *A guide to treatments that work* (pp. 127–155). New York: Oxford University Press.

O'Connor, K., Hallam, R., & Rachman, S. (1985). Fearlessness and courage: A replication experiment. *British Journal of Psychology, 76,* 187–197.

O'Donnell, L., O'Donnell, C., Wardlaw, D. M., & Stueve, A. (2004). Risk and resiliency factors influencing suicidality among urban African American and Latino youth. *American Journal of Community Psychology, 33,* 37–49.

Office of Ethnic Minority Affairs, American Psychological Association. (1993). Guidelines for providers of psychological services to ethnic, linguistic, and culturally diverse populations. *American Psychologist, 48,* 45–48.

Offord, D. R. (1997). Bridging development, prevention, and policy. In D. M. Stoff, J. Breiling, & J. D. Maser (Eds.), *Handbook of antisocial personality disorder* (pp. 357–364). New York: Wiley.

Offord, D. R., Boyle, M. H., Racine, Y. A., & Fleming, J. E. (1992). Outcome, prognosis, and risk in a longitudinal follow-up study. *Journal of the American Academy of Child & Adolescent Psychiatry, 31,* 916–923.

O'Hara, M. W., & Swain, A. M. (1996). Rates and risk of postpartum depression—A meta-analysis. *International Review of Psychiatry, 8,* 37–54.

Ohman, A., Fredrikson, M., Hugdahl, K., & Rimmo, P. (1976). The premise of equipotentiality in human classical conditioning: Conditioned electrodermal responses to potentially phobic stimuli. *Journal of Experimental Psychology: General, 105,* 313–337.

Okazaki, S., & Sue, S. (2003). Methodological issues in assessment research with ethnic minorities. In A. E. Kazdin (Ed.), *Methodological issues & strategies in clinical research* (3rd ed., pp. 349–367). Washington, DC: American Psychological Association.

O'Leary, A. (1990). Stress, emotion, and human immune function. *Psychological Bulletin, 108,* 363–382.

Olfson, M., Marcus, S., Sackheim, H. A., Thompson, J., & Pincus, H. A. (1998). Use of ECT for the inpatient treatment of recurrent major depression. *American Journal of Psychiatry, 155,* 22–29.

Olin, S. S., Raine, A., Cannon, T. D., Parnas, J., Schulsinger, F., & Mednick, S. A. (1999). Childhood behavior precursors of schizotypal personality disorder. *Schizophrenia Bulletin, 23,* 93–103.

Olivardia, R., Pope, H. G., Mangweth, B., & Hudson, J. I. (1995). Eating disorders in college men. *American Journal of Psychiatry, 152,* 1279–1285.

Olmos de Paz, T. (1990). Working-through and insight in child psychoanalysis. *Melanie Klein & Object Relations, 8,* 99–112.

Olson, H. C., Feldman, J. J., Streissguth, A. P., Sampson, P. D., & Boostein, F. L. (1998). Neuropsychological deficits in adolescents with fetal alcohol syndrome: Clinical findings. *Alcoholism: Clinical & Experimental Research, 22,* 1998–2012.

Ondersma, S. J., & Walker, C. E. (1998). Elimination disorders. In T. H. Ollendick & M. Hersen (Eds.), *Handbook of child psychopathology* (pp. 355–380). New York: Plenum Press.

Oquendo, M. A., Ellis, S. P., Greenwald, S., Malone, K. M., Weissman, M. M., & Mann, J. J. (2001). Ethnic and sex differences in suicide rates relative to major depression in the United States. *American Journal of Psychiatry, 158,* 1652–1658.

Oquendo, M. A., Malone, K. M., Ellis, S. P., Sackeim, H. A., & Mann, J. J. (1999). Inadequacy of antidepressant treatment for patients with major depression who are at risk for suicidal behavior. *American Journal of Psychiatry, 156,* 190–194.

Oquendo, M. A., & Mann, J. J. (2000). The biology of impulsivity and suicidality. *Psychiatric Clinics of North America, 23,* 11–25.

Orsillo, S. M., Weathers, F. W., Litz, B. T., Steinberg, H. R., Huska, J. A., & Keane, T. M. (1996). Current and lifetime psychiatric disorders among veterans with war zone–Related posttraumatic stress disorder. *Journal of Nervous & Mental Disease, 184,* 307–313.

Öst, L. (1992). Blood and injection phobia: Background and cognitive, physiological, and behavioral variables. *Journal of Abnormal Psychology, 101,* 68–74.

Öst, L., Svensson, L., Hellström, K., & Lindwall, R. (2001). One-session treatment of phobias in youths: A randomized clinical trial. *Journal of Consulting & Clinical Psychology, 69,* 814–824.

Öst, L. S., & Sterner, U. (1987). Applied tension: A specific behavioral method for treatment of blood phobia. *Behaviour Research & Therapy, 25,* 25–29.

Osvold, L. L., & Sodowsky, G. R. (1993). Eating disorders of white American, racial and ethnic minority American, and international women. Special issue: Multicultural health issues. *Journal of Multicultural Counseling & Development, 21,* 143–154.

Overmier, J. B., & Seligman, M. E. (1967). Effects of inescapable shock upon subsequent escape and avoidance responding. *Journal of Comparative & Physiological Psychology, 63,* 28–33.

Ozonoff, S., & Cathcart, K. (1998). Effectiveness of a home program intervention for young children with autism. *Journal of Autism & Developmental Disorders, 28,* 25–32.

P

Paffenberger, R. S., Hyde, R. T., Wing, A. L., & Hsieh, C. (1986). Physical activity, all-cause mortality, and longevity of college alumni. *New England Journal of Medicine, 314,* 605–613.

Palazzoli, M. S. (1974). *Self-starvation: From the intrapsychic to the transpersonal approach to anorexia nervosa* (A. Pomerans, Trans.). London: Chaucer.

Pappenheim, B. (1936). *Gebete. Ausgewahlt und herausgegeben vom Judischen Frauenbund.* Berlin: Philo Verlag.

Pariante, C. M., & Miller, A. H. (2001). Glucocorticoid receptors in major depression: Relevance to pathophysiology and treatment. *Biological Psychiatry, 49,* 391–404.

Parker, G., Johnston, P., & Hayward, L. (1988). Parental "expressed emotion" as a predictor of schizophrenic relapse. *Archives of General Psychiatry, 45,* 806–813.

Parks, G. A., Anderson, B. K., & Marlatt, G. A. (2001). Relapse prevention therapy. In N. Heather, T. J. Peters, & T. Stockwell (Eds.), *International handbook of alcohol dependence and problems* (pp. 575–592). New York: Wiley.

Parrott, A. C. (1998). Nesbitt's Paradox resolved? Stress and arousal modulation during cigarette smoking. *Addiction, 93,* 27–39.

Pate, J. E., Pumariega, A. J., Hester, C., & Garner, D. M. (1992). Cross-cultural patterns in eating disorders: A review. *Journal of the American Academy of Child & Adolescent Psychiatry, 31,* 802–809.

Patterson, R. (1994). *Opening remarks.* Paper presented at the National Forum on Creating Jail Mental Health Services for Tomorrow's Health Care Systems, San Francisco.

Pauli, P., Dengler, W., Wiedemann, G., Montoya, P., Flor, H., Birbaumer, N., & Buchkremer, G. (1997). Behavioral and neurophysiological evidence for altered processing of anxiety-related words in panic disorder. *Journal of Abnormal Psychology, 106,* 213–220.

Pauls, D. A., Morton, L. A., & Egeland, J. A. (1992). Risks of affective illness among first-degree relatives of bipolar I old-order Amish probands. *Archives of General Psychiatry, 49,* 703–708.

Paunovic, N., & Öst, L. (2001). Cognitive-behavior therapy vs exposure therapy in the treatment of PTSD in refugees. *Behaviour Research & Therapy, 39,* 1183–1197.

Pavlov, I. P. (1927). *Conditioned reflexes: An investigation of the physiological activity of the cerebral cortex.* London: Oxford University Press.

Pendery, M. L., Maltzman, I. M., & West, L. J. (1982). Controlled drinking by alcoholics? New findings and a reevaluation of a major affirmative study. *Science, 217,* 169–175.

Pennebaker, J. W. (1990). *Opening up: The healing power of confiding in others.* New York: William Morrow.

Pennebaker, J. W., & O'Heeron, R. C. (1984). Confiding in others and illness rates among spouses of suicide and accidental-death victims. *Journal of Abnormal Psychology, 93,* 473–476.

Perourka, S. J., Newman, H., & Harris, H. (1988). Subjective effects of 3, 4-methylenedioxymethamphetamine in recreational users. *Neuropsychopharmacology, 1,* 273–277.

Perry, J. C. (1993). Longitudinal studies of personality disorders. *Journal of Personality Disorders* (Suppl. 1), 63–85.

Perugi, G., Akiskal, H. S., Giannotti, D., Frare, F., Di Vaio, S., & Cassano, G. B. (1997). Gender-related differences in body dysmorphic disorder (dysmorphophobia). *Journal of Nervous & Mental Disease, 185,* 578–582.

Petegnief, V., Saura, J., De Gregorio-Rocasolano, N., & Paul, S. M. (2001). Neuronal injury-induced expression and release of apolipoprotein E in mixed neuron/GLIA co-cultures: Nuclear factor KB inhibitors reduce basal and lesion-induced secretion of apolipoprotein E. *Neuroscience, 104,* 223–234.

Peterson, C., & Seligman, M. E. (1984). Causal explanations as a risk factor for depression: Theory and evidence. *Psychological Review, 91,* 347–374.

Peterson, C., Seligman, M. E., & Vaillant, G. E. (1988). Pessimistic explanatory style is a risk factor for physical illness: A thirty-five-year longitudinal study. *Journal of Personality & Social Psychology, 55,* 23–27.

Peterson, C., Seligman, M. E. P., Yurko, K. H., Martin, L. R., & Friedman, H. S. (1998). Catastrophizing and untimely death. *Psychological Science, 9,* 127–130.

Peterson, G. (1991). Children coping with trauma: Diagnosis of "dissociation identity disorder." *Dissociation: Progress in the Dissociation Disorders, 4,* 152–164.

Petronis, K. R., Samuels, J. F., Moscicki, E. K., & Anthony, J. C. (1990). An epidemiologic investigation of potential risk factors for suicide attempts. *Social Psychiatry & Psychiatric Epidemiology, 25,* 193–199.

Pettit, G. S., Dodge, K. A., & Brown, M. M. (1988). Early family experience, social problem solving patterns, and children's social competence. *Child Development, 59,* 107–120.

Pfeffer, C. R. (1985). Suicidal tendencies in normal children. *Journal of Nervous & Mental Disease, 173,* 78–84.

Pfefferbaum, B., Gurwitch, R. H., McDonald, N. B., Leftwich, M. J. T., Sconzo, G. M., Messenbaugh, A. K., & Schultz, R. (2000). Posttraumatic stress among young children after the death of a friend or acquaintance in a terrorist bombing. *Psychiatric Services, 51,* 386–388.

Phares, E. J. (1992). *Clinical psychology: Concepts, methods and profession.* Pacific Grove, CA: Brooks/Cole.

Phariss, B., Millman, R. B., & Beeder, A. B. (1998). Psychological and psychiatric consequences of cannabis. In R. E. Tarter (Ed.), *Handbook of substance abuse: Neurobehavioral pharmacology* (pp. 147–158). New York: Plenum Press.

Phillips, K. A. (1991). Body dysmorphic disorder: The distress of imagined ugliness. *American Journal of Psychiatry, 148,* 1138–1149.

Phillips, K. A. (2001). *Somatoform and factitious disorders.* Washington, DC: American Psychiatric Association.

Phillips, K. A., & Diaz, S. F. (1997). Gender differences in body dysmorphic disorder. *Journal of Nervous & Mental Disease, 185,* 570–577.

Phillips, K. A., Kim, J. M., & Hudson, J. I. (1995). Body image disturbance in body dysmorphic disorder and eating disorders: Obsessions or delusions? *Psychiatric Clinics of North America, 18,* 317–334.

Phillips, K. A., & Najjar, F. (2003). An open-label study of citalophram in body dysmorphic disorder. *Journal of Clinical Psychiatry, 64,* 715–720.

Pilkonis, P. A. (1995). Commentary on avoidant personality disorder: Temperament, shame, or both? In W. J. Livesley (Ed.), *The DSM-IV personality disorders* (pp. 234–238). New York: Guilford Press.

Pipher, M. (1994). *Reviving Ophelia: Saving the selves of adolescent girls.* New York: Putnam.

Pitman, R. K. (1989). Posttraumatic stress disorder, hormones, and memory. *Biological Psychiatry, 26,* 221–223.

Pitman, R. K., Shalev, A. Y., & Orr, S. P. (2000). Posttraumatic stress disorder: Emotion, conditioning, and memory. In M. S. Gazzaniga (Ed.), *The new cognitive neurosciences* (2nd ed., pp. 1133–1147). Cambridge, MA: MIT Press.

Pitschel-Walz, G., Leucht, S., Baumi, J., Kissling, W., & Engel, R. (2001). The effect of family interventions on relapse and rehospitalization in schizophrenia—A meta-analysis. *Schizophrenia Bulletin, 27,* 73–92.

Pizzagalli, D., Pascual-Marqui, R. D., Nitschke, J. B., Oakes, T. R., Larson, C. L., et al. (2001). Anterior cingulated activity as a predictor of degree of treatment response in major depression: Evidence from brain electrical tomography analysis. *American Journal of Psychiatry, 158,* 405–415.

Plantenga, B. (1991). *Like open bright windows.* New York: Poets in Public Service.

Plassman, B. L., & Breitner, J. C. S. (1996). Recent advances in the genetics of Alzheimer's disease and vascular dementia with an emphasis on gene-environment interactions. *Journal of the American Geriatric Society, 44,* 1242–1250.

Platt, S., & Hawton, K. (2000). Repetition of suicidal behavior. In K. Hawton (Ed.), *International book of suicide and attempted suicide.* New York: Wiley.

Pliner, P., & Chaiken, S. (1990). Eating, social motives, and self-presentation in women and men. *Journal of Experimental Social Psychology, 26,* 240–254.

Plomin, R. (1994). *Genetics and experience: The interplay between nature and nurture.* Thousand Oaks, CA: Sage.

Polivy, J., & Herman, C. P. (2002). Causes of eating disorders. *Annual Review of Psychology, 53,* 187–213.

Pomerleau, O., & Kardia, S. (1999). Introduction to the featured section: Research on smoking. *Health Psychology, 18,* 3–6.

Pope, H. G., Gruber, A. J., Hudson, J. I., Huestis, M. A., & Yurgelun-Todd, D. (2001). Neuropsychological performance in long-term cannabis users. *Archives of General Psychiatry, 58,* 909–915.

Pope, H. G., Gruber, A. J., Mangweth, B., Bureau, B., deCol, C., Jouvent, R., & Hudson, J. I. (2000). Body image perception among men in three countries. *American Journal of Psychiatry, 157,* 1297–1301.

Pope, H. G., & Hudson, J. I. (1992). Is childhood sexual abuse a risk factor for bulimia nervosa? *American Journal of Psychiatry, 149,* 455–463.

Pope, H. G., Ionescu-Pioggia, M., & Pope, K. W. (2001). Drug use and lifestyle among college undergraduates: A 30-year longitudinal study. *American Journal of Psychiatry, 158,* 1519–1521.

Pope, H. G., Jacobs, A., Mialet, J., Yurgelun-Todd, D., & Gruber, S. (1997). Evidence for a sex-specific residual effect of cannabis on visuospatial memory. *Psychotherapy & Psychosomatics, 66,* 179–184.

Pope, H. G., Oliva, P. S., Hudson, J. I., Bodkin, J. A., & Grueber, A. J. (1999a). Attitudes toward DSM-IV dissociative disorders diagnoses among board-certified American psychiatrists. *American Journal of Psychiatry, 156,* 321–323.

Pope, H. G., Olivardia, R., Gruber, A., & Borowiecki, J. (1999b). Evolving ideals of male body image as seen through action toys. *International Journal of Eating Disorders, 26,* 65–72.

Pope, K. S., Tabachnick, B. G., & Keith-Spiegel, P. (1987). Ethics of practice: The beliefs and behaviors of psychologists as therapists. *American Psychologist, 42,* 993–1006.

Post, R. M., Frye, M. A., Denicoff, K. D., Leverich, G. S., Dunn, R. T., Osuch, E. A., Speer, A. M., Obrocea, G., & Jajodia, K. (2000). Emerging trends in the treatment of rapid cycling bipolar disorder: A selected review. *Bipolar Disorders, 2,* 305–315.

Powers, D. V., Thompson, L., Futterman, A., & Gallagher-Thompson, D. (2002). Depression later in life: Epidemiology, assessment, impact, and treatment. In I. H. Gotlib & C. L. Hammen (Eds.), *Handbook of depression* (pp. 560–580). New York: Guilford Press.

Prescott, C. A., & Kendler, K. S. (1999). Genetic and environmental contributions to alcohol abuse and dependence in a population-based sample of male twins. *American Journal of Psychiatry, 156,* 34–40.

Pretzer, J. (2004). Cognitive therapy of personality disorders. In G. G. Magnavita (Ed.), *Handbook of personality disorders: Theory and practice* (pp. 169–193). New York: Wiley.

Pribor, E. F., Yutzy, S. H., Dean, J. T, & Wetzel, R. D. (1993). Briquet's syndrome, dissociation, and abuse. *American Journal of Psychiatry, 150,* 1507–1511.

Price, R. W. (1998). Implications of the AIDS dementia complex viewed as an acquired genetic neurodegenerative disease. In M. F. Folstein (Ed.), *Neurobiology of primary dementia* (pp. 213–234). Washington, DC: American Psychiatric Press.

Pridal, C. G., & LoPiccolo, J. (2000). Multielement treatment of desire disorders: Integration of cognitive, behavioral, and systemic therapy. In S. R. Leiblum & R. C. Rosen (Eds.), *Principles and practice of sex therapy* (3rd ed., pp. 57–81). New York: Guilford Press.

Pritchard, J. C. (1837). *A treatise on insanity and other diseases affecting the mind.* Philadelphia: Harwell, Barrington, & Harwell.

Prochaska, J. O. (1995). Common problems: Common solutions. *Clinical Psychology: Science & Practice, 2,* 101–105.

Project MATCH Research Group. (1998). Matching alcoholism treatments to client heterogeneity: Treatment main effects and matching effects on drinking during treatment. *Journal of Studies on Alcohol, 59,* 631–639.

Pumariega, A. J., & Winters, N. C. (2003). *Handbook of child and adolescent systems of care: The new community psychology.* San Francisco: Jossey-Bass.

Purugganan, O. H., Stein, R. E. K., Silver, E. J., & Benenson, B. S. (2003). Exposure to violence and psychosocial adjustment among urban school-aged children. *Journal of Developmental & Behavioral Pediatrics, 24,* 424–430.

Putnam, F. W. (1991). Recent research on multiple personality disorder. *Psychiatric Clinics of North America, 14,* 489–502.

Putnam, F. W. (1996). Posttraumatic stress disorder in children and adolescents. In L. J. Dickstein, M. B. Riba, & J. M. Oldham (Eds.), *Review of psychiatry* (Vol. 15, pp. 447–467). Washington, DC: American Psychiatric Press.

Putnam, F. W., Guroff, J. J., Silberman, E. K., & Barban, L. (1986). The clinical phenomenology of multiple personality disorder: Review of 100 recent cases. *Journal of Clinical Psychiatry, 47,* 285–293.

Putnam, F. W., & Lowenstein, R. J. (1993). Treatment of multiple personality disorder: A survey of current practices. *American Journal of Psychiatry, 150,* 1048–1052.

Puttler, L. I., Zucker, R. A., Fitzgerald, H. E., & Bingham, C. R. (1998). Behavioral outcomes among children of alcoholics during the early and middle childhood years: Familial subtype variations. *Alcoholism: Clinical & Experimental Research, 22,* 1962–1972.

Q

Quality Assurance Project. (1990). Treatment outlines for paranoid, schizotypal, and schizoid personality disorders. *Australian & New Zealand Journal of Psychiatry, 24,* 339–350.

Quay, H. C. (1993). The psychobiology of undersocialized aggressive conduct disorder: A theoretical perspective. *Development & Psychopathology, 5,* 165–180.

R

Rachman, S. (1978). *Fear and courage.* San Francisco: W. H. Freeman.

Rachman, S. (1993). Obsessions, responsibility and guilt. *Behaviour Research & Therapy, 31,* 149–154.

Rachman, S. (1997). A cognitive theory of obsessions. *Behaviour Research & Therapy, 35,* 667–682.

Rachman, S., & deSilva, P. (1978). Abnormal and normal obsessions. *Behaviour Research & Therapy, 16,* 233–248.

Rachman, S. J., & Hodgson, R. J. (1980). *Obsessions and compulsions.* Englewood Cliffs, NJ: Prentice-Hall.

Ragin, D. F., Pilotti, M., Madry, L., Sage, R. E., Bingham, L. E., & Primm, B. J. (2002). Intergenerational substance abuse and domestic violence as familial risk factors for lifetime attempted suicide among battered women. *Journal of Interpersonal Violence, 17,* 1027–1045.

Ragland, J. D., & Berman, A. L. (1990–1991). Farm crisis and suicide: Dying on the vine? *Omega Journal of Death & Dying, 22,* 173–185.

Raikkonen, K., Matthews, K. A., Flory, J. D., Owens, J. F., & Gump, B. B. (1999). Effects of optimism, pessimism, and trait anxiety on ambulatory blood pressure and mood during everyday life. *Journal of Personality & Social Psychology, 76,* 104–113.

Raine, A. (1997). Antisocial behavior and psychophysiology: A biological perspective. In D. M. Stoff, J. Breiling, & J. D. Maser (Eds.), *Handbook of antisocial personality disorder* (pp. 289–304). New York: Wiley.

Raine, A., Venables, P. H., & Williams, M. (1996). Better autonomic conditioning and faster electrodermal half-recovery time at age 15 years as possible protective factors against crime at age 29 years. *Developmental Psychology, 32,* 624–630.

Ramchandani, P. (2004). A question of balance: How safe are the medicines that are prescribed to children? *Nature, 430,* 401–402.

Rankin, H., Hodgson, R., & Stockwell, T. (1983). Cue exposure and response prevention with alcoholics: A controlled trial. *Behaviour Research & Therapy, 21,* 435–446.

Rapee, R. M. (1994). Detection of somatic sensations in panic disorder. *Behaviour Research & Therapy, 32,* 825–831.

Rapee, R. M., & Barlow, D. H. (1993). Generalized anxiety disorder, panic disorder, and the phobias. In P. B. Sutker (Ed.), *Comprehensive handbook of psychopathology* (pp. 109–127). New York: Plenum Press.

Rapee, R. M., Brown, T. A., Antony, M. M., & Barlow, D. H. (1992). Response to hyperventilation and inhalation of 5.5% carbon dioxide-enriched air across the DSM-III-R anxiety disorders. *Journal of Abnormal Psychology, 101,* 538–552.

Rapee, R. M., & Heimberg, R. G. (1997). A cognitive-behavioral model of anxiety in social phobia. *Behaviour Research & Therapy, 35,* 741–756.

Rapoport, J. L. (1989). The biology of obsessions and compulsions. *Scientific American,* 83–89.

Rapoport, J. L. (1990). *The boy who couldn't stop washing.* New York: Plume.

Rapoport, J. L. (1991). Recent advances in obsessive-compulsive disorder. *Neuropsychopharmacology, 5,* 1–10.

Rapoport, J. L., Jensen, P. S., Inoff-Germain, G., Weissman, M. M., Greenwald, S., Narrow, W. E., Lahey, B. B., & Canino, G. (2000). Childhood obsessive-compulsive disorder in the NIMH MECA study: Parent versus child identification of cases. *Journal of Anxiety Disorders, 14,* 535–548.

Rasekh, Z., Bauer, H. M., Manos, M. M., & Iacopino, V. (1998). Women's health and human rights in Afghanistan. *Journal of the American Medical Association, 280,* 449–455.

Rauch, S. L., Phillips, K. A., Segal, E., Makris, N., Shin, L. M., Whalen, P. J., Jenike, M. A., Caviness, V. S., Jr., & Kennedy, D. N. (2003). A preliminary morphometric magnetic resonance imaging study of regional brain volumes in body dysmorphic disorder. *Psychiatry Research: Neuroimaging, 122,* 13–19.

Ray, O., & Ksir, C. (1993). *Drugs, society, and human behavior.* St. Louis: C. V. Mosby.

Read, J. D., & Lindsay, D. S. (Eds.). (1997). *Recollections of trauma: Scientific research and clinical practice.* New York: Plenum Press.

Redmond, D. E. (1985). Neurochemical basis for anxiety and anxiety disorders: Evidence from drugs which decrease human fear or anxiety. In A. H. Tuma & J. Maser (Eds.), *Anxiety and the anxiety disorders* (pp. 533–555). Hillsdale, NJ: Erlbaum.

Reed, G. M., Kemeny, M. E., Taylor, S. E., & Visscher, B. R. (1999). Negative HIV-specific expectancies and AIDS-related bereavement as predictors of symptom onset in asymptomatic HIV-positive gay men. *Health Psychology, 18,* 354–363.

Regier, D. A., Boyd, J. H., Burke, J. D., Rae, D. S., Myers, J. K., Kramer, M., Robins, L. N., George, L. K., Karno, M., & Locke, B. Z. (1988). One-month prevalence of mental disorders in the United States: Based on five epidemiologic catchment area sites. *Archives of General Psychiatry, 45,* 977–986.

Regier, D. A., Narrow, W. E., Rae, D. S., Manderscheid, R. W., Locke, B. Z., & Goodwin, F. K. (1993). The de facto U.S. mental and addictive disorders service system. *Archives of General Psychiatry, 50,* 85–94.

Rehm, L. P. (1977). A self-control model of depression. *Behavior Therapy, 8,* 787–804.

Reich, T., Edenberg, H. J., Goate, A., Williams, J. T., Rice, J. P., Van Eerdeweghm, P., Foroud, T., Hesselbrock, V., Schuckit, M. A., Bucholz, K., Porjesz, B., Li, T. K., Conneally, P. M., Nurnberger, J. I. Jr., Tischfield, J. A., Crowe, R. R., Cloninger, C. R., Wu, W., Shears, S., Carr, K., Crose, C., Willig, C., & Begleiter, H. (1998). Genome wide-research for genes affecting the risk for alcohol dependence. *American Journal of Medical Genetics, 81,* 207–215.

Reid, J. B., & Eddy, J. M. (1997). The prevention of antisocial behavior: Some considerations in the search for effective interventions. In D. M. Stoff, J. Breiling, & J. D. Maser (Eds.), *Handbook of antisocial personality disorder* (pp. 343–356). New York: Wiley.

Reissing, E. D., Binik, Y. M., & Khalife, S. (1999). Does vaginismus exist? *Journal of Nervous & Mental Disease, 187,* 261–274.

Reitan, R. M., & Davidson, L. A. (1974). *Clinical neuropsychology: Current status and applications.* Washington, DC: V. H. Winston & Sons.

Resick, P. A. (1993). The psychological impact of rape. *Journal of Interpersonal Violence, 8,* 223–255.

Resick, P. A., & Calhoun, K. S. (2001). Posttraumatic stress disorder. In D. H. Barlow (Ed.), *Clinical handbook of psychological disorders: A step-by-step treatment manual* (3rd ed., pp. 60–113). New York: Guilford Press.

Resick, P. A., & Schnicke, M. K. (1992). Cognitive processing therapy for sexual assault victims. *Journal of Consulting & Clinical Psychology, 60,* 748–756.

Resnick, H. S., Kilpatrick, D. G., Dansky, B. S., & Saunders, B. E. (1993). Prevalence of civilian trauma and posttraumatic stress disorder in a representative national sample of women. *Journal of Consulting & Clinical Psychology, 61,* 984–991.

Resnick, H. S., Yehuda, R., Pitman, R. K., & Foy, D. W. (1995). Effect of previous trauma on acute plasma cortisol level following rape. *American Journal of Psychiatry, 152,* 1675–1677.

Reynolds, C. F., Miller, M. D., Mulsant, B. H., Dew, M. A., & Pollock, B. G. (2000). Pharmacotherapy of geriatric depression: Taking the long view. In G. M. Williamson, D. R. Shaffer, & P. A. Parmelee (Eds.), *Physical illness and depression in older adults: A handbook of theory, research, and practice* (pp. 277–294).

New York: Kluwer Academic/Plenum Publishers.

Rhee, S. H., Waldman, I. D., Hay, D. A., & Levy, F. (1999). Sex differences in genetic and environmental influences on DSM-III-R attention-deficit/hyperactivity disorder. *Journal of Abnormal Psychology, 108,* 24–41.

Ricca, V., Mannucci, E., Mezzani, B., Moretti, S., Di Bernardo, M., Bertelli, M., Rotella, C. M., & Faravelli, C. (2001). Fluoxetine and fluvoxamine combined with individual cognitive-behaviour therapy in binge eating disorder: A one-year follow-up study. *Psychotherapy & Psychosomatics, 70,* 298–306.

Richards, R., Kinney, D. K., Lunde, I., & Benet, M. (1988). Creativity in manic-depressives, cyclothymes, their normal relatives, and control subjects. *Journal of Abnormal Psychology, 97,* 281–288.

Richardson, J. L., Shelton, D. R., Krailo, M., & Levine, A. M. (1990). The effect of compliance with treatment in survival among patients with hematologic malignancies. *Journal of Clinical Oncology, 8,* 356.

Rickels, K., Pollack, M. H., Sheehan, D. V., & Haskins, J. T. (2000). Efficacy of extended-release venlafaxine in nondepressed outpatients with generalized anxiety disorder. *American Journal of Psychiatry, 157,* 968–974.

Riddle, M. A., Reeve, E. A., Yaryura-Tobias, J. A., Yang, H. M., Claghorn, J. L., Gaffney, G., Greist, J. H., Holland, D., McConville, B. J., Pigott, T., & Walkup, J. T. (2001). Fluvoxamine for children and adolescents with obsessive-compulsive disorder: A randomized, controlled, multicenter trial. *Journal of the American Academy of Child & Adolescent Psychiatry, 40,* 222–229.

Rief, W., Hiller, W., & Margraf, J. (1998). Cognitive aspects of hypochondriasis and the somatization syndrome. *Journal of Abnormal Psychology, 107,* 587–595.

Riehman, K. S., Hser, Y., & Zeller, M. (2000). Gender differences in how intimate partners influence drug treatment motivation. *Journal of Drug Issues, 30,* 823–838.

Rifkin, A., Ghisalbert, D., Dimatou, S., Jin, C., & Sethi, M. (1998). Dissociative identity disorder in psychiatric inpatients. *American Journal of Psychiatry, 155,* 844–845.

Riley, K. P., Snowdon, D. A., Saunders, A. M., Roses, A. D., Mortimer, J. A., & Nanayakkara, N. (2000). Cognitive function and apolipoprotein in very old adults: Findings from the Nun Study. *Journal of Gerontology, 55B,* S69–S75.

Rimm, D. C., & Masters, J. C. (1979). *Behavior therapy: Techniques and empirical findings* (2nd ed.). New York: Academic Press.

Rimmele, C. T., Miller, W. R., & Dougher, M. J. (1989). Aversion therapies. In R. K. Hester & W. R. Miller (Eds.), *Handbook of alcoholism treatment approaches: Effective alternatives* (pp. 128–140). New York: Pergamon Press.

Rivera, G. (1988). Hispanic folk medicine utilization in urban Colorado. *Sociology & Social Research, 72,* 237–241.

Robbins, P. C., Monahan, J., & Silver, E. (2003). Mental disorder, violence, and gender. *Law and Human Behavior, 27,* 561–571.

Roberts, A. H. (1969). *Brain damage in boxers.* London: Pitman.

Roberts, J. E., Gotlib, I. H., & Kassel, J. D. (1996). Adult attachment security and symptoms of depression: The mediating roles of dysfunctional attitudes and low self-esteem. *Journal of Personality & Social Psychology, 60,* 310–320.

Roberts, M. C., Vernberg, E. M., & Jackson, Y. (2000). Psychotherapy with children and families. In C. R. Snyder & R. E. Ingram (Eds.), *Handbook of psychological change: Psychotherapy processes and practices for the 21st century* (pp. 500–519). New York: Wiley.

Robin, A. L. (2003). Behavioral family systems therapy for adolescents with anorexia nervosa. In A. E. Kazdin & J. R. Weisz (Eds.), *Evidence-based psychotherapies for children and adolescents* (pp. 358–373). New York: Guilford Press.

Robins, L. N., Helzer, J. E., Croughan, A., & Ratcliff, K. S. (1981). National Institute of Mental Health Diagnostic Interview Schedule. *Archives of General Psychiatry, 38,* 381–389.

Robins, L. N., Helzer, J. E., & Davis, D. H. (1975). Narcotic use in Southeast Asia and afterward: An interview of 898 Vietnam returnees. *Archives of General Psychiatry, 32,* 955–961.

Robins, L. N., Helzer, J. E., Weissman, M. M., Orvaschel, H., Gruenberg, E., Burke, J. D., & Regier, D. A. (1984). Lifetime prevalence of specific psychiatric disorders in three sites. *Archives of General Psychiatry, 41,* 949–958.

Robinson, L. A., Berman, J. S., & Neimeyer, R. A. (1990). Psychotherapy for the treatment of depression: A comprehensive review of controlled outcome research. *Psychological Bulletin, 109,* 30–49.

Robinson, T. E., & Berridge, K. C. (1993). The neural basis of drug craving: An incentive-sensitization theory of addiction. *Brain Research Reviews, 18,* 247–291.

Robles, T. F., & Kiecolt-Glaser, J. K. (2003). The physiology of marriage: Pathways to health. *Physiology & Behavior, 79,* 409–416.

Rockney, R. M., & Lemke, T. (1992). Casualties from a junior-senior high school during the Persian Gulf War: Toxic poisoning or mass hysteria? *Journal of Developmental & Behavioral Pediatrics, 13,* 339–342.

Rodin, J. (1992, January). Sick of worrying about the way you look? Read this. *Psychology Today,* pp. 56–60.

Rodin, J., Slochower, J., & Fleming, B. (1977). Effects of degree of obesity, age of onset, and weight loss on responsiveness to sensory and external stimuli. *Journal of Comparative & Physiological Psychology, 91,* 586–597.

Roelofs, K., Hoogduin, K. A. L., Keijsers, G. P. J., Naring, G. W. B., Moene, F. C., & Sandijck, P. (2002). Hypnotic susceptibility in patients with conversion disorder. *Journal of Abnormal Psychology, 111,* 390–395.

Rogers, C. R. (1951). *Client-centered therapy, its current practice, implications, and theory.* Boston: Houghton Mifflin.

Rogler, L. H. (1989). The meaning of culturally sensitive research in mental health. *American Journal of Psychiatry, 146,* 296–303.

Rogler, L. H. (1999). Methodological sources of cultural insensitivity in mental health research. *American Psychologist, 54,* 424–433.

Roisman, G. I., Tsai, J. L, & Chiang, K.-H. S. (2004). The emotional integration of childhood experience: Physiological, facial expressive, and self-reported emotional response during the Adult Attachment Interview. *Developmental Psychology, 40,* 776–789.

Ron, M. (2001). Explaining the unexplained: Understanding hysteria. *Brain, 124,* 1065–1066.

Rook, K. (1984). The negative side of social interaction: Impact on psychological well-being. *Journal of Personality & Social Psychology, 46,* 1097–1108.

Rorty, M., Yager, J., & Rossotto, E. (1994). Childhood sexual, physical, and psychological abuse in bulimia nervosa. *American Journal of Psychiatry, 151,* 1122–1126.

Rosen, G. (1968). *Madness in society: Chapters in the historical sociology of mental illness.* Chicago: University of Chicago Press.

Rosen, J. C., & Ramirez, E. (1998). A comparison of eating disorders and body dysmorphic disorder on body image and psychological adjustment. *Journal of Psychosomatic Research, 44,* 441–449.

Rosen, L. N., Targum, S. D., Terman, M., Bryant, M. J., Hoffman, H., Kasper, S. F., Hamovit, J. R., Docherty, J. P., Welch, B., & Rosenthal, N. E. (1990). Prevalence of seasonal affective disorder at four latitudes. *Psychiatry Research, 31,* 131–144.

Rosen, R. C. (1996). Erectile dysfunction: The medicalization of male sexuality. *Clinical Psychology Review, 16,* 497–519.

Rosen, R. C., & Ashton, A. K. (1993). Prosexual drugs: Empirical status of the "new aphrodisiacs." *Archives of Sexual Behavior, 22,* 521–543.

Rosen, R. C., & Leiblum, S. R. (1995). Treatment of sexual disorders in the 1990s: An integrated approach. *Journal of Consulting & Clinical Psychology, 63,* 877–890.

Rosenbaum, M. (1980). The role of the term schizophrenia in the decline of the diagnoses of multiple personality. *Archives of General Psychiatry, 37,* 1383–1385.

Rosenblatt, P. C. (2001). A social constructionist perspective on cultural differences in grief. In M. S. Stroebe & R. O. Hansson (Eds.), *Handbook of bereavement research: Consequences, coping and care* (pp. 285–300). Washington, DC: American Psychological Association.

Rosenhan, D. L. (1973). On being sane in insane places. *Science, 179,* 250–258.

Rosenheck, R. A. (1999). Principles for priority setting in mental health services and their implications for the least well off. *Psychiatric Services, 50,* 653–658.

Rosenman, R. H., Brand, R. J., Jenkins, C. D., Friedman, M., Straus, R., & Wrum, M. (1976). Coronary heart disease in the Western Collaborative Group Study: Final follow-up experience of 8 years. *Journal of the American Medical Association, 233,* 877–878.

Rosenstein, M. J., Milazzo-Sayre, L. J., & Manderscheid, R. W. (1989). Care of persons with schizophrenia: A statistical profile. *Schizophrenia Bulletin, 15,* 45–58.

Rosenthal, N. E. (1995, October 9–11). *The mechanism of action of light in the treatment of seasonal affective disorder.* Paper presented at the Biologic Effects of Light 1995, Atlanta.

Rosenweig, S. (1936). Some implicit common factors in diverse methods in psychotherapy. *American Journal of Orthopsychiatry, 6,* 412–415.

Ross, C. A. (1989). *Multiple personality disorder: Diagnosis, clinical features, and treatment.* New York: Wiley.

Ross, C. A. (1991). Epidemiology of multiple personality disorder and dissociation. *Psychiatric Clinics of North America, 14,* 503–517.

Ross, C. A. (1997). *Dissociative identity disorder: Diagnosis, clinical features, and treatment of multiple personality.* Toronto: Wiley.

Ross, C. A. (1999). Dissociative disorders. In T. Millon (Ed.), *Oxford textbook of psychopathology* (pp. 466–481). New York: Oxford University Press.

Ross, C. A., & Ellason, J. (1999). Comment on the effectiveness of treatment for dissociative identity disorder. *Psychological Reports, 84,* 1109–1110.

Ross, C. A., & Norton, G. R. (1989). Differences between men and women with multiple personality disorder. *Hospital & Community Psychiatry, 40,* 186–188.

Ross, C. A., Norton, G. R., & Fraser, G. A. (1989). Evidence against the iatrogenesis of multiple personality disorder. *Dissociation: Progress in the Dissociative Disorders, 2,* 61–65.

Ross, C. A., Norton, G. R., & Wozney, K. (1989). Multiple personality disorder: An analysis of 236 cases. *Canadian Journal of Psychiatry, 34,* 413–418.

Ross, C. E., & Mirowsky, J. (1984). Socially-desirable response and acquiescence in a cross-cultural survey of mental health. *Journal of Health & Social Behavior, 25,* 189–197.

Ross, C. E., Mirowsky, J., & Goldsteen, K. (1990). The impact of the family on health: The decade in review. *Journal of Marriage & the Family, 52,* 1059–1078.

Ross, L., Lepper, M. R., & Hubbard, M. (1975). Perseverance in self-perception and social preparation: Biased attributional processes in the debriefing paradigm. *Journal of Personality & Social Psychology, 32,* 880–892.

Ross, L., & Nisbett, R. E. (1991). *The person and the situation: Perspectives of social psychology.* Philadelphia: Temple University Press.

Rosselló, J., & Bernal, G. (2004). *Randomized trial of CBT and IPT in individual and group format for depression in Puerto Rican adolescents.* Paper under review.

Rost, K., Nutting, P., Smith, J., Coyne, J., Cooper-Patrick, L., & Rubenstein, L. (2000). The role of competing demands in the treatment provided primary care patients with major depression. *Archives of Family Medicine, 9,* 150–154.

Rost, K., Zhang, M., Fortney, J., Smith, J., & Smith, R. (1998). Expenditures for the treatment of major depression. *American Journal of Psychiatry, 155,* 883–888.

Rothbart, M., & Bates, J. (1998). Temperament. In W. Damon (Series Ed.) & N. Eisenberg (Vol. Ed.), *Handbook of child psychology: Vol. 3. Social, emotional, and personality development* (5th ed., pp. 105–176). New York: Wiley.

Rothbaum, B. O., & Foa, E. B. (1991). Exposure treatment of PTSD concomitant with conversion mutism: A case study. *Behavior Therapy, 22,* 449–456.

Rothbaum, B. O., Foa, E. D., Riggs, D. S., & Murdock, T. (1992). A prospective examination of post-traumatic stress disorder in rape victims. *Journal of Traumatic Stress, 5,* 455–475.

Rotter, J. B. (1954). *Social learning and clinical psychology.* Englewood Cliffs, NJ: Prentice Hall.

Rovner, B., Steele, C., Shmuely, Y., & Folstein, M. F. (1996). A randomized trial of dementia care in nursing homes. *Journal of the American Geriatric Society, 44,* 7–13.

Rovner, B. W. (1993). Depression and increased risk of mortality in the nursing home patient. *American Journal of Medicine, 94*(Suppl. 5A), 19S–22S.

Rowe, R., Maughan, B., Worthman, C. M., Costello, E. J., & Angold, A. (2004). Testosterone, antisocial behavior, and social dominance in boys: Pubertal development and biosocial interaction. *Biological Psychiatry, 55,* 546–552.

Rowse, A. L. (1969). *The early Churchills.* Middlesex, UK: Penguin Books.

Roy, A. (1992). Genetics, biology, and suicide in the family. In R. W. Maris, A. L. Berman, J. T. Maltsberger, & R. I. Yufit (Eds.), *Assessment and prediction of suicide* (pp. 574–588). New York: Guilford Press.

Rozin, P., Bauer, R., & Catanese, D. (2003). Food and life, pleasure and worry, among American college students: Gender differences and regional similarities. *Journal of Personality & Social Psychology, 85,* 132–141.

Rubin, K. H., Daniels-Beirness, T., & Hayvren, M. (1982). Social and social-cognitive correlates of sociometric status in preschool and kindergarten children. *Canadian Journal of Behavioural Science, 14,* 338–349.

Ruggiero, K. J., Morris, T. L., & Scotti, J. R. (2001). Treatment for children with posttraumatic stress disorder: Current status and future directions. *Clinical Psychology: Science & Practice, 8,* 210–227.

Russell, S. T. (2003). Sexual minority youth and suicide risk. *American Behavioral Scientist, 46,* 1241–1257.

Rutter, M. (1997). Antisocial behavior: Developmental psychopathology perspectives. In D. M. Stoff, J. Breiling, & J. D. Maser (Eds.), *Handbook of antisocial personality disorder* (pp. 115–124). New York: Wiley.

Rutter, M., Caspi, A., Fergusson, D., Horwood, L. J., Goodman, R., Maughan, B., Moffitt, T. E., Meltzer, H., & Carroll, J. (2004). Sex differences in developmental reading disability: New findings from 4 epidemiological studies. *Journal of the American Medical Association, 291,* 2007–2012.

Rutter, M., MacDonald, H., Couteur, A. L., Harrington, R., Bolton, P., & Bailey, A. (1990). Genetic factors in child psychiatric disorders: II. Empirical findings. *Journal of Child Psychology & Psychiatry, 31,* 39–83.

Rutter, M., Silberg, J., O'Connor, T., & Simonoff, E. (1999). Genetics and child psychiatry: II. Empirical research findings. *Journal of Child Psychology & Psychiatry, 40,* 19–55.

Ryan, J. J., & Lopez, S. J. (2001). Wechsler Adult Intelligence Scale–III. In W. I. Dorfman & S. M. Freshwater (Eds.), *Understanding psychological assessment* (pp. 19–42). Dordrecht, Netherlands: Kluwer Academic Publishers.

S

Sabol, S. Z., Nelson, M. L., Fisher, C., Gunzerath, L., Brody, C. L., Hu, S., Sirota, L. A., Marcus, S. E., Greenberg, B. D., Lucas, F. R., Benjamin, J., Murphy, D. L., & Hamer, D. H. (1999). A genetic association for cigarette smoking behavior. *Health Psychology, 18,* 7–13.

Sackheim, H. A., & Lisanby, S. H. (2001). Physical treatments in psychiatry: Advances in electroconvulsive therapy, transcranial magnetic stimulation, and vagus nerve stimulation. In M. Weissman (Ed.), *Treatment of depression: Bridging the 21st century* (pp. 151–174). Washington, DC: American Psychiatric Press.

Sackheim, H. A., Rush, A. J., George, M. S., Marangell, L. B., Husain, M. M., Nahas, Z., Johnson, C. R., Seidman, S., Giller, C., Haines, S., Simpson, R. K., & Goodman, R. R. (2001). Vagus nerve stimulation (VNS-super(TM)) for treatment-resistant depression: Efficacy, side effects, and predictors of outcome. *Neuropsychopharmacology, 25,* 713–728.

Salkovskis, P. M. (1998). Psychological approaches to the understanding of obsessional problems. In R. Swinson (Ed.), *Obsessive-compulsive disorder: Theory, research, and treatment* (pp. 33–50). New York: Guilford Press.

Saluja, G., Iachan, R., Scheidt, P. C., Overpeck, M. D., Sun, W., & Giedd, J. N. (2004). Prevalence of and risk factors for depressive symptoms among young adolescents. *Archives of Pediatrics & Adolescent Medicine, 158,* 760–765.

Salzman, L. (1980). *Psychotherapy of the obsessive personality.* New York: Jason Aronson.

Sampath, G., Shah, A., Krska, J., & Soni, S. D. (1992). Neuroleptic discontinuation in the very stable schizophrenic patient: Relapse rates and serum neuroleptic levels. *Human Psychopharmacology: Clinical & Experimental, 7,* 255–264.

Sampson, R. J., & Laub, J. H. (1992). Crime and deviance in the life course. *Annual Review of Sociology, 18,* 63–84.

Sanderson, W. C., Rapee, R. M., & Barlow, D. H. (1989). The influence of illusion of control on panic attacks induced via inhalation of 5.5% carbon dioxide–enriched air. *Archives of General Psychology, 46,* 157–162.

Sandnabba, N. K., Santtila, P., Alison, L., & Nordling, N. (2002). Demographics, sexual behaviour, family background and abuse experiences of practitioners of sadomasochistic sex: A review of recent research. *Sexual & Relationship Therapy, 17,* 39–55.

Sano, M., Ernesto, C., Thomas, R. G., & Klauber, M. R. (1997). A controlled trial of selegiline, alpha-tocopherol, or both as treatment for Alzheimer's disease. *New England Journal of Medicine, 336,* 1216–1222.

Sapolsky, R. M., Krey, L. C., & McEwen, B. S. (1986). The neuroendocrinology of stress and aging: The glucocorticoid cascade hypothesis. *Endocrinology Review, 7,* 284–301.

Sarason, I. G., Johnson, J. H., & Siegel, J. M. (1978). Assessing the impact of life changes: Development of the Life Experiences Survey.

Journal of Consulting & Clinical Psychology, 46, 932–946.

Sarbin, T. R., & Juhasz, J. B. (1967). The historical background of the concept of hallucination. *Journal of the History of the Behavioral Sciences, 3,* 339–358.

Sarwer, D. B., Magee, L., & Crerand, C. E. (2004). Cosmetic surgery and cosmetic medical treatments. In J. K. Thompson (Ed.), *Handbook of eating disorders and obesity* (pp. 718–737). Hoboken, NJ: Wiley.

Satir, V. (1967). Family systems and approaches to family therapy. *Journal of the Fort Logan Mental Health Center, 4,* 81–93.

Saunders, B. E., Villeponteaux, L. A., Lipovsky, J. A., Kilpatrick, D. G., et al. (1992). Child sexual assault as a risk factor for mental disorders among women: A community survey. *Journal of Interpersonal Violence, 7,* 189–204.

Saxena, S., Brody, A. L., Ho, M. L., Alborzian, S., Ho, M. K., Maidment, K. M., Huang, S.-C., Wu, H.-M., Au, S. C., & Baxter, L. R., Jr. (2001). Cerebral metabolism in major depression and obsessive-compulsive disorder occurring separately and concurrently. *Biological Psychiatry, 50,* 159–170.

Saxena, S., Brody, A. L., Ho, M. L., Zohrabi, N., Maidment, K. M., & Baxter, L. R., Jr. (2003). Differential brain metabolic predictors of response to paroxetine in obsessive-compulsive disorder versus major depression. *American Journal of Psychiatry, 160,* 522–532.

Saxena, S., Brody, A. L., Maidment, K. M., Dunkin, J. J., Colgan, M., Alborzian, S., Phelps, M. E., & Baxter, L. R. (1999). Localized orbitofrontal and subcortical metabolic changes and predictors of response to paroxetine treatment in obsessive-compulsive disorder. *Neuropsychopharmacology, 21,* 683–693.

Saxena, S., & Prasad, K. V. (1989). DSMIII subclassification of dissociative disorders applied to psychiatric outpatients in India. *American Journal of Psychiatry, 146,* 261–262.

Saxena, S., & Rauch, S. L. (2000). Functional neuroimaging and the neuroanatomy of obsessive-compulsive disorder. *Psychiatric Clinics of North America, 23,* 563–586.

Saxena, S., Winograd, A., Dunkin, J. J., Maidment, K., Rosen, R., Vapnik, T., Tarlow, G., & Bystritsky, A. (2001). A retrospective review of clinical characteristics and treatment response in body dysmorphic disorder versus obsessive-compulsive disorder. *Journal of Clinical Psychiatry, 62,* 67–72.

Scarr, S., Weinberg, R. A., & Waldman, I. D. (1993). IQ correlations in transracial adoptive families. *Intelligence, 17,* 541–555.

Schacter, D. L. (1999). The seven sins of memory. *American Psychologist, 54,* 182–203.

Schacter, D. L., Chiao, J. Y., & Mitchell, J. P. (2003). The seven sins of memory: Implications for the self. In J. LeDoux, J. Debiece, & H. Moss (Eds.), The self: From soul to brain. *Annals of the New York Academy of Sciences, 1001,* 226–239.

Schafer, W. (1992). *Stress management for wellness.* Fort Worth: Holt, Rinehart & Winston.

Scheff, T. J. (1966). *Being mentally ill: Sociological theory.* Chicago: Aldine.

Scheier, M. F., Matthews, K. A., Owens, J. F., Magovern, G. J., Lefebvre, R. C., Abbott, R. A., & Carver, C. S. (1989). Dispositional optimism and recovery from coronary artery surgery: The beneficial effects on physical and psychological well-being. *Journal of Personality & Social Psychology, 57,* 1024–1040.

Scherrer, J. F., True, W. R., Xian, H., Lyons, M. J., Eisen, S. A., Goldberg, J., Lin, N., & Tsuang, M. T. (2000). Evidence for genetic influences common and specific to symptoms of generalized anxiety and panic. *Journal of Affective Disorders, 57,* 25–35.

Schiavi, R. C. (1990). Sexuality and aging in men. *Annual Review of Sex Research, 1,* 227–249.

Schiavi, R. C., & Segraves, R. T. (1995). The biology of sexual dysfunction. *Psychiatric Clinics of North America, 18,* 7–23.

Schiavi, R. C., Stimmel, B. B., Mandeli, J., & Schreiner-Engel, P. (1995). Diabetes, psychological functioning, and male sexuality. *Journal of Psychosomatic Research, 39,* 305–314.

Schiavi, R. C., White, D., Mandeli, J., & Levine, A. (1997). Effect of testosterone administration on sexual behavior and mood in men with erectile dysfunction. *Archives of Sexual Behavior, 26,* 231–241.

Schildkraut, J. J. (1965). The catecholamine hypothesis of affective disorder: A review of supporting evidence. *American Journal of Psychiatry, 122,* 509–522.

Schlenger, W. E., Kulka, R. A., Fairbank, J. A., & Hough, R. L. (1992). The prevalence of post-traumatic stress disorder in the Vietnam generation: A multimethod, multisource assessment of psychiatric disorder. *Journal of Traumatic Stress, 5,* 333–363.

Schmahl, C. G., Vermetten, E., Elzinga, B. M., & Bremner, J. D. (2004). A positron emission tomography study of memories of childhood abuse in borderline personality disorder. *Biological Psychiatry, 55,* 759–765.

Schneider, J. A., O'Leary, A., & Jenkins, S. R. (1995). Gender, sexual orientation, and disordered eating. *Psychology & Health, 10,* 113–128.

Schneiderman, N., Antoni, M. H., Saab, P. G., & Ironson, G. (2001). Health psychology: Psychosocial and biobehavioral aspects of chronic disease management. *Annual Review of Psychology, 52,* 555–580.

Schneiderman, N., Ironson, G., & Siegel, S. D. (2005). Stress and health: Psychological, behavioral, and biological determinants. *Annual Review of Clinical Psychology, 1,* 607–628.

Schneier, F. R. (2001). Treatment of social phobia with antidepressants. *Journal of Clinical Psychiatry, 62*(Suppl. 1), 43–49.

Schnurr, P. P., Spiro, A., III, & Paris, A. H. (2000). Physician-diagnosed medical disorders in relation to PTSD symptoms in older male military veterans. *Health Psychology, 19,* 91–97.

Scholte, W. F., Olff, M., Ventevogel, P., de Vries, G.-J., Jansveld, E., Cardozo, B. L., & Crawford, C. A. G. (2004). Mental health symptoms following war and repression in eastern Afghanistan. *Journal of the American Medical Association, 292,* 585–593.

Schonfeld, L., & Dupree, L. W. (1997). Treatment alternatives for older alcohol abusers. In A. M. Gurnack (Ed.), *Older adults' misuse of alcohol, medicines, and other drugs: Research and practice issues* (pp. 113–131). New York: Springer.

Schreibman, L., & Charlop-Christy, M. H. (1998). Autistic disorder. In T. H. Ollendick & M. Hersen (Eds.), *Handbook of child psychopathology* (pp. 157–180). New York: Plenum Press.

Schuckit, M. A. (1991). A longitudinal study of children of alcoholics. In M. Galanter (Ed.), *Recent developments in alcoholism* (Vol. 9, pp. 5–19). New York: Plenum Press.

Schuckit, M. A. (1995). *Drug and alcohol abuse: A clinical guide to diagnosis and treatment.* New York: Plenum Medical Book Company.

Schuckit, M. A. (1996). Recent developments in the pharmacotherapy of alcohol dependence. *Journal of Consulting & Clinical Psychology, 64,* 669–676.

Schuckit, M. A. (1998). Biological, psychological, and environmental predictors of the alcoholism risk: A longitudinal study. *Journal of Studies on Alcohol, 59,* 485–494.

Schuckit, M. A., Daeppen, J. B., Tipp, J. E., Hesselbrock, M., & Bucholz, K. K. (1998). The clinical course of alcohol-related problems in alcohol dependent and nonalcohol dependent drinking men and women. *Journal of Studies in Alcohol, 59,* 581–590.

Schuckit, M. A., Edenberg, H. J., Kalmijn, J., Flury, L., Smith, T. L., Reich, T., Bierut, L., Goate, A., & Foroud, T. (2001). A genome-wide search for genes that relate to a low level response to alcohol. *Alcoholism: Clinical & Experimental Research, 25,* 323–329.

Schuckit, M. A., & Smith, T. L. (1996). An 8-year follow-up of 450 sons of alcoholic and control subjects. *Archives of General Psychiatry, 53,* 202–211.

Schuckit, M. A., & Smith, T. L. (1997). Assessing the risk for alcoholism among sons of alcoholics. *Journal of Studies on Alcohol, 58,* 141–145.

Schuckit, M. A., Smith, T. L., Danko, G. P., Bucholz, K. K., Reich, T., & Bierut, L. (2001). Five-year clinical course associated with DSM-IV alcohol abuse or dependence in a large group of men and women. *American Journal of Psychiatry, 158,* 1084–1090.

Schuckit, M. A., Tip, J. E., Reich, T., & Hesselbrock, V. M. (1995). The histories of withdrawal convulsions and delirium tremens in 1648 alcohol dependent subjects. *Addiction, 90,* 1335–1347.

Schultz, R., Gauthier, I., Klin, A. et al. (2000). Abnormal ventral temporal cortical activity during face discrimination among individuals with autism and Asperger syndrome. *Archives of General Psychiatry, 57,* 332–343.

Schulz, R., Bookwala, J., Knapp, J. E., Scheier, M., & Williamson, G. M. (1996). Pessimism, age, and cancer mortality. *Psychology & Aging, 11,* 304–309.

Schuster, M. A., Stein, B. D., Jaycox, L. H., Collins, R. L., Marshall, G. N., Elliott, M. N., Zhou, A. J., Kanouse, D. E., Morrison, J. L., & Berry, S. H. (2001). A national survey of stress reactions after the September 11, 2001, terrorist attacks. *New England Journal of Medicine, 345,* 1507–1512.

Schwartz, J., Stoessel, P. W., Baxter, L. R., Martin, K. M., & Phelps, M. C. (1996). Systemic changes in cerebral glucose metabolic rate after successful behavior modification treatment of obsessive-compulsive disorder. *Archives of General Psychiatry, 53,* 109–113.

Scogin, F., Floyd, M., & Forde, J. (2000). Anxiety in older adults. In S. K. Whitbourne (Ed.), *Psychopathology in later adulthood* (pp. 117–140). New York: Wiley.

Scogin, F., Rickard, H. C., Keith, S., Wilson, J., et al. (1992). Progressive and imaginal relaxation training for elderly persons with subjective anxiety. *Psychology & Aging, 7,* 419–424.

Scull, A. (1993). *The most solitary of afflictions.* New Haven: Yale University Press.

Sechehaye, M. (1951). *Autobiography of a schizophrenic girl.* New York: Grune & Stratton.

Seedat, S., Stein, M. B., & Forde, D. R. (2003). Prevalence of dissociative experiences in a community sample. *Journal of Nervous & Mental Disorders, 191,* 115–120.

Segal, S. P., Laurie, T. A., & Franskoviak, P. (2004). Ambivalence of PES patients toward hospitalization and factors in their disposition. *International Journal of Law & Psychiatry, 27,* 87–99.

Segerstrom, S. C., & Miller, G. E. (2004). Psychological stress and the human immune system: A meta-analytic study of 30 years of inquiry. *Psychological Bulletin, 130,* 601–630.

Segerstrom, S. C., Solomon, G. F., Kemeny, M. E., & Fahey, J. L. (1998). Relationship of worry to immune sequelae of the Northridge earthquake. *Journal of Behavioral Medicine, 21,* 433–450.

Segerstrom, S. C., Taylor, S. E., Kemeny, M. E., Reed, G. M., & Visscher, B. R. (1996). Causal attributions predict rate of immune decline in HIV seropositive gay men. *Health Psychology, 15,* 485–493.

Segman, R. H., & Shalev, A. Y. (2003). Genetics of posttraumatic stress disorder. *CNS Spectrums, 8,* 693–698.

Segraves, K. B., & Segraves, R. T. (1991). Multiple-phase sexual dysfunction. *Journal of Sex Education & Therapy, 17,* 153–156.

Segraves, R. T. (2003). Pharmacologic management of sexual dysfunction: Benefits and limitations. *CNS Spectrums, 8,* 225–229.

Segraves, R. T., Clayton, A., Croft, H., Wolf, A., & Warnock, J. (2004). Bupropion sustained release for the treatment of hypoactive sexual desire disorder in premenopausal women. *Journal of Clinical Psychopharmacology, 24,* 339–342.

Segraves, R. T., & Segraves, K. B. (1998). Pharmacotherapy for sexual disorders: Advantages and pitfalls. *Sexual & Marital Therapy, 13,* 295–309.

Seguin, J. R., Pihl, R. O., Harden, P. W., & Tremblay, R. E. (1995). Cognitive and neuropsychological characteristics of physically aggressive boys. *Journal of Abnormal Psychology, 104,* 614–624.

Seidman, L. J., Faraone, S. V., Goldstein, J. M., Kremen, W. S., Horton, N. J., Makris, N., Toomey, R., Kennedy, D., Caviness, V. S., &

Tsuang, M. T. (2002). Left hippocampal volume as a vulnerability indicator for schizophrenia. *Archives of General Psychiatry, 59,* 839–849.

Seidman, S. N., Roose, S. P., Menza, M. A., Shabsigh, R., & Rosen, R. C. (2001). Treatment of erectile dysfunction in men with depressive symptoms: Results of a placebo-controlled trial with sildenafil citrate. *American Journal of Psychiatry, 158,* 1623–1630.

Seligman, M. (1970). On the generality of the laws of learning. *Psychological Review, 77,* 406–418.

Seligman, M. E. (1993). *What you can change and what you can't: The complete guide to self-improvement.* New York: Knopf.

Seligman, M. E., & Maier, S. F. (1967). Failure to escape traumatic shock. *Journal of Experimental Psychology, 74,* 1–9.

Seligman, M. E. P. (1975). *Helplessness: On depression, development, and death.* San Francisco: Freeman, Cooper.

Seligman, M. E. P., & Binik, Y. M. (1977). The safety signal hypothesis. In H. Davis & H. Hurwitz (Eds.), *Pavlovian operant interactions.* Hillsdale, NJ: Erlbaum.

Selling, L. H. (1940). *Men against madness.* New York: Greenberg.

Selye, H. (1979). *The stress of life.* New York: McGraw-Hill.

Semans, J. H. (1956). Premature Ejaculation: A New Approach. *Southern Medical Journal, 49,* 353–357.

Shadish, W. R., Montgomery, L. M., Wilson, P., Wilson, M. R., Bright, I., & Okwumabua, T. (1993). Effects of family and marital psychotherapies: A meta-analysis. *Journal of Consulting & Clinical Psychology, 61,* 992–1002.

Shaffer, D., & Gould, M. (2000). Suicide prevention in the schools. In K. Hawton (Ed.), *The international handbook of suicide and attempted suicide* (pp. 585–724). New York: Wiley.

Shalev, A. Y., Peri, T., Canetti, L., & Schreiber, S. (1996). Predictors of PTSD in injured trauma survivors: A prospective study. *American Journal of Psychiatry, 153,* 219–225.

Shalev, A. Y., Tuval-Mashiach, R., & Hadar, H. (2004). Posttraumatic stress disorder as a result of mass trauma. *Journal of Clinical Psychiatry, 65*(Suppl. 1), 4–10.

Shapiro, F. (1995). *Eye movement desensitization and reprocessing: Basic principles, protocols, and procedures.* New York: Guilford Press.

Shaw, D. S., Keenan, K., & Vondra, J. I. (1994). Developmental precursors of externalizing behavior: Ages 1 to 3. *Developmental Psychology, 30,* 355–364.

Shaw, D. S., & Winslow, E. B. (1997). Precursors and correlates of antisocial behavior from infancy to preschool. In D. M. Stoff, J. Breiling, & J. D. Maser (Eds.), *Handbook of antisocial personality disorder* (pp. 148–158). New York: Wiley.

Shea, M. T. (1993). Psychosocial treatment of personality disorders. *Journal of Personality Disorders* (Suppl. 1), 167–180.

Shea, M. T., Stout, R., Gunderson, J., Morey, L. C., Grilo, C. M., McGlashan, T., Skodol, A. E., Dolan-Sewell, R., Dyck, I., Zanarini, M. C., & Keller, M. B. (2002). Short-term diagnostic stability of schizotypal, borderline, avoidant, and obsessive-compulsive personality disorders. *American Journal of Psychiatry, 159,* 2036–2041.

Sheard, M. H., Marini, J. L., Bridges, C. I., & Wagner, E. (1976). The effect of lithium on impulsive aggressive behavior in man. *American Journal of Psychiatry, 133,* 1409–1413.

Shearin, E. N., & Linehan, M. M. (1989). Dialectics and behavior therapy: A metaparadoxical approach to the treatment of borderline personality disorder. In L. M. Ascher (Ed.), *Therapeutic paradox* (pp. 255–288). New York: Guilford Press.

Sheikh, J. I. (1992). Anxiety and its disorders in old age. In J. E. Birren, K. Sloan, & G. D. Cohen (Eds.), *Handbook of mental health and aging* (pp. 410–432). New York: Academic Press.

Shenton, M. E., Frumin, M., McCarley, R. W., Maier, S. E., Westin, C.-F., Fischer, I. A., Dickey, C., & Kikinis, R. (2001). Morphometric magnetic resonance imaging studies: Findings in schizophrenia. In D. D. Dougherty & S. L. Rauch (Eds.), *Psychiatric neuroimaging research: Contemporary strategies* (pp. 1–60). Washington, DC: American Psychiatric Association.

Sher, K. J., Grekin, E. R., & Williams, N. A. (2005). The development of alcohol use disorders. In S. Nolen-Hoeksema, T. D. Cannon, & T. A. Widiger (Eds.), *Annual Review of Clinical Psychology* (Vol. 1, pp. 493–523). Palo Alto, CA: Annual Reviews.

Sher, K. J., & Trull, T. J. (1994). Personality and disinhibitory psychopathology: Alcoholism and antisocial personality disorder. *Journal of Abnormal Psychology, 103,* 92–102.

Sherrington, R., Rogaev, E. I., & Liang, Y. (1995). Cloning of a gene bearing missense mutations in early-onset familial Alzheimer's disease. *Nature, 375,* 754–760.

Sherwin, B. B. (1991). The psychoendocrinology of aging and female sexuality. *Annual Review of Sex Research, 2,* 191–198.

Shifren, J., Braunstein, G., Simon, J., Casson, P., Buster, J., Redmond, G., Burki, R., Ginsburg, E., Rosen, R., Leibum, S., Caramell, K., Mazer, N., Jones, K., & Daughery, C. (2000). Transdermal Testosterone Treatment in Women with Impaired Sexual Function after Oophorectomy. *The New England Journal of Medicine, 343,* 682–688.

Shin, L. M., Kosslyn, S. M., McNally, R. J., Alpert, N. M., Thompson, W. L., Rauch, S. L., Macklin, M. L., & Pitman, R. K. (1997). Visual imagery and perception in posttraumatic stress disorder: A positron emission tomographic investigation. *Archives of General Psychiatry, 54,* 233–241.

Shin, L. M., McNally, R. J., Kosslyn, S. M., Thompson, W. L., Rauch, S. L., Alpert, N. M., Metzger, L. J., Lasko, N. B., Orr, S. P., & Pitman, R. K. (1999). Regional cerebral blood flow during script-driven imagery in childhood sexual abuse–related PTSD: A PET investigation. *American Journal of Psychiatry, 156,* 575–584.

Shipherd, J. C., Beck, J. G., & Ohtake, P. J. (2001). Relationships between the anxiety sensitivity index, the suffocation fear scale, and responses to COsub-2 inhalation. *Journal of Anxiety Disorders, 15*(3), 247–258.

Shneidman, E. S. (1963). Orientations toward death: Subintentioned death and indirect suicide. In R. W. White (Ed.), *The study of lives.* New York: Atherton.

Shneidman, E. S. (1979). A bibliography of suicide notes: 1856–1979. *Suicide & Life-Threatening Behavior, 9,* 57–59.

Shneidman, E. S. (1981). Suicide. *Suicide & Life-Threatening Behavior, 11,* 198–220.

Shneidman, E. S. (1993). *Suicide as psychache: A clinical approach to self-destructive behavior.* Northvale, NJ: Jason Aronson.

Shneidman, E. S. (2001). *Comprehending suicide: Landmarks in 20th-century suicidology.* Washington, DC: American Psychological Association.

Shortt, A. L., Barrett, P. M., & Fox, T. L. (2001). Evaluating the FRIENDS program: A cognitive-behavioral group treatment for anxious children and their parents. *Journal of Clinical Child Psychology, 30,* 525–535.

Shrestha, N. M., Sharma, B., Van Ommeren, M., Regmi, S., Makaju, R., Komproe, I., Shrestha, G. B., & de Jong, J. T. V. M. (1998). Impact of torture on refugees displaced within the developing world. *Journal of the American Medical Association, 280,* 443–448.

Shrout, P. E., Canino, G. J., Bird, H. R., & Rubio-Stipec, M. (1992). Mental health status among Puerto Ricans, Mexican Americans, and non-Hispanic whites. *American Journal of Community Psychology, 20,* 729–752.

Siever, L. J., Bernstein, D. P., & Silverman, J. M. (1995). Schizotypal personality disorder. In W. J. Livesley (Ed.), *The DSM-IV personality disorders* (pp. 71–90). New York: Guilford Press.

Siever, L. J., & Davis, K. L. (1991). A psychobiological perspective on the personality disorders. *American Journal of Psychiatry, 148,* 1647–1658.

Siever, L. J., & Kendler, K. S. (1985). Paranoid personality disorder. In R. Michels, J. Cavenar, & H. Bradley (Eds.), *Psychiatry* (Vol. 1, pp. 1–11). New York: Basic Books.

Siever, L. J., New, A. S., Kirrane, R., Novotny, S., Koenigsberg, H., & Grossman, R. (1998). New biological research strategies for personality disorders. In K. R. Silk (Ed.), *Biology of personality disorders* (pp. 27–61). Washington, DC: American Psychiatric Press.

Silberg, J. L., Parr, T., Neale, M. C., Rutter, M., Angold, A., & Eaves, L. J. (2003). Maternal smoking during pregnancy and risk to boys' conduct disturbance: An examination of the causal hypothesis. *Biological Psychiatry, 53,* 130–135.

Silver, R. L., Boon, C., & Stones, M. H. (1983). Searching for meaning in misfortune: Making sense of incest. *Journal of Social Issues, 39,* 81–101.

Simeon, D., Guralnik, O., Schmeidler, J., Sirof, B., & Knutelska, M. (2001). The role of childhood interpersonal trauma in depersonalization disorder. *American Journal of Psychiatry, 158,* 1027–1033.

Simon, G. E., Katon, W. J., Von Korff, M., Un.tzer, J., Lin, E., Walker, E. A., Bush, T., Rutter, C., & Ludman, E. (2001). Cost-effectiveness of a collaborative care program for primary care patients with persistent depression. *American Journal of Psychiatry, 158*(10), 1638–1644.

Simonoff, E., Bolton, P., & Rutter, M. (1998). Genetic perspectives on mental retardation. In J. A. Burack, R. M. Hodapp, & E. Zigler (Eds.), *Handbook of mental retardation and development* (pp. 41–79). New York: Cambridge University Press.

Simons, J. A., & Helms, J. E. (1976). Influence of counselors' marital status, sex, and age on college and noncollege women's counselor preferences. *Journal of Counseling Psychology, 23,* 380–386.

Simpson, E. B., Yen, S., Costello, E., Rosen, K., Begin, A., Pistorello, J., & Pearlstein, T. (2004). Combined dialectical behavior therapy and fluoxetine in the treatment of borderline personality disorder. *Journal of Clinical Psychiatry, 65,* 379–385.

Sing, L. (1995). Self-starvation in context: Towards a culturally sensitive understanding of anorexia nervosa. *Social Science & Medicine, 41,* 25–36.

Singer, M. T., & Wynne, L. C. (1965). Thought disorder and family relations of schizophrenics: IV. Results and implications. *Archives of General Psychiatry, 12,* 201–212.

Singh, N. N., Oswald, D. P., & Ellis, C. R. (1998). Mental retardation. In T. H. Ollendick & M. Hersen (Eds.), *Handbook of child psychopathology* (pp. 91–116). New York: Plenum Press.

Sipahimalani, A., & Masand, P. S. (1998). Olanzapine in the treatment of delirium. *Psychosomatics, 39,* 422–430.

Siqueland, L., Kendall, P. C., & Steinberg, L. (1996). Anxiety in children: Perceived family environments and observed family interaction. *Journal of Clinical Child Psychology, 25,* 225–237.

Slate Magazine. (2004, June 3). Gender gap: What were the real reasons behind David Reimer's suicide? Retrieved February 11, 2005, from http://slate.msn.com/id/2101678/

Slater, L. (1998). *Prozac diary.* New York: Random House.

Slijper, F. M. E., Drop, S. L. S., Molenaar, J. C., & de Munick Keizer-Schrama, S. M. P. F. (1998). Long-term psychological evaluation of intersex children. *Archives of Sexual Behavior, 27,* 125–144.

Sloan, J. H., Rivara, F. P., Reay, D. T., Ferris, J. A., Path, M. R. C., & Kellerman, A. L. (1990). Firearm regulations and rates of suicide: A comparison of two metropolitan areas. *New England Journal of Medicine, 322,* 369–373.

Small, G. W. (1998). The pathogenesis of Alzheimer's disease. *Journal of Clinical Psychiatry, 59,* 7–14.

Smith, C. A., & Farrington, D. P. (2004). Continuities in antisocial behavior and parenting across three generations. *Journal of Child Psychology & Psychiatry, 45,* 230–247.

Smith, D. (2001). Sleep psychologists in demand. *Monitor on Psychology, 32,* 36–38.

Smith, D. E., & Seymour, R. B. (1994). LSD: History and toxicity. *Psychiatric Annals, 24,* 145–147.

Smith, M. L., Glass, G. V., & Miller, T. I. (1980). *The benefits of psychotherapy.* Baltimore: Johns Hopkins University Press.

Smith, T. W., Turner, C. W., Ford, M. H., & Hunt, S. C. (1987). Blood pressure reactivity in adult male twins. *Health Psychology, 6,* 209–220.

Smith, Y. L. S., van Goozen, S. H. M., & Cohen-Kettenis, P. T. (2001). Adolescents with gender identity disorder who were accepted or rejected for sex reassignment surgery: A prospective follow-up study. *Journal of the American Academy of Child & Adolescent Psychiatry, 40,* 472–481.

Smolak, L., Murnen, S. K., & Ruble, A. E. (2000). Female athletes and eating problems: A meta-analysis. *International Journal of Eating Disorders, 27,* 371–380.

Smoller, J. W., Rosenbaum, J. F., Biederman, J., Kennedy, J., Dai, D., Racette, S. R., Laird, N. M., Kagan, J., Snidman, N., Hirshfeld-Becker, D., Tsuang, M. T., Sklar, P. B., & Slaugenhaupt, S. A. (2003). Association of a genetic marker at the corticotrophin-releasing hormone locus with behavioral inhibition. *Biological Psychiatry, 54,* 1376–1381.

Snowden, J. S., Neary, D., & Mann, D. M. A. (1996). *Frontotemporal lobar degeneration: Frontotemporal dementia, progressive aphasia, semantic dementia.* New York: Churchill Livingstone.

Snowden, L. R. (2003). Challenges to consensus in preparing the supplement to the surgeon general's report on mental health. *Culture, Medicine & Psychiatry, 27,* 409–418.

Snowden, L. R., & Cheung, F. K. (1990). Use of inpatient mental health services by members of ethnic minority groups. *American Psychologist, 45,* 347–355.

Snowden, L. R., & Yamada, A. M. (2005). Cultural differences in access to care. *Annual Review of Clinical Psychology, 1,* 143–166.

Snowdon, D. A. (1997). Aging and Alzheimer's disease: Lessons from the Nun Study. *Gerontologist, 37,* 150–156.

Snowdon, D. A., Greiner, L. H., Mortimer, J. A., Riley, K. P., et al. (1997). Brain infarction and the clinical expression of Alzheimer's disease: The Nun Study. *Journal of the American Medical Association, 277,* 813–817.

Snowdon, D. A., Kemper, S. J., Mortimer, J. A., Greiner, L. H., Wekstein, D. R., & Markesbery, W. R. (1996). Linguistic ability in early life and cognitive function and Alzheimer's disease in late life: Findings from the Nun Study. *Journal of the American Medical Association, 275,* 528–532.

Snyder, C. R., Ilardi, S., Michael, S. T., & Cheavens, J. (2000). Hope theory: Updating a common process for psychological change. In C. R. Snyder & R. E. Ingram (Eds.), *Handbook of psychological change: Psychotherapy processes and practices for the 21st century* (pp. 128–153). New York: Wiley.

Sobal, J., & Stunkard, A. J. (1989). Socioeconomic status and obesity: A review of the literature. *Psychological Bulletin, 105,* 260–275.

Sobell, M. B., & Sobell, L. C. (1973). Individualized behavior therapy for alcoholics. *Behavior Therapy, 4,* 49–72.

Sobell, M. B., & Sobell, L. C. (1978). *Behavioral treatment of alcohol problems.* New York: Plenum Press.

Sobell, M. B., & Sobell, L. C. (1984). The aftermath of heresy: A response to Pendery et al.'s (1982) critique of "Individualized behavior therapy for alcoholics." *Behavior Research & Therapy, 22,* 413–440.

Sobell, M. B., & Sobell, L. C. (1995). Controlled drinking after 25 years: How important was the great debate? *Addiction, 90,* 1145–1153.

Soloff, P. H., Cornelius, J., George, A., Nathan, S., Perel, J. M., & Ulrich, R. F. (1993). Efficacy of phenelzine and haloperidol in borderline personality disorder. *Archives of General Psychiatry, 50,* 377–385.

Soloff, P. H., Meltzer, C. C., Greer, P. J., Constantine, D., & Kelly, T. M. (2000). A fenfluramine-activated FDG-PET study of borderline personality disorder. *Biological Psychiatry, 47,* 540–547.

Solomon, G. F., Segerstrom, S. C., Grohr, P., Kemeny, M., & Fahey, J. (1997). Shaking up immunity: Psychological and immunologic changes following a natural disaster. *Psychosomatic Medicine, 59,* 114–127.

Southwick, S. M., Vythilingam, M., & Charney, D. S. (2005). The psychobiology of depression and resilience to stress: Implications for prevention and treatment. *Annual Review of Clinical Psychology, 1,* 255–292.

Sowers, W. (1998). Psychological and psychiatric consequences of sedatives, hypnotics, and anxiolytics. In R. E. Tarter (Ed.), *Handbook of substance abuse: Neuro-behavioral pharmacology* (pp. 471–483). New York: Plenum Press.

Spanos, N. P. (1978). Witchcraft in histories of psychiatry: A critical analysis and an alternative conceptualization. *Psychological Bulletin, 85,* 417–439.

Spanos, N. P., Weekes, J. R., & Bertrand, L. D. (1985). Multiple personality: A social psychological perspective. *Journal of Abnormal Psychology, 94,* 362–376.

Speckens, A. E., Hengeveld, M. W., Nijeholt, G. L., & Van Hemert, A. M. (1995). Psychosexual functioning of partners of men with presumed nonorganic erectile dysfunction: Causes or consequences of the disorder? *Archives of Sexual Behavior, 24,* 157–172.

Spector, I. P., & Carey, M. P. (1990). Incidence and prevalence of the sexual dysfunctions: A critical review of the empirical literature. *Archives of Sexual Behavior, 19,* 389–408.

Sperber, K., & Shao, L. (2003). Neurologic consequences of HIV infection in the era of HAART. *AIDS Patient Care & STDs, 17,* 509–518.

Spiegel, D. (1991). Dissociation and trauma. In A. Tasman (Ed.), *American Psychiatric Press review of psychiatry* (Vol. 10, pp. 261–275). Washington, DC: American Psychiatric Press.

Spiegel, D. (2001). Mind matters—Group therapy and survival in breast cancer. *New England Journal of Medicine, 345,* 1767–1768.

Spiegel, D., Bollm, J. R., Kraemer, H. C., & Gottheil, E. (1989). Psychological support for cancer patients. *Lancet, 2,* 1447.

Spiegel, D. A. (1998). Efficacy studies of alprazolam in panic disorder. *Psychopharmacology Bulletin, 43,* 191–195.

Spierings, C., Poels, P. J., Sijben, N., Gabreels, F. J., & Renier, W. O. (1990). Conversion disorders in childhood: A retrospective follow-up study of 84 inpatients. *Developmental Medicine & Child Neurology, 32,* 865–871.

Spirito, A. (2006). Attempted and completed suicide in adolescence. *Annual Review of Clinical Psychology, 2.*

Spitzer, R. L. (1981). The diagnostic status of homosexuality in DSM-III: A reformulation of the issues. *American Journal of Psychiatry, 138,* 210–215.

Spitzer, R. L., Gibbon, M., Skodol, A. E., Williams, J. B. W., & First, M. B. (Eds.). (1994). *DSM-IV case book: A learning companion to the* Diagnostic and Statistical Manual of Mental Disorders (4th ed.). Washington, DC: American Psychiatric Association Press.

Spitzer, R. L., Skodol, A. E., Gibbon, M., & Williams, J. B. W. (1981). *DSM-III case book: A learning companion to the* Diagnostic and Statistical Manual of Mental Disorders (3rd ed.). Washington, DC: American Psychiatric Association.

Spitzer, R. L., Skodol, A. E., Gibbon, M., & Williams, J. B. W. (1983). *Psychopathology, a case book.* New York: McGraw-Hill.

Spitzer, R. L., Williams, J. B. W., Gibbon, M., & First, M. (1992). The Structured Clinical Interview for DSM-III-R (SCID): I. History, rationale, and description. *Archives of General Psychiatry, 49,* 624–636.

Spivack, G., & Shure, M. B. (1974). *Social adjustment of young children: A cognitive approach to solving real-life problems.* San Francisco: Jossey-Bass.

Sprock, J. (2000). Gender-typed behavioral examples of histrionic personality disorder. *Journal of Psychopathology and Behavioral Assessment, 22,* 107–122.

Sprock, J., Blashfield, R. K., & Smith, B. (1990). Gender weighting of DSM-IIIR personality disorder criteria. *American Journal of Psychiatry, 147,* 586–590.

Stack, S. (1987). Celebrities and suicide: A taxonomy and analysis, 1948–1983. *American Sociological Review, 52,* 401–412.

Stack, S. (1991). Social correlates of suicide by age: Media impacts. In A. A. Leenaars (Ed.), *Life span perspectives of suicide* (pp. 187–213). New York: Plenum Press.

Stahl, S. M. (1998). Basic psychopharmacology of antidepressants: Part 1. Antidepressants have seven distinct mechanisms of action. *Journal of Clinical Psychiatry 59*(Suppl. 4), 5–14.

Stahl, S. M. (2001). Dopamine system stabilizers, aripiprazole, and the next generation of antipsychotics, Part II: Illustrating their mechanisms of action. *Journal of Clinical Psychiatry, 62,* 923–924.

Stanley, M. A., & Novy, D. M. (2000). Cognitive-behavior therapy for generalized anxiety late in life: An evaluation overview. *Journal of Anxiety Disorders, 14,* 191–207.

Stark, L. J., Opipari, L. C., Donaldson, D. L., Danovsky, M. B., Rasile, D. A., & DelSanto, A. F. (1997). Evaluation of a standard protocol for retentive encopresis: A replication. *Journal of Pediatric Psychology, 22,* 619–633.

Statham, D. J., Heath, A. C., Madden, P., Bucholz, K., Bierut, L., Dinwiddie, S. H., Slutske, W. S., Dunne, M. P., & Martin, N. G. (1998). Suicidal behavior: An epidemiological study. *Psychological Medicine, 28,* 839–855.

Steadman, H. J., McGreevy, M. A., Morrissey, J. P., Callahan, L. A., Robbins, P. C., & Cirincione, C. (1993). *Before and after Hinckley: Evaluating insanity defense reform.* New York: Guilford Press.

Steadman, H. J., Mulvey, E. P., Monahan, J., Robbins, P. C., Appelbaum, P. S., Grisso, T., Roth, L. H., & Silver, E. (1998). Violence by people discharged from acute psychiatric inpatient facilities and by others in the same neighborhoods. *Archives of General Psychiatry, 55,* 393–401.

Stein, B. D., Elliott, M. N., Jaycox, L. H., Collins, R. L., Berry, S. H., Klein, D. J., & Schuster, M. A. (2004). A national longitudinal study of the psychological consequences of the September 11, 2001 terrorist attacks: Reactions, impairments, and help-seeking. *Psychiatry, 67,* 105–117.

Steinberg, M. (1990). Transcultural issues in psychiatry: The ataque and multiple personality disorder. *Dissociation: Progress in the Dissociative Disorders, 3,* 31–33.

Steiner, M., Dunn, E., & Born, L. (2003). Hormones and mood: From menarche to menopause and beyond. *Journal of Affective Disorders, 74,* 67–83.

Steketee, G., & Frost, R. (2003). Compulsive hoarding: Current status of the research. *Clinical Psychology Review, 23,* 905–927.

Stephens, S., Kenny, R. A., Rowan, E., Allan, L., Kalaria, R. N., Bradbury, M., & Ballard, C. G. (2004). Neuropsychological characteristics of mild vascular cognitive impairment and dementia after stroke. *International Journal of Geriatric Psychiatry, 19,* 1053–1057.

Sterk, C. E. (1999). *Fast lives: Women who use crack cocaine.* Philadelphia: Temple University Press.

Stern, Y., Gurland, B., Tatemichi, T. K., & Tang, M. X. (1994). Influence of education and occupation on the incidence of Alzheimer's disease. *Journal of the American Medical Association, 271,* 1004–1010.

Sternberg, R. J. (2004). Culture and intelligence. *American Psychologist, 59,* 325–338.

Stewart, S. H. (1996). Alcohol abuse in individuals exposed to trauma: A critical review. *Psychological Bulletin, 120,* 83–112.

Stewart, W. F., Ricci, J. A., Chee, E., Hahn, S. R., & Morganstein, D. (2003). Cost of lost productive work time among US workers with depression. *Journal of the American Medical Association, 289,* 3135–3144.

St. George-Hyslop, P. H., Tanzi, R. E., Polinsky, R. J., Haines, J. L., Nee, L., Watkins, P. C., & Meyers, R. H. (1987). The genetic defect causing familial Alzheimer's disease maps on chromosome 21. *Science, 235,* 885–890.

Stice, E. (2001). A prospective test of the dual-pathway model of bulimic pathology: Mediating effects of dieting and negative affect. *Journal of Abnormal Psychology, 110,* 124–135.

Stice, E. (2002). Risk and maintenance factors for eating pathology: A meta-analytic review. *Psychological Bulletin, 128,* 825–848.

Stice, E. (2003). Puberty and body image. In C. Hayward (Ed.), *Gender differences at puberty* (pp. 61–76). New York: Cambridge University Press.

Stice, E., & Agras, W. S. (1998). Predicting the onset and remission of bulimic behaviors in adolescence: A longitudinal grouping analysis. *Behavior Therapy, 29,* 257–276.

Stice, E., Agras, W. S., Telch, C. F., Halmi, K. A., Mitchell, J. E., & Wilson, T. (2001). Subtyping binge eating–disordered women along dieting and negative affect dimensions. *International Journal of Eating Disorders, 30,* 11–27.

Stice, E., Burton, E. M., & Shaw, H. (2004). Prospective relations between bulimic pathology, depression, and substance abuse: Unpacking comorbidity in adolescent girls. *Journal of Consulting & Clinical Psychology, 72,* 62–71.

Stice, E., Chase, A., Stormer, S., & Appel, A. (2001). A randomized trial of a dissonance-based eating disorder prevention program. *International Journal of Eating Disorders, 29,* 247–262.

Stice, E., & Fairburn, C. G. (2003). Dietary and dietary-depressive subtypes of bulimia nervosa show differential symptom presentation, social impairment, comorbidity, and course of illness. *Journal of Consulting & Clinical Psychology, 71,* 1090–1094.

Stice, E., Maxfield, J., & Wells, T. (2003). Adverse effects of social pressure to be thin on young women: An experimental investigation of the effects of "fat talk." *International Journal of Eating Disorders, 34,* 108–117.

Stice, E., Mazotti, L., Weibel, D., & Agras, W. S. (2000). Dissonance prevention program decreases thin-ideal internalization, body dissatisfaction, dieting, negative affect, and bulimic symptoms: A preliminary experiment. *International Journal of Eating Disorders, 27,* 206–217.

Stice, E., Presnell, K., & Spangler, D. (2002). Risk factors for binge eating onset in adolescent girls: A 2-year prospective investigation. *Health Psychology, 21,* 131–138.

Stice, E., & Shaw, H. E. (1994). Adverse effects of the media-portrayed thin-ideal on women and linkages to bulimic symptomatology. *Journal of Social & Clinical Psychology, 13,* 288–308.

Stice, E., Spangler, D., & Agras, W. S. (2001). Exposure to media-portrayed thin-ideal images adversely affects vulnerable girls: A longitudinal experiment. *Journal of Social & Clinical Psychology, 20,* 270–288.

Stocchi, F., Nordera, G., Jokinen, R., et al. (2001, May). *Efficacy and tolerability of paroxetine for long-term treatment of GAD.* Paper presented at 154th annual APA meeting, New Orleans.

Stoller, R. F. (1975). *Perversion: The erotic form of hatred.* New York: Pantheon Books.

Stoney, C. M. (2003). Gender and cardiovascular disease: A psychobiological and integrative approach. *Current Directions in Psychological Science, 12,* 129–133.

Stormer, S. M., & Thompson, J. K. (1998, November). *Challenging media messages regarding appearance: A psychoeducational program for males and females.* Paper presented at the annual meeting of the Association for the Advancement of Behavior Therapy, Washington, DC.

Storr, A. (1988). *Churchill's black dog, Kafka's mice, and other phenomena of the human mind.* New York: Grove Press.

Stouthamer-Loeber, M., Loeber, R., Homish, D. L., & Wei, E. (2001). Maltreatment of boys and the development of disruptive and delinquent behavior. *Development & Psychopathology, 13,* 941–955.

Straus, M. A., & Gelles, R. J. (1990). *Physical violence in American families: Risk factors and adaptations to violence in 8,145 families.* New Brunswick, NJ: Transaction.

Strauss, J. S. (1969). Hallucinations and delusions as points on continua function: Rating scale evidence. *Archives of General Psychiatry, 21,* 581–586.

Stravynski, A., Marks, I., & Yule, W. (1982). Social skills problems in neurotic outpatients: Social skills training with and without cognitive modification. *Archives of General Psychiatry, 39,* 1378–1385.

Streissguth, A. P., Barr, H. M., Bookstein, F. L., Sampson, P. D., & Olson, H. C. (1999). The long-term neurocognitive consequences of prenatal alcohol exposure: A 14-year study. *Psychological Science, 10,* 186–190.

Striegel-Moore, R. (1995). Psychological factors in the etiology of binge eating. *Addictive Behaviors, 20,* 713–723.

Striegel-Moore, R., Wilson, G. T., Wilfley, D. E., Elder, K. A., & Brownell, K. D. (1998). Binge eating in an obese community sample. *International Journal of Eating Disorders, 23,* 27–37.

Striegel-Moore, R. H. (1993). Etiology of binge eating: A developmental perspective. In C. G. Fairburn & G. T. Wilson (Eds.), *Binge eating: Nature, assessment, and treatment* (pp. 144–172). New York: Guilford Press.

Striegel-Moore, R. H., Dohm, F. A., Kraemer, H. C., Taylor, C. B., Daniels, S., Crawford, P. B., & Schreiber, G. B. (2003). Eating disorders in white and black women. *American Journal of Psychiatry, 160,* 1326–1331.

Striegel-Moore, R. H., & Franko, D. L. (2003). Epidemiology of binge eating disorder. *International Journal of Eating Disorders, 34*(Suppl. 1), 19–29.

Striegel-Moore, R. H., Seeley, J. R., & Lewinsohn, P. M. (2003). Psychosocial adjustment in young adulthood of women who experienced an eating disorder during adolescence. *Journal of the American Academy of Child & Adolescent Psychiatry, 42,* 587–593.

Striegel-Moore, R. H., Silberstein, L. R., & Rodin, J. (1993). The social self in bulimia nervosa: Public self-consciousness, social anxiety, and perceived fraudulence. *Journal of Abnormal Psychology, 102,* 297–303.

Stroebe, M., Gergen, M., Gergen, K., & Stroebe, W. (1992). Broken hearts or broken bonds: Love and death in historical perspective. *American Psychologist, 47,* 1205–1212.

Study Group on Anorexia Nervosa. (1995). Anorexia nervosa: Directions for future research. *International Journal of Eating Disorders, 17,* 235–241.

Stunkard, A. (1997). Eating disorders: The last 25 years. *Appetite, 29,* 181–190.

Stunkard, A. J. (1993). A history of binge eating. In C. G. Fairburn & G. T. Wilson (Eds.), *Binge eating: Nature, assessment, and treatment* (pp. 15–34). New York: Guilford Press.

Styron, W. (1990). *Darkness visible: A memoir of madness.* New York: Vintage Books.

Substance Abuse and Mental Health Services Administration (SAMHSA). (2002a). National household survey on drug abuse.

Retrieved November 1, 2004, from http://dawninfo.samhsa.gov/

Substance Abuse and Mental Health Services Administration (SAMHSA). (2002b). National survey on drug use and health. Retrieved November 1, 2004, from http://www.oas.samhsa.gov/nhsda2k2.htm

Substance Abuse and Mental Health Services Administration (SAMHSA). (2005). Overview of findings from the 2003 national survey on drug use and health. Retrieved November 1, 2004, from http://www.oas.samhsa.gov/nhsda/2k3nsduh/2k3Overview.htm

Suddath, R. L., Christison, G. W., Torrey, E. F., & Casanova, M. F. (1990). Anatomical abnormalities in the brains of monozygotic twins discordant for schizophrenia. *New England Journal of Medicine, 322,* 789–794.

Sudhansu, C., Hening, W. A., & Walters, A. S. (2003). *Sleep and movement disorders.* Burlington, MA: Butterworth-Heinemann.

Sue, D. W., Carter, R. T., Casas, J. M., Fouad, N. A., Ivey, A. E., Jensen, M., LaFromboise, T., Manese, J. E., Ponterotto, J. G., & Vazquez-Nutall, E. (1998). *Multicultural counseling competencies: Individual and organizational development.* Thousand Oaks, CA: Sage.

Sue, D. W., & Sue, D. (2003). *Counseling the culturally diverse: Theory and practice* (4th ed.). New York: Wiley.

Sue, S., & Lam, A. G. (2002). Cultural and demographic diversity. In J. C. Norcross (Ed.), *Psychotherapy relationships that work: Therapist contributions and responsiveness to patients* (pp. 401–421). London: Oxford University Press.

Sue, S., & Zane, N. (1987). The role of culture and cultural techniques in psychotherapy: A critique and reformulation. *American Psychologist, 42,* 37–51.

Suhail, K., & Cochrane, R. (2002). Effect of culture and environment on the phenomenology of delusions and hallucinations. *International Journal of Social Psychiatry, 48,* 126–138.

Suhara, T., Okubo, Y., Yasuno, F., Sudo, Y., Inoue, M., Ichimiya, T., Nakashima, Y., Nakayama, K., Tanada, S., Suzuki, K., Halldin, C., & Farde, L. (2002). Decreased dopamine D2 receptor binding in the anterior cingulated cortex in schizophrenia. *Archives of General Psychiatry, 59,* 25–30.

Sullivan, H. S. (1953). *The interpersonal theory of psychiatry.* New York: W. W. Norton.

Sullivan, P. F., Bulik, C. M., Fear, J. L., & Pickering, A. (1998). Outcome of anorexia nervosa: A case-control study. *American Journal of Psychiatry, 155,* 939–946.

Summers, M. (2000). *Everything in its place.* New York: Putnam.

Sundgot-Borgen, J. (1994). Risk and trigger factors for the development of eating disorders in female elite athletes. *Medicine & Science in Sports & Exercise, 26,* 414–419.

Suomi, S. J. (1999). Developmental trajectories, early experiences, and community consequences: Lessons from studies with rhesus monkeys. In D. P. Keating (Ed.), *Developmental health and the wealth of nations: Social, biological, and educational dynamics* (pp. 185–200). New York: Guilford Press.

Sutker, P. B., Allain, A. N., & Winstead, D. K. (1993). Psychopathology and psychiatric diagnoses of World War II Pacific theater prisoners of war and combat veterans. *American Journal of Psychiatry, 150,* 240–245.

Sutker, P. B., Davis, J. M., Uddo, M., & Ditta, S. R. (1995). Assessment of psychological distress in Persian Gulf troops: Ethnicity and gender comparisons. *Journal of Personality Assessment, 64,* 415–427.

Sutker, P. B., Winstead, D. K., Galina, Z. H., & Allain, A. N. (1991). Cognitive deficits and psychopathology among former prisoners of war and combat veterans of the Korean conflict. *American Journal of Psychiatry, 148,* 67–72.

Swartz, H. A., & Frank, E. (2001). Psychotherapy for bipolar depression: A phase-specific treatment strategy? *Bipolar Disorders, 3,* 11–12.

Swartz, M., Blazer, D., George, L., & Winfield, I. (1990). Estimating the prevalence of borderline personality disorder in the community. *Journal of Personality Disorders, 4,* 257–272.

Swazey, J. P. (1974). *Chlorpromazine in psychiatry: A study of therapeutic innovation.* Cambridge, MA: MIT Press.

Swendsen, J. D., Merikangas, K. R., Canino, G. J., Kessler, R. C., Rubio-Stipec, M., & Angst, J. (1998). The comorbidity of alcoholism with anxiety and depressive disorders in four geographic communities. *Comprehensive Psychiatry, 39,* 176–184.

Szasz, T. (1961). *The myth of mental illness.* New York: Hoeber-Harper.

Szasz, T. S. (1963a). *Law, liberty, and psychiatry: An inquiry into the social uses of mental health practice.* New York: Collier Books.

Szasz, T. S. (1963b). *The manufacture of madness.* New York: Harper & Row.

Szasz, T. S. (1971). The sane slave: An historical note on the use of medical diagnosis as justificatory rhetoric. *American Journal of Psychotherapy, 25,* 228–239.

Szasz, T. S. (1977). *Psychiatric slavery.* New York: Free Press.

Szatmari, P., Bartolucci, G., Bremner, R., & Bond, S. (1989). A follow-up study of high-functioning autistic children. *Journal of Autism & Developmental Disorders, 19,* 213–225.

Szatmari, P., Jones, M. B., Zwaigenbaum, L., & MacLean, J. E. (1998). Genetics of autism: Overview and new directions. *Journal of Autism & Developmental Disorders, 28,* 351–368.

T

Tager-Flusberg, H., Joseph, R., & Folstein, S. (2001). Current directions in research on autism. *Mental Retardation & Developmental Disabilities Research Review, 7,* 21–19.

Takahashi, Y. (1990). Is multiple personality disorder really rare in Japan? *Dissociation: Progress in the Dissociative Disorders, 3,* 57–59.

Takei, N., Sham, P. C., O'Callaghan, E., & Murray, R. M. (1992). Cities, winter birth, and schizophrenia. *Lancet, 340,* 558–559.

Takei, N., Sham, P. C., O'Callaghan, R., Glover, G., et al. (1995). Early risk factors in schizophrenia: Place and season of birth. *European Psychiatry, 10,* 165–170.

Tanay, E. (1992). The verdict with two names. *Psychiatric Annals, 22,* 571–573.

Tariot, P. N. (2003). Alzheimer disease: Current challenges, emerging treatments. *Alzheimer Disease & Associated Disorders, 17*(Suppl. 4), 98.

Tarrier, N., Pilgrim, H., Sommerfield, C., Faragher, B., Reynolds, M., Graham, E., & Barrowclough, C. (1999). A randomized trial of cognitive therapy and imaginal exposure in the treatment of chronic posttraumatic stress disorder. *Journal of Consulting & Clinical Psychology, 67,* 13–18.

Tateyama, M., Asai, M., Hashimoto, M., Bartels, M., & Kasper, S. (1998). Transcultural study of schizophrenic delusions: Tokyo versus Vienna versus Tuebingen (Germany). *Psychopathology, 31,* 59–68.

Tateyama, M., Asai, M., Kamisada, M., Hashimoto, M., Bartels, M., & Heimann, H. (1993). Comparison of schizophrenia delusions between Japan and Germany. *Psychopathology, 26,* 151–158.

Taylor, J., Iacono, W. G., & McGue, M. (2000). Evidence for a genetic etiology of early-onset delinquency. *Journal of Abnormal Psychology, 109,* 634–643.

Taylor, R. (1982). *Robert Schumann: His life and work.* London: Granada.

Taylor, S., Fedoroff, I., Koch, W. J., Thordarson, D. S., Fecteau, G., & Nicki, R. M. (2001). Posttraumatic stress disorder arising after road traffic collisions: Patterns of response to cognitive-behavior therapy. *Journal of Consulting & Clinical Psychology, 69,* 541–551.

Taylor, S. E. (1999). *Health psychology.* New York: McGraw-Hill.

Taylor, S. E., & Brown, J. D. (1988). Illusion and well-being: A social psychological perspective on mental health. *Psychological Bulletin, 103,* 193–210.

Taylor, S. E., Kemeny, M. E., Aspinwall, L. G., & Schneider, S. G. (1992). Optimism, coping, psychological distress, and high-risk sexual behavior among men at risk for acquired immunodeficiency syndrome (AIDS). *Journal of Personality & Social Psychology, 63,* 460–473.

Taylor, S. E., Klein, L. C., Lewis, B. P., Gruenwald, T. L., Gurung, R. A. R., & Updegraff, J. A. (2000). Biobehavioral responses to stress in females: Tend-and-befriend, not fight-or-flight. *Psychological Review, 3,* 411–429.

Tebartz van Elst, L., Hesslinger, B., Thiel, T., Geiger, E., Haegele, K., Lemieux, L., Lieb, K., Bohus, M., Hennig, J., & Ebert, J. (2003). Frontolimbic brain abnormalities in patients with borderline personality disorder: A volumetric magnetic resonance imaging study. *Biological Psychiatry, 54,* 163–171.

Telch, C. F., Agras, W. S., & Linehan, M. M. (2001). Dialectical behavior therapy for binge eating disorder. *Journal of Consulting & Clinical Psychology, 69,* 1061–1065.

Telch, C. F., & Stice, E. (1998). Psychiatric comorbidity in women with binge eating disorder: Prevalence rates from a non-treatment-seeking sample. *Journal of Consulting & Clinical Psychology, 66,* 768–776.

Telch, M. J., Lucas, J. A., Schmidt, N. B., Hanna, H. H., LaNae, J. T., & Lucas, R. A. (1993). Group cognitive-behavioral treatment of panic disorder. *Behaviour Research & Therapy, 31,* 279–287.

Telles, C., Karno, M., Mintz, J., Paz, G., Arias, M., Tucker, D., & Lopez, S. (1995). Immigrant families coping with schizophrenia. *British Journal of Psychiatry, 167,* 473–479.

Temple, N. (2001). Psychodynamic psychotherapy in the treatment of conversion hysteria. In P. W. Halligan, C. Bass, & J. Marshall (Eds.), *Contemporary approaches to the study of hysteria: Clinical and theoretical perspectives* (pp. 283–297). Oxford, UK: Oxford University Press.

Teplin, L. A. (1990). The prevalence of severe mental disorder among male urban jail detainees: Comparison with the Epidemiologic Catchment Area program. *American Journal of Public Health, 80,* 663–669.

Teplin, L. A., Abram, K. M., & McClelland, G. M. (1996). Prevalence of psychiatric disorders among incarcerated women. I. Pretrial jail detainees. *Archives of General Psychiatry, 53,* 505–512.

Teplin, L. A., Abram, K. M., & McClelland, G. M. (1997). Mentally disordered women in jail: Who receives services? *American Journal of Public Health, 87,* 604–609.

Teri, L., Gibbons, L. E., McCurry, S. M., Logsdon, R. G., Buchner, D. M., Barlow, W. E., Kukull, W. A., LaCroix, A. Z., McCormick, W., & Larson, E. B. (2003). Exercise plus behavioral management in patients with Alzheimer disease: A randomized controlled trial. *Journal of the American Medical Association, 290,* 2015–2022.

Terr, L. C. (1981). Psychic trauma in children: Observations following the Chowchilla school-bus kidnapping. *American Journal of Psychiatry, 138,* 14–19.

Test, M. A., & Stein, L. I. (1980). Alternative to mental hospital treatment: III. Social cost. *Archives of General Psychiatry, 37,* 409–412.

Teyber, E., & McClure, F. (2000). Therapist variables. In C. R. Snyder & R. E. Ingram (Eds.), *Handbook of psychological change: Psychotherapy processes and practices for the 21st century* (pp. 62–87). New York: Wiley.

Tharp, R. G. (1991). Cultural diversity and treatment of children. *Journal of Consulting & Clinical Psychology, 59,* 799–812.

Thase, M. E., Greenhouse, J. B., Frank, E., Reynolds, C. F., III, Pilkonis, P. A., Hurley, K., Grochocinski, V., & Kupfer, D. J. (1997). Treatment of major depression with psychotherapy or psychotherapy-pharmacotherapy combinations. *Archives of General Psychiatry, 54,* 1009–1015.

Thase, M. E., Jindal, R., & Howland, R. H. (2002). Biological aspects of depression. In I. H. Gotlib & C. L. Hammen (Eds.), *Handbook of depression* (pp. 192–218). New York: Guilford Press.

Thermenos, H. W., Seidman, L. J., Breiter, H., Goldstein, J. M., Goodman, J. M., Poldrack, R., Faraone, S. V., & Tsuang, M. T. (2004). Functional magnetic resonance imaging during auditory verbal working memory in nonpsychotic relatives of persons with schizophrenia: A pilot study. *Biological Psychiatry, 55,* 490–500.

Thienemann, M. (2004). Medications for pediatric anxiety. In H. Steiner (Ed.), *Handbook of mental health intervention in children and adolescents: An integrated developmental approach* (pp. 288–317). San Francisco: Jossey-Bass.

Thomas, A., & Chess, S. (1984). Genesis and evolution of behavioral disorders: From infancy to early adult life. *American Journal of Psychiatry, 141,* 1–9.

Thompson, J. K., Heinberg, L. J., Altabe, M. N., & Tantleff-Dunn, S. (1999). *Exacting beauty: Theory, assessment and treatment of body image disturbance.* Washington, DC: American Psychological Association.

Thompson, J. K., & Stice, E. (2001). Thin ideal internalization: Mounting evidence for a new risk factor for body image disturbance and eating pathology. *Current Directions in Psychological Science, 10,* 181–183.

Thompson, L. W., Coon, D. W., Gallagher-Thompson, D., Sommer, B., & Koin, D. (2001). Comparison of desipramine and cognitive/behavioral therapy in the treatment of late-life depression. *American Journal of Geriatric Psychiatry, 9,* 225–240.

Thoresen, C. E., Telch, M. J., & Eagleston, J. R. (1981). Altering Type A behavior. *Psychosomatics, 8,* 472–482.

Thorpe, G. L., & Olson, S. L. (1997). *Behavior therapy: Concepts, procedures, and applications* (2nd ed.). Boston: Allyn & Bacon.

Tienari, P. (1991). Interaction between genetic vulnerability and family environment: The Finnish adoptive family study of schizophrenia. *Acta Psychiatrica Scandinavica, 84,* 460–465.

Tienari, P., Wynne, L. C., Laksy, K., Moring, J., Nieminen, P., Sorri, A., Lahti, I., & Wahlberg, K.-E. (2003). Genetic boundaries of the schizophrenia spectrum: Evidence from the Finnish Adoptive Family Study of Schizophrenia. *American Journal of Psychiatry, 160,* 1587–1594.

Tiet, Q. Q., Wasserman, G. A., Loeber, R., McReynolds, L. S., & Miller, L. S. (2001). Developmental and sex differences in types of conduct problems. *Journal of Child & Family Studies, 10,* 181–197.

Tillich, P. (1952). Anxiety, religion, and medicine. *Pastoral Psychology, 3,* 11–17.

Tolan, P. H., & Gorman-Smith, D. (1997). Treatment of juvenile delinquency: Between punishment and therapy. In D. M. Stoff, J. Breiling, & J. D. Maser (Eds.), *Handbook of antisocial personality disorder* (pp. 405–415). New York: Wiley.

Tondo, L., Baldessarini, R. J., Floris, G., & Rudas, N. (1997). Effectiveness of restarting lithium treatment after its discontinuation in bipolar I and bipolar II disorders. *American Journal of Psychiatry, 154,* 548–550.

Tondo, L., Jamison, K. R., & Baldessarini, R. J. (1997). Effect of lithium maintenance on suicidal behavior in major mood disorders. *Annals of the New York Academy of Sciences, 836,* 339–351.

Torrey, E. F. (1995). *Surviving schizophrenia: A manual for families, consumers, and providers* (3rd ed.). New York: HarperPerennial.

Torrey, E. F. (1997). *Out of the shadows: Confronting America's mental illness crisis.* New York: Wiley.

Torrey, E. F., Bowler, A. E., & Clark, K. (1997). Urban birth and residence as risk factors for psychosis: An analysis of 1880 data. *Schizophrenia Research, 25,* 169–176.

Torrey, E. F., & Yolken, R. H. (1998). At issue: Is household crowding a risk factor for schizophrenia and bipolar disorder? *Schizophrenia Bulletin, 24,* 321–324.

Torti, F. M., Jr., Gwyther, L. P., Reed, S. D., Friedman, J. Y., & Schulman, K. A. (2004). A multinational review of recent trends and reports in dementia caregiver burden. *Alzheimer Disease & Associated Disorders, 18,* 99–109.

Toufexis, A. (1996, April 29). Why Jennifer got sick. *Time,* p. 70.

Treatment for Adolescents with Depression Study (TADS) Team. (2004). Fluoxetine, cognitive-behavioral therapy, and their combination for adolescents with depression: Treatment for adolescents with depression study (TADS) randomized controlled trial. *Journal of the American Medical Association, 292,* 807–820.

Trierweiler, S. J., & Stricker, G. (1998). *The scientific practice of professional psychology.* New York: Plenum Press.

Trinh, N.-H., Hoblyn, J., Mohanty, S., & Yaffe, K. (2003). Efficacy of cholinesterase inhibitors in the treatment of neuropsychiatric symptoms and functional impairment in Alzheimer disease: A meta-analysis. *Journal of the American Medical Association, 289,* 210–216.

Tronick, E. Z., Frank, D. A., Cabral, H., Mirochnick, M., & Zuckerman, B. (1996). Late dose-response effects of prenatal cocaine exposure on newborn neurobehavioral performance. *Pediatrics, 98,* 76–83.

True, W. R., Rice, J., Eisen, S. A., Heath, A. C., Goldberg, J., Lyons, M. J., & Nowak, J. (1993). A twin study of genetic and environmental contributions to liability for posttraumatic stress symptoms. *Archives of General Psychiatry, 50,* 257–264.

Trull, T. J., & Durrett, C. A. (2005). Categorical and dimensional models of personality disorder. In S. Nolen-Hoeksema, T. D. Cannon, & T. A. Widiger (Eds.), *Annual review of clinical psychology* (Vol. 1, pp. 355–380). Palo Alto, CA: Annual Reviews.

Trull, T. J., Waudby, C. J., & Sher, K. J. (2004). Alcohol, tobacco, and drug use disorders and personality disorder symptoms. *Experimental & Clinical Psychopharmacology, 12,* 65–75.

Tsai, G., & Coyle, J. T. (2002). Glutamatergic mechanisms in schizophrenia. *Annual Review of Pharmacological Toxicology, 42,* 165–179.

Tsai, J. L., Butcher, J. N., Munoz, R. F., & Vitousek, K. (2001). Culture, ethnicity, and psychopathology. In P. B. Sutker (Ed.), *Comprehensive handbook of psychopathology* (3rd ed., pp. 105–127). New York: Kluwer Academic/Plenum Publishers.

Tsai, J. L., & Chentsova-Dutton, Y. (2002). Understanding depression across cultures. In I. H. Gotlib & C. L. Hammen (Eds.), *Handbook of depression* (pp. 467–491). New York: Guilford Press.

Tseng, W. (1973). The development of psychiatric concepts in traditional Chinese medicine. *Archives of General Psychiatry, 29,* 569–575.

Tseng, W.-S. (2001). *Culture and psychotherapy: A guide to clinical practice.* Washington, DC: American Psychiatric Press.

Tsuang, M. T., Fleming, J. A., & Simpson, J. C. (1999). Suicide and schizophrenia. In D. G. Jacobs (Ed.), *The Harvard Medical School guide to suicide assessment and intervention* (pp. 287–299). San Francisco: Jossey-Bass.

Tsuang, M. T., Lyons, M. J., Meyer, J. M., Doyle, T., Eisen, S. A., Goldberg, J., True, W., Lin, N., Toomey, R., & Eaves, L. (1998). Co-occurrence of abuse of different drugs in men: The role of drug-specific and shared vulnerabilities. *Archives of General Psychiatry, 55,* 967–972.

Tugrul, C., & Kabakci, E. (1997). Vaginismus and its correlates. *Sexual & Marital Therapy, 12,* 23–34.

Tuma, J. M. (1989). Mental health services for children: The state of the art. *American Psychologist, 44,* 188–199.

Turk, C. L., Heimberg, R. G., & Hope, D. A. (2001). Social anxiety disorder. *Clinical handbook of psychological disorders: A step-by-step treatment manual* (3rd ed., pp. 114–153). New York: Guilford Press.

Turk, D. C., Meichenbaum, D. H., & Berman, W. H. (1979). Application of biofeedback for the regulation of pain: A critical review. *Psychological Bulletin, 86,* 1322–1338.

Turk, D. C., & Ruby, T. E. (1992). Cognitive factors and persistent pain: A glimpse into Pandora's box. *Cognitive Therapy & Research, 16,* 99–122.

Turkat, I. D. (1985). *Behavioral case formulation.* New York: Plenum Press.

Turkheimer, E., & Parry, C. D. (1992). Why the gap? Practice and policy in civil commitment hearings. *American Psychologist, 47,* 646–655.

Turnbull, J. E., & Gomberg, E. S. (1990). The structure of depression in alcoholic women. *Journal of Studies on Alcohol, 51,* 148–155.

Turner, R. J., & Lloyd, D. A. (2004). Stress burden and the lifetime incidence of psychiatric disorder in young adults: Racial and ethnic contrasts. *Archives of General Psychiatry, 61,* 481–488.

Turner, S. M., Beidel, D. C., & Wolff, P. L. (1996). Is behavioral inhibition related to the anxiety disorders? *Clinical Psychology Review, 16*(2) 157–172.

Turner-Cobb, J. M., Sephton, S. E., Koopman, C., Blake-Mortimer, J., & Spiegel, D. (2000). Social support and salivary cortisol in women with metastatic breast cancer. *Psychosomatic Medicine, 62,* 337–345.

Twenge, J. M., & Nolen-Hoeksema, S. (2002). Age, gender, race, SES, and birth cohort differences on the Children's Depression Inventory: A meta-analysis. *Journal of Abnormal Psychology, 111,* 578–588.

U

Ullman, L. P., & Krasner, L. (1975). *A psychological approach to abnormal behavior* (2nd ed.). Oxford, UK: Prentice Hall.

Unützer, J., Patrick, D. L., Diehr, P., Simon, G., Grembowski, D., & Katon, W. (2000). Quality adjusted life years in older adults with depressive symptoms and chronic medical disorders. *International Psychogeriatrics, 12,* 15–33.

U.S. Department of Health and Human Services (USDHHS). (1999). *Mental health: A report of the surgeon general—Executive summary.* Rockville, MD: U.S. Department of Health and Human Services, Substance Abuse and Mental Health Services Administration, Center for Mental Health Services, National Institutes of Health, National Institute of Mental Health.

U.S. Department of Health and Human Services (USDHHS). (2001). *Mental health: Culture, race, and ethnicity. A supplement to mental health: A report of the surgeon general.* Rockville, MD: U.S. Department of Health and Human Services, Public Health Services, Office of the Surgeon General.

Uva, J. L. (1995). Review: Autoerotic asphyxiation in the United States. *Journal of Forensic Sciences, 40,* 574–581.

V

Vakoch, D. A., & Strupp, H. H. (2000). Psychodynamic approaches to psychotherapy: Philosophical and theoretical foundations of effective practice. In C. R. Snyder & R. E. Ingram (Eds.), *Handbook of psychological change: Psychotherapy processes and practices for the 21st century* (pp. 200–216). New York: Wiley.

Valenstein, E. S. (1986). *Great and desperate cures: The rise and decline of psychosurgery and other radical treatments for mental illness.* New York: Basic Books.

Valenstein, R. S. (1998). *Blaming the brain: The truth about drugs and mental health.* New York: Free Press.

Van Ameringen, M. A., Lane, R. M., Walker, J. R., Bowen, R. C., Chokka, P. R., Goldner, E. M., Johnston, D. G., Lavallee, Y., Nandy, S., Pecknold, J. C., Hadrava, V., & Swinson, R. P. (2001). Sertraline treatment of generalized social phobia: A 20-week, double-blind, placebo-controlled study. *American Journal of Psychiatry, 158*(2), 275–281.

Van Etten, M. L., & Anthony, J. C. (2001). Male-female differences in transitions from first drug opportunity to first use: Searching for subgroup variation by age, race, region, and urban status. *Journal of Women's Health & Gender-Based Medicine, 10,* 797–804.

van Gorp, W. G., Altshuler, L., Theberge, D. C., Wilkins, J., & Dixon, W. (1998). Cognitive impairment in euthymic bipolar patients with and without prior alcohol dependence: A preliminary study. *Archives of General Psychiatry, 55,* 41–46.

Van Heeringen, C. (2001). Suicide in adolescents. *International Clinical Psychopharmacology, 16*(Suppl. 2), S1–S6.

Van Hemert, A. M., Hengeveld, M. W., Bolk, J. H., & Rooijmans, H. G. (1993). Psychiatric disorders in relation to medical illness among patients of a general medical outpatient clinic. *Psychological Medicine, 23,* 167–173.

van Ommeren, M., De Jong, J. T. V. M., Bhogendra, S., Komproe, I., Thapa, S. B., & Cardena, E. (2001). Psychiatric disorders among tortured Bhutanese refugees in Nepal. *Archives of General Psychiatry, 58,* 475–482.

van Os, J., Hanssen, M., Bijl, R. V., & Vollebergh, W. (2001). Prevalence of psychotic disorder and community level of psychotic symptoms. *Archives of General Psychiatry, 58,* 663–668.

van Velzen, C. J. M., Emmelkamp, P. M. G., & Scholing, A. (2000). Generalized social phobia versus avoidant personality disorder: Differences in psychopathology, personality traits, and social and occupational functioning. *Journal of Anxiety Disorders, 14,* 395–411.

Vaughn, C. E., & Leff, J. P. (1976). The influence of family and social factors on the course of psychiatric illness: A comparison of schizophrenic and depressed neurotic patients. *British Journal of Psychiatry, 129,* 125–137.

Vazquez-Nuttall, E., Avila-Vivas, Z., & Morales-Barreto, G. (1984). Working with Latin American families. *Family Therapy Collections, 9,* 74–90.

Vazquez-Nuttall, E., Romero-Garcia, I., & DeLeon, R. (1987). Sex roles and perceptions of femininity and masculinity of Hispanic women: A review of the literature. *Psychology of Women Quarterly, 11,* 409–425.

Veith, I. (1965). *Hysteria: The history of a disease.* Chicago: University of Chicago Press.

Velting, O. N., Setzer, N. J., & Albano, A. M. (2004). Update on and advances in assessment and cognitive-behavioral treatment of anxiety disorders in children and adolescents. *Professional Psychology: Research & Practice, 35,* 42–54.

Ventura, J., Neuchterlein, K. H., Lukoff, D., & Hardesty, J. P. (1989). A prospective study of stressful life events and schizophrenic relapse. *Journal of Abnormal Psychology, 98,* 407–411.

Verhulst, J., & Heiman, J. (1988). A systems perspective on sexual desire. In S. R. Leiblum & R. C. Rosen (Eds.), *Sexual desire disorders* (pp. 243–270). New York: Guilford Press.

Verma, K. K., Khaitan, B. K., & Singh, O. P. (1998). The frequency of sexual dysfunctions in patients attending a sex therapy clinic in north India. *Archives of Sexual Behavior, 27,* 309–314.

Verona, E., Patrick, C. J., Joiner, T. E. (2001). Psychopathy, antisocial personality, and suicide risk. *Journal of Abnormal Psychology, 110,* 462–470.

Veronen, L. J., & Kilpatrick, D. G. (1983). Stress management for rape victims. In D. Meichenbaum & M. E. Jaremko (Eds.), *Stress reduction and prevention.* New York: Plenum Press.

Viken, R. J., Treat, T. A., Nosofsky, R. M., McFall, R. M., & Palmeri, T. J. (2002). Modeling individual differences in perceptual and attentional processes. *Journal of Abnormal Psychology, 111,* 598–609.

Villarreal, G., Hamilton, D. A., Petropoulos, H., Driscoll, I., Rowland, L. M., Griego, J. A., Kodituwakku, P. W., Hart, B. L., Escalona, R., & Brooks, W. M. (2002). Reduced hippocampal volume and total white matter volume in posttraumatic stress disorder. *Biological Psychiatry, 52,* 119–125.

Visintainer, M. A., Volpicelli, J. R., & Seligman, M. E. (1982). Tumor rejection in rats after inescapable or escapable shock. *Science, 216,* 437–439.

Vohs, K. D., Bardone, A. M., Joiner, T. E., Jr., & Abramson, L. Y. (1999). Perfectionism, perceived weight status, and self-esteem interact to predict bulimic symptoms: A model of bulimic symptom development. *Journal of Abnormal Psychology, 108,* 695–700.

Vohs, K. D., Voelz, Z. R., Pettit, J. W., Bardone, A. M., Katz, J., Abramson, L. Y., Heatherton, T. F., & Joiner, T. E. (2001). Perfectionism, body dissatisfaction, and self-esteem: An

interactive model of bulimic symptom development. *Journal of Social & Clinical Psychology, 20,* 476–497.

Volkmar, F. G. (2001). Pharmacological intervention in autism: Theoretical and practical issues. *Journal of Clinical Child Psychology, 30,* 80–87.

Volkmar, F. R., Lord, C., Bailey, A., Schultz, R. T., & Klin, A. (2004). Autism and pervasive developmental disorders. *Journal of Child Psychology and Psychiatry, 45,* 135–170.

Volpicelli, J. R. (2001). Alcohol abuse and alcoholism: An overview. *Journal of Clinical Psychiatry, 62*(Suppl. 20), 4–10.

Volpicelli, J. R., Rhines, K. C., Rhines, J. S., Volpicelli, L. A., Alterman, A. I., & O'Brien, C. P. (1997). Naltrexone and alcohol dependence: Role of subject compliance. *Archives of General Psychiatry, 54,* 737–742.

Volz, H.-P., & Kieser, M. (1997). Kavakava extract WS 1490 versus placebo in anxiety disorders: A randomized placebo-controlled 25-week outpatient trial. *Pharmacopsychiatry, 30,* 1–5.

von Buhler, J. M. (1998). Vacuum and constriction devices for erectile disorder—An integrative view. *Sexual & Marital Therapy, 13,* 257–276.

Von Korff, M., Nestadt, G., Romanoski, A., Anthony, J., Eaton, W., Merchant, A., Chahal, R., Kramer, M., Folstein, M., & Gruenberg, E. (1985). Prevalence of treated and untreated DSMIII schizophrenia: Results of a two-stage community survey. *Journal of Nervous & Mental Disease, 173,* 577–581.

Vuilleumier, P., Chicherio, C., Assal, F., Schwartz, S., Slosmen, D., & Landis, T. (2001). Functional neuroanatomical correlates of hysterical sensorimotor loss. *Brain, 124,* 1077–1090.

Vythilingam, M., Heim, C., Newport, J., Miller, A. H., Anderson, E., Bronen, R., Brummer, M., Staib, L., Vermetten, E., Charney, D. S., Nemeroff, C. B., & Bremner, J. D. (2002). Childhood trauma associated with smaller hippocampal volume in women with major depression. *American Journal of Psychiatry, 159,* 2072–2080.

W

Wadden, T. A., Brownell, K. D., & Foster, G. D. (2002). Obesity: Responding to the global epidemic. *Journal of Consulting & Clinical Psychology, 70,* 510–525.

Wade, T., Neale, M. C., Lake, R. I. E., & Martin, N. G. (1999). A genetic analysis of the eating and attitudes associated with bulimia nervosa: Dealing with the problem of ascertainment in twin studies. *Behavior Genetics, 99,* 1–10.

Wade, T. D., Bulik, C. M., Neale, M., & Kendler, K. S. (2000). Anorexia nervosa and major depression: Shared genetic and environmental risk factors. *American Journal of Psychiatry, 157,* 469–471.

Wagner, B. M., Silverman, M. A. C., & Martin, C. E. (2003). Family factors in youth suicidal behaviors. *American Behavioral Scientist, 46,* 1171–1191.

Wahlberg, D. (1999, October 21). Binge drinking remains problem. *Ann Arbor News,* p. A1.

Waldron, H. B., Slesnick, N., Brody, J. L., Turner, C. W., & Peterson, T. R. (2001).

Treatment outcomes for adolescent substance abuse at 4- and 7-month assessments. *Journal of Consulting & Clinical Psychology, 69,* 802–813.

Walker, E., Kestler, L., Bollini, A., & Hochman, K. M. (2004). Schizophrenia: Etiology and course. *Annual Review of Psychology, 55,* 401–430.

Walker, L. E. A. (1994). Are personality disorders gender biased? In S. A. Kirk & S. D. Einbinder (Eds.), *Controversial issues in mental health* (pp. 22–29). Boston: Allyn & Bacon.

Wallace, J., Schneider, T., & McGuffin, P. (2002). Genetics of depression. In I. H. Gotlib & C. L. Hammen (Eds.), *Handbook of depression* (pp. 169–191). New York: Guilford Press.

Waller, S. J., Lyons, J. S., & Costantini-Ferrando, M. F. (1999). Impact of comorbid affective and alcohol use disorders on suicide ideation and attempts. *Journal of Clinical Psychology, 55,* 585–595.

Walters, E., & Kendler, K. (1999). Anorexia nervosa and anorexic-like syndromes in a population based female twin sample. *The American Journal of Psychiatry, 152,* 64–75.

Wampold, B. E., Mondin, G. W., Moody, M., Stich, F., Benson, K., & Ahn, H. (1997). A meta-analysis of outcome studies comparing bona fide psychotherapies: Empirically, "all must have prizes." *Psychological Bulletin, 122,* 203–215.

Wandersman, A., & Nation, M. (1998). Urban neighborhoods and mental health: Psychological contributions to understanding toxicity, resilience, and interventions. *American Psychologist, 53,* 647–656.

Warga, C. (1988, September). You are what you think. *Psychology Today,* pp. 54–58.

Warner, M. B., Morey, L. C., Finch, J. F., Gunderson, J. G., Skodol, A. E., Sanislow, C. A., Shea, M. T., McGlashan, T. H., & Grilo, C. M. (2004). The longitudinal relationship of personality traits and disorders. *Journal of Abnormal Psychology, 113,* 217–227.

Warren, J. I., Murrie, D. C., Chauhan, P., Dietz, P. E., & Morris, J. (2004). Opinion formation in evaluating sanity at the time of the offense: An examination of 5175 pre-trial evaluations. *Behavioral Sciences and the Law, 22,* 171–186.

Waschbusch, D. A. (2002). A meta-analytic examination of comorbid hyperactive-impulsive-attention problems and conduct problems. *Psychological Bulletin, 128,* 118–150.

Washington Post. (2004, August 27). Poverty rate up 3rd year in a row [Electronic version]. *Washington Post,* p. A01.

Waters, A., Hill, A., & Waller, G. (2001). Bulimics' response to food cravings: Is binge-eating a product of hunger or emotional state? *Behaviour Research & Therapy, 39,* 877–886.

Watson, C. G., & Buranen, C. (1979). The frequencies of conversion reaction symptoms. *Journal of Abnormal Psychology, 88,* 209–211.

Watson, D., & Clark, L. A. (1984). Negative affectivity: The disposition to experience aversive emotional states. *Psychological Bulletin, 96,* 465–490.

Watson, J. B. (1930). *Behaviorism.* Chicago: University of Chicago Press.

Watson, J. B., & Raynor, R. (1920). Conditioned emotional reactions. *Journal of Experimental Psychology, 3*, 1–14.

Watson, K. A., & Hayward, C. (2005). A prospective evaluation of agoraphobia and depression symptoms following panic attacks in a community sample of adolescents. *Journal of Anxiety Disorders, 19*, 87–103.

Watson, M., Haviland, J. S., Greer, S., Davidson, J., & Bliss, J. M. (1999). Influence of psychological response on survival in breast cancer: A population-based cohort study. *Lancet, 354*, 1331–1336.

Webster-Stratton, C., & Reid, M. J. (2003). The incredible years parents, teachers, and children training series: A multifaceted treatment approach for young children with conduct problems. In A. E. Kazdin & J. R. Weisz (Eds.), *Evidence-based psychotherapies for children and adolescents* (pp. 224–240). New York: Guilford Press.

Weeks, D., & James, J. (1995). *Eccentrics.* New York: Villard.

Wehr, T. A., Duncan, W. C., Sher, L., Aeschbach, D., Schwartz, P. J., Turner, E. H., Postolache, T. T., & Rosenthal, N. E. (2001). A circadian signal of change of season in patients with seasonal affective disorder. *Archives of General Psychiatry, 58*, 1108–1114.

Weine, S. M., Becker, D. F., McGlashan, T. H., Laub, D., Lazrove, S., Vojvoda, D., & Hyman, L. (1995). Psychiatric consequences of "ethnic cleansing": Clinical assessments and trauma testimonies of newly resettled Bosnian refugees. *American Journal of Psychiatry, 152*, 536–542.

Weine, S. M., Vojvoda, D., Becker, D. F., McGlashan, T. H., Hodzic, E., Laub, D., Hyman, L., Sawyer, M., & Lazrove, S. (1998). PTSD symptoms in Bosnian refugees 1 year after resettlement in the United States. *American Journal of Psychiatry, 155*, 562–564.

Weiner, B. A., & Wettstein, R. M. (1993). *Legal issues in mental health care.* New York: Plenum Press.

Weissman, M. M. (1993). The epidemiology of personality disorders: A 1990 update. NIMH Conference: Personality disorders (1990, Williamsburg, Virginia). *Journal of Personality Disorders* (Suppl. 1), 44–62.

Weissman, M. M., Bland, R. C., Canino, G. J., et al. (1996). Cross-national epidemiology of major depression and bipolar disorder. *Journal of the American Medical Association, 276*, 293–299.

Weissman, M. M., & Markowitz, J. C. (2002). Interpersonal psychotherapy for depression. In I. H. Gotlib & C. L. Hammen (Eds.), *Handbook of depression* (pp. 404–421). New York: Guilford Press.

Weisz, J. R., Donenberg, G., Han, S., & Kauneckis, D. (1995). Child and adolescent psychotherapy outcomes in experiments versus clinics: Why the disparity? *Journal of Abnormal Child Psychology, 23*, 83–106.

Weisz, J. R., & Hawley, K. M. (2002). Developmental factors in the treatment of adolescents. *Journal of Consulting & Clinical Psychology, 70*, 21–43.

Welch, S. L., & Fairburn, C. G. (1994). Sexual abuse and bulimia nervosa: Three integrated case control comparisons. 11th National Conference on Eating Disorders (1992,

Columbus, Ohio). *American Journal of Psychiatry, 151*, 402–407.

Welch, S. S. (2001). A review of the literature on the epidemiology of parasuicide in the general population. *Psychiatric Services, 52*, 368–375.

Wellman, H. M. (1994). Early understanding of mind: The normal case. In S. Baron-Cohen (Ed.), *Understanding other minds: Perspectives from autism.* New York: Oxford University Press.

Wender, P. H., Kety, S. S., Rosenthal, D., Schulsinger, F., Ortmann, J., & Lunde, I. (1986). Psychiatric disorders in the biological and adoptive families of adopted individuals with affective disorders. *Archives of General Psychiatry, 43*, 923–929.

Wentz, E., Gillberg, C., Gillberg, I. C., & Ratsam, M. (2001). Ten-year follow-up of adolescent-onset anorexia nervosa: Psychiatric disorders and overall functioning scales. *Journal of Child Psychology & Psychiatry, 42*, 613–622.

Wessely, S., & Kerwin, R. (2004). Suicide risk and the SSRIs. *Journal of the American Medical Association, 292*, 379–381.

Westen, D. (1998). The scientific legacy of Sigmund Freud: Toward a psychodynamically informed psychological science. *Psychological Bulletin, 124*, 333–371.

Westen, D., & Morrison, K. (2001). A multidimensional meta-analysis of treatments for depression, panic, and generalized anxiety disorder: An empirical examination of the status of empirically supported therapies. *Journal of Consulting & Clinical Psychology, 69*, 875–899.

Westen, D., Novotny, C. M., & Thompson-Brenner, H. (2004). The empirical status of empirically supported psychotherapies: Assumptions, findings, and reporting in controlled clinical trials. *Psychological Bulletin, 130*, 631–663.

Westermeyer, J. (1993). Cross-cultural psychiatric assessment. In A. C. Gaw (Ed.), *Culture, ethnicity, and mental illness* (pp. 125–144). Washington, DC: American Psychiatric Press.

Westermeyer, J., Bouafuely, M., Neider, J., & Callies, A. (1989). Somatization among refugees: An epidemiologic study. *Psychosomatics, 30*, 34–43.

Weston, S. C., & Siever, L. J. (1993). Biologic correlates of personality disorders. NIMH Conference: Personality disorders (1990, Williamsburg, Virginia). *Journal of Personality Disorders* (Suppl. 1), 129–148.

Wetherell, J. L., Sorrell, J. T., Thorp, S. R., & Patterson, T. L. (2005). Psychological Interventions for Late-Life Anxiety: A Review and Early Lessons From the CALM Study. *Journal of Geriatric Psychiatry & Neurology, 18*, 72–82.

Whalen, C. K., & Henker, B. (1998). Attention-deficit/hyperactivity disorder. In T. H. Ollendick & M. Hersen (Eds.), *Handbook of child psychopathology* (pp. 181–212). New York: Plenum Press.

Whaley, S. E., Pinto, A., & Sigman, M. (1999). Characterizing interactions between anxious mothers and their children. *Journal of Consulting & Clinical Psychology, 67*, 826–836.

Whitbourne, S. K. (2000). The normal aging process. In S. K. Whitbourne (Ed.),

Psychopathology in later adulthood (pp. 27–59). New York: Wiley.

White, H. R., Xie, M., & Thompson, W. (2001). Psychopathology as a predictor of adolescent drug use trajectories. *Psychology of Addictive Behaviors, 15*, 210–218.

White, K., & Barlow, D. H. (2002). Panic disorder and agoraphobia. In D. H. Barlow (Ed.), *Anxiety and its disorders: The nature and treatment of anxiety and panic* (2nd ed., pp. 328–379). New York: Guilford Press.

Whittal, M. L., Agras, W. S., & Gould, R. A. (1999). Bulimia nervosa: A meta-analysis of psychosocial and pharmacological treatments. *Behavior Therapy, 30*, 117–135.

Widiger, T. A. (1998). Invited essay: Sex biases in the diagnosis of personality disorders. *Journal of Personality Disorders, 12*, 95–118.

Widiger, T. A. (2002). Values, politics, and science in the construction of the DSMs. In J. Z. Sadler (Ed.), *Descriptions and pre-scriptions: Values, mental disorders, and the DSMs* (pp. 25–41). Baltimore: Johns Hopkins University Press.

Widiger, T. A. (2005). Classification and diagnosis: Historical development and contemporary issues. In J. E. Maddux & B. A. Winstead (Eds.), *Psychopathology: Foundations for a contemporary understanding* (pp. 63–83). Mahwah, NJ: Erlbaum.

Widiger, T. A., & Clark, L. A. (2000). Toward DSM-V and the classification of psychopathology. *Psychological Bulletin, 126*, 946–963.

Widiger, T. A., & Coker, L. A. (2003). Mental disorders as discrete clinical conditions: Dimensional versus categorical classification. In M. Hersen & S. M. Turner (Eds.), *Adult psychopathology and diagnosis* (4th ed., pp. 3–35). New York: Wiley.

Widiger, T. A., & Costa, P. T., Jr. (1994). Personality and personality disorders. Special Issue: Personality and psychopathology. *Journal of Abnormal Psychology, 103*, 78–91.

Widiger, T. A., Costa, P. T., Jr., & McCrae, R. R. (2002). A proposal for Axis II: Diagnosing personality disorders using the five-factor model. In P. T. Costa, Jr., & T. A. Widiger (Eds.), *Personality disorders and the five factor model of personality* (2nd ed., pp. 431–456). Washington, DC: American Psychological Association.

Widiger, T. A., Mangine, S., Corbitt, E. M., Ellis, C. G., & Thomas, G. V. (1995). *Personality disorder interview- IV: A semistructured interview for the assessment of personality disorders.* Odessa, FL: Psychological Assessment Resources.

Widiger, T. A., & Spitzer, R. L. (1991). Sex biases in the diagnosis of personality disorder: Conceptual and methodological issues. *Clinical Psychological Review, 11*, 1–22.

Widiger, T. A., Trull, T. J., Clarkin, J. F., Sanderson, C., & Costa, P. T. (1994). A description of the DSM-III-R and DSM-IV personality disorders with the five-factor model of personality. In P. T. Costa & T. A. Widiger (Eds.), *Personality disorders and the five-factor model of personality* (pp. 41–58). Washington, DC: American Psychological Association.

Wiggins, J. S. (1982). Circumplex models of interpersonal behavior in clinical psychology. In P. Kendall & J. Butcher (Eds.), *Handbook of research methods in clinical psychology.* New York: Wiley.

Wikan, U. (1991). *Managing turbulent hearts.* Chicago: University of Chicago Press.

Wileman, S. M., Eagles, J. M., Andrew, J. E., Howie, F. L., Cameron, I. M., McCormack, K., & Naji, S. A. (2001). Light therapy for seasonal affective disorder in primary care: Randomized controlled trial. *British Journal of Psychiatry, 178,* 311–316.

Wilens, T. E., Biederman, J., & Spencer, T. J. (2002). Attention deficit/hyperactivity disorder across the lifespan. *Annual Review of Medicine, 53,* 113–131.

Wilfley, D. E., Agras, W. S., Telch, C. F., Rossiter, E. M., Schneider, J. A., Cole, A. G., Sifford, L., & Raeburn, S. D. (1993). Group cognitive-behavioral therapy and group interpersonal psychotherapy for the nonpurging bulimic individual: A controlled comparison. *Journal of Consulting & Clinical Psychology, 61,* 296–305.

Wilfley, D. E., Welch, R. R., Stein, R. I., Spurrell, E. B., Cohen, L., R., Saelens, B. E., Dounchis, J. Z., Frank, M. A., Wiseman, C. V., & Matt, G. E. (2002). A randomized comparison of group cognitive-behavioral therapy and group interpersonal psychotherapy for the treatment of overweight individuals with binge-eating disorder. *Archives of General Psychiatry, 59,* 713–721.

Williams, J. B., & Spitzer, R. L. (1983). The issue of sex bias in DSM-III. *American Psychologist, 38,* 793–798.

Williams, J. W., Rost, K., Dietrich, A. J., Ciotti, M. C., Zyzanski, S. J., & Cornell, J. (1999). Primary care physicians' approach to depressive disorders. *Archives of Family Medicine, 8,* 58–67.

Williams, L. M. (1995). Recovered memories of abuse in women with documented child sexual victimization histories. *Journal of Traumatic Stress, 8,* 649–673.

Williams, R. B., Barefoot, J. C., Haney, T. L., & Harrell, F. E. (1988). Type A behavior and angiographically documented coronary atherosclerosis in a sample of 2,289 patients. *Psychosomatic Medicine, 50,* 139–152.

Williamson, G. L. (1993). Postpartum depression syndrome as a defense to criminal behavior. *Journal of Family Violence, 8,* 151–165.

Wilps, R. F., Jr. (1990). Male bulimia nervosa: An autobiographical case study. In A. E. Andersen (Ed.), *Males with eating disorders* (pp. 9–29). New York: Brunner/Mazel.

Wilson, G. R., Loeb, K. L., Walsh, B. T., Labouvie, R., Petkova, E., Xinhua, L., & Waternaux, C. (1999). Psychological versus pharmacological treatments of bulimia nervosa: Predictors and processes of change. *Journal of Consulting & Clinical Psychology, 67,* 451–459.

Wilson, G. T. (2005). Psychological treatment of eating disorders. *Annual Review of Clinical Psychology, 1,* 439–465.

Wilson, G. T., & Fairburn, C. G. (1998). Cognitive treatments for eating disorders. *Journal of Consulting & Clinical Psychology, 61,* 261–269.

Wilson, G. T., Fairburn, C. G., & Agras, W. S. (1997). Cognitive-behavioral treatment for anorexia nervosa. In D. M. Garner & P. E.

Garfinkel (Eds.), *Handbook of treatment for eating disorders* (pp. 67–93). New York: Guilford Press.

Wilson, G. T, Fairburn, C. C., Agras, W. S., Walsh, B. T., & Kraemer, H. (2002). Cognitive-behavioral therapy for bulimia nervosa: Time course and mechanisms of change. *Journal of Consulting & Clinical Psychology, 70,* 267–274.

Wilson, K. A., & Hayward, C. (2005). A prospective evaluation of agoraphobia and depression symptoms following panic attacks in a community sample of adolescents. *Journal of Anxiety Disorders, 19,* 87–103.

Windholz, M. J., Marmar, C. R., & Horowitz, M. J. (1985). A review of the research on conjugal bereavement: Impact on health and efficacy of intervention. *Comprehensive Psychiatry, 26,* 433–447.

Winger, G., Hofmann, F. G., & Woods, J. H. (1992). *Handbook on drug and alcohol abuse.* New York: Oxford University Press.

Winick, B. J. (2003). A therapeutic jurisprudence assessment of sexually violent predator laws. In B. J. Winick & J. Q. LaFond (Eds.), *Protecting society from sexually dangerous offenders: Law, justice, and therapy* (pp. 317–331). Washington, DC: American Psychological Association.

Winokur, G., & Clayton, P. (1967). Family history studies: II. Sex differences and alcoholism in primary affective illness. *British Journal of Psychiatry, 113,* 973–979.

Winters, J., Fals-Stewart, W., O'Farrell, T. J., Birchler, G. R., & Kelley, M. L. (2002). Behavioral couples therapy for female substance-abusing patients: Effects on substance use and relationship adjustment. *Journal of Consulting & Clinical Psychology, 70,* 344–355.

Wiseman, C. V., Gray, J. J., Mosimann, J. E., & Ahrens, A. H. (1992). Cultural expectations of thinness in women: An update. *International Journal of Eating Disorders, 11,* 85–89.

Wittchen, H.-U., & Fehm, L. (2003). Epidemiology and natural course of social fears and social phobia. *Acta Psychiatrica Scandinavica, 108*(Suppl. 417), 4–18.

Woelk, H., Burkard, G., & Grunwald, J. (1994). Benefits and risks of the hypericum extract LI 160: Drug monitoring study with 3,250 patients. *Journal of Geriatric Psychiatry and Neurology, 7* (Suppl. 1), 34–38.

Wolfe, J., Erickson, D. J., Sharkansky, R. J., King, D. W., & King, L. A. (1999). Course and predictors of posttraumatic stress disorder among Gulf War veterans: A prospective analysis. *Journal of Consulting & Clinical Psychology, 67,* 520–528.

Wolff, S., & Wolff, H. G. (1947). An experimental study of changes in gastric function in response to varying life experiences. *Review of Gastroenterology, 14,* 419–426.

Wolfner, G. D., & Gelles, R. J. (1993). A profile of violence toward children: A national study. *Child Abuse & Neglect, 17,* 197–212.

Wolitzky, D. L. (1995). The theory and practice of traditional psychoanalytic psychotherapy. In A. S. Gurman (Ed.), *Essential psychotherapies: Theory and practice* (pp. 12–54). New York: Guilford Press.

Wollstonecraft, M. (1792). *A vindication of the rights of women.* London: J. Johnson.

Wolpe, J. (1997). Thirty years of behavior therapy. *Behavior Therapy, 28,* 633–635.

Wolfsdorf, B. A., & Zlotnick, C. (2001). Affect management in group therapy for women with posttraumatic stress disorder and histories of childhood sexual abuse. *Journal of Clinical Psychology, 57,* 169–181.

Wolfson, A. R. (2002). Bridging the gap between research and practice: What will adolescents' sleep-wake patterns look like in the 21st century? In M. A. Carskadon (Ed.), *Adolescent sleep patterns: Biological, social, and psychological influences* (pp. 198–219). New York: Cambridge University Press.

Wolfson, A. R., & Carskadon, M. A. (1998). Sleep schedules and daytime functioning in adolescents. *Child Development, 69,* 875–887.

Wonderlich, S. A., de Zwaan, M., Mitchell, J. E., Peterson, C., & Crow, S. (2003). Psychological and dietary treatments of binge eating disorder: Conceptual implications. *International Journal of Eating Disorders, 34*(Suppl. 1), 58–73.

Woolf, V. (1975–1980). "Dearest I want to tell you," Virginia Woolf, March 28, 1941. In N. Nicolson & J. Trautman (Eds.), *The letters* (Vol. 6, pp. 486–487). London: Hogarth Press.

World Health Organization (WHO). (2002). Mental health: Suicide prevention. Retrieved from the World Wide Web: http://www.who.int/mental_health/suicide

World Health Organization (WHO). (2004). Distribution of suicide rates (per 100,000) by gender and age, 2000. Retrieved from: http://www.who.int/mental_health/prevention/suicide/suicidecharts/en/

World Health Organization (WHO). (2005a). WHO SUPRE suicide prevention: Live your life. Retrieved from: http://www.who.int/mental_health/management/ en/SUPRE_flyer1.pdf

World Health Organization (WHO). (2005b). *Global alcohol database.* Retrieved from the World Wide Web: http://www3.who.int/whosis.

Wurtman, J. J. (1987). Disorders of food intake: Excessive carbohydrate snack intake among a class of obese people. *Annals of the New York Academy of Sciences, 499,* 197–202.

Wurtman, R. J., & Wurtman, J. J. (1984). Nutritional control of central neurotransmitters. In K. M. Pirke & D. Plogg (Eds.), *The psychobiology of anorexia nervosa.* Berlin: Springer-Verlag.

Wurtzel, E. (1995). *Prozac nation.* New York: Berkley.

Wyatt, S. A., & Ziedonis, D. (1998). Psychological and psychiatric consequences of amphetamines. In R. E. Tarter (Ed.), *Handbook of substance abuse: Neurobehavioral pharmacology* (pp. 529–544). New York: Plenum Press.

Y

Yalom, I. D. (1985). *The theory and practice of group psychotherapy* (3rd ed.). New York: Basic Books.

Yamamoto, J. (1970). Cultural factors in loneliness, death, and separation. *Medical Times, 98,* 177–183.

Yang, J., Dai, X., Yao, S., Cai, T., Gao, B., McCrae, R. R., & Costa, P. T. (2002). Personality disorders and the five-factor model of personality in Chinese psychiatric patients. In P. T. Costa & T. A. Widiger (Eds.), *Personality Disorders and the Five-factor Model of Personality* (2nd ed., pp. 215–221). Washington, DC: American Psychological Association.

Yapko, M. D. (1997). *Breaking the patterns of depression*. New York: Golden Books.

Yeh, M., & Weisz, J. R. (2001). Why are we here at the clinic? Parent-child (dis)agreement on referral problems at outpatient treatment entry. *Journal of Consulting & Clinical Psychology, 69*, 1019–1025.

Yehuda, R. (2000). Biology of posttraumatic stress disorder. *Journal of Clinical Psychiatry, 61* (Suppl. 7), 14–21.

Yehuda, R. (2004). Risk and resilience in posttraumatic stress disorder. *Journal of Clinical Psychiatry, 65*(Suppl. 1), 29–36.

Yehuda, R., McFarlane, A. C., & Shalev, A. Y. (1998). Predicting the development of posttraumatic stress disorder from the acute response to a traumatic event. *Biological Psychiatry, 44*, 1305–1313.

Yen, S., Shea, M. T., Pagano, M., Sanislow, C. A., Grilo, C. M., McGlashan, T. H., Skodol, A. E., Bender, D. S., Zanarini, M. C., Gunderson, J. G., & Morey, L. C. (2003). Axis I and axis II disorders as predictors of prospective suicide attempts: Findings from the Collaborative Longitudinal Personality Disorders Study. *Journal of Abnormal Psychology, 112*, 375–381.

Yirmiya, N., Erel, O., Shaked, M., & Solomonica-Levi, D. (1998). Meta-analysis comparing theory of mind abilities of individuals with autism, individuals with mental retardation, and normally developed individuals. *Psychological Bulletin, 124*, 283–307.

Yonkers, K. A., & Gurguis, G. (1995). Gender differences in the prevalence and expression of anxiety disorders. In M. V. Seeman (Ed.), *Gender and psychopathology* (pp. 113–130). Washington, DC: American Psychiatric Press.

Young, E., & Korzun, A. (1998). Psychoneuroendocrinology of depression: Hypothalamic-pituitary-gonadal axis. *Psychiatric Clinics of North America, 21*, 309–323.

Z

Zaider, T. I., & Heimberg, R. G. (2003). Non-pharmacologic treatments for social anxiety disorder. *Acta Psychiatrica Scandinavica, 108*(Suppl. 417), 72–84.

Zanarini, M. C. (Ed.). (1997). *Role of sexual abuse in the etiology of borderline personality disorder*. Washington, DC: American Psychiatric Press.

Zanarini, M. C., Skodol, A.-E., Bender, D., Dolan, R., Sanislow, C., Schaefer, E., Morey, L., Grilo, C. M., Shea, M. T., McGlashan, T. H., & Gunderson, G. (2000). The Collaborative Longitudinal Personality Disorders Study: Reliability of Axis I and II diagnoses. *Journal of Personality Disorder, 14*, 291–299.

Zarit, S. H., & Haynie, D. A. (2000). Introduction to clinical issues. In S. K. Whitbourne (Ed.), *Psychopathology in later adulthood* (pp. 1–25). New York: Wiley.

Zelt, D. (1981). First person account: The Messiah quest. *Schizophrenia Bulletin, 7*, 527–531.

Zerbe, K. J. (1990). Through the storm: Psychoanalytic theory in the psychotherapy of anxiety disorders. *Bulletin of the Menninger Clinic, 54*, 171–183.

Zhou, J.-N., Hofman, M. A., & Swaab, D. F. (1995). No changes in the number of vasoactive intestinal polypeptide (VIP)-expressing neurons in the suprachiasmatic nucleus of homosexual men; comparison with vasopressin-expressing neurons. *Brain Research, 672*, 285–288.

Zhou, S., Chan, E., Pan, S.-Q., Huang, M., & Lee, E. J. D. (2004). Pharmacokinetic interactions of drugs with St. John's wort. *Journal of Psychopharmacology, 18*, 262–276.

Zigler, E., & Hodapp, R. M. (1991). Behavioral functioning in individuals with mental retardation. *Annual Review of Psychology, 42*, 29–50.

Zilboorg, G., & Henry, G. W. (1941). *A history of medical psychology*. New York: W. W. Norton.

Zimbardo, P. G. (1977). *Shyness: What it is, what to do about it*. New York: Addison-Wesley.

Zimbardo, P. G., Andersen, S. M., & Kabat, L. G. (1981). Induced hearing deficit generates experimental paranoia. *Science, 212*, 1529–1531.

Zisook, S., & Downs, N. (1998). Diagnosis and treatment of depression in late life. *Journal of Clinical Psychiatry, 59*(Suppl. 4), 80–91.

Zlotnik, C., Elkin, I., & Shea, M. T. (1998). Does the gender of a patient or the gender of a therapist affect the treatment of patients with major depression? *Journal of Consulting & Clinical Psychology, 66*, 655–659.

Zoccolillo, M. (1993). Gender and the development of conduct disorder. *Development & Psychopathology, 5*, 65–78.

Zoellner, L. A., Craske, M. G., & Rapee, R. M. (1996). Stability of catastrophic cognitions in panic disorder. *Behaviour Research & Therapy, 34*, 399–402.

Zubenko, G. S., Hughes, H. B., III, Stiffler, J. S., Zubenko, W. N., & Kaplan, B. B. (2002). D2S2944 identifies a likely susceptibility locus for recurrent, early-onset, major depression in women. *Molecular Psychiatry, 7*, 460–467.

Zubieta, J. K., & Alessi, N. E. (1992). Acute and chronic administration of trazodone in the treatment of disruptive behavior disorders in children. *Journal of Clinical Psychopharmacology, 12*, 346–351.

Zucker, K. J. (2005). Gender identity disorder in children and adolescents. In S. Nolen-Hoeksema, T. D. Cannon, & T. A. Widiger (Eds.), *Annual Review of Clinical Psychology* (Vol. 1, pp. 467–492). Palo Alto, CA: Annual Reviews.

Zucker, R. A., Chermack, S. T., & Curran, G. M. (1999). Alcoholism: A lifespan perspective on etiology and course. In M. Lewis & A. J. Sameroff (Eds.), *Handbook of developmental psychopatholgy* (2nd ed.). New York: Plenum Press.

Zucker, R. A., Ellis, D. A., Fitzgerald, H. E., Bingham, C. R., & Sanford, K. (1996). Other evidence for at least two alcoholisms: II. Life course variation in antisociality and heterogeneity of alcoholic outcome. *Development & Psychopathology, 8*, 831–848.

Zucker, R. A., Kincaid, S. B., Fitzgerald, H. E., & Bingham, C. R. (1995). Alcohol schema acquisition in preschoolers: Differences between children of alcoholics and children of nonalcoholics. *Alcoholism: Clinical & Experimental Research, 19*, 1011–1017.

CREDITS

CHAPTER 1

Opener: *People Flying* by Peter Sickles. American. Superstock. **P. 4:** © Corbis Images. **Pp. 4, 5:** Anonymous, 1992. "First-person account: Portrait of a schizophrenic." *Schizophrenia Bulletin,* 18, 333–334. **P. 5:** From *An Unquiet Mind: A Memoir of Moods and Madness* by K.R. Jamison. Copyright © 1995. Used by permission of Alfred A. Knopf, a Division of Random House, Inc. **P. 6:** © A.P./Wide World Photos. **P. 7:** © Archivo Iconografico, S.A./Corbis Images. **P. 9:** © Courtesy of Gary Holloway. Photo by Josef Astor. **P. 12:** © Sandved B. Kjell/Visuals Unlimited. **P. 13:** © The Granger Collection. **P. 14:** © Archivo Iconografico, S.A./Corbis Images. **P. 15:** © Bettmann/Corbis Images. **P. 18:** © National Library of Medicine/Science Photo Library/Photo Researchers. **P. 19:** © National Library of Medicine/Photo Researchers. **P. 20:** © Robert Fleeury/Photo Researchers. **Pp. 21, 22:** © The Granger Collection. **P. 27:** © Corbis Images.

CHAPTER 2

Opener: *Heart of the Hunter* by Michelle Puleo, B. 1967. American. Private Collection/Superstock. **P. 34:** Courtesy, Albert Ellis, Albert Ellis Institute. **Pp. 36, 37:** Adapted with permission from Damasio H, Grabowski T, Frank R, Galaburda AM, Damasio AR: The return of Phineas Gage: Clues about the brain from a famous patient. *Science,* 264:1102–1105, 1994. Department of Neurology and Image Analysis Facility, University of Iowa. Copyright © 1994 AAAS. **Figure 2.3:** Damasio H., Grabowski, T., Frank R., Galaburda A. M., Damasio A. R. (1994). The return of Phineas Gage: Clues about the brain from the skull of a famous patient. *Science, 264,* 1102–1105. Department of Neurology and Image Analysis Facility, University of Iowa. **Figure 2.5:** Adapted from Feldman, *Understanding Psychology,* 7e, Fig. 3, p. 83. Copyright © 2005 The McGraw-Hill Companies. Reprinted with permission from The McGraw-Hill Companies. **Figure 2.6:** Adapted from Feldman, *Understanding Psychology,* 7e, Fig. 4, p. 85. Copyright © 2005 The McGraw-Hill Companies. Reprinted with permission from The McGraw-Hill Companies. **Figure 2.8a&b:** Adapted from Feldman, *Understanding Psychology,* 7e, Fig. 5, p. 67. Copyright © 2005 The McGraw-Hill Companies. Reprinted with permission from The McGraw-Hill Companies. **P. 45:** © Enrico Ferorelli. **P. 47:** © Bettman/Corbis Images. **P. 49:** © Barton Silverman/NYT Pictures. **P. 52 (left):** © Wellcome Library, London. **P. 52 (right):** © Otto Kernberg. **P. 53:** © Bettman/Corbis Images. **P. 55:** © Syracuse Newspapers/Dennis Nett /Image Works. **P. 57:** Courtesy Aaron Beck. **P. 58:** National Library of Medicine. **P. 63:** ©Bruce Ayres/Getty Images. **P. 66:** Courtesy, Albert Ellis, Albert Ellis Institute.

CHAPTER 3

Opener: *The Global Seat* by Christian Pierre. American. Private Collection/Superstock. **P. 72:** © Lee Snider/Image Works. **P. 75:** From J. Giles, "The Poet of Alienation," *Newsweek,* April 18, 1994. Copyright © 1994 Newsweek, Inc. All rights reserved. Reprinted by permission. **P. 75:** © Jay Blakesberg/Corbis Sygma. **P. 80:** © Keith Brofsky/Getty Images. **P. 83:** © A.P./Wide World Photos. **P. 87:** © Michael Newman/PhotoEdit. **P. 93:** © Lee Snider/Image Works.

CHAPTER 4

Opener: *Essor* by Andrè Rouillard, 1981/Superstock. **P. 98:** From *The Unicorn and Other Poems* by Anne Morrow Lindbergh. Copyright © 1956. Used by permission of Pantheon Books, a Division of Random House, Inc. **P. 102:** © Steven Peters/Getty Images. **P. 103:** © Rhoda Sidney/PhotoEdit. **Figure 4.3:** From J. M. Sattler, *Assessment of Children,* 3rd edition. Reprinted with permission. **108 (both):** © ZEPHYR/Photo Researchers. **P. 113:** © Grantpix/Index Stock Imagery. **P. 114:** © Michael Newman/PhotoEdit. **P. 116:** © Camilla Smith/Rainbow. **P. 117:** © Michael Newman/PhotoEdit. **P. 126:** © Corbis Images. **P. 128:** © Frank Trapper/Corbis Sygma/Corbis Images.

CHAPTER 5

Opener: *Window of Opportunity* by Christian Pierre. American. Private Collection/Superstock. **Pp. 134, 135, 167, 168:** Anonymous, 1983. "First-person account," *Schizophrenia Bulletin,* 9, 152–155. **P. 139:** © 1994 Newsweek, Inc. All rights reserved. Reprinted by permission. Photo by Myko Photography. **P. 141:** © Don Farrall/Getty Images. **P. 142:** © Najlah Feanny/Stock Boston. **P. 153:** © David Young-Wolff/PhotoEdit. **P. 156:** © Michael Newman/PhotoEdit. **P. 157:** © Bob Daemmrich/Image Works. **Pp. 160, 161:** From Sue, S. & Zane, N., 1987, "The Role of Culture and Cultural Techniques in Psychotherapy: A Critique and Reformulation," *American Psychologist,* 42, pp. 37–45. Reproduced with permission. **P. 161:** © Michael Grecco/Stock Boston. **P. 162:** © David R. Frazier/Photo Researchers. **P. 165:** © Michael Newman/PhotoEdit.

Kobal Collection/20th Century Fox. **P. 286:** © Cindy Charles/Photo Edit. **Pp. 287–288:** Adapted from Steinberg, M. (1990). Transcultural issues in psychiatry: The ataque and multiple personality disorder. *Dissociation: Progress in the Dissociative Disorders, 3,* 31–32. Reprinted with permission from the Ridgeview Institute. **P. 289:** © Bettmann/Corbis Images. **P. 292:** From Hilgard, E. R. (1986). *Divided consciousness: Multiple controls in human thought and action,* p. 68. New York: Wiley. Reprinted with permission of the estate of Ernest R. Hilgard. **P. 293:** © Jeffrey Markowitz/Corbis Sygma. **P. 294:** From Loftus, E. F., 1993, "The Reality of Repressed Memories, *American Psychologist, 48,* 518–537. Copyright © 1993 by the American Psychological Association. Reproduced with permission. **P. 296:** © The Granger Collection.**P. 297:** Prayer by Bertha Pappenheim. From Pappenheim, B., 1936, Gebete, *Ausgewahlt und herausgegeben von Judischen Frauenbund,* Berline: Philo Verlag. Reproduced with permission.

CHAPTER 9

Opener: *Watching from the Steps* by Hyacinth Manning-Carner. African- American. Private Collection/ Superstock. **P. 302:** © Johns Hopkins Medicine. **Pp. 302, 303, 336, 343, 346:** From *An Unquiet Mind: A Memoir of Moods and Madness* by K.R. Jamison. Copyright © 1995. Used by permission of Alfred A. Knopf, a Division of Random House, Inc. **P. 306:** © Peter Dazeley/Corbis Images. **P. 308:** © Tom Prettyman/PhotoEdit. **P. 312 (left):** © Hulton-Deutsch Collection/Corbis Images. **P. 312 (right):** © Bettmann/Corbis Images. **Figure 9.4a-d:** From Davidson, R. J., Pizzagalli, D., Nitschke, J. B., and Putnam, K. (2002). Depression: Perspectives from affective neuroscience. *Annual Review of Psychology, 53,* 545–74. **P. 318:** © Robert Brenner/ PhotoEdit. **P. 321:** © Diaphor Agency/Index Stock Imagery. **Table 9.7:** From David H. Burns, *Feeling Good: The New Mood Therapy,* 1980, William Morrow. Copyright © 1980 HarperCollins Publishes. Used with permission. **Pp. 324, 325:** Adapted from J. Bemporad, 1995, "Long-Term Analytic Treatment of Depression," in E. E. Beckham & W. R. Leber (Eds.), *Handbook of Depression, Second Edition.* Copyright © 1995 Guilford Publications. Reprinted with permission. **P. 326:** "Rachel" Case Study from *Eating, Drinking, Overthinking: The Toxic Triangle of Food, Alcohol, and Depression— and How Women Can Break Free* by Susan Nolen-Hoeksema. Copyright © 2005 by Susan Nolen-Hoeksema. Reprinted by permission of Henry Holt and Company, LLC., Piatkus Books Ltd., and Zachary Shuster Harmsworth Literary Agency. **Figure 9.2:** From Twenge, J. & Nolen-Hoeksema, Susan. Age, gender, race, socioeconomic status, and birth cohort difference on the children's depression inventory: A meta-analysis. *Journal of Abnormal Psychology.* Vol 111(4) Nov 2002, 578–588. Copyright © 2002 by the American Psychological Association. Reproduced with permission. **Figure 9.3:** "Risk of Bipolar Disorder in Relatives of People with Bipolar and in the General Population." Reprinted, with permission, from *Annual Review of Neuroscience,* Volume 20, © 1997 by Annual Reviews www.annualreviews.org. **Figure 9.4:** From R. J. Davidson, et al., "Perspectives from Affective Neuroscience." Reprinted, with permission, from *Annual Review of Psychology,* Volume 53, © 2002 by Annual Reviews www.annualreviews.org. **P. 327:** © Gary Conner/Index Stock Imagery. **Figure 9.6:** Kessler, R. C., Berglund, P., Demler, O., Jin, R., Koretz, D., Merikangas, K. R., Rush, A. J., Walters, E. E., & Wang, P. S. (2003). The epidemiology of major depressive disorder: Results from the national comorbidity survey replication (NCS-R). *JAMA,* 2003, v. 289, pp. 3095–3105. Copyright © 2003 American Medical Association. All rights reserved. Reproduced with permission. **P. 329:** Adapted from Kleinman, A. & Kleinman, J., "Somatization: The Interconnections in Chinese Society Among Culture, Depressive Experiences, and Meanings of Pain," in A. Kleinman & B. Goods (Eds.), *Culture and Depression,* 454–455, 1986, Berkeley: University of California Press. Copyright © 1986 The Regents of the University of California. Used with permission. **P. 331:** © Bernard Annebicque/Corbis Sygma. **P. 332:** Excerpts from *Prozac Nation* by Elizabeth Wurtzel. Copyright © 1994 by Elizabeth Wurtzel. Reprinted by permission of Houghton Mifflin Company and Collins McCormick Literary Agency. All rights reserved. **P. 334:** © Will McIntyre/Photo Researchers. **P. 335:** © Pascal Goetgheluck/Photo Researchers. **Pp. 337, 338:** From *Breaking the Patterns of Depression* by Michael D. Yapko. Copyright © 1997 by Michael D. Yapko. Used by permission of Doubleday, a division of Random House, Inc. **Pp. 339, 340:** From Thorpe, G. & Olson, S. *Behavior Therapy: Concepts, Procedures and Application,* 2/e. Published by Allyn and Bacon, Boston, MA. Copyright © 1997 by Pearson Education. Reprinted/adapted by permission of the publisher. **P. 341:** © David Young-Wolff/PhotoEdit. **Figure 9.10:** From Clarke, G., Hawkins, W., Murphy, M., Sheeber, L. B., et al., 1995, "Targeted Prevention of Unipolar Depressive Disorder in an At-Risk Sample of High School Adolescents: A Randomized Trial of Group Cognitive Intervention," *Journal of the American Academy of Child and Adolescent Psychiatry, 34,* 312, 321. Copyright © 1995 Lippincott Williams and Wilkins. Used with permission. **P. 344:** © Mary Kate Denny/ PhotoEdit. **P. 346:** © Johns Hopkins Medicine.

CHAPTER 10

Opener: *Florista* by Bernadita Zegers. Kactus Foto, Santiago, Chile/Superstock. **P. 350:** "Resume" from *Dorothy Parker: Complete Poems* by Dorothy Parker. Copyright © 1999 by The National Association for the Advancement of Colored People. Used by permission of Penguin, a division of Penguin Group (USA) Inc. **P. 352:** © Douglas Kirkland/Corbis Images. **Pp. 352, 372:** From *A Darkness Visible: A Memoir of Madness* by William Styron. Copyright © 1990 by William Styron. Used by permission of Vintage Books, a Division of Random House, Inc. **Figure 10.1:** From New York Times/CBS News Poll: Teenagers' Experience with Suicide, *New York Times,* October 20, 1999, p. 1.

Copyright © 1999 The New York Times Graphics. Reprinted with permission. **P. 354:** © Reuters NewMedia/Tsafrir Abayov/Corbis Images. **Figure 10.2:** Adapted from World Health Organization (WHO). (2004). Distribution of suicide rates (per 100,000) by gender and age, 2000. Retrieved from: http://www.who.int/mental_health/prevention/suicide/suicidecharts/en/. Reprinted with permission from the World Health Organization. **Table 10.1:** *American Journal of Community Psychology,* v. 33, 2004, "Risk and resiliency factors influencing suicidality among urban African American and Latin Youth" by L. O'Donnell, C. O'Donnell, D. M. Wardlaw, & A. Stueve, copyright © 2004. Used with kind permission of Springer Science and Business Media. **P. 356:** From Pfeffer, C. R., 1985, "Suicidal Tendencies in Normal Children," *Journal of Nervous & Mental Disease,* 173, 78–84. Copyright © 1985 Lippincott Williams & Wilkins. Reprinted with permission. **Figure 10.3:** From World Health Organization (WHO). (2005). WHO SUPRE suicide prevention: Live your life. Rretrieved from: http://www.who.int/mental_health/management/en/SUPRE_flyer1.pdf. Reprinted with permission from the World Health Organization. **Figure 10.4:** Gould, M. S., Greenberg, T., Velting, D. M., & Shaffer, D. (2003). Youth suicide risk and preventive interventions: A review of the past 10 years. *Journal of the American Academy of Child & Adolescent Psychiatry,* 42, 386–405. Copyright © 2003 by Lippincott Williams & Wilkins. Used with permission. **Pp. 358–359:** From Nolen-Hoeksema S, Larson J (1999), *Coping with Loss.* Mahweh, N.J.: Lawrence Erlbaum. Reprinted with permission. **P. 359:** © Chris Niedenthal/Black Star/PictureQuest. **P. 360:** Drawing from *Night Falls Fast* by Kay Redfield Jamison. Copyright © 1999 by Kay Redfield Jamison. Used by permission of Alfred A. Knopf, a division of Random House, Inc. and Picador. **Pp. 360, 361:** *Suicide Notes: Predictive Clues and Patterns,* 1988, "I wish I could explain it" by A. A. Leenaars. Copyright © 1998. Used with kind permission of Springer Science and Business Media. **Pp. 360, 361:** Excerpts from *Prozac Nation* by Elizabeth Wurtzel. Copyright © 1994 by Elizabeth Wurtzel. Reprinted by permission of Houghton Mifflin Company and Collins McCormick Literary Agency. All rights reserved. **P. 361:** Excerpt from The Letters of Virginia Woolf, Volume VI: 1936–1941. Copyright © 1980 by Quentin Bell and Angelica Garnett, reproduced by permission of Harcourt, Inc. Published in the UK as The Letters of Virginia Woolf, edited by N. Nicolson and J. Trautman, published by Hogarth Press. Reprinted by permission of The Random House Group Ltd. **Pp. 364, 365:** From *An Unquiet Mind: A Memoir of Moods and Madness* by K.R. Jamison. Copyright © 1995. Used by permission of Alfred A. Knopf, a Division of Random House, Inc. **P. 365:** © Esbin-Anderson/Image Works. **P. 367 (left):** © Corbis/Bettmann. **P. 367 (right):** © Alain Benainous/Gamma Press. **P. 369:** © Michael Newman/Photo Edit. **P. 370:** © Gary D. Landsman/Corbis Images. **P. 372:** © Douglas Kirkland/Corbis Images.

CHAPTER 11

Opener: *My Dog and I Are One* by Patricia Schwimmer. Canadian/Superstock. **P. 376:** © Reuters/Corbis Images. **Pp. 376, 415:** Reprinted with permission of Simon & Schuster Adult Publishing Group and the author from *A Beautiful Mind* by Sylvia Nasar. Copyright © 1998 by Sylvia Nasar. **P. 378:** From *Angelhead* by Greg Bottoms, copyright © 2000 by Greg Bottoms. Used by permission of Crown Publishers, a division of Random House, Inc. **Figure 11.1:** From *Surviving Schizophrenia: A Family Manual* by E. Fuller Torrey. Copyright © 1983 by E. Fuller Torrey. Reprinted by permission of HarperCollins Publishers. **P. 384:** © A.P./Wide World Photos. **P. 387:** From R. D. Laing, *The Divided Self,* 1971, pp. 29–30. Harmondsworth: Routledge. Reprinted with permission from Taylor & Francis. **P. 387:** © Grunnitus/Photo Researchers. **P. 388:** © Bob Daemmrich/Stock Boston. **P. 389:** From McGhie, A. & Chapman, J., 1961, "Disorders in Attention and Perception in Early Schizophrenia," *British Journal of Medical Psychology,* 34, p. 104. Reproduced with permission from Psychology and Psychotherapy: Theory Research and Practice (formerly the British Journal of Medical Psychology) © The British Psychological Society. **P. 391:** Poem "Anxiety" from *Surviving Schizophrenia: A Family Manual* by E. Fuller Torrey. Copyright © 1983 by E. Fuller Torrey. Reprinted by permission of HarperCollins Publishers. **Figure 11.3:** From *Schizophrenia Genesis: The Origins of Madness* by Irving I. Gottesman. © 1991 by Irving I. Gottesman. Used with permission of Worth Publishers. **P. 397:** Courtesy, The Genain Quadruplets. **P. 398 (both):** Courtesy, Dr. Nancy Andreasen. **Figure 11.5:** Barch, D. M., "The cognitive neuroscience of schizophrenia." Reprinted, with permission, from *Annual Review of Clinical Psychology,* Volume 1, © 2005 by Annual Reviews www.annualreviews.org. **Figure 11.7:** Barch, D. M., "The cognitive neuroscience of schizophrenia." Reprinted, with permission, from *Annual Review of Clinical Psychology,* Volume 1. Copyright © 2005 by Annual Reviews www.annualreviews.org. **P. 401:** From McGhie, A. & Chapman, J., 1961, "Disorders in Attention and Perception in Early Schizophrenia," *British Journal of Medical Psychology,* 34, p. 104. Reproduced with permission from Psychology and Psychotherapy: Theory Research and Practice (formerly the British Journal of Medical Psychology) © The British Psychological Society. **P. 403:** © Joseph Nettis/Photo Researchers. **P. 406:** From Brown, T. A., O'Leary, T. A. & Barlow, D. H., 2001, in Barlow, D. H. (Ed.) "Generalized Anxiety Disorder," *Clinical Handbook of Psychological Disorders: A Step-by-Step Treatment Manual,* Third Edition, New York: The Guilford Press. Reprinted with permission. **Table 11.10:** From Liberman, R. P., Glynn, S., Blair, K. E., Ross, D., & Marder, S. R. (2002). In vivo amplified skills training: Promoting generalization of independent living skills for clients with schizophrenia. *Psychiatry: Interpersonal & Biological Processes,* 65, 137–155. Reprinted with permission from The Guilford Press. **Figure 11.9:** From G.E. Hogarty, et al., "Family Psychoeducation," in

Images. **P. 513:** Reprinted with permission from Spitzer, R. L., Gibbon, M., Skodol, A. E., Williams, J. B. W., and First, M. B. (Eds.), 1994, *DSM-IV Case Book: A Learning Companion to the Diagnostic and Statistical Manual of Mental Disorders.* Copyright © 1994 American Psychiatric Association. **P. 515:** © Bettman/Corbis Images. **Figure 14.2:** © D. Miller/Peter Arnold. **Figure 14.3a-b:** Courtesy, Dr. Arnold B. Scheibel. **P. 517:** © Judy Griesedieck/Getty Images. **P. 518:** © Science Photo Library/Photo Researchers. **P. 519:** © J. M. Loubat/Vandystadt/Photo Researchers. **P. 524:** From Gallagher-Thompson, D., Lovett, S. & Rose, J., 1991, "Psychotherapeutic Interventions for Stressed Family Caregivers." Reprinted with permission from W. A. Myers (Ed.) *New Techniques in Psychotherapy of Older Patients.* Copyright © 1991 American Psychiatric Association. **P. 528:** Reprinted with permission from Spitzer, R. L., Gibbon, M., Skodol, A. E., Williams, J. B. W., and First, M. B. (Eds.), 1994, *DSM-IV Case Book: A Learning Companion to the Diagnostic and Statistical Manual of Mental Disorders,* Copyright © 1994. American Psychiatric Association. **Pp. 529, 530:** Adapted from Scogin, F., Floyd, M. & Forde, J., 2000, Anxiety in Older Adults, in S. K. Whitbourne (Ed.)., *Psychopathology in Later Adulthood.* Copyright © John Wiley & Sons, Inc. Reprinted with permission of John Wiley & Sons, Inc. **P. 530, 531:** Adapted from D. A. King and H. W. Markus (2000). Mood Disorders in Older Adults in S. K. Whitbourne (Ed.), *Psychopathology in Later Adulthood.* Copyright © John Wiley & Sons, Inc. Reprinted with permission of John Wiley & Sons, Inc. **P. 531:** © Fritz Hoffmann/Image Works. **P. 533:** © Macduff Everton/Getty Images. **P. 533:** Lisansky-Gomberg, E. (2000). Substance Abuse Disorders, in S. K. Whitbourne (Ed.), *Psychopathology in Later Adulthood.* Copyright © John Wiley & Sons, Inc. Reprinted with permission of John Wiley & Sons, Inc. **P. 535:** © Sophie Bassouls/Sygma/Corbis Images.

CHAPTER 15

Opener: *Wednesday's Child* by John S. Bunker. American/Superstock. **P. 540:** © Tim Graham Picture Library/A.P./Wide World Photos. **Pp. 540, 541, 569:** Diana, Princess of Wales, BBC Panorama Interview, November 1995. BBC. Reproduced with permission. **P. 545:** © N.M.S.B./Custom Medical Stock Photo. **P. 545:** Excerpt from pp. 254–5 from *Wasted: A Memoir of Anorexia and Bulimia* by Marya Hornbacher. Copyright © 1998 by Marya Hornbacher-Beard. Reprinted by permission of HarperCollins Publishers. **P. 548:** © Bill Losh/Getty Images. **P. 548:** Reprinted with permission from Spitzer, R. L., Skodol, A. E., Gibbon, M. & Williams, J. B. W., 1981, *DSM-III Case Book: A Learning Companion to the Diagnostic and Statistical Manual of Mental Disorders,* Third Edition. Copyright © 1981 American Psychiatric Association. **P. 548:** Kim Hubbard, Anne-Marie O'Neill and Christina Cheakalos/*People Weekly* © 1999. Reprinted with permission. **P. 549:** From Wilps, R. F., Jr., 1990, "Male Bulimia Nervosa: An Autobiographical Case Study." Copyright © 1990 From *Males with Eating Disorders*

by A. E. Andersen (Ed). Reproduced by permission of Routledge/Taylor & Francis Group. **Figure 15.3:** From D. Garner, A. K. Cooke, H. W. Marano, "The 1997 Body Image Survey," in *Psychology Today,* pp. 30–44. Reprinted with permission from Psychology Today Magazine. Copyright © 1997 www.psychologytoday.com. **P. 551 (left):** © Petre Buzoianu/ZUMA/Corbis Images. **P. 551 (right):** © Charles O'Rear/Corbis Images. **Pp. 551, 552:** Adapted from *Social Science & Medicine,* v. 41, L. Sing, "Self-starvation in context: Towards a culturally sensitive understanding of anorexia nervosa," pp. 27–29. Copyright © 1995, with permission from Elsevier. **Pp. 552, 553:** From Stunkard, A. J., 1993, "A History of Binge Eating," in C. G. Fairburn and G. T. Wilson (Eds.), *Binge Eating: Nature, Assessment, and Treatment,* pp. 20–21. New York: Guilford Press. Reprinted with permission. **Figure 15.4:** From C. V. Wiseman, et al., "Cultural Expectations of Thinness in Women: An Update," in *International Journal of Eating Disorders,* Vol. 11. Copyright © 1992 John Wiley & Sons, Inc. Reprinted with permission of John Wiley & Sons, Inc. **Pp. 556, 557:** "Worshipping The Gods Of Thinness," from *Reviving Ophelia* by Mary Pipher, Ph.D. Copyright © 1994 by Mary Pipher, Ph.D. Used by permission of G.P. Putnam's Sons, a division of Penguin Group (USA) Inc. and by permission of the author. **P. 557:** © Bob Daemmrich/Stock Boston. **P. 569:** © Tim Graham Picture Library/A.P./Wide World Photos.

CHAPTER 16

Opener: *Shadow of Her Former Self* by Diana Ong. 1940. Chinese/USA/Superstock. **P. 574 (top):** © Corbis Images. **P. 574 (bottom):** Courtesy, HarperCollins Publishers. **Figure 16.1:** From J. S. Hyde, *Understanding Human Sexuality,* p. 199. McGraw-Hill Companies, Copyright © 1990. Reprinted with permission from The McGraw-Hill Companies. **Figure 16.2:** From J.S. Hyde, *Understanding Human Sexuality,* p. 200. McGraw-Hill Companies, Copyright © 1990. Reprinted with permission from The McGraw-Hill Companies. **Pp. 574, 613:** Excerpts from pp. 57, 262, 280 from *As Nature Made Him* by JOHN COLAPINTO. Copyright © 1999 by John Colapinto. Reprinted by permission of HarperCollins Publishers. **Pp. 581, 582, 586, 600, 601, 602, 603, 604:** Reprinted with permission from Spitzer, R. L., Gibbon, M., Skodol, A. E., Williams, J. B. W., and First, M. B. (Eds.), 1994, *DSM-IV Case Book: A Learning Companion to the Diagnostic and Statistical Manual of Mental Disorders.* Copyright © 1994 American Psychiatric Association. **Table 16.2:** From *Sex in America* by Robert T. Michael. Copyright © 1994 by CSG Enterprises, Inc., Edward O. Laumann, Robert T. Michael, and Gina Kolata. By permission of Little, Brown and Co., Inc. and Edward Laumann. **Table 16.3:** From E. O. Laumann, et al., *The Social Organization of Sexuality: Sexual Practices in the United States.* Copyright © 1994 University of Chicago Press. Reprinted with permission of the publisher, University of Chicago Press. **Pp. 582, 583:** From McCarthy, B. W., 1989, "Cognitive Behavioral Strategies and Techniques in the Treatment of Early Ejaculation," in S. R. Leiblum & R. C. Rosen (Eds.), *Principles and*

Practice of Sex Therapy: Update for the 1990s, pp. 151–152. New York: Guilford Press. Reprinted with permission. **585:** © A. Collins/Image Works. **Figure 16.4:** From Barlow, D. H., 1986, "Causes of Sexual Dysfunction: The Role of Anxiety and Cognitive Interference," *Journal of Consulting and Clinical Psychology,* 54, 140–148. Copyright © 1986 by the American Psychological Association. Reproduced with permission. **P. 589:** © Bill Bachmann/PhotoEdit. **P. 595:** © Grace/Zefa/Corbis Images. **Pp. 595, 596:** From Althof, S. E. (2000). Erectile dysfunction: Psychotherapy with men and couples. In S. R. Leiblum & R. C. Rosen (Eds.), *Principles and Practice of Sex Therapy* (3rd ed.), p. 270. New York, NY: Guilford Press. Reprinted with permission. **P. 597:** © Digital Vision. **P. 601:** © Bill Aron/Photo Researchers. **P. 603, 610:** © A.P./Wide World Photos. **Tables 16.9 and 16.10:** From "The Paraphilias: Research and Treatment" by Barry Maletsky from *A Guide to Treatments That Work,* Second Edition, edited by Peter Nathan and Jack Gorman. Copyright © 1998 2002 by Peter E. Nathan and Jack M. Gorman. Used by permission of Oxford University Press, Inc. **P. 608:** Adapted from *Archives of Sexual Behavior,* v. 24, 1995, "Female-to-Male Transsexualism Type: Two Cases" by R. Dicky and J. Stephens, copyright © 1995. Used with kind permission of Springer Science and Business Media. **Pp. 609, 610:** From Feinberg, L. 2001 "Trans health crisis: For us it's life or death." *American Journal of Public Health,* 91, pp. 897–898. Reprinted with permission from The American Public Health Association. **P. 613:** © Corbis Images.

CHAPTER 17

Opener: *The Ferryman's* by George E. Dunne. Irish. New Apollo Gallery, Dublin/Superstock. **P. 620:** © Pacha/Corbis Images. **Pp. 621, 622:** Quoted in Marlatt, 1993, from *Behavior Therapy,* 24(4), p. 462. Copyright © 1993 by the Association for Advancement of Behavior Therapy. Reprinted by permission of the publisher. **P. 622:** © Bettmann/Corbis Images. **Figure 17.2:** From Pope, H. G., Jr., Ionescu-Pioggia, M., & Pope, K. W., 2001, "Drug Use and Lifestyle Among College Undergraduates: A 30-Year Longitudinal Study." Reprinted with permission from *American Journal of Psychiatry,* 158. Copyright © 2001 American Psychiatric Association. **Pp. 625, 633, 642:** Reprinted with permission from Spitzer, R. L., Gibbon, M., Skodol, A. E., Williams, J. B. W., and First, M. B. (Eds.), 1994, *DSM-IV Case Book: A Learning Companion to the Diagnostic and Statistical Manual of Mental Disorders.* Copyright © 1994 American Psychiatric Association. **Pp. 627, 628, 657, 658:** From Inciardi, J. A., Lockwood, D. & Pottieger, A. E. *Women and Crack-Cocaine.* Published by Allyn and Bacon, Boston, MA. Copyright © 1993 by Pearson Education. Reprinted/adapted by permission of the publisher. **P. 630:** © Philip Lee Harvey/Getty Images. **P. 632:** © Christopher Brown/Stock Boston. **Figure 17.3:** From Global Status Report on Alcohol, World Health Organization, 2001, www.who.int/substance_abuse. Reprinted with permission from the World Health Organization. **Figures 17.4 and 17.5:** From the National Household Survey on Drug Abuse, 2000. Substance Abuse & Mental Health Services Administration. **P. 637:** © Kindra Clineff/Index Stock Imagery. **Figure 17.6a-b:** © Courtesy, Dr. Neil Rosenberg, Department of Medicine, University of Colorado School of Medicine and the International Institute on Inhalant Abuse. **Pp. 640, 641, 665** From Spitzer, R. L., Skodol, A. E., Gibbon, M. & Williams, J. B. W., 1983, *Psychopathology: A Case Book,* pp. 63–64. NY: McGraw-Hill. Reprinted with permission from The McGraw-Hill Companies. **P. 642:** © Tannen Maury/Image Works. **P. 643:** © A. Ramey/Stock Boston/PictureQuest. **P. 644 (left):** © Scott Camazine/Photo Researchers. **P. 644 (right):** © Dept. of Clinical Radiology, Salisbury District Hospital/Science Photo Library/Photo Researchers. **P. 45:** © A.P./Wide World Photos. **Pp. 648, 649:** From Hoffman, A. 1968, Psychotomimetic Agents, in A. Burger (Ed.) *Drugs Affecting the Central Nervous System,* Vol. 2, pp. 185–186. New York: Marcel Dekker. Copyright © 1968. Reprinted with permission of Routledge/Taylor & Francis Group, LLC. **P. 651:** © G. Baden/zefa/Corbis Images. **Pp. 653, 657:** Engel, J., *Addicted: Kids talking about drugs in their own words,* 1989, New York: Tom Doherty and Associates. Reproduced with permission of Palgrave MacMillan. **P. 656:** © Jeff Dunn/Index Stock Imagery. **P. 659:** © Tom & Dee Ann McCarthy/Corbis Images. **P. 661:** Reprinted from Hester, RK and WR Miller (Eds). *Handbook of Alcoholism Treatment Approaches: Effective Alternatives,* CT Rimmele, WR Miller, MJ Dougher, "Aversion Therapies," p. 135. Copyright © 1989, with permission from Elsevier. **Pp. 662, 663:** Adapted from *Behavioral Treatment of Alcohol Problems,* 1978, by M. B. Sobell and L. C. Sobell. Copyright © 1978. Used with kind permission of Springer Science and Business Media. **P. 663:** © Jill Sabella/Getty Images. **P. 666:** © Mary Kate Denny/PhotoEdit. **P. 669:** © Pacha/Corbis Images.

CHAPTER 18

Opener: *Sun and Moon* (Subtitled *Starker Traum*) by Paul Klee. Swiss. Bridgeman Art Library, London/Superstock. **P. 676:** Photo by William DiLillo. **Pp. 676, 677, 695:** From *Angelhead* by Greg Bottoms. Copyright © 2000 by Greg Bottoms. Used by permission of Crown Publishers, a division of Random House, Inc. **P. 679:** © Bob Daemmrich/Stock Boston. **P. 680:** © A.P./Wide World Photos. **P. 681 (left):** © Mike Stewart/Corbis Sygma. **P. 681 (right):** © A.P./Wide World Photos. **P. 687 (both):** © A.P./Wide World Photos. **P. 689:** Reprinted from Morrissey, J. and J. Monahan (eds.), *Research in Community and Mental Health,* v. 10, J. Monahan, et al., "Coercion in the Provision of Mental Health Services: The MacArthur Studies." Copyright © 2001, with permission from Elsevier. **P. 690:** © Eric Roth/Index Stock Imagery. **P. 694:** Photo by William DiLillo.

NAME INDEX

A

Aarsland, D., 520
Abbott, B. B., 173
Abbott, D. W., 564
Abel, G. G., 602, 603
Abi-Dargham, A., 434
Abram, K. M., 690, 691
Abramowitz, C. S., 467
Abramowitz, J. S., 257, 258
Abramson, L. Y., 56, 321, 322, 323
Ackerman, M. D., 585, 588
Addis, M. E., 231
Aderibigbe, Y. A., 281
Agras, S., 234
Agras, W. S., 553, 555, 556, 563, 564, 566, 567
Aguero-Torres, H., 513
Akhtar, S., 252
Akiskal, H. S., 307, 311
Albano, A. M., 481
Alexander, K. L., 493
Alexander, M. A., 606
Allain, A. N., 196
Allderidge, P., 18
Allen, J. B., 286
Allison, J., 113, 114
Alloy, L. B., 56, 322, 323
Althof, S. E., 582, 594, 595
Altman, D. G., 159
Altshuler, L. L., 316, 318
American Heart Association, 177, 178
American Law Institute, 683
American Psychiatric Association, 74, 121, 122, 123, 146, 182, 183, 184, 192, 193, 199, 222, 234, 245, 252, 271, 274, 287, 293, 304, 305, 309, 378, 382, 388, 390, 391, 424, 428, 429, 435, 448, 466, 471, 479, 483, 485, 486, 487, 490, 497, 514, 526, 532, 544, 547, 579, 583, 597, 600, 609, 623, 626, 627, 629, 639, 647, 649, 650
Ananth, J., 408
Anastopoulos, A. D., 470
Anders, S. L., 393, 406
Andersen, A. E., 544, 554
Anderson, B. K., 666
Anderson, E. M., 148
Anderson, G., 272
Anderson, G. M., 502
Anderson, N. B., 178
Anderson, R. E., 557, 558

Anderson-Hanley, C., 524
Andreasen, N., 397
Andreasen, N. C., 389, 397
Angiulo, M. J., 289
Angold, A., 308, 467, 469, 472, 474, 477, 479, 483, 484
Angst, J., 182, 251, 252, 256, 330
Anthony, J. C., 620
Anton, R. F., 660
Appelbaum, P. S., 26, 691
Arango, V., 366
Arieti, Silvano, 324, 403
Armstrong, H. E., 444
Arnold, L. M., 379
Arseneault, L., 473, 687
Asberg, M., 366
Aschenbrand, S. G., 481
Ashall, F., 518
Ashton, A. K., 590
Astin, J. A., 141
Atiya, M., 516, 517
August, G. L., 477
Avery, K., 502
Ayowa, O. B., 589

B

Bach, A. K., 580, 583, 584, 585, 588, 590
Bachrach, H. M., 147
Badia, P., 173
Baer, J. S., 667
Bagby, R. M., 454
Bagge, C., 442
Bakalar, J. B., 651
Baker, A., 193
Baker, D., 293
Baker, G. B., 223
Baker, L., 63
Baldessarini, R. J., 335, 368
Balla, D. A., 478
Ballenger, J. C., 202, 203, 208
Balon, R., 590
Bandura, Albert, 55, 56, 57, 240, 243, 244
Banks, S., 687
Banse, R., 62
Barber, J. P., 147
Barch, D. M., 386, 397, 398, 400, 401, 433, 434
Barchas, J. D., 653
Barefoot, J. C., 186, 187
Barkley, R. A., 467, 468, 469, 470

Barlow, D. H., 223, 224, 226, 228, 231, 245, 249, 259, 580, 586, 587
Baron, P., 327
Baron-Cohen, S., 500
Barrett, P. M., 481
Barry, T. D., 477
Barsky, A. J., 278
Bartlik, B., 590
Basoglu, M., 195, 198, 200
Basson, R., 591
Bastien, C. H., 183
Batchelor, I. R. C., 272
Bates, J., 462
Bates, M. E., 634
Bateson, Gregory, 404
Bauer, R., 541
Bauermeister, J. J., 469
Baum, A., 180
Baum, A. S., 25
Bauman, M. L., 501
Baxter, L. R., Jr., 254, 255
Bayley, John, 510–511, 535–536
Bayon, C., 436
Beatty, J., 516, 518, 519, 520
Beaubrun, G., 141
Beck, A. T., 110, 151, 153, 225, 243, 247, 321, 338, 366, 369, 405, 406, 430, 431, 432, 433, 434, 445, 446, 447, 449, 450, 452
Beck, J. G., 226, 585, 586, 588
Beck, R. W., 110
Becker, A. E., 355
Becker, J. V., 603
Becker-Blease, K. A., 289
Beckman, L. J., 667
Beeder, A. B., 651
Beidel, D. C., 236, 241
Beiderman, J., 241
Beiser, M., 200
Belcher, J. R., 406
Bell, C. J., 224
Bellack, A. S., 151
Bemporad, J. R., 324, 325
Bender, D. S., 442
Bender, L., 107
Benedetti, F., 444
Benet-Martinez, V., 453
Bennett, A. E., 18
Benotsch, E. G., 187
Berenbaum, S. A., 611
Bergen, A. E., 163
Berglund, P. A., 136, 236, 330
Berkman, L. F., 362
Berlin, L. J., 495

Berman, A. L., 355, 361
Berman, J. S., 342
Berman, M. E., 473
Berman, W. H., 190
Bernal, G., 161
Bernstein, D. P., 429, 430, 433
Berridge, K. C., 653
Bertrand, L. D., 293
Bettelheim, B., 500
Beutler, L. E., 167, 277
Bibring, E., 324
Biederman, J., 221, 223, 467, 468, 479, 480
Bierut, L. J., 654
Bilder, S., 25, 26
Billings, F. J., 295
Binder, R. L., 687
Binik, Y. M., 173, 239, 583
Bird, H. R., 474
Bird, T. D., 517
Birley, J. L., 90, 404
Birmaher, B., 482
Blacher, J. B., 496
Blair, A. J., 565
Blanchard, E. B., 201
Blanchard, J. J., 408
Blashfield, R. K., 427
Blatt, S. J., 113, 324, 325
Blazer, D. G., 305, 306, 328, 530
Blin, O., 255
Bliss, E. L., 287, 288
Bloch, R. M., 281
Blume, A. W., 666
Boeschen, L. E., 201
Bohart, A. C., 148, 149
Bohus, M., 444
Boland, R. J., 307
Bolte, S., 498
Bolton, P., 341, 490
Bonanno, G. A., 62, 530
Bondolfi, G., 400, 408
Bonnie, R. J., 679
Book, A. S., 473
Boon, C., 201
Booth, D. A., 565
Booth-Kewley, S., 186
Bootzin, R. R., 183
Borkovec, T. D., 149, 247, 248, 250
Born, L., 305, 318
Borys, D. S., 692
Bottoms, Greg, 378, 676–677, 695
Bouchard, T. J., 44
Bourden, K., 233
Bourin, M., 223, 224
Bouton, M. E., 223, 226
Bowen, R. C., 479
Bower, G. H., 58, 292
Bowlby, John, 62, 325
Bowler, A. E., 403
Bowman, E. S., 289
Boyd, C. J., 658
Boyle, M. F., 526, 527
Boyle, M. H., 479
Bradley, J. D. D., 468
Bradley, S. J., 609, 610, 611, 612
Bradwejn, J., 223
Brady, K., 208

Braginsky, B. M., 406
Braginsky, D. D., 406
Brain, P. F., 437
Brambilla, F., 554
Braun, B. G., 287
Bravo, M., 275
Brawman-Mintzer, O., 224
Breggin, P. R., 142
Bregman, J. D., 502
Breier, A., 393, 400
Breitner, J. C. S., 516
Bremner, J. D., 203, 316
Brenner, R., 409
Brent, D. A., 354, 362, 363, 365, 366, 370
Bretz, D. A., 180
Brevoort, P., 141
Briere, J., 294, 599
Brockington, I., 355
Brodsky, A. M., 692
Brody, A. L., 316, 342
Broidy, L. M., 471
Bromberger, J. T., 325
Brooker, C., 411
Brookman, L. I., 502
Brooks-Gunn, J., 64, 493, 494, 495
Brown, D., 294
Brown, G. K., 369
Brown, G. W., 90, 404
Brown, J. D., 323
Brown, J. E., 589
Brown, J. S., 364, 392
Brown, L. L., 154, 337
Brown, M. M., 475
Brown, M. Z., 365
Brown, R. C., 589
Brown, S. A., 656
Brown, T. A., 231, 245, 249
Brown, T. M., 526, 527
Browne, K. O., 385, 406
Brownell, K. D., 564
Bruch, Hilde, 559, 560, 561, 563
Bruch, M. A., 259
Bruck, M., 294
Brugha, T. S., 318
Bryant, B., 199
Bucholz, K. K., 654
Buchsbaum, M. S., 316
Buckwalter, J., 522
Bugental, J. F. T., 247
Buka, S. L., 362
Bulik, C. M., 553, 554, 561, 563
Bulman, R. J., 201
Bunney, W. E., 315
Burack, J. A., 489
Buranen, C., 273
Burd, L., 502
Burkard, G., 141
Burnam, A., 533
Burnam, M. A., 259
Burnes, D. W., 25
Burnette, E., 210
Burns, D., 322
Burr, J. A., 355, 361
Burton, E. M., 558
Busfield, J., 18, 19
Bustillo, J. R., 409, 411, 412

Butcher, J. N., 110
Butler, G., 250
Butzel, J. S., 289
Butzlaff, R. L., 404
Byrne, E. J., 527
Byrne, S., 542, 558
Bystritsky, A., 257

C

Cade, J., 140
Caffey, J., 492
Cahill, L., 142
Caldwell, C. B., 654
Caldwell, R., 167
Cale, E. M., 426, 427, 436, 437
Calhoun, K. S., 200, 205, 208
Callahan, H. J., 680
Cameron, N., 278
Camp, B. W., 490, 493
Campbell, C., 404, 405
Campbell, M., 491
Campo, J. V., 277
Canetto, S. S., 355, 359, 361, 371
Canino, G. J., 275
Canive, J. M., 412
Cannon, T. D., 379, 397, 399
Caplan, P. J., 125
Cardozo, B. L., 197, 200, 201
Carey, G., 437
Carey, M. P., 581, 582, 585, 588
Carmelli, D. S., 654
Carroll, J. K., 329
Carroll, K. M., 660, 661
Carroll, R. A., 588
Carskadon, M. A., 180
Carter, M. M., 226
Caspi, A., 35, 315, 462, 471, 475, 480
Castiglioni, A., 16
Castonguay, L. G., 250, 553
Catanese, D., 541
Cathcart, K., 502
Cauce, A. M., 167
Ceci, S. J., 294
Centers for Disease Control and Prevention (CDC), 353, 354, 355, 357, 358
Cervantes, R. C., 277
Chae, J.-H., 143, 334
Chambless, D. C., 259
Champoux, M., 248
Chang, C.-J., 430
Chang, K. D., 475, 476
Chang, V. W., 541
Chapman, J., 388, 401
Chapman, J. P., 385
Chapman, L. J., 385
Chapman, T. F., 260
Charlop-Christy, M. H., 502
Charney, D. S., 223, 224, 249, 313
Chase, A., 556
Chassin, L., 656
Chavira, D. A., 428, 433, 436, 442
Cheek, J. M., 259
Cheltenham, M. P., 354
Chemtob, C. M., 201
Chentsova-Dutton, Y., 329

Chermack, S. T., 657
Chess, S., 462
Cheung, F. K., 433
Chiang, K.-H. S., 62
Chodorow, N., 259
Chou, T., 645
Chouinard, G., 228
Christakis, N. A., 541
Christensen, A. J., 187
Christopherson, E. R., 241
Chronis, A. M., 470
Chun, M. R., 522
Church, S. E., 278
Cicchetti, D., 35, 195, 204, 212, 319, 461, 464
Clancy, S. A., 295
Clark, D. A., 256
Clark, D. M., 206, 225, 228, 231, 241, 244, 256
Clark, K., 403
Clark, L. A., 123, 221
Clarke, G. N., 340, 343
Classen, C., 194, 201
Clayton, P., 655
Cleckley, Hervey, 436
Clipp, E. C., 196
Cloninger, C. R., 437
Cloninger, R., 436
Coates, S., 611
Coccaro, E. F., 473
Cochran, B. N., 440
Cochran, S. D., 597
Cochrane, R., 384
Cochrane, R. E., 679
Cocores, J., 622
Cohen, J. A., 205
Cohen, S., 179
Cohen, S. A., 494
Cohen-Kettenis, P. T., 612
Coker, L. A., 123
Colapinto, John, 574–575, 613
Colas, Emily, 254, 257
Colby, D. M., 430
Cole, D. A., 307
Cole, M. G., 525, 526, 527
Cole, W., 606
Coleman, C. C., 590
Coles, M. E., 244
Collins, J. J., 690
Compton, S. N., 471, 474
Compton, W. M., 259
Comtois, K. A., 365, 566
Conklin, H. M., 399, 400
Consumer Reports, 565
Conte, J. R., 294
Conwell, Y., 370, 531
Cooke, A. K., 542, 550
Cooley, E., 558
Coons, P. M., 286, 287, 288, 289
Coontz, P. D., 688
Cooper, M. L., 635, 656
Cooper, Z., 542
Coplan, J. D., 224
Corazzini, J. G., 157
Corbitt, E. M., 454
Corder, E. H., 517
Cornelius, M. D., 492, 634

Corove, M. B., 279, 280
Cosgrove, J., 166
Costa, P. T., 424, 432, 453
Costantini-Ferrando, M. F., 365
Costello, E. J., 308, 461, 462, 471, 474
Cote, G., 690
Cott, J. M., 141, 142
Courtet, P., 366, 367
Couture, L. J., 283
Couture, M., 599
Couzin, J., 165
Coyle, J. T., 400
Coyne, J. C., 58
Crabbe, J. C., 654
Craig, T. K., 275, 276
Cranston-Cuebas, M. A., 586
Craske, M. G., 221, 222, 223, 224, 226, 231, 241, 246, 249
Creer, C., 381
Crepault, C., 599
Crerand, C. E., 542
Crick, N. R., 439, 472, 475
Crits-Christoph, P., 147, 163
Cronbach, L. J., 106
Crosby, A. E., 354, 361, 368
Cross, S. E., 188
Cross-National Collaborative Group, 329
Crowe, R. R., 241
Cruess, D. G., 181
Csernansky, J. G., 409
Culpepper, L., 223, 228
Curran, G. M., 657

D

Dadds, M. R., 481, 482
Dahl, A. A., 442, 445, 449, 450
Dahlstrom, W. G., 187
Dain, Norman, 28
Damasio, H., 37
Dana, R. H., 103, 110, 111, 112, 114, 117
D'Andrea, M., 161
Daniels, J., 161
Daniels-Bierness, T., 475
Danko, G. P., 635
Dare, C., 563
Davenport, D. S., 195
Davidson, J., 208, 250
Davidson, J. R. T., 205, 208, 244, 245, 250
Davidson, L. A., 107
Davidson, R. J., 316
Davis, C. G., 654
Davis, D. H., 657
Davis, J. M., 315
Davis, K. L., 400, 455
Davis, R. D., 454
Day, N., 492
DeFries, J. C., 468
De Jong, J. T. V. M., 211
DeKosky, S. T., 524
Delay, J., 137
DeLeon, R., 195
Dell, P. F., 285, 287, 289

Dembroski, T. M., 186
Dement, W. C., 181
Deniker, P., 137
Denison, M. E., 640
Denning, D. G., 355
Dennis, M. L., 663
DePaulo, J. R., 313
DePrince, A. P., 295
DeRubeis, R. J., 342
DeSilva, P., 240, 256
Desmond, D. W., 518
De Snyder, V. N. S., 260
Despret, V., 211
Deutsch, A., 20
Dewaraja, R., 589
De Wit, H., 651
de Zwann, M., 567
Diaz, S. F., 279, 280
Diaz-Perez, M. D., 260
DiDomenico, L., 554
Diekstra, R. F. W., 163
Dierker, L. C., 654
Dietary Supplement Health and Education Act (1994), 142
DiLillo, D., 589
Dishion, T. J., 439, 474
Dissanayake, C., 500
Dittman, R. W., 611
Dixon, D., 188
Dixon, J. F., 335
D'Lugoff, B. C., 190
Dobson, K. S., 163
Docherty, N. M., 401
Dodge, K., 475
Dodge, K. A., 437, 439, 440, 475
Dohm, F. A., 545, 549, 553
Dohrenwend, B. P., 402, 403
Donahey, K. M., 588
Donegan, N. H., 442
Dorahy, M. J., 286
Dorfman, W. I., 111
Dornbusch, S. M., 308
Dorris, M., 492
Dossenbach, M., 408, 409
Dougher, M. J., 661
Dougherty, D., 468
Downs, N., 306
Doyle, A., 227, 228
Drake, C. L., 180
Drevets, W. C., 316
Du, Y., 516
Dudley-Grant, G. R., 477
Duncan, G. J., 493
Duncan, J. J., 280
D,ndar, Y., 183
Dunkin, J. J., 524
Dunn, E., 305, 318
Dunner, D. L., 364
DuPaul, G. J., 470
Dupree, L. W., 534
Durkheim, Emil, 362
Durrett, C. A., 424, 426, 441, 453, 454, 455
Dwyer, W. O., 180
Dykens, E. M., 502

E

Eagleston, J. R., 186
Earls, F., 64
Eaton, W. W., 389, 392, 393
Eaves, L. J., 315, 345, 432, 434, 442, 468, 479
Eckert, E., 44
Eckert, E. D., 563
Eckman, T. A., 411
Eddy, J. M., 475, 476, 477
Edell, W. S., 385
Edelmann, R. J., 221, 236, 241, 252
Edenberg, H. J., 655
Edmunds, C., 197
Egeland, Janice, 64, 72, 90, 94, 329
Ehlers, A., 199, 200, 201, 206, 223
Eisenberg, L., 247
Eisenbruch, M., 211
Eisenhower, J. W., 285, 289
Ekselius, L., 429, 432, 433, 436, 445, 447, 448, 450, 452
Elder, G. H., 196, 307
Eldredge, K. L., 553
Eley, T. C., 256, 437
Elkin, I., 86, 162
Ellason, J. W., 287, 289
Elliot, R., 149
Ellis, A., 247, 338
Ellis, C. R., 493
Ellsberg, M., 197
Emery, G., 225, 243, 247
Emmelkamp, P. M. G., 241, 448
Emslie, G. J., 475
Eng, W., 236
Engel, B. T., 190
Engel, J., 653, 657
Engel, R. J., 532
Engels, G. I., 163
Entwisle, D. R., 493
Epple, D. M., 513
Epstein, J., 200
Erdelyi, M. H., 53
Erickson, M. T., 483
Erlenmeyer-Kimling, L., 394, 395
Escobar, J. I., 252, 275, 278, 379
Eshleman, S. K., 94
Essau, C. A., 307
Estrada, A. U., 166, 477
Exner, J. E., 113
Eysenck, H. J., 221, 241, 439

F

Fabrega, H., 384, 429, 432, 433, 437, 442, 445, 446, 448, 450, 452
Fagan, P. J., 604
Fahy, T. A., 288
Fairbank, J. A., 201
Fairburn, C. G., 542, 550, 553, 558, 561, 563, 564, 566
Fairly, M., 272
Fairweather, George, 412
Fallon, A. E., 543
Falloon, I. R., 411
Fals-Stewart, W., 258
Fanous, A. H., 361, 365

Fanskoviak, P., 689
Faraone, S. V., 468
Faravelli, C., 195
Farley, S. E., 470
Farrington, D. P., 437, 471, 473, 474
Fauerbach, J. A., 201
Fava, G. A., 231
Fava, M., 331
Fawzy, F. I., 191
Fear, J. L., 563
Feder, A., 275
Federoff, I. C., 564
Fehm, L., 236
Feigon, S. A., 479
Feinberg, Leslie, 609
Feinleib, M., 186
Fennell, M. J. V., 164
Fenton, W. S., 389
Fergusson, D. M., 468
Field, A. E., 558
Field, G., 605
Figley, C. R., 200
Fink, M., 332, 334
Fink, P., 271, 275, 278
Finkelhor, D., 200
Finney, J. W., 661, 666
First, M. B., 104, 105, 428
Fishbain, D. A., 273
Fisher, J., 182
Fisher, R. A., 654
Fitterling, J. M., 201
Fitzgerald, P. B., 398, 401
Fitzgerald, T. E., 185
Flakierska-Praquin, N., 479
Flaum, M., 397
Fleming, B., 564
Fleming, J. A., 365
Flemming, M., 630
Florio, C. M., 114
Floyd, M., 529
Foa, E., 258
Foa, E. B., 195, 196, 201, 205, 207, 251, 252, 258, 273
Follette, W. C., 149
Folstein, M. F., 523
Folstein, S., 499
Folstein, S. E., 523
Fombonne, E., 498, 499, 501
Forde, D. R., 281
Forde, J., 529
Forslund, K., 366
Forsyth, D. R., 157
Foster, G. D., 564
Fox, P., 524
Fox, T. L., 481
Fraley, R. C., 62
Frances, A., 336
Frances, A. J., 428
Francis, E. L., 323
Frank, E., 319, 331, 342, 343
Frank, G. K., 554
Frank, J. D., 164
Frankl, V. E., 201
Franklin, E., 251, 252, 258
Franklin, J. A., 561
Franko, D. L., 549, 553, 554
Frasure-Smith, N., 531

Fratiglioni, L., 513
Frederick, R. I., 679
Fredrickson, B. L., 172
Freeman, A., 152, 153
Freeman, A. M., 430, 431, 432, 433, 434, 445, 446, 447, 449, 450, 452
Freeston, M. H., 256
Fremont, W. P., 193
Freshwater, S. M., 107
Freud, S., 145, 201, 237, 246, 256, 324, 364, 403, 447, 452
Freyd, J. J., 292, 295
Frick, P. J., 467, 473
Fried, P. A., 492
Friedman, H. S., 186
Friedman, M., 186
Frieze, I. H., 201
Frith, C., 502
Frith, U., 502
Fritsch, S., 275
Fritz, G., 277
Fritz, G. K., 275
Fromme, K., 667
Fromm-Reichmann, Freida, 403
Frost, R., 258
Frost-Pineda, K., 652
Frye, M. A., 336
Fuchs, D. L., 287
Fugh-Berman, A., 141, 142
Furr, S. R., 358
Futterman, A., 340
Fyer, A. J., 228, 241, 260

G

Gaader, K. R., 190
Gadow, K. D., 475
Galea, S., 192, 200
Gannon, L. R., 190
Gans, M., 125
Gao, S., 522
Garb, H. N., 114
Garber, J., 275, 276, 307, 340
Gardner, C. O., 255
Gardner, H., 109
Gardner, W., 689
Garfield, S. L., 162
Garfinkel, P. E., 547, 550, 554
Garmezy, N., 461
Garnefski, N., 163
Garner, D. M., 542, 547, 550, 554, 566
Garrison, C. Z., 194
Gatley, S. J., 640
Gatz, M., 511, 531
Ge, X., 503
Geddes, J. R., 335
Geer, J. H., 173
Gelenberg, A. J., 250
Geller, B., 311
Gelles, R. J., 328
George, L., 530
George, M. S., 143, 334, 335
Gerardin, P., 605
Gerdtz, J., 502
Ghaemi, S., 311
Ghaemi, S. N., 335, 336

Gijsman, H. J., 331
Giles, J., 75
Gilger, J. W., 468
Gillberg, C., 479, 498, 499, 501
Gillespie, N. A., 276
Gillham, J. E., 344
Gillilland, R., 589
Gillis, L. S., 117
Gilman, S. E., 597
Gilvarry, C. M., 434
Ginns, E. I., 94
Giovini, G. A., 643
Gitlin, M., 331, 408
Glaser, R., 180
Glasgow, M. S., 190
Glass, G. V., 163, 173
Glass, R. M., 334
Glassman, A., 315
Gleaves, D. H., 279, 280, 292, 295
Glisky, M. L., 289
Glowinski, A. L., 366
Goate, A., 517
Goate, A. M., 518
Goff, D. C., 400
Gold, M. S., 622, 652
Gold, P. E., 142
Goldberg, E. M., 402
Goldberg, J., 590
Goldberg, M., 273
Golden, C. J., 107, 468
Golding, J. M., 252
Goldman, D., 437
Goldsmith, H. H., 428, 430, 432,
    434, 442
Goldsteen, K., 188
Goldstein, A., 621, 639, 645
Goldstein, G., 107
Goldstein, J. M., 379, 386, 393, 399
Goldstein, M. G., 644, 645
Goldstein, M. J., 404, 405
Goldstein, M. Z., 590
Gomberg, E. S., 658
Gonzalez, N. M., 491
Good, B. J., 10
Goode, S., 499
Goodwin, D. W., 666
Goodwin, F., 311
Goodwin, F. K., 309, 310, 364
Goodwin, P. J., 191
Gorman, J. M., 224, 225, 250,
    606, 607
Gorman-Smith, D., 478
Gotlib, I. H., 58, 319, 327
Gottemuller, M., 197
Gottesman, I. I., 378, 389, 394, 395,
    397, 404, 437, 654
Gould, M., 370
Gould, M. S., 357, 358, 362, 363,
    368, 369
Gould, R. A., 564
Graeff, F. G., 224
Grafton-Becker, V., 586
Graham-Hole, V., 411
Grant, B., 423, 430, 448, 450, 452
Grattan-Smith, P., 272
Gray, E., 166
Gray, G. E., 141

Gray, J. A., 221, 241
Gray, J. J., 544
Grayson, C., 324
Greaves, G. B., 287
Greden, J. F., 333
Green, A. H., 603
Green, R., 611
Greenberg, D. M., 605
Greenberg, L. S., 149
Greenberg, T., 357, 358, 368, 369
Griffin, P. A., 691
Grilo, C. M., 442, 566
Grinspoon, L., 651
Grisso, T., 679, 691
Grob, G. N., 19, 20
Grochocinski, V. J., 342
Gross, B. H., 690
Gross, R. T., 494
Grotpeter, J. K., 472
Grouchocinski, V. J., 331
Grove, W. M., 114
Gruber, A. J., 542, 558, 651
Grunwald, J., 141
Grunze, H., 336
Guarnaccia, P. J., 260, 385
Guarnaccia, P. J. J., 103
Gullone, E., 222
Gumley, A., 409
Gunderson, J. G., 442, 447
Gunnar, M., 248
Guo, Y.-J., 195
Gurguis, G., 259
Gusella, J. F., 521
Guthrie, B., 658

H

Haas, A. P., 370
Hadar, H., 200
Hadjiyannakis, K., 174
Hagengimana, A., 275
Haggerty, R. J., 159
Hagino, O., 275
Halford, W. K., 411
Hall, G. C. N., 161, 162
Hallam, R., 439
Haman, K. L., 154, 337
Hammen, C., 308, 319
Hanneman, R. A., 496
Hansen, D. J., 201
Hansen, M. S., 271
Harding, C. M., 393
Hare, R. D., 435, 440
Hare, Robert, 436
Harl, J. M., 137
Harper, R. A., 338
Harrell, J. P., 178
Harris, H., 652
Harris, M. J., 126
Harris, V. A., 425
Hart, S. D., 435, 440
Hart, T. A., 244
Harter, S., 116
Hartman, D. E., 638
Hartman, J. T., 355
Hartung, C. M., 6, 426
Harvey, A. G., 250

Harvey, J. G., 354
Harvey, M. R., 294
Harwood, D. M. J., 359, 371
Hasler, G., 315
Hatsukami, D. K., 660, 661, 663
Hauri, P., 182
Hawley, K. M., 165
Hawton, K., 361
Hayes, A., 164
Hayes, R., 411
Hayes, S. C., 149
Haynes, S. G., 186, 187
Haynie, D. A., 529
Hayvren, M., 475
Hayward, C., 223, 226, 241, 309
Hayward, L., 405
Heard, H. L., 444
Hearst-Ikeda, D., 201
Heath, A. C., 223, 345, 432, 434,
    442, 654
Heiden, L., 180
Heim, C., 204, 319
Heiman, J., 592
Heiman, J. R., 586, 594
Heimberg, R. G., 236, 241, 244, 245
Heinrichs, N., 241
Heise, L., 197
Heiser, N. A., 236
Helgeland, M. I., 443
Helgeson, V. S., 326
Helms, J. E., 162
Helzer, J. E., 533, 657
Hendin, H., 370
Hendrick, V., 318
Henker, B., 467, 468
Hennen, J., 368
Henriques, G., 369
Henry, B., 438, 439, 473
Henry, G. W., 15
Henry, M. E., 332
Herman, C. P., 545, 554, 559, 561,
    564, 567
Herman, J. L., 294
Hernandez, E., 295
Herpertz, S. C., 439
Herpertz-Dahlmann, B., 545
Hersen, M., 107, 276
Heslegrave, R., 442
Heston, Leonard, 396
Hettema, J. M., 223, 241, 255
Hewlett, W. A., 252, 257
Higgins, S. T., 667
Hilgard, Ernest, 283, 292
Hill, A. J., 561
Hiller, J. B., 404
Hiller, W., 275
Hines, M., 611
Hinshaw, S. P., 467
Hirschfeld, R., 342
Hite, S., 588
Hlastsala, S. A., 319
Hodapp, R. M., 489, 495
Hodgins, S., 690
Hodgson, R., 662
Hodgson, R. J., 256, 258
Hoek, H. W., 545
Hoffman, Albert, 648

Hoffman, R. E., 143
Hofman, M. A., 610
Hofman, S. G., 241
Hofmann, F. G., 520
Hofmann, S. G., 244
Hogarty, G. E., 411, 412
Hoge, C. W., 196, 200, 201
Hoge, S. K., 679, 689
Hokin, L. E., 335
Holden, C., 45
Hollander, E., 444
Hollenshead, J. D., 359, 361, 371
Holley, J. M., 404
Hollon, S. D., 154, 337, 340, 342
Holmes, T. H., 173
Holroyd, J. C., 692
Hooley, J. M., 404, 405
Hope, D. A., 236
Hornbacher, M., 544–545
Horney, Karen, 259, 447
Hornig, C. D., 223
Hornstein, N. L., 286, 289
Horowitz, J. L., 307, 340
Horowitz, M. J., 201, 205, 206
Horwood, J. L., 468
Hoshino, Y., 502
Hostetter, A. M., 64, 72, 90, 94
Hough, D. W., 444
Hough, R. L., 201
Houts, A. C., 483, 484
Howland, R. H., 139
Howlin, P., 499
Hser, Y., 667
Hsu, D. J., 335
Hubbard, K., 548
Hubbard, M., 84
Hudson, J. I., 279, 561
Hudson, J. L., 221, 481
Hudziak, J. J., 256
Hugdahl, K., 240
Hughes, D., 361, 530
Hughes, J. R., 654
Hunt, W. A., 623, 630
Huppert, J. D., 162
Hur, Y., 44
Hurlbert, D. F., 588
Huselid, R. F., 635
Hutton, J., 499
Hwu, H.-G., 392
Hyde, J. S., 576, 577
Hyman, I. E., 295
Hypericum Depression Trial Study
      Group, 141

I

Iacono, W. G., 286, 399, 400, 437
Inciardi, J. A., 627, 658
Infant Health and Development
      Program, 494
Ingram, R. E., 164
Insel, T. R., 252
Ionescu-Pioggia, M., 620
Ironside, R. N., 272
Ironson, G., 80, 173, 179, 181
Iwamasa, G. Y., 427, 436

J

Jablensky, A., 378, 379, 393
Jack, D. C., 326
Jack, R., 355
Jackson, B., 327
Jacobson, E., 51
Jacobson, J. L., 492, 634
Jacobson, S. W., 492, 634
James, J., 8, 9
James, William, 290
Jamieson, P., 363
Jamison, K. R., 5, 309, 310, 311, 313,
      335, 336, 343, 358, 360, 364
Jang, K. L., 453, 654
Janoff-Bulman, R., 200, 201
Jaremko, M., 207
Jarrett, R. B., 342
Jaworski, B. J., 307
Jaycox, L. H., 205, 344
Jefferson, J. W., 244
Jeffery, R. W., 565
Jellinek, E., 654
Jemmott, J. B., 189
Jemmott, L. S., 189
Jenkins, J. H., 10, 91, 393, 405, 406,
      413, 414
Jenkins, R. L., 247, 470
Jenkins, S. R., 544
Jensen, J. E., 532
Jensen, P. S., 469, 470
Ji, J., 355
Jindal, R., 139
Jobes, D. A., 355
Joe, G. W., 474
Joe, S., 355
Johannessen, D. J., 259
John, O. P., 453
Johnson, F., 366
Johnson, J. H., 173
Johnson, Virginia, 576, 578, 580,
      586, 594, 596
Johnson, W., 44
Johnston, L. D., 620, 635, 641,
      647, 650
Johnston, P., 405
Joiner, T., 172
Joiner, T. E., 365
Joiner, T. E., Jr., 307, 326, 327, 364,
      365, 366, 392
Joiner, Thomas, 363
Jones, C. G., 566
Jones, E. E., 425
Jonnal, A. H., 255
Jordan, B. D., 519
Jorge, R. E., 143
Joseph, R., 499
Joshi, S. V., 469, 470, 476
Judd, L. L., 123, 304, 307, 311
Juhasz, J. B., 16
Jun-mian, X., 275
Justice, A., 651

K

Kabakci, E., 586
Kagan, J., 479

Kaltman, S., 530
Kamen-Siegel, L., 185
Kannel, W. B., 186
Kanner, Leo, 496, 500
Kanter, J. W., 566
Kaplan, Helen Singer, 578, 580, 588
Kaplan, M., 426, 428
Kaplan, M. S., 355
Kappes, M. E., 611
Kappes, M. H., 611
Karasek, R. A., 178
Karbe, E., 394
Kardia, S., 655
Karel, M. J., 511
Karkowski-Shuman, L., 345
Karno, M., 91, 252, 393, 405, 406,
      413, 414
Karper, L. P., 440
Kasl-Godley, J. E., 511
Kaslow, N., 362
Kassel, J. D., 327
Katchadourian, H. A., 609
Katon, W., 275, 277, 333
Katz, R., 173, 314
Katzman, R., 523
Kavoussi, R. J., 473
Kaye, W. H., 567
Kazdin, A. E., 116, 164, 477
Keane, T. M., 205, 206
Keck, P. E., 311, 336
Keel, P. K., 550, 551, 552, 554
Keeler, G. P., 474
Keenan, K., 473
Keesey, R. E., 564
Kehrer, C. A., 440
Keith-Spiegel, P., 692
Keller, M. B., 307, 331, 342
Kellermann, A. L., 370
Kelley, S. J., 634
Kelly, G. F., 583, 591, 598
Kelly, K. A., 248
Kelly, S. J., 492
Kenardy, J. A., 228
Kendall, P. C., 110, 221, 481
Kendall-Tackett, K. A., 200
Kendler, K., 345
Kendler, K. S., 223, 241, 249, 315,
      345, 361, 392, 403, 430, 432, 434,
      442, 554, 650, 654
Kennedy, S. H., 316
Kerbeshian, J., 502
Kernberg, O. F., 443, 444, 447
Kerwin, R., 165
Keshavan, M., 434
Kessler, R. C., 26, 81, 123, 136, 158,
      192, 195, 200, 220, 223, 234, 235,
      236, 246, 259, 306, 307, 311, 328,
      330, 345, 428, 432, 434, 442,
      635, 654
Kety, 1994, 396
Keys, A., 561
Khaitan, B. K., 589
Khalife, S., 583
Kiecolt-Glaser, J. K., 180, 186, 188
Kieser, M., 142
Kiesler, C. A., 25

Kihlstrom, J. F., 281, 283, 289, 293, 294
Killen, J. D., 558
Kilpatrick, D. G., 197, 200, 207, 321, 328
Kim, J. M., 279
Kim, L. I. C., 252
King, D. A., 531, 532, 534
King, D. W., 200, 201
King, N. H., 222
King, R. A., 357, 358
Kinzie, J. D., 197, 208, 209
Kinzl, J. F., 561
Kirk, J. M., 651
Kirk, S. A., 119
Kirkley, B. G., 567
Kirmayer, L. J., 103, 124, 260, 276
Kirsch, I., 283
Kisiel, C. L., 289, 442
Klebanov, P. K., 493, 495
Kleespies, P., 361
Klein, D. N., 123, 311, 314, 325
Klein, Donald, 223
Klein, M., 443
Kleinman, A., 10, 329, 355
Kleinman, J., 329
Klerman, G. L., 154, 278, 325, 327
Kline, P., 114
Klosko, J. S., 231
Kluft, R. P., 285, 287, 288, 289
Klump, K. L., 550, 551, 552, 553, 554
Knable, M. B., 398
Knoke, D. M., 660
Knopman, D., 518, 522
Koegel, L. K., 502
Koegel, R. L., 502
Kohut, H., 51, 404, 447
Kolodny, R. C., 578, 580
Koopman, C., 201, 287
Koorengevel, K. M., 335
Kopelman, M. D., 291, 293
Kopelowicz, A. A., 412
Korenman, S. G., 653
Korlin, D., 612
Korszun, A., 317, 318
Kortegaard, L. S., 553
Koss, J. D., 277
Koss, M. P., 321, 328
Koss-Chioino, J. D., 162
Kosson, D. S., 467
Kouri, E. M., 651
Kozak, M., 258
Krakow, B., 205
Krakowski, M., 438
Krasner, L., 273, 276
Kraus, G., 437, 440, 442, 443, 445
Krause, K., 468
Krey, L. C., 316
Kring, A. M., 187, 387
Kroll, J., 15, 17
Krueger, R. F., 124
Kryger, M. H., 181
Krystal, H., 193
Krystal, J. H., 440
Ksir, C., 631
Kugler, K. E., 679
Kuhn, Roland, 139

Kuiper, N. A., 325
Kujawa, M. J., 315
Kupfer, D. J., 319
Kutchins, H., 119
KwaZulu-Natal Program for Survivors of Violence, 211

L

Ladd, G. W., 475
LaFromboise, T. D., 162
Lagana, L., 585
LaGreca, A. M., 193, 194, 200, 201
Lahey, B. B., 471
Laing, R. D., 386
Lalonde, J. K., 293
Lam, A. G., 159
Lamb, H. R., 24, 25, 158, 690
Lambert, M. C., 116
Lambert, M. J., 148, 163
Lambert, M. T., 370
Lane, T. J., 276
Lang, A. J., 236
Langevin, R., 604
Larimer, M., 667
Larrabee, A. L., 427
Larson, J., 157, 201, 324, 358
Laub, J. H., 475
Laudenslager, M. L., 178
Laumann, E. O., 575, 580, 581, 582, 583, 589
Laurie, T. A., 689
Lavoie, K. L., 187
Lawrie, S. M., 398
Leary, T., 61
Le Bars, P. L., 142, 522
Lee, J. K. P., 605
Lee, Y.-J., 183
Leenaars, A. A., 360, 361
Leff, J. P., 90, 404
Lèger, D., 180
Lehman, D. R., 199, 201
Leiblum, S. R., 578, 582, 586, 588, 589, 592, 596
Leit, R. A., 544
Lemaire, J., 211
Lemke, T., 17
Lendon, C. L., 518
Lenox, R. H., 335
Leon, G. R., 561
Leonard, S., 111
Lepine, J.-P., 329
Lepore, S. J., 187
Lepper, M. R., 84
Lerman, C., 654, 655
Lerner, H. D., 560
Lerner, M. J., 201
Lesperance, F., 531
Leung, P. K., 208
LeVay, S., 610
Leventhal, T., 64
Leventman, S., 200
Leverenz, J. B., 317
Levin, F. R., 660
Levy, S. M., 180, 188
Lewine, R. R. J., 379, 393

Lewinsohn, P. M., 123, 220, 307, 308, 311, 319, 338, 340, 357, 358, 361, 364, 541, 549, 635
Lewis, D. O., 478
Lewis, G., 403
Lewis, J., 565
Liang, Y., 518
Liaw, F., 495
Liberman, R. P., 409, 410, 411, 413
Liberto, J. G., 533
Liberzon, I., 202
Lichenstein, P., 437
Lichtermann, D., 394
Lidz, C. W., 688, 689
Lieberman, J., 397
Lieberman, J. A., 409
Lietaer, G., 149
Light, K. C., 178
Liker, J. K., 307
Lilienfeld, S. O., 293, 426, 427, 436, 437, 438
Lillard, A. S., 500
Lin, K.-M., 408
Lindemalm, G., 612
Lindsay, D. S., 294
Lindstrom, M., 479
Linehan, M., 355, 365, 366, 369, 440, 442, 443, 444, 566
Links, P. S., 442
Lisanby, S. H., 334
Lisansky-Gomberg, E. S., 533, 534
Livesley, W. J., 654
Lochman, J. E., 474, 477
Lockwood, D., 627
Loebel, J. P., 359
Loeber, R., 437, 471, 473, 475
Loehlin, J. C., 44
Loftus, E. F., 294, 295
Lombardi, E., 609
Long, P. W., 385
Lopez, A. D., 330
Lopez, S. J., 108
Lopez, S. R., 103, 260, 412
LoPiccolo, J., 586, 592
Lotspeich, L. J., 501
Lovaas, O. I., 502
Lowe, B., 545
Lowenstein, R. J., 289
Luborsky, L., 147, 247
Ludwig, A. M., 312
Luria, A., 107
Luthar, S. S., 461
Lyman, R., 492
Lynam, D. R., 453, 475
Lyness, J. M., 306, 532
Lynn, S. J., 283
Lynskey, M. T., 468
Lyons, J. S., 289, 365
Lytton, H., 474

M

MacArthur Research Network on Mental Health and the Law, 679
Maccoby, N., 159
MacCoun, R. J., 621, 659

MacDonald, H., 437
MacDonald, M. R., 325
Machover, K. A., 114
Macintosh, K. E., 500
Mack, D., 564
MacKinnon, D., 313, 314
MacLeod, C., 247, 248
Madden, P. A. F., 654
Madge, N., 354
Madson, L., 188
Magee, L., 542
Maguire, G. A., 487
Maher, B. A., 12, 14
Maher, W. B., 12, 14
Mahler, M., 51
Mahmoud, R., 409
Maier, S. F., 320
Maier, Steven, 88
Maier, W., 394
Maisel, E., 173
Maj, M., 335
Maletzky, B. M., 604, 605, 606, 607
Malizia, A. L., 202
Malla, A. K., 403
Maltsberger, J. T., 364
Maltzman, I. M., 663
Manderscheid, R. W., 407
Mangweth, B., 544, 557
Manicavasagar, V., 479
Manji, H. K., 335
Mann, J. J., 365, 366, 367, 370, 438
Mannino, J. D., 589, 598
Mannuzza, S., 468
Manson, S., 201, 209, 259
Manson, S. M., 635
Manu, P., 276
Manuzza, S., 260
Manwell, L. B., 630
Maramba, G. G., 161, 162
Marangell, L. B., 311, 334
Marano, H. E., 542, 550
Marantz, S., 611
March, J. S., 257
Marcos, L. R., 117
Marcus, D. K., 278
Marder, S. R., 411
Margraf, J., 225, 231, 275
Markovitz, P. J., 440, 444
Markowitz, J. C., 154, 155, 341, 342
Marks, A. P., 258
Marks, I. M., 258
Markus, H. E., 531, 532, 534
Marlatt, G. A., 622, 656, 659, 662, 664, 666, 667, 669
Marshall, G. N., 201, 287
Marshall, R. D., 208
Martenyi, F., 208
Martin, A., 165
Martin, C. S., 634
Martin, J. L. R., 143
Martin, N. G., 654
Martinez, J. M., 334
Masten, A. S., 461
Masters, J. C., 230
Masters, K., 366
Masters, W., 576, 578, 580, 585, 586, 594, 596

Mathews, A., 247, 248
Mathews, A. M., 149
Matteson, D. W., 355
Matthews, A., 187
Matthews, D. A., 276
Matthews, K. A., 318, 325
Maughan, B., 471, 472
Mausbach, B. T., 522
Max, W., 513, 515
Maxfield, J., 556
Maxmen, J. S., 526, 527
May, R., 247
Mayberg, H. S., 316
Mayeux, R., 517, 520
Mayou, R., 199, 200, 201
Mays, V. M., 597
Mazzoni, G., 295
McBride, A. A., 474
McBurnett, K., 467, 473
McCabe, M. P., 544
McCann, U. D., 567
McCarthy, Barry, 587
McCarthy, B. W., 582, 592, 594, 596
McCarthy, M., 550, 554, 558
McClelland, G. M., 690, 691
McClure, F., 161, 162
McConaghy, N., 604, 606
McConnell, C. F., 180
McCormick, M. C., 495
McCrady, B. S., 663
McCrae, R. R., 424, 453
McDonald, K., 555
McEvoy, L. T., 533
McEwen, B. S., 316
McFarlane, A. C., 203
McFarlane, W. R., 411
McGhie, A., 388, 401
McGlashan, T. H., 389, 392, 442
McGovern, C. M., 20
McGrath, M. L., 483, 484
McGreevy, M. A., 680
McGue, M., 654, 657
McGuffin, P., 313, 314
McHugh, P. R., 523
McIntosh, D. N., 201
McIntosh, J. L., 358, 359
McKay, J. R., 660, 661
McKelvey, L., 187
McLean, P. D., 258
McMillan, T. M., 439
McNally, R. J., 223, 224, 241, 294, 295
McNiel, D. E., 687
McWilliams, N., 46, 47
Mechanic, D., 25, 26
Mednick, B., 437
Mednick, S. A., 399
Meehl, P. E., 106
Megivern, D., 488
Meichenbaum, D., 207
Meichenbaum, D. H., 190
Meinlschmidt, G., 204
Mellon, M. W., 483, 484
Melnick, S. M., 467
Menza, M., 277
Merikangas, K. R., 241, 654, 656
Merrill, L. L., 200, 201

Merritt, R. D., 427
Mervaala, E., 316
Merzenich, M. M., 487
Meston, C. M., 590
Metalsky, G. I., 56, 322
Mezzich, J. E., 6
Micallef, J., 255
Michael, R. T., 579, 581, 599
Miklowitz, D. J., 343, 404
Milam, J. E., 184, 185
Milazzo-Sayre, L. J., 407
Miller, A. H., 316
Miller, G. E., 178, 180
Miller, J. B., 259
Miller, J. C., 180
Miller, N. S., 640, 641
Miller, R., 524
Miller, S. D., 285
Miller, T. I., 163
Miller, T. Q., 186
Miller, W. R., 661
Millman, R. B., 651
Millon, T., 430, 436, 440, 442, 446, 447, 450, 451, 452, 454, 455
Milne, A. A., 321
Milstein, V., 286, 289
Mineka, S., 223, 240, 248, 481
Minkea, S., 248
Minshew, N. J., 501
Mintz, L. B., 558
Minuchin, S., 62, 63, 559
Miranda, J., 160, 164
Mirowsky, J., 91, 188
Mirsalimi, H., 62, 63, 165
Mirsky, A. E., 397
Mitchell, J. E., 567
Mitler, M. M., 180
Mitropoulou, V., 434
Moffitt, T. E., 437, 438, 439, 471, 473, 475
Mohatt, G. V., 162
Molgaard, C. A., 533
Molnar, B. E., 362
Monahan, J., 687, 688, 689, 691
Money, J., 611
Monitoring the Future, 643, 650
Monroe, S. M., 174
Montgomery, S. A., 331
Mooney, M. E., 660, 661, 663
Moos, R. H., 661, 666
Morey, L. C., 438
Morgan, A. B., 438
Morgan, C. A., 281
Morokoff, P. J., 589
Morris, A. S., 473
Morris, T. L., 193
Morrison, K., 231
Morrison, N. K., 650
Morrison, R. L., 151
Morrison, S. L., 402
Morrow, J., 200, 324
Mortensen, P. B., 392
Morton, L. A., 72
Mortweet, S. L., 241
Mowrer, O. H., 149, 238
Mrazek, P. J., 159
Mueser, K. T., 151, 394

Mukherjee, S., 117
Mulholland, A. M., 558
Muller, B., 545
Mulvey, E. P., 688, 689
Munoz, R. F., 159, 343
Murden, R. A., 523
Murnen, S. K., 556, 558
Murphy, J. M., 6
Murray, C. J., 330
Murray, H. A., 113
Mustillo, S., 462
Myers, J., 241

N

Nadder, T. S., 468
Nagayama Hall, G. C., 161, 162
Najjar, F., 280
Nakao, M., 190
Napiorkowski, B., 492
Naranjo, C. A., 660
Narrow, W. E., 158, 377
Nasar, Sylvia, 376, 415
Nathan, Peter E., 606, 607
Nation, M., 64
National Depressive and Manic-
    Depressive Association, 368
National Institute of Mental Health
    (NIMH), 370
National Institute on Drug Abuse
    (NIDA), 637, 638, 640, 643, 644,
    645, 663
Neal, J. A., 221, 236, 241
Neale, J. M., 387, 408
Neale, M. C., 223, 241, 345, 432,
    434, 442
Neighbors, H. W., 117, 379, 690
Neimeyer, R. A., 342
Nelson, C. B., 635
Nemeroff, C. B., 204, 315, 319, 331,
    335, 336, 554, 555
Nemeroff, C. J., 543
Nestadt, G., 255, 445
Neugebauer, R., 14
Newcomer, R., 524
Newhill, C. E., 689
Newman, H., 652
Newman, M. G., 250
Newmann, J. P., 306, 532
Newsweek, 471, 648
Newton, T. L., 180, 188
New York Times/CBS News Poll, 353
Niazi, S. K., 334
Nicholson, R. A., 679
Nicol-Smith, L., 318
Nigg, J. T., 428, 430, 432, 434, 442
Nisbett, R. E., 425
Nitschke, J. B., 316
Nock, M. K., 116
Noga, J. T., 316
Nolen-Hoeksema, S., 92, 157, 187,
    200, 201, 307, 308, 317, 323, 324,
    326, 327, 328, 358, 633, 634, 655,
    658, 681
Nopoulos, P., 397
Norcross, J. C., 163, 167
Nordin, V., 499

Norman, R. M., 403
Norris, E. H., 195
Norris, F. H., 200
Norton, G. R., 285, 286
Novotny, C. M., 163
Novy, D. M., 530
Nowell, P. D., 182, 183
Noyes, R., 241
Nunes, E. V., 660
Nutt, D. J., 202, 224

O

O'Brien, C. P., 660, 661
O'Connor, K., 439
O'Donnell, L., 355, 356
Office of Ethnic Minority
    Affairs, 693
Offord, D. R., 471, 479
O'Hara, M. W., 318
O'Heeron, R. C., 200
Ohman, A., 240
Ohtake, P. J., 226
Ojeda, V. D., 260
Okazaki, S., 117, 118
O'Leary, A., 544
O'Leary, T. A., 245, 249
Olfson, M., 136, 330, 334
Olin, S. S., 432
Olinger, L. J., 325
Olivardia, R., 544
Oliveau, D., 234
Olmos de Paz, T., 483
Olmstead, M. P., 550
Olson, H. C., 492, 634
Olson, S. L., 115, 151, 243, 337, 338
Ondersma, S. J., 483
Oquendo, M. A., 332, 355, 356,
    365, 368
Orgogozo, J.-M., 524
Orlando, M., 201, 287
Orsillo, S. M., 201
Osborn, C., 602, 603
O'Shaughnessy, M., 547
Oslin, D. W., 533
Öst, L., 205, 235
Öst, L. S., 241, 242, 245
Osvold, L. L., 558
Oswald, D. P., 493
Overmier, Bruce, 88
Overmier, J. B., 320
Oxh-j, M.-L., 271
Ozonoff, S., 502

P

Padilla, A. M., 277
Paffenberger, R. S., 565
Paik, A., 575
Paker, L. E., 324
Palazzoli, M. S., 561
Papp, L. A., 224
Pardini, D. A., 477
Pardo, T. B., 335
Pariante, C. M., 316
Paris, A. H., 530
Parker, G., 405

Parker, K. C. H., 208
Parks, G. A., 666
Parrott, A. C., 644
Parry, C. D., 685, 686, 689, 690
Pate, J. E., 558
Patrick, C. J., 365
Patterson, G. R., 439, 474
Patterson, R., 690
Patterson, T. L., 533
Pauli, P., 226
Pauls, D. A., 72
Pauls, D. L., 656
Paunovic, N., 205
Pavlov, I. P., 241
Peixoto, N., 327
Pendery, M. L., 663, 664
Pennebaker, J, 188
Pennebaker, J. W., 200
Pennington, B. F., 468
Perlis, M. L., 183
Peroutka, S. J., 652
Perry, J. C., 437
Perugi, G., 279
Petegnief, V., 517
Peterson, C., 82, 185, 321
Peterson, G., 285, 289
Petrila, J., 691
Petronis, K. R., 364, 365
Pettit, G. S., 437, 439, 440, 475
Pfeffer, C. R., 356
Pfefferbaum, B., 193
Pfiffner, L. J., 467
Phan, K., 202
Phariss, B., 651
Phillips, K. A., 272, 276, 279, 280
Pickens, R. W., 654
Pilkonis, P. A., 449
Pincus, H. A., 428
Pinsof, W. M., 166, 477
Pinto, A., 221
Pipher, M., 556–557
Pitman, R. K., 204
Pitschel-Walz, G., 411
Pizzagalli, D., 316
Plassman, B. L., 516
Platt, S., 361
Plomin, R., 511
Polivy, J., 545, 550, 554, 559,
    564, 567
Pollack, M. H., 227, 228
Pomerleau, O., 654, 655
Pope, H. G., 293, 543, 544, 558, 561,
    620, 622, 651
Pope, K. S., 692
Pope, K. W., 620
Posluszny, D. M., 180
Post, R. M., 336
Pottash, A. C., 622
Pottieger, A. E., 627
Powell, J. L., 461
Powers, D. V., 532
Poythress, N., 689
Prasad, K. V., 287
Prescott, C. A., 241, 255, 315, 361,
    650, 654
Presnell, K., 558
Pretzer, J., 449

Pribor, E. F., 277
Price, R. W., 521
Pridal, C. G., 592
Pritchard, J. C., 435
Prochaska, J. O., 164
Procopis, P., 272
Project MATCH Research
    Group, 666
Przybeck, T., 436
Purdon, C., 256
Purugganan, O. H., 461
Putnam, F. W., 192, 285, 286, 289
Putnam, K., 316
Puttler, L. I., 633

Q

Quality Assurance Project, 432
Quay, H. C., 473
Quinsey, V. L., 473

R

Rachman, S., 240
Rachman, S. J., 206, 252, 256,
    258, 439
Ragin, D. F., 362
Ragland, J. D., 361
Rahe, R. H., 173
Raikkonen, K., 185
Raine, A., 439, 473
Ramchandani, P., 165
Ramirez, E., 280
Rankin, H., 662
Rapee, R. M., 221, 225, 226, 241,
    249, 250
Rapoport, J. L., 251, 252, 254,
    255, 257
Rasekh, Z., 196
Rauch, S. L., 254, 280
Ray, O., 631
Read, J. D., 294
Rector, Neil, 405, 406
Redmond, D. E., 223
Reed, G. M., 184
Regier, D. A., 234, 330, 413, 530
Rehm, L. P., 338
Reich, T., 655
Reid, J. B., 475, 476, 477
Reid, M. J., 477
Reif, W., 278
Reilly, J. L., 394
Reinecke, M. A., 152, 153
Reissing, E. D., 583
Reitan, R. M., 107
Resick, P. A., 200, 202, 205, 207, 208
Resnick, H. S., 195, 203
Resnick, J. S., 479
Reynolds, C. F., 532
Reynolds, D. J., 437, 440, 442,
    443, 445
Rhee, S. H., 468
Ricca, V., 566
Ricciardelli, L. A., 544
Richards, R., 312, 313
Richardson, J. L., 191
Rickels, K., 250

Riddle, M. A., 257
Rief, W., 275
Riehman, K. S., 667
Rifkin, A., 285
Riggs, D. S., 195, 196
Riley, K. P., 517
Rimm, D. C., 230
Rimmele, C. T., 661
Ring, K., 406
Rivera, G., 162
Robbins, P. C., 688, 689
Roberts, A. H., 520
Roberts, J. E., 327
Roberts, M. C., 165
Robins, L. N., 104, 252, 657
Robinson, L. A., 342
Robinson, T. E., 653
Robles, T. F., 180
Rockney, R. M., 17
Rodin, J., 542, 559, 564
Roehrs, T., 180
Roelofs, K., 273
Roerig, J. L., 567
Rogaev, E. I., 518
Rogers, Carl, 58, 86, 148
Rogler, L. H., 90, 91
Rogosch, F. A., 35, 204
Roisman, G. I., 62
Romer, D., 363
Romero-Garcia, I., 195
Romney, D. M., 474
Ron, M., 273
Ronningstam, E., 447
Rorty, M., 561
Rosen, G., 15, 19
Rosen, J. C., 280
Rosen, L. N., 306
Rosen, R. C., 575, 578, 582, 586, 588,
    589, 590, 591, 592
Rosenbaum, J. F., 331
Rosenbaum, M., 287
Rosenblatt, P. C., 6
Rosenhan, David, 125, 126
Rosenheck, R. A., 25, 158
Rosenman, R. H., 186
Rosenstein, M. J., 407
Rosenthal, N. E., 335
Rosenweig, S., 163
Rosman, B. L., 63
Ross, C. A., 272, 281, 282, 285, 286,
    287, 288, 289, 293
Ross, C. E., 91, 188
Ross, L., 84, 425
Rossello, J., 161
Rossotto, E., 561
Rost, K., 330, 333
Roth, T., 180, 181
Rothbart, M., 462
Rothbaum, B. O., 195, 273
Rothmaum, B. O., 208
Rotter, J. B., 56
Rousey, A. B., 496
Rovner, B., 522
Rovner, B. W., 531
Rowe, R., 473
Rowse, A. L., 312
Roy, A., 366

Rozin, P., 541, 542, 543, 549
Rubin, K. H., 475
Rubio-Stipec, M., 275
Ruble, A. E., 556, 558
Ruby, T. E., 277
Ruggiero, K. J., 193
Runtz, M., 599
Ruscio, A. M., 250
Ruskin, P. E., 533
Russell, R. S., 178
Russell, S. T., 358
Rutter, M., 315, 437, 438, 471, 485,
    490, 499, 657
Ryan, J. J., 108
Rychlak, J. F., 278

S

Sabol, S. Z., 655
Sackheim, H. A., 334, 335
Sacks, J. J., 354
Sakheim, D. K., 586
Sakinofsky, I., 355
Salgado de Snyder, V. N., 277
Salkovskis, P. M., 256
Saluja, G., 307, 328
Salzman, L., 256
Sampath, G., 408
Sampson, R. J., 475
Sanderson, W. C., 226
Sandnabba, N. K., 602
Sanislow, C. A., 442
Sano, M., 522
Sapolsky, R. M., 316
Sarason, I. G., 173
Sarbin, T. R., 16
Sarwer, D. B., 542
Sasaki, Y., 589
Satir, Virginia, 62, 155
Saunders, A. M., 517
Saunders, B. E., 195, 197, 200
Saxena, S., 254, 255, 280, 287, 316
Scarr, S., 490
Schacter, D. L., 295, 398
Schafer, J., 258
Schafer, W., 230
Schatzberg, A. F., 331
Scheflin, A. W., 294
Scheier, M. F., 185
Scherrer, J. F., 223
Schiavi, R. C., 578, 583, 585, 591
Schildkraut, J. J., 315
Schlenger, W. E., 196, 200, 259, 690
Schmahl, C. G., 443
Schneider, J. A., 544
Schneider, T., 313
Schneiderman, N., 80, 173, 175, 178,
    179, 186, 187, 199
Schneier, F. R., 244
Schnicke, M. K., 205
Schnurr, P. P., 530
Schoen, L. S., 173
Scholing, A., 448
Scholte, W. F., 196
Schonfeld, L., 534
Schreibman, L., 502

Schuckit, M. A., 633, 635, 637, 647, 655, 656, 657, 660, 661
Schultz, R., 502
Schulz, R., 185
Schuster, M. A., 192
Schwartz, D., 475
Schwartz, J., 254, 255, 256
Schwartz, M., 611
Scogin, F., 529, 530
Scott, W., 164
Scotti, J. R., 193
Scull, A., 18, 20
Seedat, S., 281
Seeley, J. R., 123, 311, 549
Segal, S. P., 689
Segerstrom, S. C., 178, 179, 180, 184
Segman, R. H., 204
Segraves, K. B., 583
Segraves, R. T., 578, 583, 585, 590, 591
Seguin, J. R., 473
Seidenberg, M., 467
Seidman, L. J., 398
Seidman, S. N., 590
Seligman, M., 240
Seligman, Martin, 56, 88, 89
Seligman, M. E., 82, 179, 185, 222, 320, 321
Seligman, M. E. P., 56, 173, 239
Selling, L. H., 12, 18
Semans, J. H., 596
Setzer, N. J., 481
Seymour, A., 197
Seymour, R. B., 649
Shadish, W. R., 163
Shaffer, D., 357, 369, 370
Shalev, A. Y., 200, 201, 203, 204
Shalhoub-Kevorkian, N., 193
Shanok, S. S., 478
Shao, L., 521
Shaw, D. S., 473
Shaw, H. E., 555, 558
Shea, M. T., 162, 426, 449
Shearin, E. N., 369
Sheikh, J. I., 259
Shen, W. W., 408
Shenton, M. E., 398
Sher, K. J., 435, 437, 438, 633, 634, 636, 655
Sherrington, R., 518
Sherwin, B. B., 585
Sherwood, A., 178
Shields, J., 397
Shifren, J., 591
Shin, L. M., 202
Shipherd, J. C., 226
Shneidman, Edwin, 353, 364
Shortt, A. L., 481
Shrestha, N. M., 198, 201
Shrout, P. E., 275
Shure, M. B., 475
Sibulkin, A. E., 25
Siegel, J. M., 173
Siegel, S. D., 80, 173
Siever, L. J., 429, 430, 433, 434, 442, 455
Sigman, M., 221

Silberg, J. L., 475
Silberstein, L. R., 559
Silva, P. A., 473
Silva, P. S., 370
Silver, E., 680, 688
Silver, R. L., 201, 202, 206
Silverman, J. M., 433
Silverman, W. K., 201
Simeon, D., 293
Simeonova, D. I., 476
Simon, G. E., 333
Simonoff, E., 490
Simons, J. A., 162
Simpson, D. D., 474
Simpson, E. B., 444
Simpson, J. C., 365
Sing, L., 551
Singer, J. E., 173
Singer, Margaret, 404
Singh, N. N., 493, 494
Singh, O. P., 589
Siqueland, L., 221
Slater, L., 139, 144
Slijper, F. M. E., 611
Sloan, J. H., 370
Slowchower, J., 564
Small, G. W., 518
Smith, A. P., 179
Smith, B., 427
Smith, C. A., 473, 474
Smith, D., 183
Smith, D. E., 649
Smith, L. E., 447
Smith, M. L., 163
Smith, T., 502
Smith, T. L., 635, 655
Smith, Y. L. S., 612
Smolak, L., 556, 558
Smoller, J. W., 480
Snidman, M., 479
Snowden, J. S., 523
Snowden, L. R., 6, 10, 159, 161, 166, 433
Snowdon, D. A., 517
Snyder, C. R., 164
Sobal, J., 550, 554
Sobell, Linda, 662, 663, 664
Sobell, Mark, 662, 663, 664
Soderstrom, K., 366
Sodowsky, G. R., 558
Soloff, P. H., 442, 444
Solomon, G. F., 179
Sorrell, J. T., 533
Southwick, S. M., 313, 315, 316, 317, 319
Sowers, W., 637
Spangler, D., 555
Spanos, N. P., 15, 293
Speckens, A. E., 588
Spector, I. P., 581, 582
Spencer, T. J., 467
Sperber, K., 521
Spiegel, D., 190, 191, 201
Spiegel, D. A., 201, 228
Spierings, C., 272
Spiker, D., 494
Spirito, A., 357, 358, 361, 364

Spiro, A., III, 530
Spitzer, R. L., 9, 431, 433, 448, 451, 464, 472, 496, 513, 528, 548, 581, 586, 597, 600, 601, 603, 604, 625, 633, 641, 642, 655, 665
Spivack, G., 475
Sprock, J., 426, 427
Stack, S., 363
Stahl, S. M., 331, 409
Stangler, D., 558
Stanley, M. A., 530
Stark, L. J., 484, 485
Starzyk, K. B., 473
Statham, D. J., 354, 356, 361
Steadman, H. J., 680, 684, 687, 688, 691
Stein, B. D., 192
Stein, L. I., 412, 413
Stein, M. B., 236, 281
Steinberg, L., 221
Steinberg, M., 287
Steiner, M., 305, 318
Steinhauser, C., 607
Steketee, G., 258
Stephens, S., 518
Sterk, C. E., 658
Stern, Y., 523
Sternberg, R. J., 109
Sterner, U., 242
Stevenson, J., 437
Stewart, S. H., 657
Stewart, W. F., 307
St. George-Hyslop, P. H., 517
Stice, E., 553, 554, 555, 556, 558
Stocchi, F., 250
Stockwell, T., 662
Stones, M. H., 201
Stoney, C. M., 187
Stormer, S., 556
Stormer, S. M., 556
Storr, A., 312
Stouthamer-Loeber, M., 474
Straus, M. A., 328
Strauss, J. S., 381, 393
Streissguth, A. P., 492, 634
Striegel-Moore, R., 544
Striegel-Moore, R. H., 545, 549, 553, 559, 567
Strittmatter, W. J., 517
Stroebe, M., 6
Strupp, H. H., 145
Study Group on Anorexia Nervosa, 554
Stunkard, A. J., 550, 553, 554
Substance Abuse and Mental Health Services Administration (SAMHSA), 620, 632, 636, 637, 641, 643, 648, 650, 652
Suddath, R. L., 399
Sue, D. W., 161
Sue, S., 117, 118, 159, 160
Suhail, K., 384
Suhara, T., 398
Sullivan, Harry Stack, 452
Sullivan, J. G., 597
Sullivan, M., 275, 277

Sullivan, P. F., 554, 563
Sundgot-Borgen, J., 556, 557
Suomi, S. J., 481
Suri, R., 318
Susman, E. J., 437
Sutker, P. B., 196, 200, 201
Svikis, D. S., 654
Swaab, D. F., 610
Swain, A. M., 318
Swartz, H. A., 319, 343
Swartz, M., 306, 442
Swazey, J. P., 137
Sweeney, J. A., 501
Swendsen, J. D., 656
Swettenham, J., 500
Swinson, R., 258
Sylvester, D., 234
Szasz, Thomas, 6, 125, 685
Szatmari, P., 501, 654

T

Tabachnick, B. G., 692
Tabrah, H., 652
Tager-Flusberg, H., 499, 501
Taillefer, S., 276
Takahashi, Y., 287
Takei, N., 403
Talajic, M., 531
Tanay, E., 684
Tariot, P. N., 518, 524
Tarrier, N., 205
Taylor, S., 205
Tatemichi, T. K., 518
Tateyama, M., 384
Taylor, J., 437
Taylor, S., 205
Taylor, S. E., 175, 185, 189, 323
Teasdale, J., 56
Teasdale, J. D., 164
Tebartz van Elst, L., 443
Telch, C. F., 553, 566
Telch, M. J., 186, 228
Telles, C., 412
Temple, N., 274
Teplin, L. A., 690, 691
Teri, L., 522
Terr, L. C., 193
Test, M. A., 412, 413
Teyber, E., 161, 162
Tharp, R. G., 161
Thase, M. E., 139, 316, 342
Theorell, T., 178
Thermenos, H. W., 399
Thibaut, F., 605
Thienemann, M., 482
Thomas, A., 462
Thompson, J. K., 554, 555, 556
Thompson, L. W., 532
Thompson, M. S., 493
Thompson-Brenner, H., 163
Thoresen, C. E., 186
Thorp, S. R., 533
Thorpe, G. L., 115, 151, 243, 337, 338
Tienari, P., 396
Tiet, Q. Q., 472, 473
Tillich, P., 247

Tolan, P. H., 478
Tondo, L., 335, 368
Tonge, B. J., 222
Toray, T., 558
Torgersen, S., 443
Torrey, E. Fuller, 25, 158, 316, 377, 379, 387, 391, 403, 413
Torti, F. M., Jr., 515, 522, 524
Toth, S. L., 195, 204, 212, 319, 461, 464
Toufexis, A., 270
Treatment for Adolescents with Depression Study (TADS) Team, 340, 342
Trimble, J. E., 162
Trinh, N.-H., 522
Tronick, E. Z., 492
True, W. R., 204
Trull, T. J., 424, 426, 435, 437, 438, 441, 453, 454, 455
Tsai, G., 400
Tsai, J. L., 62, 111, 117, 124, 329
Tseng, W., 12
Tseng, W.-S., 117
Tsuang, M. T., 365, 654
Tugrul, C., 586
Turk, C. L., 236, 241, 243, 244
Turk, D. C., 190, 277
Turkheimer, E., 685, 686, 689, 690
Turner, S. M., 236, 241, 276
Turner-Cobb, J. M., 188
Tuval-Mashiach, R., 200
Twenge, J. M., 92, 308
Tyrrell, D. A., 179

U

Uddenberg, N., 612
Uhl, G. A., 200
Ullman, L. P., 273, 276
Un tzer, J., 531
U.S. Department of Health and Human Services, 135, 164
Useda, D., 429

V

Vaillant, G. E., 185
Vakoch, D. A., 145
Valenstein, R. S., 45, 136, 137, 138, 139, 140, 143
Van Ameringen, M. A., 244
Van de Put, W., 211
Van Etten, M. L., 620
Van Goozen, S. H. M., 612
Van Gorp, W. G., 311
Van Heeringen, C., 353
Van Hemert, A. M., 275
Van Hoeken, D., 545
Van Ommeren, M., 277, 293
Van Os, J., 403
Van Reekum, R., 442
Van Velzen, C. J. M., 448
Vaughn, C. E., 90, 404
Vazquez-Nuttall, E., 195
Veith, I., 13, 15, 272
Velting, D. M., 357

Velting, O. N., 481
Venables, P. H., 473
Ventura, J., 403
Verhulst, J., 592
Verma, K. K., 589
Vernon, P. A., 654
Verona, E., 365
Veronen, L. J., 207
Viken, R. J., 559
Villarral, G., 203
Visintainer, M. A., 179
Vladar, K., 316
Vohs, K. D., 559
Volkmar, F. R., 500, 502
Volpicelli, J. R., 179, 660, 661
Volz, H.-P., 142
Vondra, J. I., 473
Von Korff, M., 333, 413
Vuilleumier, P., 273
Vythilingam, M., 204, 313

W

Wadden, T. A., 564, 565
Wade, T., 554
Wade, T. D., 553
Wagner, B. M., 357
Wahlberg, D., 632
Walden, J., 336
Waldman, I. D., 490
Waldron H. B., 663
Walker, C. E., 483
Walker, E., 275, 277, 378
Walker, L., 687
Walker, L. E. A., 426, 428
Walker, L. S., 275
Walker, W. R., 281
Wallace, J., 313, 314
Waller, S. J., 365
Wampold, B. E., 163
Wandersman, A., 64
Ward, N. G., 526, 527
Warga, C., 34, 66
Warner, M. B., 453
Warner, M. S., 295
Warren, J. L., 680, 684
Waschbusch, D. A., 467
Washington Post, 461
Wasserstein, S. B., 201
Waters, A. M., 221, 222, 223, 226, 241, 246, 249
Watkinson, B., 492
Watson, C. G., 273
Watson, D., 221
Watson, M., 180
Waudby, C. J., 437
Wayland, K. K., 474
Webster-Stratton, C., 477
Weekes, J. R., 293
Weeks, D., 8, 9
Wehr, T. A., 335
Weinberg, R. A., 490
Weinberger, J., 46, 47
Weinberger, L. E., 24, 25, 158, 690
Weine, S. M., 192, 197, 198
Weiner, B. A., 685

Weissman, M. M., 154, 155, 311, 327, 341, 342, 425, 432, 433, 442, 445, 447, 448, 450, 452, 656
Weisz, J. R., 116, 164, 165, 166
Welch, S. L., 561
Welch, S. S., 355, 361, 365
Wellman, H. M., 500
Wells, A., 241
Wells, T., 556
Wenk, G. L., 142
Wentz, E., 545
Wessely, S., 165
West, L. J., 663
Westen, D., 53, 163, 231
Westermeyer, J., 103, 275, 277, 384, 385
Weston, S. C., 442
Wetherell, J. L., 533
Wettstein, R. M., 685
Whalen, C. K., 467, 468
Whaley, S. E., 221
Whisman, M. A., 250
Whitbourne, S. K., 511, 534
White, H. R., 657
White, K., 223
White, K. J., 474
Whitfield, C. L., 294
Whittal, M. L., 564
Widiger, T. A., 6, 120, 123, 424, 426, 427, 428, 432, 453, 454
Wiggins, J. S., 61
Wikan, U., 6
Wileman, S. M., 335
Wilens, T. E., 467, 468, 469, 470
Wilfley, D. E., 566
Williams, A. F., 199
Williams, J. B., 655
Williams, J. W., 333
Williams, L. M., 200, 294
Williams, M., 473
Williams, R. B., 186, 187
Williamson, G. L., 681
Wilps, R. F., Jr., 549
Wilson, G. T., 223, 549, 562, 564, 566, 567

Winblad, B., 513
Wincze, J. P., 580
Winegrad, A., 280
Wing, J. K., 90, 381, 404
Wingate, L. R., 364, 392
Winger, G., 520, 630, 633, 634, 644, 647, 650, 658
Winick, B. J., 687
Winokur, G., 655
Winslow, E. B., 473
Winstead, D. K., 196
Winters, J., 668
Wiseman, C. V., 554, 555
Wittchen, H., 635
Wittchen, H.-U., 236
Woelk, H., 141
Wolf, E. S., 404
Wolfe, J., 200
Wolff, P. L., 241
Wolfsdorf, B. A., 206, 207
Wolfson, A. R., 180
Wolitzky, D. L., 147
Wolpe, J., 241
Wonderlich, S. A., 567
Woods, J. H., 520
Woolf, Virginia, 360
World Health Organization (WHO), 353, 354, 355, 356, 635
Worthman, C. M., 308
Wortman, C. B., 199
Wortman, C. G., 201
Wozney, K., 285, 286
Wurtman, J. J., 554
Wurtman, R. J., 554
Wurtzel, Elizabeth, 313, 332, 360
Wyatt, S. A., 642
Wykes, T., 173
Wynne, Lyman, 404
Wyshak, G., 278

Y

Yager, J., 561
Yalom, I., 247
Yamada, A. M., 6, 10, 166

Yamamoto, J., 6
Yang, J., 453
Yapko, M. D., 337
Yasenik, L., 272
Yeh, M., 116, 166
Yehuda, R., 203, 204
Yen, S., 365
Yirmiya, N., 500, 501
Yolken, R. H., 403
Yonkers, K. A., 224, 259
Young, E., 317, 318
Yurich, J. M., 195

Z

Zaider, T. I., 245
Zanarini, M. C., 426, 442, 443
Zane, N., 160
Zarit, S. H., 529
Zeller, M., 667
Zelt, D., 383
Zeman, J., 275
Zerbe, K. J., 246
Zhou, J.-N., 610
Zhou, S., 141
Ziedonis, D., 642
Zigler, E., 489, 495
Zilboorg, G., 15
Zimet, C. N., 113
Zinbarg, R., 248
Zisook, S., 306
Zlotnick, C., 162, 206, 207
Zoccolillo, M., 472
Zoellner, L. A., 226
Zubenko, G. S., 315
Zubin, J., 393
Zucker, K. J., 609, 610, 611, 612
Zucker, R. A., 632, 656, 657
Zuroff, D. C., 324, 325

SUBJECT INDEX

Note: Page numbers in italic type indicate figures or tables.

A

ABAB design, 88, *88*
Ability to function, 101, *123*
Abnormality; *see also* Biological theories; Interpersonal approaches; Psychological theories; Social approaches; Supernatural theories
  ancient theories, 11–14
  contemporary perspectives, 34–66
  cultural relativism, 6–7
  defining, 5–11, *123*
  discomfort, 9
  eighteenth-century moral treatment, 19–20
  historical perspectives, 11–21
  integrationist approach, 26–27, *27*, 35
  maladaptiveness, 9–10, *10*
  medieval perspectives on, 14–17
  mental illness, 9
  modern mental-health care, 24–26
  modern perspectives on, 21–24
  personal analysis, 11
  professions within abnormal psychology, 26
  Renaissance perspectives on, 17–18
  unusualness, 8–9
Abraham, Karl, 53
Abstinence violation effect, 664
Abuse; *see also* Sexual abuse; Substance abuse
  depression and, 328
  dissociative identity disorder and, 288–289
  elder, 692
  suicide and, 361–362
  as trauma source, 195–196
  women as victims of, 328
Acamprosate, 660
Acculturation, 103
Acetylcholine, 518, 522
Acquired immune deficiency syndrome (AIDS), 180
Acute disorders, 121
Acute stress disorder, 171, *193*, 193–194

Adaptive fear, 220
Adderall, 469
ADHD; *see* Attention-deficit/ hyperactivity disorder
Adjustment disorder, 171, 194
Adler, Alfred, 61
Adolescents; *see also* Children
  bipolar mood disorders, 311
  body dysmorphic disorder, 279
  depression, 307–308, *308*, 343–344
  eating disorders, 560
  suicide, 353, *353*, 356–358, *358*
Adoption studies, 44–45
  antisocial personality disorder, 437
  childhood disorders, 503
  "Jim twins," 45
  schizophrenia, 396
Adrenal-cortical system, 175
Aesculapius, 14
Affective flattening, 387–388
Affect-management therapy, 206
African Americans
  antisocial behavior, 477–478
  assessment of, 117–118
  delirium, 527
  dementia, 522
  depression, 328
  hypertension, 178
  personality disorders, 427, 433–434
  schizophrenia, 379
  suicide, 355
Age; *see also* Adolescents; Children; Older adults
  alcohol abuse, 635–636
  depression, 306
  schizophrenia, 393
  sex and, 589–590
Aggression; *see also* Violence
  antisocial personality disorder, 437, 440
  gender differences, 472–473
  psychodynamic theory, 47
  testosterone, 437, 473–474
Agnosia, 514
Agoraphobia, 13, 232–233, *239*, 239
Agranulocytosis, 408
AIDS, 180
Akathesis, 408
Akinesia, 408
Alarm, as stress response, 175

Alcohol, 628–636
  abuse and dependence, 630–632
  behavior changes, 628
  blood-alcohol level, *631*
  cultural differences, *634*, 634–635
  and death, 630
  fetal alcohol syndrome, 492, 634
  Korsakoff's syndrome, 528
  long-term effects, 634
  prenatal influence of, 492
  problems related to, *632*
  reactivity, 655
  responsible drinking, 669
  sexual dysfunctions caused by, 585
  suicide and, 355–356, 365
  withdrawal, 633
Alcohol abuse, 630
Alcohol dependence, 630
Alcoholics Anonymous, 158, 659, 664–666, 690
Alcohol-induced dementia, 634
Alcohol-induced persisting amnesic disorder, 634
Alcoholism; *see also* Substance-related disorders
  antisocial, 632–633
  controlled drinking controversy, 663–664
  defined, 630
  depression and, 655–656
  disease model, 654, 659, 664
  gender-sensitive treatment programs, 667–668
  Korsakoff's syndrome, 292
  negative affect, 633
  older adults, 533
  prevention programs for college students, 666–667
  relapse prevention, 664
Alcohol Skills Training Program (ASTP), 667
Ali, Muhammed, 520
ALI rule, 683–684
Alogia, 388
Alprazolam, 228
Alternate form reliability, 107
Alters, 285–286, 289
Altruistic suicide, 362
Alzheimer, Alois, 516
Alzheimer's Association, 525
Alzheimer's disease, 515–518
Ambien, 183
Amenorrhea, 544

American Civil Liberties Union, 686
American Heart Association, 186
American Law Institute, 683
American Psychiatric Association, 9, 119, 146
American Psychiatric Association definition of insanity, 684
Amish, 72, 93, 328–329
Amitriptylene, 331
Amnesia, 509, 527–529
   alcohol-induced, 634
   anterograde, 291, 528
   crimes and, 293
   dissociative, 283, 291–293
   dissociative fugue and, 291
   dissociative identity disorder and, 286
   feigned, 293
   organic, 291, 292
   psychogenic, 291–292, 292
   retrograde, 291–292, 528
Amok, 124
Amphetamines, 400, 641–643
Amygdala, 202, 202, 316, 442
Amyloid, 516
Anafranil, 139, 257, 590
Analogue study; see also Experimental studies
Anal stage, 50–51
Angina pectoris, 177
Anhedonia, 303, 389
Animal studies, 88–89
   ethical issues, 88, 89
   evaluation of, 89
Animal type phobias, 234
Anna O. (Bertha Pappenheim), 47, 268, 296–297
Anomic suicide, 362
Anorexia nervosa, 539, 544–547
   diagnosis, 544, 544
   prognosis, 545
   psychotherapy, 562–563
   types, 545–547
Anorgasmia, 582, 594
Antabuse, 660, 661
Antagonist drugs, 660
Anterior cingulate, 316
Anterograde amnesia, 291, 528
Antiandrogen drugs, 605
Antianxiety drugs, 140
Anticonvulsants, 140, 336
Antidepressant drugs, 138–139
   ADHD, 470
   anxiety disorders, 244–245
   enuresis, 483
   mood disorders, 331
   OCD, 257
   older adults, 530, 532
   panic disorder, 227
   personality disorders, 444
   sexual dysfunctions, 590
   substance-related disorders, 660
Antidiuretic hormone (ADH), 483
Antioxidants, 522
Antipsychotic drugs, 136–138, 336, 369, 444, 502

Antisocial behavior; see Conduct disorder; Oppositional defiant disorder
Antisocial personality disorder, 435–440
   characteristics, 435–437
   contributors to, 438
   integrative model, 440
   prevalence, 436–437
   theories, 437–439
   treatments, 439–440
Anxiety
   early tendency toward, 221
   existential, 59
   herbal medicines, 141–142
   maladaptive, 220
   moral, 246
   neurotic, 246
   psychological disorders and, 220–221
   realistic, 246
   symptoms, 220, 220
Anxiety disorders, 217–264
   cultural differences, 260
   gender differences, 259–260
   generalized anxiety disorder, 217, 245–251
   integrationist approach, 261
   interview questions and criteria, 105
   obsessive-compulsive disorder, 217, 251–258
   older adults, 529–530
   panic disorder, 217, 221–232
   phobias, 217, 232–245
   social approaches, 217, 259–260
Anxiety sensitivity, 225–226
Anxious-fearful personality disorders, 421, 447–452
   avoidant personality disorder, 447–449
   dependent personality disorder, 449–450
   obsessive-compulsive personality disorder, 451–452
   overview, 448
Aphasia, 514
Apomorphine, 590
Appetite, depression and, 303
Applied tension technique, 242
Apraxia, 514
Aretaeus, 13
Aricept, 522
Arousal levels, 439
Arousal phase (sex), 576
Asians
   dementia in, 522–523
   PTSD in Southeast, 208–209
Asperger's disorder, 499–500
Assertive community treatment programs, 412–413
Assertiveness, 340
Assessment; see also Assessment tools
   behavioral, 149
   children, 115–116

Assessment—Cont.
   defined, 100
   information gathering, 99, 101–103
   older adults, 529
   problems in, 99, 115–118
   self-, 111
Assessment tools, 99, 104–115; see also Measurement
   behavioral observation, 114–115
   brain-imaging techniques, 107–108, 108
   clinical interview, 104
   intelligence tests, 108–109
   neuropsychological tests, 107
   personality inventories, 110–112
   projective tests, 112–114
   questionnaires, 110
   reliability, 106–107
   self-monitoring, 115
   validity, 104–106
Assisted suicide, 371
Assortative relationships, 363
Asylums, 17–19, 18, 20
Ataque de nervios, 124, 260, 287
Athletes; see Sports
Atomoxetine, 469
Attachment theory, 62, 325
Attention-deficit/hyperactivity disorder (ADHD), 464–470
   adults with, 467
   antisocial personality disorder and, 438
   biological contributors, 468
   conduct disorder and, 467, 473
   learning disorders and, 467
   psychosocial factors, 468–469
   symptoms, 466
   treatments, 469–470
   types, 466–467
Atypical antipsychotic drugs, 138, 400, 408–409, 434, 444
Atypical features, depression with, 305
Auditory hallucinations, 385
Autism, 496–503
   contributors to, 500–502, 501
   diagnosis, 498–499
   schizophrenia and, 498
   symptoms, 497
   treatments, 502
Automatic thoughts, 248
Automatic thoughts record, 339
Autonomic nervous system, 175
Aversion therapy, 605
Aversive classical conditioning, 661
Avoidant personality disorder, 447–449
Avolition, 388
Axon, 39
Azaspirones, 250

B

Bandura, Albert, 24, 55, 56–57
Barbiturates, 140, 636–637
Barrett v. United States, 683

Basal ganglia, 398
Bazelon, David, 683
Beauty standards, eating disorders and, 554–556, 555
Beck, Aaron, 24, 57, 57, 151, 321
Beck Depression Inventory (BDI), 110, 110
Bedlam (Saint Mary of Bethlehem), 17, 18
Bed nucleus of stria terminalis, 610
Beers, Clifford, 20, 27–28
Behavioral assessment, 149
Behavioral assignments, 153
Behavioral inhibition, 479–480
Behavioral observation, 114–115
Behavioral theories, 53–55
    assessment of, 55
    classical conditioning, 53–54
    conversion disorder, 272
    development of, 23
    modeling, 55
    mood disorders, 319–321
    observational learning, 55
    OCD, 256–257
    operant conditioning, 54–55
    paraphilias, 605
    phobias, 238–241
    schizophrenia, 406
    substance-related disorders, 656
Behavioral undercontrol, 657
Behavior disorders, 459, 464–478
    ADHD, 464–470
    conduct disorder, 470–478
    developmental model, 476
    oppositional defiant disorder, 470–478
    overview, 465
Behavior genetics, 42
Behavior therapies, 149–151
    ADHD, 470
    anorexia nervosa, 563
    autism, 502
    body dysmorphic disorder, 280
    borderline personality disorder, 444
    bulimia nervosa, 564–566
    conduct disorder, 477
    conversion disorder, 274
    dementia, 522
    depression, 337–340, 342–343
    extinguishing unwanted behaviors, 149–150
    generalized anxiety disorder, 249–250
    hierarchy of fears, 150
    learning desirable behaviors, 150–151
    mental retardation, 493
    OCD, 258
    oppositional defiant disorder, 477
    panic disorder, 228–231
    paraphilias, 605
    phobias, 241–244
    PTSD, 205
    schizophrenia, 409

Behavior therapies—Cont.
    separation anxiety disorder, 481–482, 482
    somatization disorders, 277
    substance-related disorders, 661–662
    suicide risk, 369
    techniques for change, 150
Bell and pad method, 483–484
La belle indifference, 271, 274
Bell-shaped curve, 109
Belushi, John, 620
Bender-Gestalt test, 107, 107
Benzedrine, 641
Benzodiazepines, 140
    abuse of, 636–637
    anxiety disorders, 244, 248–249, 250
    insomnia, 183
    older adults, 530, 533
    panic disorder, 228
    PTSD, 208
Bereavement
    cultural differences, 6
    support groups, 157
Bernheim, Hippolyte-Marie, 22
Bernthsen, August, 136
Bias, sample, 79
Big 5 personality factors, 453, 453–454
Binge drinking, 632
Binge-eating disorder, 539, 552–553
Bingeing, 547
Bini, Lucio, 142, 332
Biochemical factors, 39–41
    endocrine system, 40–41
    neurotransmitter theories, 39–40
Biofeedback, 190
Biological factors
    ADHD, 468
    autism, 501–502
    conduct disorder, 473–474
    oppositional defiant disorder, 473–474
    separation anxiety disorder, 479–480
    sexual dysfunctions, 583–585
Biological theories, 11, 33, 36–46, 37
    antisocial personality disorder, 437–439
    assessment of, 45–46
    biochemical factors, 39–41
    borderline personality disorder, 442–443
    China, 12
    colonial America, 18
    drug therapies, 137
    eating disorders, 553–554
    Egypt, 13
    gender identity disorder, 610–611
    generalized anxiety disorder, 248–249
    genetic factors, 42–45
    Greece, 13, 14
    modern, 21–22
    mood disorders, 301, 313–319, 314

Biological theories—Cont.
    OCD, 254–256
    panic disorder, 223–225
    phobias, 241
    schizophrenia, 375, 394–402, 395
    schizotypal personality disorder, 434
    structural, 37–39
    substance-related disorders, 654–656
    suicide, 366, 366–367
Biological treatments, 133, 136–144; see also Drug therapies
    bulimia nervosa, 567
    electroconvulsive therapy, 142, 142
    generalized anxiety disorder, 250
    herbal medicines, 140–142
    mood disorders, 330, 330–336
    OCD, 257
    panic disorder, 227–228
    phobias, 244–245
    psychosurgery, 142–143
    PTSD, 208
    repetitive transcranial magnetic stimulation, 143
    sexual dysfunctions, 590–591
    social impact of, 143–144
    substance-related disorders, 659–661
Bipolar mood disorders, 301, 309–313
    creativity and, 311–313
    description of, 303, 309
    diagnosis of mania, 310–311
    diagnostic criteria, 310
    drug therapies, 335–336
    with postpartum onset, 305
    prevalence and course of, 311
    with seasonal pattern, 305
    symptoms of mania, 309, 309–310
Birth complications
    ADHD and, 468
    schizophrenia and, 399
Bisexuals, sexual dysfunctions among, 597
Blackout, 629
Blaming the victim, 64
Bleuler, Eugen, 389
Blood-alcohol level, 631
Blood-injection-injury type phobias, 234–235
Bloomfield, Harold, 140
Blunted affect, 387
Bobbitt, John, 681
Bobbitt, Lorena, 293, 681
Body dysmorphic disorder, 271, 279–280
Body image
    eating disorders, 541–542, 542, 544, 547, 554–556, 556, 558–559
    gender differences, 543, 543–544, 554
    puberty and, 308–309
Bonaparte, Napoleon, 311

Borderline personality disorder, 440–444
  characteristics, 441
  diagnosis, 442
  splitting, 52, 443
  theories, 442–443
  treatments, 443–444
Botox, 542
Bottoms, Greg, 676–677, 695
Bottoms, Michael, 676–677, 694–695
Bourne, Ansel, 290
Bowlby, John, 62
Brady, Jim, 680
Brain
  ADHD, 468
  Alzheimer's, 516, 516
  antisocial personality disorder, 438, 438–439
  autism, 501, 501–502
  borderline personality disorder, 442, 443
  conduct disorder, 473
  eating disorders, 554
  electroconvulsive therapy, 142, 332, 334
  fight-or-flight response, 175
  gender identity disorder, 610, 610–611
  imaging techniques, 107–108, 108
  injury, 519–520, 520
  mood disorders, 315–317, 316
  OCD, 254–255, 255, 256
  panic disorder, 223–225, 224
  PTSD, 202–204
  repetitive transcranial magnetic stimulation, 143, 334
  schizophrenia, 379, 386, 397–399, 398, 399, 400, 401
  stroke damage, 518
  structural abnormalities, 37–39
  structures, 38
  substance abuse, 638, 640, 653, 653
Breuer, Josef, 23, 47, 268, 296–297
Brown, Joyce, 686
Bulimia nervosa, 539, 547–552
  biological therapies, 567
  diagnostic criteria, 547
  psychotherapy, 564–567
Bupropion, 332, 590, 591, 645, 661
Bush, Jennifer, 270, 270
Bush, Kathleen, 270
BuSpar, 250
Buspirone, 250
Butyrophenone, 137–138, 407

C

Cade, John, 140
Caffeine, 645–646
Calcium channel blockers, 140, 336
Cancer
  stress and, 180
  support groups and, 190–191
Cannabis, 619, 650–651
Carbamazepine, 336

Caregivers
  dementia and, 524–525
  depression and, 532
Cartwright, Samuel, "Report on the Diseases and Physical Peculiarities of the Negro Race," 6–7
Case studies, 71, 74–76
Castration anxiety, 51
Cataplexy, 184
Catatonia, 305, 386–387
Catatonic excitement, 386–387
Catatonic features, depression with, 305
Catatonic schizophrenia, 392
Catecholamines, 187
Catharsis, 23, 47, 147
Caudate nucleus, 254
Causal attribution, 56, 321
Causation, correlation versus, 79, 80
Celexa, 227, 368
Cell body, 39
Cerebrovascular disease, 518
Cerletti, Ugo, 142, 332
Charcot, Jean, 22, 47
Child alters, 285
Childhood disintegrative disorder, 499
Childhood disorders, 459–506; see also Children
  behavior disorders, 459, 464–478
  communication disorders, 487
  conditions for, 461–464
  elimination disorders, 459, 483–485
  incidence of, 462
  integrationist approach, 503
  learning disorders, 485–486
  mental retardation, 459, 488–496
  motor skills disorder, 486
  overview, 463
  pervasive developmental disorders, 459, 496–503
  separation anxiety disorder, 459, 478–482
  temperament and, 462
Child molestation, 603
Children; see also Adolescents; Childhood disorders
  antisocial personality disorder, 439
  anxious, 221
  assessment of, 115–116
  bipolar mood disorders, 311
  borderline personality disorder, 443
  conversion disorder, 272
  depression, 307–308, 308, 325
  dissociative identity disorder, 285, 288, 289
  factitious disorder by proxy, 270
  family context, 116, 165–166
  gender identity disorder of childhood, 608–609
  narcissistic personality disorder, 447

Children—Cont.
  OCD, 251
  pedophilia, 603–604
  phobias, 234
  PTSD, 193, 195–196
  repressed memories, 294–295
  sexual abuse, 195–196, 288–289, 294–295, 692
  somatization disorders, 276
  suicide, 356–358
  treatment of, 133, 161, 164–167
China, 12, 13
Chlorpromazine, 136–137, 407
Cholinesterase inhibitors, 522
Chromosomal abnormalities, 490–491, 501, 517–518
Chronic disorders, 121
Chronic fatigue syndrome, 276
Churchill, Winston, 311, 312
Circadian rhythms, 335
Civil commitment, 685–690
Civil rights, 675, 690–691
  right to refuse treatment, 691
  right to treatment, 690–691
Clangs, 386
Classical conditioning, 23, 53–54, 54
Classification system, 118; see also Diagnostic and Statistical Manual of Mental Disorders
Claustrophobia, 234
Client-centered therapy (CCT), 58, 148–149, 157
Clinical interviews, 104
Clinical psychologists, 26
Clinical social workers, 26
Clinicians' duty to clients and society, 675, 691–692
Clomipramine, 257, 590
Clonazepam, 228
Clonidine, 469
Close, Glenn, 441
Clozapine, 138, 336, 408, 444
Club drugs, 619, 651–653
Cobain, Kurt, 74, 75, 363
Coca-Cola, 622
Cocaine, 640–641
  historical use of, 622
  prenatal complications from, 491–492
Cocaine Anonymous, 666
Cognitions, 56
Cognitive disorders, 511–528
  amnesia, 509, 527–529
  delirium, 509, 525–527
  dementia, 509, 512–525
Cognitive factors
  conduct disorder, 475
  paraphilias, 606
Cognitive functioning, 102
Cognitive theories, 55–58
  assessment of, 57–58
  causal attribution, 56
  control theory, 56–57
  development of, 23–24
  eating disorders, 558–559
  generalized anxiety disorder, 247–249

Cognitive theories—*Cont.*
  global assumptions, 57
  mood disorders, 321–324
  narcissistic personality
    disorder, 447
  OCD, 256–257
  panic disorder, 225–226
  paranoid personality
    disorder, 430
  phobias, 241
  schizophrenia, 405–406
  somatization disorders, 276–277
  substance-related disorders,
    656–657
  suicide, 365–366
Cognitive therapies, 151–154
  automatic thoughts record, *339*
  behavioral assignments, 153
  body dysmorphic disorder, 280
  borderline personality
    disorder, 444
  bulimia nervosa, 564–566
  conduct disorder, 477
  dementia, 512–525
  depression, 338–340, 342–343
  generalized anxiety disorder,
    249–250
  goals, 151
  OCD, 258
  oppositional defiant
    disorder, 477
  panic disorder, 228–231
  paranoid personality disorder,
    430–431
  paraphilias, 605–606
  phobias, 243–244
  PTSD, 205
  schizophrenia, 409
  schizotypal personality
    disorder, 434
  separation anxiety disorder,
    481–482, *482*
  somatization disorders, 277
  substance-related disorders,
    662–663
  suicide risk, 369
  taking control, 153–154
  techniques, *152*
Cohort effect, 327
College students
  alcohol prevention programs,
    666–667
  drug use, *622*
  with mental disorders, 488–489
Commitment; *see* Involuntary
    commitment
Communication
  autism and, 498
  disorders of, 487
  schizophrenia and, 404
  sexual dysfunction and, 588, 595
Community mental-health
    movement, 24–25
Community treatment
  centers, 158–159
  prevention programs, 159

Community treatment—*Cont.*
  schizophrenia, *410*, 412–413
  suicide risk, 367
Comorbidity, 124
Competence to stand trial, 679
Compulsions, 251
Computerized tomography (CT),
    107–108
Concordance rate, 43
Concurrent validity, 106
Conditioned avoidance
    response, 55
Conditioned response (CR), 54
Conditioned stimulus (CS), 54
Conditioning
  classical, 23, 53–54
  operant, 23, 54–55
Condoms, 189
Conduct disorder, 470–478
  ADHD and, 467, 473
  biological contributors, 473–474
  cognitive-behavioral therapy, 477
  cognitive contributors, 475
  drug therapies, 475–476
  peers and, 474–475
  social contributors, 474–475
  symptoms, *471*
  treatments, 475–478
Confidentiality, clients', 692
Conjoint Family Therapy, 155
Conscience, 49
Conscious, 49
Consent, informed, 691
Construct validity, 106
Content validity, 106
Context, 5
Contingencies of self-worth, 325
Continuous reinforcement
    schedule, 54
Continuous variable, 76–77
Control group
  experimental studies, 83
  placebo, 86
  simple, 86
  therapy outcome studies, 86
  wait list, 86
Control/lack of control
  depression, 323
  stress, 173, 178–180, *179*, 185
Controlled drinking controversy,
    663–664
Control theory, 56
Conversion disorder, 271–274
  diagnostic criteria, *271*
  physical disorders versus,
    273–274
  theories, 272–273
  treatments, 274
Coping style
  assessment of, 101
  dissociative identity disorder
    and, 288–289
  PTSD, 201–202
  schizophrenia, 134–135
Coronary heart disease (CHD),
    177–178, 186–188

Correlational studies, 71, 76–81
  continuous variable studies,
    76–77
  evaluation of, 80
  group comparison studies, 77
  measurement in, 77–79
  sample selection, 79–80
Correlation coefficient, 77–78
Correlation versus causation, 79, 80
Cortisol, 175, 203, 317, 473
Couples therapy, 592–594
Cousins, Norman, 172, 212
Cover stories, 83
Covert sensitization therapy,
    661–662
Crack babies, 491–492
Creativity, bipolar mood disorders
    and, 311–313
Crimes, amnesia and, 293
Crisis intervention programs, 367
Cross-cultural research, 71,
    90–91, 93
Cross-dressing, 601–602
Cross-sectional studies, 77
Cruise, Tom, *486*
Cue exposure and response
    prevention, 662
Cultural belief systems
  schizophrenia, 413–414
  sexual dysfunctions, 598
  somatization disorders, 277–278
Cultural differences; *see also*
    African Americans; Hispanics;
    Native Americans
  alcohol, 634–635, *635*
  antisocial behavior, 477–478
  anxiety disorders, 260
  assessment and, 103, 117–118
  body image, 308–309
  cross-cultural research and,
    90–91
  delusions, 384
  dementia, 522–523
  depression, *328*, 328–329
  dissociative identity
    disorder, 287–288
  eating disorders, 550–552
  ethical service, 693
  expressed emotion, 90–91
  expressed emotion interaction
    style, *405*
  hallucinations, 385
  intelligence tests, 109
  maladaptive behavior, 10
  personality disorders, 427
  PTSD, 195, *195*, 208–209
  schizophrenia, 384, 385, *393*,
    393–394, *405*, 406–407,
    411–412, 413–414
  sexual dysfunctions, 589,
    597–598
  somatization disorders, 275
  suicide, 355–356, *357*
  syndromes, *124*
  therapist-client match, 161–162
  treatment, 159–162, 277–278
Cultural relativism, 6–7

Culture-fair tests, 109
Curanderos/as, 162
Cyclothymic disorder, 310
Cymbalata, 332

D

Dahmer, Jeffrey, 683, *687*
Dance frenzies, 16
Dangerousness to others, 687
Dangerousness to self, 686–687
Date rape drugs, 652
Day treatment centers, 158
Death darers, 354
Death ignorers, 354
Death initiators, 354
Death seekers, 353–354
Debriefing, 84–85
Defense mechanisms, 49, *50*
Degradation, 39
Deinstitutionalization, 24–25, 158
Delay, Jean, 137, 138, 407
Delirium, 509, 525–527
    causes, 526–527
    diagnostic criteria, *526*
    substances inducing, *527*
    treatments, 527
Delirium tremens (DTs), 633
Delusion of reference, 382
Delusion of thought insertion, 382
Delusions, 304, 381–385
    delusion of reference, 382
    delusion of thought
        insertion, 382
    grandiose delusions, 382
    persecutory delusions, 382
Demand characteristics, 83
Dementia, 509, 512–525
    alcohol-induced, 634
    Alzheimer's, 515–518
    assessment, 523
    caregivers, 524–525
    causes, *515*
    depression and, 532
    head injuries, 519–520
    HIV, 520–521
    Parkinson's, 520–522
    symptoms, 513–515, *514*
    types, *515*, 515–522
    vascular, 518–519
Dementia praecox, 389
Dementia pugilistica, 519–520
Dendrites, 39
Deniker, Pierre, 137, 407
Depakene, 336
Depakote, 336
Dependence; *see* Substance
    dependence
Dependent personality disorder,
    449–450
Dependent variable, 74
Depersonalization disorder,
    283, 293
Depletion syndrome, 532

Depressants, 619, 628–638
    alcohol, 628–636
    benzodiazepines, barbiturates,
        and inhalants, 636–638
    intoxication and withdrawal
        symptoms, *629*
Depression, 303–309, 335–336; *see
    also* Mood disorders
    age differences, *306*
    alcoholism and, 655–656
    Beck Depression Inventory, 110
    childhood and adolescence,
        307–308
    cognitive errors and
        distortions, *322*
    cohort effect, 327, *328*
    control/lack of control, 323
    co-occurring disorders, 305
    dementia and, 532
    description of, 301, 303
    diagnosis, 304–306, 532
    double, 304
    ECT, 142
    Freudian theory of, 49
    Huntington's, 521–522
    integrationist approach, *65*
    learned helplessness and, 89
    major, 304, *305*
    older adults, 530–532
    Old Order Amish, 72, 93
    prevalence and course of,
        306–307
    prevention, *343*, 343–344
    primary care physicians
        treating, 333
    St. John's wort, 140–141
    subtypes, *305*
    symptoms, 303–304, *304*
    treatments, 522, 532
Depressive realism, 323
Desensitization (paraphilia), 605
Desipramine, 331
Detoxification, 659
Developmental coordination
    disorder, 486
Developmental psychology, 464
Deviance, 10
Dexedrine, 469, 641
Dhat, *124*
Diabetes, and sexual
    dysfunction, 583
Diagnosis, 99, 118–127
    dangers of, 125–127
    *Diagnostic and Statistical Manual
        of Mental Disorders* (DSM),
        119–125
    differential, 102
*Diagnostic and Statistical Manual of
    Mental Disorders* (DSM), 99
    cultural issues, 124
    development of, 125
    DSM-IV-TR issues, 123–125
    early and subsequent
        editions, 119
    multiaxial system, 120–123, *121,
        122, 123*

*Diagnostic and Statistical Manual of
    Mental Disorders* (DSM)—*Cont.*
    panic disorder diagnostic
        criteria, *120*
    personality disorders, 423–424,
        426–428, 452
    phobic disorders, *232*
    reliability, 119–120
    schizophrenia, 390
    sleep disorders, 181–182
Diagnostic Interview Schedule
    (DIS), 104
Dialectical behavior therapy, 369,
    444, 566–567
Diamond, Milton, 574, 613
Diana, Princess of Wales,
    540–541, 569
Diaries
    depression, *339*
    panic disorder, *229*
Diathesis, 319
Diathesis-stress model, 371
Dichotomous thinking, 366
Dieting, 541–542, 564–565
Differential diagnosis, 102
Dimensional models of
    personality, 454
Direct effects model, of
    physiological factors, 176
Discomfort, 9
Disease, *176; see also* Illness
Disease model of substance
    addictions, 654, 659, 664
Disorder of written expression, 485
Disorganized behavior, 386–387
Disorganized schizophrenia, 392
Disorganized thought and speech,
    385–386
Dissociation, 201, 281–282
Dissociative amnesia, *283*, 291–293
Dissociative disorders, 267, 281–296
    controversies over, 293–295
    depersonalization disorder,
        283, 293
    dissociative amnesia, *283*
    dissociative fugue, *283*, 290–291
    dissociative identity disorder,
        283, 283–289
    integrationist approach, 296
    overview, *283*
Dissociative fugue, *283*, 290–291
Dissociative identity disorder
    diagnostic criteria, 287–288
    explanations, 288–289
    symptoms, 285–286
    treatments, 289
Dissociative identity disorder
    (DID), *283*, 283–289
Dissociative symptoms, 193
Distress, 10
Disulfiram, 660, 661
Divalproex sodium, 336
Dix, Dorothea, *19*, 19
Dizygotic (DZ) twins, 43
Dodo bird verdict, 163
Donaldson, Kenneth, 686
Donaldson v. O'Connor, 686

Donepezil, 522
Dopamine, *40, 40*
  ADHD, 468, 469
  amphetamines, 642
  cocaine, *640*
  dementia, 522
  mood disorders, 315
  R. serpentina, 141
  schizophrenia, 379, 399–400, 407
  schizotypal personality
      disorder, 434
  substance use, 653, 655
Double-bind theory of
      schizophrenia, 404
Double-blind experiment, 86
Double depression, 304
Down syndrome, 490, 517
Dramatic-emotional personality
      disorders, 421, 435–447
  antisocial personality disorder,
      435–440
  borderline personality disorder,
      440–444
  histrionic personality disorder,
      444–445
  narcissistic personality disorder,
      445–447
  overview, *435*
Drapetomania, 6
Draw-a-Person Test, 114
Dreams, 147
Drug addicts, 620
Drug interactions; *see* Interactions
      of medications
Drugs; *see also* Drug therapies;
      Substance-related disorders
  assessment of, 102
  prenatal influence of, 491–492
  sexual dysfunctions caused by,
      585, 590
Drug therapies, 136–140, *137*
  ADHD, 469–470
  antianxiety, 140
  antidepressant, 138–139
  antipsychotic, 136–138
  antisocial personality
      disorder, 440
  autism, 502
  bipolar disorder, 335–336, 343
  borderline personality
      disorder, 444
  childhood anxiety disorders, 482
  children, 165
  conduct disorder, 475–476
  dementia, 522
  depression, 331–332, 342–343
  lithium and other mood
      stabilizers, 139–140
  maintenance doses, 408
  mental retardation, 493–494
  older adults and management
      of, 530
  panic disorder, 227–228
  paraphilias, 605
  schizophrenia, 407–409
  schizotypal personality
      disorder, 434

Drug therapies—*Cont.*
  sexual dysfunctions, 590–591
  substance-related disorders, *660,*
      660–661
  suicide risk, 368–369
DSM; *see Diagnostic and Statistical
      Manual of Mental Disorders*
Duloxetine, 332
Durham rule, 683
Durham v. United States, 683
Dysaesthesia Aethiopis, 7
Dysfunction, 10
Dyslexia, 485
Dyspareunia, 583
Dyssomnias, *182*
Dysthymic disorder, 304

E

Early intervention programs for
      mental retardation, 494–495
Eating Disorder Inventory, *550*
Eating disorders, 539–570
  anorexia nervosa, 539, 544–547
  athletes, 556–558
  beauty standards, 554–556
  binge-eating disorder, 539,
      552–553
  biological theories, 553–554
  body dissatisfaction, 541–542,
      542, 544, 547, 554–556,
      558–559
  body dysmorphic disorder
      and, 280
  bulimia nervosa, 539, 547–552
  comparisons, *546*
  cultural and historical trends,
      550–552
  family systems theory, 63
  integrationist approach, 567–569
  overview, *553*
  partial-syndrome, 549–550
  psychological factors, 558–561
  sociocultural factors, 554–558
  treatments, 539, *562,* 562–567
  understanding, 539, 553–562
Echolalia, 392, 498, 514
Echopraxia, 392
Economic hardship, suicide
      and, 361
Ecstasy (drug), 649, 652
ECT; *see* Electroconvulsive therapy
Educational attainment, dementia
      and, 523
Effectiveness of therapy, 87
Effect size, 91
Effexor, 139, 250, 332
Efficacy of therapy, 87
Ego, 48
Ego ideal, 49
Egoistic suicide, 362
Egypt, 13
Elavil, 139
Elder abuse, 692
Elderly; *see* Older adults
Electra complex, 51

Electroconvulsive therapy (ECT),
      142, *142,* 332, *332,* 334, 407, 532
Elimination disorders, 459, 483–485
  encopresis, 484–485
  enuresis, 483–484
  overview, *484*
Ellis, Albert, 24, *34,* 34, 57, 66
Emotion
  affective flattening, 387–388
  anhedonia, 303, 389
  bingeing and, 558
  expressed, 90–91
  expressed emotion interaction
      style, 404–405
  inappropriate affect, 388–389
Empathy training, 606
Encopresis, 484–485
Endocrine system, 40–41, *41*
Endorphins, 646
Enemy Way (healing
      ceremony), 209
Enkaphalins, 646
Enlarged ventricles, 397
Enmeshed families, 559
Enuresis, 483–484
Epidemiological studies, 71, 81–82
Epidemiology, 81
Erectile disorders, 585, 590; *see also*
      Sexual arousal disorders
Erikson, Erik, 61, *62*
Essential hypertension, 178
Estrogen, 317–318, 585
Ethical issues
  animal studies, 88, 89
  human laboratory studies, 84–85
  therapy outcome studies, 86–87
Ethnicity; *see also* African
      Americans; Cultural
      differences; Hispanics; Native
      Americans
  alcohol consumption, *636*
  antisocial behavior, 477–478
  competence to stand trial, 679
  dementia, 522
  depression, 328, *328*
  eating disorders, 558
  older population, 534
  suicide, 355–356, *356*
  violence among people with
      mental disorders, 689
Ethology, 62
European Americans
  antisocial behavior, 477–478
  dementia, 522
  depression, 328
  suicide, 355
Euthanasia, 371
Excessive reassurance seeking, 326
Excited insanity, 12
Executive functions, 438, 514
Exelon, 522
Exhaustion, as stress response, 175
Exhibitionism, 602–603
Existential anxiety, 59, 247
Existential theories, 58–59, 247
Experimental group, 83

Experimental studies, 71, 82–90
    animal studies, 88–89
    human laboratory studies, 82–85
    single-case, 87–88
    therapy outcome studies, 85–87
Expressed emotion, 90–91, 404–405
Expressive language disorder, 487
External validity, 80
Extinction, 54
Eye movement desensitization and
    reprocessing (EMDR), 207–208
Eysenck, Hans, 163

F

Face validity, 105–106
Factitious disorders, 269
Factitious disorders by proxy,
    270–271
False memories, 294–295
Familism, 161
Family doctors; see Primary care
    physicians
Family/families; see also Family
        systems theories; Family
        systems therapy;
        Parenting style
    assessment, 102–103, 116
    child therapies, 165–166
    eating disorders, 559–561, 563
    gender identity disorder, 611
    schizophrenia, 403–405, 411–412
    separation anxiety disorder,
        480–481
Family history; see also Genetics
    diagnosis and, 102
    dissociative identity disorder,
        289
    enuresis, 483
    somatization disorders, 276
    suicide, 366
Family history studies; see also
        Genetics
    ADHD, 468
    Alzheimer's, 516
    antisocial personality
        disorder, 437
    biological approaches and, 42
    borderline personality
        disorder, 442
    conduct disorder, 473
    mood disorders, 313–314, 314
    schizophrenia, 395–396
    substance-related disorders, 654
Family systems theories, 62–63
Family systems therapy,
    155–157, 563
Family therapists, 26
Farley, Chris, 620, 669
Fatal Attraction (film), 441
Feedback effects, 35, 36
Female orgasmic disorder, 582, 594
Fetal alcohol syndrome (FAS),
    492, 634
Fetishism, 600–602
Fight-or-flight response, 174, 175,
    185, 224–225

File drawer effect, 92
Filler measures, 83, 84
Flooding, 150, 243
Fluoxetine, 139, 257, 567, 590
Fluphenazine, 407
Fluvoxamine, 257
Folk remedies; see Cultural belief
    systems
Formal thought disorder, 385
Foster, Jodi, 684
Fox, George, 311
Fox, Michael J., 100, 128, 520
Fragile X syndrome, 491
Franklin, Benjamin, 18, 22
Free association, 145
Freud, Anna, 49, 49
Freud, Sigmund, 47
    and Anna O., 268–269, 297
    on anxiety, 221, 246
    and case studies, 76
    on depression, 324
    and dissociative experiences, 272
    early work, 22–23
    key concepts, 48
    on narcissism, 447
    on phobias, 237
    psychoanalytic theory, 46–53,
        60, 272
    on suicide, 364
    on treatment, 145
Friedman, Meyer, 185
Fromm, Erich, 61
Frontal lobe, 520
Frotteurism, 603
Functional analysis, 337

G

GABA; see Gamma-
    aminobutyric acid
GAD; see Generalized anxiety
    disorder
Gage, Phineas, 36–38, 37
Galantamine, 522
Galvanic skin response (GSR), 173
Gamma-aminobutyric acid
    (GABA), 40
    generalized anxiety disorder, 249
    panic disorder, 224
    schizophrenia, 400–401
    substance use, 653
Gays
    gender roles, 608
    sexual dysfunctions, 597
Gender differences
    aggression, 472–473
    agoraphobia, 241
    alcohol, 635, 654, 655, 656, 658,
        667–668
    anxiety disorders, 259–260
    assisted suicide, 371
    body dysmorphic disorder, 279
    body image, 543, 543–544, 554
    competence to stand trial, 679
    conduct disorder, 472–473
    coronary heart disease, 187–188
    dementia, 522

Gender differences—Cont.
    depression, 307, 308,
        326–327, 328
    dissociative identity
        disorder, 285
    eating disorders, 554, 560–561
    inmate treatment needs, 690–691
    maladaptive behavior, 10
    marriage, 188
    mood disorders, 317–319
    personality disorders, 426–428
    phallic stage, 51
    PTSD, 195, 195
    schizophrenia, 379, 386, 393–394
    sex and sexuality, 578, 579
    social phobia, 236
    social support seeking, 188
    stress responses, 175–176
    suicide, 355, 355–357
    treatment, 162
    Type A behavior pattern, 187–188
    violence among people with
        mental disorders, 688–689
Gender identity, 607–608
Gender identity disorder, 573,
        607–612
    contributors to, 610–611
    diagnostic criteria, 609
    integrationist approach, 612
    treatments, 611–612
Gender roles
    abnormality defined by, 6, 7
    gender identity versus, 608
General adaptation syndrome, 175
Generalizability
    animal studies, 89
    case studies, 76
    cross-cultural research, 90
    single-case designs, 88
    therapy outcome studies, 84,
        86–87
Generalized anxiety disorder
        (GAD), 217, 245–251
    older adults, 530
    symptoms, 246
    theories, 246–249, 247
    treatments, 249–250
Generalized sexual desire
        disorder, 580
General medical sector, 135
General paresis, 21
Genetics; see also Family history;
        Family history studies
    abnormality, 42–45
    adoption studies, 44–45
    Alzheimer's, 516–518
    antisocial personality
        disorder, 437
    autism, 501
    basics of, 42
    creativity and bipolar disorder,
        312–313
    degrees of relationship, 44
    family history studies, 42
    influence of, 43
    mental retardation, 490
    mood disorders, 313–315

Genetics—*Cont.*
  OCD, 255–256
  Old Order Amish, 93
  panic disorder, 223
  PTSD, 204
  schizophrenia, 394–397, *396*
  substance-related disorders,
    654–655
  suicide, 366
  twin studies, 42–44
Genital stage, 51
GHB (gamma-
    hydroxybutyrate), 652
Ghost sickness, *124*
Ginkgo biloba, 142, 522
Global assumptions, 57
Glove anesthesia, 272, *273*
Glutamate
  dementia, 522
  schizophrenia, 400–401
Gout, 139
Grandin, Temple, 460–461, 504
Grandiose delusions, 382
Grave disability, 685–686
Greece, 13–14
Grief, 532
Griesinger, Wilhelm, *The Pathology
    and Therapy of Psychic
    Disorders*, 21
Group comparison studies, 77,
    79–80
Group homes, for people with
    mental retardation, 495–496
Group therapy, 157–158, 244, 341
Guanfacine, 469
Guided mastery techniques,
    189–190
Guilty but mentally ill (GBMI), 684
Guns, and suicide, 370

H

Halcion, 636
Haldol, 137, 407
Halfway houses, 158
Hall, G. Stanley, 23
Hallucinations, 304, 385
Hallucinogens, 619, 648–649
Haloperidol, 137, 409, 434
Halstead-Reitan Test, 107
Hamilton, Alexander, 311
Hammand, William, 140
Hans, 237
Harm-reduction model, 659
Healing, traditional, 27, 162,
    413–414
Health
  interventions to improve, 171,
    188–191
  personality, 171, 184–188
  sleep, 171, 180–184
  social support and, 188
Health insurance, 25, 26, 158
Health psychology, *176*, 176–177
Heart attack; *see* Coronary heart
    disease

Heaven's Gate, 354
Heidegger, Martin, 58
Helper personality, 286
Hemingway, Ernest, 366, *367*
Hemingway, Margaux, 366, *367*
Hendrix, Jimmy, 669
Herbal medicines, 140–142
Heroin, 646–648, 657, 660, 661
Hidden observer phenomenon, 283
Hierarchy of needs, Maslow's, *59*
High blood pressure; *see*
    Hypertension
Higson-Smith, Craig, 210–211
Hinckley, John, 680, *680*, 681,
    683–684
Hippocampus, 203, *203*, 316, 398
Hippocrates, 13–14, *14*, 118
Hispanics
  anxiety disorders, 260
  borderline personality
    disorder, 442
  dementia, 522–523
  depression, 328
  healing processes, 162
  inhalants, 637–638
  somatization disorders,
    277–278
  suicide, 355–356
History
  family, 102
  patient, 101–102
Histrionic personality disorder,
    444–445
Hitler, Adolf, 6
HIV, 520–521, 609, 648
Hoffman, Albert, 648–649
Holloway, Gary, 8, *9*
Home-based treatment, for
    schizophrenia, *413*
Homeless, mental disorders of, 25
Homeostasis, 62
Homosexuality, 9, 597
Hopelessness, 366
Hopkins, Anthony, *437*
Hormones, 40, 317–319, 584–585,
    590–591, 610–611
Horney, Karen, 53, *53*, 61
Hospitals; *see* Asylums
Hostility, 186–187, *187*
Huang Ti, *Nei Ching*, 12
Human immunodeficiency virus
    (HIV), 520–521
Humanistic theories, 58–59, 247
Humanistic therapy, 148–149
Human laboratory studies, 82–85
  ethical issues, 84–85
  evaluation of, 84–85
  internal validity, 82–84
Human services, 135
Huntington's disease, 521–522
Hyperactivity; *see* Attention-
    deficit/hyperactivity disorder
    (ADHD)
Hyperreactivity, physiological,
    202–204
Hypersomnia, 183–184

Hypertension
  African Americans, 178
  alcohol and, 634
  biofeedback, 190
  stress and, 178
Hypnosis, 22–23, 283, 289, 293
Hypoactive sexual desire
    disorder, 580
Hypochondriasis, *271*, 278–279
Hypomania, 310
Hypothalamic-pituitary-adrenal
    (HPA) axis, 41, *317*
Hypothalamus, 38, 175, 554, 610
Hypothesis, 73
Hysteria, 13, 22–23, 47, 272

I

ICU/CCU psychosis, 526
Id, 47
Illness; *see also* Disease
  sexual dysfunction and, 583–584
  suicide and, 361, 371
Imipramine, 138–139, 227, 250,
    331, 483
Immigrants, somatization
    disorders of, 277
Immune system, stress and,
    178–180
Impaired social skills, 389
Implosive therapy, 150
Impotence, 581
Impulsivity; *see also* Attention-
    deficit/hyperactivity disorder
    (ADHD)
  antisocial personality disorder,
    438, 440
  borderline personality disorder,
    442–443
  suicide, 365
Inappropriate affect, 388–389
Incidence of disorder, 81
Incompetent to stand trial, 679
Independent variable, 74
Indirect effects model, of
    physiological factors, 176–177
Infant Health and Development
    Program, 494
Information gathering, 99, 101–103
  physiological and
    neurophysiological
    factors, 102
  sociocultural factors, 102–103
  symptoms and history, 101–102
Informed consent, 691
Inhalants, 637–638
Insanity defense, 679–685
  guilty but mentally ill, 684
  problems with, 684
  public perception versus
    reality, *680*
  rules, *682*, 682–684
Insanity Defense Reform Act
    (1984), 684
Insomnia, 182–183
Instability, 441

Institutionalization, 496
Instrumental conditioning; *see*
    Operant conditioning
Insulin coma therapy, 407
Insurance, 25, 26, 158
Intake interview, 104
Integrationist approach
    anxiety disorders, 261
    assessment, 127–128
    childhood disorders, 503
    depression, 65
    eating disorders, 567–569
    gender identity disorder, 612
    health and stress, 211–212
    legal issues, 692, 694
    methodology, 26–27, *27*, 35,
        92–93
    mood disorders, 345
    older adults, 534–535
    panic disorder, 226–227
    personality disorders, 454–455
    schizophrenia, 414–415
    somatoform and dissociative
        disorders, 296
    substance-related disorders, 668
    suicide, 371–372
    treatment, 167
Intellectual abilities, 102
Intelligence tests, 108–109
Interactions of medications
    older adults, 530
    St. John's wort, 141
Interactive model, of physiological
    factors, 176
Internal reliability, 107
Internal validity, 82–84
Interoceptive awareness, 226
Interpersonal approaches
    bulimia nervosa, 566
    depression, 325–327,
        340–343, *341*
    sexual dysfunctions, 587–589
    theories of abnormality, 33,
        60–62
    treatment, 133, 154–155
Interrater reliability, 107
Interviews
    clinical, 104
    intake, 104
    questions and criteria, *105*
    resistance in, 104
    structured clinical, 82, 104, 428
    unstructured, 104
Intoxication, *623*, *625*
    alcohol, legal definition of, 630
    cannabis, *650*
    depressants, *629*
    hallucinogens and PCP, *649*
    opioids, *647*
    stimulants, *639*
Introjected hostility theory of
    depression, 324
Introjection, 49
Inventories, personality, 110–112
In vivo exposure, 150

Involuntary commitment, 675,
    685–691
    criteria, 685–687, *686*
    prevalence of, *689*, 689–690
    violence among people with
        mental disorders, 687–689
Iproniazid, 138
IQ, 109
Irresistible impulse rule, 683
Isoniazid, 138

J

James, William, 212
Jamison, Kay Redfield,
    302–303, 346
Janet, Pierre, 22, 281
Janssen, Paul, 137
Japan, anxiety disorders in, 260
Johnson, Virginia, 576, 578
Joplin, Janis, 669
Journals; *see* Diaries

K

Kava, 141–142
Kaysen, Susanna, 422–423, 455
Kennedy, John F., 24, 158, 412
Kernberg, Otto, 51, *52*
Ketamine, 652
Kevorkian, Jack, 370
Khat, 622
Kierkegaard, Soren, 58
Klein, Melanie, 51, *52*
Klenke, Johann, 15
Klonopin, 636
Koch, Ed, 686
Kohut, Heinz, 51
Koro, *124*, 589
Korsakoff's psychosis, 634
Korsakoff's syndrome, 292, 528
Kraepelin, Emil, 21, *21*, 386,
    389, 633
Krafft-Ebing, Richard, 21
Kuhn, Roland, 138

L

Labeling, 125–127
Laborit, Henri, 137
Latency stage, 51
Latinos; *see* Hispanics
Laughter, 172
Learned helplessness, 56, *89*, 89,
    320–321, *321*–323
Learning disorders, 467, 485–486
Legal issues, 675–696
    accused, judgments about, 675,
        678–685
    civil rights of committed
        patients, 675, 690–691
    clinicians' duty to clients and
        society, 675, 691–692
    competence to stand trial, 679
    insanity defense, 679–685

Legal issues—*Cont.*
    integrationist approach, 692, 694
    involuntary commitment, 675,
        685–691
Lesbians
    gender roles, 608
    sexual dysfunctions, 597
Lesions, 38
Lewis, Jim, 45, *45*
Libido, 47
Librium, 140, 250, 636
Liebault, Ambroise-Auguste, 22
Light therapy, 335
Limbaugh, Rush, 648
Limbic system, *38*, 38–39, 224,
    224–225, 315, 398
Lincoln, Abraham, 311, *312*
Lindsley, Ogden, 150
Lithium, 139–140, 335–336, 368, 440
Little Albert, 238, *239*
Little Hans, 237
Lobotomy, 143
Locus ceruleus, 223–224, *224*
Lodge (residential treatment
    program), 412
Longitudinal studies, 77, 80
Lorcet, 646
Lortab, 646
Loss, suicide and, 361–362
Love, Courtney, 75
Lowell, Robert, 376
LSD, 648–649, 652
Lungs, smoking's effect on, *644*
Luria-Nebraska Test, 107
Luther, Martin, 311
Luvox, 257, 368
Lymphocytes, 178

M

Magnetic resonance imaging
    (MRI), 108
Mahler, Margaret, 51
Mainstreaming, 495
Maintenance doses, 408
Major depression, 304, *305*
Maladaptive anxiety, 220
Maladaptiveness, 9–10, *10*
Mal de ojo, *124*
Male orgasmic disorder, 583
Malingering, 269
Managed care, 25–26
Mania; *see also* Mood disorders
    creativity and, 311–313
    lithium treatment, 140, 335–336
    Old Order Amish, 72, 93
    symptoms, *309*, 309–310
Manic-depression; *see* Bipolar
    mood disorders
MAOIs; *see* Monoamine oxidase
    inhibitors
Marijuana, 650–651
Marlborough, Duke of, 311
Marriage, as social support, 188
Marriage therapists, 26
Maslow, Abraham, 58, *59*
Masochism, sexual, 602

Masters, William, 576, 578
Masturbation, 587, 589, 594
Mathematics disorder, 485
Mathews, Billy, 621–622
Measurement; *see also* Assessment
   tools
   correlational studies, 77–79
   demand characteristics and filler
     measures, 83, *84*
   reliability, 106–107
   statistical significance, 78–79
   validity, 104–106
Medicaid, 25
Medical condition; *see* Disease;
   Illness
Medication, 136; *see also*
   Interactions of medications;
   Side effects
Melancholic features, depression
   with, 305
Melatonin, 335
Mellaril, 137, 407
Memantine, 522
Memory deficit, 513
Mental disorders; *see* Mental illness
Mental health, law and; *see* Legal
   issues
Mental-health care; *see also*
   Asylums
   modern, 24–26
   sectors, 135
Mental-health care, modern
   deinstitutionalization, 24–25
   insurance for, 25, 26
   managed care, 25–26
   professions within, 26
Mental hygiene movement, 27–28
Mental illness
   as abnormality criterion, 9
   college students, 488–489
   definition of, 678
   suicide and, 364–365
Mental retardation, 459, 488–496
   biological causes, 490–493
   contributors to, *491*
   degrees of, 488–489
   diagnostic criteria, *490*
   early intervention programs,
     494–495
   group homes, 495–496
   institutionalization, 496
   mainstreaming, 495
   organic versus
     cultural/familial, 489
   social contributors, 493
   treatments, 493–496, *494*
Mental status exam, 104
Mercy killing, 371
Mesmer, Franz Anton, 22, *22*
Mesmerism, 22
Mesolimbic pathway, 400
Meta-analysis, 71, 91–92
Methadone, 661
Methadone maintenance
   program, 661

Methodology, 71–96
   case studies, 74–76
   correlational studies, 76–81
   cross-cultural research, 90–91
   epidemiological studies, 81–82
   experimental studies, 82–90
   integrationist approach, 92–93
   meta-analysis, 91–92
   multimethod approach, 73
   scientific method, 73–74
Meyer, Adolph, 27
Middle Ages
   psychic epidemics, 16–17
   theories of abnormality in, 14–17
   witchcraft, 14–16
Migraine headaches, 190
Milk, Harvey, 683
Mind-body problem, 296
Minimal brain damage, 468
Mini-Mental State Examination,
   523, *523*
Minnesota Multiphasic Personality
   Inventory (MMPI),
   110–112, *112*
Minuchin, Salvador, 155, 156
Mirtazapine, 139, 332
Mixed receptive-expressive
   language disorder, 487
M'Naghten, Daniel, 682
M'Naghten rule, 682–683, 684
Modeling
   of behavior, 55
   in behavior therapy, 149
   phobia treatment, 243
Moderate correlation, *78*, 78
Moderation Management
   (MM), 666
Money, John, 574–575
Moniz, Antonio de Egas, 143
Monoamine oxidase inhibitors
   (MAOIs), 138, 331, 522, 567
Monoamines, 315
Monozygotic (MZ) twins, 42–43
Monroe, Marilyn, 363, 669
Mood disorders, 301–348; *see also*
   Depression; Mania
   biological theories, 301,
     313–319, *314*
   biological treatments, *330*,
     330–336
   bipolar mood disorders, 301
   depression, 301
   integrationist approach, 345
   Old Order Amish, 72, 93
   psychological theories, 301,
     319–327, *320*
   psychological treatments,
     336–342, *337*
   schizophrenia and, 380–381, 390
   social approaches, 301, 327–330
   treatments, 301, 330–343
Mood-management skills, 337–338
Mood stabilizers, 139–140
Moral anxiety, 246
Moral insanity, 435
Moral treatment, 19–20
Morphine, 646

Morrison, Jim, 669
Moscone, George, 683
Motor skills disorder, 486
Multi-infarct dementia, 518
Multimethod approach, 73
Multiple personality disorder, 22,
   283; *see also* Dissociative
   identity disorder
Munchhausen's syndrome, 269
Murdoch, Iris, 510–511, 535–536
Murug, 329
Mussolini, Benito, 311
Myotonia, 576

N

Naloxone, 660
Naltrexone, 502, 660
Namenda, 522
Narcissistic personality disorder,
   445–447
Narcolepsy, 184
Narcotics Anonymous, 666, 690
Nardil, 138
Nash, John, 376–377, 415
National Alliance for the Mentally
   Ill (NAMI), 381
National and International
   Committees on Mental
   Hygiene, 28
Native Americans
   alcohol, 635
   depression, 328
   healing processes, 162, 209
   inhalants, 637
   suicide, 355
Natural disasters, as trauma
   source, 194–195
Natural environment type
   phobias, 234
Natural killer cells, 179
Nature-nurture question, 35
Navane, 407
Need for treatment, 685
Nefazodone, 332, 342
Negative cognitive triad, 321
Negative correlation, *78*, 78
Negative reinforcement, 238
Negative symptoms, 380
Neighborhood effects, 63–64
Neologisms, 386
Nervios, 260
Nervous breakdown, 402
Neurasthenia, 329
Neuroendocrine system, 317–319
Neurofibrillary tangles, 516
Neuroleptics, 137, 407–408, 434
Neuron, 39
Neurophysiological factors,
   assessment of, 102
Neuropsychological tests, 107
Neurosis, 221
Neurotic anxiety, 246
Neurotic paradox, 49
Neurotransmitters, *39*, 39–40, *40*
   Alzheimer's, 518
   mood disorders, 315

Neurotransmitters—*Cont.*
   panic disorder, 223–225
   schizophrenia, 399–401
   suicide, 366–367
Neurotransmitter theories, 39–40
Nicotine, 643–645, 660–661
Nimodipine, 336
Norepinephrine, 40
   ADHD, 469–470
   amphetamines, 642
   mood disorders, 315, 332
   panic disorder, 223–224, 227
Null hypothesis, 73

O

Object relations theory, 51–52, 443
Observational learning, 55
Obsessions, 251
Obsessive-compulsive disorder
      (OCD), 217, 251–258
   body dysmorphic disorder
      and, 280
   symptoms, 252, 252–254
   theories, 254, 254–257
   treatments, 257, 257–258
Obsessive-compulsive personality
      disorder, 451–452
OCD; *see* Obsessive-compulsive
      disorder
Odd-eccentric personality
      disorders, 421, 428–434
   overview, *429*
   paranoid personality disorder,
      428–431
   schizoid personality disorder,
      431–432
   schizophrenia and, 428
   schizotypal personality disorder,
      432–434
Oedipus complex, 51, 237
Olanzapine, 336, 409, 434, 444
Older adults
   anxiety disorders, 529–530
   assessment problems, 529
   depression, 306, 530–532
   integrationist approach, 534–535
   mental disorders, 509, 529–534
   sex, 589–590
   substance use disorders, 532–534
   suicide, 358–359, 531
Ol' Dirty Bastard, 669
Old Order Amish, 72, 93, 328–329
Old Testament, 13
One Flew over the Cuckoo's Nest
      (film), 332
Operant conditioning, 23, 54–55
Operationalization, 74
Opioids, 619, 646–648
Opium, 622
Oppositional defiant disorder,
      470–478
   biological contributors, 473–474
   cognitive-behavioral therapy, 477
   social contributors, 474–475
   symptoms, *472*
Oral stage, 50

Organic amnesia, 291, *292*
Organic brain disorders, 512
Orgasm, 577–578
Orgasmic disorders, 582–583
Oxycodone, 648
Oxycontin, 646

P

Packard, Mrs. E. P. W., 685
Pain disorders, *271*, 274–278
Palialia, 514
Panic attacks, 221–222, *222*, 232,
      239, 239
Panic disorder, 217, 221–232
   diary of panic thoughts, *229*
   DSM-IV-TR diagnostic
      criteria, *120*
   integrated model, *223*
   integrationist approach, 226–227
   interview questions and
      criteria, *105*
   kindling model, 224–225, *225*
   panic attacks, 221–222, *222*
   theories, 223–227
   treatments, 227, 227–231
Pappenheim, Bertha; *see* Anna O.
Paranoid personality disorder,
      428–431
Paranoid schizophrenia, 391–392
Paraphilias, 573, 598–607
   causes, 604–605
   defined, 599
   exhibitionism, 602–603
   fetishism, 600–602
   frotteurism, 603
   overview, *600*
   pedophilia, 603–604
   sexual sadism and
      masochism, 602
   treatments, 605–607, *607*
   voyeurism, 602
Parasomnias, *183*
Parens patriae, 686
Parenting style; *see also*
      Family/families
   depression and, 325
   schizophrenia, 403
Parker, Charlie, 669
Parkinson's disease, 400, 520
Parnate, 138
Paroxetine, 257
Partial reinforcement schedule, 54
Partial-syndrome eating disorders,
      549–550
Patients' rights movement, 24, 685
Pavlov, Ivan, 23, 53–54
Paxil, 139, 227, 250, 257, 368
PCP, 619, 648–650
Pedophilia, 603–604
Peer counseling, 157
Penis envy, 51
Percocet, 646
Percodan, 646
Performance anxiety (sex), 586
Periaqueductal gray, 224
Perinatal hypoxia, 399

Perls, Fritz, 58
Persecutor personality, 285–286
Persecutory delusions, 382
Perseveration, 386
Personality; *see also* Temperament
   defined, 423
   five-factor model, *453*, 453–454
   health and, 171, 184–188
   pessimism, 184–185
   situational influences versus,
      425–426
   social support, 188
   and substance-related
      disorders, 657
   Type A behavior pattern, 185–188
Personality disorders, 421–457
   alternative conceptualizations,
      452–454
   anxious-fearful, 421, 447–452
   defining and diagnosing, 421,
      423–428
   dramatic-emotional, 421, 435–447
   integrationist approach, 454–455
   odd-eccentric, 421, 428–434
   overview, *424*
Person-centered therapy, 148
Pervasive developmental
      disorders, 459, 496–503
   autism, 496–503
   other than autism, 499–500
   overview, *500*
Pessimism, 184–185, *185*
Peter of Herental, 16
Peyote, 623, 648
Peyronie's disease, 585
Phallic stage, 51
Phenothiazines, 24–26, 136–138,
      399–400, 407
Phenylketonuria (PKU), 490
Phobias, 217, 232–245
   agoraphobia, 232–233
   animal type, 234
   blood-injection-injury type,
      234–235
   in DSM-IV-TR, *232*
   natural environment type, 234
   situational type, 234
   social, 235–236, *236*
   specific, 233–235
   theories, 236–241, *237*
   treatments, 241–245, *242*
Phoenix, River, 669
Phonological disorder, 487
Physical examinations, 102
Physiological factors, assessment
      of, 102
Phytomedicines, 141
Pinel, Philippe, 19
Pittman, Christopher, 681
Pituitary gland, 41
Placebo control group, 86
Placebos, 86
Plaque (blood vessels), 177
Plaques (brain), 516
Plateau phase (sex), 577
Plato, 14
Playgirl (magazine), 543

Pleasure principle, 47
Poddar, Prosenjit, 692
Polygenic processes, 42
Positive correlation, 77, 77
Positive symptoms, 380
Positron-emission tomography
    (PET), 108
Postpartum depression, 305, 681
Posttraumatic stress disorder
    (PTSD), 171, 191–211
  biological factors, 202–204
  biological therapies, 208
  cognitive-behavioral therapy, 205
  contributors to, 199
  conversion disorder and, 272
  cultural differences, 195, 195
  environmental and social
      factors, 200
  eye movement desensitization
      and reprocessing, 207–208
  gender differences, 195, 195
  older adults, 530
  psychological factors, 200–202
  role of trauma, 194–199
  sociocultural approaches,
      208–211
  somatization disorders and, 277
  stress management, 206–207
  symptoms, 192, 192–193
  treatments, 204, 204–211
  vulnerability to, 199–204
Potsmokers Anonymous, 666
Poverty
  antisocial behavior and, 474
  children in, 460
  mental retardation and, 493
  schizophrenia and, 403
Preconscious, 49
Predictive validity, 106
Predisposition, 43
Prefrontal cortex, 316, 398, 399
Prefrontal lobotomy, 143
Premature ejaculation, 582, 596
Premenstrual dysphoric
    disorder, 318
Premenstrual symptoms
    (PMS), 318
Prenatal complications
  ADHD and, 468
  alcohol and, 492, 634
  mental retardation, 491–492
  schizophrenia and, 399
Prepared classical
    conditioning, 240
Prescription drugs
  abuse of, 533
  sexual dysfunction caused
      by, 585
Presley, Elvis, 669
Prevalence of disorder, 81
Primary care, 135
Primary care physicians,
    depression treated by, 333
Primary prevention, 159
Primary process thinking, 48
Prisoners, mental disorders of, 25,
    436, 690

Probands, 42
Process debriefing, 84–85
Prodromal symptoms, 390
Progesterone, 317–318
Projective tests, 112–114
Prolixin, 407
Prototypes, 61
Prozac, 139, 227, 257, 368, 567, 590
Pryor, Richard, 669
Psychiatric nurses, 26
Psychiatrists, 26
Psychic epidemics, 16–17
Psychoanalysis, 46–51
  body dysmorphic disorder, 280
  borderline personality
      disorder, 443
  conversion disorder, 272, 274
  development of, 22–23
  id, ego, and superego, 47–49
  key concepts, 48
  psychodynamic therapies
      versus, 147
  psychosexual stages, 49–51
Psychodynamic theories, 46–53
  assessment of, 52–53
  generalized anxiety disorder,
      246–247
  later, 51–53
  mood disorders, 324–325
  narcissistic personality
      disorder, 447
  OCD, 256
  phobias, 237–238
  psychoanalysis, 46–51
  schizophrenia, 403–404
  suicide, 364
Psychodynamic therapies, 145–148
  bipolar disorder, 343
  borderline personality
      disorder, 444
  depression, 341–342
  somatization disorders, 277
Psychogenic amnesia, 291–292, 292
Psychological autopsy, 364
Psychological factors
  eating disorders, 558–561
  PTSD, 200–202
  sexual dysfunctions,
      585–587, 587
Psychological theories, 11, 33, 46,
    46–60
  behavioral, 23, 53–55
  borderline personality
      disorder, 443
  cognitive, 23–24, 55–58
  eighteenth century, 19
  humanistic and existential, 58–59
  modern, 22–24
  mood disorders, 301,
      319–327, 320
  psychodynamic, 22–23, 46–53
  schizophrenia, 375, 403–407
  substance-related disorders,
      656–657
  suicide, 363, 363–366

Psychological therapies, 133,
    144–154, 145
  anorexia nervosa, 562–563
  antisocial personality
      disorder, 440
  behavior therapies, 149–151
  bulimia nervosa, 564–567
  for children, 165
  cognitive, 151–154
  conduct disorder, 477
  depression, 336–342, 337
  humanistic, 148–149
  oppositional defiant
      disorder, 477
  panic disorder, 228–231
  psychodynamic, 145–148
  PTSD, 205
  schizophrenia, 409
  schizotypal personality
      disorder, 434
  sexual dysfunctions, 591–597
  suicide risk, 369
Psychomotor agitation, 304
Psychomotor retardation, 303–304
Psychoneuroimmunology, 178
Psychopathology, defined, 4
Psychopathy, 435, 436
Psychosis
  defined, 377
  drug therapies, 136–138
Psychosocial development,
    Erikson's stages of, 62
Psychosocial factors
  ADHD, 468–469
  schizophrenia, 402, 402–407,
      409–413, 412
  separation anxiety disorder,
      480–481
Psychosomatic disorders, 269
Psychosurgery, 142–143
Psychotic disorders, overview
    of, 378
Psychotic features, depression
    with, 305
PTSD; see Posttraumatic stress
    disorder
Puberty, 308–309

Q

Quaalude, 636
Questionnaires, 110

R

Rain Man (film), 498, 499
Ramone, Dee Dee, 669
Random assignment, 83
Random sample, 79
Rape; see also Sexual abuse; Sexual
    assault
  date rape drugs, 652
  incidence of, 328
  PTSD, 195, 196
Rational deliberation, 48
Rational-emotive therapy, 24, 34
Rauwolfia serpentina, 141

Raynor, Rosalie, 238
Reading disorder, 485
Reagan, Ronald, 515, *515*, 680, 683–684
Realistic anxiety, 246
Reality principle, 48
Reasoner, Harry, 663
Recent events, 101
Receptors, 39
Reflection, 148
Reformulated learned helplessness theory, 321
Refractory period (sex), 577
Refugees
    PTSD, 196–198
    somatization disorders, 277
Reimer, David, 574–575, 613
Reinforcement, 54
Relapse prevention programs, 664
Relationship problems, 588–589
Relaxation exercises, 190, 230–231
Reliability, 106–107
    alternate form, 107
    defined, 106
    internal, 107
    interrater, 107
    test-retest, 106
    types, *106*
Religion
    Hispanic healing processes, 162
    Native American healing processes, 162
    psychic epidemics, 16–17
    substance use and, 623
    suicide and, 356
Remeron, 139, 332
Reminyl, 522
Renaissance, 17–18
Repetitive transcranial magnetic stimulation, 143, 334
Replication, 76
Representative sample, 79
Repressed memories, 294–295
Repression, 47, 272
Research; *see also* Methodology
    challenges of, 72–73
    participants' rights, 85
Residual schizophrenia, 392
Residual symptoms, 390
Resilience, 461
Resistance
    in assessment interviews, 104
    of children, 166–167
    in psychotherapy, 145
    as stress response, 175
Resolution (sex), 578
Response, 53–54
Response shaping, 151
Retrograde amnesia, 291–292, 528
Rett's disorder, 499
Reuptake, 39
Reversal design, *88*, 88
Rheumatism, 139
Richards, Keith, 669
Right to refuse treatment, 691
Right to treatment, 690

Risk factors, epidemiological studies on, 81
Risperidone, 138, 336, 408–409
Ritalin, 469
Rivastigmine, 522
Rogers, Carl, *58*, 58, 148, 247
Rohypnol, 652
Role-playing, 149, 153
Rome, 13–14
Rorschach, Hermann, 112
Rorschach Inkblot Test, 112–113
Rosenman, Ray, 185
Ruminative response styles theory, 323–324
Rush, Benjamin, 18
Ryder, Winona, 423

S

Sachs, Hanns, 53
SAD; *see* Seasonal affective disorder
Sadism, sexual, 602
Sadness, 303
Sadomasochism, 602
SAFE attitude, 380–381
Safe sex, 189–190, 593
Safety signal hypothesis, 173, 239
Saint Vitus' dance, 16
Sample
    bias, 79
    correlational studies, 79–80
    defined, 79
    group comparison studies, 79–80
    random, 79
    representative, 79
Sandwich generation, 524
Satir, Virginia, 155
Savants, 498
Schizoaffective disorder, 390, *391*
Schizoid personality disorder, 431–432
Schizophrenia, 375–418
    autism and, 498
    biological theories, 375, 394–402, *395*
    biological treatments, 407–409
    characteristics, 377
    coping, 134–135
    costs, 377–378
    diagnosis, 375, 389–392, *390*
    drug treatment for, 24
    families coping with, 380–381
    integrationist approach, 414–415
    living situations of people with, *379*
    mood disorders and, 380–381, 390
    negative symptoms, 387–388, *388*
    odd-eccentric personality disorders and, 428
    personal account of, 134–135, 167–168
    positive symptoms, 381–387, *382*
    prognosis, 375, 392–394
    psychological theories, 375

Schizophrenia—*Cont.*
    psychological treatments, 409
    psychosocial perspectives, *402*, 402–407, 409–413, *411*
    SAFE attitude, 380–381
    sociocultural factors, 393–394
    symptoms, 375, 381–389
    treatments, 375, 407–414
    types, 390–392, *391*
Schizophrenogenic mothers, 403
Schizotypal personality disorder, 432–434
Schou, Mogens, 140
Science (journal), 663
Scientific method, 71, 73–74; *see also* Experimental studies
    hypothesis statement, 73
    method selection, 73–74
    problem definition, 73
    replication, 76
Scot, Reginald, *Discovery of Witchcraft*, 16
Scripts, 61
Seasonal affective disorder (SAD), 305–306, 335
Secondary prevention, 159
Secondary process thinking, 48
Secular Organizations for Sobriety/Save Ourselves (SOS), 666
Sedatives, 637
Seduction rituals, 592
Selective serotonin reuptake inhibitors (SSRIs), 139
    body dysmorphic disorder, 280
    bulimia nervosa, 567
    depression, 331–332
    generalized anxiety disorder, 250
    OCD, 257
    panic disorder, 227–228
    paraphilias, 605
    PTSD, 208
    sexual dysfunctions, 585
    suicide risk, 368
Self-actualization, 58
Self-assessment, 111
Self-concept
    depression and, 307–308
    development of, 51–52
Self-deceptions, 381–382
Self-destructive behavior, dissociative identity disorder and, 286
Self-efficacy, 24, 56–57, 244
Self-help groups, 157
Self-Management and Recovery Training (SMART), 666
Self-monitoring, 115
Self-reports, 72
Self-stimulatory behaviors, 498
Self-worth, 325
Selye, Hans, 175, 176
Semen loss, 589
Sensate focus therapy, 594–596
Sentence Completion Test, 114

Separation anxiety disorder, 459,
    478–482
  biological contributors, 479–480
  causes, *480*
  psychosocial contributors,
    480–481
  symptoms, *479*
  treatments, *480*, 481–482
Serax, 140, 250
Serotonin, 40, *40*; *see also* Selective
    serotonin reuptake inhibitors
    (SSRIs)
  aggression, 438
  alcohol, 653
  antisocial personality disorder,
    438, 440
  autism, 502
  eating disorders, 554
  impulsivity, 438, 442–443
  mood disorders, 315, 335
  OCD, 254, 257
  panic disorder, 224, 227–228
  schizophrenia, 400
  suicide, 366–367
  violence, 473
Serotonin transporter gene, 315
Sertraline, 257, 590
Serzone, 332, 342
Set point, 564
Sex offenders, 599, 605, 687
Sex reassignment, 611–612
Sex therapy, 593–597, *594*
  premature ejaculation
    treatments, 596
  sensate focus therapy, 594–596
  vaginismus treatments, 596–597
Sexual abuse; *see also* Rape
  children, 195–196, 288–289,
    294–295, 692
  conversion disorder and, 272–273
  dissociative identity disorder
    and, 288–289
  eating disorders and, 561
  pedophilia, 603–604, 605
  repressed memories and,
    294–295
  as trauma source, 195–196, *196*
  victim response, 197
Sexual arousal disorders, 581–582
Sexual assault, sexual dysfunction
    and, 581, 589; *see also* Rape
Sexual aversion disorder, 580–581
Sexual desire, 576
  frequency of sex, *580*
  frequency of sex thoughts, *579*
Sexual desire disorders, 578–581
  generalized, 580
  hypoactive sexual desire
    disorder, 580
  sexual aversion disorder, 580–581
  situational, 580
Sexual disorders, 573–616
  gender identity disorder, 573,
    607–612
  paraphilias, 573, 598–607
  sexual dysfunctions, 573,
    575–598

Sexual dysfunctions, 573, 575–598
  biological causes, 583–585
  biological therapies, 590–591
  causes, 583–590, *584*
  interpersonal factors, 587–589
  orgasmic disorders, 582–583
  overview, *579*
  prevalence of difficulties, *578*
  psychological causes,
    585–587, *587*
  psychotherapy, 591–597
  sexual arousal disorders, 581–582
  sexual desire disorders, 578–581
  sexual pain disorders, 583
  sexual response cycle, 576–578
  sociocultural factors, 589
  treatments, 590–598, *591*
  types, 578–583
Sexuality
  desire, 576
  frequency of sex, *580*
  frequency of sex thoughts, *579*
  practices, *599*
  psychodynamic theory, 47
  psychosexual stages, 49–51
  safe sexual practices,
    189–190, 593
  scripts for sex, 592
  sexual orientation, 608
  therapist-client relations, 691–692
Sexual masochism, 602
Sexual orientation, 608
Sexual pain disorders, 583
Sexual predator law, 687
Sexual response cycle, 576–578
  female, *577*
  male, *576*
Sexual sadism, 602
Shaken baby syndrome, 492–493
Shakespeare, William, 17
Shanley, Paul, *603*
Shapiro, Francine, 206
Shinjing shuairuo, *124*
Short-term therapies, 147, 153, 154
Side effects
  anticonvulsants, 336
  antipsychotic drugs, 336
  atypical antipsychotics, 408–409
  bupropion, 332
  butyrophenone, 137–138
  lithium, 140, 336
  MAOIs, 138, 331
  neuroleptics, 408
  phenothiazines, 137–138
  sildenafil, 590
  SSRIs, 139, 227, 257, 331–332, 585
  stimulants, 469
  St. John's wort, 141
  tricyclic antidepressants, 227,
    331, 483
Sigmundson, Keith, 613
Sildenafil, 590–591
Silence of the Lambs (film), *437*
Simple control group, 86
Single-case experimental designs,
    87–88
Sister of Notre Dame, 517, *517*

Situational influences on behavior,
    425–426
Situational sexual desire
    disorder, 580
Situational type phobias, 234
60 Minutes (television show), 663
Skinner, B. F., 23, 54–55
Slaves, 6–7
Sleep
  depression and, 303
  deprivation, 181
  disorders, 181–184, *182*, *183*
  health and, 171, 180–184
  social costs of sleep
    disorders, 180
Sleep apnea, 184
Sleeping pills, 140
Sleep restriction therapy, 183
Sluggish cognitive tempo, 466
Smoking; *see* Nicotine
Smooth pursuit eye movement, 386
Social approaches
  anxiety disorders, 217
  assessment of, 64
  community treatment and
    intervention, 158–159,
    209–211
  cross-cultural issues, 159–162
  eating disorders, 554–558
  family systems theories, 62–63
  gender issues, 162
  group therapy, 157–158
  interpersonal theories, 60–62
  mental retardation, 493, 494–496
  mood disorders, 301, 327–330
  PTSD, 208–211
  schizophrenia, 402–405, 409–413
  social structural theories,
    63–64, *64*
  substance-related disorders,
    657–659
  suicide, 361–363, *362*, 369–371
  theories of abnormality, 33,
    60–64, *61*
  treatment, 133, 157–163
Social learning theory, 55, 477
Social phobia, 235–236, *236*, 448
Social resources, 102–103
Social selection, 402–403
Social skills, impaired, 389
Social skills training, 151
Social status, 328
Social structural theories, 63–64, *64*
Social support
  PTSD, 200
  stress, 188
Society, substance use and, 619,
    621–623
Sociocultural background, 103
Sociocultural health interventions,
    190–191
Socioeconomic factors; *see also*
    Poverty
  eating disorders, 558
  sexual dysfunctions, 589
Socrates, 14
Somatic hallucinations, 385

Somatization disorders, *271*,
    274–278
    conversion disorder and, 274
    diagnostic criteria, *274*
    hypochondriasis and, 278
    model of, *276*
    organic disorders versus, 276
    theories, 276–277
    treatments, 277–278
Somatoform disorders, 267,
    269–281
    body dysmorphic disorder, *271*,
        279–280
    conversion disorder, *271*, 271–274
    hypochondriasis, *271*, 278–279
    integrationist approach, 296
    overview, *271*
    pain disorders, *271*, 274–278
    related disorders versus, 269–271
    somatization disorders, *271*,
        274–278
Southeast Asians, and PTSD,
    208–209
Spectatoring, 586
Spiritual healers, 27
Splitting, 52, 443
Sports
    brain injury from, 519–520
    eating disorders and,
        556–558, *557*
Springer, Jim, *45*, 45
Squeeze technique, 596
SSRIs; *see* Selective serotonin
    reuptake inhibitors
Stanford Heart Disease
    Program, 159
Statistical significance, 78–79
Statistics; *see also* Sample
    effect size, 91
    meta-analysis, 91
    significance, 78–79
Statutory rape, 603
Stelazine, 137, 407
Stimulants, 619, 638–646
    ADHD treatment, 469
    amphetamines, 641–643
    autism treatment, 502
    caffeine, 645–646
    cocaine, 640–641
    intoxication and withdrawal
        symptoms, *639*
    nicotine, 643–645
Stimulus, 53–54
Stimulus-control therapy, 183
St. John's wort, 140–141
Stone Age, theories of abnormality
    in, 11–12
Stop-start technique, 596
Stress; *see also* Acute stress
    disorder; Adjustment disorder;
    Posttraumatic stress disorder
    control/lack of control, 173,
        178–180, *179*, 185
    coronary heart disease, 177–178
    definition of, 74, 173
    depression, 308, 319
    factors in, 173

Stress—*Cont.*
    health psychology and, 176–177
    hypertension, 178
    immune system, 178–180
    integrationist approach, 211–212
    physiological responses to, 171,
        174–180
    schizophrenia, 403
    smoking, 643
    substance-related disorders,
        657–658
Stress management, 206–207
Stressors, 74, 173
Stress responses, 173
Stroke, 518
Stroop color naming task, 248, *249*
Structural brain abnormalities,
    schizophrenia and, 397–399
Structural Family Therapy, 155–156
Structured Clinical Interview for
    DSM, 104
Structured clinical interviews, 82,
    104, 428
Stuttering, 487
Styron, William, 352, 372
Subintentional deaths, 354
Substance, 620
Substance abuse, *623*, *626*, 626
    alcohol, 630–632
Substance dependence, *623*,
    626–628, *627*
    alcohol, 630–632
Substance-induced sexual
    dysfunction, 585
Substance-related disorders,
    619–672, *623*; *see also*
    Alcoholism; Drugs
    abuse, *623*, 626
    behavior therapies, 661–662
    biological theories, 654–656
    biological treatments, 659–661
    cannabis, 619, 650–651
    club drugs, 619, 651–653
    cognitive therapies, 662–663
    definitions of, 619, 623–628
    dependence, *623*, 626–628
    depressants, 619, 628–638
    hallucinogens, 619, 648–649
    integrationist approach, 668
    intoxication, *623*, 625
    older adults, 532–534
    opioids, 619, 646–648
    other substances, *624*
    PCP, 619, 648–650
    psychological theories, 656–657
    society and, 619, 621–623
    sociocultural approaches,
        657–659
    stimulants, 619, 638–646
    substance classes and
        diagnoses, *624*
    substance-induced sexual
        dysfunction, 585
    theories, 619, 653–659
    treatments, 619, 659–669
    violence likelihood, *688*
    withdrawal, *623*, 626

Sudden sniffing death, 638
Suicide, 351–373
    assisted, 371
    biological theories, *366*, 366–367
    children and adolescents,
        356–358, *358*
    college students, 358
    contagion, 362–363
    defining and measuring, 351,
        353–359
    dissociative identity disorder
        and, 286
    Durkheim on, 362
    ethnic and cultural differences,
        355–356, *357*
    gender differences, 355–357
    integrationist approach, 371–372
    jail detainees, 690
    older adults, 358–359, 531
    psychological theories, *363*,
        363–366
    rates, 354
    right to, 370–371
    social approaches, 361–363, *362*,
        369–371
    treating and preventing, 351,
        367–371
    types, 353–354, 362
    understanding, 351, 359–367
Suicide cluster, 363
Suicide contagion, 363
Suicide hot lines, 367
Suicide notes, 359–361
Sullivan, Harry Stack, 61
Summers, Marc, 218–219, 261–262
Sundowning, 525
Superego, 49
Supernatural theories, 11
    Greece and Rome, 13–14
    Middle Ages, 14–17
    modern, 27
    Stone Age, 11–12
Support groups, 190–191, 409, 411
Supportive-expressive therapy, for
    bulimia nervosa, 566
Survivor guilt, 193
Susto, *124*
Symptom questionnaire, 110
Symptoms, 101–102, 118, *119*
    negative, 380
    positive, 380
Synapse, *39*, 39
Syndromes, 118, *119*, *124*
Syphilis, 21
Systematic desensitization therapy,
    149–150, 205, 229, 242
Szasz, Thomas, 370

T

Tactile hallucinations, 385
Taijin kyofusho, *124*
Taijin kyofu-sho, 260
Taking Psychology Personally
    abnormality, 11
    choosing a therapist, 146

Taking Psychology Personally—
    Cont.
   college students with mental
       disorders, 488–489
   dementia and caregivers,
       524–525
   dieting, 564–565
   dissociation, 281–282
   ethical service to culturally
       diverse populations, 693
   families coping with
       schizophrenia, 380–381
   genetic factors, 43
   personality disorders, 425–426
   primary care physicians treating
       depression, 333
   relaxation exercises, 230–231
   research participants' rights, 85
   responsible drinking, 669
   safe sex, 593
   self-assessment, 111
   sexual assault victims, 197
   suicidal friend, 368
Tarantism, 16
Tarasoff, Tatiana, 692
Tardive dyskinesia, 336, 408
Tay-Sachs disease, 490
Teachers, as assessment
       resource, 116
Teenagers; see Adolescents
Tegretol, 336
Temperament, childhood disorders
       and, 462–463, 479–480
Tend-and-befriend response, 176
Teresa of Avila, 16
Testosterone, 437, 473–474, 590,
       590–591
Test-retest reliability, 106
THC, 651
Thematic Apperception Test
       (TAT), 113
Theory, defined, 34
Theory of mind, 500–501
Therapeutic alliance, 147
Therapists
   choosing, 146
   duties to clients and society,
       691–692
   matching with client, 161–162
Therapy; see Treatment
Therapy outcome studies, 85–87
   control groups, 86
   ethical issues, 86–87
   evaluation of, 86–87
Thioridazine, 137, 407
Thiothixene, 434
Thioxanthenes, 407
Third variable problem, 79, 80, 83
Thorazine, 137
Thorndike, E. L., 23, 54
Thought-stopping techniques, 206
The Three Faces of Eve (film), 285
Tics, 469
Tobacco; see Nicotine
Tofranil, 139, 250
Token economy, 151, 409
Tolerance, 627

Torrey, E. Fuller, 379
Traditional healing, 413–414
Tranquilizers, 140
Transference, 145–146, 341
Transsexuals, 609
Transvestism, 601–602
Trauma, 194–199
   abuse, 195–196
   common sources of, 198–199
   natural disasters, 194–195
   sexual dysfunction and, 589
   war-related, 196–198
Trazadone, 590
Treatment, 133–169
   ADHD, 469–470
   antisocial personality disorder,
       439–440
   autism, 502
   biological, 133, 136–144
   borderline personality disorder,
       443–444
   children, 133, 161, 164–167
   common components of
       successful, 163, 163–164
   conduct disorder, 475–478
   conversion disorder, 274
   delirium, 527
   dementia, 522
   dissociative identity
       disorder, 289
   eating disorders, 539, 562,
       562–567
   evaluation of, 133, 163–164
   gender identity disorder, 611–612
   generalized anxiety disorder,
       249–250
   mental retardation, 493–496, 494
   mood disorders, 301, 330–343
   OCD, 257, 257–258
   panic disorder, 227, 227–231
   paranoid personality disorder,
       430–431
   paraphilias, 605–607, 607
   phobias, 241–245, 242
   psychological, 133, 144–154
   PTSD, 204, 204–211
   right to, 690–691
   right to refuse, 691
   schizoid personality
       disorder, 432
   schizophrenia, 375, 407–414
   schizotypal personality
       disorder, 434
   seeking, 135–136, 136
   separation anxiety disorder, 480,
       481–482
   sexual dysfunctions,
       590–598, 591
   social and interpersonal, 133,
       154–163
   somatization disorders, 277–278
   substance-related disorders, 619,
       659–669
   suicide, 351, 367–371
   therapy outcome studies, 85–87
Trephination, 12, 12, 143

Tricyclic antidepressants, 138–139,
       227, 331, 567
Trifluoperazine, 137, 407
Trisomy 13, 18, 21, 490, 491
Trotter, Hale, 415
Tuke, William, 19
Twinkie Defense, 683
Twin studies, 42–44
   antisocial personality
       disorder, 437
   autism, 501
   conduct disorder, 473
   "Jim twins," 45
   mood disorders, 314–315
   panic disorder, 223
   phobias, 241
   PTSD, 204
   schizophrenia, 396–397
   substance-related disorders, 654
   suicide, 366
Type A behavior pattern, 185–188
   components of, 185–186
   coronary heart disease,
       186–187, 187
   gender differences, 187–188
Type B behavior pattern, 186

U

Uganda, 341
Unconditional positive regard, 148
Unconditioned response (UR), 53
Unconditioned stimulus (US), 53
Unconscious, 22–23, 49
Undifferentiated
       schizophrenia, 392
Unipolar depression; see
       Depression
Unstructured interviews, 104
Unusualness, 8–9
Urban areas, schizophrenia
       and, 403

V

Vaginismus, 583, 596–597
Vagus nerve stimulation (VNS),
       334–335
Valerian, 141
Validity, 104–106
   concurrent, 106
   construct, 106
   content, 106
   defined, 104
   external, 80
   face, 105–106
   internal, 82–84
   predictive, 106
   types, 106
Valium, 140, 250, 636
Valproate, 336
Valproic acid, 336
Variable
   continuous, 76–77
   defined, 73–74
   dependent, 74

Variable—*Cont.*
  independent, 74
  third variable problem, 79, 80, 83
Vascular dementia, 518–519
Vasocongestion, 576
Venlafaxine, 139, 250, 332
Ventricles, enlarged, 397, *398*
Verapamil, 336
Veterans Administration, 25
Viagra, 590
Vicodin, 646
Violence; *see also* Aggression
  among people with mental
    disorders, 687–689
  serotonin and, 473
Visual hallucinations, 385
Voluntary support network, 135
Voyeurism, 602
Vulnerability-stress models, 35, *35*,
  261, 371

W

Wait list control group, 86
War, as trauma source, 196–198

Watson, John, 23, 238
Wellbutrin, 332, 590
Wernicke's encephalopathy, 634
Weyer, Johann, *The Deception of
  Dreams*, 16
White, Dan, 683
Wish fulfillment, 48
Witchcraft, 14–16, *15*
Withdrawal, *623*, 626
  alcohol, 633
  depressants, *629*
  opioids, *647*
  stimulants, *639*
Witmer, Lightner, 23
Wollstonecraft, Mary, 296
Woolf, Virginia, 360–361
Word salad, 386
Working memory, 386
Working through, 147
World Trade Center attacks,
  191–192
Wundt, Wilhelm, 23
Wyatt, Ricky, 690
Wyatt v. Stickney, 690

X

Xanax, 250, 636

Y

Yates, Andrea, *681*
Yohimbine, 590

Z

Zero correlation, *78*, 78
Zoloft, 139, 227, 257, 368, 590
Zoloft defense, 681
Zolpidem, 183
Zyban, 332, 590, 661

DSM-IV-TR Classification

- **MULTIAXIAL SYSTEM (ABBREVIATED)**

  Axis I Clinical Disorders
  Other Conditions That May Be a Focus of Clinical Attention (Conditions that do not meet precise diagnostic criteria are designated "NOS" ["Not Otherwise Specified"])

  Axis II Personality Disorders
  Mental Retardation

  Axis III General Medical Conditions

  Axis IV Psychosocial and Environmental Problems

  Axis V Global Assessment of Functioning

- **DISORDERS USUALLY FIRST DIAGNOSED IN INFANCY, CHILDHOOD, OR ADOLESCENCE**

Mental Retardation (Axis II)
Mild Mental Retardation
Moderate Mental Retardation
Severe Mental Retardation
Profound Mental Retardation
Mental Retardation, Severity Unspecified

Learning Disorders
Reading Disorder
Mathematics Disorder
Disorder of Written Expression

Motor Skills Disorder
Developmental Coordination Disorder

Communication Disorders
Expressive Language Disorder
Mixed Receptive-Expressive Language Disorder
Phonological Disorder
Stuttering

Pervasive Developmental Disorders
Autistic Disorder
Rett's Disorder
Childhood Disintegrative Disorder
Asperger's Disorder

Attention-Deficit and Disruptive Behavior Disorders
Attention-Deficit/Hyperactivity Disorder
Conduct Disorder
Oppositional Defiant Disorder

Feeding and Eating Disorders of Infancy or Early Childhood
Pica
Rumination Disorder
Feeding Disorder of Infancy or Early Childhood

Tic Disorders
Tourette's Disorder
Chronic Motor or Vocal Tic Disorder
Transient Tic Disorder

Elimination Disorders
Encopresis
Enuresis

Other Disorders of Infancy, Childhood, or Adolescence
Separation Anxiety Disorder
Selective Mutism
Reactive Attachment Disorder of Infancy or Early Childhood
Stereotypic Movement Disorder

- **DELIRIUM, DEMENTIA, AND AMNESTIC AND OTHER COGNITIVE DISORDERS**
Delirium Due to a General Medical Condition
Substance Intoxication Delirium
Substance Withdrawal Delirium
Delirium Due to Multiple Etiologies

Dementia
Dementia of the Alzheimer's Type, with Early Onset
Dementia of the Alzheimer's Type, with Late Onset
Vascular Dementia
Dementia Due to HIV Disease
Dementia Due to Head Trauma
Dementia Due to Parkinson's Disease
Dementia Due to Huntington's Disease
Dementia Due to Pick's Disease
Dementia Due to Creutzfeldt-Jakob Disease
Dementia Due to a General Medical Condition
Substance-Induced Persisting Dementia
Dementia Due to Multiple Etiologies

Amnestic Disorders
Amnestic Disorder Due to a General Medical Condition
Substance-Induced Persisting Amnestic Disorder

- **MENTAL DISORDERS DUE TO A GENERAL MEDICAL CONDITION NOT ELSEWHERE SPECIFIED**
Catatonic Disorder Due to a General Medical Condition
Personality Change Due to a General Medical Condition
Mental Disorder NOS Due to a General Medical Condition

- **SUBSTANCE-RELATED DISORDERS**

Alcohol-Related Disorders
Alcohol Use Disorders
Alcohol-Induced Disorders

Amphetamine-Related Disorders
Amphetamine Use Disorders
Amphetamine-Induced Disorders

Caffeine-Related Disorders
Caffeine-Induced Disorders

Cannabis-Related Disorders
Cannabis Use Disorders
Cannabis-Induced Disorders

Cocaine-Related Disorders
Cocaine Use Disorders
Cocaine-Induced Disorders

Hallucinogen-Related Disorders
Hallucinogen Use Disorders
Hallucinogen-Induced Disorders

Inhalant-Related Disorders
Inhalant Use Disorders
Inhalant-Induced Disorders

Nicotine-Related Disorders
Nicotine Use Disorders
Nicotine-Induced Disorders

Opioid-Related Disorders
Opioid Use Disorders
Opioid-Induced Disorders

Phencyclidine-Related Disorders
Phencyclidine Use Disorders
Phencyclidine-Induced Disorders

Sedative-, Hypnotic-, or Anxiolytic-Related Disorders
Sedative, Hypnotic, or Anxiolytic Use Disorders
Sedative-, Hypnotic-, or Anxiolytic-Induced Disorders

Polysubstance-Related Disorder
Polysubstance Use Disorders
Polysubstance-Induced Disorders

Other (or Unknown) Substance-Related Disorders
Other (or Unknown) Substance Use Disorders
Other (or Unknown) Substance-Induced Disorders

- **SCHIZOPHRENIA AND OTHER PSYCHOTIC DISORDERS**

Schizophrenia
  Paranoid Type
  Disorganized Type
  Catatonic Type
  Undifferentiated Type
  Residual Type
Schizophreniform Disorder
Schizoaffective Disorder
Delusional Disorder
Brief Psychotic Disorder